What's New in This Edition

This edition updates *Alison Balter's Mastering Access 95 Development*, Premier Edition to include the new features available in Access 97 (Office Developer's Edition).

New topics and examples address

- Making your Access 97 applications Internet-aware (the new HyperLink field type; saving forms and reports as HTML; importing, linking to, and exporting HTML tables; adding a hyperlink to a report; and addinghyperlinks to labels, images, and command buttons)
- Integration between Access and Office 97
- Enhancements to the development environment, including right-click enhancements such as Quick Info, Parameter Info, Complete Word, List Properties and Methods, List Constants, Definition, and Last Position
- Language enhancements such as class modules
- Changes to the object model
- Changes surrounding menu bars and toolbars
- The addition of a built-in tab control
- Changes and enhancements to the Jet Engine
- ODBC-Direct
- SourceSafe integration
- Changes to the Debugger
- Removing source code from databases

This edition also includes expanded coverage of

- Parameter queries
- Collections
- The generic error handler

Above all, we hope that *Alison Balter's Mastering Access 97 Development*, Second Edition will be your definitive guide for your Access 97 development efforts.

Alison Balter's Mastering Access 97 Development, Second Edition

Alison Balter

SAMS
PUBLISHING

201 West 103rd Street
Indianapolis, Indiana 46290

I dedicate this book to my husband, Dan; my daughter, Alexis; my parents, Charlotte and Bob; and to my real father, Herman. Dan, you are my partner in life and the wind beneath my wings. Your support of my endeavors is relentless. Alexis, you are the sweet little girl that I always dreamed for. You are everything that I could have ever wanted and so very much more. Mom and Dad, without all that you do to help out with life's chores, the completion of this book would never have been possible.

To my real father, Herman, I credit my ability to soar in such a technical field to you. I hope that I inherited just a small part of your intelligence, wit, and fortitude. I am sorry that you did not live to see this accomplishment. I hope that you can see my work and that you are proud of it. More than anyone else, I dedicate this book to you.

Copyright © 1997 by Sams Publishing

SECOND EDITION

International Standard Book Number: 0-672-30999-8

Library of Congress Catalog Card Number: 96-72230

2000 99 98 97   4   3   2   1

Interpretation of the printing code: the leftmost number is the year of the book's printing; the rightmost single digit the number of the book's printing. For example, a printing code of 97-1 shows that the first printing of the book occurred in 1997.

Composed in AGaramond, Optima, and MCPdigital by Macmillan Computer Publishing

Printed in the United States of America

Trademarks

Publisher and President:	*Richard K. Swadley*
Publishing Manager:	*Rosemarie Graham*
Director of Editorial Services:	*Cindy Morrow*
Assistant Marketing Managers:	*Kristina Perry, Rachel Wolfe*

Acquisitions Editor
Grace M. Buechlein

Development Editor
Kristi Asher

Software Development Specialist
John Warriner

Production Editors
Fran Blauw
Lisa M. Lord

Indexer
Tom Dinse

Technical Reviewers
Karen Jaskolka
John Nelson
Paul Cassel
Nick Malik
Chris Rothberg
David Shank

Editorial Coordinator
Katie Wise

Technical Edit Coordinator
Lorraine Schaffer

Resource Coordinator
Deborah Frisby

Editorial Assistants
Carol Ackerman
Andi Richter
Rhonda Tinch-Mize

Cover Designer
Tim Amrhein

Book Designer
Alyssa Yesh

Copy Writer
Peter Fuller

Production Team Supervisors
Brad Chinn
Charlotte Clapp

Production
Rick Bond
Carol Bowers
Brad Lenser
Chris Livengood
Carl Pierce

Overview

	Introduction	xlv
Part I	**Building a Foundation for Your Access Applications**	**1**
1	Introduction to Access Development	3
2	A Strategy to Developing Access Applications	25
3	What Every Developer Needs to Know About Tables	39
4	Relationships: Your Key to Data Integrity	69
5	What Every Developer Needs to Know About Query Basics	85
6	What Every Developer Needs to Know About Form Basics	117
7	What Every Developer Needs to Know About Report Basics	165
8	VBA 101: The Basics of VBA	207
9	Advanced VBA Techniques	243
10	The Real Scoop on Objects, Properties, and Events	279
11	What Are Macros and When Do You Need Them?	305
12	Advanced Query Concepts	331
13	Let's Get More Intimate with Forms: Advanced Techniques	373
14	Let's Get More Intimate with Reports: Advanced Techniques	425
15	What Are Data Access Objects and Why Are They Important?	453
Part II	**What To Do When Things Don't Go As Planned**	**491**
16	Debugging: Your Key to Successful Development	493
17	Handling Those Dreaded Runtime Errors	515
Part III	**Preparing Your Applications for a Multiuser Environment**	**539**
18	Developing for a Multiuser Environment	541
19	Using External Data	567
20	Client/Server Techniques	599
21	Client/Server Strategies	629
22	Transaction Processing	639
23	Optimizing Your Application	655
24	Replication Made Easy	677
Part IV	**Extending the Power of Access**	**711**
25	Automation: Communicating with Other Applications	713
26	Using ActiveX Controls	739
27	Access and the Internet	765
28	Managing Application Development with Visual SourceSafe	781
29	Leveraging Your Application: Creating Your Own Libraries	795
30	Using Builders, Wizards, and Menu Add-Ins	811

Part V	**Putting the Final Polish on Your Application**	**835**
31	Using External Functions: The Windows API	837
32	Database Security Made Easy	859
33	Complex Security Issues	885
34	Documenting Your System	909
35	Database Maintenance Techniques	923
36	Developing a Help File	931
37	Distributing Your Application with ODE	957
Part VI	**Appendixes**	**991**
A	Table Structures	993
B	Naming Conventions	1045
	Index	1051

Contents

Part I **Building a Foundation for Your Access Applications**   **1**

1 **Introduction to Access Development**   **3**

What Types of Applications Can You Develop in Access? 4
  Access as a Development Platform for Personal Applications .. 4
  Access as a Development Platform for Small-Business
    Applications 4
  Access as a Development Platform for Departmental
    Applications 5
  Access as a Development Platform for Corporation-Wide
    Applications 5
  Access as a Development Platform for Enterprise-Wide
    Client/Server Applications 6
  Access as a Scalable Product 6
What Exactly Is a Database? 7
Getting to Know the Database Objects 7
  Tables: A Repository for Your Data 8
  Queries: Stored Questions or Actions to be Applied to Your
    Data 10
  Forms: A Means of Displaying, Modifying, and Adding
    Data 11
  Reports: Turning Data Into Information 12
  Macros: A Means of Automating Your System 13
  Modules: The Foundation to the Application Development
    Process 14
Object Naming Conventions 15
Hardware Requirements 16
  What Hardware Does Your System Require? 16
  What Hardware Does the User's System Require? 17
How Do I Get Started Developing an Access Application? 17
  Task Analysis 17
  Data Analysis and Design 17
  Prototyping 20
  Testing 20
  Implementation 21
  Maintenance 21
  A Practical Example of Application Design: A Computer
    Consulting Firm 21
Summary 23

2   **A Strategy for Developing Access Applications**   **25**
Why Strategize? 26
Splitting Tables and Other Objects 26
Basing Forms and Reports on Queries 28
Understanding the Access Runtime Engine 28
    Features of the ODE 29
    Differences Between the Standard and Runtime Versions of
      Access 30
    Preparing an Application for Distribution 31
    RESOURCE 34
    The Access Runtime Engine: Summing It Up 34
EXE Versus Access Database: What It Means to You 34
The Importance of Securing Your Database 34
Using Access as a Front-End 35
    Things You Need to Worry About in Converting to
      Client/Server 36
    Benefits and Costs of Client/Server Technology 36
    Your Options When Using Access as a Front-End 37
    What All This Means to You Right Now 38
Applying the Strategy to the Computer Consulting Firm
    Application 38
Summary 38

3   **What Every Developer Needs to Know About Tables**   **39**
Building a New Table 40
    Building a Table with a Wizard 41
    Designing a Table from Scratch 43
    Building a Table from a Datasheet 44
Selecting the Appropriate Field Type for Your Data 46
    Text Fields: The Most Common Field Type 49
    Memo Fields: For Those Long Notes and Comments 49
    Number Fields: When You Need to Calculate 49
    Date/Time Fields: Tracking When Things Happened 49
    Currency Fields: Storing Money 50
    AutoNumber Fields: For Unique Record Identifiers 50
    Yes/No Fields: When One of Two Answers Is Correct 50
    OLE Object Fields: The Place to Store Just About
      Anything 50
    Hyperlink Fields: Your Link to the Internet 51
Working with Field Properties 51
    Field Size: Limiting What's Entered into a Field 51

TRY IT 51
   Format: Determining How Data Is Displayed 52
TRY IT 52
   Input Mask: Determining What Data Goes into a Field 52
TRY IT 53
   Caption: A Great Timesaver 54
   Default Value: Saving Data-Entry Time 54
TRY IT 54
   Validation Rule: Controlling What's Entered in a Field 55
TRY IT 55
   Validation Text: Providing Error Messages to the User 56
TRY IT 56
Required: Make the User Enter a Value 57
TRY IT 57
   Allow Zero Length: Accommodate Situations with
   Nonexistent Data 57
TRY IT 57
Indexed: Speeding Up Searches 58
TRY IT 58
The All-Important Primary Key 59
Working with the Lookup Feature 59
Working with Table Properties 61
Using Indexes to Improve Performance 62
Access Tables and the Internet 62
   The Hyperlink Field Type 62
   Saving Table Data as HTML 63
Practical Examples: Designing the Tables Needed for the
   Computer Consulting Firm's Time and Billing Application.... 65
Summary... 68

4   Relationships: Your Key to Data Integrity   69
Understanding Relationships... 70
Examining the Types of Relationships 70
   One-to-Many 70
   One-to-One... 71
   Many-to-Many 72
Establishing Relationships 72
   Establishing a Relationship Between Two Tables 73
   Looking At Guidelines for Establishing Relationships 73
TRY IT 74
   Modifying an Existing Relationship 75

Establishing Referential Integrity 75
TRY IT 77
   Cascade Update Related Fields 77
   Cascade Delete Related Records.. 78
TRY IT 79
Looking At the Benefits of Relationships 80
Examining Indexes and Relationships 80
Practical Examples: Establishing the Relationships Between
   the Tables Included in the Time and Billing Database 81
Summary.. 83

**5   What Every Developer Needs
to Know About Query Basics   85**
What Is a Query and When Should You Use One? 86
Everything You Need to Know About Selecting Fields 86
TRY IT 88
   Removing a Field from the Query Grid 88
TRY IT 89
   Inserting a Field After the Query Is Built 89
TRY IT 89
   Moving a Field to a Different Location on the Query Grid ... 89
TRY IT 90
   Saving Your Query 90
Ordering Your Query Result 90
TRY IT 91
   Sorting by More than One Field 91
TRY IT 91
   Refining Your Query with Criteria 92
TRY IT 93
Working with Dates in Criteria 94
Understanding How Query Results Can Be Updated................ 95
Building Queries Based on Multiple Tables 96
TRY IT 97
   Pitfalls of Multitable Queries 98
TRY IT 98
   Row Fix-up in Multitable Queries 99
Creating Calculated Fields... 101
TRY IT 102
Getting Help from the Expression Builder 103
Summarizing Data with Totals Queries..................................... 104
TRY IT 107

Excluding Fields from the Output 107
Nulls and Query Results 108
Refining Your Queries with Field and Query Properties 110
   Field Properties: Changing the Behavior of a Field 110
Field List Properties 111
   Query Properties Changing the Behavior of the Overall
   Query 111
Building Parameter Queries When You Don't Know the
  Criteria at Design Time 112
TRY IT 113
Practical Examples: Building Queries Needed by the Time
  and Billing Application for the Computer Consulting Firm .. 115
Summary.. 116

6   What Every Developer Needs to Know About Form Basics   117

Uses of Forms 118
Anatomy of a Form 119
Creating a New Form 120
   Creating a Form with the Form Wizard 121
   Creating a Form from Design View 122
Working with the Form Design Window 123
   Understanding and Working with the Form Design Tools   123
   Adding Fields to the Form 125
   Selecting, Moving, Aligning, and Sizing Form Objects 125
   Modifying Object Tab Order 130
Selecting the Correct Control for the Job 131
   Labels 131
   Text Boxes 132
   Combo Boxes 132
   List Boxes 135
   Checkboxes... 135
   Option Buttons 136
   Toggle Buttons 136
   Option Groups 136
Control Morphing 138
   Text Box to Combo Box 138
   Combo Box to List Box 139
What Form Properties Are Available and
  Why Use Them? 139
   Working with the Properties Window 140
   Working with the Important Form Properties 140

Data Properties of a Form 143
Other Properties of a Form 144
What Control Properties Are Available and
  Why Use Them? 145
Format Properties of a Control 145
Data Properties of a Control 147
Other Properties of a Control 149
Bound, Unbound, and Calculated Controls 150
Using Expressions to Enhance Your Forms 150
The Command Button Wizards: Programming Without
  Typing 151
Building Forms Based on More Than One Table 153
Creating One-to-Many Forms 153
Working with Subforms 156
Basing Forms on Queries: The Why and How 157
Embedding SQL Statements Versus Stored Queries 157
Access Forms and the Internet 158
Adding a Hyperlink to a Form 158
Saving a Form as HTML 159
Saving a Form as Microsoft IIS 1-2 160
Practical Examples: Designing Forms for Your Application 160
Designing the Clients Form 160
Designing the Time Cards Form 162
Designing the Payments Form 162
Designing the Projects Form 163
What's Ahead 164
Summary 164

7 **What Every Developer Needs to Know About Report
   Basics**   **165**

Types of Reports Available 166
Detail Reports 166
Summary Reports 167
Cross Tabulation Reports 167
Reports with Graphics and Charts 168
Reports with Forms 169
Reports with Labels 169
Anatomy of a Report 170
Creating a New Report 171
Creating a Report with the Report Wizard 172
Creating a Report from Design View 174

Working with the Report Design Window 174
    Understanding the Report Design Tools 174
    Adding Fields to the Report 175
    Selecting, Moving, Aligning, and Sizing Report Objects 175
Selecting the Correct Control for the Job 178
    Labels 178
    Text Boxes 178
    Lines 179
    Rectangles 179
    Bound Object Frames 179
    Unbound Object Frames 180
    Image Controls 181
    Other Controls 181
What Report Properties Are Available and Why Use Them 181
    Working with the Properties Window 182
    The Report's Format Properties 182
    The Report's Data Properties 183
    Other Report Properties 183
What Control Properties Are Available and Why Use Them ... 184
    The Control's Format Properties 185
    The Other Control Properties 186
Inserting Page Breaks 187
Unbound, Bound, and Calculated Controls 187
Using Expressions to Enhance Your Reports 187
Building Reports Based on More Than One Table 187
    Creating One-to-Many Reports 188
    Working with Subreports 193
Working with Sorting and Grouping 193
    Adding Sorting and Grouping 194
    Sorting and Grouping Properties 195
    What Are Group Header and Footer Properties and Why
        Use Them 196
Improving Performance and Reusability by Basing Reports
    on Stored Queries 197
Access Reports and the Internet 198
    Adding a Hyperlink to a Report 198
    Saving a Report as HTML 199
Practical Examples: Building Reports Needed for Your
    Application 199
    Designing the rptClientListing Report 199
    Designing the rptTimeSheet Report 202
Summary 205

8	**VBA 101: The Basics of VBA**	**207**
	VBA Explained	208
	Access Class Modules, Standard Modules, Form Modules, and Report Modules Explained	210
	Anatomy of a Module	210
	Option Explicit	212
	Event Procedures Made Easy	213
	Creating Functions and Subroutines	213
	Calling Event and User-Defined Procedures	214
	Scope and Lifetime of Procedures	215
	Naming Conventions for Procedures	217
	Working with Variables	218
	Declaring Variables	218
	VBA Data Types	219
	Scope and Lifetime of Variables: Exposing Your Variables as Little as Possible	220
	Adding Comments to Your Code	222
	Using the Line-Continuation Character	222
	Using the VBA Control Structures	223
	If...Then...Else	223
	Immediate If (IIf)	224
	The Conditional If: Conditional Compilation	225
	Select Case	226
	Looping	227
	For...Next	228
	With...End With	229
	For Each...Next	229
	Passing Parameters and Returning Values: An Introduction	230
	Working with Built-In Functions	231
	Format	231
	Instr	232
	Left	232
	Right	232
	Mid	232
	UCase	232
	DatePart	233
	DateDiff	233
	DateAdd	233
	Functions Made Easy with the Object Browser	233
	Tools for Working with the Module Window	235
	List Properties and Methods	235
	List Constants	236

Quick Info 237

Parameter Information 238

Complete Word 238

Definition 238

Practical Examples: Event Routines, User-Defined Functions,
and Subroutines Needed for the Time and Billing
Application 239

Summary 240

9   Advanced VBA Techniques   243

Navigation Tips and Tricks 244

Mysteries of the Coding Environment Solved 244

Zoom Shift+F2 245

Find and Replace 246

Help 247

Splitting the Code Window 248

Full Module View 249

Using Bookmarks to Save Your Place 249

Executing Procedures from the Module Window 250

The DoCmd Object: Performing Macro Actions 250

What Are User-Defined Types and Why Would You Use
Them? 252

Declaring a User-Defined Type 252

Creating a Type Variable 252

Storing Information from a Record in a Form into a
Type 253

Retrieving Information from the Elements of a Type 253

Working with Constants 253

Defining Your Own Constants 254

Working with Intrinsic Constants 256

Working with Arrays 257

Declaring and Working with Fixed Arrays 257

Declaring and Working with Dynamic Arrays 258

Advanced Function Techniques 259

Passing by Reference Versus Passing by Value 260

Optional Parameters: Building Flexibility into Functions ... 261

Named Parameters: Eliminate the Need to Count
Commas 263

Property Let and Get: Working with Custom Properties 264

Property Let 264

Property Get 264

Class Modules 265
Working with `Empty` and `Null` 268
 Working with `Empty` 268
 Working with `Null` 269
Understanding and Effectively Using Compilation Options 273
 Compile On Demand 273
 Compile Loaded Modules 273
 Compile All Modules 274
Customizing the IDE 274
 Code Color, Fonts, and Sizes 274
 Coding Options 275
Practical Examples: Putting Advanced Techniques to Use in
 the Time and Billing Application 276
 Examples of `Null`, the DoCmd Object, and Intrinsic
  Constants 276
 An Example of Using a Type Structure 277
Summary 278

10 The Real Scoop on Objects, Properties, and Events   279
Understanding Access's Object Model 280
 The Application Object 280
The Forms Collection 280
 The Reports Collection 281
 The Modules Collection 281
 The Screen Object 281
 The DoCmd Object 281
Understanding Objects, Properties, Events, and Methods 282
 What Exactly Are Objects? 282
 What Exactly Are Properties? 282
 What Exactly Are Events? 284
 What Exactly Are Methods? 285
Using the Object Browser to Learn About Access's Objects 286
 How to Use the Object Browser 287
 Pasting Code Templates into a Procedure 288
Referring to Objects 288
Properties and Methods Made Easy 289
 Default Properties 291
Declaring and Assigning Object Variables 291
 Object Variables Versus Regular Variables 291
 Generic Versus Specific Object Variables 292
 Cleaning Up After Yourself 292

Understanding the Differences Between Objects and
   Collections 293
     Manipulating a Single Object 293
     Manipulating a Collection of Objects 293
     Collections Versus Containers and Documents 294
     Creating Custom Collections 295
Using the New Keyword 297
Passing Objects to Functions and Subroutines 298
Returning to a Unique Item in a Collection 299
Determining the Type of a Control 300
Special Properties That Refer to Objects 301
Practical Examples of Working with Objects 302
     Bringing Up Multiple Instances of the Projects Form 302
     Enabling and Disabling Command Buttons 302
Summary 304

11   What Are Macros and When Do You Need Them?   305
Why Learning About Macros Is Important 306
The Basics of Creating and Running a Macro 306
     Macro Actions 307
     Macro Action Arguments 309
     Macro Names 311
     Macro Conditions 312
Running an Access Macro 314
     Running a Macro from the Macro Design Window 314
     Running a Macro from the Macros Tab 315
     Triggering a Macro from a Form or Report Event 315
TRY IT 316
Modifying an Existing Macro 318
     Inserting New Macro Actions 318
     Deleting Macro Actions 319
     Moving Macro Actions 319
     Copying Macro Actions 320
Documenting Your Macro: Adding Comments 321
Testing a Macro 322
TRY IT 323
When You Should Use Macros and When You Shouldn't 323
Converting a Macro to VBA Code 324
Creating an AutoExec Macro 325
Creating an AutoKeys Macro 326
The DoCmd Object 328

Practical Examples: Adding an AutoExec Macro to the Time
and Billing Application 328
Summary... 329

12   Advanced Query Concepts   331
Action Queries 332
Update Queries.. 332
Delete Queries 334
Append Queries 336
Make Table Queries.. 337
Special Notes About Action Queries 339
Action Queries Versus Processing Records with Code......... 340
Special Query Properties 340
Unique Values 341
Unique Records 342
Top Values 342
Optimizing Queries 344
The Query Compilation Process 344
Analyzing a Query's Performance 344
Things You Can Do to Improve a Query's Performance 345
Rushmore Technology 346
Crosstab Queries 347
Creating a Crosstab Query with the Crosstab Query
Wizard.. 348
Creating a Crosstab Query Without the Crosstab Query
Wizard.. 351
Fixed Column Headings 352
Important Notes About Crosstab Queries 353
Outer Joins 353
Self-Joins 355
Understanding SQL 356
What Is SQL and Where Did It Come From? 356
What Do You Need to Know About SQL? 357
SQL Syntax 357
The SELECT Clause 357
The FROM Clause 357
The WHERE Clause 358
The ORDER BY Clause 358
The JOIN Clause 358
ALL, DISTINCTROW, and DISTINCT Clauses 359
The GROUP BY Clause 359
Applying What You Have Learned 360

Union Queries 362
Pass-Through Queries 362
The Propagation of Nulls and Query Results 364
Subqueries 364
Using the Result of a Function as the Criteria
  for a Query 365
Passing Parameter Query Values from a Form 367
Practical Examples: Applying These Techniques in Your
  Application 368
    Archive Payments 368
    Show All Payments 370
    Create State Table 370
Summary 371

13 **Let's Get More Intimate with Forms:**
    Advanced Techniques   **373**
What Are the Form Events and When Do You Use Them? 374
    Current 374
    BeforeInsert 374
    BeforeUpdate 375
    AfterUpdate 375
    AfterInsert 375
    Delete 376
    BeforeDelConfirm 376
    AfterDelConfirm 376
    Open 376
    Load 377
    Resize 377
    Unload 377
    Close 378
    Activate 378
    Deactivate 378
    GotFocus 379
    LostFocus 379
    Click 379
    DblClick 379
    MouseDown 379
    MouseMove 380
    MouseUp 380
    KeyDown 380
    KeyUp 380
    KeyPress 380

Error 380

Filter 381

ApplyFilter 381

Timer 381

Understanding the Sequence of Form Events 381

What Are the Section and Control Events and When
Do You Use Them? 383

BeforeUpdate 383

AfterUpdate 383

Updated 384

Change 384

NotInList 384

Enter 384

Exit 385

GotFocus 385

LostFocus 385

Click 385

DblClick 386

MouseDown 387

MouseMove 387

MouseUp 387

KeyDown 387

KeyUp 387

KeyPress 387

Understanding the Sequence of Control Events 388

Referring to Me 388

What Types of Forms Can I Create and When Are They
Appropriate? 389

Single Forms: Viewing One Record at a Time 389

Continuous Forms: View Multiple Records at a Time 390

Multipage Forms: When Everything Doesn't Fit on One
Screen 391

Tabbed Forms: Conserving Screen Real-Estate 393

Switchboard Forms: Controlling Your Application 395

Splash Screen Forms: A Professional Opening to Your
Application 396

Dialog Forms: Gathering Information 397

Using Built-In Dialog Boxes 397

Message Boxes 397

Input Boxes 400

Common Dialog Boxes 400

Adding Custom Menus, Toolbars, and Shortcut Menus to
    Your Forms 400
    Designing a Menu 400
Taking Advantage of Built-in Form-Filtering Features 405
Including Objects from Other Applications: Linking Versus
    Embedding 406
    Bound OLE Objects 406
    Unbound OLE Objects 407
OpenArgs 408
Switching a Form's Record Source 408
Power Combo Box and List Box Techniques 410
    Handling the NotInList Event 410
    Populating a Combo or List Box with a Callback Function 412
    Handling Multiple Selections in a List Box 414
Power Subform Techniques 416
    Referring to Subform Controls 416
Synchronizing a Form with Its Underlying Recordset 417
Creating Custom Properties and Methods 417
    Creating Custom Properties 417
    Creating Custom Methods 421
Practical Examples: Applying Advanced Techniques to Your
    Application 422
    Building an AutoExec Routine to Launch the Application 422
    Building a Splash Screen 423
    Summary 424

14   Let's Get More Intimate with Reports: Advanced
     Techniques   425
Events Available for Reports and When to Use Them 426
    The Open Event 426
    The Close Event 426
    The Activate Event 427
    The Deactivate Event 427
    The NoData Event 428
    The Page Event 428
    The Error Event 428
Order of Events for Reports 429
Events Available for Report Sections and When to Use Them   429
    The Format Event 429
    The Print Event 431
    The Retreat Event 432
    Order of Section Events 433

Special Report Properties 433
    MoveLayout 433
    NextRecord 433
    PrintSection 433
    Interaction of MoveLayout, NextRecord, and PrintSection 434
    FormatCount... 434
    PrintCount 435
    HasContinued 435
    WillContinue 435
Practical Applications of Report Events and Properties............ 435
    Changing a Report's RecordSource 435
    Using the Same Report to Display Summary,
        Detail, or Both 437
    Printing Multiple Labels 438
    Determining Where a Label Prints.. 439
    Building a Report from a Crosstab Query 440
    Printing the First and Last Page Entries in the Page Header 446
    Creating a Multifact Crosstab Report 448
Practical Examples... 450
Summary.. 451

**15 What Are the Data Access Objects and Why Are They
    Important?   453**
Understanding Data Access Objects 454
Examining the Data Access Object Model................................. 454
    Workspaces 456
    Users 456
    Groups.. 456
    Databases 456
    TableDefs 457
    Indexes 458
    QueryDefs 458
    Fields 458
    Parameters 459
    Recordsets 460
    Relations 460
    Containers 460
    Documents 461
    Properties 461
    Errors 462
Getting to Know DBEngine 462
Using CurrentDB() 463

Understanding Recordset Types 463
    Dynasets 464
    Snapshots 464
    Tables 464
Selecting Among the Types of `Recordset` Objects Available 465
Working with Recordset Properties and Methods 465
    Creating a `Recordset` Variable 465
    Using Arguments to Open a Recordset 467
    Examining Record-Movement Methods 468
    Detecting the Limits of a Recordset 469
    Counting the Number of Records in a Recordset 470
    Sorting, Filtering, and Finding Records 471
    Using the AbsolutePosition Property 474
    Using the Bookmark Property 475
    Using the RecordsetClone Property 476
    Running Parameter Queries 476
Modifying Table Data Using Code 477
    Changing Record Data One Record at a Time 477
    Making Bulk Changes 478
    Deleting an Existing Record 478
    Adding a New Record 479
    Using the LastModified Property 480
Creating and Modifying Database Objects Using Code 480
    Adding a Table Using Code 481
    Removing a Table Using Code 481
    Establishing Relationships Using Code 482
    Creating a Query Using Code 482
Using the Containers Collection 483
Practical Examples: Applying These Techniques to Your
  Application 484
    Creating a Report Selection Form 484
    Using Recordset Methods on a Data-Entry Form 486
Summary 489

Part II   What To Do When Things Don't Go As Planned   491

16   Debugging: Your Key to Successful Development   493

Understanding the Importance of Debugging 494
Avoiding Bugs 494
    Option `Explicit` 494
    Strong-Typing 494
    Naming Standards 494

Variable Scoping 495
Bugs Happen! 495
Harnessing the Power of the Debug Window 495
Testing Values of Variables and Properties 496
Setting Values of Variables and Properties 496
Clearing the Debug Window 497
Practicing with the Built-In Functions 498
Executing Subroutines, Functions, and Methods 498
Printing to the Debug Window at Runtime 499
Invoking the Debugger 500
Using Breakpoints to Troubleshoot 500
TRY IT 501
Stepping Through Code 502
Using Step Into 502
TRY IT 502
Executing Until the Next Breakpoint Is Reached 503
TRY IT 504
Using Step Over 504
TRY IT 504
Using Step Out 505
TRY IT 505
Setting the Next Statement to Execute 505
TRY IT 505
Using the Calls Window 506
TRY IT 506
Working with the Locals Pane 507
Working with Watch Expressions 507
Using Auto Data Tips 508
Using Quick Watch 508
Adding a Watch Expression 508
TRY IT 510
Editing a Watch Expression 510
Breaking When an Expression Is True 510
Breaking When an Expression Changes 511
Continuing Execution After a Runtime Error 512
Looking At Gotchas with the Debug Window 513
Practical Examples: Debugging Real Applications 513
Summary 514

17 **Handling Those Dreaded Runtime Errors**   515
Implementing Error Handling 516
Working with Error Events 517

Using On Error Statements 518
  Using On Error Goto 519
  Including the Error Number and Description in the Error
    Handler 519
  Using On Error Resume Next 520
  Using On Error Goto 0 520
Using Resume Statements 521
  The Resume Statement 521
  The Resume Next Statement 522
  The Resume <LineLabel> Statement....................................... 522
Clearing an Error 523
Examining the Cascading Error Effect...................................... 523
Using the Err Object 524
Raising an Error 525
  Generating an Error on Purpose 525
  Creating User-Defined Errors 526
Using the Errors Collection 526
Creating a Generic Error Handler 527
  Logging the Error 530
  Determining the Appropriate Response to an Error 531
  Creating an Error Form 534
  Printing the Error Form 536
Preventing Your Own Error Handling from Being Invoked 537
Practical Examples: Incorporating Error Handling 537
Summary.. 538

Part III Preparing Your Applications for a Multiuser Environment 539

18 Developing for a Multiuser Environment 541
Designing Your Application with Multiuser Issues in Mind 542
  Multiuser Design Strategies 542
  Strategies for Installing Your Application 543
  The Basics of Linking to External Data 545
Understanding Access's Locking Mechanisms 546
Locking and Refreshing Strategies 547
  Default Record Locking... 548
  Default Open Mode 549
  Number of Update Retries 549
  ODBC Refresh Interval 550
  Refresh Interval... 550
  Update Retry Interval 550
  Refreshing Versus Requerying Data 550

Form Locking Strategies 551
    No Locks 551
    All Records 551
    Edited Record 552
Recordset Locking 552
    Pessimistic Locking 553
    Optimistic Locking 554
Effectively Handling Locking Conflicts 555
    Errors with Pessimistic Locking 555
    Coding Around Pessimistic Locking Conflicts 556
    Errors with Optimistic Locking or New Records 558
    Coding Around Optimistic Locking Conflicts 558
    Testing to See Who Has a Record Locked 561
Testing a Record for Locking Status 562
Using Code to Refresh or Requery 563
Understanding the .LDB File 563
Creating Custom Counters 564
Using Unbound Forms 564
Using Replication to Improve Performance 565
Practical Examples: Making an Application Multiuser Ready .. 565
Summary 566

19   **Using External Data**   **567**
Understanding External Data 568
Importing, Linking, and Opening: When and Why 568
    Selecting an Option 569
    Looking At Supported File Formats 570
Importing External Data 571
    Importing External Data via the User Interface 571
    Importing External Data Using Code 572
Creating a Link to External Data 575
    Creating a Link Using the User Interface 575
    Creating a Link Using Code 579
Opening an External Table 582
    Providing Connection Information 583
    Opening the Table 583
Understanding Windows Registry Settings 584
Using the Connection String 585
Working with Passwords 585
Refreshing and Removing Links 586
    Updating Links That Have Moved 587
    Deleting Links 588

Creating an External Table 588
Looking At Special Considerations 589
   dBASE 589
   FoxPro 590
   Text Data 591
Troubleshooting... 591
   Connection Problems 591
   Temp Space 591
Looking At Performance Considerations and Links 591
Working with HTML Documents 592
Practical Examples: Working with External Data from within
   Your Application 594
   Splitting the Database By Using the Database Splitter 595
   Refreshing Links 595
Summary 598

20   Client/Server Techniques   599
Understanding the Client/Server Model 600
Deciding Whether to Use the Client/Server Model 600
   Dealing With a Large Volume of Data 602
   Dealing With a Large Number of Concurrent Users 602
   Demanding Faster Performance 603
   Handling Increased Network Traffic 603
   Implementing Backup and Recovery 603
   Focusing on Security 604
   Sharing Data among Multiple Front-End Tools 604
   Understanding What It All Means 604
Roles Access Plays in the Application Design Model 605
   The Front-End and Back-End 605
   The Front-End Using Links to Communicate to a
     Back-End 605
   The Front-End Using SQL Pass-Through to
     Communicate to a Back-End 606
   The Front-End Using ODBCDirect to Communicate to a
     Back-End 607
Learning the Client/Server Buzzwords 608
Upsizing: What to Worry About 609
   Indexes 610
   AutoNumber Fields 610
   Default Values 610
   Validation Rules 610
   Relationships 611

Security 611
Table and Field Names 611
Reserved Words 611
Case-Sensitivity 611
Properties 612
Visual Basic Code 612
Proactively Preparing for Upsizing 612
Defining an ODBC Data Source 612
Connecting to a Database Server 615
Working with Linked Tables 616
Linking to External Tables via the User Interface 616
Linking to External Tables via Code 618
Linking to Views Rather Than Tables 619
Using Pass-Through Queries 620
Opening a Server Table Directly 624
Using ODBCDirect to Access Client/Server Data 624
Summary 628

21   Client/Server Strategies   629
Developing Client/Server Strategies 630
Selecting the Best Recordset Type 630
Using Forward-Scrolling Snapshots 631
Using Key Set Fetching 631
Using Pass-Through Queries and Stored Procedures 631
Using ODBCDirect 632
Preconnecting to the Server 632
Reducing the Number of Connections 633
Optimizing Data Handling 633
Optimizing Queries and Forms 633
Optimizing Queries 634
Optimizing Forms 634
Practical Examples: Using Client/Server Strategies 637
Summary 638

22   Transaction Processing   639
Understanding Transaction Processing 640
Understanding the Benefits 640
Modifying the Default Behavior 642
Implementing Explicit Transaction Processing 643
Looking At Transaction Processing Issues 644
Realizing That Transactions Occur in a Workspace 644
Making Sure the Data Source Supports Transactions 645

Nesting Transactions 646
Neglecting to Explicitly Commit Transactions 646
Checking Available Memory 646
Using Forms with Transactions 647
Using Transaction Processing in a Multiuser Environment 647
Using Transaction Processing in a Client/Server
    Environment 651
Implicit Transactions 651
Explicit Transactions 651
Nested Transactions 652
Lock Limits 652
Negative Interactions with Server-Specific Transaction
    Commands 652
Practical Examples: Improving the Integrity of the Time and
    Billing Application Using Transaction Processing 653
Summary 654

23   Optimizing Your Application   655

Understanding Optimization 656
Modifying Hardware and Software Configurations 656
Hardware, Hardware, More Hardware Please! 657
Change Access's Software Settings 659
Understanding What Jet 3.5 Does to Improve Performance.... 660
Letting the Performance Analyzer Determine Problem Areas .. 661
Designing Tables to Optimize Performance 662
Why Be Normal? 662
I Thought You Just Told Me to Normalize 663
Index, Index, Index! 663
Select the Correct Data Type 663
Designing Queries to Optimize Performance 664
Changing Code to Improve Performance 664
Eliminate Variants and Use the Smallest Data Type
    Possible 665
Use Specific Object Types 665
Use Inline Code 666
Toggle Booleans Using Not 666
Use the Built-In Collections 666
Use the Length Function 667
Use True and False Instead of Zero 667
Use Transactions... Sometimes? 668
Eliminate Unused Dim and Declare Statements 668
Eliminate Unused Code.. 668

Use Variables to Refer to Properties, Controls, and Data
  Access Objects 668
Use With...End With 669
Use the Me Keyword 669
Use String Functions When Possible 670
Use Dynamic Arrays 670
Use Constants When Possible 670
Use Bookmarks 670
Set Object Variables Equal to Nothing 671
Use Action Queries Instead of Looping Through
  Recordsets 671
Deliver Your Application with the Modules Compiled 672
Retaining the Compiled State 672
Distribute Your Application as an MDE 673
Organize Your Modules 673
Designing Forms and Reports to Improve Performance 673
Designing Forms 673
Designing Reports 675
Practical Examples: Improving the Performance of the Time
  and Billing Application 675
Summary 675

24 **Replication Made Easy**   **677**
What Is Replication? 678
Uses of Replication 678
Sharing Data Among Offices 678
Sharing Data Among Dispersed Users 678
Reducing Network Load 679
Distributing Application Updates 679
Backing Up the Data in Your Application 679
Understanding When Replication Isn't Appropriate 679
An Overview of the Implementation of Replication 680
The Access User Interface 680
Briefcase Replication 680
The Replication Manager 680
DAO Code 681
Programs That Support Replication Using DAO 681
The Replication Architecture: What Makes Replication
  Tick? 681
The Tracking Layer 681
The Microsoft Replication Manager 682
The Synchronizer 682

File System Transport 683
The Briefcase Reconciler 683
Registry Entries 683
Understanding Replication Topologies 683
Star Topology 684
Ring Topology 684
Fully Connected Topology 685
Linear Topology 685
Hybrid Topology 685
Changes That Replication Makes to Your Database 685
Fields Added to Each Replicated Table 686
System Tables Added to the Database 686
Properties Added to the Database Objects 686
Changes to Sequential AutoNumber Fields 687
Changes to the Size of the Database 687
Making a Database Replicable 687
Rendering a Database Replicable with the Access User
Interface 688
Rendering a Database Replicable with the Windows 95
Briefcase 689
Preventing Objects from Being Replicated 690
Creating Additional Replicas 690
Creating Additional Replicas with the Access User
Interface 691
Creating Additional Replicas with the Windows 95
Briefcase 691
Synchronizing Replicas 691
Synchronizing Databases with the Access User Interface 691
Synchronizing Databases with the Windows 95 Briefcase ... 692
Resolving Replication Conflicts 693
Using the Replication Manager 695
Running the Replication Manager for the First Time 695
Replicating a Database with the Replication Manager 698
Creating Replicas with the Replication Manager 701
Partial Replication 702
Synchronizing Replicas with the Replication Manager 702
Reviewing the Synchronization History 704
Working with Synchronization Properties 705
Implementing Replication by Using Code 705
Making a Database Replicable by Using Code 705
Flagging an Object as Local 706

Creating a Replica by Using Code 706
Creating a Partial Replica Using Code 707
Synchronizing a Database by Using Code 707
Handling Conflicts by Using Code 708
Practical Examples: Managing the Time and Billing
Application with Replication 708
Summary 709

Part IV   Extending the Power of Access   711

25   Automation: Communicating with Other Applications   713
Understanding Automation 714
Defining Some Automation Terms 714
Declaring an Object Variable to Reference Your Application .. 715
Using CreateObject and GetObject 717
CreateObject 717
GetObject 718
Manipulating an Automation Object 719
Setting and Retrieving Properties 719
Executing Methods 719
Controlling Excel from Access 719
Closing an Automation Object 722
Creating a Graph from Access 723
Controlling Word from Access 726
Controlling PowerPoint from Access 728
Controlling Access from Other Applications 730
Practical Examples: Using Automation to Extend the
Functionality of the Time and Billing Application 733
Summary 737

26   Using ActiveX Controls   739
ActiveX Controls Explained 740
Incorporating ActiveX Controls in Access 97 740
Registering an ActiveX Control 741
Adding ActiveX Controls to Forms 742
Understanding and Managing the Control Reference in
Your Access Application 744
Setting Properties of an ActiveX Control at Design Time 745
Coding Events of an ActiveX Control 746
The Calendar Control 747
Properties of a Calendar Control 747
Methods of a Calendar Control 748

The UpDown Object 750
The StatusBar Control 751
The Common Dialog Control 753
The Rich Textbox Control 755
The TabStrip Control 758
The ImageList Control 760
Licensing and Distribution Issues 761
Practical Examples: Implementing ActiveX Controls 762
Adding a Calendar to the Report Criteria Dialog 762
Summary 763

27   Access and the Internet   765
What's New with Access and the Internet 766
Saving Database Objects as HTML 766
Saving Table Data as HTML 766
Saving Query Results as HTML 767
Saving Forms as HTML 768
Saving Reports as HTML 768
Linking to HTML Files 769
Importing HTML Files 771
Static Versus Dynamic HTML Formats 772
The Publish to the Web Wizard 773
Working with HTML Templates 775
Sending Data to an FTP or HTTP Server 776
Importing or Linking to Data on FTP and HTTP Servers .. 776
Exporting an Object to an FTP Server 776
Taking Advantage of Hyperlinks 777
Storing Hyperlinks in Tables 777
Placing Hyperlinks on Forms and Reports 777
The Microsoft WebBrowser Control 778
The Web Toolbar 778
Replication Over the Internet 779
Summary 779

**28   Managing Application Development with Visual
SourceSafe   781**
What Is Visual SourceSafe? 782
How Do I Install Visual SourceSafe? 782
Using Visual SourceSafe: An Overview 783
The Logistics of Managing a Project with Visual SourceSafe ... 783
Adding a Database to Visual SourceSafe 783
Creating a Database from a SourceSafe Project 787

Checking in and Checking out Database Objects 787

Getting the Latest Version 789

Adding Objects to Visual SourceSafe 789

Refreshing an Object's Status 790

Leveraging the Power of Visual SourceSafe 790

Showing Differences Between Modules 790

Showing an Object's History 790

Reverting to an Object's Previous Version 791

Changes Visual SourceSafe Makes to Access's Behavior 791

The Compact Command 791

Opening a Database 791

Closing a Database 791

Opening an Object in Design View 792

Saving a New Object or Using Save As on an Existing

Object 792

Renaming an Object 792

Deleting an Object 792

Understanding the Limitations of Visual SourceSafe 793

Practical Examples: Putting the Time and Billing Application

Under SourceSafe Control 793

Summary 793

29   Leveraging Your Application: Creating Your Own

Libraries   795

Understanding Library Databases 796

Preparing a Database to Be a Library 796

Structuring Code Modules for Optimal Performance 797

Writing Library Code that Runs 797

Compiling the Library 798

Creating a Reference 798

Creating a Library Reference 798

Using the LoadOnStartup Key 800

Creating an Explicit Reference 801

Creating a Reference Using VBA Code 805

Debugging a Library Database 805

Securing an Access Library 806

Practical Examples: Building a Library for Your Application ... 807

Summary 809

30   Using Builders, Wizards, and Menu Add-Ins   811

Defining Builders, Wizards, andMenu Add-Ins, Builders 812
Using Builders 812
  Looking At Design Guidelines 812
  Creating a Builder 813
  Writing a Builder Function 813
  Designing a Builder Form 815
  Registering a Builder 816
Using Wizards 822
  Looking At Design Guidelines 822
  Creating a Wizard 823
  Getting the Wizard Ready to Go 826
Using Menu Add-Ins 827
  Looking At Design Guidelines 827
  Creating a Menu Add-In 828
Practical Examples: Designing Your Own Add-Ins 829
Summary 833

Part V   Putting the Final Polish on Your Application   835

31   Using External Functions: The Windows API   837

Using the Win32 API 838
Declaring an External Function to the Compiler 838
  Passing by Reference versus Passing by Value 839
  Passing String Parameters 839
  Aliasing a Function 841
Working with Constants and Types 843
  Working with Constants 843
  Working with Types 844
  Using the Windows API Text Viewer 845
  Loading a Text File 845
  Loading a Database File 846
  Pasting API Declares, Types, and Constants 847
Calling DLL Functions: Important Issues 848
Examining the Differences Between 16-Bit and 32-Bit APIs ... 849
Using API Functions 849
Getting Information about the Operating Environment 849
Determining Drive Types and Available Drive Space 854
Practical Examples: Applying What You Have Learned to
  the Time and Billing Application 857
Summary 857

32 Database Security Made Easy   **859**
Reviewing Your Options for Securing a Database 860
Implementing Share-Level Security: Establishing a Database
  Password 860
Encrypting a Database 861
Establishing User-Level Security 863
  Step 1: Creating a Workgroup 864
  Step 2: Creating an Administrative User 867
  Step 3: Making the Administrative User a Member of the
    Admins Group 869
  Step 4: Changing the Password for the Admin User 869
  Step 5: Removing the Admin User from the Admins
    Group 870
  Step 6: Exiting Access and Logging On as the System
    Administrator 871
  Step 7: Assigning a Password to the System Administrator .. 871
  Step 8: Opening the Database You Want to Secure 871
  Step 9: Running the Security Wizard 871
  Step 10: Creating Users and Groups 873
  Step 11: Assigning Rights to Users and Groups 875
Providing an Additional Level of Security: Creating an
  MDE File 877
Looking At Special Issues 878
  Passwords 878
  Security and Linked Tables 879
  Ownership 879
  Printing Security 880
Practical Examples: Securing the Time and Billing
  Application 880
Summary 883

33 Complex Security Issues   **885**
Controlling Security Via Code 886
Maintaining Groups Using Code 886
  Adding a Group 886
  Removing a Group 888
Maintaining Users Using Code 889
  Adding Users 889
  Assigning Users to a Group 890
  Removing Users from a Group 891
  Removing Users 893

Listing All Groups and Users 894
   Listing All Groups 894
   Listing All Users 895
Working with Passwords 896
   Assigning Passwords to Users 896
   Listing Users without Passwords 897
   Ensuring That Users Have Passwords 899
Assigning and Revoking Permissions to Objects Using Code .. 900
Encrypting a Database By Using Code 902
Accomplishing Field-Level Security By Using Queries 902
Prohibiting Users from Creating Objects 904
   Prohibiting Users from Creating Databases 904
   Prohibiting Users from Creating Other Objects 905
Accomplishing Prohibited Tasks By Logging on a Different
   User 906
Securing Client/Server Applications 906
Examining Security and Replication 906
Practical Examples: Applying Advanced Techniques to Your
   Application 906
Summary 907

34   Documenting Your System   909

Understanding Why You Should Document 910
Preparing Your Application to Be Self-Documenting 910
   Documenting Your Tables 910
   Documenting Your Queries 911
   Documenting Your Forms 912
   Documenting Your Reports 913
   Documenting Your Macros 913
   Documenting Your Modules 914
Using Database Properties to Document the Overall
   Database 914
Using the Database Documenter 916
   Using the Documenter Options 917
   Producing Documentation in Other Formats 919
Writing Code to Create Your Own Documentation 920
Practical Examples: Applying What You Learned to the
   Time and Billing Application 921
Summary 921

35 Database Maintenance Techniques   **923**

Understanding What Database Maintenance Is All About 924

Compacting Your Database 924

    Using the User Interface 925

    Using a Shortcut 926

    Using Code 927

Repairing Your Database 928

    Using the User Interface 929

    Using a Shortcut 929

    Using Code 930

Summary 930

36 Developing a Help File   **931**

Deciding To Create a Help File 932

Looking at Help from a User's Perspective 932

    The Contents Tab 932

    The Index Tab 933

    The Find Tab 934

    The Office Assistant 934

    Button Bars 935

    Hotspots 935

    Hypergraphics 936

    Authorable Buttons 936

Planning the Help File 936

Building the Help Components 937

    Creating a Topic File 938

    Creating a Map File 945

    Creating a Contents File 946

    Creating the Help Project File 946

    Preparing the Help Project to be Compiled 948

    Compiling the Project 952

Adding Custom Help to Your Applications 952

Getting Help with Help: Authoring Tools 953

Practical Examples: Adding Help to the Time and Billing

    Application 954

Summary 955

37   Distributing Your Application with ODE   957

Distributing Your Application: An Introduction 958
Looking At the ODE 958
    Royalty-Free Runtime License 959
    Setup Wizard 959
    Replication Manager 959
    Two-Volume Language Reference 959
    32-Bit ActiveX Controls 959
    Win32 API Text Viewer 960
    Help Workshop for Windows 95 960
    Microsoft Access Developer Sample CD-ROM 960
    Microsoft Graph Runtime Executable 960
Distributing Your Application to Run with a Full Copy of
Access 960
Using Full Versions versus Runtime Versions of Access 961
    Hidden Database Window 962
    Hidden Design Views 962
    Built-In Toolbars Not Supported 962
    Unavailable Menu Items 962
    Disabled Keys 963
Preparing Your Database for Use with the Access Runtime
Version 964
    Creating the Application 964
    Distributing Your Application as an MDE 973
    Adding Custom Help to the Application 973
    Testing and Debugging the Application 973
    Running and Testing the Application with the /Runtime
    Command Line Switch 973
    Running the Setup Wizard 974
    Packaging and Distributing the Application 982
Looking At Other Issues 984
    Automating the Process of Linking to Tables 984
    Using Replication to Efficiently Distribute Your
    Application 989
Practical Examples: Distributing the Time and Billing
Application 989
Summary 989

Part VI Appendixes   **991**

   A   **Table Structures**   **993**

        The tblClients table 994

        The tblCompanyInfo Table 1004

        The tblEmployees Table 1009

        The tblErrorLog Table 1014

        The tblErrors Table 1018

        The tblExpenseCodes Tables 1019

        The tblPaymentMethods Table 1020

        The tblPayments Table 1022

        The tblProjects Table 1026

        The tblTimeCardExpenses Table 1031

        The tblTimeCardHours Table 1036

        The tblTimeCards Table 1041

        The tblWorkCodes Table 1043

   B   **Naming Conventions**   **1045**

        Index   **1051**

Acknowledgments

Writing a book is a monumental task. Without the support and understanding of those close to me, my dreams for this book would have never come to fruition. Special thanks go to the following special people who helped to make this book possible:

Dan Balter (My Incredible Husband) for his ongoing support, love, encouragement, friendship, and for staying up many nights proofreading this book. Dan, words cannot adequately express the love and appreciation that I feel for all that you are and all that you do for me. Thank you for being the phenomenal person that you are. I enjoy sharing not only our career successes, but even more I enjoy sharing the life of our beautiful child, Alexis. There is no one I'd rather spend forever with than you.

Alexis Balter (My Precious Daughter) for giving life a special meaning. Alexis, you make all of my hard work worth it. No matter how bad my day, when I look at you, sunshine fills my life. You are the most special gift that anyone has ever given me.

Charlotte and Bob Roman (Mom & Dad) for believing in me and sharing in both the good times and the bad. Mom and Dad, without your special love and support, I never would have become who I am today. Without all of your help, I could never get everything done. Words can never express how much I appreciate all that you do!

Maureen and Herb Balter (Mom- & Dad-in-law) for their willingness to be the mother- and father-in-law that I missed for so long and, most of all, for accepting and appreciating me for who I am! Mom and Dad, your appreciation for my success and accomplishments makes them more meaningful to me. I am glad that I could help to give you a grandchild that you can love and cherish forever.

Roz, Ron, and Charlie Carriere for supporting my endeavors and for encouraging me to pursue my writing. It means a lot to know that you guys are proud of me for what I do.

Steven Chait for being a special brother. I want you to know how much you mean to me. When I was a little girl, I was told about your gift to write. You might not know this, but my desire to write was started as a little girl wanting to be like her big brother.

John Hawkins, Jeanne Banfield, Mike Groh, Geri Bahr, Dana Gardner, and all of the rest of **Advisor Publications'** wonderful staff for giving me a chance as an author. I enjoy both the professional and personal relationships that I have developed with all of you. Thanks for believing in me!

Greggory Peck, Clint Argle, and the Folks at Keystone Learning Systems for their contribution to my success in this industry. I believe that the opportunities you have given me have helped me reach a level in this industry that would have been much more difficult for me to reach on my own.

Paul Sheriff for inspiring and encouraging me to reach my potential as a trainer and developer. Paul, you are a special friend. I appreciate all that you have taught me as a friend rather than a competitor.

Grace Buechlein for doing her best to get through both the good times and the trying times. Grace, I know you always do your best to smooth the rough edges. You take your job as an acquisitions editor quite seriously and help to produce the best book possible.

Janet Reyes for being the person responsible for getting me started with computers. Janet, you were a tough boss, but now you are an incredible friend. I credit my beginnings as a computer nerd to you. Thanks for believing in me and pushing me to reach my potential.

About the Author

Alison Balter is the president of Marina Consulting Group, a firm based in Westlake Village, California. Alison is a highly experienced independent trainer and consultant, specializing in Windows applications training and development. During her 14 years in the computer industry, she has trained and consulted with many corporations and government agencies. Since Alison founded Marina Consulting Group in 1990, its client base has expanded to include major corporations and government agencies such as Northrop, the Drug Enforcement Administration, Prudential Insurance, Transamerica Insurance, Fox Broadcasting, the United States Navy, and others.

Alison is a Microsoft Solution Provider and Certified Professional. Most recently, she became one of the first professionals in the computer industry to become a Microsoft Certified Solutions Developer.

Alison is the author of more than 100 internationally marketed computer training videos for Keystone Learning Systems Corporation, including seven Access 2.0, 11 Access 95, 12 Access 97, nine Visual Basic for Applications, and 14 Visual FoxPro videos. She travels throughout North America giving training seminars in Microsoft Access, Visual Basic, and Visual FoxPro.

Alison is a regular contributing columnist for *Databased Advisor* and *Access/Visual Basic Advisor,* as well as other computer publications. She is also a regular on the Access and Visual Basic national speaker circuit. She was one of four speakers on the Visual Basic 4.0 World Tour, a seminar series co-sponsored by Application Developers Training Company and Microsoft.

Alison is also a co-author of three other Access books published by Sams: *Essential Access 95, Access 95 Unleashed,* and *Access 97 Unleashed.*

An active participant in many user groups and other organizations, Alison is a former president of the Independent Computer Consultants Association of Los Angeles, and of the Los Angeles Clipper Users' Group.

Tell Us What You Think!

As a reader, you are the most important critic and commentator of our books. We value your opinion and want to know what we're doing right, what we could do better, what areas you'd like to see us publish in, and any other words of wisdom you're willing to pass our way. You can help us make strong books that meet your needs and give you the computer guidance you require.

Do you have access to CompuServe or the World Wide Web? Then check out our CompuServe forum by typing **GO SAMS** at any prompt. If you prefer the World Wide Web, check out our site at http://www.mcp.com.

> **NOTE**
>
> If you have a technical question about this book, call the technical support line at (800) 571-5840, ext. 3668.

As the publishing manager of the group that created this book, I welcome your comments. You can fax, e-mail, or write me directly to let me know what you did or didn't like about this book—as well as what we can do to make our books stronger. Here's the information:

Fax: 317/581-4669

E-mail: enterprise_mgr@sams.mcp.com

Mail: Rosemarie Graham
           Publishing Manager
           Sams Publishing
           201 W. 103rd Street
           Indianapolis, IN 46290

Introduction

Many excellent books about Access are available. So why write another one? While talking to the many students that I meet in my travels around the country, I have heard one common complaint. Instead of the several great books available for the user community or the host of wonderful books available for expert Access developers, my students yearn for a book targeted toward the intermediate to advanced *developer*. They yearn for a book that starts at the beginning, ensures that they have no gaps in their knowledge, and takes them through some of the most advanced aspects of Access development. Along the way, they want to be provided with volumes of practical code that they easily can port into their own applications. *Alison Balter's Mastering Access 97 Development*, Second Edition is specifically written with those requests in mind.

This book begins by providing you with an introduction to Access development. It alerts you to the types of applications that can be developed in Access and introduces you to the components of an Access application. After you understand what an Access application is and when it is appropriate to develop one, you explore the steps involved in building an actual Access application. Several strategies are covered before the first application component is built. This ensures that you, as the developer of the application, are aware of the design issues that might affect you in your particular environment.

After you discover the overall picture, you are ready to venture into the specific details of each object in an Access database. Chapters 3 through 7 cover the basics of tables, relationships, queries, forms, and reports. These chapters provide you with an approach to developing these database objects from a developer's perspective. Although this text starts at the beginning, it provides you with many tips, tricks, and caveats not readily apparent from the documentation or from books targeted toward end-users.

After you have a strong foundation of knowledge on how to build tables, queries, forms, and reports, you are ready to plunge into coding full-force. Chapters 8 through 10 provide you with an extremely strong grasp of the VBA language. Once again, starting with the basics, you are gently taken to the most complex intricacies of the VBA language and Access object model. Many practical examples are provided in the text to ensure that you thoroughly digest each topic.

Chapter 11 introduces you to macros. Because this book is targeted toward developers, this chapter is the only one in which macros are discussed. The chapter focuses on why you as a developer might opt or need to use macros to complete certain tasks.

Chapters 12 through 14 provide you with an advanced discussion of queries, forms, and reports. By the time you reach this point in the text, you should be familiar with all the basics of creating database objects. These chapters combine the basics of table, query, form, and report design with the VBA and object techniques covered in Chapters 8 through 10. The power techniques covered in Chapters 12 through 14 provide you with the expertise you need in order to design the most complex types of queries, forms, and reports required by your applications.

Before you are ready to ride through the frontier of the many intricacies of the Access development environment, one basic topic remains. Chapter 15 introduces you to data access objects. After reading Chapter 15, you will see how you can move away from bound objects, manipulating the data in your database using code.

Unfortunately, things don't always go as planned. No matter what your level of expertise, you often will find yourself stumped over a piece of code and looking for answers. Chapter 16 shows you how to effectively employ the debugger to solve any coding problems you might have. Every aspect of the debugger is covered here. Even after your application has been thoroughly debugged, you still must responsibly provide a means by which errors are handled in your application. Chapter 17 shows you everything you need to know to implement error handling in your application. Included in the text and on the sample code CD-ROM is a generic error handler that you easily can build into any of your own applications.

With the foundation provided by the first 17 chapters, you are ready to move into the more rich and complex aspects of the VBA language and the Access development environment. Chapters 18 through 24 cover all aspects of developing applications for a multiuser or client/server environment. You explore locking strategies, how to interact with non-native Access file formats, and how to use ODBC to design client/server applications. Transaction processing, application optimization, and replication also are covered in these chapters.

As an Access developer, your world is not limited to just Access. To be effective and productive as an Access developer, you must know how to interact with other applications and how to use ActiveX controls, libraries, menu add-ins, wizards, and builders to assist you with the application development process. Chapters 25 through 30 cover OLE, using ActiveX controls, Access and the Internet, managing application development with Visual SourceSafe, and library and add-in techniques. After reading these chapters, you will understand how to use external objects and functionality to add richness to your applications without too much effort on your part.

At last, you are ready to put the final polish on your application. Chapters 31 through 37 cover the Windows API, security, documentation, maintenance, help, and distribution. You learn how to properly secure your application so that the investment you have put into the application development process is not compromised in any way. You also discover how easy it is to put into your application the final touches that provide it with a professional polish and make it stand out from the rest.

The Access development environment is robust and exciting. With the keys to deliver all that it offers, you can produce applications that provide you with much satisfaction as well as many financial rewards. After poring over this hands-on guide and keeping it nearby for handy reference, you too can become masterful at Access 97 development. This book is dedicated to demonstrating how you can fulfill the promise of making Access 97 perform up to its lofty capabilities. As you will see, you have the ability to really make Access 97 shine in the everyday world!

Building a Foundation for Your Access Applications

CHAPTER

1

Introduction to Access Development

- What Types of Applications Can You Develop in Access?, 4
- What Exactly Is a Database?, 7
- Getting to Know the Database Objects, 7
- Object Naming Conventions, 15
- Hardware Requirements, 16
- How Do I Get Started Developing an Access Application?, 17

What Types of Applications Can You Develop in Access?

I often find myself explaining exactly what types of applications can be built with Microsoft Access. Access offers a variety of features for different database needs. It can be used to develop five general types of applications:

- Personal applications
- Applications used to run a small business
- Departmental applications
- Corporation-wide applications
- As a front-end for enterprise-wide client/server applications

Access as a Development Platform for Personal Applications

At its most basic level, Access can be used to develop simple personal database-management systems. I caution people against this idea, though. People who buy Access hoping to auto-mate everything from their wine collections to their home finances are often disappointed. The problem is that Access is deceptively easy to use. Its wonderful built-in wizards make Access look like a product anyone can use. After answering a series of questions, you have a finished application—switchboards, data-entry screen, reports, and all. In fact, when Access was first released, many people asked if I was concerned that my business as a computer programmer and trainer would diminish because Access seemed to let absolutely anyone write a database application. Although it's true that the simplest of Access applications can be produced without any thought of design and without a single line of code written by the user, most applications require at least some designing and custom code.

As long as you're satisfied with a wizard-generated personal application with only minor modifications, no problems should occur. It's when you want to substantially customize a personal application that problems can happen.

Access as a Development Platform for Small-Business Applications

Access is an excellent platform for developing an application that can run a small business. Its wizards let developers quickly and easily build the application's foundation, the ability to build code modules allows developers to create code libraries of reusable functions, and the ability to add code behind forms and reports allows them to create powerful custom forms and reports.

The main limitation of using Access for developing a custom small-business application is the time and money involved in the development process. Many people use Access Wizards to begin the development process but find they need to customize their application in ways they can't accomplish on their own, and small-business owners often have this problem on an even greater scale. The demands of a small-business application are usually much higher than those of a personal application. I have been called in many times after a doctor, attorney, or other professional reaches a dead-end in the development process. They're always dismayed at how much money it costs to make their application usable.

Access as a Development Platform for Departmental Applications

Access is perfect for developing applications for departments in large corporations. It's relatively easy to upgrade departmental users to the appropriate hardware—for example, it's much easier to buy additional RAM for 15 users than it is for 4,000! Furthermore, Access's performance is adequate for most departmental applications without the need for client/server technology. Finally, most departments in large corporations have the development budgets to produce well-designed applications.

Fortunately, most departments usually have a PC guru who is more than happy to help design forms and reports. This gives the department a sense of ownership, since they have contributed to the development of their application. It also makes my life as a developer much easier. I can focus on the hard-core development issues, leaving some of the simpler tasks to the local talent.

Access as a Development Platform for Corporation-Wide Applications

Although Access might be best suited for departmental applications, it can also be used to produce applications that are distributed throughout the organization. How successful this endeavor is depends on the corporation. There's a limit to the number of users who can concurrently share an Access application while maintaining acceptable performance, and there's also a limit to the number of records that each table can contain without a significant performance drop. These numbers vary depending on factors such as the following:

- How much traffic already exists on the network.
- How much RAM and how many processors the server has.
- What the server is already being used for; for example, are applications such as Microsoft Office being loaded from the server or from local workstations?
- What types of tasks the users of the application are performing; are they querying, entering data, running reports, and so on?
- Where Access and your Access application are run from (the server or the workstation).
- What network operating system is in place.

My general rule of thumb for an Access application that's not client/server is that with more than 10–15 concurrent users and more than 100,000 records, poor performance generally results. Remember, this number varies immensely depending on the factors mentioned, as well as on the definition of acceptable performance by you and your users.

Developers often misunderstand what Access is and what it isn't when it comes to client/server. I'm often asked "Isn't Access client/server?" The answer is that Access is an unusual product because it's a file server application out of the box, but it can act as a front-end to a client/server database. In case you're lost, here's an explanation: If you buy Access and develop an application that stores the data on a file server in an Access database, all data processing is performed on the workstation. This means that every time the user runs a query or report, all the data is brought over to the workstation. The query is then run on the workstation machine, and the results are displayed in a datasheet or on a report. This process generates a significant amount of network traffic, particularly if multiple users are running reports and queries at the same time on large Access tables. In fact, such operations can bring the entire network to a crawl.

A client/server database, such as Microsoft SQL Server or Oracle, processes queries on the server machine and returns results to the workstation. The server software itself can't display data to the user, so this is where Access comes to the rescue. Acting as a front-end, Access can display the data retrieved from the database server in reports, datasheets, or forms. If the data is updated by the user in an Access form, the update is sent to the back-end database. This is all generally done by linking to these external databases so that they appear to both you and the user as Access tables. This process is covered in detail in Chapter 20, "Client/Server Techniques."

Access as a Development Platform for Enterprise-Wide Client/Server Applications

When you reduce the volume of network traffic by moving the processing of queries to the back-end, Access becomes a much more powerful development solution. When data isn't stored in an Access database, and is instead stored on a database server, Access can serve quite well as the front-end to a system with huge volumes of data and many concurrent users. The main issue usually faced by developers who want to deploy such a widescale Access application is the type of hardware each user has. Although processing queries is done at the server, which significantly reduces network traffic, the application itself still must reside in the memory of each user's PC. The hardware requirements for an Access application are covered later in this chapter. Before you decide to deploy a widescale Access application, you need to know the hardware configurations of all your system's users.

Access as a Scalable Product

One of Access's biggest strong points is its scalability. An application that begins as a small-business application running on a standalone machine can be scaled to an enterprise-wide client/server application. If you design your application properly, scaling can be done with little to no rewriting of your application. This feature makes Access an excellent choice for growing businesses, as well as for applications being tested at a departmental level with the idea that they might eventually be distributed corporation-wide.

The great thing about Access is that even acting as both the front-end and back-end with data stored on a file server in Access tables, it still provides excellent security and the ability to establish database rules previously available only on back-end databases. As you will see in Chapters 32, "Database Security Made Easy," and 33, "Complex Security Issues," security can be assigned to every object in a database at either a user or group level. Referential integrity rules can be applied at the database level, ensuring that orders aren't entered for customers who don't exist. Data validation rules can be enforced at either a field or record level, maintaining the integrity of the data in your database. In other words, many of the features previously available only on high-end database servers are now available by using Access's own proprietary data-storage format.

What Exactly Is a Database?

The term *database* means different things to different people. For many years, in the world of xBase (dBASE, FoxPro, CA-Clipper), *database* was used to describe a collection of fields and records. In a client/server environment, *database* refers to all the data, schema, indexes, rules, triggers, and stored procedures associated with a system. In Access terms, a database is a collection of all the tables, queries, forms, reports, macros, and modules that compose a complete system.

Getting to Know the Database Objects

Access databases are made up of tables, queries, forms, reports, macros, and modules. Each of these objects has its own special function. The Access environment also consists of several miscellaneous objects, including relationships, command bars, database properties, and import/export specifications. With these objects, you can create a powerful, user-friendly, integrated application. Figure 1.1 shows the Access Database window. Notice the six tabs, one for each main type of object in a database. The following sections take you on a tour of the objects that make up an Access database.

Figure 1.1.

The Access Database window, with tabs for each type of database object.

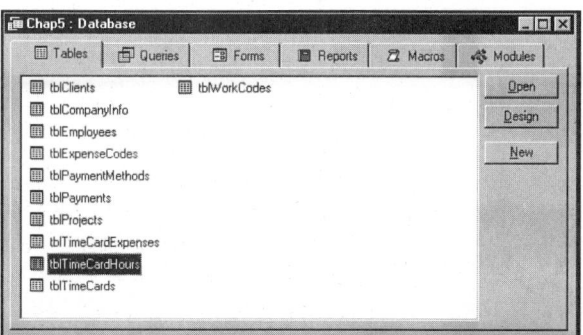

Tables: A Repository for Your Data

Tables are the starting point for your application. Whether your data is stored in the Access format or you are referencing external data by using linked tables, all the other objects in your database either directly or indirectly reference your tables.

To view all the tables that are part of your database, click on the Tables tab of the Database window. If you want to view the data in a table, double-click on the name of the table you want to view (you can also select the table, then click the Open button). The table's data is displayed in a datasheet, which includes all the table's fields and records. (See Figure 1.2.) Notice that you can modify many of the datasheet's attributes and that you can search for and filter data from within the datasheet. These techniques aren't covered in this book but can be found in the Access user manual or any introductory Access book, such as *Teach Yourself Access 97 in 14 Days*.

Figure 1.2.

Datasheet view of the tblTimeCardHours table.

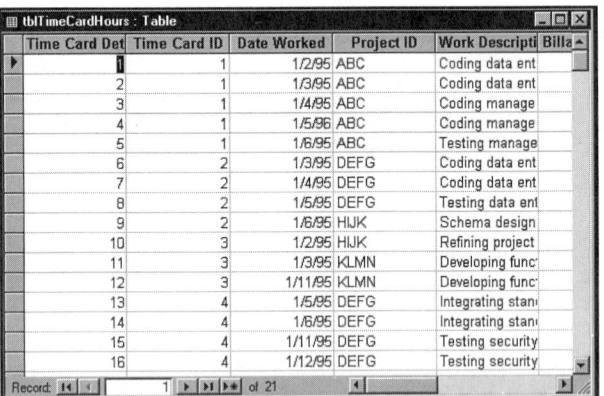

As a developer, you most often want to view the table's design, which is the blueprint or template for the table. To view a table's design, click Design with the table selected. (See Figure 1.3.) In Design view, you can view or modify all the field names, data types, and field and table properties. Access gives you the power and flexibility you need to customize the design of your tables. These topics are covered in Chapter 3, "What Every Developer Needs to Know About Tables."

Relationships: Tying the Tables Together

To properly maintain your data's integrity and ease the process of working with other objects in the database, you must define relationships among the tables in your database. This can be done by using the Relationships window. To view the Relationships window, choose Tools | Relationships or click Relationships on the toolbar. (See Figure 1.4.) In this window, you can view and maintain the relationships in the database. If you or a fellow developer have set up some relationships, but you don't see any in the Relationships dialog box, choose Relationships | Show All to reveal any hidden tables and relationships.

Figure 1.3.
The design of the tblTimeCardHours table.

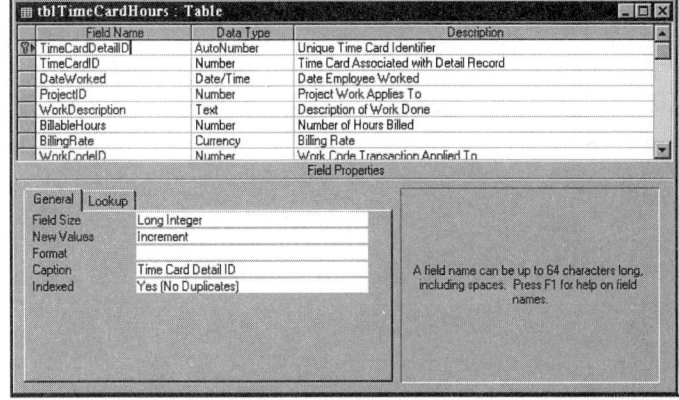

Figure 1.4.
The Relationships window, where you view and maintain the relationships in the database.

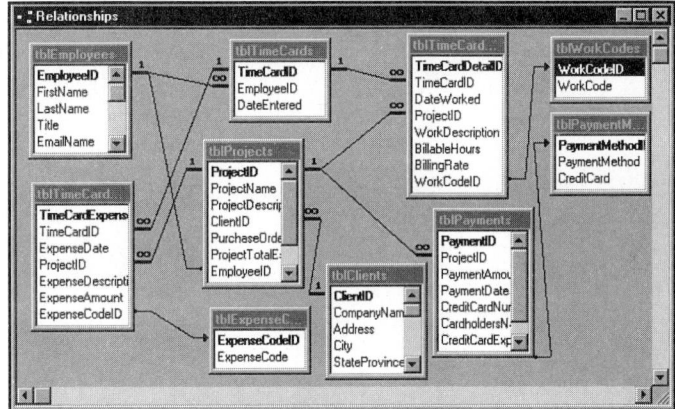

Notice that many of the relationships in Figure 1.4 have a join line between tables with a number *1* and an infinity symbol. This indicates a one-to-many relationship between the tables. If you double-click on the join line, the Relationships dialog box opens. (See Figure 1.5.) In this dialog box, you can specify the exact nature of the relationship between tables. The relationship between tblClients and tblProjects, for example, is a one-to-many relationship with referential integrity enforced. This means that projects can't be added for clients who don't exist. Notice that the checkboxes to Cascade Update Related Fields and Cascade Delete Related Records are both checked. This means that if a client is deleted, its projects are deleted, too; for example, if a ClientID is updated in tblClients, all records containing that ClientID in tblProjects are automatically updated.

Figure 1.5.

The Relationships dialog box, which lets you specify the nature of the relationship between tables.

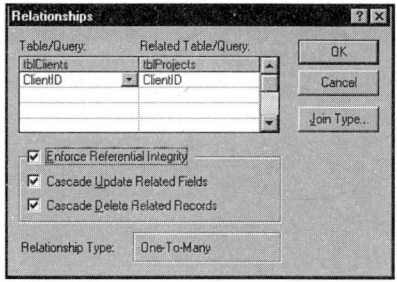

Chapter 4, "Relationships: Your Key to Data Integrity," extensively covers the process of defining and maintaining relationships. For now, remember that relationships should be established both conceptually and literally as early in the design process as possible. They are integral to successfully designing and implementing your application.

Queries: Stored Questions or Actions to be Applied to Your Data

Queries in Access are powerful and multifaceted. Select queries allow you to view, summarize, and perform calculations on the data in your tables. Action queries let you add to, update, and delete table data. To run a query, select the Queries tab, choose the query you want to run, and then click Open. A datasheet appears, containing all the fields specified in the query and all the records meeting the query's criteria. (See Figure 1.6.) In general, the data in a query result can be updated because the result of a query is actually a dynamic set of records, called a *dynaset*, based on your tables' data.

Figure 1.6.

The result of running the qryCustomerOrderInfo query.

Country	City	Order Date	Unit Price	Quantity	TotalPrice
Germany	Berlin	22-Aug-94	$45.60	15	$684.00
Germany	Berlin	22-Aug-94	$18.00	21	$378.00
Germany	Berlin	22-Aug-94	$12.00	2	$24.00
Germany	Berlin	13-Mar-95	$25.00	16	$400.00
Germany	Berlin	13-Mar-95	$45.60	2	$91.20
Germany	Berlin	30-Sep-94	$43.90	20	$878.00
Germany	Berlin	12-Jan-95	$55.00	15	$825.00
Germany	Berlin	12-Jan-95	$13.00	2	$26.00
Germany	Berlin	06-Apr-95	$13.25	40	$530.00
Germany	Berlin	06-Apr-95	$21.50	20	$430.00
Germany	Berlin	10-Oct-94	$10.00	6	$60.00
Germany	Berlin	10-Oct-94	$18.00	15	$270.00
Mexico	México D.F.	25-Nov-94	$32.00	10	$320.00
Mexico	México D.F.	01-Mar-95	$21.00	2	$42.00

Record: 1 of 2155

When you store a query, only its definition, layout or formatting properties, and datasheet are actually stored in the database. Access offers an intuitive, user-friendly tool for you to design your queries. Figure 1.7 shows the Query Design window. To open this window, select the Queries tab, choose the query you want to modify, and click Design. The query pictured in the figure selects data from tblClients, tblProjects, and tblTimeCardHours. It groups the query results by client name, displaying the name of each client and the amount of sales generated from the client within a certain period of time. This special type of query is called a *parameter query*. It prompts for criteria at runtime, using the criteria to determine what records are included in the output. Queries are covered in Chapters 5, "What Every Developer Needs to Know About Query Basics," and 12, "Advanced Query Concepts." Because queries are the foundation for most forms and reports, they're covered throughout this book as they apply to other objects in the database.

Figure 1.7.

The design of a query that displays data from the tblClients, tblProjects, and tblTimeCardHours tables.

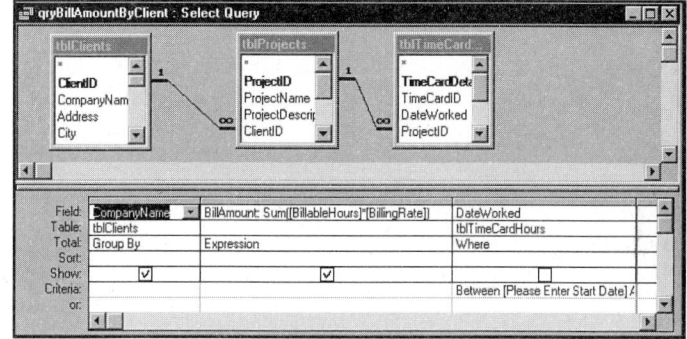

Forms: A Means of Displaying, Modifying, and Adding Data

Although you can enter and modify data in a table's Datasheet view, you can't control the user's actions very well, nor can you do much to facilitate data entry. This is where forms come in. Access forms can take on many traits, and they're very flexible and powerful.

To view any form, select the Forms tab, choose the form you want to view, and then click Open. Figure 1.8 illustrates a data-entry form in Form view. This form is actually three forms in one: one main form and two subforms. The main form displays information from the Time Cards table, and the subforms display information from the Time Card Hours table and the Time Card Expenses table. A combo box is used to help select the employee associated with a particular time card.

Figure 1.8.

The Time Cards data-entry form includes time worked and expenses for an employee in a given time period.

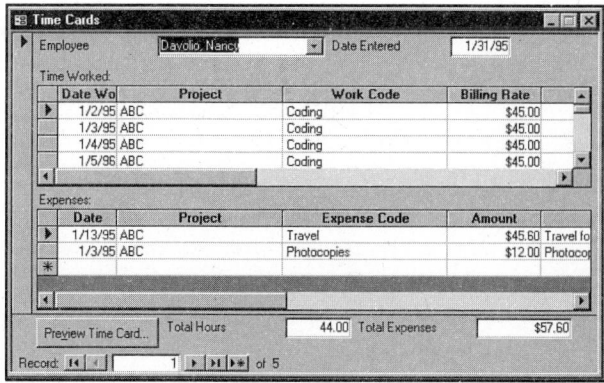

Like tables and queries, forms can also be viewed in Design view. To view the design of a form, select the Forms tab, choose the form whose design you want to modify, and then click Design. Figure 1.9 shows the Time Cards form in Design view. Notice the two subforms within the main form. The main form has three sections: Form Header, Detail, and Form Footer. Nothing is contained in the header; most of this form's content is in the Detail section. The Form Footer, which isn't visible in the figure, has a command button that lets the user preview a printed time card with all the information on the form. Forms are covered in more detail in Chapters 6, "What Every Developer Needs to Know About Form Basics," and 13, "Let's Get More Intimate with Forms: Advanced Techniques." They're also covered throughout the text as they apply to other examples of building an application.

Figure 1.9.

The design of the Time Cards form, showing two subforms.

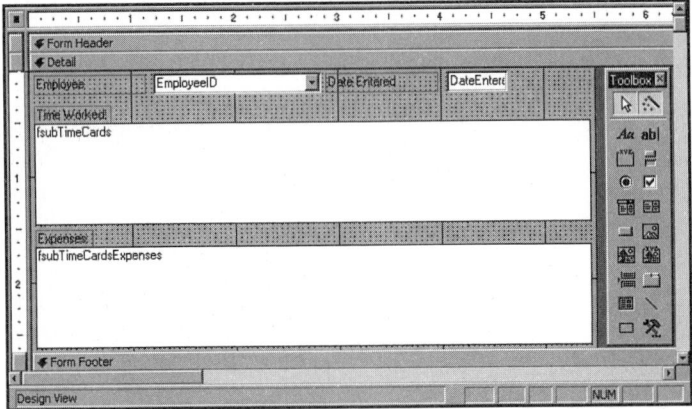

Reports: Turning Data Into Information

Forms allow you to enter and edit information, but with reports, you can display information, usually to a printer. Figure 1.10 shows a report being previewed. To preview any report, select the Reports tab, choose the report you want to preview, and then click Preview. Notice the graphic in the report, as well as other details, such as the thick horizontal line. Like forms, reports can be elaborate and exciting yet contain valuable information.

If you haven't guessed yet, reports can be viewed in Design view, as shown in Figure 1.11. To view the design of any report, select the Reports tab and click Design after selecting the report you want to view. Figure 1.11 illustrates a report with many sections; you can see a Report Header, Page Header, TimeCardID Group Header, and Detail section—just a few of the many sections available on a report. Just as a form can contain subforms, a report can contain subreports. The Detail section of this report has two subreports, one for hours and the other for expenses. Reports are covered in Chapters 7, "What Every Developer Needs to Know About Report Basics," and 14, "Let's Get More Intimate with Reports: Advanced Techniques," and throughout the book as they apply to other examples.

Figure 1.10.

A preview of the Time Sheet report.

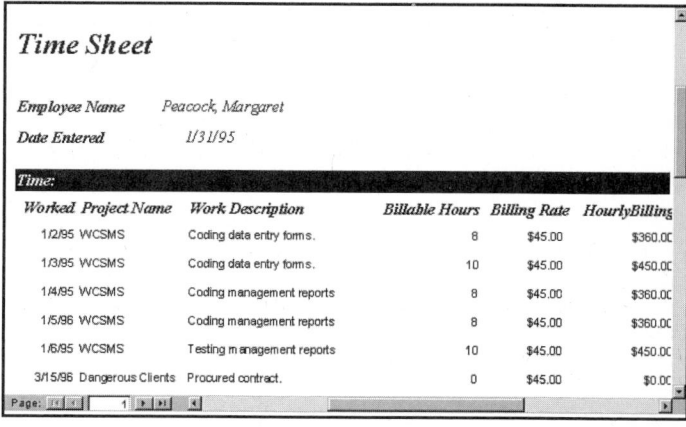

Figure 1.11.

The Report Design view of the Time Sheet report.

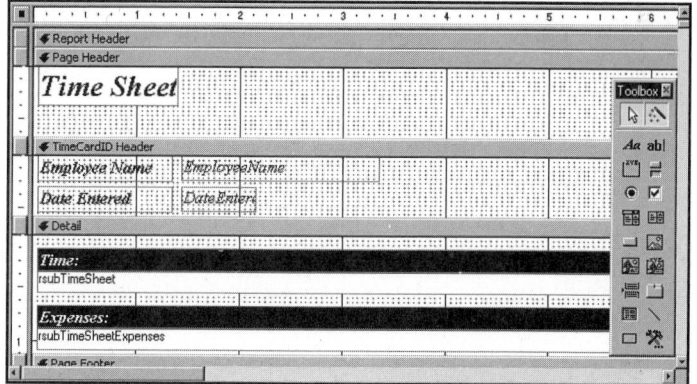

Macros: A Means of Automating Your System

Macros in Access aren't like the macros in other languages. They can't be recorded, as they can in Microsoft Word or Excel. With Access macros, you can perform most of the tasks you can manually perform from the keyboard, menus, and toolbars, and they provide for conditions, allowing you to build logic into your application flow. Generally, you use VBA (Visual Basic for Applications) code contained in modules, rather than macros, to do the tasks your application must perform because VBA code modules give you more flexibility and power than macros do. However, certain tasks can be performed only by using macros, so most applications include a few macros. Chapter 11, "What Are Macros and When Do You Need Them?" covers macros and their uses in detail.

To run a macro, select the Macros tab, click on the macro you want to run, then click Run. The actions in the macro are then executed. To view a macro's design, select the Macros tab, select the macro you want to modify, and click Design to open the Macro Design window.

(See Figure 1.12.) The macro pictured has four columns. The first column is the Macro Name column where you can specify the name of a subroutine within a macro. The second column allows you to specify a condition. The action in the macro's third column won't execute unless the condition for that action evaluates to true. The fourth column lets you document the macro. In the bottom half of the Macro Design window, you specify the arguments that apply to the selected action. In Figure 1.12, the selected action is `MsgBox`, which accepts four arguments: `Message`, `Beep`, `Type`, and `Title`.

Figure 1.12.

The design of the Customers macro, containing macro names, conditions, actions, and comments.

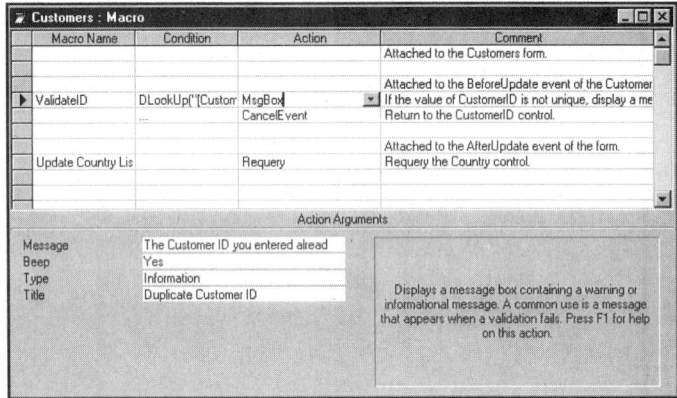

Modules: The Foundation to the Application Development Process

Modules, the foundation of any application, let you create libraries of functions that can be used throughout your application. Modules are usually made up of subroutines and functions. Functions always return a value; subroutines do not. By using Code modules, you can do the following:

- Perform error handling
- Declare and use variables
- Loop through and manipulate recordsets
- Call Windows API and other library functions
- Create and modify system objects, such as tables and queries
- Perform transaction processing
- Perform many functions not available with macros
- Test and debug complex processes
- Create library databases

These are just a few of the tasks you can accomplish with modules. To view the design of an existing module, select the Modules tab, choose the module you want to modify, and click Design to open the Module Design window. (See Figure 1.13.) The module in Figure 1.13

contains a General Declarations section and one function called IsLoaded. Modules and VBA are discussed in Chapters 8, "VBA 101: The Basics of VBA," and 9, "Advanced VBA Techniques," and are covered extensively throughout this book.

Figure 1.13.
The Global Code module in Design view, showing the General Declarations section and IsLoaded function.

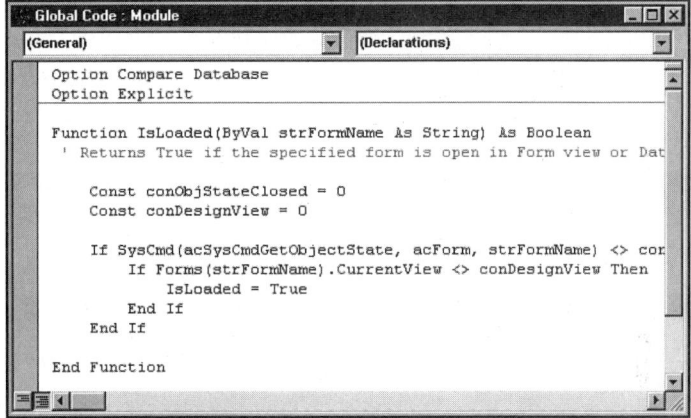

```
Global Code : Module                                              _ □ X
(General)                        ▼   (Declarations)                    ▼
Option Compare Database
Option Explicit

Function IsLoaded(ByVal strFormName As String) As Boolean
    ' Returns True if the specified form is open in Form view or Dat

        Const conObjStateClosed = 0
        Const conDesignView = 0

        If SysCmd(acSysCmdGetObjectState, acForm, strFormName) <> con
            If Forms(strFormName).CurrentView <> conDesignView Then
                    IsLoaded = True
            End If
        End If

End Function
```

Object Naming Conventions

Finding a set of naming conventions—and sticking to it—is one of the keys to successful development in Access or any other programming language. When you're choosing a set of naming conventions, look for three characteristics:

- Ease of use
- Readability
- Acceptance in the developer community

The Leszynski naming convention, proposed by Stan Leszynski of Leszynski Company, Inc., and Kwery Corporation, is by far the best set of naming conventions currently published in the development world.

The Leszynski naming conventions supply a standardized approach for naming objects. They were derived from the Leszynski/Reddick naming conventions that were prominent in Access versions 1.x and 2.0. These standards were adopted and used extensively by the development community and can be found in most good development books and magazine articles written in the past couple of years. The new Leszynski naming conventions have been revised to deal with issues faced by people developing concurrently in Access, Visual Basic, Excel, and other Microsoft products that use the VBA language. These conventions give you an easy-to-use, consistent methodology for naming the objects in all these environments.

A summarized and slightly modified version of the Leszynski conventions for naming objects is published in Appendix B, "Naming Conventions." I'll be using them throughout the book and highlighting certain aspects of them as they apply in each chapter.

Hardware Requirements

One of the downsides of Access is the amount of hardware resources it requires. The requirements for a developer are different from those for an end-user, so I have broken the system requirements into two parts. As you read through these requirements, be sure to note actual versus recommended requirements.

What Hardware Does Your System Require?

According to Microsoft documentation, these are the *official* minimum requirements to run Microsoft Access 7.0 for Windows 95:

- 386DX processor (486 recommended)
- Windows 95 or Windows NT 3.51 or later
- 12M of RAM on a Windows 95 machine, 16M of RAM on a Windows NT machine
- VGA or higher resolution (SVGA 256-color recommended)
- pointing device

As if all that hardware isn't enough, my personal recommendations for a development machine are much higher because you'll probably be running other applications along with Microsoft Access. You also want to greatly reduce the chance of hanging or other problems caused by low-memory conditions. I recommend the following for a development machine (in addition to Microsoft's requirements):

- 486 or higher processor (Pentium or Pentium Pro, if possible)
- 20M of RAM for Windows 95, 24M for Windows NT (or even higher if you like to run multiple applications simultaneously)
- high-resolution monitor—the larger, the better, and SVGA if possible

> **WARNING**
>
> A word of caution: If you're developing on a high-resolution monitor, you should design your forms so that they will display properly on a low-resolution monitor. Although you can take advantage of the high-resolution in your development endeavors, don't forget that many of your users will be running your application on a 640×480 display.

The bottom line for hardware is the more, the better. You just can't have enough memory. The more you have, the happier you will be using Access.

What Hardware Does the User's System Require?

Although the user's PC doesn't need to be as sophisticated as the developer's, I still recommend the following in addition to Microsoft's requirements:

- 486 or higher processor
- 16M of RAM for Windows 95, 20M for Windows NT (or even higher if your application supports OLE or your user will be running your application along with other programs)

How Do I Get Started Developing an Access Application?

Many developers believe that because Access is such a rapid application-development environment, there's absolutely no need for system analysis or design when creating an application. I couldn't disagree more. As mentioned earlier in this chapter, Access applications are deceptively easy to create, but without proper planning, they can become a disaster.

Task Analysis

The first step in the development process is *task analysis*, or considering each and every process that occurs during the user's workday—a cumbersome but necessary task. When I first started working for a large corporation as a mainframe programmer, I was required to carefully follow a task-analysis checklist. I had to find out what each user of the system did to complete his or her daily tasks, document each procedure and determine the flow of each task to the next, relate each task of each user to his or her other tasks as well as to the tasks of every other user of the system, and tie each task to corporate objectives. In this day and age of rapid application development and changing technology, this step in the development process seems to have gone out the window. I maintain that if care isn't taken to complete this process at least at some level, the developer will have to rewrite large parts of the application.

Data Analysis and Design

After you have analyzed and documented all the tasks involved in the system, you're ready to work on the data analysis and design phase of your application. In this phase, you must identify each piece of information needed to complete each task. These data elements must be assigned to subjects, and each subject will become a separate table in your database. For example, a subject might be a client; then every data element relating to that client would become a field in the client table. The name, address, phone, credit limit, and any other pertinent information about the client would become fields within the client table.

You should determine the following for each data element:

- Appropriate data type
- Required size
- Validation rules

You should also determine whether each data element can be updated and whether it's entered or calculated; then you can figure out whether your table structures are normalized.

Normalization Made Easy

Normalization is a fancy term for the process of testing your table design against a series of rules that ensure your application will operate as efficiently as possible. These rules are based on set theory and were originally proposed by Dr. E. F. Codd. Although you could spend years studying normalization, its main objective is to make sure you have an application that runs efficiently, with as little data manipulation and coding as possible. Here are six of the rules:

1. Fields should be atomic; that is, each piece of data should be broken down as much as possible. For example, rather than creating a field called Name, you would create two fields: one for the first name and the other for the last name. This method makes the data much easier to work with. If you need to sort or search by first name separately from the last name, for example, you can do so without any extra effort.

2. Each record should contain a unique identifier so that you have a way of safely identifying the record. For example, if you're changing customer information, you can make sure you're changing the information associated with the correct customer. This unique identifier is called a *primary key.*

3. The primary key is a field or fields that uniquely identify the record. Sometimes you can assign a natural primary key. For example, the social security number in an employee table should serve to uniquely identify that employee to the system. At other times, you might need to create a primary key. Because two customers could have the same name, for example, the customer name might not uniquely identify the customer to the system. It might be necessary to create a field that would contain a unique identifier for the customer, such as a customer ID.

4. A primary key should be short, stable, and simple. Short means it should be small in size (not a 50-character field); stable means the primary key should be a field whose value rarely, if ever, changes. For example, although a customer ID would rarely change, a company name is much more likely to change. Simple means it should be easy for a user to work with.

5. Every field in a table should supply additional information about the record the primary key serves to identify. For example, every field in the customer table describes the customer with a particular customer ID.

6. Information in the table shouldn't appear in more than one place. For example, the customer name shouldn't appear in more than one record.

Take a look at an example. The datasheet shown in Figure 1.14 is an example of a table that hasn't been normalized. Notice that the CustInfo field is repeated for each order, so if the customer address changes, it has to be changed in every order assigned to that customer. In other words, the CustInfo field is not atomic. If you want to sort by city, you're out of luck because the city is in the middle of the CustInfo field. If the name of an inventory item changes, you need to make the change in every record where that inventory item was ordered. Probably the worst problem in this example involves items ordered. With this design, you must create four fields for each item the customer orders: name, supplier, quantity, and price. This design would make it extremely difficult to build sales reports and other reports your users need to effectively run the business.

Figure 1.14.
A table that hasn't been normalized.

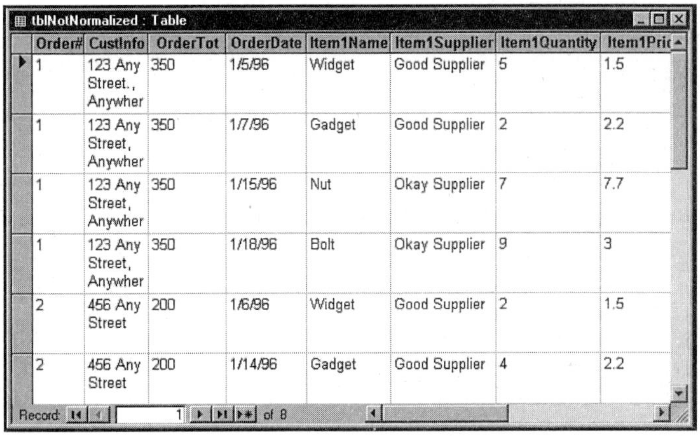

Order#	CustInfo	OrderTot	OrderDate	Item1Name	Item1Supplier	Item1Quantity	Item1Pric
1	123 Any Street., Anywher	350	1/5/96	Widget	Good Supplier	5	1.5
1	123 Any Street, Anywher	350	1/7/96	Gadget	Good Supplier	2	2.2
1	123 Any Street, Anywher	350	1/15/96	Nut	Okay Supplier	7	7.7
1	123 Any Street, Anywher	350	1/18/96	Bolt	Okay Supplier	9	3
2	456 Any Street	200	1/6/96	Widget	Good Supplier	2	1.5
2	456 Any Street	200	1/14/96	Gadget	Good Supplier	4	2.2

Figure 1.15 shows the same data normalized. Notice that it's been broken out into several different tables: tblCustomers, tblOrders, tblOrderDetails, and tblSuppliers. The tblCustomers table contains data that relates only to a specific customer. Each record is uniquely identified by a contrived CustID field, which is used to relate the orders table, tblOrders, to tblCustomers. The tblOrders table contains only information that applies to the entire order, rather than to a particular item that was ordered. This table contains the CustID of the customer who placed the order and the date of the order, and it's related to the tblOrderDetails table based on the OrderID. The tblOrderDetails table holds information about each item ordered for a particular OrderID. There's no limit to the potential number of items that can be ordered. As many items can be ordered as needed, simply by adding more records to the tblOrderDetails table. Finally, supplier information has been placed in a separate table, tblSuppliers, so that if any of the supplier information changes, it has to be changed in only one place.

Figure 1.15.

A table with a normalized design.

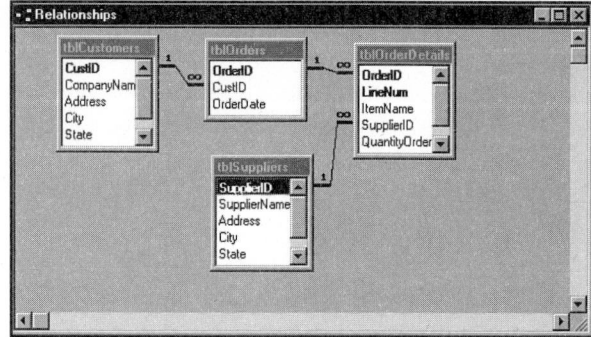

Prototyping

Although the task analysis and data analysis phases of application development haven't changed much since the days of mainframes, the prototyping phase has changed. In working with mainframes or DOS-based languages, it was important to develop detailed specifications for each screen and report. I remember requiring users to sign off on every screen and report. Even a change such as moving a field on a screen meant a change order and approval for additional hours. After the user signed off on the screen and report specifications, the programmers would work arduously for days to develop each screen and report. They would return to the user after many months only to hear that everything was wrong. This meant back to the drawing board for the developer and many additional hours before the user could once again review the application.

The process is quite different now. As soon as the tasks have been outlined and the data analysis finished, the developer can design the tables and establish relationships among them. The form and report prototype process can then begin. Rather than the developer working for weeks or months before having further interaction with the user, the developer needs only a few days, using the Access Wizards to quickly develop form prototypes.

Testing

As far as testing goes, you just can't do enough. I recommend that if your application is going to be run in both Windows 95 and Windows NT, you test in both environments. I also suggest you test your application extensively on the lowest common denominator piece of hardware—the application might run great on your machine but show unacceptable performance on your users' machines.

It usually helps to test your application both in pieces and as an integrated application. Recruit several people to test your application and make sure they range from the most savvy of users to the least computer-adept person you can find. These different types of users will probably find completely different sets of problems. Most important, make sure you're not the only tester of your application because you're the least likely person to find errors in your own programs.

Implementation

Your application is finally ready to go out into the world, or at least you hope so! Distribute your application to a subset of your users and make sure they know they're the test case. Make them feel honored to participate as the first users of the system, but warn them that problems might occur and it's their responsibility to make you aware of them. If you distribute your application on a widescale basis and it doesn't operate exactly as it should, it will be difficult to regain the confidence of your users. That's why it is so important to roll out your application slowly.

Maintenance

Because Access is such a rapid application-development environment, the maintenance period tends to be much more extended than the one for a mainframe or DOS-based application. Users are much more demanding; the more you give them, the more they want. For a consultant, this is great. Just don't get into a fixed-bid situation—you could very well end up on the losing end of that deal.

There are three categories of maintenance activities: bug fixes, specification changes, and frills. Bug fixes need to be handled as quickly as possible. The implications of specification changes need to be clearly explained to the user, including the time and cost involved in making the requested changes. As far as frills, try to involve the users as much as possible in adding frills by teaching them how to enhance forms and reports and by making the application as flexible and user-defined as possible. Of course, the final objective of any application is a happy group of productive users.

A Practical Example of Application Design: A Computer Consulting Firm

Your goal throughout this book is to build an application that will be a time and billing system for a computer consulting firm. First, look at the application from a design perspective.

The system will track client contacts and the projects associated with those clients. It will allow the users to record all hours billed to and expenses associated with each client and project. It will also let users track pertinent information about each employee or subcontractor. The tables in the system are based on the tables produced by the Database Wizard. They have been modified somewhat, and their names have been changed to follow the Leszynski naming conventions. The system you build will be far more powerful and flexible than the one supplied by the

Database Wizard. Ten tables will be included in the system. Some of these tables are built in Chapter 3, and they can all be found in the application databases on the sample code CD-ROM:

- **tblClients:** This table contains all the pertinent information about each client; it's related to tblProjects, the table that will track the information about each project associated with a client.

- **tblProjects:** This table holds all the pertinent information about each project; it's related to several other tables: tblClients, tblPayments, tblEmployees, tblTimeCardHours, and tblTimeCardExpenses.

- **tblTimeCardHours:** This table tracks the hours associated with each project and employee; it's related to tblProjects, tblTimeCards, and tblWorkCodes.

- **tblPayments:** This table tracks all payments associated with a particular project; it's related to tblProjects and tblPaymentMethods.

- **tblTimeCardExpenses:** This table tracks the expenses associated with each project and employee; it's related to tblProjects, tblTimeCards, and tblExpenseCodes.

- **tblEmployees:** This table tracks employee information; it's related to tblTimeCards and tblProjects.

- **tblTimeCards:** This table tracks each employee's hours; it's actually a bridge between the many-to-many relationship between Employees and Time Card Expenses, as well as between Employees and Time Card Hours, and it's related to tblEmployees, tblTimeCardHours, and tblTimeCardExpenses.

- **tblExpenseCodes:** This table is a lookup table for valid expense codes; it's related to tblTimeCardExpenses.

- **tblWorkCodes:** This table is a lookup table for valid work codes; it's related to tblTimeCardHours.

- **tblPaymentMethods:** This table is a lookup table for valid payment methods; it's related to tblPayments.

The relationships among the tables are covered in more detail in Chapter 4, but they're also shown in Figure 1.16.

Figure 1.16.

Relationships among tables in the Time and Billing system.

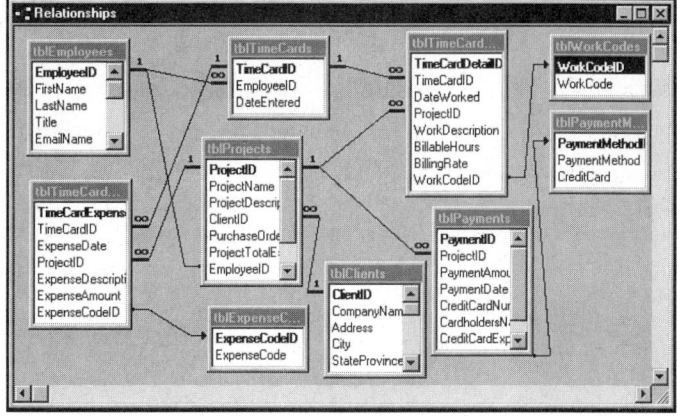

Summary

Before you learn about the practical aspects of Access development, you need to understand what Access is and how it fits into the application development world. Access is an extremely powerful product with a wide variety of uses; Access applications can be found on everything from the home PC to the desks of many corporate PC users going against enterprise-wide client/server databases.

Once you understand what Access is and what it does, you're ready to learn about its many objects. Access applications are made up of tables, queries, forms, reports, macros, modules, command bars, relationships, and other objects. When designed properly, an Access application effectively combines these objects to give the user a powerful, robust, utilitarian application.

2

A Strategy for Developing Access Applications

- Why Strategize?, 26
- Splitting Tables and Other Objects, 26
- Basing Forms and Reports on Queries, 28
- Understanding the Access Runtime Engine, 28
- EXE Versus Access Database: What It Means to You, 34
- The Importance of Securing Your Database, 34
- Using Access as a Front-End, 35
- Applying the Strategy to the Computer Consulting Firm Application, 38

Why Strategize?

You should know about several tricks of the trade that can save you a lot of time in the development process and help make sure your applications are as optimized as possible for performance. This chapter addresses these strategies and also explains several commonly misunderstood aspects of the Jet Engine, Access Runtime Engine, and security. All the topics covered in this chapter should be kept in mind when developing your Access applications. When reading this chapter, think of the general strategy outlined rather than the details of each topic. Each topic is covered in depth in later chapters of the book.

Splitting Tables and Other Objects

In a multiuser environment, it's almost imperative that the tables that make up your system be placed in one database and the rest of the system objects be placed in another database. For simplicity, I'll refer to the database containing the tables as the Table database and the database with the other objects as the Application database. The two databases are connected by linking from the Application database to the Table database. Here are the reasons for this strategy:

- Maintainability
- Performance
- Scalability

Assume for a moment that you distribute your application as one MDB file. Your users work with your application for a week or two, writing down all problems and changes. It's time for you to make modifications to your application. Meanwhile, live data has been entered into the application for two weeks. You make a copy of the database (which includes the live data) and make all the fixes and changes. This process takes a week. You're ready to install your copy of the database on the network. Now what? The users of the application have been adding, editing, and deleting records all week. Data replication, covered in Chapter 24, "Replication Made Easy," could help you with this problem.

The simplest solution is to split the database objects so that the tables (your data) are in one MDB file, and the rest of your database objects (your application) are in a second MDB file. When you're ready to install the changes, all you need to do is copy the Application database to the file server. The new Application database can then be installed on each client machine from the file server. In this way, users can run new copies of the application from their machines. The database containing your data tables remains intact and is unaffected by the process.

The second benefit of splitting the database objects has to do with performance. Your Table database obviously needs to reside on the network file server so the data can be shared among the system's users; however, there's no good reason why the other database components need to be shared. Access gives you optimal performance if the Application database is stored on each local machine. This method not only improves performance, but greatly reduces network traffic. If the Application database is stored on the file server, the application objects and code will need to be sent over the network each time an object in the database is opened. If the Application database is stored on each local machine, only the data will need to be sent over the network. The only complication of this scenario is that each time the Application database is updated, it will need to be redistributed to the users—a small inconvenience compared to the performance benefits gained from this structural split.

The third benefit of splitting tables from the other database objects has to do with scalability. Because the tables are already linked, it's easy to change from a link to a table stored in Access's own proprietary format to any ODBC database, such as Microsoft SQL Server. This capability gives you quick-and-dirty access to client/server databases. If you have already thought through your system's design with linked tables in mind, the transition will be that much easier. Don't be fooled, though, by how easy this sounds. There are many issues associated with using Access as a front-end to client/server data that go far beyond a matter of simply linking to the external tables. Some of these issues are covered in this chapter, and others are covered in Chapter 20, "Client/Server Techniques."

TIP

A few special types of tables should be stored in the Application database rather than the Table database. Tables that rarely change should be stored in the Application database on each user's local machine. For example, a State table rarely, if ever, changes, but it's continually accessed to populate combo boxes, participate in queries, and so on. Placing the State table on each local machine, therefore, improves performance and reduces network traffic.

Temporary tables should also be placed on each local machine—this is more a necessity than an option. If two users are running the same process at the same time and that process uses temporary tables, a conflict will occur when one user overwrites the other's temporary tables. Placing temporary tables on each local machine improves performance and eliminates the chance of potentially disastrous conflicts.

If you have already designed your application and included all the tables in the same database as the rest of your database objects, don't despair; Access 97 includes a Database Splitter Wizard. You can find this valuable tool by choosing Tools | Add-ins | Database Splitter. The Database Splitter, as well as linked tables, is covered in Chapter 19, "Using External Data."

NOTE

I split *all* the applications I build into two databases. However, you might notice when looking at the sample databases that none of them are split in the manner I recommend until Chapter 19. This is because until you learn all you need to know about splitting database objects, I don't think it's helpful to split the sample databases. Each chapter, from Chapter 19 on, uses the strategy recommended in this chapter.

Basing Forms and Reports on Queries

The record source for a form or report can be based on a table object, a query object, or an SQL statement. By basing forms and reports on stored queries, you can improve the performance and flexibility of your applications. In most cases, you don't need to display all fields and all records on a form or report. By basing a form or report on a query, you can better limit the data transferred over the network. These benefits are most pronounced in a client/server environment. When you base a form or report on a table object, Access sends an SQL statement that retrieves all fields and all records from the database server. On the other hand, if the record source for the form or report is a query, just the fields and records specified within the query are returned to the workstation.

Many developers don't realize that basing a form or report on a stored query is more efficient than basing it on an SQL statement. When you save a query, the Access database Jet Engine creates a Query Plan, which contains information on the most efficient method of executing the query. When the query is saved, the Jet Engine looks at the volume of data as well as available indexes, determines the optimal method of executing the query, and stores the method as the Query Plan. This plan is used whenever a form or report based on that query is executed. When a form or report is based on an SQL statement, the optimization process happens when the form or report is opened, and the Query Plan is executed on-the-fly.

When basing a form on table data, you can't control the order of the records in the form, nor can you base the form on more than one table. You can't limit the records displayed on the form until after the form is opened, unless you are using Access's OpenForm method with a Where argument. By basing a form on a query, you can control the criteria for the form as well as the default order in which the records are displayed. Everything just mentioned applies to reports as well, except the order of the records, which is determined by the sorting and grouping of the report itself.

> **TIP**
>
> Many other techniques are available to you when displaying a form based on a large record set. My favorite involves basing the form on only a single record at a time and changing the form's RecordSource property each time the user wants to view a different record. This technique, and others, are covered in detail in Chapter 13, "Let's Get More Intimate with Forms: Advanced Techniques."

Understanding the Access Runtime Engine

Many developers misunderstand what Access has to offer out of the box and what the Office Developer Edition (ODE) tools can add to the picture. They often tell me "I can't develop applications in Access because my company refuses to buy each user a copy of Access," or "I'm going to buy the ODE so that I can compile my applications with the ODE tools." These are just two of the many misconceptions about exactly what the ODE tools do and don't have to offer.

Features of the ODE

You no longer need to buy a separate product to create runtime versions of your Access applications. As a developer, you will likely buy the ODE, which includes a license for Office Professional plus all the features from the old Access Developer's Toolkit (ADT). An important feature of the ODE is a royalty-free distribution license that allows you to distribute unlimited copies of your Access application without your users having to own copies of Access. This means that by using the ODE tools, you can create applications you distribute to your users, who can run the application with the runtime engine you distribute to them. The ODE tools also include the following:

- *The Microsoft Access Language Reference* and *Microsoft Office 97 Data Access Reference.*
- A Setup Wizard that helps you create disks containing compressed files with everything you need to install and run your application. The Setup Wizard is covered in Chapter 37, "Distributing Your Application," and is pictured in Figure 2.1.

Figure 2.1.

The Setup Wizard used for application distribution.

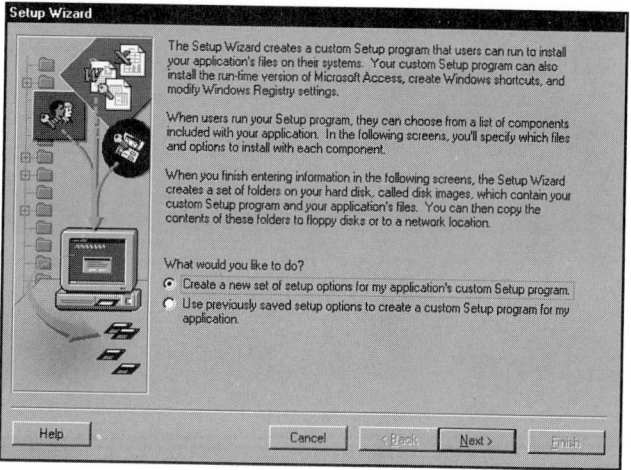

- A host of ActiveX custom controls that can be used to enhance your application's functionality and distributed to your users as part of your ODE license. ActiveX custom controls are covered in Chapter 26, "Using ActiveX Controls."
- The Microsoft Replication Manager helps you with the replication process by letting you schedule updates between replicas, determine which objects in the database are replicated, display all the replicas in a replica set, and manage multiple replica sets. The Replication Manager is covered in Chapter 24 and shown in Figure 2.2.

Figure 2.2.

The Replication Manager tool, used to help with the replication process.

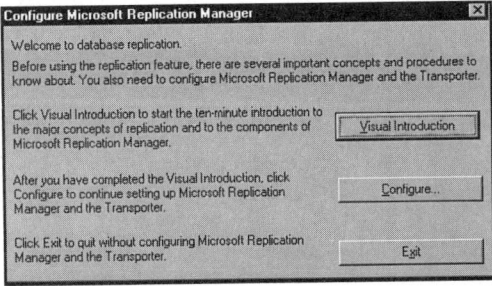

- The Windows 95 Help Compiler and accompanying documentation, covered in more depth in Chapter 36, "Developing a Help File."
- The Windows API Viewer has all the declares, constants, and type structures used with the 32-bit Windows application programming interface (API). It allows you to easily copy the function, constant, and type declarations into your Code modules. The Windows API Viewer is covered in Chapter 31, "Using External Functions: The Windows API," and shown in Figure 2.3.

Figure 2.3.

The Windows API Viewer with the declares, constants, and type structures required by API calls.

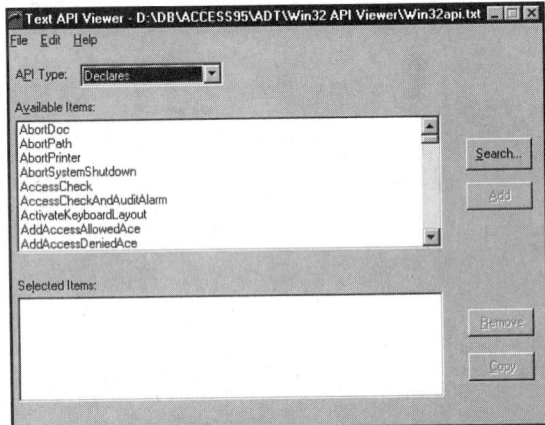

Differences Between the Standard and Runtime Versions of Access

It's important to understand the differences between the standard and runtime versions of Access. The following differences have definite implications for the way you develop any applications you expect to run from the runtime version:

- The Database, Macro, and Module windows aren't available in the runtime environment.
- No Design views are available in the runtime environment.
- No built-in toolbars are available in the runtime environment.

- Many windows, menus, and commands are invisible in the runtime environment. For example, the Window | Hide and Window | Unhide commands are invisible. Although these and other commands aren't visible, their functions are generally accessible by using code.
- You must build error handling into your runtime applications. If you don't, when an error occurs the application displays a standard Access dialog box, indicating an irrecoverable error, and then exits to the desktop.
- You must build your own custom help files for each runtime application.
- Some keystrokes aren't available in your application.

Some of the disabled features protect your applications. For example, the absence of the Database and Design windows means that your users can't modify your application while running it under Access's runtime version. Other disabled features translate into additional coding chores for you, such as the absence of command bars. If you want your application to offer toolbars, you have to build your own and then assign them to the forms and reports in your database.

Preparing an Application for Distribution

With all the features absent from the runtime version of Access, it's not surprising that you must take some special steps to prepare your application for distribution. Some of the steps are specific to running from the runtime version, but most are steps you'll probably want to take so your application seems professional to the user. There are six steps to prepare your application for distribution with the runtime version of Access:

- Basing your application around forms
- Adding start-up options to your database
- Securing the objects in your application
- Building error handling into your application
- Adding a help file to your application
- Building custom command bars to be associated with your application's forms and reports

Your application should be based on and controlled through forms. It should generally begin with a main switchboard that lets the user get to the other components of your application. The main switchboard can bring the user to additional switchboards, such as a data-entry switchboard, a report switchboard, or a maintenance switchboard. You can build switchboards by using an add-in called the Switchboard Manager or by designing them as custom dialog boxes. Building a switchboard as a custom dialog box is covered in Chapter 13, and using the Switchboard Manager to create switchboards is covered in Chapter 37. The main advantage of using the Switchboard Manager is that it lets you quickly and easily create a polished application interface, but the primary advantage of custom switchboards is the flexibility and freedom they offer.

You set a form as the starting point for your application by modifying the start-up options for your database. Set these options by choosing Tools | Startup to open the Startup dialog box. (See Figure 2.4.) In this dialog box, you can set start-up options, such as a start-up form, an application title, and an icon that appears when your application is minimized. These options are covered in detail in Chapter 37.

Figure 2.4.

The Startup dialog box lets you control many aspects of your application environment.

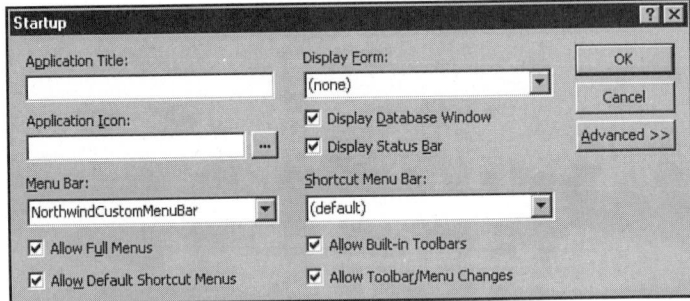

As you will learn in the next section, a database isn't secure just because you're running it from a runtime version of Access. Without security, your application can be modified by anyone with a full copy of Access, so securing your database objects is an important step in preparing your application for distribution. Security is covered in Chapters 32, "Database Security Made Easy," and 33, "Complex Security Issues."

In addition to security, Access 97 offers you the ability to remove the source code from your applications. This protects your intellectual property *and* improves the performance of your application. The resulting database is called an MDE (covered in Chapter 37).

If error handling isn't built into your application and an error occurs while your user is running your application from Access's runtime version, the user will be rudely exited out of the program. He or she won't get an appropriate error message and will be left wondering what happened, so it's essential that you add error handling to your application's procedures. Error handling is covered in Chapter 17, "Handling Those Dreaded Runtime Errors."

In most cases, you want your users to have custom help specific to your application. To add custom help to your application, you must build a help file, then attach parts of it to forms and controls in your application. Help files are covered in Chapter 36.

Finally, because built-in toolbars aren't available in the runtime version and most of the features on the standard built-in menus are disabled, you should build your own command bars associated with specific forms and reports. Creating custom command bars adds both polish and functionality to your application.

After you complete these steps, you'll be ready for the final phase of preparing your application for distribution, which includes the following:

- Test your application by using the /Runtime switch.
- Create setup disks or perform a network install with the Setup Wizard.
- Install your application on a machine that has never run a copy of either the standard or runtime version of Access.
- Test your application on the machine to make sure it runs as expected.

Before you bother running the Setup Wizard (a somewhat lengthy process), it's best that you run your application using the /Runtime switch. This switch simulates the runtime environment, allowing you to simulate user actions under the runtime version of Access. Taking this step saves you a lot of time and energy. It will find most, if not all, of the problems associated with running under the runtime version.

After you test your application with the /Runtime switch, you're ready to run the Setup Wizard, which lets you create setup disks or perform a network install. When your users are ready to install your application, they run the installation program by using A:Setup (or the appropriate network drive and path) to get a professional-looking, familiar setup program similar to those included with most Microsoft products.

After you run the Setup Wizard, you must test your application by running the install on a machine that has never had a copy of either the standard or runtime version of Access. I suggest you use a compression utility such as PKZIP to zip all the files in the test machine's Windows System directory or back up the entire Windows directory to another directory. Install and fully test your application; make sure you experiment with every feature. When you're done testing, delete everything but the zip file, then unzip the zip file into the Windows System directory (so that it holds all the files it contained before your program's installation). The whole idea is to test your application on a machine containing no Access-related files. This ensures that all the required files are included on your setup disks. After you test your application, restore the machine to its original state so that you can use it to test your next installation.

> **WARNING**
>
> Although this process cleans up much of what was changed as a result of installing the application, it doesn't fully restore the machine to its original state. This is because the registry is modified during the install process. If you want to *fully* restore the machine to its original state, you must back up the registry before the install and restore it once you're done testing the application.

PKZIP is a shareware utility you can get from PKWARE, Inc., and you must properly register the utility once you start using it. This involves sending the appropriate fee to PKWARE, Inc. in Brown Deer, Wisconsin. You can find out the fee and full address by typing PKZIP /? at the DOS prompt after switching to the correct directory.

The Access Runtime Engine: Summing It Up

You have just read an overview of the differences between the full and runtime versions of Access. The process of preparing an application for distribution with the runtime version of Access is covered in detail in Chapter 37. If you plan to distribute an application with the runtime version of Access, remember which features will be available to your users; otherwise, you and your users will be in for some big surprises.

EXE Versus Access Database: What It Means to You

Many developers mistakenly think that distributing an application with the runtime version of Access is equivalent to distributing an EXE. A database distributed with the runtime version of Access can be modified just like any other database.

Users can run your application using Access's runtime version, and all the rules of running an application under the runtime version apply. This means that while running under the runtime version of Access, users can't go into Design view, can't create their own objects, don't have access to the built-in toolbars, and so on.

These same users can install their own copies of the standard Access product. Using the standard version of Access, they can open the same database. If the objects in the database haven't been secured, users can modify the application at will.

In short, a database prepared with the Setup Wizard is no different from any other database. The Setup Wizard doesn't modify an MDB file in any way. It simply compresses all the files needed to run your application, including the database and runtime engine, and creates a network install or distribution disks containing the compressed files. Two ways to protect the design of your application are to set up security and to distribute your application as an MDE file.

The Importance of Securing Your Database

By now, you should understand the importance of securing your application. Setting up security is a complex but worthwhile process that can be done at either a group or user level. You can assign rights to objects, and those rights can be assigned to either individual users or a group of users. Figure 2.5 shows the User and Group Permissions dialog box. As you can see, rights can be assigned for each object. For a table, the user or group can be assigned rights to read, insert, update, and delete data as well as read, modify, or administer the table's design. Different groups of users can be assigned different rights to an object. For example, one group can be assigned rights to add, edit, and delete data. Another group can be assigned rights to edit only, another group to view only, and another can be denied the right to even view the data.

Figure 2.5.

The User and Group Permissions dialog box lets you assign user and group rights to each database object.

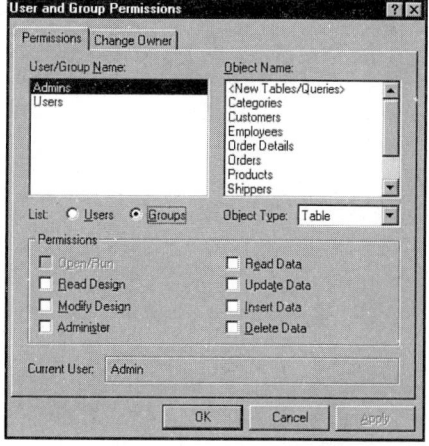

Available rights differ for tables, queries, forms, reports, macros, and modules. The types of rights that can be assigned are appropriate to each particular type of object. When security has been properly invoked, it can't be violated, no matter how someone tries to access the database objects (including using the runtime version of Access, a standard copy of Access, programming code, or even a Visual Basic application). If properly secured, the database is as difficult to access illegally as an executable file. ˙

Using Access as a Front-End

If you're planning to use Access as a front-end to other databases, then you need to consider a few issues. In fact, the whole design methodology of your system will differ depending on whether you plan to store your data in an Access database or on a back-end database server.

In a system where your data is stored solely in Access tables, the Jet Engine part of Access supplies all data retrieval and management functions. The Jet Engine also handles security, data validation, and enforcing referential integrity.

In a system where Access acts as a front-end to client/server data, the server handles the data management functions. It's responsible for retrieving, protecting, and updating data on the back-end database server. When Access acts as a front-end, the local copy of Access is responsible only for sending requests and getting either data or pointers to data back from the database server. If you're creating an application in which Access acts as a front-end, capitalizing on the strengths of both Access and the server can be a challenging endeavor.

Things You Need to Worry About in Converting to Client/Server

The transition to client/server isn't always a smooth one. You need to consider several factors if you're developing a client/server application or planning to eventually move your application from an Access database to a back-end structured query language (SQL) database server:

- Not all field types supported in Access are supported in every back-end database.
- Any security you set up in Access won't be converted to your back-end database.
- Validation rules you set up in Access need to be re-established on the back-end.
- Referential integrity isn't supported on all back-ends. If it is on yours, it won't automatically be carried over from Access.
- Queries involving joins that could be updated in Access can't be updated on the back-end server.

This list is just an overview of what you need to think about when moving an application from an Access database with linked tables to a back-end server or when developing an application specifically for a back-end. Many of these issues have far-reaching implications. For example, if you set up validation rules and validation text in your application, the rules will need to be rewritten as triggers on the back-end, but that isn't your only problem. If a validation rule is violated on the back-end, you will get a returnable error code. You have to handle this returnable error code by using error handling in your application, displaying the appropriate message to your user. The Validation Text property can't be used.

> **TIP**
>
> Some of the issues covered in this chapter can be handled by the Upsizing Wizard. This tool, available from Microsoft, automates the migration of data from the native Access data format to Microsoft SQL Server. The Upsizing Wizard is covered in Chapter 20, "Client/Server Techniques."

Benefits and Costs of Client/Server Technology

With all the issues discussed in the previous section, you might ask "Why bother with client/server?" Client/server technology offers important benefits but requires high costs in time and money if it's to be used properly. In each case, you need to evaluate whether the benefits of client/server technology outweigh the costs. The major benefits include the following:

- Greater control over data integrity
- Increased control over data security
- Increased fault tolerance
- Reduced network traffic

- Improved performance
- Centralized control and management of data

These are some of the major costs:

- Increased development costs
- Hardware costs for the server machine
- Setup costs for the server database
- Full- or part-time database administrator (DBA)

These lists summarize the major costs and benefits of client/server technology; they are meant only to alert you to what you need to think about when evaluating your data's movement to a back-end database server. These and other issues are covered in more detail in Chapter 20.

Your Options When Using Access as a Front-End

Client/server is not an all-or-none proposition, nor is there only one way to implement it using Access as a front-end. One option is to use Access as a true front-end, which means all data is stored on the server and all queries are processed on the server. This is done by using pass-through queries rather than stored Access queries. With pass-through queries (covered in Chapter 21, "Client/Server Strategies"), a back-end–specific SQL statement is passed to the back-end instead of being processed by Access. To make Access a true front-end, you must also disable its natural ability to bind data to forms and reports. After you've done all this, though, you have eliminated all the features that make Access a strong product in the first place. Unfortunately, you haven't eliminated all the overhead associated with the functionality you removed. If you want to use this approach, you're better off developing the entire application in a lower-overhead environment, such as Visual Basic.

Another approach is a hybrid method in which you use a combination of linked tables, SQL pass-through queries, and local Access tables. The idea is that you take advantage of Access's features and strong points whenever possible. Pass-through queries are used to perform functions that are done more efficiently by communicating directly to the back-end or that aren't available at all with Access SQL. To further improve performance, many tasks can be performed locally and then communicated to the server as one transaction, after any initial validation has been done. A new feature called ODBCDirect allows you to communicate with the back-end database without loading the Microsoft Jet Engine. With ODBCDirect, you can improve both the performance and functionality of a client/server application. Furthermore, data can also be downloaded to Access in bulk so that additional processing is done locally. Many possibilities exist, and each is appropriate in different situations. It takes experience and experimentation to determine the combination of methods that will optimize performance in a given situation.

What All This Means to You Right Now

The preceding sections have given you an overview of the issues you need to consider when building an application for client/server or considering moving it to client/server in the future. More detailed information is given in Chapters 20 and 21. The issues behind developing client/server applications are highlighted here to reduce the chances of unexpected grief in the future. If you read this book with these issues in mind, you will be a much happier developer. If you're using Access as a front-end, make sure as you read through this book, particularly the more advanced chapters, that you take special note of any warnings about developing client/server applications.

Applying the Strategy to the Computer Consulting Firm Application

When it's finished, the Time and Billing application for the computer consulting firm introduced in Chapter 1, "Introduction to Access Development," will be made up of two databases: one containing the majority of the tables, and the other with the remainder of the database objects, including static and temporary tables. The application will be developed with the idea that the data might eventually be moved to a back-end database server and designed so that the transition to client/server will be as smooth as possible. The forms and reports that make up the application will be based on stored queries to maximize their flexibility and efficiency. Finally, the application will be designed so that it can easily run from Access's runtime version and will be secured so that its data and other objects can't be accessed by unauthorized users. As you move through the chapters in the book, each of these design strategies will be carried out.

Summary

It's important that you have a strategy before you begin the application development process. This chapter has introduced many strategic issues, such as splitting tables and other objects and using Access as a front-end. It has also covered converting to client/server, the benefits and costs of client/server technology, and the different options available to you. These concepts have then been tied together by explaining what you can do to prepare your applications for future growth.

Many people don't fully understand the Access runtime engine, so this chapter has explained what it is and what it isn't. It has also explained what you need to be concerned about in preparing an application for distribution, including the importance of properly securing your databases.

3

CHAPTER

What Every Developer Needs to Know About Tables

- Building a New Table, 40
- Selecting the Appropriate Field Type for Your Data, 46
- Working with Field Properties, 50
- The All-Important Primary Key, 59
- Working with the Lookup Feature, 59
- Working with Table Properties, 61
- Using Indexes to Improve Performance, 62
- Access Tables and the Internet, 62
- Practical Examples: Designing the Tables Needed for the Computer Consulting Firm's Time and Billing Application, 65

Building a New Table

There are several ways to add a new table to an Access 97 database: using a wizard to help you with the design process, designing the table from scratch, building the table from a spreadsheet-like format, importing the table from another source, and linking to an external table. The first three methods are discussed in this chapter; the other two, importing and linking, are covered extensively throughout this book.

Regardless of which method you choose, start by selecting the Table tab of the Database window, then clicking the New button. (See Figure 3.1.) This opens the New Table dialog box, shown in Figure 3.2, which allows you to choose the method you want to use to build your table.

Figure 3.1.

To create a new table, select the Tables tab of the Database window.

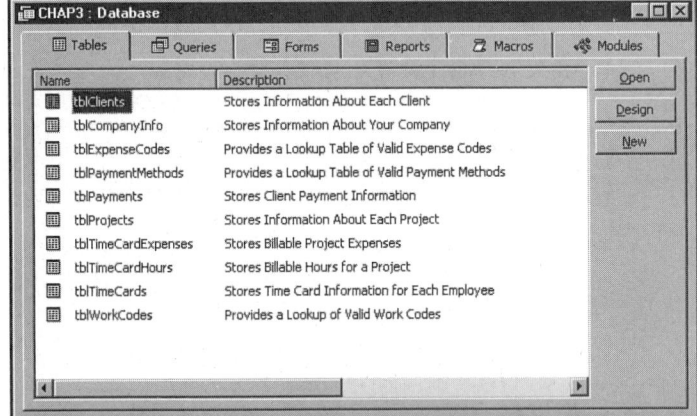

Figure 3.2.

The New Table dialog box lets you choose the method for creating the new table.

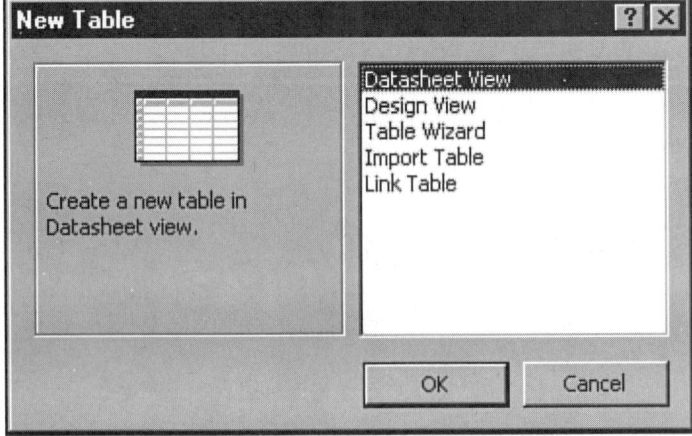

Building a Table with a Wizard

If you select Table Wizard from the New Table dialog box, the Table Wizard dialog box opens. The first step in the Table Wizard dialog box lets you choose specific fields from one of many predefined tables. The tables are categorized as either Business or Personal. If you select the Business option, you'll see a set of business-related tables; if you select Personal, you'll see a set of tables for personal topics. After you have selected a table, you can specify which fields you want to include in your table. To do this, double-click on the field you want or click the > button. In Figure 3.3, I have selected the EmployeeID, FirstName, LastName, Title, Extension, DateHired, and Salary fields from the table called Employees.

Figure 3.3.

The Table Wizard: In Step 1, you choose a sample table and designate which fields you want to include in your table.

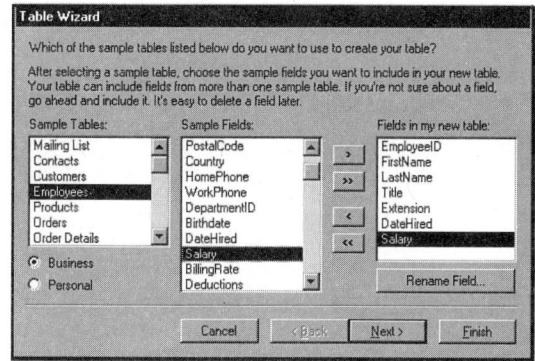

After you have selected the table and fields you want, click Next to open the dialog box shown in Figure 3.4. In this step of the Table Wizard, you name your table and indicate whether you want Access to set the primary key for you. (Primary keys are covered in more detail later in this chapter.) It's always a good idea for a table to have a primary key, which is used to uniquely identify each record. If you don't tell Access to set a primary key, you have the opportunity later to designate your unique field as the primary key. If you haven't entered a unique identifier (some field that differentiates each record from the next) for the table, select Yes. Access will add an AutoNumber field to your table and designate it as the primary key. It's a good idea to let Access set the primary key, but if you don't, the primary key or any other attributes of the table can be modified at any time.

> **NOTE**
>
> The naming conventions for table names are similar to those for field names, except the standard for table names is that they should begin with the tag *tbl*. Naming conventions are covered in detail in Chapter 1, "Introduction to Access Development," and in Appendix B, "Naming Conventions."

Figure 3.4.
The Table Wizard: In Step 2,
you name your new table.

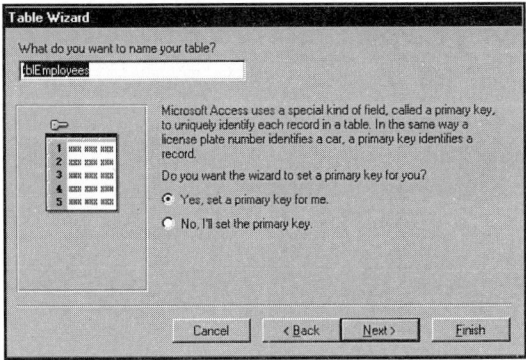

In the third step of the Table Wizard, Access tries to identify relationships between the new table and any existing tables. This step is shown in Figure 3.5. The process of establishing relationships is an important part of Access development. Relationships allow you to normalize your database and to once again "flatten out" the data structure at runtime. They also help you ensure the integrity of your application's data. For example, you can define a relationship so that orders can't be entered for customers who don't exist. Although Access automatically identifies relationships if it can, you can modify or add relationships by clicking the Relationships button. When you're satisfied with the relationships that have been established, click Next.

Figure 3.5.
The Table Wizard: In Step 3,
you designate relationships
between the new table and any
existing tables.

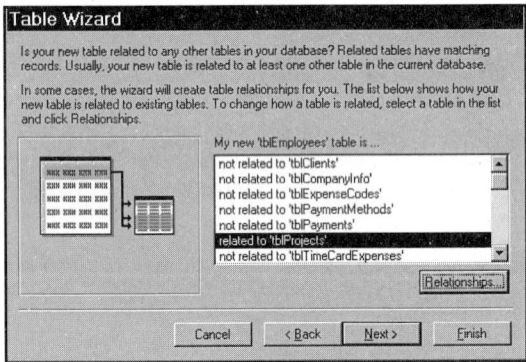

The final dialog box, shown in Figure 3.6, allows you to indicate whether you want to view the design of the table, enter data into the table, or let Access automatically build both the table and a data-entry form for you.

Figure 3.6.

The Table Wizard: In Step 4, you specify what you want the wizard to do when it has finished processing.

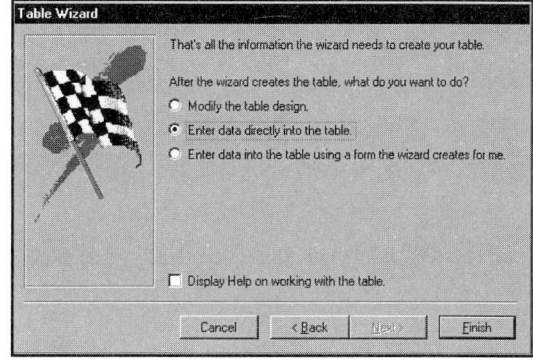

Designing a Table from Scratch

Designing tables from scratch offers flexibility and encourages good design principles. Select Design View from the New Table dialog box to open the Table Design View window, pictured in Figure 3.7. Follow these steps:

Figure 3.7.

The Table Design View window is used to enter field names, data types, and descriptions for all the fields in a table.

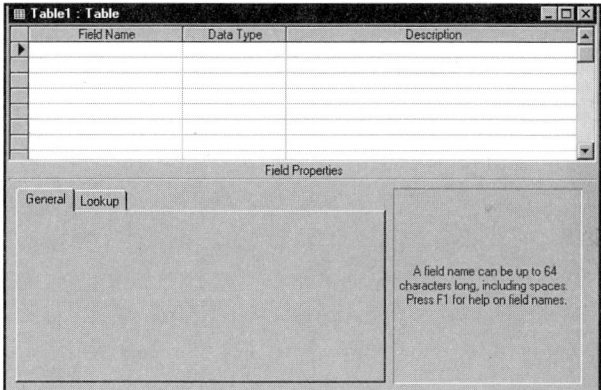

1. Define each field in the table by typing its name in the Field Name column. If you prefer, you can click the build button on the toolbar to open the Field Builder dialog box, shown in Figure 3.8. This builder lets you select from predefined fields with predefined properties. Of course, the properties can be modified at any time.

2. Tab to the Data Type column. Select the default field type, which is Text, or use the drop-down combo box to select another field type. You can find details on which field type is appropriate for your data in the "Selecting the Appropriate Field Type for Your Data" section of this chapter. Note that if you use the Field Builder, it sets a field type value for you that you can modify.

Figure 3.8.

The Field Builder dialog box lets you select from predefined fields with predefined properties.

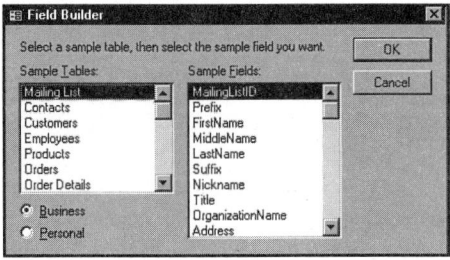

3. Tab to the Description column. What you type in this column appears on the status bar when the user is entering data into the field. This column is also great for documenting what data is actually stored in the field.

4. Continue entering fields. If you need to insert a field between two existing fields, click the Insert Rows button on the toolbar. The new field is inserted above the field you were on. To delete a field, click the Delete Rows button.

> **NOTE**
>
> Field names can be up to 64 characters long. For practical reasons, you should try to limit them to 10–15 characters—enough to describe the field without making the name difficult to type.
>
> Field names can include any combination of letters, numbers, spaces, and other characters, excluding periods, exclamation points, accents, and brackets. I recommend that you stick to letters. Spaces in field names can be inconvenient when you're building queries, modules, and other database objects.
>
> Field names can't begin with leading spaces. As mentioned, field names shouldn't contain any spaces, so this shouldn't be a problem.
>
> Try not to duplicate property names or the names of other Access objects when naming your fields. Although your code might work in some circumstances, you'll get unpredictable results in others.
>
> To make a potential move to client/server as painless as possible, you should be aware that not all field types are supported by every back-end database. Furthermore, most back-end databases impose stricter limits than Access does on the length of field names and the characters that are valid in field names. To reduce the number of problems you'll encounter if you migrate your tables to a back-end database server, these issues should be considered when you're naming the fields in your Access tables.

Building a Table from a Datasheet

Building a table from a datasheet might seem simple, but it isn't a very good way to build a table because it's all too easy to introduce severe design flaws into your table. Although this method was added as an "enhancement" to Access, it was added primarily for spreadsheet users getting their feet wet in the database world. I suggest you use one of the other methods to design your tables. If you decide to use the datasheet method, follow these steps:

1. Select Datasheet View from the New Table dialog box. A window similar to that shown in Figure 3.9 appears.

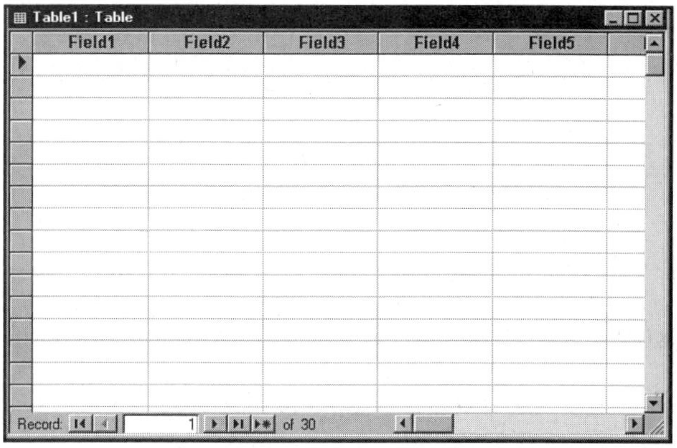
Table1 : Table
Field1
Field2
Field3
Field4
Field5
Record:
1
of 30

Figure 3.9.
Building a table from a datasheet.

2. Rename each column by double-clicking on the column heading (for example, Field1) you want to change, or by right-clicking on the column and selecting Rename Column from the shortcut menu. Type the name for your field, then press Enter.
3. Enter data into the datasheet. Be sure to enter the data in a consistent format. For example, if your table includes a column for the hire date, make sure all entries in that column are valid dates and all dates are entered in the same format. (See Figure 3.10.) Access uses the contents of each column to determine the data type for each field, so inconsistent data entry confuses Access and causes unpredictable results.

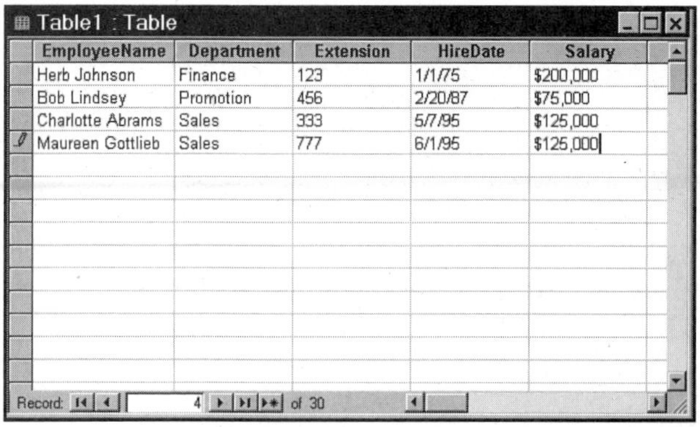
Table1 : Table
EmployeeName
Department
Extension
HireDate
Salary
Herb Johnson
Finance
123
1/1/75
$200,000
Bob Lindsey
Promotion
456
2/20/87
$75,000
Charlotte Abrams
Sales
333
5/7/95
$125,000
Maureen Gottlieb
Sales
777
6/1/95
$125,000
Record:
4
of 30

Figure 3.10.
Data entered in a datasheet is used to determine the new table's structure.

4. After you have added all the columns and data you want, click the Save button on the toolbar. You are then prompted for a table name.

5. Access asks whether you want to add a primary key.

6. Access assigns data types to each field based on the data you have entered. When Access is done, click the Table View button on the toolbar to look at the design of the resulting table.

7. Add a description to each field to help make your table self-documenting. Your table should look something like Figure 3.11.

Figure 3.11.

The table design results from building a table with the datasheet method.

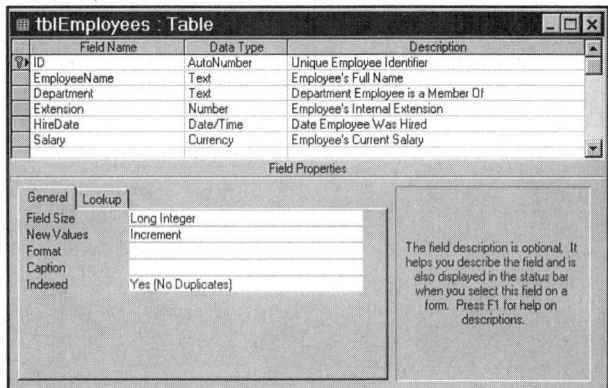

Adding descriptions to your table, query, form, report, macro, and module objects goes a long way toward making your application self-documenting. This helps you, or anyone who modifies your application, perform any required maintenance on the application's objects. Documenting your application is covered in detail in Chapter 34, "Documenting Your System."

If you forget a field and need to insert it later, right-click on the column heading to the right of where you want to insert the new column. In the context-sensitive menu that appears, select Insert Column. A column is inserted that can be renamed by double-clicking on the column heading.

Selecting the Appropriate Field Type for Your Data

The data type you select for each field can greatly affect the performance and functionality of your application. Several factors can influence your choice of data type for each field in your table:

- The type of data that's stored in the field
- Whether the field's contents need to be included in calculations
- Whether you need to sort the data in the field
- The way you want to sort the data in the field
- How important storage space is to you

The type of data you need to store in a field has the biggest influence on which data type you select. For example, if you need to store numbers beginning with leading zeros, you can't select a Number field because leading zeros entered into a Number field are ignored. This rule affects data such as ZIP codes (some begin with leading zeros) and department codes.

If the contents of a field need to be included in calculations, you must select a Number or Currency data type. You can't perform calculations on the contents of fields defined with the other data types. The only exception to this rule is Date fields, which can be included in date/time calculations.

You also need to consider whether you will sort or index the data in a field. Memo, OLE, and Hyperlink fields can't be sorted, so don't select these field types if the data in the field must be sorted or indexed. Furthermore, you must think about the *way* you want the data to be sorted. For example, in a Text field, a set of numbers would be sorted in the order in which they appear (that is, 1, 10, 100, 2, 20, 200) because data in the Text field is sorted in a standard ASCII sequence. On the other hand, in a Number or Currency field. the numbers would be sorted as expected (that is, 1, 2, 10, 20, 100, 200). You might think you would never want data sorted in a standard ASCII sequence, but sometimes it makes sense to sort certain information, such as department codes, in this fashion.

Finally, you should consider how important disk space is to you. Each field type takes up a different amount of storage space on your hard disk, which could be a factor when you're selecting a data type for a field.

Nine field types are available in Access: Text, Memo, Number, Date/Time, Currency, AutoNumber (known as Counter in Access 2.0), Yes/No, OLE Object, and Hyperlink. Table 3.1 summarizes information on the appropriate uses for each field type and the amount of storage space each type needs.

Table 3.1. Appropriate uses and storage space for Access field types.

Field Type	Appropriate Uses	Storage Space
Text	Data containing text, a combination of text and numbers, or numbers that don't need to be included in calculations; examples are names, addresses, department codes, phone numbers	Based on what's actually stored in the field; ranges from 0 to 255 bytes

continues

Table 3.1. continued

Field Type	Appropriate Uses	Storage Space
Memo	Long text and numeric strings; examples are notes and descriptions	Ranges from 0 to 64,000 bytes
Number	Data that's included in calculations (excluding money); examples are ages, codes, such as employee ID, or payment methods	1, 2, 4, or 8 bytes, depending on the field size selected
Date/Time	Dates and times; examples are date ordered and birthdate	8 bytes
Currency	Currency values; examples are amount due and price	8 bytes
AutoNumber	Unique sequential or random numbers; examples are invoice numbers and project numbers	4 bytes (16 bytes for replication ID)
Yes/No	Fields that contain one of two values (yes/no, true/false); examples are indicating bills paid and tenure status	1 bit
OLE Object	Objects like Word documents or Excel spreadsheets; examples are employee reviews and budgets	0 bytes to 1 gigabyte, depending on what's stored within the field
Hyperlink	Text, or a combination of text and numbers, stored as text and used as a hyperlink address; examples are Web pages or network files	0 to 2048 bytes for each of the three parts that compose the address

> **NOTE**
>
> The Hyperlink field type consists of three parts. The first part is called the *displaytext*; it's the text that appears in the field or control. The second part is the actual *file path* (UNC) or *page* (URL) the field is referring to. The third part is the *subaddress*, a location within the file or page.

The most difficult part of selecting a field type is knowing which type is best in each situation. The following detailed descriptions of each field type and when it's used should help you with this process.

Text Fields: The Most Common Field Type

Most fields are Text fields. Many developers don't realize that it's best to use Text fields for any numbers not used in calculations. Examples are phone numbers, part numbers, and ZIP codes. Although the default size for a Text field is 50 characters, up to 255 characters can be stored in a Text field. Because Access allocates disk space dynamically, a large field size doesn't use hard-disk space, but you can improve performance if you allocate the smallest field size possible. The maximum number of characters allowed in a Text field can be controlled by the FieldSize property.

Memo Fields: For Those Long Notes and Comments

Memo fields can store up to 64K of text, which can hold up to 16 pages of text for each record. Memo fields are excellent for any types of notes you want to store with table data. Remember, you can't sort by a Memo field.

Number Fields: When You Need to Calculate

Number fields are used to store data that must be included in calculations. If currency amounts are included in calculations or if your calculations require the highest degree of accuracy, you should use a Currency field rather than a Number field. The Number field is actually several types of fields in one because Access 97 offers six sizes of numeric fields. Byte can store integers from 1 to 255, Integer can hold whole numbers from −32768 to 32767, and Long Integer can hold whole numbers ranging from less than −2 billion to more than 2 billion. Although all three of these sizes offer excellent performance, each type requires an increasingly larger amount of storage space. Two of the other numeric field sizes, Single and Double, offer floating decimal points and, therefore, much slower performance. Single can hold fractional numbers to seven significant digits; Double extends the precision to 14 significant digits. The final size, Replication ID, supplies a unique identifier required by the data synchronization process.

Date/Time Fields: Tracking When Things Happened

The Date/Time field type is used to store valid dates and times. Data/Time fields allow you to perform date calculations and make sure dates and times are always sorted properly. Access actually stores the date or time internally as an 8-byte floating-point number. Time is represented as a fraction of a day.

NOTE

Any date and time settings you establish in the Windows Control Panel are reflected in your data.

Currency Fields: Storing Money

The Currency field type is a special type of number field used when currency values are being stored in a table. Currency fields prevent rounding off data during calculations. They hold 15 digits of whole dollars, plus accuracy to the hundredths of a cent. Although very accurate, this type of field is quite slow.

> **NOTE**
>
> Any changes to the currency format made in the Windows Control Panel are reflected in your data. Of course, Access doesn't automatically perform any actual conversion of currency amounts.

AutoNumber Fields: For Unique Record Identifiers

The AutoNumber field in Access 95 and 97 is equivalent to the Counter field in Access 2.0. AutoNumber field values are automatically generated when a record is added. In Access 2.0, counter values had to be sequential. The AutoNumber field type in Access 97 can be either sequential or random. The random assignment is useful when several users are adding records offline because it's unlikely that Access will assign the same random value to two records. A special type of AutoNumber field is a Replication ID. This randomly produced, unique number helps with the replication process by generating unique identifiers used to synchronize database replicas.

You should note a few important points about sequential AutoNumber fields. If a user deletes a record from a table, its unique number is lost forever. Likewise, if a user is adding a record but cancels, the unique counter value for that record is lost forever. If this behavior is unacceptable, you can generate your own counter values. This process is covered in Chapter 18, "Developing for a Multiuser Environment."

Yes/No Fields: When One of Two Answers Is Correct

You should use Yes/No fields to store a logical true or false. What's actually stored in the field is -1 for Yes and 0 for No. The display format for the field determines what the user actually sees (Yes/No, True/False, On/Off). Yes/No fields work efficiently for any data that can have only a true or false value. Not only do they limit the user to valid choices, they take up only 1 bit of storage space.

OLE Object Fields: The Place to Store Just About Anything

OLE Object fields are designed to hold data from any OLE server application registered in Windows, including spreadsheets, word processing documents, sound, and video. There are many business uses for OLE fields, such as storing resumes, employee reviews, budgets, or videos.

Hyperlink Fields: Your Link to the Internet

Hyperlink fields are used to store Uniform Resource Locator addresses (URLs), which are links to World Wide Web pages on the Internet, or Universal Naming Convention paths (UNCs), which are links to a file path. The Hyperlink field type is broken into three parts: (1) what the user sees, (2) the URL or UNC, and (3) a subaddress, such as a range name or bookmark. Once an entry is placed in a Hyperlink field, the entry serves as a direct link to the file or page it's referring to. Hyperlinks are covered in more detail later in this chapter, in the section "Access Tables and the Internet."

Working with Field Properties

After you have added fields to your table, you need to customize their properties. Field properties let you control how data is stored as well as what data can be entered into the field. The available properties differ depending on which field type is selected. The most comprehensive list of properties is found under the Text field type. (See Figure 3.12.) The following sections describe each field property.

Figure 3.12.
Field properties available for a Text field.

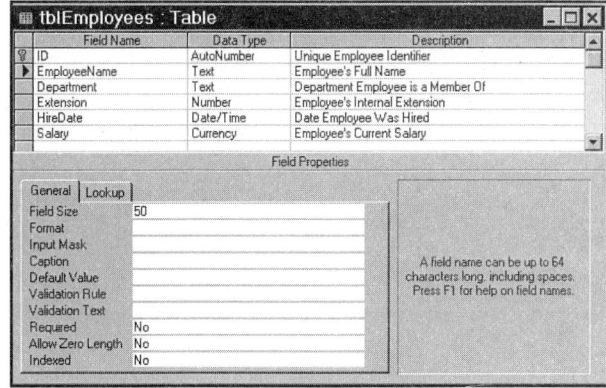

Field Size: Limiting What's Entered into a Field

The first property is Field Size, available for Text and Number fields only. As mentioned previously, it's best to set the field size to the smallest type possible. For Number fields, a small size means lower storage requirements and faster performance.

Build a table with the following fields and types:

CompanyID: AutoNumber

CompanyName: Text

State: Text

PhoneNumber: Text

TRY IT

ContactDate: Date/Time

CreditLimit: Currency

To set the Field Size property of the State field to two characters, click anywhere in the field, then type **2** in the Field Size property. Switch to Datasheet view and name the table **tblCustomers**. When you try to enter data into the State field, notice that only two characters can be entered.

> **NOTE**
>
> This example, and all others in this chapter, can be found in the Chap3TryIt.MDB file included on the book's sample code CD-ROM.

Format: Determining How Data Is Displayed

The second property is Format, available for all but OLE Object fields. It allows you to specify how Access displays your data. Access lets you select from predefined formats or create your own custom formats. The available formats differ depending on the field's data type. For example, with Access you can select from a variety of Date/Time formats, including Short Date (7/7/96), Long Date (Sunday, July 7, 1996), Short Time (7:17), and Long Time (7:17:11AM). The formats for a Currency field include Currency ($1,767.25), Fixed (1767.25), and Standard (1,767.25).

TRY IT   Set the Format property of the ContactDate field to Medium Date. Switch to Datasheet view and enter some dates in different formats, such as 07/08/96 and July 8, 1996. Notice that no matter how you enter the dates, they appear in the format mm/dd/yy as 08-Jul-96.

Input Mask: Determining What Data Goes into a Field

Another important property is Input Mask, available for Text, Number, Date/Time, and Currency fields. The Format property affects how data's displayed, but the Input Mask property controls what data is stored in a field. You can use the Input Mask property to control, on a character-by-character basis, what type of character (numeric, alphanumeric, and so on) can be stored and whether a particular character is required. The Input Mask Wizard, shown in Figure 3.13, helps you create commonly used input masks for Text and Date fields only.

> **NOTE**
>
> The Input Mask Wizard is available only if you selected the Advanced Wizards component in Setup.

Figure 3.13.

The Input Mask Wizard helps
you enter an input mask.

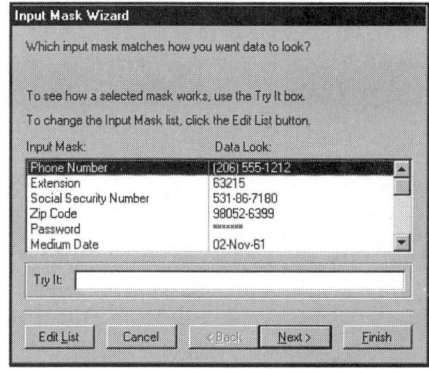

For example, the input mask 000-00-0000;;_ forces the entry of a valid social security number. Everything that precedes the first semicolon designates the actual mask. The character you enter between the first and second semicolon determines whether literal characters (the dashes in this case) are stored in the field. The zeros force the entry of the digits 0 through 9. The dashes are literals that appear within the control as the user enters data. If you enter a 0 in this position, literal characters are stored in the field; if you enter a 1 or leave this position blank, the literal characters aren't stored. The final position (after the second semicolon) indicates what character is displayed to indicate the space where the user types the next character (in this case, the underscore).

Here's a more detailed example: In the mask \(999") "000\-0000;;_, the first backslash causes the character that follows it (the parenthesis) to be displayed as a literal. The three nines allow optional numbers or spaces to be entered. The parenthesis and space within the quotation marks are displayed as literals. The first three zeros require values 0 through 9. The dash that follows the next backslash is displayed as a literal. Four additional numbers are then required. The two semicolons have nothing between them, so the literal characters aren't stored in the field. The second semicolon is followed by an underscore, so an underscore is displayed to indicate the space where the user types the next character.

Use the Input Mask Wizard to add a mask for the PhoneNumber field, which you should have set up as a Text field. To do this, click anywhere in the PhoneNumber field, then click in the Input Mask property. Click on the ellipsis to the right of the Input Mask property. Select Phone Number from the list of available masks and choose not to store the literal characters in the field. Switch to Datasheet view and enter a phone number. Notice how your cursor skips over the literal characters. Try leaving the area code blank; Access should allow you to do this. Now try to enter a letter in any position—Access should prohibit you from doing this. Next, try to leave any character from the seven-digit phone number blank. Access shouldn't let you do this, either.

TRY IT

> **TIP**
>
> When you use an input mask, the user is always in Overtype mode. This behavior is a feature of the product and can't be altered.

Caption: A Great Timesaver

The next available property is Caption. The text placed in this property becomes the caption for fields in Datasheet view. It's also used as the caption for the attached label added to data-bound controls when you add them to forms and reports. The Caption property becomes important whenever you name your fields without spaces. Whatever is in the Caption property overrides the field name for use in Datasheet view, on forms, and on reports.

> **TIP**
>
> It's important to set the Caption property for fields *before* you build any forms or reports that use them. When a form or report is produced, Access looks at the current caption. If the caption is added or modified at a later time, captions for that field on existing forms and reports aren't modified.

Default Value: Saving Data-Entry Time

Another important property is the Default Value property, used to specify the default value that Access will place in the field when the user adds new records to the table. Default values, which can be either text or expressions, can save the data-entry person a lot of time. However, they do not in any way validate what's entered into a field.

> **TIP**
>
> Default values are automatically carried into any queries and forms containing the field. Unlike what happens with the Caption property, this occurs whether the default value was created before or after the query or form.

TRY IT Enter the following default values for the State, ContactDate, and CreditLimit fields:

State: `CA`

ContactDate: `=Date()`

CreditLimit: `1000`

Switch to Datasheet view and add a new record. Notice that default values appear for the State, ContactDate, and CreditLimit fields. You can override these defaults, if you want.

Validation Rule: Controlling What's Entered in a Field

The Default Value property suggests a value to the user, but the Validation Rule property actually limits what the user can place in the field. Validation rules can't be violated; the database engine strictly enforces them. As with the Default Value property, this property can contain either text or a valid Access expression, but user-defined functions can't be included in the Validation Rule property. You also can't include references to forms, queries, or tables in the Validation Rule property.

> **TIP**
>
> If you set the Validation Rule property but not the Validation Text property, Access automatically displays a standard error message whenever the validation rule is violated. To display a custom message, you must enter something in the Validation Text property.

Add the following validation rules to the fields in your table:

TRY IT

State: `In (CA, AZ, NY, MA, UT)`

ContactDate: `<= Date()`

CreditLimit: `Between 0 And 5000`

Switch to Datasheet view. After you save the table, the message shown in Figure 3.14 will appear. If you select Yes, Access tries to validate all existing data using the new rules. If any errors are found, you're notified that errors occurred, but you aren't informed of the offending records. (See Figure 3.15.) You have to build a query to find all the records violating the new rules. If you select No, Access doesn't try to validate your existing data, and you aren't warned of any problems. After you have entered Datasheet view, try to enter an invalid state in the State field; you should see the message box displayed in Figure 3.16. As you can see, this isn't the most friendly message, which is why you should create a custom message by using the Validation Text property.

Figure 3.14.

The message box asking whether you want to validate existing data.

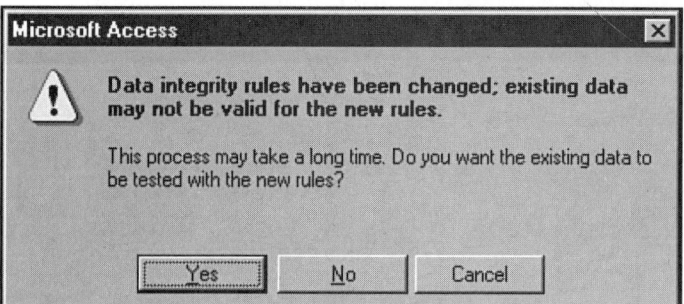

Figure 3.15.

A warning that all data did not validate successfully.

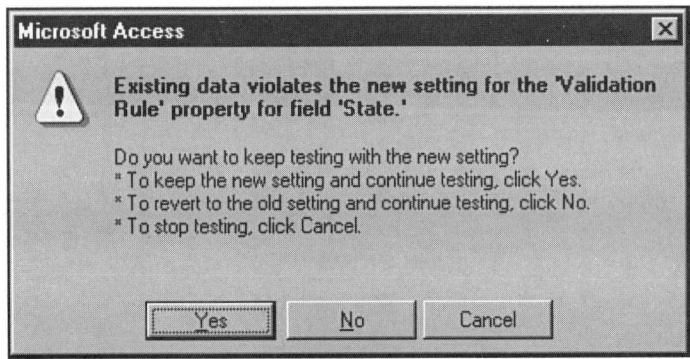

Figure 3.16.

The message displayed when a validation rule is violated and no validation text has been entered.

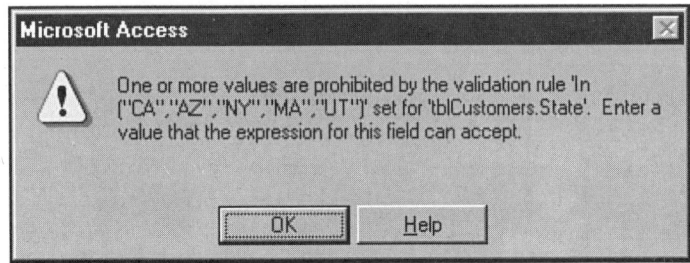

TIP

Validation rules entered at a table level are automatically applied to forms and queries built from the table. This occurs whether the rule was entered before or after the query or form was built. If you create a validation rule for a field, Access won't allow Null values to be entered in the field, which means the field can't be left blank. If you want to allow the field to be left Null, you must add the Null to the validation expression:

```
In (CA, AZ, NY, MA, UT) or Is Null
```

Validation Text: Providing Error Messages to the User

Use the Validation Text property to specify the error message users see when they violate the validation rule. The Validation Text property must contain text; expressions aren't valid in this property.

TRY IT   Add the following to the Validation Text properties of the State, ContactDate, and CreditLimit fields:

State: `The State Must Be CA, ZA, NY, MA, or UT`

ContactDate: `The Contact Date Must Be On or Before Today`

CreditLimit: **The Credit Limit Must Be Between 0 and 5000**

Try entering invalid values for each of the three fields, and observe the error messages.

Required: Make the User Enter a Value

The Required property is very important—it determines whether you require that a value be entered into the field. This property is useful for foreign key fields, when you want to make sure data is entered into the field. It's also useful for any field containing information that's needed for business reasons (company name, for example).

Set the Required property of the CompanyName and PhoneNumber fields to **Yes**. Switch to Datasheet view and try to add a new record, leaving the CompanyName and PhoneNumber fields blank. Make sure you enter a value for at least one of the other fields in the record. When you try to move off the record, the error message shown in Figure 3.17 appears.

TRY IT

Figure 3.17.
This message appears when you leave a field blank with the Required property set to Yes.

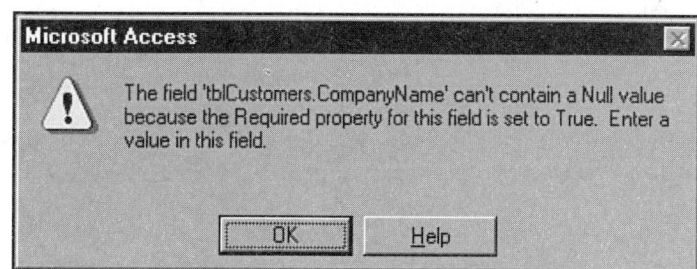

Allow Zero Length: Accommodate Situations with Nonexistent Data

The Allow Zero Length property is similar to the Required property. Use it to determine whether you will allow the user to enter a zero-length string (" "). A zero-length string isn't the same as a Null (absence of an entry); it indicates that the data doesn't exist for that particular field. For example, a foreign employee might not have a social security number. By entering a zero-length string, the data-entry person can indicate that the social security number doesn't exist.

Add a new field called ContactName and set its Required property to **Yes**. Try to add a new record and enter two quotes ("") in the ContactName field. You should get the error message shown in Figure 3.18. Return to the design of the table. Change the Allow Zero Length Property to **Yes**, then go to Datasheet view and try to enter two quotes in the ContactName field. This time you should be successful. Your zero-length string will appear blank once you move off the field.

TRY IT

Figure 3.18.

The result of entering " " when the Allow Zero Length property is set to No.

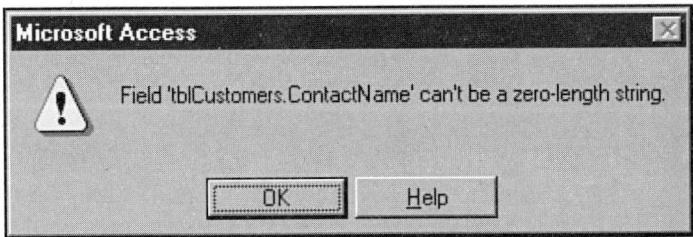

Microsoft Access

⚠ Field 'tblCustomers.ContactName' can't be a zero-length string.

OK   Help

> **TIP**
>
> The Required and Allow Zero Length properties interact with each other. If the Required property is set to Yes and the Allow Zero Length property to No, you're being as strict as possible with your users. Not only must they enter a value, but that value can't be a zero-length string.
>
> If the Required property is set to Yes and the Allow Zero Length property to Yes, you're requiring users to enter a value, but that value can be a zero-length string. However, if the Required property is set to No and the Allow Zero Length property to No, you're allowing users to leave the field Null (blank), but not to enter a zero-length string.
>
> Finally, if you set the Required property to No and the Allow Zero Length property to Yes, you're being the most lenient with your users. In this case, they can leave the field Null or enter a zero-length string.

Indexed: Speeding Up Searches

The final property is Indexed. Indexes are used to improve performance when the user searches a field. It's generally best to include too many indexes rather than too few.

TRY IT Set the Indexed property of the CompanyName, ContactName, and State fields to Yes – (Duplicates OK). Click the Indexes button on the toolbar. Your screen should look like Figure 3.19. Notice the Index Name of PrimaryKey. This is the name for the Primary Key index. Note that the Primary and Unique properties for this index are both set to True.

> **TIP**
>
> To create multifield indexes, you must use the Indexes window; you create an index with one name and more than one field. See Figure 3.20, which shows an index called StateByCredit that's based on the combination of the CreditLimit and State fields. Notice that only the first field in the index has an index name. The second field, State, appears on the line below the first field but doesn't have an index name.
>
> Indexes speed up searching, sorting, and grouping data. The downside is that they take up hard-disk space and slow down the process of editing, adding, and deleting data. Although the

benefits of indexing outweigh the detriments in most cases, you should *not* index every field in each table. Create indexes only for fields, or combinations of fields, on which the user will search or sort. Finally, never index Yes/No fields. They are only 1 bit and can take on only one of two values. For these reasons, indexes offer no benefits with Yes/No fields.

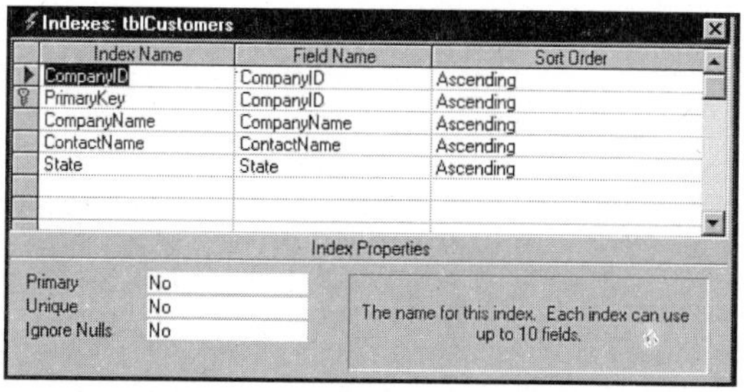

Figure 3.19.

The Indexes window shows you all the indexes defined for a table.

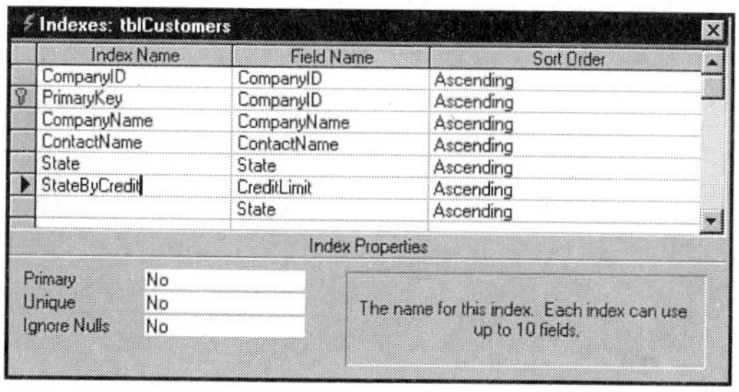

Figure 3.20.

A multiField index called StateByCredit, based on a combination of the CreditLimit and State fields.

The All-Important Primary Key

The most important index in a table is called the Primary Key index; it ensures uniqueness of the fields that make up the index and also gives the table a default order. You must set a primary key for the fields on the one side of a one-to-many relationship. To create a Primary Key index, select the fields you want to establish as the primary key, then click the Primary Key button on the toolbar.

Working with the Lookup Feature

Using the Lookup Wizard, you can instruct a field to look up its values in another table or query or from a fixed list of values. You can also display the list of valid values in a combo or list box. A lookup is generally created from the foreign key (many side) to the primary key (one side) of a one-to-many relationship.

The Lookup Wizard can be invoked by selecting Lookup Wizard from the list of data types for the field. The first dialog box of the wizard asks whether you want to look up the values in a table or query or whether you want to input the values. I recommend that you always look up the values in a table or query; this makes your application easy to maintain. The second dialog box asks you to indicate the table or query used to look up the values. Select a table or query and click Next to open the third dialog box. This step of the Lookup Wizard asks you which field in the table or query will be used for the lookup. The fourth step of the Lookup Wizard, shown in Figure 3.21, gives you the opportunity to control the width of the columns in your combo or list box.

> **NOTE**
>
> If you select more than one field for your lookup and one is a key column, such as an ID, the Hide Key Column checkbox appears. You should leave this checked; it automatically hides the key column in the lookup, even though the end result will be bound to the key field.

Figure 3.21.
In the fourth step of the Lookup Wizard, you adjust the field width.

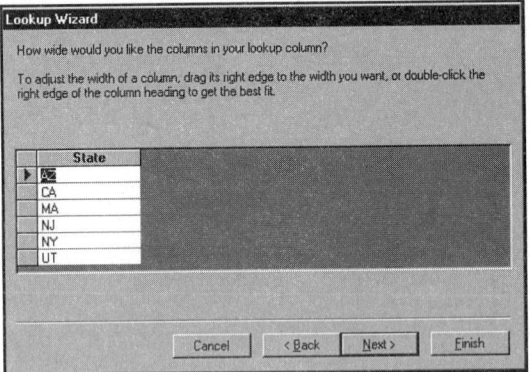

Finally, the wizard lets you specify a title for your combo box. When you click Finish, all the appropriate properties are filled in by the wizard; they appear on the Lookup tab of the field. (See Figure 3.22.) The Display Control property is set to Combo Box, indicating that a combo box is used to display the valid values. This occurs whether the user is in Datasheet view or in a form. The Row Source Type indicates that the source for the combo box is a table or query and shows the actual SQL Select statement used to populate the combo box. Other properties show which column in the combo box is bound to data, how many columns are in the combo box, the width of the combo box, and the width of each column in the combo box. These properties are covered in more detail in Chapter 6, "What Every Developer Needs to Know About Form Basics."

Figure 3.22.

The field properties set by the Lookup Wizard.

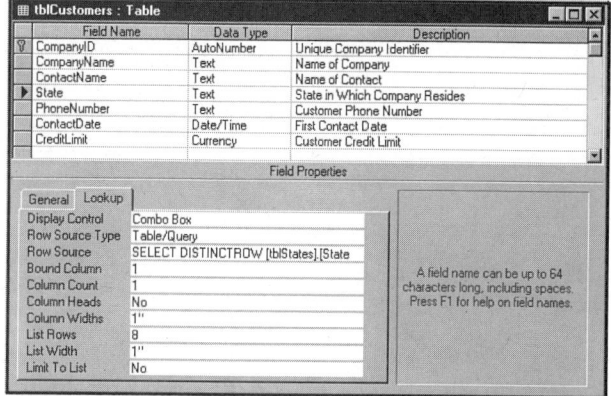

Working with Table Properties

With table properties, you can specify properties that apply to the table as a whole. To access them, click the Properties button on the toolbar while in a table's Design view. The available table properties are shown in Figure 3.23. The Description property is used mainly for documentation purposes. The Validation Rule property is used to specify validations that must occur at a record level rather than a field level. For example, credit limits might differ depending on what state a customer is in. In that case, what's entered in one field depends on another field. By entering a table-level validation rule, it doesn't matter in what order the user enters the data. A table-level validation rule ensures that the proper dependency between fields is enforced. The validation rule might look something like this:

```
[State] In ("CA","NY") And [CreditLimit]<=2500 Or _
    [State] In ("MA","AZ") And [CreditLimit]<=3500
```

Figure 3.23.

Viewing the available table properties.

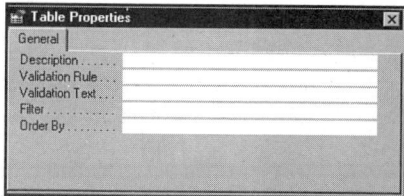

This validation rule requires a credit limit of $2,500 or less for California and New York and a limit of $3,500 or less for Massachusetts and Arizona, but it doesn't specify a credit limit for any other states. Table-level validation rules can't be in conflict with field-level validation rules.

The Validation Text property determines the message that appears when the user violates the validation rule. If it's left blank, a default message appears.

The Filter property is used to indicate a subset of records that appears in a datasheet, form, or query. The Order By property is used to specify a default order for the records. The Filter and Order By properties aren't generally applied as properties of a table.

Using Indexes to Improve Performance

As mentioned, indexes can help you improve your application's performance. You should create indexes on any fields you sort, group, join, or set criteria for. Queries can greatly benefit from indexes, especially when created for fields included in your criteria, fields used to order the query, and fields used to join two tables included in the query. In fact, you should always create indexes for fields on both sides of a join. If your users are using the Find dialog box, indexes can help reduce the search time. Remember, the downsides to indexes are the disk space they require and the amount of time it takes to update them when adding, deleting, and updating records. You should always perform benchmarks with your own application, but you will probably find indexes helpful in many situations.

Access Tables and the Internet

Microsoft has made it easier to develop Internet-aware applications by adding a Hyperlink field type and by allowing users to save table data as HTML. The Hyperlink field type lets your users easily store UNC or URL addresses within their tables. The ability to save table data makes it easy for you or your users to publish table data on an Internet or intranet site. These features are covered in the following sections.

The Hyperlink Field Type

By using the Hyperlink field type, your users can store a different UNC or URL address for each record in the table. Although a UNC or URL address can be typed directly into a field, it's much easier to enter the address by using the Insert Hyperlink dialog box. (See Figure 3.24.) Here, users can graphically browse hyperlink addresses and subaddresses and enter the address for them when they exit the dialog box. To invoke the Insert Hyperlink dialog box, choose Insert I Hyperlink with the cursor placed in the Hyperlink field.

The "Link to file or URL" combo box allows you to enter a UNC or URL address or click Browse to locate the path to the document you want to link to. The combo box has a list of UNCs and URLs you have previously linked to. The optional "Named location in file" text box lets you designate a specific location in the selected document you want to jump to. Examples of a subaddress are a range name in Microsoft Excel, a bookmark in Microsoft Word, or a database object in an Access database. If the address refers to an Access database, the Browse button for the Named location invokes a Select Location dialog box. (See Figure 3.25.) Here, the user can choose a database object in the database cited as the address.

Figure 3.24.
With the Insert Hyperlink dialog box, users can designate UNC and URL address and subaddress information.

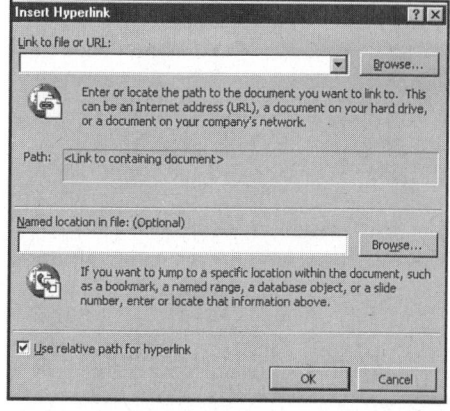

Figure 3.25.
The Select Location dialog box lets the user designate an Access object to open when the hyperlink is selected.

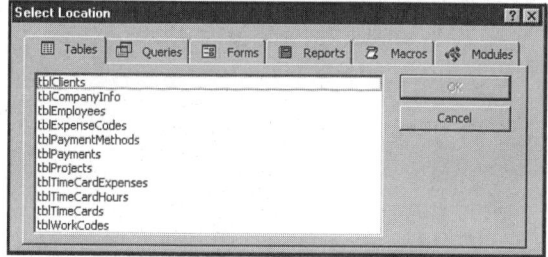

Another option in the Insert Hyperlink dialog box is the "Use relative path for hyperlink" check box, which lets the user designate whether a UNC path will be absolute or relative. An example of a relative path is ..\..\MyFiles\Customer.XLS; an absolute path is m:\MyFiles\Customer.XLS.

Once all the required information has been entered, the link is established, and the hyperlink is entered in the field. If a UNC was entered, clicking the hyperlink invokes the application associated with the file. The selected file is opened, and the user is placed in the part of the document designated in the subaddress. If a URL is entered, and the user is logged onto the Internet or connected to his or her company's intranet, the user is taken directly to the designated page. If the user isn't currently connected to the Internet or an intranet, the Connect To dialog appears, allowing him or her to log on to the appropriate network.

Saving Table Data as HTML

Table data can be easily saved as HTML so that it can be published on an Internet or intranet site. You can save a file as HTML by using the File | Save As/Export menu item. The steps are as follows:

1. Choose File | Save As/Export.
2. Select "To an External File or Database."

3. Select HTML Documents (*.htm; *.html) from the "Save as type" combo box.

4. Select a name and location for the .HTM file and click Export. Saving a file as HTML with this procedure does *not* load the browser.

Figure 3.26 shows you what your published Access table might look like, and Figure 3.27 displays the underlying HTML that can be edited by using any HTML editor.

You can also use the Publish to Web Wizard to publish your tables as HTML. The Wizard can be invoked by choosing File | Save to HTML. See Chapter 27, "Access and the Internet," for more detailed information.

Figure 3.26.

Viewing an HTML document in Internet Explorer after a table was saved as HTML.

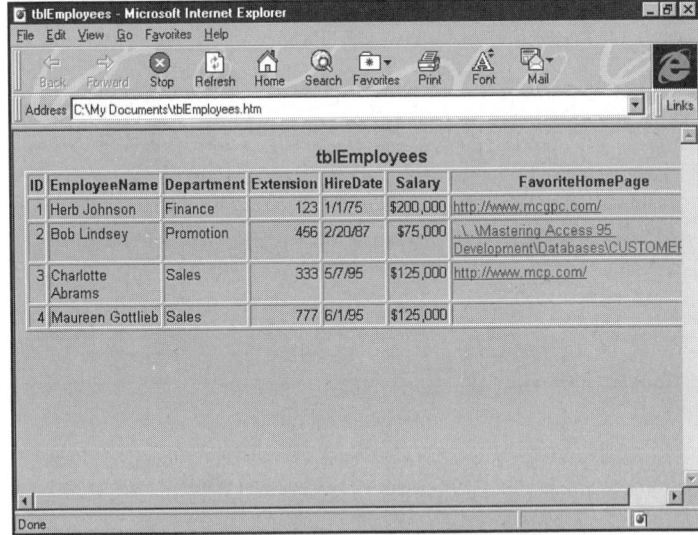

Figure 3.27.

Viewing HTML generated when a table is saved as HTML.

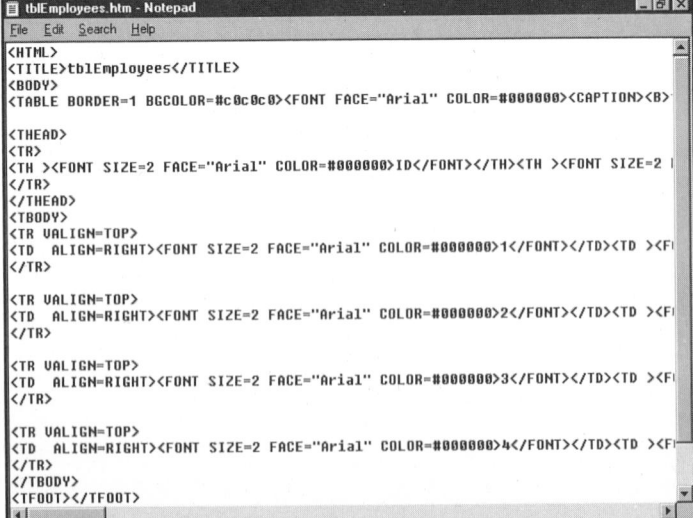

NOTE

Building applications for the Internet is covered extensively in Chapter 27.

Practical Examples: Designing the Tables Needed for the Computer Consulting Firm's Time and Billing Application

Now try designing a few of the tables needed by the computer consulting firm's Time and Billing application. You will build tblClients and tblProjects; tblClients is the main table for the application. It will be used to track the key information about each client. The second table, tblProjects, will be used to hold all the key information users need to store on the projects they're working on for each client. Table 3.2 shows the field names, data types, and sizes for each field in tblClients. You should include indexes for all fields except Notes. Table 3.3 shows the properties that need to be set for these fields. Table 3.4 shows the fields, data types, and sizes for the fields in tblProjects, and Table 3.5 shows the properties that need to be set for these fields. You should include indexes for all fields except ProjectDescription.

Table 3.2. Field names, data types, and sizes for the fields in tblClients.

Field Name	Data Type	Size
ClientID	AutoNumber	4
CompanyName	Text	50
Address	Text	255
City	Text	30
StateProvince	Text	20
PostalCode	Text	20
Country	Text	20
ContactFirstName	Text	30
ContactLastName	Text	50
ContactTitle	Text	50
OfficePhone	Text	30
Fax	Text	30
Cellular	Text	30
Home	Text	30

continues

Table 3.2. continued

Field Name	Data Type	Size
EMailAddress	Text	30
ReferredBy	Text	30
AssociatedWith	Text	30
IntroDate	Date/Time	8
DefaultRate	Currency	8
Notes	Memo	-
HomePage	Hyperlink	-

Table 3.3. Properties that need to be set for the fields in tblClients.

Field Name	Property	Value
ClientID	Caption	Client ID
ClientID	Set as primary key	
CompanyName	Caption	Company Name
CompanyName	Required	Yes
StateProvince	Caption	State/Province
StateProvince	DefaultValue	CA
PostalCode	Caption	Postal Code
ContactFirstName	Caption	Contact First Name
ContactLastName	Caption	Contact Last Name
ContactTitle	Caption	Contact Title
OfficePhone	Caption	Office Phone
OfficePhone	Input Mask	!\(999\)000\-0000
Fax	Input Mask	!\(999\)000\-0000
Cellular	Input Mask	!\(999\)000\-0000
Home	Input Mask	!\(999\)000\-0000
EMailAddress	Caption	E-Mail Address
ReferredBy	Caption	Referred By
AssociatedWith	Caption	Associated With
IntroDate	Caption	Intro Date
IntroDate	Default Value	=Date()
IntroDate	Validation Rule	<=Date()

Field Name	Property	Value
IntroDate	Validation Text	Date Entered Must Be On Or Before Today
IntroDate	Required	Yes
DefaultRate	Caption	Default Rate
DefaultRate	Default Value	125
DefaultRate	Validation Rule	Between 75 an 150
DefaultRate	Validation Text	Rate Must Be Between 75 and 150
HomePage	Caption	Home Page

Table 3.4. Field names, data types, and sizes for the fields in tblProjects.

Field Name	Data Type	Size
ProjectID	AutoNumber	4
ProjectName	Text	50
ProjectDescription	Memo	–
ClientID	Number (Long)	4
PurchaseOrderNumber	Text	30
ProjectTotalEstimate	Currency	8
EmployeeID	Number (Long)	4
ProjectBeginDate	Date/Time	8
ProjectEndDate	Date/Time	8

Table 3.5. Properties that need to be set for the fields in tblProjects.

Field Name	Property	Value
ProjectID	Caption	Project ID
ProjectID	Set as primary key	
ProjectName	Caption	Project Name
ProjectName	Required	Yes
ProjectDescription	Caption	Project Description
ClientID	Caption	Client ID

continues

Table 3.5. continued

Field Name	Property	Value
ClientID	Set lookup to ClientID in tblClients	
ClientID	Required	Yes
PurchaseOrderNumber	Caption	Purchase Order Number
ProjectTotalEstimate	Caption	Project Total Estimate
EmployeeID	Caption	Employee ID
ProjectBeginDate	Caption	Project Begin Date
ProjectEndDate	Caption	Project End Date

The remainder of the tables needed by the Time and Billing application are listed in Appendix A, "Table Structures." The finished table structures can be found in CHAP3.MDB; this file, and all files referred to in this book, can be found on the book's sample code CD-ROM.

Summary

Tables are the foundation for your application. A poorly designed table structure can render an otherwise well-designed application useless. This chapter begins by walking you through several methods for creating tables. It then discusses theoretical issues, such as selecting the correct field type and effectively using field properties. Each property, and its intended use, is discussed in detail. Finally, table properties and indexes are covered. After reading this chapter, you should be ready to harness the many features the Access table designer has to offer.

Relationships: Your Key to Data Integrity

- Understanding Relationships, 70
- Examining the Types of Relationships, 70
- Establishing Relationships, 72
- Establishing Referential Integrity, 75
- Looking At the Benefits of Relationships, 80
- Examining Indexes and Relationships, 80
- Practical Examples: Establishing the Relationships Between the Tables Included in the Time and Billing Database, 81

Understanding Relationships

A relationship exists between two tables when a key fields from one table is matched to a key fields in another table. The fields in both tables usually have the same name, data type, and size. Relationships are a necessary by-product of the data-normalization process. Data normalization is covered in Chapter 1, "Introduction to Access Development;" it is the process of eliminating duplicate information from your system by splitting information into several tables, each containing a unique value. Although data normalization brings many benefits, you need to relate the tables in your system so that your users can view the data in the system as a single entity. After you define relationships between tables, you can build queries, forms, and reports that combine information from multiple tables. In this way, you can reap all the benefits of data normalization while ensuring that your system provides users with all the information they need.

Examining the Types of Relationships

Three types of relationships can exist between tables in a database: one-to-many, one-to-one, and many-to-many. Setting up the proper type of relationship between two tables in your database is imperative. The right type of relationship between two tables ensures

- Data integrity
- Optimal performance
- Ease of use in designing system objects

The reasons behind these benefits are covered throughout this chapter. Before you can understand the benefits of relationships, though, you must understand the types of relationships available.

One-to-Many

A one-to-many relationship is by far the most common type of relationship. In a *one-to-many relationship*, a record in one table can have many related records in another table. A common example is a relationship set up between a Customers table and an Orders table. For each customer in the Customers table, you want to have more than one order in the Orders table. On the other hand, each order in the Orders table can belong to only one customer. The Customers table is on the *one side* of the relationship, and the Orders table is on the *many side*. In order for this relationship to be implemented, the field joining the two tables on the one side of the relationship must be unique. In the Customers and Orders tables example, the CustomerID field that joins the two tables must be unique in the Customers table. If more than one customer in the Customers table has the same customer ID, it is not clear which customer belongs to which order in the Orders table. For this reason, the field that joins the two tables on the one side of the one-to-many relationship must be a primary key or have a unique index.

In almost all cases, the field relating the two tables is the *primary key* of the table on the one side of the relationship. The field relating the two tables on the many side of the relationship is called a *foreign key*.

One-to-One

In a *one-to-one relationship*, each record in the table on the one side of the relationship can have only one matching record in the table on the many side of the relationship. This relationship is not common and is used only in special circumstances. Usually, if you have set up a one-to-one relationship, you should have combined the fields in both tables into one table. You should create a one-to-one relationship for one of these reasons:

- The amount of fields required for a table exceeds the number of fields allowed in an Access table.
- Certain fields that are included in a table need to be much more secure than other fields included in the same table.
- Several fields in a table are required for only a subset of records in the table.

The maximum number of fields allowed in an Access table is 255. There are very few reasons why a table should ever have more than 255 fields. In fact, before you even get close to 255 fields, you should take a close look at the design of your system. On the rare occasion when having more than 255 fields is appropriate, you can simulate a single table by moving some of the fields to a second table and creating a one-to-one relationship between the two tables.

The second reason to separate data that logically would belong in the same table into two tables involves security. An example is a table containing employee information. Certain information, such as employee name, address, city, state, ZIP code, home phone, and office extension, might need to be accessible by many users of the system. Other fields, including the hire date, salary, birth date, and salary grade, might be highly confidential. Field-level security is not available in Access. You can simulate field-level security by using a special attribute of queries called *Run with Owner's permissions*. This feature is covered in Chapter 12, "Advanced Query Concepts." The alternative to this method is to place all the fields that can be accessed by all users in one table and the highly confidential fields in another. Only a special Admin user (not actually named Admin) is given access to the table containing the confidential fields. *Data Access Object* (DAO) code is used to display the fields in the highly confidential table when needed. This is done using a query with Run with Owner's permissions, based on the special Admin user's permission to the highly secured table. This technique is covered in Chapter 33, "Complex Security Issues."

The last reason to define one-to-one relationships is when certain fields in a table are going to be used for only a relatively small subset of records. An example is an Employee table and a Vesting table. Certain fields are required only for employees who are vested. If only a small percentage of the company's employees are vested, it is not efficient in terms of performance or disk space to place all the fields containing information about vesting in the Employee table.

This is especially true if the vesting information requires a large volume of fields. By breaking the information into two tables and creating a one-to-one relationship between them, you can reduce disk-space requirements and improve performance. This improvement is particularly pronounced if the Employee table is large.

Many-to-Many

In a *many-to-many relationship*, records in both tables have matching records in the other table. A many-to-many relationship cannot be defined in Access; you must develop this type of relationship by adding a table called a *junction table*. The junction table is related to each of the two tables as one-to-many relationships. An example is an Orders table and a Products table. Each order probably will contain multiple products, and each product is found on many different orders. The solution is to create a third table called Order Details. The Order Details table is related to the Orders table in a one-to-many relationship based on the OrderID field. It is related to the Products table in a one-to-many relationship based on the ProductID field.

Establishing Relationships

Relationships between Access tables are established in the Relationships window, as shown in Figure 4.1. To open the Relationships window, click Relationships on the toolbar with the Database window active or choose Relationships from the Tools menu. In the Relationships window, you can see the type of relationship that exists for each table. All the one-to-many relationships defined in a database are represented with a join line. If referential integrity has been enforced between the tables involved in a one-to-many relationship, the join line between the tables appears with the number 1 on the one side of the relationship and with an infinity symbol on the many side of the relationship.

Figure 4.1.

The Relationships window enables you to view, add, modify, and remove relationships between tables.

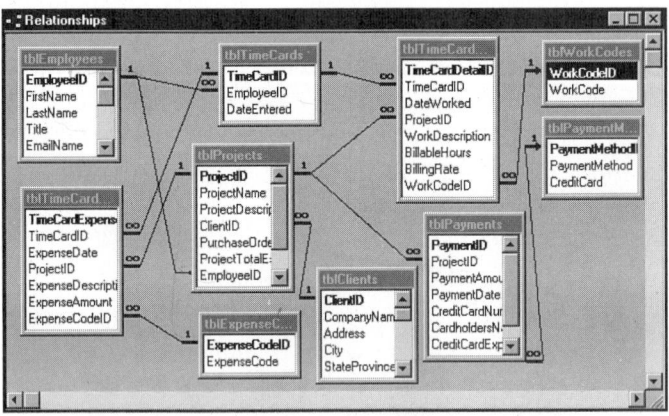

Establishing a Relationship Between Two Tables

To establish a relationship between two tables, follow these steps:

1. Open the Relationships window.

2. If you have never opened the Relationships window of a particular database, the Show Table dialog box appears. Select each table you want to relate and click Add.

3. If you already established relationships in the current database, the Relationships window appears. If the tables you want to include in the relationship do not appear, click the Show Table button on the toolbar or choose Show Table from the Relationships menu. To add the desired tables to the Relationships window, click to select a table and then click Add. Repeat this process for each table you want to add. To select multiple tables at once, press Shift while clicking to select contiguous tables, or press Ctrl while clicking to select noncontiguous tables, then click Add. Click Close when you are done.

4. Click-and-drag the field from the table on the one side of the relationship to the matching field in the table on the many side of the relationship. The Relationships dialog box appears, as shown in Figure 4.2.

Figure 4.2.
The Relationships dialog box enables you to view and modify the relationships between the tables in a database.

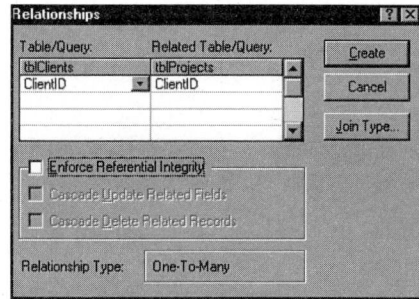

5. Determine whether you want to establish referential integrity (covered in the next section) and whether you want to cascade update related fields or cascade delete related records (covered in the next section) by enabling the appropriate checkboxes.

6. Click Create.

Looking At Guidelines for Establishing Relationships

You need to remember a few important things when establishing relationships. If you are not aware of these important gotchas, you could find yourself in some pretty hairy situations:

• It is important to understand the correlation between the Relationships window and the actual relationships you have established in the database. You use the Relationships window to view and modify the existing relationships. When you establish relationships, the actual relationship is created the moment you click Create. You can delete the tables from the Relationships window (by selecting them and pressing Delete), but the relationships still will exist. The Relationships window provides a visual blueprint of the relationships that have been established. If you modify the layout of the window by moving tables, adding tables to the window, or removing tables from the window, you are prompted to save the layout after you close the Relationships window. Access is not asking whether you want to save the relationships you have established; it is simply asking whether you want to save the visual layout of the window.

- When adding tables to the Relationships window using the Show Tables dialog box, it is easy to accidentally add the same table to the window many times. This is because the tables you are adding can hide behind the Show Tables dialog box or appear below the portion of the Relationships window you are viewing. If this occurs, you see multiple occurrences of the same table when you close the Show Tables dialog box. Each occurrence of the table is given a different alias. You must remove the extra occurrences.

- You also can add queries to the Relationships window by using the Show Tables dialog box. Although you will rarely use this capability, it might be useful if you regularly include the same queries within other queries and want to permanently establish a relationship between them.

- If you remove tables from the Relationships window (this does not delete the relationships) and you want to once again show all relationships that exist in the database, click Show All Relationships on the toolbar or choose Show All from the Relationships menu. This button shows all existing relationships.

TRY IT Create a new database and add a table called tblCustomers, another called tblOrders, and another called tblOrderDetails. Each table should have the following fields:

tblCustomers: CustomerID, CompanyName, Address, City, State, ZipCode

tblOrders: OrderID, CustomerID, OrderDate, ShipVIA

tblOrderDetails: OrderID, LineNumber, ItemID, Quantity, Price

In the tblCustomers table, set the CustomerID field as the primary key. Set the size of the field to 5. You can leave all other fields with their default properties.

In the tblOrders table, set OrderID to the AutoNumber field type. Make the OrderID the primary key field. Set the length of the CustomerID field to 5. Add an index to this field. Set the field type of the OrderDate field to Date.

In the tblOrderDetails table, set the field type of the OrderID field to Number and make sure that the size is Long Integer. Add an index to this field. Set the type of the LineNumber field to Number with a size of Long Integer. The primary key of the table should be based on the combination of the OrderID and LineNumber fields. The ItemID and Quantity fields should be Number type with a size of Long Integer. The Price field should be Currency type.

To open the Relationships window, click Relationships on the toolbar with the Database window active. With the tblCustomers table in the Show Table dialog box selected, hold down your Shift key and click to select the tblOrderDetails table. Click Add. All three tables should be added to the Relationships window. Click Close. Click-and-drag from the CustomerID field in the tblCustomers table to the CustomerID field in the tblOrders table. After the Relationships dialog box appears, click Create. Repeat the process, clicking and dragging the OrderID field from the tblOrders table to the OrderID field in the tblOrderDetails table.

> **NOTE**
>
> You can find this example, and all examples included in this chapter, in the .5 file included with the sample code on the accompanying CD-ROM.

Modifying an Existing Relationship

Modifying an existing relationship is easy. Access gives you the capability to delete an existing relationship or to simply modify the nature of the relationship. To permanently remove a relationship between two tables, follow these steps:

1. With the Database window active, click Relationships on the toolbar.
2. Click on the line joining the two tables that have the relationship you want to delete.
3. Press Delete. You are asked to verify your actions. Click Yes.

You often will want to modify the nature of a relationship rather than remove it. To modify a relationship, follow these steps:

1. With the Database window active, click Relationships on the toolbar.
2. Double-click on the line joining the two tables that have the relationship you want to modify.
3. Make the required changes.
4. Click OK. All the ordinary rules regarding the establishment of relationships will apply.

Establishing Referential Integrity

As you can see, establishing a relationship is quite easy. Establishing the right kind of relationship is a little more difficult. When you attempt to establish a relationship between two tables, Access makes some decisions based on a few predefined factors:

- A one-to-many relationship is established if one of the related fields is a primary key or has a unique index.
- A one-to-one relationship is established if both the related fields are primary keys or have unique indexes.

- An indeterminate relationship is created if neither of the related fields is a primary key and neither has a unique index. Referential integrity cannot be established in this case.

Referential integrity consists of a series of rules that are applied by the Jet Database Engine to ensure that the relationships between tables are maintained properly. At its most basic level, referential integrity rules prevent the creation of orphan records in the table on the many side of the one-to-many relationship. After establishing a relationship between a Customers table and an Orders table, for example, all orders in the Orders table must be related to a particular customer in the Customers table. Before you can establish referential integrity between two tables, the following conditions must be met:

- The matching field on the one side of the relationship must be a primary key field or have a unique index.
- The matching fields must have the same data types. With the exception of text fields, they also must have the same size. Number fields on both sides of the relationship must have the same size (Long Integer), for example.
- Both tables must be part of the same Access database.
- Both tables must be stored in the proprietary Access file (MDB) format (they cannot be external tables from other sources).
- The database containing the two tables must be open.
- Existing data in the two tables cannot violate any referential integrity rules. All orders in the Orders table must relate to existing customers in the Customers table, for example.

WARNING

Although text fields involved in a relationship do not have to be the same size, it is prudent to make them the same size. Otherwise, you will degradate performance as well as risk the chance of unpredictable results when creating queries based on the two tables.

After referential integrity is established between two tables, the following rules are applied:

- You cannot enter a value in the foreign key of the related table that does not exist in the primary key of the primary table. You cannot enter a value in the CustomerID field of the Orders table that does not exist in the CustomerID field of the Customers table, for example.
- You cannot delete a record from the primary table if corresponding records exist in the related table. You cannot delete a customer from the Customers table, for example, if related records exist in the Orders table (records with the same value in the CustomerID field).

- You cannot change the value of a primary key on the one side of a relationship if corresponding records exist in the related table. You cannot change the value in the CustomerID field of the Customers table if corresponding orders exist in the Orders table, for example.

If any of these three rules are violated and referential integrity is being enforced between the tables, an appropriate error message is displayed, as shown in Figure 4.3.

Figure 4.3.
An error message when attempting to add an order for a customer who doesn't exist.

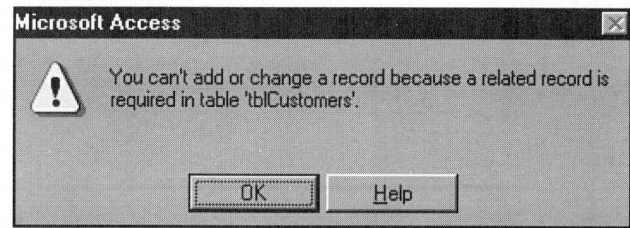

Access's default behavior is to prohibit the deletion of parent records that have associated child records and to prohibit the change of a primary key value of a parent record when that parent has associated child records. You can override these restrictions by using the two checkboxes available in the Relationships dialog box when you establish or modify a relationship.

To open the Relationships window, select the Database window and click Relationships on the toolbar. Double-click on the join line between tblCustomers and tblOrders. Enable the Enforce Referential Integrity checkbox. Click OK. Repeat the process for the relationship between tblOrders and tblOrderDetails.

TRY IT

Go into tblCustomer and add a couple of records. Take note of the customer IDs. Go into tblOrders. Add a couple of records, taking care to assign customer IDs of customers who exist in the tblCustomers table. Now try to add an order for a customer whose customer ID does not exist in tblCustomers. You should get an error message.

Attempt to delete a customer from tblCustomers who does not have any orders. You should get a warning message, but you should be allowed to complete the process. Now try to delete a customer who does have orders. You should be prohibited from deleting the customer. Attempt to change the customer ID of a customer who has orders. You should not be able to do this.

Cascade Update Related Fields

The Cascade Update Related Fields option is available only if referential integrity has been established between the tables. If this option is selected, the user is not prohibited from changing the primary key value of the record on the one side of the relationship. Instead, when an attempt is made to modify the field joining the two tables on the one side of the relationship, the change is cascaded down to the foreign key field on the many side of the relationship.

NOTE

There is no need to enable the Cascade Update Related Fields checkbox when the related field on the one side of the relationship is an AutoNumber field. An AutoNumber field can never be modified. The Cascade Update Related Fields option has no effect on AutoNumber fields.

WARNING

It is very easy to accidentally introduce a loophole into your system. If you create a one-to-many relationship between two tables but forget to set the Required property of the foreign key field to Yes, you allow the addition of orphan records. Figure 4.4 illustrates this point. An order was added to tblOrders without a customer ID being entered. This record is an orphan record because no records in tblCustomers have a customer ID of Null. You can eliminate this problem by setting the Required property of the foreign key field to Yes.

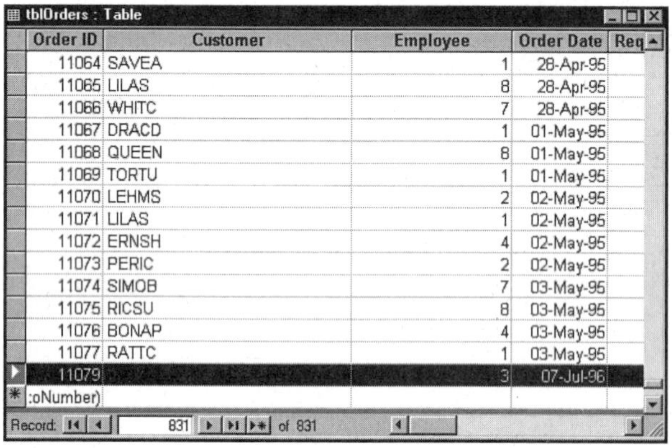

tblOrders : Table

Order ID	Customer	Employee	Order Date	Req
11064	SAVEA	1	28-Apr-95	
11065	LILAS	8	28-Apr-95	
11066	WHITC	7	28-Apr-95	
11067	DRACD	1	01-May-95	
11068	QUEEN	8	01-May-95	
11069	TORTU	1	01-May-95	
11070	LEHMS	2	02-May-95	
11071	LILAS	1	02-May-95	
11072	ERNSH	4	02-May-95	
11073	PERIC	2	02-May-95	
11074	SIMOB	7	03-May-95	
11075	RICSU	8	03-May-95	
11076	BONAP	4	03-May-95	
11077	RATTC	1	03-May-95	
11079		3	07-Jul-96	
:oNumber)				

Record: 831 of 831

Figure 4.4.
An orphan record with Null in foreign key field.

Cascade Delete Related Records

The Cascade Delete Related Records option is available only if referential integrity has been established between the tables. If this option is selected, the user can delete a record on the one side of a one-to-many relationship, even if related records exist in the table on the many side of the relationship. A customer can be deleted even if the customer has existing orders, for example. Referential integrity is maintained between the tables because Access automatically deletes all related records in the child table.

If you attempt to delete a record from the table on the one side of a one-to-many relationship, you get the usual warning message, as shown in Figure 4.5. One the other hand, if you attempt to delete a record from the table on the one side of a one-to-many relationship and related records exist in the child table, you are warned that you are about to delete the record from the parent table and any related records in the child table. (See Figure 4.6.)

Figure 4.5.

A message that appears after the user attempts to delete a parent record without related child records.

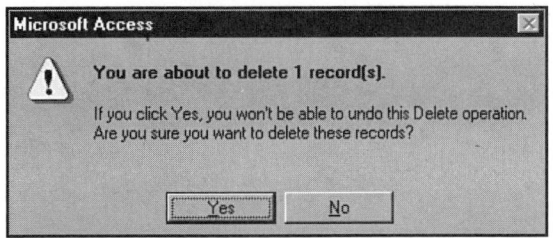

Figure 4.6.

A message that appears after the user attempts to delete a parent record with related child records.

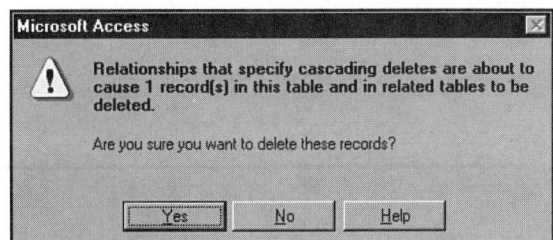

TIP

The Cascade Delete Related Records option is not always appropriate. It is an excellent feature, but you should use it prudently. Although it usually is appropriate to cascade delete from an Orders table to an Order Details table, for example, it generally is not appropriate to cascade delete from a Customers table to an Orders table. This is because you generally do not want all your order history to be deleted from the Orders table if for some reason you want to delete a customer. Deleting the order history causes important information, such as your profit and loss history, to change. It therefore is appropriate to prohibit this type of deletion and handle the customer in some other way, such as marking him as inactive. On the other hand, if you delete an order because it was canceled, you probably want the corresponding order detail information to be removed as well. In this case, the Cascade Delete Related Records option is appropriate. You need to make the appropriate decision in each situation, based on business needs. The important thing is to carefully consider the implications of each option before making your decision.

Modify the relationship between tblCustomers and tblOrders. Enable the Cascade Update Related Fields checkbox. Modify the relationship between tblOrders and tblOrderDetails. Enable the Cascade Delete Related Records checkbox. There is no need to enable Cascade Update Related Fields because the OrderID field in tblOrders is an AutoNumber field.

TRY IT

Attempt to delete a customer who has orders. You still should be prohibited from doing this, because you did not enable Cascade Delete Related Records. Change the customer ID of a customer who has orders in tblCustomers. This change should be allowed. Take a look at the tblOrders table. The customer ID of all corresponding records in the table now should be updated to reflect the change in the parent record.

Add some order details to the tblOrderDetails table. Try to delete any order that has detail in the tblOrderDetails table. You should receive a warning, but you should be allowed to complete the process.

Looking At the Benefits of Relationships

The primary benefit of relationships is the data integrity they provide. Without the establishment of relationships, users are free to add records to child tables without regard to entering required parent information. After referential integrity is established, you can enable Cascade Update Related Fields or Cascade Delete Related Records, as appropriate, which will save you quite a bit of code in maintaining the integrity of the data in your system. Most relational database management systems require that you write the code to delete related records when a parent record is deleted or to update the foreign key in related records when the primary key of the parent is modified. By enabling the Cascade Update and Cascade Delete checkboxes, you are sheltered from having to write a single line of code to accomplish these common tasks.

Relationships automatically are carried into your queries. This means that each time you build a new query, the relationships between the tables within it automatically are established based on the relationships you have set up in the Relationships window. Furthermore, each time you build a form or report, relationships between the tables included on the form or report are used to assist with the design process. Whether you delete or update data using a datasheet or a form, all referential integrity rules automatically apply, even if the relationship is established after the form is built.

Examining Indexes and Relationships

The field that joins two tables on the one side of a one-to-many relationship must be a primary key field or have a unique index so that referential integrity can be maintained. If the index on the one side of the relationship is not unique, there is no way to determine to which parent a child record belongs.

An index on the field on the many side of the one-to-many relationship is optional. It improves the performance of any processing involving the relationship. Make sure that you set the index to Yes (Duplicates OK); otherwise, you will have a one-to-one rather than a one-to-many relationship.

Practical Examples: Establishing the Relationships Between the Tables Included in the Time and Billing Database

In this example, you'll establish the relationships you need to set up for the tables included in the Time and Billing database:

- **tblClients to tblProjects:** tblClients and tblProjects need to be related in a one-to-many relationship based on the ClientID field. You must enforce referential integrity to ensure that projects cannot be added for clients who do not exist. There is no need to set Cascade Update Related Fields, because the client ID that relates the two tables is an AutoNumber field in tblClients. You do not want to enable Cascade Delete Related Records, because you do not want any billing information to change if a client is deleted. Instead, you want to prohibit the deletion of clients who have projects by establishing referential integrity between the two tables.

- **tblProjects to tblPayments:** tblProjects and tblPayments need to be related in a one-to-many relationship based on the ProjectID field. You must enforce referential integrity to ensure that payments cannot be added for projects that do not exist. There is no need to set Cascade Update Related Fields, because the ProjectID that relates the two tables is an AutoNumber field in tblProjects. You do not want to enable Cascade Delete Related Records, because you do not want any payment information to change if a client is deleted. Prohibit the deletion of clients who have projects by establishing referential integrity between the two tables.

- **tblProjects to tblTimeCardHours:** tblProjects and tblTimeCardHours need to be related in a one-to-many relationship based on the ProjectID field. You must enforce referential integrity to ensure that hours cannot be added for projects that do not exist. There is no need to enable Cascade Update Related Fields, because the ProjectID that relates the two tables is an AutoNumber field in tblProjects. Enable Cascade Delete Related Records so that hours are deleted if a project is deleted.

- **tblProjects to tblTimeCardExpenses:** tblProjects and tblTimeCardExpenses need to be related in a one-to-many relationship based on the ProjectID field. You must enforce referential integrity to ensure that expenses cannot be added for projects that do not exist. There is no need to enable Cascade Update Related Fields, because the ProjectID field that relates the two tables is an AutoNumber field in tblProjects. Enable Cascade Delete Related Records so that expenses are deleted if a project is deleted.

- **tblEmployees to tblTimeCards:** tblEmployees and tblTimeCards need to be related in a one-to-many relationship based on the EmployeeID field. You must enforce referential integrity to ensure that time cards cannot be added for employees who do not exist. There is no need to set Cascade Update Related Fields, because the

EmployeeID that relates the two tables is an AutoNumber field in tblEmployees. You do not want to enable Cascade Delete Related Records, because if an employee is deleted, all the employee's time cards are deleted.

- **tblEmployees to tblProjects:** tblEmployees and tblProjects need to be related in a one-to-many relationship based on the EmployeeID field. You must enforce referential integrity to ensure that projects cannot be assigned to employees who do not exist. There is no need to set Cascade Update Related Fields, because the employee ID that relates the two tables is an AutoNumber field in tblEmployees. You do not want to enable Cascade Delete Related Records, because if an employee is deleted, all the employee's projects are deleted.

- **tblTimeCards to tblTimeCardHours:** tblTimeCards and tblTimeCardHours need to be related in a one-to-many relationship based on the TimeCardID field. You must enforce referential integrity to ensure that time card hours cannot be added for time cards that do not exist. There is no need to set Cascade Update Related Fields, because the time card ID that relates the two tables is an AutoNumber field in tblTimeCards. You do want to enable Cascade Delete Related Records, because if a time card is deleted, you want the corresponding hours to be deleted.

- **tblTimeCards to tblTimeCardExpenses:** tblTimeCards and tblTimeCardExpenses need to be related in a one-to-many relationship based on the TimeCardID field. You must enforce referential integrity to ensure that time card expenses cannot be added for time cards that do not exist. There is no need to set Cascade Update Related Fields, because the time card ID that relates the two tables is an AutoNumber field in tblTimeCards. You do want to enable Cascade Delete Related Records, because if a time card is deleted, you want the corresponding expenses to be deleted.

- **tblExpenseCodes to tblTimeCardExpenses:** tblExpenseCodes and tblTimeCardExpenses need to be related in a one-to-many relationship based on the ExpenseCodeID field. You must enforce referential integrity to ensure that time card expenses cannot be added with expense codes that do not exist. There is no need to set Cascade Update Related Fields, because the expense code ID that relates the two tables is an AutoNumber field in tblExpenseCodes. You do not want to enable Cascade Delete Related Records, because if an expense code is deleted, you do not want the corresponding expenses to be deleted.

- **tblWorkCodes to tblTimeCardHours:** tblWorkCodes and tblTimeCardHours need to be related in a one-to-many relationship based on the WorkCodeID field. You must enforce referential integrity to ensure that time card hours cannot be added with work codes that do not exist. There is no need to set Cascade Update Related Fields, because the work code ID that relates the two tables is an AutoNumber field in tblWorkCodes. You do not want to enable Cascade Delete Related Records, because if a work code is deleted, you do not want the corresponding hours to be deleted.

- **tblPaymentMethods to tblPayments:** tblPaymentMethods and tblPayments need to be related in a one-to-many relationship based on the PaymentMethodID field. You must enforce referential integrity to ensure that payments cannot be added with a payment method that does not exist. There is no need to set Cascade Update Related Fields, because the PaymentMethodID field that relates the two tables is an AutoNumber field in tblPaymentMethods. You do not want to enable Cascade Delete Related Records, because if a payment method is deleted, you do not want the corresponding payments to be deleted.

Summary

Relationships enable you to normalize your database. Using relationships, you can divide your data into separate tables, once again combining the data at runtime. This chapter began by describing the types of relationships that you can define. It then covered the details of establishing and modifying relationships between tables and described all the important aspects of establishing relationships.

The capability to easily establish and maintain referential integrity between tables is an important strength of Microsoft Access. This chapter described the referential integrity options and highlighted when each option is appropriate. Finally, this chapter summarized the benefits of relationships.

5

CHAPTER

What Every Developer Needs to Know About Query Basics

- What Is a Query and When Should You Use One?, 86
- Everything You Need to Know About Selecting Fields, 86
- Ordering Your Query Result, 90
- Refining Your Query with Criteria, 92
- Working with Dates in Criteria, 94
- Understanding How Query Results Can Be Updated, 95
- Building Queries Based on Multiple Tables, 96
- Creating Calculated Fields, 101
- Getting Help from the Expression Builder, 103
- Summarizing Data with Totals Queries, 104
- Excluding Fields from the Output, 107
- Nulls and Query Results, 108
- Refining Your Queries with Field and Query Properties, 110
- Field List Properties, 111
- Practical Examples: Building Queries Needed by the Time and Billing Application for the Computer Consulting Firm, 115

What Is a Query and When Should You Use One?

A *Select query* is a stored question about the data stored in your database's tables, and Select queries are the foundation of much of what you do in Access. They underlie most of your forms and reports, allowing you to view the data you want, when you want. You use a simple Select query to define the tables and fields whose data you want to view and also to specify the criteria to limit the data the query's output displays. A Select query is simply a query of a table or tables that just displays data; it doesn't modify data in any way. More advanced Select queries are used to summarize data, supply the results of calculations, or cross-tabulate your data. You can use Action queries to add, edit, or delete data from your tables, based on selected criteria, but this chapter covers Select queries. Other types of queries are covered in Chapter 12, "Advanced Query Concepts."

Everything You Need to Know About Selecting Fields

Creating a basic query is easy because Microsoft has given you a user-friendly drag-and-drop interface. There are two ways to start a new query in Access 97. The first way is to select the Query tab from the Database window, then click New to open the New Query dialog box. (See Figure 5.1.) This dialog box lets you select whether you want to build the query from scratch or use one of the wizards to help you. The Simple Query Wizard walks you through the steps for creating a basic query. The other wizards help you create three specific types of queries: Crosstab, Find Duplicates, or Find Unmatched.

Figure 5.1.
Use the New Query dialog box to select a wizard for the query you want to create, or choose Design View to make a query on your own.

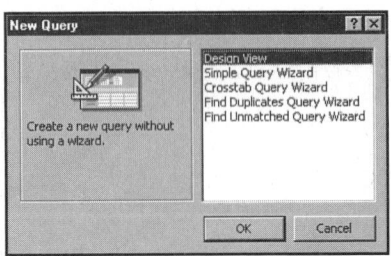

If you select Design View rather than one of the wizards, the Show Table dialog box appears. (See Figure 5.2.) Here, you can select the tables or queries that supply data to your query. Access doesn't care whether you select tables or queries as the foundation for your queries. You can select them by double-clicking on the name of the table or query you want to add or by clicking on the table and then clicking Add. You can select multiple tables or queries by using the Shift key to select a contiguous range of tables or the Ctrl key to select noncontiguous tables. After you have selected the tables or queries you want, click Add and then click Close. This brings you to the Query Design window shown in Figure 5.3.

Figure 5.2.

Selecting Design View displays the available tables in your database on which you can create a query.

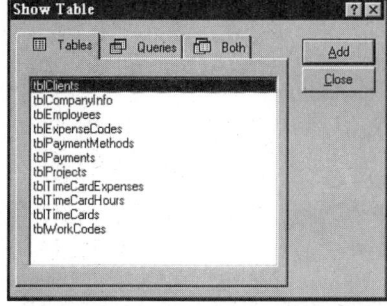

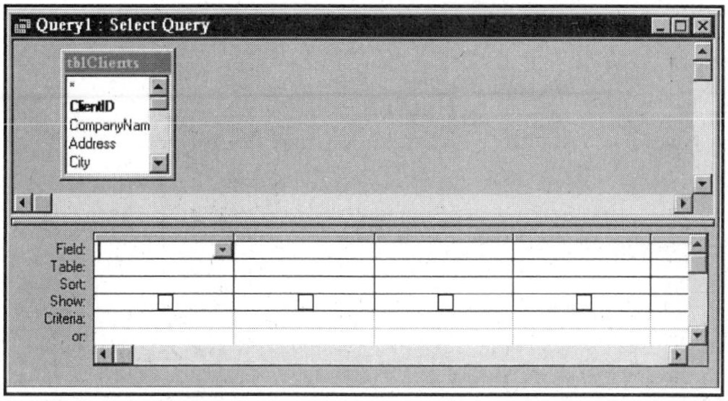

Figure 5.3.

The Query Design window contains an easy-to-use (and learn) Query By Design grid.

TIP

An alternative to the method just described is to select a table from the Tables tab, then select New Query from the New Object drop-down list on the toolbar or choose Query from the Insert menu. This is an efficient method of starting a new query based on only one table because the Show Table dialog box never appears.

You're now ready to select the fields you want to include in the query. The query shown in Figure 5.3 is based on the tblClients table included in the CHAP5.MDB database on the sample code CD-ROM. Notice that the query window is divided into two sections. The top half of the window shows the tables or queries that underlie the query you're designing; the bottom half shows any fields that will be included in the query output. A field can be added to the query design grid on the bottom half of the query window in several ways:

- Double-click on the name of the field you want to add.
- Click and drag a single field from the table in the top half of the query window to the query grid below.

- Select multiple fields at the same time by using your Shift key (for a contiguous range of fields) or your Ctrl key (a noncontiguous range). You can double-click the title bar of the field list to select all fields, then click and drag any one of the selected fields to the query grid.

TRY IT Open the Northwind database that comes with Access. If you want to prevent the Startup form from appearing, hold down your Shift key as you open the database. Click on the Query tab and then click New. Add the Customers table to the query. Follow these steps to select the CustomerID, CompanyName, ContactName, ContactTitle, Region, and Phone fields from Customers:

1. Click on the CustomerID field.
2. Hold down your Shift key and click on the ContactTitle field. This should select the CustomerId, CompanyName, ContactName, and ContactTitle fields.
3. Scroll down the list of fields, using the vertical scrollbar, until the Region field is visible.
4. Hold down your Ctrl key and click on the Region field.
5. With the Ctrl key still held down, click on the Phone field. All six fields should now be selected.

Click and drag any of the selected fields from the table on the top half of the query window to the query grid on the bottom. All six fields should appear in the query grid. You might need to use the horizontal scrollbar to view some of the fields on the right.

> **TIP**
>
> The easiest way to run a query is to click the Run button on the toolbar (which looks like an exclamation point). You can click the Query View button to run a query, but this method works only for Select queries, not for Action queries. The Query View button has a special meaning for Action queries (explained in Chapter 12). Clicking Run is preferable because you don't have to worry about what type of query you're running. After running a Select query, you should see what looks like a datasheet, with only the fields you selected. To return to the query's design, click the Query View button.

Removing a Field from the Query Grid

To remove a field from the query grid, follow these steps:

1. Find the field you want to remove.
2. Click the small gray button (column selector) immediately above the name of the field. The entire column of the query grid should become black. (See Figure 5.4.)
3. Press the Delete key or select Delete from the Edit menu.

Figure 5.4.

Removing a field from the query grid.

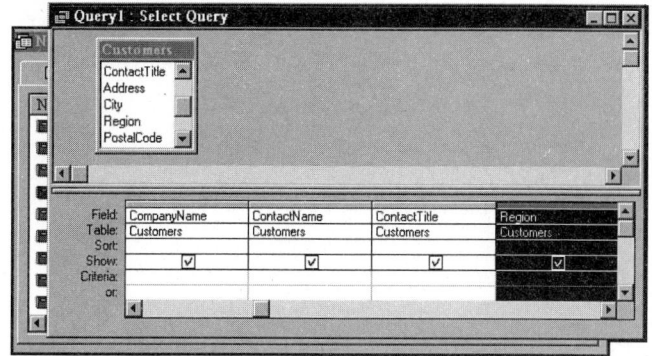

Suppose you have decided to remove the Region field from the query grid. Use the horizontal scrollbar to see the Region field on the query grid.

TRY IT

1. Click on the column selector immediately above the Region field. The entire column of the query grid should become black.

2. Press the Delete key to remove the Region field from the query grid.

Inserting a Field After the Query Is Built

The process for inserting a field after a query is built differs, depending on where you want the new field to be inserted. If you want the new field to be inserted after the existing fields, it's easiest to double-click on the name of the field you want to add. If you prefer to insert the new field between two existing fields, it's best to click and drag the field you want to add, dropping it on the column you want to appear to the right of the inserted column.

To insert the Country field between the ContactTitle and Phone fields, click and drag the Country field from the table until it's on top of the Phone field. This inserts the field in the correct place. To run the query, click Run on the toolbar.

TRY IT

Moving a Field to a Different Location on the Query Grid

Although the user can move a column while in a query's Datasheet view, sometimes you want to permanently alter the position of a field in the query output. This can be done as a convenience to the user or, more important, because you will use the query as a foundation for forms and reports. The order of the fields in the query becomes the default order of the fields on any forms and reports you build using any of the wizards. You can save yourself quite a bit of time by setting up your queries effectively.

Follow these steps to move a single column:

1. To select a column while in the query's Design view, click on its column selector (the button immediately above the field name).

2. Click the selected column a second time, then drag it to a new location on the query grid.

Follow these steps to move more than one column at a time:

1. Drag across the column selectors of the columns you want to move.

2. Click any of the selected columns a second time, then drag them to a new location on the query grid.

TRY IT Move the ContactName and ContactTitle fields so that they appear before the CompanyName field. Do this by clicking and dragging from ContactName's column selector to ContactTitle's column selector. Both columns should be selected. Click again on the column selector for either column, then click and drag until the thick black line jumps to the left of the CompanyName field.

> **NOTE**
>
> Moving a column in the Datasheet view doesn't modify the query's underlying design. If you move a column in Datasheet view, subsequent reordering in the Design view isn't reflected in the Datasheet view. In other words, Design view and Datasheet view are no longer synchronized, and you must reorder both by hand.

Saving Your Query

To save your query at any time, click the Save button on the toolbar. You're then prompted to name your query. Query names should begin with the tag *qry* so that you can easily recognize and identify them as queries. It's important to understand that when you save a query, you're saving only the query's definition, not the actual query result.

Return to the design of the query. To save your work, click Save on the toolbar. When prompted for a name, call the query qryCustomers.

Ordering Your Query Result

When you run a new query, notice that the query output appears in no particular order, but generally, you want to order it. You can do this by using the Sort row of the query grid. To order your query result, follow these steps:

1. Click within the query grid in the Sort cell of the column you want to sort. (See Figure 5.5.)

2. Use the drop-down combo box to select an ascending or descending sort.

Figure 5.5.
*Changing the order
of the query result.*

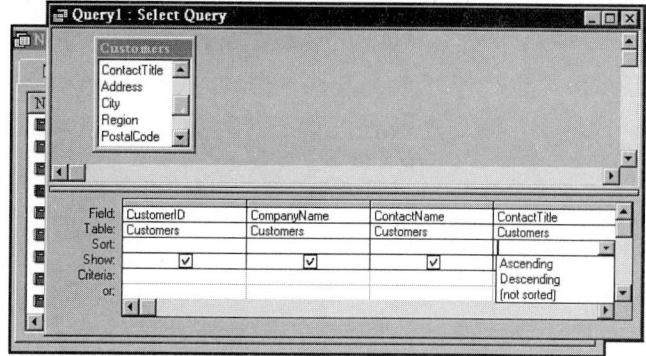

To sort in ascending order by the ContactTitle field, follow these steps:

1. Click in the Sort row of the query grid for the ContactTitle field.

2. Open the Sort drop-down combo box.

3. Select Ascending.

4. Run your query and view the results. Your records should now be in order by the ContactTitle field.

5. If you want to return to the query's design, click Query View on the toolbar.

Sorting by More than One Field

Quite often you want to sort your query output by more than one field. The columns you want to sort must be placed in order from left to right on the query grid, with the column you want to act as the primary sort on the far left and the secondary, tertiary, and any additional sorts following to the right. If you want the columns to appear in a different order in the query output, they need to be moved manually after the query is run.

Sort the query output by the Country field and, within country, by the ContactTitle field. Because sorting always occurs from left to right, you must place the Country field before the ContactTitle field. Therefore, you must move the Country field. Follow these steps:

1. Select the Country field from the query grid by clicking the thin gray button above the Country column.

2. After you have selected the Country field, move your mouse back to the thin gray button and click and drag to the left of ContactTitle. A thick gray line should appear to the left of the ContactTitle field.

3. Release the mouse button.

4. Change the sort of the Country field to Ascending.

5. Run the query. The records should be in alphabetical order by country and, within Country, by contact title.

91

Refining Your Query with Criteria

So far, you have learned how to select the fields you want and how to indicate the sort order for your query output. One of the important features of queries is the ability to limit your output by selection criteria. Access allows you to combine criteria by using any of several operators to limit the criteria for one or more fields. The operators and their meanings are covered in Table 5.1.

Table 5.1. Access operators and their meanings.

Operator	Meaning	Example	Result
=	Equal to	="Sales"	Finds only those records with "Sales" as the field value.
<	Less than	<100	Finds all records with values less than 100 in that field.
<=	Less than or equal to	<=100	Finds all records with values less than or equal to 100 in that field.
>	Greater than	>100	Finds all records with values greater than 100 in that field.
>=	Greater than or equal to	>=100	Finds all records with values greater than or equal to 100 in that field.
<>	Not equal	<>"Sales"	Finds all records with values other than Sales in the field.
And	Both conditions must be true	Created by adding criteria on the same line of the query grid to more than one field	Finds all records where the conditions in both fields are true.
Or	Either condition can be true	"CA" or "NY" or "UT"	Finds all records with the value of "CA", "NY", or "UT" in the field.
Like	Compares a string expression to a pattern	Like "Sales*"	Finds all records with the value of "Sales" at the beginning of the field.
Between	Finds a range of values	Between 5 and 10	Finds all records with the values of 5 through 10 (inclusive) in the field.

Operator	Meaning	Example	Result
In	Same as Or	In("CA", "NY","UT")	Finds all records with the value of "CA", "NY", or "UT" in the field.
Not	Same as not equal	Not "Sales"	Finds all records with values other than Sales in the field.
Is Null	Finds nulls	Is Null	Finds all records where no data has been entered in the field.
Is Not Null	Finds all records not null	Is Not Null	Finds all records where data has been entered in the field.

Criteria entered for two fields on a single line of the query grid are considered an And, which means that both conditions need to be true for the record to appear in the query output. Entries made on separate lines of the query grid are considered an Or, which means that either condition can be true for the record to be included in the query output. Take a look at the example in Figure 5.6; this query would output all records in which the ContactTitle field begins with either Marketing or Owner, regardless of the customer ID. It outputs the records in which the ContactTitle field begins with Sales only for the customers whose IDs begin with the letters *M* through *R* inclusive.

Figure 5.6.
Adding criteria to a query.

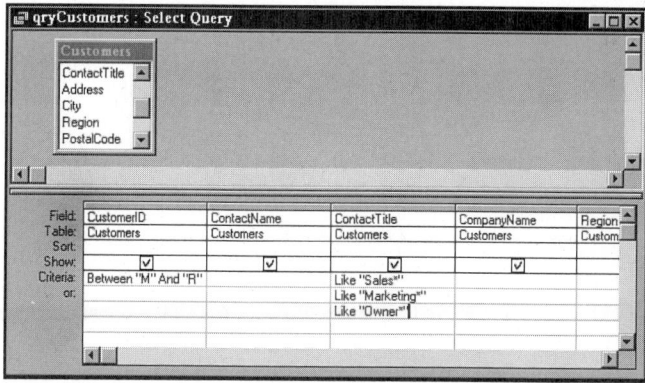

Design a query to find all the sales agents in Brazil or France. The criteria you build should look like those in Figure 5.7.

TRY IT

1. Notice that the criterion for the Country field is "Brazil" Or "France" because you want both Brazil and France to appear in the query output. The criterion for the ContactTitle field is "Sales Agent". Because the criteria for both the Country and ContactTitle fields are entered on the same line of the query grid, both must be true

for the record to appear in the query output. In other words, the customer must be in either Brazil or France and must also be a sales agent.

2. Modify the query so that you can output all the customers for whom the contact title begins with Sales. Try changing the criteria for the ContactTitle field to Sales. Notice that no records appear in the query output because no contact titles are just Sales. You must enter "Like Sales*" for the criteria. Now you get the Sales Agents, Sales Associates, Sales Managers, and so on. You still don't see the Assistant Sales Agents because their titles don't begin with Sales. Try changing the criteria to "Like *Sales*". Now all the Assistant Sales Agents appear.

Figure 5.7.

The criteria to select sales agents whose country is either Brazil or France.

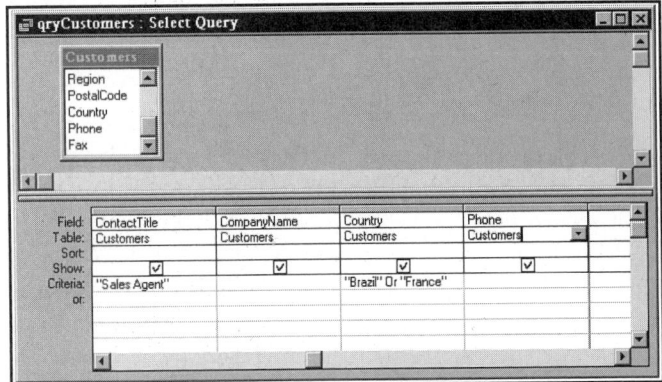

Working with Dates in Criteria

Access gives you significant power for adding date functions and expressions to your query criteria. Using these criteria, you can find all records in a certain month, on a specific weekday, or between two dates. Table 5.2 lists several examples.

Table 5.2. Sample date criteria.

Expression	Meaning	Example	Result
Date()	Current date	Date()	Records with the current date within a field.
Day(Date)	The day of a date	Day ([OrderDate])=1	Records with the order on the first day of the month.
Month(Date)	The month of a date	Month ([OrderDate])=1	Records with the order in January.
Year(Date)	The year of a date	Year ([OrderDate]) =1991	Records with the order in 1991.

Expression	Meaning	Example	Result
Weekday(Date)	The weekday of a date	Weekday ([OrderDate])=2	Records with the order on a Monday.
Between Date And Date	A range of dates	Between #1/1/95# and #12/31/95#	All records in 1995.
DatePart (Interval, Date)	A specific part of a date	DatePart ("q", [OrderDate])=2	All records in the second quarter.

The Weekday(Date, [FirstDayOfWeek]) function works based on your locale and how your system defines the first day of the week. Weekday() used without the optional FirstDayOfWeek argument defaults to vbSunday as the first day. A value of 0 defaults the FirstDayOfWeek to the system definition. Other values can be set, too. (See the online help for Weekday().)

Figure 5.8 illustrates the use of a date function. Notice that the expression DatePart("q",[OrderDate]) is entered as the field name, and the value of 2 is entered for the criterion. The expression Year([OrderDate]) is entered as another field name with the number 1995 as the criterion. Therefore, this query outputs all records in which the order date is in the second quarter of 1995.

Figure 5.8.

Using the DatePart() *and* Year() *functions in a query.*

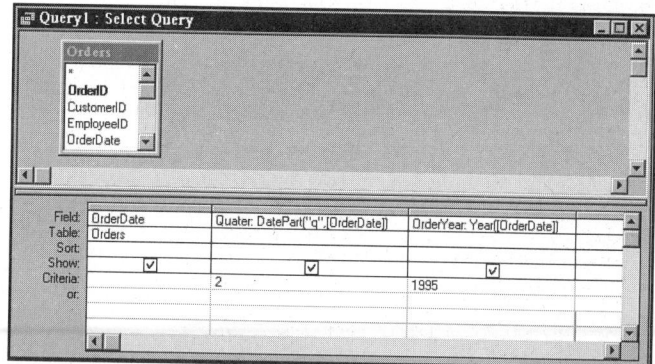

Understanding How Query Results Can Be Updated

If you haven't realized it yet, the results of your query can usually be updated. This means that if you modify the data in the query output, the data in the tables underlying the query is permanently modified.

Build a query based on the Customers table. Add the CustomerID, CompanyName, Address, City, and Region fields to the query grid, then run the query. Change the address of a particular customer, and make a note of the customer ID of the customer whose address you changed.

Make sure you move off the record so that the change is written to disk. Close the query, open the actual table in Datasheet view, and find the record whose address you modified. Notice that the change you made was written to the original table—this is because a query result is a dynamic set of records that maintains a link back to the original data. This happens whether you're on a standalone machine or on a network.

> ### WARNING
>
> It's essential that you understand how query results are updated; otherwise, you might mistakenly update table data without even realizing you did so. Updating multitable queries is covered later in this chapter in the sections "Pitfalls of Multitable Queries" and "Row Fix-up in Multitable Queries."

Building Queries Based on Multiple Tables

If you have properly normalized your table data, you probably want to bring the data from your tables back together by using queries. Fortunately, you can do this quite easily with Access queries.

The query in Figure 5.9 joins the Customers, Orders, and Order Details tables, pulling fields from each. Notice that the CustomerID and CompanyName fields are selected from the Customers table, the OrderID and OrderDate from the Orders table, and the UnitPrice and Quantity from the Order Details table. After running this query, you should see the results shown in Figure 5.10. Notice that you get a record in the query's result for every record in the Order Details table. In other words, there are 2,155 records in the Order Details table, and that's how many records appear in the query output. By creating a multitable query, you can look at data from related tables, along with the data from the Order Details table.

Figure 5.9.

A query joining the Customers, Orders, and Order Details tables.

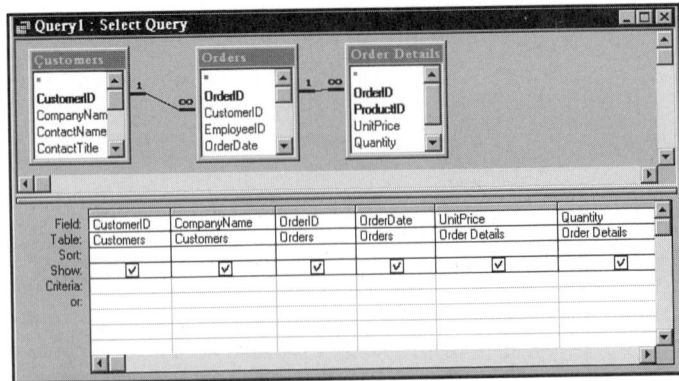

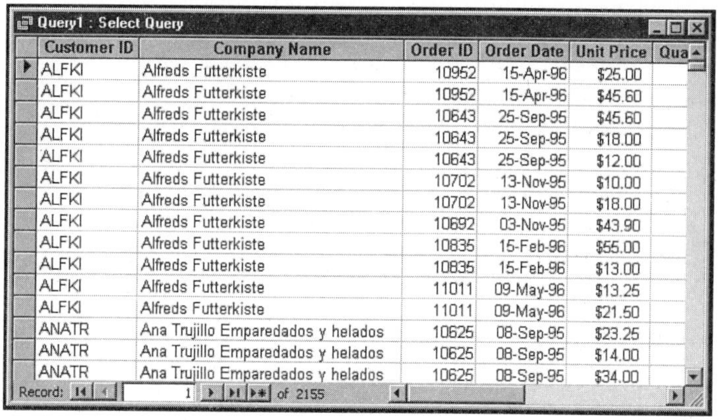

Query1 : Select Query

	Customer ID	Company Name	Order ID	Order Date	Unit Price	Qua
▶	ALFKI	Alfreds Futterkiste	10952	15-Apr-96	$25.00	
	ALFKI	Alfreds Futterkiste	10952	15-Apr-96	$45.60	
	ALFKI	Alfreds Futterkiste	10643	25-Sep-95	$45.60	
	ALFKI	Alfreds Futterkiste	10643	25-Sep-95	$18.00	
	ALFKI	Alfreds Futterkiste	10643	25-Sep-95	$12.00	
	ALFKI	Alfreds Futterkiste	10702	13-Nov-95	$10.00	
	ALFKI	Alfreds Futterkiste	10702	13-Nov-95	$18.00	
	ALFKI	Alfreds Futterkiste	10692	03-Nov-95	$43.90	
	ALFKI	Alfreds Futterkiste	10835	15-Feb-96	$55.00	
	ALFKI	Alfreds Futterkiste	10835	15-Feb-96	$13.00	
	ALFKI	Alfreds Futterkiste	11011	09-May-96	$13.25	
	ALFKI	Alfreds Futterkiste	11011	09-May-96	$21.50	
	ANATR	Ana Trujillo Emparedados y helados	10625	08-Sep-95	$23.25	
	ANATR	Ana Trujillo Emparedados y helados	10625	08-Sep-95	$14.00	
	ANATR	Ana Trujillo Emparedados y helados	10625	08-Sep-95	$34.00	

Record: 1 of 2155

Figure 5.10.
The results of querying multiple tables.

TRY IT

Build a query that combines information from the Customers, Orders, and Order Details tables. To do this, build a new query by following these steps:

1. Select the Query tab from the Database window.
2. Click New.
3. Select Design view.
4. From the Show Table dialog box, select Customers, Orders, and Order Details by holding down the Ctrl key and clicking on each table name. Then select Add.
5. Click Close.
6. Some of the tables included in the query might be hiding below. If so, scroll down with the vertical scrollbar to view any tables that aren't visible. Notice the join lines between the tables; they're based on the relationships set up in the Relationships window.
7. Select the following fields from each table:

   Customers: Country, City

   Orders: Order Date

   Order Details: UnitPrice, Quantity
8. Sort by Country and then City. Your finished query design should look like the one in Figure 5.11.
9. Run the query. Data from all three tables should be included in the query output.

NOTE

To remove a table from a query, click anywhere on the table in the top half of the query grid and press the Delete key. You can add tables to the query at any time by clicking the Show Table button from the toolbar. If you prefer, you can also click and drag tables directly from the Database window to the top half of the query grid.

Figure 5.11.

The query design from the example.

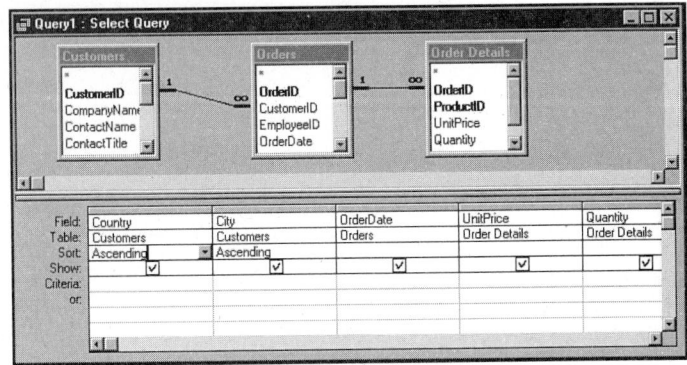

Pitfalls of Multitable Queries

You should be aware of some pitfalls of multitable queries; they concern updating as well as which records you see in the query output.

It's important to remember that certain fields in a multitable query can't be updated—these are the join fields on the "one" side of a one-to-many relationship (unless the Cascade Update referential integrity feature has been activated). You also can't update the join field on the "many" side of the relationship after you've updated data on the "one" side. More important, which fields can be updated, and the consequences of updating them, might surprise you. If you update the fields on the "one" side of a one-to-many relationship, you must be aware of that change's impact. You're actually updating that record in the original table on the "one" side of the relationship; several records on the "many" side of the relationship will be affected.

For example, Figure 5.12 shows the result of a query based on the Customers, Orders, and Order Details tables. I have changed `"Alfreds Futterkiste"` to `"Waldo Futterkiste "` on a specific record of my query output. You might expect this change to affect only that specific order detail item. Pressing the down-arrow key to move off the record shows that all records associated with Alfreds Futterkiste have been changed. (See Figure 5.13.) This happened because all the orders for Alfreds Futterkiste were actually getting their information from one record in the Customers table—the record for customer ID ALFKI. This is the record I modified while viewing the query result.

TRY IT

To get this experience firsthand, try changing the data in the City field for one of the records in the query result. Notice that the record (as well as several other records) is modified. This happens because the City field actually represents data from the "one" side of the one-to-many relationship. In other words, when you're viewing the Country and City fields for several records in the query output, the data for the fields might be originating from one record. The same goes for the Order Date field because it's also on the "one" side of a one-to-many relationship. The only field in the query output that can't be modified is TotalPrice, a calculated field. Practice modifying the data in the query result, then returning to the original table and noticing what data has changed.

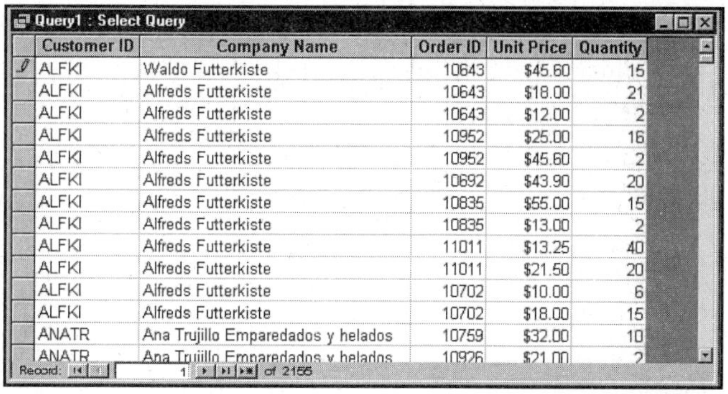

Query1 : Select Query

Customer ID	Company Name	Order ID	Unit Price	Quantity
ALFKI	Waldo Futterkiste	10643	$45.60	15
ALFKI	Alfreds Futterkiste	10643	$18.00	21
ALFKI	Alfreds Futterkiste	10643	$12.00	2
ALFKI	Alfreds Futterkiste	10952	$25.00	16
ALFKI	Alfreds Futterkiste	10952	$45.60	2
ALFKI	Alfreds Futterkiste	10692	$43.90	20
ALFKI	Alfreds Futterkiste	10835	$55.00	15
ALFKI	Alfreds Futterkiste	10835	$13.00	2
ALFKI	Alfreds Futterkiste	11011	$13.25	40
ALFKI	Alfreds Futterkiste	11011	$21.50	20
ALFKI	Alfreds Futterkiste	10702	$10.00	6
ALFKI	Alfreds Futterkiste	10702	$18.00	15
ANATR	Ana Trujillo Emparedados y helados	10759	$32.00	10
ANATR	Ana Trujillo Emparedados y helados	10926	$21.00	2

Record: 1 of 2155

Figure 5.12.
Changing a record on the "one" side of a one-to-many relationship. After updating the company name, all records with the same customer ID are affected.

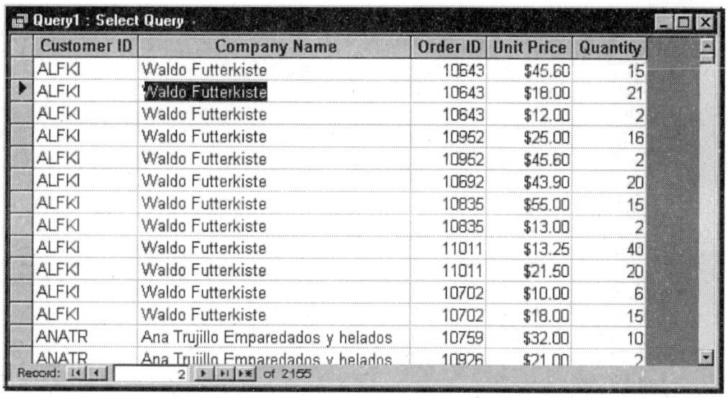

Query1 : Select Query

Customer ID	Company Name	Order ID	Unit Price	Quantity
ALFKI	Waldo Futterkiste	10643	$45.60	15
ALFKI	Waldo Futterkiste	10643	$18.00	21
ALFKI	Waldo Futterkiste	10643	$12.00	2
ALFKI	Waldo Futterkiste	10952	$25.00	16
ALFKI	Waldo Futterkiste	10952	$45.60	2
ALFKI	Waldo Futterkiste	10692	$43.90	20
ALFKI	Waldo Futterkiste	10835	$55.00	15
ALFKI	Waldo Futterkiste	10835	$13.00	2
ALFKI	Waldo Futterkiste	11011	$13.25	40
ALFKI	Waldo Futterkiste	11011	$21.50	20
ALFKI	Waldo Futterkiste	10702	$10.00	6
ALFKI	Waldo Futterkiste	10702	$18.00	15
ANATR	Ana Trujillo Emparedados y helados	10759	$32.00	10
ANATR	Ana Trujillo Emparedados y helados	10926	$21.00	2

Record: 2 of 2155

Figure 5.13.
The result of changing a record on the "one" side of a one-to-many relationship. Notice that the Company Name field has been updated for all records with `ALFKI` *as the customer ID.*

The second pitfall of multitable queries is figuring out what records result from such a query. So far, you have learned how to build only inner joins. Join types are covered in detail in Chapter 12, but for now, it's important to understand that the query output contains only customers who have orders and orders that have order detail. This means that not all the customers or orders might be listed. In Chapter 12, you learn how to build queries in which you can list all customers, regardless of whether they have orders. You also learn how to list only the customers without orders.

Row Fix-up in Multitable Queries

The row fix-up feature is automatically available to you in Access. As you fill in key values on the "many" side of a one-to-many relationship in a multitable query, the non-key values are automatically looked up in the parent table. Most database developers refer to this as *enforced referential integrity*. When a foreign key is entered on the "many" side of a query, it must first exist on the "one" side of the query to be entered successfully on the "many" side. As you can imagine, you don't want to be able to add an order to your database for which no customer record exists.

For example, the query in Figure 5.14 is based on the Customers and Orders tables. The fields included in the query are CustomerID from the Orders table; CompanyName, Address, and City from the Customers table; and OrderID and OrderDate from the Orders table. If the CustomerID associated with an order is changed, the CompanyName, Address, and City are looked up from the Customers table and immediately displayed in the query result. Notice in Figure 5.15 how the information for Alfreds Futterkiste is displayed in the query result. Figure 5.16 shows that the CompanyName, Address, and City change automatically when the CustomerID is changed. Don't be confused by the combo box used to select the customer ID. This is a result of Access's auto-lookup feature, covered in Chapter 3, "What Every Developer Needs to Know About Tables." The customer ID associated with a particular order is actually being modified in the query. If a new record is added to the query, the customer information is filled in as soon as the customer ID associated with the order is selected.

Figure 5.14.

This query illustrates the use of Auto Fix Up in a query with multiple tables.

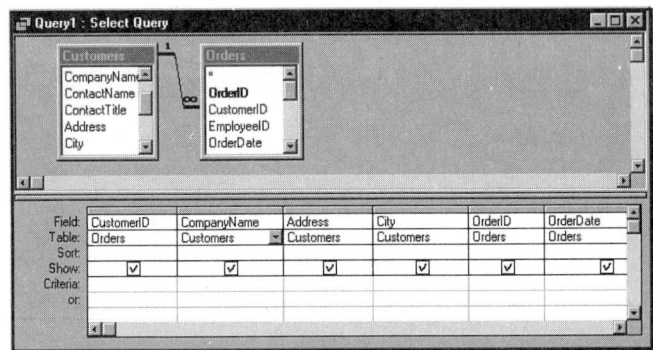

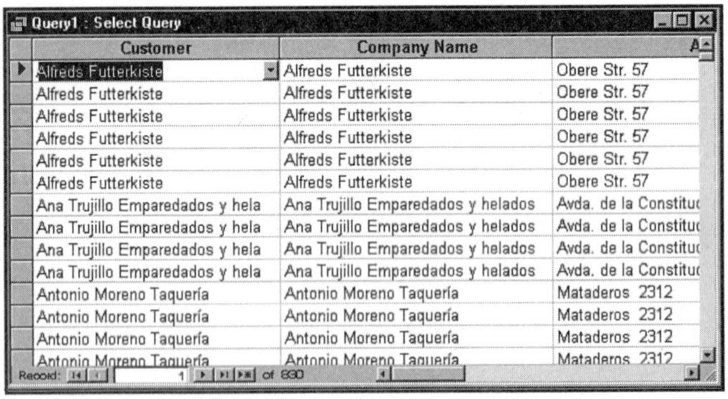

Figure 5.15.

The query result before selecting another customer ID.

Figure 5.16.
The result of an auto-lookup after the customer ID is changed. The information on the "one" side of the relationship is "fixed up" to display information for the appropriate customer.

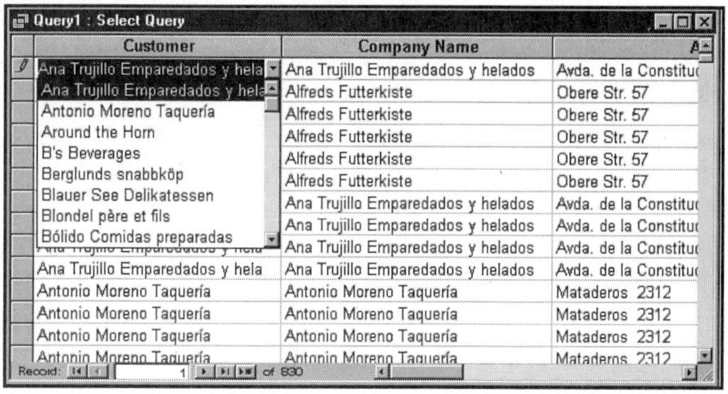

Creating Calculated Fields

One of the rules of data normalization is that the results of calculations shouldn't be included in your database. You can output the results of calculations by building those calculations into your queries, and you can display the results of the calculations on forms and reports by making the query the foundation for a form or report. You can also add controls to your forms and reports containing the calculations you want. In certain cases, this can improve performance. (This topic is covered in more detail in Chapter 12.)

The columns of your query result can hold the result of any valid expression, including the result of a user-defined function. This makes your queries extremely powerful. For example, the following expression could be entered:

```
Left([FirstName],1) & "." & Left([LastName],1) & "."
```

This expression would give you the first character of the first name followed by a period, the first character of the last name, and another period. An even simpler expression would be this one:

```
[UnitPrice]*[Quantity]
```

This calculation would simply take the UnitPrice field and multiply it by the Quantity field. In both cases, Access would automatically name the resulting expression. For example, the calculation that results from concatenating the first and last initials is shown in Figure 5.17. To give the expression a name, such as Initials, you must enter it as follows:

```
Initials:Left([FirstName],1) & "." & Left([LastName],1) & "."
```

The text preceding the colon is the name of the expression—in this case, Initials. If you don't explicitly give your expression a name, it defaults to Expr1.

Figure 5.17.

The result of the expression
`Initials:Left([FirstName],1)`
`& "." &`
`Left([LastName],1) & "."`
in the query.

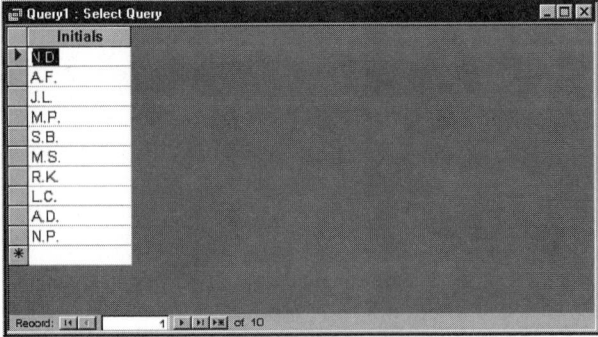

TRY IT Follow these steps to add a calculation that shows the unit price multiplied by the quantity:

1. Scroll to the right on the query grid until you can see a blank column.

2. Click in the Field row for the new column.

3. Type **TotalPrice:UnitPrice*Quantity**. If you want to see more easily what you're typing, press Shift+F2 (Zoom). The dialog box shown in Figure 5.18 appears.

Figure 5.18.

Expanding the field with the Zoom function (Shift+F2).

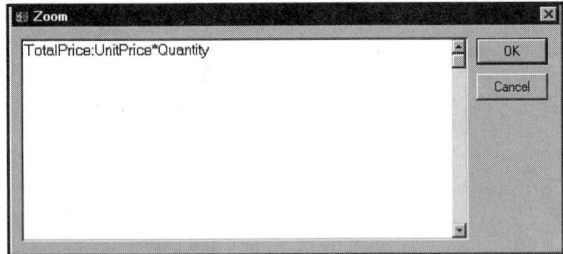

4. Click OK to close the Zoom window.

5. Run the query. The total sales amount should appear in the far-right column of the query output. The query output should look like the one in Figure 5.19.

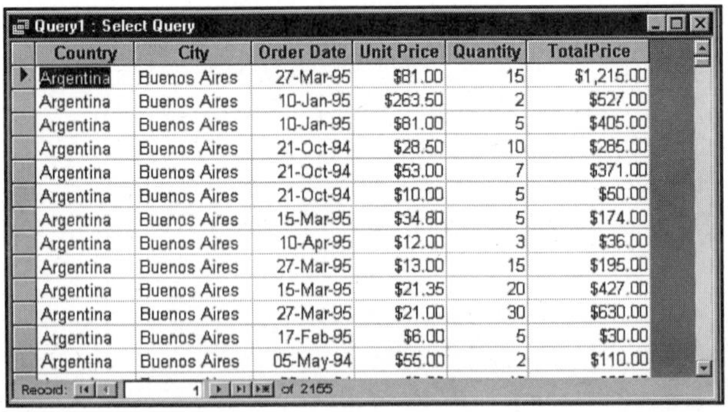

Figure 5.19.

The result of the total sales calculation.

Country	City	Order Date	Unit Price	Quantity	TotalPrice
Argentina	Buenos Aires	27-Mar-95	$81.00	15	$1,215.00
Argentina	Buenos Aires	10-Jan-95	$263.50	2	$527.00
Argentina	Buenos Aires	10-Jan-95	$81.00	5	$405.00
Argentina	Buenos Aires	21-Oct-94	$28.50	10	$285.00
Argentina	Buenos Aires	21-Oct-94	$53.00	7	$371.00
Argentina	Buenos Aires	21-Oct-94	$10.00	5	$50.00
Argentina	Buenos Aires	15-Mar-95	$34.80	5	$174.00
Argentina	Buenos Aires	10-Apr-95	$12.00	3	$36.00
Argentina	Buenos Aires	27-Mar-95	$13.00	15	$195.00
Argentina	Buenos Aires	15-Mar-95	$21.35	20	$427.00
Argentina	Buenos Aires	27-Mar-95	$21.00	30	$630.00
Argentina	Buenos Aires	17-Feb-95	$6.00	5	$30.00
Argentina	Buenos Aires	05-May-94	$55.00	2	$110.00

Record: 1 of 2155

> **NOTE**
>
> You can enter any valid expression in the Field row of your query grid. Notice that field names included in an expression are automatically surrounded by square brackets. This happens automatically unless your field name has spaces. If a field name includes any spaces, you must enclose the field name in brackets; otherwise, your query won't run properly, which is just one of the many reasons why field and table names shouldn't contain spaces.

Getting Help from the Expression Builder

The Expression Builder is a helpful tool for building expressions in your queries, as well as in many other situations in Access. To invoke the Expression Builder, click in the Field cell of your query grid and then click Builder on the toolbar. (See Figure 5.20.) Notice that the Expression Builder is divided into three columns. The first column shows the objects in the database. After selecting an element in the leftmost column, select the elements you want to paste from the middle and rightmost columns.

Figure 5.20.

The Expression Builder makes it easier for you to create expressions in your query.

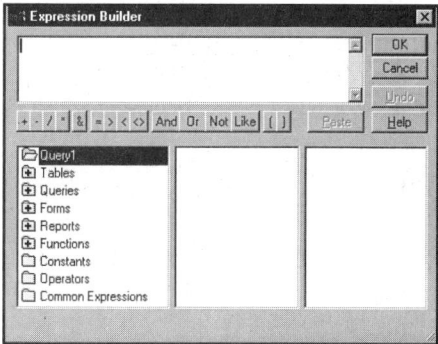

The example in Figure 5.21 shows Functions selected in the leftmost column. Within Functions, both user-defined and built-in functions are listed; here, the Functions object is expanded with Built-In Functions selected. In the center column, Date/Time is selected. After selecting Date/Time, all the built-in date and time functions appear in the rightmost column. If you double-click on a particular function—in this case, the DatePart function—the function and its parameters are placed in the text box at the top of the Expression Builder window. Notice that the DatePart function has four parameters: Interval, Date, FirstWeekDay, and FirstWeek. If you know what needs to go into each of these parameters, you can simply replace the parameter place markers with your own values. If you need more information, you can invoke help on the selected function and learn more about the required parameters. In Figure 5.22, two parameters are filled in: the interval and the name of the field being evaluated. After clicking OK, the expression is placed in the Field cell of the query.

Figure 5.21.
The Expression Builder with the DatePart *function selected.*

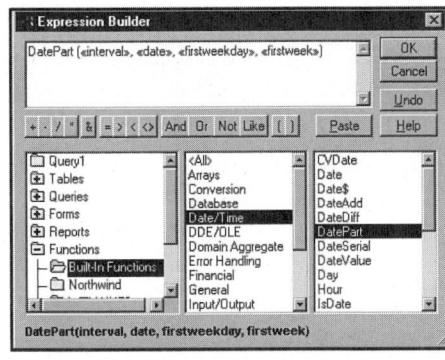

Figure 5.22.
A function pasted by Expression Builder.

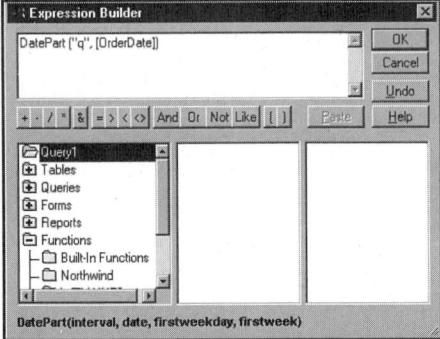

Summarizing Data with Totals Queries

With Totals queries, you can easily summarize numeric data. Totals queries can be used to calculate the Sum, Average, Count, Minimum, Maximum, and other types of summary calculations for the data in your query result. These queries let you calculate one value for all the records in your query result or group the calculations as desired. For example, you could determine the total sales for every record in the query result, as shown in Figure 5.23, or you could output the total sales by country and city. (See Figure 5.24.) You could also calculate the total, average, minimum, and maximum sales amounts for all customers in the United States. The possibilities are endless.

Figure 5.23.

Total sales for every record in the query result.

Figure 5.24.

Total sales by country and city.

Country	City	TotalSales
Argentina	Buenos Aires	$8,119.10
Austria	Graz	$113,236.68
Austria	Salzburg	$26,259.95
Belgium	Bruxelles	$10,430.58
Belgium	Charleroi	$24,704.40
Brazil	Campinas	$8,702.23
Brazil	Resende	$6,480.70
Brazil	Rio de Janeiro	$53,999.18
Brazil	São Paulo	$45,786.37
Canada	Montréal	$32,203.90
Canada	Tsawassen	$22,607.70
Canada	Vancouver	$522.50
Denmark	Århus	$16,643.80

Here are the steps for creating a Totals query:

1. Add to the query grid the fields or expressions you want to summarize. It's important that you add the fields in the order in which you want them grouped. For example, Figure 5.25 shows a query grouped by country, then city.

2. Click Totals on the toolbar or choose View|Totals to add a Total row to the query. Each field in the query has Group By in the total row.

3. Click in the Total row on the design grid.

4. Open the combo box and choose the calculation you want. (See Figure 5.25.)

5. Leave Group By in the Total cell of any fields you want to group by, as shown in Figure 5.25. Remember to place the fields in the order in which you want them grouped. For example, if you want the records grouped by country, then by sales representative, the Country field must be placed to the left of the Sales Representative field on the query grid. On the other hand, if you want records grouped by sales representative, then by country, the Sales Representative field must be placed to the left of the Country field on the query grid.

Figure 5.25.

Selecting the type of calculation from a drop-down list.

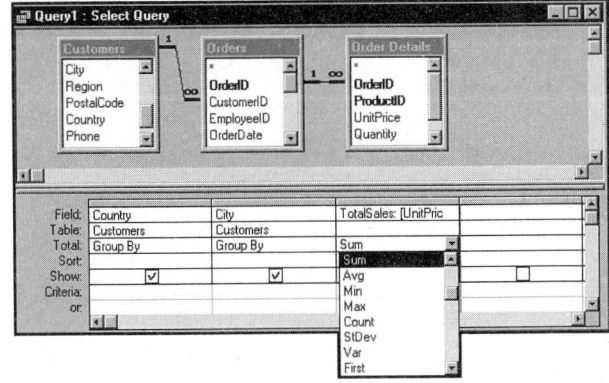

6. Add the criteria you want to the query.

Figure 5.26 shows the design of a query that finds the total, average, maximum, and number of sales by country; Figure 5.27 shows the results of running the query. As you can see, Totals queries can give you valuable information.

Figure 5.26.

A query that finds the total, average, maximum, and number of sales by country.

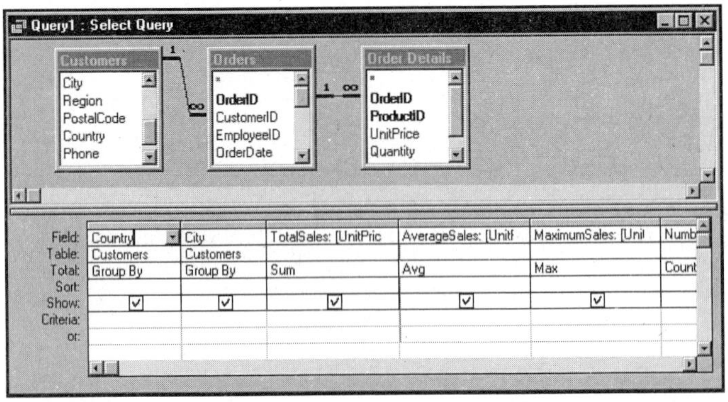

Figure 5.27.

The result of running a query with many aggregate functions.

Country	City	TotalSales	AverageSales	MaximumSales	NumberOfSales
Argentina	Buenos Aires	$8,119.10	$238.80	$1,215.00	34
Austria	Graz	$113,236.68	$1,110.16	$6,360.00	102
Austria	Salzburg	$26,259.95	$1,141.74	$10,540.00	23
Belgium	Bruxelles	$10,430.58	$613.56	$2,200.00	17
Belgium	Charleroi	$24,704.40	$633.45	$2,750.00	39
Brazil	Campinas	$8,702.23	$458.01	$1,600.00	19
Brazil	Resende	$6,480.70	$341.09	$1,552.00	19
Brazil	Rio de Janeiro	$53,999.18	$650.59	$15,810.00	83
Brazil	São Paulo	$45,786.37	$558.37	$8,432.00	82
Canada	Montréal	$32,203.90	$1,006.37	$10,329.20	32
Canada	Tsawassen	$22,607.70	$645.93	$2,958.00	35
Canada	Vancouver	$522.50	$65.31	$154.00	8
Denmark	Århus	$16,643.80	$536.90	$2,736.00	31
Denmark	København	$18,138.45	$1,209.23	$10,540.00	15
Finland	Helsinki	$3,161.35	$185.96	$550.00	17

If you save this query and reopen it, you'll see that Access has made some changes in its design. The Total cell for the Sum is changed to Expression, and the Field cell is changed to the following:

```
TotalSales: Sum([UnitPrice]*[Quantity])
```

If you look at the Total cell for the Avg, it's also changed to Expression. Its Field cell is changed to the following:

```
AverageSales: Avg([UnitPrice]*[Quantity])
```

Access modifies the query in this way when it determines you're using an aggregate function on an expression having more than one field. You can enter the expression either way. Access stores and resolves the expression as noted.

Modify the query to show the total sales by country, city, and order date. Before you continue, save your query as qryCustomerOrderInfo, then close it. With the Query tab of the Database window visible, click qryCustomerOrderInfo. Choose Copy from the toolbar, then Paste. Access should prompt you for the name of the new query. Type **qryCustomerOrderSummary** and click OK. With qryCustomerOrderSummary selected, click the Design command button. Delete both the UnitPrice and Quantity fields from the query output. To turn your query into a Totals query, follow these steps:

1. Click Totals on the toolbar. Notice that an extra line, called the Total line, is added to the query grid; this line says Group By for all fields.

2. You want to group by country, city, and order date but total by the total price (the calculated field). Click the Total row for the TotalPrice field and use the drop-down list to select Sum. (Refer back to Figure 5.25.)

3. Run the query. Your result should be grouped and sorted by country, city, and order date, with a total for each unique combination of the three fields.

4. Return to the query's design and remove the order date from the query grid.

5. Rerun the query. Notice that now you're summarizing the query by country and city.

6. Change the Total row to Avg. Now you're seeing the average price times quantity for each combination of country and city. Change it back to Sum, and save the query.

As you can see, Totals queries are both powerful and flexible. Their output can't be edited, but you can use them to view the sum, minimum, maximum, average, and count of the total price, all at the same time. You can easily modify whether you're viewing this information by country, country and city, and so on, all at the click of your mouse.

Excluding Fields from the Output

At times, you need to include a column in your query that you don't want displayed in the query output; this is often the case with columns used solely for criteria. Figure 5.28 shows an example. If this query were run, you would get the total, average, and maximum sales grouped by both country and order date. However, you want to group only by country and use the order date only for criteria. Therefore, you need to set the Total row of the query to Where, as shown in Figure 5.29. The column used in the Where has been excluded from the query result.

Figure 5.28.
A query with criteria for the order date, before excluding fields from the query output.

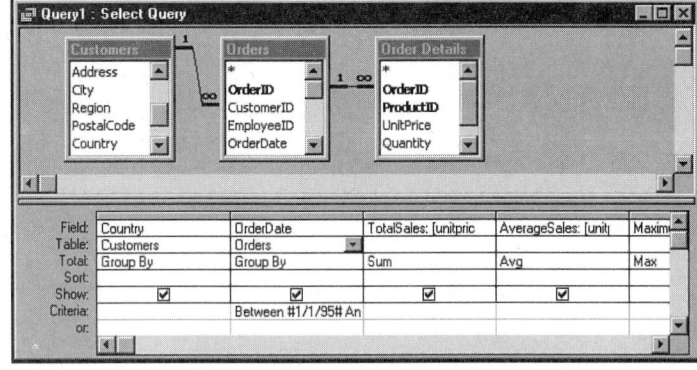

Figure 5.29.
The Total row of the OrderDate field is set to Where.

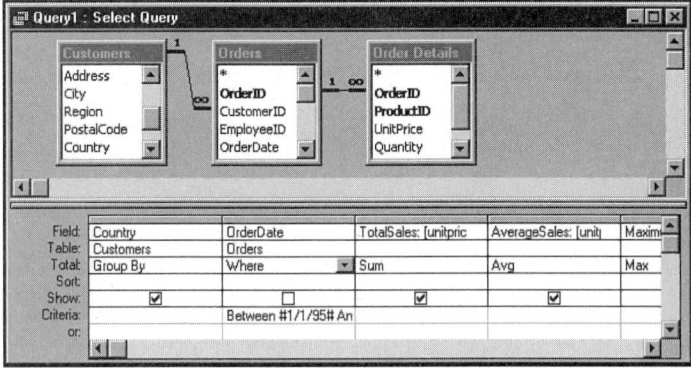

Nulls and Query Results

Null values in your table's fields can noticeably affect query results. A Null value is different from a zero or a zero-length string; a field contains a Null value when no value has yet been stored in the field. As discussed in Chapter 3, a zero-length string is entered in a field by typing two quotation marks.

Null values can affect the results of multitable queries, queries including aggregate functions (Totals queries), and queries with calculations. By default, when a multitable query is built, only records that have non-Null values on the "many" side of the relationship appear in the query result (discussed earlier in this chapter, in the "Pitfalls of Multitable Queries" section).

Null values can also affect the result of aggregate queries. For example, if you perform a count on a field containing Null values, only records having non-Null values in that field are included in the count. If you want to get an accurate count, it's best to perform the count on a Primary Key field or some other field that can't have Null values.

Probably the most insidious problem with Nulls happens when they're included in calculations. A Null value, when included in a calculation containing a numeric operator (+, -, /, *, and so on), results in a Null value. In Figure 5.30, for example, notice that the query includes a calculation that adds the values in both the Parts and Labor fields. These fields have been set to have no default value and, therefore, contain Nulls unless something has been explicitly entered into them. Running the query gives you the results shown in Figure 5.31. Notice that all the records having Nulls in either the Parts or Labor fields contain a Null in the result.

Figure 5.30.

The Design view of a query that propagates Nulls in the query result.

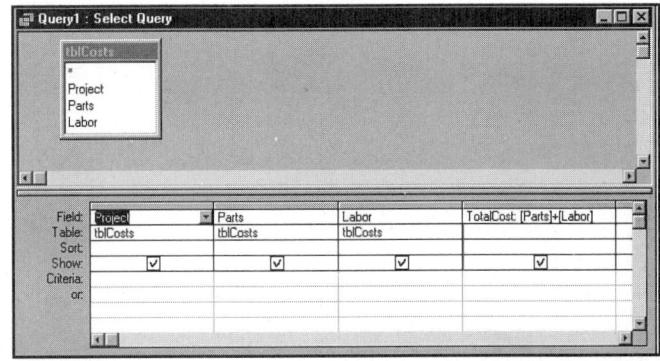

Figure 5.31.

The result of running a query illustrating Nulls.

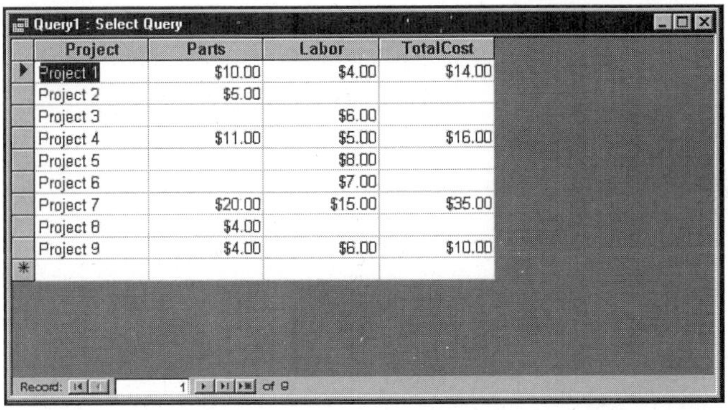

The solution to this problem is constructing an expression that converts the Null values to zero. The expression looks like this:

```
TotalCost: IIf(IsNull([Parts]),0,[Parts])+IIf(IsNull([Labor]),0,[Labor])
```

The Immediate If statement (IIf) is used along with the IsNull function to determine whether the Parts field contains a Null value. If the Parts field contains a Null value, it's converted to a zero and included in the calculation; otherwise, the field's value is used in the calculation. The same expression is used to evaluate the Labor field. The result of the modified query is shown in Figure 5.32.

Figure 5.32.

The query with an expression to eliminate Nulls.

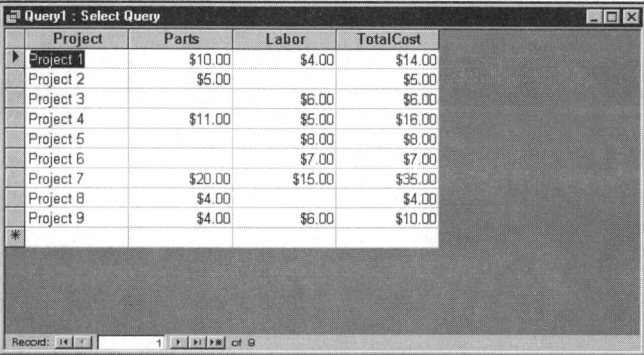

Project	Parts	Labor	TotalCost
Project 1	$10.00	$4.00	$14.00
Project 2	$5.00		$5.00
Project 3		$6.00	$6.00
Project 4	$11.00	$5.00	$16.00
Project 5		$8.00	$8.00
Project 6		$7.00	$7.00
Project 7	$20.00	$15.00	$35.00
Project 8	$4.00		$4.00
Project 9	$4.00	$6.00	$10.00

Record: 14 ◄ | 1 | ► ►I ►* of 9

> **WARNING**
>
> Nulls really cause trouble when the results of one query containing Nulls are used in another query—a snowball effect occurs. It's easy to miss the problem and output reports with inaccurate results. Using the IsNull() function eliminates this kind of problem. You can use the IsNull() function to replace the Null values with zeros or zero-length strings. Be careful when doing this, though, because it might affect other parts of your query that use this value for another calculation. Also, be sure to use any function in a query on the top level of the query tree only, because functions at lower levels might hinder query performance.

Refining Your Queries with Field and Query Properties

Field and query properties can be used to refine and control the behavior and appearance of the columns in your query and of the query itself. Here's how:

1. Click in a field to select it, click in a field list to select a field, or click in the Query Design window anywhere outside a field or the field list to select the query.

2. Click Properties on the toolbar.

3. Modify the desired property.

Field Properties: Changing the Behavior of a Field

The properties of a field in your query include the Description, Format, Input Mask, and Caption of the column. The Description property is used for documentation and to control what appears on the status bar when the user is in that column in the query result. The Format property is the same as the Format property in a table's field; it controls the display of the field in the query result. The Input Mask property, like its table counterpart, actually controls how data is entered and modified in the query result. Just as the Caption property of a field sets the caption for the column in Datasheet view and the default label for forms and reports, the Caption property in the query does the same thing.

You might be wondering how the properties of the fields in a query interact with the same properties of a table. For example, how does the Caption property of a table's field interact with the Caption property of the same field in a query? All properties of a table's field are automatically inherited in your queries. Properties explicitly modified in the query override those same properties of the table's fields. Any objects based on the query inherit the properties of the query, not of the original table.

Field List Properties

Field List properties are used to specify attributes of each table participating in the query. The two Field List properties are Alias and Source. The Alias property is used most often when the same table is used more than once in the same query. This is done in self-joins, covered in Chapter 12. The Source property is used to specify a connection string or database name when you're dealing with external tables that aren't linked to the current database.

Query Properties Changing the Behavior of the Overall Query

Microsoft offers many properties, shown in Figure 5.33, that allow you to affect the behavior of the overall query. Some of the properties are discussed here; the rest are covered as applicable throughout this book.

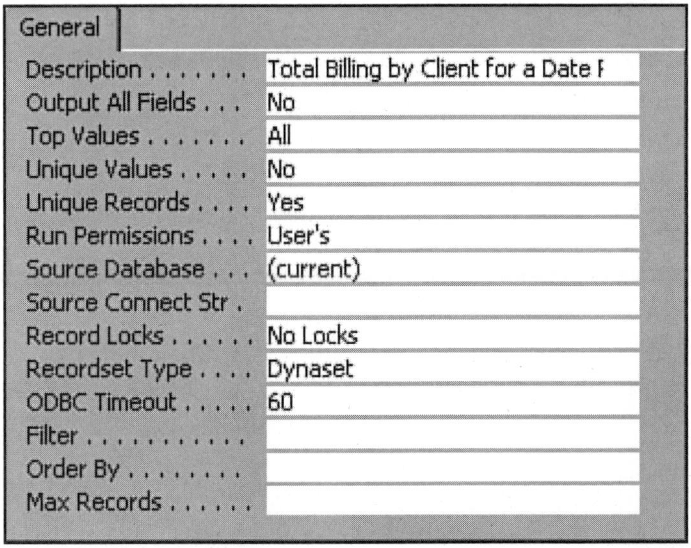

Figure 5.33.
Query properties that affect the behavior of a given query.

General	
Description	Total Billing by Client for a Date F
Output All Fields . . .	No
Top Values	All
Unique Values	No
Unique Records	Yes
Run Permissions	User's
Source Database . . .	(current)
Source Connect Str .	
Record Locks	No Locks
Recordset Type	Dynaset
ODBC Timeout	60
Filter	
Order By	
Max Records	

The Description property is used to document what the query does. Top Values lets you specify the top *x* number or *x* percent of values in the query result. Output All Fields shows all the fields in the query results, regardless of the contents of the Show check box in each field. Filter displays a subset that you determine, rather than the full result of the query. Order By determines the sort order of the query. The Unique Values and Unique Records properties are used to determine whether only unique values or unique records are displayed in the query's output. (These properties are also covered in detail in Chapter 12.) The Recordset Type property determines whether updates can be made to the query output. By default, this is set to the Dynaset type allowing updates to the underlying data. The Run Permissions property has to do with security and is covered in Chapter 33, "Complex Security Issues." Source Database, Source Connect String, ODBC Timeout, and MaxRecords all have to do with client/server issues and are covered in Chapter 20, "Client/Server Techniques." The Record Locks property concerns multiuser issues and is covered in Chapter 18, "Developing for a Multiuser Environment."

Building Parameter Queries When You Don't Know the Criteria at Design Time

You, or your application's user, might not always know the parameters for the query output when designing the query. Parameter queries let you specify different criteria at runtime so that you don't have to modify the query each time you want to change the criteria.

For example, say you have a query, like the one shown in Figure 5.34, for which you want users to specify the date range they want to view each time they run the query. The following clause has been entered as the criterion for the OrderDate field:

```
Between [Enter Starting Date] And [Enter Ending Date]
```

Figure 5.34.
This Parameter query prompts for a starting date and an ending date.

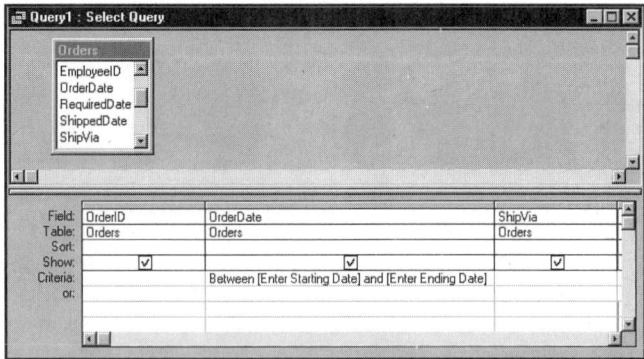

This criterion causes two dialog boxes to appear when the query is run. The first one, shown in Figure 5.35, prompts the user with the text in the first set of brackets. The text the user types is substituted for the bracketed text. A second dialog box appears, prompting the user for whatever is in the second set of brackets. The user's responses are used as criteria for the query.

Figure 5.35.
This dialog box appears when the Parameter query is run.

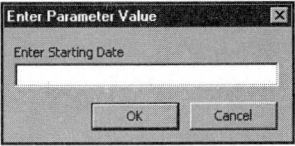

Add a parameter to the query qryCustomerOrderSummary so that you can view only TotalPrice summaries within a specific range. Go to the criteria for TotalPrice and type **Between [Please Enter Starting Value] and [Please Enter Ending Value]**. This allows you to view all the records in which the total price is within a specific range. The bracketed text is replaced by actual values when the query is run. Click OK and run the query. You're then prompted to enter both a starting and an ending value.

TRY IT

To make sure Access understands what type of data should be placed in these parameters, you must define the parameters. Do this by selecting Parameters from the Query menu to open the Parameters window. Another way to display the Parameters window is to right-click on a gray area in the top half of the query grid, then select Parameters from the context-sensitive pop-up menu.

The text typed in the brackets for each parameter must be typed exactly as it appears within the brackets to define each parameter, and the type of data in the brackets must be defined in the Data Type column. Figure 5.36 shows an example of a completed Query Parameters dialog box.

Figure 5.36.
This completed Query Parameters dialog box declares two date parameters.

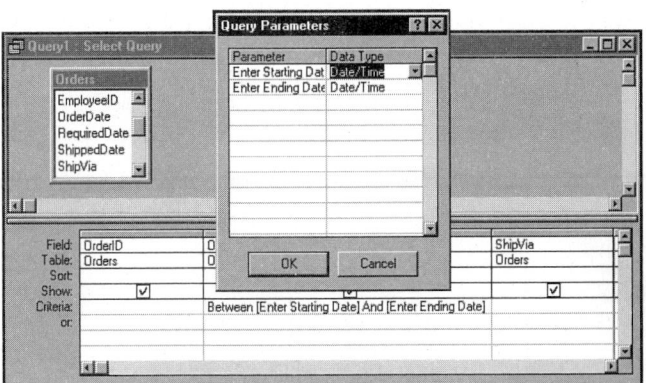

You can easily create parameters for as many fields as you want, and parameters are added just as you would add more criteria. For example, the query shown in Figure 5.37 has parameters for the Title, HireDate, and City fields in the Employees table from the NorthWind database. Notice that all the criteria are on one line of the query grid, which means that all the parameters entered must be satisfied for the records to appear in the output. The criteria for the title is [Please Enter a Title]. This means that the records in the result must match the title entered when the query is run. The criteria for the HireDate field is >=[Please Enter Starting Hire Date]. Only records with a hire date on or after the hire date entered when the query is run will appear in the output. Finally, the criterion for the City field is [Please Enter a City]. This means that only records with the City entered when the query is run will appear in the output.

The criteria for a query can also be the result of a function; this technique is covered in Chapter 12.

Figure 5.37.

The Query Design window showing a query with parameters for three fields.

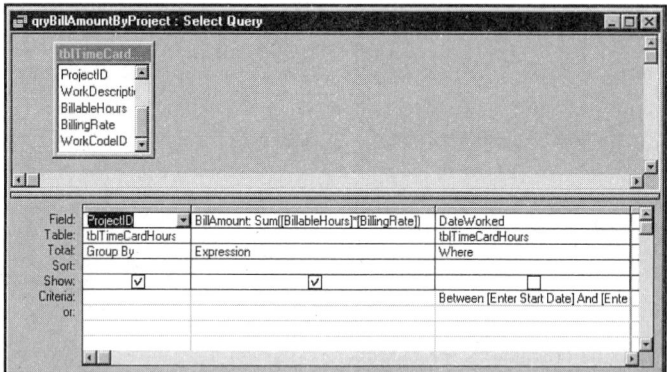

NOTE

Parameter queries offer significant flexibility; they allow the user to enter specific criteria at runtime. What's typed in the Query Parameters dialog box must exactly match what's typed within the brackets; otherwise, Access prompts the user with additional dialog boxes.

TIP

You can add as many parameters as you like to a query, but the user might become bothered if too many dialog boxes appear. Instead, build a custom form that feeds the Parameter query. This technique is covered in Chapter 12.

Practical Examples: Building Queries Needed by the Time and Billing Application for the Computer Consulting Firm

Build a query based on tblTimeCardHours. This query gives you the total billing amount by project for a specific date range. The query's design is shown in Figure 5.38. Notice that it's a Totals query that groups by project and totals by using the following expression:

```
BillAmount: Sum([BillableHours]*[BillingRate])
```

The DateWorked field is used as the Where clause for the query; here's the criteria for the Where clause:

```
Between [Enter Start Date] And [Enter End Date]
```

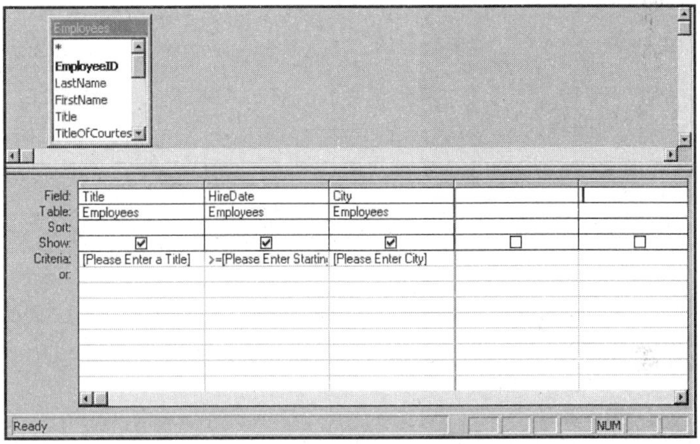

Figure 5.38.

The design of the qryBillAmountByProject query.

The two parameters of the criteria are declared in the Parameters dialog box. (See Figure 5.39.) Save this query as qryBillAmountByProject.

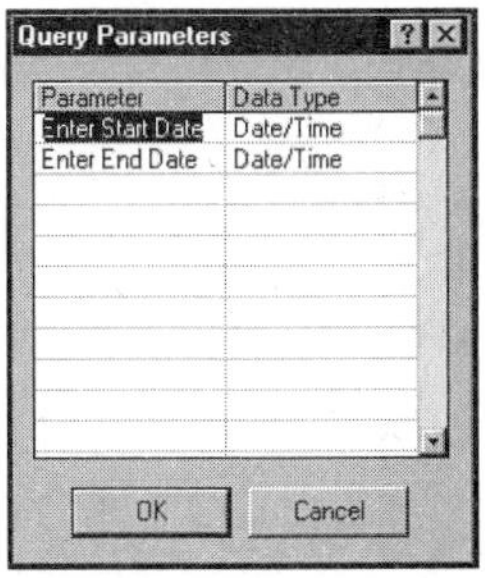

Figure 5.39.

The Parameters window for qryBillAmountByProject.

115

The second query is based on tblClients, tblProjects, and tblTimeCardHours. This query gives you the total billing amount by client for a specific date range. The query's design is shown in Figure 5.40. This query is a Totals query that groups by the company name from the tblClients table and totals by using the following expression:

```
BillAmount: Sum([BillableHours]*[BillingRate])
```

Figure 5.40.

The design of the qryBillAmountByClient query.

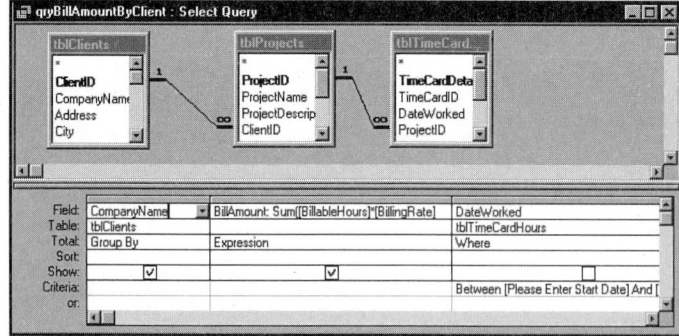

As with the first query, the DateWorked field is used as the Where clause for the query, and the parameters are defined in the Parameters window. Save this query as qryBillAmountByClient.

These queries are included on the sample CD-ROM in a database called CHAP5.MDB. You will build many other queries as part of the computer consulting firm's Time and Billing system.

Summary

This chapter has covered the foundations of perhaps the most important function of a database: getting data from the database in a usable form. You have learned about the Select query used to retrieve data from a table, how to retrieve data from multiple tables, and how to use functions in your queries to make them more powerful by synthesizing data. In later chapters, you will extend your abilities with Action queries and queries based on other queries (also known as *nested queries*).

6

CHAPTER

What Every Developer Needs to Know About Form Basics

- Uses of Forms, 118
- Anatomy of a Form, 119
- Creating a New Form, 120
- Working with the Form Design Window, 123
- Selecting the Correct Control for the Job, 131
- Control Morphing, 138
- What Form Properties Are Available and Why Use Them?, 139
- What Control Properties Are Available and Why Use Them?, 145
- Bound, Unbound, and Calculated Controls, 150
- Using Expressions to Enhance Your Forms, 150
- The Command Button Wizards: Programming Without Typing, 151
- Basing Forms on Queries: The Why and How, 157
- Access Forms and the Internet, 158
- Practical Examples: Designing Forms for Your Application, 160

Uses of Forms

Developers often think that forms exist solely for the purpose of data entry. On the contrary, forms serve many different purposes in Access 97:

- data entry—displaying and editing data
- application flow—navigation through your application
- custom dialog boxes—providing messages to your user
- printing information—hard copies of data-entry information

Probably the most common use of an Access form is as a vehicle for displaying and editing existing data or for adding new data. Fortunately, Access offers many features that allow you to build forms that ease data entry for your users. Access also makes it easy for you to design forms that let your users view and modify data, view data but not modify it, or add new records only.

Although not everyone immediately thinks of an Access form as a means of navigating through an application, forms are quite strong in this area. Figure 6.1 shows a form created with the Switchboard Manager in Access 97; Figure 6.2 shows a "home-grown" switchboard form. Although the Switchboard Manager makes designing a switchboard form very simple, you will find any type of switchboard easy to develop. You can be creative with switchboard forms by designing forms that are both utilitarian and exciting. Switchboard forms are covered in detail in Chapter 13, "Let's Get More Intimate with Forms: Advanced Techniques."

Figure 6.1.
Form created with the Switchboard Manager.

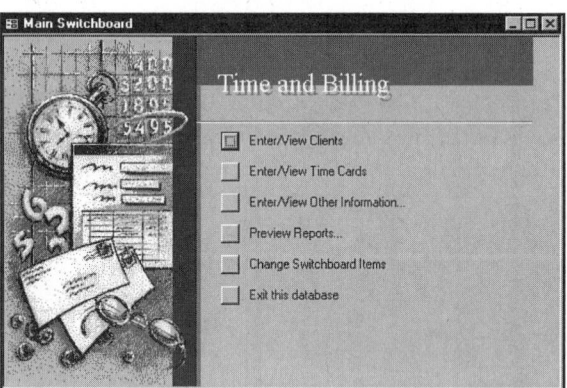

You can also use Access to create custom dialog boxes used to display information or retrieve information from your users. The custom dialog box shown in Figure 6.3 gets the information needed to run a report. The user must fill in the required information before he or she can proceed.

Figure 6.2.
A custom switchboard with tooltips and bitmaps.

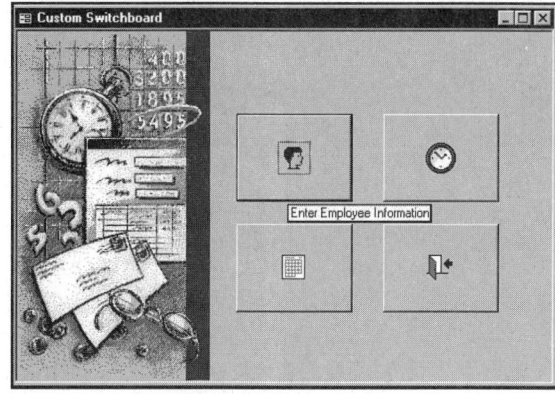

Figure 6.3.
A custom dialog box that lets the user specify a date range for a report.

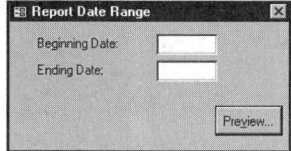

Another strength of Access is its ability to produce professional-looking printed forms. With many other products, it's difficult to print a data-entry form; sometimes the entire form needs to be re-created as a report. In Access, printing a form is simply a matter of clicking a button. You have the option of creating a report that displays the information your user is entering or of printing the form itself.

Access offers many styles of forms. The data in a form can be displayed one record at a time, or you can let the user view several records at once. Forms can be displayed *modally*, meaning that the user must respond and close the form before continuing, or displayed so that the user can move through the open forms at will. The important thing to remember is that there are many uses and styles of forms. You will learn about them throughout this chapter, in Chapter 13, and throughout the book. As you read this chapter, remember that your forms are limited only by your imagination.

Anatomy of a Form

Access forms comprise a few sections; each one has its own function and behavior. These are the three sections of an Access form:

- Header
- Detail
- Footer

The Detail section of a form is the main section; it's the one used to display the data of the table or query underlying the form. As you will see, the Detail section can take on many different looks. It's quite flexible and robust.

The Header and Footer sections of the form are used to display information that doesn't change from record to record. Command buttons—such as one used to let users view all the projects associated with a particular client—that control the form are often placed in the form's header or footer. Controls can also be used to help the user navigate around the records associated with the form. In the example shown in Figure 6.4, the user can select from a valid list of clients. After a client has been selected from the combo box, the user is moved to the appropriate record.

Figure 6.4.

Record navigation using a combo box placed in the form header.

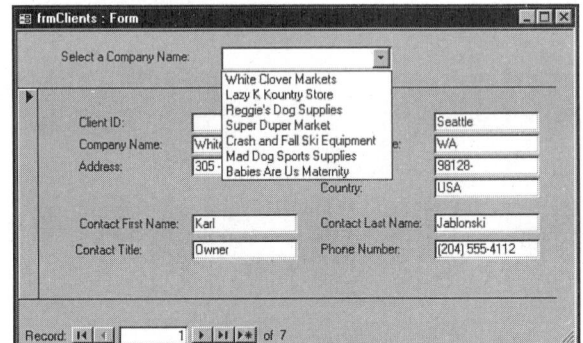

Creating a New Form

You can create a new form in several ways. The most common way is to select the Forms tab of the Database window and click New. In the New Form dialog box that appears, you can select from the multitude of options available for creating a new form. (See Figure 6.5.) Forms can also be created from scratch by using Design view or created with the help of six wizards. The wizards will be covered briefly before you move on to the process of creating a form from scratch. Even the most experienced developers use the Form Wizard to perform certain tasks.

Figure 6.5.

The New Form dialog box lets you specify the table or query to underlie the form and choose the method for creating the form.

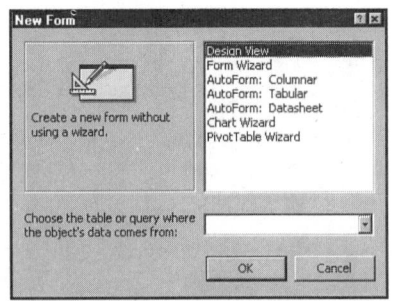

Creating a Form with the Form Wizard

To create a form with the Form Wizard, select Form Wizard from the New Form dialog and click OK to launch it. The first step of the Form Wizard prompts you for the name of the table or query you want to use as the form's foundation. Whether you're creating a form with Form Wizard or from Design view, it's generally better to base a form on a query. Using a query as the foundation for a form offers better performance (unless your form requires all fields and all records), allows for more flexibility, and lets you create a form based on data from several tables.

Figure 6.6 shows the Tables/Queries drop-down list. You can see that all the tables are listed, followed by all the queries. After you select a particular table or query, its fields are displayed in the list box on the left. (See Figure 6.7.) To select the fields you want to include on the form, double-click on the name of the field or click on the field, then click the > button. In the example shown in Figure 6.7, several fields have been selected from the qryClients query.

Figure 6.6.
List of available tables and queries.

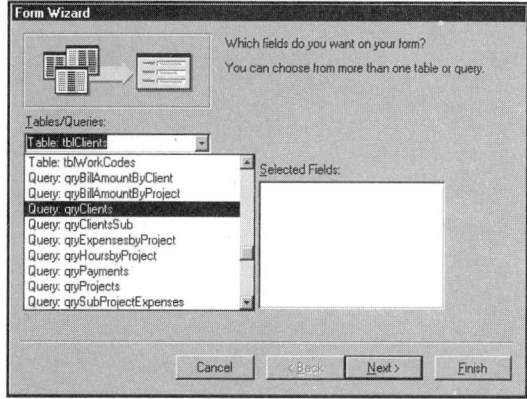

Figure 6.7.
Selected fields from qryClients.

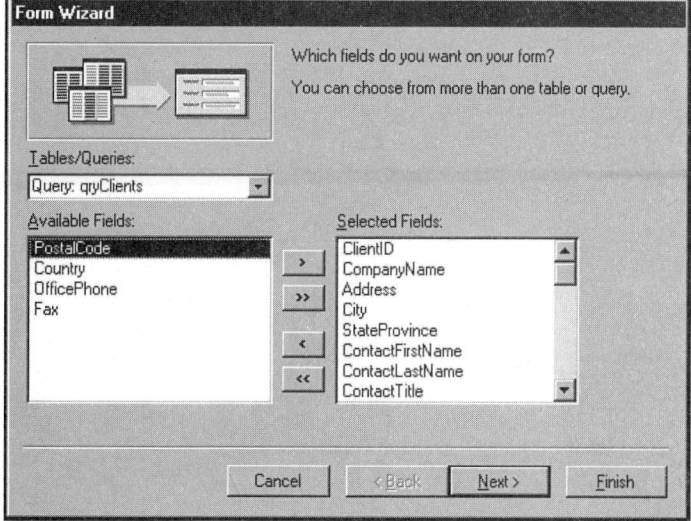

121

After you've selected the fields you want, click Next. The second step of the Form Wizard allows you to specify the layout for the form you're designing. You can select from Columnar, Tabular, Datasheet, or Justified; the most common choice is Columnar. Click Next after selecting a form layout. In the third step of the Form Wizard, you can select a style for your form from several predefined styles. (See Figure 6.8.) Although all the properties set by the wizard can be modified in Design view once the form has been created, to save time, it's best to select the appropriate style now. Click Next after selecting a style.

Figure 6.8.

Selecting a form style.

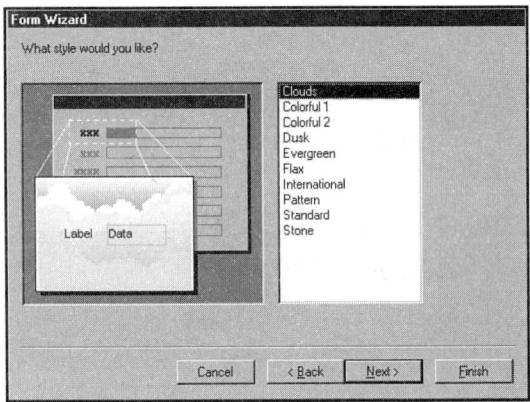

In the final step of the Form Wizard, you supply a title for your form. Unfortunately, the form's title becomes the name of the form, as well. For this reason, type the text you want to use as the name of the form. You can worry about changing the title in Design view of the form. This step of the Form Wizard also lets you specify whether you want to view the results of your work or open the form in Design view. It's usually best to view the results and then modify the form's design after you have taken a peek at what the Form Wizard has done.

> **TIP**
>
> Another way to start the Form Wizard is to click on the Tables or Queries tab, then click on the table or query you want the form to be based on. Use the New Object drop-down list on the toolbar to select New Form; this opens the New Form dialog box. Select Form Wizard. You won't have to use the Tables/Queries drop-down list to select a table or query. The table or query you selected before invoking the wizard is automatically selected for you.

Creating a Form from Design View

Although the Form Wizards are both powerful and useful, in many cases you'll prefer building a form from scratch, especially if you're building a form that's not bound to data. To create a form without using a wizard, click the Forms tab and then click New to open the New Form dialog box. Select Design view (the default choice). If your form will be bound to data, use the drop-down list in the New Form dialog box to select the table or query that will serve as the form's foundation. Click OK, and the Form Design window appears. (See Figure 6.9.)

Figure 6.9.

Use the Form Design window to build and customize a form.

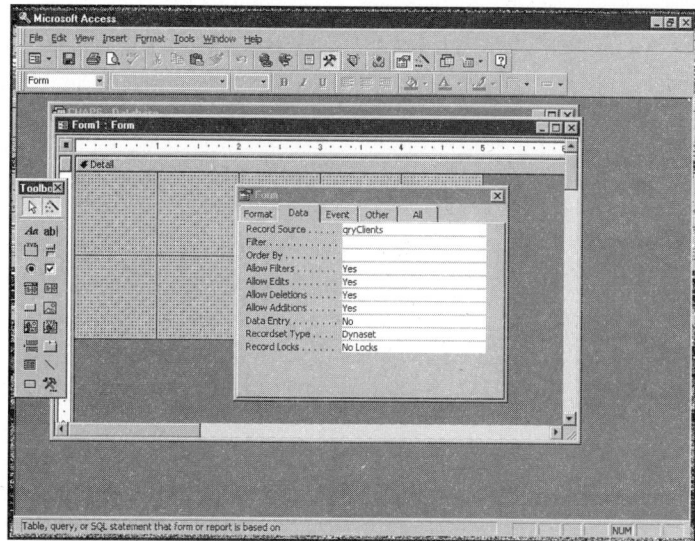

Working with the Form Design Window

The Form Design window is used to build and customize a form. Using this window, you can add objects to a form and customize them by using the Properties window. Microsoft has supplied many form and control properties. After gaining a command of these properties, you can customize the look and feel of your forms.

Understanding and Working with the Form Design Tools

Even the best developer needs the right tools for the job. Fortunately, Microsoft has given you tools to help you build exciting and utilitarian forms. The Form Design window includes a toolbar, a toolbox, and the actual form you're designing. Other tools are available to help you with the design process, including the Field List and Properties window.

By default, two toolbars appear when you're in a form's Design view: the Form Design toolbar and the Formatting toolbar. The Form Design toolbar has buttons you use to save, print, copy, cut, paste, and perform other standard Windows tasks within the form. It also includes buttons that allow you to toggle the different design windows (such as the toolbox). The Formatting toolbar contains tools for graphically modifying the form's properties and objects. You can modify the font, font size, and color of selected objects on the form. With the Formatting toolbar, you can also add bold, underline, and italic; change the alignment; and add special effects to the selected objects.

Toggling the Tools to Get What You Want

Many windows are available to help you with the design process when you're in a form's Design view. Depending on whether you have a high-resolution monitor, you'll probably find it annoying to have all the windows open at once. In fact, with all the windows open at once on a low-resolution monitor, the form is likely to get buried underneath all the windows. This is why Microsoft has made each window open and close in a toggle-switch–like fashion. The Form Design toolbar has tools for the Field List, Toolbox, and Properties windows, and each of these toolbar buttons is a toggle. Clicking once on the button opens the appropriate window; clicking a second time closes it.

Figure 6.10 shows a form with the Field List, Toolbox, and Properties windows open. Although each of these windows can be sized however you want, the design environment in this low-resolution display is rather cluttered with all these windows open. One of the tricks in working with Access is knowing when it's appropriate to have each set of tools available. The goal is to have the right windows open at the right time as often as possible.

Figure 6.10.

The Form Design toolbar with design windows visible.

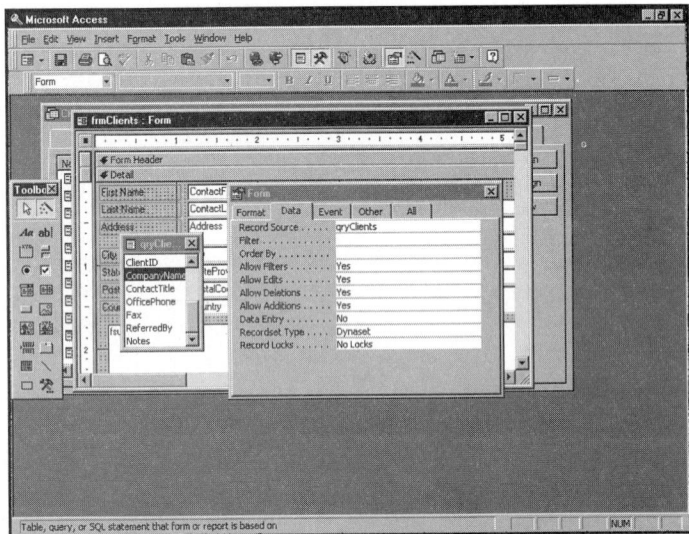

> **NOTE**
>
> The Field List, Toolbox, and Properties windows can be closed by using the toolbar buttons. In addition, they can be closed by using the Close button on each window or toggled with the View menu.

Adding Fields to the Form

Fields can be easily added to a form by using the Field List window, which contains all the fields that are part of the form's record source. The *record source* for the form is the table or query that underlies the form. For example, in Figure 6.10, the form's record source is qryClients. The fields listed in the Field List window are the fields that are part of the query. To add fields to a form, use these two steps:

1. Make sure the Field List window is visible. If it isn't, click the Field List button on the toolbar.

2. Locate the field you want to add to the form, then click and drag the field from the field list to the place on the form where you want it to appear. The location you select becomes the upper-left corner of the text box, and the attached label appears to the left of where you dropped the control.

> **NOTE**
>
> To add multiple fields to a form at the same time, select several fields from the field list. Use the Ctrl key to select noncontiguous fields or the Shift key to select contiguous fields. For example, hold down your Ctrl key and click on three noncontiguous fields. Each field will be selected. Now click a field, hold down your Shift key and click another field. All fields between the two fields will be selected. If you want to select all fields, double-click the field list title bar. Click and drag any of the selected fields to the form, and all of them will be added to the form at once.

Selecting, Moving, Aligning, and Sizing Form Objects

You need to know several important tricks of the trade when selecting, moving, aligning, and sizing form objects. These tips will save you hours of frustration and wasted time.

Selecting Form Objects

The easiest way to select a single object on a form is to click on it. Once the object is selected, you can move it, size it, or change any of its properties. Selecting multiple objects is a bit trickier, but can be done in several ways. Different methods are more efficient in different situations. To select multiple objects, you can hold down the Shift key and click on each object you want to select. Each selected object is surrounded by selection handles, indicating that it's selected.

Figure 6.11 shows a form with four selected objects; it's important to understand which objects are actually selected. The ClientID text box, the Address label and text box, and the Company Name label are all selected; however, the Client ID label and CompanyName text box aren't selected. If you look closely at the figure, you can see that the selected objects are completely surrounded by selection handles. The Client ID label and CompanyName text box have single selection handles because they're attached to objects that are selected. If you change any properties of the selected objects, the Client ID label and CompanyName text box will be unaffected.

Figure 6.11.

Selecting objects on a form.

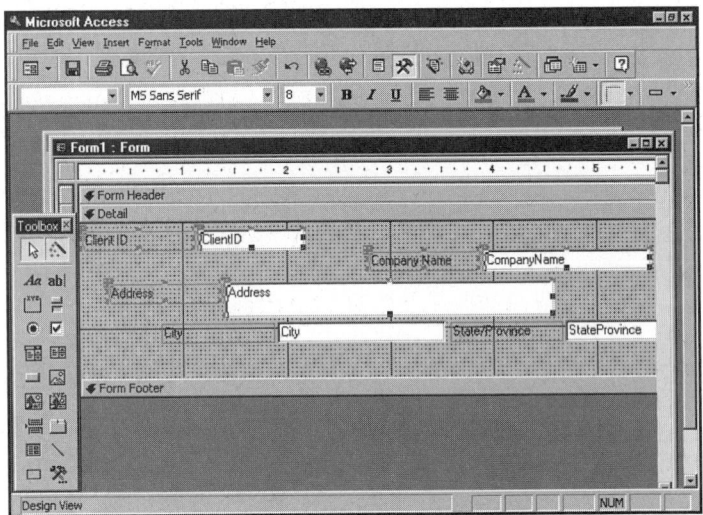

You can also select objects by lassoing them. To lasso objects, they must be located close to one another on the form. Place your mouse pointer on a blank area of the form (not over any objects), then click and drag. You can see a thin line around the objects your mouse pointer is encircling. When you let go, any objects that were within the lasso, including those only partially surrounded, are selected. If you want to deselect any of these objects to exclude them, hold down your Shift key and click on the object you want to deselect.

One of my favorite ways to select multiple objects is to use the horizontal and vertical rulers that appear at the edges of the Form Design window. Click and drag within the ruler. Notice that as you click and drag on the vertical ruler, two horizontal lines appear, indicating which objects are selected. As you click and drag across the horizontal ruler, two vertical lines appear, indicating the selection area. When you let go of your mouse, any objects within the lines are selected. As with the process of lassoing, to remove any objects from the selection, hold down your Shift key and click on the object you want to deselect.

Moving Things Around

To move a single control with its attached label, you don't need to select it first. Place your mouse over the object and click and drag. An outline appears, indicating the object's new location. When the object reaches the position you want, release the mouse. The attached label automatically moves with its corresponding control.

To move more than one object at a time, you must first select the objects you want to move. Select the objects using one of the methods outlined in the previous section. Place your mouse over any of the selected objects and click and drag. An outline appears, indicating the proposed new position for the objects. Release the mouse when you have reached the position you want for the objects.

Sometimes you want to move a control independent of its attached label, which requires a special technique. If you click on a control, such as a text box, as you move your mouse over the border of the control, a hand icon with five fingers pointing upward appears. If you click and drag, both the control and the attached label move as a unit, and the relationship between them is maintained. If you place your mouse pointer over the larger handle in the upper-left corner of the object, the mouse pointer appears as a hand with only the index finger pointing upward. If you click and drag here, the control moves independently of its attached label, and the relationship between the objects changes.

Aligning Objects with One Another

Access makes it easy to align objects. Figure 6.12 shows several objects that aren't aligned. Notice that the attached labels of three of the objects are selected. If you align the attached labels, the controls (in this case, text boxes) remain in their original positions. If you select the text boxes as well, they will try to align with the attached labels. Because Access doesn't allow the objects to overlap, the text boxes end up immediately next to their attached labels. To left-align any objects (even objects of different types), select the objects you want to align and then choose Format | Align | Left. The selected objects are then aligned. (See Figure 6.13.) You can align the left, right, top, or bottom edges of any objects on a form; you can also align the center of each object.

Figure 6.12.
The form before aligning objects.

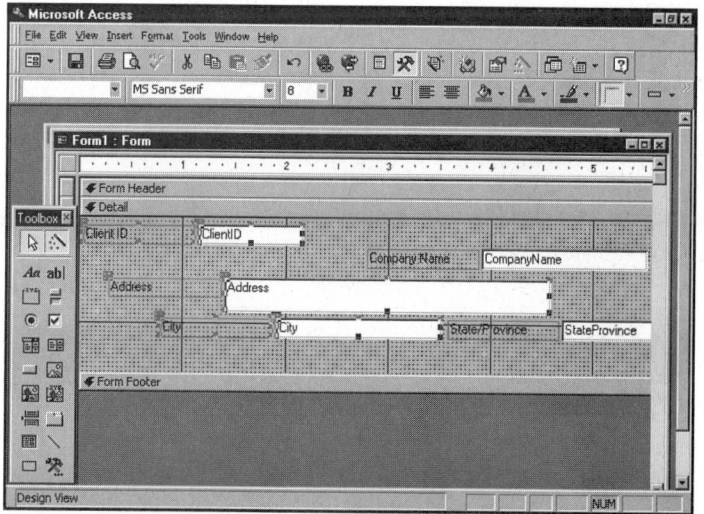

Figure 6.13.

The form after aligning objects.

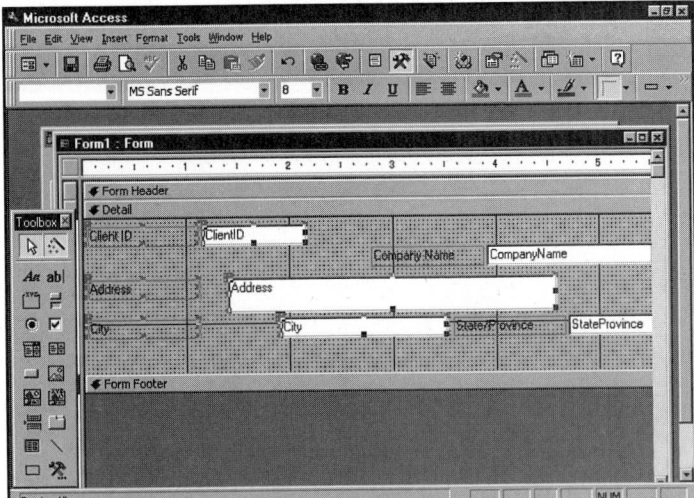

Don't confuse the Format|Align feature with the Align tools on the Formatting toolbar. The Format|Align feature aligns objects with each other, but the Align tools on the Formatting toolbar align the text of an object within its borders.

Snap to Grid

The Snap to Grid feature determines whether objects snap to the gridlines on the form as you move and size them. This feature is found under the Format menu. If you turn this feature off (it's a toggle), objects can be moved and sized without regard for the gridlines.

I prefer to leave the Snap to Grid feature on at all times. I use a special trick to temporarily deactivate the feature when needed—hold down your Ctrl key as you click and drag to move objects. The Snap to Grid setting is then ignored.

Power Sizing Techniques

Just as there are several ways to move objects, you have several options for sizing objects. When an object is selected, each handle, except for the handle in the upper-left corner of the object, can be used to size the object. The handles at the top and bottom of the object allow you to change the object's height, and the handles at the left and right of the object let you change the object's width. You can use the handles in the upper-right, lower-right, and lower-left corners of the object to change the width and height of the object simultaneously. To size an object, place your mouse pointer over a sizing handle and click and drag. You can select several objects and size them at once. Each of the selected objects increases or decreases in size by the same amount; their relative sizes stay intact.

Access offers several powerful methods of sizing multiple objects, found under the Format | Size menu:

- **To Fit:** Sizes the selected objects to fit the text within them.
- **To Grid:** Sizes the selected objects to the nearest gridlines.
- **To Tallest:** Sizes the selected objects to the height of the tallest object in the selection.
- **To Shortest:** Sizes the selected objects to the height of the shortest object in the selection.
- **To Widest:** Sizes the selected objects to the width of the widest object in the selection.
- **To Narrowest:** Sizes the selected objects to the width of the narrowest object in the selection.

Probably the most confusing of the options is Format | Size | To Fit. This option is somewhat deceiving because it doesn't perfectly size text boxes to the text within them. In today's world of proportional fonts, it isn't possible to perfectly size a text box to the largest possible entry it contains. Generally, however, you can visually size text boxes to a sensible height and width. Use the field's Size property to limit what's typed in the text box. If the entry is too large to fit in the allocated space, the user can scroll to view the additional text.

> **TIP**
>
> To quickly size a label to fit the text within it, select the label and then double-click any of its sizing handles, except the sizing handle in the upper-left corner of the label.

Controlling Object Spacing

Access gives you excellent tools for spacing the objects on your form an equal distance from one another. Notice in Figure 6.14 that the ClientID, Address, and City text boxes aren't equally spaced vertically from one another. To make the vertical distance between selected objects equal, choose Format | Vertical Spacing | Make Equal. In Figure 6.15, you can see the result of using this command on the selected objects in Figure 6.14.

Figure 6.14.

The form before modifying vertical spacing.

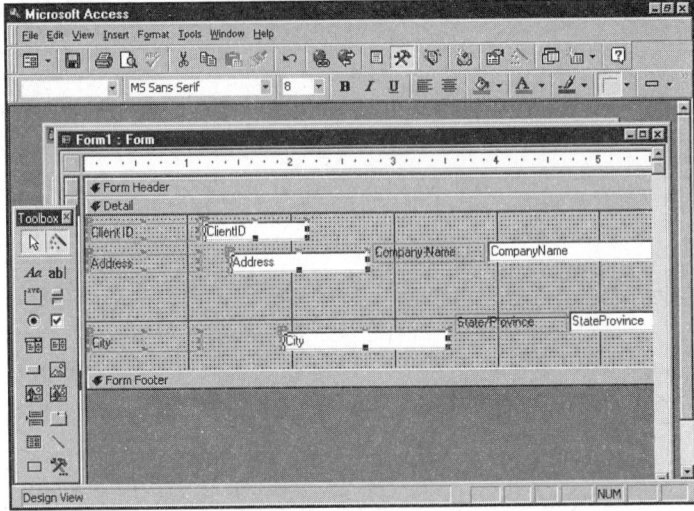

Figure 6.15.

The form after modifying vertical spacing.

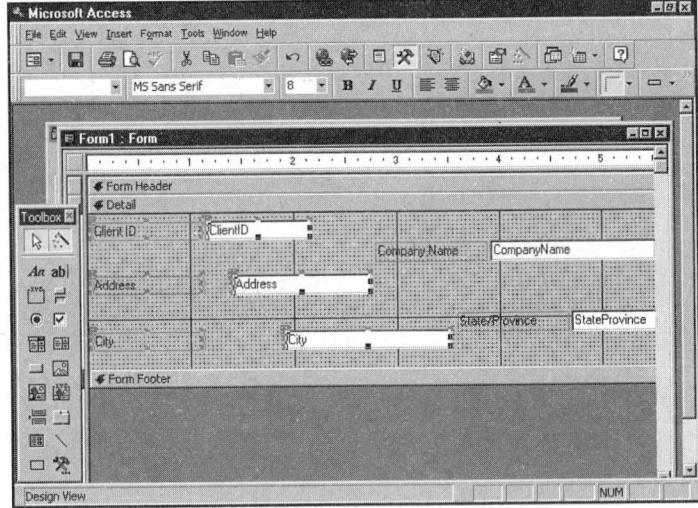

The horizontal distance between objects can be made equal by choosing Format | Horizontal Spacing | Make Equal. Other related commands that are useful are Format | Vertical Spacing | Increase (or Decrease) and Format | Horizontal Spacing | Increase (or Decrease). These commands maintain the relationship between objects while proportionally increasing or decreasing the distance between them.

Modifying Object Tab Order

The tab order for the objects on a form is determined by the order in which you add the objects to the form. However, this order isn't necessarily appropriate for the user. You might need to modify the tab order of the objects on the form. To do so, select View|Tab Order to open the Tab Order dialog box, shown in Figure 6.16. This dialog box offers two options. Use the Auto Order command button to tell Access to set the tab order based on the each object's location in a section on the form. However, if you want to customize the order of the objects, click and drag the gray buttons to the left of the object names listed under the Custom Order heading to specify the objects' tab order.

> **NOTE**
>
> You must set the tab order for the objects in each section of the form separately. To do this, select the appropriate section from the Tab Order dialog box, then set the order of the objects in the section. If your selected form doesn't have a header or footer, the Form Header and Form Footer sections are unavailable.

Figure 6.16.
Use the Tab Order dialog box to select the tab order of the objects in each section of a form.

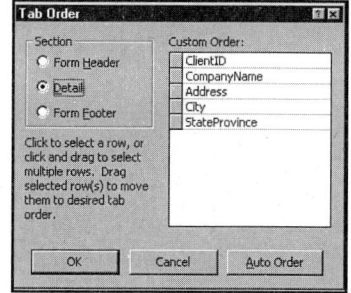

Selecting the Correct Control for the Job

Windows programming in general, and Access programming in particular, isn't limited to just writing code. Your ability to design a user-friendly interface can make or break the success of your application. Access and the Windows programming environment offer a variety of controls, and each one is appropriate in different situations. The following sections discuss each control, outlining when and how it should be used.

Labels

Labels are used to display information to your users. Attached labels are automatically added to your form when you add other controls, such as text boxes, combo boxes, and so on, and they can be deleted or modified as necessary. Their default captions are based on the Caption property of the field that underlies the control they're attached to. If nothing has been entered into the field's Caption property, the field name is used for the label's caption.

The Label tool, found in the toolbox, can be used to add any text to the form. Click the Label tool, then click and drag the label to place it on the form. Labels are often used to provide a description of the form or to supply instructions to users. Labels can be customized by modifying their font, size, color, and so on. Although developers can use VBA code to modify label properties at runtime, users don't have this ability.

Text Boxes

Text boxes are used to get information from the user. Bound text boxes display and retrieve field information; unbound text boxes gather information from the user that's not related to a specific field in a specific record. For example, a text box can be used to gather information about report criteria from a user.

Text boxes are automatically added to a form when you click and drag a field from the field list to the form and the Display control for the field is set to Text Box. Another way to add a text box is to select the Text Box tool from the toolbox, then click and drag to place the text box on the form. This process adds an unbound text box to the form. If you want to bind the text box to data, you must set its Control Source property.

Combo Boxes

Access offers several easy ways to add a combo box to a form. If a field's Display Control property has been set to Combo Box, a combo box is automatically added to a form when the field is added. The combo box automatically knows the source of its data as well as all its other important properties.

If a field's Display Control property hasn't been set to Combo Box, the easiest way to add a combo box to a form is to use the Control Wizard. The Control Wizard, when selected, helps you add combo boxes, list boxes, option groups, and subforms to your forms. Although all the properties set by the Combo Box Wizard can be set manually, using the wizard saves both time and energy. If you want the Combo Box Wizard to be launched when you add a combo box to the form, make sure the Control Wizards tool in the toolbox has been clicked (switched on) before you add the combo box.

To add a combo box to a form, select the Combo Box tool in the toolbox, then click and drag to place the combo box on the form. This launches the Combo Box Wizard; its first step is shown in Figure 6.17. You're asked whether you want the combo box to look up the values in a table or query, whether you prefer to type the values yourself, or whether the combo box is going to be used to search for a particular record. Use the first option if your combo box will select the data that's stored in a field, such as the state associated with a particular client. I rarely, if ever, use the second option, which requires that you type the values for the combo box, because populating a combo box this way makes it difficult to maintain. Every time you want to add an entry to the combo box, your application must be modified. The third and final option is appropriate when you want the combo box to be used as a tool to find a specific record. For example, a combo box can be placed in the form's header to display a list of valid customers. After selecting a customer, the user is then moved to the appropriate record. This option is available only when the form is bound to a record source.

Figure 6.17.
The first step of the Combo Box Wizard.

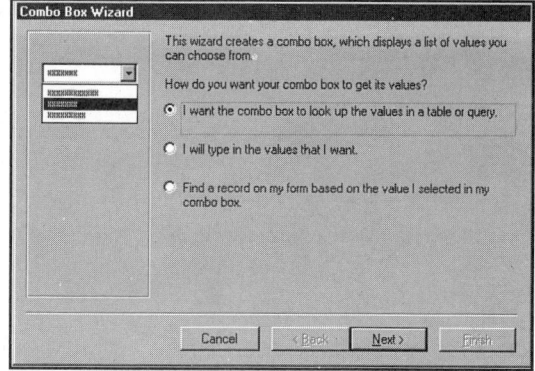

In the second step of the Combo Box Wizard, you select a table or query to populate the combo box. For optimal performance, you should select a query. The third step of the Combo Box Wizard allows you to select the fields that appear in your combo box. (See Figure 6.18.) The combo box being built in the example will be used to select the client associated with a particular project. Although the CompanyName field will be the only field visible in the combo box, ClientID and CompanyName have both been selected because ClientID is a necessary element of the combo box. Once a company name has been selected from the combo box, the client ID associated with the company name will be stored in the ClientID field of the tblProjects table.

Figure 6.18.
The third step of the Combo Box Wizard: selecting fields.

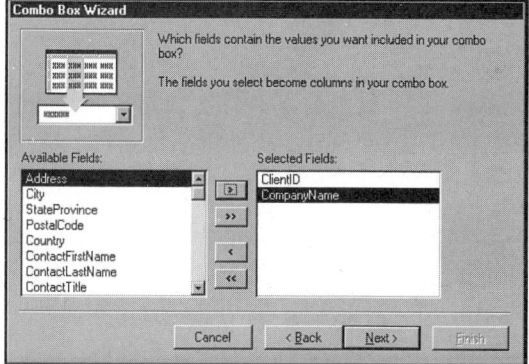

The fourth step of the Combo Box Wizard lets you specify the width of each field in the combo box. Notice in Figure 6.19 that Access recommends that the key column, ClientID, be hidden. The idea is that the user will see the meaningful English description while Access worries about storing the appropriate key value into the record.

In the Combo Box Wizard's fifth step, you specify whether you want Access to simply remember the selected value or store it in a particular field in a table. In the example shown in Figure 6.20, the selected combo box value will be stored in the ClientID field of the tblProjects table.

Figure 6.19.

The fourth step of the Combo Box Wizard: setting column widths.

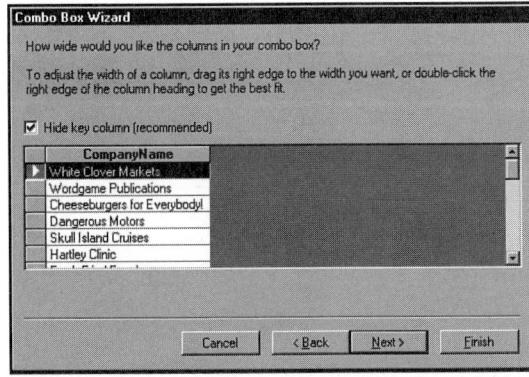

Figure 6.20.

The fifth step of the Combo Box Wizard: indicating where the selected value will be stored.

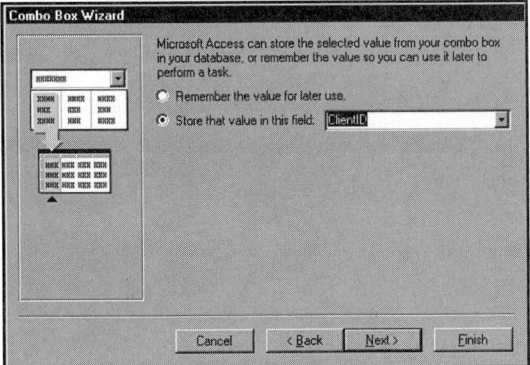

The sixth and final step of the Combo Box Wizard prompts for the text that will become the attached label for the combo box. The Finish button completes the process, building the combo box and filling in all its properties with the appropriate values.

Although the Combo Box Wizard is a helpful tool, it's important to understand the properties it sets. Figure 6.21 shows the Properties window for a combo box. Many of the Combo Box properties are covered in other chapters, but take a moment to go over the properties set by the Combo Box Wizard here.

The Control Source property indicates the field in which the selected entry is stored. In Figure 6.21, the selected entry will be stored in the ClientID field of the tblProjects table. The Row Source Type property specifies whether the source used to populate the combo box is a table/query, value list, or field list. In the example, the Row Source Type is Table/Query. The Row Source is the name of the actual table or query used to populate the combo box. In the example, the Row Source is qryClients. The Column Count property designates how many columns are in the combo box, and the Column Widths property indicates the width of each column. In the example, the width of the first column is zero, which renders the column invisible. Finally, Bound Column is used to specify which column in the combo box is being used to store data into the Control Source. In the example, this is column 1.

Figure 6.21.

Properties of a combo box, showing that the ClientID field has been selected as the control source for the Combo13 combo box.

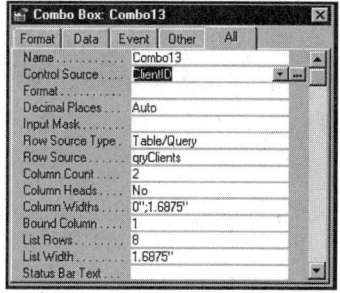

Combo boxes are very powerful controls, but you need to know many other things about them to leverage their power. The advanced aspects of combo boxes are covered in Chapter 13.

List Boxes

List boxes are very similar to combo boxes, but differ from them in three major ways:

- List boxes consume more screen space.
- They allow you to select only from the list that's displayed. This means you can't type new values into a list box (as you can with a combo box).
- They can be configured to let you select multiple items.

As with a combo box, the Display Control of a field can be set to List Box. If the Display Control has been set to List Box, a list box is added to the form when the field is clicked and dragged from the field list to the form.

The List Box Wizard is almost identical to the Combo Box Wizard. After running the List Box Wizard, the List Box properties affected by the wizard are the same as the Combo Box properties. Advanced list box techniques are covered in Chapter 13.

Checkboxes

Checkboxes are used when you want to limit your user to entering one of two values. The values entered can be limited to Yes/No, True/False, or On/Off. You can add a checkbox to a form in several ways:

- Set the Display Control of the underlying field to Check Box, then click and drag the field from the field list to the form.
- Click the Check Box tool in the toolbox, then click and drag a field from the field list to the form. This method adds a checkbox to the form even if the Display Control of the underlying field isn't a checkbox.
- Click the Check Box tool in the toolbox, then click and drag to add a checkbox to the form. The checkbox you have added will be unbound. To bind the checkbox to data, you must set the control's Control Source property.

Option Buttons

Option buttons can be used alone or as part of an option group. An option button alone can be used to display a True/False value, but this isn't a standard use of an option button (checkboxes are standard for this purpose). As part of an option group, option buttons force the user to select from a mutually exclusive set of options, such as choosing from American Express, MasterCard, Visa, or Discover for a payment type. This use of option buttons is covered in the section "Option Groups."

Toggle Buttons

Like option buttons, toggle buttons can be used alone or as part of an option group. A toggle button by itself can display a True/False value, but this isn't a standard use. Toggle buttons are more commonly used as part of an option group, as discussed in the next section.

Option Groups

Option groups allow the user to select from a mutually exclusive set of options. They can include check boxes, toggle buttons, or option buttons, but the most common implementation of an option group is option buttons.

The easiest way to add an option group to a form is to use the Option Group Wizard. To ensure that the Option Group Wizard will run, make sure the Control Wizards button in the toolbox is selected. Click Option Group in the toolbox, then click and drag to add the option group to the form; this launches the Option Group Wizard.

The first step of the Option Group Wizard, shown in Figure 6.22, allows you to type the text associated with each item in the option group. The second step gives you the option of selecting a default choice for the option group. This choice comes into effect when a new record is added to the table underlying the form. The third step of the wizard lets you select values associated with each option button. (See Figure 6.23.) The text displayed with the option button isn't stored in the record; instead, the underlying numeric value is stored in the record. In the example shown in Figure 6.23, the number 2 is stored in the field if Check is selected. The fourth step of the Option Group Wizard asks whether you want to remember the option group value for later use or store the value in a field. In the example in Figure 6.24, the option group value is stored in the PaymentMethodID field. In the fifth step of the Option Group Wizard, you can select from a variety of styles for the option group buttons, including option buttons, checkboxes, and toggle buttons. You can also select from etched, flat, raised, shadowed, or sunken effects for your buttons. The wizard lets you preview each option. The sixth and final step of the wizard allows you to add an appropriate caption to the option group. The completed group of option buttons is shown in Figure 6.25.

Figure 6.22.

Step 1 of the Option Group Wizard: adding text to options.

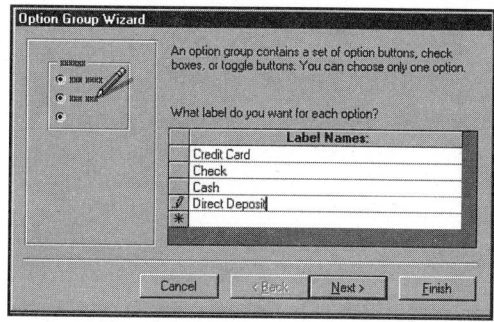

Figure 6.23.

Step 3 of the Option Group Wizard: selecting values for options.

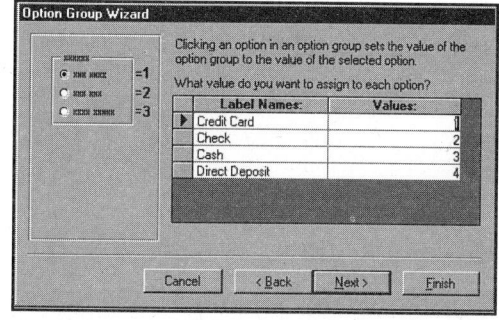

Figure 6.24.

Step 4 of the Option Group Wizard: tying the group to data.

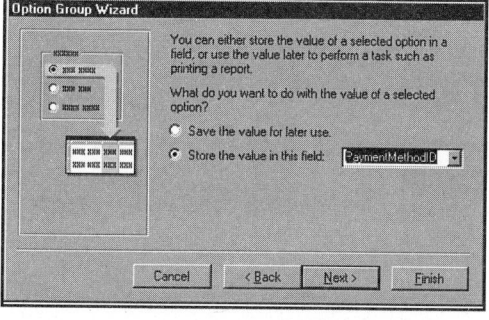

Figure 6.25.

The results of running the Option Group Wizard.

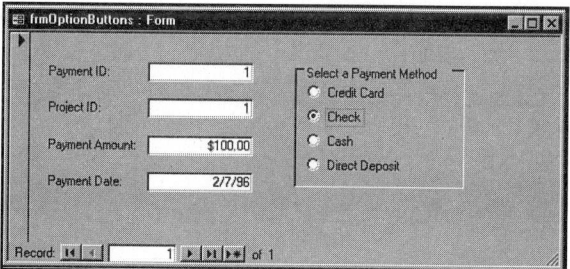

It's important to understand that the Option Group Wizard sets properties of the frame, the option buttons within the frame, and the labels attached to the option buttons. The properties of the frame are shown in Figure 6.26. The control source of the frame and default value of the option group are set by the Option Group Wizard. Each individual option button is assigned a value, and the caption of the attached labels associated with each button is set.

Figure 6.26.

An option group frame, showing the properties of the selected button.

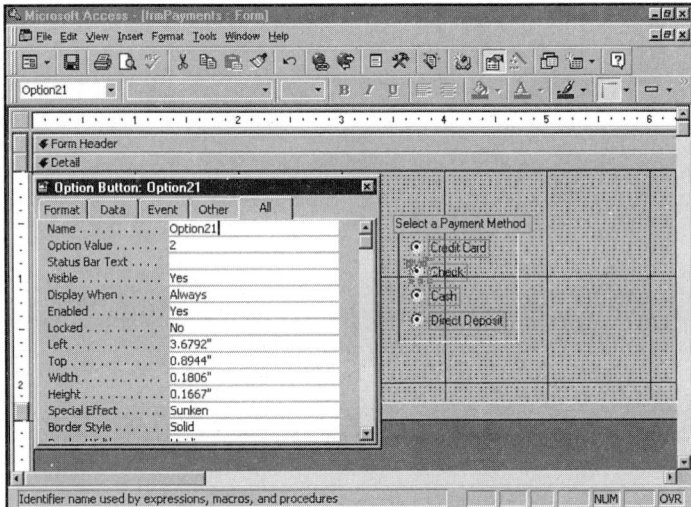

Control Morphing

When you first build a form, you might not always choose the best type of control to display each field on the form, or you might make what you think is the best choice for the control, only to find out later that it wasn't exactly what your user had in mind. In Access, it's easy to "morph," or convert, the type of control. For example, you can morph a list box into a combo box.

Text Box to Combo Box

One of the most common types of conversions is from a text box to a combo box. To morph a text box to a combo box, right-click on the text box. Choose Change To, then select the type of control you want to morph the text box to. The types of controls available depend on the type of control you're morphing. For example, a text box can be converted to a label, list box, or combo box. (See Figure 6.27.)

Figure 6.27.

Morphing a text box.

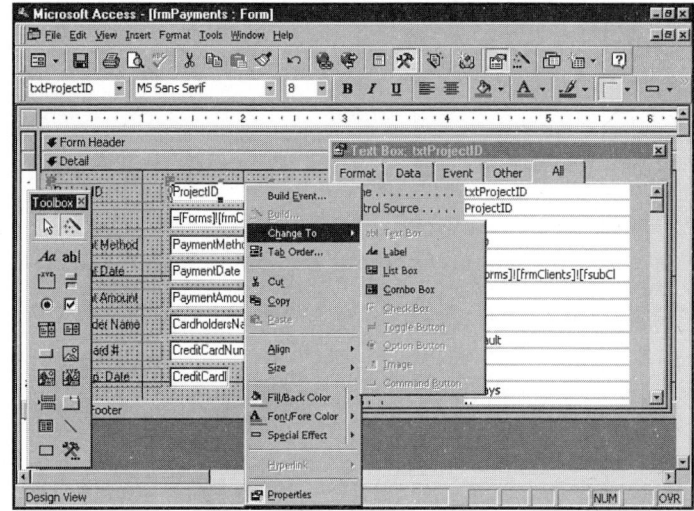

After morphing a text box to a combo box, you modify the appropriate Control properties. The Row Source, Bound Column, Column Count, and Column Widths properties need to be filled in. For the row source, you must select the appropriate table or query. If you select a table and then click on the ellipse, you are prompted to create a query based on the table. After selecting Yes, you can build a query containing only the fields you want to include in the combo box. You're then ready to select the bound column, which is used to store data in the underlying table. For example, the user might select the name of a project that a payment is being applied to, but the ProjectID will be stored in the Payments table. Set the column count to the number of columns selected in the underlying query; the column widths can be set so that the key column is hidden.

Combo Box to List Box

Converting a combo box to a list box is a much simpler process than converting a text box to a combo box or list box because combo boxes and list boxes share so many properties. To morph a combo box into a list box, simply right-click on the combo box and choose Change To | List Box.

What Form Properties Are Available and Why Use Them?

Forms have many properties that can be used to affect their look and behavior. The properties are broken down into categories: Format, Data, Event, and Other. To view a form's properties, you must select the form in one of two ways:

- Click the Form Selector (the small gray button at the intersection of the horizontal and vertical rulers).
- Choose Edit | Select Form.

Working with the Properties Window

Once a form has been selected, click the Properties button on the toolbar to view its properties. The Properties window, shown in Figure 6.28, consists of five tabs: Format, Data, Event, Other, and All. Many developers prefer to view all properties at once, but a form has a total of 77 properties! Rather than viewing all 77 properties at once, try viewing the properties by category. The Format category includes all the physical attributes of the form, the ones that affect the form's appearance (such as background color, for example). The Data category includes all the properties that relate to the data the form is bound to, such as the form's underlying record source. The Event category contains all the Windows events to which a form can respond. For example, you can write code that executes in response to the form being loaded, becoming active, displaying a different record, and so on. The Other category has a few properties that don't fit into the other three categories.

Figure 6.28.

Viewing the Format properties of a form.

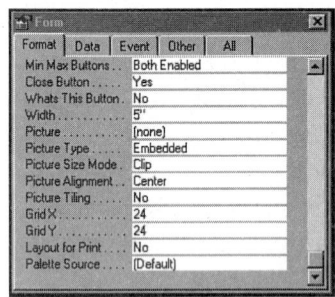

Working with the Important Form Properties

As mentioned, forms have 77 properties, and of those, 31 are Event properties, covered in Chapter 13. This section covers the Format, Data, and Other properties of forms.

Format Properties of a Form

The Format properties of a form affect its physical appearance. Forms have 24 Format properties:

Caption: The Caption property sets the text that appears on the form's title bar. This property can be customized at runtime. For example, you could include the name of the current user or specify the name of the client for whom an invoice is being generated.

Default View: The Default View property allows you to select three options:

- `Single Form`—only one record can be viewed at a time.
- `Continuous Forms`—as many records as will fit within the form window are displayed at one time, each displayed as the detail section of a single form.
- `Datasheet`—displays the records in a spreadsheet-like format, with the rows representing records and the columns representing fields.

The selected option becomes the default view for the form.

Views Allowed: The Views Allowed property determines whether the user is allowed to switch from Form view to Datasheet view or vice versa. The Default View property determines the default display mode for the form, but Views Allowed determines whether the user is permitted to switch out of the default view.

Scroll Bars: The Scroll Bars property determines whether scrollbars appear if the controls on the form don't fit within the form's display area. You can select from vertical and horizontal, neither vertical nor horizontal, just vertical, or just horizontal.

Record Selectors: A record selector is the gray bar to the left of a record in Form view or the gray box to the left of each record in Datasheet view. It's used for selecting a record to be copied or deleted. The Record Selectors property determines whether the record selectors appear. If you give the user a custom menu, you can opt to remove the record selector to make sure the user copies or deletes records using only the features specifically built into your application.

Navigation Buttons: Navigation buttons are the controls that appear at the bottom of a form; they allow the user to move from record to record within the form. The Navigation Buttons property determines whether the navigation buttons are visible. You should set it to `No` for any dialog forms, and you might want to set it to `No` for data-entry forms, too, and add your own toolbar or command buttons that enhance or limit the standard buttons' functionality. For example, in a client/server environment, you might not want to give users the ability to move to the first or last record because that type of record movement can be inefficient in a client/server architecture.

Dividing Lines: The Dividing Lines property indicates whether you want a line to appear between each record when the default view of the form is set to `Continuous Forms`.

Auto Resize: The Auto Resize property determines whether the form is automatically sized to display a complete record.

Auto Center: The Auto Center property specifies whether you want the form to automatically be centered within the Application window whenever it's opened.

Border Style: The Border Style property is far more powerful than its name implies. The options for the Border Style property are `None`, `Thin`, `Sizable`, and `Dialog`. The border style is often set to `None` for splash screens, which means the form has no border. A `Thin` border is not resizable; the Size command isn't available in the Control menu. This setting is a good choice for pop-up forms, which remain on top even when other forms are given the focus. A `Sizable`

border is standard for most forms. It includes all the standard options in the Control menu. A `Dialog` border is thick. A form with a border style of Dialog can't be maximized, minimized, or resized. Once the border style of a form is set to `Dialog`, the Maximize, Minimize, and Resize options aren't available in the form's Control menu. The `Dialog` border >is often used along with the Pop Up and Modal properties to create custom dialog boxes.

Control Box: The Control Box property determines whether a form has a Control menu. You should use this option sparingly. One of your responsibilities as an Access programmer is to make your applications comply with Windows standards. If you look at the Windows programs you use, you'll find very few forms without Control menu boxes. This should tell you something about how to design your own applications.

Min Max Buttons: The Min Max Buttons property indicates whether the form has minimize and maximize buttons. The available options are `None`, `Min Enabled`, `Max Enabled`, and `Both Enabled`. If you remove one or both buttons, the appropriate options also become unavailable in the Control menu. The Min Max property is ignored for forms with a border style of `None` or `Dialog`. As with the Control Box property, I rarely use this property. To make my applications comply with Windows standards, I set the Border Style property, then inherit the standard attributes for each border style.

Close Button: The Close Button property determines whether the user can close the form by using the Control menu or double-clicking on the Control icon. If you set the value of this property to `No`, you must give your user another way to close the form; otherwise, the user might have to reboot his or her computer to close your application.

Whats This Button: The Whats This Button property specifies whether you want the Whats This button added to the form's title bar. This feature works only when the form's Min Max Buttons property is set to `No`. When set to `Yes`, the user can click on the Whats This button and then click on an object on the form to display Help for that object. If the selected object has no Help associated with it, Help for the form is displayed, and if the form has no Help associated with it, Microsoft Access Help is displayed.

Width: The Width property is used to specify the form's width. This option is most often set graphically by clicking and dragging to select an appropriate size for the form. You might want to set this property manually when you want more than one form to be the exact same size.

Picture, Picture Type, Picture Size Mode, Picture Alignment, and Picture Tiling: The Picture properties let you select and customize the attributes of a bitmap used as the background for a form.

Grid X, Grid Y: The Grid X and Grid Y properties can be used to modify the spacing of the horizontal and vertical lines that appear in the form when in Design view. By setting these properties, you can affect how precisely you place objects on the form when the Snap to Grid option is active.

Layout for Print: The Layout for Print property specifies whether screen or printer fonts are used on the form. If you want to optimize the form for printing rather than display, set this property to Yes.

Palette Source: The Palette Source property determines the source for selecting colors for a form.

Data Properties of a Form

The Data properties of a form are used to control the source for the form's data, what sort of actions the user can take on the data in the form, and how the data in the form is locked in a multiuser environment. There are 10 Data properties of a form:

Record Source: The Record Source property indicates the Table, Stored Query, or SQL statement on which the form's records are based. Once you have selected a record source for a form, the controls on the form can be bound to the fields in the record source.

> **NOTE**
>
> The Field List window is unavailable until the record source of the form has been set.

> **TIP**
>
> The record source of a form can be changed at runtime. With this aspect of the Record Source property, you can create generic, reusable forms for many situations.

Filter: The Filter Property is used to automatically load a stored filter along with the form. I prefer to base a form on a query that limits the data displayed on the form. The query can be passed parameters at runtime to customize exactly what data is displayed.

Order By: The Order By property specifies in what order the records on a form appear. This property can be modified at runtime to change the order in which the records appear.

Allow Filters: The Allow Filters property allows you to control whether records can be filtered at runtime. When this option is set to No, all filtering options become disabled to the user.

Allow Edits, Allow Deletions, Allow Additions: These properties let you specify whether the user can edit data, delete records, or add records from within the form. These options can't override any permissions that have been set for the form's underlying table or queries. Security is covered in Chapters 32, "Database Security Made Easy," and 33, "Complex Security Issues."

Data Entry: The Data Entry property determines whether your users can only add records within a form. Set this property to Yes if you don't want your users to view or modify existing records but want them to be able to add new records.

Recordset Type: The Recordset Type property gives you three options: `Dynaset`, `Dynaset (Inconsistent Updates)`, and `Snapshot`. Each offers different performance and updating ability. The `Dynaset` option creates a fully updatable recordset. The only exceptions to this rule involve records or fields that can't be updated for some other reason. An example is a form based on a query involving a one-to-many relationship. The join field on the "one" side of the relationship can be updated only if the Cascade Update Related Records feature has been enabled. The `Dynaset (Inconsistent Updates)` option allows all tables and bound data to be edited. This may result in inconsistent updating of data in the tables involved in the query. The `Snapshot` option doesn't allow any updating.

Record Locks: The Record Locks property specifies the locking mechanism to be used for the data underlying the form's recordset. Three options are available. The `No Locks` option—the least restrictive locking mechanism—provides *optimistic locking*; that is, Access doesn't try to lock the record until the user moves off it. This option can lead to potential conflicts when two users simultaneously make changes to the same record. The `All Records` option locks all records underlying the form the entire time the form is open. This is the most restrictive option and should be used only when it's necessary for the form's user to make sure other users can view, but not modify, the form's underlying recordset. The `Edited Record` option locks a 2K page of records as soon as a user starts editing the data in the form. This option provides *pessimistic locking*. Although it averts conflicts by prohibiting two users from modifying a record at the same time, it can lead to potential locking conflicts. These three locking options are covered in detail in Chapter 18, "Developing for a Multiuser Environment."

Other Properties of a Form

Pop Up: The Pop Up property indicates whether the form always remains on top of other windows. This property is often set to `Yes`, along with the Modal property, for custom dialog boxes.

Modal: The Modal property indicates whether focus can be removed from a form while it's open. When the Modal property is set to `Yes`, the form must be closed before the user can continue working with the application. As mentioned, this property is used with the Pop Up property to create custom dialog boxes.

Cycle: The Cycle property controls the behavior of the Tab key in the form. The options are `All Records`, `Current Record`, and `Current Page`. When the Cycle property is set to `All Records`, the user is placed on the next record when he or she presses Tab from the last control on the form. With `Current Record`, the user is moved from the last control on a form to the first control on the same record. The `Current Page` option refers only to multipage forms; when the Cycle property is set to `Current Page`, the user tabs from the last control on the page to the first control on the same page. All three options are affected by the tab order of the objects on the form.

Menu Bar: The Menu Bar property specifies a menu bar associated with the form. The menu bar, sometimes referred to as a command bar in Access 97, is created by using the Customize dialog box, available by choosing Toolbars from the View menu, then selecting Customize. Menus are covered in Chapter 13.

Toolbar: The Toolbar property designates a toolbar associated with the form. The toolbar, sometimes referred to as a *command bar* in Access 97, is created by using the Customize dialog box. The toolbar you select is displayed whenever the form has the focus. Toolbars are covered in Chapter 13.

Shortcut Menu, Shortcut Menu Bar: The Shortcut Menu property indicates whether a shortcut menu is displayed when the user clicks with the right mouse button over an object on the form. The Shortcut Menu Bar property lets you associate a custom menu with a control on the form or with the form itself. As with a standard menu bar, a shortcut menu bar is created by choosing Toolbars from the View menu, then selecting Customize. Shortcut menus are covered in Chapter 13.

Fast Laser Printing: The Fast Laser Printing property determines whether lines and rectangles print along with the form. When this property is set to Yes, you'll notice a definite improvement when printing the form to a laser printer.

Help File, Help Context ID: The Help File and Help Context ID properties are used to associate a specific Help file and topic with a form.

Tag: The Tag property is an extra property used to store miscellaneous information about the form. This property is often set and monitored at runtime to store necessary information about the form.

Has Module: The Has Module property determines whether the form has a class module. If no code is associated with your form, setting this property to No can noticeably decrease load time and improve your form's performance while decreasing the database's size.

What Control Properties Are Available and Why Use Them?

Available Control properties vary quite a bit, depending on the type of control that's been selected. The more common properties are covered in this section; individualized properties are covered throughout the book as they apply to a specific topic.

Format Properties of a Control

Format: The Format property of a control determines the way the data in the control is displayed. A control's format is automatically inherited from its underlying data source. This property is used in only two situations:

- When you want to override the Format setting set for the field
- When you want to apply a format to an unbound control

You can select from a multitude of predefined values for a control's format, or you can create a custom format. I often modify this property at runtime to vary the format of a control depending on a certain condition. For example, the format for a Visa card number is different from the format for an ATM card number.

Decimal Places: The Decimal Places property specifies how many decimal places you want to appear in the control. This property is used with the Format property to determine the control's appearance.

Caption: The Caption property is used to specify information helpful to the user. It's available for labels, command buttons, and toggle buttons.

Hyperlink Address: The Hyperlink Address property is available only for command buttons, images, and unattached labels. It contains a string used to specify the UNC (path to a file) or URL (Web page address) associated with the control. When the form is active and the cursor is placed over the control, clicking the control displays the specified object or Web page.

Hyperlink SubAddress: Like the Hyperlink Address property, the Hyperlink SubAddress property is available only for command buttons, images, and unattached labels. The Hyperlink SubAddress property is a string representing a location in the document specified in the Hyperlink Address property.

Visible: The Visible property indicates whether a control is visible. This property can be toggled at runtime, depending on specific circumstances. For example, a question on the form might apply only to records in which the gender is set to Female; if the gender is set to Male, the question shouldn't be visible.

Display When: The Display When property is used when you want certain controls on the form to be sent only to the screen or only to the printer. The three options are Always, Print Only, or Screen Only. An example of the use of the Display When property is a label containing instructions. You might want the instructions to appear on the screen but not on the printout.

Scroll Bars: The Scroll Bars property determines whether scrollbars appear when the data in the control doesn't fit within the control's size. The options are None and Vertical. I often set the Scroll Bars property to Vertical when the control is used to display data from a Memo field. The scrollbar makes it easier for the user to work with a potentially large volume of data in the Memo field.

Can Grow, Can Shrink: The Can Grow and Can Shrink properties apply only to the form's printed version. The Can Grow property, when set to Yes, expands the control when printing so that all the data in the control fits on the printout. The Can Shrink property applies when no data has been entered into the control. When this property is set to Yes, the control shrinks when no data has been entered so that blank lines won't be printed.

Left, Top, Width, Height: These properties are used to set the control's position and size.

Back Style, Back Color: The Back Style property can be set to Normal or Transparent. When set to Transparent, the form's background color shows through the control. This is often the preferred setting for an option group. The control's Back Color property specifies the background color (as opposed to text color) for the control.

> **WARNING**
>
> If the Back Style of a control is set to Transparent, the control's back color is ignored.

Special Effect: The Special Effect property adds 3-D effects to a control. The options for this property are Flat, Raised, Sunken, Etched, Shadowed, and Chiseled. Each of these effects gives the control a different look.

Border Style, Border Color, Border Width: These properties affect the look, color, and thickness of a control's border. The border style options are Transparent, Solid, Dashes, Short Dashes, Dots, Sparse Dots, Dash Dot, and Dash Dot Dot. The Border Color property specifies the color of the border; you can select from a variety of colors. The Border Width property can be set to one of several point sizes.

> **WARNING**
>
> If the Border Style of a control is set to Transparent, the control's Border Color and Border Width are ignored.

Fore Color, Font Name, Font Size, Font Weight, Font Italic, Font Underline: These properties control the appearance of the text in a control. As their names imply, they let you select a color, font, size, and thickness for the text and determine whether the text is italicized or underlined. These properties can be modified in response to a runtime event, such as modifying a control's text color if the value in that control exceeds a certain amount.

Text Align: The Text Align property is often confused with the ability to align controls. The Text Align property affects how the data is aligned *within* a control.

Data Properties of a Control

Control Source: The Control Source property specifies the field from the record source that's associated with that particular control. A control source can also be any valid Access expression.

Input Mask: The Format and Decimal Places properties affect the appearance of the control, but the Input Mask property affects what data can be entered into the control. The input mask of the field underlying the control is automatically inherited into the control. If no input mask is entered as a field property, the input mask can be entered directly in the form.

If a control's Format property and Input Mask property are different, the Format property affects the display of the data in the control until the control gets focus. Once the control gets focus, the Input Mask property prevails.

Default Value: The Default Value property of a control determines the value assigned to new records entered in the form. This property can be set within the field properties. A default value set at the field level is automatically inherited into the form. The default value set for the control overrides the default value set at the field level.

Validation Rule, Validation Text: The validation rule and validation text of a control perform the same function as they do for a field.

Because the validation rule is enforced at the database engine level, the validation rule set for a control can't be in conflict with the validation rule set for the field to which the control is bound. If the two rules conflict, the user can't enter data into the control.

Enabled: The Enabled property determines whether you allow a control to get focus. If set to No, the control appears dimmed.

Locked: The Locked property determines whether the data in the control can be modified. When the Locked property is set to Yes, the control can get focus but can't be edited. The Enabled and Locked properties of a control interact with one another. Table 6.1 summarizes their interactions.

Table 6.1. How Enabled and Locked properties interact.

Enabled	Locked	Effect
Yes	Yes	The control can get focus; its data can be copied but not modified.
Yes	No	The control can get focus, and its data can be edited.
No	Yes	The control can't get focus.
No	No	The control can't get focus; its data appears dimmed.

Filter Lookup: The Filter Lookup property indicates whether you want the values associated with a bound text box to appear in the Filter By Form window.

Other Properties of a Control

Name: The Name property allows you to name the control. This name is used when you refer to the control in code and is also displayed in various drop-down lists that show all the controls on a form. It's important to name your controls because named controls improve your code's readability and make working with Access forms and other objects easier. The naming conventions for controls are in Appendix B, "Naming Conventions."

Status Bar Text: The Status Bar Text property specifies the text that appears in the status bar when the control gets focus. This property setting overrides the Description property that can be set in a table's design.

Enter Key Behavior: The Enter Key Behavior property determines whether the Enter key causes the cursor to move to the next control or add a new line in the current control. This setting is often changed for text boxes used to display the contents of Memo fields.

Allow AutoCorrect: The Allow AutoCorrect property specifies whether the AutoCorrect feature is available in the control. The AutoCorrect feature automatically corrects common spelling errors and typos.

Auto Tab: The Auto Tab property, when set to Yes, automatically advances the cursor to the next control when the last character of an input mask has been entered. Some users like this option and others find it annoying, especially if they must tab out of some fields but not others.

Default: The Default property applies to a command button or ActiveX control and specifies whether the control is the default button on a form.

Cancel: The Cancel property applies to a command button or ActiveX control. It indicates that you want the control's code to execute when the Esc key is pressed while the form is active.

Auto Repeat: The Auto Repeat property specifies whether you want an event procedure or macro to execute repeatedly while the command button is being pressed.

Status Bar Text: The Status Bar Text property specifies the message that appears in the status bar when the control has the focus.

Tab Stop: The Tab Stop property determines whether the Tab key can be used to enter a control. It's appropriate to set this property to No for controls whose values rarely get modified. The user can always opt to click in the control when necessary.

Tab Index: The Tab Index property sets the tab order for the control. I generally set the Tab Index property by using View|Tab Order, rather than by setting the value directly in the control's Tab Index property.

Shortcut Menu Bar: The Shortcut Menu Bar attaches a specific menu to a control. The menu bar appears when the user right-clicks on the control.

ControlTip Text: The ControlTip Text property specifies the tooltip associated with a control. The tooltip automatically appears when the user places the mouse pointer over the control and leaves it there for a moment.

Help Context ID: The Help Context ID property designates the Help topic associated with a particular control.

Tag: The Tag property is an extra property you can use to store information about a control. Your imagination determines how you use this property. The Tag property can be read and modified at runtime.

Bound, Unbound, and Calculated Controls

There are important differences between bound and unbound controls. *Unbound controls* display information to the user or gather information from the user that's not going to be stored in your database. Here are some examples of unbound controls:

- A label providing instructions to the user
- A logo placed on a form
- A combo or text box placed on a form so that the user can enter report criteria
- A rectangle placed on the form to logically group several controls

Bound controls are used to display and modify information stored in a database table. A bound control automatically appears in the form specified in its Display Control property; the control automatically inherits many of the attributes assigned to the field the control is bound to.

A *Calculated control* is a special type of control that displays the results of an expression. The data in a Calculated control can't be modified by the user. The control's value automatically changes as the values in its expression are changed. For example, the Sales Total changes as the Price or Quantity is changed.

Using Expressions to Enhance Your Forms

As mentioned in the previous section, a control can contain any valid expression as its control source. When entering an expression as a control source, the expression must be proceeded by an equal sign. The control source can be manually typed, or you can use the Expression Builder to make the process easier.

To add an expression to a control source, start by adding an unbound control to the form. To use the Expression Builder, click in the control's Control Source property, then click the ellipse. The Expression Builder appears. (See Figure 6.29.) In the list box on the left, select the type of object you want to include in the expression. The middle and right list boxes let you select the specific element you want to paste into your expression. The Expression Builder is useful when you're not familiar with the specific syntax required for the expression. An expression can also be entered directly into the text box for the Control Source property. To view the expression more easily, you can use the Zoom feature (Shift+F2). The Zoom dialog box for the control source is pictured in Figure 6.30; the expression shown in the figure evaluates the PaymentAmount. If the PaymentAmount is greater than or equal to 1,000, the message "Big Hitter" is displayed; otherwise, nothing is displayed.

Figure 6.29.
The Expression Builder helps you add an expression as a control's control source.

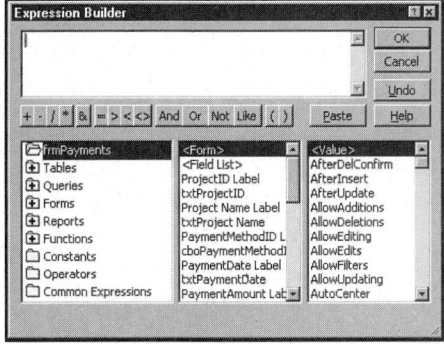

Figure 6.30.
The Zoom dialog box for a control source.

The Command Button Wizards: Programming Without Typing

With the Command Button Wizard, you can quickly and easily add functionality to your forms. It writes the code to perform 32 commonly required tasks. The tasks are separated into record navigation, record operations, form operations, report operations, application operations, and other miscellaneous tasks. The first step of the Command Button Wizard is shown in Figure 6.31; here, you specify the category of activity and specific action you want the command button to perform. The subsequent wizard steps vary, depending on the category and action you select.

Figure 6.32 shows the second step of the Command Button Wizard when the Form Operations category and Open Form action are selected in the first step. Notice that this step asks which form you want to open. After selecting a form and clicking Next, you're asked whether you want Access to open the form and find specific data to display or whether you want the form to be opened and all records displayed. If you indicate that you want only specific records displayed, the dialog box shown in Figure 6.33 appears. This dialog box asks you to select fields relating the two forms. In the next step of the wizard, you select text or a picture for the button. The final step of the wizard asks you to name the button.

Figure 6.31.
The first step of the Command Button Wizard.

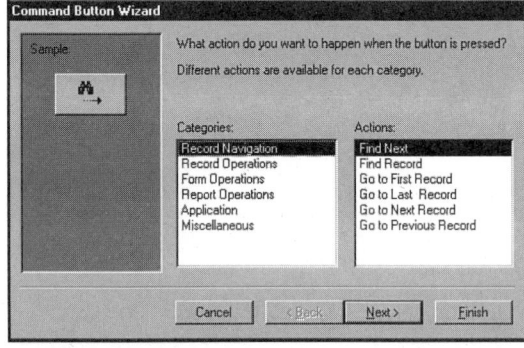

Figure 6.32.
The Command Button Wizard requesting the name of a form to open.

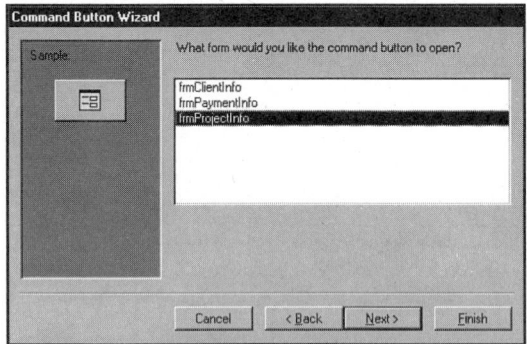

Figure 6.33.
The Command Button Wizard asking for the fields that relate each form.

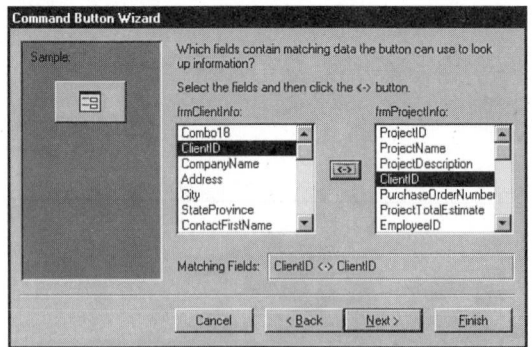

What's surprising about the Command Button Wizard is how much it varies depending on the features you select. It allows you to add somewhat sophisticated functionality to your application without writing a single line of code. The code generated by the example just outlined is shown in Figure 6.34; it will make a lot more sense after you read the next couple of chapters. The advantage to the code generated by the Command Button Wizard is that it can be fully modified after it's written; this means you can have Access do some of the dirty work for you, then customize the work to your liking.

Figure 6.34.
The code generated from the Command Button Wizard.

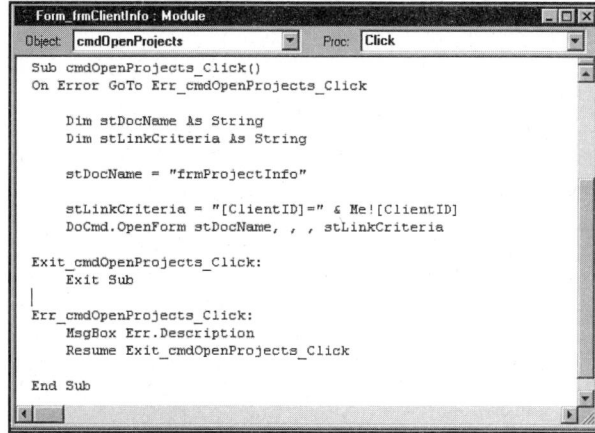

```
Sub cmdOpenProjects_Click()
On Error GoTo Err_cmdOpenProjects_Click

    Dim stDocName As String
    Dim stLinkCriteria As String

    stDocName = "frmProjectInfo"

    stLinkCriteria = "[ClientID]=" & Me![ClientID]
    DoCmd.OpenForm stDocName, , , stLinkCriteria

Exit_cmdOpenProjects_Click:
    Exit Sub

Err_cmdOpenProjects_Click:
    MsgBox Err.Description
    Resume Exit_cmdOpenProjects_Click

End Sub
```

Building Forms Based on More Than One Table

Many forms are based on more than one table. A form, for example, that shows a customer at the top and the orders associated with that customer at the bottom is considered a One-to-Many form. Forms can also be based on a query that joins more than one table. Rather than see a one-to-many relationship in such a form, you see the two tables displayed as one, with each record on the "many" side of the relationship appearing with its parent's data.

Creating One-to-Many Forms

There are several ways to create One-to-Many forms. As with many other types of forms, you can use a wizard to help you or build the form from scratch. Because all the methods for creating a form are useful to users and developers alike, the available options are covered in this section.

Building a One-to-Many Form by Using the Form Wizard

Building a One-to-Many form by using the Form Wizard is a simple process with 11 steps:

1. Click on the Forms tab and click New.
2. Select Form Wizard from the New Form dialog box.

3. Use the Tables/Queries drop-down list to select the table or query that will appear on the "one" side of the relationship.

4. Select the fields you want to include from the "one" side of the relationship.

5. Use the Tables/Queries drop-down list to select the table or query that will appear on the "many" side of the relationship.

6. Select the fields you want to include from the "many" side of the relationship.

7. Click Next.

8. Select whether you want the parent form to appear with subforms or the child forms to appear as linked forms. (See Figure 6.35.) Click Next.

Figure 6.35.
The Form Wizard creating a One-to-Many form.

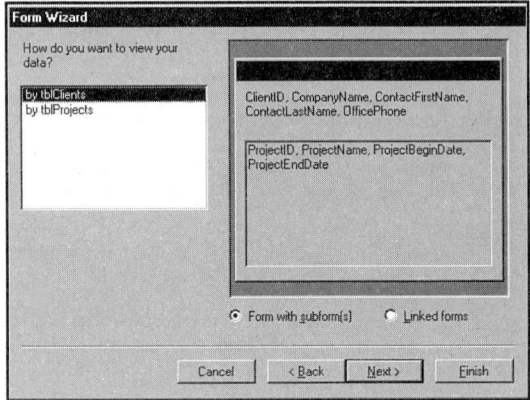

9. If you select the Subform option, indicate whether you want the subform to appear in a tabular format or as a datasheet. Click Next.

10. Select a style for the form, then click Next.

11. Name both the form and the subform and click Finish.

The result is a main form that contains a subform. An example is shown in Figure 6.36.

Figure 6.36.
The result of creating a One-to-Many form with the Form Wizard.

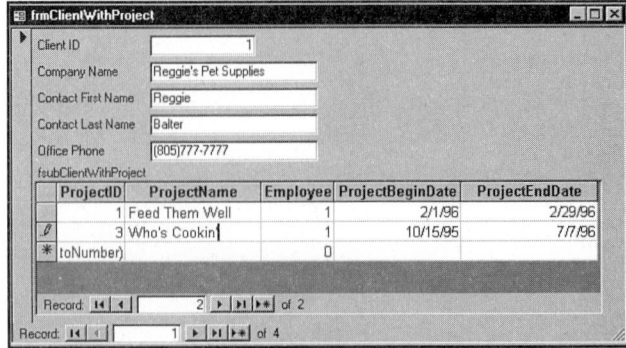

Building a One-to-Many Form with the Subform/Subreport Wizard

A One-to-Many form can also be created by building the parent form, then adding a Subform/Subreport control, which is found in the toolbox. If you want to use the Subform Subreport Wizard, make sure the Control Wizards tool is selected before you add the Subform/ Subreport control to the main form, then follow these six steps:

1. Click to select the Subform/Subreport control.

2. Click and drag to place the Subform/Subreport control on the main form; this invokes the Subform/Subreport Wizard.

3. Indicate whether you want to use an existing form as the subform or build a new subform from a table or query.

4. If you select Table/Query, the next step of the Subform/Subreport Wizard prompts you to select a table or query and which fields you want to include from it. (See Figure 6.37.) Select the fields, then click Next.

Figure 6.37.

Selecting fields to include in the subform.

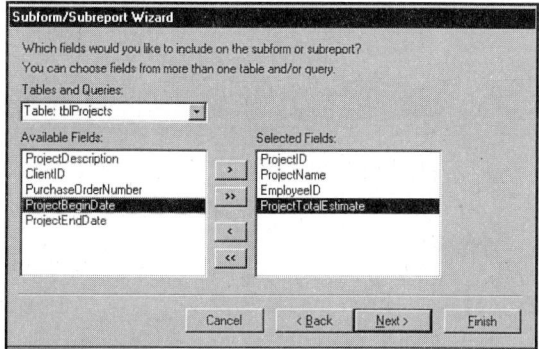

5. The next step of the Subform/Subreport Wizard prompts you to select the relationship between the fields in the two forms. You can select from the ones suggested or define your own. (See Figure 6.38.) Select the appropriate relationship and click Next.

6. Name the subform and click Finish.

Figure 6.38.

Defining the relationship between the main form and the subform.

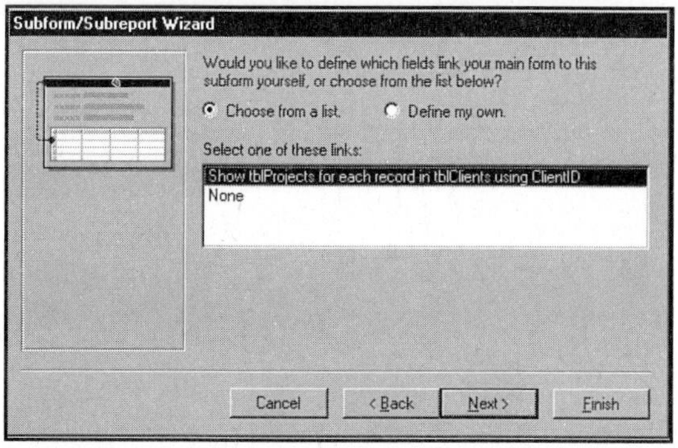

155

The resulting form should look like the form created with the Form Wizard. Creating a One-to-Many form this way is simply an alternative to the Form Wizard.

> **TIP**
>
> Another way to add a subform to a main form is to click and drag a form from the Database window onto the main form. Access then tries to identify the relationship between the two forms.

Working with Subforms

Once a subform has been added, you need to understand how to work with it. To begin, familiarize yourself with a few properties of a Subform control:

Source Object: The name of the form that's being displayed in the control.

Link Child Fields: The field(s) from the child form that link the child form to the master form.

Link Master Fields: The fields(s) from the master form that link the child form to the master form.

You should also understand how to make changes to the subform. One option is to open the subform as you would open any other form. After closing and saving the form, all the changes automatically appear in the parent form. The other choice is to modify the subform from within the main form. With the main form open, start by making sure the subform isn't selected, then double-click on the subform; it should open.

The default view of the subform is Datasheet or Continuous Forms, depending on how you added the subform and what options you selected. If you want to modify the default view, simply change the subform's Default View property.

> **NOTE**
>
> If the subform is displayed in Datasheet view, the order of the columns in the datasheet depends on the tab order of the fields in the subform. When the subform is displayed in Datasheet view, the order of the fields in the subform has no bearing on the datasheet that appears in the main form. You must modify the tab order of the fields in the subform to change the order of the fields in the resulting datasheet.

Basing Forms on Queries: The Why and How

Chapter 2, "A Strategy for Developing Access Applications," covered strategies for developing Access applications. One strategy is basing forms on queries; by doing this, you generally get optimal performance and flexibility. Rather than bring all fields and all records over the network, you bring only the fields and records you need. The benefits are even more pronounced in a client/server environment where the query is run on the server. Even in an environment where data is stored in the proprietary Access file format (.MDB) on a file server, a form based on a stored query can better take advantage of Access's indexing and paging features. By basing a form on a query, you also have more control over which records are included in the form and in what order they appear. Finally, you can base a form on a query containing a one-to-many join, viewing parent and child information as if it were one record. Notice in Figure 6.39 that the client and project information appear on one form as if they were one record.

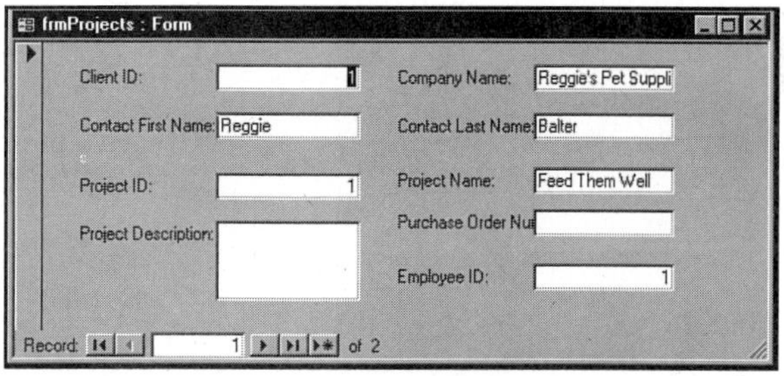

Figure 6.39.
A form based on a one-to-many query.

Embedding SQL Statements Versus Stored Queries

Most developers are unaware that a stored query usually offers better performance than an embedded SQL statement. When a query is saved, Access compiles the query and creates a Query Plan, which has information on the best way to execute the query based on available indexes and the volume of data. If a form is based on an embedded SQL statement, the SQL statement is compiled and optimized *each time* the form is opened. The difference in performance is particularly apparent with forms that are opened frequently.

NOTE

Basing a form on a stored query can actually degrade performance if the volume of data in the table(s) underlying the form varies greatly. This is because the stored Query Plan will be inaccurate. If the amount of data in the table(s) underlying a form isn't relatively stable, it's better to base the form on an embedded SQL statement rather than a stored query. In this case, recompiling the query and re-creating the query plan each time the form is opened actually improves performance.

Access Forms and the Internet

Microsoft has made it easier to develop Internet-aware applications by adding hyperlinks to forms and allowing you to save an Access form as HTML or in the Microsoft IIS 1-2 format. These features are covered in the following sections.

Adding a Hyperlink to a Form

Hyperlinks can be added to unattached labels (labels not attached to a text box or other object), command buttons, and image controls. Once added, they let the user jump to a document (UNC) or home page (URL) simply by clicking on the control containing the hyperlink. To add a hyperlink to a label, command button, or image control, follow these steps:

1. Click to select the control.
2. View the control's properties.
3. Select the Format tab of the Properties window.
4. Click in the Hyperlink Address property.
5. Click the build button (the ellipses) to open the Insert Hyperlink dialog box. (See Figure 6.40.)

Figure 6.40.

Establishing a link to a file or URL by using the Insert Hyperlink dialog box.

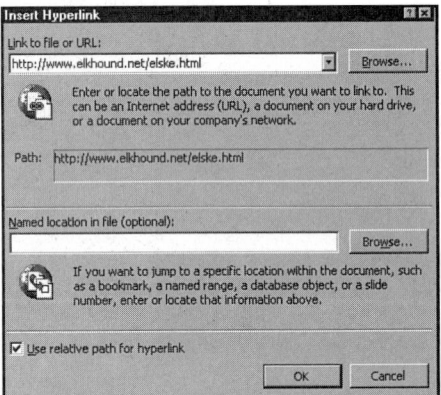

6. Enter a file path or URL in the combo box or click Browse to locate the file or URL.
7. Enter an optional location in the specified document. This must be a recognized item, such as a bookmark in Microsoft Word, a named range in Microsoft Excel, or a slide number in Microsoft PowerPoint. If the hyperlink address is an Access database, you can use the Browse button in the Insert Hyperlink dialog box to select the object in the database you want to link to. (See Figure 6.41.)

Figure 6.41.
Setting the location within an Access database for your hyperlink.

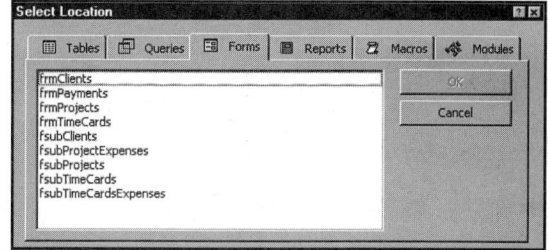

8. If you want the path for the hyperlink to be relative to the directory containing the current database, rather than absolute, make sure the "Use relative path for hyperlink" checkbox is marked. An example of a relative path is ...\MySpreadsheets; an absolute path is F:\MyFiles\MySpreadsheets.

9. Click OK to finish the process. The contents of the "Link to file or URL" combo box become the Hyperlink Address, and the contents of the "Named location in file" combo box become the Hyperlink SubAddress. (See Figure 6.42.)

Figure 6.42.
Hyperlink address and subaddress defined for a label control.

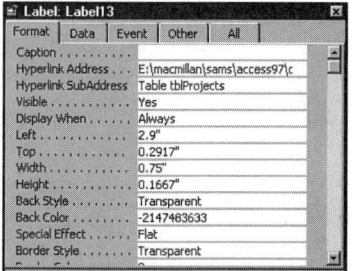

TIP

Using a Hyperlink Address to open an object in an Access database, rather than using the Click event of the command button and VBA code, allows you to remove the class module associated with the form, thereby optimizing the form's performance.

Saving a Form as HTML

Forms can be saved as HTML documents in one of two ways. The first method is to save a form as HTML by choosing File | Save As/Export. Select To an External File or Database and click OK. When the Save Form dialog box appears, use the "Save as type" drop-down list to select HTML. You can then select a location and name for the .HTM file. The system's default browser won't be loaded unless you select the AutoStart option on the Save Form As dialog box. Only the datasheet associated with the form is saved as HTML; the format of the form itself isn't saved.

The other method is to choose File|Save As HTML. This invokes the Publish to Web Wizard, which will walk you through publishing one or more Access objects as HTML. See Chapter 27, "Access and the Internet," for more detailed information.

Saving a Form as Microsoft IIS 1-2

Forms can also be saved in the Microsoft IIS 1-2 format, which creates dynamic forms. This means that the Microsoft Information Server uses the .HTX and .IDC files the process creates to build an .HTM file with the current data. The .IDC file contains data source information, including the data source name, user name, password, and the query that returns the record source of the form being created. The .HTX file is an HTML file that includes merge codes indicating where the data being returned should be inserted.

> **NOTE**
>
> These topics, and others, on creating Access applications for the Internet are covered in more detail in Chapter 27.

Practical Examples: Designing Forms for Your Application

Several forms are required by the Time and Billing application. The more important ones are designed in this section; they're included in the CHAP6.MDB file on the CD-ROM.

Designing the Clients Form

Figure 6.43 shows the frmClients form, a One-to-Many form containing a subform called fsubClients. The main form is based on a query called qryClients, and the subform is based on a query called qryClientsSub.

Figure 6.43.

The frmClients form shows all the projects associated with the selected client.

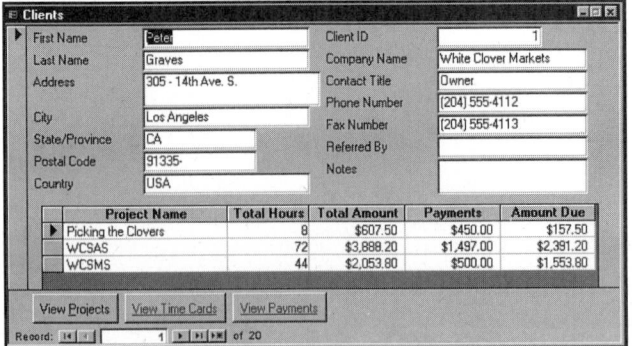

The form footer has three command buttons. The View Projects command button opens the frmProjects form with a Where condition, showing only the projects associated with the client being displayed on the main form. The frmPayments form is opened for the project selected in the fsubClients subform. Rather than use a Where condition on the OpenForm statement, the criteria is set in the query underlying the frmPayments form. A hyperlink is used to open the frmPayments form. The frmTimeCards form is opened without regard for the selected client by clicking the View Time Cards command button. It allows time cards to be entered for any project, regardless of the client. It's also opened with a hyperlink.

Now take a look at the steps required for adding a command button, such as the View Projects command button. It can be added by using the Command Button Wizard. Select the category Form Operations and the action Open Form. Make sure you open the frmProjects form with a Where condition by selecting "Open the form and find specific data to display" on the third step of the Command Button Wizard. Name the command button cmdProjects.

One important line needs to be added to the piece of code the Command Button Wizard wrote. To add this line of code, click the command button whose code you want to modify while you're in Design view for frmClients. View the command button's Event properties, then click the ellipses to the right of the Click event for the command button. Add the following line of code before the DoCmd.OpenForm line:

```
DoCmd.DoMenuItem acFormBar, acRecordsMenu, acSaveRecord, acMenuVer70
```

This line of code saves the current client record before opening any of the other forms. An example of the completed routine looks like this:

```
Sub cmdProjects_Click()
On Error GoTo Err_cmdProjects_Click

    Dim stDocName As String
    Dim stLinkCriteria As String

    DoCmd.DoMenuItem acFormBar, acRecordsMenu, acSaveRecord, , acMenuVer70

    stDocName = "frmProjects"

    stLinkCriteria = "[ClientID]=" & Me![txtClientID]
    DoCmd.OpenForm stDocName, , , stLinkCriteria

Exit_cmdProjects_Click:
    Exit Sub

Err_cmdProjects_Click:
    MsgBox Err.Description
    Resume Exit_cmdProjects_Click

End Sub
```

Name the other two buttons cmdPayments and cmdTimeCards. Fill in the Hyperlink Address property for each of the command buttons to refer to the current database. Set the Hyperlink SubAddress property of cmdPayments to open the frmPayment form and the Hyperlink SubAddress property of cmdTimeCards to open the frmTimeCards form.

Designing the Time Cards Form

The frmTimeCards form is based on a query called qryTimeCards and contains two subforms. (See Figure 6.44.) The first subform is fsubTimeCards and the second is fsubTimeCardsExpenses. The fsubTimeCards subform is based on the qrySubTimeCards query and has a Calculated control in its footer. The control is called txtTotalHoursWorked and holds the expression =Sum(BillableHours), which totals the billable hours in the subform. The fsubTimeCardsExpenses subform is based on the qrySubTimeCardsExpenses query and has a Calculated control in its footer. The control is called txtTotalExpenses and holds the expression =Sum(ExpenseAmount), which totals the expense amounts in the subform.

Figure 6.44.

The frmTimeCards form shows all the time and expenses entered for a particular employee.

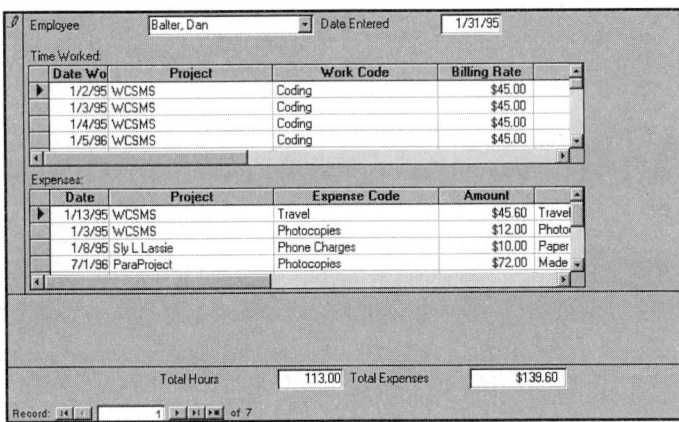

The footer of the frmTimeCards form contains two controls: txtTotalBillableHours and txtTotalExpenses. The txtTotalBillableHours control contains the following expression:

```
=[fsubTimeCards].[Form]![txtTotalHoursWorked]
```

This expression pulls the result of the calculation of the txtTotalHoursWorked control on the fsubTimeCards subform. The txtTotalExpenses control contains the following expression:

```
=[fsubTimeCardsExpenses].[Form]![txtTotalExpenses]
```

This expression pulls the result of the calculation of the txtTotalExpenses control on the fsubTimeCardsExpenses form.

Designing the Payments Form

The frmPayments form is based on a query called qryPayments, which contains the following criteria for the ProjectID:

```
[Forms]![frmClients]![fsubClients].[Form]![ProjectID]
```

This criteria looks at the ProjectID field from the subform fsubClients that's part of the frmClients form. It ensures you'll be looking only at payments relating to the selected project. The Payments form is shown in Figure 6.45. The Project Name text box contains this expression:

```
=[Forms]![frmClients]![fsubClients].[Form]![txtProject Name]
```

Figure 6.45.

The frmPayments form is used to enter payments associated with a project.

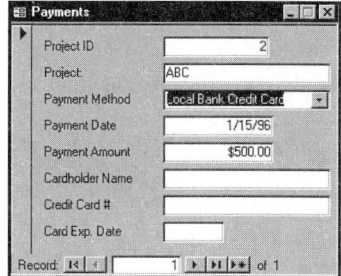

This expression displays the ProjectName from the subform called fsubClients on the frmClients form.

Designing the Projects Form

The frmProjects form is more complex than the others; it contains two subforms, one on top of the other. The View Expenses button is a toggle that lets the user view both expenses and hours. (See Figure 6.46.)

Figure 6.46.

The frmProjects form allows the user to view the expenses and hours associated with the selected project.

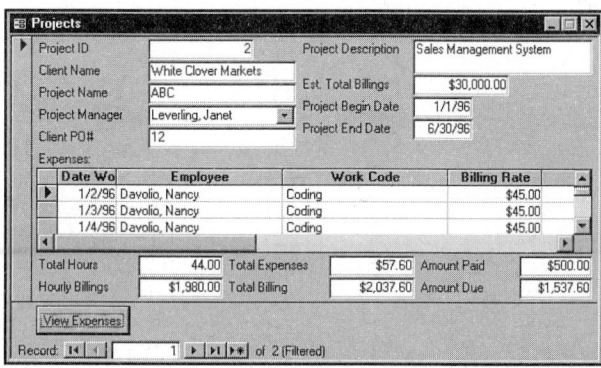

The frmProjects form is based on a query called qryProjects, which has the following expression as the criteria for the ClientID:

```
[Forms]![frmClients]![txtClientID]
```

This means that only projects with the ClientID displayed in the frmClients form are shown. The two subforms are fsubProjects and fsubProjectExpenses. The code that toggles their visibility is covered in Chapter 10, "The Real Scoop on Objects, Properties, and Events." The fsubProjects form is based on qrySubProjects, and the fsubProjectExpenses form is based on qrySubProjectExpenses. The frmProjects form, as well as the subforms, contains several Calculated controls.

What's Ahead

The application you're building is modeled after the time and billing application created by the Database Wizard. You will build the application from scratch so you can learn about all its components. You'll also be adding considerably more functionality to the application. When you're done, your application will be far more powerful than the application built by the Database Wizard.

Summary

Microsoft Access gives you rich, powerful tools you can use to build even the most sophisticated form. This chapter has given you an overview of what Access forms are capable of and shown you the many options you have for creating a new form.

Regardless of how a form has been created, you need to know how to modify all the attributes of a form and its controls. This chapter has shown you how to work with form objects, modifying both their appearance and how they're tied to data. Each control type and its properties have been discussed in detail, and all the properties of the form itself have been covered. Using the techniques in this chapter, you can control both the appearance and functionality of a form and its objects.

7

CHAPTER

What Every Developer Needs to Know About Report Basics

- Types of Reports Available, 166
- Anatomy of a Report, 170
- Creating a New Report, 171
- Working with the Report Design Window, 174
- Selecting the Correct Control for the Job, 178
- What Report Properties Are Available and Why Use Them, 181
- What Control Properties Are Available and Why Use Them, 184
- Inserting Page Breaks, 187
- Unbound, Bound, and Calculated Controls, 187
- Using Expressions to Enhance Your Reports, 187
- Building Reports Based on More Than One Table, 187
- Working with Sorting and Grouping, 193
- Improving Performance and Reusability, 197
- Access Reports and the Internet, 198
- Practical Examples: Building Reports Needed for Your Application, 199

Types of Reports Available

The reporting engine of Microsoft Access is very powerful, with a wealth of features. Many types of reports are available in Access 97:

- Detail reports
- Summary reports
- Cross-tabulation reports
- Reports containing graphics and charts
- Reports containing forms
- Reports containing labels
- Reports including any combination of the above

Detail Reports

A Detail report supplies an entry for each record included in the report. As you can see in Figure 7.1, there's an entry for each order in the Orders table during the specified period (1994). The report's detail is grouped by country and within country by salesperson and gives you subtotals by salesperson and country. The bottom of the report has grand totals for all records included in the report. The report is based on a Parameter query that limits the data displayed on the report based on criteria supplied by the user at runtime.

Figure 7.1.

An example of a Detail report.

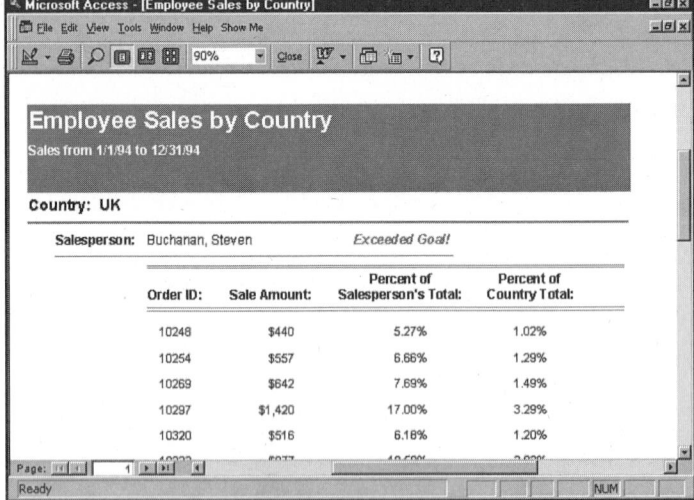

Summary Reports

A Summary report gives you summary data for all the records included in the report. In Figure 7.2, only total sales by quarter and year are displayed in the report. The underlying detail records that compose the summary data aren't displayed in the report. The report is based on a query that summarizes the net sales by OrderID. The report itself contains no controls in its Detail section. All controls are placed in report Group Headers and Footers that are grouped on the quarter and year of the ship date. Because no controls are found in the report's Detail section, Access prints summary information only.

Figure 7.2.

An example of a Summary report.

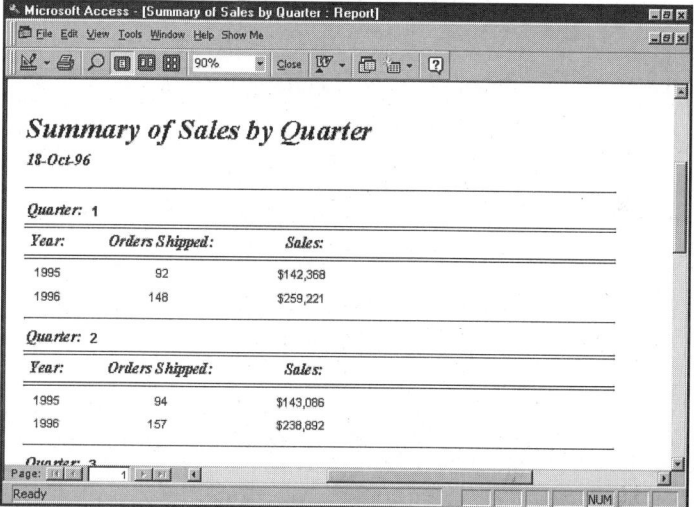

Cross Tabulation Reports

Cross Tabulation reports display summarized data grouped by one set of information on the left side of the report and another set across the top. The report shown in Figure 7.3 shows total sales by product name and employee. The report is based on a Crosstab query and is generated using a fair amount of VBA code. This code is required because each time the report is run, a different number of employees might need to be displayed in the report's columns. In other words, the number of columns needed might be different each time the report is run. This report and the techniques needed to produce it are covered in Chapter 14, "Let's Get More Intimate with Reports: Advanced Techniques."

Figure 7.3.

An example of a Cross Tabulation report.

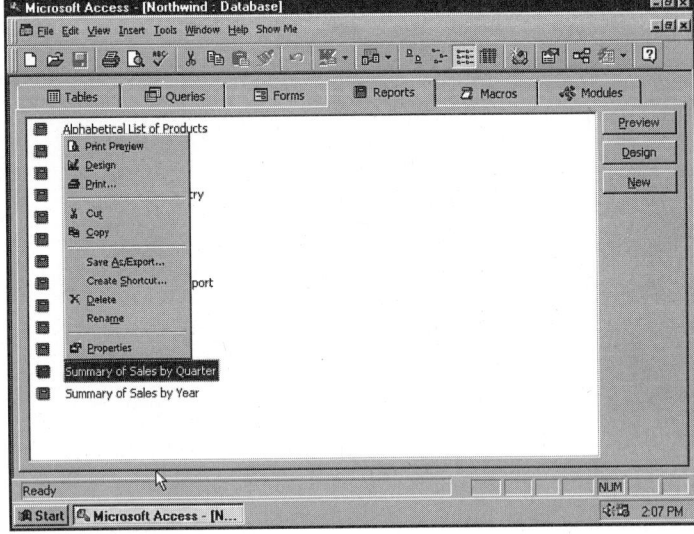

Reports with Graphics and Charts

Although the statement "A picture paints a thousand words" is a cliché, it's also quite true—research proves that you retain data much better when it's displayed as pictures rather than numbers. Fortunately, Access makes including graphics and charts in your reports quite easy. As shown in Figure 7.4, a report can be designed to combine both numbers and charts. The report in Figure 7.4 shows the sales by product, both as numbers and as a bar chart. The main report is grouped by product category and contains a subreport based on a query that summarizes sales by CategoryID, CategoryName, and ProductName for a specific date range. The chart totals product sales by product name, displaying the information graphically.

Figure 7.4.

An example of a report with a chart.

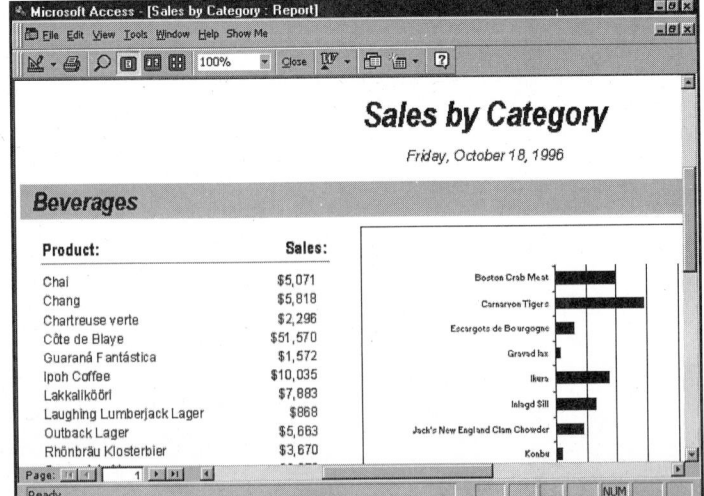

Reports with Forms

A report that looks like a printed form is a common need. The Access Report Builder, with its many graphical tools, allows you to quickly produce reports that emulate the most elegant data-entry form. The report shown in Figure 7.5 produces an invoice for a customer. The report is based on a query that draws information from the Customers, Orders, Order Details, Products, Employees, and Shippers tables. The report's Filter property is filled in, limiting the data that appears on the report to the last six records in the Orders table. Using graphics, color, fonts, shading, and other special effects gives the form a professional look.

Figure 7.5.
An example of a report containing a form.

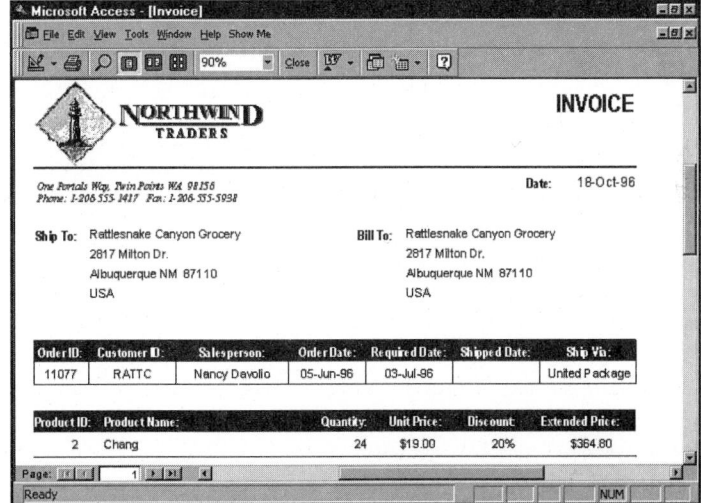

Reports with Labels

Creating mailing labels in Access 97 is easy using the Label Wizard. Mailing labels are simply a special type of report with a page setup indicating the number of labels across the page and the size of each label. An example of a mailing label report created by using the Label Wizard is shown in Figure 7.6. This report is based on the Customers table but could have just as easily been based on a query that limits the mailing labels produced.

Figure 7.6.

An example of a report containing mailing labels.

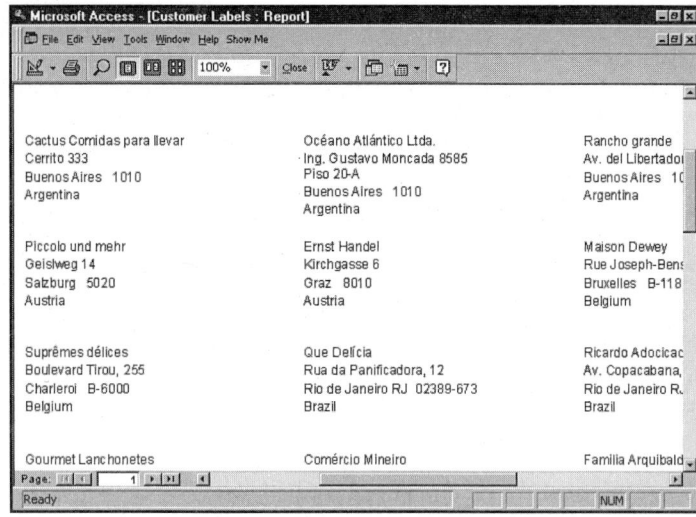

Anatomy of a Report

Reports can have many parts. These parts are referred to as *sections* of the report. A new report is automatically made up of the following three sections, shown in Figure 7.7:

- Page Header Section
- Detail Section
- Page Footer Section

Figure 7.7.

Sections of a report.

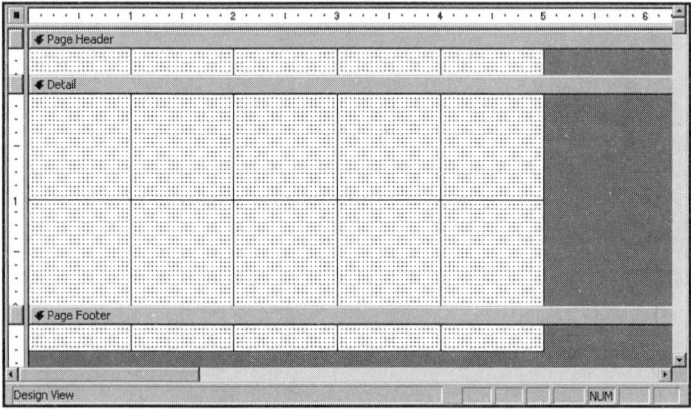

The Detail section is the main section of the report; it's used to display the detailed data of the table or query underlying the report. Certain reports, such as Summary reports, have nothing in the Detail section. Instead, Summary reports contain data in Group Headers and Footers (discussed at the end of this section).

The Page Header is the portion that automatically prints at the top of every page of the report. It often includes information such as the report's title. The Page Footer automatically prints at the bottom of every page of the report and usually contains information such as the page number and date. Each report can have only one Page Header and one Page Footer.

In addition to the three sections automatically added to every report, a report can have the following sections:

- Report Header
- Report Footer
- Group Headers
- Group Footers

A Report Header is a section that prints once, at the beginning of the report; the Report Footer prints once, at the end of the report. Each Access report can have only one Report Header and one Report Footer. The Report Header is often used to create a cover sheet for the report. It can include graphics or other fancy effects, adding a professional look to a report. The most common use of the Report Footer is for grand totals, but it can also include any other summary information for the report.

In addition to Report and Page Headers and Footers, an Access report can have up to 10 Group Headers and Footers. Report groupings separate data logically and physically. The Group Header prints before the detail for the group, and the Group Footer prints after the detail for the group. For example, you can group customer sales by country and city, printing the name of the country or city for each related group of records. If you total the sales for each country and city, you can place the country and city names in the country and city Group Headers and the totals in the country and city Group Footers.

Creating a New Report

You can create a new report in several ways—the most common is to select the Reports tab in the Database window and click New to open the New Report dialog box. (See Figure 7.8.) Here, you can select from many options available for creating reports. Reports can be created from scratch by using Design view; they can also be created with the help of five wizards. Three of the wizards help you build standard reports, one helps you build reports with charts, and the last wizard automates the process of creating mailing labels. The Report Wizards are so powerful that I use one of them to build the initial foundation for almost every report I create.

Figure 7.8.

In the New Report dialog box, you can designate Design view or select from one of five wizards.

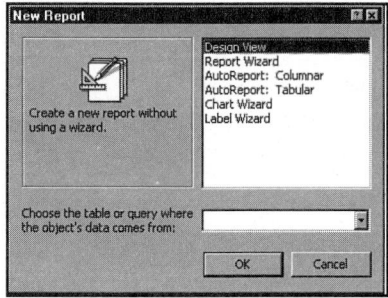

Creating a Report with the Report Wizard

To create a report with the Report Wizard, select Report Wizard from the New Report dialog box and click OK. This launches the Report Wizard. The first step is to select the table or query that will supply data to the report. I prefer to base my reports on queries. This generally improves performance because it returns as small a dataset as possible. In a client/server environment, this is *particularly* pronounced, since the query is usually run on the server and only the results are sent over the network wire. Basing reports on queries also enhances your ability to produce reports based on varying criteria.

Once you have selected a table or query, you can select the fields you want to include on the report. The fields included in the selected table or query are displayed in the list box on the left. To add fields to the report, double-click on the name of the field you want to add or click on the field name and click the > button. In the example in Figure 7.9, six fields have been selected from the tblClients table.

Figure 7.9.

The first step of the Report Wizard: table/field selection.

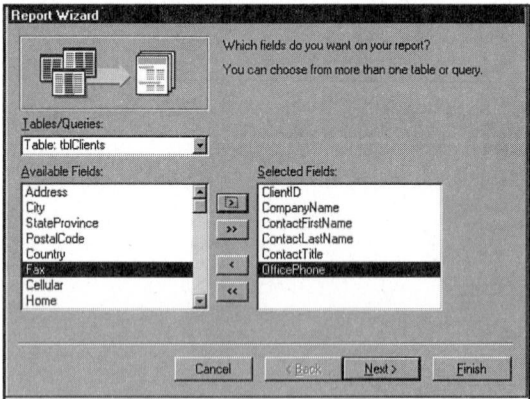

After you have selected a table or query and the fields you want to include on the report, click Next. You're then prompted to add group levels, which add report groupings, to the report. Add group levels if you need to visually separate groups of data or include summary calculations (subtotals) in your report. Report groupings are covered later in this chapter. If your report doesn't require groupings, click Next.

In the third step of the Report Wizard, you choose sorting levels for your report. Because the order of a query underlying a report is overridden by any sort order designated in the report, it's a good idea to designate a sort order for the report. You can add up to four sorting levels with the wizard. In the example shown in Figure 7.10, the report is sorted by the ClientID field. After you select the fields you want to sort on, click Next.

Figure 7.10.

The third step of the Report Wizard: sorting report data.

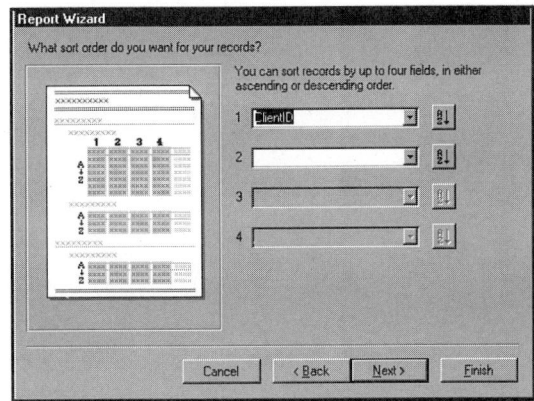

In the fourth step of the Report Wizard, you decide on the report's layout and orientation. The layout options vary depending on what selections have been made in the wizard's previous steps. The orientation can be Portrait or Landscape. This step of the Report Wizard also allows you to specify whether you want Access to try to adjust the width of each field so that all the fields fit on each page. After supplying Access with this information, click Next.

You choose a style for your report in the Report Wizard's fifth step. The available choices are Bold, Casual, Compact, Corporate, Formal, and Soft Gray. You can preview each look before you make a decision. Any of the style attributes applied by the Report Wizard, as well as other report attributes defined by the wizard, can be modified in Report Design view anytime after the wizard has produced the report. After you have selected a style, click Next.

The final step of the Report Wizard prompts you for the report's title. This title is used as both the name and the caption for the report. I supply a standard Access report name and modify the caption after the Report Wizard has finished its process. You're then given the opportunity to preview the report or modify the report's design. If you opt to modify the report's design, you're placed in Design view. (See Figure 7.11.) The report can then be previewed at any time.

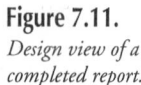

Figure 7.11.
Design view of a completed report.

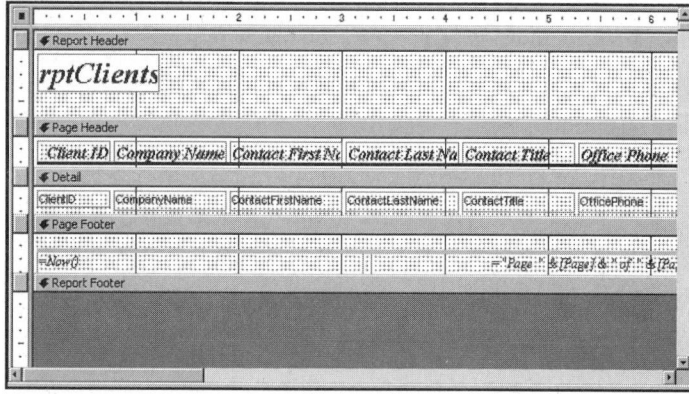

> **NOTE**
>
> Another way to start the Report Wizard is to click on the Tables or Queries tab in the Database Container, then click on the table or query you want the report to be based on. Use the New Object drop-down list on the toolbar to select Report. In the New Report dialog box, select Report Wizard. You don't have to use the Tables/Queries drop-down menu to select a table or query because the one you selected before invoking the wizard is automatically selected for you.

Creating a Report from Design View

Although you usually get started with most of your reports by using a Report Wizard, you should understand how to create a new report from Design view. To create a report without using a wizard, click the Reports tab and then click New to open the New Report dialog box. Click Design View, use the drop-down list to select the table or query on which the report will be based, then click OK. The Report Design window appears.

Working with the Report Design Window

The Report Design window is used to build and modify a report. Using this window, you can add objects to a report and modify their properties. Microsoft provides numerous Report, Report Grouping, and Control properties. By modifying these properties, you can create reports with diverse looks and functionality.

Understanding the Report Design Tools

To help you with designing reports, several report design tools are available, including the Properties, Toolbox, Field List, and Sorting and Grouping windows. Two toolbars are also available to make developing and customizing your reports easier: the Report Design toolbar and the Formatting toolbar. The Report Design toolbar offers tools for saving, previewing, and printing your report and for cutting, copying, and pasting report objects. The Formatting toolbar is specifically designed to help you customize the look of your report. It includes tools for changing the font, font size, alignment, color, shading, and other physical attributes of the report objects.

The Properties, Toolbox, Field List, and Sorting and Grouping windows are all designed as toggles. This means that buttons on the Report Design toolbar alternately hide and show these valuable windows. If you have a high-resolution monitor, you might want to leave the windows open at all times. If you have a low-resolution monitor, you need to get a feel for when it's most effective for each window to be opened or closed.

Adding Fields to the Report

Fields can most easily be added to a report by using the Field List window. With the Field List window open, click and drag a field from the field list onto the appropriate section of the report. Several fields can be added at one time, just as they can in forms. Use the Ctrl key to select noncontiguous fields, use the Shift key to select contiguous fields, or double-click the field list's title bar to select all the fields, then click and drag them to the report as a unit.

WARNING

One problem with adding fields to a report is that both the fields and the attached labels are placed in the same section of the report. This means that if you click and drag fields from the Field List window to the Detail section of the report, both the fields and the attached labels appear in the Detail section. If you're creating a tabular report, this isn't acceptable, so you must cut the attached labels and paste them into the report's Page Header section.

Selecting, Moving, Aligning, and Sizing Report Objects

Microsoft Access offers several techniques to help you select, move, align, and size report objects. Different techniques are effective in different situations. Experience will tell you which technique you should use and when. Selecting, moving, aligning, and sizing report objects are quite similar to performing the same tasks with form objects. The techniques are covered briefly in this chapter; for a more detailed explanation of each technique, refer to Chapter 6, "What Every Developer Needs to Know About Form Basics."

Selecting Report Objects

To select a single report object, click on it; selection handles appear around the selected object. Once the object is selected, you can modify any of its attributes (properties), or you can size, move, or align it.

To select multiple objects so you can manipulate them as a unit, use one of the following techniques:

- Hold down the Shift key as you click on multiple objects. Each object you click on is then added to the selection.

- Place your mouse pointer in a blank area of the report. Click and drag to lasso the objects you want to select. When you let go of the mouse, any object even partially within the lasso is selected.

- Click and drag within the horizontal or vertical ruler. As you click and drag, lines appear indicating the potential selection area. When you release the mouse, all objects within the lines are selected.

> **NOTE**
>
> Make sure you understand which objects are actually selected; attached labels can cause some confusion. Figure 7.12 shows a report with four objects selected: the rptClients label, the Contact First Name label, the City text box, and the ContactFirstName text box. The City label is *not* selected. It's surrounded by one selection handle because it's attached to the City text box. If you were to modify the properties of the selected objects, the City label would be unaffected.

Figure 7.12.
Selecting objects in an Access report.

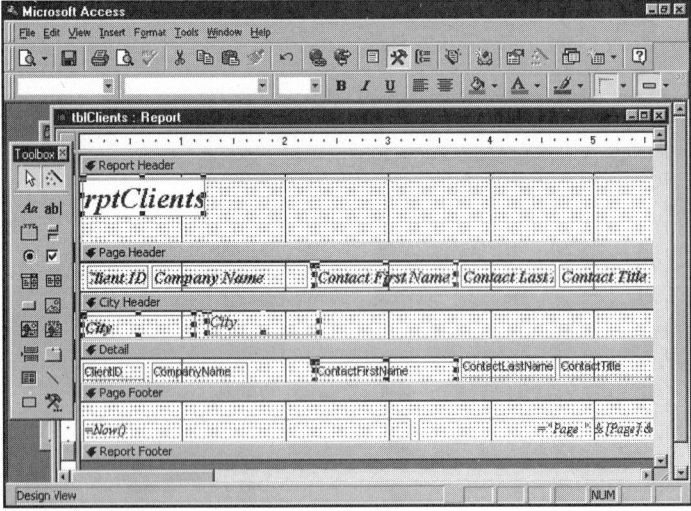

Moving Things Around

If you want to move a single control along with its attached label, click on the object and drag it to a new location. The object and the attached label move as a unit. To move multiple objects, use one of the methods explained in the previous section to select the objects you want to move. After the objects are selected, click and drag any of them; the selected objects and their attached labels move as a unit.

Moving an object without its attached label is a trickier process. When placed over the center or border of a selected object (not on a sizing handle), the mouse pointer looks like a hand with all five fingers pointing upward. This indicates that the selected object and its attached label move as a unit, maintaining their relationship to one another. However, if you place your mouse pointer directly over the selection handle in the object's upper-left corner, the mouse pointer looks like a hand with the index finger pointing upward. This indicates that the object and the attached label move independently of one another so that you can alter the distance between them.

Aligning Objects with One Another

To align objects with one another, you must select them first. Choose Format|Align, then select Left, Right, Top, Bottom, or To Grid. The selected objects then align in relation to each other.

WARNING

Watch out for a few "gotchas" when you're aligning report objects. If you select several text boxes and their attached labels and align them, Access tries to align the left sides of the text boxes with the left sides of the labels. To avoid this problem, you have to align the text boxes separately from their attached labels.

During the alignment process, Access never overlaps objects. For this reason, if the objects you're aligning don't fit, Access can't align them. For example, if you try to align the bottom of several objects horizontally and they don't fit across the report, Access aligns only the objects that fit on the line.

Using Snap to Grid

The Snap to Grid feature is a toggle found under the Format menu. When Snap to Grid is selected, all objects that you're moving or sizing snap to the report's grid lines. To temporarily disable the Snap to Grid feature, hold down your Ctrl key while sizing or moving an object.

Using Power Sizing Techniques

Access offers many techniques to help you size report objects. A selected object has eight sizing handles, and all of them, except for the upper-left handle, can be used to size the object. Simply click and drag one of the sizing handles. If multiple objects are selected, they are sized by the same amount.

The Format|Size menu can also help you to size objects. It has six options: To Fit, To Grid, To Tallest, To Shortest, To Widest, and To Narrowest. These options are discussed in detail in Chapter 6.

> **TIP**
>
> Access offers a great trick that can help size labels to fit. Simply double-click on any sizing handle, and the object is automatically sized to fit the text within it.

Controlling Object Spacing

Access also makes it easy for you to control object spacing. Both the horizontal and vertical distances between selected objects can be made equal. Select the objects, then choose Format | Horizontal Spacing | Make Equal or Format | Vertical Spacing | Make Equal. You can also maintain the relative relationship between selected objects while increasing or decreasing the space between them. To do this, choose Format | Horizontal/Vertical Spacing | Increase/Decrease.

Selecting the Correct Control for the Job

Reports usually contain labels, text boxes, lines, rectangles, image controls, and bound and unbound object frames. The other controls are generally used for reports that emulate data-entry forms. The different controls that can be placed on a report, as well as their uses, are discussed briefly in the following sections.

Labels

Labels are used to display information to your users. They're commonly used as report headings, column headings, or group headings for your report. Although the text they display can be modified at runtime by using VBA code, they can't be directly bound to data.

To add a label to a report, select the Label tool in the toolbox, then click and drag to place the label on the report.

Text Boxes

Text boxes are used to display field information or the result of an expression. They are used throughout a report's different sections. For example, in a Page Header, a text box might contain an expression showing the date range that's the criteria for the report. In a Group Header, a text box might be used to display a heading for the group. The possibilities are endless because a text box can hold any valid expression.

To add a text box to a report, select the Text Box tool from the toolbox. Click and drag the text box to place it on the report. A text box can also be added to a report by dragging a field from the field list to a report. This works as long as the field's Display control property is a text box.

Lines

Lines can be used to visually separate objects on your report. For example, a line can be placed at the bottom of a section or underneath a subtotal. To add a line to a report, click the Line tool to select it, then click and drag to place the line on your report. Once added, the line has several properties that can be modified to customize its look.

> **TIP**
>
> To make sure the line you draw is perfectly straight, hold down the Shift key while you click and drag to draw the line.

Rectangles

Rectangles can be used to visually group items on the report that logically belong together. They can also be used to make certain controls on your report stand out. I often draw rectangles around important subtotal or grand total information that I want to make sure the report's reader notices.

To add a rectangle to a report, select the Rectangle tool from the toolbox, then click and drag to place the rectangle on the report.

> **WARNING**
>
> The rectangle might obscure objects that have already been added to the report. To rectify this problem, the rectangle's Back Style property can be set to Transparent. This setting is fine unless you want the rectangle to have a background color. If so, choose Format | Send to Back to layer the objects so that the rectangle lies behind the other objects on the report.

Bound Object Frames

Bound object frames let you display the data in OLE fields, which contain objects from other applications, such as pictures, spreadsheets, and word processing documents.

To add a bound object frame to a report, click the Bound Object Frame tool in the toolbox, then click and drag the frame onto the report. Set the Control Source property of the frame to the appropriate field. You can also add a bound object frame to a report by dragging and dropping an OLE field from the field list onto the report.

Unbound Object Frames

Unbound object frames can be used to add logos and other pictures to a report. Unlike bound object frames, however, they aren't tied to underlying data.

To add an unbound object frame to a report, click the Unbound Object Frame tool in the toolbox. Click and drag the object frame to place it on the report. This opens the Insert Object dialog box, shown in Figure 7.13, which you use to create a new OLE object or insert an existing OLE object from a file on disk. If you click on Create From File, the Insert Object dialog box changes to look like Figure 7.14. Click Browse and locate the file you want to include in the report. The Insert Object dialog box gives you the option of linking to or embedding an OLE object. If you select Link, a reference is created to the OLE object. Only the bitmap of the object is stored in the report, and the report continues to refer to the original file on disk. If you don't select Link, the object you select is copied and embedded in the report and becomes part of the Access MDB file; no link to the original object is maintained.

Figure 7.13.

Use the Insert Object dialog box to insert a new or an existing object into an unbound object frame.

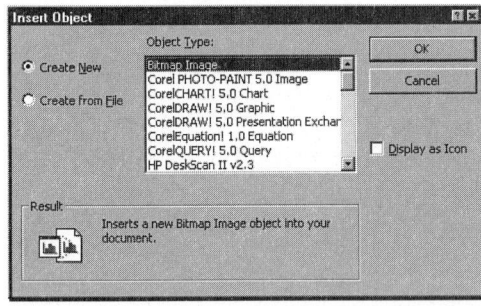

Figure 7.14.

The Insert Object dialog box with Create from File selected.

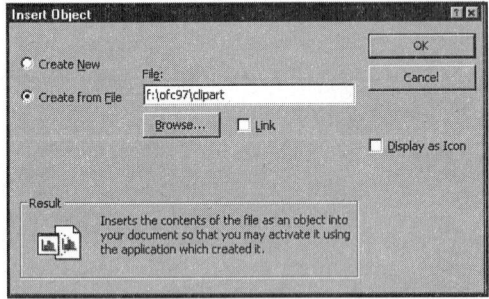

> **NOTE**
>
> It's usually preferable to use an image control rather than an unbound object frame for static information like a logo because the image control requires much fewer resources than an unbound object frame does. Image controls are covered in the next section; Figure 7.15 shows a report with an image control.

Figure 7.15.

A report with an unbound object frame.

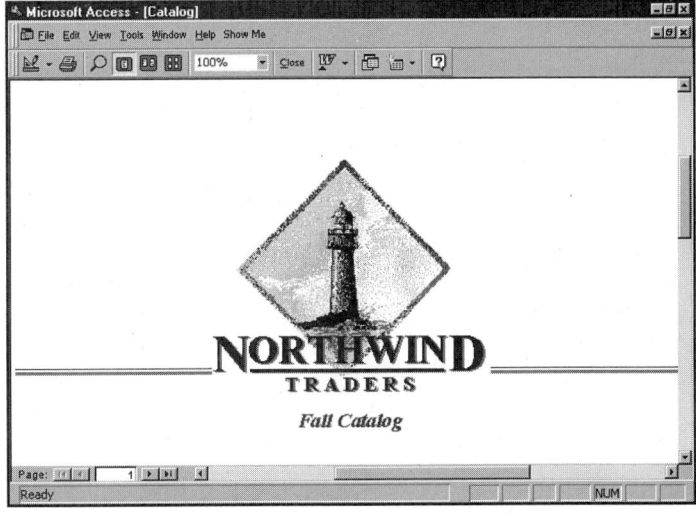

Image Controls

Image controls are your best option for displaying static images, such as logos, on a report. An unbound object can be modified after it's placed on a report, but you can't open the object application and modify an image once it's placed on a report. This limitation, however, means far fewer resources are needed, so performance improves noticeably.

Other Controls

As mentioned earlier in this section, it's standard to include mostly labels and text boxes on your reports, but other controls can be added when appropriate. To add any other type of control, click to select the control, then click and drag to place it on the report.

What Report Properties Are Available and Why Use Them

Reports have many different properties that can be modified to change how the report looks and performs. Like Form properties, Report properties are divided into the categories Format, Data, Event, and Other. To view a report's properties, first select the report, rather than a section of the report, in one of two ways:

- Click the Report Selector, the small gray button at the intersection of the horizontal and vertical rulers.
- Choose Edit | Select Report.

Once a report has been selected, you can view and modify its properties.

Working with the Properties Window

When the report is selected, the Properties window shows all the properties associated with the report. To select the report and open the Properties window at the same time, double-click on the Report Selector. A report has 37 properties available on the property sheet (there are additional properties available only from code) broken down into the appropriate categories in the Properties window. Thirty of the properties relate to the report's format, data, and other special properties; the remaining seven relate to the events that occur when a report is run. The format, data, and other properties are covered here, and the event properties are covered in Chapter 14.

The Report's Format Properties

A report has 15 Format properties for changing the report's physical appearance:

Caption: The Caption property of the report is the text that appears in the Report window's title bar when the user is previewing the report. It can be modified at runtime to customize it for a particular situation.

Page Header, Page Footer: The Page Header and Page Footer properties determine on what pages these sections appear. The options are All Pages, Not with Rpt Hdr, Not with Rpt Ftr, and Not with Rpt Hdr/Ftr. Since you might not want the Page Header or Page Footer to print on the Report Header or Report Footer pages, these properties give you control over where those sections print.

Grp Keep Together: In Access, you can keep a group of data together on the same page by using the Grp Keep Together property. The Per Page option forces the group of data to remain on the same page, and the Per Column option forces the group of data to remain within a column. A *group of data* refers to all the data within a report grouping (for example, all the customers in a city).

Width: The Width property specifies the width of the report sections.

Picture, Picture Type, Picture Size Mode, Picture Alignment, Picture Tiling, and Picture Pages: The background of a report can be a picture. The Picture properties determine what picture is used as a background for the report and what attributes are applied to it.

Grid X / Grid Y: The Grid X and Grid Y properties determine the density of the gridlines in the Report Design window.

Layout for Print: The Layout for Print property specifies whether screen or printer fonts are used in the report. If you want to optimize reports for preview, select No; if you want to optimize reports for the printer, select Yes. This option is not as important if you select True Type Fonts because True Type Fonts usually print equally well to the screen and printer.

Palette Source: The Palette Source property determines the source for the report's selectable color.

The Report's Data Properties

A report has five Data properties used to supply information about the data underlying the report:

Record Source: The Record Source property specifies the table or query whose data underlies the report. The record source of a report can be modified at runtime. This aspect of the Record Source property makes it easy for you to create generic reports that use different record sources in different situations.

Filter: The Filter property allows you to open the report with a specific filter set. I usually prefer to base a report on a query rather than apply a filter to it. At other times, it's more appropriate to base the report on a query but then apply and remove a filter as required, based on the report's runtime conditions.

Filter On: The Filter On property determines whether a report filter is applied. If the value of this property is set to No, the Filter property of the report is ignored.

Order By: The Order By property determines how the records in a report are sorted when the report is opened.

Order By On: The Order By On property determines whether the Order By property of the report is used. If the value of this property is No, the report's Order By property is ignored.

Other Report Properties

A report has ten Other properties; these miscellaneous properties allow you to control other important aspects of the report:

Record Locks: The Record Locks property determines whether the tables used in producing the report are locked while the report is being run. The two values for this property are No Locks and All Records. No Locks is the default value; it means that no records in the tables underlying the report are locked while the report is being run. Users can modify the underlying data as the report is run, which can be disastrous when running sophisticated reports. The data in the report can be changed as the report is being run, which would make figures for totals and percent of totals invalid. Although the All Records option for this property locks all records in all tables included in the report (thereby preventing data entry while the report is being run), it might be a necessary evil for producing an accurate report.

Date Grouping: The Date Grouping property determines how grouping of dates occurs in your report. The US Defaults option means that Access uses United States defaults for report groupings; therefore, Sunday is the first day of the week, the first week begins January 1, and so on. The Use System Settings option means that date groupings are based on the locale set in the Control Panel's Regional Settings, rather than on U.S. defaults.

Menu Bar: The Menu Bar property allows you to associate a custom menu bar with the report that's visible when the user is previewing the report. Adding a custom menu to your report lets you control what the user can do while the report is active.

Toolbar: The Toolbar property lets you associate a custom toolbar with the report that's visible when the user is previewing the report.

Shortcut Menu Bar: The Shortcut Menu Bar property determines what shortcut menu is associated with the report while the report is being previewed. The shortcut menu bar appears when the user clicks the right mouse button over the preview window.

Fast Laser Printing: The Fast Laser Printing property determines whether lines and rectangles are replaced with text character lines when you print a report with a laser printer. If fast printing is your objective and you're using a laser printer, you should set this property to Yes.

Help File, Help Context ID: The Help File and Help Context ID properties let you associate a help file and help topic with the report.

Tag: The Tag property is an extra property for storing information defined by the user at either design time or runtime. It is Microsoft Access's way of giving you an extra property. Access makes no use of this property; if you don't take advantage of it, it will never be used.

HasModule: The HasModule property determines whether the report contains an associated class module. If no code will be included in the report, eliminating the class module can both improve performance and reduce the size of the application database. A report without a class module is considered a "lightweight object," which loads and displays faster than an object with an associated class module.

WARNING

A couple of the HasModule property's behaviors deserve special attention. When a report is created, the default value for the HasModule property is No. Access automatically sets the HasModule property to Yes as soon as you try to view a report's module. If you set the HasModule property of an existing report to No, Access deletes the object's class module and all the code it contains!

What Control Properties Are Available and Why Use Them

Just as reports have properties, so do controls. Most control properties can be changed at design time or at runtime, allowing you to easily build flexibility into your reports. For example, certain controls are visible only when specific conditions are true.

The Control's Format Properties

You can modify several formatting properties of the selected objects by using the formatting toolbar. If you prefer, you can set all the properties in the Properties window.

Format: The Format property determines how the data in the control is displayed. This property is automatically inherited from the underlying field. If you want the control's format on the report to differ from the underlying field's format, you must set the Format property of the control.

Caption: The Caption property specifies the text displayed for labels and command buttons. A caption is a string containing up to 2048 characters.

Hyperlink Address: The Hyperlink Address property is a string representing the path to a UNC (network path) or URL (Web page). Command buttons, image controls, and labels all contain the Hyperlink Address property.

Hyperlink SubAddress: The Hyperlink SubAddress property is a string representing a location within the document specified in the Hyperlink Address property. Command buttons, image controls, and labels all contain the Hyperlink SubAddress property.

Decimal Places: The Decimal Places property defines the number of decimal places displayed for numeric values

Visible: The Visible property determines whether a control is visible. In many cases, you want to toggle the visibility of a control in response to different situations.

Hide Duplicates: The Hide Duplicates property hides duplicate data values in a report's Detail section. Duplicate data values occur when one or more consecutive records in a report contain the same value in one or more fields.

Can Grow, Can Shrink: The Can Grow property, when set to Yes, allows a control to expand vertically to accommodate all the data in it. The Can Shrink property eliminates blank lines when no data exists in a field for a particular record. For example, if you have a second address line on a mailing label, but there's no data in the Address2 field, you don't want a blank line to appear on the mailing label.

Left, Top, Width, Height: These properties set the size and position of the controls on a report.

Back Style, Back Color: The Back Style property can be set to Normal or Transparent. When set to Transparent, the color of the report shows through to the control. When set to Normal, the control's Back Color property determines the object's color.

Special Effect: The Special Effect property adds 3-D effects to a control.

Border Style, Border Color, Border Width: These properties set the physical attributes of a control's border.

Font Color, Font Name, Font Size, Font Weight, Font Italic, Font Underline: The border properties affect the control's border, but the font properties affect the appearance of the text within the control.

Text Align: The Text Align property sets the alignment of the text within the control. It can be set to Left, Center, Right, or General. When set to General, text aligns to the left, and numbers and dates align to the right.

The Control's Data Properties

The Data properties of a control specify information about the data underlying a particular report control.

Control Source: The Control Source property specifies the field in the report's record source that's used to populate the control. A control source can also be a valid expression.

Running Sum: The Running Sum property is quite powerful. It can be used to calculate a record-by-record or group-by-group total. It can be set to No, Over Group, or Over All. When set to Over Group, the value of the text box accumulates from record to record within the group but is reset each time the group value changes. An example is a report that shows deposit amounts for each state with a running sum for the amount deposited within the state. Each time the state changes, the amount deposited is set to zero. When set to Over All, the sum continues to accumulate over the entire report.

The Other Control Properties

The Other properties of a control designate properties that don't fit into any other category.

Name: The Name property gives you an easy and self-documenting way to refer to the control in VBA code and in many other situations. You should name all your controls. Naming conventions for report controls are the same as those for form controls. Refer to Appendix B, "Naming Conventions," for more detailed information.

Tag: Like the Tag property of a report, the Tag property of a control gives you a user-defined slot for the control. You can place any extra information in the Tag property.

> **WARNING**
>
> A common mistake many developers make is giving controls names that conflict with Access names. This type of error is very difficult to track down. Make sure you use distinctive names for both fields and controls. Furthermore, don't give a control the same name as the name of a field within its expression. For example, the expression =ClientName & Title shouldn't have the name "ClientName"; that would cause an #error# message when the report is run. Finally, don't give a control the same name as its control source. Once again, this can cause problems. Following these simple warnings will spare you a lot of grief!

Inserting Page Breaks

Page breaks can be set to occur before, within, or at the end of a section. The way you set each type of page break is quite different. To set a page break within a section, you must use the Page Break tool in the toolbox. Click the Page Break tool in the toolbox, then click the report where you want the page break to occur. To set a page break before or after a section, set the Force New Page property of the section to Yes. The Force New Page property applies to Group Headers, Group Footers, and the report's Detail section.

> **WARNING**
>
> Be careful not to place a page break within a control on the report. The page break will occur in the middle of the control's data.

Unbound, Bound, and Calculated Controls

Three types of controls can be placed on a report: Bound, Unbound, and Calculated. Unbound controls, such as logos placed on reports, aren't tied to data. Bound controls are tied to data within a field of the table or query underlying the report. Calculated controls contain valid expressions; they can hold anything from a page number to a sophisticated financial calculation. Most complex reports have a rich combination of Bound, Unbound, and Calculated controls.

Using Expressions to Enhance Your Reports

Calculated controls are made up of expressions, which are the control sources for Calculated controls. To create a Calculated control, you must first add an Unbound control to the report. Expressions must be preceded by an equal sign (=); an example of a report expression is =Sum([BillableHours]). This expression, if placed in the Report Footer, totals the contents of the BillableHours control for all detail records in the report. You can build an expression by typing it directly into the control source or by using the Expression Builder, covered in Chapter 6.

Building Reports Based on More Than One Table

The majority of reports you create will probably be based on more than one table. This is because a properly normalized database usually requires that you bring table data back together to give your users valuable information. For example, a report that combines data from a Customers table, an Orders table, and an Order Details table can supply the following information:

- Customer information: company name and address
- Order information: order date and shipping method
- Order detail information: quantity ordered, price
- Product table: product description

A multitable report can be based directly on the tables whose data it displays, or it can be based on a query that has already joined the tables, providing a flat table structure.

Creating One-to-Many Reports

You can create One-to-Many reports by using a Report Wizard, or you can build the report from scratch. Different situations require different techniques, some of which are covered in the following sections.

Building a One-to-Many Report with the Report Wizard

Building a One-to-Many report with the Report Wizard is quite easy; just follow these steps:

1. Click the Reports tab and click New.
2. Select Report Wizard from the New Report dialog box and click OK.
3. Use the Tables/Queries drop-down list to select the first table or query whose data will appear on the report.
4. Select the fields you want to include from that table.
5. Select each additional table or query you want to include on the report, selecting the fields you need from each.
6. Click Next after selecting all the fields you want to include from all the tables and queries. Step 2 of the Report Wizard offers a suggested layout for your data. (See Figure 7.16.) You can accept Access's suggestion, or you can choose from any of the available layout options. Click Next.

Figure 7.16.
Step 2 of the Report Wizard: selecting a layout.

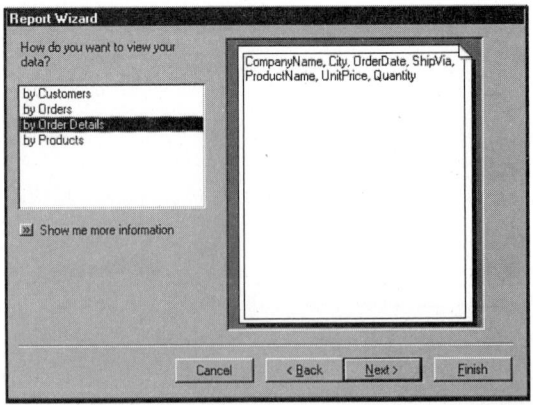

7. Step 3 of the Report Wizard asks whether you want to add any grouping levels. Grouping levels can be used to visually separate data and to provide subtotals. In the example in Figure 7.17, the report is grouped by city. After you select grouping levels, click Next.

Figure 7.17.

Step 3 of the Report Wizard: selecting groupings.

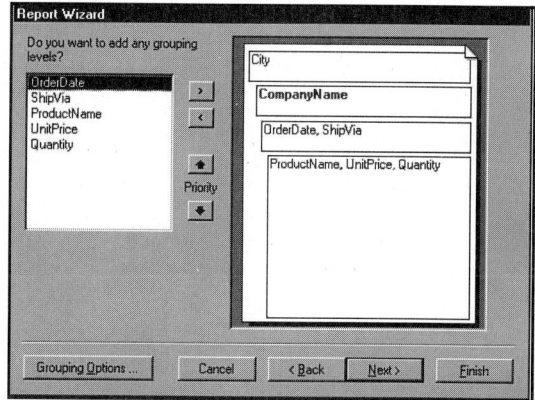

8. Step 4 of the Report Wizard lets you select how you want the records in the report's Detail section to be sorted. (See Figure 7.18.) This step of the wizard also allows you to specify any summary calculations you want to perform on the data. (See Figure 7.19.) You can even opt to include the percent of total calculations.

Figure 7.18.

Step 4 of the Report Wizard: selecting a sort order.

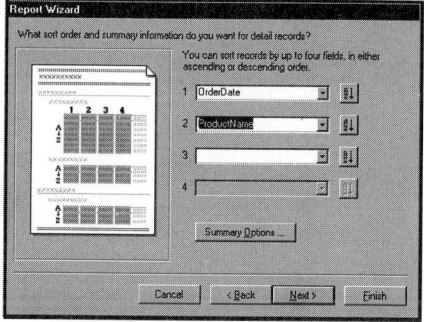

9. In Step 5 of the Report Wizard, you select the layout and orientation of your report. Layout options include Stepped, Blocked, Outline 1, Outline 2, Align Left 1, and Align Left 2.

10. Step 6 of the Report Wizard lets you select from predefined styles for your report. The styles include Bold, Casual, Compact, Corporate, Formal, and Soft Gray. You can preview each style to see what it looks like.

Figure 7.19.
Adding summary calculations.

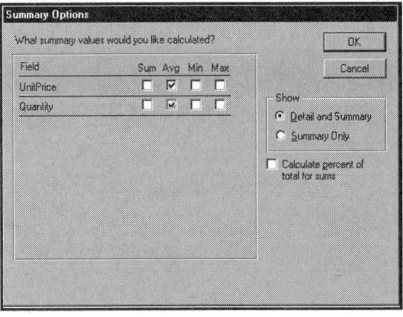

11. In Step 7 of the Report Wizard, you select a title for your report. The title also becomes the name for the report. I select an appropriate name and change the title after the wizard is finished. The final step also allows you to determine whether you want to immediately preview the report or to see the report's design first.

The report created in the previous example is shown in Figure 7.20. Notice that the report is sorted and grouped by City and CompanyName. The report's data is in order by OrderDate within a CompanyName grouping.

Figure 7.20.
A completed One-to-Many report.

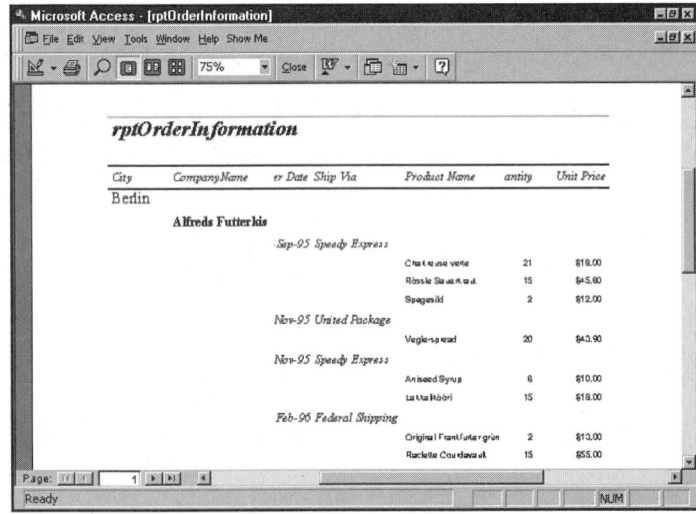

This method of creating a One-to-Many report is by far the easiest. In fact, the "background join" technology that the wizards use when they allow you to pick fields from multiple tables, figuring out how to build the complex queries needed for the report or form, was one of the major enhancements in Access for Windows 95. It's a huge timesaver and helps hide unnecessary complexity from you as you build a report. Although you should take advantage of this feature, it's important that, as a developer, you know what's happening under the covers. The following two sections give you this necessary knowledge.

Building a Report Based on a One-To-Many Query

Another popular method of building a One-to-Many report is from a one-to-many query. A One-to-Many report built in this way is constructed as though it were based on the data within a single table. First, you build the query that will underlie the report. (See Figure 7.21.)

Figure 7.21.
An example of a query underlying a One-to-Many report.

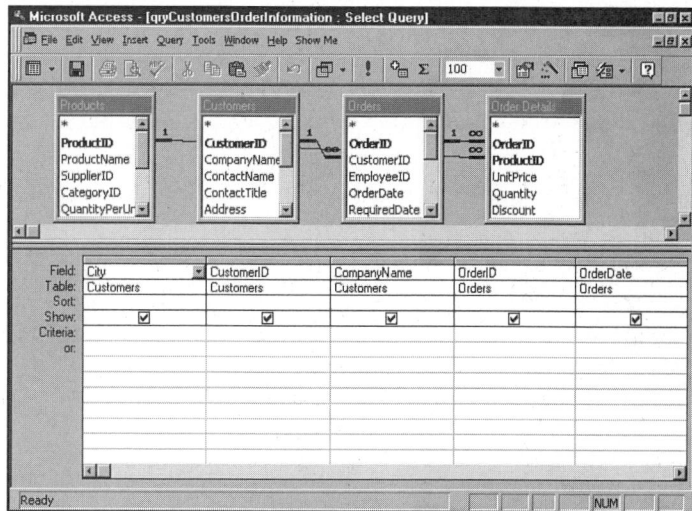

Once you have finished the query, you can select it rather than select each individual table (as was done in the previous section). After the query is selected, creating the report is the same process as the one used for the previous report.

Building a One-to-Many Report with the Subreport Wizard

A One-to-Many report can also be created by building the parent report and then adding a Subform/Subreport control. This is often the method used to create reports such as invoices that show the report's data in a one-to-many relationship rather than in a denormalized format (as shown in Figure 7.20). If you want to use the Subform/Subreport Wizard, you must make sure that the Control Wizards tool is selected before you add the Subform/Subreport control to the main report. Here is the process:

1. Click to select the Subform/Subreport control.

2. Click and drag to place the Subform/Subreport control on the main report. The Subform/Subreport control is usually placed in the report's Detail section. Once you have placed the Subform/Subreport control on the report, the Subform/Subreport Wizard is invoked.

3. Indicate whether you want the Subreport to be based on an existing report or you want to build a new subreport based on a query or table. Click Next.

4. If you select Table or Query, you have to select the table or query on which the subreport will be based. You can then select the fields you want to include on the subreport. You can even select fields from more than one table or query. When you're done, click Next.

5. The next step of the Subform/Subreport Wizard suggests a relationship between the main report and the subreport. (See Figure 7.22.) You can accept the selected relationship, or you can define your own. When you're done, click Next.

6. The final step of the Subform/Subreport Wizard asks you to name the subreport. To follow standards, the name should begin with the prefix *rsub*. Click Finish when you're done.

Figure 7.22.

The Subform/Subreport Wizard: identifying the relationship.

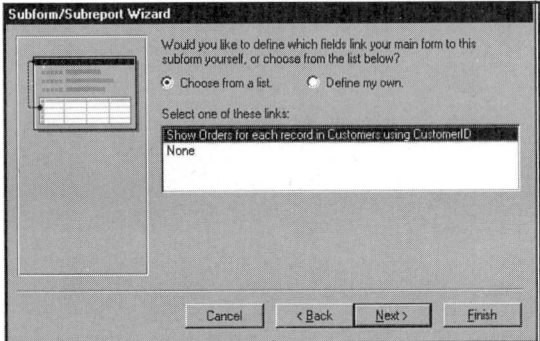

As you can see in Figure 7.23, the one-to-many relationship between two tables is clearly highlighted by this type of report. In the example, each customer is listed. All the detail records reflecting the orders for each customer are listed immediately following each customer's data.

Figure 7.23.

A completed One-to-Many report created with the Subform/Subreport Wizard.

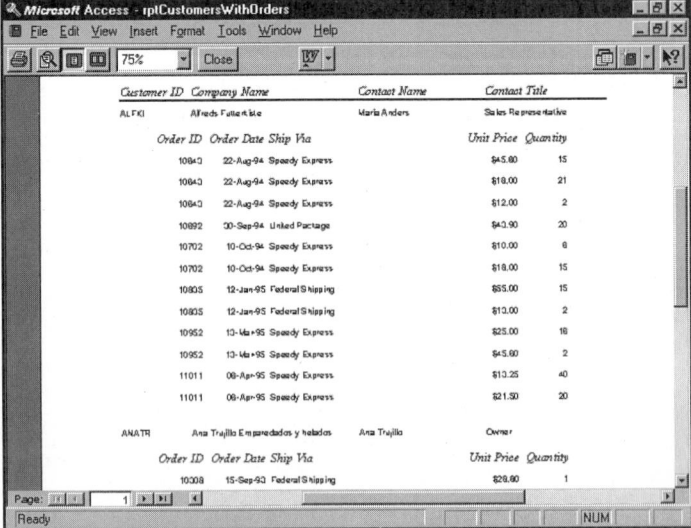

Working with Subreports

Once a subreport has been added to a report, it's important to understand what properties have been set by the Subform/Subreport Wizard so that you can modify the Subreport control, if needed. You should become familiar with a few properties of a subreport:

Source Object: The name of the report that's being displayed within the control.

Link Child Fields: The field(s) from the Child report that links the Child report to the Master report.

Link Master Fields: The field(s) from the Master report that links the Master report to the Child report.

Can Grow: Determines whether the control can expand vertically to accommodate data in the subreport.

Can Shrink: Determines whether the control can shrink to eliminate blank lines when no data is found in the subreport.

Not only should you know how to work with the properties of a Subreport object, but you should also be able to easily modify the subreport from within the main report. You can always modify the subreport from the Reports tab of the Database window. To do this, click on the report you want to modify, then click Design. Here's a much easier way to modify a subreport from within the main report:

1. Make sure the Subreport control isn't already selected.
2. Double-click on the Subreport control; this loads the subreport.
3. Make the changes you want to the subreport.
4. Close and save the subreport. All the changes made to the subreport will be reflected when you run the main report.

Working with Sorting and Grouping

As opposed to sorting within forms, sorting the data within a report isn't determined by the underlying query. In fact, the underlying query affects the report's sort order only when no sort order has been specified for the report. Any sort order specified in the query is completely overwritten by the report's sort order, which is determined by the report's Sorting and Grouping window. (See Figure 7.24.) The sorting and grouping of the report is affected by what options you select when you run a Report Wizard. The Sorting and Grouping window can then be used to add, remove, or modify sorting and grouping options for the report. Sorting simply affects the order of the records on the report. Grouping adds Group Headers and Footers to the report.

Figure 7.24.

The Sorting and Grouping window, showing grouping by city and company name and sorting by order date and product name.

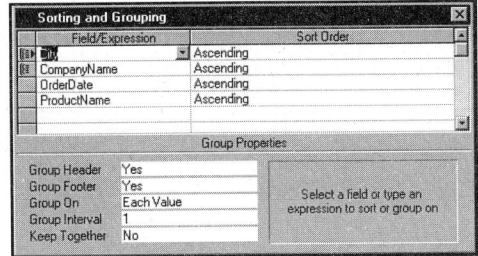

Adding Sorting and Grouping

Often, you want to add sorting or grouping to a report. To do so, follow these four steps:

1. Click Sorting and Grouping on the Report Design toolbar to open the Sorting and Grouping window.

2. Click on the selector of the line above where you want to insert the sorting or grouping. In Figure 7.25, a sorting or grouping level is being added above the City grouping. Press the Insert key to insert a blank line in the Sorting and Grouping window.

Figure 7.25.

Inserting a sorting or grouping level.

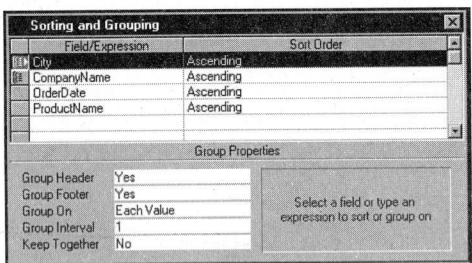

3. Click in Field/Expression and use the drop-down list to select the field on which you want to sort or group.

4. Set the properties to determine the nature of the sorting or grouping (see the next section).

> **NOTE**
>
> To remove a sorting or grouping that has been added, click to select the field in the Sorting and Grouping window, then press the Delete key. You will be warned that any controls in the Group Header or Footer will be lost.

Sorting and Grouping Properties

Each grouping in a report has properties that define the group's attributes. Each group has five properties that determine whether the field is used as a sorting, a grouping, or both. (See Figure 7.26.) They are also used to specify details about the grouping options. Here are the Sorting and Grouping properties:

Figure 7.26.

The Sorting and Grouping window, showing the five Sorting and Grouping properties.

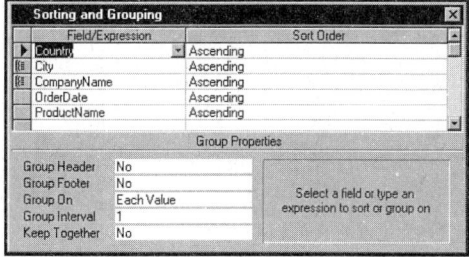

Group Header: The Group Header property specifies whether the selected group contains a header band. When you set the Group Header property to Yes, an additional band appears in the report that can be used to display information about the group. For example, if you're grouping by country, the Group Header is used to display the name of the country you're about to print. If the Group Header and Group Footer properties are both set to No, the field is used only to determine the sort order of the records in the report.

Group Footer: The Group Footer property specifies whether the selected group contains a footer band. When you set the Group Footer property to Yes, an additional band appears in the report. The Group Footer band can be used to display summary information about the group; it's often used to display subtotals for the group.

Group On: The Group On property specifies what constitutes a new group. It's often used for situations such as departmental roll-ups. Rather than grouping on the entire department number, you might want to group on the first three digits, for example.

The Group On choices for text fields are Each Value and Prefix Characters. For Date fields, the choices are much more complex. They include Each Value Year, Qtr, Month, Week, Day, Hour, and Minute. This means you could group by a Date field and have Access subtotal and begin a new group each time the week changes in the field. For AutoNumber, Currency, and Number fields, the choices are Each Value and Interval.

Group Interval: The Group Interval property is used with the Group On property to specify an interval value that data is grouped by. If, for example, the Group On property for a text field is set to Prefix Characters and the Group Interval is set to 3, the field's data is grouped on the first three characters.

Keep Together: The Keep Together property determines whether Access tries to keep an entire group together on one page. The three choices for the property are `No`, `Whole Group`, and `With First Detail`. The `Whole Group` option means that Access tries to keep the entire group together on one page. This includes the Group Header, Group Footer, and Detail sections. The `With First Detail` option means that Access prints the group header on a page only if it can also print the first detail record on the same page.

> **NOTE**
>
> If you have set Keep Together to `Whole Group` and the group is too large to fit on a page, Access ignores the property setting. Furthermore, if you set Keep Together to `With First Detail` and either the group header or detail record is too large to fit on one page, that setting is ignored, too.

What Are Group Header and Footer Properties and Why Use Them

Each Group Header and Footer has its own properties that determine the behavior of the Group Header or Footer:

Force New Page: The Force New Page property can be set to `None`, `Before Section`, `After Section`, or `Before and After`. When set to `None`, no page break occurs either before or after the report section. If set to `Before Section`, a page break occurs before the report section prints; if set to `After Section`, a page break occurs after the report section prints. When set to `Before and After`, a page break occurs before the report section prints as well as after it prints.

New Row or Col: The New Row or Col property determines whether a column break occurs whenever the report section prints. This property applies only to multicolumn reports. The choices are `None`, `Before Section`, `After Section`, and `Before and After`. Like the Force New Page property, this property determines whether the column break occurs before the report section prints, after it prints, or before and after, or whether it's affected by the report section break at all.

Keep Together: The Keep Together property specifies whether you want Access to try to keep an entire report section together on one page. If this property is set to `Yes`, Access starts printing the section at the top of the next page if it can't print the entire section on the current page. When set to `No`, Access prints as much of the section as possible on the current page, inserting each page break as necessary. If a section exceeds the page length, Access starts printing the section on a new page and continues printing it on the following page.

Visible: The Visible property indicates whether the section is visible. It's common to hide the visibility of a particular report section at runtime in response to different situations. This can easily be done by changing the value of the report section's Visible property with VBA code.

Can Grow, Can Shrink: The Can Grow property determines whether the section stretches vertically to accommodate the data in it. The Can Shrink property specifies whether you want the section to shrink vertically, eliminating blank lines.

Repeat Section: The Repeat Section property is a valuable property; it lets you specify whether the group header is repeated on subsequent pages if a report section needs more than one page to print.

Improving Performance and Reusability by Basing Reports on Stored Queries

It's usually best to base your Access reports on stored queries. This option offers you several benefits:

- Reports based on stored queries open more quickly.
- The query underlying the report can be used by other forms and reports.
- Sophisticated calculations need to be built only once—they don't need to be re-created for each report (or form).

Reports based on stored queries open more quickly than reports based on embedded SQL statements because when you build and save a query, it compiles and creates a Query Plan. This Query Plan is a plan of execution that's based on the amount of data in the query's tables as well as all the indexes available in each table. If you run a report based on an embedded SQL statement, the query is compiled and the Query Plan is built at runtime, slowing the query's execution.

> **NOTE**
>
> The one situation where basing a report on an embedded query might be preferable is when the volume of data, or the available indexes, might vary each time the report is run. In this specific case, you could get a more optimized query if the query is compiled—and the Query Plan is built—at runtime.

Often, you want to build several reports and forms all based on the same information. An embedded SQL statement can't be shared by multiple database objects. At the very least, you must copy the embedded SQL statement for each form and report you build. Basing reports and forms on stored queries eliminates this problem. You build the query once and modify it once if changes need to be made to it. Many forms and reports can all use the same query (including its criteria, expressions, and so on).

Reports often contain complex expressions. If a particular expression is used in only one report, nothing is lost by building the expression into the embedded SQL statement. On the other hand, many complex expressions are used in multiple reports and forms. By building these expressions into queries on which the reports and forms are based, you have to create the expression only one time.

> **TIP**
>
> It's easy to save an embedded SQL statement as a query. This allows you to use the Report Wizard to build a report using several tables; you can then save the resulting SQL statement as a query. With the report open in Design view, bring up the Properties window. Click the Data tab, then click in the RecordSource property and click the ellipsis. The embedded SQL statement appears as a query. Select File Save As/Export, enter a name for the query, and click OK. Close the Query window, indicating that you want to update the RecordSource property. Your query is now based on a stored query instead of an embedded SQL statement.

Access Reports and the Internet

Microsoft has made it easier to develop Internet-aware applications by adding hyperlinks to reports and by allowing you to save an Access report as an HTML document. These features are covered in the following sections.

Adding a Hyperlink to a Report

Hyperlinks can be added to reports in the form of labels. Once added, they serve as a direct link to a UNC or URL. To add a hyperlink to a report, follow these steps:

1. With the report open in Design view, add a label to the report.
2. Set the Hyperlink Address property to the UNC or URL you want to link to. The easiest way to do this is to click in the Hyperlink Address property, then click the ellipsis to open the Insert Hyperlink dialog box.
3. Enter the UNC or URL in the "Link to file or URL" combo box. You can use the Browse button to locate the UNC or URL.
4. If you want to enter a Hyperlink SubAddress, enter it in the "Named location in file" combo box. The Hyperlink SubAddress can be a range name, bookmark, slide number, or any other recognized location in the document specified in the "Link to file or URL" combo box.
5. Click OK. The Hyperlink Address and Hyperlink SubAddress properties are filled in with the information supplied in the Insert Hyperlink dialog box.

The Hyperlink Address and Hyperlink SubAddress properties come into play only when a report is saved as HTML and viewed in a Web browser, such as Internet Explorer 3.0. Saving a report as an HTML document is covered in the following section.

Saving a Report as HTML

Access gives you two methods for saving a report as an HTML document. The first method is to choose File | Save to HTML/Web Formats | Save to HTML while viewing the report's design or previewing the report. Access generates an HTML file, which is given the name of the report, followed by the .HTM extension. The file is placed in the folder specified as the Default Database Folder on the General tab of the Options dialog box. The system's default browser is loaded, and the file is displayed in the browser. Most Web browsers allow you to view the source HTML code associated with the file. There is a separate HTML file created for each page of the report.

The second method is to choose File | Save As/Export, then select To an External File or Database and click OK. Use the "Save as type" drop-down list to select HTML Documents (*.htm, *.html). Pick a location and name for the file, then click Export. The document is saved as HTML and assigned the name and location you specified. The default Web browser isn't automatically loaded when the report is saved as HTML in this way.

> **NOTE**
>
> Once a file is saved as HTML, you probably want to publish it on the Web. This can be done by using the Publish to the Web Wizard, covered in Chapter 27, "Access and the Internet."

Practical Examples: Building Reports Needed for Your Application

The Time and Billing application requires several reports that you'll design throughout the book. A couple of the simpler ones are built here.

Designing the rptClientListing Report

The rptClientListing report lists all the clients in the tblClients table. The report includes the company name, contact name, city, state, ZIP code, and office phone of each customer and is sorted by company name.

The rptClientListing report is based on a query called qryClientListing, which is shown in Figure 7.27. The query includes the CompanyName, City, State, OfficePhone, and Fax fields. It also includes an expression called ContactName that concatenates the ContactFirstName and ContactLastName fields. The expression looks like this:

```
ContactName: [ContactFirstName] & " " & [ContactLastName]
```

Figure 7.27.
The qryClientListing query—a foundation for the rptClientListing report.

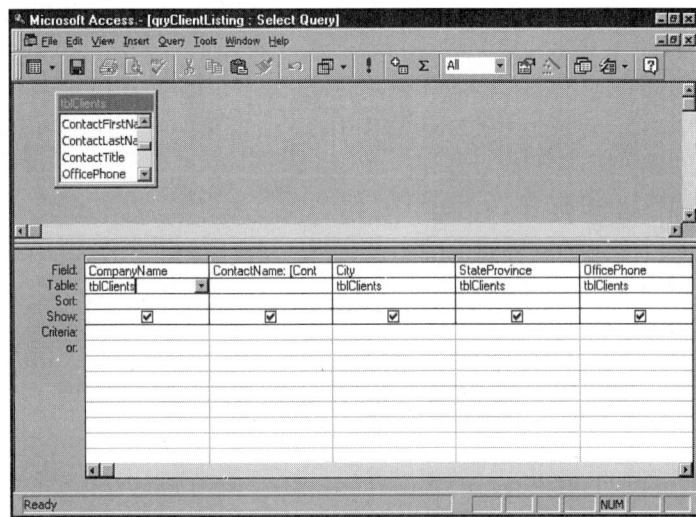

To build the report, follow these nine steps:

1. Select the Reports tab and click New.

2. Select Report Wizard and use the drop-down list to select the qryClientListing query. (See Figure 7.28.) Click OK.

Figure 7.28.
Selecting the qryClientListing query.

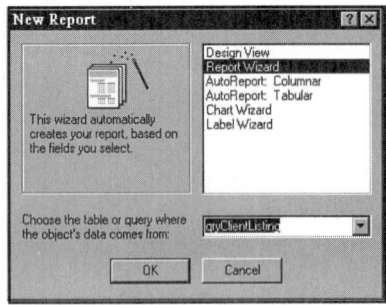

3. Click the >> button to select all the fields in the query you want to include in the report. Click Next.

4. Do not add any grouping to the report. Click Next.

5. Use the drop-down list to select CompanyName as the sort field. (See Figure 7.29.) Click Next.

Figure 7.29.
Selecting CompanyName as the sort order.

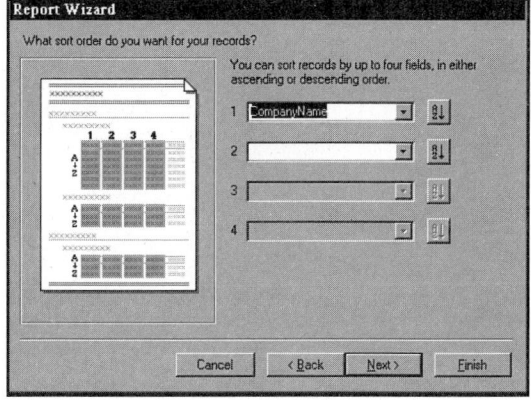

6. Select Landscape for the orientation and click Next.

7. Select a style for the report and click Next.

8. Give the report the title rptClientListing, then click Finish.

9. The completed report should look like Figure 7.30. Close the report and reopen it in Design view. Notice that both the name and title of the report are rptClientListing. Modify the title of the report so that it reads Client Listing By Company Name. (See Figure 7.31.)

Figure 7.30.
A preview of the completed report.

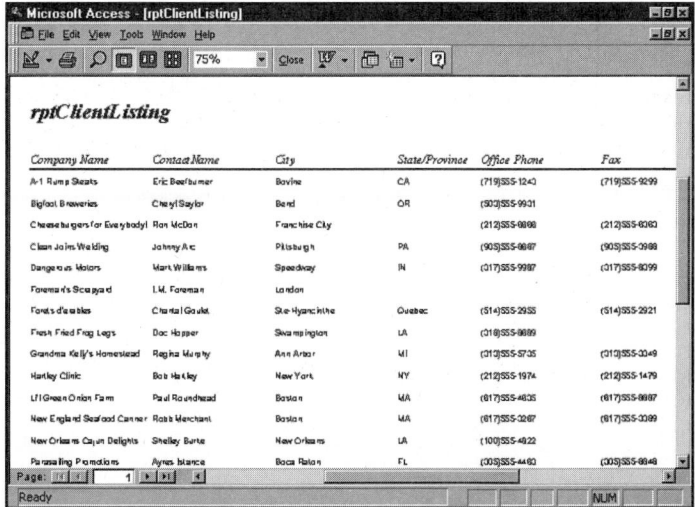

Figure 7.31.

Changing the report caption.

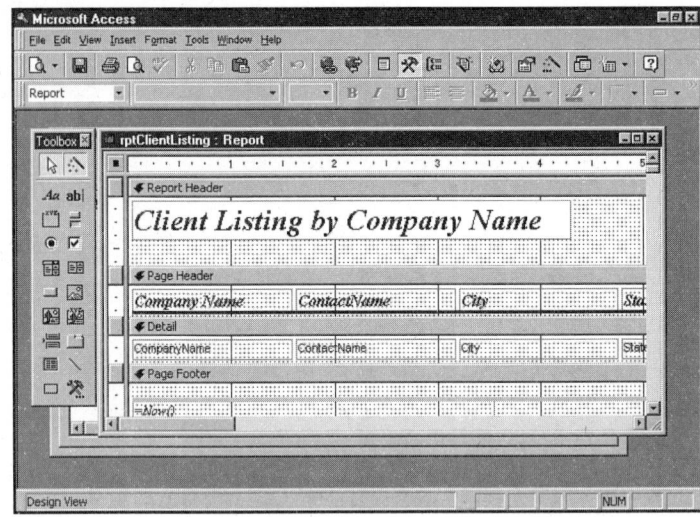

Designing the rptTimeSheet Report

The rptTimeSheet report is much more complex than the rptClientListing report. It includes two subreports: rsubTimeSheet and rsubTimeSheetExpenses.

The rptTimeSheet report is shown in Figure 7.32. It's based on a query called qryTimeSheet. (See Figure 7.33.) It contains fields from both tblClients and tblEmployees.

Figure 7.32.

The rptTimeSheet report in Design view.

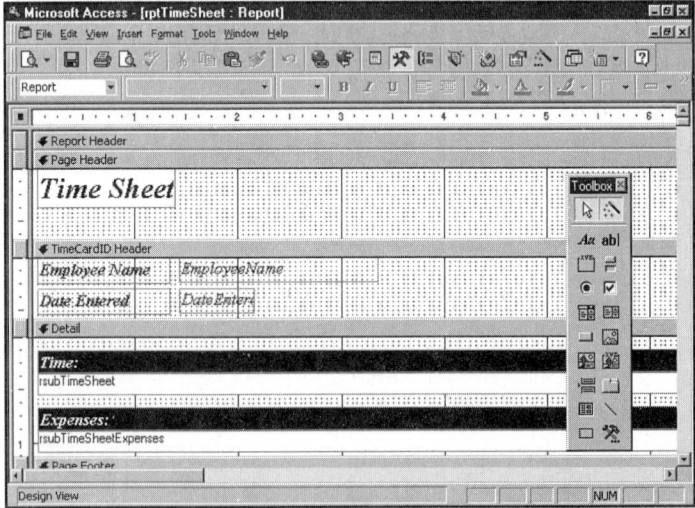

Figure 7.33.
The qryTimeSheet query in Design view.

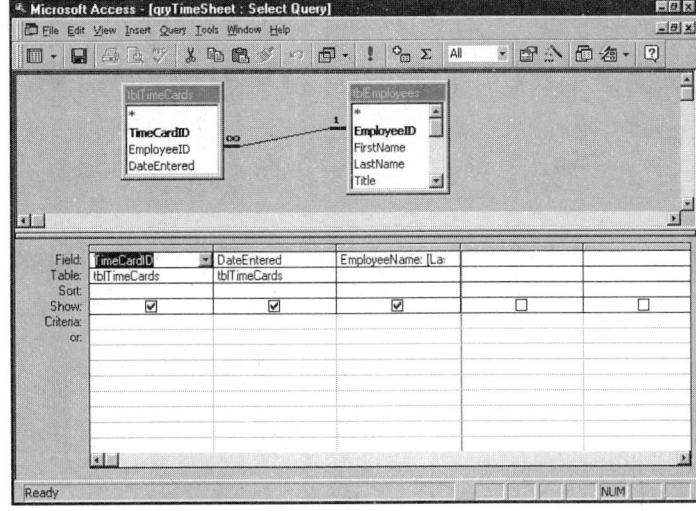

The rptTimeSheet report has a Page Header that includes the title of the report, but nothing else is found within the Page Header. The TimeCardID header contains the EmployeeName and DateEntered from the qryTimeSheet query. The report's Detail section contains the two subreports rsubTimeSheet and rsubTimeSheetExpenses. The Page Footer holds two expressions, one for the date and another for the page number. They look like this:

```
=Now()
="Page " & [Page] & " of " & [Pages]
```

The rsubTimeSheet report is based on qrySubTimeSheet; this query contains the following fields from the tblProjects and tblTimeCardHours tables:

> tblProjects: ProjectName
>
> tblTimeCardsHours: TimeCardID, TimeCardDetailID, DateWorked, WorkDescription, BillableHours, BillingRate, and the expression `HourlyBillings:` `[tblTimeCardHours].[BillingRate]*[BillableHours]`

The design of rsubTimeSheet is shown in Figure 7.34. This subreport can easily be built from a wizard. Select all fields except TimeCardID and TimeCardDetailID from qrySubTimeSheets. View the data by tblTimeCardHours. Don't add any groupings, and don't sort the report. When you're done with the wizard, modify the design of the report. Remove the caption from the Report Header, and move everything from the Page Header to the Report Header. Collapse the Page Header, remove everything from the Page Footer, and add a Report Footer with the expression `=Sum([HourlyBillings])`.

Figure 7.34.

The rsubTimeSheet report in Design view.

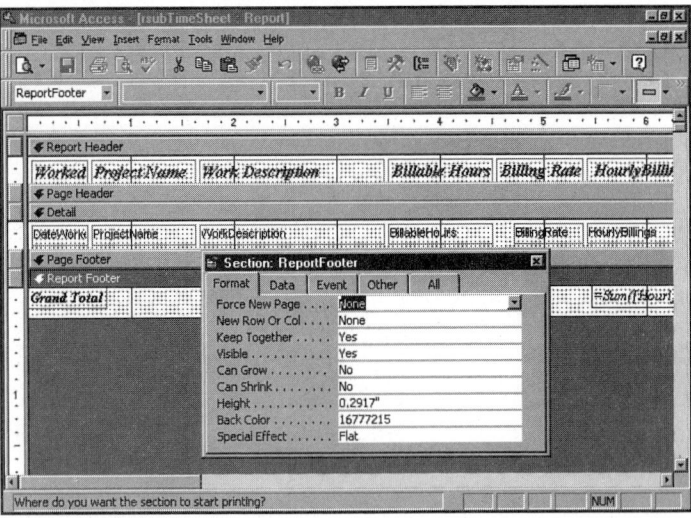

Change the format of the HourlyBillings and the TotalHourlyBillings controls to Currency. Use the Sorting and Grouping window to sort by TimeCardID and TimeCardDetailID.

The rsubTimeSheetExpenses report is based on qrySubTimeSheetExpense, which contains the following fields from the tblProjects, tblExpenseCodes, and tblTimeCardExpenses tables:

> tblProjects: ProjectName
>
> tblTimeCardExpenses: TimeCardExpenseID, ExpenseDate, ExpenseDescription, and ExpenseAmount
>
> tblExpenseCodes: ExpenseCode

The design of rsubTimeSheetExpenses is shown in Figure 7.35. This subreport can easily be built from a wizard. Select all fields except TimeCardID and TimeCardExpenseID from qrySubTimeSheetExpense. View the data by tblTimeCardExpenses. Don't add any groupings, and don't sort the report. When you're done with the wizard, modify the design of the report. Remove the caption from the Report Header, and move everything from the Page Header to the Report Header. Collapse the Page Header, remove everything from the Page Footer, and add a Report Footer with the expression =Sum([ExpenseAmount]).

Change the format of the ExpenseAmount and the TotalExpenseAmount controls to Currency, and use the Sorting and Grouping window to sort by TimeCardID and TimeCardExpenseID.

Figure 7.35.

The rsubTimeSheetExpenses report in Design view.

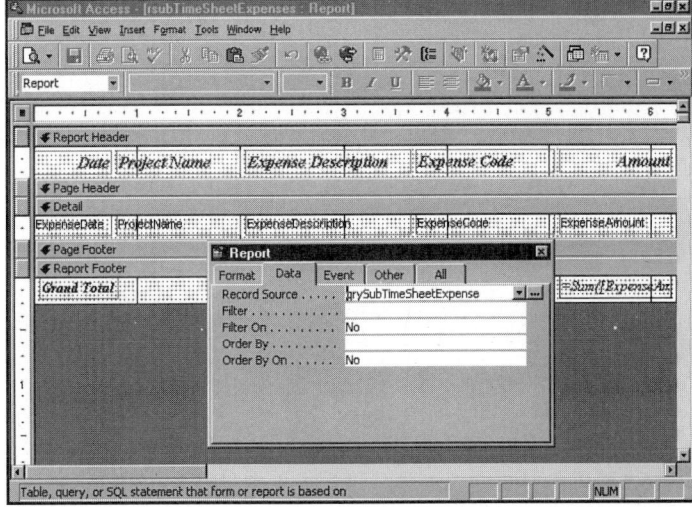

Summary

Reports give you valuable information about the data stored in your database. Many types of reports can be built in Access 97, including Detail reports, Summary reports, reports that look like printed forms, and reports containing graphs and other objects. Access offers many properties for customizing the look and behavior of each report to fit your users' needs. Understanding how to work with each property is integral to the success of your application-development projects.

8

VBA 101: The Basics of VBA

- VBA Explained, 208
- Access Class Modules, Standard Modules, Form Modules, and Report Modules Explained, 210
- Working with Variables, 218
- Adding Comments to Your Code, 222
- Using the Line-Continuation Character, 222
- Using the VBA Control Structures, 223
- Passing Parameters and Returning Values: An Introduction, 230
- Working with Built-In Functions, 231
- Tools for Working with the Module Window, 235
- Practical Examples: Event Routines, User-Defined Functions, and Subroutines Needed for the Time and Billing Application, 239

VBA Explained

Visual Basic for Applications (VBA) is the development language for Microsoft Access 97. It offers a consistent language for application development in the Microsoft Office suite. The core language, its constructs, and the environment are the same in Microsoft Access 97, Microsoft Visual Basic, Microsoft Excel, Microsoft Word, and Microsoft Project. What's different among these environments are the built-in objects specific to each application. For example, Access has a Recordset object, but Excel has a Workbook object. Each application's objects have appropriate properties (attributes) and methods (actions) associated with them. This chapter gives you an overview of the VBA language and its constructs.

Simple Access applications can be written by using macros, covered in Chapter 11, "What Are Macros and When Do You Need Them?" Although macros are great for quick prototyping and very basic application development, most serious Access development is done by using the VBA language. Unlike macros, VBA gives you the ability to do the following:

- Work with complex logic structures (case statements, loops, and so on).
- Use constants and variables.
- Take advantage of functions and actions not available in macros.
- Loop through and perform actions on recordsets.
- Perform transaction processing.
- Programmatically create and work with database objects.
- Implement error handling.
- Create libraries of user-defined functions.
- Call Windows API functions.
- Perform complex DDE and OLE automation commands.

The VBA language allows you to use complex logic structures. Macros allow you to perform only simple If...Then...Else logic, but the VBA language offers a wealth of logic and looping constructs, which are covered later in this chapter. The VBA language also lets you declare and work with variables and constants. These variables can be scoped appropriately and passed as parameters to subroutines and functions. As you will see later in this chapter, variables and constants are an integral part of any Access application. These features, however, aren't available in macros.

Many important features of the VBA language aren't available through macro actions. If you try to develop an application using only macros, you can't take advantage of many of the rich features available in the VBA language. In addition, many of the actions available in both macros and modules can be done much more efficiently with VBA code.

Complex Access applications often require you to loop through a recordset, performing some action on each member of the set. There's no way to do this by using Access macros. However, with the VBA language and Data Access Objects, you can add, delete, update, and manipulate data. Data Access Objects are covered in Chapter 15, "What Are Data Access Objects and Why Are They Important?"

When manipulating sets of records, you want to ensure that all processing finishes successfully before your data is permanently updated. Macros don't allow you to protect your data with transaction processing. Using the `BeginTrans`, `CommitTrans`, and `Rollback` methods, you can make sure your data is updated only if all parts of a transaction finish successfully. Transaction processing, if done properly, can substantially improve your application's performance because no data is written to disk until the process is finished. Transaction processing and its benefits are covered in Chapter 22, "Transaction Processing."

With Access macros, you can't create or modify database objects at runtime. Using VBA, you can create databases, tables, queries, and other database objects; you can also modify existing objects. There are many practical applications of this ability to create or modify database objects (discussed in more detail in Chapter 15). When users are allowed to build queries on the fly, for example, you might want to give them the ability to design a query by using a front-end form you provide and store the query so they can run it again later.

Access macros don't allow you to implement error handling. If an error occurs while an Access macro is executing in Access's runtime version, the user is exited out of the application (and, therefore, the Access runtime). By using error-handling techniques, you can determine exactly what will happen when an error occurs during the execution of your application. Error handling is covered in more depth in Chapter 17, "Handling Those Dreaded Runtime Errors."

VBA also makes it easier for the developer to write code libraries of reusable functions and to design and debug complex processes. If you're developing even moderately complex applications, you want to be able to create generic function libraries that can be used with all your Access applications. It's extremely difficult, if not impossible, to do this using macros.

Many powerful functions not available with the VBA language are available as part of Windows itself. The Windows API (Application Programming Interface) refers to the nearly 1,000 Windows functions Microsoft has for use by Access programmers. You can't take advantage of these functions from an Access macro; however, by using VBA code, you can declare and call these functions, improving both the performance and functionality of your applications.

DDE (Dynamic Data Exchange)and Automation allow you to communicate between your Access applications and other applications. Although DDE is an older technology than Automation, it's still used to communicate with many applications that don't support Automation. Automation is used to control Automation server applications, such as Excel and Project, and their objects. Automation is covered in Chapter 25, "Automation: Communicating with Other Applications."

Although macros can offer a quick fix to a simple problem, their limitations require using the VBA language for developing complex solutions. To make the transition from macros to modules easier, Microsoft has given you a feature that allows you to convert any macro to VBA code (discussed in Chapter 11).

Access Class Modules, Standard Modules, Form Modules, and Report Modules Explained

VBA code is written in units called subroutines and functions that are stored in modules. Microsoft Access modules are either Standard modules or Class modules. Standard modules are created by clicking the New button on the Modules tab of your Database window. Class modules can be standalone objects or can be associated with a form or report. To create a standalone Class module, you choose the Class Module command from the Insert menu. In addition, whenever you add code behind a form or report, Microsoft Access creates a Class module associated with that form or report that contains the code you create.

Modules specific to a form or report are generally called *Form and Report Class modules*, and their code is often referred to as Code Behind Forms (CBF). CBF is created and stored in that form or report and triggered from events occurring within it.

A *subroutine* (subprocedure) is a routine that responds to an event or performs some action. An Event procedure is a special type of subroutine that automatically executes in response to an event, such as a mouse click on a command button or the loading of a form. A *function* is a special type of routine because it can return a value; a subroutine can't return a value. Like a subroutine, a function can be triggered from an event.

Anatomy of a Module

Whether you're dealing with a Standard module or a Class module, all modules contain a General Declarations section. (See Figure 8.1.) As the name implies, this is where you can declare variables and constants that you want to be visible to all the functions and subroutines in the module. These variables are referred to as *module-level* or *Private variables*. You can also declare Public variables in the General Declarations section of a module. Public variables can be seen and modified by *any* function or procedure in *any* module in the database.

> **NOTE**
>
> Public variables in Access 97 replace Access 2.0's Global variables. Although Global variables are still supported in Access 97, subtle differences exist between Public and Global variables. These differences are discussed later in this chapter.

A module is also made up of user-defined subroutines and functions. Figure 8.2 shows a subroutine called SayHello. Notice that the Object drop-down list pictured in the figure says "General." This is because the subroutine called SayHello isn't associated with a particular object.

Figure 8.1.

The General Declarations section of a module is used to declare Private and Public variables.

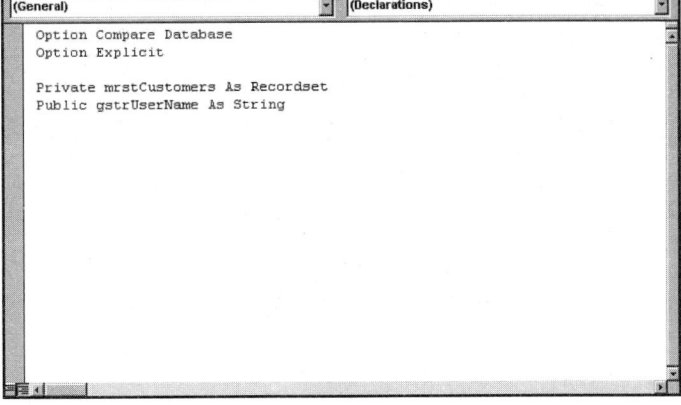

Figure 8.2.

An example of a user-defined subroutine called SayHello.

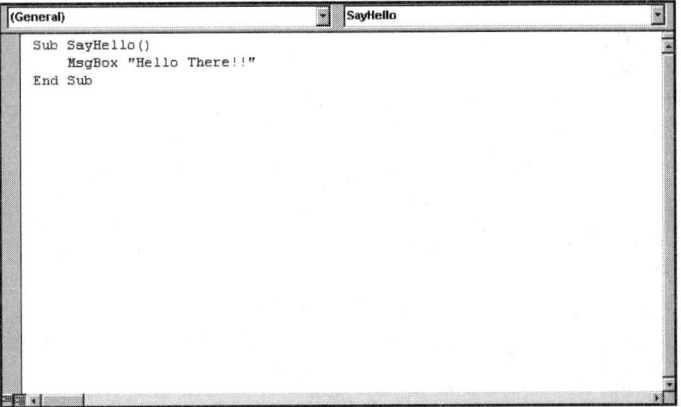

TIP

Access 97 has an environment option called Full Module view. This option, when checked, allows you to see several subroutines and functions in a module at one time. Notice the difference between Figure 8.2 and Figure 8.3. In the code window shown in Figure 8.2, only one subroutine is visible at a time. The code window shown in Figure 8.3 illustrates the effects of Full Module view—multiple subroutines are visible, each separated by a thin horizontal line. To use the Full Module view environmental setting, choose Tools | Options, click the Module tab, and check Full Module View or click the Full Module View button in the lower-left corner of a module window.

Figure 8.3.

In Full Module view, you can view several procedures simultaneously.

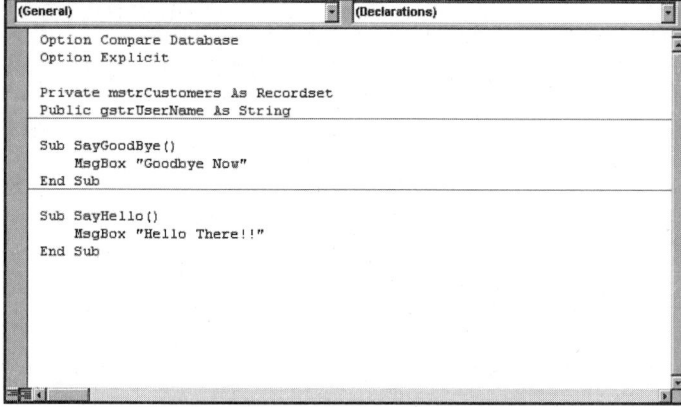

```
(General)                              (Declarations)

Option Compare Database
Option Explicit

Private mstrCustomers As Recordset
Public gstrUserName As String

Sub SayGoodBye()
    MsgBox "Goodbye Now"
End Sub

Sub SayHello()
    MsgBox "Hello There!!"
End Sub
```

Option Explicit

Option Explicit is a statement that can be included in the General Declarations section of a module, form, or report. When Option Explicit is placed in a General Declarations section, all variables in that module, form, or report must be declared before they're used.

> **TIP**
>
> In Access 2.0, you had to manually enter the Option Explicit statement into each module, form, and report. However, you can globally instruct Access 97 to insert the Option Explicit statement in all new modules, forms, and reports. To do this, choose Tools | Options. Under the Modules tab, click Require Variable Declaration. It's important that the Option Explicit statement be placed in all your modules, so make sure you set this option to True. It will save you hours of debugging and prevent your beeper from going off once your application has been distributed to your users.

In addition to a General Declarations section and user-defined procedures, forms and reports also contain event procedures that are associated with a particular object on a form. Notice in Figure 8.4 that the Object drop-down list says cmdHello. This is the name of the object whose event routines you are viewing. The drop-down list on the right shows all the events that can be coded for a command button; each of these events creates a separate event routine. You will have the opportunity to write many event routines as you read through this book.

Figure 8.4.

An Event routine for the Click *event of the cmdHello command button.*

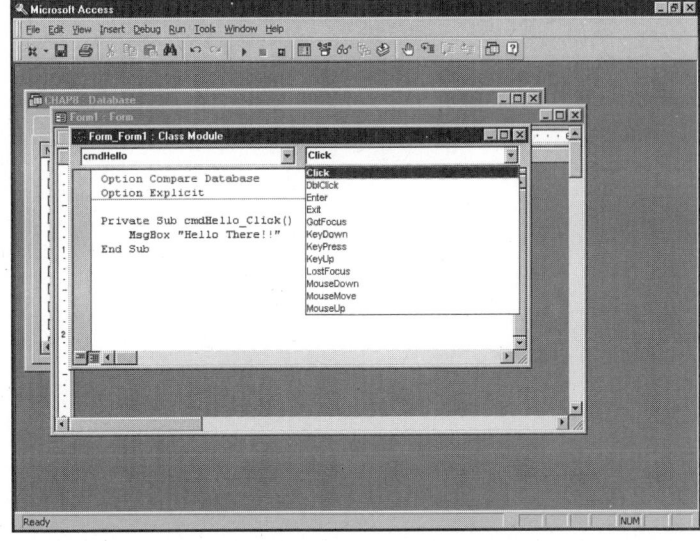

Event Procedures Made Easy

Event procedures are automatically created when you write event code for an object. For example, the routine Private Sub cmdHello_Click is created when you place code in the Click event of the cmdHello command button, shown in Figure 8.4.

To get to the event code of an object, follow these steps:

1. Click on the object in Design view and click the Properties button on the toolbar, or right-click on the object and choose Properties from the context-sensitive menu.

2. Click on the Event properties tab.

3. Select the property you want to write code for (for example, the On Click event).

4. Select [Event Procedure] from the drop-down list.

5. Click on the ellipsis button, which places you in the event code for that object.

Creating Functions and Subroutines

You can also create your own procedures that aren't tied to a particular object or event. Depending on how and where they're declared, they can be called from anywhere in your application or from a particular Code module, Form module, or Report module.

To create a user-defined routine in a Code module, follow these steps:

1. Click on the Modules tab of the Database window.

2. Start a new module or select an existing module and click Design.

3. Select Insert Procedure from the toolbar or choose Procedure from the Insert menu to open the dialog box shown in Figure 8.5.

213

Figure 8.5.

In the Insert Procedure dialog box, you specify the name, type, and scope of the procedure you're creating.

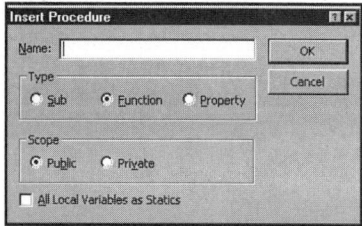

4. Type the name of the procedure, then indicate whether you're creating a function, subroutine, or property and whether you want the procedure to be public to your entire application or private to this module only. Finally, indicate whether you want all the variables in the routine to be static. (Static variables are discussed in this chapter under "Scope and Lifetime of Variables: Exposing Your Variables as Little as Possible.") Then click OK.

To create a user-defined routine in a Form or Report Class module, follow these steps:

1. While in Design view of a form or report, view the code behind the form or report by clicking the Code button on the toolbar or by choosing Code from the View menu.

2. Select Insert Procedure from the toolbar or choose Procedure from the Insert menu to open the Insert Procedure dialog box.

3. Type the name of the procedure, then indicate whether you're creating a function, subroutine, or property, whether you want the procedure to be public or private, and whether you want all the variables to be static. When you're done, click OK.

TIP

Whether you're creating a procedure in a Standard module or a Class module, you're now ready to enter the code for your procedure. A great shortcut for creating a procedure is to type **Sub *Whatever*** or **Function *Whatever*** directly in the code window; this creates a new subroutine or function as soon as you press Return.

Calling Event and User-Defined Procedures

Event procedures are automatically called when an event occurs for an object. For example, when a user clicks a command button, the `Click` event code for that command button executes.

The standard method for calling user-defined procedures is to use the `Call` keyword—`Call SayHello`, for example. You can also call the same procedure without using the `Call` keyword: `SayHello`.

Although not required, using the `Call` keyword makes the statement self-documenting and easier to read. A user-defined procedure can be called from an event routine or from another user-defined procedure or function.

Scope and Lifetime of Procedures

Procedures can be declared Public, Private, or Static, which determines their scope (where they can be called from) and their lifetime (how long they reside in memory). The placement of a procedure can noticeably affect your application's functionality and performance.

Public Procedures

A Public procedure can be called from anywhere in the application. Procedures declared in a module are automatically Public. This means that unless you specify otherwise, procedures you place in any Code module can be called from anywhere within your application.

You might think that two Public procedures can't have the same name. Although this was true in earlier versions of Access, it isn't true in Access 97. If two Public procedures share a name, the procedure that calls them must explicitly state which of the two routines it's calling. This is illustrated by the following code snippet:

```
Private Sub cmdSayGoodBye_Click()
   Call basUtils.SayGoodBye
End Sub
```

The `SayGoodBye` routine is found in two Access code modules; however, the prefix `basUtils` indicates that the routine you want to execute is in the Standard module named basUtils.

Procedures declared in Form or Report Class modules are also automatically Public, so they can be called from anywhere within the application. The procedure called `cbfIAmPublic`, shown in Figure 8.6, is found in the form called frmHello. Although the procedure is found in the form, it can be called from anywhere within the application. The only requirement is that the form containing the procedure must be open. The following `cbfIAmPublic` procedure can be called from anywhere within the application by using the following syntax:

```
Sub PublicFormProc()
   Call Forms.frmHello.cbfIAmPublic
End Sub
```

> **TIP**
>
> Although all procedures are by default Public, the `Public` keyword should be used to show that the procedure is visible to any subroutine or function in the database.

Figure 8.6.

A Public Form procedure visible to any subroutine or function in the database.

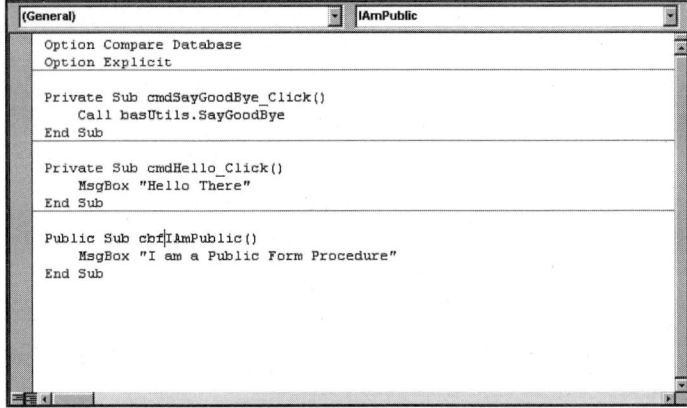

Private Procedures

As mentioned, all procedures are automatically Public. If you want a procedure declared in a module to have the scope of that module only, meaning that it can be called only from another routine within the module, you must explicitly declare it as Private. (See Figure 8.7.)

Figure 8.7.

A Private procedure visible only to subroutines and functions in the basAnother module.

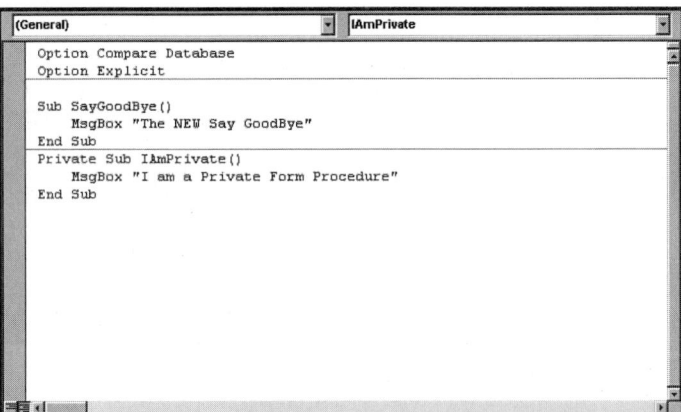

The procedure shown in Figure 8.7, called IAmPrivate, is in the Standard module named basUtils. Because the procedure is Private, it can be called only from other procedures in the basUtils module.

Scope Precedence

Private procedures always take precedence over Public procedures. If a Private procedure has the same name as a Public procedure, the Private procedure's code is executed if it's called by any routine in the module where it was declared. Naming conflicts don't occur between Public and Private procedures.

Developers often wonder where to place code: in form or report Class modules or in Standard modules? There are pros and cons to each method. Placing code in Standard modules means that the code can be easily called from anywhere in your application, without loading a specific form or report. Public routines placed in Standard modules can also be called from other databases. For this reason, Standard modules are a great place to put generic routines that you want readily available as part of a library.

Access 97 loads modules on a demand-only basis, which means that procedures no longer take up memory unless they're being used. This is especially true if you plan your modules carefully (see Chapter 23, "Optimizing Your Application"). Regardless of when the code is loaded, an advantage of placing code behind forms and reports (rather than within modules) is that the form or report is very self-contained and, therefore, portable. You can import the form or report into any other database and it still operates as expected. This "object-oriented" approach means that the form requires nothing from the outside world.

As you can see, there are pluses and minuses to each method. As a general rule, if a routine is specific to a particular form or report, place that routine in the form or report; if it's widely used, place it in a module.

Static Procedures

If a procedure is declared as Static, all the variables declared in the procedure maintain their values between calls to the procedure. This is an alternative to explicitly declaring each variable in the procedure as Static; here's an example of a Static procedure:

```
Static Sub IncrementThem()
    Dim intCounter1 As Integer
    Dim intCounter2 As Integer
    Dim intCounter3 As Integer
    intCounter1 = intCounter1 + 1
    intCounter2 = intCounter2 + 1
    intCounter3 = intCounter3 + 1
    MsgBox intCounter1 & " - " & intCounter2 & " - " & intCounter3
End Sub
```

Ordinarily, each variable in this procedure would be reinitialized to zero each time the procedure is run. This means that all *1*s would appear in the message box each time the procedure is run. Because the procedure is declared as Static, the variables in it retain their values from call to call. Each time the procedure is run, the values in the message box would increase. This factor should become much clearer after the discussion of variables later in this chapter.

Naming Conventions for Procedures

The LNC (Leszynski) naming conventions suggest that all form and report procedure names be prefixed with the tag cbf. LNC standards add an optional scoping tag of *s* for Static procedures, *m* for Private procedures, and *p* for Public procedures; these standards suggest you use the scoping tag only if you're creating software that will be widely distributed or released as public domain.

Working with Variables

You need to consider many issues when creating VBA variables. The way you declare a variable determines its scope, its lifetime, and more. The following topics will help you better understand declaring variables in VBA.

Declaring Variables

There are several ways to declare variables in VBA: three are nonstandard and one is standard. For example, you could simply declare x=10. With this method of variable declaration, you really aren't declaring your variables at all; you're essentially declaring them as you use them. This method is quite dangerous; it lends itself to typos and other problems. If you follow the previously recommended practice of always using the `Option Explicit` statement, Access will not allow you to declare variables in this manner.

You could also type `Dim intCounter`; the `Dim` statement declares the variable. The only problem with this method is that you haven't declared the type of the variable to the compiler, so it's declared as a variant variable.

Another common mistake is declaring multiple variables on the same line, as in this example:

```
Dim intCounter, intAge, intWeight As Integer.
```

In this line, only the last variable is explicitly declared as an integer variable. The other variables are implicitly declared as variants. If you're going to declare multiple variables on one line, make sure each variable is specifically declared, as in the following example:

```
Dim intCounter As Integer, intAge As Integer, intWeight As Integer
```

The most efficient and bug-proof way to declare your variables is to strong type them to the compiler and declare only one variable per line of code, as in this example:

```
Dim intCounter As Integer
Dim strName As String
```

As you can see, strong typing declares the name of the variable as well as the type of data it can contain. This allows the compiler to catch errors, such as storing a string into an integer variable, before your program runs. If implemented properly, by selecting the smallest practical data type for each variable, this method can also reduce the resources needed to run your programs.

NOTE

You should try to eliminate using variants whenever possible. Besides requiring a significant amount of storage space, variants are also slow, since they must be resolved by the compiler at runtime. However, certain situations warrant using a variant, such as including variables that need to contain different types of data at different times, and being able to differentiate between an empty variable (one that hasn't been initialized) and a variable having a zero or a zero-length string. Also, variant variables are the only type of variable that can hold the special value of Null. Empty and Null values are covered in Chapter 9, "Advanced VBA Techniques."

VBA Data Types

VBA offers several data types for variables. Table 8.1 shows a list of the available data types, the standard for naming them, the amount of storage space they require, the data they can store, and their default values.

Table 8.1. Data types and naming conventions.

Data Type	Naming Conv.	Example	Storage of Data	Range	Default Value
Byte	byt	bytValue	1 byte	0 to 255	0
Boolean	bln	blnAnswer	2 bytes	True or False	False
Integer	int	intCounter	2 bytes	-32768 to 32767	0
Long Integer	lng	lngAmount	4 bytes	-2147483648 to 2147483647	0
Single	sng	sngAmount	4 bytes	Very large	0
Double	dbl	dblValue	8 bytes	Extremely large	0
Currency	cur	curSalary	8 bytes	Very large	0
Date	dtm	dtmStartDate	8 bytes	1/1/100 to 12/31/9999	
Object Reference	obj	objExcel	4 bytes	Any object	
Fixed String	str	strName	10 bytes + String	0 to 2 billion	""
Var. String	str	strName	String	1 to 65,400	""
Variant /w Numbers	var	varData	16 bytes	Any numeric to double	Empty

continues

Table 8.1. continued

Data Type	Naming Conv.	Example	Storage of Data	Range	Default Value
Variant /w Characters	var	varData	22 bytes	Same as var. string	Empty
Type	typ	typEmp	Varies	Based on Elements	
Hyperlink	hyp	hypHomePage	Varies	0 to 6,144	Empty

Scope and Lifetime of Variables: Exposing Your Variables as Little as Possible

You have read about the different types of variables available in VBA. Variables can be declared as Local, Private (Module), or Public in scope. You should try to use Local variables in your code because they're shielded from being accidentally modified by other routines. In the following sections, take a closer look at how you can determine the scope and lifetime of variables.

Local Variables

Local variables are available only in the procedure where they are declared. Consider this example:

```
Private Sub cmdOkay_Click
  Dim strAnimal As String
  strAnimal = "Dog"
  Call ChangeAnimal
  Debug.Print strAnimal ''Still Dog
End Sub

Private Sub ChangeAnimal
  strAnimal = "Cat"
End Sub
```

This code would behave in one of two ways. If Option Explicit were in effect, meaning that all variables must be declared before they're used, this code would generate a compiler error. If the Option Explicit statement isn't used, strAnimal would be changed to Cat only within the context of the subroutine ChangeAnimal.

Static Variables: A Special Type of Local Variable

The following examples illustrate the difference between Local and Static variables. Local variables are reinitialized each time the code is called. Each time you run the following procedure, for example, the numeral *1* is printed in the Debug window:

```
Private Sub cmdLocal_Click()
   Dim intCounter As Integer
   intCounter = intCounter + 1
   Debug.Print intCounter
End Sub
```

Each time this code runs, the `Dim` statement reinitializes `intCounter` to zero. This is quite different from the following code, which illustrates the use of a Static variable:

```
Private Sub cmdStatic_Click()
   Static sintCounter As Integer
   sintCounter = sintCounter + 1
   Debug.Print sintCounter
End Sub
```

Each time this code executes, the variable called `sintCounter` is incremented and its value retained.

Private Variables

So far, this discussion has been limited to variables that have scope within a particular procedure. Private (module-level) variables can be seen by any routine in the module they were declared in. Private variables are declared by placing a `Private` statement, such as the following, in the General Declarations section of a Form, Report, or Access module:

```
[General Declarations]
Option Explicit
Private mintCounter As Integer
```

The value of a variable declared as Private can be changed by any subroutine or function within that module. For example, the following subroutine changes the value of the Private variable `mintCounter` to 20:

```
Private Sub cmdModule_Click()
   mintCounter = 20
   Debug.Print mintCounter
End Sub
```

Notice the naming convention of using the letter *m* to prefix the name of the variable, which denotes the variable as a Private module-level variable. You should use Private declarations only for variables that need to be seen by multiple procedures in the same module; aim for making most of your variables Local to make your code modular and more bullet-proof.

Public Variables

Public variables can be accessed from anywhere within your application. They're usually limited to things such as log-in IDs, environment settings, and other variables that must be seen by your entire application. Declarations of Public variables can be placed in the General Declarations section of a module. The declaration of a Public variable looks like this:

```
Option Explicit
Public gintCounter As Integer
```

Notice the prefix *g*, the proper prefix for a Public variable declared in a Standard module. This standard is used because Public variables declared in a Standard module are visible not only to the database they were declared in but to other databases. The prefix *p*, used for Public variables declared in a Form or Report Class module, indicates that the variable is Public to the database but not visible to other databases. The following code, placed in the Click event of the cmdPublic command button, changes the value of the Public variable pintCounter to 50:

```
Private Sub cmdPublic_Click()
  pintCounter = 50
  Debug.Print pintCounter
End Sub
```

Adding Comments to Your Code

Comments, which are color-coded in Access 97, are added to modules by using an apostrophe. The keyword Rem can also be used, but the apostrophe is generally preferred. The apostrophe can be placed at the beginning of the line of code or anywhere within it. Anything following the apostrophe is considered a comment. Figure 8.8 shows code containing comments.

Figure 8.8.

Code containing comments that clarify what the subroutine is doing.

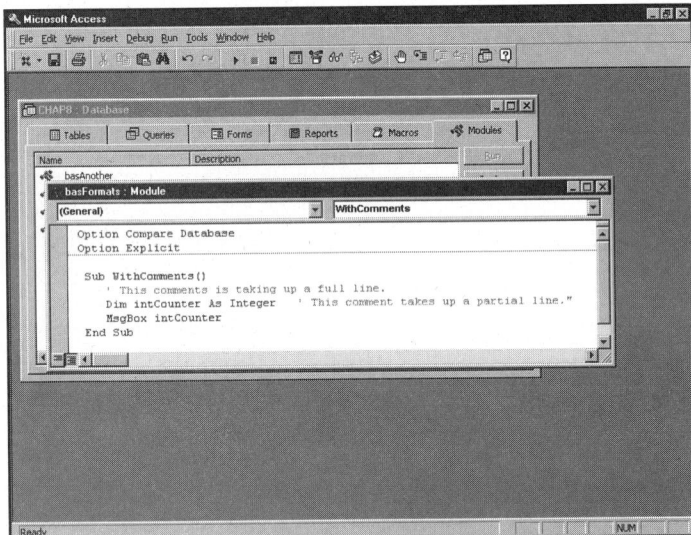

Using the Line-Continuation Character

Access Basic code didn't have a line-continuation character, which meant you had to scroll a lot, as well as pull out a bag of tricks to simulate continuing a line of code. With VBA, Access 97 solves this problem; the line-continuation character is an underscore. Figure 8.9 illustrates the use of this character.

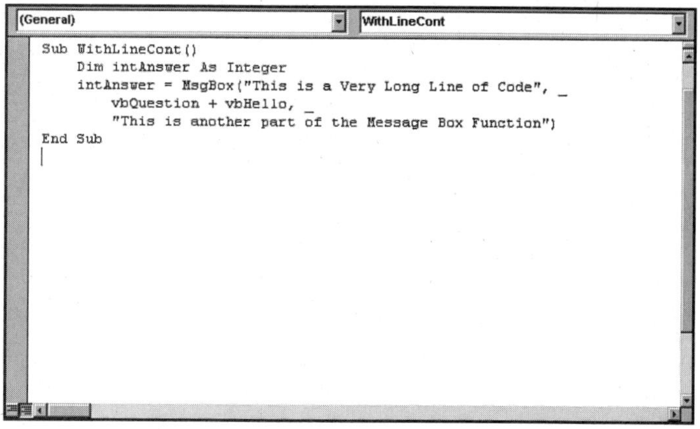

Figure 8.9.

The line-continuation character is used to improve the readability of a long line of code.

```
(General)                              ▼   WithLineCont                          ▼
Sub WithLineCont()
    Dim intAnswer As Integer
    intAnswer = MsgBox("This is a Very Long Line of Code", _
        vbQuestion + vbHello, _
        "This is another part of the Message Box Function")
End Sub
```

Using the VBA Control Structures

VBA gives the developer several different constructs for looping and decision processing. The most commonly used ones are covered in the following sections.

If...Then...Else

The `If...Then...Else` construct evaluates whether a condition is true. In the following example, anything between `If` and `Else` will occur if the statement evaluates to `True`, and any code between `Else` and `End If` will be executed if the statement evaluates to `False`. The `Else` is optional.

```
Private Sub cmdIf_Click()
 If IsNull(Me!txtValue) Then
    MsgBox "You must Enter a Value"
  Else
    MsgBox "You entered " & Me!txtValue
  End If
End Sub
```

This code tests whether the text box called `txtValue` contains a null. A different message is displayed depending on whether the text box value is null.

One-line `If` statements are also permitted; they look like this:

```
If IsNull(Me!txtvalue) Then MsgBox "You must Enter a Value"
```

However, this format for an `If` statement isn't recommended because it reduces readability.

Another valid part of an `If` statement is `ElseIf`, which allows you to evaluate an unlimited number of conditions in one `If` statement. The following code gives you an example:

```
Sub MultipleIfs(intNumber As Integer)
   If intNumber = 1 Then
      MsgBox "You entered a One"
   ElseIf intNumber = 2 Then
```

223

```
        MsgBox "You entered a Two"
    ElseIf intNumber >= 3 And intNumber <= 10 Then
        MsgBox "You entered a Number Between 3 and 10"
    Else
        MsgBox "You Entered Some Other Number"
    End If
End Sub
```

The conditions in an `If` statement are evaluated in the order in which they appear. For this reason, it's best to place the most common conditions first. Once a condition is met, execution continues immediately after `End If`. If no conditions are met, and there's no `Else` statement, execution will also continue immediately after `End If`.

> **NOTE**
>
> If multiple conditions exist, it's almost always preferable to use a `Select Case` statement rather than an `If` statement. The exception to this rule is when you're using the `TypeOf` keyword to evaluate the type of an object. The `TypeOf` keyword is covered in Chapter 10, "The Real Scoop on Objects, Properties, and Events."

Immediate If (`IIf`)

An Immediate If (`IIf`) is a variation of an `If` statement; it's a function that returns one of two values, depending on whether the condition being tested is true or false. Here's an example:

```
Function EvalSales(curSales As Currency) As String
    EvalSales = IIf(curSales >= 100000, "Great Job", "Keep Plugging")
End Function
```

This function evaluates the `curSales` parameter to see whether its value is greater than or equal to $100,000. If it is, the string `"Great Job"` is returned from the function; otherwise, the string `"Keep Plugging"` is returned.

> **WARNING**
>
> Both the true and false portions of the `IIf` are evaluated, so if there's a problem with either part of the expression (for example, a divide-by-zero condition), an error occurs.

The `IIf` function is most often used in a calculated control on a form or report. Probably the most common example is an `IIf` expression that determines whether the value of a control is null. If it is, you can have the expression return a zero or an empty string; otherwise, you can have the expression return the value in the control. The following expression, for example, evaluates the value of a control on a form:

8

```
=IIf(IsNull(Forms!frmOrders!Freight),0,Forms!frmOrders!Freight)
```

This expression displays either a zero or the value for freight in the control called `Freight`.

The Conditional `If`: Conditional Compilation

Conditional compilation allows you to selectively execute blocks of code. This feature is useful in several situations:

- When you want certain blocks of code to execute in the demo version of your product and other blocks to execute in your product's retail version
- When you're distributing your application in different countries and want certain blocks of code to apply to some countries but not to others
- When you want certain blocks of code to execute only during the testing of your application

Conditional compilation is done by using the `#If...Then...#Else` directive, as shown here:

```
Sub ConditionalIf()
    #If Language = "Spanish" Then
        MsgBox "Hola, Que Tal?"
    #Else
        MsgBox "Hello, How Are You?"
    #End If
End Sub
```

The compiler constant, in this case, `Language`, can be declared in one of two places: in a module's General Declarations section or in the Advanced tab of the Tools|Options dialog box. A compiler constant declared in the General Declarations section of a module looks like this:

```
#Const Language = "Spanish"
```

The disadvantage of this constant is that it can't be declared as Public. It isn't possible to create Public compiler constants by using the `#Const` directive. This means that any constants declared in a module's Declarations section can be used only within that module. The major advantage of declaring this type of compiler constant is that it can contain a string. For example, the compiler constant `Language`, defined in the previous paragraph, is given the value `"Spanish"`.

Public compiler constants can be declared only by choosing Tools|Options. Because they're Public in scope, compiler constants defined in Tools|Options can be referred to from anywhere in your application. The major limitation on compiler directives set up in Tools|Options is that they can contain only integers. For example, you would have to say `"Spanish = 1"`.

To set up a compiler directive by using Tools|Options, select the Advanced tab, shown in Figure 8.10, from the Options dialog box. Add the compiler directive to the Conditional Compilation Arguments text box. You can add more than one directive by separating each one with a colon. As mentioned, compiler directives entered in this way can contain only integers.

Figure 8.10.

Adding compiler directives by using Tools | Options.

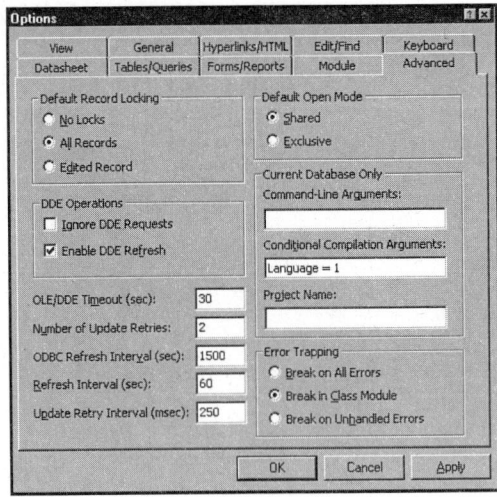

With the compiler directive that appears in the dialog box, the code would look like this:

```
Sub ConditionalIf()
    #If Language = 1 Then
        MsgBox "Hola, Que Tal?"
    #Else
        MsgBox "Hello, How Are You?"
    #End If
End Sub
```

Notice that `ConditionalIf` now evaluates the constant `Language` against the integer of 1.

It's important to understand that using conditional constants isn't the same as using regular constants or variables with the standard `If...Then...Else` construct. Although regular constants or variables are evaluated at runtime, which requires processing time each time the application is run, conditional constants and conditional `If...Then...Else` statements control which sections of code are actually compiled. All resolution is completed at compile time; this eliminates the need for unnecessary processing at runtime.

Select Case

Rather than using multiple `If...Then...Else` statements, it's often much clearer to use a `Select Case` statement, as shown here:

```
Private Sub cmdCase_Click()
    Dim intResponse As Integer
    If IsNull(Me!txtValue) Then
        intResponse = 0
    Else
        intResponse = Val(Me!txtValue)
    End If
    Select Case intResponse
```

```
     Case 0
       MsgBox "You Must Enter a Number"
     Case 1 To 5
       MsgBox "You Entered a Value Between 1 and 5"
     Case 7, 11, 21
       MsgBox "You Entered 7, 11, or 21"
     Case Else
       MsgBox "You Entered an Invalid Number"
   End Select
End Sub
```

This subroutine first uses an `If` statement to evaluate whether the txtValue control contains a null. If txtValue contains a null, the routine stores a zero in the `intResponse` variable; otherwise, the value in txtValue is stored in `intResponse`. The `Select Case` statement then evaluates `intResponse`. If the value is `0`, a message box is displayed with `You Must Enter a Number`. If the value is between 1 and 5 inclusive, a message box is displayed saying `You Entered a Value Between 1 and 5`. If the user enters 7, 11, or 21, an appropriate message is displayed; otherwise, the user gets a message indicating that he or she entered an invalid number.

Looping

Several looping structures are available in VBA; most are discussed in this section. Take a look at the following example of a looping structure:

```
Sub DoWhileLoop()
  Dim intCounter As Integer
    intCounter = 1
    Do While intCounter < 5
      MsgBox intCounter
      intCounter = intCounter + 1
    Loop
End Sub
```

In this structure, if `intCounter` is greater than or equal to 5, the code in the loop is not executed. If you want the code to execute unconditionally at least one time, you need to use the following construct:

```
Sub DoLoopWhile()
  Dim intCounter As Integer
    intCounter = 5
    Do
        MsgBox intCounter
        intCounter = intCounter + 1
    Loop While iCounter < 5
End Sub
```

This code will execute one time, even though `intCounter` is set to 5. The `Do While...Loop` in the previous example evaluates before the code is executed, so it doesn't ensure code execution. The `Do...Loop While` is evaluated at the end of the loop and is, therefore, guaranteed execution.

Alternatives to the `Do While...Loop` and the `Do...Loop While` are `Do Until...Loop` and `Do...Loop Until`. `Do Until...Loop` works like this:

```
Sub DoUntilLoop()
   Dim intCounter As Integer
   intCounter = 1
   Do Until intCounter = 5
      MsgBox intCounter
      intCounter = intCounter + 1
   Loop
End Sub
```

This loop sets `intCounter` equal to 1. It continues to execute until `intCounter` becomes equal to 5. The `Do...Loop Until` construct is another variation:

```
Sub DoLoopUntil()
   Dim intCounter As Integer
   intCounter = 1
   Do
      MsgBox intCounter
      intCounter = intCounter + 1
   Loop Until intCounter = 5
End Sub
```

As with the `Do...Loop While` construct, the `Do...Loop Until` construct doesn't evaluate the condition until the end of the loop, so the code in the loop is guaranteed to execute at least once.

WARNING

It's easy to unintentionally cause a loop to execute endlessly, as shown in this example:

```
Sub EndlessLoop()
   Dim intCounter As Integer
   intCounter = 5
   Do
      Debug.Print intCounter
      intCounter = intCounter + 1
   Loop Until intCounter = 5
End Sub
```

This code snippet sets `intCounter` equal to 5. The code in the loop increments `intCounter`, then tests to see whether `intCounter` equals 5. If it doesn't, the code in the loop executes another time. Because `intCounter` will never become equal to 5, the loop executes endlessly. You need to use Ctrl+Break to exit out of the loop; however, Ctrl+Break doesn't work in Access's runtime version.

For...Next

The `For...Next` construct is used when you have an exact number of iterations you want to perform. It looks like this:

```
Sub ForNext()
    Dim intCounter As Integer
    For intCounter = 1 To 5
        MsgBox intCounter
    Next intCounter
End Sub
```

Note that `intCounter` is self-incrementing. The start value and the stop value can both be variables. A `For...Next` construct can also be given a step value, as shown here:

```
Sub ForNextStep()
    Dim intCounter As Integer
    For intCounter = 1 To 5 Step 2
        MsgBox intCounter
    Next intCounter
End Sub
```

With...End With

The `With...End With` statement executes a series of statements on a single object. Here's an example:

```
Private Sub cmdWithEndWith_Click()
    With Me!txtHello
        .BackColor = 16777088
        .ForeColor = 16711680
        .Value = "Hello World"
        .FontName = "Arial"
    End With
End Sub
```

This code performs four operations on the txtHello text box, found on the form it's run on. The BackColor, ForeColor, Value, and FontName properties of the txtHello text box are all modified by the code.

> **TIP**
>
> The `With...End With` statement offers two main benefits. The first is simply less typing—you don't need to repeat the object name for each action you want to perform on the object. The second, and more important, benefit involves performance. Because the object is referred to once rather than multiple times, this code runs much more efficiently. The benefits are even more pronounced when the `With...End With` construct is found in a loop.

For Each...Next

The `For Each...Next` statement executes a group of statements on each member of an array or collection. The following example illustrates the use of this powerful construct:

```
Private Sub cmdForEachNext_Click()
    Dim ctl As Control
    For Each ctl In Controls
```

```
      ctl.ForeColor = 16711680
   Next ctl
End Sub
```

This code loops through each control on a form; the ForeColor property of each control on the form is modified. The With...End With construct is often used with the For Each...Next construct. Here's an example:

```
Private Sub cmdForEachWith_Click()
   Dim ctl As Control
   For Each ctl In Controls
      With ctl
         .ForeColor = 16711680
         .FontName = "Arial"
         .FontSize = 14
      End With
   Next ctl
End Sub
```

This code loops through each control on the form. Three properties are changed for each control: ForeColor, FontName, and FontSize.

> **WARNING**
>
> Before you put all this good information to use, remember that no error handling has been implemented in the code yet. If one of the controls on the form in the example doesn't have a ForeColor, FontName, or FontSize property, the code would cause an error. In Chapter 10, you will learn how to determine the type of an object before you perform a command on it. Knowing the type of an object before you try to modify its properties can help you prevent errors.

Passing Parameters and Returning Values: An Introduction

Both subroutines and functions can receive arguments (parameters), but only functions can return values. The following subroutine receives two parameters, txtFirst and txtLast. It then displays a message box with the first character of each of the parameters that was passed.

```
Private Sub cmdSendNames_Click()
   Call Initials(Me!txtFirstName, Me!txtLastName)
End Sub

Sub Initials(strFirst As String, strLast As String)
   MsgBox "Your Initials Are: " & Left$(strFirst, 1) _
     & Left$(strLast, 1)
End Sub
```

Notice that the text in the controls txtFirstName and txtLastName from the current form (represented by the Me keyword) is passed to the subroutine called Initials. The parameters are received as `strFirst` and `strLast`. The first left character of each parameter is displayed in the message box.

The preceding code simply passes values and then operates on those values. This next example uses a function to return a value.

```
Private Sub cmdNameFunc_Click()
    Dim strInitials As String
    strInitials = ReturnInit(Me!txtFirstName, _
        Me!txtLastName)
    MsgBox "Your initials are: " & strInitials
End Sub

Function ReturnInit(strFName As String, strLName As String) As String
    ReturnInit = Left$(strFName, 1) & Left(strLName, 1)
End Function
```

Notice that this example calls the function `ReturnInit`, sending values contained in the two text boxes as parameters. The function sets `ReturnInit` (the name of the function) equal to the first two characters of the strings. This returns the value back to the calling routine (`cmdNameFunc_Click`) and sets `strInitials` equal to the return value.

> **NOTE**
>
> Notice that the function `ReturnInit` is set to receive two string parameters. You know this because of the `As String` keywords that follow each parameter. The function is also set to return a string. You know this because the keyword `As String` follows the list of the parameters, outside the parentheses. If you don't explicitly state that the function will return a particular type of data, it will return a variant.

Working with Built-In Functions

Visual Basic for Applications has a rich and comprehensive function library. Some of the more commonly used functions and examples are listed in the following sections. On some rainy day, go through the online Help or the *Microsoft Access Language Reference* to become familiar with the rest.

Format

The `Format` function formats expressions in the style specified. The first parameter is the expression you want to format; the second is the type of format you want to apply. Here's an example of using the `Format` function:

```
Sub FormatData()
    Debug.Print Format$(50, "Currency")
    'Prints $50.00
    Debug.Print Format$(Now, "Short Date")
```

```
    'Prints the current date
    Debug.Print Format$(Now, "DDDD")
    'Displays the word for the day
    Debug.Print Format$(Now, "DDD")
    'Displays 3 - CHAR Day
    Debug.Print Format$(Now, "YYYY")
    'Displays 4 - digit Year
    Debug.Print Format$(Now, "WW")
    'Displays the Week Number
End Sub
```

Instr

The Instr function returns the position where one string begins within another string:

```
Sub InstrExample()
  Debug.Print InStr("Alison Balter", "Balter") 'Returns 8
  Debug.Print InStr("Hello", "l") 'Returns 3
End Sub
```

Left

Left returns the leftmost number of characters in a string:

```
Sub LeftExample()
  Debug.Print Left$("Hello World", 7) 'Prints Hello W
End Sub
```

Right

Right returns the rightmost number of characters in a string:

```
Sub RightExample()
 Debug.Print Right$("Hello World", 7) 'Prints o World
End Sub
```

Mid

Mid returns a substring of a specified number of characters in a string. This example starts at the fourth character and returns five characters:

```
Sub MidExample()
    Debug.Print Mid$("Hello World", 4, 5) ''Prints lo Wo
End Sub
```

UCase

UCase returns a string that is all uppercase:

```
Sub UCaseExample()
    Debug.Print UCase$("Hello World") 'Prints HELLO WORLD
End Sub
```

DatePart

DatePart returns the specified part of a date:

```
Sub DatePartExample()
    Debug.Print DatePart("YYYY", Now)
    'Prints the Year
    Debug.Print DatePart("M", Now)
    'Prints the Month Number
    Debug.Print DatePart("Q", Now)
    'Prints the Quarter Number
    Debug.Print DatePart("Y", Now)
    'Prints the Day of the Year
    Debug.Print DatePart("WW", Now)
    'Prints the Week of the Year
End Sub
```

DateDiff

DateDiff returns the interval of time between two dates:

```
Sub DateDiffExample()
  Debug.Print DateDiff("d", Now, "12/31/99")
  ''Days until 12/31/99
  Debug.Print DateDiff("m", Now, "12/31/99")
  ''Months until 12/31/99
  Debug.Print DateDiff("yyyy", Now, "12/31/99")
  ''Years until 12/31/99
  Debug.Print DateDiff("q", Now, "12/31/99")
  ''Quarters until 12/31/99
End Sub
```

DateAdd

DateAdd returns the result of adding or subtracting a specified period of time to a date:

```
Sub DateAddExample()
    Debug.Print DateAdd("d", 3, Now)
    'Today plus 3 days
    Debug.Print DateAdd("m", 3, Now)
    'Today plus 3 months
    Debug.Print DateAdd("yyyy", 3, Now)
    'Today plus 3 years
    Debug.Print DateAdd("q", 3, Now)
    'Today plus 3 quarters
    Debug.Print DateAdd("ww", 3, Now)
    'Today plus 3 weeks
End Sub
```

Functions Made Easy with the Object Browser

With the Object Browser, you can view members of an ActiveX component's type library. In plain English, the Object Browser allows you to easily browse a component's methods, properties, and constants. You can also copy information and add it to your code. It even adds a method's parameters for you. The following steps let you browse the available methods, copy the method you want, and paste it into your code:

1. Select Object Browser from the toolbar or press F2 to open the Object Browser window. (See Figure 8.11.)

2. Use the Project/Library drop-down list to select the project or library whose classes and members you want to view.

3. The Object Browser window is divided into two parts. Select the class from the left-hand list box, which lists class modules, templates for new objects, Standard modules, and modules containing subroutines and functions.

4. Select a related property, method, event, constant, function, or statement from the "Members of" list box. In Figure 8.11, the basAnother module is selected from the list box on the left, and the EvalSales function is selected from the list box on the right. Notice that the function and its parameters appear below the list boxes.

5. Click the Copy to Clipboard button to copy the function and its parameters to the Clipboard so that you can easily paste it into your code.

Figure 8.11.

The Object Browser showing all the classes in the Chapter8Figures database and all the members in the basAnother module.

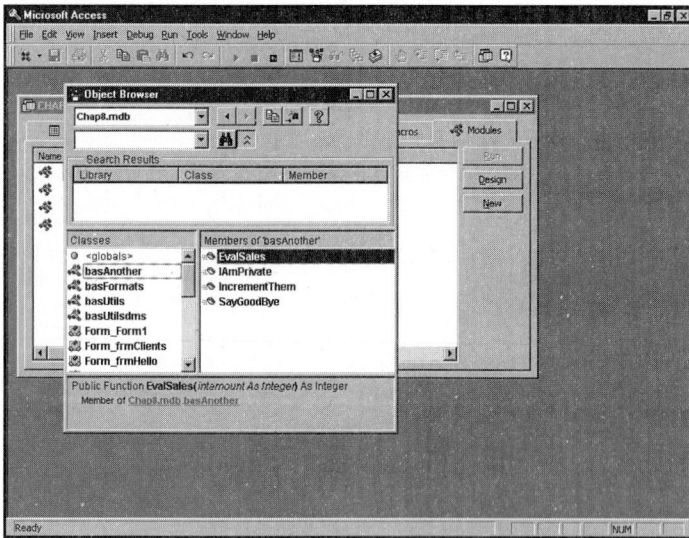

The example in Figure 8.11 shows choosing a user-defined function selected from a module in a database, but you can also select any built-in function. Figure 8.12 shows an example in which the DatePart function is selected from the Visual Basic for Applications library. The Object Browser exposes all libraries referred to by the database and is covered in more detail in Chapters 10 and 25.

Figure 8.12.
The Object Browser with the VBA library selected.

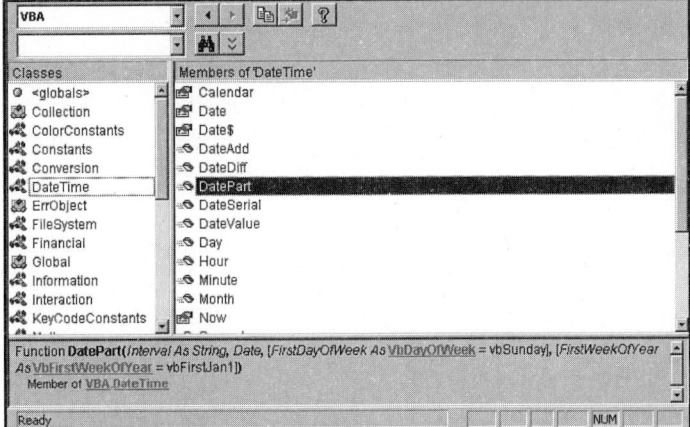

Tools for Working with the Module Window

The Access 97 development environment is better than its predecessors. Several features have been added to make coding easier and more pleasant for you. These enhancements include the ability to do the following:

- List properties and methods
- List constants
- Get quick information on a command or function
- Get parameter information
- Allow Access to finish a word for you
- Get a definition of a function

All these features that help you with coding are available with a right-click when you place your cursor within the Module window.

List Properties and Methods

With the List Properties and Methods feature, you can view all the objects, properties, and methods available for the current object. To invoke this feature, right-click after the name of the object and select List Properties/Methods (you can also press Ctrl+J). The applicable objects, properties, and methods appear in a list box. (See Figure 8.13.) To find the appropriate object, property, or method in the list, use one of these methods:

1. Begin typing the name of the object, property, or method.
2. Use the up-arrow and down-arrow keys to move through the list.
3. Scroll through the list and select your choice.

Figure 8.13.
A list of properties and methods for the Recordset object.

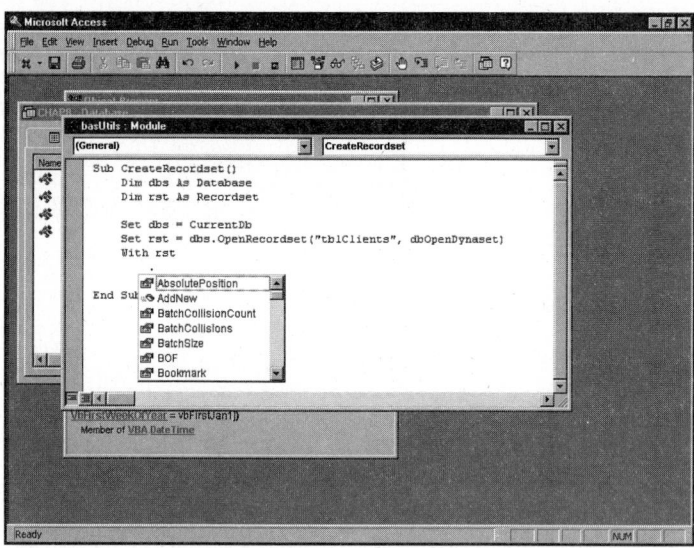

Use one of these methods to insert your selection:

- Double-click the entry.
- Click to select the entry, then press Tab to insert it or Enter to insert it and move to the next line.

> **TIP**
>
> The Auto List Members option, available in the Options dialog box, causes the List Properties and Methods feature, as well as the List Constants feature, to be invoked automatically each time you type the name of an object or property.

List Constants

The List Constants feature opens a drop-down list displaying valid constants for a property you have typed and for functions with arguments that are constants. It works like the List Properties and Methods feature. To invoke it, right-click after the name of the property or argument and select List Constants (or press Ctrl+Shift+J). A list of valid constants appears. (See Figure 8.14.) You can use any of the methods listed in the previous section to select the constant you want.

Figure 8.14.

A list of constants for the vbMsgBoxStyle *parameter.*

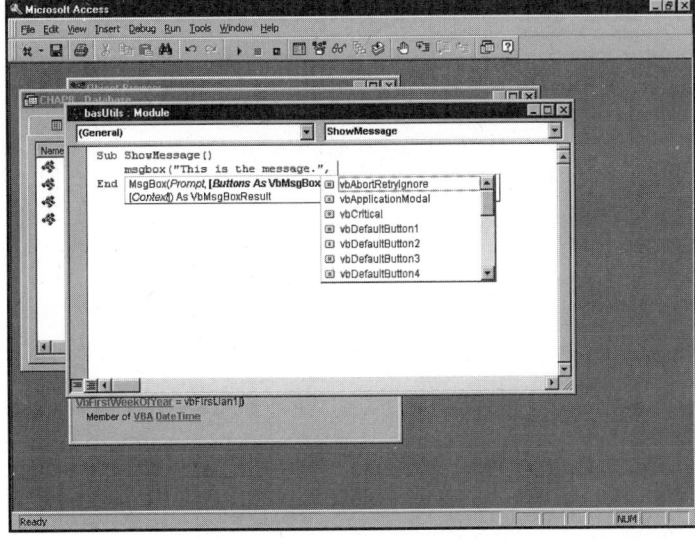

Quick Info

The Quick Info feature gives you the full syntax for a function, statement, procedure, method, or variable. To use this feature, right-click after the name of the function, statement, procedure, method, or variable and select Quick Info (or press Ctrl+I). A tip appears, showing the valid syntax for the item. (See Figure 8.15.) As you type each parameter in the item, it's displayed in boldface type until you type the comma that delineates it from the next parameter.

Figure 8.15.

The syntax for the MsgBox *function.*

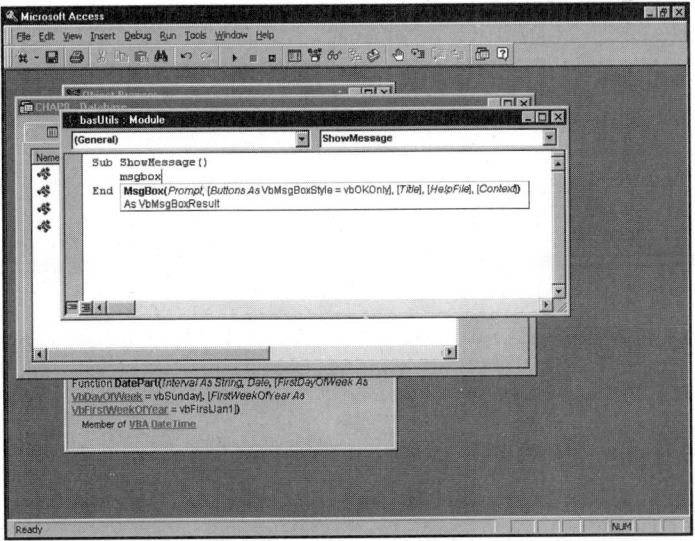

TIP

The Auto Quick Info option, available in the Options dialog box, causes the Quick Info feature to be invoked automatically each time you type the name of an object or property.

Parameter Information

The Parameter Info feature gives you information about the parameters of a function or statement. To use this feature, right-click and select Parameter Info (or press Ctrl+Shift+I). A pop-up list appears with information about the parameters of the function or statement. This list doesn't close until all the required parameters are entered, the function is completed without any optional parameters, or the Esc key is pressed.

NOTE

The Parameter Info feature supplies information about the initial function only. If parameters of a function are themselves functions, you must use Quick Info to find information about the embedded functions.

Complete Word

The Complete Word feature completes a word you're typing. To use this feature, you must first type enough characters for Visual Basic to recognize the word you want. Next, right-click and select Complete Word (or press Ctrl+Spacebar). Visual Basic then finishes the word you're typing.

Definition

The Definition feature shows the place in the Code window where the selected variable or procedure is defined. To get a definition of the selected variable or procedure, right-click in the Code window and select Definition (or press F2). Your cursor is moved to the module and location where the variable or procedure was defined.

NOTE

If the definition is in a referenced library, the Object Browser is invoked and the definition is displayed.

Practical Examples: Event Routines, User-Defined Functions, and Subroutines Needed for the Time and Billing Application

This example uses a form, a query, and a report to retrieve criteria and then preview sales information by client for a specific date range. The rptClientInformationByProject report is based on a query called qryBillingDetailByClient; this query requires information from a form named frmPrintClientBilling. The frmPrintClientBilling form, shown in Figure 8.16, must be open for the process to finish successfully because the criteria for the query is gathered from the report. The code for the two command buttons looks like this:

```
Sub cmdRunReport_Click()
    If IsNull(Me!txtStartDate) Or IsNull(Me!txtEndDate) Then
        MsgBox "Both the Start Date and End Date Must Be Filled In"
    Else
        Call RunReport("rtpClientInformationByProject")
    End If
End Sub

Sub cmdClose_Click()
    DoCmd.Close
End Sub
```

Figure 8.16.

The Report Criteria form, requesting required information for the query underlying the Billing Detail Report.

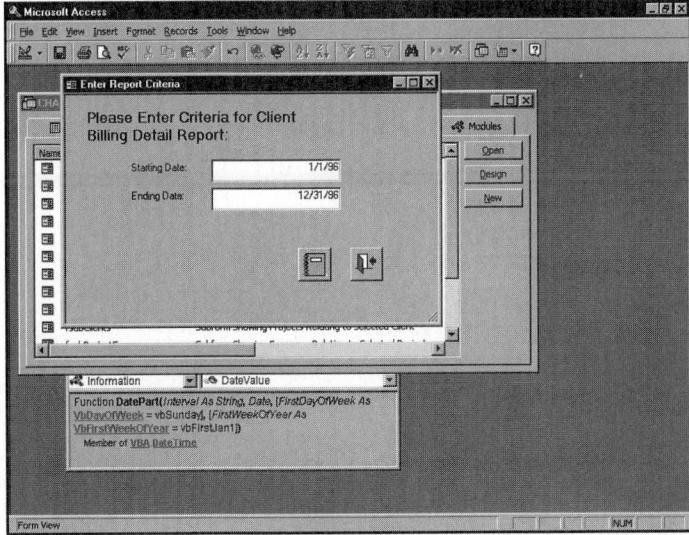

The first routine evaluates the two text boxes to make sure they're filled in. If either text box contains a null, a message is displayed, but if neither one does, a user-defined routine called RunReport is executed. The second routine simply closes the criteria form.

The RunReport subroutine is included in a module called basUtils; RunReport looks like this:

```
Sub RunReport(strReportName As String)
     DoCmd.OpenReport strReportName, acPreview
End Sub
```

This routine receives the name of any report as a parameter and runs the report whose name is passed as the parameter.

The other code, found in the report itself, is placed in the report's Open event and looks like this:

```
Private Sub Report_Open(Cancel As Integer)
    If Not IsLoaded("frmPrintClientBilling") Then
        MsgBox "Print Client Billing Form Must Be Open to Run This Report", _
            vbCritical, "Error!!"
        Cancel = True
    End If
End Sub
```

This routine calls the user-defined function IsLoaded. If the function returns a false, indicating that the required criteria form isn't open, a message is displayed and the report is canceled. The IsLoaded function looks like this:

```
Function IsLoaded(ByVal strFormName As String) As Integer
    IsLoaded = False
    Dim frm As Form
    For Each frm In Forms
      If frm.Name = strFormName Then
          IsLoaded = True
          Exit Function
      End If
    Next frm
 End Function
```

This function loops through the Forms collection. It tries to match the name of each open form with the name of the report criteria form. If a match is found, a True is returned; otherwise, a False is returned.

Summary

A strong knowledge of the VBA language is imperative for the Access developer. This chapter has covered all the basics of the VBA language. You have learned the differences between Code, Form, and Report modules and how to effectively use each. You have also learned the difference between event procedures and user-defined subroutines and functions. To get the most mileage out of your subroutines and functions, you have learned how to pass parameters to, and receive return values from, procedures.

Variables are used throughout your application code. Declaring each variable with the proper scope and lifetime helps make your application bullet-proof and easy to maintain. Furthermore, selecting an appropriate variable type ensures that the minimal amount of memory is consumed and that your application code protects itself. Finally, effectively using control structures and built-in functions gives you the power, flexibility, and functionality required by even the most complex of applications.

9

Advanced VBA Techniques

- Navigation Tips and Tricks, 244
- Executing Procedures from the Module Window, 250
- The DoCmd Object: Performing Macro Actions, 250
- What Are User-Defined Types and Why Would You Use Them, 252
- Working with Constants, 253
- Working with Arrays, 257
- Advanced Function Techniques, 259
- Property Let and Get: Working with Custom Properties, 264
- Class Modules, 265
- Working with Empty and Null, 268
- Understanding and Effectively Using Compilation Options, 273
- Customizing the IDE, 274
- Practical Examples: Putting Advanced Techniques to Use in the Time and Billing Application, 276

The Visual Basic for Applications (VBA) language is extremely rich and comprehensive. VBA is covered throughout this book as it applies to different topics, but this chapter focuses on some advanced application development techniques. Some of the techniques are tips and tricks of the trade; others are advanced aspects of the language that weren't covered in Chapter 8, "VBA 101: The Basics of VBA." An understanding of the concepts in this chapter is essential to learning about the more advanced topics covered in the rest of this book.

Navigation Tips and Tricks

Using the tips and tricks of the trade (many of which are highlighted in this chapter) effectively can save you hours of time. These tricks help you to navigate around the coding environment as well as quickly and easily modify your code. They include the ability to easily zoom to a user-defined procedure, search and replace within modules, get help on VBA functions and commands, and split the Code window so that two procedures can be viewed simultaneously.

Mysteries of the Coding Environment Solved

If you're a developer who's new to VBA, you might be confused by the coding environment. The Code window has two combo boxes, shown in Figure 9.1. The combo box on the left lists objects. For a form or report, the list includes all its objects; for a module, which has no objects, only `(General)` appears.

Figure 9.1.

The Code window with the Object combo box.

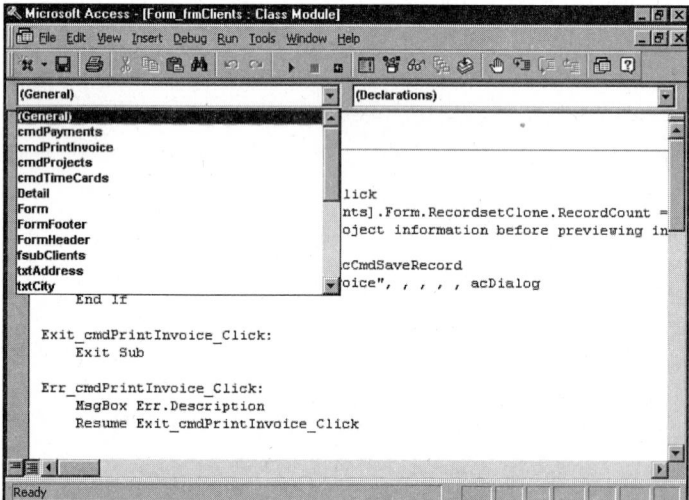

The combo box on the right lists all the event procedures associated with a particular object. Figure 9.2 shows all the event procedures associated with a command button. Notice that the Click event is the only one that appears in bold because it's the only event procedure that has been coded.

Figure 9.2.

The Code window with the Procedure combo box.

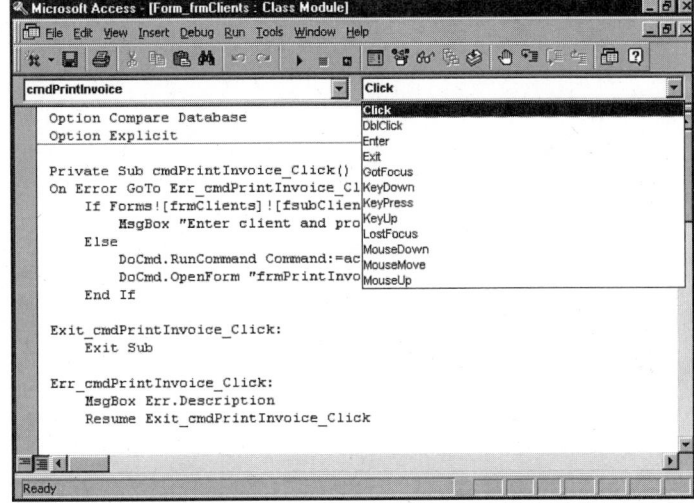

Zoom Shift+F2

As you become more advanced with VBA, you can create libraries of VBA functions and sub-routines. When you're viewing a call to a particular subroutine or function, you usually want to view the code behind that function. Fortunately, VBA gives you a quick and easy way to navigate from procedure to procedure. Assume that the following code appears in your application:

```
Private Sub cmdOkay_Click()
    Dim iAgeInTen As Integer
    If IsNull(Me!txtName) Or IsNull(Me!txtAge) Then
        MsgBox "You must fill in name and age"
        Exit Sub
    Else
        MsgBox "Your Name Is: " & Me!txtName & " and Your Age Is: " & Me!txtAge
        Call EvaluateAge(Val(Me!txtAge))
        iAgeInTen = AgePlus10(Fix(Val(Me!txtAge)))
        MsgBox "In 10 Years You Will Be " & iAgeInTen
    End If
End Sub
```

Say you want to quickly jump to the procedure called `EvaluateAge` so that you can take a better look at it. All you need to do is place your cursor anywhere within the call to `EvaluateAge` and then press Shift+F2. This immediately moves you to the `EvaluateAge` procedure. Ctrl+Shift+F2 takes you back to the routine you came from (in this case, `cmdOkay_Click`). This procedure works for both functions and subroutines.

> **TIP**
>
> If you prefer, you can right-click on the name of the routine you want to jump to and select Definition. To return to the original procedure, right-click again and select Last Position.

Find and Replace

Often, you name a variable only to decide later that you want to change the name. VBA comes with an excellent find-and-replace feature to help you with this change. You can simply search for data, or you can search for a value and replace it with some other value. To invoke the Find dialog box, shown in Figure 9.3, choose Edit | Find or use Ctrl+F.

Figure 9.3.
The Find dialog box is set up to search for `typCompanyInfo` *in the current module.*

Type the text you want to find in the Find What text box. Notice that you can search in the Current Procedure, Current Module, Current Database, or Selected Text. The option Find Whole Word Only doesn't find the text if it's part of another piece of text. For example, if you check Find Whole Word Only, then search for "Count," VBA doesn't find "Counter." Other options include toggles for case sensitivity and pattern matching.

You use the Replace dialog box to search for text and replace it with another piece of text. (See Figure 9.4.) It offers all the features of the Find dialog box, but also allows you to enter Replace With text. In addition, you can select Replace or Replace All. Replace asks for confirmation before each replacement, but Replace All replaces text without this prompt. I recommend you take the time to confirm each replacement because it's all too easy to miscalculate the pervasive effects of a global search-and-replace.

Figure 9.4.
The Replace dialog box is set to find typCompanyInfo *and replace it with* typCompanyInformation *in the current module.*

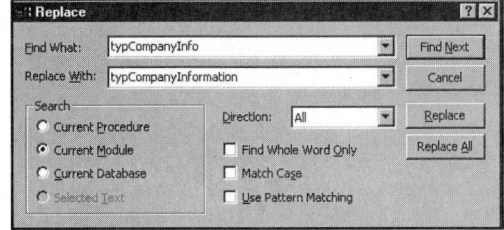

Help

A very useful but little-known feature of VBA is getting context-sensitive help while coding. With your cursor placed anywhere in a VBA command or function, press the F1 key to get context-sensitive help on that command or function. Most of the help topics let you view practical examples of the function or command within code. Figure 9.5 shows help on the With...End With construct. Notice that the Help window includes the syntax for the command, a detailed description of each parameter included in the command, and remarks about using the command. At the top of the window, you can see hypertext links to related topics (See Also), as well as a link to an example of using the With...End With construct. If you click on Example, a specific example of the construct appears that you can copy and place into a module. (See Figure 9.6.) This feature is a great way to learn about the various parts of the VBA language.

Figure 9.5.
Help on With...End With.

Visual Basic Reference

Help Topics | Back | Options

With Statement

See Also   Example   Specifics

Executes a series of statements on a single object or a user-defined type.

Syntax

With *object*
  [*statements*]
End With

The **With** statement syntax has these parts:

Part	Description
object	Required. Name of an object or a user-defined type.
statements	Optional. One or more statements to be executed on *object*.

Remarks

The **With** statement allows you to perform a series of statements on a specified object without requalifying the name of the object. For example, to change a number of different properties on a single object, place the property assignment statements within the **With** control structure, referring to the object once instead of referring to it with each property assignment. The following example illustrates use of the **With** statement to assign values to several properties of the same object.

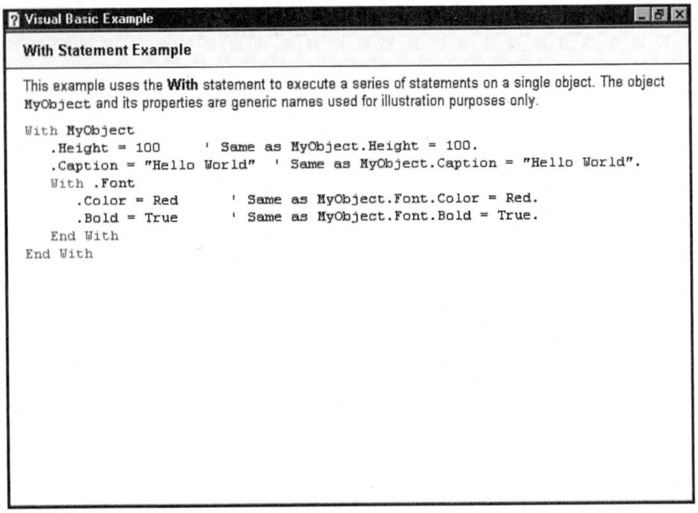

Figure 9.6.

An example of
With...End With.

```
Visual Basic Example                                                _ □ ×

With Statement Example

This example uses the With statement to execute a series of statements on a single object. The object
MyObject and its properties are generic names used for illustration purposes only.

With MyObject
    .Height = 100       ' Same as MyObject.Height = 100.
    .Caption = "Hello World"  ' Same as MyObject.Caption = "Hello World".
    With .Font
        .Color = Red        ' Same as MyObject.Font.Color = Red.
        .Bold = True        ' Same as MyObject.Font.Bold = True.
    End With
End With
```

Splitting the Code Window

The VBA Code window can be split so that you can look at two routines in the same module
at the same time. This option is useful if you're trying to solve a problem involving two procedures or event routines in a large module. An example of a split Code window is shown in
Figure 9.7. To split your Code window, choose Window | Split.

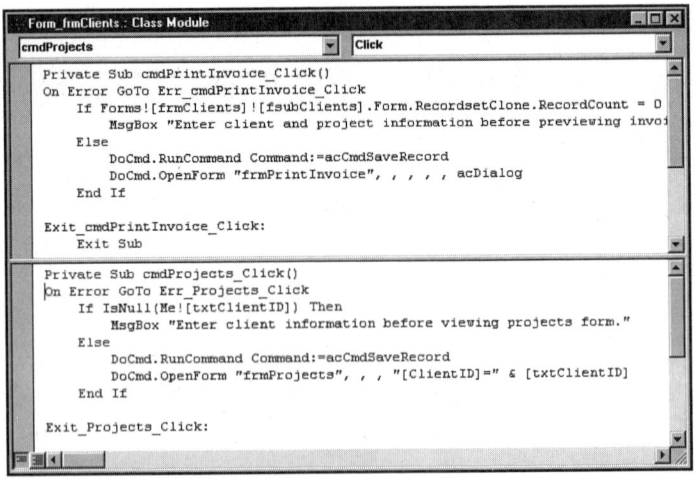

Figure 9.7.

A split Code window lets you
view two routines.

```
Form_frmClients : Class Module                                      _ □ ×

cmdProjects                              ▼   Click                    ▼

Private Sub cmdPrintInvoice_Click()
On Error GoTo Err_cmdPrintInvoice_Click
    If Forms![frmClients]![fsubClients].Form.RecordsetClone.RecordCount = 0
        MsgBox "Enter client and project information before previewing invoi
    Else
        DoCmd.RunCommand Command:=acCmdSaveRecord
        DoCmd.OpenForm "frmPrintInvoice", , , , , acDialog
    End If

Exit_cmdPrintInvoice_Click:
    Exit Sub

Private Sub cmdProjects_Click()
On Error GoTo Err_Projects_Click
    If IsNull(Me![txtClientID]) Then
        MsgBox "Enter client information before viewing projects form."
    Else
        DoCmd.RunCommand Command:=acCmdSaveRecord
        DoCmd.OpenForm "frmProjects", , , "[ClientID]=" & [txtClientID]
    End If

Exit_Projects_Click:
```

Notice the splitter. By placing your mouse cursor on the gray splitter button just above the Code window's vertical scrollbar and clicking and dragging, you can size each half of the window. The window can be split into only two parts. After it has been split, you can use the Object and Procedure drop-down lists to navigate to the procedure of your choice.

> **NOTE**
>
> Only routines in the same module can be viewed in a particular Code window, but several Code windows can be open at the same time. Each time you open an Access, Form, or Report module, you're placed in a different window. Each module window can then be sized, moved, and split.

Full Module View

Another way to view multiple routines at the same time is to work in Full Module view (briefly discussed in Chapter 8). You use it to view all the code in a module as though you were in a normal text editor. To activate Full Module view so that it appears automatically each time you open a Code window, choose Tools | Options. Click on the Module tab, then place an × in the Full Module View checkbox under Window Settings. This global setting affects all the modules in all your databases, but can be changed at any time.

Full Module view has a slightly different effect than splitting a Code window does. Full Module View allows you to view multiple contiguous code routines, but splitting the Code window lets you view two nonconsecutive routines in the same module.

> **TIP**
>
> You can easily toggle back and forth between Full Module view and Procedure view while working in the Module window by using the Procedure View and Full Module View buttons in the lower-left corner.

Using Bookmarks to Save Your Place

The Access 97 coding environment allows you to create placemarkers—called *bookmarks*—so that you can easily return to key locations in your modules. To add a bookmark, right-click on the line of code where the bookmark will be placed and choose Toggle | Bookmark or either Bookmarks | Bookmark from the Edit menu. You can add as many bookmarks as you like.

To navigate between bookmarks, choose Edit | Bookmarks | Next Bookmark or Edit | Bookmarks | Previous Bookmark. A bookmark is a toggle; to remove one, you simply choose Toggle | Bookmark from the shortcut menu or Bookmarks | Bookmark from the Edit menu. If you want to clear all bookmarks, choose Edit | Bookmarks | Clear All Bookmarks. All bookmarks are automatically removed when you close the database.

Executing Procedures from the Module Window

It's easy to test procedures from the Module window in Access 97—simply place your cursor in the routine you want to execute, then press the F5 key or click the Go/Continue button on the toolbar. The procedure you're in will execute as though you had called it from code or from the Immediate pane of the Debug window.

The DoCmd Object: Performing Macro Actions

The Access environment is rich with objects that have built-in properties and methods. By using VBA code, you can modify the properties and execute the methods. One of the objects available in Access is the DoCmd object, used to execute macro actions in Visual Basic procedures. The macro actions are executed as methods of the DoCmd object. The syntax looks like this:

```
DoCmd.ActionName [arguments]
```

Here's a practical example:

```
DoCmd.OpenReport strReportName, acPreview
```

The OpenReport method is a method of the DoCmd object; it runs a report. The first two parameters the OpenReport method receives are the name of the report you want to run and the view in which you want the report to appear (Preview, Normal, or Design). The name of the report and the view are both arguments of the OpenReport method.

Most macro actions have corresponding DoCmd methods that can be found in Help, but some don't. They are AddMenu, MsgBox, RunApp, RunCode, SendKeys, SetValue, StopAllMacros, and StopMacro. The SendKeys method is the only one that has any significance to you as a VBA programmer. The remaining macro actions either have no application to VBA code or can be performed more efficiently by using VBA functions and commands. The VBA language includes a MsgBox function, for example, that's far more robust than its macro action counterpart.

Many of the DoCmd methods have optional parameters, such as the OpenForm method shown in Figure 9.8. If you don't supply an argument, its default value is assumed. You must use commas as placemarkers to designate the position of missing arguments, as shown here:

```
DoCmd.OpenForm "frmOrders", , ,"[OrderAmount} > 1000"
```

Figure 9.8.

The OpenForm *method of the* *DoCmd object in Help.*

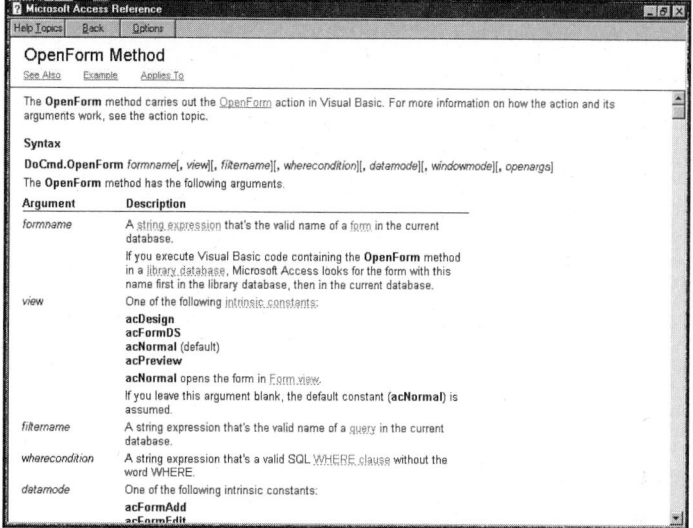

The OpenForm method of the DoCmd object receives seven parameters; the last six parameters are optional. In the example, two parameters are explicitly specified. The first is the name of the form, a required parameter. The second and third parameters have been omitted, meaning that you're accepting their default values. The commas, used as placemarkers for the second and third parameters, are necessary because one of the parameters following them is explicitly designated. The fourth parameter is the Where condition for the form, which has been designated as the records in which the OrderAmount is greater than 1,000. The remaining four parameters haven't been referred to, so default values are used for these parameters.

> **TIP**
>
> Named parameters, covered later in this chapter, can greatly simplify the preceding syntax. With named parameters, the arguments don't need to be placed in a particular order, nor do you need to worry about counting commas. The preceding syntax can be changed to the following:
>
> ```
> DoCmd.OpenForm FormName:="frmOrders", _
>    WhereCondition:=[OrderAmount]>1000
> ```
>
> For more about named parameters, see the "Advanced Function Techniques" section of this chapter.

What Are User-Defined Types and Why Would You Use Them?

A user-defined type, known as a *struct* or *record*, allows you to create a variable containing several pieces of information. User-defined types are often used to hold information from one or more records in memory. Because each element of a user-defined type can be instructed to hold a particular type of data, each element in the type can be defined to correspond to the type of data stored in a specific field of a table. A user-defined type might look like this:

```
Public Type TimeCardInfo
    TimeCardDetailID As Long
    TimeCardID As Long
    DateWorked As Date
    ProjectID As Long
    WorkDescription As String * 255
    BillableHours As Double
    BillingRate As Currency
    WorkCodeID As Long
End Type
```

Notice that the type of data stored in each element has been explicitly declared. The element containing the string WorkDescription has been declared with a length of 255. User-defined types make code cleaner by storing related data as a unit. A user-defined type exists only in memory and is, therefore, temporary. It's excellent for information that needs to be temporarily tracked at runtime. Because it's in memory, it can be quickly and efficiently read from and written to.

Declaring a User-Defined Type

You declare a user-defined type by using a Type statement that must be placed in the module's Declarations section. Types can be declared as Public or Private, but types can't be placed in Form or Report modules.

Creating a Type Variable

A Type variable is an instance of the type in memory; it must be declared before you can use the type. To declare a Type variable, create a Local, Private, Module-Level, or Public variable based on the type. Depending on where you place this declaration and how you declare it (Dim, Private, or Public), you determine its scope. The same rules for any other kind of variable apply to Type variables. The Dim statement in the code that follows creates a variable called typTimeCardData. If you place this Dim statement in the module's General section, it's visible to all routines in that module. If you place it in a subroutine or function, it's local to that particular routine:

```
Dim typTimeCardData As TimeCardInfo
```

Storing Information from a Record in a Form into a Type

After a Type variable has been declared, you can store data into each of its elements. The following code stores information from the frmTimeCardHours form into a Type variable called typTimeCardData, declared in basDataHandling:

```
Private Sub cmdWriteToType_Click()
    Dim typTimeCardData As TimeCardInfo
    typTimeCardData.TimeCardDetailID = Me!TimeCardDetailID
    typTimeCardData.TimeCardID = Me!TimeCardID
    typTimeCardData.DateWorked = Me!DateWorked
    typTimeCardData.ProjectID = Me!ProjectID
    typTimeCardData.WorkDescription = Me!WorkDescription
    typTimeCardData.BillableHours = Me!BillableHours
    typTimeCardData.BillingRate = Me!BillingRate
    typTimeCardData.WorkCodeID = Me!WorkCodeID
End Sub
```

The code for this chapter can be found in the CHAP9EX.MDB database on the book's CD-ROM. The advantage of this code is that rather than creating eight variables to store these eight pieces of related information, it creates one variable with eight elements. This method keeps things nice and neat.

Retrieving Information from the Elements of a Type

To retrieve information from your Type variable, simply refer to its name, followed by a period, then the name of the element. The following code displays a message box containing all the time-card hour information:

```
Private Sub cmdDisplayFromType_Click()
    MsgBox "Timecard Detail ID Is " & typTimeCardData.TimeCardDetailID & Chr(13) & _
        "Timecard ID Is " & typTimeCardData.TimeCardID & Chr(13) & _
        "Date Worked Is " & typTimeCardData.DateWorked & Chr(13) & _
        "Project ID Is " & typTimeCardData.ProjectID & Chr(13) & _
        "Work Description Is " & Trim(typTimeCardData.WorkDescription) & Chr(13) _
        & _
        "Billable Hours Is " & typTimeCardData.BillableHours & Chr(13) & _
        "Billing Rate Is " & typTimeCardData.BillingRate & Chr(13) & _
        "Workcode ID Is " & typTimeCardData.WorkCodeID
End Sub
```

Working with Constants

A *constant* is a meaningful name given to a meaningless number or string. Constants can be used only for values that don't change at runtime. A tax rate or commission rate, for example, might be constant throughout your application. There are three types of constants in Access:

- Symbolic
- Intrinsic
- System-defined

Symbolic constants, created by using the Const keyword, are used to improve the readability of your code and make code maintenance easier. Rather than referring to the number .0875 every time you want to refer to the tax rate, you can refer to the constant mccurTaxRate. If the tax rate changes and you need to modify the value in your code, you'll make the change in only one place. Furthermore, unlike the number .0875, the name mccurTaxRate is self-documenting.

Intrinsic constants are built into Microsoft Access; they are part of the language itself. As an Access programmer, you can use constants supplied by Microsoft Access, Visual Basic, and Data Access Objects (DAO). You can also use constants provided by any object libraries you're using in your application.

There are only three system-defined constants, available to all applications on your computer: True, False, and Null.

Defining Your Own Constants

As mentioned, a Symbolic constant is declared by using the Const keyword. A constant can be declared in a subroutine or function or in the General section of a Form or Report module. Unlike in previous versions of Access, constants can be strong-typed in Access 97. The naming convention for constants is to use a suitable scoping prefix, the letter *c* to indicate you're working with a constant rather than a variable, and then the appropriate tag for the data type. The declaration and use of a Private constant would look like this:

```
Private Const mccurTaxRate As Currency = .0875
```

This code, when placed in a module's Declarations section, creates a Private constant called mccurTaxRate and sets it equal to .0875. Here's how the constant is used in code:

```
Function TotalAmount(curSaleAmount As Currency)
    TotalAmount = curSaleAmount * mccurTaxRate
End Function
```

This routine multiplies the curSaleAmount, received as a parameter, by the constant mccurTaxRate. It returns the result of the calculation by setting the function name equal to the product of the two values. The advantage of the constant in this example is that the code is more readable than TotalAmount = curSaleAmount * .0875 would be.

Scoping Symbolic Constants

Just like regular variables, user-defined constants have scope. In the preceding example, you created a Private constant. The following statement, when placed in a module's Declarations section, creates a Public constant:

```
Public Const pccurTaxRate = 0.0875 As Currency
```

Because this constant is declared as Public, it can be accessed from any subroutine or function (including event routines) in your entire application. To better understand the benefits of a Public constant, say you have many functions and subroutines all making reference to the constant pccurTaxRate. Imagine what would happen if the tax rate were to change. If you hadn't used a constant, you would need to search your entire application, replacing the old tax rate with the new tax rate. However, because your Public constant is declared in one place, you can easily go in and modify the one line of code where this constant is declared.

NOTE

By definition, the value of constants can't be modified at runtime. If you try to modify the value of a constant, you get this VBA compiler error:

```
Variable Required—can't assign to this expression
```

Figure 9.9 illustrates this message box. You can see that an attempt was made to modify the value of the constant called pccurTaxRate, which resulted in a compile error.

If you need to change the value at runtime, you should consider storing the value in a table rather than declaring it as a constant. You can read the value into a variable when the application loads, then modify the variable if necessary. If you choose, you can write the new value back to the table.

Figure 9.9.
Trying to modify the value of a constant.

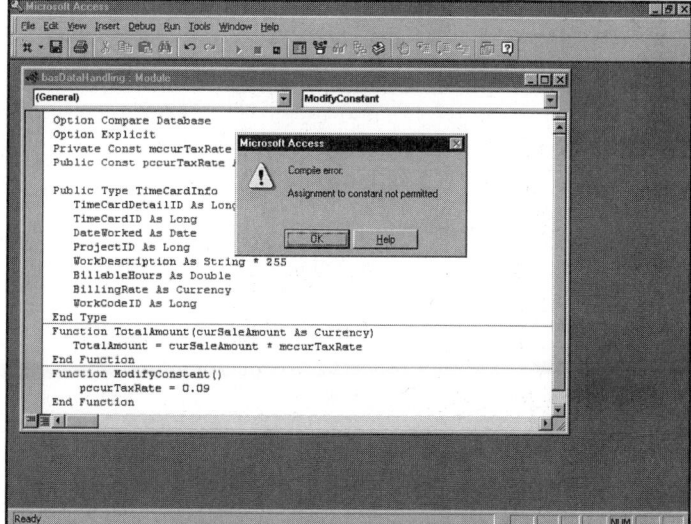

Working with Intrinsic Constants

Microsoft Access declares a number of intrinsic constants that can be used in Code, Form, and Report modules. Because they're reserved by Microsoft Access, you can't modify their values or reuse their names; however, they can be used at any time without being declared.

You should use intrinsic constants whenever possible in your code. Besides making your code more readable, they make your code more portable to future releases of Microsoft Access. Microsoft might change the value associated with a constant, but it isn't likely to change the constant's name. All intrinsic constants appear in the Object Browser; to activate it, simply click the Object Browser tool on the Visual Basic toolbar. To view the constants that are part of the VBA language, select VBA from the Object Browser's Project/Library drop-down list. Click Constants in the Classes list box, and a list of those constants are displayed in the "Members of 'Constants'" list box. (See Figure 9.10.)

In the list shown in Figure 9.10, all the constant names begin with *vb*. All VBA constants are prefixed with *vb*, all Data Access Object constants are prefixed with *db*, and all constants that are part of the Access language are prefixed with *ac*. To view the Access language constants, select Access from the Project/Library drop-down list and Constants from the Classes list box. To view the Data Access Object constants, select DAO from the Project/Library drop-down list. The constants are categorized by their function into various classes (for example, DAOCollatingOrderConstants, DAOCursorDriverConstants). Select the appropriate class from the Classes list box, and its members appear in the "Members of..." list box.

Figure 9.10.

Using the Object Browser to view intrinsic constants.

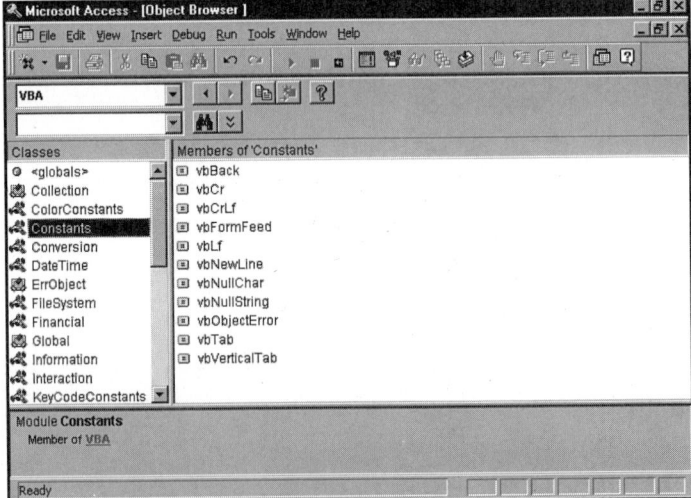

Another way to view constants is within the context of the parameter you're working with in the Code window. Right-click after the name of a parameter and select List Constants to display the constants associated with the parameter. This feature is covered in detail in Chapter 8.

Working with Arrays

An *array* is a series of variables referred to by the same name. Each element of the array is differentiated by a unique index number, but all the elements must be of the same data type. Arrays help make coding more efficient. It's easy to loop through each element of an array, performing some process on each element. Arrays have a lower bound, which is zero by default, and an upper bound, and all array elements must be contiguous.

The scope of an array can be Public, Module, or Local. As with other variables, this depends on where the array is declared and whether the Public, Private, or Dim keyword is used.

Declaring and Working with Fixed Arrays

When declaring a *fixed array*, you give VBA the upper bound and the type of data it will contain. The following code creates an array that holds six string variables:

```
Dim astrNames(5) As String
```

Fixed means that this array's size can't be altered at runtime. The following code gives an example of how you can loop through the array:

```
Sub FixedArray()
    Dim astrNames(5) As String
    Dim intCounter As Integer
    astrNames(0) = "Dan"
    astrNames(1) = "Reggie"
    astrNames(2) = "Alexis"
    astrNames(3) = "Joshua"
    For intCounter = 0 To UBound(astrNames)
        Debug.Print astrNames(intCounter)
    Next intCounter
End Sub
```

This code starts by storing values into the first four elements of a six-element array. It then loops through each element of the array, printing the contents. Notice that the For...Next loop starts at zero and goes until the upper bound of the array, which is (5). Because the array is made up of strings, the last two elements of the array contain zero-length strings. If the array were composed of integers, the last two elements would contain zeros.

Another way to traverse the array is to use the `For Each...Next` construct. Your code would look like this:

```
Sub ArrayWith()
    Dim astrNames(5) As String
    Dim intCounter As Integer
    Dim vntAny As Variant
    astrNames(0) = "Dan"
    astrNames(1) = "Reggie"
    astrNames(2) = "Alexis"
    astrNames(3) = "Joshua"
    For Each vntAny In astrNames
        Debug.Print vntAny
    Next vntAny
End Sub
```

This code declares a Variant variable called `vntAny`. Instead of using a loop with `Ubound` as the upper delimiter to traverse the array, the example uses the `For Each...Next` construct.

Declaring and Working with Dynamic Arrays

Often, you don't know how many elements your array needs. In this case, you should consider declaring a *dynamic array*, which can be resized at runtime. Using this type of array can make your code more efficient because VBA preallocates memory for all elements of a fixed array, regardless of whether data is stored in each of the elements. However, if you aren't sure how many elements your array will contain, preallocating a huge amount of memory can be quite inefficient.

To create a dynamic array, you declare it without assigning an upper bound. You do this by omitting the number between the parentheses when declaring the array, as shown in this example:

```
Sub DynamicArray()
    Dim astrNames() As String
    Dim intCounter As Integer
    Dim vntAny As Variant
    ReDim astrNames(1)
    astrNames(0) = "Dan"
    astrNames(1) = "Reggie"
    For Each vntAny In astrNames
        Debug.Print vntAny
    Next vntAny
End Sub
```

However, there's a potential problem when you try to resize the array:

```
Sub ResizeDynamic()
    Dim astrNames() As String
    Dim intCounter As Integer
    Dim vntAny As Variant
    ReDim astrNames(1)
    astrNames(0) = "Dan"
    astrNames(1) = "Reggie"
```

```
    ReDim astrNames(3)
    astrNames(2) = "Alexis"
    astrNames(3) = "Joshua"
    For Each vntAny In astrNames
        Debug.Print vntAny
    Next vntAny
End Sub
```

You might expect that all four elements will contain data. Instead, the `ReDim` statement reinitializes all the elements, and only elements two and three contain values. This problem can be avoided by using the `Preserve` keyword. The following code behaves quite differently:

```
Sub ResizePreserve()
    Dim astrNames() As String
    Dim intCounter As Integer
    Dim vntAny As Variant
    ReDim astrNames(1)
    astrNames(0) = "Dan"
    astrNames(1) = "Reggie"
    ReDim Preserve astrNames(3)
    astrNames(2) = "Alexis"
    astrNames(3) = "Joshua"
    For Each vntAny In astrNames
        Debug.Print vntAny
    Next vntAny
End Sub
```

In this example, all values already stored in the array are preserved. The `Preserve` keyword brings its own difficulties, though. It can temporarily require huge volumes of memory because during the `ReDim` process, VBA creates a copy of the original array. All the values from the original array are copied to a new array. The original array is removed from memory when the process is complete. The `Preserve` keyword can cause problems if you're dealing with very large arrays in a limited memory situation.

> **TIP**
>
> Each type of array complements the other's drawbacks. As a VBA developer, you have the flexibility of choosing the right type of array for each situation. Fixed arrays are the way to go when the number of elements doesn't vary widely, but dynamic arrays should be used when the number varies widely and you're sure you have enough memory to resize even the largest possible arrays.

Advanced Function Techniques

The advanced function techniques covered in this section allow you to get the most out of the procedures you build. First, you learn the difference between passing your parameters by reference and passing them by value, and see that the default method of passing parameters isn't necessarily the most prudent method.

The second part of this section shows you how to work with optional parameters, which help you build flexibility into your functions. They let you omit parameters, but named parameters allow you to add readability to your code. Named parameters also shelter you from having to worry about the order in which the parameters must appear. After reading this section, you can build much more robust and easy-to-use functions.

Passing by Reference Versus Passing by Value

By default, parameters in Access are passed by reference. This means that a memory reference to the variable being passed is received by the function. This process is best illustrated by an example:

```
Sub PassByRef()
    Dim strFirstName As String
    Dim strLastName As String
    strFirstName = "Alison"
    strLastName = "Balter"
    Call FuncByRef(strFirstName, strLastName)
    Debug.Print strFirstName
    Debug.Print strLastName
End Sub
Sub FuncByRef(strFirstParm As String, strSecondParm As String)
    strFirstParm = "Bill"
    strSecondParm = "Gates"
End Sub
```

You might be surprised that the Debug.Print statements found in the subroutine PassByRef print "Bill" and "Gates". This is because strFirstParm is actually a reference to the same location in memory as strFirstName, and strSecondParm is a reference to the same location in memory as strLastName. This violates the concepts of *black-box processing*, in which a variable can't be changed by any routine other than the one it was declared in. The following code eliminates this problem:

```
Sub PassByVal()
    Dim strFirstName As String
    Dim strLastName As String
    strFirstName = "Alison"
    strLastName = "Balter"
    Call FuncByVal(strFirstName, strLastName)
    Debug.Print strFirstName
    Debug.Print strLastName
End Sub
Sub FuncByVal(ByVal strFirstParm As String, ByVal strSecondParm As String)
    strFirstParm = "Bill"
    strSecondParm = "Gates"
End Sub
```

This FuncByVal subroutine receives the parameters by value. This means that only the values in strFirstName and strLastName are passed to the FuncByVal routine. The strFirstName and strLastName variables, therefore, can't be modified by the FuncByVal subroutine. The Debug.Print statements print "Alison" and "Balter".

Although I try to avoid passing parameters by reference, sometimes it makes good sense to do so. Take a look at the following example:

```
Sub GoodPassByRef()
    Dim blnSuccess As Boolean
    Dim strName As String
    strName = "Microsoft"
    blnSuccess = GoodFunc(strName)
    Debug.Print blnSuccess
End Sub
Function GoodFunc(strName As String)
    If Len(strName) Then
        strName = UCase$(strName)
        GoodFunc = True
    Else
        GoodFunc = False
    End If
End Function
```

In essence, the GoodFunc function needs to return two values. Not only does the function need to return the uppercase version of the string passed to it, but it also needs to return a success code. Because a function can return only one value, you need to be able to modify the value of strName within the function. As long as you're aware of what you're doing and why you're doing it, there's no problem with passing a parameter by reference.

> **TIP**
>
> I use a special technique to help readers of my code see whether I'm passing parameters by reference or by value. When passing parameters by reference, I refer to the parameters by using the same name in both the calling routine and the actual procedure that I'm calling. On the other hand, when passing parameters by value, I refer to the parameters by using different names in the calling routine and in the procedure that's being called.

Optional Parameters: Building Flexibility into Functions

Access 97 allows you to use optional parameters. In other words, it isn't necessary to know how many parameters will be passed. The ReturnInit function in the following code receives the second two parameters as optional, then evaluates whether the parameters are missing and responds accordingly:

```
Function ReturnInit(ByVal strFName As String, _
        Optional ByVal strMI, Optional ByVal strLName)
    If IsMissing(strMI) Then
        strMI = InputBox("Enter Middle Initial")
    End If
    If IsMissing(strLName) Then
        strLName = InputBox("Enter Last Name")
    End If
    ReturnInit = strLName & "," & strFName & " " & strMI
End Function
```

This function could be called as follows:

```
strName = ReturnInit("Bill",,"Gates")
```

As you can see, the second parameter is missing. Rather than causing a compiler error, as in earlier versions of Access, this code compiles and runs successfully. The IsMissing function, built into Access, determines whether a parameter has been passed. After identifying missing parameters, you must decide how to handle the situation in code. In the example, the function prompts for the missing information, but here are some other possible choices:

- Insert default values when parameters are missing
- Somehow accommodate for the missing parameters in your code

The following two examples illustrate how to carry out these two alternatives:

Listing 9.1. Inserting default values when parameters are missing.

```
Function ReturnInit2(ByVal strFName As String, _
     Optional ByVal strMI, Optional ByVal strLName)
   If IsMissing(strMI) Then
      strMI = "B"
   End If
   If IsMissing(strLName) Then
      strLName = "Jones"
   End If
   ReturnInit2 = strLName & "," & strFName & " " & strMI
End Function
```

This example uses a default value of "B" for the middle initial and a default last name of "Jones". Now take a look at Listing 9.2, which illustrates another method of handling missing parameters.

Listing 9.2. Accommodating for missing parameters in your code.

```
Function ReturnInit3(ByVal strFName As String, _
     Optional ByVal strMI, Optional ByVal strLName)
   Dim strResult As String
   If IsMissing(strMI) And IsMissing(strLName) Then
      ReturnInit3 = strFName
   ElseIf IsMissing(strMI) Then
      ReturnInit3 = strLName & ", " & strFName
   ElseIf IsMissing(strLName) Then
      ReturnInit3 = strFName & " " & strMI
   Else
      ReturnInit3 = strLName & "," & strFName & " " & strMI
   End If
End Function
```

This example manipulates the return value, depending on which parameters it receives. If neither optional parameter is passed, just the first name displays. If the first name and middle initial are passed, the return value contains the first name followed by the middle initial. If the first name and last name are passed, the return value contains the last name, a comma, and the first name. If all three parameters are passed, the function returns the last name, a comma, a space, and the first name.

Named Parameters: Eliminate the Need to Count Commas

In all the examples you've seen so far, the parameters to a procedure have been supplied positionally. Named parameters allow you to supply parameters without regard for their position, which is particularly useful with procedures that receive optional parameters. Take a look at this example:

```
strName = ReturnInit("Bill",,"Gates")
```

Because the second parameter isn't supplied, and the parameters are passed positionally, a comma must be used as a placemarker for the optional parameter. This requirement can become unwieldy when you're dealing with several optional parameters. The following example greatly simplifies the process of passing the parameters and also better documents what's happening:

```
strName = ReturnInit3(strFName:= "Bill",strLName:= "Gates")
```

When parameters are passed by name, it doesn't even matter in what order the parameters appear, as shown in the following example:

```
strName = ReturnInit3(strLName:= "Gates",strFName:="Bill")
```

This call to the ReturnInit3 function yields the same results as the call to the function in the previous example.

> **NOTE**
>
> When using named parameters, each parameter name must be exactly the same as the name of the parameter in the function being called. Besides requiring thorough knowledge of the function being called, this method of specifying parameters has one important disadvantage: If the author of the function modifies a parameter's name, all routines that use the named parameter when calling the function will fail.

Property Let and Get: Working with Custom Properties

With property procedures, you can create custom runtime properties of user-defined objects. After you have defined custom properties, you can use `Property Let` and `Get` to assign values to and retrieve values from custom properties. Custom properties give you more flexibility in creating your applications; you can create reusable objects that expose properties to other objects.

Custom properties are Public by default and are placed in Class, Form, or Report modules, making them visible to other modules in the current database. They aren't visible to other databases.

Property Let

The `Property Let` routine defines a property procedure that assigns a value to a user-defined object's property. Using a `Property Let` is similar to assigning a value to a Public variable, but a Public variable can be written to from anywhere in the database, with little or no control over what's written to it. With a `Property Let` routine, you can control exactly what happens when a value is assigned to the property. Here's an example:

```
Property Let TextEnabled(blnEnabled As Boolean)
    Dim ctl As Control
    For Each ctl In Controls
        If TypeOf ctl Is TextBox Then
            ctl.Enabled = blnEnabled
        End If
    Next ctl
End Property
```

This routine receives a Boolean parameter. It loops through each control in the controls collection, setting the Enabled property of each text box to `True` or `False`, depending on the value of the Boolean variable that was passed to it. You might be thinking this code looks just like a subroutine, and you're somewhat correct. It's a special type of subroutine that executes automatically in response to the change in a custom property's value. The following line of code causes the code in the `Property Let` to execute:

```
Me.TextEnabled = False
```

The value `False` is received as a parameter to the `Property Let` routine, so all the text boxes become disabled. The TextEnabled property of the form can be called from any module in the database, causing the `Property Let` routine to execute.

Property Get

`Property Let` sets the value of a custom property, but `Property Get` defines a property procedure that retrieves a value from a user-defined object's property. This example illustrates how `Property Get` is used:

```
Property Get TextBoxValues()
   Dim ctl As Control
   For Each ctl In Controls
      If TypeOf ctl Is TextBox Then
         TextBoxValues = TextBoxValues & ctl.Name & _
            " = " & ctl.Value & Chr(13)
      End If
   Next ctl
End Property
```

The Property Get routine loops through each control on the form. It retrieves the name and value of each text box, building a return value that's a concatenated string with the names and values of all the text boxes. The call to the Property Get routine looks like this:

```
MsgBox Me.TextBoxValues
```

When the MsgBox command executes, it retrieves the value of the form's TextBoxValues property. The Property Get routine automatically executes whenever the code tries to retrieve the value of the property. This routine can be executed by retrieving the property from anywhere in the database.

Class Modules

Access 97 offers two types of modules: standard modules and class modules. Access 95 introduced class modules for forms and reports, but Access 97 is the first version of Access to offer the ability to create class modules from the Database window. To create a class module, simply choose Insert | Class Module.

A class module is similar to a code module. The subroutines and functions in the class module become the methods of the class. The Property Let and Property Get routines become the properties of the class, and the class module's name becomes the name of the custom object. A class module is a great way to encapsulate related functions into a portable, self-contained object.

Say that you regularly open databases and recordsets and traverse those recordsets by using code. You have decided that you want to simplify performing all the functions needed for these tasks. By building class modules, you can make accessing the table data much simpler. The class called clsRecordsets has eight methods:

- **OpenDB:** Opens the database
- **OpenRS:** Opens the recordset
- **GoTop:** Moves to the top of the recordset
- **GoPrev:** Moves to the previous record
- **GoNext:** Moves to the next record
- **GoBott:** Moves to the bottom of the recordset
- **GetFieldValue:** Gets the value from the first field of the current record
- **CleanUp:** Closes the database and recordset objects

265

Listing 9.3 shows you what the methods of the `clsRecordsets` class look like:

Listing 9.3. The methods for `clsRecordsets`.

```
Public Function OpenDB()
    'Point module level workspace variable at first workspace
    Set mWS = DBEngine.Workspaces(0)
    'Point module level workspace variable to the database with the
    'name specified in the DBName property
    Set mDB = mWS.OpenDatabase(mDBName)
End Function
Public Function OpenRS()
    'Point recordet variable to the recordset name
    'contained in the RSName property
    Set mRS = mDB.OpenRecordset(Name:=mRSName)
End Function
Public Function GoTop()
    'Move to the first record in the recordset
    mRS.MoveFirst
End Function
Public Function GoBott()
    'Move to the last record in the recordset
    mRS.MoveLast
End Function
Public Function GoPrev()
    'Check for beginning of file
    'If not at beginning of file, move to the
    'previous record.  If still not at beginning
    'of file, return true. Otherwise, move next and
    'return false
    If Not mRS.BOF Then
        mRS.MovePrevious
        If mRS.BOF Then
            mRS.MoveNext
            GoPrev = False
        Else
            GoPrev = True
        End If
    Else
        GoPrev = False
    End If
End Function
Public Function GoNext()
    'Check for end of file
    'If not at end of file, move to the
    'next record.  If still not at end
    'of file, return true. Otherwise, move previous and
    'return false
    If Not mRS.EOF Then
        mRS.MoveNext
        If mRS.EOF Then
            mRS.MovePrevious
            GoNext = False
        Else
            GoNext = True
        End If
```

```
    Else
        GoNext = False
    End If
End Function
Public Function GetFieldValue()
    'Return the value from the first field of the
    'current record
    GetFieldValue = mRS.Fields(0).Value
End Function
Public Function CleanUp()
    'Close recordset and database objects
    mRS.Close
    mDB.Close
End Function
```

The eight methods are explained by the comments in each method. Several methods require the values of properties contained in the class. These properties are DBName and RSName; their declarations are as follows:

```
Public Property Let DBName(ByVal strDBName As String)
    mDBName = strDBName
End Property
Public Property Let RSName(ByVal strRSName As String)
    mRSName = strRSName
End Property
```

Notice that each Property Let receives a string as a parameter and sets a module-level variable equal to that string. The idea is that only the properties are exposed to the outside world. The module-level variables used by the class methods are protected by the Property Let procedures. The Property Let procedures can easily be enhanced to validate the parameters or to manipulate their values before they're placed in the module-level variables. The following module-level variables are declared in the module's General Declarations section; they're all used by the methods of the class:

```
Private mWS As Workspace
Private mDB As Database
Private mRS As Recordset
Private mDBName As String
Private mRSName As String
```

The mWS, mDB, and mRS variables are set in the class methods, and the mDBName and mRSName variables are set by using the Property Let routines.

The class is used to contain all the functionality needed to access and manipulate recordset data. Once you have created the class, it's easy for a routine in a standard module to call the class methods and to set the class properties. The TraverseRecordSet method in basRecordsets illustrates how to use the clsRecordsets class. It looks like this:

```
Sub TraverseRecordSet()
    clsRecordsets.DBName = CurrentDb.Name
    clsRecordsets.RSName = "tblClients"
    clsRecordsets.OpenDB
```

```
    clsRecordsets.OpenRS
    Debug.Print clsRecordsets.GetFieldValue
    Do While clsRecordsets.GoNext()
        Debug.Print clsRecordsets.GetFieldValue
    Loop
    clsRecordsets.CleanUp
End Sub
```

The routine begins by setting the DBName property of the clsRecordsets class to the name of the current database. This has the indirect effect of setting the mDBName variable in the class to the name of the current database. It then sets the RSName property of the class to tblClients, which has the indirect effect of setting the mRSName variable in the class to tblClients. Next, the OpenDB method of the class is issued, opening the database specified in the DBName property. The OpenRS method of the class opens the recordset found in the RSName property. The GoNext method of the class is called recursively until it returns a False because no further records can be found. After the GoNext method is called, the GetFieldValue method is called to get the value from the first field in the record. Finally, the CleanUp method is called to close the recordset and database object.

This example illustrates how you can create custom methods that help you through the complexities of the task at hand. Whenever you want to take advantage of the functionality supplied by the class, you simply set the class properties and call the class methods.

Working with Empty and Null

Empty and Null are values that can exist only for Variant variables. They're different from one another and different from zero or a zero-length string. At times, you need to know whether the value stored in a variable is zero, a zero-length string, Empty, or Null. You can make this differentiation only with Variant variables.

Working with Empty

Variant variables are initialized to the value of Empty. Often, you need to know whether a value has been stored in a Variant variable. If a Variant has never been assigned a value, its value is Empty. As mentioned, the Empty value is not the same as zero, Null, or a zero-length string.

It's important to be able to test for Empty in a runtime environment. This can be done by using the IsEmpty function, which determines whether a variable has the Empty value. The following example tests a String variable for the Empty value:

```
Sub StringVar()
    Dim sName As String
    Debug.Print IsEmpty(sName) 'Prints False
    Debug.Print sName = "" 'Prints True
End Sub
```

The `Debug.Print` statement prints `False`. This variable is equal to a zero-length string because the variable is initialized as a String variable. All String variables are initialized to a zero-length string. The next example tests a Variant variable to see whether it has the `Empty` value:

```
Sub EmptyVar()
    Dim vntName As Variant
    Debug.Print IsEmpty(vntName) 'Prints True
    vntName = ""
    Debug.Print IsEmpty(vntName) 'Prints False
    vntName = Empty
    Debug.Print IsEmpty(vntName) 'Prints True
End Sub
```

A Variant variable loses its `Empty` value when any value has been stored in it, including zero, `Null`, or a zero-length string. It can become `Empty` again only by storing the keyword `Empty` in the variable.

Working with `Null`

`Null` is a special value that indicates unknown or missing data. `Null` is not the same as `Empty`, nor is one `Null` value equal to another one. Variant variables can contain the special value called `Null`.

Often, you need to know whether specific fields or controls have ever been initialized. Uninitialized fields and controls have a default value of `Null`. By testing for `Null`, you can make sure fields and controls contain values.

If you want to make sure that all fields and controls in your application have data, you need to test for `Null`s. This can be done by using the `IsNull` function:

```
Sub NullVar()
    Dim vntName As Variant
    Debug.Print IsEmpty(vntName) 'Prints True
    Debug.Print IsNull(vntName) 'Prints False
    vntName = Null
    Debug.Print IsNull(vntName) 'Prints True
End Sub
```

Notice that `vntName` is equal to `Null` only after the value of `Null` is explicitly stored in it. It's important to know not only how variables and `Null` values interact, but also how to test for `Null` within a field in your database. A field contains a `Null` if data hasn't yet been entered in the field and the field has no default value. In queries, you can test for the criteria `"Is Null"` to find all the records in which a particular field contains a Null value. When dealing with recordsets (covered in Chapter 15, "What Are Data Access Objects and Why Are They Important?"), you can also use the `IsNull` function to test for a `Null` value in a field. Here's an example:

```
Sub LoopProjects()
    Dim db As DATABASE
    Dim rs As Recordset
```

```
   Set db = CurrentDb
   Set rs = db.OpenRecordset("tblProjects", dbOpenDynaset)
   Do While Not rs.EOF
      Debug.Print rs![ProjectID], rs![ProjectName]
      If IsNull(rs!ProjectBeginDate) Then
        Debug.Print "Project Begin Date Contains No Value!!"
      End If
      rs.MoveNext
   Loop
End Sub
```

All the concepts of recordset handling are covered in Chapter 15. For now, you need to understand only that this code loops through each record in tblProjects. It uses the IsNull function to evaluate whether the ProjectBeginDate field contains a Null value. If the field does contain a Null, a warning message is printed to the Debug window:

```
Private Sub Form_Current()
   Dim ctl As Control
   For Each ctl In Controls
      If TypeOf ctl Is TextBox Then
         If IsNull(ctl.Value) Then
            ctl.BackColor = 16776960
         Else
            ctl.BackColor = 16777215
         End If
      End If
   Next ctl
End Sub
```

The code in this example (found in the frmProjects form in CHAP9EX.MDB) loops through every control on the current form. If the control is a text box, the routine checks to see whether the value in the text box is Null. If it is, the BackColor property of the text box is set to Aqua; otherwise, it's set to White.

You should know about some idiosyncrasies of Null:

- Expressions involving Null always result in Null. (See the next example.)
- A function that's passed a Null usually returns a Null.
- Null values propagate through built-in functions that return variants.

The following example shows how Null values are propagated:

```
Sub PropNulls()
   Dim db As DATABASE
   Dim rs As Recordset
   Set db = CurrentDb
   Set rs = db.OpenRecordset("tblProjects", dbOpenDynaset)
   Do While Not rs.EOF
      Debug.Print rs![ProjectID], rs![ProjectBeginDate] + 1
      rs.MoveNext
   Loop
End Sub
```

9

Figure 9.11 illustrates the effects of running this routine on a table in which the first and third records contain Null values. Notice that the result of the calculation is Null for those records because the Null propagated within those records.

Figure 9.11.
The result of running the
PropNulls *routine.*

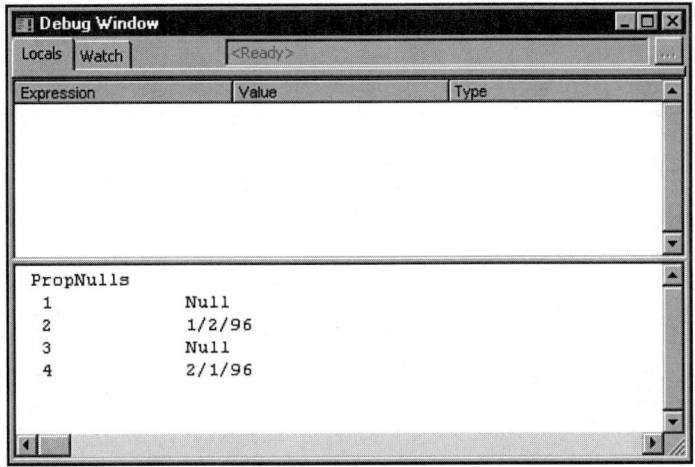

Notice the difference if the value in the field is Empty:

```
Sub EmptyVersusNull()
    Dim db As DATABASE
    Dim rs As Recordset
    Set db = CurrentDb
    Set rs = db.OpenRecordset("tblProjects", dbOpenDynaset)
    Do While Not rs.EOF
        Debug.Print rs![ProjectID], rs![PurchaseOrderNumber] + "Hello"
        rs.MoveNext
    Loop
End Sub
```

In this example, the tblProjects table has four records. The PurchaseOrderNumber for the first record contains a Null; for the third record, it contains an Empty. Notice the different effects of the two values, as shown in Figure 9.12.

Looking at Figure 9.12, you can see that Null printed for the first record, and Hello printed for the third record.

> **NOTE**
>
> The EmptyVersusNull routine uses a numeric operator (+). As discussed, the effect of Null used in a calculation is a resulting Null. In text strings, you can use an ampersand (&) instead of a plus (+) to eliminate this problem. Figure 9.13 illustrates the same code with an ampersand to concatenate rather than add. You can see that no Null values result from the concatenation.

271

Figure 9.12.

The result of running the EmptyVersusNull *routine.*

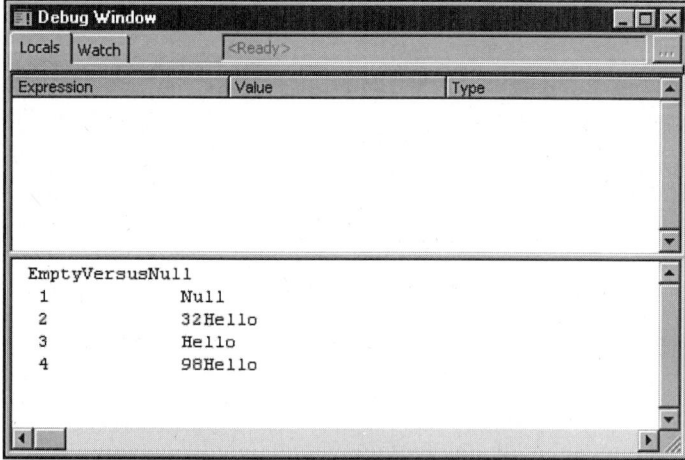

Figure 9.13.

The result of changing plus (+) in the EmptyVersusNull *routine to ampersand (&).*

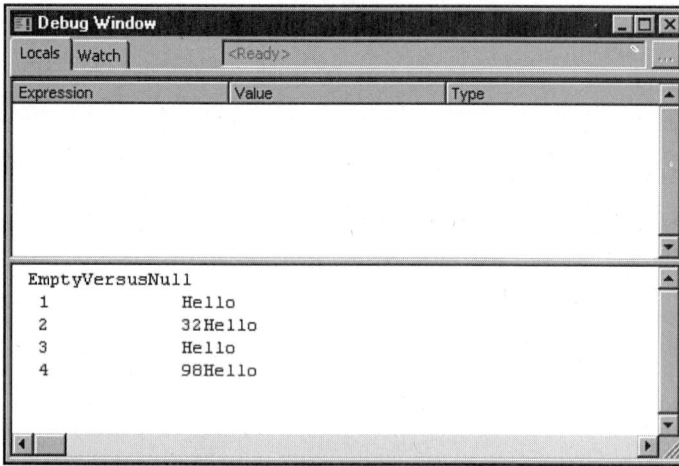

It's very common to create a generic routine that receives any value, tests to see whether it's Null, and returns a non-Null value. An example is the CvNulls function:

```
Function CvNulls(vntVar1 As Variant, vntVar2 As Variant) _
    As Variant
    CvNulls = IIf(IsNull(vntVar1), vntVar2, vntVar1)
End Function
```

This routine would be called as follows:

```
Sub TestForNull(vntSalary As Variant, vntCommission As Variant)
    Dim curTotal As Currency
    curTotal = CvNulls(vntSalary, 0) + CvNulls(vntCommission, 0)
    MsgBox curTotal
End Sub
```

The `TestForNull` routine receives two parameters: `salary` and `commission`. It adds the two values to determine the total of salaries plus commissions. Ordinarily, if the value of either parameter is `Null`, the expression results in `Null`. This problem is eliminated by the `CvNulls` function, which also receives two parameters. The first parameter is the variable being tested for `Null`; the second is the value you want the function to return if the first parameter is determined to be `Null`. The routine combines the Immediate If (`IIf`) function and the `IsNull` function to evaluate the first parameter and return the appropriate value.

Understanding and Effectively Using Compilation Options

Microsoft Access gives you a few alternatives for compilation. Understanding them can help you decide whether compilation speed or trapping compilation errors is more important to you.

Compile On Demand

By default, VBA compiles your code only when the code in the module changes or when a procedure in one module is called by another module. Although this default setting can dramatically speed up the compilation process, it can also leave you wondering whether you have a hidden timebomb lurking somewhere in your application.

Here's a typical scenario: You open a form, make some simple changes, save the changes, and close the form. You repeat this process for a few additional forms. You also open a couple of modules to make some equally simple changes. During the testing process, you forget to test one or more of the forms and one or more of the modules. With the Compile On Demand option set to `True` (its default value), errors aren't identified until the offending code is accessed.

To disable the Compile On Demand feature, choose Tools | Options. Click the Module tab and remove the check from Compile On Demand. You might notice some degradation in performance each time your code compiles, but this is time well spent.

Compile Loaded Modules

Whether the Compile On Demand feature is on or off, the Compile Loaded Modules tool, found on the Visual Basic toolbar, compiles only loaded modules. This means that all open Access, Form, and Report modules are compiled, but the code in any closed modules, forms, and reports is *not* compiled. If an error is found in any open module, the compilation process terminates, an error message is displayed, and your cursor is placed on the offending line of code.

Compile All Modules

The Compile All Modules and Compile and Save All Modules features are found under the Debug menu. These menu items, when selected, compile every module in the database, regardless of whether it's open.

The Compile and Save All Modules selection takes an additional step and saves all code in the database in its fully compiled state. This procedure not only ensures that the modules compile successfully, it makes sure they're saved in their compiled state so that they don't need to be compiled again when the application is run.

Customizing the IDE

Before Access 95, Access programmers had little opportunity to customize the look and behavior of the interactive development environment (IDE). Fortunately, Access 95 and Access 97 offer major improvements in this area. To view the environment options, choose Tools | Options, then click the Module tab. Figure 9.14 shows the Module tab of the Options dialog box; its different aspects are discussed in detail in the rest of this section.

Figure 9.14.

The Module tab of the Options dialog box.

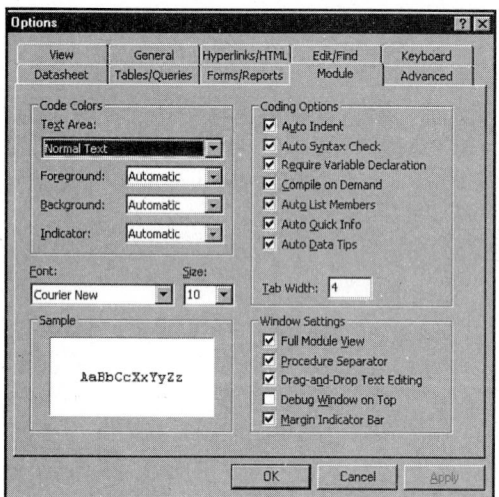

Code Color, Fonts, and Sizes

In Access 97, you can customize code colors, font, size, and tab width within the coding environment. You can also specify the foreground and background colors for the Code window text, selection text, syntax error text, comment text, keyword text, and more. You can select from any of the Windows fonts and sizes for the text in the Code window. Finally, you can specify how many characters your text is indented each time the Tab key is pressed.

Coding Options

The coding options available to you include Auto Indent, Auto Syntax Check, Require Variable Declaration, Compile On Demand (discussed in the previous section), Auto List Members, Auto Quick Info, and Auto Data Tips. The Auto Indent feature invokes the automatic indenting of successive lines of code. This means that when you indent one line, all other lines are indented to the same position until you specify otherwise.

The Auto Syntax Check feature determines whether Access performs a syntax check each time you press Enter after typing a single line of code. Many developers find this option annoying. It's not uncommon to type a line of code and notice a typo in a previous line of code, so you want to rectify the error before you forget. You move off the incomplete line of code you're typing, only to get an error message that your syntax is incorrect. Although I find this aspect of Auto Syntax Check annoying, I would still rather identify any syntax errors sooner instead of later.

The Require Variable Declaration option is a must. If this option is turned on, all variables must be declared before they are used. This important feature, when set, places the Option Explicit line in the Declarations section of every module. You're then forced to declare all variables before they're used. Many innocent typos are identified by the compiler at compile time rather than by your users at runtime.

The Auto List Members option determines whether the List Properties/Methods and List Constants features are automatically invoked as you type code in the Code window. They help you in your coding endeavors by presenting a valid list of properties, methods, and constants. For more about these features, see Chapter 8.

The Auto Quick Info feature determines whether the syntax of a procedure or method is automatically displayed. If this option is selected, the syntax information is displayed as soon as you type a procedure or method name followed by a space, period, or opening parenthesis.

The Auto Data Tips feature is used when you're debugging. It displays the current value of a selected value when you place your mouse pointer over the variable in Break mode. This feature is discussed in Chapter 16, "Debugging: Your Key to Successful Development."

Practical Examples: Putting Advanced Techniques to Use in the Time and Billing Application

The Time and Billing application will put into practice all that you have learned throughout this chapter. The following examples cover the use of Null, the DoCmd object, intrinsic constants, and type structure.

Examples of Null, the DoCmd Object, and Intrinsic Constants

The following event routine is used to view all the projects associated with the selected client. It illustrates the importance of the ability to work with Null values, the DoCmd object, and intrinsic constants.

```
Private Sub cmdProjects_Click()
On Error GoTo Err_Projects_Click
    If IsNull(Me![txtClientID]) Then
        MsgBox "Enter client information before viewing projects form."
    Else
        DoCmd.RunCommand Command:=acSaveRecord
        DoCmd.OpenForm "frmProjects", , , "[ClientID]=" & [txtClientID]
    End If
Exit_Projects_Click:
    Exit Sub
Err_Projects_Click:
    MsgBox Err.Description
    Resume Exit_Projects_Click
End Sub
```

The routine first invokes error handling (discussed in Chapter 17, "Handling Those Dreaded Runtime Errors"), then uses the IsNull function to test whether a ClientID has been entered. The IsNull function returns a True if the value in the txtClientID control is Null. If it is, an error message is displayed. If the txtClientID control contains a non-Null value, two methods are performed on the DoCmd object.

The first method performed on the DoCmd object is the RunCommand method. This method receives the constant associated with the name of the menu command you want to execute. The use of intrinsic constants makes this code more readable, and the RunCommand method makes it much easier now to call menu commands from code.

The second method performed on the DoCmd object is `OpenForm`, which opens the frmProjects form. Two optional parameters, `View` and `FilterName`, are omitted. The fourth parameter, the `WhereCondition`, is set to the ClientID that's displayed on the Client form.

An Example of Using a Type Structure

Many parts of the Time and Billing application require the company information stored in the tblCompanyInfo table. It would be inefficient to read the data from this table each time the application needs it. It would be much more efficient to read this data once, when the application loads, and store it in a type structure. Because it remains in memory at all times, you can efficiently retrieve it whenever needed. The type structure is defined and a Public Type variable based on the type structure is declared in a module's Declarations section. It looks like this:

```
Type CompanyInfo
    SetUpID As Long
    CompanyName As String * 50
    Address As String * 255
    City As String * 50
    StateProvince As String * 20
    PostalCode As String * 20
    Country As String * 50
    PhoneNumber As String * 30
    FaxNumber As String * 30
    DefaultPaymentTerms As String * 255
    DefaultInvoiceDescription As String
End Type
Public typCompanyInfo As CompanyInfo
```

A subroutine is invoked when the client form (your startup form) is first loaded. This routine populates all the elements of the type structure. The routine looks like this:

```
Sub GetCompanyInfo()
    Dim db As DATABASE
    Dim rs As Recordset
    Set db = CurrentDb
    Set rs = db.OpenRecordset("tblCompanyInfo", dbOpenSnapshot)
    typCompanyInfo.SetUpID = rs!SetUpID
    typCompanyInfo.CompanyName = rs!CompanyName
    typCompanyInfo.Address = rs!Address
    typCompanyInfo.City = rs!City
    typCompanyInfo.StateProvince = rs!StateProvince
    typCompanyInfo.PostalCode = rs!PostalCode
    typCompanyInfo.Country = rs!Country
    typCompanyInfo.PhoneNumber = rs!PhoneNumber
    typCompanyInfo.FaxNumber = rs!PhoneNumber
    rs.Close
    db.Close
End Sub
```

Don't be concerned with the recordset handling included in this routine. Instead, notice that the value from each field in the first (and only) record of the tblCompanyInfo table is being loaded into the elements of the Global Type variable. Here's an example of how the Type variable is used:

```
Sub PopulateControls()
    txtCompanyName.Value = Trim(typCompanyInfo.CompanyName)
    txtAddress.Value = Trim(typCompanyInfo.Address)
    txtCityStateZip.Value = Trim(typCompanyInfo.City) & ", " & _
        Trim(typCompanyInfo.StateProvince) & _
        " " & Format(Trim(typCompanyInfo.PostalCode), "!&&&&&-&&&&")
    txtPhoneFax.Value = "PHONE: " & _
        Format(Trim(typCompanyInfo.PhoneNumber), "(&&&)&&&-&&&&") & _
        "      FAX: " & _
        Format(Trim(typCompanyInfo.FaxNumber), "(&&&)&&&-&&&&")
End Sub
```

This routine is called by the Activate event of rptInvoice. It populates four different controls on the form with the company information retrieved from the elements of the Global Type variable.

Summary

As an Access developer, you spend much of your time writing VBA code. Knowing the tricks and tips of the trade and understanding the more advanced aspects of the language will save you much time and help you streamline your application code.

This chapter has shown you tricks and tips you can use to help you effectively navigate the VBA environment and delved into more advanced aspects of the VBA language, such as the DoCmd object, user-defined types, constants, and arrays. You have seen the important difference between passing parameters by reference and passing them by value, and learned about other advanced function techniques, such as optional and named parameters. Other important topics covered in this chapter include Property Let and Property Get, classes modules, collections, Empty versus Null, and compilation options. Understanding these valuable aspects of the VBA language will help you get the most out of the code you write.

10

CHAPTER

The Real Scoop on Objects, Properties, and Events

- Understanding Access's Object Model, 280
- The Forms Collection, 280
- Understanding Objects, Properties, Events, and Methods, 282
- Using the Object Browser to Learn About Access's Objects, 286
- Referring to Objects, 288
- Properties and Methods Made Easy, 289
- Declaring and Assigning Object Variables, 291
- Understanding the Differences Between Objects and Collections, 293
- Using the New Keyword, 297
- Passing Objects to Functions and Subroutines, 298
- Returning to a Unique Item in a Collection, 299
- Determining the Type of a Control, 300
- Special Properties That Refer to Objects, 301
- Practical Examples of Working with Objects, 302

10

Understanding Access's Object Model

Objects are the components of a database. They include the tables, queries, forms, reports, macros, and modules that appear in the database window. They also include the controls (text boxes, list boxes, and so on) on a form or report. The key to successful programming lies in your ability to manipulate the database objects by using VBA code at runtime. It's also very useful to be able to add, modify, and remove application objects at runtime.

The Application Object

An overview of the superficial Access Object Model is shown in Figure 10.1. At the top of the model, you can see the Application object, which refers to the active Access application. It contains all of Access's other objects and collections, including the Forms collection, the Reports collection, the Modules collection, the Screen object, and the DoCmd object. The Application object can be used to modify the properties of, or execute commands on, the Access application itself, such as specifying whether Access's built-in toolbars are available while the application is running.

Figure 10.1.

An overview of Access's superficial objects.

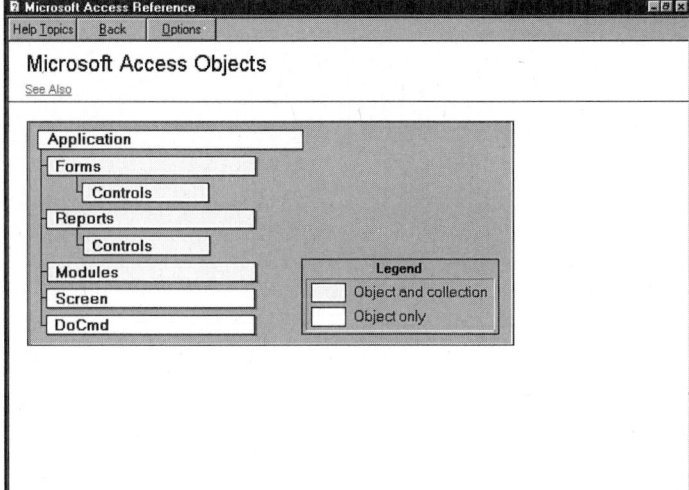

The Forms Collection

The Forms collection contains all the currently open forms in the database. Using the Forms collection, you can perform an action, such as changing the color, on each open form.

The Reports Collection

Just as the Forms collection contains all the currently open forms, the Reports collection contains all the currently open reports. Using the Reports collection, you can perform an action on each open report.

The Modules Collection

The Modules collection contains all the standard and class modules that are open. All open modules are included in the Modules collection, regardless of whether they're compiled and whether they contain code that's currently running.

The Screen Object

The Screen object can be used to refer to the form, report, or control that has the focus. The Screen object contains properties that refer to the active form, active report, active control, and previous control. Using these properties, you can manipulate the currently active form, report, or control, as well as the control that was active just before the current control. If you try to refer to the Screen object when no form or report is active, a runtime error occurs.

The DoCmd Object

The DoCmd object is used to perform macro commands or Access actions from VBA code; it's followed by a period and the name of an action. Most of the DoCmd actions—the OpenQuery action, for example—also require arguments. The OpenQuery action is used to execute an Access query. It receives the following arguments:

- **Query Name:** The name of the query you want to execute
- **View:** Normal, design, or preview
- **Data Mode:** Add, edit, or read only

Here's an example of the OpenQuery action of the DoCmd object:

```
DoCmd.OpenQuery "qryCustomers", acNormal, acReadOnly
```

The OpenQuery action is performed by the DoCmd object. The first argument, the query name, is "qryCustomers". This is the name of the query that's opened in Datasheet view (rather than Design view or Print preview). It's opened in read-only mode, meaning the resulting data can't be modified.

Understanding Objects, Properties, Events, and Methods

Many people, especially those used to a procedural language, don't understand the concept of objects, properties, and events. You need a thorough knowledge of Access's objects, their properties, and the events each object can respond to if you want to be a productive and successful Access programmer.

What Exactly Are Objects?

As mentioned earlier in this chapter, *objects* are all the things that make up your database. They include tables, queries, forms, reports, macros, and modules, as well as the components of those objects. For example, a Table object contains Field and Index objects. A Form contains various controls (text boxes, combo boxes, list boxes, and so on). Each object in the database has specific properties that determine its appearance or behavior. Each object also has specific methods, which are actions that can be taken on it.

What Exactly Are Properties?

A *property* is an attribute of an object, and each object has many properties. Often, different types of objects share the same properties; at other times, an object's properties are specific to that particular object. Forms, combo boxes, and text boxes all have Width properties, for example, but a form has a RecordSource property that the combo box and text box don't have.

Most properties can be set at design time and modified at runtime; however, some can't be modified at runtime, and others can't be accessed at design time (just modified at runtime). Access's built-in Help for each property tells you one of the following:

- You can set the property in the object's property sheet, a macro, or Visual Basic.
- You can set this property only in Design view.
- You can access this property by using Visual Basic or a macro.

Each of these descriptions indicates when the property can be modified.

As a developer, you set the values of many objects' properties at design time; the ones you set at design time are the starting values at runtime. Much of the VBA code you write modifies the values of these properties at runtime in response to different situations. For example, a text box has a Visible property. If a client is paying by cash, you might not want the text box for the credit-card number to be visible. If they're paying by credit card, you might want to set the Visible property of the text box with the credit-card number to True. This is just one of the many things you can do to modify the value of an object's property at runtime in response to an event or action that has occurred.

You might wonder how you can determine all the properties associated with a particular object (both those that can be modified at design time and those that can be modified at runtime). Of course, to view the properties that can be set at design time, you can select the object and then view its property sheet. Viewing all the properties associated with an object is actually quite easy to do; just invoke Help by pressing F1. Click the Index tab in the Help Topics dialog box and type the name of the object whose properties you want to view. In Figure 10.2, combo boxes has been typed into the text box. Notice that one of the entries in the list box at the bottom of the dialog box is "properties." If you double-click on that entry, the Topics Found dialog box opens. (See Figure 10.3.) When you select Combo Box Control Properties, you're given a complete list of properties associated with a combo box. (See Figure 10.4.) To find out about a specific property, click the property you want to view.

Figure 10.2.

The Help Topics dialog box.

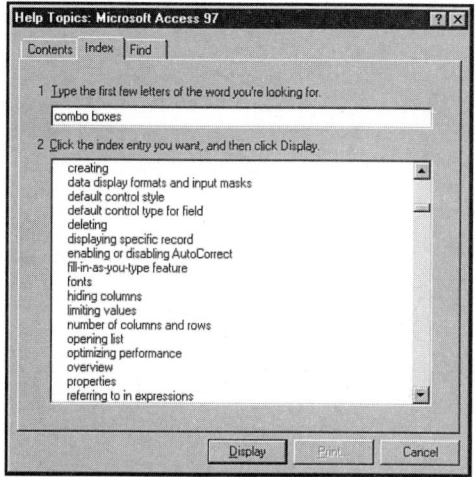

Figure 10.3.

The Topics Found dialog box.

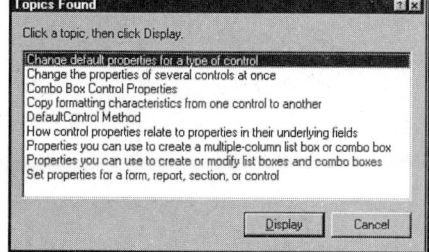

Figure 10.4.

A list of properties associated with a combo box.

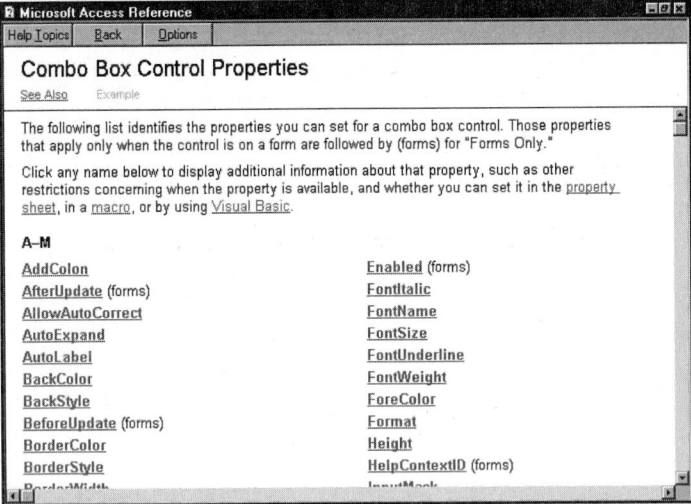

What Exactly Are Events?

Windows is an event-driven operating system; in other words, the operating system responds to many events that are triggered by actions the user takes and by the operating system itself. Access exposes many of these events through its Object Model. An *event* in an Access application is something your application can respond to. Events include mouse movements, changes to data, a form opening, a record being added, and much more. Users initiate events, as does your application code. It's up to you to determine what happens in response to the events that are occurring. You respond to events by using macros or VBA code. Each Access object responds to different events. If you want to find out all the events associated with a particular object, take the following steps:

1. Select the object (for example, a text box).
2. Open the Properties window.
3. Click the Event tab, shown in Figure 10.5.
4. Scroll through the available list of events.

Figure 10.5.

The list of events associated with a text box.

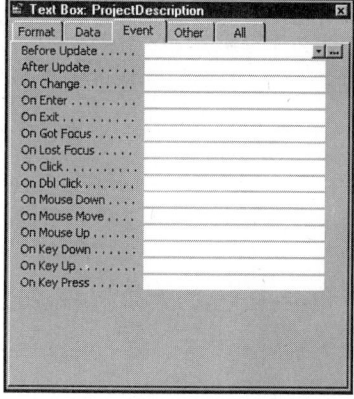

What Exactly Are Methods?

Methods are actions that can be taken on the objects in your database. As with properties and events, different objects have different methods associated with them. A method is like a function or subroutine, except that it's specific to the object it applies to. For example, a form has a `GoToPage` method that doesn't apply to a text box or any other object. If you search for help on methods, you see that you can get help on reference topics. (See Figure 10.6.) If you select methods, reference topics, a Methods Reference appears. (See Figure 10.7.) When a particular method is selected, you get specific help on that method and how it's used. (See Figure 10.8.) If you click the "Applies To hypertext" entry, you get a list of all objects the selected method applies to. You can click the "Example hypertext" entry to view sample code that includes an appropriate implementation of the selected method.

Figure 10.6.

Getting help on methods.

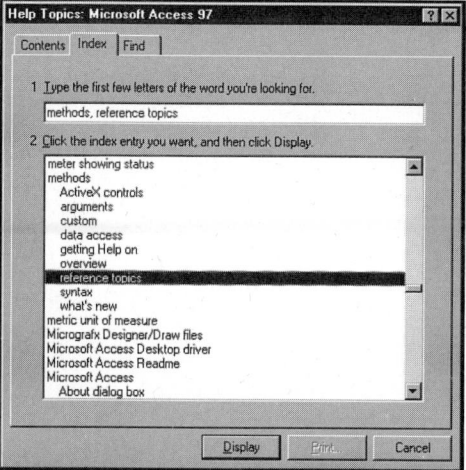

Figure 10.7.
The Methods Reference provides help on all Access methods and collections.

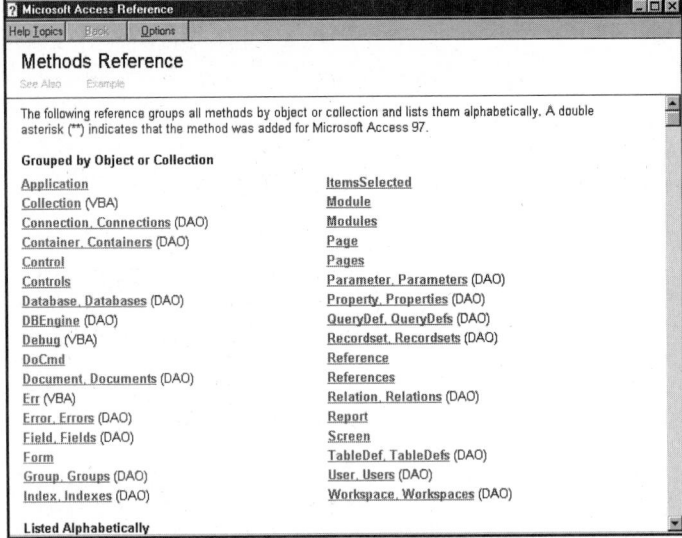

Figure 10.8.
Getting help on a specific method.

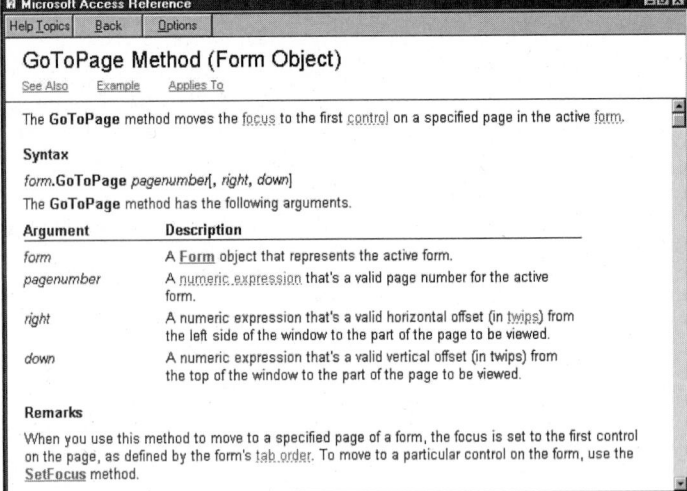

Using the Object Browser to Learn About Access's Objects

The Object Browser is a powerful tool that can help you learn about and work with the objects that are part of both Access 97 and the Microsoft Windows environment. The Object Browser displays information about Microsoft Access and other objects and can help you with coding by showing you all the properties and methods associated with a particular object.

Access objects are complex—they have many properties and methods. The Object Browser helps you to understand and use objects, properties, and methods by doing the following:

- Displaying the types of objects available
- Allowing you to quickly navigate between application procedures
- Displaying the properties and methods associated with a particular object
- Finding and pasting code into your application

How to Use the Object Browser

The Object Browser can easily be invoked from the Module window. You can click the Object Browser button on the toolbar, press F2, or choose View | Object Browser. The dialog box shown in Figure 10.9 appears.

Figure 10.9.
The Object Browser dialog box with the database object selected.

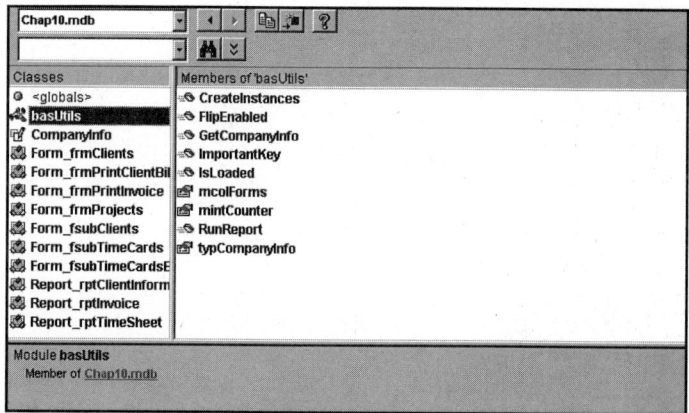

The Object Browser displays two levels of information about the selected library or database. If you select the CHAP10.MDB database from this book's CD-ROM, your screen will look similar to Figure 10.9. The Classes list box displays all modules, including Form and Report modules, in the database. The "Members of" list box displays any procedures that have been defined in the selected module. Notice the basUtils module, which is part of the CHAP10.MDB database. Looking at the list box on the right, you can see the functions included in the basUtils module. You can click to select each Form and Report module in the list box on the left and view the associated methods and properties in the list box on the right.

You can use the Project/Library drop-down list to select a different object library. The Classes list box displays the types of objects available in the selected library or database. The "Members of" list box displays the methods, properties, and data elements defined for the selected object. (See Figure 10.10.) The Access item has been selected from the Library combo box, so the list box on the left shows all of Access 97's classes. The list box on the right shows all the members of the selected object—in this case, the Application object. You can even add other libraries to the Library drop-down list by referring to other type libraries. This method is covered in Chapter 25, "Automation: Communicating with Other Applications."

Figure 10.10.
Selecting the Access 97 library in the Object Browser.

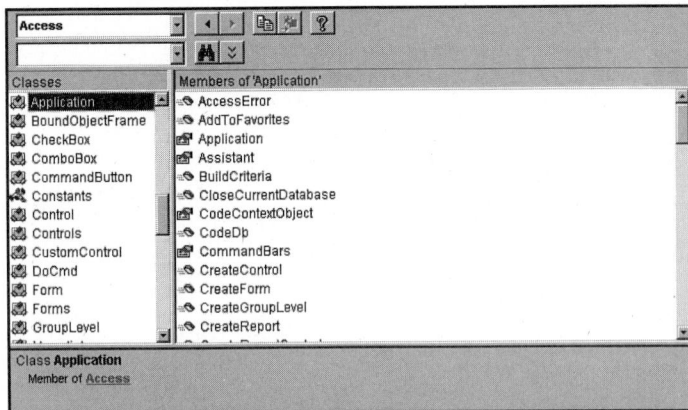

Pasting Code Templates into a Procedure

After you have located the method or property you're interested in, you have the option of pasting it into your application. With the member selected in the list box, simply click the Copy button in the Object Browser, then paste it in the appropriate module. If you want to get more information about a particular method or property, just click the Help button in the Object Browser or press F1.

Referring to Objects

Access objects are categorized into *collections*, which are groupings of objects of the same type. The Forms collection, for example, is a grouping of all the open forms in a database. Each form has a Controls collection that includes all the controls on that form. Each control is an object, and you must refer to an object through the collection it belongs to. For example, you refer to a form through the Forms collection. VBA offers three ways to refer to an object; if you want to refer to the frmProjects form, for example, you can choose from the following options:

- `Forms!frmProjects`
- `Forms("frmProjects")`
- `Forms(0)`

Referring to the form as `Forms(0)` assumes that frmProjects was the first form opened. However, you need to understand that although an element number is assigned as each form is loaded, this element number changes as forms are loaded and unloaded at runtime. For example, the third form that's loaded can initially be referred to as "element two," but if the second form is unloaded, that third form becomes element one. In other words, you can't rely on the element number assigned to a form; that number is a moving target.

You must refer to a control on a form first through the Forms collection, then through the specific form. The reference looks like this:

```
Forms!frmProjects!txtClientID
```

In this example, Forms is the name of the collection, frmProjects is the name of the specific form, and txtClientID is the name of a control on the frmProjects form. If this code is found in the Code module of frmProjects, it could be rewritten like this:

```
Me!txtClientID
```

Me refers to the current form or report. It's generic because the code could be copied to any form having a txtClientID control and it would still run properly. Referring to a control on a report is very similar to referring to a control on a form. Here's an example:

```
Reports!rptTimeSheet!txtHoursBilled
```

This example refers to the txtHoursBilled text box on the rptTimeSheet report, part of the Reports collection. After you know how to refer to an object, you're ready to write code that modifies its properties and executes its methods.

Properties and Methods Made Easy

To modify an object's properties and execute its methods, you must refer to the object and then supply an appropriate property or method, as shown in this example:

```
Forms!frmHello!cmdHello.Visible = False
```

This line of code refers to the Visible property of cmdHello, found in the frmHello form, which is in the Forms collection. Notice that you must identify the object name "frmHello" as being associated with the Forms collection. If you want to change the Caption property of frmHello to say "Hello World", you would use the following code:

```
Forms!frmHello.Caption = "Hello World"
```

> ### TIP
>
> You might be confused about whether you're looking at an object's property or method, but there are a couple of quick ways to tell. A property is always used in some type of an expression. For example, you might be setting a property equal to some value:
>
> ```
> Forms!frmClients!txtAddress.Visible = False
> ```
>
> Here, you're setting the Visible property of the txtAddress text box on the frmClients form from True to False. You also might retrieve the value of a property and place it in a variable:
>
> ```
> strFirstName = Forms!frmClients!txtFirstName.Value
> ```

You also might use the value of a property in an expression, as in the following example:

```
MsgBox Forms!frmClients!txtFirstName.Value
```

The pattern here is that a property is always used somewhere in an expression. It can be set equal to something, something can be set equal to its value, or it's otherwise used in an expression.

A method, however, is an action taken on an object. The syntax for a method is `Object.Method`. A method isn't set equal to something, nor is anything set equal to it. A method looks like this:

```
Forms!frmHello!txtHelloWorld.SetFocus
```

In this example, the `SetFocus` method is being executed on the text box called txtHelloWorld.

A method that returns an object variable looks like this:

```
Dim cbr As CommandBar
Set cbr = CommandBars.Add("MyNewCommandBar")
```

In this example, the CommandBars collection `Add` method is used to set the value of the CommandBar object variable named `cbr`. For more information, see the section "Declaring and Assigning Object Variables" later in this chapter

NOTE

Many people are confused about when to use a bang (!) and when to use a period. You should use a bang whenever you're separating an object from its collection, as shown in these two examples:

```
Forms!frmClients
```

```
Forms!frmClients!txtClientID
```

In the first example, `frmClients` is part of the Forms collection. In the second example, `txtClientID` is part of the Controls collection of the frmClients form.

The period is used to separate an object from a property or method, like so:

```
Forms!frmClients.RecordSource = "tblClients"
```

```
Forms!frmClients!txtClientID.Visible = False
```

The first example sets the RecordSource property of frmClients to `tblClients`, and the second example sets the Visible property of the txtClientID on the frmClients form to `False`.

Many people are in the habit of separating objects from their collections by using periods rather than bangs. However, following the standard of using bangs to separate objects from their collections and periods to separate a property or method from an object makes your code much easier to read. Furthermore, when using data access objects (covered in Chapter 15), you must include the Microsoft DAO 2.5/3.5 Compatibility Layer if you want backward compatibility for the `Collection.Object` syntax of referring to objects.

Default Properties

Each object has a default property, and if you're working with an object's default property, you don't have to explicitly refer to it in code. Take a look at the following two code samples:

```
Forms!frmHello!txtHello.Value = "Hello World"

Forms!frmHello!txtHello = "Hello World"
```

The Value property is the default property of a text box, so you don't need to explicitly refer to it in code. However, I prefer to always explicitly state the property—this practice contributes to the code's readability and keeps novice Access programmers who work with my code from having to guess which property I'm changing.

Declaring and Assigning Object Variables

Object variables are variables that reference an object of a specific type, such as databases, record sets, forms, controls, and even objects created in other applications. They allow you to create shortcut references to objects and pass objects to subroutines and functions. You can use them to streamline code by using short names to refer to objects with long names and to optimize code by supplying a direct pointer to a particular object.

First, you must declare an object variable; then, you assign—or *point*—the object variable to a particular object, as shown in the following code:

```
Private Sub cmdChangeCaption_Click()
    Dim cmdAny As CommandButton
    Set cmdAny = Me!cmdHello
    cmdAny.Caption = "Hello"
End Sub
```

This code creates an object variable called cmdAny of the type CommandButton. You then use the Set statement to point your CommandButton object variable toward the cmdHello object on the current form, using the Me keyword. Finally, you modify the caption of the cmdAny object variable. Because an object variable is a reference to the original object, you're actually changing the caption of the cmdHello command button.

Object Variables Versus Regular Variables

The difference between object variables and regular variables is illustrated by the following code:

```
Dim intVar1 As Integer
Dim intVar2 As Integer
intVar1 = 5
intVar2 = intVar1
intVar1 = 10
Debug.Print intVar1 'Prints 10
Debug.Print intVar2 'Prints 5
```

This code uses ordinary variables. When you dimension these variables, each one is assigned a separate memory location. Although intVar2 is initially assigned the value of intVar1, changing the value of intVar1 has no effect on intVar2. This differs from the following code, which uses an object variable:

```
Private Sub Command5_Click()
    Dim ctlText As TextBox
    Set ctlText = Forms!frmSales!txtProductID
    ctlText.Text = "New Text"
    Debug.Print Forms!frmSales!txtProductID.Text 'Prints New Text
End Sub
```

This routine creates an object variable called ctlText of type TextBox. It then associates the object variable with Forms!frmSales!txtProductID. Next, it modifies the Text property of the object variable. Because the object variable is actually pointing to the text box on the form, the Debug.Print statement prints the new text value.

Generic Versus Specific Object Variables

Access supports the use of generic object variables, including Application, Control, Form, and Report. Generic object variables can be used to refer to any object of that generic type:

```
Private Sub ChangeVisible_Click()
    Dim ctlAny As Control
    Set ctlAny = Me!txtCustomerID
    ctlAny.Visible = False
End Sub
```

In this example, ctlAny can be used to point to any control. Compare that with the following code:

```
Private Sub cmdChangeVisible_Click()
    Dim txtAny As TextBox
    Set txtAny = Me!txtCustomerID
    txtAny.Visible = False
End Sub
```

Here, your object variable can be used only to point to a text box.

Cleaning Up After Yourself

After you're done working with an object variable, you should set its value to Nothing. As used in the following example, this statement frees up all memory and system resources associated with the object:

```
Set frmNew = Nothing
```

Understanding the Differences Between Objects and Collections

Many people get confused about the differences between an object and a collection. Think of an object as a member of a collection. For example, frmHello is a form that's a member of the Forms collection; cmdHello, a command button on frmHello, is a member of the Controls collection of frmHello. Sometimes you want to manipulate a specific object, but other times you want to manipulate a collection of objects.

Manipulating a Single Object

You have already learned quite a bit about manipulating a single object, such as setting the Enabled property of a text box:

```
txtCustomerID.Enabled = False
```

This line of code affects only one text box and only one of its properties. However, when you're manipulating a single object, you might want to affect several properties at the same time. In that case, it's most efficient to use the With...End With construct, explained in the following section.

With...End With: Performing Multiple Commands on an Object

One method you can use to modify several properties of an object is to modify the value of each property, one at a time:

```
txtCustomerID.Enabled = False
txtCustomerID.SpecialEffect = 1
txtCustomerID.Fontsize = 16
txtCustomerID.FontWeight = 700
```

Contrast this with the following code:

```
With txtCustomerID
.Enabled = False
.SpecialEffect = 1
.Fontsize = 16
.FontWeight = 700
End With
```

This code uses the With...End With statement to assign multiple properties to an object. In addition to improving the readability of your code, the With...End With construct results in a slight increase in performance.

Manipulating a Collection of Objects

A *collection* is like an array of objects. What makes the array special is that it's defined and maintained by Access. Every collection in Microsoft Access is an object, each with its own properties and methods. The VBA language makes it easy for you to manipulate Access's collections of objects; you simply use the `For Each...Next` construct, covered in the following section.

For Each...NEXT: Performing the Same Command on Multiple Objects

In the "Determining the Type of a Control" section of this chapter, you learn how to loop through the collection of controls on a form, performing actions on all the command buttons. This illustrates a practical use of a collection. In the following example, you loop through all the open forms, changing the caption of each form:

```
Sub FormCaptions()
    Dim frm As Form
    For Each frm In Forms
        frm.Caption = frm.Caption & " - " & CurrentUser
    Next frm
End Sub
```

This routine uses the `For...Each` construct to loop through each form in the Forms collection, setting the caption of each form to the form's caption concatenated with the current user name. As you travel through the loop, the code `frm.Caption` refers to each individual member of the Forms collection.

Collections Versus Containers and Documents

The Jet Engine maintains information about all the components of an Access 97 database. This information is stored in both container and document objects. Access 97 ships with eight containers: Databases, Forms, Modules, Relationships, Reports, Scripts, Tables, and SysRel. Every container object is made up of a collection of documents, which are the *instances* of the objects in the container.

It's easy to confuse the Forms container with the Forms collection. The Forms *container* comprises all the saved forms that are part of the database; the Forms *collection* comprises only the forms currently running in memory. If you want to see a list of all the forms that make up a database, you must use the Forms container, but if you want to change the caption of all the open forms, you must use the Forms collection.

To view all the forms stored in the database, you must loop through the Forms container and list the documents, as shown in the following code:

```
Sub FormList()
    Dim db As DATABASE
    Dim cnt As Container
    Dim doc As Document

    Set db = CurrentDb()
    Set cnt = db.Containers("Forms")

    For Each doc In cnt.Documents
        Debug.Print doc.Name
    Next doc
End Sub
```

This code creates a database object variable and a container object variable. It uses the `CurrentDB()` function (discussed in Chapter 15) to point the database object variable to the current database. It then points the `Container` object variable to the Forms container. Next, it uses the Document object to loop through each document in the Documents collection of the Forms container and print out the name of each form in the database.

Creating Custom Collections

You can create custom collections in addition to the built-in collections. Custom collections are similar to arrays, but they offer several advantages:

- Collections are dynamically allocated. They take up memory based only on what's in them at a given time. This is different from arrays, whose size must be either predefined or redimensioned at runtime. When an array is redimensioned, Access actually makes a copy of the array in memory, taking up substantial resources. By using custom collections, you can avoid that.

- A collection always knows how many elements it has, and elements can easily be added and removed.

- Each element of a collection can contain a different type of data.

- Elements can be added into any element of a collection.

Defining Custom Collections

Defining a custom collection is easy—simply use the `Dim` keyword to create an object of the type `Collection`, as shown here:

```
Dim colSports As New Collection
```

The `Dim` statement tells the compiler you want to declare a variable, and the `As New` keywords indicate that you're creating a new instance of something. Specifically, you're creating a new instance of a Collection object. The `New` keyword is covered in more detail later in the chapter. For now, take a look at how you can add items to, and remove items from, a custom collection.

Adding Items to and Removing Items from a Custom Collection

The `Add` method adds a new item to a custom collection. It looks like this:

```
colSports.Add "Basketball"
```

This line of code adds the text `"Basketball"` to the colSports collection. The `Add` method has three optional arguments: `Key`, `Before`, and `After`. `Key` is a string name you can use to uniquely identify an element; the `Before` and `After` arguments allow you to specify where in the collection the new item will be placed. Here's an example:

```
Sub NewCollection()
   Dim colSports As New Collection
```

```
    colSports.Add "Basketball"
    colSports.Add "Skiing"
    colSports.Add "Skating", Before:=1
    colSports.Add "Hockey", After:=2
End Sub
```

This code creates a new collection called colSports and adds two consecutive elements to the collection: Basketball and Skiing. It then adds Skating before Basketball. Skating becomes Element 1 and Basketball becomes Element 2. Finally, it adds Hockey after Element 2 (Basketball).

> **WARNING**
>
> Unlike almost every other array or collection in VBA, custom collections are one-based rather than zero-based. This is a big change if you're used to relying on arrays and collections being zero-based.

Removing objects from a custom collection is just as easy as adding them. You use the Remove method, which looks like this:

```
Sub RemoveElements()
    Dim colSports As New Collection
    colSports.Add "Basketball"
    colSports.Add "Skiing"
    colSports.Add "Skating"
    colSports.Add "Hockey"
    colSports.Remove 2
End Sub
```

This routine removes Element 2 (Skiing) from the collection.

Looping Through the Elements of a Custom Collection

Just as you can loop through built-in collections, you can also loop through a custom collection. The code looks like this:

```
Sub LoopThroughCollection()
    Dim colSports As New Collection
    Dim varSport As Variant
    colSports.Add "Basketball"
    colSports.Add "Skiing"
    colSports.Add "Skating", Before:=1
    colSports.Add "Hockey", After:=2
    For Each varSport In colSports
        Debug.Print varSport
    Next varSport
End Sub
```

This code uses a For Each...Next loop to loop through each element of colSports. Notice that the routine declares a variant variable as the type of object in the collection. This is done so that different types of values can be stored in each object in the collection. Access refreshes any collection when you first open a database and specifically refer to it.

Referring to a Specific Item in a Collection

When you add an item to a collection, you can specify a custom key for the object. This makes it easy to return to the item in the collection whenever necessary. The code that follows illustrates how to specify a custom key:

```
Sub CustomKey()
   Dim colSports As New Collection
   colSports.Add "Basketball", "B"
   colSports.Add "Skiing", "S1"
   colSports.Add "Skating", "S2"
   colSports.Add "Hockey", "H"
   Debug.Print colSports.Item("S1")
End Sub
```

This code adds several items to the colSports collection. As each item is added, it's assigned a unique key. Each item in the collection can then be easily accessed by using its unique key. The Item method is often used when adding several instances of a form, such as a Customer form to a collection. The Customer ID of each customer is added as the unique key for each form in the collection. This unique identifier allows you to readily return to a specific instance of the Customer form. This technique is illustrated in the TrackInstances procedure found in the section "Returning to a Unique Item in a Collection" later in this chapter.

Using the New Keyword

The New keyword creates a new instance of an existing object. For example, you might want to display information about several customers, each customer on its own form, so you want each instance of the Customer form to contain the same objects, variables, and code. You might also want to create multiple instances of a form called frmSales; each instance would show information about a different customer.

There are a couple of ways you can use the New keyword. The first way looks like this:

```
Dim frmNew As New Form_frmCustomers
frmNew.Visible = True
```

This method creates a new instance of frmCustomers, using an object variable called frmNew. It then sets the Visible property of the new instance to True.

In the second method, you create an object variable of the specific type of your form, then point the object variable to a new instance of the form:

```
Dim frmNew As Form_frmCustomers
Set frmNew = New Form_frmCustomers
frmNew.Visible = True
```

Notice that you first create an object variable specifically of the type frmCustomers, then point the object variable to a new instance of frmCustomers. The object variables used to hold the new instances of the form have a scope just like any other variable. This means that if you place the object variable in a procedure, the variable goes out of scope as soon as the Exit Sub or Exit Function is reached, causing the new instance of the form to vanish. For this reason, object variables that hold new instances of forms are generally module-level or public in scope. Here's an example (frmMultiInstance from CHAP10EX.MDB):

```
Private colForms As New Collection

Private Sub cmdNewInstance_Click()
    Static intCounter As Integer
    Dim frm As Form
    Set frm = New Form_frmMultiInstance
    intCounter = intCounter + 1
    colForms.Add frm
    frm.Caption = "New Instance " & intCounter
    frm.Visible = True
End Sub
```

The `Private` declaration for the collection called colForms is placed in the General Declarations section of frmMultiInstance. The `cmdNewInstance_Click` event routine maintains a Static variable that's incremented each time the command button is clicked. A Local form variable called `frm` is declared and set equal to a new instance of the frmMultiInstance form. The new instance is added to the Private collection; next, its caption is set and its Visible property is set equal to `True`. This example illustrates two important points:

- Each instance of the form maintains its own Static variable, so if you create more than one instance from the same parent, the number in the title increments. If you create a child form from one of the new instances, the new instance increments and maintains its own Static variable.

- All the child forms close if you close the original parent because the collection called colForms is Private to frmMultiInstance.

Both of these "idiosyncrasies" are remedied in the following section, after you learn to pass objects to functions and subroutines.

Passing Objects to Functions and Subroutines

One of the beauties of object variables is that you can easily pass them to a subroutine or function. They are always passed by reference, meaning that when you change the object's property in a routine, you're changing the property in the original example, too. As you will see, the ability to pass an object to a function or subroutine solves the problems created when building multiple instances of a form in the preceding example. The following code is found in CHAP10EX.MDB in the frmPassedToSub form and the basExamples module:

```
Private Sub cmdNewInstance_Click()
    Call NewInstance(Me)
End Sub
```

The cmdNewInstance command button, found in frmPassedToSub, passes the current form (Me) to a routine called `NewInstance` (found in basExamples). The `NewInstance` routine looks like this:

```
Private mcolForms As New Collection
Private mintCounter As Integer

Sub NewInstance(frmAny As Form)
   Dim frm As Form
   Set frm = New Form_frmPassedToSub
   mintCounter = mintCounter + 1
   mcolForms.Add frm
   frm.Caption = "New Instance " & mintCounter
   frm.Visible = True
End Sub
```

Returning to a Unique Item in a Collection

The techniques you've learned so far don't allow you to return to a specific item in a collection. Using the Collection object's Key property, covered earlier in the chapter, you can easily return to a specific item in a collection. The code that follows illustrates this useful technique found in the frmTrackInstances form:

```
Private Sub cmdMore_Click()
   Call LocateInstance
End Sub

Sub LocateInstance()
   On Error Resume Next
   mcolForms.Item("" & PaymentID & "").SetFocus
   If Err.Number Then
      Call TrackInstances
   End If
End Sub
```

The mcolForms is a Private collection declared in the General Declarations section of the frmTrackInstances form. The LocateInstance routine tries to set focus to a specific form in the mcolForms custom collection. If an error occurs, no instance exists for the selected payment. The TrackInstances routine that follows is then called:

```
Sub TrackInstances()
   On Error GoTo Track_Err
   Dim frm As Form_frmPmtInfo, colItem As Object
   Const conKeyInUseErr = 457
   Set frm = New Form_frmPmtInfo
   mcolForms.Add Item:=frm, key:=PaymentID & ""
   frm.Caption = "Payment ID " & PaymentID
   frm.RecordSelectors = False
   frm.NavigationButtons = False
   frm.RecordSource = "Select * from tblPayments Where " & _
      "tblPayments!PaymentID = " & Me!PaymentID & ";"
   frm.Visible = True
Track_Bye:
   Exit Sub
Track_Err:
   If Err = conKeyInUseErr Then
      mcolForms.Remove (PaymentID)
      Resume
   Else
```

299

```
        Resume Track_Bye
    End If
End Sub
```

The `TrackInstances` routine creates a new instance of the frmPmtInfo form. As each instance is created, the subroutine adds the PaymentID of the selected record to the new element of the collection. This unique key is used by the `LocateInstance` routine called by the `Click` event of the cmdMore command button. When the user clicks the cmdMore command button, the `LocateInstance` routine tries to set focus to the form in the collection containing the unique key. If the user closes one of the pop-up forms and then tries to open it again by clicking the More button, code in the `TrackInstances` procedure error handler removes the item from the collection before trying to again add it to the collection.

Determining the Type of a Control

When writing generic code, you may need to determine the type of a control. For example, you might want to loop through all the controls on a form and flip the Enabled property of all the command buttons. To do this, use the `TypeOf` keyword, which is actually part of the `If` statement. Here's an example of how it's used (you can find this in CHAP10EX.MDB in the module called basExamples):

```
Sub FlipEnabled(frmAny As Form, ctlAny As Control)
    Dim ctl As Control
    'Loop through the Controls collection using the For..Each Construct
    ctlAny.Enabled = True
    ctlAny.SetFocus
    For Each ctl In frmAny.Controls
        'Evaluate the type of the control
        If TypeOf ctl Is CommandButton Then
            'Make sure that we don't try to disable the command button _
            that invoked this routine
            If ctl.Name <> ctlAny.Name Then
                ctl.Enabled = Not ctl.Enabled
            End If
        End If
    Next ctl
End Sub
```

The `FlipEnabled` procedure is called from the form frmTypeOf. Each command button on the form (Add, Edit, Delete, and so on) sends the form and the name of a control to the `FlipEnabled` routine:

```
Private Sub cmdAdd_Click()
    Call FlipEnabled(Me, Me!cmdSave)
End Sub
```

The `FlipEnabled` routine receives the form and control as parameters. It begins by enabling the command button that was passed to it and setting focus to it. The `FlipEnabled` routine then uses the VBA construct `For...Each` to loop through all the controls on a form. The `For...Each` construct repeats a group of statements for each object in an array or collection—in this case, the Controls collection. The code evaluates each control on the form to determine whether it's a command button. If it is, and it isn't the command button that was passed to the routine, the routine flips the control's Enabled property. The following VBA keywords are specific object types that can be evaluated by the `TypeOf` statement:

BoundObjectFrame	OptionButton	Label
CheckBox	OptionGroup	PageBreak
ComboBox	Rectangle	Image
CommandButton	Subform	CustomControl
Chart	Subreport	UnboundObjectFrame
Line	TextBox	Tab
ListBox	ToggleButton	Page

Besides using the `TypeOf` statement described previously, you can also use a control's ControlType property to determine what kind of control it is.

Special Properties That Refer to Objects

VBA offers the convenience of performing actions on the active control, the active form, and other specially recognized objects. The following is a list of special properties that refer to objects in the Access Object Model:

- The ActiveControl property refers to the control that has focus on a screen object, form, or report.
- The ActiveForm property refers to the form that has focus.
- The ActiveReport property refers to the report that has focus.
- The Form property refers to the form that a subform is contained in or to the form itself.
- Me refers to the form or report where code is currently executing.
- Module refers to the module of a form or report.
- The Parent property refers to the form, report, or control that contains a control.
- PreviousControl refers to the control that had focus immediately before the ActiveControl.
- RecordsetClone refers to a clone of the form's underlying recordset.
- The Report property refers to the report that a subform is contained in or to the report itself.
- The Section property refers to the section in a form or report where a particular control is located.

The following example of using the Screen.ActiveForm property shows how a subroutine can change the caption of the active form:

```
Sub ChangeCaption()
    Screen.ActiveForm.Caption = Screen.ActiveForm.Caption & _
        " - " & CurrentUser()
End Sub
```

This subroutine modifies the caption of the active form, appending the value of the CurrentUser property onto the end of the existing caption.

Practical Examples of Working with Objects

Objects are used throughout the Time and Billing application. Almost every aspect of the application uses the skills explained in this chapter. The examples that follow apply the techniques you learned to open multiple instances of the Projects form and to enable and disable command buttons in response to the user's making changes to the data on the frmClients form.

Bringing Up Multiple Instances of the Projects Form

While viewing a project, a user might want to see information from another project. This can be done by creating multiple instances of the Projects form. The cmdViewOtherProjects command button on the frmProjects form calls the CreateInstances routine:

```
Private Sub cmdViewOtherProjects_Click()
        Call CreateInstances(Me)
End Sub
```

The CreateInstances routine is a generic routine that can create multiple instances of any form. It's found in basUtils and looks like this:

```
Sub CreateInstances(frmAny As Form)
    Dim frm As Form
    Set frm = New Form_frmTimeCards
    mintCounter = mintCounter + 1
    mcolForms.Add frm
frm.Filter = frmAny.Filter
    frm.Visible = True
End Sub
```

The CreateInstances routine receives a reference to the form that was passed to it. It then dimensions a form object variable and sets it equal to a new instance of the frmTimeCards form. It increments a Private variable (mintCounter) and adds the form to a Private custom collection called mcolForms. The Filter of the new instance is set to match the filter of the instance that the form came from. This ensures that the new instance shows only projects associated with the client selected on the frmClients form. Finally, the new instance of the form is made visible.

Enabling and Disabling Command Buttons

When a user is in the middle of modifying form data, there's really no need for him or her to use the Project, Time Cards, Payments, and Invoice portions of the application. It makes sense to disable these features until the user has opted to save the changes to the Client data. The "clean" form begins with the Project, Time Cards, Payments, and Invoice command buttons enabled and the Save button disabled. The KeyPreview property of the form is set to Yes so that the form previews all keystrokes before the individual controls process them. The `KeyDown` event of the form looks like this:

```
Private Sub Form_KeyDown(KeyCode As Integer, Shift As Integer)
    If Not cmdSave.Enabled Then
        If ImportantKey(KeyCode, Shift) Then
            Call FlipEnabled(Me, ActiveControl)
        End If
    End If
End Sub
```

The `KeyDown` event automatically receives the code of the key that was pressed and whether Shift, Alt, or Ctrl was pressed along with that key. The event routine checks to determine whether the Save button is already enabled. If it is, there's no reason to continue; the Enabled property of the command buttons has already been flipped. If Save isn't already enabled, the `ImportantKey` function is called. It receives the key that was pressed and detects whether Shift, Alt, or Control was used. The `ImportantKey` function looks like this:

```
Function ImportantKey(KeyCode, Shift)
    ImportantKey = False
    If Shift = 4 Then
        Exit Function
    End If
    If KeyCode = vbKeyDelete Or KeyCode = vbKeyBack Or (KeyCode > 31 _
    And KeyCode < 256) Then
        If KeyCode >= 37 And KeyCode <= 40 Then
            ' Right, Left, Up And Down Arrows
        Else
            ImportantKey = True
        End If
    End If
End Function
```

This generic function, found in basUtils, sets its default return value to `False`. It tests to see whether the Alt key was pressed. If so, the user was accessing a menu or accelerator key, which means there's no reason to flip the command buttons, so the function is exited. If Alt wasn't pressed, the key that was pressed is evaluated. If the Delete key, Backspace key, or any key with an ANSI value between 31 and 256 (excluding values 37 to 40—the arrow keys) was pressed, a `True` is returned from this function. The `Keydown` event of the form then calls the `FlipEnabled` routine. It looks like this:

```
Sub FlipEnabled(frmAny As Form, ctlAny As Control)
    Dim ctl As Control
    If TypeOf ctlAny Is CommandButton Then
        ctlAny.Enabled = True
        ctlAny.SetFocus
    End If
    For Each ctl In frmAny.Controls
        If TypeOf ctl Is CommandButton Then
            If ctl.Name <> ctlAny.Name Then
                ctl.Enabled = Not ctl.Enabled
            End If
        End If
    Next ctl
End Sub
```

This generic routine, also found in basUtils, flips the Enabled property of every command button

303

in the form except the one that was passed to it. The `FlipEnabled` routine receives a form and a control as parameters. It begins by creating a control object variable, then tests to see whether the type of control that was passed to it is a command button. If so, it enables the control and sets focus to it. The routine then loops through every control on the form that was passed to it. It tests to see whether each control is a command button. If it finds a command button, and the name of the command button isn't the same as the name of the control that was passed to it, it flips the Enabled property of the command button. The idea is this: When the user clicks Save, you can't immediately disable the Save button because it still has focus. You must first enable a selected control (the one that was passed to the routine) and set focus to the enabled control. After the control is enabled, you don't want to disable it again, so you need to eliminate it from the processing loop.

You need a way to flip the command buttons back the other way. The `Click` event of the Save button has the following code:

```
Private Sub cmdSave_Click()
    DoCmd.RunCommand Command:=acCmdSaveRecordacMenuVer70
    Call FlipEnabled(Me, Me!Projects)
End Sub
```

This code saves the current record and calls the `FlipEnabled` routine. The `FlipEnabled` routine flips the command buttons back to their original state. You probably want to add a Cancel button that issues an `Undo` and also flips the command buttons. You should also either prohibit users from moving to other records until they select Save, or flip the command buttons if the Save button is enabled and the user moves to another record. If you fail to do this, users move to another record, their changes are automatically saved (by Access), and the command buttons still reflect a "dirty" state of the form.

Summary

The ability to successfully work with objects and understand their properties, methods, and events is fundamental to your success as an Access programmer. Working with properties involves setting properties at design time and changing their values in response to events that occur at runtime. The ability to create multiple form instances and pass forms and other objects to subroutines and functions makes the VBA language extremely robust and flexible.

11

CHAPTER

What Are Macros and When Do You Need Them?

- Why Learning About Macros Is Important, 306
- The Basics of Creating and Running a Macro, 306
- Running an Access Macro, 314
- Modifying an Existing Macro, 318
- Documenting Your Macro: Adding Comments, 321
- Testing a Macro, 322
- When You Should Use Macros and When You Shouldn't, 323
- Converting a Macro to VBA Code, 324
- Creating an AutoExec Macro, 325
- Creating an AutoKeys Macro, 326
- The DoCmd Object, 328
- Practical Examples: Adding an AutoExec Macro to the Time and Billing Application, 328

Why Learning About Macros Is Important

Although macros shouldn't be used to develop the routines that control your applications, it's a good idea for you to have a general understanding of macros and how they work. In fact, one task—reassigning a keystroke—can be done only by using macros, so it's important to understand at least the basics of how macros work. Furthermore, using Access 97 macros can often help you get started with developing applications because these macros can be converted to VBA code. This means you can develop part of your application using macros, convert the macros to VBA code, and then continue developing your application. Although I don't recommend this approach for serious developers, it offers a great jump-start for those new to Access or Windows development in general.

The Basics of Creating and Running a Macro

To create a Macro, click on the Macros tab from the Database window, then click New to open the Macro Design window shown in Figure 11.1. In this window, you can build a "program" by adding macro actions, arguments, names, and conditions to the macro.

Figure 11.1.

The Macro Design window, showing the macro Action and Comment columns.

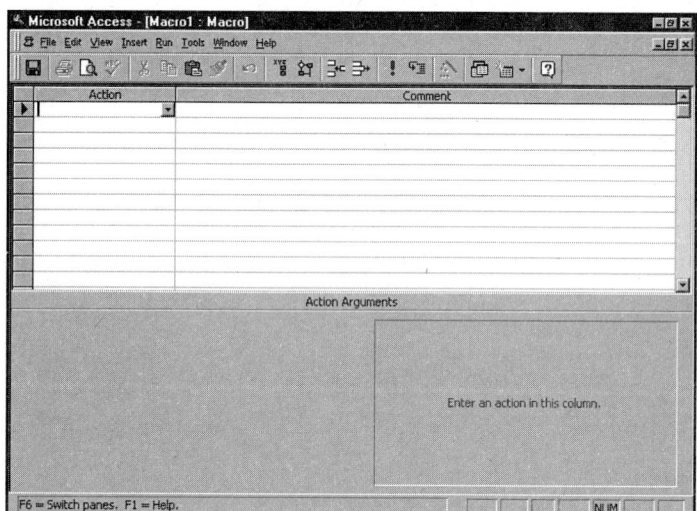

Macro *actions* are like programming commands or functions. They instruct Access to take a specific action—for example, to open a form. Macro *arguments* are like parameters to a command or function; they give Access specifics on the selected action. For example, if the macro action instructs Access to open a form, the arguments for that action tell Access which form should be opened and how it should be opened (Form, Design, or Datasheet view or Print Preview). Macro *names* are like subroutines, and several subroutines can be included in one Access macro. Each of these routines is identified by its macro name. Macro *conditions* allow you to determine when a specific macro action will execute. For example, you might want one form to open in one situation and a second form to open in another situation.

Macro Actions

As mentioned, macro actions instruct Access to perform a task. You can add a macro action to the Macro Design window in several ways. One method is to click in a cell in the Macro Action column, then click to open the drop-down list. (See Figure 11.2.) A list of all the macro actions appears. Select the one you want from the list, and it's instantly added to the macro. Use this method of selecting a macro action if you aren't sure of the macro action's name and want to browse the available actions.

Figure 11.2.

The Macro Action drop-down list, showing all the available macro actions.

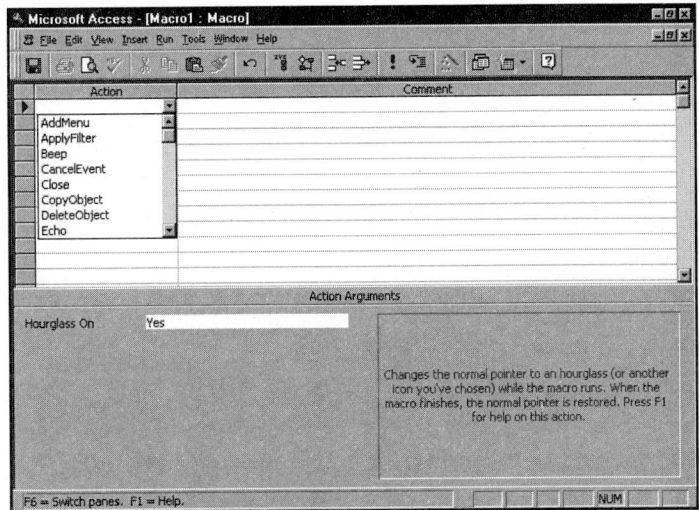

After you have worked with macros for a while, you will know which actions you want to select. Rather than open the drop-down list and scroll through the entire list of actions, you can click a cell in the Action column and then start typing the name of the macro action you want to add. Access will find the first macro action beginning with the character(s) you type.

The OpenTable, OpenQuery, OpenForm, OpenReport, and OpenModule actions are used to open a table, query, form, report, or module, respectively. These actions and associated arguments can all be filled in quite easily with a drag-and-drop technique:

1. Tile the Database window and the Macro Design window on the desktop. (See Figure 11.3.)

2. Select the appropriate tab from the Database window. For example, if you want to open a form, select the Forms tab.

3. Click and drag the object you want to open over to the Macro Design window. The appropriate action and arguments are automatically filled in. Figure 11.4 shows the effects of dragging and dropping the frmClients form onto the Macro Design window.

Figure 11.3.

The Database window and Macro Design window tiled.

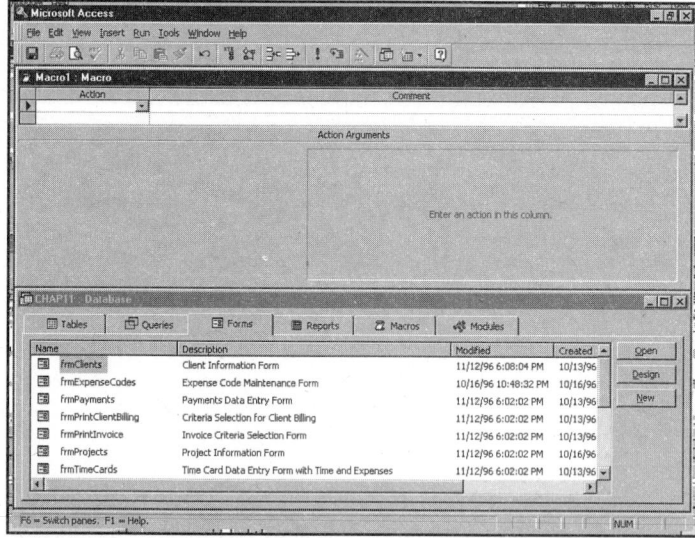

Figure 11.4.

The Macro Design window after the frmClients form was dragged and dropped on it.

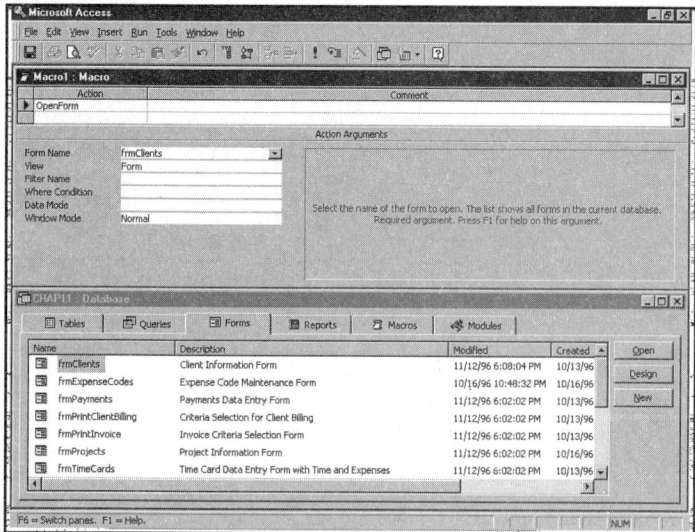

Dragging and dropping a table, query, form, report, or module onto the Macro Design window saves you time because all the macro action arguments are automatically filled in for you. Notice in Figure 11.4 that six action arguments are associated with the OpenForm action: Form Name, View, Filter Name, Where Condition, Data Mode, and Window Mode. Three of the arguments for the OpenForm action have been filled in: the name of the form (frmClients), the view (Form), and the window mode (Normal). Macro action arguments are covered more thoroughly in the next section.

Macro Action Arguments

As mentioned, macro action arguments are like command or function parameters: They give Access specific instructions on how to execute the selected macro action. The available arguments differ depending on what macro action has been selected. Some macro action arguments force you to select from a drop-down list of appropriate choices; others allow you to enter a valid Access expression. Macro action arguments are automatically filled in when you click and drag a Table, Query, Form, Report, or Module object to the Macro Design window. In all other situations, you must supply Access with the arguments required to properly execute a macro action. To specify a macro action argument, follow these five steps:

1. Select a macro action.

2. Press the F6 function key to jump down to the first macro action argument for the selected macro action.

3. If the macro action argument requires selecting from a list of valid choices, click to open the drop-down list of available choices for the first macro action argument associated with the selected macro action. Figure 11.5 shows all the available choices for the Form Name argument associated with the OpenForm action. Because the selected argument is Form Name, the names of all the forms included in the database are displayed in the drop-down list.

Figure 11.5.

Available choices for the FormName argument.

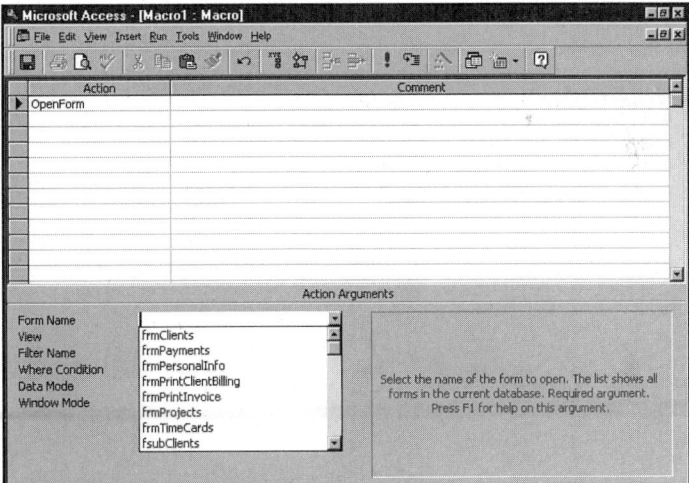

4. If the macro action argument requires entering a valid expression, you can type the argument into the appropriate text box or get help from the Expression Builder. Take a look at the Where Condition argument of the OpenForm action, for example. After you click in the Where Condition text box, an ellipsis appears. If you click on the ellipsis, the Expression Builder dialog box is invoked. (See Figure 11.6.)

Figure 11.6.

The Expression Builder dialog box allows you to easily add complex expressions to your macros.

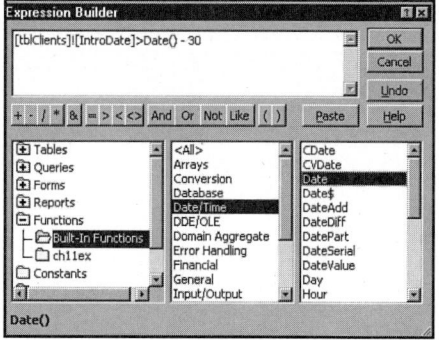

5. To build an appropriate expression, select a database object from the list box on the left, then select a specific element from the center and right-hand list boxes. Click Paste to paste the element into the text box. In Figure 11.6, the currently selected database object is Built-in Functions, and the currently selected elements are Date/Time and Date. Click OK to close the Expression Builder. The completed expression appears in Figure 11.7.

Figure 11.7.

The completed expression for the Where *argument of the* OpenForm *action.*

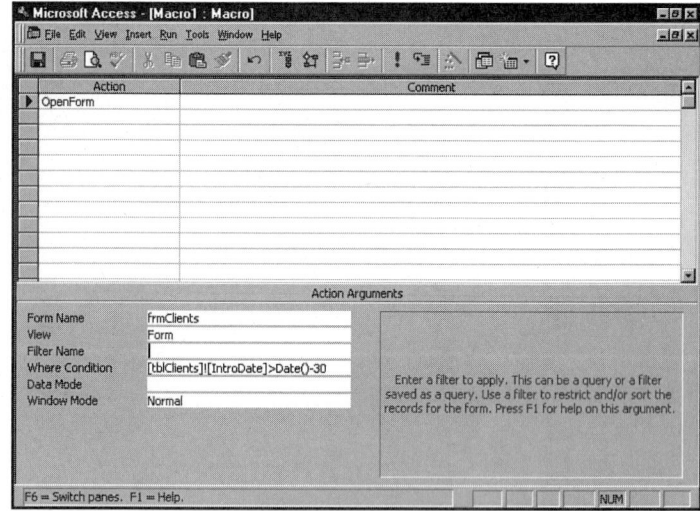

Remember that each macro action has different macro action arguments. Some of the arguments associated with a particular macro action are required, and others are optional. If you need help on a particular macro action argument, click in the argument and Access gives you a short description of that argument. If you need more help, press F1 to see Help for the macro action and all its arguments. (See Figure 11.8.)

Figure 11.8.

Help on the OpenForm *action.*

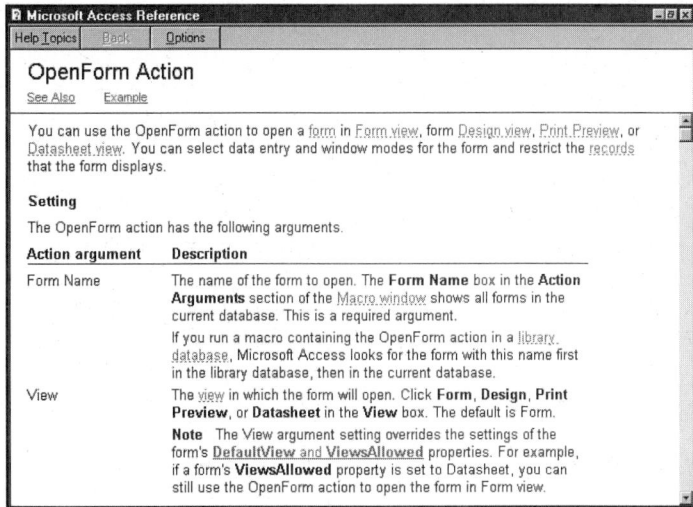

Macro Names

Macro names are like subroutines—they allow you to place more than one routine in a macro. This means you can create many macro routines without having to create several separate macros. You should include macros that perform related functions within one particular macro. For example, you might build a macro that contains all the routines required for form handling and another that has all the routines needed for report handling.

Only two steps are needed to add macro names to a macro:

1. Click the Macro Names button on the Macro Design toolbar or choose View | Macro Names. The Macro Name column appears. (See Figure 11.9.)

Figure 11.9.

The Macro Name column allows you to create subroutines within a macro.

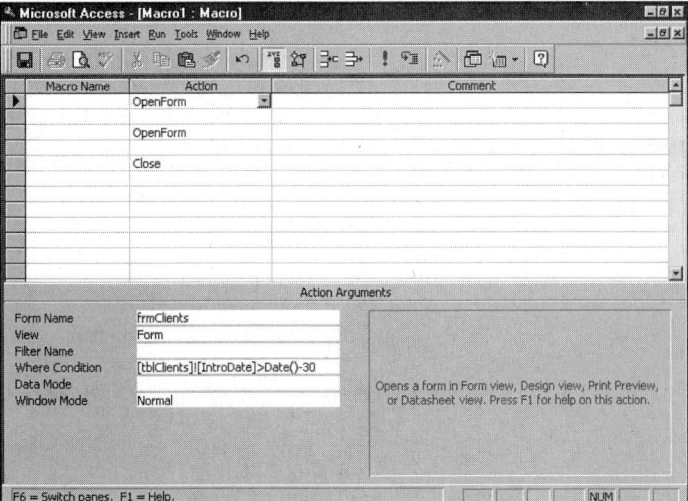

2. Add macro names to each macro subroutine. Figure 11.10 shows a macro with three subroutines: `OpenFrmClients`, `OpenFrmTimeCards`, and `CloseAnyForm`. The `OpenFrmClients` subroutine opens the frmClients form, showing all the clients added in the last 30 days. The `OpenFrmTimeCards` subroutine opens the frmTimeCards form, and the `CloseAnyForm` subroutine displays a message to the user, then closes the active form.

Figure 11.10.

A macro with three subroutines.

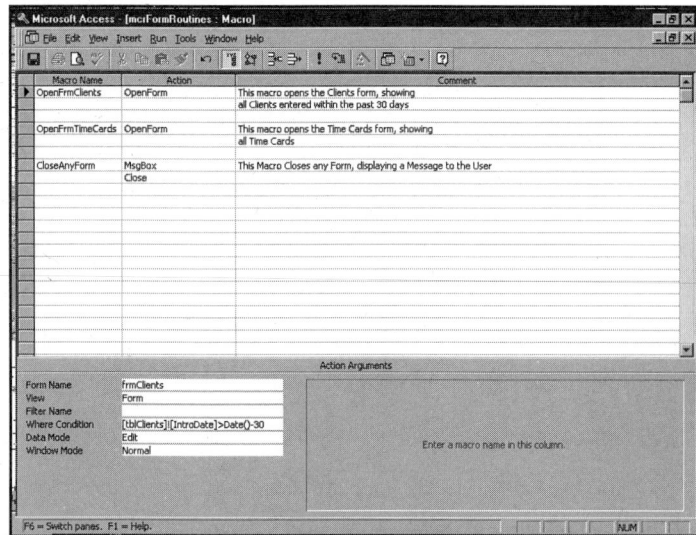

> **NOTE**
>
> The Macro Name column is a toggle. You can hide it and show it at will, without losing the information in the column.

Macro Conditions

At times, you want a macro action to execute only when a certain condition is true. Fortunately, Access allows you to specify the conditions under which a macro action executes:

1. Click the Conditions button on the Macro Design toolbar or choose View | Conditions. The Condition column appears. (See Figure 11.11.)

2. Add the conditions you want to each macro action.

Figure 11.11.

You can designate the condition under which a macro action executes in the Condition column of a macro.

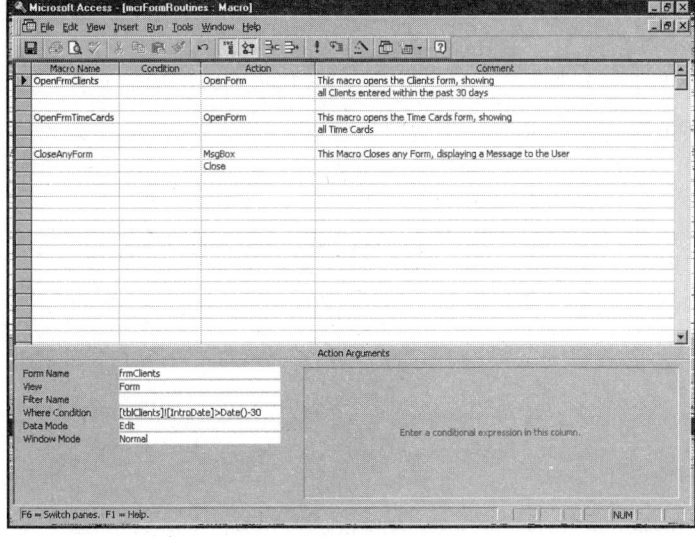

The macro pictured in Figure 11.12 evaluates information entered on a form. The CheckBirthDate subroutine evaluates the date entered in the txtBirthDate text box. Here's the expression entered in the first condition:

```
DateDiff("yyyy",[Forms]![frmPersonalInfo]![txtBirthDate],Date()) Between 25 And 49
```

Figure 11.12.

An example of a macro containing conditions.

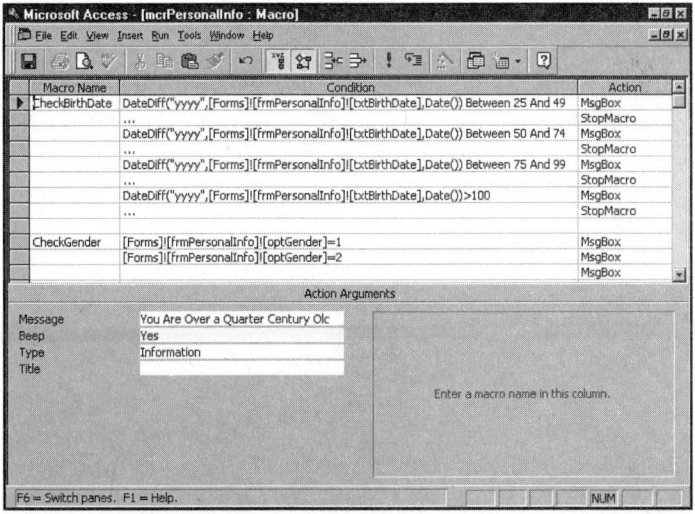

This expression uses the DateDiff function to determine the difference between the date entered in the txtBirthDate text box and the current date. If the difference between the two dates is between 25 and 49 years, a message box is displayed indicating that the person is over a quarter century old.

The ellipsis on the second line of the `CheckBirthDate` subroutine indicates to Access that the macro action should be executed only if the condition entered on the previous line is true. In this case, if the condition is true, the macro is terminated.

If the first condition isn't satisfied, the macro continues evaluating each condition in the subroutine. The `CheckBirthDate` subroutine displays an age-specific message for each person 25 years of age and older. If the person is younger than 25, none of the conditions is met, and no message is displayed.

The `CheckGender` subroutine works a little bit differently. It evaluates the value of the `optGender` option group. One of the first two lines of the subroutine executes, depending on whether the first or second option button is selected. The third line of the subroutine executes regardless of the Option Group value because no ellipsis is entered in the macro action's Condition column. If no ellipsis is found on any line of the subroutine, the macro action executes unconditionally. If an ellipsis is placed before the line, the macro action will execute only if the value of `OptGender` is 2.

Running an Access Macro

You have learned quite a bit about macros but haven't yet learned how to execute them. This process varies depending on what you're trying to do. A macro can be run from the Macro Design window or the Macros tab, triggered from a Form or Report event, or invoked by selecting a menu or toolbar option. The first three methods are covered here in the following sections, but invoking a macro from a menu or toolbar option is covered in Chapter 13, "Let's Get More Intimate with Forms: Advanced Techniques."

Running a Macro from the Macro Design Window

A macro can be executed easily from the Macro Design window. It's simple to run a macro without subroutines; just click Run on the Macro Design toolbar or choose Run | Run. Each line of the macro is executed unless conditions have been placed on specific macro actions. After you click the Run button of mcrOpenClients (shown in Figure 11.13), the frmClients form is opened.

From Macro Design view, you can run only the first subroutine in a macro. To run a macro with subroutines, click Run on the Macro Design toolbar to execute the first subroutine in the macro. As soon as the second macro name is encountered, the macro execution terminates. The section "Triggering a Macro from a Form or Report Event" explains how to execute subroutines other than the first one in a macro.

Figure 11.13.

Running a macro from the Macro Design window.

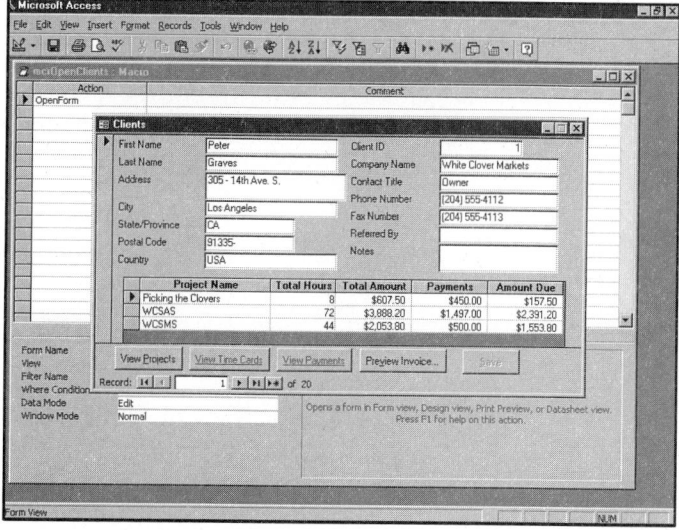

Running a Macro from the Macros Tab

To run a macro from the Macros tab of the Database window, follow these two steps:

1. Click on the Macros tab of the Database window.

2. Double-click on the name of the macro you want to execute or click on the name of the macro and click Run.

> **NOTE**
>
> If the macro you execute contains macro names, only the macro actions with the first subroutine are executed.

Triggering a Macro from a Form or Report Event

Chapter 10, "The Real Scoop on Objects, Properties, and Events," introduced the concept of executing code in response to an event. Here, you will learn how to associate a macro with a command button.

The form in Figure 11.14 illustrates associating a macro with the Click event of a form's command button. Four steps are needed to associate a macro with a Form or Report event:

1. Select the object you want to associate the event with. In the example, the cmdCheckGender command button is selected.

2. Open the Properties window and click the Event tab.

3. Click the event you want the macro to execute in response to. In the example, the Click event of the command button is selected.

4. Use the drop-down list to select the name of the macro you want to execute. If the macro has macro names, make sure you select the correct macro name subroutine. In the example, the macro mcrPersonalInfo and the macro name CheckGender have been selected. Notice the period between the name of the macro and the name of the macro name subroutine. The period is used to differentiate the macro group (mcrPersonalInfo, in this case) from the macro name (CheckGender, in this example).

Figure 11.14.

Associating a macro with a Form or Report event.

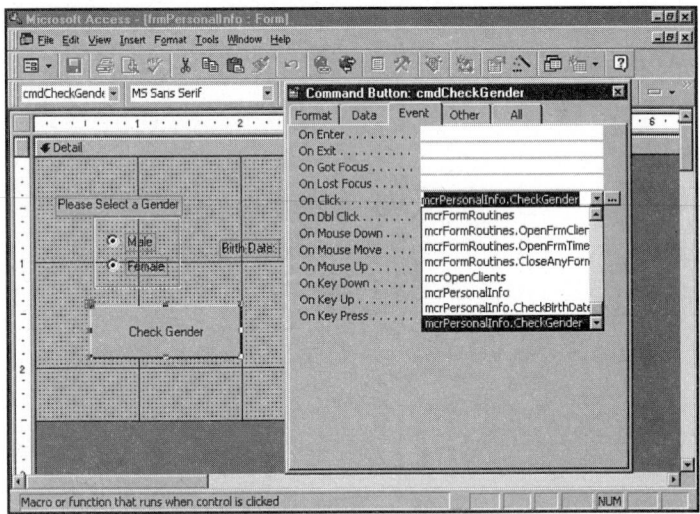

TRY IT   To practice the techniques you have learned, build the macro shown in Figure 11.12.

1. Click the Macros tab of the Database window.

2. Click New.

3. Click the Macro Name and Condition buttons on the Macro Design toolbar to show both the Macro Name and Condition columns of the Macro Design window.

4. Enter all the macro names, actions, arguments, and conditions shown in Table 11.1.

5. Save and name the macro **mcrPersonalInfo**.

6. Build a form.

7. Add an option group with two option buttons. Set one of their Text properties to Male and the other to Female, then set one of their values to 1 and the other to 2. Name the option group **optGender**.

8. Add a text box for the birth date. Set the Format and Input Mask properties to Short Date. Name the text box **txtBirthDate**.

Table 11.1. The mcrPersonalInfo macro.

Macro Name	Macro Condition	Macro Action	Argument	Value
CheckBirthDate	DateDiff("yyyy", [Forms]! [frmPersonalInfo]! [txtBirthDate], Date()) Between 25 And 49	MsgBox	Message	You Are Over a Quarter Century Old
	...	StopMacro		
	DateDiff("yyyy", [Forms]! [frmPersonalInfo]! [txtBirthDate],Date()) Between 50 And 74	MsgBox	Type Message	Information You Are Over a Half Century Old
	...	StopMacro		
	DateDiff("yyyy",[Forms]! [frmPersonalInfo]! [txtBirthDate],Date()) Between 75 And 99	MsgBox	Type Message	Information You Are Over Three Quarters of a Century Old
	...	StopMacro		Warning
	DateDiff("yyyy",[Forms]! [frmPersonalInfo]! [txtBirthDate], Date())>100	MsgBox	Type Message	You Are Over a Century Old!!
	...	StopMacro		Warning
CheckGender	[Forms]![frmPersonalInfo]! [optGender]=1	MsgBox	Type Message Type	You Are Male Information
	[Forms]![frmPersonalInfo]! [optGender]=2	MsgBox	Message Type	You Are Female Information
		MsgBox	Message	Thank You for the Information

9. Add two command buttons to the form. Name the first button **cmdCheckGender** and set its Text property to Check Gender; name the second button **cmdCheckBirthDate** and set its Text property to Check Birth Date. Set the Click event of the first command button to mcrPersonalInfo.CheckGender and the second command button to mcrPersonalInfo.CheckBirthDate.

10. Save the form as **frmPersonalInfo**.

11. Test the macros by clicking each of the command buttons after selecting a gender and entering a birth date.

Modifying an Existing Macro

You have learned how to create a macro, add macro actions and their associated arguments, create macro subroutines by adding macro names, and conditionally execute the actions in the macro by adding macro conditions. However, once a macro has been created, you might want to modify it. First, you must enter Design view for the macro:

1. Click the Macros tab of the Database window.

2. Select the macro you want to modify.

3. Click Design.

When the design of the macro appears, you're then ready to insert new lines, delete existing lines, move the macro actions around, or copy macro actions to the macro you're modifying or to another macro.

Inserting New Macro Actions

To insert a macro action, follow these steps:

1. Click on the line above where you want the macro action to be inserted.

2. Press your Insert key, click the Insert Rows button on the toolbar, or choose Insert | Rows. A new line is inserted in the macro at the cursor.

To insert multiple macro actions, follow these steps:

1. Place your cursor on the line above where you want the new macro action lines to be inserted. Click on the Macro Action Selector, which is the gray box to the left of the macro's Action column.

2. Click and drag to select the same number of Macro Action Selectors as the number of macro actions you want to insert.

3. Press the Insert key, click the Insert Rows button on the toolbar, or choose Insert | Rows. All the new macro lines are inserted above the macro actions that were selected.

Deleting Macro Actions

Follow these steps to delete a macro action:

1. Click on the Macro Action Selector of the macro action you want to delete.

2. Press the Delete key, click Delete Rows on the toolbar, or choose Edit | Delete Rows.

Follow these steps to delete multiple macro actions:

1. Click and drag to select the Macro Action Selectors of all the macro actions you want to delete. All the macro actions should become black. (See Figure 11.15.)

2. Press the Delete key, click Delete Rows, or choose Edit | Delete Rows.

Figure 11.15.

Selecting and deleting macro actions.

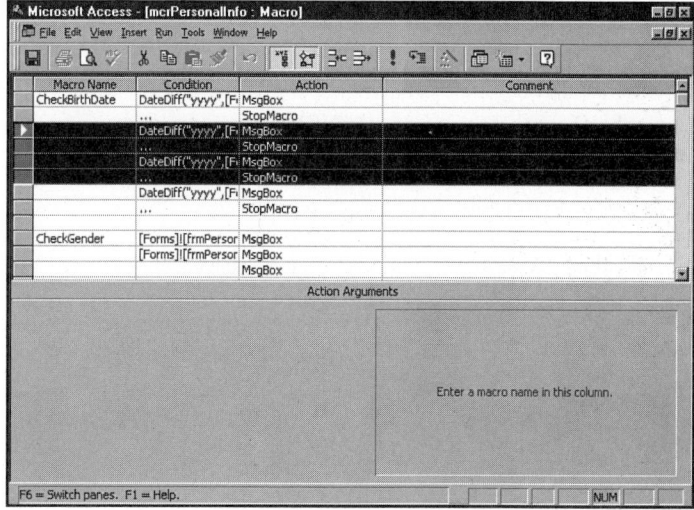

Moving Macro Actions

You can move macro actions in a few ways, including dragging and dropping, and cutting and pasting. To move macro actions by dragging and dropping, follow these steps:

1. Click and drag to select the macro action(s) you want to move.

2. Release the mouse button.

3. Place your mouse cursor over the Macro Action Selector of any of the selected macro actions.

4. Click and drag. A black line appears, indicating where the selected macro actions will be moved.

5. Release the mouse button.

> **TIP**
>
> If you accidentally drag and drop the selected macro actions to an incorrect place, use the Undo button on the Macro Design toolbar or choose Edit | Undo to reverse your action.

To move macro actions by cutting and pasting, follow these steps:

1. Click and drag to select the Macro Action Selectors of the macro actions you want to move.
2. Click Cut on the Macro Design toolbar (or use Ctrl+X).
3. Click in the line above where you want the cut macro actions to be inserted. Don't click the Macro Action Selector.
4. Click Paste. The macro actions you cut are inserted at the cursor.

> **WARNING**
>
> Don't click the Macro Action Selector of the row where you want to insert the cut macro actions, unless you want to overwrite the macro action you have selected. If you don't click to select the Macro Action Selectors, the cut lines are inserted into the macro without overwriting any other macro actions; if you click to select Macro Action Selectors, existing macro actions are overwritten.

Copying Macro Actions

Macro actions can be copied within a macro or to another macro. Follow these steps to copy macro actions within a macro:

1. Click and drag to select the Macro Action Selectors of the macro actions you want to copy.
2. Click Copy on the Macro Design toolbar (or use Ctrl+C).
3. Click in the line above where you want the copied macro actions to be inserted. Don't click on any Macro Action Selectors unless you want to overwrite existing macro actions. (See the Warning preceding this section.)
4. Click Paste. The macro actions you copied are inserted at the cursor.

Follow these steps to copy macro actions to another macro:

1. Click and drag to select the Macro Action Selectors of the macro actions you want to copy.
2. Click Copy on the Macro Design toolbar (or use Ctrl+C).
3. Open the macro that will include the copied actions.

4. Click in the line above where you want the copied macro actions to be inserted.

5. Click Paste. The macro actions you copied are inserted at the cursor.

Documenting Your Macro: Adding Comments

Just as it's useful to document any program, it's also useful to document what you're trying to do in your macro. These comments can be used when you or others are trying to modify your macro later. They can also be used as documentation because they print when you print the macro.

To add a comment to a macro, click in the Comment column of the macro and begin to type. Figure 11.16 shows a macro with comments. As you can see in Figure 11.17, these comments appear in the printed macro.

Figure 11.16.

Adding comments to a macro.

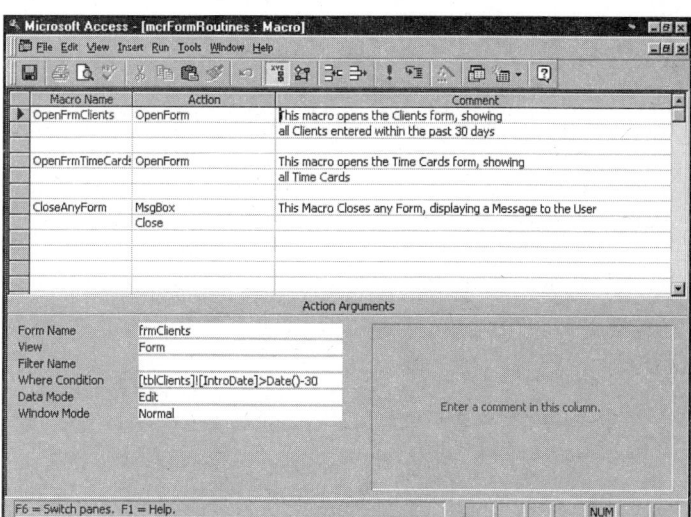

You can add comments to a macro action by placing FALSE in the Condition column of the macro line you're commenting on. This is a useful tip when you're testing or debugging a macro.

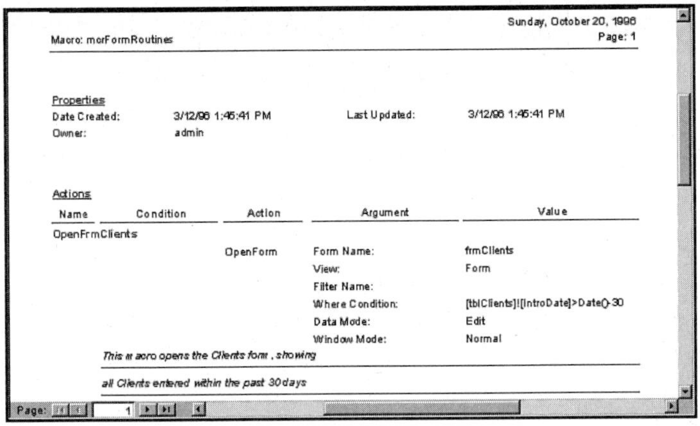

Figure 11.17.
Comments included in the printed macro.

Testing a Macro

Although Access doesn't offer very sophisticated tools for testing and debugging your macros, it does give you a method for stepping through each line of a macro:

1. Open the macro in Design view.

2. Click Single Step on the toolbar or choose Run | Single Step.

3. To execute the macro, click Run. The first line of the macro is executed, and the Macro Single Step dialog box appears, showing you the Macro Name, Condition, Action Name, and Arguments. (See Figure 11.18.) In the figure, the Macro Name is mcrPersonalInfo, the Condition evaluates to False, and the Action Name is MsgBox. The MsgBox arguments are You Are Over a Quarter Century Old, Yes, and Information.

4. To continue stepping through the macro, click the Step button on the Macro Single Step dialog box. If you want to halt the execution of the macro without proceeding, click the Halt button. To continue normal execution of the macro without stepping, click the Continue button.

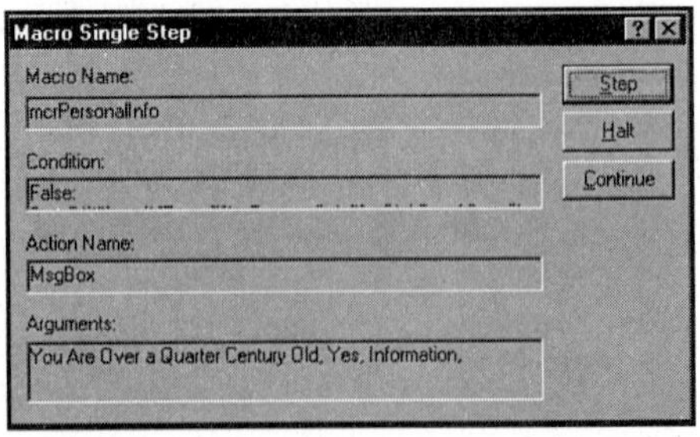

Figure 11.18.
In the Macro Single Step dialog box, you can view the macro name, condition, action name, and arguments for the current step of the macro.

TRY IT

It's easiest to learn about stepping through a macro by doing it yourself. To begin, open the mcrPersonalInfo macro that you created in the last example in Design view. Click the Single Step button on the Macro Design toolbar. Run the frmPersonalInfo form, also created in the last example. Select a gender and type in a birthdate. Click the Check Gender command button; this should invoke the Macro Single Step dialog box. Step through the macro one step at a time. View the Macro Name, Condition, Action Name, and Arguments for each step. Change the gender and run the macro again. Carefully observe how this affects the macro's execution.

Now click the Check Birth Date command button. Step through the macro one step at a time, viewing whether the condition evaluates to True or False. After the macro ends, try entering a different value for the birthdate. Step through the macro again and carefully observe whether the condition evaluates to True or False for each step.

As you can see, although Microsoft supplies some tools to help you debug your macro, you will probably agree that they're quite limited. That's one reason why most developers prefer to develop applications by using VBA code.

> **NOTE**
>
> The Single Step button on the Macro Design toolbar is a toggle. Once you activate Step Mode, it's activated for all macros in the current database and all other databases until you either turn the toggle off or exit Access. This can be quite surprising if you don't expect it. You might have invoked Step Mode in another database quite a bit earlier in the day, only to remember that you forgot to click the toggle button when some other macro unexpectedly goes into Step Mode.

When You Should Use Macros and When You Shouldn't

In Access 97, there's just one task that can be performed only by using macros—reassigning key combinations (the AutoKeys macro). This chapter gives you many other examples of macros, but that's just so you can have a basic understanding of macros and how they work. Developers should use macros *only* to create an AutoKeys macro. As you will see later in this section, VBA code is much more appropriate for most of the tasks your application must perform.

A second common use of macros is as a starting point for your application. Although macros aren't your only choice for this in Access 97, the AutoExec macro is one of two choices for this task. For more about the AutoExec macro, see the section "Creating an AutoExec Macro" in this chapter.

However, macros aren't the best tool for creating code that controls industrial-strength applications because they're quite limited in both function and capability. Access macros are limited in the following ways:

- You can't include error handling in an Access macro.
- You can't create user-defined functions by using macros.
- Access macros don't allow you to create variables or pass parameters.
- Access macros provide no method of processing table records one at a time.
- When using Access macros, you can't use Object Linking and Embedding Automation or Dynamic Data Exchange to communicate with other applications.
- It's more difficult to debug Access macros than it is to debug VBA code.
- Transaction processing can't be done with Access macros.
- You can't call Windows API functions by using Access macros.
- You can't perform any replication by using Access macros.
- Access macros don't allow you to create database objects at runtime.

Converting a Macro to VBA Code

Now that you have discovered all the limitations of macros, you might be thinking about all the macros you've already written that you wish you had developed by using VBA code, or, after seeing how easy it is to do certain tasks by using macros, you might be disappointed to learn how limited macros are. Fortunately, Access 97 comes to the rescue. It's easy to convert an Access macro to VBA code—once the macro has been converted to VBA code, the code can be modified just like any VBA module. Follow these seven steps to convert an Access macro to VBA code:

1. Open the macro you want to convert in Design view.
2. Choose File | Save As/Export.
3. Click the Save as Visual Basic Module option button. (See Figure 11.19.)

Figure 11.19.
The macro File | Save As/Export dialog box allows you to save a macro as a Visual Basic module.

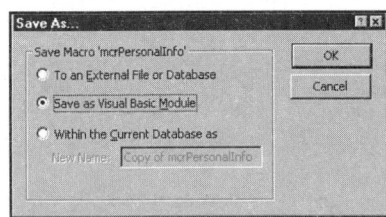

4. Click OK; this opens the Convert Macro dialog box. (See Figure 11.20.)

Figure 11.20.
Use the Convert Macro dialog box to indicate whether error handling and comments will be added to the Visual Basic module.

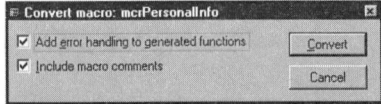

5. Indicate whether you want to add error handling and comments to the generated code, then click Convert.

6. After you get an indication that the conversion is finished, click OK.

7. The converted macro appears under the list of modules with "Converted Macro:" followed by the name of the macro. Click Design to view the results of the conversion.

Figure 11.21 shows a macro that's been converted into distinct subroutines, one for each macro name. The macro is complete with logic, comments, and error handling. All macro conditions are converted into If...Else...End If statements, and all the macro comments are converted into VBA comments. Basic error-handling routines are automatically added to the code.

Figure 11.21.
A converted macro as a module.

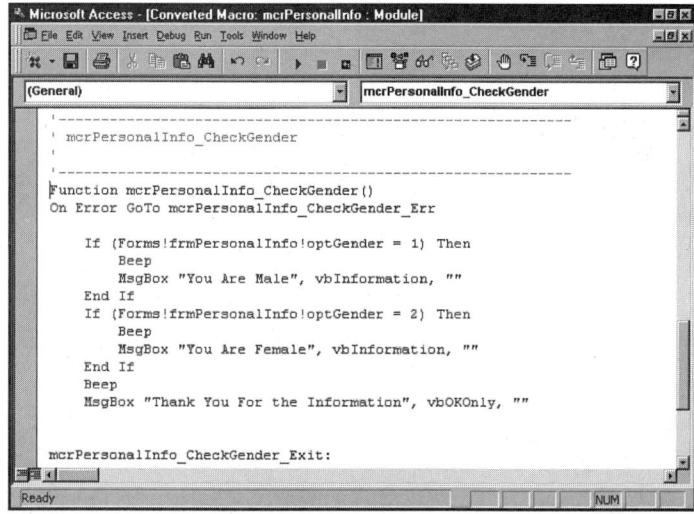

WARNING

When you convert a macro to a Visual Basic module, the original macro remains untouched. Furthermore, all the objects in your application will still call the macro. To effectively use the macro conversion options, you must find all the places where the macro was called and replace the macro references with calls to the VBA function.

Creating an AutoExec Macro

In earlier versions of Access, the only way to have something happen when a database was opened was to use an AutoExec macro. With Access 97, you can use either an AutoExec macro or Startup options to determine what occurs when a database is opened. Nevertheless, using an AutoExec macro to launch the processing of your application is certainly a viable option.

> **NOTE**
>
> I prefer to include as few macros as possible in my application. For this reason, I tend to designate a Startup form for my application that calls a custom "AutoExec" routine when it's opened. This method is covered in Chapter 37, "Distributing Your Application with ODE."

Creating an AutoExec macro is quite simple; it's just a normal macro saved with the name *AutoExec*. An AutoExec macro usually performs tasks such as hiding or minimizing the Database window and opening a Startup form or switchboard. The macro shown in Figure 11.22 hides the Database window, displays a welcome message, and opens the frmClients form.

Figure 11.22.

An example of an AutoExec macro.

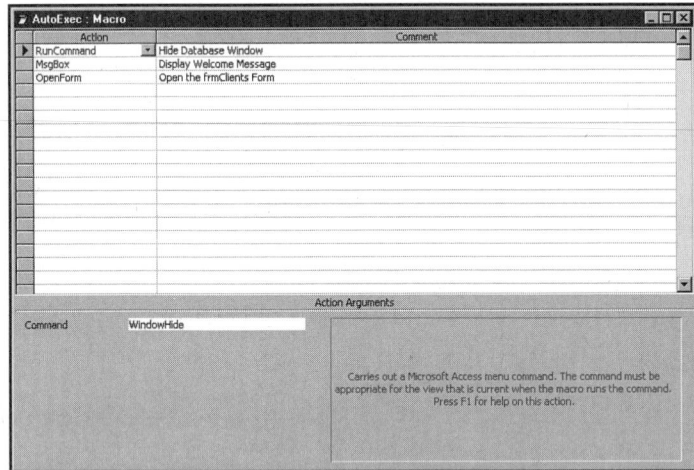

> **TIP**
>
> When you're opening your own database to make changes or additions to the application, you probably won't want the AutoExec macro to execute. To prevent it from executing, hold down your Shift key as you open the database.

Creating an AutoKeys Macro

An AutoKeys macro allows you to redefine keystrokes within your database. You can map selected keystrokes to a single command or to a series of commands. Follow these six steps to build an AutoKeys macro:

1. Open a new macro in Design view.
2. Make sure the Macro Name column is visible.

3. Enter a key name in the Macro Name column. Allowable key names are defined in Access Help and can be seen in Figure 11.23.

Figure 11.23.

A list of valid key names for the AutoKey macro.

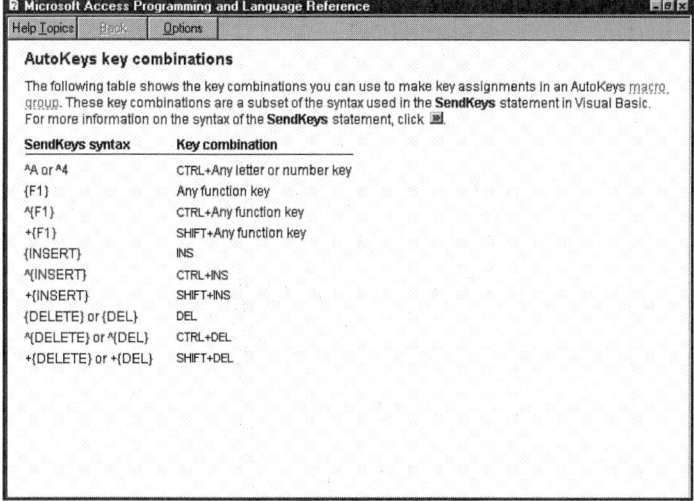

4. Select the macro action you want to associate with the key name. You can apply conditions and arguments just as you do for a normal macro. You can have Access execute multiple commands in one of three ways: Associate multiple macro actions with a key name, perform a `RunCode` action, or perform a `RunMacro` action.

5. Continue adding key names and macro actions to the macro as desired. Separate each key name by one blank line to improve readability.

6. Save the macro as **AutoKeys**. The moment you save the macro, the key names are in effect, and the keystrokes will be remapped. The AutoKeys macro comes into effect automatically each time you open the database.

WARNING

Generally, it's not a good idea to remap common Windows or Access keystrokes. Your users become accustomed to certain keystrokes having certain meanings in all Windows applications. If you try to change the definition of these common keystrokes, your users will become confused and frustrated. That's why it's important to use keystroke combinations that are rarely, if ever, used in Windows.

The DoCmd Object

Most macro commands can be performed in VBA code by using the DoCmd object. The macro action becomes a method of the DoCmd object, and the arguments associated with each macro action become the arguments of the method. For example, the following method of the DoCmd object is used to open a form:

```
DoCmd.OpenForm "frmClients", acNormal, "", "[tblClients]![IntroDate]>Date()-30", _
               acEdit, acNormal
```

The OpenForm method of the DoCmd object that opens the form appears as the first argument to the method. The second argument indicates the view in which the form is opened. The third and fourth arguments specify a filter and Where condition, respectively. The fifth argument of the OpenForm method specifies the Data mode for the form (Add, Edit, or Read Only). The sixth argument indicates the Window mode (Normal, Hidden, Minimized, or Dialog).

Notice the intrinsic constants used for the OpenForm arguments; they help make the code more readable. You can find them in the Help for each DoCmd method.

Practical Examples: Adding an AutoExec Macro to the Time and Billing Application ·

In Chapter 13, you will learn how to add a switchboard to your application. In Chapter 37, you will learn how to use Startup options to designate a Startup form for your application. For now, you'll build an AutoExec macro that acts as the launching point for your application. The macro will start the application by hiding the Database window, displaying a message to the user, and opening the frmClients form.

Build the macro shown in Figure 11.22. Start by opening a new macro in Design view. Set the first action of the macro to RunCommand, then set the Command argument to WindowHide. This will hide the Database window when it's run. Set the second action of the macro to MsgBox, and set the Message to Welcome to the Client Billing Application. Set Beep to No, the Type to Information, and the Title to Welcome. The final action of the macro opens the frmClients form. Set the action to OpenForm, and set the FormName to frmClients. Leave the rest of the arguments at their default values.

Close and reopen the database. The AutoExec macro should automatically execute when the database is opened. Close the database and open it again, holding down the Shift key to prevent the macro from executing.

Summary

Many end-users try to develop entire applications by using macros. Although this is possible, it is *not* appropriate. Macros don't give the developer adequate control or the error handling, debugging capabilities, and other features needed for successful application development.

However, reassigning keystrokes can be done *only* by using macros. Furthermore, an AutoExec macro is one of two ways you can determine what happens when an application loads. Unless you're using a macro to perform one of these tasks, you should always automate your application by using VBA code.

12

CHAPTER

Advanced Query Concepts

- Action Queries, 332
- Special Query Properties, 340
- Optimizing Queries, 344
- Crosstab Queries, 347
- Outer Joins, 353
- Self-Joins, 355
- Understanding SQL, 356
- Union Queries, 362
- Pass-Through Queries, 362
- The Propagation of Nulls and Query Results, 364
- Subqueries, 364
- Using the Result of a Function as the Criteria for a Query, 365
- Passing Parameter Query Values from a Form, 367
- Practical Examples: Applying These Techniques in Your Application, 368

You learned the basics of query design in Chapter 5, "What Every Developer Needs to Know About Query Basics," but Access has a wealth of query capabilities. In addition to the relatively simple Select queries covered in Chapter 5, you can create Crosstab queries, Union queries, Self-Join queries, and many other complex selection queries. You can also easily build Access queries that modify rather than retrieve information. This chapter covers these topics and the more advanced aspects of query design.

Action Queries

With Action queries, you can easily modify data without writing any code, and these queries are often more efficient than performing the same task by using code. Four types of Action queries are available: Update, Delete, Append, and Make Table. You use Update queries to modify data in a table, Delete queries to remove records from a table, Append queries to add records to an existing table, and Make Table queries to create an entirely new table. Each type of query and its appropriate uses are explained in the following sections.

Update Queries

Update queries are used to modify all records or any records meeting specific criteria. They can be used to modify the data in one field or several fields (or even tables) at one time, such as a query that increases the salary of everyone in California by 10 percent. As mentioned, using Update queries is usually more efficient than performing the same task with VBA code, so they're considered a respectable way to modify table data.

To build an Update query, follow these steps:

1. Click the Queries tab of the Database window, then click New.

2. Select Design View and click OK.

3. In the Show Table dialog box, select the tables or queries that will participate in the Update query and click Add. Click Close when you're ready to continue.

4. To let Access know you're building an Update query, open the Query Type drop-down list on the toolbar and select Update. You can also choose Query | Update Query from the menu.

5. Add fields to the query that will either be used for criteria or be updated as a result of the query. In Figure 12.1, StateProvince has been added to the query grid because it will be used as criteria for the update. DefaultRate has been included because it's the field that's being updated.

6. Add any further criteria, if you want. In Figure 12.1, the criteria for StateProvince has been set to CA.

7. Add the appropriate Update expression. In Figure 12.1, the DefaultRate is being increased by 10 percent.

Figure 12.1.

An Update query that increases the DefaultRate for all clients in California.

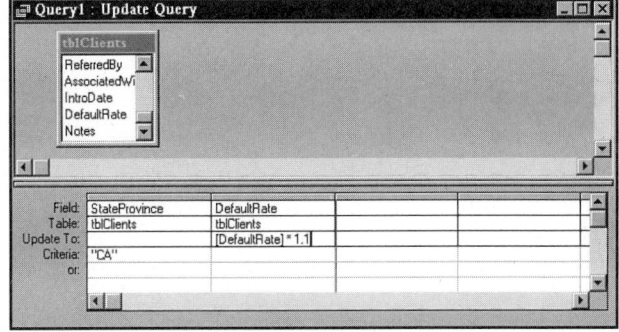

8. Click Run on the toolbar. The message box shown in Figure 12.2 appears. (See the section "Special Notes About Queries" for how to suppress this message by programming.) Click Yes to continue. All records meeting the selected criteria are updated.

Figure 12.2.

The confirmation message you see when running an Update query.

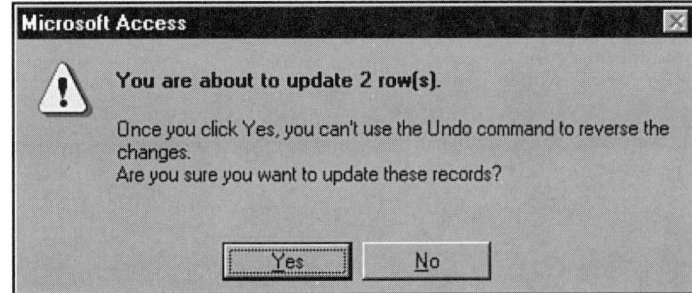

Access Update queries should be named with the prefix *qupd*. Each type of Action query should be given a prefix indicating what type of query it is. Table 12.1 lists all the proper prefixes for Action queries.

Table 12.1. Naming prefixes for Action queries.

Type of Query	Prefix	Example
Update	qupd	qupdDefaultRate
Delete	qdel	qdelOldTimeCards
Append	qapp	qappArchiveTimeCards
Make Table	qmak	qmakTempSales

All Access queries are stored as SQL (Structured Query Language) statements. (Access SQL is discussed later in this chapter in the "Understanding SQL" section.) The SQL behind an Access Update query looks like this:

```
UPDATE DISTINCTROW tblClients SET tblClients.DefaultRate = [DefaultRate]*1.1
    WHERE (((tblClients.StateProvince)="CA"));
```

WARNING

The actions taken by an Update query, as well as by all Action queries, can't be reversed. You must exercise extreme caution when running any Action query.

WARNING

It's important to remember that if the Cascade Update Related Fields Referential Integrity setting is turned on and the Update query tried to modify a primary key field, the foreign key of all corresponding records in related tables is updated. If the Cascade Update Related Fields option isn't turned on and referential integrity is being enforced, the Update query doesn't allow the offending records to be modified.

Delete Queries

Rather than simply modify table data, Delete queries permanently remove records meeting specific criteria from a table; they're often used to remove old records from a table. You might want to delete all orders from the previous year, for example. Follow these four steps to build a Delete query:

1. While in a query's Design view, use the Query Type drop-down list on the toolbar to select Delete. You can also choose Query | Delete Query from the menu.

2. Add the criteria you want to the query grid. The query shown in Figure 12.3 deletes all time cards more than 365 days old.

Figure 12.3.
A Delete query used to delete all time cards entered over a year ago.

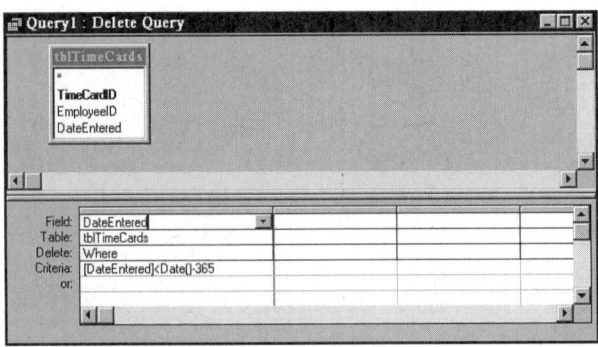

3. Click Run on the toolbar. The message box shown in Figure 12.4 appears. You can suppress this message by using the programming techniques explained in the section "Special Notes About Action Queries."

Figure 12.4.
The Delete query confirmation message box.

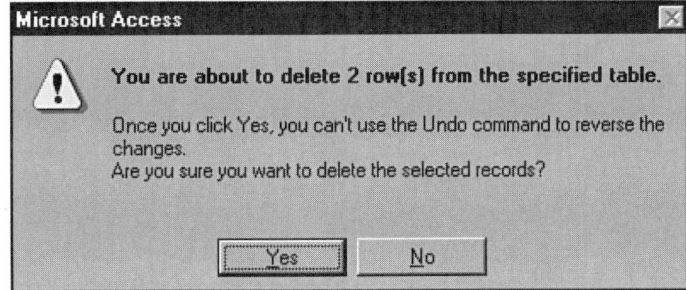

4. Click Yes to permanently remove the records from the table.

The SQL behind a Delete query looks like this:

```
DELETE DISTINCTROW tblTimeCards.DateEntered
    FROM tblTimeCards
    WHERE (((tblTimeCards.DateEntered)<Date()-365));
```

NOTE

It's often useful to view the results of an Action query before you actually affect the records included in the criteria. To view the records affected by the Action query, click the Query View button on the toolbar before you select Run. All records that will be affected by the Action query appear in Datasheet view. If necessary, you can temporarily add key fields to the query to get more information about the records that are about to be affected.

WARNING

Remember that if the Cascade Delete Related Records Referential Integrity setting is turned on, all corresponding records in related tables are deleted. If the Cascade Delete Related Records option isn't turned on and referential integrity is being enforced, the Delete query doesn't allow the offending records to be deleted. If you want to delete the record(s) on the "one" side of the relationship, first you need to delete all the related records on the "many" side.

Append Queries

With Append queries, you can add records to an existing table. This is often done during an archive process. First, the records to be archived are appended to the history table by using an Append query, then they're removed from the master table by using a Delete query. To build an Append query, follow these steps:

1. While in Design view of a query, use the Query Type drop-down list on the toolbar to select Append or choose Query | Append Query from the menu. The dialog box shown in Figure 12.5 appears.

Figure 12.5.
Identifying which table to append and which database to append it to.

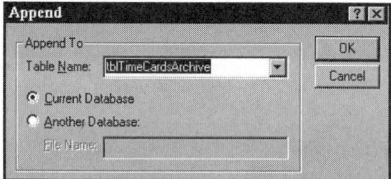

2. Select the table you want the data appended to.
3. Drag all the fields whose data you want included in the second table to the query grid. If the field names in the two tables match, Access automatically matches the field names in the source table to the corresponding field names in the destination table. (See Figure 12.6.) If the field names in the two tables don't match, you need to explicitly designate which fields in the source table match which fields in the destination table.

Figure 12.6.
An Append query that appends the TimeCardID, EmployeeID, and DateEntered of all employees entered in the year 1995 to another table.

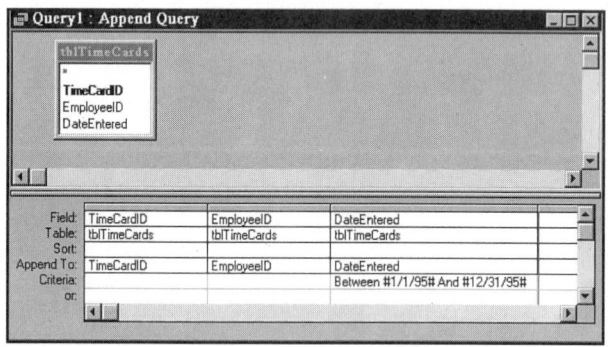

4. Enter any criteria in the query grid. Notice in Figure 12.6 that all records with a DateEntered in 1995 are appended to the destination table.

   To run the query, click Run on the toolbar. The message box shown in Figure 12.7 appears. Click Yes to finish the process.

Figure 12.7.

The Append Query confirmation message box.

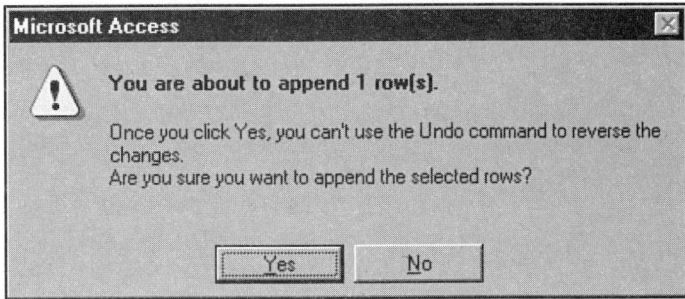

The SQL behind an Append query looks like this:

```
INSERT INTO tblTimeCardsArchive ( TimeCardID, EmployeeID, DateEntered )
    SELECT DISTINCTROW tblTimeCards.TimeCardID, tblTimeCards.EmployeeID,
    tblTimeCards.DateEntered
    FROM tblTimeCards
    WHERE (((tblTimeCards.DateEntered) Between #1/1/95# And #12/31/95#));
```

WARNING

Append queries don't allow you to introduce any primary key violations. If you're appending any records that duplicate a primary key value, the message box shown in Figure 12.8 appears. If you go ahead with the append process, only those records without primary key violations are appended to the destination table.

Figure 12.8.

The warning message you see when an Append query and conversion, primary key, lock, or validation rule violation occur.

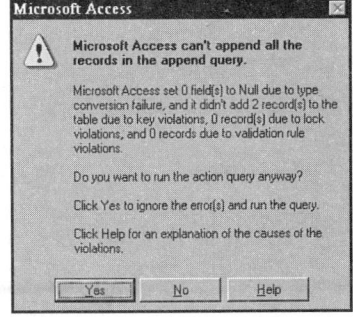

Make Table Queries

An Append query adds records to an existing table, but a Make Table query creates a new table, which is often a temporary table used for intermediary processing. A temporary table is often created to freeze data while a report is being run. By building temporary tables and running the report from those tables, you make sure users can't modify the data underlying the report during the reporting process. Another common use of a Make Table query is to supply a subset of fields or records to another user. Six steps are needed to create a Make Table query:

1. While in the query's Design view, use the Query Type drop-down list on the toolbar to select Make Table or choose Query | Make Table Query from the menu. The dialog box shown in Figure 12.9 appears.

Figure 12.9.

Entering a name for the new table and selecting which database to place it in.

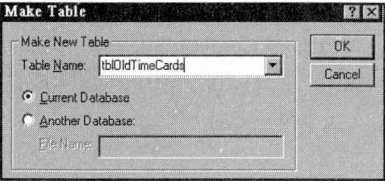

2. Enter the name of the new table and click OK.

3. Move all the fields you want included in the new table to the query grid. The result of an expression is often included in the new table. (See Figure 12.10.)

Figure 12.10.

Adding an expression to a Make Table query.

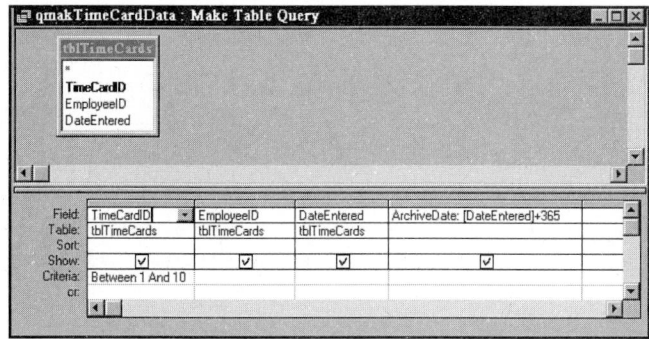

4. Add the criteria you want to the query grid.

5. Click Run on the toolbar to run the query. The message shown in Figure 12.11 appears.

Figure 12.11.

The Make Table query confirmation message box.

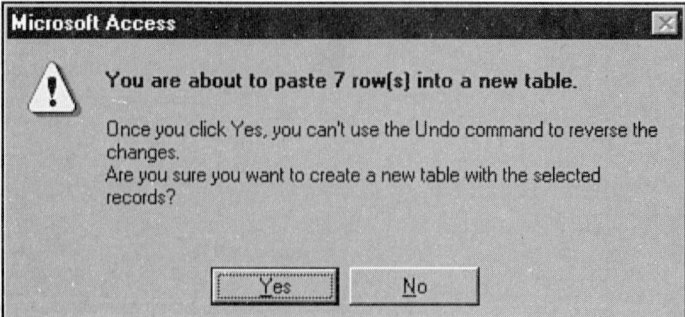

6. Click Yes to finish the process.

WARNING

If you try to run the same Make Table query more than one time, the table with the same name as the table you're creating is permanently deleted. (See the warning message in Figure 12.12.)

Figure 12.12.
The Make Table query warning message you get when a table already exists.

The SQL for a Make Table query looks like this:

```
SELECT DISTINCTROW tblTimeCards.TimeCardID, tblTimeCards.EmployeeID,
    tblTimeCards.DateEntered, [DateEntered]+365 AS ArchiveDate
    INTO tblOldTimeCards
    FROM tblTimeCards
    WHERE (((tblTimeCards.TimeCardID) Between 1 And 10));
```

Special Notes About Action Queries

Additional warning messages, such as the one shown in Figure 12.13, appear when you're running Action queries from the Database window or using code. This message, and all other query messages, can be suppressed programmatically by using the SetWarnings method of the DoCmd object. The code looks like this:

```
DoCmd.SetWarnings False.
```

Figure 12.13.
The warning message you see when running an Action query from code.

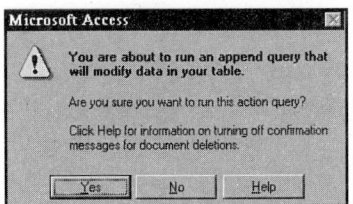

339

To suppress warnings by modifying the Access environment, choose Tools | Options and click the Edit/Find tab. Remove the checkmark from the Action Queries Confirm checkbox.

> **NOTE**
>
> There's a major difference between suppressing warnings by using the DoCmd object and doing so by choosing Tools | Options. Suppressing warnings by using the DoCmd object centralizes control within the application. On the other hand, using Tools | Options to suppress warnings affects all applications run by a particular user.

Action Queries Versus Processing Records with Code

As mentioned, Action queries can be far more efficient than VBA code. Take a look at this example:

```
Sub ModifyPrice()
    Dim db As DATABASE
    Dim rs As Recordset
    Set db = CurrentDb()
    Set rs = db.OpenRecordset("tblOrderDetails")
    Do Until rs.EOF
        If rs!UnitPrice > 1 Then
            rs.Edit
            rs!UnitPrice = rs!UnitPrice - 1
            rs.UPDATE
        End If
        rs.MoveNext
    Loop
End Sub
```

This subroutine loops through tblOrderDetails. If the UnitPrice of a record is greater than 1, the price is reduced by 1. Compare the ModifyPrice subroutine to the following code:

```
Sub RunActionQuery()
    DoCmd.OpenQuery "qupdUnitPrice"
End Sub
```

As you can see, the RunActionQuery subroutine is much easier to code. The qupdUnitPrice query, shown in Figure 12.14, performs the same tasks as the ModifyPrice subroutine. In most cases, the Action query runs more efficiently.

Special Query Properties

Access 97 queries have several properties that can dramatically change their behavior. To look up a query's properties, right-click on a blank area in the top half of the Query window and select Properties to open the Properties window. (See Figure 12.15.) Many of these properties are discussed in Chapter 5, but Unique Values, Unique Records, and Top Values are covered in the following sections.

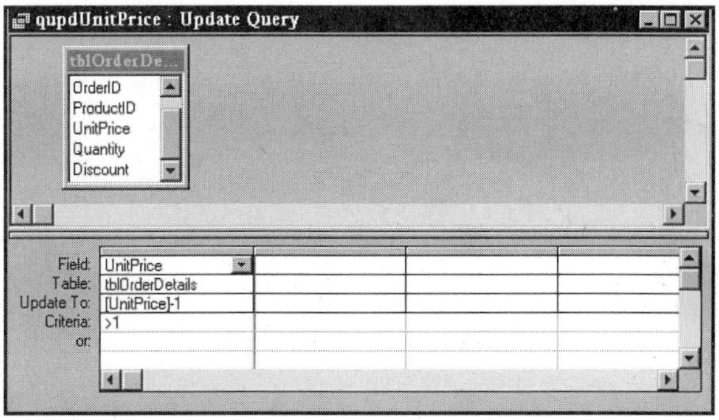

Figure 12.14.
The qupdUnitPrice query decrements the UnitPrice for all records in which the UnitPrice is greater than 1.

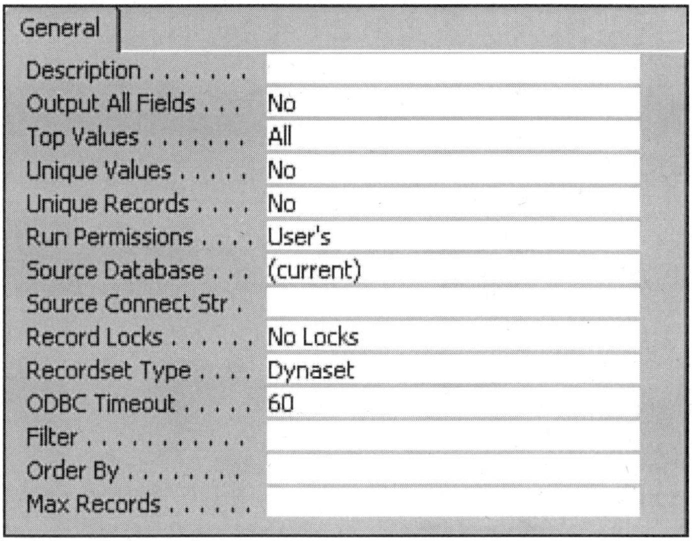

Figure 12.15.
Viewing the general properties for a query.

Unique Values

The Unique Values property, when set to Yes, causes the query output to contain no duplicates for the combination of fields included in it. Figure 12.16, for example, shows a query that includes the Country and City fields from tblCustomers. The Unique Values property in this example is set to No, its default value. Notice that many combinations of countries and cities appear more than once. This happens whenever more than one customer is found in a particular country and city. Compare this with Figure 12.17, in which the Unique Values property is set to Yes. Each combination of country and city appears only once.

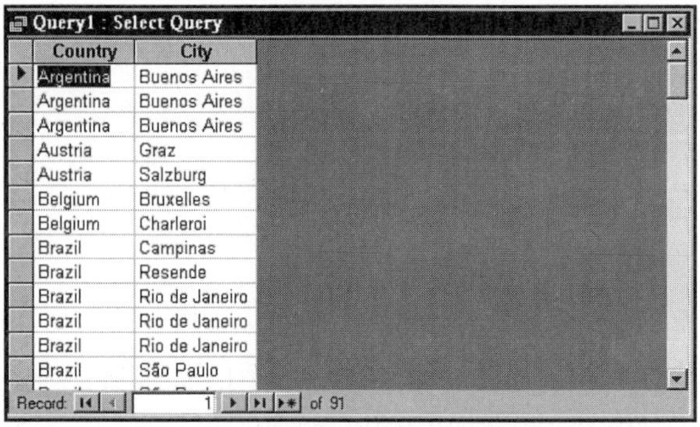

Figure 12.16.

A query with the Unique Values property set to No.

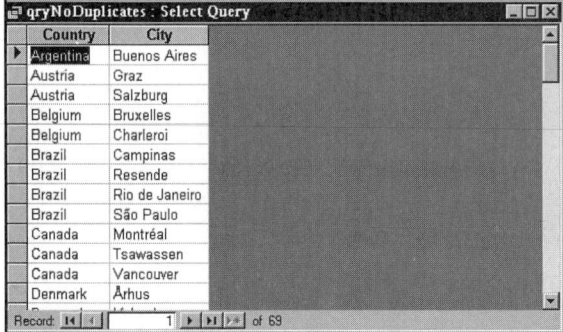

Figure 12.17.

A query with the Unique Values property set to Yes.

Unique Records

The default value for the Unique Records property is Yes, which causes the DISTINCTROW statement to be included in the SQL statement underlying the query. The Unique Records property applies only to multitable queries; it's ignored for queries that include only one table. The DISTINCTROW statement allows the results of a multitable query to be updated by making sure each record in the query output is unique.

Top Values

The Top Values property allows you to specify a certain percentage or a specific number of records that the user wants to view in the query result. For example, you can build a query that outputs the country/city combinations having the top 10 sales amounts. You can also build a query that shows the country/city combinations whose sales ranked in the top 50 percent. You can specify the Top Values property in a few different ways; here are two examples:

- Click Top Values on the toolbar and choose from the predefined list of choices.
- Type a number or a number with a percent sign directly into the Top Values property in the Query Properties window.

Figure 12.18 illustrates the design of a query showing the country/city combinations with the top 10 percent of sales. This Totals query summarizes the result of the price multiplied by the quantity for each combination of country and city. Notice that the Top Values property is set to 10%. The output of the query is sorted in descending order by the result of the SaleAmount calculation. (See Figure 12.19.) If the SaleAmount field were sorted in ascending order, the bottom 10 percent of the sales amount would be displayed in the query result. Remember that the field being used to determine the top values must appear as the leftmost field in the query's sort order.

Figure 12.18.

A Totals query that retrieves the top 10 percent of the sales amounts.

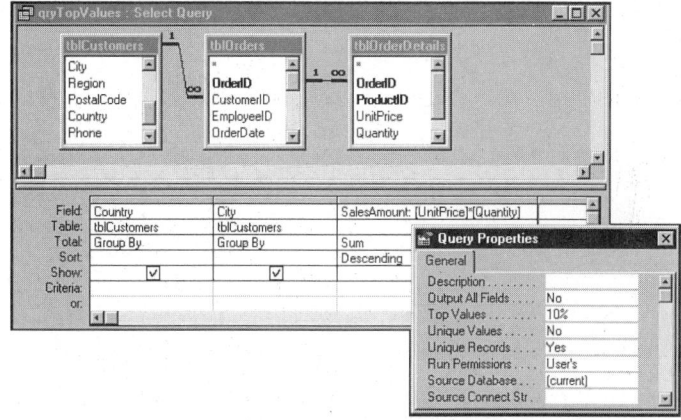

Figure 12.19.

The result of a Totals query showing the top 10 percent of the sales amounts.

Country	City	SaleAmount
Germany	Cunewalde	$229,402.78
USA	Boise	$224,658.78
Austria	Graz	$219,613.36
Ireland	Cork	$111,944.78
UK	London	$105,604.42
Brazil	Rio de Janeiro	$105,554.36
USA	Albuquerque	$102,039.80

Record: |◄| ◄ | 1 | ► | ►| | ►* | of 7

NOTE

You might be surprised to discover that the Top Values property doesn't always seem to accurately display the correct number of records in the query result. This is because all records with values that match the value in the last record are returned as part of the query result. In a table with 100 records, for example, the query asks for the top 10 values. Twelve records will appear in the query result if the 10th, 11th, and 12th records all have the same value in the field being used to determine the top value.

Optimizing Queries

The Microsoft Jet Engine includes an Optimizer that looks at how long it takes to perform each task needed to produce the required query results. It then produces a plan for the shortest path to getting the results you want; this plan is based on several statistics:

- The amount of data in each table included in the query
- How many data pages are in each table
- The location of each table included in the query
- What indexes are available in each table
- Which indexes are unique
- Other statistics

The Query Compilation Process

These statistics are updated whenever the query is compiled. For a query to be compiled, it must be flagged as needing to be compiled—this happens when any of the following occurs:

- Changes are saved to the query.
- Changes are saved to any tables underlying a query.
- The database is compacted.

After a query has been flagged as needing to be compiled, it isn't compiled until the next time the query is run. During compiling, which takes one to four seconds, all statistics are updated, and a new optimization or Query Plan is produced.

> **NOTE**
>
> Because a Query Plan is based on the number of records in each table included in the query, you should open and save your queries each time the volume of data in a table changes significantly. This is especially true when you're moving your query from a test environment to a production environment. If you test your application with a few records in each table and the table's production data soon grows to thousands of records, your query will be optimized for only a few records and won't run efficiently.

Analyzing a Query's Performance

When you're analyzing the time it takes for a particular query to run, it's important to time two tasks:

- How long it takes for the first screen of data to display
- How long it takes to get the last record in the query result

The first measurement is fairly obvious; it measures the amount of time it takes from the moment the Run button is clicked on the toolbar until the first screen of data is displayed. The second measurement is a little less obvious; it involves waiting until the "N" value in "Record 1 of N" at the bottom of the query result displays. The two measurements might be the same if the query returns only a small number of records. This is because the Jet Engine decides whether it's more efficient to run the query, then display the query results, or to display partial query results, then continue running the query in the background.

TIP

The Performance Analyzer can analyze your queries to determine whether additional indexes will improve query performance. It's important to run the Performance Analyzer with the volume of data that will be present in your tables' production version. The Performance Analyzer is covered in Chapter 23, "Optimizing Your Application."

Things You Can Do to Improve a Query's Performance

You can do many things to improve a query's performance. These include, but aren't limited to, the following techniques:

- Index fields on both sides of a join.
- Add only the fields you actually need in the query results to the query grid. If a field is required for criteria but doesn't need to appear in the query result, clear the Show checkbox on the query grid.
- Add as many indexes as possible. This slows down inserting, updating, and deleting records, but the tradeoff is usually well worth it.
- Always index on fields used in the criteria of the query.
- Compact the database often. During compacting, Access tries to reorganize a table's records so that they reside in adjacent database pages, ordered by the table's primary key. This improves performance when the table is being scanned during a query.
- When running a multitable query, test to see whether the query runs faster with the criteria placed on the "one" side or the "many" side of the join.
- Avoid adding criteria to calculated or nonindexed fields.
- Select the smallest field types possible for each field. For example, create a Long Integer CustID field rather than specifying the CompanyName field as the primary key for the table.
- Avoid calculated fields in nested queries. It's always preferable to add calculations to the higher level queries.

- Rather than including all expressions in the query, include some expressions on form and report controls. The downside to this is that the expression will need to be repeated and maintained on each form and report.

- Use Make Table queries to build tables out of query results based on tables that rarely change. In a State table, for example, rather than displaying a unique list of states on all the states currently included in the Customer table, build a separate State table and use that in your queries.

- When using Like in the query criteria, try to place the asterisk at the end of the character string rather than at the beginning. When the asterisk is placed at the end of a string, as in Like Th*, an index can be used to improve query performance. If the asterisk is placed at the beginning of a string, as in Like *Sr, no index can be used.

- Use Count(*) rather than Count([fieldname]) when counting how many records meet a particular set of criteria. Count(*) simply tallies up the total number of records, but Count([fieldname]) actually checks to see whether the value is Null, which would exclude the record from the total computation. Furthermore, as mentioned in the next section on Rushmore technology, the Count(*) function is highly optimized by Rushmore.

- Use Group By as little as possible. When possible, use First instead. For example, if you're totaling sales information by order date and order number, you can use First for the order date and group by order number. This is because all records for a given order number automatically occur on the same order date.

- Use Rushmore technology to speed query performance whenever possible. Rushmore technology—a data-access technology "borrowed" from Microsoft's FoxPro PC database engine—improves the performance of certain queries. Rushmore technology is discussed in the following section.

Probably one of the most important things to learn from the tips listed here is that they shouldn't be followed blindly. Query optimization is an art rather than a science. What helps in some situations might actually do harm in others, so it's important to do benchmarks with your actual system and data.

Rushmore Technology

As mentioned, Rushmore is a data-access technology that can help improve processing queries. Rushmore technology can be used only when certain types of expressions are included in the query criteria. It won't automatically speed up all your queries. A query must be constructed in a certain way for the query to benefit from Rushmore.

A query with an expression and comparison operator as the criteria for an indexed field can be optimized by Rushmore. The comparison operator must be <, >, =, <=, >=, <>, Between, Like, or In.

The expression can be any valid expression, including constants, functions, and fields from other tables. Here are some examples of expressions that can be optimized:

```
[Age] > 50
[OrderDate] Between #1/1/96# And #12/31/96#
[State] = "CA"
```

Rushmore can also be used to optimize queries that include complex expressions combining the And and Or operators. If both expressions are fully optimizable, the query will be fully optimized. However, if only one expression is fully optimizable and the expressions are combined with an And, the query will be partially optimized; if only one expression is fully optimizable and the expressions are combined with an Or, the query won't be optimized.

Important Notes About Rushmore

You should remember a few important notes about Rushmore:

- Queries containing the Not operator can't be optimized.
- The Count(*) function is highly optimized by Rushmore.
- Descending indexes cannot be used by Rushmore unless the expression is =.
- Queries on ODBC data sources can't use Rushmore.
- Multifield indexes can be used by Rushmore only when the criteria is in the order of the index. For example, if an index exists for the LastName field in combination with the FirstName field, the index can be used to search on LastName or on a combination of LastName and FirstName, but it can't be used in an expression based on the FirstName field.

Crosstab Queries

A Crosstab query summarizes query results by displaying one field in a table down the left side of the datasheet and additional facts across the top of the datasheet. A Crosstab query can, for example, summarize the number of orders placed each month by a salesperson. The name of each salesperson can be placed in the query output's leftmost column, and each month can be displayed across the top. The number of orders placed would appear in the appropriate cell of the query output. (See Figure 12.20.)

Crosstab queries are probably one of the most complex and difficult queries to create. For this reason, Microsoft offers a Crosstab Query Wizard. The methods for creating a Crosstab query with and without the Crosstab Query Wizard are explained in the following sections.

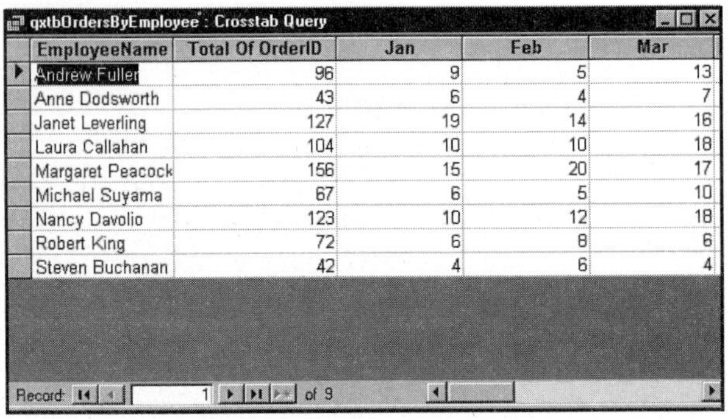

Figure 12.20.

An example of a Crosstab query that shows the number of orders placed by each employee by month.

EmployeeName	Total Of OrderID	Jan	Feb	Mar
Andrew Fuller	96	9	5	13
Anne Dodsworth	43	6	4	7
Janet Leverling	127	19	14	16
Laura Callahan	104	10	10	18
Margaret Peacock	156	15	20	17
Michael Suyama	67	6	5	10
Nancy Davolio	123	10	12	18
Robert King	72	6	8	6
Steven Buchanan	42	4	6	4

(qxtbOrdersByEmployee : Crosstab Query — Record: 1 of 9)

Creating a Crosstab Query with the Crosstab Query Wizard

Follow these eight steps to design a Crosstab query with the Crosstab Query Wizard:

1. Select the Queries tab from the Database window and click New.
2. Select Crosstab Query Wizard and click OK.
3. Select the table or query that will act as a foundation for the query. If you want to include fields from more than one table in the query, you'll need to base the Crosstab query on another query that has the tables and fields you want. Click Next.
4. Select the field(s) whose values you want to use as the row headings for the query output. In Figure 12.21, the EmployeeName expression is selected as the row heading. Click Next.

Figure 12.21.

Specifying the rows of a Crosstab query.

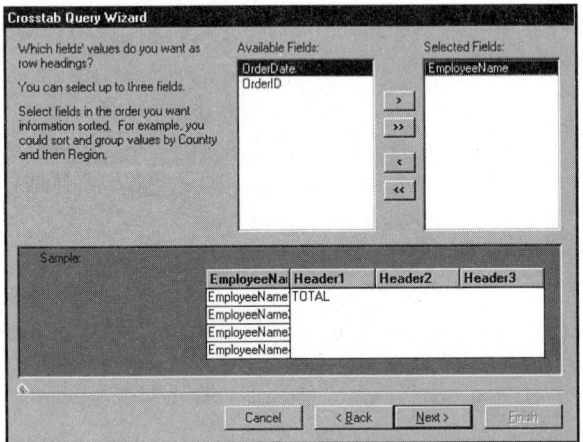

5. Select the field whose values you want to use as the column headings for the query output. In Figure 12.22, the OrderDate field is selected as the column heading. Click Next.

Figure 12.22.

Specifying the columns of a Crosstab query.

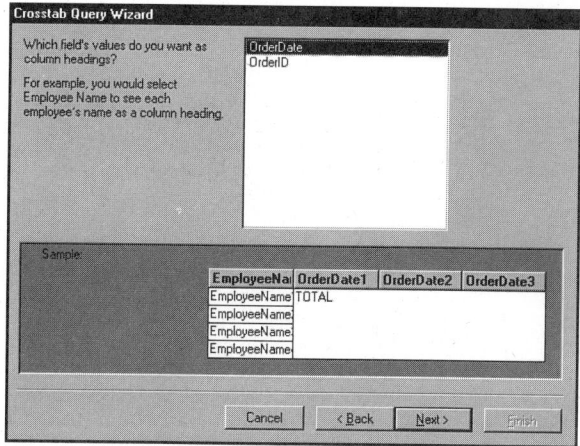

6. If the field you selected for a heading is a Date field, the Crosstab Query Wizard asks that you specify the interval you want to group by. In Figure 12.23, the OrderDate field is grouped by month. Select the desired date interval and click Next.

Figure 12.23.

Specifying the interval for a Date field of a Crosstab query.

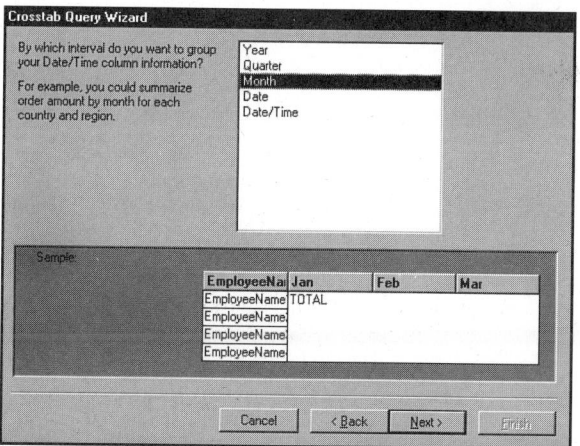

7. The next step of the Crosstab Query Wizard asks you to specify what number you want calculated for each column and row intersection. In Figure 12.24, the OrderID is counted by month for each employee. Click Next.

Figure 12.24.

Specifying the number you want the Crosstab query to calculate.

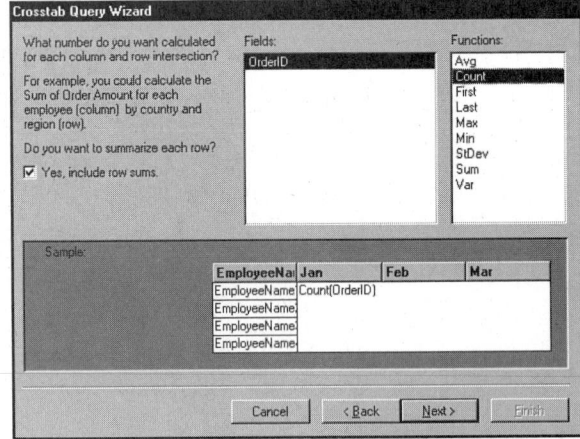

8. In the final step of the wizard, you specify a name for your query. When you're done, click Finish.

Figure 12.25 shows a completed Crosstab query in Design view; take a look at several important attributes. Notice the Crosstab row of the query grid. The EmployeeName field is specified as a row heading and is used as a Group By for the query. The following expression is included as a Column Heading:

```
Format([OrderDate],"mmm").
```

This expression returns the order date formatted to display only the month. This expression is also used as a Group By for the query. The OrderID is specified as a value. The Total cell for the column indicates that this field will be counted (as opposed to being summed, averaged, and so on).

Notice the column labeled "Total of OrderID." This column displays the total of all the columns in the query; it's identical to the column containing the value except for the alias in the field name and the fact that the Crosstab cell is set to Row Heading rather than Value.

Figure 12.25.

A completed Crosstab query in Design view.

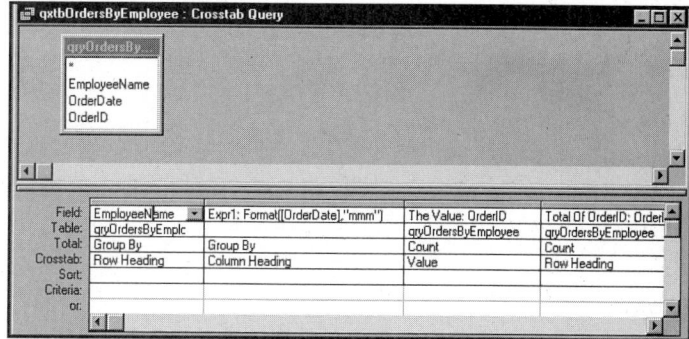

Creating a Crosstab Query Without the Crosstab Query Wizard

Although you can create many of your Crosstab queries by using the Crosstab Query Wizard, you should know how to build one without the wizard. This knowledge lets you modify existing Crosstab queries and gain ultimate control over creating new queries. To build a Crosstab query without using the Crosstab Query Wizard, follow these steps:

1. Click the Queries tab of the Database window and click New.
2. Select Design View and click OK.
3. Select the table or query that will be included in the query grid. Click Add to add the table or query, then click Close.
4. Use the Query Type drop-down list to select Crosstab Query.
5. Add the fields you want to include in the query output to the query grid.
6. Click the Crosstab row of each field you want to include as a row heading. Select Row Heading from the drop-down list.
7. Click the Crosstab row of the field you want to include as a column heading. Select Column Heading from the drop-down list.
8. Click the Crosstab row of the field whose values you want to cross-tabulate. Select Value from the Crosstab drop-down list, then select the appropriate aggregate function from the Total drop-down list.
9. Add any date intervals or other expressions you want to include.
10. Specify any criteria for the query.
11. Change the sort order of any of the columns, if you like.
12. Run the query when you're ready.

Figure 12.26 shows a query in which the column heading is set to the month of the OrderDate field; the row heading is set to the ProductName field. The sum of the TotalAmount field is the value for the query. The OrderDate is also included in the query grid as a WHERE clause for the query. Figure 12.27 shows the results of running the query.

Figure 12.26.

A Crosstab query designed without a wizard, showing the total dollars sold by product and month.

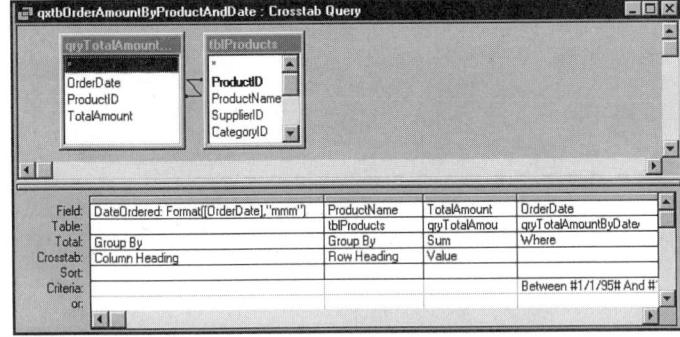

Figure 12.27.

The result of running the Crosstab query shown in Figure 12.26.

Product Name	Jan	Feb	Mar	Apr
Alice Mutton	$3,648.00	$5,168.00	$912.00	$6,764.
Aniseed Syrup	$1,580.00			$500.
Boston Crab Meat	$2,958.00	$4,280.40	$348.00	$1,914.
Camembert Pierrot	$10,296.00	$8,910.00	$5,214.00	$11,220.
Carnarvon Tigers	$6,765.00	$3,075.00	$2,214.00	$6,519.
Chai	$3,328.00	$4,160.00	$672.00	$3,328.
Chang	$2,988.00	$1,440.00	$2,160.00	$5,436.
Chartreuse verte	$4,448.00	$1,696.00	$960.00	
Chef Anton's Cajun Seasoning	$882.00	$1,260.00	$210.00	$1,050.
Chef Anton's Gumbo Mix	$1,221.00		$814.00	$4,070.
Chocolade	$204.00			
Côte de Blaye	$68,250.00	$21,000.00	$34,125.00	$13,125.
Escargots de Bourgogne	$2,703.00	$795.00	$795.00	$1,060.

Record: 14 ◄ 1 ► ►► ►* of 76

Fixed Column Headings

If you don't use fixed column headings, all the columns are included in the query output in alphabetical order. For example, if you include month names in the query result, they appear as Apr, Aug, Dec, Feb, and so on. By using fixed column headings, you tell Access the order in which each column appears in the query result. Column headings can be specified by setting the query's Column Headings. (See Figure 12.28.)

> **NOTE**
>
> All fixed column headings must match the underlying data exactly; otherwise, information will be omitted inadvertently from the query result. For example, if the column heading for the month of June was accidentally entered as June, and the data output by the format statement included data for the month of "Jun," all June data would be omitted from the query output.

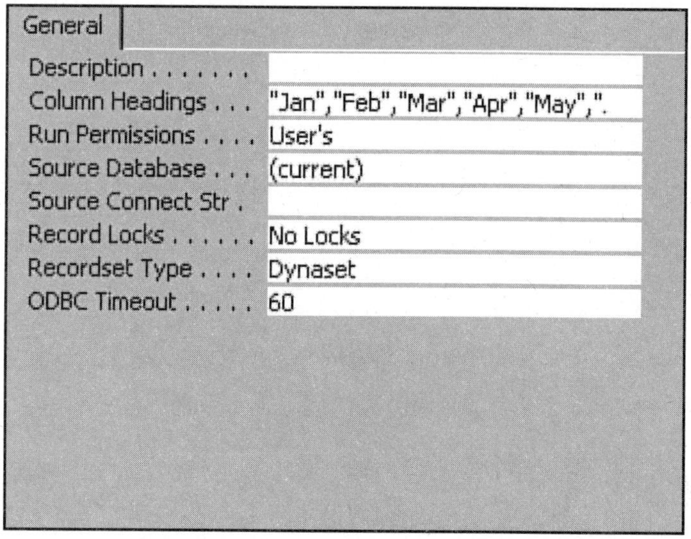

Figure 12.28.

A query's Column Headings property.

General	
Description	
Column Headings . . .	"Jan","Feb","Mar","Apr","May","
Run Permissions	User's
Source Database . . .	(current)
Source Connect Str .	
Record Locks	No Locks
Recordset Type	Dynaset
ODBC Timeout	60

Important Notes About Crosstab Queries

Regardless of how Crosstab queries are created, you should be aware of some special caveats when working with them:

- You can select only one value and one column heading for a Crosstab query, but multiple row headings can be selected.

- The results of a Crosstab query can't be updated.

- You can't define criteria on the Value field. If you do, you get the error message "You can't specify criteria on the same field for which you enter Value in the Crosstab row." If you must specify criteria for the Value field, you must build a Crosstab query based on a Totals query. The criteria is then placed in the Totals query on which the Crosstab query is based.

- All parameters used in a Crosstab query must be explicitly declared in the Query Parameters dialog box.

Outer Joins

Outer Joins are used when you want the records on the "one" side of a one-to-many relation-ship to be included in the query result regardless of whether there are matching records in the table on the "many" side. With a customers table and an orders table, for example, users often want to include only customers with orders in the query output. An Inner Join (the default join type) does this. In other situations, users want *all* customers to be included in the query result whether they have orders or not—this is when an Outer Join is necessary.

NOTE

There are two types of Outer Joins: Left Outer Joins and Right Outer Joins. A Left Outer Join occurs when all records on the "one" side of a one-to-many relationship are included in the query result regardless of whether any records exist on the "many" side. A Right Outer Join means all records on the "many" side of a one-to-many relationship are included in the query result regardless of whether there are any records on the "one" side. A Right Outer Join should never occur, unless referential integrity isn't being enforced.

To establish an Outer Join, you must modify the join between the tables included in the query:

1. Double-click the line joining the tables in the query grid.

2. The Join Properties window appears. (See Figure 12.29.) Select the type of join you want to create. To create a Left Outer Join between the tables, select Option 2 (Option 3 if you want to create a Right Outer Join). Notice in Figure 12.29 that the description is "Include ALL records from 'tblCustomers' and only those records from 'tblOrders' where the joined fields are equal."

Figure 12.29.

Establishing a Left Outer Join.

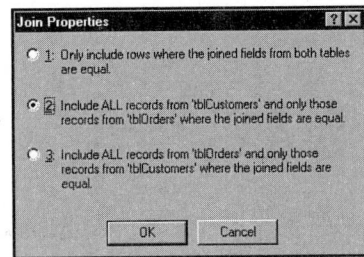

3. Click OK to accept the join. An Outer Join should be established between the tables.

The SQL statement produced when a Left Outer Join is established looks like this:

```
SELECT DISTINCTROW tblCustomers.CustomerID, tblCustomers.CompanyName
FROM tblCustomers
LEFT JOIN tblOrders ON tblCustomers.CustomerID = tblOrders.CustomerID;
```

A Left Outer Join can also be used to identify all the records on the "one" side of a join that don't have any corresponding records on the "many" side. To do this, simply enter **Is Null** as the criteria for any field on the "many" side of the join. In the query shown in Figure 12.30, only customers without orders are displayed in the query result.

Figure 12.30.

A query showing customers without orders.

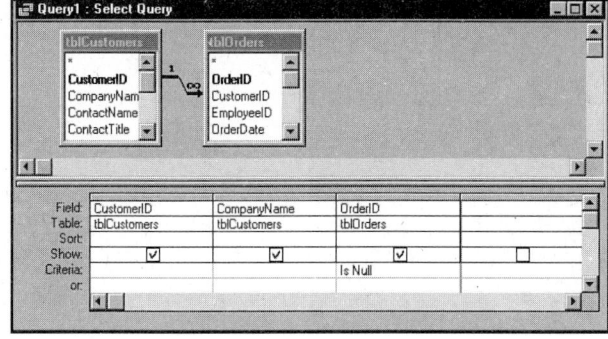

Self-Joins

A Self-Join allows you to join a table to itself, which is often done so that information in a single table can appear to exist in two separate tables. A classic example is seen with employees and supervisors. Two fields are included in the employees table; one field includes the EmployeeID of the employee being described in the record, and the other field specifies the EmployeeID of the employee's supervisor. If you want to see a list of employees and their supervisors, you'll need to use a Self-Join. To build a Self-Join query, follow these steps:

1. Click the Queries tab of the Database window and then click New.

2. Select Design View and click OK.

3. From the Show Tables dialog box, add the table to be used in the Self-Join to the query grid two times. Click Close. Notice that the second instance of the table appears with an underscore and the number *1*.

4. To change the alias of the second table, right-click on top of the table in the query grid and select Properties. Change the Alias property as desired. In Figure 12.31, the alias has been changed to Supervisors.

Figure 12.31.

Building a Self-Join.

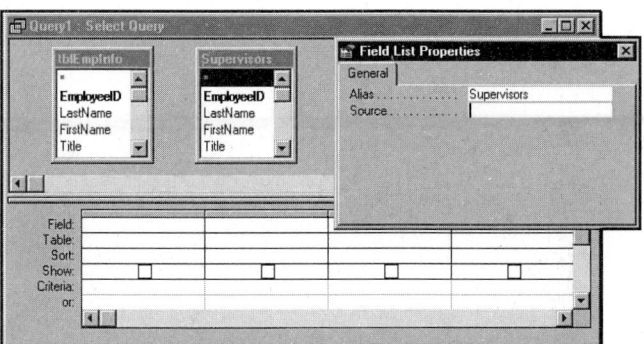

5. To establish a join between the table and its alias, click and drag from the field in one table that corresponds to the field in the aliased table. In Figure 12.32, the ReportsTo field of the tblEmpInfo table has been joined with the EmployeeID field from the aliased table.

6. Drag the appropriate fields to the query grid. In Figure 12.32, the FirstName and LastName fields are included from the tblEmpInfo table. The SupervisorName expression (a concatenation of the supervisor's first and last names) is supplied from the copy of the table with the Supervisors alias.

Figure 12.32.

Establishing a Self-Join between the table and its alias.

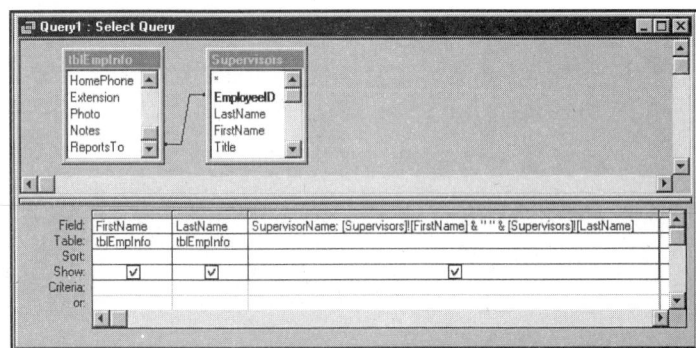

Understanding SQL

Access SQL is the language that underlies Access queries, so you need to understand a little bit about it, where it came from, and how it works. Access SQL allows you to construct queries without using the Access QBE (Query By Example) grid, such as when you must build an SQL statement on-the-fly in response to user interaction with your application. Furthermore, certain operations supported by Access SQL aren't supported by the graphical QBE grid. You must build these SQL statements in the Query Builder's SQL view.

What Is SQL and Where Did It Come From?

SQL is a standard from which many different dialects have emerged. It was developed at an IBM research laboratory in the early 1970s and first formally described in a research paper released in 1974 at an Association for Computing Machinery meeting. Access SQL, a dialect of SQL, is a hybrid of the SQL-86 and SQL-92 standards.

What Do You Need to Know About SQL?

At the very least, you need to understand SQL's basic constructs, which allow you to select, update, delete, and append data by using SQL commands and syntax. SQL is actually made up of very few verbs. The most commonly used verbs are discussed in the following sections.

SQL Syntax

SQL is easy to learn. When retrieving data, you simply build a SELECT statement. SELECT statements are composed of clauses that determine the specifics of how the data is selected. When they're executed, SELECT statements select rows of data and return them as a recordset.

The SELECT Clause

The SELECT clause specifies what columns you want to retrieve from the table whose data is being returned to the recordset. The simplest SELECT clause looks like this:

```
SELECT *
```

This SELECT clause retrieves all columns from a table. Here's another example that retrieves only the ClientID and CompanyName columns from a table:

```
SELECT ClientID, CompanyName
```

Not only can you include columns that exist in your table, you can include expressions in a SELECT clause. Here's an example:

```
SELECT ClientID, [City] & ", " & [State] & "  " & [PostalCode] AS Address
```

This SELECT clause retrieves the ClientID column as well as a pseudo-column called Address, which includes an expression that concatenates the City, State, and PostalCode columns.

The FROM Clause

The FROM clause specifies the tables or queries from which the records should be selected. It can include an alias you use to refer to the table. The FROM clause looks like this:

```
FROM tblClients AS Clients
```

In this case, the name of the table is tblClients, and the alias is Clients. If you combine the SELECT clause with the FROM clause, the SQL statement looks like this:

```
SELECT ClientID, CompanyName FROM tblClients
```

This SELECT statement retrieves the ClientID and CompanyName columns from the tblClients table.

The WHERE Clause

The WHERE clause limits the records retrieved by the SELECT statement. A WHERE clause can include up to 40 columns combined by the keywords AND and OR. A simple WHERE clause looks like this:

```
WHERE Country = "USA"
```

Using an AND to further limit the criteria, the WHERE clause looks like this:

```
WHERE Country = "USA" AND ContactTitle Like "Sales*"
```

This WHERE clause limits the records returned to those in which the country is equal to "USA" and the ContactTitle begins with "Sales." Using an OR, the SELECT statement looks like this:

```
WHERE Country = "USA" OR Country = "Canada"
```

This WHERE clause returns all records in which the country is equal to either "USA" or "Canada." Compare that with the following example:

```
WHERE Country = "USA" OR ContactTitle Like "Sales*"
```

This WHERE clause returns all records in which the country is equal to "USA" or the ContactTitle begins with "Sales." For example, the salespeople in China will be returned from this WHERE clause. The WHERE clause combined with the SELECT and FROM clauses looks like this:

```
SELECT ClientID, CompanyName FROM tblClients
    WHERE Country = "USA" OR Country = "Canada"
```

The ORDER BY Clause

The ORDER BY clause determines the order in which the returned rows are sorted. It's an optional clause and looks like this:

```
ORDER BY ClientID
```

The ORDER BY clause can include more than one field:

```
ORDER BY Country, ClientID
```

When more than one field is specified, the leftmost field is used as the primary level of sort. Any additional fields are the lower sort levels. Combined with the rest of the SELECT statement, the ORDER BY clause looks like this:

```
SELECT ClientID, CompanyName FROM tblClients
    WHERE Country = "USA" OR Country = "Canada"
    ORDER BY ClientID
```

The JOIN Clause

Often you'll need to build SELECT statements that retrieve data from more than one table. When building a SELECT statement based on more than one table, you must join the tables with a JOIN clause. The JOIN clause differs depending on whether you join the tables with an INNER JOIN, a LEFT OUTER JOIN, or a RIGHT OUTER JOIN. Here's an example of an INNER JOIN:

```
SELECT DISTINCTROW tblClients.ClientID,
    tblClients.CompanyName, tblProjects.ProjectName,
    tblProjects.ProjectDescription
    FROM tblClients
    INNER JOIN tblProjects ON tblClients.ClientID = tblProjects.ClientID
```

Notice that four columns are returned in the query result. Two columns are from tblClients and two are from tblProjects. The SELECT statement uses an INNER JOIN from tblClients to tblProjects based on the ClientID field. This means that only clients who have projects are displayed in the query result. Compare this with the following SELECT statement:

```
SELECT DISTINCTROW tblClients.ClientID,
    tblClients.CompanyName, tblProjects.ProjectName,
    tblProjects.ProjectDescription
    FROM tblClients
    LEFT JOIN tblProjects ON tblClients.ClientID = tblProjects.ClientID
```

This SELECT statement joins the two tables using a LEFT JOIN from tblClients to tblProjects based on the ClientID field. All clients are included in the resulting records whether they have projects or not.

> **NOTE**
>
> The word OUTER is assumed in the LEFT JOIN clause used when building a Left Outer Join.

ALL, DISTINCTROW, and DISTINCT Clauses

The ALL clause of a SELECT statement means that all rows meeting the WHERE clause are included in the query result. When the DISTINCT keyword is used, Access eliminates duplicate rows, based on the fields included in the query result. This is the same as setting the Unique Values property to Yes in the graphical QBE grid. When the DISTINCTROW keyword is used, Access eliminates any duplicate rows based on all columns of all tables included in the query (whether they appear in the query result or not). This is the same as setting the Unique Records property to Yes in the graphical QBE grid.

The GROUP BY Clause

The GROUP BY clause is used to calculate summary statistics; it's created when you build a Totals query by using the graphical QBE grid. In the following example, the SELECT statement returns the country, city, and total freight for each country/city combination:

```
SELECT DISTINCTROW tblCustomers.Country, tblCustomers.City,
    Sum(tblOrders.Freight) AS SumOfFreight
    FROM tblCustomers
    INNER JOIN tblOrders ON tblCustomers.CustomerID = tblOrders.CustomerID
    GROUP BY tblCustomers.Country, tblCustomers.City
```

The GROUP BY clause indicates that detail for the selected records isn't displayed. Instead, the fields indicated in the GROUP BY clause are displayed uniquely. One of the fields in the SELECT statement must include an aggregate function. This result of the aggregate function is displayed along with the fields specified in the GROUP BY clause.

The HAVING Clause

A HAVING clause is similar to a WHERE clause but differs in one major respect: It's applied after the data is summarized rather than before. In the following example, the criteria > 1000 will be applied after the aggregate function SUM is applied to the grouping:

```
SELECT DISTINCTROW tblCustomers.Country, tblCustomers.City,
    Sum(tblOrders.Freight) AS SumOfFreight
    FROM tblCustomers
    INNER JOIN tblOrders ON tblCustomers.CustomerID = tblOrders.CustomerID
    GROUP BY tblCustomers.Country, tblCustomers.City
    HAVING (((Sum(tblOrders.Freight))>1000))
```

Applying What You Have Learned

You can practice entering and working with SQL statements in two places:

- In a query's SQL View window
- In VBA code

Now take a look at both these techniques.

Using the Graphical QBE Grid as a Two-Way Tool

A great place to practice writing SQL statements is in the SQL View window of a query. It works like this:

1. Start by building a new query.
2. Add a couple of fields, and maybe even some criteria.
3. Use the Query View drop-down list on the Query Design toolbar to select SQL View.
4. Try changing the SQL statement by using what you have learned in this chapter.
5. Use the Query View drop-down list on the Query Design toolbar to select Design View. As long as you haven't violated any Access SQL syntax rules, you can easily switch to the query's Design view and see the graphical result of your changes. If you've introduced any syntax errors into the SQL statement, an error occurs when you try to return to the query's Design view.

Including SQL Statements in VBA Code

SQL statements can also be executed directly from VBA code. You can run an SQL statement from VBA code in a couple of ways:

- You can build a temporary query, then execute it.
- You can open a recordset with the SQL statement as the foundation for the recordset.

The VBA language allows you to build a query on-the-fly, execute it, and never store it. The parentheses are omitted in the following CurrentDB function because VBA doesn't require parentheses with functions that have no arguments. You can decide whether to include them. The code looks like this:

```
Sub CreateTempQuery()
    Dim db As DATABASE
    Dim qry As QueryDef
    Dim rst As Recordset

    Set db = CurrentDb
    Set qry = db.CreateQueryDef("", _
        "Select ProjectID, ProjectName FROM tblProjects " _
        & "Where ProjectTotalEstimate > 30000")
    Set rst = qry.OpenRecordset()
    Do Until rst.EOF
        Debug.Print rst!ProjectID & " - " & rst!ProjectName
        rst.MoveNext
    Loop
End Sub
```

Working with recordsets is covered extensively in Chapter 15, "What Are Data Access Objects and Why Are They Important?" For now, you need to understand that this code creates a query definition using an SQL statement. Because the first parameter of the database object's CreateQueryDef method is set to a zero-length string, the query definition is never added to the database. Instead, the SQL statement is executed but never stored.

An SQL statement can also be used as part of the database's OpenRecordset method. The code looks like this:

```
Sub OpenRSWithSQL()
    Dim db As DATABASE
    Dim rst As Recordset

    Set db = CurrentDb
    Set rst = db.OpenRecordset("Select ProjectID, " _
        & "ProjectName FROM tblProjects " _
        & "Where ProjectTotalEstimate > 30000", _
        dbOpenDynaset)
    Do Until rst.EOF
        Debug.Print rst!ProjectID & " - " & rst!ProjectName
        rst.MoveNext
    Loop
End Sub
```

Again, this code is discussed more thoroughly in Chapter 15. Notice that the OpenRecordset method of the database object receives two parameters: The first is a SELECT statement, and the second is a constant that indicates what type of recordset you're opening.

Union Queries

A Union query allows you to combine data from two tables with similar structures; data from each table is included in the output. For example, say you have a tblTimeCards table containing active time cards and a tblTimeCardsArchive table containing archived time cards. The problem occurs when you want to build a report that combines data from both tables. To do this, you must build a Union query as the record source for the report:

1. Click the Queries tab of the Database window and click New.
2. Select Design View and click OK.
3. Click Close from the Show Tables dialog box without selecting a table.
4. Choose Query | SQL Specific | Union to open an SQL window.
5. Type in the SQL UNION clause. Notice that you can't switch back to the query's Design view. (See Figure 12.33.)
6. Click the Run button on the toolbar to execute the query.

Figure 12.33.

An example of a Union query that joins tblTimeCards with tblTimeCardsArchive.

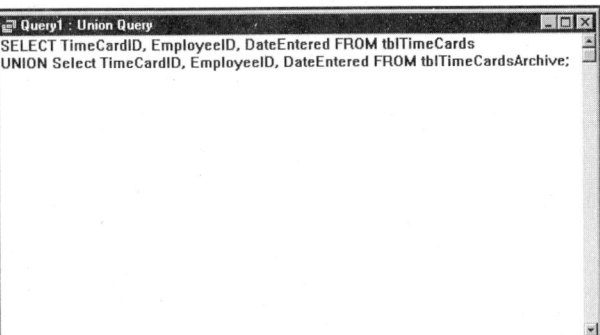

Pass-Through Queries

Pass-Through queries allow you to send uninterpreted SQL statements to your back-end database when you're using something other than the Jet Engine. These uninterpreted statements are in the SQL that's specific to your particular back-end. Although the Jet Engine sees these SQL statements, it makes no attempt to parse or modify them. Pass-Through queries are used in several situations:

- The action you want to take is supported by your back-end database server but not by Access SQL or ODBC SQL.
- Access or the ODBC driver is doing a poor job parsing the SQL statement and sending it in an optimized form to the back-end database.
- You want to execute a stored procedure on the back-end database server.
- You want to make sure the SQL statement is executed on the server.

- You want to join data from more than one table residing on the database server. If you execute the join without a Pass-Through query, the join is done in the memory of the user's PC after all the required data has been sent over the network.

Although Pass-Through queries offer many advantages, they aren't a panacea; they do have a few disadvantages:

- Because you're sending SQL statements specific to your particular database server, you'll need to rewrite all the SQL statements if you switch to another back-end.
- The results returned from a Pass-Through query can't be updated.
- The Jet Engine does no syntax checking of the query before passing it on to the back-end.

Now that you know all the advantages and disadvantages of Pass-Through queries, you can learn how to build one:

1. Click the Queries tab of the Database window, then click New.
2. Select Design View and click OK.
3. Click Close from the Show Tables dialog box without selecting a table.
4. Choose Query | SQL Specific | Pass-Through to open the SQL Design window.
5. Type in the SQL statement in the dialect of your back-end database server.
6. View the Query Properties window and enter an ODBC connect string. (See Figure 12.34.)

Figure 12.34.
The SQL Pass-Through query that selects specific fields from the Sales table, which resides in the PublisherInfo data source.

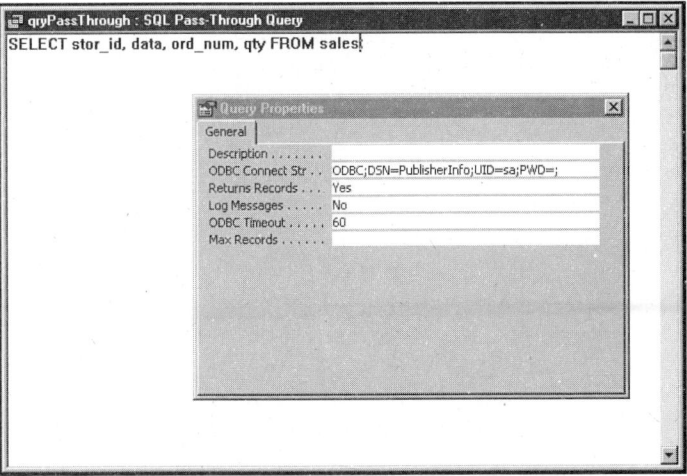

7. Click the Run button on the toolbar to run the query.

The Propagation of Nulls and Query Results

Null values can wreak havoc with your query results because they propagate. Take a look at the query in Figure 12.35. Notice that when parts and labor are added, and either the parts or labor field contains a Null, the result of adding the two fields is Null. In Figure 12.36, the problem is rectified. Notice the expression that adds the two values:

```
TotalPrice:IIF(IsNull([Parts]),0,[Parts]+IIF(IsNull([Labor]),0,[Labor])
```

This expression uses the IIF function to convert the Null values to zero before the two field values are added together.

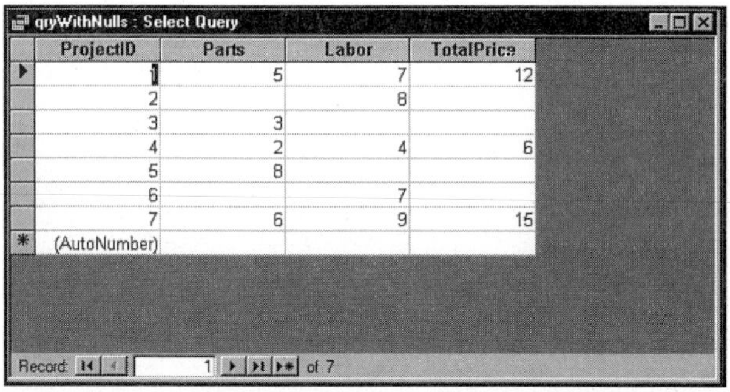

Figure 12.35.

Propagation of Nulls in a query result.

Figure 12.36.

A solution to eliminate propagation of Nulls.

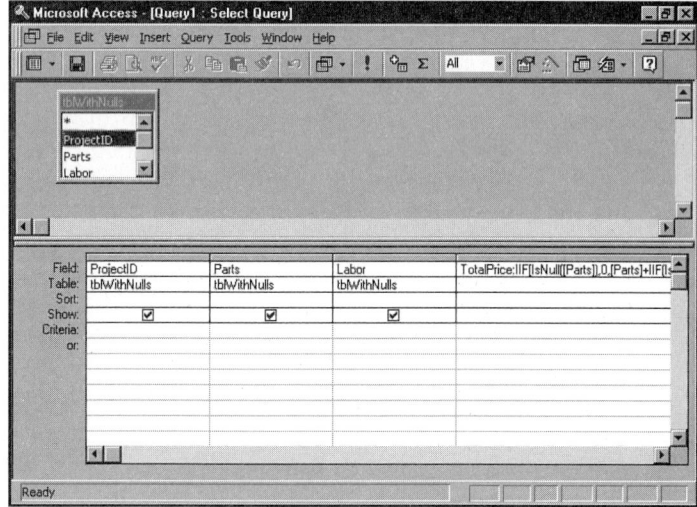

Subqueries

Subqueries allow you to embed one SELECT statement within another. By placing a subquery in a query's criteria, you can base one query on the result of another. Figure 12.37 shows an example. The query pictured finds all the customers without orders. The SQL statement looks like this:

```
SELECT DISTINCTROW tblCustomers.CustomerID,
    tblCustomers.CompanyName, tblCustomers.ContactName
    FROM tblCustomers
    WHERE (((tblCustomers.CustomerID) Not In (Select CustomerID from _
    tblOrders )))
```

This query first runs the SELECT statement Select CustomerID from tblOrders. It uses the result as criteria for the first query.

Figure 12.37.

A query containing a subquery.

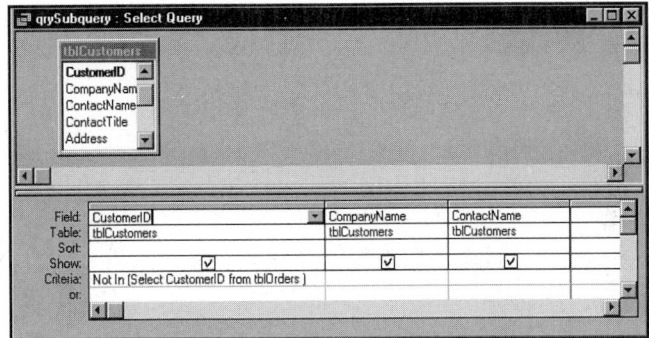

Using the Result of a Function as the Criteria for a Query

Many people are unaware that the result of a function can serve as an expression in a query or as a parameter to a query. The query shown in Figure 12.38 evaluates the result of a function called Initials. The return value from the function is evaluated with criteria to determine whether the employee is included in the result. The Initials function shown below (it's also in the basUtils module of CHAP12EX.MDB, found on the sample code CD-ROM) receives two strings and returns the first character of each string followed by a period:

```
Function Initials(strFirstName As String, _
    strLastName As String) As String
  Initials = Left(strFirstName, 1) & "." & _
    Left(strLastName, 1) & "."
End Function
```

The return value from a function can also be used as the criteria for a query. (See Figure 12.39.) The query in the figure uses a function called HighlyPaid to determine which records appear in the query result. Here's what the HighlyPaid function looks like (it's also in the basUtils module of CHAP12EX.MDB, found on the sample code CD-ROM):

```
Function HighlyPaid(strTitle) As Currency
    Dim curHighRate As Currency
    Select Case strTitle
      Case "Sr. Programmer"
```

365

```
            curHighRate = 60
        Case "Systems Analyst"
            curHighRate = 80
        Case "Project Manager"
            curHighRate = 100
        Case Else
            curHighRate = 50
    End Select
    HighlyPaid = curHighRate
End Function
```

The function receives the employee's title as a parameter. It then evaluates the title and returns a threshold value to the query that's used as the criteria for the query's Billing Rate column.

Figure 12.38.

A query that uses the result of a function as an expression.

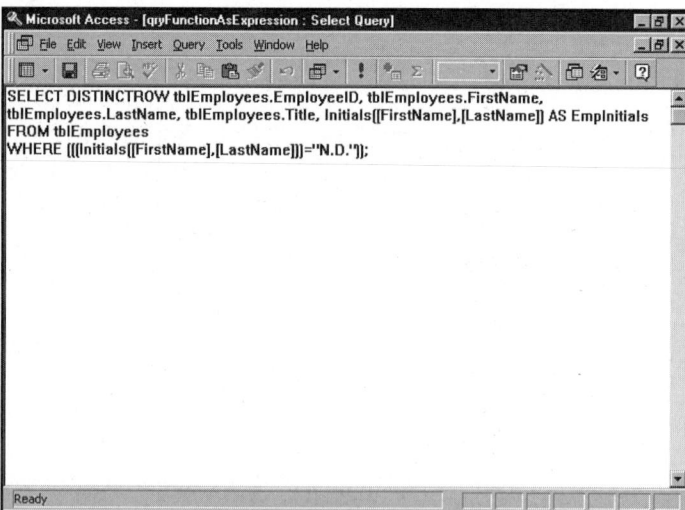

Figure 12.39.

A query that uses the result of a function as criteria.

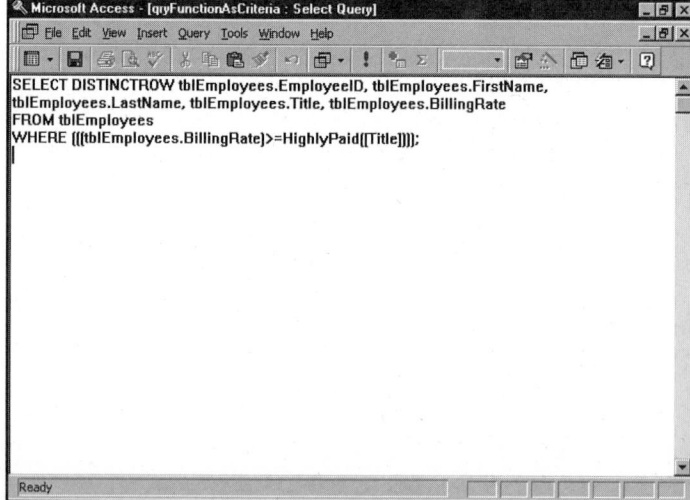

Passing Parameter Query Values from a Form

The biggest frustration with Parameter queries occurs when multiple parameters are required to run the query. The user is confronted with multiple dialog boxes, one for each parameter in the query. The following steps explain how to build a Parameter query that receives its parameter values from a form:

1. Create a new unbound form.

2. Add text boxes or other controls to accept the criteria for each parameter added to your query.

3. Name each control so that you can readily identify the data it contains.

4. Add a command button to the form and instruct it to call the Parameter query. (See Figure 12.40.)

Figure 12.40.

The command button that calls the Parameter query.

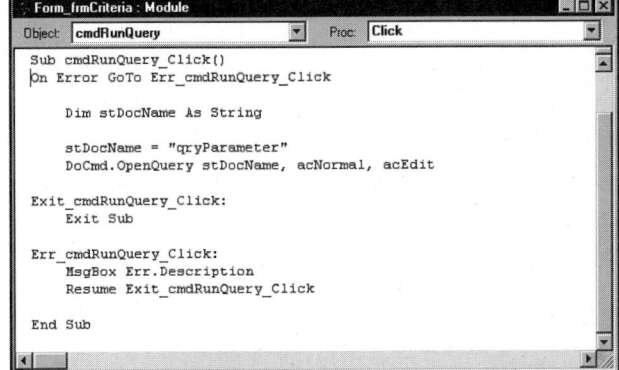

5. Save the form.

6. Add the parameters to the query. Each parameter should refer to a control on the form. (See Figure 12.41.)

7. Right-click the top half of the Query Design grid and select Parameters. Define a data type for each parameter in the Query Parameters dialog box. (See Figure 12.42.)

8. Save and close the query.

9. Fill in the values on the criteria form and click the command button to execute the query. It should execute successfully.

Figure 12.41.

Parameters that refer to controls on a form.

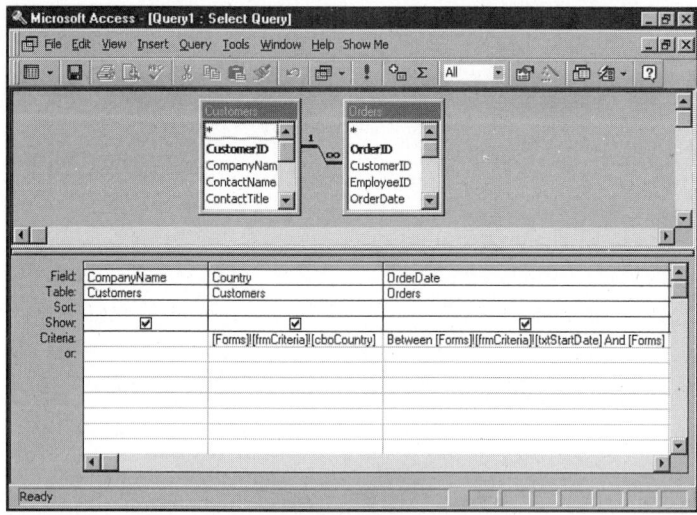

Figure 12.42.

The Query Parameters dialog box lets you select the data type for each parameter in the query.

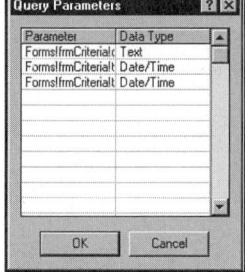

Practical Examples: Applying These Techniques in Your Application

The advanced query techniques you have learned will be used while you're creating the Time and Billing application. Take a look at several practical applications of these advanced techniques.

Archive Payments

After a while, you might need to archive some of the data in the tblPayment table. Two queries archive the payment data. The first, called qappAppendToPaymentArchive, is an Append query that sends all data in a specified date range to an archive table called tblPaymentsArchive. (See Figure 12.43.) The second query, called qdelRemoveFromPayments, is a Delete query that deletes all the data archived from the tblPayments table. (See Figure 12.44.) The archiving is run from a form called frmArchivePayments, where the date range can be specified by the user at runtime. (See Figure 12.45.)

Figure 12.43.

The Append query
qappAppendToPaymentArchive.

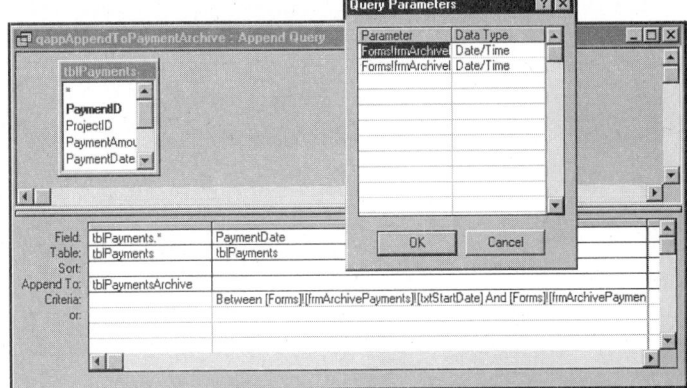

Figure 12.44.

The Delete query
qdelRemoveFromPayments.

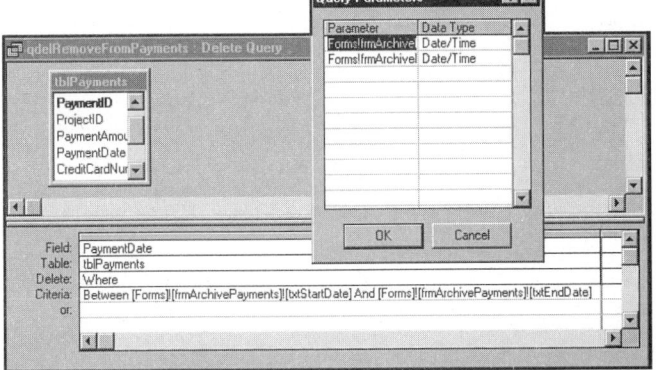

Figure 12.45.

The form that supplies criteria
for the archive process.

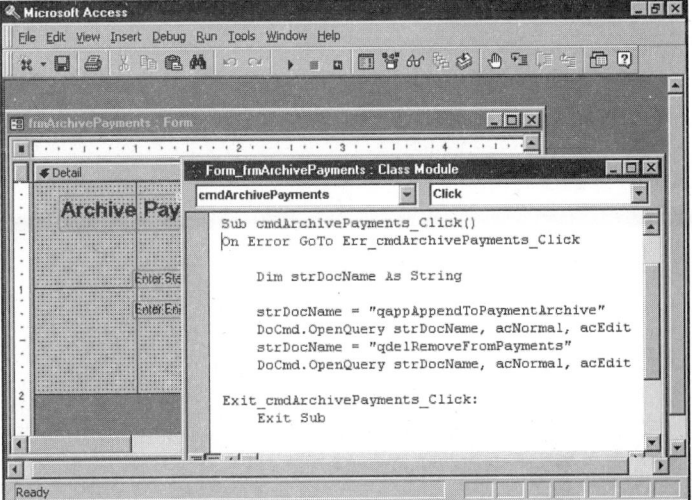

NOTE

The examples shown in this section are included in the CHAP12.MDB database on the sample code CD-ROM.

Show All Payments

At times you might want to combine data from both tables. To do this, you'll need to create a Union query that joins tblPayments to tblPaymentsArchive. The query's design is shown in Figure 12.46.

Figure 12.46.

Using a Union query to join tblPayments to tblPaymentsArchive.

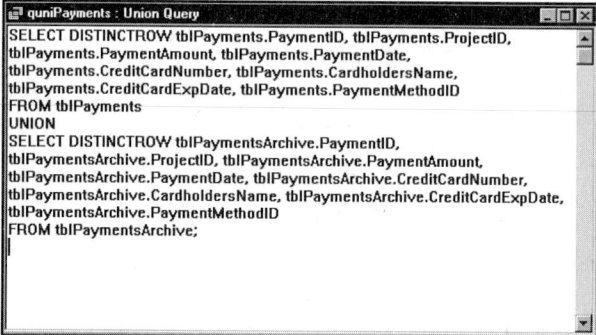

Create State Table

Because you'll regularly be looking up the states and provinces, you want to build a unique list of all the states and provinces your clients are currently located in. The query needed to do this is shown in Figure 12.47. The query uses the tblClients table to come up with all the unique values for the StateProvince field. The query is a Make Table query that takes the unique list of values and outputs it to a tblStateProvince table.

Figure 12.47.

A Make Table query that creates a tblStateProvince table.

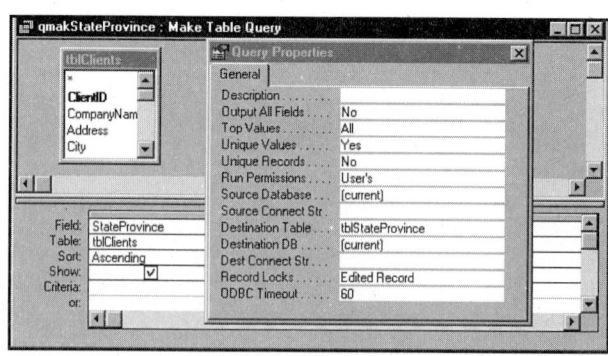

Summary

As you can see, Microsoft gives you a sophisticated query builder for constructing complex and powerful queries. Action queries let you modify table data without writing code; these highly efficient queries can be used to add, edit, or delete table data. The Unique Values and Top Values properties of a query offer you flexibility in determining exactly what data is returned in your query result.

Many things can be done to improve your queries' efficiency. A little attention to the details covered in this chapter can give you dramatic improvements in your application's performance.

Other special types of queries covered in this chapter include Crosstab queries, Outer Joins, and Self-Joins. Whatever can't be done by using the graphical QBE grid can be accomplished by typing the required SQL statement directly into the SQL View window. In this window, you can type Access SQL statements or use SQL Pass-Through to type SQL statements in the SQL dialect that's specific to your back-end database.

13

Let's Get More Intimate with Forms: Advanced Techniques

- What Are the Form Events?, 374
- What Are the Section and Control Events?, 383
- What Types of Forms Can I Create?, 389
- Using Built-In Dialog Boxes, 397
- Adding Custom Menus, Toolbars, and Shortcut Menus, 400
- Taking Advantage of Built-in Form-Filtering Features, 405
- Including Objects from Other Applications: Linking Versus Embedding, 406
- OpenArgs, 408
- Switching a Forms's Record Source, 408
- Power Combo Box and List Box Techniques, 410
- Power Subform Techniques, 416
- Synchronizing a Form with Its Underlying Recordset, 417
- Creating Custom Properties and Methods, 417
- Practical Examples: Applying Advanced Techniques to Your Application, 422

Given Access's graphical environment, your development efforts are often centered on forms, so you must understand all the Form and Control events and know which event you should code to perform each task. You should also know what types of forms are available and how you can get the look and behavior you want for them.

Often, you won't need to design your own form because you can make use of one of the built-in dialog boxes that are part of the VBA language or supplied as part of the Microsoft Office 97 Developer Edition tools. Whatever types of forms you create, you should take advantage of all the tricks and tips of the trade covered throughout this chapter, including adding menu bars and toolbars to your forms.

What Are the Form Events and When Do You Use Them?

Microsoft Access traps for 29 Form events, each of which has a distinct purpose. Access also traps events for Form sections and controls. The following sections cover the Form events and when you should use them.

Current

A form's Current event is one of the more commonly coded events. It happens each time focus moves from one record to another. The Current event is a great place to put code you want to execute whenever a record is displayed. For example, you might want the company name to appear with a special background if the client is an important one. The following code is placed in the Current event of the frmClients form that's part of the Time and Billing application:

```
Private Sub Form_Current()
    If IsNull(Me![txtClientID]) Then
      DoCmd.GoToControl "txtContactFirstName"
    End If
End Sub
```

This code moves focus to the txtContactFirstName control if the txtClientID of the record the user is moving to happens to be Null; this happens if the user is adding a new record.

BeforeInsert

The BeforeInsert event occurs when the first character is typed in a new record, but before the new record is actually created. If the user is typing in a text or combo box, the BeforeInsert event occurs even before the Change event of the text or combo box. The frmProjects form of the Time and Billing application has an example of a practical use of the BeforeInsert event:

```
Private Sub Form_BeforeInsert(Cancel As Integer)
    Me![txtClientID] = Forms![frmClients]![txtClientID]
End Sub
```

The frmProjects form is always called from the frmClients form. The BeforeInsert event of frmProjects sets the value of the txtClientID text box equal to the value of the txtClientID text box on frmClients.

BeforeUpdate

The BeforeUpdate event runs before a record is updated. It occurs when the user tries to move to a different record or when the Records | Save Record command is executed. The BeforeUpdate event can be used to cancel the update process when you want to perform complex validations. When a user adds a record, the BeforeUpdate event occurs after the BeforeInsert event. The NorthWind database that comes with Access has an excellent example of using a BeforeUpdate event:

```
Private Sub Form_BeforeUpdate(Cancel As Integer)
' Display a message box that says that product name is required.

    Dim strMsg As String, strTitle As String
    Dim intStyle As Integer

    If IsNull(Me![ProductName]) Then
        strMsg = "You must enter a product name before you leave the _
        record."    ' Define message.
        intStyle = vbOKOnly + vbInformation ' Define buttons.
        strTitle = "Product Name Required"   ' Define title.
        MsgBox strMsg, intStyle, strTitle
        DoCmd.CancelEvent
    End If
End Sub
```

This code from the Products form determines whether the product name is Null. If it is, a message is displayed and the CancelEvent method is executed, canceling the update process.

AfterUpdate

The AfterUpdate event occurs after the changed data in a record is updated. You might use this event to requery combo boxes on related forms or perhaps log record changes. Here's an example:

```
Private Sub Form_AfterUpdate()
    Me!cboSelectProduct.Requery
End Sub
```

This code requeries the cboSelectProduct combo box after the current record is updated.

AfterInsert

The AfterInsert event occurs after the record has actually been inserted. It can be used to requery a recordset when a new record is added.

Here's the order of events when a user begins to type data into a new record:

    BeforeInsert'BeforeUpdate'AfterUpdate'AfterInsert

The BeforeInsert event occurs when the user types the first character, the BeforeUpdate event happens when the user updates the record, the AfterUpdate event takes place when the record is updated, and the AfterInsert event occurs when the record that's being updated is a new record.

Delete

The Delete event occurs when a user tries to delete a record but before the record is actually removed from the table. This is a great way to place code that allows deleting a record only under certain circumstances. If the Delete event is canceled, the BeforeDelConfirm and AfterDelConfirm events never execute, and the record is never deleted.

When the user deletes multiple records, the Delete event happens after each record is deleted. This allows you to evaluate a condition for each record and decide whether each record should be deleted.

BeforeDelConfirm

The BeforeDelConfirm event takes place after the Delete event but before the Delete Confirm dialog box is displayed. If you cancel the BeforeDelConfirm event, the record being deleted is restored from the delete buffer, and the Delete Confirm dialog box is never displayed.

AfterDelConfirm

The AfterDelConfirm event occurs after the record is actually deleted, even if the deletion is canceled. If the BeforeDelConfirm is *not* canceled, the AfterDelConfirm event takes place after the Confirmation dialog box is displayed.

Open

The Open event occurs when a form is opened but before the first record is displayed. With this event, you can control exactly what happens when the form first opens. The Open event of the Time and Billing application's frmProjects form looks like this:

```
Private Sub Form_Open(Cancel As Integer)
    If Not IsLoaded("frmClients") Then
        MsgBox "Open the Projects form using the Projects button on the _
        Clients form."
        Cancel = True
    End If
End Sub
```

This code checks to make sure the frmClients form is loaded. If it isn't, a message box is displayed, and the Cancel parameter is set to True, which prohibits the form from loading.

Load

The Load event happens when a form is opened and the first record is displayed; it occurs after the Open event. A form's Open event can cancel the opening of a form, but the Load event can't. The following routine is placed in the Load event of the Time and Billing application's frmProjects form:

```
Private Sub Form_Load()
    If Me.OpenArgs = "GotoNew" And Not IsNull([txtProjectID]) Then
        DoCmd.RunCommand acCmdRecordsGoToNew
    End If
End Sub
```

This routine looks at the string that's passed as an opening argument to the form. If the OpenArg string is "GotoNew" and the ProjectID isn't Null (the user is not already on a new record), a new record is inserted.

Resize

The Resize event takes place when a form is opened or whenever the form's size changes.

Unload

The Unload event happens when a form is closed, but before the form is actually removed from the screen. It's triggered when the user chooses Close from the File menu, quits the application by choosing End Task from the task list, quits Windows, or when your code closes the form. You can place code that makes sure it's okay to unload the form in the Unload event, and you can also use the Unload event to place any code you want executed whenever the form is unloaded. Here's an example:

```
Private Sub Form_Unload(Cancel As Integer)

    '   If EnterorEditProducts form is loaded,
    '   select it, requery CategoryID combo box,
    '   and set value of CategoryID combo box.
    Dim ctl As Control
```

```
    If IsLoaded("EnterOrEditProducts") Then
        Set ctl = Forms!EnterOrEditProducts!cboCategoryID
        DoCmd.SelectObject acForm, "EnterOrEditProducts"
        ctl.Requery
        ctl = Me!CategoryID
    End If

End Sub
```

This code is placed in the Load event of the AddCategory form from the Solutions database that's included with Access. It checks whether the EnterOrEditProducts form is loaded. If it is, the EnterOrEditProducts form is selected, the CategoryID combo box is requeried, and the combo box's value is set equal to the CategoryID of the AddCategory form.

Close

The Close event occurs when a form is closed and removed from the screen, *after* the Unload event. Remember, you can cancel the Unload event but not the Close event.

The following code is placed in the Close event of the Suppliers form that's part of the NorthWind database:

```
Private Sub Form_Close()

    ' Close Product List form and Products form if they are open.
    If IsLoaded("Product List") Then DoCmd.Close acForm, "Product List"
    If IsLoaded("Products") Then DoCmd.Close acForm, "Products"

End Sub
```

When the Suppliers form is closed, the code tests whether the Product List and Products forms are open. If they are, it closes them.

Activate

The Activate event takes place when the form gets focus and becomes the active window. It's triggered when the form is opened, when a user clicks on the form or one of its controls, and when the SetFocus method is applied by using VBA code. The following code, found in the Activate event of the Time and Billing application's frmClients form, requeries the fsubClients subform whenever the frmClients main form is activated:

```
Private Sub Form_Activate()
    Me![fsubClients].Requery
End Sub
```

Deactivate

The Deactivate event occurs when the form loses focus, which happens when a table, query, form, report, macro, module, or the Database window becomes active. However, the

Deactivate event isn't triggered when a dialog, pop-up form, or another application becomes active. The following example is code from the EnterOrEditProducts form that's part of the Solutions database:

```
Private Sub Form_Deactivate()
    ' Use AllowEdits property setting to determine which toolbar to hide.
    ' Show Form View toolbar.
    If Me.AllowEdits = True Then
        DoCmd.ShowToolbar "Enter Or Edit Products 2", acToolbarNo
    Else
        DoCmd.ShowToolbar "Enter Or Edit Products 1", acToolbarNo
    End If
    DoCmd.ShowToolbar "Form View", acToolbarWhereApprop
End Sub
```

This code evaluates the AllowEdits property to determine which custom toolbar is currently active. It hides the appropriate toolbar and shows the standard Form View toolbar.

GotFocus

The GotFocus event happens when a form gets focus, but only if there are no visible, enabled controls on the form. This event is rarely used for a form.

LostFocus

The LostFocus event occurs when a form loses focus, but only if there are no visible, enabled controls on the form. This event, too, is rarely used for a form.

Click

The Click event takes place when the user clicks on a blank area of the form, on a disabled control on the form, or on the form's record selector.

DblClick

The DblClick event happens when the user double-clicks on a blank area of the form, on a disabled control on the form, or on the form's record selector.

MouseDown

The MouseDown event occurs when the user clicks on a blank area of the form, on a disabled control on the form, or on the form's record selector, but it happens *before* the Click event fires. It can be used to determine which mouse button was pressed.

MouseMove

The MouseMove event takes place when the user moves the mouse over a blank area of the form, over a disabled control on the form, or over the form's record selector. It's generated continuously as the mouse pointer moves over the form. The MouseMove event occurs *before* the Click event fires.

MouseUp

The MouseUp event occurs when the user releases the mouse button. Like the MouseDown event, it happens before the Click event fires and can be used to determine which mouse button was pressed.

KeyDown

The KeyDown event happens if there are no controls on the form or if the form's KeyPreview property is set to Yes; if the latter condition is true, all keyboard events are previewed by the form and occur for the control that has focus. If the user presses and holds down a key, the KeyDown event occurs repeatedly until the key is released.

KeyUp

Like the KeyDown event, the KeyUp event occurs if there are no controls on the form or if the form's KeyPreview property is set to Yes. The KeyUp event takes place only once, though, regardless of how long the key is pressed. The keystroke can be canceled by setting KeyCode to zero.

KeyPress

The KeyPress event occurs when the user presses and releases a key or key combination that corresponds to an ANSI code. It takes place if there are no controls on the form or if the form's KeyPreview property is set to Yes. The keystroke can be canceled by setting KeyCode to zero.

Error

The Error event is triggered whenever an error happens while the user is in the form. Microsoft Jet Engine errors are trapped, but Visual Basic errors aren't. This event can be used to suppress the standard error messages. Visual Basic errors must be handled by using standard On Error techniques. Both the Error event and handling Visual Basic errors are covered in Chapter 17, "Handling Those Dreaded Runtime Errors."

Filter

The Filter event takes place whenever the user selects the Filter By Form or Advanced Filter/Sort options. You can use this event to remove the previous filter, enter default settings for the filter, invoke your own custom filter window, or prevent certain controls from being available in the Filter By Form window.

ApplyFilter

The ApplyFilter event occurs when the user selects the Apply Filter/Sort, Filter By Selection, or Remove Filter/Sort options. It also takes place when the user closes the Advanced Filter/Sort window or the Filter By Form window. You can use this event to make sure the filter being applied is correct, to change the form's display before the filter is applied, or to undo any changes you made when the Filter event occurred.

Timer

The Timer event occurs at regular intervals, but only when the form's TimerInterval property is set. How often the Timer event triggers depends on the value set in the TimerInterval property.

Understanding the Sequence of Form Events

One of the mysteries of events is the order in which they occur. One of the best ways to figure this out is to place Debug.Print statements in the events you want to learn about. This technique is covered in Chapter 16, "Debugging: Your Key to Successful Development." Keep in mind that event order isn't an exact science; it's nearly impossible to guess when events will happen in all situations. It's helpful, though, to understand the basic order in which certain events do take place.

What Happens When a Form Is Opened?

When the user opens a form, the following events occur:

```
Open➡Load➡Resize➡Activate➡Current
```

After these Form events take place, the Enter and GotFocus events of the first control occur. Remember that the Open event is the only place you can cancel opening the form.

What Happens When a Form Is Closed?

When the user closes a form, the following events take place:

`Unload➡Deactivate➡Close`

Before these events occur, the `Exit` and `LostFocus` events of the active control are triggered.

What Happens When a Form Is Sized?

When the user resizes a form, what happens depends on whether the form is minimized, restored, or maximized. When the form is minimized, here's what happens:

`Resize➡Deactivate`

When the user restores a minimized form, these events take place:

`Activate➡Resize`

When the user maximizes a form or restores a maximized form, then just the `Resize` event occurs.

What Happens When Focus Shifts from One Form to Another?

When the user moves from one form to another, the `Deactivate` event occurs for the first form, then the `Activate` event occurs for the second form. Remember that the `Deactivate` event doesn't take place if focus moves to a dialog box, a pop-up form, or another application.

What Happens When Keys Are Pressed?

When the user types a character and the form's KeyPreview property is set to `True`, the following events occur:

`KeyDown➡KeyPress➡Change➡KeyUp`

If you trap the `KeyDown` event and set the KeyCode to zero, the remaining events never happen. The `KeyPress` and `Change` events capture only ANSI keystrokes. These events are the easiest to deal with; however, you must handle the `Keydown` and `KeyUp` events when you need to trap for non-ANSI characters, such as Shift, Alt, and Ctrl.

What Happens When Mouse Actions Take Place?

When the user clicks the mouse button, the following events occur:

`MouseDown➡MouseUp➡Click`

What Are the Section and Control Events and When Do You Use Them?

Sections have only five events: Click, DblClick, MouseDown, MouseMove, and MouseUp. These events rarely play a significant role in your application.

Each control type has its own set of events it responds to. Many events are common to most controls, but others are specific to certain controls. Furthermore, some controls respond to very few events. The following sections cover all the Control events. As each event is covered, you learn which controls the event applies to.

BeforeUpdate

The BeforeUpdate event applies to text boxes, option groups, combo boxes, list boxes, and bound object frames. It occurs before changed data in the control is updated. The following code example is found in the BeforeUpdate event of the SelectProduct control on the EditProducts form from the Solutions database:

```
Private Sub SelectProduct_BeforeUpdate(Cancel As Integer)
    If IsNull([SelectProduct]) Then
        MsgBox "You must select a product."
        DoCmd.CancelEvent
    End If
End Sub
```

This code tests whether the value of the SelectProduct control is Null. If it is, a message box is displayed, and the Update event is canceled.

AfterUpdate

The AfterUpdate event applies to text boxes, option groups, combo boxes, list boxes, and bound object frames. It occurs after changed data in the control is updated. The following code example is from the AfterUpdate event of the SelectProduct control on the EditProducts form found in the Solutions database:

```
Private Sub SelectProduct_AfterUpdate()

    '  Find record for product selected in SelectProduct combo box.
    '  Enable controls in detail section and disable ProductID text box.
    '  Go to SupplierID combo box.

    Dim varTmp As Variant

    DoCmd.ApplyFilter , "ProductID = Forms!EditProducts!SelectProduct"
    varTmp = EnableControls("Detail", True)
    Me!ProductID.Enabled = False
    Me!SupplierID.SetFocus

End Sub
```

This code begins by applying a filter to the form based on the product selected from the SelectProduct combo box. It then runs a function that enables all the controls in the form's Detail section. It disables the ProductID control and sets focus to the SupplierID control.

Updated

The Updated event applies to a bound object frame only. It occurs when the OLE (Object Linking and Embedding) object's data has been modified.

Change

The Change event applies to text and combo boxes and takes place when data in the control changes. For a text box, this event occurs when a character is typed; for a combo box, it happens when a value is selected from the list. You use this event when you want to trap for something happening on a character-by-character basis.

NotInList

The NotInList event applies only to a combo box and happens when the user enters a value in the text box portion of the combo box that's not in the combo box list. By using this event, you can allow the user to add a new value to the combo box list. For this event to be triggered, the LimitToList property must be set to Yes. Here's an example from the Time and Billing application's frmPayments form:

```
Private Sub cboPaymentMethodID_NotInList(NewData As String, Response As Integer)
    MsgBox "Double-click this field to add an entry to the list."
    Response = acDataErrContinue
End Sub
```

This code is executed when the user enters a payment method that's not in the cboPaymentMethodID combo box. It instructs the user to double-click to add the entry as a payment method and suppresses the normal error message. The NotInList event is covered in more detail later in the "Handling the NotInList Event" section.

Enter

The Enter event applies to text boxes, option groups, combo boxes, list boxes, command buttons, object frames, and subforms. It occurs before a control actually gets focus from another control on the same form and takes place *before* the GotFocus event. Here's an example from the Time and Billing application's frmTimeCards form:

```
Private Sub fsubTimeCards_Enter()
    If IsNull(Me![EmployeeID]) Then
        MsgBox "Enter employee before entering time or expenses."
        DoCmd.GoToControl "cboEmployeeID"
    End If
End Sub
```

When the user moves into the fsubTimeCards subform control, its Enter event tests whether the EmployeeID has been entered on the main form. If it hasn't, a message box is displayed, and focus is moved to the cboEmployeeID control on the main form.

Exit

The Exit event applies to text boxes, option groups, combo boxes, list boxes, command buttons, object frames, and subforms. It occurs just before the LostFocus event.

GotFocus

The GotFocus event applies to text boxes, toggle buttons, options buttons, checkboxes, combo boxes, list boxes, and command buttons. It takes place when focus moves to a control in response to a user action or when the SetFocus, SelectObject, GoToRecord, GoToControl, or GoToPage methods are issued in code. Controls can get focus only if they're visible and enabled.

LostFocus

The LostFocus event applies to text boxes, toggle buttons, options buttons, checkboxes, combo boxes, list boxes, and command buttons. It occurs when focus moves away from a control in response to a user action or when the SetFocus, SelectObject, GoToRecord, GoToControl, or GoToPage methods are issued in code.

> **NOTE**
>
> The difference between GotFocus/LostFocus and Enter/Exit lies in when they occur. If focus is moved to another form or returned to the current form, the control's GotFocus and LostFocus events are triggered. The Enter and Exit events don't take place when the form loses or regains focus.

Click

The Click event applies to labels, text boxes, option groups, combo boxes, list boxes, command buttons, and object frames. It occurs when the user presses, then releases a mouse button over a control. Here's an example from the Time and Billing application's frmProjects form:

```
Private Sub cmdToggleView_Click()
    If Me![cmdToggleView].Caption = "&View Expenses" Then
        Me![fsubProjects].Visible = False
        Me![fsubProjectExpenses].Visible = True
        Me![cmdToggleView].Caption = "&View Hours"
```

```
    Else
        Me![fsubProjectExpenses].Visible = False
        Me![fsubProjects].Visible = True
        Me![cmdToggleView].Caption = "&View Expenses"
    End If
End Sub
```

This code checks the caption of the cmdToggleView command button. If the caption reads
"&View Expenses" (with the ampersand indicating a hotkey), the fsubProjects subform is hidden, the fsubProjectExpenses subform is made visible, and the caption of the cmdToggleView
command button is modified to read "&View Hours". Otherwise, the fsubProjectsExpenses
subform is hidden, the fsubProjects subform is made visible, and the caption of the
cmdToggleView command button is modified to read "&View Expenses".

> **NOTE**
>
> The `Click` event is triggered when the user clicks the mouse over an object, as well as in the
> following situations:
>
> - When the spacebar is pressed while a command button has focus
> - When a command button's Default property is set to Yes and the Enter key is pressed
> - When a command button's Cancel property is set to Yes and the Escape key is pressed
> - When an accelerator key for a command button is used

DblClick

The `DblClick` event applies to labels, text boxes, option groups, combo boxes, list boxes, command buttons, and object frames. It occurs when the user presses, then releases the left mouse
button twice over a control. Here's an example from the Time and Billing application's
frmPayments form:

```
Private Sub cboPaymentMethodID_DblClick(Cancel As Integer)
    Dim lngPaymentMethodID As Long

    If IsNull(Me![cboPaymentMethodID]) Then
        Me![cboPaymentMethodID].Text = ""
    Else
        lngPaymentMethodID = Me![cboPaymentMethodID]
        Me![cboPaymentMethodID] = Null
    End If
    DoCmd.OpenForm "frmPaymentMethods", , , , , acDialog, "GotoNew"
    Me![cboPaymentMethodID].Requery
    If lngPaymentMethodID <> 0 Then Me![cboPaymentMethodID] = lngPaymentMethodID
End Sub
```

In this example, the code evaluates the cboPaymentMethodID combo box control to see whether it's Null. If it is, the text of the combo box is set to a zero-length string. Otherwise, a long integer variable is set equal to the combo box value, and the combo box value is set to Null. The frmPaymentMethods form is opened modally. When it's closed, the cboPaymentMethods combo box is requeried. If the long integer variable doesn't contain a zero, the combo box value is set equal to the long integer value.

MouseDown

The MouseDown event applies to labels, text boxes, option groups, combo boxes, list boxes, command buttons, and object frames. It takes place when the mouse button is pressed over a control, *before* the Click event fires.

MouseMove

The MouseMove event applies to labels, text boxes, option groups, combo boxes, list boxes, command buttons, and object frames. It occurs as the mouse is moved over a control.

MouseUp

The MouseUp event applies to labels, text boxes, option groups, combo boxes, list boxes, command buttons, and object frames. It occurs when the mouse is released over a control, *before* the Click event fires.

KeyDown

The KeyDown event applies to text boxes, toggle buttons, option buttons, checkboxes, combo boxes, list boxes, and bound object frames. It happens when the user presses a key while within a control and occurs repeatedly until the key is released. It can be canceled by setting KeyCode equal to zero.

KeyUp

The KeyUp event applies to text boxes, toggle buttons, option buttons, checkboxes, combo boxes, list boxes, and bound object frames. It occurs when a key is released within a control. It occurs only once, no matter how long a key is pressed down.

KeyPress

The KeyPress event applies to text boxes, toggle buttons, option buttons, checkboxes, combo boxes, list boxes, and bound object frames. It occurs when the user presses and releases an ANSI key while the control has focus. It can be canceled by setting KeyCode equal to zero.

Understanding the Sequence of Control Events

Just as Form events take place in a certain sequence when the form is opened, activated, and so on, Control events occur in a specific sequence. When writing the event code for a control, you need to understand the order in which Control events happen.

What Happens When Focus Is Moved to or from a Control?

When focus is moved to a control, the following events occur:

```
Enter➡GotFocus
```

If focus is moving to a control as the form is opened, the Form and Control events take place in the following sequence:

```
Open(form)➡Activate(form)➡Current(form)➡Enter(control)➡GotFocus(control)
```

When focus leaves a control, the following events occur:

```
Exit➡LostFocus
```

When focus leaves the control because the form is closing, the following events happen:

```
Exit(control)➡LostFocus(control)➡Unload(form)➡Deactivate(form)➡Close(form)
```

What Happens When the Data in a Control Is Updated?

When you change data in a control and then move focus to another control, the following events occur:

```
BeforeUpdate➡AfterUpdate➡Exit➡LostFocus
```

After every character that's typed in a text or combo box, the following events take place before focus is moved to another control:

```
KeyDown➡KeyPress➡Change➡KeyUp
```

For a combo box, if the NotInList event is triggered, it occurs after the KeyUp event.

Referring to Me

The Me keyword is like an implicitly declared variable; it's available to every procedure in a Form or Report module. Using Me is a great way to write generic code in a form or report. You can change the name of the form or report, and the code will be unaffected. Here's an example:

```
Me.RecordSource = "qryProjects"
```

It's also useful to pass Me (the current form or report) to a generic procedure in a module, as shown in the following example:

```
Call ChangeCaption(Me)
```

The ChangeCaption procedure looks like this:

```
Sub ChangeCaption(frmAny As Form)
   If IsNull(frmAny.Caption) Then
      frmAny.Caption = "Form For - " & CurrentUser
   Else
      frmAny.Caption = frmAny.Caption & " - " & CurrentUser
   End If
End Sub
```

The ChangeCaption procedure in a Code module receives any form as a parameter. It evaluates the caption of the form that was passed to it. If the caption is Null, ChangeCaption sets the caption to "Form for -", concatenated with the user's name. Otherwise, it takes the existing caption of the form passed to it and appends the user's name.

What Types of Forms Can I Create and When Are They Appropriate?

You can design a variety of forms with Microsoft Access. By working with the properties available in Access's form designer, you can create forms with many different looks and types of functionality. This chapter covers all the major categories of forms, but remember that you can create your own forms. Of course, don't forget to maintain consistency with the standards for Windows applications.

Single Forms: Viewing One Record at a Time

One of the most common types of forms allows you to view one record at a time. The form shown in Figure 13.1, for example, lets the user view one customer record, then move to other records as needed.

Figure 13.1.

A Single form.

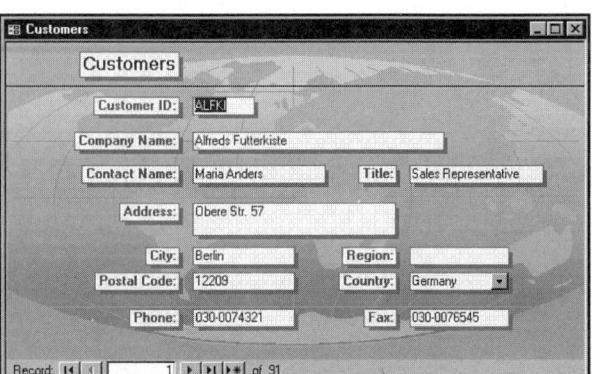

Creating a Single form is easy—simply set the form's Default View property to `Single Form`. (See Figure 13.2.)

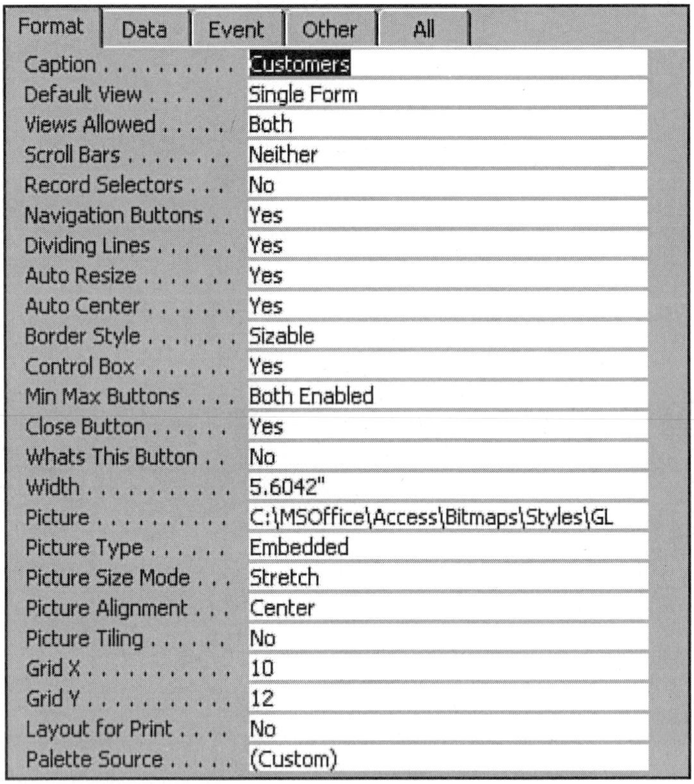

Figure 13.2.
Setting the form's Default View property.

Format	Data	Event	Other	All
Caption		Customers		
Default View		Single Form		
Views Allowed		Both		
Scroll Bars		Neither		
Record Selectors . . .		No		
Navigation Buttons . .		Yes		
Dividing Lines		Yes		
Auto Resize		Yes		
Auto Center		Yes		
Border Style		Sizable		
Control Box		Yes		
Min Max Buttons		Both Enabled		
Close Button		Yes		
Whats This Button . .		No		
Width		5.6042"		
Picture		C:\MSOffice\Access\Bitmaps\Styles\GL		
Picture Type		Embedded		
Picture Size Mode . . .		Stretch		
Picture Alignment . . .		Center		
Picture Tiling		No		
Grid X		10		
Grid Y		12		
Layout for Print		No		
Palette Source		(Custom)		

Continuous Forms: View Multiple Records at a Time

Often, the user wants to be able to view multiple records at a time. which requires creating a Continuous form, like the one shown in Figure 13.3. To do this, just set the Default View property to `Continuous Forms`.

A subform is a common use of a Continuous form; generally, you should show multiple records in a subform. The records displayed in the subform are all the records that relate to the record displayed in the main form. An example is pictured in Figure 13.4, which shows two subforms, each with its Default View property set to `Continuous Forms`. One subform shows all the orders relating to a specific customer, and the other shows all the order detail items for the selected order.

Figure 13.3.

A Continuous form.

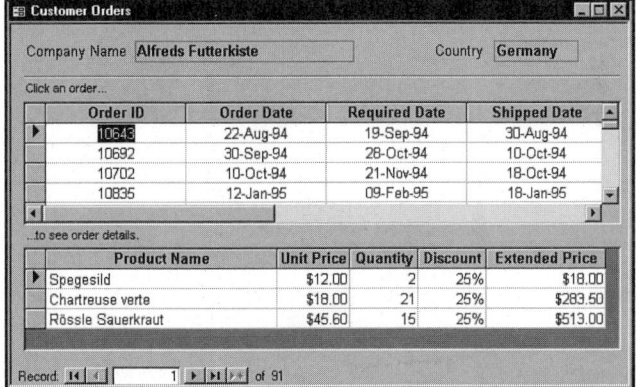

Figure 13.4.

A form containing two Continuous subforms.

Multipage Forms: When Everything Doesn't Fit on One Screen

Scarcity of screen real-estate is a never-ending problem, but a multipage form can be a good solution. Figures 13.5 and 13.6 show the two pages of the multipage Employee form, which can be found in the Northwind.MDB database. When looking at the form in Design view, you can see a Page Break control placed just before the 3-inch mark on the form. (See Figure 13.7.) To insert a Page Break control, select it from the toolbox, then click and drag to place it on the form.

Figure 13.5.

The first page of a multipage form.

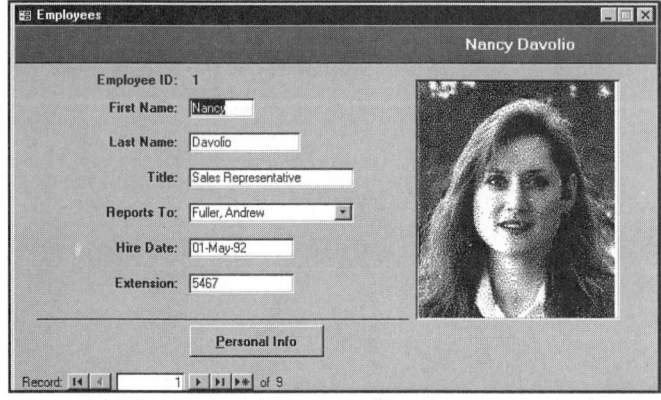

Figure 13.6.

The second page of a multipage form.

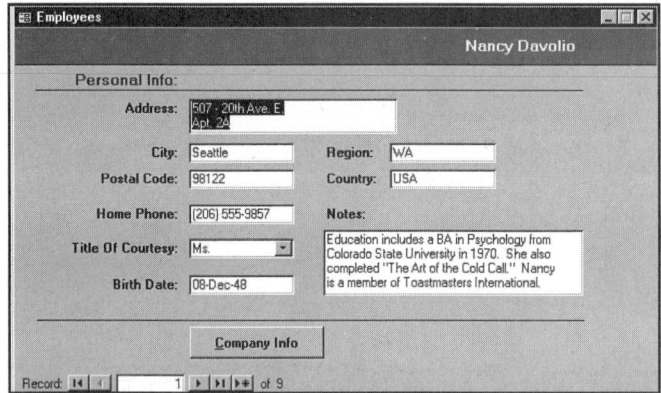

Figure 13.7.

A multipage form in Design view.

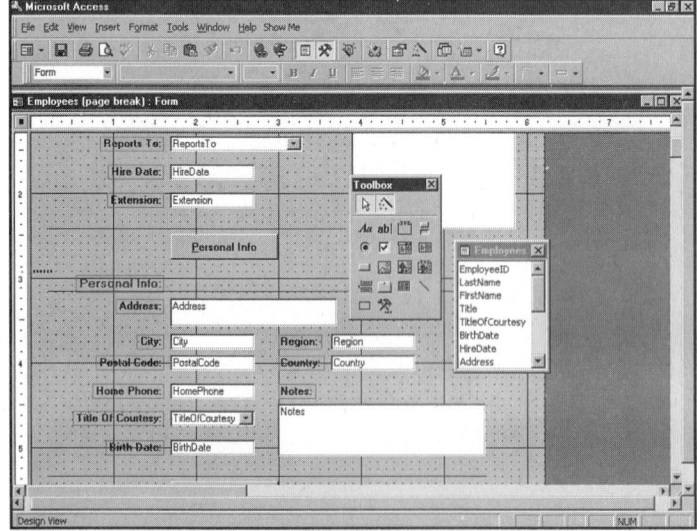

When creating a multipage form, remember a few important steps:

- Set the Default View property of the form to `Single Form`.
- Set the Scrollbars property of the form to `Neither` or `Horizontal Only`.
- Set the AutoResize property of the form to `No`.
- Place the Page Break control exactly halfway down the form's Detail section if you want the form to have two pages. If you want more pages, divide the total height of the Detail section by the number of pages and place Page Break controls at the appropriate positions on the form.
- Size the Form window to fit exactly one page of the form.

Tabbed Forms: Conserving Screen Real-Estate

A tabbed form is an alternative to a multipage form. Access 97 includes a built-in Tab control that allows you to easily group sets of controls together. A tabbed form could, for example, show customers on one tab, orders for the selected customer on another tab, and order detail items for the selected order on a third tab.

The form shown in Figure 13.8 uses a Tab control. This form, called frmTabbed, is included in the CHAP13EX.MDB database on your sample code CD-ROM. It shows clients on one tab and the selected client's projects on the second tab. No code is needed to build the example.

Figure 13.8.
A multipage tabbed form.

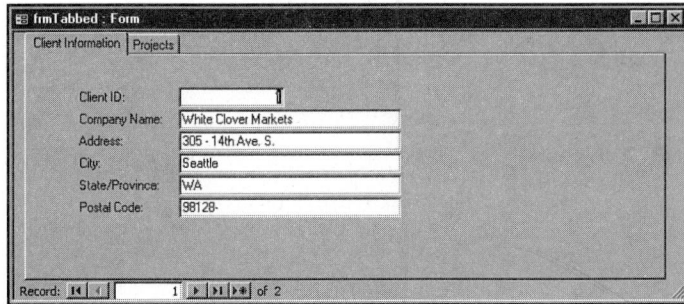

Adding a Tab Control and Manipulating Its Pages

To add a Tab control to a form, simply select it from the toolbox and drag and drop it onto the form. By default, two tab pages appear. To add more tabs, right-click the control and select Insert Page. The new page is inserted before the selected page. To remove tabs, right-click the page you want to remove and select Delete Page. To change the order of pages, right-click any page and select Page Order.

Adding Controls to Tab Pages

You can add controls to each tab just as you would add them directly to the form. However, remember to select a tab by clicking it before you add the controls. If you don't select a specific tab, the controls you add will appear on every page.

Modifying the Tab Order of Controls

The controls on each page have their own tab order. To modify their tab order, right-click the page and select Tab Order. You can then reorder the controls in whatever way you want on the page.

Changing the Properties of the Tab Control

To change the properties of the Tab control, click to select it rather than a specific page. You can tell whether you've selected the Tab control because the words Tab Control appear in the upper-left corner of the Properties window. (See Figure 13.9.) A Tab control's properties include its name, the text font on the tabs, and more.

Figure 13.9.

Viewing properties of a Tab control.

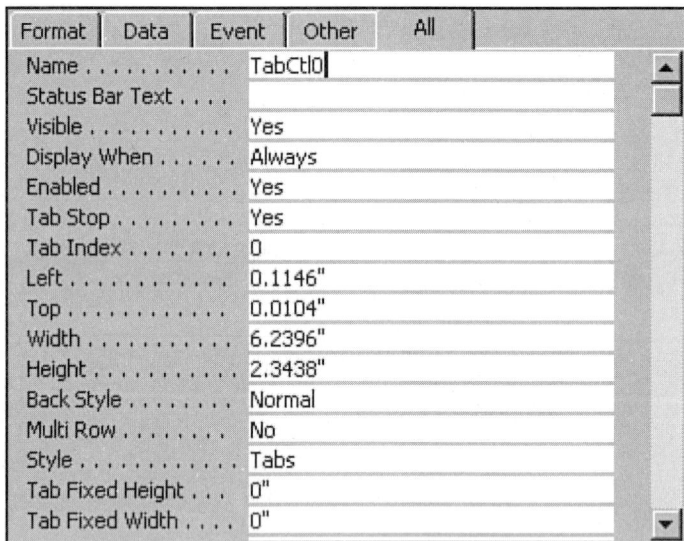

Changing the Properties of Each Page

To change the properties of each page, select a specific page of the Tab control. You can tell whether you've selected a specific page because the word Page is displayed in the upper-left corner of the Properties window. (See Figure 13.10.) Here you can select a name for the page, the page's caption, a picture for the page's background, and more.

Figure 13.10.

Viewing properties of a Tab page.

Format	Data	Event	Other	All	
Name				pgClients	
Caption				Client Information	
Picture				(none)	
Picture Type				Embedded	
Page Index				0	
Status Bar Text					
Visible				Yes	
Enabled				Yes	
Left				0.2083"	
Top				0.2917"	
Width				6.0521"	
Height				1.9688"	
Shortcut Menu Bar . .					
ControlTip Text					
Help Context Id				0	
Tag					

Switchboard Forms: Controlling Your Application

A Switchboard form is a great way to control your application. The Switchboard Manager, a tool designed to help you create switchboards, is covered in Chapter 37, "Distributing Your Application with ODE." In this section, you learn how to create a custom Switchboard form. A Switchboard form is simply a form with command buttons that navigate you to other Switchboard forms or to the forms and reports that make up your system.

The form shown in Figure 13.11 is a Switchboard form. Each tab on the form lets the user work with different components of the database. What differentiates a Switchboard form from other forms is that its purpose is limited to navigating through the application. It usually has a border style of `Dialog`, and it has no scrollbars, record selectors, or navigation buttons. Other than these characteristics, a Switchboard form is a normal form. There are many styles of Navigation forms; which one you use depends on your users' needs.

Figure 13.11.

An example of a tabbed Switchboard form.

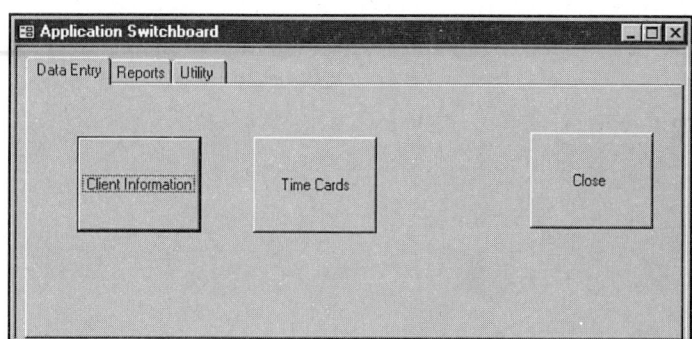

Splash Screen Forms: A Professional Opening to Your Application

Splash screens add professional polish to your applications and give your users something to look at while your programming code is setting up the application. Just follow these steps to create a Splash Screen form:

1. Create a new form.

2. Set the Scrollbars property to Neither, the Record Selectors property to No, the Navigation Buttons property to No, the Auto Resize property to Yes, the AutoCenter property to Yes, and the Border Style to None.

3. Make the form Popup and Modal.

4. Add a picture to the form and set the picture's properties.

5. Add any text you want to put on the form.

6. Set the form's timer interval to the number of seconds you want the splash screen to be displayed.

7. Code the form's Timer event for DoCmd.Close.

8. Code the form's Unload event to open your main Switchboard form.

Because the Timer event of the Splash Screen form closes the form after the amount of time specified in the timer interval, the Splash Screen form unloads itself. While it's unloading, it loads the Switchboard form. The Splash Screen form included in CHAP13EX.MDB is called frmSplash. When it unloads, it opens the frmSwitchboard form.

You can implement your Splash Screen form in many other ways. For example, you can call the Splash Screen form from a Startup form; its Open event simply needs to open the Splash Screen form. The problem with this method is that if your application loads and unloads the switchboard while the application is running, the splash screen is displayed again.

Another popular method is to build a function that's called from an AutoExec macro. This Startup function can display the splash screen, execute all the tasks needed to set up your application, then unload the splash screen. Here's an example that opens the frmSplash form:

```
Function AutoExec()
    DoCmd.OpenForm "frmSplash"
    DoCmd.Hourglass True
    '*** Code to set up your application is placed here  ***
    '*** End of Setup Code ***
    DoCmd.OpenForm "frmSwitchboard"
    DoCmd.Close acForm, "frmSplash"
    DoCmd.Hourglass False
End Function
```

This code then displays an hourglass and continues with any setup processing. When it's done with all the setup processing, it opens the frmSwitchboard form, closes the splash screen, and gets rid of the hourglass.

TIP

You can also display a splash screen by including a bitmap file with the same name as your database (MDB) in the same directory as the database file. When the application is loaded, the splash screen is displayed for a couple of seconds. The only disadvantage to this method is that you have less control over when, and how long, the splash screen is displayed.

Dialog Forms: Gathering Information

Dialog forms are typically used to gather information from the user. What makes them Dialog forms is that they're modal, meaning that the user can't go ahead with the application until the form is handled. Dialog forms are generally used when you must get specific information from your user before your application can continue processing. A custom Dialog form is simply a regular form that has a Dialog border style and has its Modal property set to Yes. Remember to give users a way to close the form; otherwise, they might close your modal form with the famous "Three-Finger Salute" (Ctrl+Alt+Del) or, even worse, by using the PC's Reset button. The frmArchivePayments form in CHAP13EX.MDB is a custom Dialog form.

Using Built-In Dialog Boxes

Access comes with two built-in dialog boxes: the standard Windows message box and the input box. The ODE also includes the Common Dialog OLE control, which gives you access to other commonly used dialog boxes.

Message Boxes

A message box is a predefined dialog box that you can incorporate into your applications; however, it can be customized by using parameters. The VBA language has a MsgBox statement—that just displays a message—and a MsgBox function, which can display a message and return a value based on the user's response.

The message box in the VBA language is the same message box that's standard in most Windows applications, so it's already familiar to most Windows users. Rather than create your own dialog boxes to get standard responses from your users, you can use an existing, standard interface.

The MsgBox Statement

The MsgBox statement receives five parameters: the message, the type of icon you want, the message box's title, and the Help file and context ID you want available if the user selects Help while the dialog box is displayed. The MsgBox statement looks like this:

```
MsgBox "This is a Message", vbInformation, "This is a Title"
```

This example displays the message `"This is a Message"` and the information icon. The title for the message box is `"This is a Title"`. The message box also has an OK button that's used to close the dialog box.

The MsgBox Function

The `MsgBox` statement is normally used to display just an OK button, but the `MsgBox` function lets you select from a variety of standard button combinations and returns a value indicating which button the user selected. The `MsgBox` function receives the same five parameters as the `MsgBox` statement. The first parameter is the message you want to display, and the second is a numeric value indicating which buttons and icon you want to display. Tables 13.1 and 13.2 list the values that can be numerically added to create the second parameter. The intrinsic constants in the table can be substituted for the numeric values, if you like.

Table 13.1. Values indicating the buttons you want to display.

Buttons	Value	Intrinsic Constant
OK button only	0	vbOKOnly
OK and Cancel	1	vbOKCancel
Abort, Retry, and Ignore	2	vbAbortRetryIgnore
Yes, No, and Cancel	3	vbYesNoCancel
Yes and No	4	vbYesNo
Retry and Cancel	5	vbRetryCancel

The values in Table 13.1 must be numerically added to one of the values in Table 13.2 if you want to include an icon other than the dialog box's default icon.

Table 13.2. Values indicating the icons you want to display.

Icon	Value	Intrinsic Constant
Critical (Stop Sign)	16	vbCritical
Warning Query (Question)	32	vbQuestion
Warning Exclamation (!)	48	vbExclamation
Information (I)	64	vbInformation

In the following example, the message box displays Yes, No, and Cancel buttons:

```
Sub MessageBoxFunction()
    Dim intAnswer As Integer
    intAnswer = MsgBox("Are You Sure?", vbYesNoCancel + vbQuestion, _
        "Please Respond")
End Sub
```

This message box also displays the Question icon. (See Figure 13.12.) The `Function` call returns a value stored in the Integer variable `iAnswer`.

Figure 13.12.

The dialog box displayed by the `MsgBox` *function.*

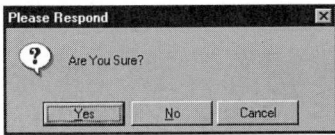

After you have placed the return value in a variable, you can easily introduce logic into your program to respond to the user's selection, as shown in this example:

```
Sub MessageBoxAnswer()
    Dim intAnswer As Integer
    intAnswer = MsgBox("Are You Sure?", vbYesNoCancel + vbQuestion, _
        "Please Respond")
    Select Case intAnswer
        Case vbYes
            MsgBox "I'm Glad You are Sure!!"
        Case vbNo
            MsgBox "Why Aren't You Sure??"
        Case vbCancel
            MsgBox "You Coward! You Bailed Out!!"
    End Select
End Sub
```

This code evaluates the user's response and displays a message based on his or her answer. Of course, in a real-life situation, the code in the `Case` statements would be more practical. Table 13.3 lists the values returned from the `MsgBox` function, depending on which button the user selected.

Table 13.3. Values returned from the `MsgBox` function.

Response	Value	Intrinsic Constant
OK	1	vbOK
Cancel	2	vbCancel
Abort	3	vbAbort
Retry	4	vbRetry
Ignore	5	vbIgnore
Yes	6	vbYes
No	7	vbNo

399

Input Boxes

The InputBox function displays a dialog box containing a simple text box. It returns the text the user typed in the text box and looks like this:

```
Sub InputBoxExample()
    Dim strName As String
    strName = InputBox("What is Your Name?", _
                "This is the Title", "This is the Default")
    MsgBox "You Entered " & strName
End Sub
```

This subroutine displays the input box shown in Figure 13.13. Notice that the first parameter is the message, the second is the title, and the third is the default value. The second and third parameters are optional.

Figure 13.13.

An example of using the InputBox *function to gather information.*

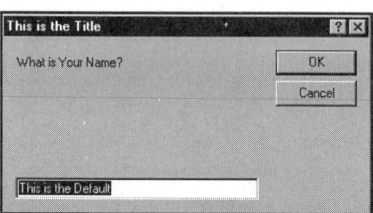

Common Dialog Boxes

As mentioned, the Common Dialog control is an OCX control that's included as part of the ODE. You can use it to display Windows common dialog boxes, including File Save, File Open, File Print, File Print Setup, Fonts, and Colors. The Common Dialog control is covered in Chapter 26, "Using ActiveX Controls."

Adding Custom Menus, Toolbars, and Shortcut Menus to Your Forms

You can create custom menus to display with your forms and reports; there's no limit on how many you can use. Each menu can be attached to one or more forms or reports.

Quite often, you want to restrict what users can do while they're working with a form or report. By creating a custom menu, you can restrict and customize what they're allowed to do.

Designing a Menu

In previous versions of Access, you created a custom menu bar by setting the MenuBar property to the name of a menu bar macro. This function is supported for backward compatibility only. In Access 97, custom menu bars, toolbars, and pop-up menus are all referred to as *command bars*. To create any of these three objects, choose View | Toolbars and then select Customize. Once a custom menu bar, toolbar, or pop-up menu has been created, you can easily associate it with forms and reports by using the Menubar, Toolbar, and Shortcut Menu Bar properties.

Follow these steps to create a custom menu bar:

1. Choose View | Toolbars and click Customize, or right-click any toolbar and select Customize.

2. When the Customize dialog box opens, click New. (See Figure 13.14.)

Figure 13.14.

Using the Customize dialog box to create a new command bar.

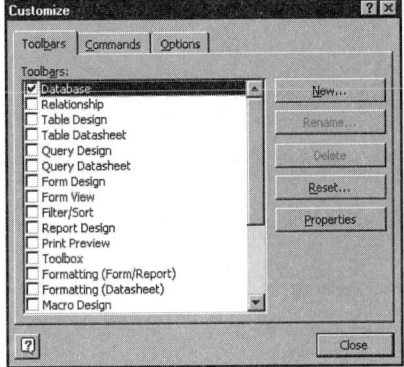

3. Assign a name to the new menu bar, toolbar, or pop-up menu. The new command bar then appears.

4. Click the Properties button on the Customize dialog box to view the properties for your newly created toolbar. In the Toolbar Properties dialog box, you name the toolbar, select the toolbar type, indicate the type of docking that's allowed, and set other options for the command bar. The Type drop-down list allows you to select Menu Bar, Toolbar, or Popup. The Docking options are Allow Any, Can't Change, No Vertical, and No Horizontal. You can also choose whether the user will be allowed to customize or move the menu or toolbar.

5. Select the options you want and click Close.

Now you're ready to add items to the toolbar, menu bar, or pop-up menu. The process differs slightly, depending on which type of command bar you selected. To add items to a command bar, click the Commands tab of the Customize dialog box, shown in Figure 13.15, and drag and drop command icons onto your new command bar.

Figure 13.15.

*Use the Commands tab to add
items to a command bar.*

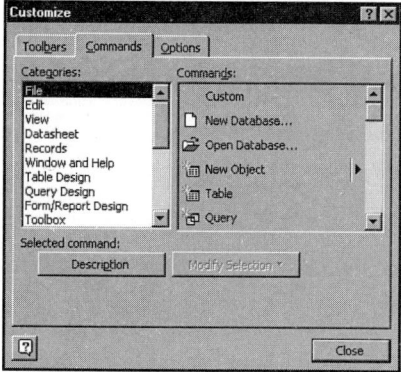

Here are some tips to help you create custom menu bars, toolbars, and pop-up menus:

- To add an entire built-in menu to the menu bar, select Built-in Menus from the Categories list box. Click and drag a menu pad from the Commands list box over to the menu bar to add the entire built-in menu pad to the custom menu.

- To create a custom menu pad, select New Menu from the Categories list box. Click and drag the New Menu option to the menu bar. To modify the text on the menu pad, right-click the menu pad and type a new value in the Name text box.

- To add a built-in command to the menu, select a category from the Categories list box, then click and drag the appropriate command to the menu pad. The new item will appear underneath the menu pad.

- To add a separator bar to a menu, right-click on the menu item that will follow the separator bar and select Begin a Group. To remove the separator bar, select Begin a Group again.

- Menu items can contain Text Only or Image and Text. To select one, right-click a menu item and select Default Style, Text Only (Always), Text Only (in Menus), or Image and Text. To customize an image, right-click a menu item and select Change Button Image. Choose one of the available images. To modify the button image, right-click a menu item and select Edit Button Image; this opens the Button Editor dialog box. (See Figure 13.16.) If you want to reset the button to its original image, right-click the menu item and select Reset Button Image.

- If you want to modify several properties of a menu item at once, you can right-click the menu item and select Properties to open the Menu Bar Control Properties dialog box. (See Figure 13.17.) Here you can select attributes for the menu item, such as the Caption, Tooltip, Style, Help File, and Help Context ID. You can also associate an action with a custom menu item (covered in the next section).

Figure 13.16.

Modifying or creating button images with the Button Editor.

Figure 13.17.

Modifying menu item properties with the Menu Bar Control Properties dialog box.

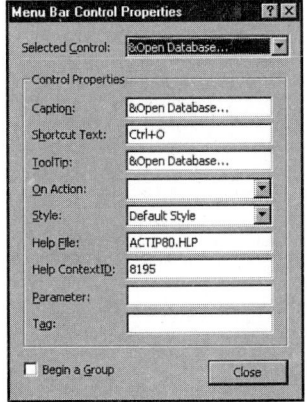

Associating a Command with a Menu Item

In Access, it's easy to customize your menus with both built-in commands and custom-built functions. For built-in commands, you can simply drag and drop commands onto your command bars. To have a command bar item run a custom-built function, you need to create a custom item and set its properties, as explained in the following steps:

1. Select the File category from the Categories list box in the Customize dialog box.

2. Click and drag the Custom option from the Commands list box to the position you want for the menu.

3. Right-click the new menu item and select Properties.

4. Type the name of the function or subroutine you want to call in the On Action drop-down list. If the procedure you're calling is a function, you must precede the function name with an equal sign and include any parameters in parentheses following the function name.

5. Click Close to close the Control Properties dialog box.

6. Click Close to close the Customize dialog box.

Deleting and Renaming Menus

You can also use the Customize dialog box to delete and rename menus by following these steps:

1. Right-click any command bar and select Customize.
2. Click in the Toolbars list box to select the command bar you want to delete or rename.
3. Click either Delete to delete the command bar or Rename to rename it.

Manipulating Command Bars by Using Code

Command bars can be added, modified, and removed by using VBA code, which allows you to build flexibility into your application. You can easily modify a command bar in response to different conditions in your application. You can even give your user a front-end to customize the command bars in your application, as shown in this example:

```
Sub CreateCustomCommandBar()
    On Error Resume Next
    Dim cbr As CommandBar
    Dim btn As CommandBarButton

    Set cbr = CommandBars("My Command Bar")
    If Err <> 0 Then
        Set cbr = CommandBars _
          .Add(Name:="My Command Bar", Position:=msoBarTop)
    End If

    Set btn = cbr.Controls("Get Initials")

    If Err <> 0 Then
        ' Custom button doesn't already exist, so create it.
        Set btn = cbr.Controls.Add(msoControlButton, , , , True)
    End If
    With btn
        .Caption = "Are You Sure?"
        .BeginGroup = True
        .OnAction = "MessageBoxAnswer"
        .Style = msoButtonCaption
    End With
End Sub
```

This code illustrates that by using the VBA language, you have full control over command bar objects. It begins by creating CommandBar and CommandBarButton object variables, then sets the CommandBar object variable to a command bar called "My Command Bar." If this causes an error, then you know that the "My Command Bar" command bar doesn't exist. The Add method is used to add the command bar, which will be placed at the top of the screen. The routine then tries to point at a command bar button called "Are You Sure?". If this causes an error, the Add method of the Controls collection of the CommandBar object is used to add a command button to the collection. The button's caption is set to "Are You Sure?", a group is added, and the command button's action is to call the subroutine MessageBoxAnswer. The command button's style is set to display just a caption.

Taking Advantage of Built-in Form-Filtering Features

Access has several form-filtering features that are part of the user interface. You can opt to include these features in your application, omit them from your application entirely, or control their behavior. For your application to control their behavior, it needs to respond to the Filter event, which it does by detecting when a filter is placed on the data in the form. When it has detected the filter, the code in the Filter event executes.

Sometimes you might want to alter the standard behavior of a filter command. You might want to display a special message to the user, for example, or take a specific action in your code. You might also want your application to respond to a Filter event because you want to alter the form's display before the filter is applied. For example, if a certain filter is in place, you may want to hide or disable certain fields. When the filter is removed, you could then return the form's appearance to normal.

Fortunately, Access not only lets you know that the Filter event occurred, but it also lets you know how the filter was invoked. Armed with this information, you can intercept and change the filtering behavior as needed.

When a user chooses Filter By Form or Advanced Filter/Sort, the FilterType parameter is filled with a value that indicates how the filter was invoked. If the user invokes the filter by selecting Filter By Form, the FilterType parameter equals the constant acFilterByForm; however, if he or she selects Advanced Filter/Sort, the FilterType parameter equals the constant acFilterAdvanced. The following code demonstrates how to use these constants:

```
Private Sub Form_Filter(Cancel As Integer, FilterType As Integer)
    Select Case FilterType
        Case acFilterByForm
            MsgBox "You Just Selected Filter By Form"
        Case acFilterAdvanced
            MsgBox "You Are Not Allowed to Select Advanced Filter/Sort"
            Cancel = True
    End Select
End Sub
```

This code, placed in the form's Filter event, evaluates the filter type. If Filter By Form was selected, a message box is displayed and the filtering proceeds as usual, but if the user selects Advanced Filter/Sort, she's told she can't do this and the filter process is canceled.

Not only can you check how the filter was invoked, but you can also intercept the process when the filter is applied. You do this by placing code in the form's ApplyFilter event, as shown in this example:

```
Private Sub Form_ApplyFilter(Cancel As Integer, ApplyType As Integer)
    Dim intAnswer As Integer
    If ApplyType = acApplyFilter Then
        intAnswer = MsgBox("You just selected the criteria: & _
                    Chr(13) & Chr(10) & Me.Filter & _
                    Chr(13) & Chr(10) & Are You Sure You Wish to Proceed?", _
                    vbYesNo + vbQuestion)
```

```
        If intAnswer = vbNo Then
            Cancel = True
        End If
    End If
End Sub
```

This code evaluates the value of the `ApplyType` parameter. If it's equal to the constant `acApplyFilter`, a message box is displayed, verifying that the user wants to apply the filter. If the user responds Yes, the filter is applied; otherwise, the filter is canceled.

Including Objects from Other Applications: Linking Versus Embedding

Microsoft Access is an OLE client application, meaning it can contain objects from other applications. Access 97 is also an OLE server application. Using Access as an OLE server is covered in Chapter 25, "Automation: Communicating with Other Applications." Access's ability to control other applications with programming code is also covered in Chapter 25. In the following sections, you learn how to link to and embed objects in your Access forms.

Bound OLE Objects

Bound OLE objects are tied to the data in an OLE field within a table in your database. An example is the Photo field that's part of the Employees table in the NorthWind database. The field type of the Employees table that supports multimedia data is OLE object. This means that each record in the table can contain a unique OLE object. The Employees form contains a bound OLE control whose control source is the Photo field from the Employees table.

If you double-click on the photo of an employee, the OLE object can be edited *In-Place*. The picture of the employee is actually embedded in the Employees table. This means that the data associated with the OLE object is actually stored as part of the Access database (MDB) file, within the Employees table. Embedded objects, if they support the OLE 2.0 standard, can be modified In-Place. This is called *In-Place activation.*

To insert a new object, take the following steps:

1. Move to the record that will contain the OLE object.
2. Right-click on the OLE Object control and select Insert Object to open the Insert Object dialog box.
3. Select an object type. Select Create New if you want to create an embedded object, or select Create from File if you want to link to or embed an existing file.
4. If you select Create from File, the Insert Object dialog box changes to look like the one shown in Figure 13.18.

Figure 13.18.
The Insert Object dialog box as it appears when you select Create from File.

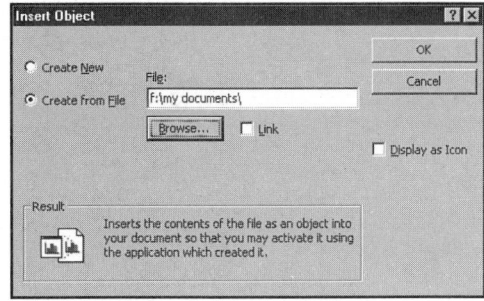

5. Select Link if you want to link to the existing file. Don't click Link if you want to embed the existing file. If you link to the file, the Access table will have a reference to the file as well as presentation data (a bitmap) for the object. If you embed the file, Access copies the original file, placing the copy in the Access table.

6. Click Browse and select the file you want to link to or embed.

7. Click OK.

If you double-click on a linked object, you launch its source application; you don't get In-Place activation. (See Figure 13.19.)

Figure 13.19.
Editing a linked object.

Unbound OLE Objects

Unbound OLE objects aren't stored in your database. Instead, they are part of the form they were created in. Like bound OLE objects, unbound OLE objects can be linked or embedded. You create an unbound OLE object by adding an unbound object frame to the form.

OpenArgs

The OpenArgs property gives you a way to pass information to a form as it's being opened. The OpenArgs argument of the OpenForm method is used to populate a form's OpenArgs property at runtime. It works like this:

```
DoCmd.OpenForm "frmPaymentMethods", , , , , acDialog, "GotoNew"
```

This code is found in the Time and Billing application's frmPayments form. It opens the frmPaymentMethods form when a new method of payment is added to the cboPaymentMethodID combo box. It sends the frmPaymentMethods form an OpenArg of "GotoNew". The Load event of the frmPaymentMethods form looks like this:

```
Private Sub Form_Load()
    If Me.OpenArgs = "GotoNew" And Not IsNull(Me![PaymentMethodID]) Then
        DoCmd.RunCommand acCmdRecordsGoToNew
    End If
End Sub
```

This code evaluates the form's OpenArgs property, moving to a new record if the OpenArgs property contains the text string "GoToNew" and the PaymentMethodID of the current record isn't Null. The OpenArgs property can be evaluated and used anywhere in the form.

Switching a Form's Record Source

Many developers don't realize how easy it is to switch a form's record source at runtime. This is a great way to use the same form to display data from more than one table or query containing the same fields. It's also a great way to limit the data that's displayed in a form at a particular moment. Using the technique of altering a form's record source at runtime, you can dramatically improve performance, especially for a client/server application. Here's an example found in the ShowSales form of the Solutions database. (See Figure 13.20 and Listing 13.1.)

Figure 13.20.

Changing the record source of a form at runtime.

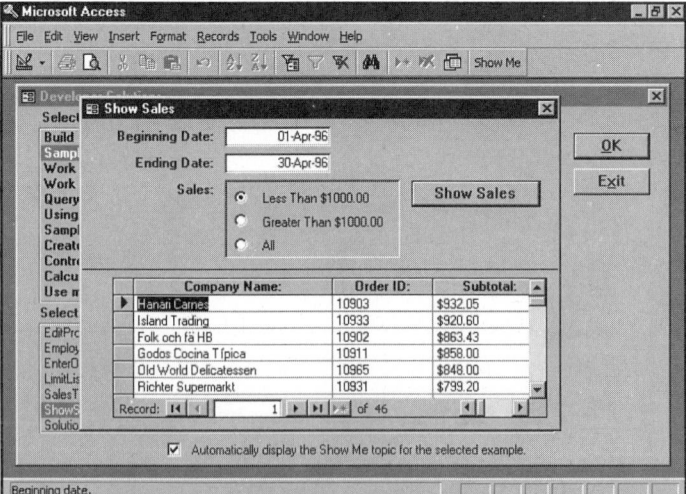

Listing 13.1. Altering a form's record source at runtime.

```
Private Sub ShowSales_Click()
    ' Create an SQL statement using
    ' search criteria entered by user and
    ' set RecordSource property of ShowSalesSubform.

    Dim strSQL As String, strRestrict As String
    Dim lngX As Long
    Dim varTmp As Variant

    lngX = Forms!ShowSales!Sales.Value
    strRestrict = ShowSalesValue(lngX)

    ' Create SELECT statement.
    strSQL = "SELECT DISTINCTROW Customers.CompanyName, " & _
            "OrderSubtotals.OrderID, "
    strSQL = strSQL & "OrderSubtotals.Subtotal , " & _
            "Orders.ShippedDate "
    strSQL = strSQL & "FROM Customers INNER JOIN " & _
            "(OrderSubtotals INNER JOIN Orders ON "
    strSQL = strSQL & "OrderSubtotals.OrderID = Orders.OrderID) ON "
    strSQL = strSQL & "Customers.CustomerID = Orders.CustomerID "
    strSQL = strSQL & "WHERE (Orders.ShippedDate Between " & _
            "Forms!ShowSales!BeginningDate "
    strSQL = strSQL & "And Forms!ShowSales!EndingDate) "
    strSQL = strSQL & "And " & strRestrict
    strSQL = strSQL & " ORDER BY OrderSubtotals.Subtotal DESC;"

    ' Set RecordSource property of ShowSalesSubform.
    Me!ShowSalesSubform.Form.RecordSource = strSQL

    ' If no records match criteria,
    ' reset subform's RecordSource property,
    ' display message, and move focus to BeginningDate text box.
    If Me!ShowSalesSubform.Form.RecordsetClone.RecordCount = 0 Then
        Me!ShowSalesSubform.Form.RecordSource = _
            "SELECT CompanyName FROM Customers WHERE False;"
        MsgBox "No records match the criteria you entered.", _
            48, "No Records Found"
        Me!BeginningDate.SetFocus
    Else
        ' Enable control in detail section.
        varTmp = EnableControls("Detail", True)
        ' Move insertion point to ShowSalesSubform.
        Me!ShowSalesSubform.SetFocus
    End If

End Sub

Private Function ShowSalesValue(lngOptionGroupValue As Long) As String

    ' Return value selected in Sales option group.

    ' Define constants for option group values.
    Const conSalesUnder1000 = 1
    Const conSalesOver1000 = 2
    Const conAllSales = 3
```

continues

409

Listing 13.1. continued

```
    '  Create restriction based on value of option group.
    Select Case lngOptionGroupValue
        Case conSalesUnder1000:
            ShowSalesValue = "OrderSubtotals.Subtotal < 1000"
        Case conSalesOver1000:
            ShowSalesValue = "OrderSubtotals.Subtotal >= 1000"
        Case Else
            ShowSalesValue = "OrderSubtotals.Subtotal = True"
    End Select
End Function
```

This code begins by storing the value of the Sales option group on the ShowSales main form into a Long Integer variable. It then calls the ShowSalesValue function, which declares three constants, then evaluates the parameter that was passed to it (the Long Integer variable containing the option group value). Based on the value of the option group, it builds a selection string for the subtotal value. This selection string becomes part of the SQL statement used for the subform's record source and limits the range of sales values displayed on the subform.

The ShowSales routine then builds a string containing a SQL statement, which selects all required fields from the Customers table and OrderSubtotals query. It builds a WHERE clause that includes the BeginningDate and EndingDate from the main form as well as the string returned from the ShowSalesValue function.

When the SQL statement has been built, the RecordSource property of the ShowSalesSubform control is set equal to the SQL statement. The RecordCount property of the RecordsetClone (the form's underlying recordset) is evaluated to determine whether any records meet the criteria specified in the record source. If the record count is zero, no records are displayed in the subform and the user is warned that no records met the criteria. However, if records are found, the form's Detail section is enabled, and focus is moved to the subform.

Power Combo Box and List Box Techniques

Combo boxes and list boxes are very powerful. Being able to properly respond to a combo box's NotInList event, to populate a combo box by using code, and to select multiple entries in a list box are essential skills of an experienced Access programmer. They're covered in detail in the following sections.

Handling the NotInList Event

As discussed, the NotInList event occurs when a user types a value in the text box portion of a combo box that's not found in the combo box list. This event takes place only if the LimitToList property of the combo box is set to True. It's up to you whether you want to respond to this event.

You might want to respond with something other than the default error message when the LimitToList property is set to True and the user tries to add an entry. For example, if a user is entering an order and she enters the name of a new customer, you could react by displaying a message box asking whether she really wants to add the new customer. If the user responds affirmatively, you can display a customer form.

After you have set the LimitToList property to True, any code you place in the NotInList event is executed whenever the user tries to type an entry that's not found in the combo box. The following is an example:

```
Private Sub cboCompany_NotInList(NewData As String, Response As Integer)
    Dim intAnswer As Integer
    intAnswer = MsgBox("Company Does Not Exist.  Add (Yes/No)", _
        vbYesNo + vbQuestion)
End Sub
```

The problem with this code is that it warns the user of the problem but doesn't rectify it; therefore, this code runs and then the default error handling kicks in.

The NotInList event procedure accepts a response argument, which is where you can tell VBA what to do *after* your code executes. Any one of the following three constants can be placed in the response argument:

- acDataErrAdded: This constant is used if your code adds the new value into the record source for the combo box. This code requeries the combo box, adding the new value to the list.

- AcDataErrDisplay: This constant is used if you want VBA to display the default error message.

- AcDataErrContinue: This constant is used if you want to suppress VBA's own error message, using your own instead. Access still requires that a valid entry be placed in the combo box.

The following code, when placed in the NotInList event procedure of your combo box, displays a message asking the user whether she wants to add the customer. If the user responds No, she is returned to the form without the standard error message being displayed, but she still must enter a valid value in the combo box. If the user responds Yes, she is placed in the customer form, ready to add the customer whose name she typed.

```
Private Sub cboCompany_NotInList(NewData As String, Response As Integer)
    Dim iAnswer As Integer
    iAnswer = MsgBox("Company Does Not Exist.  Add (Yes/No)", _
        vbYesNo + vbQuestion)
    If iAnswer = vbYes Then
        DoCmd.OpenForm "frmCustomer", acNormal, , , acAdd, acDialog
        Response = acDataErrAdded
    Else
        Response = acDataErrContinue
    End If
End Sub
```

Populating a Combo Box or List Box with a `Callback` Function

It's easy to populate a combo box or list box by setting the control's properties. This method is enough for many situations; however, there are times when you might want to populate a combo or list box programmatically—with values from an array, for example. You might also want to populate the box with table or report names or some other database component.

To populate a combo box or list box using code, you create a `Callback` function, which tells Access how many rows and columns will be in the box and what data will be used to fill the box. This function becomes the Row Source type for your combo box or list box. Access calls the function, then uses its information to populate the box. The following example is found in the CustomersDialog form that's part of the Solutions database:

Listing 13.2. Filling a list box by using a `Callback` function.

```
Function lstForms_Fill(ctl As Control, lngID As Long, lngRow As Long, _
        lngCol As Long, intCode As Integer) As Variant
    Dim frm As Form_Customers

    'Error if CustomerPhoneList form isn't open.
    Const conFormNotOpen = 2450

    On Error GoTo Fill_Error

    Select Case intCode
        Case acLBInitialize     'Initialize the listbox.
            Set colCustomerForms = Forms![CustomerPhoneList].ReturnCollection
            lstForms_Fill = True

        Case acLBOpen           'Open.
            lstForms_Fill = Timer

        Case acLBGetRowCount        'Get the number of rows.
            lstForms_Fill = colCustomerForms.Count

        Case acLBGetColumnCount     'Get the number of columns.
            lstForms_Fill = 1

        Case acLBGetColumnWidth     'Get the column width.
            lstForms_Fill = -1      'Use the default width.

        Case acLBGetValue           'Get the data.
            Set frm = colCustomerForms(lngRow + 1)
            lstForms_Fill = frm![CompanyName]

    End Select
    Exit Function

Fill_Error:
    If Err = conFormNotOpen Then
        Exit Function
    Else
        MsgBox Err.Description
        Exit Function
    End If
End Function
```

The function must contain five predetermined arguments. The first argument must be declared as a control, and the remaining arguments must be declared as variants. The function itself must return a variant. The parameters are listed in Table 13.4.

Table 13.4. Five predetermined arguments of a `Callback` function.

Argument	Description
fld	A control variable that refers to the combo or list box being filled
id	A unique value that identifies the control being filled. It's useful when you're using the same function to populate more that one combo or list box
row	The row being filled (zero-based)
col	The column being filled (zero-based)
code	A value specifying the information being requested

The `List` function is called several times. Each time it's called, Access automatically supplies a different value for the code, indicating the information it's requesting. The code item can have the values shown in Table 13.5.

Table 13.5. Code item values.

Code	Intrinsic Constant	Meaning	Returns
0	acLBInitialize	Initialize	Nonzero if the function can fill the list; False or Null if a problem occurs
1	acLBOpen	Open	Nonzero ID value if the function can fill the list; False or Null if a problem occurs
3	acLBGetRowCount	Number of rows	Number of rows in the list
4	acLBGetColumnCount	Number of columns	Number of columns in the list
5	acLBGetColumnWidth	Column width	Width of the column specified
6	acLBGetValue	List entry	List entry to be displayed in the column and row specified
7	acLBGetFormat	Format string	Format string used to format the list entry
8	acLBClose	Not used	
9	acLBEnd	End (last call)	Nothing

The function is automatically called once for codes 0, 1, 3, and 4. These calls initiate the process and determine the number of rows and columns that the combo or list box contains. The function is called twice for code 5: once to determine the total width of the box, and again to set the column width. The number of times that codes 6 and 7 are executed varies depending on the number of rows contained in the box (code 3). Code 9 is called when the form is closed or the combo box or list box is queried.

Armed with this knowledge, take a good look at the lstForms_Fill function, the Callback function that's used to populate the list box. The purpose of this function is to populate the list box with a list of forms opened by the Customer Phone List form, which allows multiple instances of the Customer form to be opened and added to a collection. When the user closes the Customer Phone List form, the CustomersDialog form is opened, asking the user which instances of the Customers form he or she wants to leave open.

The Callback function begins by creating a form object variable based on the Customers form. Each element of the case structure seen in the routine is called as each code is sent by Access. Here's what happens:

- When Access sends the code of 0, the colCustomerForms variable is set equal to the ReturnCollection method of the CustomerPhoneList form. This ReturnCollection method contains a collection of open Customer forms. The function then returns a True.

- When Access sends the code of 1, the return value is a unique value equal to the return value of the Timer function.

- When Access sends the code of 3, the return value is set equal to the count of forms in the colCustomerForms collection.

- When Access sends the code of 4, the return value is set to 1 (one column).

- When Access sends the code of 5, the return value is set to -1, forcing a default width for the combo or list box.

- Access then automatically calls code 6 by the number of times that was returned for the number of rows in the combo box or list box. Each time code 6 is called, the form object variable is set equal to a different element of the form collection. The CompanyName from each form is returned from the function. The CompanyName return value is the value that's added to the list box.

All this work might seem difficult at first. After you have populated a couple of combo boxes or list boxes, though, it's quite easy. In fact, all you need to do is copy the case structure you see in the lstForms_Fill function and use it as a template for all your Callback routines.

Handling Multiple Selections in a List Box

Access 97 list boxes have a Multi-select property. When set to True, this property lets the user select multiple elements from the list box. Your code can then evaluate which elements are selected and perform some action based on the selected elements. The example in the previous section ("Populating a Combo or List Box with a `Callback` Function") demonstrates the use of a Multi-select list box. The form shows all the instances of the Customer form that are currently open. It allows users to select which instances of the Customer form they want to keep open when the CustomersPhoneList form is closed. The code under the `Click` event of the OK button looks like this:

Listing 13.3. Evaluating which items are selected in the multi-select list box.

```
Private Sub cmdOk_Click()
    Dim intIndex As Variant
    Dim frm As Form_Customers
    Dim varFormName As Variant

    Const conObjectRequired = 424

    On Error GoTo Close_Error

    'Set the value of the user-defined KeepMeAlive property
    'of the forms that should stay open.
    intIndex = 1
    'Determine which listbox items are selected.
    For Each intIndex In lstForms.ItemsSelected
        Set frm = colCustomerForms(intIndex + 1)
        frm.KeepMealive frm
    Next intIndex

    DoCmd.Close acForm, "CustomersDialog"

    Exit Sub

Close_Error:
    If Err = conObjectRequired Then
        DoCmd.Close acForm, "CustomersDialog"
        Exit Sub
    Else
        MsgBox Err.Description
        Exit Sub
    End If
End Sub
```

This code uses the `For Each...Next` construct, along with the ItemsSelected property of the list box to loop through each selected item in the list box. The routine sets a form object variable equal to a specific form in the collection. The routine uses `intIndex + 1` as the index in the collection because the collection of forms is one-based. The KeepMeAlive custom property of each form is set to `True`, and the CustomersDialog form is closed. The KeepMeAlive property, when set to `True`, makes sure the particular instance of the form is not closed.

Power Subform Techniques

Many new Access developers don't know the ins and outs of creating and modifying a subform and referring to subform controls, so first look at some important points you should know when working with subforms:

- The easiest way to add a subform to a main form is to open the main form, then drag and drop the subform onto the main form.

- The easiest way to edit a subform after it has been added to the main form is to double-click on the subform control within the main form. If your double-click isn't successful, you need to click off the subform object, then double-click on it again.

- The subform control's LinkChildFields and LinkMasterFields properties determine which fields in the main form link to which fields in the subform. A single field name, or a list of fields separated by semicolons, can be entered into these properties. When they are properly set, these properties make sure all records in the child form relate to the currently displayed record in the parent form.

Referring to Subform Controls

Many developers don't know how to properly refer to subform controls. You must refer to any objects on the subform through the subform control on the main form, as shown in this example:

```
Forms!frmCustomer!fsubOrders
```

This example refers to the fsubOrders control on the frmCustomer form. If you want to refer to a specific control on the fsubOrders subform, you can then point at its controls collection. Here's an example:

```
Forms!frmCustomer!fsubOrders!txtOrderID
```

You can also refer to the control on the subform implicitly, as shown in this example:

```
Forms!frmCustomer!subOrders!txtOrderID
```

Both of these methods refer to the txtOrderID control on the form in the fsubOrder control on the frmCustomer form. To change a property of this control, you would extend the syntax to look like this:

```
Forms!frmCustomer!fsubOrders!txtOrderID.Enabled = False
```

This code sets the Enabled property of the txtOrderID control on the form in the fsubOrders control to `False`.

Synchronizing a Form with Its Underlying Recordset

A form's RecordsetClone property is used to refer to its underlying recordset. You can manipulate this recordset independently of what's currently being displayed on the form. Here's an example:

```
Private Sub cboCompany_AfterUpdate()
    Me.RecordsetClone.FindFirst "[ClientID] = " & cboCompany.Value
    If Me.RecordsetClone.NoMatch Then
        MsgBox "Client Not Found"
    Else
        Me.Bookmark = Me.RecordsetClone.Bookmark
    End If
End Sub
```

This example issues the FindFirst method on the form's RecordsetClone. It searches for a record in the form's underlying recordset whose ClientID is equal to the current combo box value. If a match is found, the form's bookmark is synchronized with the bookmark of the form's underlying recordset. This code can be rewritten, using an object variable to point at the RecordsetClone:

```
Private Sub cboCompany_AfterUpdate()
    Dim rs As Recordset
    Set rs = Me.RecordsetClone
    rs.FindFirst "[ClientID] = " & cboCompany.Value
    If rs.NoMatch Then
        MsgBox "Client Not Found"
    Else
        Me.Bookmark = rs.Bookmark
    End If
End Sub
```

This code creates an object variable that points at the form's RecordsetClone. The recordset object variable can then be substituted for Me.RecordsetClone, because it references the form's underlying recordset.

Creating Custom Properties and Methods

Forms and reports are called *Class modules*, which means they act as templates for objects you create instances of at runtime. Public procedures of a form and report become Custom properties and methods of the form object at runtime. Using VBA code, you can set the values of a form's Custom properties and execute its methods.

Creating Custom Properties

Custom properties of a form or report can be created in one of two ways:

- Create Public variables in the form or report.
- Create PropertyLet and PropertyGet routines.

417

Creating and Using a Public Variable as a Form Property

The following steps are used to create and access a Custom form or report property based on a Public variable. The example is included in CHAP13EX.MDB in the forms frmPublicProperties and frmChangePublicProperty:

1. Begin by creating the form that will contain the Custom property (Public variable).

2. Place a Public variable in the General Declarations section of the form or report. (See Figure 13.21.)

3. Place code in the form or report that accesses the Public variable. The code in Figure 13.21 creates a Public variable called CustomCaption. The code behind the Click event of the cmdChangeCaption command button sets the form's (frmPublicProperties) Caption property equal to the value of the Public variable.

Figure 13.21.

Creating a Public variable in the Declarations section of a Class module.

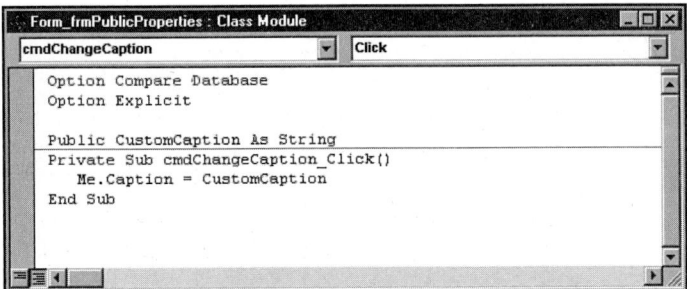

4. Create a form, report, or module that modifies the value of the Custom property. Figure 13.22 shows a form called frmChangePublicProperty.

Figure 13.22.

Viewing the form frmChangePublicProperty.

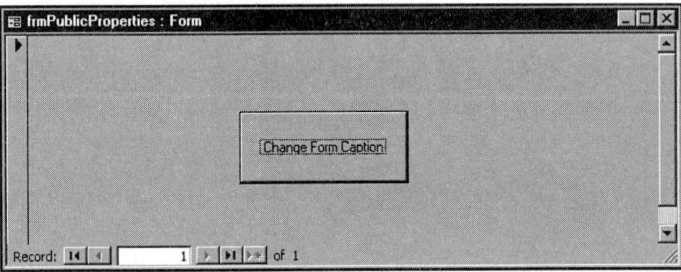

5. Add the code that modifies the value of the Custom property. The code behind the ChangeCaption button, as seen in Figure 13.21, modifies the value of the Custom property called CustomCaption that's found on the form called frmPublicProperties.

To test the Custom property created in the preceding example, run the form called frmPublicProperties, which is in the database called CHAP13EX.MDB, found on your sample code CD-ROM. Click the Change Form Caption command button. Nothing happens because the value of the `Custom` property hasn't been set. Open the form called frmChangePublicProperty and click the Change Form Property command button. Return to frmPublicProperties and again click the Change Form Caption command button. The form's caption should now change.

Close the frmPublicProperties form and try clicking the Change Form Property command button. A runtime error occurs, indicating that the form you're referring to is not open. You can eliminate the error by placing the following code in the `Click` event of cmdPublicFormProperty:

```
Private Sub cmdPublicFormProperty_Click()
   Form_frmPublicProperties.CustomCaption = _
       "This is a Custom Caption"
   Forms!frmPublicProperties.Visible = True
End Sub
```

This code modifies the value of the `Public` property by using the syntax `Form_FormName.Property`. If the form isn't loaded, this syntax loads the form but leaves it hidden. The next command sets the form's Visible property to `True`.

Creating and Using Custom Properties with `PropertyLet` and `PropertyGet` Routines

A `PropertyLet` routine is a special type of subroutine that automatically executes whenever the property's value is changed. A PropertyGet routine is another special subroutine that automatically executes whenever the value of the Custom property is retrieved. Instead of using a Public variable to create a property, you insert two special routines: `PropertyLet` and `PropertyGet`. This example is found in CHAP13EX.MDB in the frmPropertyGetLet and frmChangeWithLet forms. To insert the `PropertyLet` and `PropertyGet` routines, follow these steps:

1. Choose Insert | Procedure. The dialog box shown in Figure 13.23 appears.

Figure 13.23.

Starting a new procedure with the Insert Procedure dialog box.

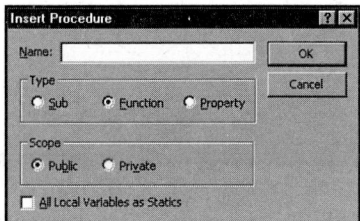

2. Type the name of the procedure in the Name text box.
3. Select Property from the Type option buttons.
4. Select Public as the Scope so that the property is visible outside the form.
5. Click OK. The `PropertyGet` and `PropertyLet` subroutines are inserted in the module. (See Figure 13.24.)

13

Figure 13.24.

Subroutines created using the Insert Procedure dialog.

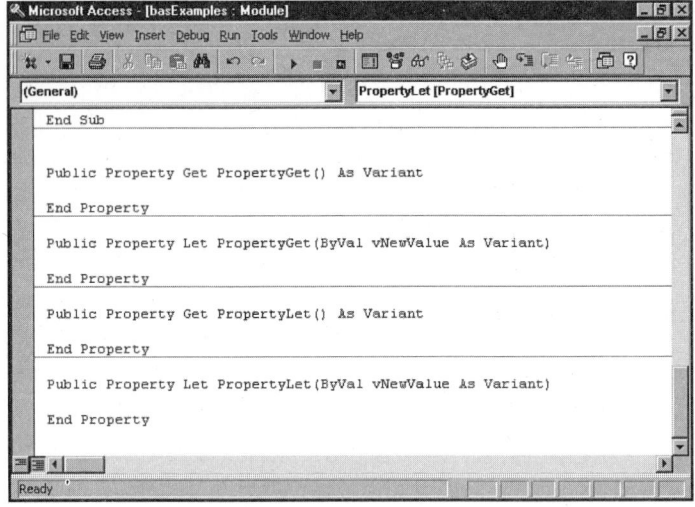

Notice that the Click event code for the cmdChangeCaption command button hasn't changed. The PropertyLet routine, which automatically executes whenever the value of the CustomCaption property is changed, takes the uppercase value of what it's being sent and places it in a Private variable called mstrCustomCaption. The PropertyGet routine takes the value of the Private variable and returns it to whomever asked for the value of the property. The sequence of events is as follows—the following code is placed in the form called frmChangeWithLet:

```
Private Sub cmdPublicFormProperty_Click()
   Form_frmPropertyGetLet.CustomCaption = "This is a Custom Caption"
   Forms!frmPropertyGetLet.Visible = True
End Sub
```

This routine tries to set the value of the Custom property called CustomCaption to the value "This is a Custom Caption". Because the property's value is being changed, the PropertyLet routine in frmPropertyGetLet is automatically executed. It looks like this:

```
Public Property Let CustomCaption(ByVal CustomCaption As String)
   mstrCustomCaption = UCase$(CustomCaption)
End Property
```

The PropertyLet routine receives the value "This is a Custom Caption" as a parameter. It uses the UCase function to manipulate the value it was passed and convert it to uppercase. It then places the manipulated value into a Private variable called mstrCustomCaption. The PropertyGet routine isn't executed until the user clicks the cmdChangeCaption button in the frmPropertyGetLet form. The Click event of cmdChangeCaption looks like this:

```
Private Sub cmdChangeCaption_Click()
   Me.Caption = CustomCaption
End Sub
```

Because this routine needs to retrieve the value of the Custom property CustomCaption, the PropertyGet routine automatically executes:

```
Public Property Get CustomCaption() As String
   CustomCaption = mstrCustomCaption
End Property
```

The PropertyGet routine takes the value of the Private variable, set by the PropertyLet routine, and returns it as the value of the property.

You might wonder why this method is preferable to declaring a Public variable. Using the UCase function within PropertyLet should illustrate why. Whenever you expose a Public variable, you can't do much to validate or manipulate the value you receive. The PropertyLet routine gives you the opportunity to validate and manipulate the value the property is being set to. By placing the manipulated value in a Private variable and then retrieving the Private variable's value when the property is returned, you gain full control over what happens internally to the property.

Creating Custom Methods

Custom methods are simply Public functions and subroutines placed in a form module or a report module. As you will see, they can be called by using the Object.Method syntax. Here are the steps involved in creating a Custom method; they are found in CHAP13EX.MDB in the forms frmMethods and frmExecuteMethod:

1. Open the form or report that will contain the Custom method.
2. Create a Public function or subroutine. (See Figure 13.25.)

Figure 13.25.

Using the Custom method ChangeCaption.

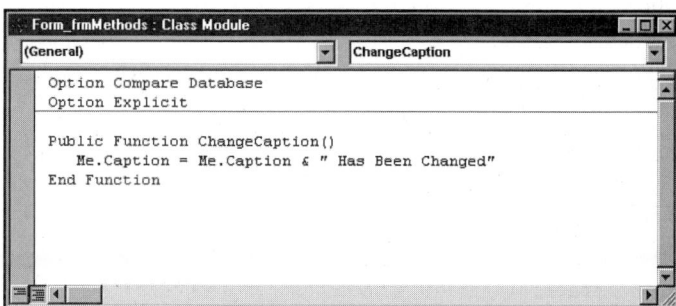

3. Open the form module, report module, or code module that executes the Custom method.
4. Use the Object.Method syntax to invoke the Custom method. (See Figure 13.26.)

Figure 13.26.

The Click *event code behind the Execute Method button.*

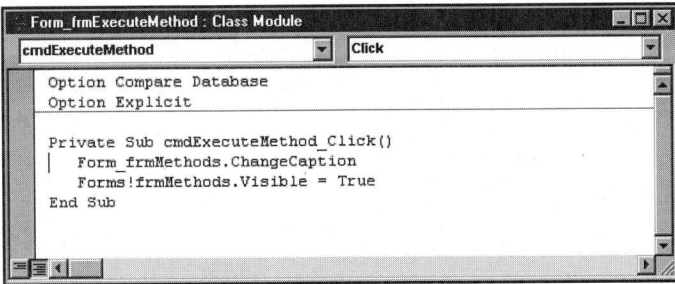

Figure 13.25 shows the Custom method ChangeCaption found in the frmMethods form. The method changes the form's caption. Figure 13.26 shows the Click event of cmdExecuteMethod found in the frmExecuteMethod form. It issues the ChangeCaption method of the frmMethods form, then sets the form's Visible property to True.

Practical Examples: Applying Advanced Techniques to Your Application

Many of the examples in this chapter are taken directly from the Time and Billing application. To add polish to your application, build an AutoExec routine that will be called from the AutoExec macro. It displays a splash screen, perform some setup functions, then load the frmClients form (the starting point for the application). The CHAP13.MDB file contains all these changes.

Building an AutoExec Routine to Launch the Application

Begin by modifying the AutoExec macro so that it hides the Database window and then calls an AutoExec function. In Chapter 37, you will remove the AutoExec macro and perform the tasks that the macro performs by using the database's StartUp properties. The AutoExec function is found in basAutoExec and looks like this:

```
Function AutoExec()
    DoCmd.OpenForm "frmSplash"
    DoEvents
    DoCmd.Hourglass True
    Call GetCompanyInfo
    DoCmd.Hourglass False
    DoCmd.OpenForm "frmClients"
    If IsLoaded("frmSplash") Then
        DoCmd.Close acForm, "frmSplash"
    End If
End Function
```

The AutoExec routine opens the frmSplash form. It issues a DoEvents to give the form time to load before the routine continues processing. It then calls the GetCompanyInfo routine, developed in Chapter 9, "Advanced VBA Techniques," to fill in the CompanyInfo type structure used throughout the application. It turns off the hourglass, opens the frmClients form, and unloads frmSplash if it's still loaded.

Remove the call to CompanyInfo from the frmClients form. This routine is now called from the AutoExec function.

> **NOTE**
>
> The AutoExec routine is one way to launch an application. Chapter 37 shows you how to use the Startup property to designate a starting point for your application, which is the method I prefer.

Building a Splash Screen

The splash screen, shown in Figure 13.27, is called frmSplash. Its timer interval is set to 3000 (3 seconds), and its Timer event looks like this:

```
Private Sub Form_Timer()
   DoCmd.Close acForm, Me.Name
End Sub
```

The Timer event unloads the form. The frmSplash Popup property is set to Yes, and its border is set to None. Record selectors and navigation buttons have been removed.

Figure 13.27.

Using an existing form as a splash screen.

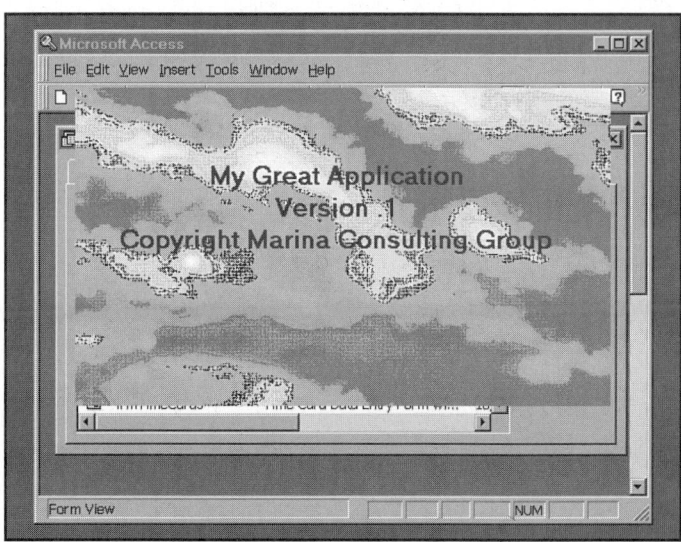

Summary

Forms are the centerpiece of most Access applications, so it's vital that you're able to fully harness their power and flexibility. The techniques covered in this chapter have shown you how to work with Form and Control events. You have seen many examples of when and how to leverage the event routines associated with forms and specific controls. You have also learned about the types of forms available, their uses in your applications, and how you can build them. Finally, you have learned several power techniques that will help you develop complex forms.

14

CHAPTER

Let's Get More Intimate with Reports: Advanced Techniques

- Events Available for Reports and When to Use Them, 426
- Order of Events for Reports, 429
- Events Available for Report Sections and When to Use Them, 429
- Special Report Properties, 433
- Practical Applications of Report Events and Properties, 435
- Practical Examples, 450

Chapter 7, "What Every Developer Needs to Know About Report Basics," covers all the basics of report design. Reports are an integral part of almost every application, so fortunately for you, the Access 97 report design tool is very powerful. Although it's easy to create most reports, as you mature as an Access developer, you'll probably want to learn the intricacies of Access report design. This chapter covers report events, advanced techniques, and tips and tricks of the trade.

Events Available for Reports and When to Use Them

Although report events aren't as plentiful as form events, the report events you can trap for allow you to control what happens as your report runs. This section discusses report events, and the section "Events Available for Report Sections and When to Use Them" covers events specific to report sections.

The Open Event

The Open event is the first event that occurs for a report, before the report begins printing or displaying. In fact, it happens even before the query underlying the report is run. Here's an example of using the Open event:

```
Private Sub Report_Open(Cancel As Integer)
    DoCmd.OpenForm "frmReportDateRange", , , , , acDialog, _
    "Project Billings by Work Code"
    If Not IsLoaded("frmReportDateRange") Then
        Cancel = True
    End If
End Sub
```

This code can be found in rptProjectBillingsByWorkCode in CHAP14.MDB on the sample code CD-ROM. It tries to open the frmReportDateRange form, the criteria form used to supply the parameters for the query underlying the report. If the form can't be loaded, the report is canceled.

The Close Event

The Close event occurs as the report is closing, before the Deactivate event occurs. The following example illustrates the use of the Close event:

```
Private Sub Report_Close()
    DoCmd.Close acForm, "frmReportDateRange"
End Sub
```

This code is found in the rptProjectBillingsByWorkCode report in CHAP14.MDB on the sample code CD-ROM. It closes the criteria form frmReportDateRange when the report is closing.

The Activate Event

A report's Activate event happens when the report becomes the active window. It occurs after the Open event and before the report starts printing and is often used to display a custom toolbar that will be visible whenever the report is active. Here's an example:

```
Private Sub Report_Activate()

    '  Used by Solutions to show toolbar with Show Me button.

    '  Hide built-in Print Preview toolbar.
    '  Show Custom Print Preview toolbar.
    DoCmd.ShowToolbar "Print Preview", acToolbarNo
    DoCmd.ShowToolbar "Custom Print Preview", acToolbarYes

End Sub
```

This code is found in the Activate event of the EmployeeSales report, which is part of the SOLUTIONS.MDB database that ships with Access. It hides the Print Preview toolbar and shows the custom toolbar called Custom Print Preview. As you will see, this event works with the Deactivate event to show and hide the custom report toolbars when the report becomes the active window and the user moves the focus to another window.

The Deactivate Event

The Deactivate event occurs when you move to another Access window or close the report, *not* when focus is moved to another application. Here's an example of how the Deactivate event is used:

```
Private Sub Report_Deactivate()

    '  Used by Solutions to hide toolbar that includes Show Me button.

    '  Hide Custom Print Preview toolbar.
    '  Show built-in Print Preview toolbar.
    DoCmd.ShowToolbar "Custom Print Preview", acToolbarNo
    DoCmd.ShowToolbar "Print Preview", acToolbarWhereApprop

End Sub
```

This routine hides the custom toolbar displayed during the Activate event and indicates that the Print Preview toolbar should once again display where appropriate. You don't want to show the Print Preview toolbar here; instead, you just "reset" it to display whenever Access's default behavior would tell it to display.

> **NOTE**
>
> The sample code used in the sections on the Activate and Deactivate events illustrates one way to hide and show custom toolbars. The Toolbar property of a report can be used to perform the same task. However, when you need to display more than one toolbar while the report is active, you must place the code to hide and show the toolbars in the Activate and Deactivate events.

The NoData Event

If no records meet the criteria of the recordset underlying a report's RecordSource, the report prints without any data and displays #Error in the report's Detail section. To eliminate this problem, you can code the NoData event of the report, as shown here:

```
Private Sub Report_NoData(Cancel As Integer)
    MsgBox "There is no data for this report. Canceling report..."
    Cancel = True
End Sub
```

This code is found in the NoData event of rptProjectBillingsByWorkCode in CHAP14.MDB on the sample code CD-ROM. In case no data is returned by the report's underlying recordset, a message is displayed to the user and Cancel is set equal to True. This exits the report without running it.

The Page Event

The Page event gives you the opportunity to do something immediately before the formatted page is sent to the printer, such as placing a border around a page. Here's an example:

```
Private Sub Report_Page()

    'Draw a page border around this report.
    Me.Line (0, 0)-(Me.LogicalPageWidth, Me.LogicalPageHeight), , B
End Sub
```

This code is found in the SalesLetter report, part of the SOLUTIONS.MDB database that comes with Access. It draws a line on the report, starting in the upper-left corner and going to the lower-right corner. It uses the LogicalPageWidth and LogicalPageHeight properties to determine where the lower-right corner of the report's printable area is.

The Error Event

If a Jet Engine error occurs when the report is formatting or printing, the Error event is triggered. This error usually occurs if there's no RecordSource for the report or if someone else has exclusive use of the report's RecordSource. Here's an example:

```
Private Sub Report_Error(DataErr As Integer, Response As Integer)
    If DataErr = 2580 Then
        MsgBox "Record Source Not Available for This Report"
        Response = acDataErrContinue
    End If
End Sub
```

This code responds to a DataErr of 2580, which means that the report's RecordSource isn't available. A custom message is displayed to the user, and the Access error is suppressed.

Order of Events for Reports

It's important to understand the order of events for reports. When the user opens a report, previews it, and then closes it, the following sequence of events occurs:

```
Open∏Activate∏Close∏Deactivate
```

When the user switches to another report *or* to a form, the following sequence occurs:

```
Deactivate(Current Report)∏Activate(Form or Report)
```

> **NOTE**
>
> The Deactivate event doesn't occur when the user switches to a dialog box, to a form whose PopUp property is set to Yes, or to a window of another application.

Events Available for Report Sections and When to Use Them

Just as the report itself has events, so does each section of the report. The three section events are the Format event, Print event, and Retreat event, covered in the following sections.

The Format Event

The Format event happens after Access has selected the data to be included in a report section, but before it formats or prints the data. With the Format event, you can affect the layout of the section or calculate the results of data in the section, before the section actually prints. Here's an example:

Listing 14.1. An example of using the Format event to affect the report layout.

```
Private Sub Detail2_Format(Cancel As Integer, FormatCount As Integer)

    '  Determine whether to print detail record or "Continued."

    '  Show Continued text box if at maximum number of
    '  detail records for page.
    If (Me!Row = Me!OrderPage * (Me!RowsPerPage - 1) + 1) And Me!Row <> _
        Me!RowCount Then
        Me!Continued.Visible = True
    End If

    ' Show page break and hide controls in detail record.
    If Me!Continued.Visible Then
        Me!DetailPageBreak.Visible = True
        Me!ProductID.Visible = False
```

continues

429

Listing 14.1. continued

```
        Me!ProductName.Visible = False
        Me!Quantity.Visible = False
        Me!UnitPrice.Visible = False
        Me!Discount.Visible = False
        Me!ExtendedPrice.Visible = False

        ' Increase value in Order Page.
        Me.NextRecord = False
        Me!OrderPage = Me!OrderPage + 1

    ' Increase row count if detail record is printed.
    Else
        Me!Row = Me!Row + 1
    End If

End Sub
```

> **NOTE**
>
> You might notice that not all the code in this chapter adheres to the naming standards I've proposed. This is because many of the examples are pulled from the Northwind and Solutions databases that are included with Access.

This code is found in the Invoice report included in the SOLUTIONS.MDB database that comes with Access. The report has controls that track how many rows of detail records should be printed on each page. If the maximum number of rows has been reached, a control with the text Continued on Next Page... is visible. If the control is visible, the page break control is also made visible, and all the controls that display the detail for the report are hidden. The report is kept from advancing to the next record.

Another example of the Format event is found in the Page Header of the EmployeeSales report, part of Access's SOLUTIONS.MDB database. Because the report is an unbound report whose controls are populated by using VBA code at runtime, the report needs to determine what's placed in the report header. This varies depending on the result of the Crosstab query on which the report is based. The code looks like this:

```
Private Sub PageHeader0_Format(Cancel As Integer, FormatCount As Integer)

    Dim intX As Integer

    ' Put column headings into text boxes in page header.
    For intX = 1 To intColumnCount
        Me("Head" + Format$(intX)) = rstReport(intX - 1).Name
    Next intX

    ' Make next available text box Totals heading.
    Me("Head" + Format$(intColumnCount + 1)) = "Totals"
```

```
  '  Hide unused text boxes in page header.
    For intX = (intColumnCount + 2) To conTotalColumns
        Me("Head" + Format$(intX)).Visible = False
    Next intX
End Sub
```

The code loops through each column of the recordset that results from executing the Crosstab query. The controls in the report's Page Header are populated with the name of each column in the query result. The final column header is set equal to `Totals`. Finally, any remaining (extra) text boxes are hidden. More examples of using the `Format` event are covered throughout this chapter.

TIP

By placing logic in the `Format` event of a report's Detail section, you can control what happens as each line of the Detail section is printed.

The `Print` Event

The code in the `Print` event is executed when the data has been formatted to print in the section, but before it's actually printed. The `Print` event occurs at the following times for different sections of the report:

Detail Section: Just before the data is printed.

Group Headers: Just before the Group Header is printed; the Group Header's `Print` event has access to both the Group Header and the first row of data in the group.

Group Footers: Just before the Group Footer is printed; the `Print` event of the Group Footer has access to both the Group Footer and the last row of data in the group.

The following code is found in the `Print` event of the EmployeeSales report's Detail section; this report is included in Access's SOLUTIONS.MDB database:

Listing 14.2. An example of using the `Print` event to calculate column and row totals.

```
Private Sub Detail1_Print(Cancel As Integer, PrintCount As Integer)

    Dim intX As Integer
    Dim lngRowTotal As Long

  '  If PrintCount is 1, initialize rowTotal variable.
  '  Add to column totals.
    If Me.PrintCount = 1 Then
        lngRowTotal = 0

        For intX = 2 To intColumnCount
          '  Starting at column 2 (first text box with crosstab value),
          '  compute total for current row in detail section.
```

continues

Listing 14.2. continued

```
            lngRowTotal = lngRowTotal + Me("Col" + Format$(intX))
            '  Add crosstab value to total for current column.
            lngRgColumnTotal(intX) = lngRgColumnTotal(intX) + Me("Col" + _
            Format$(intX))
        Next intX

        '  Place row total in text box in detail section.
        Me("Col" + Format$(intColumnCount + 1)) = lngRowTotal
        '  Add row total for current row to grand total.
        lngReportTotal = lngReportTotal + lngRowTotal
    End If
End Sub
```

The code begins by evaluating the PrintCount property. If it's equal to one, meaning this is the first time the Print event has occurred for the Detail section, then the row total is set equal to zero. The code then loops through each control in the section, accumulating totals for each column of the report and a total for the row. After the loop has been exited, the routine places the row total in the appropriate control and adds the row total to the report's grand total. The report's Detail section is now ready to be printed.

> **NOTE**
>
> Many people are confused about when to place code in the Format event and when to place code in the Print event. If you're doing something that doesn't affect the page layout, you should use the Print event. However, if you're doing something that affects the report's physical appearance (the layout), use the Format event.

The Retreat Event

Sometimes Access needs to move back to a previous section when printing, such as when a group's Keep Together property is set to With First Detail or Whole in the Sorting and Grouping dialog box. Access needs to format the Group Header and the first detail record or, in the case of Whole, the entire group. It then determines whether it can fit the section on the current page. It retreats from the two sections, then formats and prints them; a Retreat event occurs for each section. Here's an example of the Retreat event for a report's Detail section:

```
Private Sub Detail1_Retreat()

    ' Always back up to previous record when detail section retreats.
    rstReport.MovePrevious

End Sub
```

This code is placed in the `Retreat` event of the EmployeeSales report that's part of the SOLUTIONS.MDB. Because the report is an unbound report, it needs to return to the previous record in the recordset whenever the `Retreat` event occurs.

> **WARNING**
>
> Whenever you're working with an unbound report, you need to be careful that the record pointer remains synchronized with the report. For example, if the record pointer has been advanced and the `Retreat` event occurs, the record pointer must be moved back to the previous record.

Order of Section Events

Just as report events have an order, report sections also have an order of events. All the `Format` and `Print` events for each section happen after the report's `Open` and `Activate` events, but before the report's `Close` and `Deactivate` events. The sequence looks like this:

```
Open(Report)∏Activate(Report)∏Format(Report Section)∏Print(Report Section)∏
Close(Report)∏Deactivate(Report)
```

Special Report Properties

Several report properties are available only at runtime. They let you refine your report's processing significantly.

MoveLayout

The MoveLayout property indicates to Access whether it should move to the next printing location on the page. By setting the property to `False`, the printing position is not advanced.

NextRecord

The NextRecord property specifies whether a section should advance to the next record. By setting this property to `False`, you suppress advancing to the next record.

PrintSection

The PrintSection property indicates whether the section is printed. By setting this property to `False`, you can suppress printing the section.

Interaction of MoveLayout, NextRecord, and PrintSection

By using the MoveLayout, NextRecord, and PrintSection properties in combination, you can determine exactly where, how, and whether data is printed. Table 14.1 illustrates this point.

Table 14.1. Interaction of MoveLayout, NextRecord, and PrintSection.

MoveLayout	NextRecord	PrintSection	Effect
True	True	True	Move to the next position, get the next record, and print the data.
True	False	True	Move to the next position, remain on the same record, and print the data.
True	True	False	Move to the next position, get the next record, and don't print the data. This has the effect of skipping a record and leaving a blank space.
True	False	False	Move to the next position, remain on the same record, and don't print. This causes a blank space to appear without moving to the next record.
False	True	True	Remain in the same position, get the next record, and print the data. This has the effect of overlaying one record on another.
False	False	True	Not allowed.
False	True	False	Remain in the same position, get the next record, and refrain from printing. This has the effect of skipping a record without leaving a blank space.
False	False	False	Not allowed.

FormatCount

The FormatCount property evaluates the number of times the Format event has occurred for the report's current section. The Format event happens more than once whenever the Retreat event occurs. By checking the FormatCount property, you can make sure that complex code placed in the Format event is executed only once.

PrintCount

The PrintCount property identifies the number of times the Print event has occurred for the report's current section. The Print event happens more than once whenever the Retreat event occurs. By checking the value of the PrintCount property, you can make sure that logic in the Print event is executed only once.

HasContinued

The HasContinued property determines whether part of the current section is printed on a previous page. You can use this property to hide or show certain report controls (for example, Continued From...), depending on whether the section is continued.

WillContinue

The WillContinue property determines whether the current section continues on another page. You can use this property as you do the HasContinued property to hide or display certain controls when a section continues on another page.

Practical Applications of Report Events and Properties

When developing reports, you should make sure the report can be used in as many situations as possible—that you build as much flexibility into the report as you can. Using the events and properties covered in this chapter will help you do just that. This might involve changing the report's RecordSource at runtime; using the same report to print summary data, detail data, or both; changing the print position; or even running a report based on a Crosstab query with unbound controls. All these aspects of report design are covered in the following sections.

Changing a Report's RecordSource

There are many times when you might want to change a report's RecordSource at runtime. By doing this, you can allow your users to alter the conditions for your report and transparently modify the query on which the report is based. The rptClientListing report in CHAP14.MDB has the following code in its Open event:

```
Private Sub Report_Open(Cancel As Integer)
   DoCmd.OpenForm "frmClientListingCriteria", WindowMode:=acDialog
   If Not IsLoaded("frmClientListingCriteria") Then
      Cancel = True
   Else
      Select Case Forms!frmClientListingCriteria!optCriteria.Value
         Case 1
            Me.RecordSource = "qryClientListingCity"
```

```
        Case 2
            Me.RecordSource = "qryClientListingStateProv"
        Case 3
            Me.RecordSource = "qryClientListing"
      End Select
   End If
End Sub
```

This code begins by opening the frmClientListingCriteria form, if it isn't already loaded. It loads the form modally and waits for the user to select the report criteria. (See Figure 14.1.) After the user clicks to preview the report, the form sets its own Visible property to False. This causes execution to continue in the report, but leaves the form in memory so that its controls can be accessed with VBA code. The value of the form's optCriteria option button is evaluated. Depending on which option button is selected, the report's RecordSource property is set to the appropriate query. The following code is placed in the Close event of the report:

```
Private Sub Report_Close()
   DoCmd.Close acForm, "frmClientListingCriteria"
End Sub
```

Figure 14.1.

The criteria selection used to determine the RecordSource.

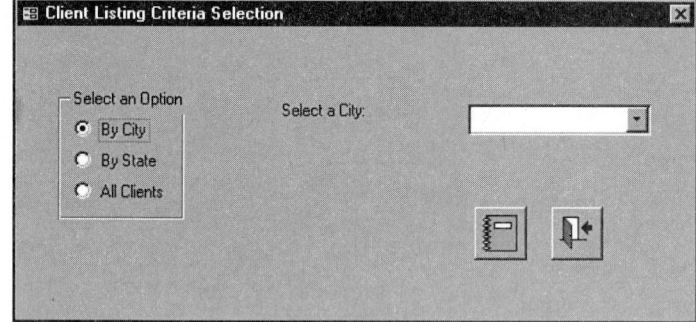

This code closes the criteria form as the report is closing. The frmClientListingCriteria form has some code that's important to the processing of the report. It's found in the After Update event of the optCriteria option group:

```
Private Sub optCriteria_AfterUpdate()
   Select Case optCriteria.Value
      Case 1
         Me!cboCity.Visible = True
         Me!cboStateProv.Visible = False
      Case 2
         Me!cboStateProv.Visible = True
         Me!cboCity.Visible = False
      Case 3
         Me!cboCity.Visible = False
         Me!cboStateProv.Visible = False
   End Select
End Sub
```

This code evaluates the value of the option group. It hides and shows the visibility of the cboCity and cboState combo boxes, depending on which option button is selected. The cboCity and cboState combo boxes are then used as appropriate criteria for the queries that underlie the rptClientListing report.

Using the Same Report to Display Summary, Detail, or Both

Many programmers create three reports for their users: one that displays summary only, one that displays detail only, and another that displays both. This is totally unnecessary. Because report sections can be optionally hidden or displayed at runtime, you can create *one* report that meets all three needs. The rptClientBillingsByProject report included in the CHAP14.MDB database illustrates this point. Place the following code in the report's Open event:

```
Private Sub Report_Open(Cancel As Integer)
    DoCmd.OpenForm "frmReportDateRange", WindowMode:=acDialog, OpenArgs:= _
    "rptClientBillingsbyProject"
    If Not IsLoaded("frmReportDateRange") Then
        Cancel = True
    Else
        Select Case Forms!frmReportDateRange!optDetailLevel.Value
            Case 1
                Me.Caption = Me.Caption & " - Summary Only"
                Me!lblTitle.Caption = Me.lblTitle.Caption & " - Summary Only"
                Me.Detail.Visible = False
            Case 2
                Me.Caption = Me.Caption & " - Detail Only"
                Me!lblTitle.Caption = Me.lblTitle.Caption & " - Detail Only"
                Me.GroupHeader0.Visible = False
                Me.GroupFooter1.Visible = False
                Me!CompanyNameDet.Visible = True
            Case 3
                Me.Caption = Me.Caption & " - Summary and Detail"
                Me!lblTitle.Caption = Me.lblTitle.Caption & " - Summary and _
                Detail"
                Me!CompanyNameDet.Visible = False
        End Select
    End If
End Sub
```

The code begins by opening frmReportDateRange included in CHAP14.MDB. (See Figure 14.2.). The form has an option group asking users whether they want a Summary report, Detail report, or report that contains both Summary and Detail. If Summary is selected, the caption of the Report window and the lblTitle label are modified, and the Visible property of the Detail section is set to False. If the user selects Detail, the captions of the Report window and the lblTitle label are modified, and the Visible property of the Group Header and Footer sections is set to False. A control in the Detail section containing the company name is made visible. The CompanyName control is visible in the Detail section when the Detail Only report is printed, but it's invisible when the Summary and Detail report is printed. When Both is selected as the level of detail, no sections are hidden. The captions of the Report window and the lblTitle label are modified, and the CompanyName control is hidden.

Figure 14.2.

The criteria selection used to
determine detail level.

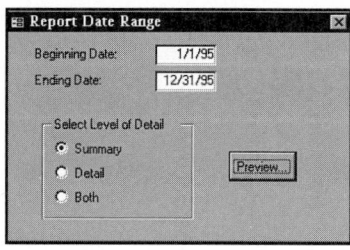

The code behind the form's Preview button looks like this:

```
Private Sub cmdPreview_Click()
    If IsNull([txtBeginDate]) Or IsNull([txtEndDate]) Then
        MsgBox "You must enter both beginning and ending dates."
        DoCmd.GoToControl "txtBeginDate"
    Else
        If [txtBeginDate] > [txtEndDate] Then
            MsgBox "Ending date must be greater than Beginning date."
            DoCmd.GoToControl "txtBeginDate"
        Else
            Me.Visible = False
        End If
    End If
End Sub
```

This code makes sure that both the beginning date and the ending date are filled in, and that the beginning date comes before the ending date. If both of these rules are fulfilled, the Visible property of the form is set to False. Otherwise, an appropriate error message is displayed.

Printing Multiple Labels

Many times, users want to print multiple copies of the same label. This can be done by using the report's MoveLayout, NextRecord, PrintSection, and PrintCount properties. The form shown in Figure 14.3 is called frmClientLabelCriteria and is found in CHAP14.MDB. It asks that the users select a company and the number of labels they want to print for that company. The code for the Print Labels command button looks like this:

```
Sub cmdPrintLabels_Click()
On Error GoTo Err_cmdPrintLabels_Click

    Dim strDocName As String

    strDocName = "lblClientMailingLabels"
    DoCmd.OpenReport strDocName, acPreview, , "CompanyName = '" _
            & Me!cboCompanyName.Value & "'"

Exit_cmdPrintLabels_Click:
    Exit Sub

Err_cmdPrintLabels_Click:
    MsgBox Err.Description
    Resume Exit_cmdPrintLabels_Click

End Sub
```

Figure 14.3.

The criteria selection used to specify company name and number of labels to print.

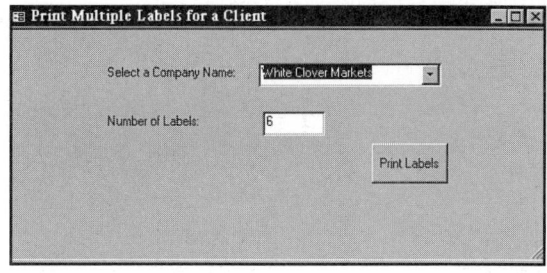

Notice that the routine uses the company name selected from the combo box as criteria to run the lblClientMailingLabels report. The Open event of lblClientMailingLabels looks like this:

```
Private Sub Report_Open(Cancel As Integer)
   If Not IsLoaded("frmClientLabelCriteria") Then
      MsgBox "You Must Run This Report From Label Criteria Form"
      Cancel = True
   End If
End Sub
```

This code tests to make sure the frmClientLabelCriteria form is open. If it's not, a message is displayed and the report is canceled. The key to the whole process is found in the Detail section's Print event:

```
Private Sub Detail_Print(Cancel As Integer, PrintCount As Integer)
   If PrintCount < Forms!frmClientLabelCriteria!txtNumberOfLabels Then
      Me.NextRecord = False
   End If
End Sub
```

This code compares the PrintCount property to the number of labels the user wants to print. As long as the PrintCount is less than the number of labels requested, the record pointer is not advanced. This causes multiple labels to be printed for the *same* record.

Determining Where a Label Prints

Users often want to print several copies of the same label, but they might also want to print mailing labels in a specific position on the page. This is done so that they can begin the print process on the first unused label. The frmClientLabelPosition form from CHAP14.MDB lets the user specify the first label location on which to print by designating the number of labels that need to be skipped. (See Figure 14.4) The Open event of the lblClientMailLabelsSkip looks like this:

```
Private Sub Report_Open(Cancel As Integer)
   If Not IsLoaded("frmClientLabelPosition") Then
      MsgBox "You Must Run This Report From Label Criteria Form"
      Cancel = True
   Else
      mfFirstLabel = True
   End If
End Sub
```

439

Figure 14.4.

The criteria selection used to indicate the number of labels to skip.

The code tests to make sure that the frmClientLabelPosition form is loaded. It also sets a private variable, mfFirstLabel, equal to True. The Detail section's Print event looks like this:

```
Private Sub Detail_Print(Cancel As Integer, PrintCount As Integer)
    If PrintCount <= Forms!frmClientLabelPosition!txtLabelsToSkip _
              And mfFirstLabel = True Then
        Me.NextRecord = False
        Me.PrintSection = False
    Else
        mfFirstLabel = False
    End If
End Sub
```

This routine checks to see whether the PrintCount property of the report is less than or equal to the number of the labels to skip. It also checks to make sure that the mfFirstLabel variable is equal to True. If both conditions are true, the report doesn't move to the next record and doesn't print anything. The print position *is* advanced. When the PrintCount becomes greater than the number of labels to skip, the mfFirstLabel variable is set to False and printing proceeds as usual. If mfFirstLabel is *not* set to False, the designated number of labels is skipped between each record. One additional event makes all this work—the Print event of the Report Header:

```
Private Sub ReportHeader_Format(Cancel As Integer, FormatCount As Integer)
    mfFirstLabel = True
End Sub
```

The ReportHeader Format event sets mfFirstLabel back to True. You must include this step in case the user previews and then prints the labels. If the mfFirstLabel variable is *not* reset to True, the selected number of labels isn't skipped on the printout because the condition that skips the labels is never met.

Building a Report from a Crosstab Query

It's difficult to base a report on the results of a Crosstab query, because its number of columns usually varies. Take a look at the example shown in Figure 14.5. Notice that the employee names appear across the top of the report as column headings, and the products are listed down the side of the report. This report is based on the crosstab query called EmployeeSales, part of the SOLUTIONS.MDB database that ships with Access. (See Figure 14.6.) The problem is that the number of employees—and, therefore, column headings—can vary. This report is coded to handle such an eventuality.

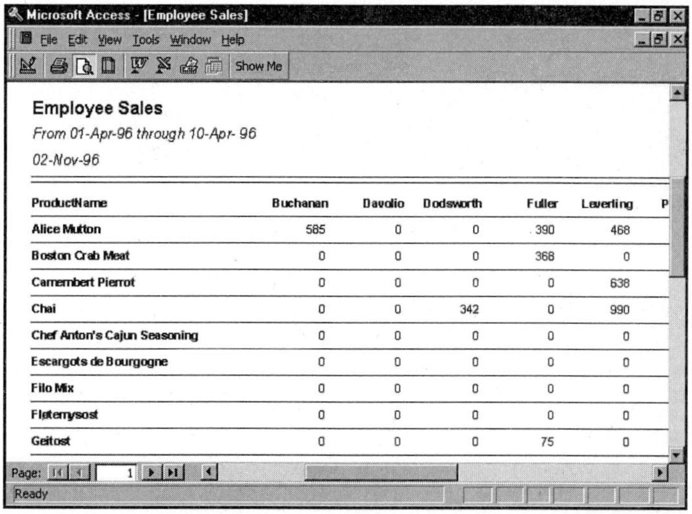

Figure 14.5.

A report based on a Crosstab query.

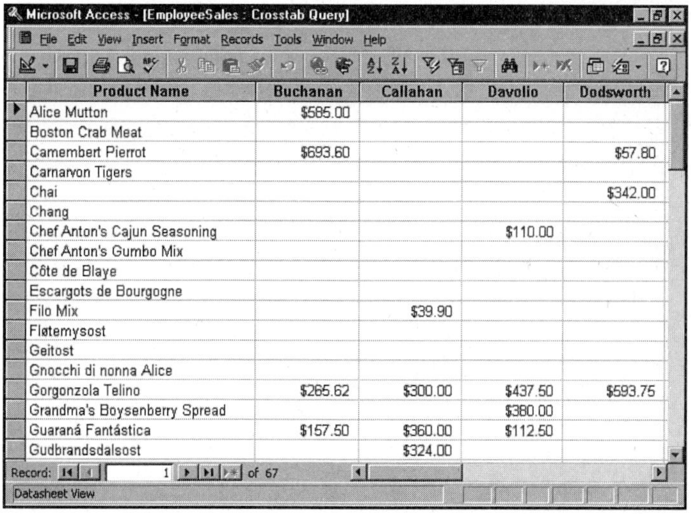

Figure 14.6.

A Crosstab query underlying a report.

When the report runs, its Open event is executed:

```
Private Sub Report_Open(Cancel As Integer)
    ' Create underlying recordset for report using criteria entered in
    ' EmployeeSalesDialogBox form.

    Dim intX As Integer
    Dim qdf As QueryDef

    ' Don't open report if EmployeeSalesDialogBox form isn't loaded.
    If Not (IsLoaded("EmployeeSalesDialogBox")) Then
        Cancel = True
        MsgBox "To preview or print this report, you must open the Employee _
```

441

```
      Sales Dialog Box in Form view.", 48, "Must Open Dialog Box"
      Exit Sub
   End If

   ' Set database variable to current database.
   Set dbsReport = CurrentDb()

   ' Open QueryDef.
   Set qdf = dbsReport.QueryDefs("EmployeeSales")
   ' Set parameters for query based on values entered in _
      EmployeeSalesDialogBox form.
   qdf.Parameters("Forms!EmployeeSalesDialogBox!BeginningDate") = _
   Forms!EmployeeSalesDialogBox!BeginningDate
   qdf.Parameters("Forms!EmployeeSalesDialogBox!EndingDate") = _
   Forms!EmployeeSalesDialogBox!EndingDate

   ' Open Recordset.
   Set rstReport = qdf.OpenRecordset()

   ' Set a variable to hold number of columns in crosstab query.
   intColumnCount = rstReport.Fields.Count


End Sub
```

The code first checks to make sure the criteria form, EmployeeSalesDialogBox, is open. This form supplies the criteria for the EmployeeSales query that underlies the report. The Open event then sets a database object variable to the current database. It opens the EmployeeSales query definition and passes it the parameters from the EmployeeSalesDialogBox criteria form. Next, it opens a recordset based on the query definition, using the criteria found on the EmployeeSalesDialogBox form. The number of columns returned from the Crosstab query is very important; this number is stored in a Private variable called intColumnCount and is used throughout the remaining functions to determine how many columns to fill with data.

After the Open event happens, the Activate event displays the Custom Print Preview toolbar that appears whenever the report is the active object:

```
Private Sub Report_Activate()

   ' Used by Solutions to show toolbar that includes Show Me button.

   ' Hide built-in Print Preview toolbar.
   ' Show Custom Print Preview toolbar.
   DoCmd.ShowToolbar "Print Preview", acToolbarNo
   DoCmd.ShowToolbar "Custom Print Preview", acToolbarYes

End Sub
```

Next, the Report Header Format event occurs. It moves to the first record in the recordset created during the Open event. It also calls an InitVars routine:

```
Private Sub ReportHeader3_Format(Cancel As Integer, FormatCount As Integer)

   ' Move to first record in recordset at beginning of report
   ' or when report is restarted. (A report is restarted when
   ' you print a report from Print Preview window, or when you return
```

```
'   to a previous page while previewing.)
rstReport.MoveFirst

'Initialize variables.
InitVars

End Sub
```

The `InitVars` routine initializes some variables used in the report:

```
Private Sub InitVars()

    Dim intX As Integer

    ' Initialize lngReportTotal variable.
    lngReportTotal = 0

    ' Initialize array that stores column totals.
    For intX = 1 To conTotalColumns
        lngRgColumnTotal(intX) = 0
    Next intX

End Sub
```

The `lngReportTotal` variable is used for the report grand total (all products, all salespeople), and the `lngRgColumnTotal` array contains the total for each salesperson. After the `Report Header Format` event occurs, the `Page Header Format` event takes place:

```
Private Sub PageHeader0_Format(Cancel As Integer, FormatCount As Integer)

    Dim intX As Integer

    '   Put column headings into text boxes in page header.
    For intX = 1 To intColumnCount
        Me("Head" + Format$(intX)) = rstReport(intX - 1).Name
    Next intX

    '   Make next available text box Totals heading.
    Me("Head" + Format$(intColumnCount + 1)) = "Totals"

    '   Hide unused text boxes in page header.
    For intX = (intColumnCount + 2) To conTotalColumns
        Me("Head" + Format$(intX)).Visible = False
    Next intX
End Sub
```

The `PageHeader Format` event uses the names of the fields in the query results as column headings for the report. This essential routine is "smart" because, after it fills in all the column headings, it hides all the extra controls on the report.

Next, the `Detail Section Format` event occurs:

```
Private Sub Detail1_Format(Cancel As Integer, FormatCount As Integer)
'   Place values in text boxes and hide unused text boxes.

    Dim intX As Integer
    '   Verify that you are not at end of recordset.
If Not rstReport.EOF Then
```

```
     ' If FormatCount is 1, place values from recordset into text boxes
     ' in Detail section.
     If Me.FormatCount = 1 Then
         For intX = 1 To intColumnCount
             ' Convert null values to 0.
             Me("Col" + Format$(intX)) = xtabCnulls(rstReport(intX - 1))
         Next intX

         ' Hide unused text boxes in Detail section.
         For intX = intColumnCount + 2 To conTotalColumns
             Me("Col" + Format$(intX)).Visible = False
         Next intX

         ' Move to next record in recordset.
         rstReport.MoveNext
     End If
  End If


End Sub
```

The `Detail Section Format` event checks the recordset's EOF property to determine whether the last record in the query has already been read. If not, the section's FormatCount property is tested to see whether it's equal to 1. If so, each column in the current record of the recordset is read. Each control in the Detail section is filled with data from a column in the recordset, and any unused text boxes in the report's Detail section are hidden. Finally, the code moves to the next record in the recordset, readying the report to print the next line of detail. The `xtabCnulls` function, which converts `Null` values into zeros, is called each time the recordset underlying the report is read:

```
Private Function xtabCnulls(varX As Variant)

    ' Test if a value is null.
    If IsNull(varX) Then
        ' If varX is null, set varX to 0.
        xtabCnulls = 0
    Else
        ' Otherwise, return varX.
        xtabCnulls = varX
    End If

End Function
```

The `xtabCnulls` function evaluates each value sent to it to check whether the value is `Null`. If so, a zero is returned from the function; otherwise, the value that was passed to the function is returned.

After the `Detail Section Format` event is executed, the `Detail Section Print` event occurs:

```
Private Sub Detail1_Print(Cancel As Integer, PrintCount As Integer)

    Dim intX As Integer
    Dim lngRowTotal As Long

    ' If PrintCount is 1, initialize rowTotal variable.
    ' Add to column totals.
```

```
     If Me.PrintCount = 1 Then
         lngRowTotal = 0

         For intX = 2 To intColumnCount
              '  Starting at column 2 (first text box with crosstab value),
              '  compute total for current row in Detail section.
              lngRowTotal = lngRowTotal + Me("Col" + Format$(intX))
              '  Add crosstab value to total for current column.
              lngRgColumnTotal(intX) = lngRgColumnTotal(intX) + Me("Col" + _
              Format$(intX))
         Next intX

         '  Place row total in text box in Detail section.
         Me("Col" + Format$(intColumnCount + 1)) = lngRowTotal
         '  Add row total for current row to grand total.
         lngReportTotal = lngReportTotal + lngRowTotal
     End If
End Sub
```

The Detail Print event generates the row total value, placing it in the last column of the report, accumulating column totals, and accumulating the lngReportTotal value, which is the grand total for all columns and rows. It does this by making sure the PrintCount of the section is 1. If so, it resets the lngRowTotal variable to 0. Starting at column 2 (column 1 contains the product name), it begins accumulating a row total by looking at each control in the row, adding its value to lngRowTotal. As it traverses each column in the row, it also adds the value in each column to the appropriate element of the lngRgColumnTotal private array, which maintains all the column totals for the report. It prints the row total and adds the row total to the report's grand total.

When the Retreat event occurs, the following code executes:

```
Private Sub Detail1_Retreat()

     ' Always back up to previous record when Detail section retreats.
     rstReport.MovePrevious

End Sub
```

This code forces the record pointer to be moved back to the previous record in the recordset. Finally, the report footer prints, which causes the Report Footer Format event to execute:

```
Private Sub ReportFooter4_Print(Cancel As Integer, PrintCount As Integer)

     Dim intX As Integer

     '  Place column totals in text boxes in report footer.
     '  Start at Column 2 (first text box with crosstab value).
     For intX = 2 To intColumnCount
         Me("Tot" + Format$(intX)) = lngRgColumnTotal(intX)
     Next intX

     '  Place grand total in text box in report footer.
     Me("Tot" + Format$(intColumnCount + 1)) = lngReportTotal

     '  Hide unused text boxes in report footer.
     For intX = intColumnCount + 2 To conTotalColumns
```

```
        Me("Tot" + Format$(intX)).Visible = False
    Next intX
End Sub
```

The `Report Footer Format` event loops through each control in the footer, populating each control with the appropriate element of the `lngRgColumnTotal` array. This gives you the column totals for the report. Finally, the grand total is printed in the next available column. Any extra text boxes are hidden from display.

Printing the First and Last Page Entries in the Page Header

Another useful technique is printing the first *and* last entries from a page in the report's header. This is illustrated in the CustomerPhoneList report, part of the SOLUTIONS.MDB database that ships with Access. (See Figure 14.7.) The code for this report relies on Access making two passes through the report. During the first pass, a variable called `gLastPage` is equal to `False`. The `gLastPage` variable becomes `True` only when the Report Footer's `Format` event is executed at the end of the first pass through the report. Keep this in mind as you review the code behind the report.

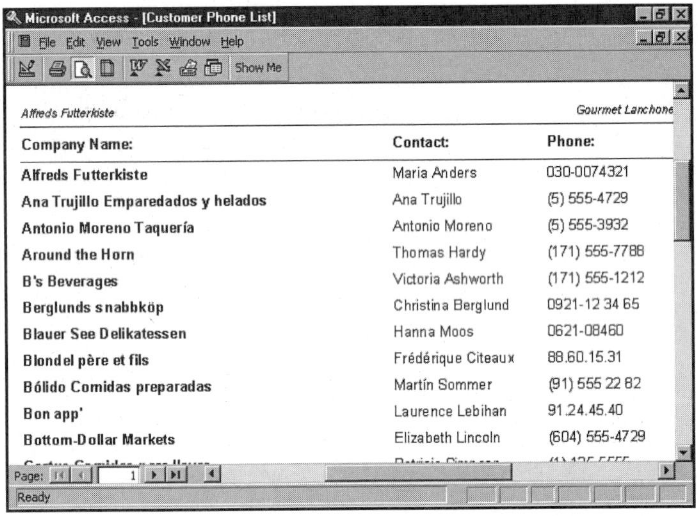

Figure 14.7.

The first and last entry printed in the report header.

The first routine that affects the report processing is the `Report Header Format` event routine:

```
Private Sub PageHeader0_Format(Cancel As Integer, FormatCount As Integer)

    ' During second pass, fill in FirstEntry and LastEntry text boxes.
    If gLastPage = True Then
        Reports!CustomerPhoneList!FirstEntry = _
                    Reports!CustomerPhoneList!CompanyName
        Reports!CustomerPhoneList!LastEntry = _
                    gLast(Reports!CustomerPhoneList.Page)
    End If

End Sub
```

The Page Header Format routine tests to see whether the gLastPage variable is equal to True. During the first pass through the report, the gLastPage variable is equal to False. During the second pass, the FirstEntry and LastEntry text boxes (both of which appear in the report's header) are populated with data. The FirstEntry text box is filled with the value in the CompanyName control of the current record (the first record on the page), and the LastEntry text box is populated with the appropriate element number from the CustomerPhoneList array. Each element of the CustomerPhoneList array is populated by the Format event of the Page Footer for that page during the first pass through the report.

Next, the Page Footer Format event is executed:

```
Private Sub PageFooter2_Format(Cancel As Integer, FormatCount As Integer)

    ' During first pass, increase size of array and enter last record on _
    page into array.
    If Not gLastPage Then
        ReDim Preserve gLast(Reports!CustomerPhoneList.Page + 1)
        gLast$(Reports!CustomerPhoneList.Page) = _
        Reports!CustomerPhoneList!CompanyName
    End If

End Sub
```

The Page Footer Format event determines whether the gLastPage variable is equal to False. If so (which it is during the first pass through the report) the gLast array is redimensioned to add an element. The value from the CompanyName control of the last record on the page is stored in the new element of the gLast array. This value eventually appears in the Page Header of that page as the last company name that appears on the page. Finally, the Report Footer Format event executes:

```
Private Sub ReportFooter4_Format(Cancel As Integer, FormatCount As Integer)

    Dim dbs As Database
    Dim rst As Recordset

    ' Set flag after first pass has been completed.
    gLastPage = True

    ' Open recordset for report.
    Set dbs = CurrentDb()
    Set rst = dbs.OpenRecordset("Customers")
    ' Move to last record in recordset.
    rst.MoveLast
    ' Enter last record into array.
    ReDim Preserve gLast(Reports!CustomerPhoneList.Page + 1)
    gLast(Reports!CustomerPhoneList.Page) = rst!CompanyName

End Sub
```

The Report Footer routine sets the gLastPage variable equal to True and opens a recordset based on the Customers table. This is the recordset on which the report is based. It moves to the last record in the recordset and adds the CompanyName value from the recordset's last record in an additional element of the array.

Now the first pass of the report has finished. As the user moves to each page of the report during a print preview, or as each page is printed to the printer, the Format event executes for the Page Header. The company name from the first record on the page is placed in the FirstEntry control, and the appropriate element from the gLast array is placed in the LastEntry control.

Creating a Multifact Crosstab Report

By nature, Crosstab queries are limited because they don't allow you to place multiple rows of data in the result. For example, you can't display months as column headings and then show the minimum, average, and maximum sales for each employee as row headings. The report shown in Figure 14.8 solves this problem.

Figure 14.8.

An example of a multifact crosstab report.

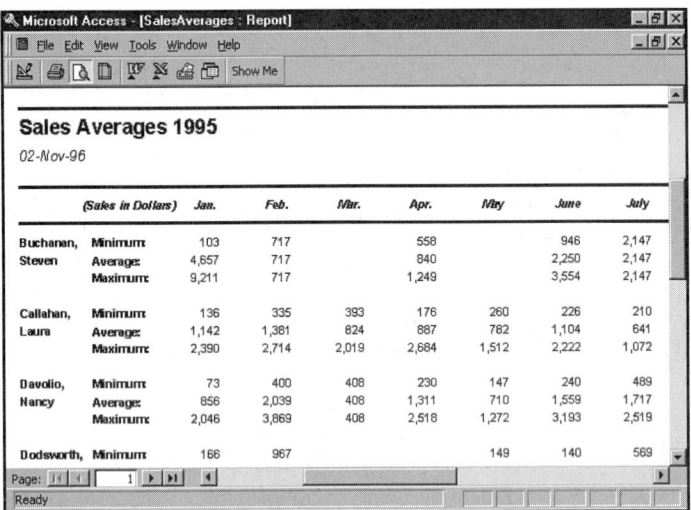

Each time the Format event of the Page Header executes, the value of a control on the report, called PrintWhat, is reset to 0:

```
Private Sub PageHeader1_Format(Cancel As Integer, FormatCount As Integer)

    ' Set PrintWhat text box to 0 at top of page.
    Me!PrintWhat = 0

End Sub
```

After the Page Header Format event executes, the Group Header Format event launches:

```
Private Sub GroupHeader2_Format(Cancel As Integer, FormatCount As Integer)
    ' Print information in row headings in correct order.

    ' Print SalespersonLastName and FirstName text boxes,
    ' hide Minimum, Average, and Maximum labels,
    ' set PrintWhat text box to -1, and don't advance to next record.
    If Me!PrintWhat = 0 Then
       Me!SalespersonLastName.Visible = True
```

```
        Me!FirstName.Visible = True
        Me!LMinimum.Visible = False
        Me!LAverage.Visible = False
        Me!LMaximum.Visible = False
        Me!PrintWhat = -1
        Me.NextRecord = False

  '  Hide SalespersonLastName and FirstName text boxes,
  '  print Minimum, Average, and Maximum labels,
  '  and set PrintWhat text box to 0.
  Else
        Me!SalespersonLastName.Visible = False
        Me!FirstName.Visible = False
        Me!LMinimum.Visible = True
        Me!LAverage.Visible = True
        Me!LMaximum.Visible = True
        Me!PrintWhat = 0
  End If

End Sub
```

The first time the `Format` event for LastName Group Header (GroupHeader2) executes, the value of the `PrintWhat` is equal to `0`. The `SalePersonLastName` and the `FirstName` controls are made visible, and the `LMinimum`, `LAverage`, and `LMaximum` controls are hidden. The `PrintWhat` control's value is set to `-1`, and movement to the next record is suppressed by setting the value of the NextRecord property to `0`.

The second time the `Format` event for the LastName Group Header executes, the `SalepersonLastName` and `FirstName` controls are hidden. The `LMinimum`, `LAverage`, and `LMaximum` controls are made visible, and the value of the `PrintWhat` control is reset to `0`.

The only other code for the report is in the `Format` event of the Shipped Date Header (GroupHeader3):

```
Private Sub GroupHeader3_Format(Cancel As Integer, FormatCount As Integer)
    '  Print data in correct column.

    ' Don't advance to next record or print next section.
    If Me.Left < Me!LeftMargin + (Month(Me!ShippedDate) + 1) * _
    Me!ColumnWidth Then
        Me.NextRecord = False
        Me.PrintSection = False
    End If
End Sub
```

This code compares the report's Left property to the result of an expression. The Left property is the amount that the current section is offset from the page's left edge. This number is compared with the value in the `LeftMargin` control added to the current month plus one, and then it's multiplied by the value in the `ColumnWidth` control. If this expression evaluates to `True`, the NextRecord and PrintSection properties of the report are both set to `False`. This causes the printer to move to the next printing position, but to remain on the same record and not print anything, which forces a blank space in the report. You might wonder what the complicated expression is all about. Simply put, it's an algorithm that makes sure printing occurs and that Access moves to the next record only when the data for January is ready to print.

Practical Examples

Almost every report in the Time and Billing application implements at least one of the techniques discussed in this chapter. In fact, the rptClientListing, rptClientBillingsByProject, lblClientMailingLabels, and lblClientMailingLabelsSkip reports discussed in this chapter are an integral part of the Time and Billing application.

One report not covered in the chapter is the rptEmployeeBillingsByProject report. This report has the following code in its NoData event:

```
Private Sub Report_NoData(Cancel As Integer)
    MsgBox "There is no data for this report. Canceling report..."
    Cancel = -1
End Sub
```

If there's no data in the report's RecordSource, a message box is displayed and the report is canceled. The Open event of the report looks like this:

```
Private Sub Report_Open(Cancel As Integer)
    DoCmd.OpenForm "frmReportDateRange", , , , , acDialog, _
    "Employee Billings by Project"
    If Not IsLoaded("frmReportDateRange") Then
        Cancel = True
    End If
End Sub
```

The report's Open event opens a form called frmReportDateRange. (See Figure 14.9.) This form is required because it supplies criteria to the query underlying the report. If the form isn't loaded successfully, the report is canceled.

Figure 14.9.

A criteria selection form.

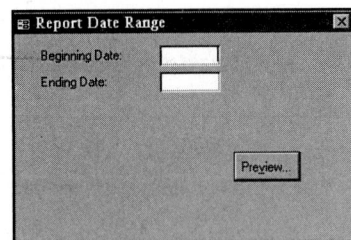

Finally, the report's Close event looks like this:

```
Private Sub Report_Close()
    DoCmd.Close acForm, "frmReportDateRange"
End Sub
```

The report cleans up after itself by closing the criteria form.

Summary

To take full advantage of what the Access report writer has to offer, you must understand—and be able to work with—report and section events. This chapter has gone through the report and section events, giving you detailed examples of when to use each event.

In addition to the report events, several special properties are available to you only at runtime. By manipulating these properties, you can have more control over your reports' behavior. After covering the report and section events, this chapter has covered the properties you can manipulate only at runtime. Examples have been given to highlight the appropriate use of each property.

There are many tips and tricks of the trade that help you do things you might otherwise think are impossible to accomplish. This chapter has given you several practical examples of these tips and tricks, making it easy for you to use them in your own application development.

15

CHAPTER

What Are the Data Access Objects and Why Are They Important?

- Understanding Data Access Objects, 454
- Examining the Data Access Object Model, 454
- Getting to Know DBEngine, 462
- Using CurrentDB(), 463
- Understanding Recordset Types, 463
- Selecting Among the Types of Recordset Objects Available, 465
- Working with Recordset Properties and Methods, 465
- Modifying Table Data Using Code, 477
- Creating and Modifying Database Objects Using Code, 480
- Using the Containers Collection, 483
- Practical Examples: Applying These Techniques to Your Application, 484

Understanding Data Access Objects

Data access objects are used to create, modify, and remove Jet Engine objects via code. They give you the flexibility to move beyond the user interface to manipulate data and Jet Engine objects. You can use data access object to perform these tasks:

- Analyze the structure of an existing database.
- Add or modify tables and queries.
- Create new databases.
- Change the underlying definitions for queries by modifying the SQL on which the query is based.
- Traverse through sets of records.
- Modify table data.

Examining the Data Access Object Model

Figure 15.1 shows an overview of the data access object model for the Jet 3.5 Database Engine. At the top of the hierarchy is the Microsoft Jet Database Engine, referred to as the DBEngine object. The DBEngine object contains all the other objects that are part of the hierarchy. It is the only object that does not have an associated collection.

Each object in the data access object model is important, because you will manipulate the various objects at runtime using code to accomplish the tasks required by your application. The following sections describe each major object and how it affects your programming endeavors.

WHAT ARE THE DATA ACCESS OBJECTS AND WHY ARE THEY IMPORTANT?

15

Figure 15.1.
The data access object model.

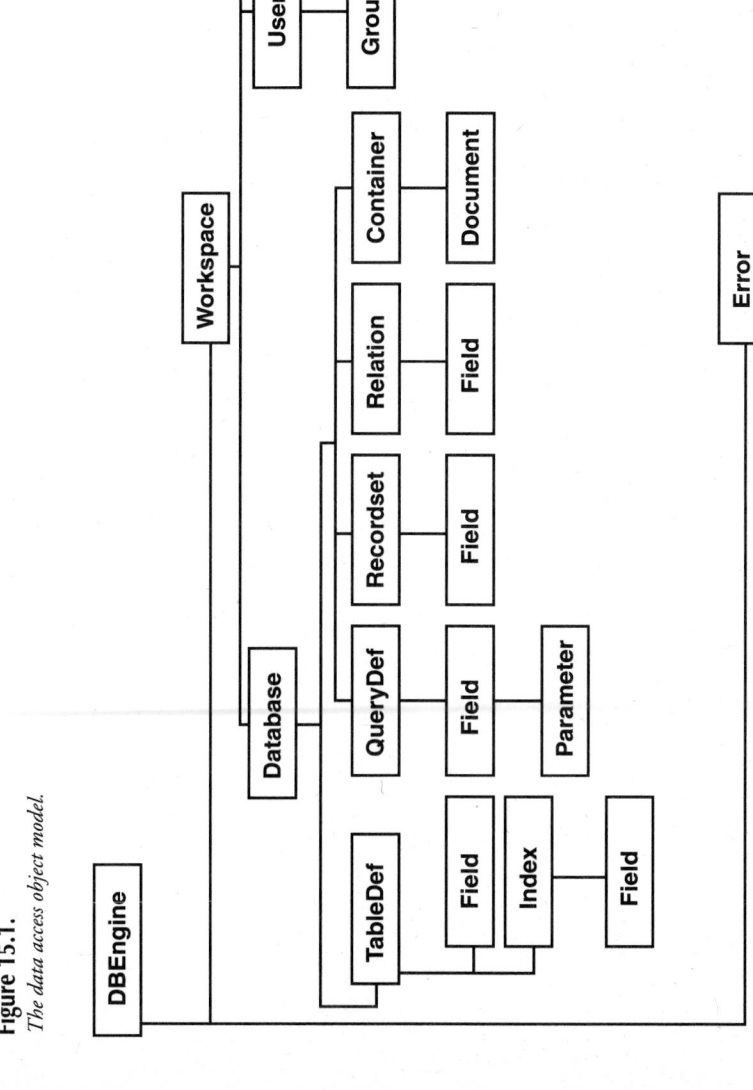

Workspaces

The Workspaces collection contains `Workspace` objects. Each `Workspace` object defines the area in which a particular user operates. All security and transaction processing for a given user takes place in a particular workspace. You can programmatically create multiple workspaces. This is of great value because, by using this technique, you can log on as another user behind the scenes and accomplish tasks not allowed by the security level of the current user. You can log on as a member of the Admins group, for example, change the structure of a table that the current user does not have rights to, and log back out without the user of the system ever knowing that anything happened.

Users

The Users collection contains the `User` objects for a particular workspace. Each `User` object is a user account defined by a workgroup database. Because each user is a member of one or more groups, each `User` object contains a Groups collection that consists of each group of which a particular user is a member. `User` objects easily can be added and manipulated at runtime.

Groups

The Groups collection contains all `Group` objects for a particular workspace. Each `Group` object is a group defined by a workgroup database. Because each group contains users, the `Group` object contains a Users collection that consists of each user who is a member of the group. Like `User` objects, `Group` objects can be added and manipulated at runtime.

Databases

The Databases collection contains all the databases that are currently open in a particular workspace. You can open multiple databases at a time. These open databases can be Jet databases or external databases. A `Database` object refers to a particular database in the Databases collection. It is easy to loop through the Databases collection, printing the name of each `Database` object contained in the collection, as shown in Listing 15.1.

Listing 15.1. Printing the name of each database in a workspace.

```
Sub EnumerateDBs()
    Dim ws As Workspace
    Dim db As DATABASE
    Dim db1 As DATABASE
    Dim db2 As DATABASE

    Set ws = DBEngine(0)
    Set db1 = CurrentDb
    Set db2 = ws.OpenDatabase("Chap9.MDB")

    For Each db In ws.Databases
        Debug.Print db.Name
    Next db
End Sub
```

WHAT ARE THE DATA ACCESS OBJECTS AND WHY ARE THEY IMPORTANT?

15

This code loops through each open database in the current workspace and prints the name of each open database. It also is easy to perform all the other tasks required to build, modify, and manipulate `Database` objects at runtime.

> **NOTE**
>
> Listing 15.1 and most of the code in this chapter is located in the CHAP15EX.MDB file included with this book's CD-ROM.

TableDefs

The TableDefs collection contains all the tables contained in a particular database. This includes all tables—whether or not they are open. The TableDefs collection also includes linked tables. It contains detailed information about each table. It is easy to loop through the TableDefs collection, printing various properties (for example, the name) of each `Table` object contained in the collection. Listing 15.2 shows an example of using the TableDefs collection to print the properties of each `Table` object, in addition to printing the properties of each index on the table.

Listing 15.2. Using the TableDefs and Indexes collections.

```
Sub EnumerateTablesAndIndexes()
   Dim db As DATABASE
   Dim tbl As TableDef
   Dim idx as Index
   Dim fld as Field

   Set db = CurrentDb

   For Each tbl In db.TableDefs
      Debug.Print "Table: "; tbl.Name
      For Each idx in tbl.Indexes
         Debug.Print "   Index: "; idx.Name
         Debug.Print "      Primary="; idx.Primary; ", Unique="; idx.Unique
         For Each fld in idx
            Debug.Print "      Field:" ; fld.Name
         Next fld
      Next idx
   Next tbl
End Sub
```

This code loops through each `TableDef` in the current database and prints the name of each table in the database. It then prints the name of every index on the table and every field in the index. It is easy to write code that adds, deletes, modifies, and otherwise manipulates tables and indexes at runtime.

Indexes

Each `TableDef` object contains an Indexes collection, which enumerates all the indexes on the table. Each index contains a Fields collection to describe the fields in the index.

QueryDefs

The QueryDefs collection contains all the queries contained in a particular database. It contains information about each query. It is easy to loop through the QueryDefs collection, printing various pieces of information about each query, as Listing 15.3 shows.

Listing 15.3. Printing information about each query using the QueryDefs collection.

```
Sub EnumerateQueries()
    Dim db As DATABASE
    Dim qry As QueryDef

    Set db = CurrentDb

    For Each qry In db.QueryDefs
        Debug.Print qry.Name
        Debug.Print qry.SQL
    Next qry
End Sub
```

This code loops through each `QueryDef` in the current database and prints the name and SQL statement associated with each `QueryDef`. It is easy to write code that adds, deletes, modifies, and otherwise manipulates queries at runtime.

Fields

Fields collections are contained in the `TableDef`, `QueryDef`, `Index`, `Relation`, and `Recordset` objects. The Fields collection of an object is the collection of `Field` objects in the parent object. A `TableDef` object contains `Field` objects that are contained in the specific table, for example. Using the parent object, you can get information about its Fields collection, as shown in Listing 15.4.

Listing 15.4. Getting information from the Fields collection.

```
Sub EnumerateFields()
    Dim db As DATABASE
    Dim tbl As TableDef
    Dim fld As Field

    Set db = CurrentDb

    For Each tbl In db.TableDefs
        For Each fld In tbl.Fields
```

WHAT ARE THE DATA ACCESS OBJECTS AND WHY ARE THEY IMPORTANT?

15

```
                Debug.Print fld.Name
                Debug.Print fld.Type
        Next fld
    Next tbl
End Sub
```

This code loops through each `TableDef` in the current database. As it loops through each `TableDef`, it prints the name and type of each field contained in the Fields collection of the `TableDef`. Code also can be used to add, delete, or change the attributes of fields at runtime. With a large database, this code is likely to output more information than can be contained in the Debug window buffer. You might want to pause the code at some point to view the contents of the Debug window.

> **NOTE**
>
> Notice that the Type property is an integer value. Each integer returned from this property represents a different field type. You might want to write a case statement that converts the integer value to a more meaningful text string.

Parameters

Access queries can contain parameters. These parameters are created so that users can supply information required by the query at runtime. Each `QueryDef` object has a Parameters collection, which consists of `Parameter` objects. You can write code to manipulate these parameters at runtime, as Listing 15.5 shows.

Listing 15.5. Listing the parameters of every query.

```
Sub EnumerateParameters()
    Dim db As DATABASE
    Dim qry As QueryDef
    Dim prm As Parameter

    Set db = CurrentDb

    For Each qry In db.QueryDefs
        Debug.Print "*****" & qry.Name & "*****"
        For Each prm In qry.PARAMETERS
            Debug.Print prm.Name
        Next prm
    Next qry
End Sub
```

This code loops through each `QueryDef` object in the current database. It prints the name of the `QueryDef` object and then loops through its Parameters collection, printing the name of each parameter. `Parameter` objects can be added, deleted, and manipulated through code at runtime.

459

Recordsets

Recordset objects exist only at runtime. A Recordset object is used to reference a set of records coming from one or more tables. The Recordsets collection contains all the Recordset objects that currently are open in the current Database object. Recordset objects are covered extensively in "Understanding Recordset Types," later in this chapter.

Relations

The Relations collection contains all the Relation objects that describe the relationships established in a Database object. The code in Listing 15.6 loops through the current database, printing the Table and ForeignTable of each Relation object.

Listing 15.6. Using the Relations collection.

```
Sub EnumerateRelations()
    Dim db As DATABASE
    Dim rel As Relation

    Set db = CurrentDb

    For Each rel In db.Relations
        Debug.Print rel.TABLE & " Related To: " & rel.ForeignTable
    Next rel
End Sub
```

Relationships can be created, deleted, and modified at runtime using VBA code.

Containers

The Containers collection contains information about each saved Database object. Using the Containers collection, you can view and modify all the objects contained in the current database, as demonstrated in Listing 15.7.

Listing 15.7. Listing every container in a database.

```
Sub EnumerateContainers()
    Dim db As DATABASE
    Dim cnt As Container

    Set db = CurrentDb

    For Each cnt In db.Containers
        Debug.Print cnt.Name
    Next cnt
End Sub
```

This code loops through the Containers collection, printing the name of each `Container` object. The results are `Database`, `Form`, `Module`, `Relationship`, `Report`, `Script`, `SysRel`, and `Table` objects.

Documents

A `Document` object represents a specific object in the Documents collection. You can loop through the Documents collection of a `Container` object, as shown in Listing 15.8.

Listing 15.8. Printing the names of `Document` objects.

```
Sub EnumerateForms()
    Dim db As DATABASE
    Dim cnt As Container
    Dim doc As Document

    Set db = CurrentDb
    Set cnt = db.Containers!Forms

    For Each doc In cnt.Documents
        Debug.Print doc.Name
    Next doc

End Sub
```

This code points a `Container` object to the forms in the current database. It then loops through each document in the `Container` object, printing the name of each `Document` object (in this case, the name of each form).

> **NOTE**
>
> It is important to understand the difference between the Forms container and the Forms collection. The *Forms container* is part of the Containers collection; it contains all the forms that are part of the database. The *Forms collection* contains all the forms open at runtime. The properties of each form in the Forms container differ from the properties of a form in the Forms collection.

Properties

Each data access object has a Properties collection. The Properties collection of an object is a list of properties associated with that particular object. This gives you a generic way to view and modify the properties of any object, as shown in Listing 15.9.

You can use this collection to create generic routines to handle common tasks. You could write a routine to set the font size of any control to 8 points, for example. Your routine could use the

Properties collection to verify that the control has a Font property before attempting to set the size.

Listing 15.9. Printing every property of Document objects.

```
Sub EnumerateProperties()
    Dim db As DATABASE
    Dim cnt As Container
    Dim doc As Document
    Dim prp As Property

    Set db = CurrentDb
    Set cnt = db.Containers!Forms

    For Each doc In cnt.Documents
        Debug.Print doc.Name
        For Each prp In doc.Properties
            Debug.Print prp.Name & " = " & prp.Value
        Next prp
    Next doc
End Sub
```

This code loops through each form in the current database, printing all the properties of each Form object.

Errors

The Errors collection consists of Error objects. An Error object contains information about the most recent error that occurred. Each time an operation generates an error, the Errors collection is cleared of any previous errors. Sometimes a single operation can cause more than one error, so one or more Error objects might be added to the Errors collection when a single data access error occurs.

Getting to Know DBEngine

As mentioned, the DBEngine object refers to the Jet Database Engine, which is at the top of the data access object hierarchy. The DBEngine object contains only two collections: Workspaces and Errors. When referring to the current database, you can use the CurrentDB() function discussed in the next section. When referring to any database other than the current database, you must refer to the DBEngine object, as shown in Listing 15.10.

Listing 15.10. Accessing the properties of the `DBEngine` object.

```
Sub ReferToCurrentDB()
    Dim ws As Workspace
    Dim db As DATABASE
    Dim err as Error

    Set ws = DBEngine(0)
    Set db = ws.OpenDatabase("Chap11")
    Debug.Print db.Version
End Sub
```

This code creates a `Workspace` object variable that points to the current workspace. The OpenDatabase method of the `Workspace` object then is used to open another database. The version of the database is printed by the routine.

Using `CurrentDB()`

Microsoft offers a shortcut you can use when creating an object variable that points to the current database. Using the `CurrentDB()` function, you do not need to first point to the workspace; nor do you need to issue the OpenDatabase method. Instead, you set the `Database` object variable equal to the result from the `CurrentDB()` function, as shown in Listing 15.11.

Listing 15.11. Listing the errors in the current database.

```
Sub UseCurrentDBFunc()
    Dim db As DATABASE
    Dim erx as Error

    Set db = CurrentDB()
    Debug.Print db.Version
    For Each erx in db.Errors
        Debug.print erx.Number, erx.Description
    Next
End Sub
```

This code sets the `Database` object variable so that it points to the current `Database` object. It then prints the version of the database engine and each of the errors in the Errors collection.

The `CurrentDB()` function cannot be used to refer to objects that are not part of the current database. As with all VBA functions that do not require arguments, the parentheses after `CurrentDB` are optional.

Understanding Recordset Types

A `Recordset` object represents the records in a table or the records returned by a query. A `Recordset` object can be a direct link to the table, a dynamic set of records, or a snapshot of the data at a certain time. `Recordset` objects are used to directly manipulate data in a database. They enable you to add, edit, delete, and move through data as required by your application. Access 97 supports three types of `Recordset` objects: dynasets, snapshots, and tables.

Dynasets

You can use a `Recordset` object of the dynaset type to manipulate local or linked tables or the results of queries. A *dynaset* is actually a set of references to table data. Using a dynaset, you can extract and update data from multiple tables—even tables from other databases. In fact, the tables containing the data included in a dynaset can even come from databases that are not of the same type (for example, Microsoft SQL Server, FoxPro, Paradox, and dBASE).

True to its name, a dynaset is a dynamic set of records. This means that changes made to the dynaset are reflected in the underlying tables, and changes made to the underlying tables by other users of the system are reflected in the dynaset. Although a dynaset is not the fastest type of `Recordset` object, it is definitely the most flexible.

Snapshots

A `Recordset` object of the snapshot type is similar to a dynaset. The major difference is that the data included in the snapshot is fixed at the time it is created. The data in the snapshot, therefore, cannot be modified and is not updated when other users make changes to the underlying tables. This trait can be an advantage or a disadvantage. It is a disadvantage, of course, if it is necessary for the data in the recordset to be updatable. It is an advantage if you are running a report and want to ensure that the data does not change during the time in which the report is being run. You therefore can create a snapshot and build the report from the `Snapshot` object.

> **NOTE**
>
> With small result sets, snapshots are more efficient than dynasets because a `Snapshot` object creates less processing overhead. Regardless of their reduced overhead, snapshots actually are less efficient than dynasets when returning a result set with a large volume of data (generally more than 500 records). This is because, when you create a `Snapshot` object, all fields are returned to the user as each record is accessed. On the other hand, a `Dynaset` object contains a set of primary keys for the records in the result set. The other fields are returned to the user only when they are required for editing or display.

Tables

A `Recordset` object of the table type often is used to manipulate local or linked tables created using Microsoft Access or the Jet Database Engine. When you open a table type of recordset, all operations are performed directly on the table.

Certain operations, such as a Seek, can be performed only on a table type of recordset. You get the best performance for sorting and filtering records when using a table type of recordset.

The downside of a table type of recordset is that it can contain the data from only one table. It cannot be opened using a join or union query. It also cannot be used with tables created by using engines other than Jet (for example, ODBC and other ISAM data sources).

Selecting Among the Types of **Recordset** Objects Available

Deciding which type of recordset to use involves looking at the task to determine which type of recordset is most appropriate. When fast searching is most important and it is not a problem to retrieve all the records, a table is the best choice. If you must retrieve the results of a query and your result set needs to be editable, a dynaset is the best choice. If there is no need for the results to be updated, but they must consist of a relatively small subset of the data, a snapshot is most appropriate.

Working with Recordset Properties and Methods

Like other objects, Recordset objects have properties and methods. The properties are the attributes of the Recordset objects, and the methods are the actions you can take on the Recordset objects. Some properties are read only at runtime; others can be read from and written to at runtime.

Creating a Recordset Variable

When working with a recordset, you first must create a Recordset variable. You use the OpenRecordSet method to create a Recordset object variable. You first must declare a generic Recordset variable and then point a specific recordset at the variable using a Set statement, as shown in the example in Listing 15.12.

Listing 15.12. Opening a recordset.

```
Sub OpenTable()
    Dim dbInfo As DATABASE
    Dim rstClients As Recordset

    Set dbInfo = CurrentDb()
    Set rstClients = dbInfo.OpenRecordset("tblClients")

    Debug.Print rstClients.Updatable
End Sub
```

This code creates a `Database` object variable and a `Recordset` object variable. It then uses the `CurrentDB` function to point the `Database` object variable to the current database. Next, it uses the OpenRecordSet method to assign the recordset based on `tblClients` to the object variable `rstClients`.

The type of recordset that is created is determined by the default type for the object or by a second parameter of the OpenRecordSet method. If the OpenRecordSet method is executed on a table and no second parameter is specified, the recordset is opened as the table type. If the OpenRecordSet method is performed on a query and no second parameter is specified, the recordset is opened as the dynaset type. You can override this default behavior by passing a second parameter to the OpenRecordSet method, as Listing 15.13 shows.

Listing 15.13. Opening a dynaset type of recordset on a table.

```
Sub OpenDynaSet()
    Dim dbInfo As DATABASE
    Dim rstClients As Recordset

    Set dbInfo = CurrentDb()
    Set rstClients = dbInfo.OpenRecordset("tblClients", dbOpenDynaset)

    Debug.Print rstClients.Updatable
End Sub
```

This code opens the recordset as a dynaset. `dbOpenTable`, `dbOpenDynaset`, and `dbOpenSnapshot` are all intrinsic constants that can be used to open a `Recordset` object. A query can be opened only as a dynaset or snapshot `Recordset` object. Listing 15.14 shows the code to open a recordset based on a query.

Listing 15.14. Opening a recordset based on a query.

```
Sub OpenQuery()
    Dim dbInfo As DATABASE
    Dim rstClients As Recordset

    Set dbInfo = CurrentDb()
    Set rstClients = dbInfo.OpenRecordset("qryHoursByProject", dbOpenSnapshot)

    Debug.Print rstClients.Updatable
End Sub
```

> **NOTE**
>
> As was the case with Access 95, the proper method to create a Recordset object in Access 97 differs from that of earlier versions of Access. In earlier versions, it was appropriate to dimension a dynaset, snapshot, or table type of object variable and then use the CreateDynaset, CreateSnapshot, and OpenTable methods of the Database object to create the appropriate type of recordset. This method for creating recordsets is included in Access 97 for backward compatibility only. It should be avoided and replaced with the code included in this section.

Using Arguments to Open a Recordset

Microsoft provides several arguments that control the way in which a recordset is opened. The arguments and their uses follow:

- **dbAppendOnly:** When this option is used, records can be added to the recordset only. Existing data cannot be displayed or modified. This option is useful when you want to ensure that existing data is not affected by the processing. This option applies to dynasets only.

- **dbConsistent:** This argument applies to dynasets. It allows consistent updates only. This means that, in a one-to-many join, you can update only those fields that are not duplicated in other records in the dynaset. This is the default argument for dynasets.

- **dbDenyRead:** This argument prevents other users from even reading the data contained in the recordset as long as the recordset remains open. You can use this option only on table recordsets.

- **dbDenyWrite:** When creating a dynaset or snapshot, this option prevents all other users from modifying the records contained in the recordset until the recordset is closed. Other users still are able to view the data contained in the recordset. When this option is applied to a table type of recordset, other users are prevented from opening the underlying table.

- **dbForwardOnly:** This argument creates a forward-scrolling snapshot. This type of recordset is fast, but limited, because you can use only the Move and MoveNext methods to move directly through the snapshot.

- **dbInconsistent:** This argument allows for inconsistent updates. This means that, in a one-to-many join, you can update all columns in the recordset.

- **dbReadOnly:** This option prevents your recordset from modifying data. If you don't want the data in the recordset to be updatable, but you expect a large number of records to be returned and you want to take advantage of the record paging offered by dynasets, you might want to open the recordset as a dynaset.

- **dbSeeChanges:** This option ensures that a user receives an error if the code issues an Edit method and another user modifies the data before an Update method is used.

This option is useful in a high-traffic environment when it is likely that two users will modify the same record at the same time. This option applies to dynaset and table recordsets only.

- **dbSQLPassThrough:** When the source of the recordset is an SQL statement, this argument passes the SQL statement to an ODBC database for processing. This option does not completely eliminate Jet; it simply prevents Jet from making any changes to the SQL statement before passing it to the ODBC Drive Manager. You can use the dbSQLPassThrough argument only with snapshots and read-only dynasets.

The arguments described here can be used in combination to accomplish the desired objectives. Listing 15.15 shows the use of an OpenRecordSet argument.

Listing 15.15. Using an OpenRecordset argument.

```
Sub OpenRecordsetArgs()
    Dim db As DATABASE
    Dim rst As Recordset

    Set db = CurrentDb
    Set rst = db.OpenRecordset("tblProjects", dbOpenDynaset, dbReadOnly)

    Debug.Print rst.Updatable
End Sub
```

This code opens a recordset as read-only.

Examining Record-Movement Methods

When you have a Recordset object variable set, you probably want to manipulate the data in the recordset. Table 15.1 shows several methods you can use to traverse through the records in a recordset.

Table 15.1. Methods for moving through the records in a recordset.

Method	Moves
MoveFirst	To the first record in a recordset
MoveLast	To the last record in a recordset
MovePrevious	To the preceding record in a recordset
MoveNext	To the next record in a recordset
Move[0]	Forward or backward a specified number of records

Listing 15.16 shows an example of using the record-movement methods on a dynaset.

Listing 15.16. Using the Move methods.

```
Sub RecordsetMovements()
    Dim db As DATABASE
    Dim rst As Recordset

    Set db = CurrentDb
    Set rst = db.OpenRecordset("tblProjects", dbOpenDynaset)

    Debug.Print rst!ProjectID
    rst.MoveNext
    Debug.Print rst!ProjectID
    rst.MoveLast
    Debug.Print rst!ProjectID
    rst.MovePrevious
    Debug.Print rst!ProjectID
    rst.MoveFirst
    Debug.Print rst!ProjectID
    rst.Close
End Sub
```

This code opens a dynaset. The record pointer automatically is placed on the first record of the dynaset when the recordset is opened. The routine prints the contents of the ProjectID field and then moves to the next record, printing its ProjectID. It then moves to the last record of the dynaset, printing its ProjectID; moves to the previous record, printing its ProjectID; and moves to the first record, printing its ProjectID. The Close method is applied to the Recordset object. It is a good idea to always close an open recordset before exiting a routine. After changes are made to the recordset, the Close method closes the recordset, ensuring that all changes are written to disk.

Detecting the Limits of a Recordset

Before you begin to traverse through recordsets, you need to understand two recordset properties: BOF and EOF. The names of these properties are outdated acronyms, which stand for *beginning of file* and *end of file*.

These properties determine whether you have reached the limits of your recordset. The BOF property is True when the record pointer is before the first record, and the EOF property is True when the record pointer is after the last record.

You commonly will use the EOF property when moving forward through your recordset with the MoveNext method. This property becomes True when your most recent MoveNext has moved you beyond the bounds of the recordset. Similarly, BOF is most useful when using the MovePrevious method.

You need to keep in mind some important characteristics of the BOF and EOF properties:

- If a recordset contains no records, both the BOF and EOF properties evaluate to True.

- When you open a recordset containing at least one record, the BOF and EOF properties are set to False.

- If the record pointer is on the first record in the recordset and the MovePrevious method is issued, the BOF property is set to True. If you attempt to use MovePrevious again, a runtime error occurs.

- If the record pointer is on the last record in the recordset and the MoveNext method is issued, the EOF property is set to True. If you attempt to use MoveNext again, a runtime error occurs.

- When the BOF and EOF properties are set to True, they remain True until you move to a valid record.

- When the only record in a recordset is deleted, the BOF and EOF properties remain False until you attempt to move to another record.

Listing 15.17 shows a code sample that uses the EOF property with the MoveNext method.

Listing 15.17. Using the EOF property with MoveNext.

```
Sub DetermineLimits()
    Dim db As DATABASE
    Dim rstClients As Recordset

    Set db = CurrentDb()
    Set rstClients = db.OpenRecordset("tblClients", dbOpenSnapshot)
    Do While Not rstClients.EOF
        Debug.Print rstClients![ClientID]
        rstClients.MoveNext
    Loop
    rstClients.Close
End Sub
```

This code traverses through a snapshot recordset, printing the value of the ClientID field for each record until it reaches the position after the last record in the recordset. It then exits the loop and closes the recordset.

Counting the Number of Records in a Recordset

The RecordCount property of a recordset returns the number of records in a recordset that have been accessed. The problem with this is evident if you open a recordset and view the RecordCount property. You will discover that the count is equal to 0 if no records exist in the recordset or equal to 1 if there are records in the recordset. The record count is accurate only if you visit all the records in the recordset, which you can do by using the MoveLast method, as Listing 15.18 shows.

Listing 15.18. Demonstrating the limitations of RecordCount.

```
Sub CountRecords()
    Dim db As DATABASE
    Dim rstProjects As Recordset

    Set db = CurrentDb()
    Set rstProjects = db.OpenRecordset("tblProjects", dbOpenSnapshot)
    Debug.Print rstProjects.RecordCount   'Prints 0 Or 1
    rstProjects.MoveLast
    Debug.Print rstProjects.RecordCount 'Prints an accurate record Count
    rstProjects.Close
End Sub
```

The MoveLast method has its problems, though. It is slow and inefficient, especially in a client/server environment. Furthermore, in a multiuser environment, the RecordCount property becomes inaccurate as other people add and remove records from the table. This means that if determining the record count is not absolutely necessary, you should avoid it.

The RecordCount property has one good use, though: You can use it to see whether there are any records in a recordset. If you are performing an operation that might return an empty recordset, you easily can use the RecordCount property to determine whether records were returned, as Listing 15.19 shows.

Listing 15.19. Checking for an empty recordset using RecordCount.

```
Sub CheckARecordset()
    Dim db As Database
    Dim rstProjects As Recordset

    Set db = CurrentDb()
    Set rstProjects = db.OpenRecordset("tblEmpty", dbOpenSnapshot)
    If Not AreThereRecords(rstProjects) Then
      MsgBox "Recordset Empty...Unable to Proceed"
    End If
End Sub

Function AreThereRecords(rstAny As Recordset) As Boolean
    AreThereRecords = rstAny.RecordCount
End Function
```

The CheckARecordset procedure opens a recordset based on the tblEmpty table. It then calls the AreThereRecords function to determine whether any records are found in the recordset. If the AreThereRecords function returns False, an error message is displayed to the user.

Sorting, Filtering, and Finding Records

Sometimes you might need to sort or filter an existing recordset. You also might want to locate each record in the recordset that meets some specified criteria. The following techniques enable you to sort, filter, and find records in a Recordset object.

Sorting a Recordset

You can't actually change the sort order of an existing dynaset or snapshot. Instead, you create a second recordset based on the first recordset. The second recordset is sorted in the desired order. Listing 15.20 shows how this process works.

Listing 15.20. Sorting an existing recordset.

```
Sub SortRecordset()
    Dim db As DATABASE
    Dim rstTimeCardHours As Recordset
    Set db = CurrentDb
    Set rstTimeCardHours = db.OpenRecordset("tblTimeCardHours", dbOpenDynaset)
    Debug.Print "NOT Sorted!!!"
    Do While Not rstTimeCardHours.EOF
        Debug.Print rstTimeCardHours![DateWorked]
        rstTimeCardHours.MoveNext
    Loop
    Debug.Print "Now Sorted!!!"
    rstTimeCardHours.Sort = "[DateWorked]"
    Set rstTimeCardHours = rstTimeCardHours.OpenRecordset
    Do While Not rstTimeCardHours.EOF
        Debug.Print rstTimeCardHours![DateWorked]
        rstTimeCardHours.MoveNext
    Loop
End Sub
```

In this case, you are sorting a dynaset based on the tblTimeCardHours table. The first time you loop through the recordset and print each date worked, the dates are in the default order (usually the primary key order). After using the Sort method to sort the recordset, the records appear in order by the date worked.

Filtering a Recordset

Filtering a recordset is a useful technique when you want to select a subset of the records in your recordset. This is especially useful for allowing users to "drill-down" on a set of records to find the subset they need.

The process of filtering an existing recordset is similar to sorting one. Listing 15.21 is a variation of the example in Listing 15.20. Instead of sorting an existing recordset, it filters an existing recordset.

Listing 15.21. Filtering an existing recordset.

```
Sub FilterRecordSet()
    Dim db As DATABASE
    Dim rstTimeCardHours As Recordset
    Set db = CurrentDb
    Set rstTimeCardHours = db.OpenRecordset("tblTimeCardHours", dbOpenDynaset)
    Debug.Print "Without Filter"
```

What Are the Data Access Objects and Why Are They Important?

15

```
    Do While Not rstTimeCardHours.EOF
        Debug.Print rstTimeCardHours![DateWorked]
        rstTimeCardHours.MoveNext
    Loop
    rstTimeCardHours.Filter = "[DateWorked] Between #1/1/95# and #1/5/95#"
    Debug.Print "With Filter"
    Set rstTimeCardHours = rstTimeCardHours.OpenRecordset
    Do While Not rstTimeCardHours.EOF
        Debug.Print rstTimeCardHours![DateWorked]
        rstTimeCardHours.MoveNext
    Loop
End Sub
```

The first time the code loops through the recordset, no filter is set. The filter is set and the code loops through the recordset again. The second time, only the records meeting the filter criteria are displayed.

Finding a Specific Record in a Recordset

The Seek method enables you to find records in a table recordset. It is usually the quickest method of locating data, because it uses the current index to locate the requested data. Listing 15.22 shows how the Seek method works.

Listing 15.22. Using the Seek method.

```
Sub SeekProject(lngProjectID As Long)
    Dim db As DATABASE
    Dim rstProjects As Recordset

    Set db = CurrentDb()
    Set rstProjects = db.OpenRecordset("tblProjects", dbOpenTable)

    rstProjects.INDEX = "PrimaryKey"
    rstProjects.Seek "=", lngProjectID

    If rstProjects.NoMatch Then
        MsgBox lngProjectID & " Not Found"
    Else
        MsgBox lngProjectID & " Found"
    End If
End Sub
```

This code uses the primary key index to locate the first project with the project number that was passed to the function. It then displays a message box to indicate whether the value was found.

You cannot use the Seek method to locate data in a dynaset or snapshot. Furthermore, you cannot use Seek to search for records in a linked table, regardless of whether the linked table is an Access table or a client/server table. In this case, you must use the FindFirst, FindLast, FindNext, and FindPrevious methods. The FindFirst method finds the first occurrence of data

473

that meets the criteria, and FindLast finds the last occurrence of such data. The FindNext and FindPrevious methods enable you to find additional occurrences of the data.

The code in Listing 15.23 uses the FindFirst method to find the first occurrence of the parameter that was passed in. Again, it displays an appropriate message box.

Listing 15.23. Using the FindFirst method.

```
Sub FindProject(lngValue As Long)
    Dim db As DATABASE
    Dim rstProjects As Recordset
    Dim sSQL As String

    Set db = CurrentDb()
    Set rstProjects = db.OpenRecordset("tblProjects", dbOpenDynaset)
    sSQL = "[ProjectID] = " & lngValue

    rstProjects.FindFirst sSQL

    If rstProjects.NoMatch Then
        MsgBox lngValue & " Not Found"
    Else
        MsgBox lngValue & " Found"
    End If
End Sub
```

> **TIP**
>
> You can use another trick to search a linked table. You can open the database that contains the linked table and seek directly on the table data. This works only if the linked table is in another Access database.

Using the AbsolutePosition Property

The AbsolutePosition property returns the position of the current record. It is a zero-based value. You can use it to specify where in a recordset a specific record was found, as shown in Listing 15.24.

Listing 15.24. Specifying where a record was found.

```
Sub FindPosition(lngValue As Long)
    Dim db As DATABASE
    Dim rstProjects As Recordset
    Dim sSQL As String

    Set db = CurrentDb()
    Set rstProjects = db.OpenRecordset("tblProjects", dbOpenDynaset)
    sSQL = "[ProjectID] = " & lngValue
```

```
    rstProjects.FindFirst sSQL

    If rstProjects.NoMatch Then
        MsgBox lngValue & " Not Found"
    Else
        Debug.Print rstProjects.AbsolutePosition
    End If
End Sub
```

This code finds the first record with a ProjectID equal to the long integer received as a parameter. If the ProjectID is found, the value in the AbsolutePosition property of the record is printed.

WARNING

Do not assume that the AbsolutePosition property of a particular record will stay the same. The AbsolutePosition property of a record changes as records are added or deleted, or as their order is changed as the records are modified.

Using the Bookmark Property

A *bookmark* is a system-generated byte array that uniquely identifies each record in a recordset. The Bookmark property of a recordset changes as you move to each record in the recordset. It often is used if you need to store the current position in the recordset so that you can perform some operation and then return to the position after the operation is completed. Three steps are involved in this process:

1. Storing the current bookmark of the recordset to a Variant variable.
2. Performing the desired operation.
3. Setting the Bookmark property of the recordset to the value contained in the Variant variable.

Listing 15.25 shows an example of using a bookmark.

Listing 15.25. Using a bookmark.

```
Sub UseBookMark()
    Dim db As DATABASE
    Dim rstProjects As Recordset
    Dim sSQL As String
    Dim vntPosition As Variant

    Set db = CurrentDb()
    Set rstProjects = db.OpenRecordset("tblProjects", dbOpenDynaset)

    vntPosition = rstProjects.Bookmark
```

continues

Listing 15.25. continued

```
    Do Until rstProjects.EOF
        Debug.Print rstProjects!ProjectID
        rstProjects.MoveNext
    Loop

    rstProjects.Bookmark = vntPosition
    Debug.Print rstProjects!ProjectID
End Sub
```

This code begins by opening a recordset and storing the bookmark and prints of the first record into a `Variant` variable. It then loops through each record in the recordset, the value in `ProjectID`. After the loop completes, the Bookmark property of the recordset is set equal to the `Variant` variable, setting the current position of the recordset back to where it was before the loop began processing.

Using the RecordsetClone Property

You use the RecordsetClone property of a form to refer to the recordset underlying the form. This property often is used when you want to perform an operation and then synchronize the form with its underlying recordset. Listing 15.26 shows an example of using the RecordsetClone property.

Listing 15.26. Using the RecordsetClone property.

```
Private Sub cmdFindClient_Click()
    Me.RecordsetClone.FindFirst "ClientID = " & Me!txtClientID
    If Me.RecordsetClone.NoMatch Then
        MsgBox Me!txtClientID & " Not Found"
    Else
        Me.Bookmark = Me.RecordsetClone.Bookmark
    End If
End Sub
```

This routine performs the FindFirst method on the RecordsetClone property of the current form. If the record is found, the Bookmark property of the form is set equal to the bookmark of the recordset. This matches the form's position to the underlying recordset's position.

Running Parameter Queries

Access parameter queries are very powerful. They enable the user to specify criteria at runtime. This capability often is helpful if your user wants to fill out a form at runtime and have the values on that form fed to the query. This also can be a useful way to protect your code from changes in the database schema. Creating a parameterized query is like writing a subroutine, where the details of implementing that routine are hidden from the caller. This programming technique is called *encapsulation*. Listing 15.27 shows an example of using parameter queries.

15

WHAT ARE THE DATA ACCESS OBJECTS AND WHY ARE THEY IMPORTANT?

Listing 15.27. Using parameter queries.

```
Sub RunParameterQuery(datStart As Date, datEnd As Date)
    Dim db As DATABASE
    Dim qd As QueryDef
    Dim rs As Recordset

    Set db = CurrentDb
    Set qd = db.QueryDefs("qryBillAmountByClient")
    qd.PARAMETERS("Please Enter Start Date") = datStart
    qd.PARAMETERS("Please Enter End Date") = datEnd
    Set rs = qd.OpenRecordset
    Do While Not rs.EOF
        Debug.Print rs![CompanyName], rs![BillAmount]
        rs.MoveNext
    Loop
End Sub
```

This subroutine receives two `Date` variables as parameters. It just as easily could receive form controls as parameters. It opens a query definition called `qryBillAmountByClient`. It then sets the values of the parameters called `Please Enter Start Date` and `Please Enter End Date` to the `Date` variables passed into the subroutine as parameters. The query then is executed by issuing the OpenRecordset method on the `Recordset` object.

Modifying Table Data Using Code

So far, you have learned how to loop through and work with `Recordset` objects. Now you will learn how to change the data contained in a recordset.

Changing Record Data One Record at a Time

Often, you want to loop through a recordset, modifying all the records that meet a specific set of criteria. Listing 15.28 shows the code required to accomplish this task.

Listing 15.28. Updating records that meet a set of criteria.

```
Sub IncreaseEstimate()
    Dim db As DATABASE
    Dim rstProjectst As Recordset
    Dim sSQL As String
    Dim intUpdated As Integer

    Set db = CurrentDb()
    Set rstProjectst = db.OpenRecordset("tblProjectsChange", dbOpenDynaset)
    sSQL = "ProjectTotalEstimate < 30000"
    intUpdated = 0

    rstProjectst.FindFirst sSQL
```

continues

Listing 15.28. continued

```
    Do While Not rstProjectst.NoMatch
        intUpdated = intUpdated + 1
        rstProjectst.Edit
        rstProjectst!ProjectTotalEstimate = rstProjectst!ProjectTotalEstimate _
        * 1.1
        rstProjectst.UPDATE
        rstProjectst.FindNext sSQL
    Loop
    Debug.Print intUpdated & " Records Updated"
    rstProjectst.Close
End Sub
```

This code finds the first record with a ProjectTotalEstimate less than 30,000. It uses the Edit method to prepare the current record in the dynaset for editing. It replaces the ProjectTotalEstimate with the ProjectTotalEstimate multiplied by 1.1. It then issues the Update method to write the changes to disk. Finally, it uses the FindNext method to locate the next occurrence of the criteria.

Making Bulk Changes

Many of the tasks you can perform by looping through a recordset also be can accomplished with an Update query. Executing an Update query often is more efficient than the process of looping through a recordset. If nothing else, it takes much less code. Therefore, it is important to understand how to execute an Update query through code.

Suppose that you have a query called qryChangeTotalEstimate that increases the ProjectTotalEstimate for all projects where the ProjectTotalEstimate is less than 30,000. The query is an Update query. The code in Listing 15.29 executes the stored query definition.

Listing 15.29. Making bulk changes using a predefined Action query.

```
Sub RunUpdateQuery()
    Dim db As DATABASE
    Dim qd As QueryDef
    Set db = CurrentDb
    Set qd = db.QueryDefs("qryIncreaseTotalEstimate")
    qd.Execute
End Sub
```

Notice that the Execute method operates on the query definition, executing the Action query.

Deleting an Existing Record

The Delete method enables you to programmatically delete records from a recordset, as shown in Listing 15.30.

WHAT ARE THE DATA ACCESS OBJECTS AND WHY ARE THEY IMPORTANT?

15

Listing 15.30. Deleting records with the Delete method.

```
Sub DeleteCusts(lngProjEst As Long)
    Dim db As DATABASE
    Dim rstProjects As Recordset
    Dim intCounter As Integer
    Set db = CurrentDb
    Set rstProjects = db.OpenRecordset("tblProjectsChange", dbOpenDynaset)
    intCounter = 0
    Do While Not rstProjects.EOF
        If rstProjects!ProjectTotalEstimate < lngProjEst Then
            rstProjects.Delete
            intCounter = intCounter + 1
        End If
        rstProjects.MoveNext
    Loop
    Debug.Print intCounter & " Customers Deleted"
End Sub
```

This code loops through the rstProjects recordset. If the `ProjectTotalEstimate` amount is less than the value passed in as a parameter, the record is deleted. This task also can be accomplished with a Delete query.

Adding a New Record

The AddNew method enables you to programmatically add records to a recordset, as shown in Listing 15.31.

Listing 15.31. Adding records to a recordset.

```
Private Sub cmdAddRecord_Click()
    Dim db As DATABASE
    Dim rstProject As Recordset

    Set db = CurrentDb()
    Set rstProject = db.OpenRecordset("tblProjectsChange", DB_OPEN_DYNASET)
    With rstProject
        .AddNew
        !ProjectName = Me!txtProjectName
        !ProjectDescription = Me!txtProjectDescription
        ![ClientID] = Me!cboClientID
        .UPDATE
    End With
    Me!txtProjectID = rstProject!ProjectID
End Sub
```

This code is used on an Unbound form called frmUnbound. The code issues an AddNew method, which creates a buffer ready to accept data. Each field in the recordset then is populated with the values from the controls on the form. The Update method writes the data to disk. If you forget to include the Update method, the record is never written to disk.

The last line of code does not work. The ProjectID field is an AutoNumber field, so Access will assign its value during the update. The offending line is supposed to copy the newly created `ProjectID` value into a text field on the form. The line is there to illustrate a problem: When an AddNew method is issued, the record pointer is not moved within the dynaset. Even after the Update method is issued, the record pointer remains at the record it was on prior to the AddNew method.

Therefore, this code will add a record, but it will place the `ProjectID` value of the previously existing record into the txtProjectId text box on the form. To get around this, you must explicitly move to the new record before populating the text box. This can be accomplished easily by using the LastModified property.

Using the LastModified Property

The LastModified property contains a bookmark of the most recently added or modified record. By setting the bookmark of the recordset to the LastModified property, the record pointer is moved to the most recently added record. Listing 15.32 is a modified version of Listing 15.31, using the LastModified property to fix the problem described previously.

Listing 15.32. Using the LastModified property after AddNew.

```
Private Sub cmdLastModified_Click()
    Dim db As DATABASE
    Dim rstProject As Recordset

    Set db = CurrentDb()
    Set rstProject = db.OpenRecordset("tblProjectsChange", DB_OPEN_DYNASET)
    With rstProject
        .AddNew
        !ProjectName = Me!txtProjectName
        !ProjectDescription = Me!txtProjectDescription
        ![ClientID] = Me!cboClientID
        .UPDATE
        .Bookmark = rstProject.LastModified
    End With
    Me!txtProjectID = rstProject!ProjectID
End Sub
```

Notice that the bookmark of the recordset is set to the LastModified property of the recordset.

Creating and Modifying Database Objects Using Code

When developing an Access application, it might be useful to add tables or queries, define or modify relationships, change security, or perform other data-definition techniques at runtime. You can accomplish all this by manipulating the various data access objects.

Adding a Table Using Code

Many properties and methods are available for adding and modifying Jet Engine objects. The code in Listing 15.33 creates a table, adds some fields, and then adds a primary key index.

Listing 15.33. Creating a table, adding fields, and adding a primary key index.

```
Sub CreateTable()
    Dim db As Database
    Dim td As TableDef
    Dim fld As Field
    Dim idx As Index

    Set db = CurrentDb()
    ' Create new TableDef.
    Set td = db.CreateTableDef("tblFoods")
    ' Add field to Table Definition
    Set fld = td.CreateField("FoodID", DB_TEXT, 5)
    td.Fields.Append fld
    Set fld = td.CreateField("Description", DB_TEXT, 25)
    td.Fields.Append fld
    Set fld = td.CreateField("Calories", DB_INTEGER)
    td.Fields.Append fld
    db.TableDefs.Append td
    'Designate the FoodID field as the Primary Key Index
    Set idx = td.CreateIndex("PrimaryKey")
    Set fld = idx.CreateField("FoodID")
    idx.Primary = True
    idx.Unique = True
    idx.Fields.Append fld
    'Add the index to the Indexes collection
    td.Indexes.Append idx
End Sub
```

This code first creates a table definition called tblFoods. Before it can add the table definition to the TableDefs collection, it must add fields to the table. Three fields are added to the table. Notice that the field name, type, and length are specified. After the table definition is added to the database, indexes can be added to the table. The index added in Listing 15.33 is a primary key index.

Removing a Table Using Code

Just as you can add a table using code, you can remove a table using code, as shown in Listing 15.34.

Listing 15.34. Removing a table.

```
Sub DeleteTable()
    Dim db As DATABASE

    Set db = CurrentDb
    db.TableDefs.Delete "tblFoods"
End Sub
```

The Delete method is issued on the TableDefs collection. The table you want to delete is passed to the Delete method as an argument.

Establishing Relationships Using Code

When you create tables using the Access environment, you normally create relationships between the tables at the same time. If you are creating tables using code, you probably want to establish relationships between those tables using code as well. Listing 15.35 shows an example.

Listing 15.35. Establishing relationships between Database objects.

```
Sub CreateRelation()
    Dim db As DATABASE
    Dim rel As Relation
    Dim fld As Field

    Set db = CurrentDb
    Set rel = db.CreateRelation()

    With rel
        .Name = "PeopleFood"
        .TABLE = "tblFoods"
        .ForeignTable = "tblPeople"
        .Attributes = dbRelationDeleteCascade
    End With

    Set fld = rel.CreateField("FoodID")
    fld.ForeignName = "FoodID"
    rel.Fields.Append fld
    db.Relations.Append rel
End Sub
```

This code begins by creating a new Relation object. It then populates the Name, Table, Foreign Table, and Attributes properties of the relationship. After the properties of the relationship are set, the field is added to the Relation object. Finally, the Relation object is appended to the Relations collection.

Creating a Query Using Code

If you are running your application from the Access runtime, your users won't be able to design their own queries unless they have their own full copies of Access. You might want to build your own query designer into your application and then allow the users to save the queries they build. This requires that you build the queries yourself, using code, after the user designs them. Listing 15.36 shows the code needed to build a query.

Listing 15.36. Building a query.

```
Sub CreateQuery()
    Dim db As DATABASE
    Dim qdf As QueryDef
    Dim strSQL As String

    Set db = CurrentDb
    Set qdf = db.CreateQueryDef("qryBigProjects")
    strSQL = "Select ProjectID, ProjectName, ProjectTotalEstimate " _
        & "From tblProjects " _
        & "Where ProjectTotalEstimate >= 30000"
    qdf.SQL = strSQL
End Sub
```

This code uses the CreateQueryDef method of the Database object to create a new query definition. It then sets the SQL statement associated with the query definition. This serves to build and store the query.

> **NOTE**
>
> It is important to understand that the CreateTableDef method does not immediately add the table definition to the database, unlike the CreateQueryDef method of the Database object, which immediately adds the query definition to the database. You must use the Append method of the TableDefs collection to actually add the table definition to the database.

> **TIP**
>
> You can create a temporary query definition by using a zero-length string for the name argument of the CreateQueryDef method.

Using the Containers Collection

A Container object maintains information about saved Database objects. The types of objects in the Containers collection are databases, tables (included queries), relationships, system relationships, forms, reports, scripts (macros), and modules. The Container object is responsible for letting Jet know about the user interface objects. Databases, tables, relationships, and system relationships have Jet as their parent object. Forms, reports, scripts, and modules have the Access application as their parent object.

Each `Container` object possesses a collection of `Document` objects. These are the actual forms, reports, and other objects that are part of your database. The `Document` objects contain only summary information about each object (date created, owner, and so on); they do not contain the actual data of the objects. To refer to a particular document within a container, you must use one of two techniques:

```
Containers("Name")
```

or

```
Containers!Name
```

To list each `Container` object and its associated `Document` objects, you need to use the code shown in Listing 15.37.

Listing 15.37. Listing each `Container` object and its associated `Document` objects.

```
Sub ListAllDBObjects()
    Dim db As DATABASE
    Dim con As Container
    Dim doc As Document

    Set db = CurrentDb
    For Each con In db.Containers
        Debug.Print "*** " & con.Name & " ***"
        For Each doc In con.Documents
            Debug.Print doc.Name
        Next doc
    Next con
End Sub
```

This code loops through all the documents in all the containers, listing each one.

Practical Examples: Applying These Techniques to Your Application

The potential applications for the methodologies learned in this chapter are endless. This section explores just a few of the ways you can apply these techniques. The examples here are located in CHAP15.MDB on the accompanying CD-ROM.

Creating a Report Selection Form

This section shows you how to create a Report Selection Form dialog box. The dialog box will contain a list box to display the name of every report in the database. After the user selects a report name and clicks the Preview Report button, the selected report runs. Figure 15.2 shows the form.

WHAT ARE THE DATA ACCESS OBJECTS AND WHY ARE THEY IMPORTANT?

15

Figure 15.2.

The Report Selection Form dialog box.

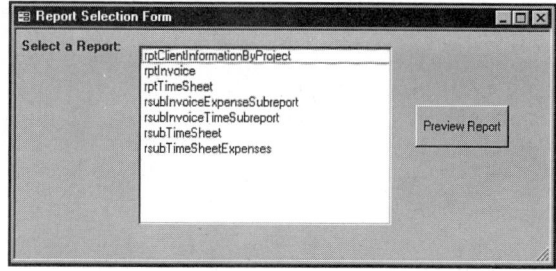

The trick here is the population of the list box that displays all the reports in the database. Chapter 13, "Let's Get More Intimate with Forms: Advanced Techniques," covers how to populate a list box using a `callback` function. Here, you learn how the `callback` function uses the Document collection to identify all the reports contained in the database.

Listing 15.38 contains the code for a `callback` function that returns a list of reports. The `acLBIntialize` case of the `Case` statement uses the Containers collection of the `Database` object to loop through each `Report` object and add its name to a static array. This function is called repeatedly, with the `intCode` parameter set to `acLBGetValue`, to return the values for the list box.

After the list box is loaded, the user can select any report in the list. The code under the `Click` event of the Preview Report button uses the value of the selected item in the list box as an argument to the OpenReport method of the `DoCmd` object. If you use this technique of report selection, you must be careful. Some reports might need to be run from forms that populate parameter queries underlying the reports. If this is the case, these reports must cancel themselves or load the required form when they are run.

Listing 15.38. A `callback` function listing all reports in the database.

```
Function FillWithReportList(ctl As Control, vntID As Variant, _
        lngRow As Long, lngCol As Long, intCode As Integer) _
        As Variant

    Dim db As DATABASE
    Dim cnt As Container
    Dim doc As Document
    Dim intCounter As Integer
    Static sastrReports() As String
    Static sintNumReports As Integer
    Dim varRetVal As Variant

    varRetVal = Null

    Select Case intCode
        Case acLBInitialize        ' Initialize.
            Set db = CurrentDb
            Set cnt = db.Containers!Reports
            sintNumReports = cnt.Documents.Count
            ReDim sastrReports(sintNumReports - 1)
            For Each doc In cnt.Documents
```

continues

Listing 15.38. continued

```
            sastrReports(intCounter) = doc.Name
            intCounter = intCounter + 1
        Next doc
        varRetVal = sintNumReports
    Case acLBOpen                        'Open
        varRetVal = Timer                'Generate unique ID for control.
    Case acLBGetRowCount                 'Get number of rows.
        varRetVal = sintNumReports
    Case acLBGetColumnCount              'Get number of columns.
        varRetVal = 1
    Case acLBGetColumnWidth              'Get column width.
        varRetVal = -1                   '-1 forces use of default width.
    Case acLBGetValue                    'Get the data.
        varRetVal = sastrReports(lngRow)
    End Select
    FillWithReportList = varRetVal
End Function
```

Using Recordset Methods on a Data-Entry Form

At times, you might want to disable the default record movement and add, edit, or delete functionality from a form and code all the functionality yourself. You might want to perform these
actions if you are going against client/server data and want to execute additional control over
the data-entry environment. You also might want to use these techniques when you are developing applications for both the Access and Visual Basic environments and are striving for
maximum code compatibility. Regardless of your reasons for using the following techniques,
it is a good idea to know how to use a form's underlying recordset to display and modify data.

Figure 15.3 shows a form in which the navigation buttons and record selectors have been removed. The form contains six command buttons: Move Previous, Move Next, Add, Delete,
Find, and Exit. All the buttons use the recordset underlying the form to move from record to
record in the form and to modify the data contained in the form.

Listing 15.39 shows the code for the Move Previous button.

Listing 15.39. Code for the Move Previous button.

```
Private Sub cmdPrevious_Click()
    Me.RecordsetClone.MovePrevious
    If Me.RecordsetClone.BOF Then
        Me.RecordsetClone.MoveNext
        MsgBox "Already at First Record!!"
    End If
    Me.Bookmark = Me.RecordsetClone.Bookmark
End Sub
```

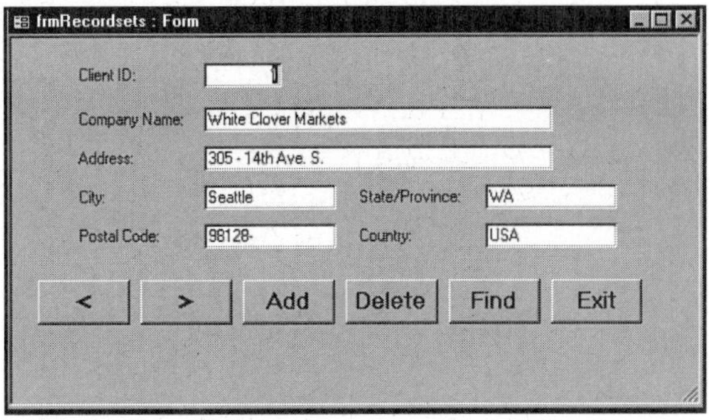

WHAT ARE THE DATA ACCESS OBJECTS AND WHY ARE THEY IMPORTANT?

15

Figure 15.3.

The frmRecordsets dialog box.

This routine performs the MovePrevious method on the RecordsetClone property of the form. If the BOF property becomes True, indicating that the record pointer is before the first valid record, the MoveNext method is performed on the RecordsetClone property of the form to return the record pointer to the first record in the recordset. Finally, the bookmark of the form is synchronized with the bookmark of the RecordsetClone property. Listing 15.40 shows the code for the Move Next button.

Listing 15.40. Code for the Move Next button.

```
Private Sub cmdNext_Click()
   Me.RecordsetClone.MoveNext
   If Me.RecordsetClone.EOF Then
      Me.RecordsetClone.MovePrevious
      MsgBox "Already at Last Record!!"
   End If
   Me.Bookmark = Me.RecordsetClone.Bookmark
End Sub
```

The code for the Add button is a little tricky, as Listing 15.41 shows.

Listing 15.41. Code for the Add button.

```
Private Sub cmdAdd_Click()
   Me.RecordsetClone.AddNew
   Me.RecordsetClone!CompanyName = "New Company"
   Me.RecordsetClone.UPDATE
   Me.Bookmark = Me.RecordsetClone.LastModified
End Sub
```

The AddNew method is performed on the RecordsetClone property of the form. This method creates a buffer in memory that is ready to accept the new data. The record pointer is not actually moved, so it remains over whatever record you were on before you began the Add process. You need to write the new record to disk so that it becomes a valid record and the user can move to it. Because the CompanyName field is a required field, you must populate it with data before issuing the Update method on the RecordsetClone property.

487

Even after the Update method is issued, the record pointer still remains over the record that the user was on before you began the Add process. By setting the bookmark of the form to the LastModified property of the recordset, you synchronize the form with the new record. In a production environment, you would want to clear out all the text boxes and force the user to save or cancel before the AddNew or Update method is issued.

The process of deleting a record is quite simple, as Listing 15.42 shows.

Listing 15.42. Deleting a record.

```
Private Sub cmdDelete_Click()
   Dim intAnswer As Integer
   intAnswer = MsgBox("Are You Sure???", vbYesNo + vbQuestion, _
   "Delete Current Record?")
   If intAnswer = vbYes Then
      Me.RecordsetClone.Delete
      Call cmdNext_Click
      Me.Bookmark = Me.RecordsetClone.Bookmark
   End If
End Sub
```

This code verifies that the user actually wants to delete the record and then issues the Delete method on the RecordsetClone property of the form. Because the current record no longer is valid, the code calls the Click event of the cmdNext button. Finally, it sets the bookmark of the form to the bookmark of the RecordsetClone property to synchronize the form with its underlying recordset.

The last piece of code involved in the form is the code for the Find button, as shown in Listing 15.43.

Listing 15.43. Code for the Find button.

```
Private Sub cmdFind_Click()
   Dim strClientID As String
   Dim strBookmark As String
   strBookmark = Me.Bookmark
   strClientID = InputBox("Enter Client ID of Client You Want to Locate")
   Me.RecordsetClone.FindFirst "ClientID = " & strClientID
   If Me.RecordsetClone.NoMatch Then
      MsgBox "Client ID " & strClientID & " Not Found!!"
      Me.Bookmark = strBookmark
   Else
      Me.Bookmark = Me.RecordsetClone.Bookmark
   End If
End Sub
```

This routine begins by storing the bookmark of the current record to a `String` variable. Users are prompted for the client ID they want to locate, and then the FindFirst method is issued on the RecordsetClone property of the form. If no match is found, the user is warned and the bookmark of the form is set to the value within the `String` variable, returning the record pointer to the position it was in prior to the search. If the client ID is found, the bookmark of the form is synchronized with the bookmark of the RecordsetClone property.

Summary

In this chapter, you learned how to manipulate recordsets via code. The chapter began by introducing you to the data access object model. It described the various collections in the database and showed how you easily can list the members of each collection. It then explored the different types of recordsets available in Access, highlighting why you would want to use each type.

Next, you learned how to manipulate recordsets using code. The capability to manipulate recordsets behind the scenes is an important aspect of the VBA language. It frees you from the user interface and enables you to control what is going on programmatically. Finally, you learned how to create and modify database objects using code. This is important if the application you are creating requires you to create or modify tables, queries, or other objects at runtime.

What To Do When Things Don't Go As Planned

16

Debugging: Your Key to Successful Development

- Understanding the Importance of Debugging, 494
- Avoiding Bugs, 494
- Harnessing the Power of the Debug Window, 495
- Invoking the Debugger, 500
- Using Breakpoints to Troubleshoot, 500
- Stepping Through Code, 502
- Setting the Next Statement to Execute, 505
- Using the Calls Window, 506
- Working with the Locals Pane, 507
- Working with Watch Expressions, 507
- Continuing Execution After a Runtime Error, 512
- Looking At Gotchas with the Debug Window, 513
- Practical Examples: Debugging Real Applications, 513

Understanding the Importance of Debugging

A good programmer is not necessarily one who can get things right the first time. To be fully effective as a VBA programmer, you need to master the art of *debugging*—the process of trouble-shooting your application. Debugging involves locating and identifying problem areas in your code and is a mandatory step in the application-development process. Fortunately, the Access 97 environment provides excellent tools to help you with the debugging process. Using the Access 97 debugging tools, you can step through your code, setting watchpoints and breakpoints as needed.

Using the VBA debugging tools is significantly more efficient than taking random stabs at fixes to your application. A strong command of the Access 97 debugging tools can save you hours of trial and error. In fact, it can be the difference between a successfully completed application-development process and one that continues indefinitely with problems left unsolved.

Avoiding Bugs

The best way to deal with bugs is to avoid them in the first place. Proper coding techniques can really aid you in this process. Using `Option Explicit`, strong-typing, naming standards, and tight scoping can help you eliminate bugs in your code.

Option Explicit

`Option Explicit` requires that all your variables be declared before they are used. Including `Option Explicit` in each form, code, and report module helps the VBA compiler find typos in the names of variables.

As discussed in detail in Chapter 8, "VBA 101: The Basics of VBA," the `Option Explicit` statement is a command that can be placed in the General Declarations section of any code, form, or report module. The `Option Explicit` command can be inserted manually into each program, or it can be inserted automatically by selecting Require Variable Declaration from the Modules tab after choosing Tools|Options.

Strong-Typing

Strong-typing your variables is discussed in Chapter 8. To *strong-type* a variable means to indicate what type of data is stored in a variable at the time it is declared. For example, `Dim intCounter As Integer` initializes a variable that contains integers. If elsewhere in your code you assign a character string to `intCounter`, the compiler will catch the error.

Naming Standards

Naming standards also can go a long way toward helping you to eliminate errors. The careful naming of variables makes your code easier to read and makes the intended use of the variable more obvious. Problem code tends to stand out when naming conventions have been followed judiciously. Naming standards are covered in Chapter 1, "Introduction to Access Development," and are outlined in detail in Appendix B, "Naming Conventions."

Variable Scoping

Finally, giving your variables the narrowest scope possible reduces the chances of one piece of code accidentally overwriting a variable in another piece of code. You should use local variables whenever possible. Use module-level and global variables only when it is necessary to see the value of a variable from multiple subroutines or multiple modules. For more information about the issues surrounding variable scoping, see Chapter 8.

Bugs Happen!

Unfortunately, no matter what you do to prevent problems and errors, they still creep into your code. Probably the most insidious type of error is a logic error. A *logic error* is sneaky because it escapes the compiler; your code compiles but simply does not execute as planned. This type of error might become apparent when you receive a runtime error or when you don't get the results you expected. This is where the debugger comes to the rescue.

Harnessing the Power of the Debug Window

The Debug window serves several purposes. It provides you with a great way to test VBA and user-defined functions, it enables you to inquire about and change the value of variables while your code is running, and it enables you to view the results of Debug.Print statements. To open the Debug window while in a code, form, or report module, do one of three things:

- Click the Debug Window tool on the toolbar.
- Choose View|Debug window.
- Press Ctrl+G.

The Debug window is shown in Figure 16.1.

Figure 16.1.

The Debug window enables you to test functions and to inquire about and change the value of variables.

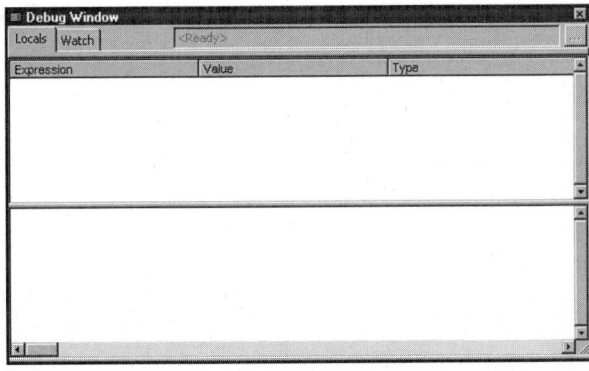

Testing Values of Variables and Properties

The Debug window enables you to test the values of variables and properties as your code executes. This can be quite enlightening as to what is actually happening in your code.

To practice with the Debug window, you do not even need to be executing code. While in a form, report, or module, all you need to do is press Ctrl+G to invoke the Debug window. To see how this works, follow these steps:

1. Run the frmClients form from the CHAP16EX.MDB database on the accompanying CD-ROM.

2. Press Ctrl+G to open and activate the Debug window. The cursor appears in the bottom half of the Debug window. This is called the *immediate pane*.

3. Type **?Forms!frmClients!txtClientID.Value**. The client ID of the current client appears on the next line.

4. Type **?Forms!frmClients!txtCompanyName.Visible**. The word True appears on the next line, indicating that the control is visible.

5. Type **?Forms!frmClients!txtAddress.BackColor**. The number -2147483643 appears on the next line, specifying the background color of the address control.

Your screen should look like the one shown in Figure 16.2. You can continue to request the values of properties or variables in your VBA code.

Figure 16.2.

Using the Debug window to test the values of properties.

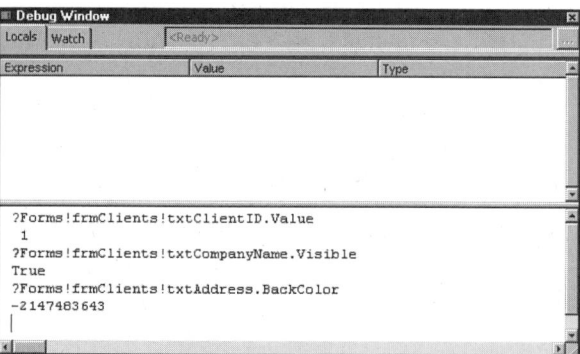

Setting Values of Variables and Properties

> **NOTE**
>
> You can invoke the Debug window in three ways. You can click the Debug Window button on the toolbar, press Ctrl+G, or choose View | Debug Window. An advantage of pressing Ctrl+G is that it invokes the Debug window without the Code window being active. You can click the Debug Window toolbar button or choose View | Debug only from a Module window.

Not only can you display things in the Debug window—you can use the Debug window to modify the values of variables and controls as your code executes. This feature becomes even more valuable when you realize that you can re-execute code in a procedure after changing the value of a variable. Here's how this process works:

1. Invoke the Debug window if necessary. Remember that you can do this by pressing Ctrl+G from any form, report, or code module.

2. Type **`Forms!frmClients!txtContactTitle.Value`** = **`"Hello"`** in the immediate pane. The contact title of the current record changes to `Hello`.

3. Type **`Forms!frmClients!txtCompanyName.Visible`** = **`False`**. The txtCompanyName control on the frmClients form becomes hidden.

4. Type **`Forms!frmClients!txtAddress.BackColor`** = **`123456`**. The background color of the txtAddress control on the frmClients forms turns green. The Debug window and your form now look like those shown in Figure 16.3.

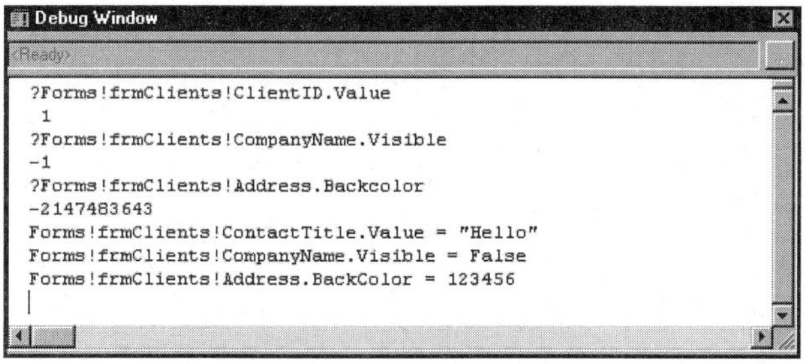

Figure 16.3.
Setting the values of properties using the Debug window.

The Debug window is an extremely valuable testing and debugging tool. The examples here barely begin to illustrate its power and flexibility.

> **WARNING**
>
> Changes you make to data while working in the Debug window are permanent. On the other hand, changes you make to the properties of controls or the values of variables are not saved with the form or report.

Clearing the Debug Window

The Debug window displays the last 200 lines of output. As additional lines of code are added to the immediate pane of the Debug window, older lines disappear. When you exit completely from Access and return to the Debug window, it is cleared. If you want to clear the immediate pane of the Debug window at any other time, follow these steps:

1. Press Ctrl+Home to go to the top of the Debug window.
2. Press Shift+Ctrl+End to go to the last statement in the Debug window.
3. Press Delete.

Practicing with the Built-In Functions

In addition to being able to test and set the values of properties and variables using the Debug window, you can test any VBA function. To test a VBA function, type the function and its arguments in the Debug window, preceded by a question mark. This code returns the month of the current date, for example:

```
?datepart("m",date)
```

This tells you the date one month after today's date:

```
?dateadd("m",1,date)
```

This tells you how many days exist between the current date and the end of the millennium:

```
?datediff("d",date(),#12/31/99#)
```

Executing Subroutines, Functions, and Methods

In addition to enabling you to test any VBA function, the Debug window enables you to test any user-defined subroutine, function, or method. This is a great way to debug your user-defined procedures. To see how this works, follow these steps:

1. Open the basExamples module found in the CHAP16EX.MDB database on the accompanying CD-ROM.
2. Invoke the Debug window if it is not already visible.
3. Type `?ReturnInitsFunc("Bill","Gates")`. This calls the user-defined function `ReturnInitsFunc`, sending "Bill" as the first parameter and "Gates" as the second parameter. The value `B.G.` appears in the Debug window. This is the return value from the function.
4. Type `Call ReturnInitsSub("Bill","Gates")`. This calls the user-defined subroutine `ReturnInitsSub`, sending "Bill" as the first parameter and "Gates" as the second parameter. The value `B.G.` appears in a message box.

Notice the difference between how you call a function and how you call a subroutine. Because the function returns a value, you must call it using a question mark. On the other hand, when calling a subroutine, you use the `Call` keyword.

You also can call a subroutine from the Debug window by using this syntax:

```
RoutineName Parameter1, Parameter2, ....
```

Notice that when you omit the Call keyword, the parameters do not need to be enclosed in parentheses.

Printing to the Debug Window at Runtime

The capability to print to the Debug window is useful because you can test what is happening as your code executes without having to suspend code execution. It also is valuable to be able to print something to a window when you are testing, without interfering with the user-interface aspect of your code. You can test a form without being interrupted and then go back and view the values of variables and so on. Here's how the process works:

1. Type **Call LoopThroughCollection**. This calls the user-defined subroutine LoopThroughCollection. The values Skating, Basketball, Hockey, and Skiing appear. These values were printed to the Debug window by the routine.

2. Open the frmDebugPrint form in Form view.

3. Press Tab to move from the First Name field to the Last Name field.

4. Press Tab to move back to the First Name field.

5. Type your first name.

6. Open the Debug window. Notice all the statements that were printed to the Debug window. (See Figure 16.4.) These Debug.Print statements were coded in all the appropriate form and control events.

Figure 16.4.

Using Debug.Print statements to print values to the Debug window.

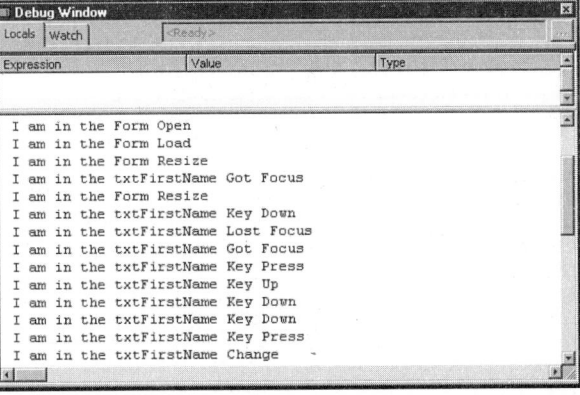

499

Invoking the Debugger

You can invoke the Access debugger in several ways:

- Place a breakpoint in your code.
- Place a watch in your code.
- Press Ctrl+Break while the code is running.
- Insert a Stop statement in your code.

A *breakpoint* is an unconditional point at which you want to suspend code execution. It is temporary because it is in effect only while the database is open. In other words, breakpoints are not saved with the database.

A *watch* is a condition under which you want to suspend code execution. You might want to suspend code execution when a counter variable reaches a specific value, for example. A watch also is temporary; it is removed after you close the database.

A Stop statement is permanent. In fact, if you forget to remove Stop statements from your code, your application stops execution while the user is running it.

Using Breakpoints to Troubleshoot

As mentioned, a breakpoint is a point at which execution of code is halted unconditionally. You can set multiple breakpoints in your code. You can add and remove breakpoints as your code executes.

A breakpoint enables you to halt your code execution at a suspicious area of code. This enables you to examine everything that is going on at that point in your code execution. By strategically placing breakpoints in your code, you quickly can execute sections of code that already are debugged, stopping only at problem areas.

To set a breakpoint, follow these steps:

1. Place your cursor on the line of code where you want to invoke the debugger.
2. You can insert a breakpoint in one of four ways:

    Press the F9 function key.

    Click in the gray margin area to the left of the line of the code that will contain the breakpoint.

    Click the Breakpoint button on the toolbar.

    Choose Debug|Toggle Breakpoint.

    The line of code containing the breakpoint appears in a different color, and a dot appears that indicates the breakpoint.

3. Run the form, report, or module containing the breakpoint. VBA suspends execution just before executing the line of code where you placed the breakpoint. The statement that is about to execute appears in a contrasting color (the default is yellow).

Now that your code is suspended, you can step through it one line at a time, change the value of variables, and view your call stack, among other things.

Keep in mind that a breakpoint is actually a toggle. If you want to remove a breakpoint, press F9 or click Breakpoint on the toolbar. Breakpoints are removed when the database is closed, when another database is opened, or when you exit Access.

It is easiest to get to know the debugger by actually using it. The following example gives you hands-on experience in setting and stopping code execution at a breakpoint. The example is developed further later in the chapter.

Start by creating a form called frmDebug that contains a command button called cmdDebug. Give the button the caption Test Code. Place the following code in the Click event of the command button:

TRY IT

```
Sub cmdDebug_Click ()
    Call Func1
End Sub
```

Create a module called basFuncs. Enter three functions in the module:

```
Sub Func1 ()
   Dim intTemp As Integer

   intTemp = 10
   Debug.Print "We Are Now In Func1()"
   Debug.Print intTemp
   Call Func2
End Sub

Sub Func2 ()
   Dim strName As String

   strName = "Bill Gates"
   Debug.Print "We Are Now In Func2()"
   Debug.Print strName
   Call Func3

End Sub

Sub Func3 ()
   Debug.Print "We Are Now In Func3()"
   MsgBox "Hi There From The Func3() Sub Procedure"
End Sub
```

Now you should debug. Start by placing a breakpoint in the Click event of cmdDebug on the line called Call Func1. Here are the steps:

1. Click anywhere on the line of code that says Call Func1.

2. Press the F9 function key, click the Breakpoint button on the toolbar, or choose Debug|Toggle Breakpoint.

501

3. Go into Form view and click the Test Code button. Access suspends execution just before executing the line where you placed the breakpoint. VBA displays the line that reads Call Func1 in a different color (by default, red), indicating that it is about to execute that line. (See Figure 16.5.)

Figure 16.5.

Code execution halted at a breakpoint.

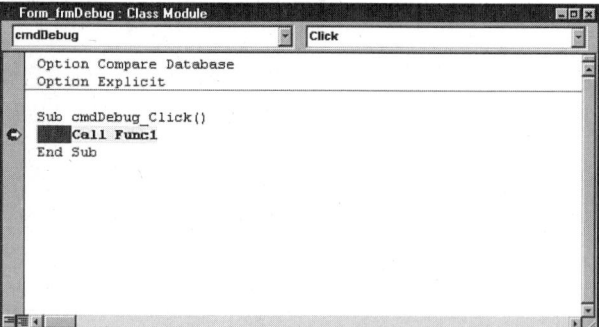

Stepping Through Code

Access 97 gives you three main options for stepping through your code. Each one is slightly different. The Step Into option enables you to step through each line of code in a subroutine or function, whereas the Step Over option executes a procedure without stepping through each line of code in it. The Step Out option runs all code in nested procedures and then returns you to the procedure that called the line of code that you are on. Knowing the right option to use to solve a particular problem is an acquired skill that comes with continued development experience.

Using Step Into

When you reach a breakpoint, you can continue executing your code one line at a time or continue execution until another breakpoint is reached. To step through your code one line at a time, click Step Into on the toolbar, press F8, or choose Debug|Step Into.

The following example illustrates the process of stepping through your code, printing the values of variables to the Debug window, and modifying the values of variables using the Debug window.

TRY IT

You can continue the debug process from the breakpoint you set in the previous example. Step two times (press F8). You should find yourself in Func1, about to execute the line of code intTemp = 10. (See Figure 16.6.) Notice that VBA did not stop on the line Dim intTemp As Integer. The debugger does not stop on variable declarations.

The Debug statements are about to print to the Debug window. Take a look by opening the Debug window. None of your code has printed anything to the Debug window yet. Press F8 (step) three more times until you have executed the line Debug.Print intTemp. Your screen should look like Figure 16.7. Notice the results of the Debug.Print statements.

Figure 16.6.

The Debug window halted in Func1.

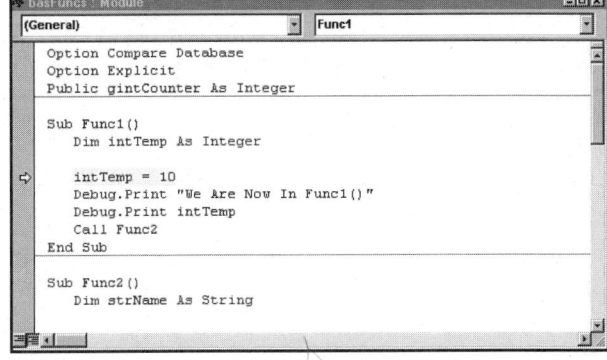

Figure 16.7.

The Debug window with entries generated by Debug.Print statements.

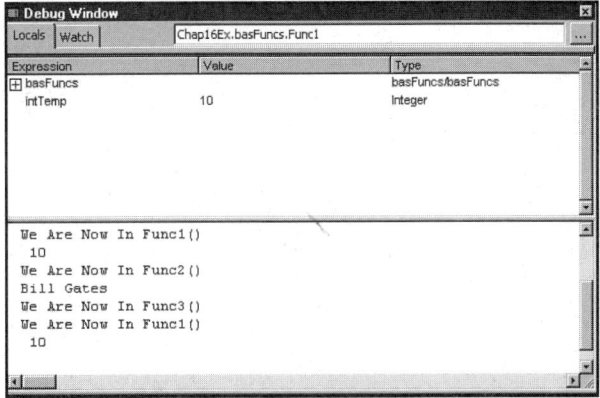

Now that you have seen how you can display variables and the results of expressions to the Debug window, take a look at how you can use the Debug window to modify values of variables and controls. Start by changing the value of intTemp. Click the Debug window and type **intTemp = 50**. When you press Enter, you actually modify the value of intTemp. Type **?intTemp**, and you'll see that Access echoes back the value of 50. You also can see the value of intTemp on the Locals tab of the Debug window. Notice in Figure 16.7 that the Locals tab is selected. The intTemp variable appears along with its value and type.

Executing Until the Next Breakpoint Is Reached

Suppose that you have reached a breakpoint but you realize that your problem is further down in the code execution. In fact, the problem is actually in a different function. You might not want to continue to move one step at a time down to the offending function. Use the Procedure drop-down menu to locate the questionable function, and then set a breakpoint on the line where you want to continue stepping. You now are ready to continue code execution until Access reaches this line. To do this, click Continue on the toolbar, press F5, or choose Run|Go/ Continue. Your code continues to execute, stopping at the next breakpoint. To see how this works, continue the Debug process with the next example.

TRY IT

Suppose that you realize your problem might be in Func3. You do not want to continue to move one step at a time down to Func3. No problem. Use the Procedure drop-down menu to view Func3, as shown in Figure 16.8. Set a breakpoint on the line that reads Debug.Print "We Are Now In Func3()". You now are ready to continue code execution until Access reaches this line. To continue execution, click Continue on the toolbar, press F5, or choose Run|Go/Continue. Your code continues to execute, stopping on the breakpoint you just set. Press F5 again. The code finishes executing. Return to the Form View window.

Figure 16.8.

Using the Procedure drop-down menu to view another function.

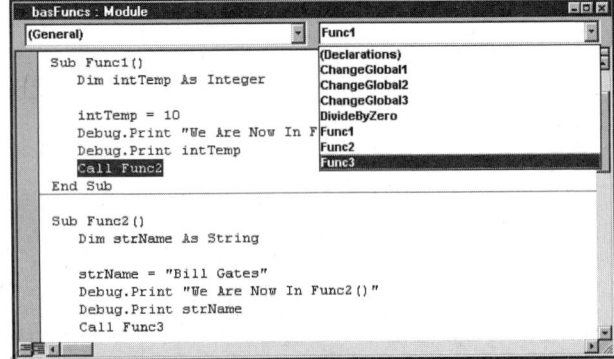

Using Step Over

Sometimes you already have a subroutine fully tested and debugged. You want to continue stepping through the routine that you are in, but you don't want to watch the execution of subroutines. In this case, you use Step Over. To step over a subroutine or function, click Step Over on the toolbar, press Shift+F8, or choose Debug|Step Over. The code in the subroutine or function you are stepping over executes, but you do not step through it. To experiment with the Step Over feature, follow the next example.

TRY IT

Click back on the open form and click one more time on the Test Code button. Because your breakpoints are still set, you are placed on the line of code that reads Call Func1. Press F9 to remove this breakpoint. Move to the basFuncs module window, which should still be open, and use the Procedure drop-down menu to move to Func3. If the basFuncs module is no longer open, you can press Shift+F2 to move to Func1, which is also in basFuncs, and then use the Procedure drop-down menu to move to Func3. Remove the breakpoint from that routine as well. Step (press F8) five times until you are about to execute the line Call Func2. Suppose that you have tested Func2 and Func3 and know that they are not the cause of the problems in your code. With Func2 highlighted as the next line to be executed, click Step Over on the toolbar. Notice that Func2 and Func3 are both executed but that you now are ready to continue stepping in Func1. In this case, you are placed on the End Sub line immediately following the call to Func2.

Using Step Out

You use the Step Out feature to step out of the procedure you are in and to return to the procedure that called the line of code you are on. You use this feature when you have accidentally stepped into a procedure that you realize is fully tested. You want to execute all the code called by the procedure you are in and then step out to the calling procedure so that you can continue with the debugging process. To test how this works, follow this example:

TRY IT

1. Place a breakpoint on the call to Func2.
2. Click the End button on the toolbar to halt code execution.
3. Activate the frmDebug form and click the Start Debug Process command button.
4. Step once to place yourself on the first line of Func2.
5. Suppose that you realize you just stepped one step too far. You really intended to step over Func2 and all the procedures it calls. No problem! Click the Step Out button to step out of Func2 and return to the line following the line of code that called Func2. In this case, you should find yourself on the End Sub statement of Func1.

Setting the Next Statement to Execute

After you have stepped through your code, watched the logical flow, and modified some variables, you might want to re-execute the code beginning at a prior statement. To do this, you can click anywhere in the line of code where you want to commence execution. Choose Debug|Set Next Statement. Notice the contrasting color (usually yellow) indicating that the next line of code to be executed now is placed over that statement. You then can step through the code by pressing F8, or you can continue normal code execution by pressing F5. Access enables you to set the next line to be executed in a procedure only. You can use this feature to re-execute lines of code or to skip over a problem line of code.

The following example walks you through the process of changing the value of a variable and then re-executing code after the value is changed.

The preceding example left you at the last line of code (the End Sub statement) in Func1. You want to change the value of intTemp and re-execute everything. Go to the Debug window and type **intTemp = 100**. You need to set the next statement to print on the line that reads Debug.Print "We Are Now in Func1()". To do this, click anywhere in the line of code that says Debug.Print "We Are Now In Func1()". Open the Debug menu and choose Set Next Statement. Notice the contrasting color (yellow), indicating that the next line of code to be executed is now over that statement. Press F8 (step) two times. The code now executes with intTemp set to 100. Observe the Debug window again. Notice how the results have changed.

TRY IT

Using the Calls Window

You have learned how to set breakpoints, step through and over code, use the Debug window, set the next line to be executed, and continue to run until the next breakpoint is reached. When you reach a breakpoint, it often is important to see which functions were called to bring you to this point. This is where the Calls feature can help.

To bring up the Call Stack window, click the Call Stack button on the toolbar or choose View|Call Stack. The window in Figure 16.9 appears. If you want to see the line of code that called a particular function or subroutine, double-click that particular function or click the function and then click Show. Although your execution point is not moved to the calling function or subroutine, you are able to view the code within the procedure. If you want to continue your code execution, press F8. You move back to the procedure through which you were stepping, and the next line of code executes. If you press F5, your code executes until another breakpoint or watch is reached. If you want to return to where you were without executing additional lines of code, choose Debug|Show Next Statement. To test this process, perform the next example.

Figure 16.9.

Viewing the stack with the Call Stack window.

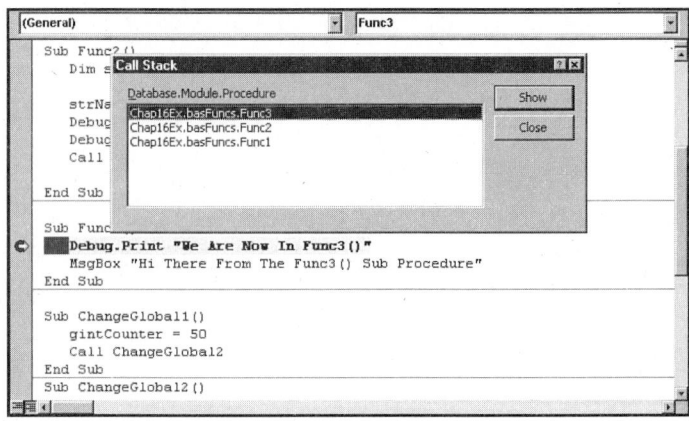

TRY IT   Click the End button to stop your code execution if you are still in Break mode. Remove the breakpoint on the call to Func2. Move to the procedure called Func3 in basFuncs. Set a breakpoint on the line Debug.Print "We Are Now in Func3()". Run the frmDebug form and click the command button. You are placed in Func3 on the line where the breakpoint is set. Bring up the Call Stack window by clicking the Call Stack button on the toolbar. If you want to see the line of code that called Func2 from Func1, double-click Func1. Although your execution point is not moved to Func1, you are able to view the code in the procedure. To return to the next line of code to execute, choose Debug|Show Next Statement. Press F5, and the remainder of your code executes.

Working with the Locals Pane

The Locals pane of the Debug window enables you to see all the variables on the current stack frame and to view and modify their values. To access the Locals pane, open the Debug window and verify that the Locals tab is selected. Three columns appear: Expression, Value, and Type. The Expression column shows you the variables, user-defined types, arrays, and other objects visible in the current procedure. The Value column displays the current value of the variable or expression. The Type column tells you what type of data the variable contains. Variables that contain hierarchical information—arrays, for example—are displayed with an Expand/Collapse button.

The information contained in the Locals pane is dynamic. It is updated automatically as the code executes and as you move from routine to routine. Figure 16.10 illustrates how you can use the Locals pane to view the elements of a collection object. As you can see in the figure, you easily can view the value of each item in the collection. To try this example yourself, step through the NewCollection procedure found in basExamples of Chap16Ex.mdb. Expand the colSports hierarchy and view the value of each item in the collection.

Figure 16.10.
Viewing the Locals pane of the Debug window.

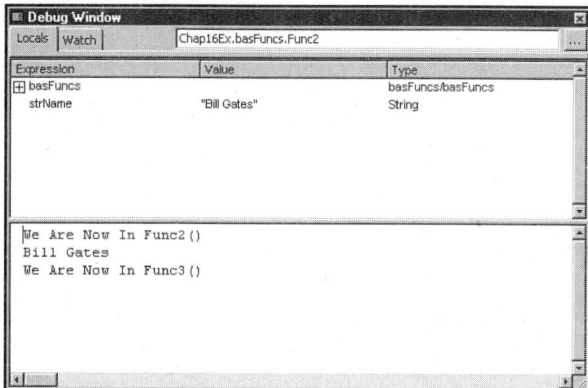

> **NOTE**
>
> You can change the value of a variable in the Locals pane, but you cannot change its name or type.

Working with Watch Expressions

Sometimes it is not enough to use the Debug window to test the value of an expression or variable. You might want to keep a constant eye on the expression's value. A feature introduced in

Access 95 was the capability to set watches. You can set a watch before running a procedure or while code execution is suspended. After a `Watch` expression is added, it appears in the Debug window. As you'll see, you can create several types of watches.

Using Auto Data Tips

The quickest and easiest way to view the value contained in a variable is to use Auto Data Tips, which is an available option for working with modules. This feature is available only when your code is in Break mode. While in Break mode, simply move your mouse over the variable or expression containing the value you want to check. A tip appears with the current value. To set the Auto Data Tips option, choose Tools|Options, click the Module tab, and check the option for Auto Data Tips, which is under the Coding options.

Using Quick Watch

A *quick watch* is the most basic type of watch. To add a quick watch, highlight the name of the variable or expression you want to watch and click the Quick Watch button on the toolbar. The Quick Watch dialog box shown in Figure 16.11 appears. You can click Add to add the expression as a permanent watch or choose Cancel to view the current value without adding it as a watch. If you click Add, the Debug window looks like the one in Figure 16.12. This window is discussed in more detail in the next section.

Figure 16.11.
The Quick Watch dialog box enables you to quickly view the value of a variable or add an expression as a permanent watch.

Adding a `Watch` Expression

As you saw, you can add a `Watch` expression by using a quick watch. Adding a watch this way does not give you full control over the nature of the watch, however. If you need more control over the watch, you must choose Debug|Add Watch. The Add Watch dialog box appears, as shown in Figure 16.13.

Figure 16.12.

The Debug window with a Watch expression.

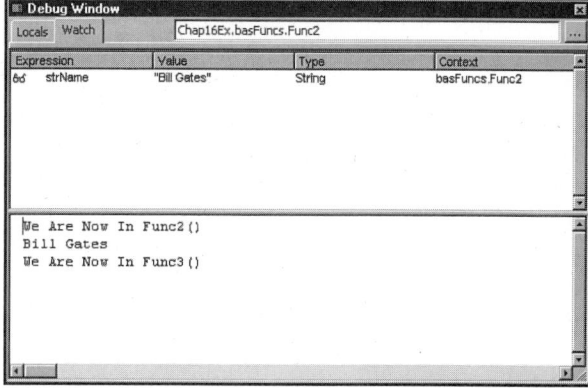

If you add a quick watch or you add a watch by choosing Debug|Add Watch, you easily can customize the specifics of the watch by right-clicking the watch in the Debug window. Then choose Debug|Edit Watch.

Figure 16.13.

The Add Watch dialog box enables you to easily designate all the specifics of a Watch *expression.*

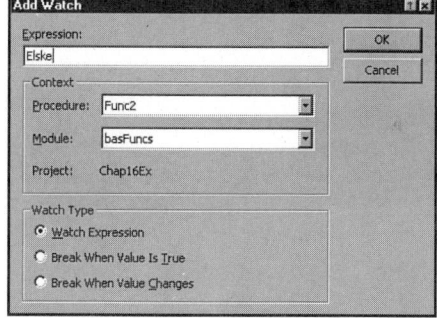

You use the Expression text box to enter a variable, property, function call, or any other valid expression. It is important to select the procedure and module in which you want the expression to be watched. Next, indicate whether you want to simply watch the value of the expression in the Debug window, break when the expression becomes True, or break whenever the value of the expression changes. The two latter options are covered in detail in the following sections.

The next example walks you through the process of adding a watch and viewing the Watch variable as you step through your code. It illustrates how a variable goes in and out of scope and changes value during code execution.

TRY IT

To begin, stop code execution if your code is running, and remove any breakpoints you have set. Click in the `strName` variable in `Func2`. Right-click and choose Add Watch. Click OK to accept the `Func2` procedure as the context for the variable and basFuncs as the module for the variable. Set a breakpoint on the line `strName = "Bill Gates"`. Run the frmDebug form and click the command button. View the Debug window and notice that `strName` has the value of a zero-length string. Step one time and notice that `strName` is equal to `Bill Gates`. Step three more times. Notice that, although you are in the `Func3` routine, `strName` still has the value `Bill Gates`. This is because the variable is still in memory in the context of `basFuncs.Func2`. Step four more times until you are back on the `End Sub` statement of `Func2`. The `strName` variable is still in context. Step one more time. The `strName` variable is finally out of context because `Func2` has been executed.

Editing a `Watch` Expression

After you add a watch, you might want to edit the nature of the watch or remove it entirely. You use the Edit Watch dialog box to edit or delete a `Watch` expression. Follow these steps:

1. Activate the Debug window.

2. Select the expression you want to edit.

3. Choose Debug|Edit Watch or right-click and choose Edit Watch. The dialog box in Figure 16.14 appears.

4. Make changes to the watch or click Delete to remove it.

Figure 16.14.

You can use the Edit Watch dialog box to modify the specifics of a watch after you add it.

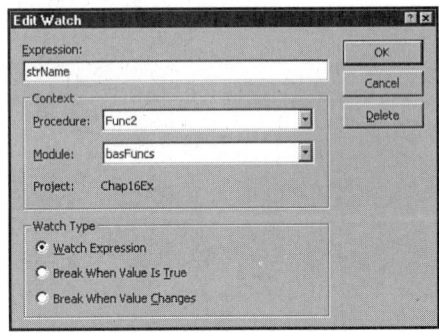

Breaking When an Expression Is True

A powerful aspect of a `Watch` expression is that you can break whenever an expression becomes True. You can break whenever a public variable reaches a specific value, for example. You might want to do this when a public or private variable somehow is being changed and you want to find out where. Consider the following code, located in the basFuncs module of CHAP16EX.MDB:

```
Sub ChangeGlobal1()
    gintCounter = 50
    Call ChangeGlobal2
End Sub

Sub ChangeGlobal2()
    gintCounter = gintCounter + 10
    Call ChangeGlobal3
End Sub

Sub ChangeGlobal3()
    Dim intCounter As Integer
    For intCounter = 1 To 10
        gintCounter = gintCounter + intCounter
    Next intCounter
End Sub
```

You might find that `gintCounter` somehow is reaching a number greater than 100 and you are not sure how. To solve the problem, add the watch shown in Figure 16.15. Notice that the expression you are testing for is `gintCounter > 100`. You have set the breakpoint to break the code whenever the expression becomes True. To test the code, type **ChangeGlobal1** in the Debug window. The code should break in the `ChangeGlobal3` routine, indicating that this routine is the culprit.

Figure 16.15.

Defining a watch that will cause the code execution to break whenever the expression is True.

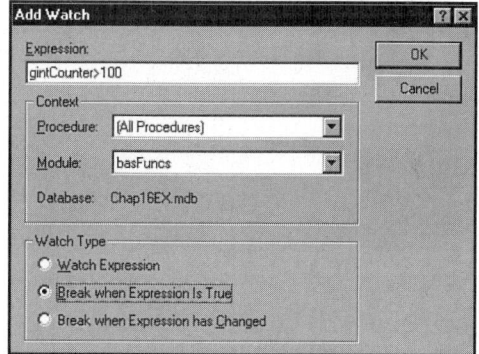

Breaking When an Expression Changes

Instead of breaking when an expression becomes True, you might want to break whenever the value of the expression changes. This is a great way to identify the place where the value of a variable is mysteriously altered. Like Break When Expression Is True, the Break when Expression Has Changed option is great for tracking down problems with public and private variables. Notice the watch being set in Figure 16.16. It is in the context of all procedures in all modules. It is set to break whenever the value of `gintCounter` changes. If you execute the `ChangeGlobal1` routine, you'll find that the code halts execution in `ChangeGlobal1` immediately after the value of `gintCounter` is set to 50. If you press F5 to continue execution, the code halts in `ChangeGlobal2` immediately after `gintCounter` is incremented by 10. In other words, every time the value of `gintCounter` is modified, the code execution breaks.

Figure 16.16.

Creating a watch that will cause code execution to break whenever the value of an expression changes.

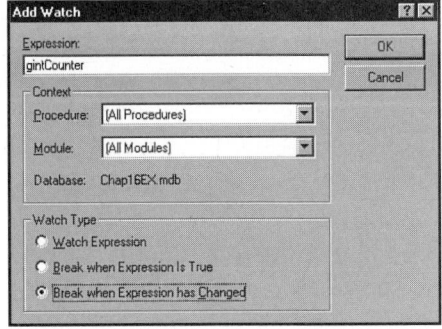

Continuing Execution After a Runtime Error

As you are testing, you often discover runtime errors that are quite easy to fix. When a runtime error occurs, a dialog box similar to the one shown in Figure 16.17 appears.

Figure 16.17.

The Runtime Error dialog box.

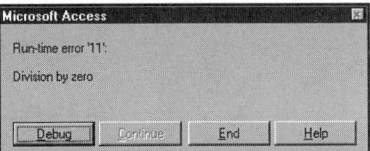

If you click Debug, you are placed in the Code window on the line that generated the error. After rectifying the problem, click the Continue button on the toolbar or choose Run|Go/Continue.

Figure 16.18 shows a divide-by-zero error, for example. After Debug was clicked from the Runtime Error dialog box, the value of int2 was set to 20. Code execution now can continue without error.

Figure 16.18.

Debug mode after a divide-by-zero error.

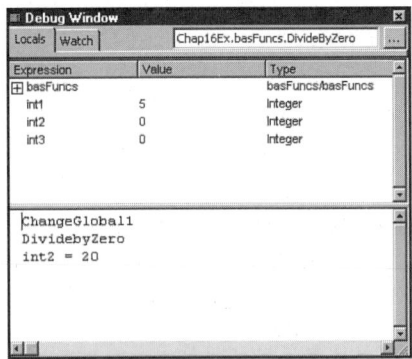

Often, after an error occurs, VBA displays a message giving you the option of resetting your code. If you opt to reset your code, all variables (including publics and statics) lose their values. You also can click Reset on the toolbar. You must decide whether it is better to proceed with your variables already set or to reset the variables and then proceed.

Looking At Gotchas with the Debug Window

Although the Access debugger is excellent, the debugging process itself is wrought with an array of potential problems:

- The debugging process can interrupt code execution, especially when forms are involved. When this occurs, the best bet is to place Debug.Print statements in your code and examine what happens after the code executes.

- Along the lines of the previous problem, it is difficult to debug code where GotFocus and LostFocus events are coded. Moving to the Debug window triggers the LostFocus event. Returning to the form causes the GotFocus event to be triggered. Once again, a great solution is Debug.Print. You also might consider writing information to an error log for perusal after the code executes.

- Code that uses Screen.ActiveForm and Screen.ActiveControl wreaks havoc on the debugging process. When the Debug window is active, there is no active form and no active control. Avoiding these lines in your code wherever possible alleviates this problem.

- Finally, be aware that resetting code can cause problems. If you are modifying environmental settings, you are left with whatever environmental settings your application code changed. If you continue execution after the error without resetting, all sorts of other problems can occur. It is a good idea to code a special utility routine that resets your environment.

Practical Examples: Debugging Real Applications

As you develop the Time and Billing application, use the techniques you learned to help solve any problems you encounter. For now, use the debugger to step through and learn more about the debugging process with one of the routines found in the Time and Billing application.

Open the frmClients form in CHAP16.MDB in Design view. Place a breakpoint on the line of code If IsNull(Me![ClientID]) Then found in the View Project's button Click event. (See Figure 16.19.) Run the form and click the View Projects command button. Step through the code and watch it execute. After a couple of steps, you should get the error shown in Figure 16.20. This error is a great example of the debugger interacting negatively with the environment. In fact, if you continue to step through the code, you will find yourself in an endless loop. The code is attempting to issue a command from the Form menu bar while you are in the Debug window. Remove the breakpoint and add a breakpoint on the DoCmd.OpenForm line.

Run the form again. You should be launched into the Form_Open event of frmProjects. Continue stepping while watching the code execution. Test the value of expressions if you want.

Figure 16.19.

Setting a breakpoint in frmClients.

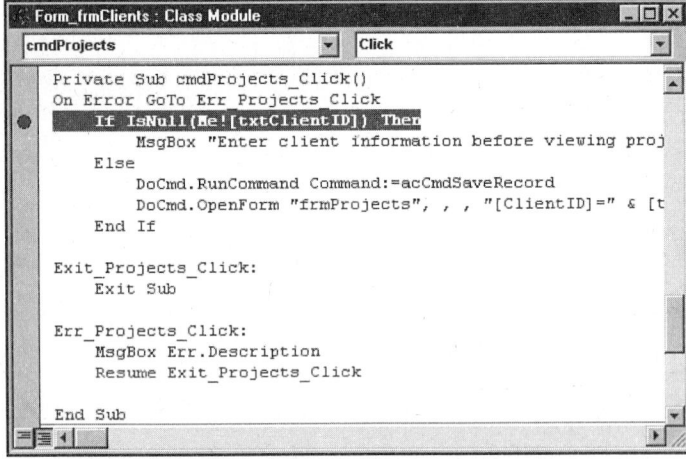

Figure 16.20.

An example of an error while stepping through frmClients.

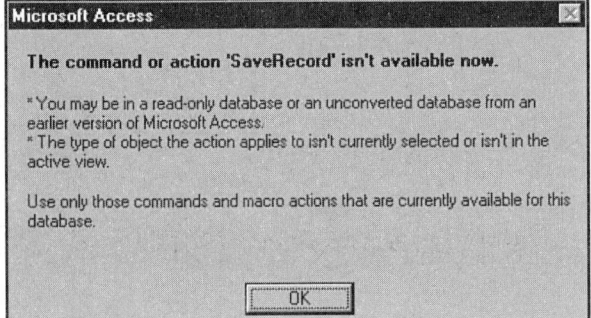

Summary

If programming were a perfect science, there would be no reason to use a debugger. Given the reality of the challenges of programming, a thorough understanding of the use of the debugger is imperative. Fortunately, Access 97 provides an excellent tool to help you with the debugging process.

This chapter began by showing you how you can reduce the chance of bugs in your application in the first place. It then taught you how to use the Debug window to test and change the values of variables and properties. You learned how to use watches and breakpoints, as well as how to view the call stack. All these techniques help make the process of testing and debugging your application a pleasant experience.

17

CHAPTER

Handling Those Dreaded Runtime Errors

- Implementing Error Handling, 516
- Working with Error Events, 517
- Using On Error Statements, 518
- Using Resume Statements, 521
- Clearing an Error, 523
- Examining the Cascading Error Effect, 523
- Using the Err Object, 524
- Raising an Error, 525
- Using the Errors Collection, 526
- Creating a Generic Error Handler, 527
- Preventing Your Own Error Handling from Being Invoked, 537
- Practical Examples: Incorporating Error Handling, 537

Implementing Error Handling

Errors happen, even in the absence of programmer error. You need to protect your programs and your data from the adverse effects of errors by practicing error handling.

Error handling is also known as error trapping. *Error handling* is the process of intercepting Jet's or VBA's response to an error. It enables the developer to determine the severity of an error and to take the appropriate action in response to the error.

Without error handling, the user of your application is forced to exit abruptly from your application code. Consider the example in Listing 17.1.

Listing 17.1. An example of code without error handling.

```
Private Sub cmdCallError_Click()
    Call TestError(txtValue1, txtValue2)
End Sub

Sub TestError(Numerator As Integer, Denominator As Integer)
    Debug.Print Numerator / Denominator
    MsgBox "I am in Test Error"
End Sub
```

The Click event behind the command button calls the routine TestError, passing it the values from two text boxes. TestError accepts those parameters and attempts to divide the first parameter by the second parameter. If the second parameter is equal to 0, a runtime error occurs. Because no error handling is in effect, the program terminates.

Figure 17.1 shows the error message the user receives. As you can see, the choices are Debug, Continue, End, and Help. If users choose Debug, the module window appears and they are placed in Debug mode on the line of code causing the error. Choosing Continue (this is not always available), tells Access to ignore the error and continue with the execution of the program. Clicking End terminates execution of the programming code. If the application is running with the runtime version of Access, it shuts down and users are returned to Windows. With error handling in effect, you can attempt to handle the error in a more appropriate way whenever possible.

Figure 17.1.
Default error handling.

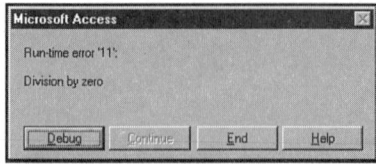

You can add error-handling code to the error event procedure of a form or report. You also can add it to any VBA subroutine, function, or event routine. You easily can modify the code in Listing 17.1 to handle the error gracefully. The code in Listing 17.2 shows a simple error-handling routine.

Listing 17.2. A simple error-handling routine.

```
Sub TestError(Numerator As Integer, Denominator As Integer)
On Error GoTo TestError_Err
    Debug.Print Numerator / Denominator
    MsgBox "I am in Test Error"

    Exit Sub

TestError_Err:
    If Err = 11 Then
        MsgBox "Variable 2 Cannot Be a Zero", , "Custom Error Handler"
    End If
    Exit Sub

End Sub
```

This code is located in the basError module, which is in the CHAP17EX.MDB database on the accompanying CD-ROM.

The routine now invokes error handling. If a divide-by-zero error occurs, a message box alerts the user to the problem, as Figure 17.2 shows.

Figure 17.2.

A custom error handler.

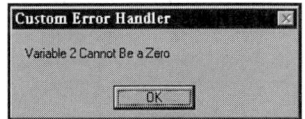

Working with Error Events

Every form and report contains an error event procedure. This event is triggered by any interface or Jet Database Engine error. It is not triggered by a programming error made by the Access developer.

Errors often occur in the interface of a form or report, as well as in the Jet Database Engine. A user might try to enter an order for a customer who doesn't exist, for example. Instead of displaying Access's default error message, you might want to intercept and handle the error in a particular way.

After an error occurs in a form, its error event is triggered. In Listing 17.3, you can see Sub Form_Error. It contains two parameters. The first parameter is the number of the error. The second parameter is the way you want to respond to the error. The error number is an Access-generated number.

This code, which is located in the frmOrders form in the CHAP17EX.MDB database, tests to see whether a referential integrity error has occurred. If it has, a message box asks whether the user wants to add the customer. If the user answers Yes, the customer form is displayed.

517

Listing 17.3. Viewing `Sub Form_Error` from the frmOrders form.

```
Private Sub Form_Error(DataErr As Integer, Response As Integer)
    Dim intAnswer As Integer
    If DataErr = 3201 Then   'Referential Integrity Error
        intAnswer = MsgBox("Customer Does Not Exist... _
                    Would You Like to Add Them Now", vbYesNo)
        If intAnswer = vbYes Then
            DoCmd.OpenForm "frmCustomer", , , , acAdd, acDialog
        End If
    End If
    Response = acDataErrContinue
End Sub
```

> **WARNING**
>
> Be aware that the sample in Listing 17.3 traps only referential integrity errors. It does not handle any other error.

The `Response = acDataErrContinue` line is very important. It instructs Access to continue the code execution without displaying the standard error message. The other option for `Response` is `AcDataErrDisplay`, which tells Access to display the default error message.

> **NOTE**
>
> If you want to get a list of all the errors that can occur in Access, as well as a description of what each error number means, search for `Error Codes` in the Help index. A list appears, containing each error number and a description of each error. You can click on an error description to get a more detailed explanation of the error.

Using `On Error` Statements

`On Error` statements activate error handling. Each routine must contain its own `On Error` statement if you want that routine to do its own error handling. Otherwise, error handling is cascaded up the call stack. If no `On Error` statements are found in the call stack, VBA's own error handling is invoked.

Suppose that `Func1` calls `Func2`, and `Func2` calls `Func3`. Only `Func1` contains error handling. An error occurs in `Func3`. `Func3` passes control up to `Func2`. `Func2` has no error handling, so it passes control up to `Func1`. `Func1` handles the error. Needless to say, the error handler found in `Func1` is not necessarily appropriate to handle the error that occurred in `Func3`.

Using an `On Error` statement, you can cause the application to branch to error-handling code, resume on the line immediately following the error, or attempt to re-execute the problem line of code.

You must decide the most appropriate response to a particular error. Sometimes it is most appropriate for your application to halt in response to an error. At other times, it is best if the routine skips the offending line entirely. By combining the use of `On Error Goto`, `On Error Resume Next`, and `On Error Resume`, you can handle each error appropriately.

Using `On Error Goto`

The statement `On Error Goto <label>` tells VBA that, from this point forward in the subroutine or function, if an error occurs, it should jump to the label specified in the statement. This is the most common form of error handling.

The label specified in the `On Error` statement must be located in the current procedure, and it must be unique within a module. Listing 17.4 shows a simple example of error handling.

Listing 17.4. An example of error handling using the `On Error GoTo` statement.

```
Sub SimpleErrorHandler(iVar1 As Integer, iVar2 As Integer)
    On Error GoTo SimpleErrorHandler_Err

    Dim sngResult As String
    sngResult = iVar1 / iVar2

    Exit Sub

SimpleErrorHandler_Err:
    MsgBox "Oops!"
    Exit Sub

End Sub
```

You can learn some important things from this simple routine. The routine receives two integer values. It then invokes the error handler. When an error occurs, execution continues at the label. Notice that this routine contains two `Exit Sub` statements. If you remove the first `Exit Sub` statement, the code falls through to the label regardless of whether an error occurred. The `Exit Sub` statement at the bottom gracefully exits the procedure, setting the error code back to 0.

Including the Error Number and Description in the Error Handler

The error-handling code in Listing 17.4 did not give a very descriptive message to users. The Description and Number properties of the `Err` object give users more meaningful error messages. The `Err` object is covered in detail later in this chapter in the section "Using the `Err` Object." For now, take a look at the Description and Number properties to see how you can use them to enhance an error-handling routine. To display the error number and description, you must modify the error-handling code to look like this:

```
SimpleErrorHandler_Err:
    MsgBox "Error #" & Err.Number & ": " & Err.Description
    Exit Sub
```

This time, instead of hard-coding the error message, you display the error number and VBA's internal error string. Figure 17.3 shows the resulting error message. The `SimpleErrorHandler` routine and all the following examples are located in the basError module of the CHAP17EX.MDB database.

Figure 17.3.

An error message with an error number and error string.

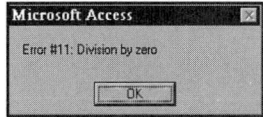

Using On Error Resume Next

`On Error Resume Next` continues program execution on the line immediately following the error. This construct generally is used when it is acceptable to ignore an error and continue code execution. Listing 17.5 shows an example of such a situation.

Listing 17.5. Ignoring an error and continuing execution.

```
Sub TestResumeNext()
    On Error Resume Next
    Kill "AnyFile"
    MsgBox "We Didn't Die, But the Error Was: " & Err.Description
End Sub
```

You use the `Kill` statement to delete a file from disk. If the specified file is not found, an error results. You delete the file only if it exists, so you are not concerned about an error. `On Error Resume Next` is very appropriate in this situation, because no harm is done by resuming execution after the offending line of code.

Using On Error Goto 0

You use `On Error Goto 0` for two purposes:

- When you want Access to return to its default error handler
- To have Access return to the error handler of a routine above the current routine

Generally, you don't want Access to return to its default error handler. You might do this only if you are unable to handle the error or if you are in the testing phase and not yet ready to implement your own error handler.

The reason why you want Access to return the error to a higher level routine is much clearer. You do this if you want to *centralize* the error handling, meaning that one routine might call several others. Instead of placing error-handling code in each routine that is called, you can place the error handling in the calling routine.

Using Resume Statements

While you are in your error-handling code, you can use the Resume, Resume Next, and Resume *<LineLabel>* statements to specify how you want VBA to respond to the error. Resume attempts to re-execute the offending line of code, Resume Next resumes execution after the offending line of code, and Resume *<LineLabel>* continues execution at a specified line label. The following sections cover these statements in detail.

The Resume Statement

The Resume statement resumes code execution on the line of code that caused the error. You must use this statement with extreme care, because it can throw the code into an unrecoverable endless loop. Listing 17.6 shows an example of an inappropriate use of the Resume statement.

Listing 17.6. Using Resume inappropriately.

```
Function BadResume(sFileName As String)
    On Error GoTo BadResume_Err
    Dim strFile As String
    strFile = Dir(sFileName)
    If strFile = "" Then
      BadResume = False
    Else
      BadResume = True
    End If
    Exit Function

BadResume_Err:
    MsgBox Error
    Resume
End Function
```

This function is passed a file name. The Dir function searches for the file name and returns True or False, depending on whether the specified file name is found. The problem occurs when the drive requested is not available or does not exist. This code throws the computer into an endless loop. To remedy the problem, you should modify your code to look like the code in Listing 17.7.

Listing 17.7. Using Resume conditionally based on user feedback.

```
Function GoodResume(sFileName As String)
    On Error GoTo GoodResume_Err
    Dim strFile As String
    strFile = Dir(sFileName)
    If strFile = "" Then
      GoodResume = False
    Else
      GoodResume = True
```

continues

Listing 17.7. continued

```
    End If
    Exit Function

GoodResume_Err:
    Dim intAnswer As Integer
    intAnswer = MsgBox(Error & ", Would You Like to Try Again?", vbYesNo)
    If intAnswer = vbYes Then
        Resume
    Else
        Exit Function
    End If
End Function
```

In this example, the error handler enables the user to decide whether to try again. The Resume occurs only if the user's response is affirmative.

The Resume Next Statement

Just as you can invoke error handling using an On Error Resume Next statement, you can place a Resume Next statement in your error handler, as Listing 17.8 shows.

Listing 17.8. Placing a Resume Next statement in your error handler.

```
Sub TestResumeNextInError()
    On Error GoTo TestResumeNextInError_Err
    Kill "AnyFile"
    MsgBox "We Didn't Die!"
    Exit Sub

TestResumeNextInError_Err:
    Resume Next
End Sub
```

In this example, the code is instructed to go to the label called TestResumeNextInError_Err when an error occurs. The TestResumeNextInError_Err label issues a Resume Next statement. This clears the error and causes execution to continue on the line after the line on which the error occurred.

The Resume <LineLabel> Statement

The Resume <LineLabel> statement enables you to specify a line of code where you want code execution to continue after an error occurs. This is a great way to eliminate the two Exit Sub or Exit Function statements required by the error-handling routines you have looked at so far. Listing 17.9 shows an example.

Listing 17.9. Specifying where code execution should continue after an error occurs.

```
Sub TestResumeLineLabel(iVar1 As Integer, iVar2 As Integer)
    On Error GoTo TestResumeLineLabel_Err

    Dim sngResult As String
    sngResult = iVar1 / iVar2

TestResumeLineLabel_Exit:
    Exit Sub

TestResumeLineLabel_Err:
    MsgBox "Error #" & Err.Number & ": " & Err.Description
    Resume TestResumeLineLabel_Exit

End Sub
```

Notice that this routine contains only one Exit Sub statement. If no error occurs, Access drops through the TestResumeLineLabel_Exit label to the Exit Sub statement. If an error *does* occur, the code in the TestResumeLineLabel_Err label executes. Notice that the last line of the label resumes execution at the TestResumeLineLabel_Exit label.

This method of resolving an error is useful because any code required to execute as the routine is exited can be written in one place. Object variables might need to be set equal to Nothing as the routine is exited, for example. You can place these lines of code in the exit routine.

Clearing an Error

When an error occurs, the Err object remains set with the error information until one of the following clears the error:

- Resume, Resume Next, or Resume *<LineLabel>*
- Exit Sub, Exit Function, or Exit Property
- Any Goto statement
- Explicitly using the Clear method on the Err object

Until the error is cleared somehow, all the information remains set in the Err object. After the error is cleared, no information is found in the Err object.

Examining the Cascading Error Effect

As mentioned earlier in this chapter, if Access does not find any error handling in a particular subroutine or function, it looks up the call stack for a previous error handler. Listing 17.10 shows an example of this process.

Listing 17.10. Looking up the call stack for a previous error handler.

```
Sub Func1()
    On Error GoTo Func1_Err
    Debug.Print "I am in Function 1"
    Call Func2
    Debug.Print "I am back in Function 1"
    Exit Sub

Func1_Err:
    MsgBox "Error in Func1"
    Resume Next
End Sub

Sub Func2()
    Debug.Print "I am in Func 2"
    Call Func3
    Debug.Print "I am still in Func2"
End Sub

Sub Func3()
    Dim sngAnswer As Single
    Debug.Print "I am in Func 3"
    sngAnswer = 5 / 0
    Debug.Print "I am still in Func3"
End Sub
```

In this situation, the error occurs in `Func3`. Because `Func3` does not have its own error handling, it refers back to `Func2`. `Func2` does not have any error handling either, so `Func2` relinquishes control to `Func1`. VBA executes the error code in `Func1`. The real problem occurs because of the `Resume Next` statement. The application continues executing within `Func1` on the `Debug.Print` `"I am back in Function 1"` statement. This type of error handling is dangerous and confusing. It therefore is best to develop a generic error-handling routine that is accessed throughout your application.

Using the Err Object

The `Err` object contains information about the most recent error that occurred. As with all Access objects, it has its own built-in properties and methods. Table 17.1 lists the properties of the `Err` object.

Table 17.1. Properties of the `Err` object.

Property	Description
Description	Description of the error that occurred
HelpContext	Context ID for the Help file
HelpFile	Path and file name of the Help file
LastDLLError	Last error that occurred in a 32-bit DLL

Property	Description
Number	Number of the error that was set
Source	System in which the error occurred (which is extremely useful when you are using OLE automation to control another application, such as Excel)

The Err object has only two methods: Clear and Raise. The Clear method enables you to clear an error condition explicitly. It is used primarily when you write code that uses the On Error Resume Next statement. This statement does not clear the error condition. Remember that there is no reason to issue the Clear method explicitly with any type of Resume, Exit Sub, Exit Function, Exit Property, or On Error Goto statement. The Clear method is implicitly issued when these constructs are used. The Raise method of the Err object is covered in the next section.

Raising an Error

You use the Raise method of the error object in these situations:

- When you want to generate an error on purpose (for example, in testing)
- When you want to generate a user-defined error
- When no code in the error routine handles the current error and you want to allow other parts of the call stack to attempt to handle the error
- When you want to nest an error handler

Using the Raise method to generate an error on purpose and create a user-defined error is covered in the following sections.

Generating an Error on Purpose

Many times, you want to generate an error when testing so that you can test out your own error handling. Instead of figuring out how to "cause" the error condition, you can use the Raise method of the Err object to accomplish this task, as Listing 17.11 shows.

Listing 17.11. Raising an error.

```
Sub TestRaiseError()
    On Error GoTo TestRaiseError_Err

    Dim sngResult As String
    Err.Raise 11

    Exit Sub

TestRaiseError_Err:
    MsgBox "Error #" & Err.Number & ": " & Err.Description
    Exit Sub

End Sub
```

This code invokes an error 11 (divide by 0). By generating the error, you can test the effectiveness of your error-handling routine.

Creating User-Defined Errors

Another important use of the Raise method of the Err object is the generation of a custom error condition. This is useful when you want to have something that does not generate an Access error generate a user-defined error that you send through the normal error-handling process. Because the Raise method enables you to set *all* the properties of the Err object, you can create a user-defined error complete with a number, description, source, and so on, as shown in Listing 17.12.

Listing 17.12. Creating a user-defined error.

```
Sub TestCustomError()
   On Error GoTo TestCustomError_Err
   Dim strName As String
   strName = InputBox("Please Enter Your Name")
   If Len(strName) < 5 Then
      Err.Raise Number:=11111, _
             Description:="Length of Name is Too Short"
   Else
      MsgBox "You Entered " & strName
   End If
   Exit Sub

TestCustomError_Err:
      MsgBox "Error # " & Err.Number & _
             " - " & Err.Description
      Exit Sub
End Sub
```

Although it is very simple, this example illustrates an important use of generating user-defined errors. The code tests to see whether the value entered has less than five characters. If it does, a user-defined error (number 11111) is generated. The routine drops into the normal error-handling routine. The section "Creating a Generic Error Handler," later in this chapter, explores how to put together a generic error handler. By passing user-defined errors through your generic error handler, all errors—user-defined or not—are handled in the same way.

Using the Errors Collection

The Errors collection is part of Access's Jet Engine. It stores the most recent *set* of errors that have occurred. This is important when dealing with DAO and ODBC, when one operation can result in multiple errors. If you are concerned with each error that was generated by one operation, you need to look at the Errors collection. The Errors collection has the same properties as the Err object. If you want to view the errors stored in the Errors collection, you must loop through it, viewing the properties of each Err object. Listing 17.13 shows the code you can use to accomplish this.

Listing 17.13. Viewing the errors stored in the Errors collection.

```
Sub TestErrorsCollection()
    On Error GoTo TestErrorsCollection_Err
    Dim db As Database
    Set db = CurrentDb
    db.Execute ("qryNonExistent")
    Exit Sub

TestErrorsCollection_Err:
    Dim ErrorDescrip As Error
    For Each ErrorDescrip In Errors
        Debug.Print ErrorDescrip.Description
    Next ErrorDescrip
    Exit Sub
End Sub
```

This routine loops through each `Err` object in the Errors collection, printing the description of each error contained in the collection.

Creating a Generic Error Handler

A generic error handler is an error handler that can be called from anywhere in your application. It is capable of responding to any type of error.

A generic error handler prevents you from having to write specific error handling in each of your subroutines and functions. This enables you to invoke error handling throughout your application in the most efficient manner possible.

You can take many approaches to create a generic error handler. A generic error handler should give users information about the error, enable users to print this information, and log the information to a file. A generic error handler should be able to be called from every procedure within your application.

The `On Error` routine (in this case, the label AnySub_Err) of every procedure that performs error handling should look like the error-handling routine contained in the subroutine in Listing 17.14.

Listing 17.14. A generic error handler for all your functions and subroutines.

```
Sub AnySub()
    Dim strSubName As String
    strSubName = "AnySub"
    On Error GoTo AnySub_Err

    MsgBox "This is the rest of your code...."
    Err.Raise 11
    MsgBox "We are Past the Error!!"

    Exit Sub
```

continues

Listing 17.14. continued

```
AnySub_Err:
    Dim intAction As Integer
    intAction = ErrorHandler(intErrorNum:=Err.Number, _
                    strErrorDescription:=Err.Description, _
                    strModuleName:=mstrModuleName, _
                    strRoutineName:=strSubName)

    Select Case intAction
        Case ERR_CONTINUE
            Resume Next
        Case ERR_RETRY
            Resume
        Case ERR_EXIT
            Exit Sub
        Case ERR_QUIT
            Quit
    End Select
End Sub
```

This error-handling routine in AnySub creates an Integer variable that holds the return value from the error system. The intAction variable holds an appropriate response to the error that occurred. The error routine calls the generic error-handling function ErrorHandler, passing it the error number (Err.Number), a description of the error (Err.Description), the name of the module containing the error, and the name of the subroutine or function containing the error. The name of the module is stored in a Private constant called mstrModuleName. The Private constant is declared in the General section of the module and needs to be created for every module you make. The name of the subroutine or function is stored in a local variable called strSubName. With this approach, you create a local string and assign it the name of the sub at the beginning of each procedure. This requires upkeep, because procedure names can change, and you need to remember to change your string. When the code returns from the ErrorHandler function, a return value is placed in the intAction variable. This return value is used to determine the fate of the routine.

Now that you have seen how to implement error handling in your procedures, take a look at the function that is called when an error occurs, as shown in Listing 17.15.

Listing 17.15. A type structure declaration to be used for generic error handling.

```
Type typErrors
    intErrorNum As Integer
    strMessage As String
    strModule As String
    strRoutine As String
    strUserName As String
    datDateTime As Variant
End Type

Public ptypError As typErrors
```

```
Public Const ERR_CONTINUE = 0   'Resume Next
Public Const ERR_RETRY = 1 'Resume
Public Const ERR_QUIT = 2   'End
Public Const ERR_EXIT = 3   'Exit Sub or Func
```

This code is placed in the General section of basHandleErrors. The type structure declared holds all the pertinent information about the error. The Public variable ptypError holds all the information from the type structure. The constants are used to help determine the fate of the application after an error occurs. Listing 17.16 shows the ErrorHandler function.

Listing 17.16. Using the ErrorHandler function.

```
Function ErrorHandler(intErrorNum As Integer, _
strErrorDescription As String, _
                strModuleName As String, _
                strRoutineName As String) As Integer
    ptypError.intErrorNum = intErrorNum
    ptypError.strMessage = strErrorDescription
    ptypError.strModule = strModuleName
    ptypError.strRoutine = strRoutineName
    ptypError.strUserName = CurrentUser()
    ptypError.datDateTime = Now

    Call LogError

    Dim db As Database
    Dim snp As Snapshot
    Set db = CurrentDb()
    Set snp = db.OpenRecordset("Select Response from tblErrors Where _
    ErrorNum = " & intErrorNum)
    If snp.EOF Then
        DoCmd.OpenForm "frmError", WindowMode:=acDialog, _
            OpenArgs:=ErrorHandler
        ErrorHandler = ERR_QUIT
    Else
        Select Case snp.Response
            Case ERR_QUIT
                DoCmd.OpenForm "frmError", WindowMode:=acDialog, _
                    OpenArgs:="Critical Error:  Application will Terminate"
                ErrorHandler = ERR_QUIT
            Case ERR_RETRY
                ErrorHandler = ERR_RETRY
            Case ERR_EXIT
                DoCmd.OpenForm "frmError", WindowMode:=acDialog, _
                    OpenArgs:="Severe Error:  Processing Did Not Complete"
                ErrorHandler = ERR_EXIT
            Case ERR_CONTINUE
                ErrorHandler = ERR_CONTINUE
        End Select
    End If

End Function
```

The ErrorHandler function receives the error number, error description, module name, and subroutine or function name as parameters. It then fills in the ptypError type structure with the information that it was passed, as well as the current user and date. Next, it calls a routine that logs the error into an Access table. The routine looks up the severity of the error code in an Access table called tblErrors to decide the most appropriate way to handle the error. If the error code is not found in the error table, an error form is displayed and a return value is sent to the calling function, indicating that application execution is to be terminated. If the error code is found in the tblErrors table and determined to be critical or severe, an error form appears before control is returned to the calling routine. In any case, a severity code for the error is returned to the calling function. The following section discusses the details involved in each step of the process.

Logging the Error

The LogError routine is responsible for logging all the error information into an Access table. Because users often decide not to print the error form or provide you with inaccurate information about what was happening when the error occurred (or neglect to tell you about the error), it is important that you log each error so that you can review the error log at any time. Errors can be logged to a text file or a data table. This section shows you both methods of logging your error. Start with logging your errors to a table. Listing 17.17 shows the LogError routine.

Listing 17.17. Using the LogError routine.

```
Sub LogError()
    Dim sSQL As String
    DoCmd.SetWarnings False
    sSQL = "INSERT INTO tblErrorLog (ErrorDate, ErrorTime, UserName, _
    ErrorNum, ErrorString, Module, Routine) "
    sSQL = sSQL & "VALUES ( #" & ptypError.datDateTime & "#, #" _
                          & ptypError.datDateTime & "#, '" _
                          & ptypError.strUserName & "', " _
                          & ptypError.intErrorNum & ", '" _
                          & ptypError.strMessage & "', '" _
                          & ptypError.strModule & "', '" _
                          & ptypError.strRoutine & "')"
    DoCmd.RunSQL sSQL
    DoCmd.SetWarnings True
End Sub
```

This routine uses an SQL statement to add a record to your error table. The record contains all the information from the structure called ptypError. The information is logged to a table called tblErrorLog. Figure 17.4 shows the structure of this table.

Figure 17.4.
The tblErrorLog table.

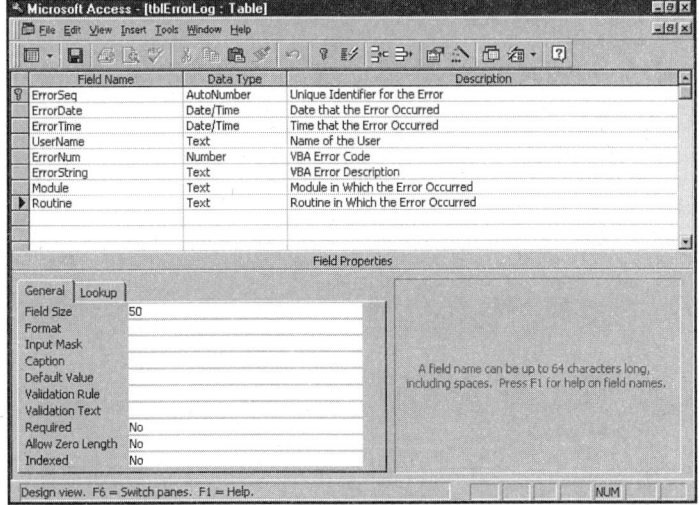

The alternative is to write the information to a textual error log file, as shown in Listing 17.18.

Listing 17.18. Writing information to a textual error log file.

```
Sub LogErrorText()
    Dim intFile As Integer
    intFile = FreeFile
    Open CurDir & "\ErrorLog.Txt" For Append Shared As intFile
    Write #intFile, "LogErrorDemo", Now, Err, Error, CurrentUser()
    Close intFile
End Sub
```

This code uses the low-level file functions `Open` and `Write` to open and write to an ASCII text file. All the pertinent information about the error is written to this text file. The routine then uses the `Close` command to close the text file. The potential advantage of this routine is that, if the problem is with the database (for example, the network is down), the error logging process still succeeds.

Determining the Appropriate Response to an Error

After the error is logged, you are ready to determine the best way to respond to the error. By making your error system data-driven, you can handle each error a little differently. Figure 17.5 shows the structure of the tblErrors table. This table should contain a list of all the error numbers you want to trap. It contains three fields: ErrorNum, ErrorDescription, and Response. When an error occurs, the `ErrorHandler` function searches for a record with a value in the ErrorNum field that matches the number of the error that occurred. The `ErrorHandler` function uses the code in Listing 17.19 to locate the error code in the tblErrors table.

Figure 17.5.

The structure of tblErrors.

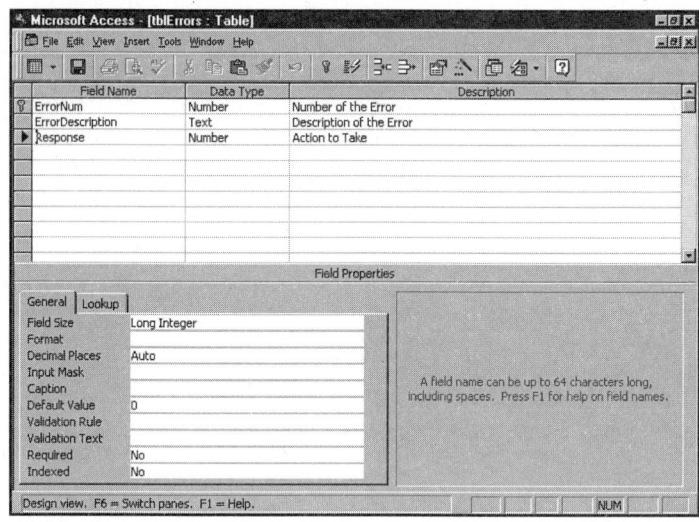

Listing 17.19. Using the `ErrorHandler` function.

```
Dim db As Database
    Dim snp As Recordset
    Set db = CurrentDb()
    Set snp = db.OpenRecordset("Select Response from tblErrors Where _
    ErrorNum = " & intErrorNum, dbOpenSnapshot)
    If snp.EOF Then
        DoCmd.OpenForm "frmError", WindowMode:=acDialog, _
            OpenArgs:="ErrorHandler"
        ErrorHandler = ERR_QUIT
    Else
        Select Case snp!Response
            Case ERR_QUIT
                DoCmd.OpenForm "frmError", WindowMode:=acDialog, _
                    OpenArgs:="Critical Error:  Application will Terminate"
                ErrorHandler = ERR_QUIT
            Case ERR_RETRY
                ErrorHandler = ERR_RETRY
            Case ERR_EXIT
                DoCmd.OpenForm "frmError", WindowMode:=acDialog, _
                    OpenArgs:="Severe Error:  Processing Did Not Complete"
                ErrorHandler = ERR_EXIT
            Case ERR_CONTINUE
                ErrorHandler = ERR_CONTINUE
        End Select
    End If
```

This part of the `ErrorHandler` function creates both a `Database` and a `Recordset` object variable. It opens a snapshot type of recordset using a `Select` statement. The `Select` statement searches a table called tblErrors. If a match is found, the Response column is used to determine the response to the error. Notice in Listing 17.19 that, if the error number is not found in tblErrors, default error handling occurs, which means that the code handles all other errors as a group. (This is my default error handling, not Access's.) If the error number is found, the

Response field is evaluated and the appropriate action is taken (via the case statement). If it is not found, the frmError form is opened and the ERR_QUIT constant value is returned from the ErrorHandler function. By using this method, you need to add to the table only specific errors that you want to trap.

If no records are found in tblErrors that match the SQL statement, the frmError form is opened, and the return value for the function is set equal to the constant value ERR_QUIT. If the error number is found in tblErrors, the Response field from the snapshot is evaluated. If the Response field contains the constant value ERR_QUIT or ERR_EXIT, the frmError form appears before the constant value is returned to the offending function or subroutine. If the Response field contains the constant value for ERR_RETRY or ERR_CONTINUE, the constant value is returned without displaying the frmError form.

> ### NOTE
>
> The tblErrors table is included in CHAP17EX.MDB on the sample code CD-ROM. To take full advantage of this table, you must add all errors that you want to trap for along with the action(s) that you want the error handler to take when that error occurs.

The return value from the ErrorHandler function is used as shown in Listing 17.20.

Listing 17.20. Using the return value from the ErrorHandler function.

```
Sub AnySub()
    Dim strSubName As String
    strSubName = "AnySub"
    On Error GoTo AnySub_Err

    MsgBox "This is the rest of your code...."
    Err.Raise 11
    MsgBox "We are Past the Error!!"

    Exit Sub

AnySub_Err:
    Dim intAction As Integer
    intAction = ErrorHandler(intErrorNum:=Err.Number, _
                strErrorDescription:=Err.Description, _
                strModuleName:=mstrModuleName, _
                strRoutineName:=strSubName)

    Select Case intAction
        Case ERR_CONTINUE
            Resume Next
        Case ERR_RETRY
            Resume
        Case ERR_EXIT
            Exit Sub
        Case ERR_QUIT
            Quit
    End Select
End Sub
```

In this example, the AnySub routine generates an error 11 (divide by 0). Because tblErrors contains the number 0 in the Response column and the ERR_CONTINUE constant is equal to 3, the error form is displayed and the AnySub routine is exited with an Exit Sub statement.

> **NOTE**
>
> To test what happens when the error code is not found in the tblErrors table, run the SubWithUnknownError routine found in basError. To test what happens when the ERR_CONTINUE code is returned, execute the SubWithContinue routine.

Creating an Error Form

The code in the error form's Load event calls two subroutines: GetSystemInfo and GetErrorInfo, as shown here:

```
Private Sub Form_Load()
    Call GetSysInfo(Me)
    Call GetErrorInfo(Me)
    Me!lblAction.Caption = Me.OpenArgs
End Sub
```

The first subroutine is called GetSystemInfo. It performs several Windows API calls to fill in the system information on your form. The code is shown in Listing 17.21, and it is discussed in Chapter 31, "Using External Functions: The Windows API."

Listing 17.21. Getting system information through code.

```
Sub GetSysInfo (frmAny As Form)
'Get Free Memory
    Dim MS As MEMORYSTATUS
    MS.dwLength = Len(MS)
    GlobalMemoryStatus MS

    frmAny!lblMemoryTotal.Caption = Format(MS.dwTotalPhys, "Standard")
    frmAny!lblMemoryAvail.Caption = Format(MS.dwAvailPhys, "Standard")

    'Get Version Information
    Dim OSInfo As OSVERSIONINFO
    OSInfo.dwOSVersionInfoSize = Len(OSInfo)
    If GetVersionEx(OSInfo) Then
        frmAny!lblOSVersion.Caption = OSInfo.dwMajorVersion & "." _
            & OSInfo.dwMinorVersion
        frmAny!lblBuild.Caption = OSInfo.dwBuildNumber And &HFFFF&
        If OSInfo.dwPlatformId = 0 Then
            frmAny!lblPlatform.Caption = "Windows 95"
        Else
            frmAny!lblPlatform.Caption = "Windows NT"
        End If
    End If
```

```
    'Get System Information
    Dim SI As SYSTEM_INFO
     GetSystemInfo SI
    frmAny!lblProcessor.Caption = SI.dwProcessorType
End Sub
```

These API calls require the Declare statements and constants shown in Listing 17.22. They are placed in a module called basAPI.

Listing 17.22. Declaring Windows API calls.

```
Option Compare Database
Option Explicit

Private Declare Sub GlobalMemoryStatus Lib "Kernel32" (lpBuffer As MEMORYSTATUS)

Private Type MEMORYSTATUS
    dwLength As Long
    dwMemoryLoad As Long
    dwTotalPhys As Long
    dwAvailPhys As Long
    dwTotalPageFile As Long
    dwAvailPageFile As Long
    dwTotalVirtual As Long
    dwAvailVirtual As Long
End Type

Private Declare Function GetVersionEx Lib "Kernel32" Alias "GetVersionExA" _
     (lpOSInfo As OSVERSIONINFO) As Boolean

Type OSVERSIONINFO
    dwOSVersionInfoSize As Long
    dwMajorVersion As Long
    dwMinorVersion As Long
    dwBuildNumber As Long
    dwPlatformId As Long
    strReserved As String * 128
End Type

Private Declare Sub GetSystemInfo Lib "Kernel32" (lpSystemInfo As SYSTEM_INFO)

Private Type SYSTEM_INFO
    dwOemID As Long
    dwPageSize As Long
    lpMinimumApplicationAddress As Long
    lpMaximumApplicationAddress As Long
    dwActiveProcessorMask As Long
    dwNumberOrfProcessors As Long
    dwProcessorType As Long
    dwAllocationGranularity As Long
    dwReserved As Long
End Type
```

The second subroutine, `GetErrorInfo`, fills in the labels on the error form with all the information from your structure, as shown in Listing 17.23.

Listing 17.23. Using the `GetErrorInfo` subroutine.

```
Sub GetErrorInfo(frmAny As Form)
    frmAny!lblErrorNumber.Caption = ptypError.intErrorNum
    frmAny!lblErrorString.Caption = ptypError.strMessage
    frmAny!lblUserName.Caption = ptypError.strUserName
    frmAny!lblDateTime.Caption = Format(ptypError.datDateTime, "c")
    frmAny!lblModuleName.Caption = ptypError.strModule
    frmAny!lblRoutineName.Caption = ptypError.strRoutine
End Sub
```

Finally, the disposition of the error, sent as an `OpenArg` from the `ErrorHandler` function, is displayed in a label on the form. Figure 17.6 shows the error form.

Figure 17.6.

The frmErrors form created by the Form Load *routine.*

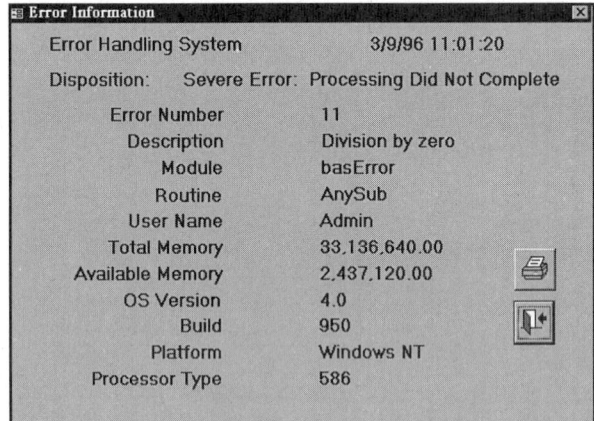

Printing the Error Form

Users often are not very accurate in describing an error and its corresponding error message. It therefore is important to give them the capability to print their error message. The code in Listing 17.24 prints your error form.

Listing 17.24. Printing your error form.

```
Sub cmdPrint_Click()
On Error GoTo Err_cmdPrint_Click


    DoCmd.PrintOut
```

```
Exit_cmdPrint_Click:
    Exit Sub

Err_cmdPrint_Click:
    MsgBox Err.Description
    Resume Exit_cmdPrint_Click

End Sub
```

Preventing Your Own Error Handling from Being Invoked

When you are testing your application, you do not want your own error handling to be triggered. Instead, you want VBA's error handling to be activated. The trick is in the Options dialog box. Choose Tools | Options and click the Advanced tab. Enable the option Break on All Errors located in the Error Trapping section. As long as this option is set, your error handling is ignored and Access's default error handling is invoked. Using this setting, you can turn error handling on and off from one central location.

Practical Examples: Incorporating Error Handling

Error-handling code should be added throughout the Time and Billing application. The following example shows you how to incorporate the generic error handler into the Time and Billing application.

The Time and Billing application contains a routine called GetCompanyInfo. This routine reads all the company information from the tblCompanyInfo table. The information is read from the type structure, as needed, while the application is running. This routine, like any routine, has the potential for error. The original routine has been modified to incorporate the generic error handler, as shown in Listing 17.25.

Listing 17.25. Incorporating the generic error handler into your code.

```
Sub GetCompanyInfo()
    On Error GoTo GetCompanyInfo_Err
    Dim strSubName As String
    Dim db As DATABASE
    Dim rs As Recordset
    strSubName = "GetCompanyInfo"
    Set db = CurrentDb
    Set rs = db.OpenRecordset("tblCompanyInfo", dbOpenSnapshot)
    typCompanyInfo.SetUpID = rs!SetUpID
    typCompanyInfo.CompanyName = rs!CompanyName
    typCompanyInfo.Address = rs!Address
    typCompanyInfo.City = rs!City
```

continues

Listing 17.25. continued

```
    typCompanyInfo.StateProvince = rs!StateProvince
    typCompanyInfo.PostalCode = rs!PostalCode
    typCompanyInfo.Country = rs!Country
    typCompanyInfo.PhoneNumber = rs!PhoneNumber
    typCompanyInfo.FaxNumber = rs!PhoneNumber
    rs.Close
    db.Close
    Exit Sub

GetCompanyInfo_Err:
    Dim intAction As Integer
    intAction = ErrorHandler(intErrorNum:=Err.Number, _
                strErrorDescription:=Err.Description, _
                strModuleName:=mstrModuleName, _
                strRoutineName:=strSubName)

    Select Case intAction
        Case ERR_CONTINUE
            Resume Next
        Case ERR_RETRY
            Resume
        Case ERR_EXIT
            Exit Sub
        Case ERR_QUIT
            Quit
    End Select

End Sub
```

Notice the On Error Goto statement at the beginning of the routine and that the local variable strSubName has been declared and set equal to GetCompanyInfo. The error handler GetCompanyInfo_Err calls the ErrorHandler function and then evaluates its return value.

Summary

In this chapter, you learned the alternatives for handling errors in your Access applications. Regardless of the amount of testing done on an application, errors will occur. It is important that you trap properly for those errors.

This chapter covered how you can use the Error event to trap for application and Jet Engine errors in forms and reports. You also learned how to use the On Error statement. Finally, you learned how to build a generic error system.

PART

III

Preparing Your Applications for a Multiuser Environment

18

Developing for a Multiuser Environment

- Designing Your Application with Multiuser Issues in Mind, 542
- Understanding Access's Locking Mechanisms, 546
- Locking and Refreshing Strategies, 547
- Form Locking Strategies, 551
- Recordset Locking, 552
- Effectively Handling Locking Conflicts, 555
- Testing a Record for Locking Status, 562
- Using Code to Refresh or Requery, 563
- Understanding the .LDB File, 563
- Creating Custom Counters, 564
- Using Unbound Forms, 564
- Using Replication to Improve Performance, 565
- Practical Examples: Making an Application Multiuser Ready, 565

Designing Your Application with Multiuser Issues in Mind

When you develop applications that will be accessed over the network by multiple users, you must make sure they effectively handle sharing data and other application objects. Many options are available for developers when they design multiuser applications, and this chapter covers the pros and cons of these options.

Multiuser issues revolve around locking data; they include deciding where to store database objects, when to lock data, and how much data to lock. In a multiuser environment, having several users simultaneously trying to modify the same data can cause conflicts. As a developer, you need to handle these conflicts. Otherwise, your users will experience unexplainable errors.

Multiuser Design Strategies

There are many methods for handling concurrent access to data and other application objects by multiple users; each one offers both solutions and limitations. It's important to select the best solution for your particular environment.

Strategies for Installing Access

There are two strategies for installing Access:

- Running Access from a file server
- Running a separate copy of Access on each workstation

Each of these strategies has associated pros and cons. The advantages of running Access from a file server are as follows:

- Allows for central administration of the Access software.
- Potentially reduces the licensing requirements. This is true because when Access is installed on a file server, the licensing requirements deal with concurrent users. When Access is installed locally, each user must have her own license, even if she rarely uses any Access applications. If all users won't be working with Access applications at the same time, it might be more cost-effective to buy a LAN license and install Access on the file server.
- Reduces hard disk requirements. The Access software takes up between 14M and 42M of hard disk space, depending on the type of installation. Although this can be reduced by using the Access runtime engine, local hard-disk space can definitely be a problem. Installing Access on the file server at least partially eliminates this problem. It can totally eliminate the problem if dynamic link libraries are also installed on the file server.

- Allows Access applications to be installed on diskless workstations.

Although the advantages of installing Access on a file server might seem compelling, there are serious drawbacks to a file server installation, including the following:

- Every time the user launches an Access application, the Access EXE, DLLs, and any other files required to run Access are *all* sent over the network wire to the local machine. Obviously, this generates a significant volume of network traffic.
- Performance is generally degraded to unacceptable levels.

Because the disadvantages of running Access from a file server are so pronounced, I strongly recommend that Access, or at least the runtime engine, be installed on each user's machine.

Strategies for Installing Your Application

Just as there are different strategies for installing Access, there are also various strategies for installing your application, such as the following:

- Install both the application and data on a file server.
- Install the data on the file server and the application on each workstation.

In other words, after you have created an application, you can place the entire application on the network, which means that all the tables, queries, forms, reports, macros, and modules that make up the system reside on the file server. Although this method of shared access keeps everything in the same place, you will see many advantages to placing only the database's data tables on the file server. The remainder of the objects are placed in a database on each user's machine, and each local application database is linked to the tables on the network. In this way, users share data but not the rest of the application objects.

The advantages of installing one database with data tables on the file server and installing another database with the other application objects locally are as follows:

- Because each user has a copy of the local database objects (queries, forms, reports, macros, and modules), load time and network traffic are both reduced.
- It's very easy to back up data without having to back up the rest of the application objects.
- When redistributing new versions of the application, you don't need to worry about overwriting the application's data.
- Multiple applications can all be designed to use the same centrally located data.
- Users can add their own objects (such as their own queries) to their local copies of the database.

In addition to storing the queries, forms, reports, macros, and modules that make up the application in a local database, I also recommend that you store the following objects in each local database:

- Temporary tables
- Static tables
- Semistatic tables

Temporary tables should be stored in the database that's on each workstation, because if two users are performing operations that build the same temporary tables, you don't want one user's process to interfere with the other user's process. The potential conflict of one user's temporary tables overwriting the other's can be eliminated by storing all temporary tables in each user's local copy of the database.

You should also place static lookup tables, such as state tables, on each workstation. Because the data doesn't change, maintenance isn't an issue. The benefit is that Access doesn't need to pull that data over the network each time it's needed.

Semistatic tables—tables that are rarely updated—can also be placed on the local machine. As with static tables, the major benefit of having these tables in a local database is that reduced network traffic means better performance, not only for the user needing the data, but also for anyone sharing the same network wire. Changes made to the semistatic tables can be transported to each workstation by using replication (covered in Chapter 24, "Replication Made Easy").

The configuration described throughout this section is shown in Figure 18.1.

Figure 18.1.

An example of a configuration with database objects split, storing temporary and static tables locally and shared tables remotely (on the file server).

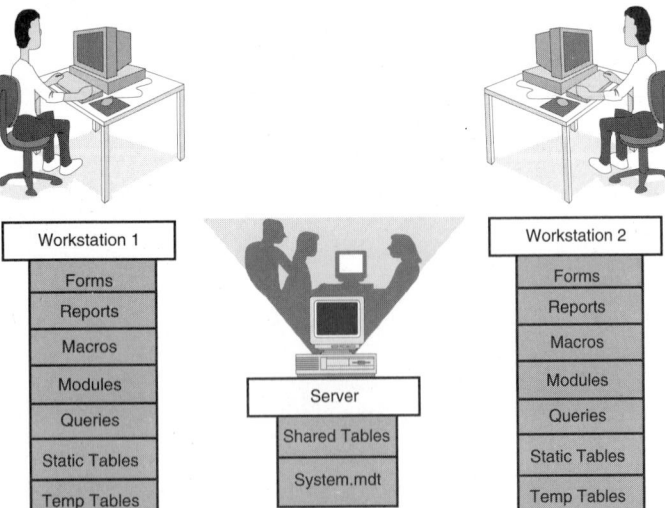

The Basics of Linking to External Data

Linking to external data, including data not stored in another Access database, is covered extensively in Chapter 19, "Using External Data." Three options are available to you:

- Design the databases separately from the start.
- Include all objects in one database, then split them manually when you're ready to distribute your application.
- Include all objects in one database, then split them by using the Database Splitter Wizard.

The first two options are covered in Chapter 19. The last option, the Database Splitter Wizard, is covered here. To split the objects in a database into two separate .MDB files, follow these steps:

1. Open the database whose objects you want to split.
2. Choose Tools | Add-Ins | Database Splitter to open the Database Splitter dialog box, shown in Figure 18.2.

Figure 18.2.
The Database Splitter Wizard helps you split the data tables that should reside on the server.

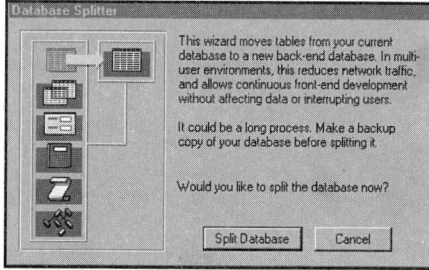

3. Click Split Database; this opens the Create Back-end Database dialog box. (See Figure 18.3.)

Figure 18.3.
Entering a name for the new shared database.

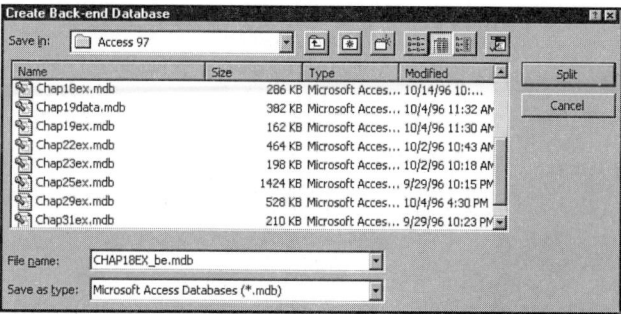

545

4. Enter the name for the database that will contain all the tables. Click Split. The Database Splitter Wizard creates a new database holding all the tables, and links are created between the current database and the database containing the tables. (See Figure 18.4.)

Figure 18.4.
The database that has been split.

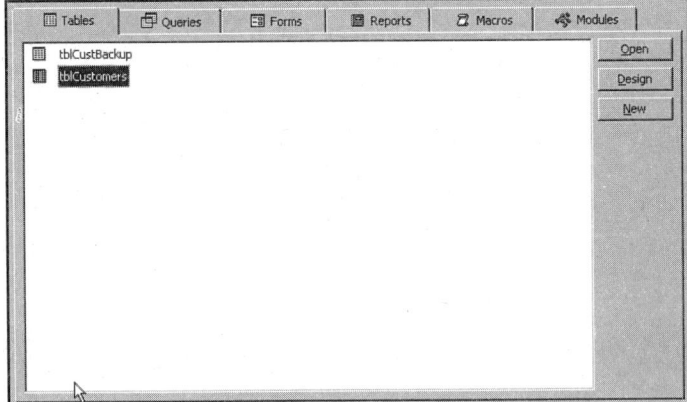

Be aware that when you're distributing an application using linked tables, you must write code to make sure the data tables can be located from each application database on the network. If each user has the same path to the file server, this isn't a problem. However, if the path to the file server varies, you need to write a routine that makes sure the tables can be located. If they can't, the routine prompts the user for the data's location. This routine is covered in Chapter 19.

Understanding Access's Locking Mechanisms

Although the preceding tips for designing network applications reduce network traffic, they in no way reduce locking conflicts. To protect shared data, Access locks a page of data as the user edits a record. In this way, multiple users can read the data, but only one user can make changes to it. Data can be locked through a form and also through a recordset that isn't bound to a form.

Here are the three methods of locking for an Access application:

- Page locking
- Table and Recordset locking
- Opening an entire database with Exclusive Access

With Page locking, only the page with the record being edited is locked. On the other hand, in Table and Recordset locking, the entire table or recordset with the record being edited is locked. With Database locking, the entire database is locked, unless the user opening the database has opened it for read-only access. If the user opens the database for read-only access, other users can also open the database for read-only access. The ability to get exclusive use of a database can be restricted through security.

It's important to note that the locking scheme you adhere to depends on the source providing the data. If you're using client/server data through ODBC, you inherit the locking scheme of the particular back-end you're using. If you're manipulating ISAM data over a network, you get any record locking that the particular ISAM database supports. For example, if you're working with a FoxPro database, you can use record locking or any other locking scheme that FoxPro supports.

Locking and Refreshing Strategies

Access has several tools for controlling locking methods in datasheets, forms, and reports. To configure the global multiuser settings, choose Tools | Options, then click on the Advanced tab. The dialog box shown in Figure 18.5 appears.

Figure 18.5.

The Advanced Options dialog box.

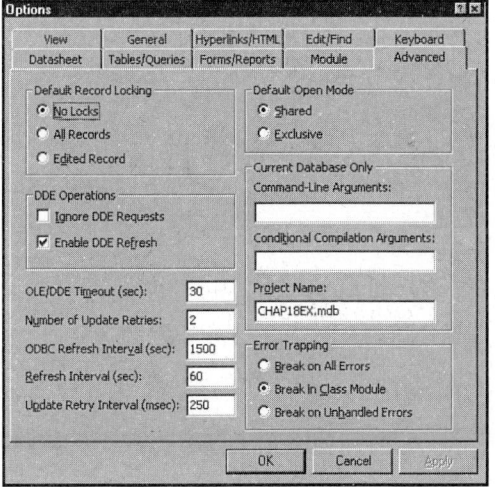

The following multiuser settings can be configured from this dialog box:

- Default Record Locking
- Default Open Mode
- Number of Update Retries
- ODBC Refresh Interval
- Refresh Interval
- Update Retry Interval

Default Record Locking

The Default Record Locking option lets you specify the default record locking as No Locks (optimistic), All Records (locks entire table or dynaset), or Edited Record (pessimistic). This is where you can affect settings for all the objects in your database. Modifying this option doesn't affect any existing queries, forms, and reports, but it does affect any new queries, forms, and reports. These options are discussed later in this chapter as they apply to forms and recordsets.

Determining the Locking Mechanism for a Query

If you want to determine the locking method for a particular query, you can do this by modifying the Record Locks query property. Once again, the options are No Locks, All Records, and Edited Record. The Query Properties window can be seen in Figure 18.6.

Figure 18.6.
Setting the locking method for a query.

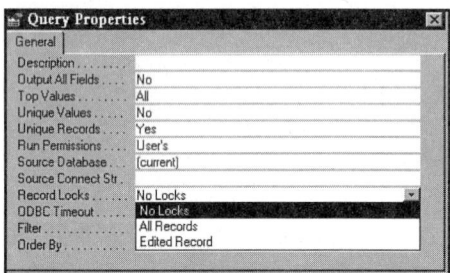

Determining the Locking Mechanism for a Form or Report

Just as you can configure the locking mechanism for a query, you can also configure the locking mechanism for each form and report. Forms and reports have Record Locks properties. (See Figure 18.7.) Changing these properties modifies the locking mechanism for that particular form or report.

Figure 18.7.

Setting the locking method for a form.

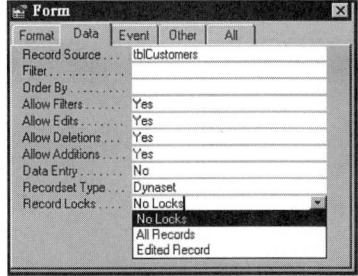

Reports don't offer the Edited Records choice for locking because report data can't be modified.

Default Open Mode

The Default Open Mode option allows you to configure the default open mode for databases. By encouraging users to set this option in their own copies of Access, you prevent people from inadvertently opening up a database exclusively. Take a good look at the Access File Open dialog box, shown in Figure 18.8. Whether the Exclusive checkbox is selected is determined by the Default Open Mode set in the Advanced Options dialog box.

Figure 18.8.

The Exclusive checkbox in the File Open dialog box is directly below the Advanced button.

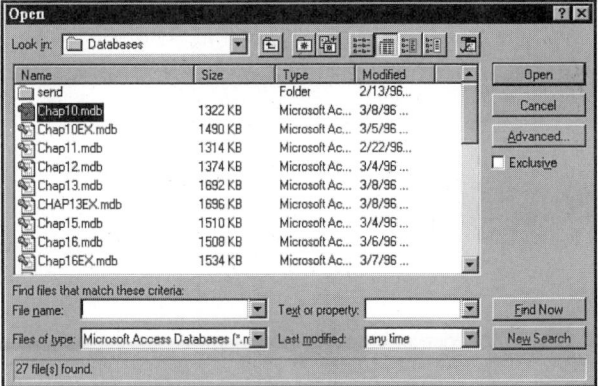

Number of Update Retries

The Number of Update Retries option specifies how many times Access will try to save data to a locked record. The higher this number is, the greater the chance that the update will succeed. The downside is that the user has to wait while Access continues trying to update the data, even when there's no hope that the update will be successful. The default for this setting is 2; the value can range from 0 to 10.

ODBC Refresh Interval

The ODBC Refresh Interval option determines how often your form or datasheet is updated with changes made to data stored in ODBC data sources. For example, assume that two users are viewing the same data stored in a back-end Microsoft SQL Server database. User 1 makes a change to the data, and the ODBC refresh interval determines how long it is before User 2 sees the change. The higher this number is, the less likely it is that User 2 will see the current data. The lower this number is, the more network traffic will be generated. The default for this setting is 500 seconds (just over eight minutes), and the value can range from 1 to 3,600 seconds.

Refresh Interval

The Refresh Interval option specifies how long it takes for a form or datasheet to be updated with changed data from an Access database. This is very similar to the ODBC refresh interval, but the ODBC refresh interval applies only to ODBC data sources, and the refresh interval applies only to Access data sources. As with the ODBC refresh interval, the higher this number is, the lower the chance that the data seen by the user is current. The lower this number is, the more network traffic is generated. The default for this setting is 60 seconds; the value can range from 1 to 32,766 seconds.

> **NOTE**
>
> Access automatically refreshes the data in a record whenever the user tries to edit the record. The benefit of a shorter refresh interval is that the user sees the record has been changed or locked by another user before he or she tries to edit it.

Update Retry Interval

The Update Retry Interval option determines how many seconds Access waits before once again trying to update a locked record. The default for this setting is 250 milliseconds, and the value can range from 0 to 1,000 milliseconds (one second).

Refreshing Versus Requerying Data

It's important to understand the difference between refreshing and requerying a recordset. *Refreshing* a recordset updates changed data and indicates any deleted records. It doesn't try to bring a new recordset over the network wire; instead, it *refreshes* the data in the existing recordset. This means that records aren't reordered, new records don't appear, and deleted records aren't removed from the display. The record pointer remains on the same record.

Requerying, on the other hand, gets a new set of records. This means that the query is run again, and all the resulting data is sent over the network wire. The data is reordered, new records appear, and deleted records are no longer displayed. The record pointer is moved to the first record in the recordset.

Form Locking Strategies

Earlier in the chapter, you learned about the locking strategies for forms: No Locks, All Records, and Edited Record. Using the three locking strategies as appropriate, you can develop a multiuser application with little to no multiuser programming. You won't gain the same power, flexibility, and control that you get out of recordsets, but you can quickly and easily implement multiuser techniques. In this section, you will see how all three of these strategies affect the bound forms in your application.

No Locks

The No Locks option means that the page of data with the edited record won't be locked until Access tries to write the changed data to disk. This happens when there's movement to a different record or the data in the record is explicitly saved. The No Locks option is the least restrictive locking option for forms.

Several users can be editing data in the same 2K page of data at the same time, but the conflict occurs when two users try to modify the same record. Say, for example, that User 1 tries to modify data in the record for customer ABCDE, and User 2 tries to modify the *same* record. No error occurs because the No Locks option is specified for the form both users are accessing. Next, User 1 makes a change to the address, and User 2 makes a change to the Contact Title. User 1 moves off the record, saving her changes. No error occurs because Access has no way of knowing that User 2 is modifying the record. Now User 2 tries to move off the record, and the Write Conflict dialog box, shown in Figure 18.9, appears. User 2 has the choice of saving her changes, thereby overwriting the changes that User 1 made; copying User 1's changes to the Clipboard so she can make an educated decision as to what to do; or dropping her own changes and accepting the changes User 1 made.

Figure 18.9.
The Write Conflict dialog box appears when two users edit the same record.

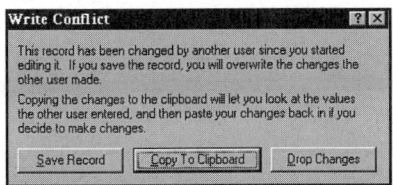

All Records

The All Records locking option is the most restrictive. When All Records is in effect, other users can only view the data in the tables underlying the form. They can't make any changes to the data, regardless of their own locking options. When they open the form, they see a quick status bar message that the data can't be updated. If they try to modify data in the form, the computer beeps and a message is displayed in the status bar.

551

Edited Record

The Edited Record option is used when you want to prevent the conflicts that happen when the No Locks option is in place. Instead of getting potential conflicts for changed data, users are much more likely to experience locking conflicts, because every time a user begins editing a record, the entire 2K page of data surrounding the record is locked.

Consider this scenario. User 1 begins editing a record, and User 2 tries to modify the same record. The computer beeps and a lock symbol appears in the form's record selector. (See Figure 18.10.) Now User 2 moves to another record. If the other record is in the same 2K page as the record User 1 has locked, the locking symbol appears and User 2 can't edit that record either until User 1 has saved the record she was working on, thereby releasing the lock.

Figure 18.10.

The lock symbol on an edited record.

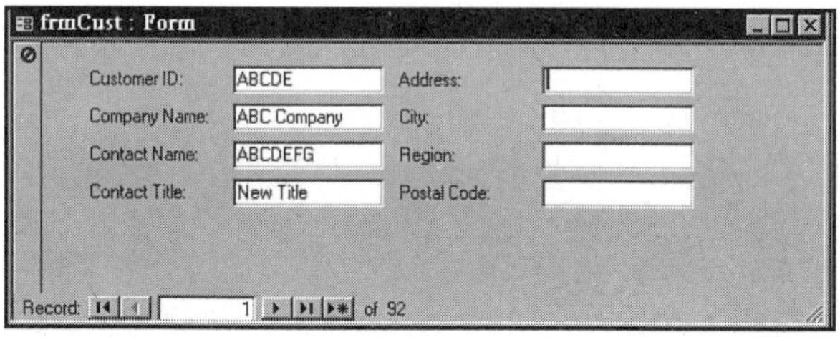

NOTE

If you want to override any of the default locking error dialogs that appear when you're in a form, you must code the form's Error event. Although you can use this method to replace any error message that appears, you can't trap for the situation with pessimistic locking when another user has the record locked. Users are cued that the record is locked only by viewing the locking symbol and hearing the beep when they try to edit the record. If you want to inform users that the record is locked before they try to edit it, you need to place code in the form's Timer event that checks whether the record is locked. This technique is covered in the "Testing a Record for Locking Status" section of this chapter.

Recordset Locking

Recordset locking locks pages of data found in a recordset. By using Recordset locking, you can control when and for how long the data is locked. This is different from locking data through bound forms, which gives you little control over the specifics of the locking process.

When you're traversing through a recordset, editing and updating data, locking occurs regardless of whether you intervene, so you must understand when the locking occurs and whether you need to step in to intercept the default behavior. If you do nothing, an entire page of records will be locked each time you issue an Edit method from your VBA code. This record page is 2048 bytes (2K) and surrounds the record being edited. If an OLE object is found in the record being edited, it isn't locked with the record because it occupies its own space.

Pessimistic Locking

VBA lets you determine when and for how long a page is locked. The default behavior is called *pessimistic locking*, which means that the page is locked when the Edit method is issued. The following code illustrates this process:

```
Sub PessimisticLock(strCustID As String)
    Dim db As Database
    Dim rst As Recordset
    Dim strCriteria As String

    Set db = CurrentDb()
    Set rst = db.OpenRecordSet("tblCustomers", dbOpenDynaset)
    rst.Lockedits = True   'Invoke Pessimistic Locking
    strCriteria = "[CustomerID] = '" & strCustID & "'"
    rst.FindFirst strCriteria
    rst.Edit    'Lock Occurs Here
    rst!City = "Thousand Oaks"
    rst.Update  'Lock Released Here
End Sub
```

> **NOTE**
>
> This code, and the rest of the code in this chapter, can be found in CHAP18EX.MDB on this books's CD-ROM.

In this scenario, although the lock occurs for a very short period of time, it's actually being issued at the edit, then released at the update.

The advantage of this method of locking is that you can make sure no changes are made to the data between the time the Edit method is issued and the time the Update method is issued. Furthermore, when the Edit method succeeds, you are ensured write access to the record. The disadvantage is that the time between the edit and the update might force the lock to persist for a significant period of time, locking other users out of not only that record, but also the entire page of records the edited record is in.

This phenomenon is exacerbated when transaction processing (covered in Chapter 22, "Transaction Processing") is invoked. Basically, transaction processing ensures that when you make multiple changes to data, all changes are made successfully or no changes occur. For now, take a look at how pessimistic record locking affects transaction processing:

```
Sub PessimisticTrans(strOldCity As String, strNewCity As String)
    Dim wrk As Workspace
    Dim db As Database
    Dim rst As Recordset
    Dim strCriteria As String

    Set wrk = DBEngine(0)
    Set db = CurrentDb()
    Set rst = db.OpenRecordSet("tblCustomers", dbOpenDynaset)
    rst.Lockedits = True   'Pessimistic Locking
```

```
    strCriteria = "[City] = '" & strOldCity & "'"
    rst.FindFirst strCriteria
    wrk.BeginTrans
    Do Until rst.NoMatch
        rst.Edit    'Lock Occurs Here
        rst!City = strNewCity
        rst.Update
        rst.FindNext strCriteria
    Loop
    wrk.CommitTrans  'Lock released here
End Sub
```

Here you can see that the lock is in place from the very first edit that happens until the CommitTrans is issued. This means that no one can update any pages of data involving the edited records until the CommitTrans is issued. This can be prohibitive during a long process.

Optimistic Locking

Optimistic locking delays the time at which the record is locked. The lock is issued upon update rather than edit. The code looks like this:

```
Sub OptimisticLock(strCustID As String)
    Dim db As Database
    Dim rst As Recordset
    Dim strCriteria As String

    Set db = CurrentDb()
    Set rst = db.OpenRecordSet("tblCustomers", dbOpenDynaset)
    rst.Lockedits = False 'Optimistic Locking
    strCriteria = "[CustomerID] = '" & strCustID & "'"
    rst.FindFirst strCriteria
    rst.Edit
    rst!City = "Thousand Oaks"
    rst.Update 'Lock Occurs and is Released Here
End Sub
```

As you can see, the lock doesn't happen until the Update method is issued. The advantage of this method is that the page is locked very briefly. However, the disadvantage occurs when two users grab the record for editing at the same time. When one user tries to update, no error occurs. When the other user tries to update, she gets an error indicating that the data has changed since her edit was first issued. Handling this error message is covered in "Coding Around Optimistic Locking Conflicts," later in this chapter.

Optimistic locking with transaction handling isn't much different from pessimistic locking. As the code reaches the Update method for each record, the page containing that record is locked, and it remains locked until the transaction is committed. Here's what the code looks like:

```
Sub OptimisticTrans(strOldCity As String, strNewCity As String)
    Dim wrk As Workspace
    Dim db As Database
    Dim rst As Recordset
    Dim strCriteria As String
```

```
        Set db = CurrentDb()
        Set rst = db.OpenRecordSet("tblCustomers", dbOpenDynaset)
        rst.Lockedits = False   'Optimistic Locking
        strCriteria = "[City] = '" & strOldCity & "'"
        rst.FindFirst strCriteria
        wrk.BeginTrans
        Do Until rst.NoMatch
            rst.Edit
            rst!City = strNewCity
            rst.Update    'Lock Occurs
            rst.FindNext strCriteria
        Loop
        wrk.CommitTrans   'Locks are Released Here
    End Sub
```

Effectively Handling Locking Conflicts

If a user has a page locked and another user tries to view data on that page, no conflict occurs. On the other hand, if other users try to edit data on that same page, they get an error.

You won't always want Access's own error handling to take over when a locking conflict occurs. For example, rather than having Access display its generic error message indicating that a record is locked, you might want to display your own message and then try to lock the record a couple of additional times. To do something like this, you must learn to interpret each locking error generated by VBA, so you can make a decision about how to respond.

Locking conflicts happen in the following situations:

- A user tries to edit or update a record that's already locked.
- A record has changed or been deleted since the user first started to edit it.

These errors can occur whether you're editing bound data through a form or accessing the records through VBA code.

Errors with Pessimistic Locking

To begin the discussion of locking conflicts, take a look at the types of errors that occur when pessimistic locking is in place. With pessimistic locking, you generally need to code for the following errors:

- 3260: This error occurs when the current record is locked by another user. It's usually enough to wait a short period of time and then try the lock again.
- 3197: This error occurs when a record has been changed since the user last accessed it. It's best to refresh the data and try the Edit method again.
- 3167: This error occurs when the record has been deleted since the user last accessed it. In this case, it's best to refresh the data.

Coding Around Pessimistic Locking Conflicts

It's fairly simple to write code to handle pessimistic locking conflicts. Here's an example of what your code should look like:

Listing 18.1. Handling pessimistic locking errors.

```
Sub PessimisticRS(strCustID As String)
    On Error GoTo PessimisticRS_Err
    Dim db As Database
    Dim rst As Recordset
    Dim strCriteria As String
    Dim intChoice As Integer

    Set db = CurrentDb()
    Set rst = db.OpenRecordSet("tblCustomers", dbOpenDynaset)
    rst.LockEdits = True    'Invoke Pessimistic Locking
    strCriteria = "[CustomerID] = '" & strCustID & "'"
    rst.FindFirst strCriteria
    rst.Edit    'Lock Occurs Here
    rst!City = "Thousand Oaks"
    rst.Update 'Lock Released Here
    Exit Sub

PessimisticRS_Err:
    Select Case Err.Number
        Case 3197
            rst.Move 0
            Resume
        Case 3260
            intChoice = MsgBox(Err.Description, vbRetryCancel + vbCritical)
            Select Case intChoice
                Case vbRetry
                    Resume
                Case Else
                    MsgBox "Couldn't Lock"
            End Select
        Case 3167
            MsgBox "Record Has Been Deleted"
        Case Else
            MsgBox Err.Number & ": " & Err.Description
    End Select

End Sub
```

The error-handling code for this routine handles all the errors that can happen with pessimistic locking. If a 3197 Data Has Changed error occurs, the data is refreshed by the rs.Move 0, and the code resumes on the line causing the error, forcing the Edit to be reissued. If a 3260 Record Is Locked error occurs, the user is asked whether she wants to try again. If she responds affirmatively, the Edit is reissued; otherwise, the user is informed that the lock failed. If the record being edited has been deleted, an error 3167 occurs, and the user is informed that the record has been deleted. Here's what the situation looks like when transaction processing is involved:

Listing 18.2. Handling pessimistic locking errors in transactions.

```
Sub PessimisticRSTrans()
    On Error GoTo PessimisticRSTrans_Err
    Dim wrk As Workspace
    Dim db As Database
    Dim rst As Recordset
    Dim intCounter As Integer
    Dim intTry As Integer
    Dim intChoice As Integer

    Set wrk = DBEngine(0)
    Set db = CurrentDb
    Set rst = db.OpenRecordSet("tblCustomers", dbOpenDynaset)

    rst.LockEdits = True
    wrk.BeginTrans
    Do While Not rst.EOF
        rst.Edit
        rst![CompanyName] = rst![CompanyName] & "1"
        rst.Update
        rst.MoveNext
    Loop
    wrk.CommitTrans
    Exit Sub

PessimisticRSTrans_Err:
    Select Case Err.Number
        Case 3197
            rst.Move 0
            Resume
        Case 3260
            intCounter = intCounter + 1
            If intCounter > 2 Then
                intChoice = MsgBox(Err.Description, vbRetryCancel + vbCritical)
                Select Case intChoice
                    Case vbRetry
                        intCounter = 1
                    Case vbCancel
                        Resume CantLock
                End Select
            End If
            DoEvents
            For intTry = 1 To 100: Next intTry
            Resume
        Case Else
            MsgBox "Error: " & Err.Number & ": " & Err.Description
    End Select

CantLock:
    wrk.Rollback
    Exit Sub
End Sub
```

This code tries to lock the record. If it's unsuccessful (that is, an error 3260 is generated), it tries three times, then prompts the user for a response. If the user selects Retry, the process repeats. Otherwise, a rollback occurs and the subroutine is exited. If a 3197 Data Has Changed error occurs, the subroutine refreshes the data and tries again. If any other error occurs, the Rollback is issued and none of the updates are accepted.

Errors with Optimistic Locking or New Records

Now that you have seen what happens when a conflict occurs with pessimistic locking, see what happens when optimistic locking is in place or when users are adding new records. These are the three most common error codes generated by locking conflicts when optimistic locking is in place:

- 3186: This error occurs when the Update method is used to save a record on a locked page. This error generally occurs when a user tries to move off a record that she is adding onto a locked page. It also can occur when optimistic locking is used and a user tries to update a record on the same page as a record that's locked by another machine. It's generally enough to wait a short period of time and then try the lock again.

- 3197: (Data Has Changed) This error occurs with optimistic locking when someone else has updated a record in the time since you first started viewing it. You have two options: You can requery the recordset, losing your changes, or you can resume and issue the Update method again, overwriting the other user's changes.

- 3260: This error usually occurs when the Edit method is issued and the page with the current record is locked. It's best to wait a short period of time, then try the lock again.

Coding Around Optimistic Locking Conflicts

Remember that with optimistic locking, VBA tries to lock the page when the Update method is issued. There's a strong chance that a 3197 Data Has Changed error could occur. This needs to be handled in your code, so here's how to modify the preceding subroutine for optimistic locking:

Listing 18.3. Handling optimistic locking errors.

```
Sub OptimisticRS(strCustID)
    On Error GoTo OptimisticRS_Err
    Dim db As Database
    Dim rst As Recordset
    Dim strCriteria As String
    Dim intChoice As Integer

    Set db = CurrentDb()
    Set rst = db.OpenRecordSet("tblCustomers", dbOpenDynaset)
    rst.Lockedits = False 'Optimistic Locking
```

```
        strCriteria = "[CustomerID] = '" & strCustID & "'"
        rst.FindFirst strCriteria
        rst.Edit
        rst!City = "Thousand Oaks"
        rst.Update 'Lock Occurs and is Released Here
        Exit Sub

OptimisticRS_Err:
    Select Case Err.Number
        Case 3197
            If rst.EditMode = dbEditInProgress Then
                intChoice = MsgBox("Overwrite Other User's Changes?", _
                vbYesNoCancel + vbQuestion)

                Select Case intChoice
                    Case vbCancel, vbNo
                        MsgBox "Update Cancelled"
                    Case vbYes
                        rst.Update
                        Resume
                End Select
            End If
        Case 3186, 3260   'Locked or Can't Be Saved
            intChoice = MsgBox(Err.Description, vbRetryCancel + vbCritical)
                Select Case intChoice
                    Case vbRetry
                        Resume
                    Case vbCancel
                        MsgBox "Udate Cancelled"
                End Select
        Case Else
            MsgBox "Error: " & Err.Number & ": " & Err.Description
    End Select

End Sub
```

As with pessimistic error handling, this routine traps for all potential errors that can occur with optimistic locking. In a 3197 Data Has Changed conflict, the user is warned of the problem and asked whether she wants to overwrite the other user's changes or cancel her own changes. In the case of a locking conflict, the user is asked whether she wants to try again. Here's what it looks like with transaction processing involved:

Listing 18.4. Handling optimistic locking errors in transactions.

```
Sub OptimisticRSTrans()
    On Error GoTo OptimisticRSTrans_Err
    Dim db As Database
    Dim rs As Recordset
    Dim iCounter As Integer
    Dim iTry As Integer
    Dim iChoice As Integer

    Set db = CurrentDb
    Set rs = db.OpenRecordSet("tblCustBackup", dbOpenDynaset)
```

Listing 18.4. continued

```
    rs.Lockedits = False
    BeginTrans
    Do While Not rs.EOF
        rs.Edit
        rs![CompanyName] = rs![CompanyName] & "1"
        rs.Update
        rs.MoveNext
    Loop
    CommitTrans
    Exit Sub

OptimisticRSTrans_Err:
    Select Case Err.Number
        Case 3197
            If rs.EditMode = dbEditInProgress Then
                iChoice = MsgBox("Overwrite Other User's Changes?", _
                vbYesNoCancel + vbQuestion)
                Select Case iChoice
                    Case vbCancel, vbNo
                        Resume RollItBack
                    Case vbYes
                        'rs.Update
                        Resume
                End Select
            End If
        Case 3186, 3260  'Locked or Can't Be Saved
            iCounter = iCounter + 1
            If iCounter > 2 Then
                iChoice = MsgBox(Err.Description, vbRetryCancel + vbCritical)
                Select Case iChoice
                    Case vbRetry
                        iCounter = 1
                    Case vbCancel
                        Resume RollItBack
                End Select
            End If
            DoEvents
            For iTry = 1 To 100: Next iTry
            Resume
        Case Else
            MsgBox "Error: " & Err.Number & ": " & Err.Description
    End Select

RollItBack:
    Rollback
    Exit Sub
End Sub
```

If a 3197 Data Has Changed conflict occurs and the user opts to not overwrite the other user's changes, the entire processing loop is canceled (a rollback occurs). If a locking error occurs, the lock is retried several times. If it's still unsuccessful, the entire transaction is rolled back.

Testing to See Who Has a Record Locked

Regardless of what type of error occurs, it's often useful to find out who has locked a particular record. This can easily be done with VBA code—it's simply a matter of parsing the Description property of the Err object, as shown here:

Listing 18.5. Discovering who has locked the page.

```
Sub WhoLockedIt()
    On Error GoTo WhoLockedIt_Err
    Dim db As Database
    Dim rst As Recordset
    Set db = CurrentDb
    Set rst = db.OpenRecordset("tblCustomers", dbOpenDynaset)
    rst.Edit
    rst!CompanyName = "Hello"
    rst.Update
    Exit Sub

WhoLockedIt_Err:
    Dim strName As String
    Dim strMachine As String
    Dim intMachineStart As Integer

    intMachineStart = InStr(43, Err.Description, " on machine ") + 13
    If Err = 3260 Then
        strName = Mid(Err.Description, 44, _
                INStr(44, Err.Description, "'") - 44)
        strMachine = Mid(Err.Description, intMachineStart, _
                Len(Err.Description) - intMachineStart - 1)
    End If
    MsgBox strName & " on " & strMachine & " is the culprit!"
End Sub
```

The error description when a locking conflict occurs is shown in Figure 18.11. The preceding routine simply parses the standard error description, pulling out the user name and machine name. The custom error message appears in Figure 18.12.

Figure 18.11.

The standard locking error message with machine and description.

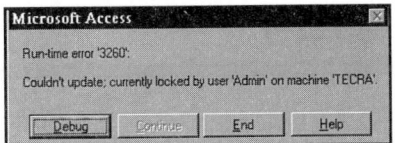

Figure 18.12.

The custom locking error message with machine and description.

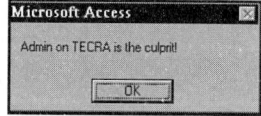

Testing a Record for Locking Status

Often, you want to determine the locking status of a record *before* you attempt an operation with it. By setting the LockEdits property of the recordset to True and trying to modify the record, you can determine whether the current row is locked. The code looks like this:

Listing 18.6. Determining whether a record is locked before editing it.

```
Sub TestLocking()
    Dim db As Database
    Dim rst As Recordset
    Dim fLocked As Boolean

    Set db = CurrentDb
    Set rst = db.OpenRecordset("tblCustomers", dbOpenDynaset)
    fLocked = IsItLocked(rst)
    MsgBox fLocked

End Sub

Function IsItLocked(rstAny As Recordset) As Boolean
    On Error GoTo IsItLocked_Err
    IsItLocked = False

    With rstAny
        .LockEdits = True
        .Edit
        .MoveNext
        .MovePrevious
    End With
    Exit Function

IsItLocked_Err:
    If Err = 3260 Then
        IsItLocked = True
        Exit Function
    End If
End Function
```

The TestLocking routine sends its recordset to the IsItLocked() function, which receives the recordset as a parameter and sets its LockEdits property to True. It then issues an Edit method on the recordset. If an error occurs, the record is locked. The error handler sets the return value for the function to True. In production code, you want to save the previous value of LockEdits before setting it to True. This allows you to set LockEdits back to its previous value before returning from the IsItLocked() function. Note that this function is useful only if you're using optimistic locking.

Using Code to Refresh or Requery

Throughout this chapter, I've mentioned the need to requery a recordset. In this section, you'll see how to requery by using code.

The `Requery` method makes sure the user gets to see any changes to existing records, as well as any records that have been added. It also ensures that deleted records are removed from the recordset. It's easiest to understand the `Requery` method by looking at the data underlying a form:

```
Private Sub cmdRequery_Click()
    If Me.RecordsetClone.Restartable Then
        Me.RecordsetClone.Requery
    Else
        MsgBox "Requery Method Not Supported on this Recordset"
    End If
End Sub
```

This code first tests the Restartable property of the recordset underlying the form. If the Restartable property is `True`, the recordset supports the `Requery` method that's performed on the form's recordset. Of course, the Restartable property and `Requery` method work on any recordset, not just the recordset underlying a form. The only reason a recordset might not be restartable is because some back-end queries can't be restarted.

Before running this code, new records don't appear in the recordset, and deleted records appear with `#Deleted`. (See Figure 18.13.) After the `Requery` method is issued, all new records appear, and deleted records are removed.

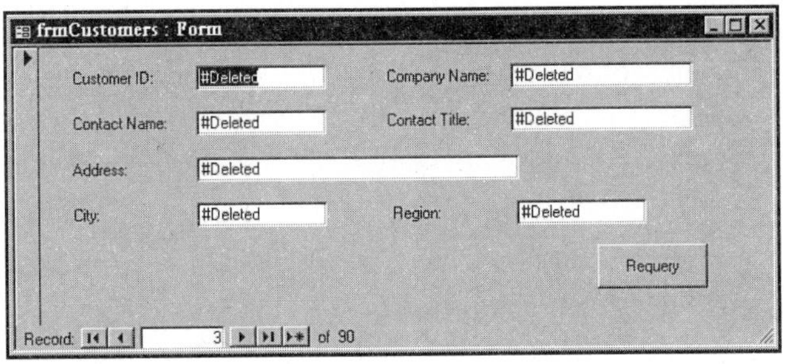

Figure 18.13.
A recordset that hasn't been requeried yet.

Understanding the .LDB File

Every database opened for shared use has a corresponding .LDB file, a locking file created to store computer and security names and to place byte range locks on the recordset. The .LDB file always has the same name and location as the databases whose locks it's tracking, and it's automatically deleted when the last user exits the database file. There are two times when the .LDB file is *not* deleted:

- The database is marked as damaged (politically correct term).
- The last user out doesn't have delete rights in the folder with the database and .LDB files.

The Jet Engine writes an entry to the .LDB file for every user who opens the database. The entry is 64 bytes; the first 32 bytes contain the user's computer name, and the last 32 bytes contain his or her security name. Because the maximum number of users for an Access database is 255, the .LDB file can't get larger than 16K. The .LDB file information prevents users from writing data to pages that other users have locked and determines who has the pages locked.

When a user exits an Access database, his or her entry in the .LDB file isn't removed. Instead, the entry is overwritten by the next person accessing the database. For this reason, the .LDB file doesn't give you an accurate picture of who's currently accessing the database.

Creating Custom Counters

Access offers an AutoNumber field type that can be set to automatically generate sequential or random values. Although the AutoNumber field type is adequate for most situations, you might want to home-grow your own AutoNumber fields for any of the following reasons:

- You want an increment value other than 1.
- You don't like the AutoNumber field discarding values from canceled records.
- The primary key value needs to be some algorithm of the other fields in the table (the first few characters from a couple of fields, for example).
- The primary key value needs to contain an alphanumeric string.

To generate your own automatically numbered sequential value, you should probably build a system table that holds the next available value for your custom AutoNumber field. You must lock this table while a user is grabbing the next available sequential value, or else two users might be assigned the same value.

Using Unbound Forms

One solution to locking conflicts is to use unbound forms. By doing this, you can greatly limit the amount of time a record is locked and fully control when Access tries to secure the lock. Unbound forms require significantly more coding than bound forms, so you should make sure the benefits you get from using unbound forms outweigh the coding and maintenance involved. With improvements to both forms and the Jet Engine in Access 97, the reasons to use unbound forms with Access data are less compelling. Unbound forms are covered in more detail in Chapter 20, "Client/Server Techniques."

Using Replication to Improve Performance

Replication, covered in Chapter 24, can be used to improve performance in a multiuser application. Using replication, you can place multiple copies of the database containing the tables out on the network, each on a different file server. Different users can be set up to access data from the different file servers, thereby better distributing network traffic. Using the Replication Manager, which ships with the Microsoft Office Developer Edition Tools for Windows 95 (ODE), the databases can be synchronized at regular intervals. Although this isn't a viable solution when the data that users are viewing needs to be fully current, there are many situations in which this type of solution might be adequate. It's often the only solution when limited resources don't allow migrating an application's data to a client/server database.

> **NOTE**
>
> The Replication Manager comes only in the ODE.

Practical Examples: Making an Application Multiuser Ready

The Time and Billing application is built mostly around forms. Because it's unlikely that two users will update the data in the same record at the same time, you can opt for optimistic locking. This reduces the chance of a page of records inadvertently being locked for a long period of time. The following example illustrates how you can use the form's Error event to override the default locking error messages:

Listing 18.7. Overriding default error handling under a form.

```
Private Sub Form_Error(DataErr As Integer, Response As Integer)
   On Error GoTo Form_Error_Err:
   Dim intAnswer As Integer
   If DataErr = 7787 Then  'Data Has Changed Error
      intAnswer = MsgBox("Another User Has Modified This Record " & vbCrLf & _
         "Since You Began Editing It. " & vbCrLf & vbCrLf & _
         "Do You Want To Overwrite Their Changes? " & vbCrLf & _
         "Select YES to Overwrite, NO to Cancel Your Changes", _
         vbYesNo, "Locking Conflict")
   End If
   If intAnswer = vbYes Then
      Dim db As DATABASE
      Dim rst As Recordset
      Dim strSQL As String
      Dim fld As Field

      strSQL = "Select * from tblClients Where ClientID = " & Me!ClientID
      Set db = CurrentDb
      Set rst = db.OpenRecordset(strSQL, dbOpenDynaset)
      For Each fld In rst.Fields
```

565

continues

Listing 18.7. continued

```
        rst.Edit
        If Nz(fld) <> Nz(Me(fld.Name)) Then
            fld.Value = Me(fld.Name).Value
        End If
        rst.UPDATE
    Next fld
  End If
  Response = acDataErrContinue
  Exit Sub

Form_Error_Err:
    MsgBox "Error # " & Err.Number & ": " & Err.Description
    Exit Sub
End Sub
```

This code is placed in the Error event of the frmClients form in the CHAP18.MDB database. It begins by checking to see whether the DataErr is equal to 7787. This is the error code for DataErr when a Data Has Changed error has occurred in a form. If a 7787 has occurred, the user sees a message box notifying her of the conflict and asking whether she wants to overwrite the other user's changes or cancel her own changes. (See Figure 18.14.)

Figure 18.14.

The custom message box displayed when trapping for a locking conflict.

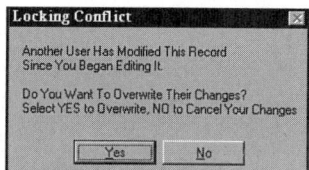

This routine could be enhanced to let the user view the other user's changes. If the user responds that she wants to overwrite the other user's changes, a new recordset is created based on the ClientID of the current record. This recordset contains all the values the other user has entered. The code loops through each field in the recordset and issues an Edit method on the recordset. Next, it tests to see whether the value of the current field matches the value of the control on the form with the same name. If there is a match, the value of the field is replaced with the value in the form. Regardless of whether the user responds Yes or No, the Response is set equal to acDataErrContinue so that the normal error message is suppressed.

Summary

VBA offers several alternative locking strategies for the developer, ranging from locking the entire database to locking one page of records at a time. In addition, VBA lets you control how long data will be locked. You use this feature through the techniques of optimistic and pessimistic locking. The developer must select which combination of strategies should be used in each particular application. The decision about which method to use is influenced by many factors, including the volume of traffic on the network and the importance of making sure collisions never happen.

19

CHAPTER

Using External Data

- Understanding External Data, 568
- Importing, Linking, and Opening: When and Why, 568
- Importing External Data, 571
- Creating a Link to External Data, 575
- Opening an External Table, 582
- Understanding Windows Registry Settings, 584
- Using the Connection String, 585
- Working with Passwords, 585
- Refreshing and Removing Links, 586
- Creating an External Table, 588
- Looking At Special Considerations, 589
- Troubleshooting, 591
- Looking At Performance Considerations and Links, 591
- Working with HTML Documents, 592
- Practical Examples: Working with External Data from within Your Application, 594

Understanding External Data

Microsoft Access is very capable of interfacing with data from other sources. It can use data from any ODBC data source, as well as data from FoxPro, dBASE, Paradox, Lotus, Excel, and many other sources. In this chapter, you will learn how to interface with external data sources through the user interface and by using code.

External data is data stored outside the current database. It can refer to data stored in another Microsoft Access database, as well as data stored in a multitude of other file formats—including ODBC, ISAM, spreadsheet, ASCII, and more. This chapter focuses on accessing data sources other than ODBC data sources. ODBC data sources are covered extensively in Chapter 20, "Client/Server Techniques," and Chapter 21, "Client/Server Strategies."

Access is an excellent *front-end* product, which means that it provides a powerful and effective means of presenting data—even data from external sources. Data is stored in places other than Access for many reasons. Large databases, for example, can be managed more effectively on a back-end database server such as Microsoft SQL Server. Data often is stored in a FoxPro, dBASE, or Paradox file format because the data is being used by a legacy application written in one of those environments. Text data often has been downloaded from a mainframe. Regardless of the reason why data is stored in another format, it is necessary that you understand how to manipulate this external data in your VBA modules. With the capability to access data from other sources, you can create queries, forms, and reports.

When accessing external data, you have three choices. You can import the data into an Access database, access the data by linking to it from your Access database, or open a data source directly. Importing the data is the best route (except with ODBC data sources) but not always possible. If you can't import external data, you should link to external files, because Microsoft Access maintains a lot of information about these linked files. This optimizes performance when manipulating the external files. Sometimes a particular situation warrants accessing the data directly. You therefore should know how to work with linked files, as well as how to open and manipulate files directly.

Importing, Linking, and Opening: When and Why

When you import data into an Access table, a copy is made of the data and is placed in an Access table. After data is imported, it is treated like any other native Access table. In fact, neither you nor Access has any way of knowing from where the data came. As a result, imported data offers the same performance and flexibility as any other Access table.

Linking to external data is quite different from importing data. Linked data remains in its native format. By establishing a link to the external data, you can build queries, forms, and reports that present the data. After you create a link to external data, the link remains permanently established unless you explicitly remove it. The linked table appears in the database window just like any other Access table. The only difference is that you cannot modify its structure from within Access. In fact, if the data source permits multiuser access, the users of your application can modify the data along with the users of applications written in the data source's native database format (such as FoxPro, dBASE, or Paradox).

Opening an external table is similar to linking to a table, except that a permanent relationship is not created. When you *link* to an external table, connection information is maintained from session to session. When you *open* a table, you create a recordset from the table, and no permanent link is established.

Selecting an Option

It is important that you understand when to import external data, when to link to external data, and when to open an external table directly. You should import external data in either of these circumstances:

- You are migrating an existing system into Access.
- You want to use external data to run a large volume of queries and reports, and you will not update the data. You want the added performance that native Access data provides.

When you are migrating an existing system to Access and you are ready to permanently migrate test or production data into your application, you import the tables into Access. Another good reason to import external data is if the data is downloaded from a mainframe into ASCII format on a regular basis, and you want to use the data for reports. Instead of attempting to link to the data and suffering the performance hits associated with such a link, you can import the data each time it is downloaded from the mainframe.

You should link to external data in any of the following circumstances:

- The data is used by a legacy application requiring the native file format.
- The data resides on an ODBC-compliant database server.
- You will access the data on a regular basis.

Often, you won't have the time or resources to rewrite an application written in FoxPro, Paradox, or some other language. You might be developing additional applications that will share data with the legacy application, or you might want to use the strong querying and reporting capabilities of Access instead of developing queries and reports in the native environment.

By linking to the external data, users of existing applications can continue to work with the applications and their data. Your Access applications can retrieve and modify data without corrupting or harming the data.

If the data resides in an ODBC database such as Microsoft SQL Server, you want to reap the data-retrieval benefits provided by a database server. By linking to the ODBC data source, you can take advantage of Access's ease of use as a front-end tool, while taking advantage of client/server technology at the same time.

Finally, if you intend to access data on a regular basis, linking to the external table instead of temporarily opening the table directly provides you with ease of use and performance benefits. After you create the link, Access treats the table just like any other Access table.

You should open an external table directly in either of these circumstances:

- You rarely need to establish a connection to the external data source.
- You have determined that performance actually improves by opening the data source directly.

If you rarely need to access the external data, it might be appropriate to open it directly. Links increase the size of your MDB file. This size increase is not necessary if you rarely will access the data. Furthermore, in certain situations, when accessing ISAM data, you might find that opening the table directly provides better performance than linking to it.

Although this chapter covers the process of importing external data, this is essentially a one-time process and doesn't require a lot of discussion. It is important to note, however, that after data is imported into an Access table, it no longer is accessed by the application in its native format. The majority of this chapter focuses on linking to or directly opening external data tables.

Looking At Supported File Formats

Microsoft Access enables you to import, link to, and open files in these formats:

- Microsoft Jet databases (including previous versions of Jet)
- ODBC databases
- HTML documents
- Microsoft Exchange/OutLook
- Microsoft FoxPro 2.0, 2.5, 2.6, 3.0, and DBC (Visual FoxPro)
- dBASE III, dBASE IV, and dBASE 5.0
- Paradox 3.x, 4.x, and 5.x
- Microsoft Excel spreadsheets, versions 3.0, 4.0, 5.0, and 8.0
- Lotus WKS, WK1, WK3, and WK4 spreadsheets
- ASCII text files stored in a tabular format

> **NOTE**
>
> Drivers for Lotus 1-2-3, Paradox, and Microsoft Exchange/OutLook are not available through Access Setup. They are included in the Office 97 ValuPack, which is on the Microsoft Office Professional Edition 97 CD-ROM. To install these drivers, run the dataacc.exe program located in the \ValuPack\DataAcc directory. The ValuPack contains a variety of useful information and tools.

Importing External Data

The process of importing external data is quite simple. You can import external data through the user interface or by using VBA code. If you are planning to import the data only once or twice, you should use the user interface. If you are importing data on a regular basis (for example, from a downloaded mainframe file), you should write code that accomplishes the task transparently to the user.

Importing External Data via the User Interface

To import an external data file using the user interface, follow these steps:

1. Right-click on any tab of the database window.

2. Choose Import (or choose File | Get External Data | Import). The Import dialog box appears, as shown in Figure 19.1.

Figure 19.1.

The Import dialog box.

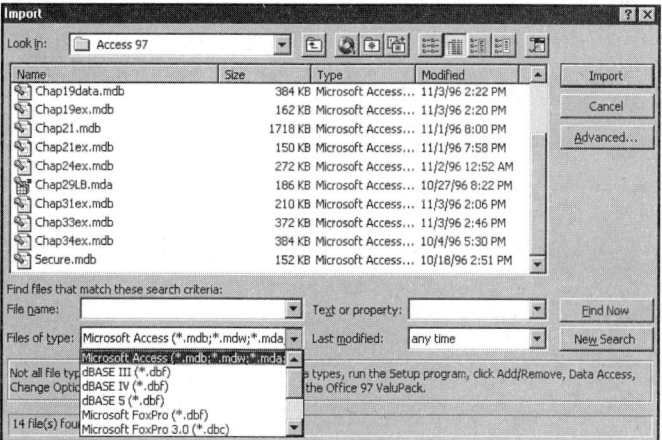

3. From the Files of Type drop-down list, select the type of file you are importing.

4. Select the file you want to import and click Import.

5. Depending on the type of file you select, the import process finishes, or you see additional dialog boxes. If you select Excel Spreadsheet, the Import Spreadsheet Wizard appears, as shown in Figure 19.2. This Wizard walks you through the process of importing spreadsheet data.

Figure 19.2.

The Import Spreadsheet Wizard.

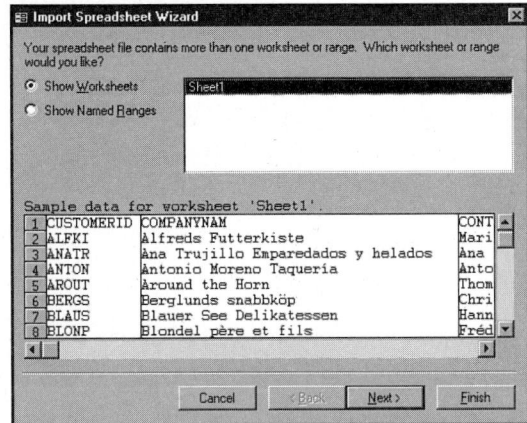

> **WARNING**
>
> Although this procedure is correct, if you find that you can't bring a text file directly into a large (4M–5M) Access database, change the text file into an Excel spreadsheet first and then import that file.

Importing External Data Using Code

The DoCmd object has three methods that assist you with importing external data. They are TransferDatabase, TransferText, and TransferSpreadsheet, each of which is covered in this section.

Importing Database Data Using Code

You use the TransferDatabase method of the DoCmd object to import data from a database such as FoxPro, dBASE, Paradox, or another Access database. A public constant called APPPATH has been declared in the General Declarations section of basImport. You need to change the value of this constant if you run the sample code from this chapter in a different directory. Listing 19.1, included in basImport, shows an example that uses the TransferDatabase method.

Listing 19.1. Using the TransferDatabase method.

```
Sub ImportDatabase()
  DoCmd.TransferDatabase _
    TransferType:=acImport, _
    DatabaseType:="FoxPro 2.5", _
    DatabaseName:=APPPATH, _
    ObjectType:=acTable, _
```

```
            Source:="Customers", _
            Destination:="tblCustomers", _
            StructureOnly:=False
End Sub
```

NOTE

This code and all the code in this chapter are located in the CHAP19EX.MDB file on the sample code CD-ROM.

Table 19.1 lists the arguments for the TransferDatabase method.

Table 19.1. TransferDatabase arguments.

Argument	Specifies
TransferType	Type of transfer being performed.
DatabaseType	Type of database being imported.
DatabaseName	Name of the database. If the table is a separate file (as is the case with dBASE, Paradox, and earlier versions of FoxPro), the database name is the name of the directory that contains the table file. Do *not* include a backslash after the name of the directory.
ObjectType	Type of object you want to import. This argument is ignored for all but Access objects.
Source	Name of the object you are importing. Do *not* include the file extension.
Destination	Name of the imported object.
StructureOnly	Whether you want the structure of the table only or the structure and data.
SaveLoginID	Whether you want to save the login ID and password for an ODBC database in the connection string for linked tables.

Importing Text Data Using Code

You use the TransferText method of the DoCmd object to import text from a text file. Listing 19.2 shows an example of this method.

Listing 19.2. Using the TransferText method.

```
Sub ImportText()
  DoCmd.TransferText _
    TransferType:=acImportDelim, _
    TableName:="tblCustomerText", _
    FileName:=APPPATH & "\Customer.Txt"
End Sub
```

Table 19.2 lists the arguments for the TransferText method.

Table 19.2. TransferText arguments.

Argument	Specifies
TransferType	Type of transfer you want to make.
SpecificationName	Name for the set of options that determines how the file is imported.
TableName	Name of the Access table that will receive the imported data.
FileName	Name of the text file to import from.
HasFieldHeadings	Whether the first row of the text file contains field headings.

Importing Spreadsheet Data Using Code

You use the TransferSpreadsheet method of the DoCmd object to import data from a spreadsheet file. Listing 19.3 shows an example that uses the TransferSpreadsheet method.

Listing 19.3. Using the TransferSpreadsheet method.

```
Sub ImportSpreadsheet()
  DoCmd.TransferSpreadsheet _
    TransferType:=acImport, _
    SpreadsheetType:=5, _
    TableName:="tblCustomerSpread", _
    FileName:=APPPATH & "\Customer.Xls", _
    HasFieldNames:=True
End Sub
```

Table 19.3 lists the arguments for the TransferSpreadsheet method.

Table 19.3. TransferSpreadsheet arguments.

Argument	Specifies
TransferType	Type of transfer you want to make.
SpreadsheetType	Type of spreadsheet to import from. The default is Excel 3.0.
TableName	Name of the Access table that will receive the imported data.
FileName	Name of the spreadsheet file to import from.
HasFieldNames	Whether the first row of the spreadsheet contains field headings.
Range	Range of cells to import.

Creating a Link to External Data

If you need to keep the data in its original format but want to treat the data just like any other Access table, linking is the best solution. All the information required to establish and maintain the connection to the remote data source is stored in the linked table definition. You can create links through the user interface and by using code. This section covers both alternatives.

One of the most common types of links is a link to another Access table. This type of link is created so that the application objects (queries, forms, reports, macros, and modules) can be placed in a local database and the tables can be stored in another database on a file server. Numerous benefits are associated with such a configuration. Chapter 18, "Developing for a Multiuser Environment," discusses these benefits in detail.

Creating a Link Using the User Interface

It is very common to create a link using the user interface. If you know what links you want to establish at design time, this is probably the easiest way to establish links to external data. You can establish links by using the Database Splitter or by establishing them manually.

Using the Database Splitter to Create Links

The Database Splitter was designed to split databases that already have been built with the tables and other database objects all in one physical MDB database file. It automates the process of moving the data tables to another database. The Database Splitter is covered in detail in Chapter 18.

Creating Links to Access Tables

To create a link to an Access table, follow these steps:

1. Right-click on any tab of the Database window.
2. Choose Link Tables. The Link dialog box appears, as shown in Figure 19.3.

Figure 19.3.

The Link dialog box.

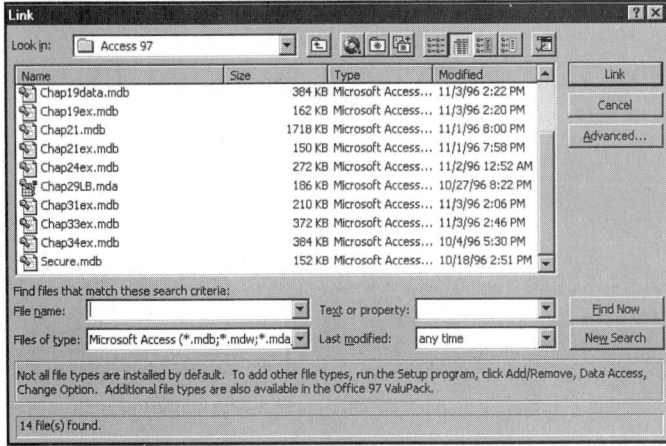

3. Select the name of the database containing the table to which you want to link.
4. Click the Link button. The Link Tables dialog box appears, as shown in Figure 19.4.

Figure 19.4.

The Link Tables dialog box.

5. Select the tables to which you want to establish a link.
6. Click OK. The link process finishes. Notice the arrows in Figure 19.5, which indicate that the tables are linked tables instead of tables stored in the current database.

Figure 19.5.

Linked tables in the Database window.

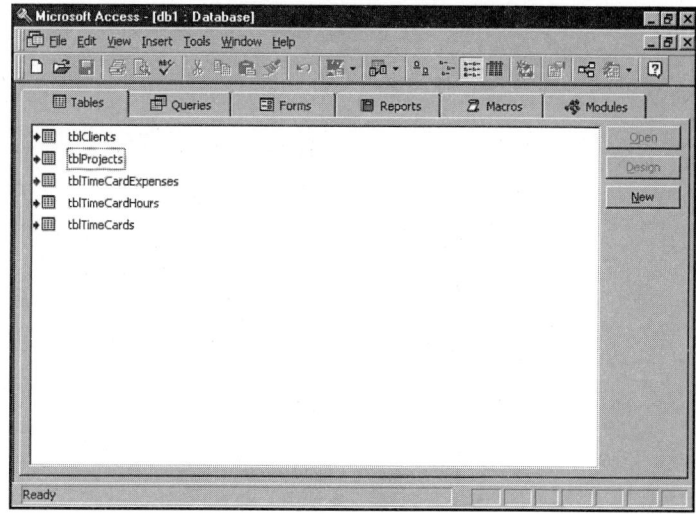

Creating Links to Other Types of Tables

The process of creating links to other types of database files is a little different. It works like this:

1. Right-click on any tab of the Database window.

2. Choose Link Tables. The Link dialog box appears.

3. From the Files of Type drop-down list, select the type of table to which you are linking.

4. Select the external file containing the data to which you will be linking.

5. Click the Link button. The next dialog box that appears varies, depending on the type of table to which you want to link. With a FoxPro file, for example, the Select Index Files dialog box appears, as shown in Figure 19.6. It is important that you select any index files associated with the data file. These indexes are updated automatically by Access as you add, change, and delete table data from Access.

6. You receive a message indicating that the index was added successfully and that you can add other indexes if you choose. Click OK.

7. Add any additional indexes and click Close.

Figure 19.6.

The Select Index Files dialog box.

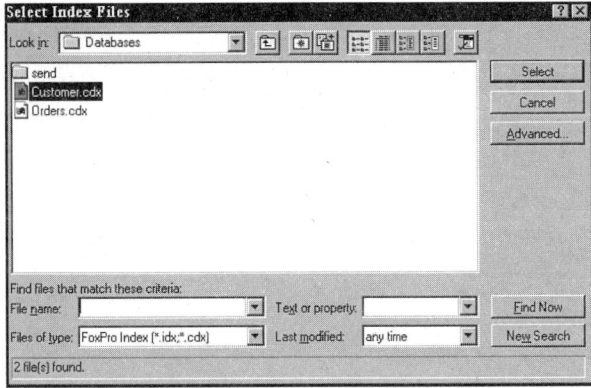

8. The Select Unique Record Identifier dialog box appears, as shown in Figure 19.7. This dialog box enables you to select a unique identifier for each record in the table. Select a unique field and click OK.

Notice the icon indicating the type of file you linked to, as shown in Figure 19.8.

Figure 19.7.

The Select Unique Record Identifier dialog box.

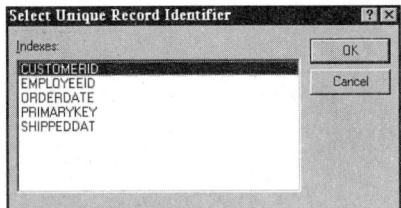

Figure 19.8.

An icon indicating that the file database is linked to a FoxPro database file.

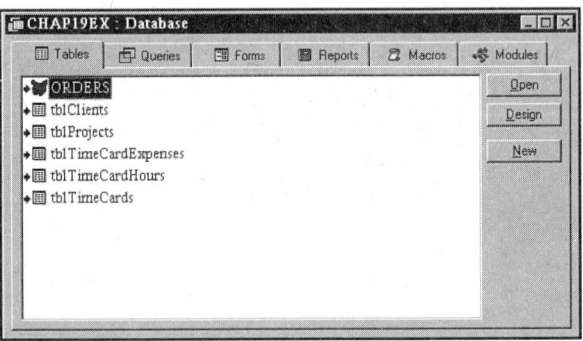

Creating a Link Using Code

Creating a link to an external table using code is a five-step process. Here are the steps involved in establishing the link:

1. Open the Microsoft Access database that will contain the link to the external file.
2. Create a new table definition using the external data source.
3. Set connection information for the external database and table.
4. Provide a name for the new table.
5. Link the table by appending the table definition to the database.

Listing 19.4 shows the code for linking to an external table, which in this case exists in another Microsoft Access database.

Listing 19.4. Linking to an external table.

```
Sub LinkToAccessTableProps()
   Dim db As DATABASE
   Dim tdf As TableDef
   Set db = CurrentDb
   Set tdf = db.CreateTableDef("tblLinkedTable")
   tdf.Connect = ";Database=" & APPPATH & "\Chap19Data.MDB"
   tdf.SourceTableName = "tblClients"
   db.TableDefs.Append tdf
End Sub
```

In Listing 19.4, the source database (Chap19Data.MDB) does not need to be opened, because you are adding a table definition to the current database. The CreateTableDef method is used to create the new table definition. The Connect property is set, and the SourceTableName is defined. Finally, the table definition is appended to the TableDefs collection of the database. This process is discussed in further detail in the following sections.

Providing Connection Information

When you link to an external table, you must provide information about the type, name, and location of the external database. This can be accomplished in one of two ways:

- Setting the SourceTableName and Connect properties of the TableDef object.
- Including the Source and Connect values as arguments to the CreateTableDef method.

The process of setting the SourceTableName and Connect properties is illustrated by these three lines of code:

```
Set tdf = db.CreateTableDef("tblLinkedTable")
tdf.Connect = ";Database=" & APPPATH & "\Chap19Data.MDB"
tdf.SourceTableName = "tblClients"
```

Including the `Source` and `Connect` values as arguments to the CreateTableDef method looks like this:

```
Set tdf = db.CreateTableDef("tblLinkedTable", _
    0, "tblClients", _
    ";Database=" & APPPATH & "\Chap19Data")
```

As you can see from the example, which is extracted from `Sub LinkToAccessTableArgs()` in basLinks, both the `Source` (`tblClients`) and the `Connect` values are included as arguments to the CreateTableDef method.

The connect string actually is composed of several pieces. These include the source database type, database name, password, and data source name. The database name is used for tables that are not ODBC-compliant, and the data source name is used for ODBC tables.

The source database type is the ISAM format that will be used for the link. Each source database type is a different folder in the Windows Registry. The folders are located in the HKEY_LOCAL_MACHINE\SOFTWARE\Microsoft\Jet\3.5\ISAM Formats section of the Registry.

Valid source database types follow:

dBASE	dBASE III, dBASE IV, and dBASE 5.0
Excel	Excel 3.0, Excel 4.0, Excel 5.0, and Excel 8.0
FoxPro	FoxPro 2.0, FoxPro 2.5, FoxPro 2.6, FoxPro 3.0, and FoxPro DBC
HTML	HTML Export and HTML Import
Jet 2.*x*	
Lotus	Lotus WK1, Lotus WK3, and Lotus WK4
Paradox	Paradox 3.*x*, Paradox 4.*x*, and Paradox 5.*x*
Text	

You must enter the source database type exactly as it is specified in the preceding list. Spaces and punctuation must be *exact* in order for the connection to be successful.

The database name must include a fully qualified path to the file. You can specify the path with a drive letter and directory path or by using *universal naming conventions* (UNCs). For a local database, you must specify the path like this:

```
Database=c:\Databases\Chap19Data
```

For a file server, you can specify the UNC path or the drive letter path. The UNC path looks like this:

```
\\FILESERVERNAME\Databases\Chap19Data
```

In this case, the database called Chap19Data is stored on the databases share of a particular file server.

The password is used to supply a password to a database (Access or another) that has been secured. It is best to fill in this part of the connection string from a variable at runtime instead of hard-coding it into the VBA code. Sending a password is covered in further detail in the "Working with Passwords" section of this chapter.

The completed connection string looks like this:

```
tdf.Connect = "FoxPro 2.6;Database=c:\Databases;PWD="
```

In this example, the connection string is set up to link to a FoxPro 2.6 database in the c:\Databases directory. No password is specified.

Creating the Link

Listing 19.5 shows how you put all the connection information together to establish a link to an external table.

Listing 19.5. Establishing a link to an external table.

```
Sub LinkToFox25(strDirName As String, strTableName As String, strAccessTable)
    Dim db As DATABASE
    Dim tdf As TableDef
    Set db = CurrentDb
    Set tdf = db.CreateTableDef(strAccessTable)
    tdf.Connect = "FoxPro 2.5;Database=" & strDirName
    tdf.SourceTableName = strTableName
    db.TableDefs.Append tdf
End Sub
```

Here is an example of how this subroutine is called:

```
Call LinkToFox25("c:\customer\data","customer","tblCustomers")
```

The LinkToFox25 subroutine receives three parameters:

- The name of the directory in which the FoxPro file is stored.
- The name of the file (the name of the table, without the DBF extension) to which you want to connect.
- The name of the Access table that you are creating.

The subroutine creates two object variables: a database object variable and a table definition object variable. The subroutine points the database object variable at the current database. Next, it creates a table definition called tblCustomers. It establishes a connection string for that table definition. The connection string specified in the subroutine indicates that you will link to a FoxPro 2.5 table. The directory name acts as the database to which you are linked. After you set the Connect property of the table definition, you are ready to indicate the name of the table with which you are establishing the link. This is the name of the FoxPro file. Finally, you are ready to append the table definition to the database.

Listing 19.6 shows an alternative to Listing 19.5.

Listing 19.6. An alternative for establishing a link to an external table.

```
Sub LinkToFoxAlt(strDirName As String, strTableName As String, strAccessTable)
    Dim db As DATABASE
    Dim tdf As TableDef
    Set db = CurrentDb
    Set tdf = db.CreateTableDef(strAccessTable, 0, strTableName, _
        "FoxPro 2.5;Database=" & strDirName)
    db.TableDefs.Append tdf
End Sub
```

Notice that here you are specifying the Access table name, the source table name, and the source database type and name—all as parameters to the CreateTableDef method.

You have seen how you can link to a FoxPro table. Listing 19.7 puts together everything you have learned in this chapter by creating a link to an Access table stored in another database.

Listing 19.7. Creating a link to an Access table stored in another database.

```
Sub LinkToAccess(strDBName As String, strTableName As String, strAccessTable)
    Dim db As DATABASE
    Dim tdf As TableDef
    Set db = CurrentDb
    Set tdf = db.CreateTableDef(strAccessTable)
    tdf.Connect = ";DATABASE=" & strDBName
    tdf.SourceTableName = strTableName
    db.TableDefs.Append tdf
End Sub
```

Notice that the connection string no longer specifies the type of database to which you are connecting. Everything else in this routine is the same as the routine that connected to FoxPro. Also notice the parameters passed to this routine:

```
Call LinkToAccess("C:\databases\northwind","Customers","tblCustomers")
```

The database passed to the routine is an actual Access database (as opposed to a directory), and the table name is the name of the Access table in the other database (instead of the DBF filename).

Opening an External Table

It generally is preferable to link to, rather than open, an external table. Linking provides additional performance and ease of use when dealing with an external table. After you link to a table, it is treated just like any other Access table. Occasionally, though, it is necessary to open an external table without creating a link to it. Opening an external table is a two-step process:

1. Open the database using the OpenDatabase method.
2. Create a `Recordset` object based on the external table.

Providing Connection Information

The connection information you provide when you open an external table is similar to the information you provide when you link to the table. The connection information is provided as arguments of the OpenDatabase method. Here's an example:

```
OpenDatabase("c:\customer\data", False, False, "FoxPro 2.5")
```

Here, the connection string is to the c:\customer\data database using the FoxPro 2.5 ISAM.

Opening the Table

The OpenDatabase method receives the following arguments:

```
OpenDatabase(DBname, Exclusive, Read-Only, Source)
```

DBname is the name of the database you are opening. The `Exclusive` and `Read-Only` parameters specify whether you are opening the database exclusively or as read-only. The `Source` argument specifies the database type and connection string. Listing 19.8 shows what the OpenDatabase method looks like in code.

Listing 19.8. Using the OpenDatabase method.

```
Sub OpenExternalFox(strDBName As String, strTableName As String)
    Dim db As DATABASE
    Dim rst As Recordset
    Set db = DBEngine.Workspaces(0).OpenDatabase(strDBName, False, _
        False, "FoxPro 2.5")
    Set rst = db.OpenRecordset(strTableName)
    Do While Not rst.EOF
        Debug.Print rst.Fields(0).Value
        rst.MoveNext
    Loop
End Sub
```

Listing 19.8 is called with this code:

```
Call OpenExternalFox("c:\customer\data","Customer")
```

Notice that you are not appending a table definition here. Instead, you are creating a temporary recordset that refers to the external data. After the external table is opened as a recordset, the code traverses through each record of the table, printing the value of the first field. Of course, after the recordset is opened, you can manipulate it in any way you want. The table does not show up as a linked table in the database window. In fact, when the routine completes and the local variable goes out of scope, the recordset no longer exists.

Now that you have seen how you can link to external tables as well as open them, you are ready to take a look at how you can refine both these processes. This involves learning the Windows Registry settings that affect the linking process, learning more about the parameters that are available to you when specifying connection information, learning how to specify passwords, learning how to refresh and remove links, and learning how to create an external table using VBA code.

Understanding Windows Registry Settings

Each ISAM driver has a separate key in the Windows Registry. These keys are located in the appropriate ISAM driver in the HKEY_LOCAL_MACHINE\SOFTWARE\Microsoft\Jet\ 3.5\ISAM Formats section of the Registry. These keys are used to configure the driver after initialization. As you can see in Figure 19.9, the Setup program has created keys for several data sources. If you look at a specific data source (in this case, FoxPro 2.6), you can see all the settings that exist for the FoxPro 2.6 driver. The `IndexFilter` is set to `FoxPro Index(*.idx;*.cdx)`, for example. At times, you will need to modify one of the Registry settings to customize the behavior of the ISAM driver; this is covered later in this chapter in the section "Looking At Special Considerations."

Figure 19.9.

The Windows Registry with keys for ISAM drivers.

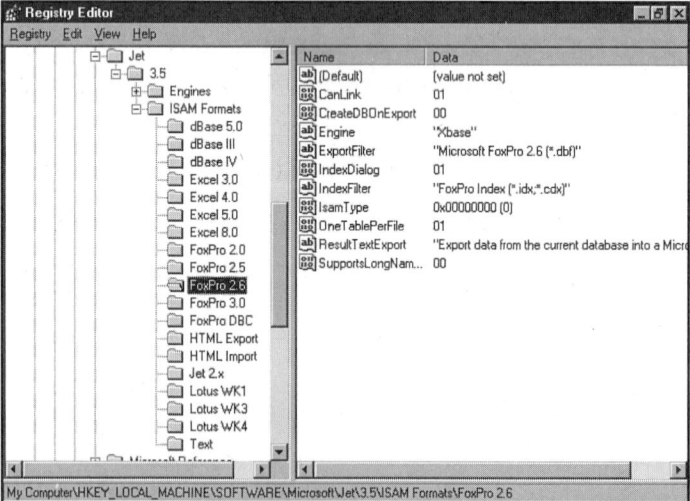

Using the Connection String

The connection string includes the source database type, database name, user ID, password, and *dataset name* (DSN). Each part of the connection string must be separated by a semicolon.

Each source database type has a valid name. This is the name that must be used when accessing that type of data. These database types are listed in Help in the Connect Property section. This is the name found in the Windows Registry under HKEY_LOCAL_MACHINE\Software\ Microsoft\Jet\3.5\ISAM Formats.

You must accurately specify the source database type, or you will be unable to access the external data.

The source database name is the name of the database to which you are linking. In the case of ISAM files, this is the name of the directory in which the file is contained. The Database keyword is used to specify the database name.

The user ID is used whenever a user name must be specified in order to successfully log onto the data source. This is most common when dealing with back-end databases such as Oracle, Sybase, or Microsoft SQL Server. This part of the parameter string can be required to log the user onto the system where the source data resides. The UID keyword is used to refer to the user ID.

As with the user ID, the password most often is included when dealing with back-end data. It also can be used on other database types that support passwords, such as Paradox, or when linking to an external Access table. The PWD keyword is used when specifying the password.

Finally, the dataset name is used to refer to a defined ODBC data source. Communicating with an ODBC data source is covered in detail in Chapter 20. The DSN keyword is used when referring to the dataset name in the connection string.

Working with Passwords

When working with passwords, you probably won't want to hard-code the password into your application because it defeats the purpose of placing a password on your database. In Listing 19.9, the database's password is included in the code, allowing the link to be made to the secured table without any password validation.

Listing 19.9. Embedding a database password in code.

```
Sub LinkToSecured()
    Dim db As DATABASE
    Dim tdf As TableDef
    Set db = CurrentDb
    Set tdf = db.CreateTableDef("tblSecuredTable")
    tdf.Connect = ";Database=" & APPPATH & "\secure.mdb;PWD=alison"
    tdf.SourceTableName = "tblClients"
    db.TableDefs.Append tdf
End Sub
```

Although an invalid password results in a message such as the one in Figure 19.10, it is best to require the user to supply the password at runtime. In Listing 19.10, the password argument is left blank, which causes the user to be prompted for a database.

Listing 19.10. Requiring password validation.

```
Sub ReallySecure()
    Dim db As DATABASE
    Dim tdf As TableDef
    Dim strPassword As String
    Set db = CurrentDb
    Set tdf = db.CreateTableDef("tblSecuredTable")
    strPassword = InputBox("Please Enter Your Password", "Database Security!!")
    tdf.Connect = ";Database=" & APPPATH & "\secure.mdb;PWD=" _
        & strPassword
    tdf.SourceTableName = "tblClients"
    db.TableDefs.Append tdf
End Sub
```

Figure 19.10.

The message that appears after an invalid password is provided.

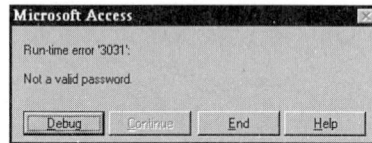

The password is retrieved from the user and stored in a variable called strPassword. This strPassword variable is included in the connection string at runtime.

Refreshing and Removing Links

Refreshing links refers to updating links to an external table. Links need to be refreshed when the location of an external table has changed. *Removing links* refers to the process of permanently removing links to an external table.

Access cannot find external tables if their locations have moved. You need to accommodate for this in your VBA code. Furthermore, there might be times when you want to remove a link to external data—when it is no longer necessary to use the data, or when the data has been imported permanently into Access.

Updating Links That Have Moved

To refresh a link using VBA code, follow these steps:

1. Redefine the connection string.
2. Perform a RefreshLink method on the table definition.

Listing 19.11 shows the code to refresh a link.

Listing 19.11. Refreshing a link.

```
Sub RefreshLink()
    Dim db As Database
    Set db = CurrentDb
    db.TableDefs!FoxCusts.Connect = "FoxPro 2.6;DATABASE=d:\newdir"
    db.TableDefs!FoxCusts.RefreshLink
End Sub
```

You can modify this routine to prompt the user for the directory containing the data tables, as Listing 19.12 shows.

Listing 19.12. Prompting the user for the database path and name.

```
Sub RefreshLink()
    On Error GoTo RefreshLink_Err
    Dim db As DATABASE
    Dim tdf As TableDef
    Dim strNewLocation As String
    Set db = CurrentDb
    Set tdf = db.TableDefs("tblClients")
    tdf.RefreshLink
    Exit Sub

RefreshLink_Err:
    strNewLocation = InputBox("Please Enter Database Path and Name")
    db.TableDefs!tblClients.Connect = ";DATABASE=" & strNewLocation
    Resume
End Sub
```

This routine points a `TableDef` object to the tblClients table. It then issues a RefreshLink method on the table definition object. The RefreshLink method attempts to refresh the link for the table. If an error occurs, an input box prompts the user for the new location of the database. The Connect property for the database is modified to incorporate the new location. The code then resumes on the offending line of code (the RefreshLink). You should modify this routine to give the user a way out. `Resume` throws the user into an endless loop if the database is not available. An enhanced routine (Listing 19.15) is presented later in the "Practical Examples: Working with External Data from within Your Application" section of this chapter.

Deleting Links

To remove a link using VBA code, simply execute a Delete method on the Table Definition collection of the database, as shown in Listing 19.13.

Listing 19.13. Removing a link.

```
Sub RemoveLink()
    Dim db As Database
    Set db = CurrentDb
    db.TableDefs.Delete "FOXCUSTS"
End Sub
```

Creating an External Table

Not only can you link to existing tables, but you can even create new external tables. This means that you actually can design a FoxPro, Paradox, or other type of table using VBA code. The table resides on disk as an independent entity and can be used by its native application and as an external linked table in Access.

Sometimes, it is necessary for your application to provide another application with a data file. That other application might not be capable of reading an Access table. Therefore, you must create the file in a format native to the application that needs to read it.

Creating a "foreign" table is not as difficult as you might think. It's actually not very different from creating an Access table using VBA code, as Listing 19.14 shows.

Listing 19.14. Creating a foreign table.

```
Sub CreateFoxTable()
    Dim db As DATABASE
    Dim rst As Recordset
    Dim fld As Field
    Dim dbFox As DATABASE
    Dim tdfFox As TableDef
```

```
    Set dbFox = DBEngine.Workspaces(0).OpenDatabase_
    ("c:\databases", False, False, "FoxPro 2.6")
    Set tdfFox = dbFox.CreateTableDef("PayMeth")
    Set db = CurrentDb
    Set rst = db.OpenRecordset("tblPaymentMethods", dbOpenSnapshot)
    For Each fld In rst.Fields
        Set fld = tdfFox.CreateField(fld.Name, _
                           fld.Type, _
                           fld.Size)
        tdfFox.Fields.Append fld
    Next fld
    dbFox.TableDefs.Append tdfFox
End Sub
```

This example reads an Access table and writes its structure to a FoxPro table. It uses two `Database` object variables, one `Recordset` object variable, a `TableDef` object variable, and a `Field` object variable. It opens a table called tblPaymentMethods as a snapshot. This is the table that contains the structure you will send to FoxPro. Looking at each field in the table, it grabs that field's Name, Type, and Size properties. It uses those properties as parameters to the CreateField method of the FoxPro table definition, appends each FoxPro field as it loops through each field in the Access table definition, and appends the table definition to create the FoxPro table.

Looking At Special Considerations

When dealing with different types of external files, various problems and issues arise. If you understand these stumbling blocks before they affect you, you will get a great head start in dealing with these potential obstacles.

dBASE

The major concerns you will have when dealing with dBASE files surround deleted records, indexes, data types, and Memo fields. When you delete a record from a dBASE table, it is not actually removed from the table. Instead, it is just marked for deletion. A Pack process must be completed in order for the records to actually be removed from the table. If records are deleted from a dBASE table using an Access application, the records are not removed. Because you cannot pack a dBASE database from within an Access application, the records still remain in the table. In fact, they are not automatically filtered from the Access table. In order to filter deleted records so that they cannot be seen in the Access application, the deleted value in the \HKEY_LOCAL_MACHINE\SOFTWARE\Microsoft\Jet\3.5\Engines\Xbase section of the Registry must be set to 01 (True).

Access can use the dBASE indexes to improve performance. After you link to a dBASE table and select an index, an INF file is created. This file has the same name as your dBASE database with an INF extension. It contains information about all the indexes being used. Here's an example of an INF:

```
[dBASE III]
NDX1=CUSTID.NDX
UNDX1=CUSTID.NDX
```

dBASE III is the database type identifier. NDX1 is an index number for the first index. The UNDX1 entry specifies a unique index.

The data types available in dBASE files are different from those available in Access files. It is important to understand how the field types are mapped. Table 19.4 shows how each dBASE data type is mapped to a Jet data type.

Table 19.4. Mapping of dBASE data types.

dBASE Data Type	Jet Data Type
Character	Text
Numeric, Float	Double
Logical	Boolean
Date	Date/Time
Memo	Memo
OLE	OLE Object

Finally, it is important to ensure that the dBASE memo files are stored in the same directory as the table. Otherwise, Access is unable to read the data in the memo file.

FoxPro

Like dBASE files, the major concerns you will have when dealing with FoxPro files surround deleted records, indexes, data types, and Memo fields. You handle deleted records in the same way you handle dBASE files. You filter deleted records by setting the deleted value in the \HKEY_LOCAL_MACHINE\SOFTWARE\Microsoft\Jet\3.5Engines\Xbase section of the Registry to 01.

As with dBASE indexes, the Access Jet Engine can take advantage of FoxPro indexes. The format of an INF file for a FoxPro file is identical to that of a dBASE file.

FoxPro field types are mapped to Jet field types in the same way that dBASE fields are mapped. The only difference is that FoxPro 3.0 supports Double, Currency, Integer, and DateTime field types. These map to the corresponding Jet field types. As with dBASE, make sure that the Memo files are stored in the same directory as the data tables.

Text Data

When linking to an ASCII text file, Jet can determine the format of the file directly, or it can use a schema information file, which resides in the same directory as the text file. It always is named SCHEMA.INI, and it contains information about the format of the file, the column names, and the data types. The schema information file is optional for delimited files, but it is required for fixed-length files. It is important to understand that ASCII files can never be opened for shared use.

Troubleshooting

Unfortunately, working with external data is not always a smooth process. Many things can go wrong, including connection problems and a lack of temporary disk space.

Connection Problems

Difficulties with accessing external data can be caused by any of the following circumstances:

- The server on which the external data is stored is down.
- The user does not have rights to the directory in which the external data is stored.
- The user does not have rights to the external data source.
- The external data source was moved.
- The UNC path or network share name was modified.
- The connection string is incorrect.
- The installable ISAM driver has not been installed.

Temp Space

Access requires a significant amount of disk space in order to run complex queries on large tables. This disk space is required whether the tables are linked tables stored remotely in another format, or they reside on the local machine. If not enough disk space is available to run a query, the application behaves unpredictably. It therefore is necessary to ensure that all users have enough disk space to meet the requirements of the queries that are run.

Looking At Performance Considerations and Links

Because your application has to go through an extra translation layer (the installable ISAM), performance is not nearly as good with ISAM files as it is with native Jet data. It always is best to import ISAM data whenever possible. If it is not possible to import the data, you need to accept the performance that linking offers or consider linking the best solution to an otherwise unsolvable problem. Opening the recordset using the OpenDatabase method might alleviate the problem, but remember that you cannot use this option with bound forms.

Working with HTML Documents

Access 97 enables you to import, export, and link to HTML documents. Although working with HTML documents is similar to working with other files types, HTML documents deserve special mention. To import an HTML document, follow these steps:

1. Right-click the Tables tab and choose Import.

2. From the Files of type drop-down list, select HTML Documents.

3. Select the document you want to import and click Import. The Import HTML Wizard dialog box appears, as shown in Figure 19.11.

Figure 19.11.
The first step of the HTML Wizard.

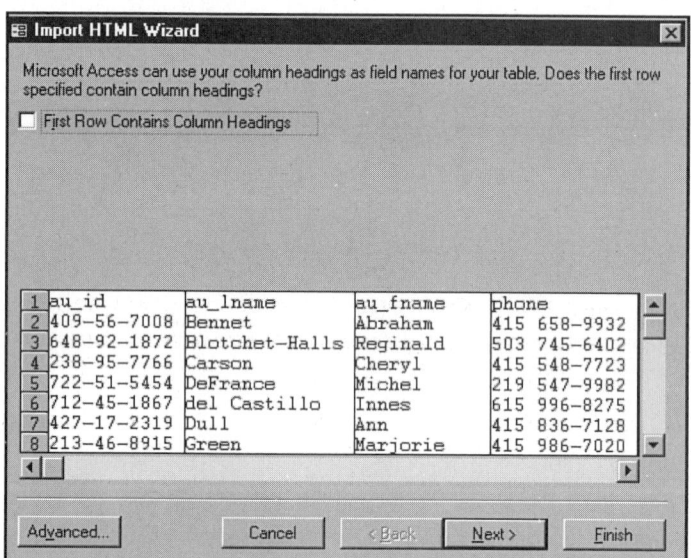

4. The first step of the Wizard attempts to parse the HTML document into fields. You can accept what the Wizard has done or click Advanced. The Web Import Specification dialog box that appears enables you to designate field names, data types, and indexes for each field; and to select any fields you want to eliminate from the imported file. (See Figure 19.12.) This dialog box also enables you to modify the date order, date delimiter, and more.

Figure 19.12.

The Web Import Specification dialog box enables you to designate the specifics of the import.

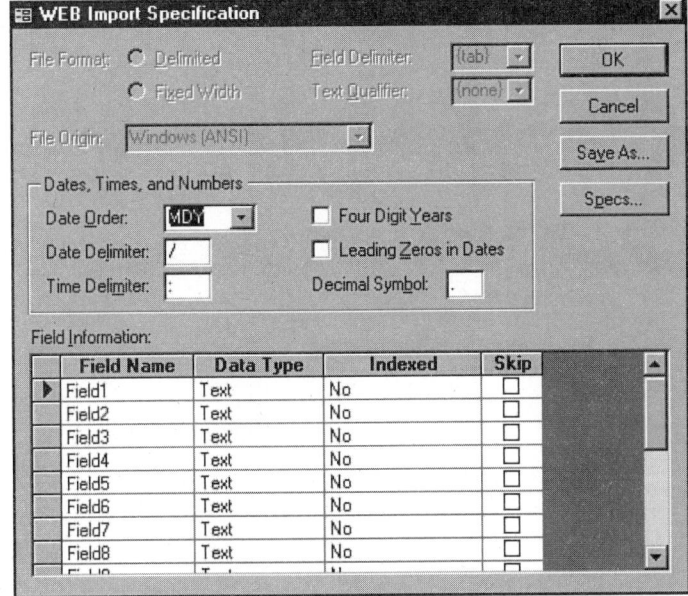

5. After you make any required changes to the import specifications, click OK to return to the HTML Wizard. Click Next to advance to the next step of the Wizard, which enables you to select whether the imported data is stored in a new table or in an existing table. Make your selection and then click Next.

6. The third step of the Wizard enables you to designate a field name, data type, and index for each field, as shown in Figure 19.13. Make any desired changes here and click Next.

7. The fourth step of the Wizard enables you to indicate that you want Access to add a primary key to the table, that you want to select your own primary key, or that you don't want the imported table to have a primary key. Make your selection and click Next.

8. The final step of the Wizard enables you to assign a name to the table. You even can have the Wizard analyze the table after importing it. Click Finish after you make your selection.

Figure 19.13.

Customizing the properties of each imported field.

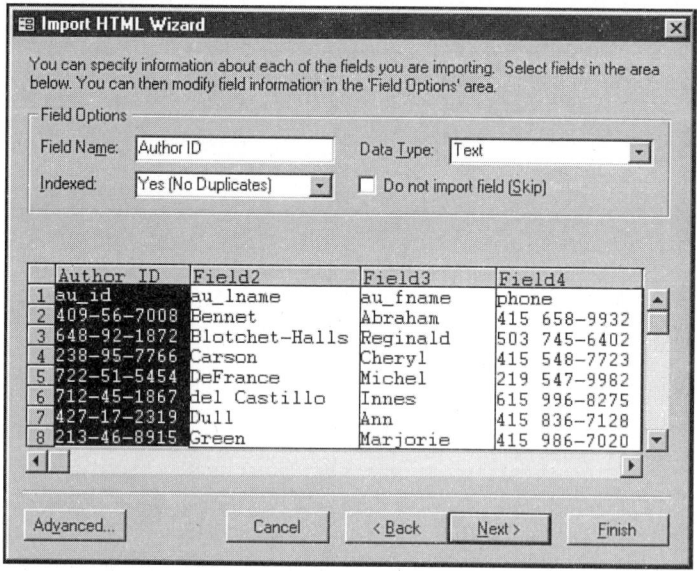

Not only can you import an HTML document, but you also can link to one. To link to an HTML document, follow these steps:

1. Right-click the Tables tab and choose Link Tables.
2. From the Files of Type drop-down list, select HTML Documents.
3. Select the table you want to link to and click Link. The Link HTML Wizard appears.
4. Click the Advanced button to modify any link specifications and return to the first step of the Wizard. Click Next to move to the second step of the Wizard.
5. The second step of the Link HTML Wizard enables you to specify information about each field you are importing. Make any required changes and click Next.
6. Supply a name for the linked table and click Finish.

Whereas an imported HTML document acts like any other Access table, the data in a linked HTML document is not modifiable from within Access. You can use the linked document to create queries, reports, and forms.

Practical Examples: Working with External Data from within Your Application

It's time to split the data tables from the remainder of the application objects. You easily can accomplish this by using the Database Splitter. After you split the tables from the rest of the database objects, you need to write code to refresh links. Both these topics are covered in this section.

Splitting the Database By Using the Database Splitter

Begin by using the Database Splitter to separate the tables from the rest of the database objects. The CHAP19.MDB and CHAP19DATA.MDB files are on the sample code CD-ROM. The CHAP19DATA.MDB file contains all the tables, and CHAP19.MDB contains the rest of the database objects.

Refreshing Links

If you distributed the Time and Billing application and all users did not have the same path to the CHAP19DATA.MDB file, the application would not load successfully. The AutoExec function ensures that the tables are successfully linked, as Listing 19.15 shows.

Listing 19.15. Loading the application and checking table attachments.

```
Function AutoExec()
  On Error GoTo AutoExec_Err:

  Dim fAnswer As Boolean
  Dim dblStartTime As Double
  Dim dblTimeElapsed As Double

  'Open splash screen form
  DoCmd.OpenForm "frmSplash"
  DoEvents
  'Invoke hourglass
  DoCmd.Hourglass True
  'Call routine that checks if tables are properly attached
  fAnswer = AreTablesAttached()
  'Test return value and proceed only if tables were
  'successfully attached
  If Not fAnswer Then
    MsgBox "You Cannot Run This App Without Locating Data Tables"
    DoCmd.Close acForm, "frmSplash"
    DoCmd.Close acForm, "frmGetTables"
  End If
  Call GetCompanyInfo
  DoCmd.Hourglass False
  DoCmd.OpenForm "frmClients"
  'If splash screen is still loaded, unload it
  If IsLoaded("frmSplash") Then
    DoCmd.Close acForm, "frmSplash"
  End If
  Exit Sub

AutoExec_Err:
    MsgBox "Error # " & Err.Number & ": " & Err.Description
    Exit Sub
End Function
```

Notice that the `AreTablesAttached` routine is called from the `AutoExec` routine. If the `AreTablesAttached` routine returns `False`, a message is displayed and the application is exited. Listing 19.16 shows the `AreTablesAttached` routine.

Listing 19.16. The `AreTablesAttached` routine.

```
Function AreTablesAttached() As Boolean
    ' Update connection information in attached tables.
    '
    ' Number of attached tables for progress meter.
    Const MAXTABLES = 8
    Const NONEXISTENT_TABLE = 3011
    Const DB_NOT_FOUND = 3024
    Const ACCESS_DENIED = 3051
    Const READ_ONLY_DATABASE = 3027

    Dim intTableCount As Integer
    Dim intResponse As Integer
    Dim strFilename As String
    Dim strAppDir As String
    Dim vntReturnValue As Variant
    Dim tdf As TableDef
    Dim db As DATABASE
    Dim rst As Recordset

    Set db = CurrentDb

    AreTablesAttached = True
    ' Continue if attachments are broken.
    On Error Resume Next
    ' Open attached table to see if connection information is correct.
    Set rst = db.OpenRecordset("tblClients")
    ' Exit if connection information is correct.
    If Err.Number = 0 Then
     rst.Close
     Exit Function
    Else
     'Otherwise, determine location of current database
     strAppDir = Left(db.Name, LastOccurence(db.Name, "\"))
     'Try to establish the connection searching for the linked
     'tables in the same folder as the application database
     If TryAgain(strAppDir) Then
        rst.Close
        Exit Function
     End If
     'If connection still cannot be established, continue
     'Warn the user
     MsgBox "You Must Locate the Data Tables"
     DoEvents
     Forms!frmGetTables!dlgCommon.DialogTitle = _
         "Please Locate the Database Containing the Data Tables"
     Forms!frmGetTables!dlgCommon.ShowOpen
     strFilename = Forms!frmLogon!dlgCommon.filename
    End If
    If strFilename = "" Then
       GoTo Exit_Failed ' User pressed Cancel.
    End If
```

```
' Initialize progress meter.
vntReturnValue = SysCmd(SYSCMD_INITMETER, "Attaching tables", MAXTABLES)

' Loop through all tables, reattaching those with
' nonzero-length Connect strings.
intTableCount = 1 ' Initialize TableCount for status meter.
For Each tdf In db.TableDefs
    If tdf.Connect <> "" Then
        tdf.Connect = ";DATABASE=" & strFilename
        Err.Number = 0
        tdf.RefreshLink
        If Err.Number <> 0 Then
            If Err.Number = NONEXISTENT_TABLE Then
                MsgBox "File '" & strFilename & _
                    "' does not contain required table '" & _
                    tdf.SourceTableName & "'", 16, "Can't Run This App"
            ElseIf Err.Number = DB_NOT_FOUND Then
                MsgBox "You can't run FSG Main Application " & vbCrLf & _
                    "Until you locate Data File", 16, "Can't Run Application"
            ElseIf Err.Number = ACCESS_DENIED Then
                MsgBox "Couldn't open " & strFilename & _
                    " because it is read-only or it is located " & _
                    "on a read-only share.", 16, "Can't Run This App"
            ElseIf Err.Number = READ_ONLY_DATABASE Then
                MsgBox "Can't reattach tables because Data File " & _
                    "is read-only or is located on a read-only share.", _
                    16, "Can't Run This App"
            Else
                MsgBox Error, 16, "Can't Run This App"
            End If
            intResponse = MsgBox(tdf.Name & " Not Found. " & _
                vbCrLf & "Would You Like to Locate it?", _
                vbQuestion + vbYesNo)
            If intResponse = vbYes Then
                Forms!frmLogon!dlgCommon.DialogTitle = "Please Locate " & _
                    tdf.Name
                Forms!frmLogon!dlgCommon.ShowOpen
                strFilename = Forms!frmLogon!dlgCommon.filename
            Else
                AreTablesAttached = False
                GoTo Exit_Final
            End If
        End If
        intTableCount = intTableCount + 1
        vntReturnValue = SysCmd(SYSCMD_UPDATEMETER, intTableCount)
    End If
Next tdf
GoTo Exit_Final
Exit_Failed:
    MsgBox "You can't run this example until " & _
        "you locate Data File", 16, "Can't Run This Example"
    AreTablesAttached = False
Exit_Final:
    vntReturnValue = SysCmd(SYSCMD_REMOVEMETER)
End Function
```

The `AreTablesAttached` function begins by pointing the `DB` object variable to the current database and setting its default return value to True. It issues an `On Error Resume Next` statement, instructing Access to proceed with the next line of code if an error is encountered. Next, it attempts to open a recordset based on the tblClients table. If the tables are not properly linked, an error occurs. The `If Err.Number = 0` statement tests to see whether an error occurred. If the `Err.Number` is equal to 0, no error occurred and the function can be exited. Otherwise, the application attempts to locate the data file in the directory that contains the application database. If this is not successful, the ShowOpen method is applied to a Common Dialog control, which is placed on a hidden form called frmGetTables.

The *Common Dialog control* is an ActiveX control that is included as part of the Office Developer Edition Tools for Windows 95. It is covered in detail in Chapter 26, "Using ActiveX Controls." In this case, the control invokes the File Open common dialog box. The filename the user selects in the File Open dialog box is returned to the variable `strFilename`. After a potential new location for the tables is identified by the user, Access attempts to issue the RefreshLink method on each table found in the Table Definitions collection of the current database. If the link to any table is not refreshed properly, another error occurs and a return value of `False` is returned from the `AreTablesAttached` function.

Summary

The capability to link to external data is one of Access 97's strongest attributes. It is important that you understand how to link to external data via the user interface and by using VBA code. This chapter taught you how to link to external tables, open external data sources directly, refresh and remove links, and create external tables using VBA code. Many of the techniques covered in this chapter are explored further in Chapter 20.

20

Client/Server
Techniques

- Understanding the Client/Server Model, 600
- Deciding Whether to Use the Client/Server Model, 600
- Looking At Roles Access Plays in the Application Design Model, 605
- Learning the Client/Server Buzzwords, 608
- Upsizing: What to Worry About, 609
- Proactively Preparing for Upsizing, 612
- Defining an ODBC Data Source, 612
- Connecting to a Database Server, 615
- Working with Linked Tables, 616

Understanding the Client/Server Model

Client/server is one of the hot computing terms of the '90s. It refers to distributed processing of information. It involves the storage of data on database servers dedicated to the tasks of processing data and storing it. These database servers are referred to as *back-ends*. A front-end tool such as Microsoft Access accomplishes the presentation of the data. Microsoft Access, with its tools that assist in the rapid development of queries, forms, and reports, provides an excellent front-end for the presentation of back-end data. As more and more applications are downsized from mainframes and upsized from personal computers, more users need to understand the details of client/server technology.

For years, most information professionals have worked with traditional programming languages. These languages are responsible for both processing and maintaining data integrity in the application. This means that data-validation rules must be embedded in the programming code. Furthermore, these types of applications are record-oriented. All records are read into memory and processed. This scenario has several drawbacks:

- If the underlying data structure changes, every application that uses the data structure must be changed.
- Data-validation rules must be placed in *every* application that accesses a data table.
- Presentation, processing, and storage are handled by one program.
- Record-oriented processing results in an extraordinary amount of unnecessary network traffic.

The client/server model introduces a separation of functionality. The *client*, or front-end, is responsible for presenting the data and doing some processing. The *server*, or back-end, is responsible for storing, protecting, and performing the bulk of the data processing.

Deciding Whether to Use the Client/Server Model

Client/server technology was not as necessary when there was a clear delineation between mainframe applications and personal computer applications. Today, the line of demarcation has blurred. Personal computer applications are beginning to take over many applications that had been relegated to mainframe computers in the past. The problem is that users still are very limited by the bandwidth of network communications. This is one place where client/server technology can really help.

Many developers are confused about what client/server architecture really is. (In fact, I have participated in many debates in which other developers have insisted that Access itself is a database server application. Well, it's not.) Access is a front-end application that can process data stored on a back-end. In this scenario, the Access application runs on the client machine accessing data stored on a database server running software such as Microsoft SQL Server. Access does an excellent job acting as the client-side, front-end software in this scenario. The confusion lies in Access's capability to act as a database server.

Many people mistakenly believe that an Access MDB database file stored on a file server acts as a database server. This is *not* the case. The difference is in the way in which data is retrieved when Access is acting as the front-end to a database server versus when the data is stored in an Access MDB file. Suppose that you have a table with 500,000 records. A user runs a query based on the 500,000-record table stored in an Access database on a file server. The user wants to see a list of all the Californians who make more than $75,000 per year. With the data stored on the file server in the Access MDB file format, all records are sent over the network to the workstation, and the query is performed on the workstation. (See Figure 20.1.) This results in significant network traffic.

Figure 20.1.
Access as a front-end and a back-end.

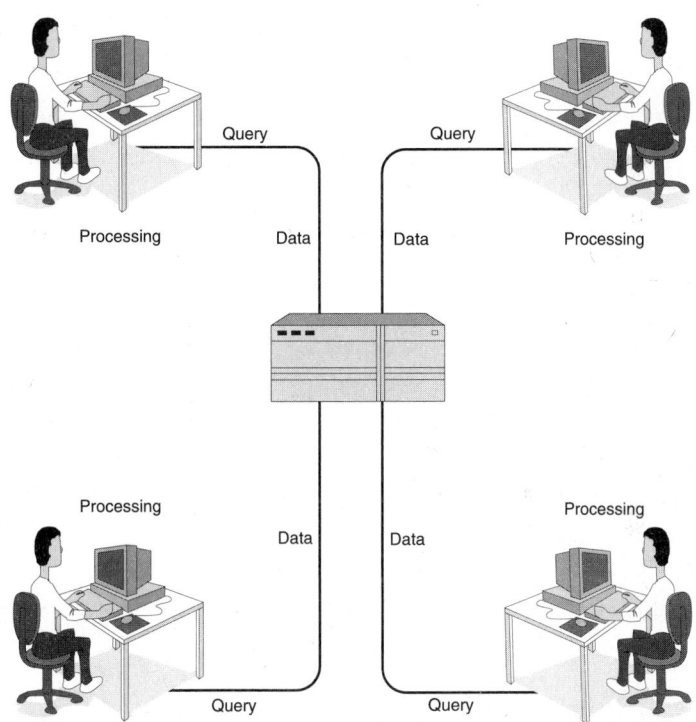

On the other hand, assume that these 500,000 records are stored on a database server such as Microsoft SQL Server. The user runs the same query. In this case, only the names of the Californians who make more than $75,000 per year are sent over the network. In fact, if you request only specific fields, only the fields you request are retrieved. (See Figure 20.2.)

What does this mean to you? When should you become concerned with client/server technology, and what it can offer you? The following sections present some reasons why you might want to upsize.

Figure 20.2.
Access as a front-end using a true back-end.

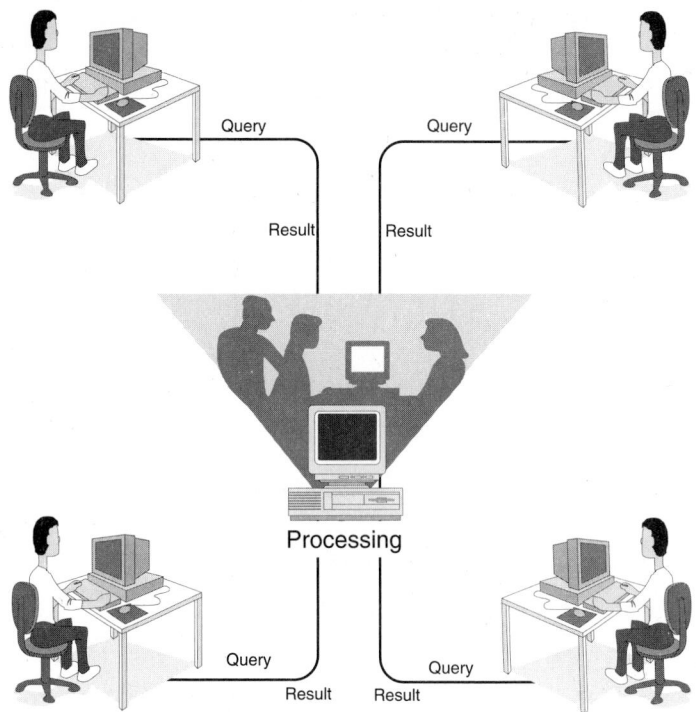

Dealing With a Large Volume of Data

As the volume of data in an Access database increases, you probably will notice a degradation in performance. Many people say that 100M is the magic number for the maximum size of an Access database, but many back-end database servers can handle databases containing multiple gigabytes of data. Although a maximum size of 100M for an Access database is a good general guideline, it is *not* a hard-and-fast rule. You might find that the need to upsize occurs when your database is significantly larger or smaller than 100M. The magic number for you depends on all the factors discussed in the following sections, as well as on how many tables are included in the database. Generally, Access performs better with large volumes of data stored in a single table rather than in multiple tables.

Dealing With a Large Number of Concurrent Users

Just as a large volume of data can be a problem, so can a large number of concurrent users. In fact, more than 10 users concurrently accessing an Access database can really degrade performance. As with the amount of data, this is not a magic number. I have seen applications with fewer than 10 users where performance was awful, and I have seen applications with significantly more than 10 users where performance was acceptable. It often depends on how the application is designed, as well as what tasks the users are performing.

Demanding Faster Performance

Certain applications demand better performance than others. An *On-line Transaction Processing* system (OLTP) generally requires significantly better performance than a *Decision Support System* (DSS), for example. Suppose that 100 users are simultaneously taking phone orders. It would not be appropriate for the users of the system to ask their customers to wait 15 seconds between entering each item that is ordered. On the other hand, asking users to wait 60 seconds to process a management report that users run once each month is not an unreasonable request (although many still will complain about the minute). Not only does the client/server architecture itself lead to better performance, but most back-end database servers can use multithreaded operating systems with multiple processors; Access cannot.

Handling Increased Network Traffic

As a file server in an organization experiences increasing demands, the Access application simply might exacerbate an already growing problem. By moving the application data to a database server, the overall reduced demands on the network might give all users on the network better performance, regardless of whether they are using the Access application.

Probably one of the most exaggerated situations I have seen was one in which all the workstations were diskless. Windows and all application software were installed on a file server. All the users were concurrently loading Microsoft Word, Microsoft Excel, and Microsoft PowerPoint over the network. In addition, they had large Access applications with many database objects and large volumes of data. All this was stored on the file server as well. Needless to say, performance was abysmal. You can't expect an already overloaded file server to be able to handle sending large volumes of data over a small bandwidth. The benefits offered by client/server technology can help alleviate this problem.

Implementing Backup and Recovery

The backup and recovery options offered with an Access MDB database stored on a file server simply do not rival the options for backup and recovery on a database server. Any database server worth its salt sports very powerful *uninterruptible power sources* (UPSs). Many have hot-swappable disk drives with disk mirroring, disk duplexing, or disk striping with parity (RAID Level 5). With disk mirroring and duplexing, data can be written to multiple drives at one time, providing instantaneous backups. Furthermore, some database server tape backup software enables backups to be completed while users are accessing the system. Many offer automatic transaction logging. All these options mean that there is less chance of data loss or downtime. With certain applications, this type of backup and recovery is overkill. With other applications, it is imperative. Although some of what back-ends have to offer in terms of backup and recovery can be mimicked by using code and replication, it is nearly impossible to get the same level of protection from an Access database stored on a file server that you can get from a database stored on a database server.

Focusing on Security

Access offers what can be considered the best security for a desktop database. Although this is the case, the security offered by an Access database cannot compare with that provided by most database servers. Database server security often works in conjunction with the network operating system. This is the case, for example, with Microsoft SQL Server and Windows NT Server. Remember that no matter how much security you place on an Access database, this does not prevent a user from deleting the entire MDB file from the network disk. It is very easy to offer protection against this potential problem, and others, on a database server. Furthermore, many back-end application database server products offer field-level security not offered in an Access MDB file. Finally, many back-ends offer integrated security with one logon for both the network and the database.

Sharing Data among Multiple Front-End Tools

The Access MDB file format is proprietary. Very few other products can read data stored in the Access database format. With a back-end database server that supports *open database connectivity* (ODBC), front-end applications can be written in a variety of front-end application software, all concurrently using the same back-end data.

Understanding What It All Means

You need to evaluate the specific environment in which your application will run:

- How many users are there?
- How much data exists?
- What is the network traffic already like?
- What type of performance is required?
- How disastrous is downtime?
- How sensitive is the data?
- What other applications will use the data?

After you answer all these questions, as well as additional ones, you can begin to make decisions about whether the benefits of the client/server architecture outweigh the costs involved. The good news is that it is not an all-or-none decision. Various options are available for client/server applications using Access as a front-end. Furthermore, if you design your application with upsizing in mind, moving to client/server technology will not require you to throw out what you have done and start again. In fact, Microsoft provides an Upsizing Wizard, which makes upsizing to an SQL Server database an almost painless process.

Roles Access Plays in the Application Design Model

Before you move on to learn more about client/server technology, take a look at the different roles Access can take in an application design. Several options are available, which are explored in this section.

The Front-End and Back-End

Earlier in this book, you learned about using Access as both the front-end and the back-end. The Access database is not acting as a true back-end because it is not doing any processing. Figure 20.3 shows the architecture in this scenario. The Access application resides on the workstation. Access uses the Microsoft Jet Engine to communicate with data stored in an Access MDB database file stored on the file server.

Figure 20.3.

Access as a front-end using an MDB file for data storage.

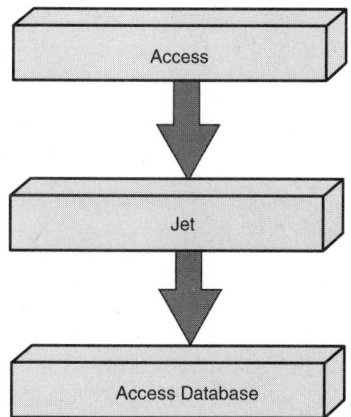

The Front-End Using Links to Communicate to a Back-End

In the second scenario, back-end tables can be linked to the front-end application database. The process of linking to back-end tables is almost identical to that of linking to tables in other Access databases or to external tables stored in FoxPro, Paradox, or dBASE. After the back-end tables are linked to the front-end application database, they can be treated like any other linked tables. Access uses ODBC to communicate with the back-end tables. (See Figure 20.4.) Your application sends an Access SQL statement to the Access Jet Engine. Jet translates the Access SQL statement into ODBC SQL. The ODBC SQL statement then is sent to the ODBC Manager. The ODBC Manager locates the correct ODBC driver and passes it the ODBC SQL statement. The ODBC driver, supplied by the back-end vendor, translates the ODBC SQL statement into the back-end's specific dialect. The back-end-specific query then is sent to the SQL server and to the appropriate database. As you might imagine, all this translation takes quite a bit of time. That is why one of the two alternatives that follow might be a better solution.

Figure 20.4.

Access as a front-end using links to back-end tables.

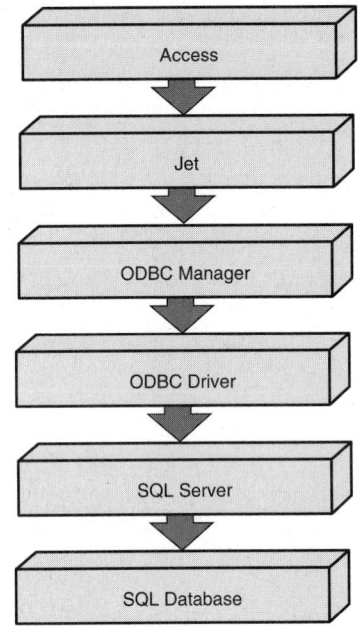

The Front-End Using SQL Pass-Through to Communicate to a Back-End

One of the bottlenecks of linked tables is the translation of the Access SQL statement by Jet to ODBC SQL, which then is translated by the ODBC driver to a generic SQL statement. Not only is the translation slow, but there might be other reasons why you want to bypass the translation process:

- Access SQL might not support some operation that is supported by the native query language of the back-end.
- Either the Jet Engine or the ODBC driver might produce a SQL statement that is not optimized for the back-end.
- You might want a process performed in its entirety on the back-end.

Pass-through queries are covered in more detail in the "Using Pass-Through Queries" section of this chapter. For now, look at what happens when a pass-through query is executed. The pass-through query is written in the syntax specific to the back-end database server. Although the query does pass through the Jet Engine, Jet does not perform any translation on the query. Neither does ODBC. The ODBC Manager sends the query to the ODBC driver. The ODBC driver passes the query to the back-end without performing any translation. In other words, exactly what was sent from Access is what is received by the SQL database. Figure 20.5 illustrates this scenario. Notice that the Jet Engine, the ODBC Manager, and the ODBC driver are not eliminated entirely. They are still there, but they have much less impact on the process than they do with attached tables. As you will see later in this chapter, pass-through queries are not a panacea, although they are very useful. The results of a pass-through query are not updatable, for example. Furthermore, because pass-through queries are written in the back-end's specific SQL dialect, you need to rewrite them if you swap out your back-end. For these reasons and others, pass-through queries generally are used with other solutions.

Figure 20.5.

Access sending a pass-through query to a back-end database.

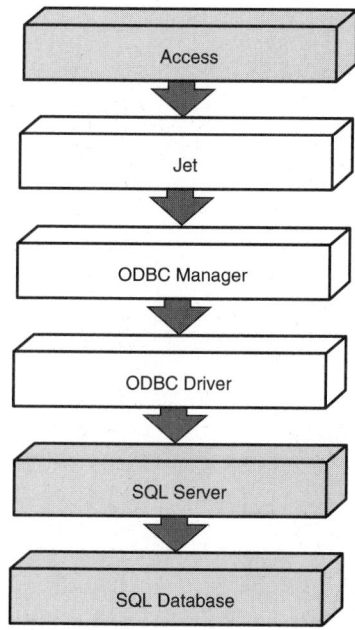

The Front-End Using ODBCDirect to Communicate to a Back-End

An additional, very viable solution is available when working with a back-end database server. This involves using ODBCDirect, which now is available with Access 97. By using ODBCDirect, you bypass the Jet Engine entirely. SQL statements are written in ODBC SQL. Figure 20.6 illustrates this scenario. Although this might look like a lot of layers, ODBCDirect is a very thin wrapper on the ODBC API calls. The SQL statement travels quickly through all the layers to the back-end database. From a performance standpoint, this solution puts Jet to shame. The major advantage of ODBCDirect over pass-through queries is that you write the SQL statements in ODBC SQL instead of the back-end-specific SQL. This means that your application easily is portable to other back-end database servers. You can swap out your back-end with little modification to your application. Furthermore, ODBCDirect is very similar to DAO, so the transition to this great technology is not a difficult one. The major disadvantage of ODBCDirect is that it cannot be used with bound forms or reports. This means a lot more coding for you. As with pass-through queries, this option can be used with the other solutions in order to gain required performance benefits in mission-critical parts of the application. ODBCDirect is covered in detail later in this chapter in "Using ODBCDirect to Access Client/Server Data."

Figure 20.6.

Access using ODBCDirect to communicate to a back-end.

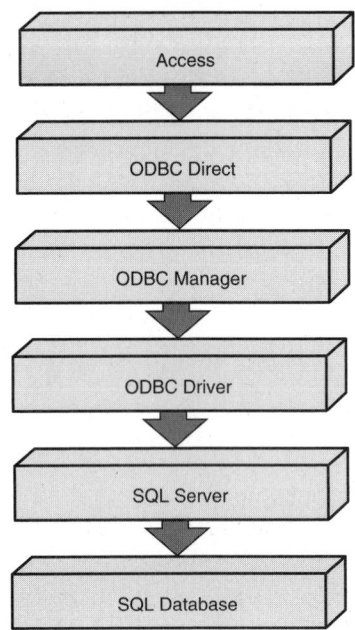

Learning the Client/Server Buzzwords

People who talk about client/server technology use many terms that are unfamiliar to the average database developer. To get a full appreciation of client/server technology and what it offers, you must have at least a general understanding of the terminology. Table 20.1 lists the most commonly used terms.

Table 20.1. Client/server terms.

Term	Definition
Column	A field.
DDL	*Data-definition language* used to define and describe the database structure.
Foreign key	A value in one table that must be looked up in another table for validation.
ODBC (Open Database Connectivity)	A standard proposed by Microsoft that provides access to a variety of back-end databases through a common interface. In essence, ODBC is a translator.
Primary key	A set of fields that uniquely identify a row.
Row	A record.

Term	Definition
Schema	Blueprint of the entire database. Includes table definitions, relationships, security, and other important information about the database.
SQL (Structured Query Language)	Type of data-manipulation language commonly used to talk to tables residing on a server.
Stored procedures	Compiled SQL statements, such as queries, stored on the database server. Can be called by an application.
Transaction	A set of actions that must be performed on a database. If any one action fails, all the actions are discarded.
Triggers	Pieces of code that execute in response to an action occurring on a table (insert, edit, or delete).

Many books are devoted solely to client/server technology; one good book is *Visual Basic/SQL Server Primer*, by Heng Tan. Most magazines targeted at developers contain numerous articles on client/server technology: *DBMS* always contains many excellent articles, and *Databased Advisor* usually offers numerous articles specifically about client/server connectivity using Access as a front-end. Another excellent source of information is the Microsoft Developer Network CD-ROM. Offered as a subscription by Microsoft, it includes numerous articles and white papers on client/server technology, ODBC, and using Access as a front-end to a database server.

Upsizing: What to Worry About

Suppose that your database is using Microsoft Access as both the front-end and back-end. Although an Access database on a file server might have been sufficient for a while, the need for better performance, enhanced security, or one of the other benefits that a back-end database provides compels your company (or your client's company) to upsize to a client/server architecture. The Access tables already have been created and even contain volumes of data. In this scenario, it might make sense to upsize.

Because all the tables have been designed as Access tables, they need to be upsized to the back-end database server. Upsizing involves moving tables from a local Access database (or from any PC database) to a back-end database server that usually runs on UNIX, Windows NT Server, or OS/2 LAN Server; or as a Novell NetWare NLM.

Another reason why tables are upsized from Access to a back-end server is that many developers prefer to design their tables from within the Access environment. Access offers a more user-friendly environment for table creation than do most server applications.

Regardless of your reasons for upsizing, you need to understand several issues regarding the movement, or upsizing, of Access tables to a database server. Indeed, because of the many caveats involved when moving tables from Access to a back-end, many people opt to design the tables directly on the back-end. If you do design your tables in Access, you should export them to the back-end and then link them to your local database. As you export your tables to the database server, you need to be aware of the issues covered in the following sections.

> **NOTE**
>
> If you are updating to an SQL Server database, most of the concerns regarding upsizing are handled by the Upsizing Wizard available from Microsoft.

Indexes

When exporting a table to a server, no indexes are created. All indexes need to be re-created on the back-end database server. If your database server is running Microsoft SQL Server, you can use the Access Upsizing Wizard for Access 97. This tool creates indexes for server tables in the place where the indexes exist in your Access tables.

AutoNumber Fields

AutoNumber fields are exported as Long integers. Because most database servers do not support autonumbering, you have to create an insert trigger on the server that provides the next key value. You also can achieve autonumbering by using form-level events, but this is not desirable, because the numbering will not be enforced if other applications access the data. As with indexes, if you are upsizing to Microsoft SQL Server, the Upsizing Wizard for Access 97 can build triggers for all your AutoNumber fields.

Default Values

Default values are not automatically moved to the server, even if the server supports them. You can set up default values directly on the server, but these values do *not* automatically appear when new records are added to the table unless the record is saved without data being added to the field containing the default value. As with autonumbering, default values can be implemented at the form level, with the same drawbacks. The Upsizing Wizard for Access 97 exports default values to your server database.

Validation Rules

Validation rules are not exported to the server. You must re-create these rules by using triggers on the server. No Access-defined error messages are displayed when a server validation rule is violated. You should code your application to provide the appropriate error messages. You also can perform validation rules at the form level, but they are enforced if the data is accessed by other means. The Upsizing Wizard for Access 97 exports validation rules to the server database.

Relationships

Relationships need to be enforced using server-based triggers. Access's default error messages do not appear when referential integrity is violated. You need to respond to and code for these error messages in your application. You can enforce relationships at the form level, but as with other form-level validations, this method of validation does not adequately protect your data. The Upsizing Wizard for Access 97 builds triggers that mimic all relationships and referential integrity that you have set up in your Access database.

Security

Security features that you have set up in Access do not carry forward to the server. You need to re-establish table security on the server. After security is set up on the server, Access is unaware that the security exists until the Access application attempts to violate the server's security. Then, error codes are returned to the application. You must handle these errors by using code and displaying the appropriate error message to users.

Table and Field Names

Servers often have much more stringent rules than Access regarding the naming of fields. When you export a table, all characters that are not alphanumeric are converted to underscores. Most back-ends do not allow spaces in field names. Furthermore, most back-ends limit the length of object names to 30 characters or fewer. If you already have created queries, forms, reports, macros, and modules that use spaces and very long field and table names, these database objects might become unusable when you move your tables to a back-end database server.

Reserved Words

Most back-ends have many reserved words. It is important to be aware of the reserved words of your specific back-end. It is quite shocking when you upsize a table and find that field names that you have been using are reserved words on your database server. If this is the case, you need to rename all the fields in which a conflict occurs. Once again, this means modifying all the queries, forms, reports, macros, and modules that reference the original field names.

Case-Sensitivity

Many back-end databases are case-sensitive. If this is the case with your back-end, you might find that your queries and application code don't process as expected. Queries or code that refers to the field or table name by using the wrong case is not recognized by the back-end database and does not process correctly.

Properties

Most properties cannot be modified on remote tables. Any properties that can be modified are lost upon export, so you need to set them up again when the table is exported.

Visual Basic Code

Certain properties and methods that work on Access tables might not work on remote tables. This might necessitate some coding changes after you export your tables.

Proactively Preparing for Upsizing

If you set up your tables and code modules with upsizing in mind, you can eliminate many of the preceding pitfalls. Despite the problems that upsizing can bring, the scalability of Access is one of its stronger points. Sometimes resources are not available to implement client/server technology in the early stages of an application. If you think through the design of the project with the possibility of upsizing in mind, you will be pleased at how relatively easy it is to move to client/server technology when the time is right. With the Access 97 Upsizing Wizard, which is designed to take an Access application and upsize it to Microsoft SQL Server, the process is relatively simple. The Access 97 version of this tool is available on www.msn.com. The upsizing tool for Access 97 performs a lot of the work involved in upsizing a database with just the click of a few buttons.

Defining an ODBC Data Source

Before you can use Microsoft Access with a database server, you need to load the ODBC drivers. These drivers come with Access and are installed with the product. You also need to load drivers for the specific back-end database servers to which you want to connect. These drivers usually are purchased from the back-end database vendor and often come with a per-seat charge. This means that you must purchase a client license for each user who will connect to the remote data.

An ODBC data source is a user-defined name that points to a remote source of data. It contains all the properties of the data source that are necessary to communicate with data stored on a database server.

Before you can access a remote table from Access, you must define it by using the ODBC Data Source Administrator. If you do not define that data source, or if it is not defined correctly, you will be unable to access the data.

You set up ODBC data sources in the ODBC Data Source Administrator. (See Figure 20.7.) Depending on your installation, the ODBC Data Source Administrator could be a stand-alone application, or it could appear as a control-panel icon. By default, this icon appears as 32-bit ODBC. It enables you to create, modify, and delete data sources, and to obtain information about existing drivers. Remember that a data source is simply a user-definable name that stores settings that can be used to access a back-end located on a particular server using a specified driver.

Figure 20.7.
The User Data Sources window in the ODBC Data Source Administrator.

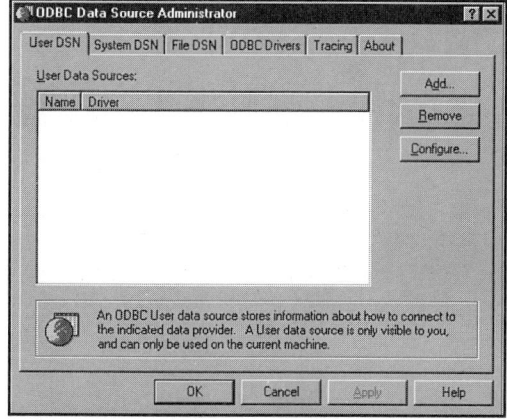

The ODBC Data Source Administrator is a tabbed dialog box. Table 20.2 describes how you use these tabs.

Table 20.2. Using the ODBC Data Source Administrator.

Tab	Function
User DSN	Enables you to add, delete, and set up data sources that are local to a computer and can be used only by the current user.
System DSN	Enables you to add, delete, and set up data sources that are local to a computer but are not specific to a particular user.
File DSN	Enables you to add, delete, and set up data sources that are file-based and can be shared between all users who have the same drivers installed. File DSNs are not limited to a specific machine.
ODBC Drivers	Displays information about installed ODBC drivers.
Tracing	Enables you to specify how the ODBC Driver Manager traces calls to ODBC functions. The available options are all of the time, for one connection only, dynamically, or by a custom trace DLL.
About	Gives information about core components, such as the location of files and version numbers.

After you enter the ODBC Data Source Administrator, you probably should set up a new data source. To define a new data source, click the Add button on the User DSN or System DSN tab, or click New on the File DSN tab of the dialog box. The Create New Data Source dialog box appears, from which you must select the name of the driver that the data source will use. (See Figure 20.8.)

Figure 20.8.

The Create New Data Source dialog box.

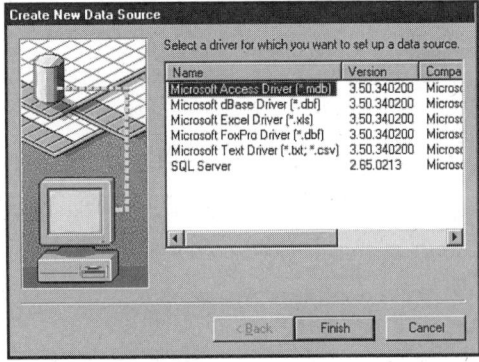

The list of available drivers varies, depending on which client drivers have been installed on the machine. After you select a data source and click Finish, another dialog box appears, which varies depending on which driver you selected. You use this dialog box to define specific information about the data source you are creating. An example is the ODBC SQL Server Setup dialog box shown in Figure 20.9. As you can see, this dialog box enables you to specify information, such as the data source name, server name, network address, and so on. If you click the Options button, the dialog box expands to appear as shown in Figure 20.10.

Figure 20.9.

The ODBC SQL Server Setup dialog box.

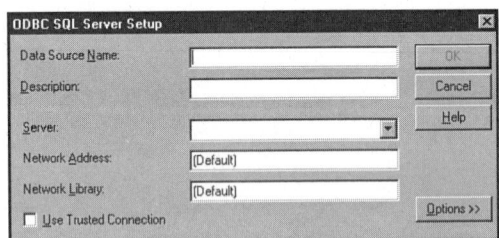

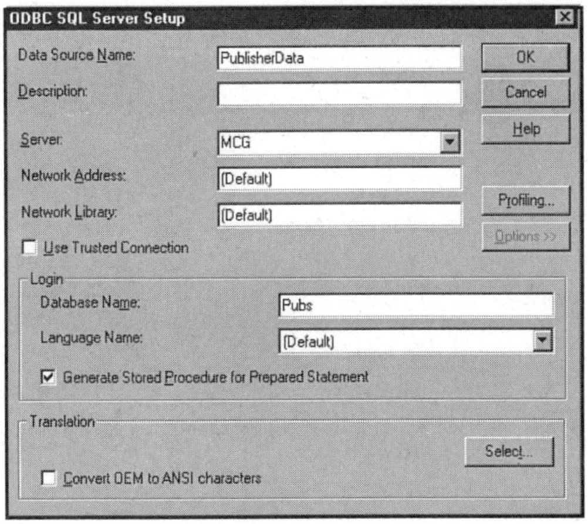

Figure 20.10.

The expanded ODBC SQL Server Setup dialog box.

The expanded dialog box enables you to specify additional information, such as the database name and language name. After you fill out this dialog box and click OK, the data source name is added to the list of data sources listed in the ODBC Data Source Administrator.

NOTE

You might be wondering how you can possibly go through the process of defining data sources on thousands of user machines in a large installation. Fortunately, you can automate the process of defining data sources by using DLL functions. It is a matter of using the ODBC Data Source Administrator DLL function calls to set up the data source by using code. The alternative is to set up file DSNs that are available to all your users.

Connecting to a Database Server

After you define a data source, you are ready to connect to it. You can use these methods to access server data:

- Link to tables residing on the server.
- Link to views residing on the server.
- Use pass-through queries to send SQL statements directly to the server.
- Use VBA code to open the server tables directly.
- Use ODBCDirect to open and manipulate the server tables.

Working with Linked Tables

The easiest method of accessing data on the server is to link to the external tables. These linked tables act almost exactly like native Access tables. When you link to remote tables, Access analyzes the fields and indexes contained in the tables so that it can achieve optimal performance. It is important to relink the tables if the structures of the remote tables change. This section discusses how you can link to remote tables through the user interface and by using code.

Linking to External Tables via the User Interface

To link to a remote table through the user interface, right-click on the Tables tab of the Database window, and then select Link Tables. From the Files of Type drop-down list, select ODBC Databases. The Select Data Source dialog box shown in Figure 20.11 appears. This dialog box has two tabs: File Data Source and Machine Data Source. You use the File Data Source tab to select from the file DSNs that have been defined. These are the data sources available to all users on all machines. You use the Machine Data Source tab to select from the user and system data sources you have defined. These data sources are available to just one user and just one machine.

Figure 20.11.

The Select Data Source dialog box.

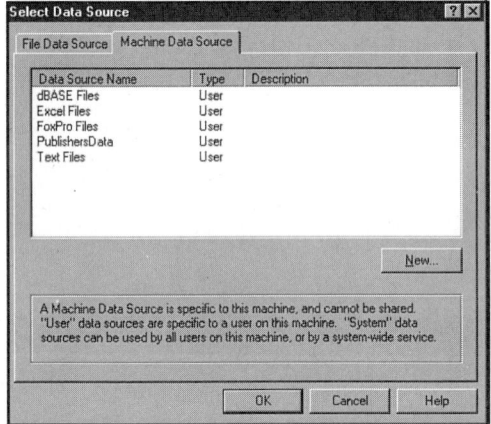

You can select an existing data source or define a new data source directly from the Select Data Source dialog box. After you select a data source, you are prompted with a Login dialog box. You can't obtain access to the server data unless you have a valid login ID and password. Figure 20.12 shows the SQL Server Login dialog box.

If you successfully log onto the server, you are presented with a list of tables contained in the database that the data source is referencing. Here, you must select the table to which you want to link. Figure 20.13 shows the Link Tables dialog box.

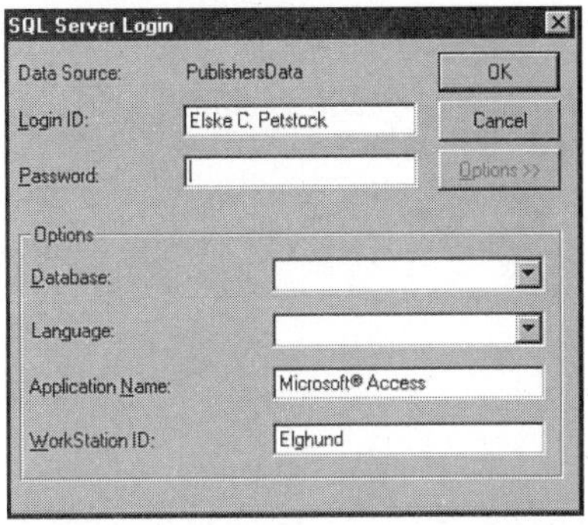

Figure 20.12.

The SQL Server Login dialog box.

Figure 20.13.

The Link Tables dialog box.

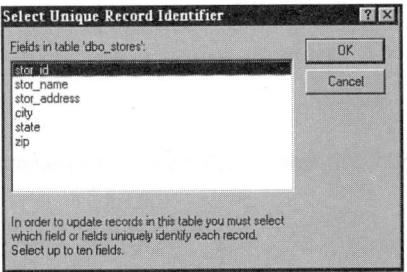

After you select one or more tables and click OK, you might be prompted with the Select Unique Record Identifier dialog box, as shown in Figure 20.14. Selecting a unique identifier for the table enables you to update records on the back-end data source. Select a unique identifier and click OK. The linked tables appear in the Database window, as shown in Figure 20.15. These tables can be treated like any other table (with a few exceptions that are covered later in this chapter).

Figure 20.14.

The Select Unique Record Identifier dialog box.

Figure 20.15.

The Database window with links to ODBC tables.

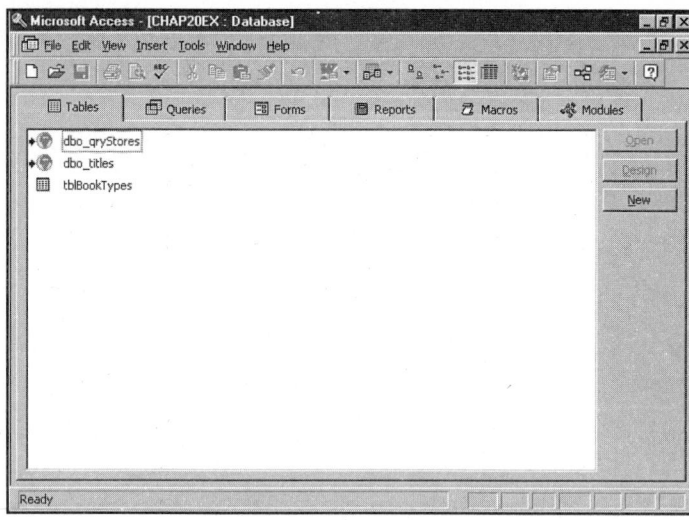

Linking to External Tables via Code

You just learned how you can link to a remote table by using Access's user interface. Now take a look at how you can link to the same table by using code. The subroutine in Listing 20.1 accepts six parameters: the name for the Access table, the name of the server database, the name of the server table, the dataset name, the user ID, and the password.

Listing 20.1. VBA code for linking to an external table.

```
Sub LinkToSQL(strAccessTable, strDBName, strTableName, _
    strDataSetName, strUserID, strPassWord)
    Dim db As DATABASE
    Dim tdf As TableDef
    Set db = CurrentDb
    Set tdf = db.CreateTableDef(strAccessTable)
    tdf.Connect = "ODBC;Database=" & strDBName _
                & ";DSN=" & strDataSetName _
                & ";UID=" & strUserID _
                & ";PWD=" & strPassWord
    tdf.SourceTableName = strTableName
    db.TableDefs.Append tdf
End Sub
```

Here is an example of how you call the subroutine. The Access table you are creating is called tblStores. The database name on the server is Pubs. The table to which you are linking is called dbo.Stores, and the dataset name is PublisherData. You are logging on as SA (database System Administrator) without a password. The user ID and password could have been supplied as the user logged onto your application and could have been stored in variables until needed for logging onto the server, as this code shows:

```
Call LinkToSQL("tblStores", "Pubs", "dbo.Stores", "PublisherData", "SA", "")
```

Linking to Views Rather Than Tables

Views on a database server are similar to Access queries. Views provide a form of security by limiting which rows and columns a user can see. Access is given to the view rather than directly to the underlying table. By default, views are not updatable. You can make a view updatable by including all the fields that comprise the primary key in the view and building a unique index on the primary key. You can create views in one of two ways:

- Using the SQL Server Enterprise Manager for SQL 6.0 or 6.5 (or the equivalent option for your back-end database server)
- Using the Create View statement in Access

To create a remote view from Access, follow these steps:

1. Create a new query.
2. When you are prompted with the Show Table dialog box, click Close *without* selecting a table.
3. Choose Query|SQL Specific|Pass-Through.
4. Type the Create View statement, as shown in Figure 20.16.

Figure 20.16.

Creating a query for a remote view.

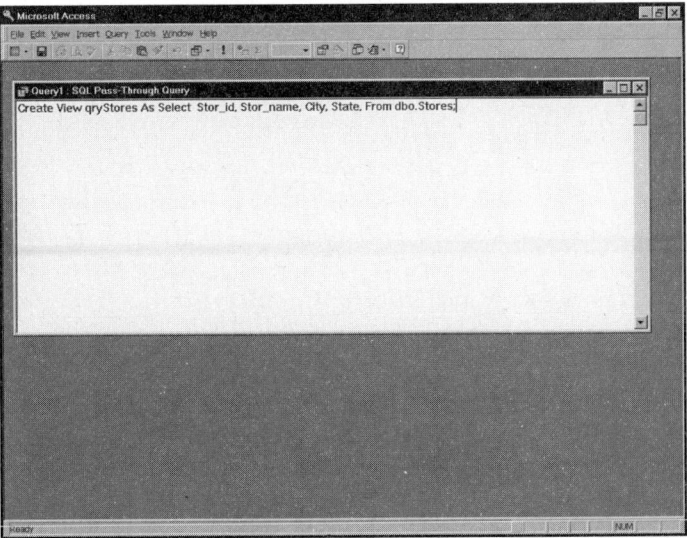

5. Click Run.

6. Select a SQL data source and click OK.

7. Supply the logon information and click OK. You might receive the message shown in Figure 20.17. This message, and how to avoid it, are explained in the section "Executing a Stored Procedure," later in this chapter.

Figure 20.17.

The error message received when creating a remote view.

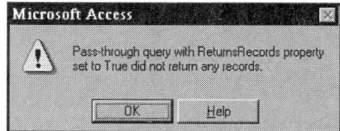

After you create a remote view, you can link to it like any other table. If you link to the view, you are prompted with the Select Unique Record Identifier dialog box, as shown in Figure 20.18. It is very important to supply Access with a unique index. Otherwise, the results of the view will not be updatable. The view then can be treated as though it were a link to a table.

Figure 20.18.

The Select Unique Record Identifier dialog box after selecting a view.

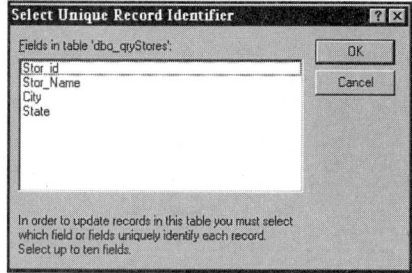

Using Pass-Through Queries

Ordinarily, when you store and execute a query in Access, even if it is running on remote data, Access compiles and optimizes the query. In many cases, this is exactly what you want. On other occasions, however, it might be preferable for you to execute a pass-through query, because pass-through queries are not analyzed by Access's Jet Engine. These queries are passed directly to the server, and this reduces the time Jet needs to analyze the query and enables you to pass server-specific syntax to the back-end. Furthermore, pass-through queries can log informational messages returned by the server. Finally, bulk update, delete, and append queries are faster using pass-through queries than they are using Access action queries based on remote tables.

Pass-through queries do have their downside. They always return a snapshot, rendering them not updatable. You also must know the exact syntax the server requires, and you must type the statement into the Query window instead of painting it graphically. Finally, you cannot parameterize a query so that it prompts the user for a value.

Creating a Pass-Through Query with the User Interface

To create a pass-through query, you can build the query in the Access Query Builder. Choose Query | SQL Specific | Pass-Through. You are presented with a text-editing window in which you can enter the query statement. The SQL statement you enter must be in the SQL flavor specific to your back-end.

Executing a Pass-Through Query Using Code

You also can perform a pass-through query by using VBA code. In fact, you must create the pass-through query by using VBA code if you want the query to contain parameters that you will pass to the server. Here's one way you can create a pass-through query by using VBA code:

1. Use the OpenDatabase method of the workspace object to open the SQL server database. You must supply the connect string as the fourth parameter to the OpenDatabase function.

2. Use the Execute method to execute the SQL statement on the back-end database server. As with an SQL statement created by choosing Query | SQL Specific | Pass-Through, the statement you create must be in the syntax specific to your particular back-end.

Listing 20.2 shows the code for this procedure.

Listing 20.2. Executing a pass-through query using code.

```
Sub PassThroughQuery(strDBName As String, _
              strDataSetName As String, _
              strUserID As String, _
              strPassWord As String)
    Dim ws As Workspace
    Dim db As DATABASE
    Dim strConnectString As String

    strConnectString = "ODBC;DATABASE=" & strDBName & _
                    ";DSN=" & strDataSetName & _
                    ";UID=" & strUserID & _
                    ";PWD=" & strPassWord
    Set ws = DBEngine(0)
    Set db = ws.OpenDatabase( "", False, False, strConnectString)
    db.Execute "Update dbo.Sales Set Qty = Qty + 1", _
        dbSQLPassThrough
End Sub
```

The routine is called as shown in this code:

```
Call PassThroughQuery("Pubs", "PublisherData", "SA","" )
```

This subroutine uses a connect string that connects to a database called Pubs, with a data source named PublisherData, a user ID of SA, and no password. It then executes a pass-through query that updates the Qty field of each record to Qty+1.

As you saw, one method of executing a pass-through query is to open the database using the OpenDatabase method and then execute the query using the Execute method on the database object. The limitation of this method is that the Execute method does not enable you to execute queries that return data. You can use another method of executing a pass-through query when you want to return records. It involves creating a query definition in the local database and opening a recordset using a pass-through query or a stored procedure as the SQL property for the query definition. This method is covered in the next section.

Executing a Stored Procedure

You also can execute a stored procedure on a back-end database server. A stored procedure is similar to a query or program stored on the back-end, and it performs some action. An example is the SQL Server 6.0 stored procedure called sp_columns. This stored procedure returns information on the fields in a table. Figure 20.19 shows how you execute the sp_columns stored procedure from the Query Design window. You simply type the name of the stored procedure and any parameters it must receive. Take a good look at the Query Properties window shown in Figure 20.19. If you enter a valid ODBC connect string, the user is not prompted to log on at runtime. The Return Records property is another important property. In this case, you want to set the value of the property to Yes so that you can see the results of the stored procedure. If the stored procedure does not return records, as is the case with the Create View pass-through query created in the "Linking to Views Rather Than Tables" section, it is important to set this property to No. Otherwise, you receive an error message indicating that no rows were returned. Figure 20.20 shows the results of running the stored procedure.

Figure 20.19.

Executing a stored procedure from the Query Design window by typing the name of the stored procedure and any parameters it must receive.

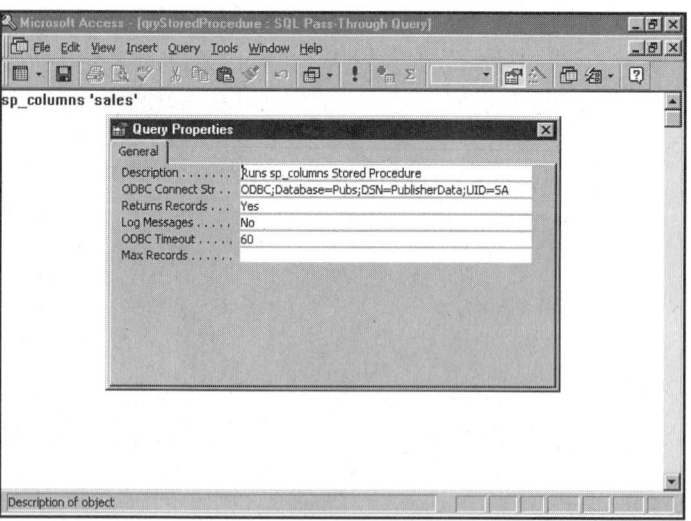

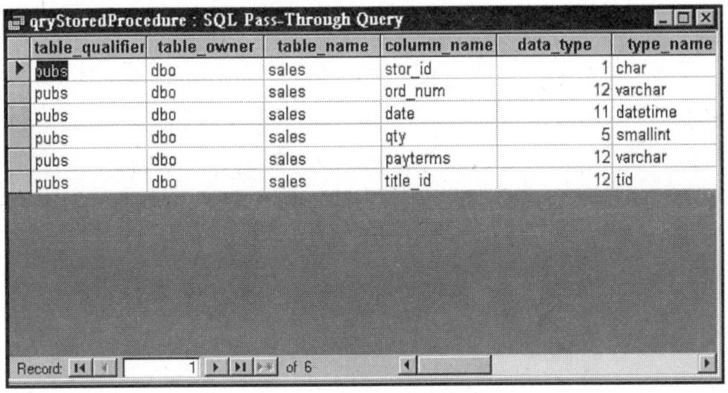

Figure 20.20.

The result of running the sp_columns stored procedure.

table_qualifier	table_owner	table_name	column_name	data_type	type_name
pubs	dbo	sales	stor_id	1	char
pubs	dbo	sales	ord_num	12	varchar
pubs	dbo	sales	date	11	datetime
pubs	dbo	sales	qty	5	smallint
pubs	dbo	sales	payterms	12	varchar
pubs	dbo	sales	title_id	12	tid

Listing 20.3 shows the procedure that executes the sp_columns stored procedure using code.

Listing 20.3. Executing the sp_columns stored procedure.

```
Sub StoredProcedure()
    Dim ws As Workspace
    Dim db As DATABASE
    Dim dbAccess As DATABASE
    Dim qdf As QueryDef
    Dim rst As Recordset

    Set dbAccess = CurrentDb
    Set ws = DBEngine(0)
    Set db = ws.OpenDatabase("", False, False, _
        "ODBC;DATABASE=Pubs;DSN=PublisherData;UID=SA;PWD=")
    Set qdf = dbAccess.CreateQueryDef("")
    qdf.Connect = "ODBC;DATABASE=Pubs;DSN=PublisherData;UID=SA;PWD="
    qdf.SQL = "sp_columns 'sales'"
    qdf.ReturnsRecords = True
    Set rst = qdf.OpenRecordset(dbOpenSnapshot)
    Do While Not rst.EOF
        Debug.Print rst!Column_Name
        rst.MoveNext
    Loop
End Sub
```

Here's how it works. Because you want to return records, you cannot use the Execute method (covered in the "Executing a Pass-Through Query Using Code" section, earlier in this chapter). Another way to execute a pass-through query is to first create an Access QueryDef object. In this case, the QueryDef object is temporary (notice the quotation marks). The Connect property is set for the QueryDef object. Instead of specifying a back-end-specific SQL statement, the SQL property of the QueryDef object is set to the name of the stored procedure and any parameters it expects to receive. The ReturnsRecords property of the QueryDef object is set to True. The OpenRecordset method then is issued on the QueryDef object. This returns the snapshot from the stored procedure. The Do While loop goes through the resulting recordset, printing the Column_Name column of each row returned from the sp_columns stored procedure.

623

Opening a Server Table Directly

As you saw earlier, you can use the OpenDatabase method of the Workspace object to execute pass-through queries. This is a very valid use of the OpenDatabase method. You also can use this method in place of linking to tables to access server data directly. This generally is extremely inefficient, because the data structure is not analyzed and maintained in the Access Database Engine. With linked tables, the fields, indexes, and server capabilities are cached in memory so that they are readily available when needed. Regardless, you occasionally might want to open a database directly. One reason is to preconnect to a server so that you will be connected when you need access to the data. The subroutine in Listing 20.4 shows how you can use the OpenDatabase function to connect to a remote server database.

Listing 20.4. Using OpenDatabase to connect to a remote server database.

```
Sub OpenRemoteDB(strDBName As String, _
                strDataSetName As String, _
                strUserID As String, _
                strPassWord As String)
    Dim ws As Workspace
    Dim db As DATABASE
    Dim tdf As TableDef
    Dim intCounter As Integer
    Dim strConnectString As String

    Set ws = DBEngine(0)
    strConnectString = "ODBC;DATABASE=" & strDBName & _
                    ";DSN=" & strDataSetName & _
                    ";UID=" & strUserID & _
                    ";PWD=" & strPassWord
    Set db = ws.OpenDatabase( "", False, False, strConnectString)
    For Each tdf In db.TableDefs
        Debug.Print tdf.Name
    Next tdf
End Sub
```

The routine is called like this:

```
Call OpenRemoteDB("Pubs", "PublisherData", "SA", "")
```

This routine uses the OpenDatabase method of the Workspace object to open the database called Pubs with the connect string specified. It then loops through the collection of table definitions, listing all the tables found in the remote server database.

Using ODBCDirect to Access Client/Server Data

As mentioned earlier in this chapter, ODBCDirect enables you to work with ODBC databases without loading the Microsoft Jet Database Engine. ODBCDirect has the following advantages over the other methods of accessing client/server data covered in this chapter:

- It gives you direct access to ODBC data sources.

- Fewer resources are required on the client side.

- The server is responsible for all query processing.

- You are able to access functionality not available when accessing ODBC via Jet.

- You can execute asynchronous queries. This means that you don't have to wait for a query to complete execution before you begin another operation.

- You can perform batch updates. This means that you can cache changes locally and then submit them to the server as a batch.

- You can run queries that return multiple result sets.

- You easily can limit the number of records returned in a result set.

- You easily can monitor messages and errors generated by the remote data source.

The disadvantages of ODBCDirect follow:

- Updatable joins are not available with ODBCDirect. Jet, however, gives you the capability to update recordsets based on multi-table joins.

- You cannot join tables located on different data sources.

- Using ODBCDirect, you cannot create and modify table structures.

- You cannot bind ODBCDirect recordsets to forms and reports.

To use ODBCDirect, you must create an ODBCDirect workspace. You do this by specifying the dbUseODBC constant in the Type argument of the CreateWorkspace method. After the ODBCDirect workspace is created, you use DAO code to manipulate it, as Listing 20.5 shows.

Listing 20.5. Creating an ODBCDirect workspace.

```
Sub CreateODBCWorkspace()

    Dim wrkODBC As Workspace
    Dim db As Database
    Dim rst As Recordset
    Dim prp As Property
    Dim fld As Field

    ' Create an ODBCDirect workspace
    Set wrkODBC = CreateWorkspace("ODBCWorkspace", "SA", _
        "", dbUseODBC)
    Workspaces.Append wrkODBC

    'Open an ODBC data source
    Set db = wrkODBC.OpenDatabase("PublisherData")
    Set rst = db.OpenRecordset("dbo.Stores")

    'Loop through the fields collection of the dbo.Stores
    'table found on the ODBC data source
    For Each fld In rst.Fields
        Debug.Print fld.Name
```

continues

Listing 20.5. continued

```
Next fld

'Display field values from the dbo.Stores table on
'the ODBC data source
Do While Not rst.EOF
   Debug.Print rst!stor_id & " - " & _
      rst!stor_name
   rst.MoveNext
Loop

rst.Close
wrkODBC.Close


End Sub
```

This code should look strikingly similar to Jet DAO code, and it is! In this example, the only difference between the ODBCDirect code and Jet DAO code is the dbUseODBC constant passed to the CreateWorkspace method and the ODBC data source name used as the database name parameter of the OpenDatabase method. The rest of the code looks exactly like any other DAO code. Listing 20.5 illustrates how you can loop through the fields collection of a table to display names and values of various fields. The code required is the same code required to accomplish these tasks using Jet.

Along with the introduction of ODBCDirect, Microsoft introduced many new properties and methods designed to take advantage of the power of ODBC databases. The code in Listing 20.6 loops through the properties of an ODBC workspace, an ODBC database, and an ODBC recordset and displays their properties.

Listing 20.6. Code to list and display ODBCDirect properties.

```
Sub ListODBCWorkspaceProps()

   Dim wrkODBC As Workspace
   Dim prp As Property
   Dim db As Database
   Dim rst As Recordset

   ' Create an ODBCDirect workspace
   Set wrkODBC = CreateWorkspace("ODBCWorkspace", "SA", _
      "", dbUseODBC)
   Workspaces.Append wrkODBC

   With wrkODBC
      ' Enumerate Properties collection of ODBCDirect
      ' workspace.
      Debug.Print "Properties of " & .Name
      On Error Resume Next

      For Each prp In .Properties
         Debug.Print prp.Name & " = " & prp
```

```
      Next prp
      On Error GoTo 0
   End With

   Set db = wrkODBC.OpenDatabase("PublisherData")
   With db
      Debug.Print "Properties of " & .Name
      On Error Resume Next

      For Each prp In .Properties
         Debug.Print prp.Name & " = " & prp
      Next prp
   End With

   Set rst = db.OpenRecordset("dbo.sales")
   With rst
      Debug.Print "Properties of " & .Name
      On Error Resume Next

      For Each prp In .Properties
         Debug.Print prp.Name & " = " & prp
      Next prp
   End With

   rst.Close
   db.Close
   wrkODBC.Close


End Sub
```

If you look at the list of properties in the Debug window, you probably will notice that many properties are available that are not available using Jet DAO. An example of a property available through ODBCDirect is the StillExecuting property of a recordset. This property is used to determine whether an asynchronous query is still executing. Another example is the Prepare property. This property lets you know whether a query should be prepared on the server with the SQLPrepare function as a temporary stored procedure or whether it can be executed directly using the SQLExecDirect function.

In addition to an expanded list of properties, ODBCDirect also adds a new list of methods. The NextRecordset method retrieves the next set of records returned from a multi-recordset query, for example. The RegisterDatabase method enters connection information for an ODBC data source in the Windows Registry.

The bottom line is that ODBCDirect provides you with significant power over ODBC data sources. This power comes with only a small learning curve beyond a basic knowledge of DAO. Combined with the other methods of accessing client/server applications, ODBCDirect can go a long way toward helping you develop applications that take full advantage of client/server functionality and performance.

Summary

In this chapter, you learned to be concerned with client/server technology when dealing with large volumes of data, large numbers of concurrent users, a demand for faster performance, problems with increased network traffic, backup and recovery, security, and a need to share data among multiple front-end tools. You also learned the roles Access can play in the application design model. Some client/server buzzwords also were introduced.

21

Client/Server Strategies

- Developing Client/Server Strategies, 630
- Selecting the Best Recordset Type, 630
- Using Forward-Scrolling Snapshots, 631
- Using Key Set Fetching, 631
- Using Pass-Through Queries and Stored Procedures, 631
- Using ODBCDirect, 632
- Preconnecting to the Server, 632
- Reducing the Number of Connections, 633
- Optimizing Data Handling, 633
- Optimizing Queries and Forms, 633
- Practical Examples: Using Client/Server Strategies, 637

Developing Client/Server Strategies

As you saw in the preceding chapter, it is very easy to implement client/server strategies ineffectively. This can result in worse performance rather than better performance. The developer's task is to intelligently apply appropriate techniques that deploy client/server systems effectively.

This chapter discusses strategies to help you develop smart client/server applications.

Selecting the Best Recordset Type

Sometimes it is best to create a dynaset, and at other times it is more efficient to create a snapshot. It is very important that you understand which choice is the most appropriate for a given circumstance.

In essence, a *dynaset* is a collection of bookmarks that enable each record on the server to be identified uniquely. Each bookmark corresponds to one record on the server and generally is equivalent to the primary key of the record. Because the bookmark is a direct pointer back to the original data, a dynaset is an updatable set of records. When you create a dynaset, you create a set of bookmarks of all rows that meet the query criteria. If you open a recordset using code, only the first bookmark is returned to the user PC's memory. The remaining columns from the record are brought into memory only if they are referenced directly using code. This means that large fields, such as OLE and Memo, are not retrieved from the server unless they are accessed explicitly using code. Access uses the primary key to fetch the remainder of the columns. As the code moves from record to record in the dynaset, additional bookmarks and columns are retrieved from the server.

> **NOTE**
>
> You can't be sure you've retrieved all the bookmarks unless you use the MoveLast method or you loop through each record in the recordset by using code.

Although this keyset method of data retrieval is relatively efficient, dynasets carry significant overhead associated with their editability. This is why snapshots often are more efficient.

> **NOTE**
>
> A *snapshot* is a static set of records returned from a query.

When you open a snapshot type of recordset, all columns from the first row are retrieved into memory. As you move to each row, all columns in the row are retrieved. If you issue a MoveLast method, all rows and all columns meeting the query criteria immediately are retrieved into the client machine's memory. Because a snapshot is not editable and maintains no link back to the server, it can be more efficient. This generally is true only for relatively small recordsets. The caveat lies in the fact that all rows and all columns in the result set are returned to the user's memory regardless of whether they are accessed. If your result set contains more than 500 records, the fact that all columns are returned to the user's memory outweighs the benefits provided by a snapshot. In these cases, you might want to create a read-only dynaset.

Using Forward-Scrolling Snapshots

If your data does not need to be updated and it is sufficient to move forward through a recordset, you might want to use a forward-scrolling snapshot. Forward-scrolling snapshots are extremely fast and efficient. You create a forward-scrolling snapshot by using the dbForwardOnly option of the OpenRecordset method. This renders the recordset forward-scrolling only, which means that you cannot issue a MovePrevious or MoveFirst method. You also cannot use a MoveLast method, because only one record is retrieved at a time. There is no concept of a set of records, so Access cannot move to the last record. This method of data retrieval provides significantly better performance than regular snapshots with large recordsets.

Using Key Set Fetching

The fact that dynasets return a set of primary keys causes problems with forms. With a very large set of records and a large primary key, sending just the primary keys over the network wire can generate a huge volume of network traffic. When you open a form, Access retrieves just enough data to display on the form. It then continues to fetch the remainder of the primary keys that satisfy the query criteria. When keyboard input is sensed, the fetching process stops until idle time is available. Access then continues to fetch the remainder of the primary keys. To prevent the huge volume of network traffic associated with this process, you must carefully limit the size of the dynasets that are returned. The section "Optimizing Forms," later in this chapter, explores methods you can use to limit the size of your dynasets.

Using Pass-Through Queries and Stored Procedures

It is important to remember that executing pass-through queries and stored procedures is much more efficient than returning a recordset to be processed by Access. Pass-through queries and the details of how they are implemented were covered in Chapter 20, "Client/Server Techniques." The difference with pass-through queries lies in where the processing occurs. With pass-through queries and stored procedures, all the processing is completed on the server. When operations are performed using VBA code, all the records that will be affected by the process must be returned to the user's memory, modified, and then returned to the server. This generates a significant amount of network traffic and slows down processing immensely.

Using ODBCDirect

ODBCDirect is a technology that enables you to access ODBC data without loading the Microsoft Jet Database Engine. It provides dramatic increases in performance by eliminating the bottlenecks that the Jet Engine imposes. Queries are sent directly to ODBC instead of being parsed and translated by Jet. ODBCDirect was covered in detail in Chapter 20. The main drawback of ODBCDirect is that you cannot use it with bound forms and reports. Instead, it returns a set of records that you must process programmatically. Despite this limitation, the performance ODBCDirect offers you may not only be worth the trouble, but necessary in order for you to achieve satisfactory performance with an application that uses client/server data.

Preconnecting to the Server

When dealing with ODBC databases, connections to the server are handled transparently by Jet. After you issue a command, a connection is established with the server. When you finish an operation, Jet keeps the connection open in anticipation of the next operation. The ConnectionTimeout setting in the Windows Registry determines the amount of time the connection is cached. You might want to use the fact that a connection is cached to connect to the back-end when your application first loads, before the first form or report even opens. The connection and authentication information will be cached and used when needed.

As you saw in the LinkToSQL routine in Chapter 20, you can send password information stored in variables as parameters when creating a link to a server. These values easily could have come from a logon form. The code in Listing 21.1 pre-connects to the server. You generally would place this in the startup form for your application.

Listing 21.1. Preconnecting to the server.

```
Sub PreConnect(strDBName As String, _
            strDataSetName As String, _
            strUserID As String, _
            strPassWord As String)
    Dim db As DATABASE
    Dim strConnectString As String
    strConnectString = "ODBC;DATABASE=" & strDBName & _
                    ";DSN=" & strDataSetName & _
                    ";UID=" & strUserID & _
                    ";PWD=" & strPassWord
    Set db = OpenDatabase("", False, False, strConnectString)
    db.Close   'Closes the database but maintains the connection
End Sub
```

The trick here is that the connection and authentication information are maintained even after the database is closed.

Reducing the Number of Connections

Some database servers are capable of running multiple queries on one connection. Other servers, such as Microsoft SQL Server, are capable of processing only one query per connection. You should try to limit the number of connections required by your application. This section looks at some ways you can reduce the number of connections your application requires.

Dynasets containing more than 100 records require two connections—one to fetch the key values from the server and the other to fetch the data associated with the first 100 records. Therefore, try to limit query results to fewer than 100 records wherever possible.

If connections are at a premium, you should close connections that you are no longer using. You can do this by moving to the last record in the result set or by running a Top 100 Percent query. Both techniques have dramatic negative effects on performance, because all the records in the result set are fetched. You therefore should use these techniques only if reducing connections is more important than optimizing performance.

Finally, you might want to set a *connection timeout*. This means that if no action is performed for a specified period of time, the connection is closed. The default value for the connection timeout is 10 minutes. You can modify this value in the My Computer\ HKEY_LOCAL_MACHINE\SOFTWARE\Microsoft\Jet\3.5\Engines\ODBC key of the Windows Registry by changing the ConnectionTimeout setting. The timeout occurs even if a form is open. Fortunately, Access automatically reestablishes the connection when it is needed.

Optimizing Data Handling

One of the best things you can do to optimize data handling—such as edits, inserts, and deletes—is to add a Version field (timestamp) to each remote table. This Version field is employed when users update the data on the remote table to avoid overwrite conflicts. If this field does not exist, the server compares every field to see whether it has changed since the user first began editing the record. This is quite inefficient and is much slower than evaluating a timestamp.

Using transactions is another way to improve performance significantly, because transactions enable multiple updates to be written as a single batch. As an added benefit, transactions protect your data by ensuring that everything has executed successfully before changes are committed to disk.

Optimizing Queries and Forms

On the whole, the movement to client/server architecture improves performance. If you are not careful when designing your queries, forms, and reports, this movement actually can degrade performance, however. You can do several things to ensure that the movement to client/ server applications is beneficial. These techniques are broken down into query techniques and form techniques.

Optimizing Queries

Servers cannot perform many of the functions offered by the Access query builder. The functions that cannot be processed on the server are performed on the workstation. This often results in a large amount of data being sent over the network wire. You can eliminate this extra traffic if you design your queries so that they can be processed solely by the server.

Examples of problem queries that cannot be performed on the server follow:

- Top N% queries
- Queries containing user-defined or Access functions
- Queries that involve tables from two different data sources—for example, a query that joins tables from two servers or from an Access table and a server table

Optimizing Forms

You can use the techniques in this section to design forms that capitalize on the benefits of the client/server architecture. The idea is to design your forms so that they request the minimal amount of data from the server and obtain additional data only if requested by the user. This means that you request as few records and fields as possible from the server. You can accomplish this by basing forms on queries instead of directly on the tables. You can further refine this process by designing your forms specifically with data retrieval in mind. A form can be opened initially with no RecordSource, for example. The form can require that users limit the criteria before any records are displayed.

You should store static tables, such as a state table, locally. This practice reduces network traffic and requests to the server. Furthermore, you should not base combo boxes and list boxes on server data. Whenever possible, you should base the row source for combo boxes and list boxes on local static tables. If this is not possible, you can use a text box with a combo box. The row source of the combo box initially is left blank. The user must enter the first few characters in the text box. The row source of the combo box then is based on a Select statement using the characters entered in the text box.

Furthermore, OLE object and Memo fields are large and therefore significantly increase network traffic. It is best not to display the contents of these fields unless they are requested specifically by the user. You can do this by setting the Visible property of OLE and Memo fields to False, or by placing these fields on another page of the form. You can add a command button that enables users to display the additional data when required.

Figure 21.1 shows a form that illustrates the implementation of several of these methods. The detail section of the form initially is not visible. The form has no RecordSource, and the data that underlies the combo box that appears on the form is stored in a local table.

Figure 21.1.

A form using the After Update *event of the combo box to populate* RecordSource *and make detail visible.*

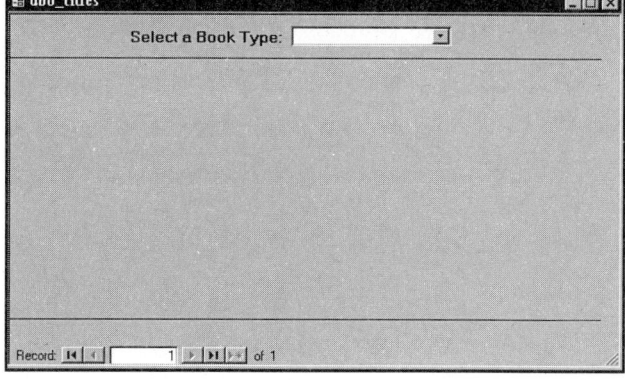

The After Update event of the combo box looks like this:

```
Private Sub cboBookType_AfterUpdate()
   Me.RecordSource = "Select * From dbo_titles Where Type Like '" & _
            cboBookType.Value & "*';"
   Me.Detail.Visible = True
End Sub
```

The Visible property of the Detail section of the form initially is set to False. After the user selects an entry from the combo box, the RecordSource of the form is set equal to a Select statement, which selects specific titles from the dbo_titles table database. The Detail section of the form then is made visible, as shown in Figure 21.2.

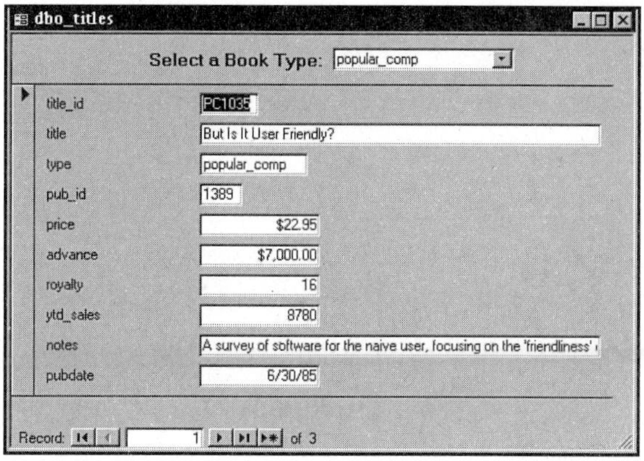

Figure 21.2.

A form using the After Update *event of the combo box to populate* RecordSource *with detail visible.*

Finally, you might want to use unbound forms. This involves creating a form and then removing its RecordSource. Users are provided with a combo box that enables them to select one record. A recordset is built from the client/server data with the row the user selected. When using this method of form design, everything must be coded. Your form needs to handle all adds, edits, and deletes. Figure 21.3 shows an example of such a form. None of the controls on the form has its control source filled in. The name of each control corresponds with a field in the database server table.

Figure 21.3.

An unbound form displaying one row of data.

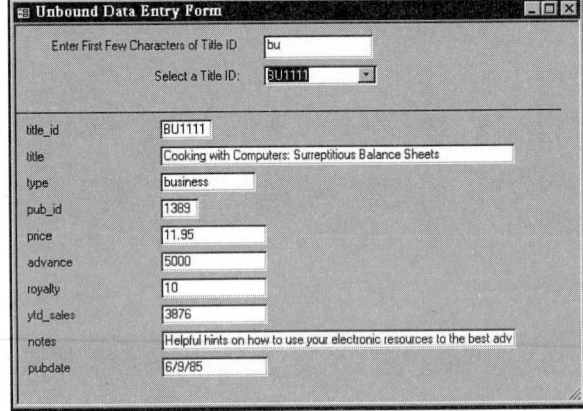

The Open event of the form looks like this:

```
Private Sub Form_Open(Cancel As Integer)
    Set mdb = CurrentDb
    Me.txtTitle.SetFocus
End Sub
```

This code sets a module-level database variable to the current database and sets focus to the txtTitle text box. The After Update event of the text box looks like this:

```
Private Sub txtTitle_AfterUpdate()
    Me!cboTitle.RowSource = "SELECT DISTINCTROW [dbo_titles].[title_id] " _
        & "FROM [dbo_titles] " _
        & "WHERE [dbo_titles].[title_id] Like '" & Me!txtTitle.Text & "*';"
End Sub
```

This code sets the RowSource property of the combo box to a Select statement that selects all records from the titles table where the title_id field begins with the first few characters the user typed. In this way, the combo box is not populated with all the titles from the server. The After Update event of the combo box looks like this:

```
Private Sub cboTitle_AfterUpdate()
    Dim fSuccess As Boolean
    Set mrst = mdb.OpenRecordset("Select * From dbo_Titles " _
        & "Where Title_ID = '" & Me!cboTitle.Value & "';")
    fSuccess = PopulateForm(Me, mrst)
    If Not fSuccess Then
        MsgBox "Record Not Found"
    End If
End Sub
```

The OpenRecordset method is used to open a recordset based on the linked table called dbo_Titles. Notice that only the records with the matching `Title_ID` are retrieved. Because the `Title_ID` is the primary key, only one record is returned. The `PopulateForm` function then is called, as shown here:

```
Function PopulateForm(frmAny As Form, rstAny As Recordset)
    If rstAny.EOF Then
        PopulateForm = False
    Else
        Dim fld As Field
        For Each fld In rstAny.Fields
            frmAny(fld.Name) = fld
        Next fld
        PopulateForm = True
    End If
End Function
```

The `PopulateForm` function checks to ensure that the recordset that was passed has records. It then loops through each field on the form, matching field names with controls on the form. It sets the value of each control on the form to the value of the field in the recordset with the same name as the control name.

Note that these changes to the data in the form do not update the data on the database server. Furthermore, the form does not provide for inserts or deletes. You need to write code to issue updates, inserts, and deletes, and you have to provide command buttons to give your users access to that functionality.

Practical Examples: Using Client/Server Strategies

Suppose that the Employees table is probably going to be moved to a database server in the near future because it contains sensitive data. You therefore must design the Employees form with client/server architecture in mind. The form limits the data displayed in the form. The form opens with only an option group containing the letters of the alphabet, as Figure 21.4 shows. After the user selects a letter, the Detail section of the form is displayed, and the `RecordSource` for the form is populated with a `Select` statement, as Figure 21.5 shows.

Figure 21.4.

The Employees form with an option group to select the employee's last name.

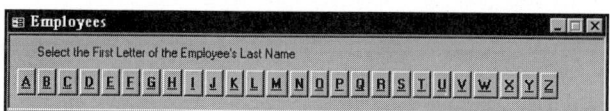

The `Open` event of the form looks like this:

```
Private Sub Form_Open(Cancel As Integer)
    Me.Detail.Visible = False
End Sub
```

The Visible property of the Detail section of the form is set to False. The `AfterUpdate` event of the option group looks like this:

```
Private Sub optEmpName_AfterUpdate()
    Me.RecordSource = "Select * from tblEmployees Where LastName Like '" _
        & Chr$(Me![optEmpName].Value) & "*';"
    Me.NavigationButtons = True
    Me.Detail.Visible = True
    DoCmd.DoMenuItem acFormBar, 7, 6, , acMenuVer70
End Sub
```

This code populates the RecordSource of the form using a Select statement. It makes the navigation buttons and the Detail section of the form visible. Finally, it resizes the window to the form.

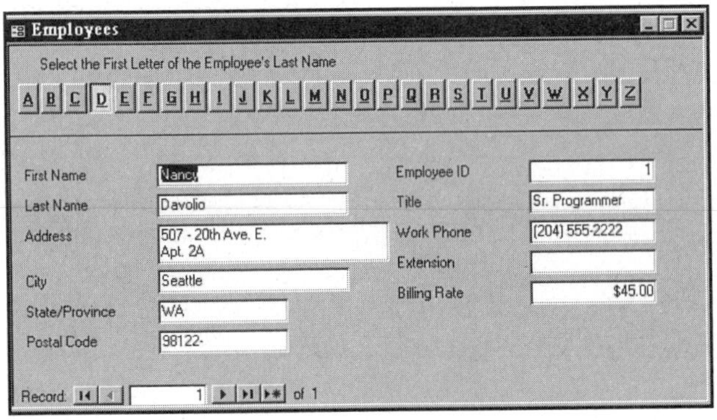

Figure 21.5.

The full view of the Employees form.

Summary

In this chapter, you learned client/server strategies and optimization techniques that will improve the performance and maintainability of your applications. You were instructed about methods for selecting the best recordset type and using key set fetching. You learned how to use pass-through queries, stored procedures, preconnecting, and connection timeouts. Finally, you learned how to optimize data handling, queries, and forms.

22

CHAPTER

Transaction Processing

- Understanding Transaction Processing, 640
- Understanding the Benefits, 640
- Modifying the Default Behavior, 642
- Implementing Explicit Transaction Processing, 643
- Looking At Transaction Processing Issues, 644
- Using Transaction Processing in a Multiuser Environment, 647
- Using Transaction Processing in a Client/Server Environment, 651
- Practical Examples: Improving the Integrity of the Time and Billing Application Using Transaction Processing, 653

Understanding Transaction Processing

Transaction processing refers to the grouping of a series of changes into a single batch. The entire batch of changes is either accepted or rejected as a group. One of the most common implementations of transaction processing is a bank automated teller machine (ATM) transaction. Imagine that you go to the ATM to deposit your paycheck. In the middle of processing, a power outage occurs. Unfortunately, the bank recorded the incoming funds prior to the outage, but the funds had not yet been credited to *your* account when the power outage occurred. You would not be very pleased with the outcome of this situation. Transaction processing would prevent this scenario from occurring. With transaction processing, the whole process succeeds or fails as a unit.

A group of operations is considered a transaction if it meets the following criteria:

- **It is atomic.** The group of operations should complete as a unit or not at all.
- **It is consistent.** The group of operations, when completed as a unit, retains the consistency of the application.
- **It is isolated.** The group of operations is independent of anything else going on in the system.
- **It is durable.** After the group of operations is committed, the changes persist, even if the system crashes.

If your application contains a group of operations that are atomic and isolated, and if, in order to maintain the consistency of your application, all changes must persist even if the system crashes, you should place the group of operations in a transaction loop. With Access 97, the primary benefit of transaction processing is data integrity. As you will see in the next section, with versions prior to Access 95, transaction processing also provided performance benefits.

Understanding the Benefits

In Access 2.0, there were many marginal benefits of added transaction processing, because Access 2.0 did no implicit transaction processing itself. Listing 22.1 shows code that, when run in Access 2.0, writes the data to disk each time the Update method occurs in the loop. These disk writes were costly in terms of performance, especially if the tables were not located on a local machine.

Listing 22.1. Transaction processing using Access Basic as seen in Access 2.0.

```
Sub IncreaseQuantity()

    On Error GoTo IncreaseQuantity_Err
    Dim db As DATABASE
    Dim rst As Recordset

    Set db = CurrentDb
    Set rst = db.OpenRecordset("Select OrderId, Quantity From tblOrderDetails", _
            dbOpenDynaset)
```

```
   'Loop through recordset increasing Quantity field by 1
   Do Until rst.EOF
      rst.Edit
      rst!Quantity = rst!Quantity + 1
      rst.UPDATE
      rst.MoveNext
   Loop

IncreaseQuantity_Exit:
   Set db = Nothing
   Set rst = Nothing
   Exit Sub

IncreaseQuantity_Err:
   MsgBox "Error # " & Err.Number & ": " & Error.Description
   Resume IncreaseQuantity_Exit
End Sub
```

> **NOTE**
>
> This code, and all the code in this chapter, is located in the CHAP22EX.MDB database on the sample code CD-ROM in the basTrans module.

The same code as found in Listing 22.1 performs much differently when run in Access 97. In addition to any *explicit* transaction processing you might implement for data-integrity reasons, Access 97 does its own behind-the-scenes transaction processing. This *implicit* transaction processing is done solely to improve the performance of your application. As the processing loop in the IncreaseQuantity routine executes, Access buffers and then periodically writes the data to disk. In a multiuser environment, Jet (implicitly) commits transactions every 50 milliseconds by default. This period of time is optimized for concurrency rather than performance. If you feel that it is necessary to sacrifice concurrency for performance, you can modify a few Windows Registry settings to achieve the specific outcome you want. These settings are covered in the next section.

Although implicit transaction processing, along with the modifiable Windows Registry settings, generally gives you better performance than explicit transaction processing, it is not a cut-and-dried situation. Many factors impact the performance benefits gained by *both* implicit and explicit transaction processing:

- Amount of free memory
- Number of columns and rows being updated
- Size of the rows being updated
- Network traffic

If you plan to implement explicit transaction processing solely to improve performance, you should make sure that you benchmark performance using both implicit and explicit transactions. It is critical that your application-testing environment be as similar as possible to the production environment in which the application will run.

Modifying the Default Behavior

Before you learn how to implement transaction processing, take a look at what you can do to modify the default behavior of the transaction processing built into Access 97. Three Registry settings affect *implicit* transactions in Access 97: ImplicitCommitSync, ExclusiveAsyncDelay, and SharedAsyncDelay. These keys are located in the \HKEY_LOCAL_MACHINES\ SOFTWARE\Microsoft\Jet\3.5\Engines\Jet 3.5 Registry folder.

The ImplicitCommitSync setting determines whether the system waits for a commit to finish before proceeding with application processing. The default is No. This means that the system will proceed without waiting for the commit to finish. You generally won't want to change this setting; using No dramatically improves performance. The danger of accepting the value of No is that you will increase the amount of time during which the data is vulnerable. Before the data is flushed to disk, the user might turn off the machine, compromising the integrity of the data.

The ExclusiveAsyncDelay setting specifies the maximum number of milliseconds that elapse before Jet commits an implicit transaction when a database is opened for exclusive use. The default value for this setting is 2000 milliseconds. This setting does not in any way affect databases that are open for shared use.

The SharedAsyncDelay setting is similar to the ExclusiveAsyncDelay setting. It determines the maximum number of milliseconds that elapse before Jet commits an implicit transaction when a database is opened for shared use. The default value for this setting is 0. The higher this value, the greater the performance benefits reaped from implicit transactions, but the higher the chances that concurrency problems will result. These concurrency issues are discussed in detail in the section "Using Transaction Processing in a Multiuser Environment," later in this chapter.

In addition to the settings that affect implicit transaction processing in Access 97, an additional Registry setting affects explicit transaction processing. The UserCommitSync setting controls whether explicit transactions are completed synchronously or asynchronously. With the default setting of Yes, control doesn't return from a `CommitTrans` statement until the transactions actually are written to disk. When this value is changed to No, a series of changes is queued, and control returns before the changes are complete.

> **NOTE**
>
> The UserCommitSync setting, when set to Yes, can be overridden for a particular transaction using the `dbFlushOSCacheWrites` constant with the CommitTrans method.

You can modify the values of these Registry settings and other Jet settings by using Regedit.exe (the Registry Editor) for Windows 95 or RegEdt32.exe for Windows NT. Changes to this section of the Registry affect all applications that use the Jet 3.51 Engine. If you want to affect only your application, you can export the Microsoft Jet portion of the Registry tree and import it into your application's Registry tree. You then can customize the Registry settings for your application. To force your application to load the appropriate Registry tree, you must set the INIPath property of the DBEngine object.

A much simpler approach is to modify the Registry values at runtime using the SetOption method; you can specify new settings at runtime for all the previously mentioned Registry entries as well as additional entries. A further advantage of this approach is that it will modify (temporarily) Registry entries for any machine under which your application runs. Any values you change at runtime temporarily override the Registry values that are set, enabling you to easily control and maintain specific settings for each application. This code illustrates the use of the SetOption method:

```
Sub ChangeOptions()
   DBEngine.SetOption dbExclusiveAsyncDelay, 1000
   DBEngineSetOption dbSharedAsyncDelay, 50
End Sub
```

Implementing Explicit Transaction Processing

Now that you are aware of the settings that affect transaction processing, you are ready to learn how to implement transaction processing. Three methods of the Workspace object control transaction processing:

- BeginTrans
- CommitTrans
- Rollback

The BeginTrans method of the Workspace object begins the transaction loop. The moment that BeginTrans is encountered, Access begins writing all changes to a log file in memory. Unless the CommitTrans method is issued on the Workspace object, the changes are never actually written to the database file. After the CommitTrans method is issued, the updates are written permanently to the Database object. If a Rollback method of the Workspace object is encountered, the log in memory is released. Listing 22.2 shows an example of how transaction processing works under Access 97. Compare this to Listing to 22.1.

Listing 22.2. Transaction processing in Access 97 using BeginTrans, logging, CommitTrans, and Rollback.

```
Sub IncreaseQuantityTrans()
   On Error GoTo IncreaseQuantityTrans_Err
   Dim wrk As Workspace
   Dim db As DATABASE
   Dim rst As Recordset
```

continues

Listing 22.2. continued

```
    Set wrk = DBEngine(0)
    Set db = CurrentDb
    Set rst = db.OpenRecordset("Select OrderId, Quantity From tblOrderDetails", _
              dbOpenDynaset)

    'Begin the Transaction Loop
    wrk.BeginTrans
    'Loop through recordset increasing Quantity field by 1
    Do Until rst.EOF
        rst.Edit
        rst!Quantity = rst!Quantity + 1
        rst.UPDATE
        rst.MoveNext
    Loop
    'Commit the Transaction; Everything went as Planned
    wrk.CommitTrans

IncreaseQuantityTrans_Exit:
    Set wrk = Nothing
    Set db = Nothing
    Set rst = Nothing
    Exit Sub

IncreaseQuantityTrans_Err:
    MsgBox "Error # " & Err.Number & ": " & Error.Description
    'Rollback the Transaction; An Error Occurred
    wrk.Rollback
    Resume IncreaseQuantityTrans_Exit
End Sub
```

This code uses a transaction loop to ensure that everything completes as planned or not at all. Notice that the loop that moves through the recordset, increasing the Quantity field in each record by 1, is placed in a transaction loop. If all processing in the loop completes successfully, the CommitTrans method executes. If the error-handling code is encountered, the Rollback method is issued, ensuring that none of the changes are written to disk.

Looking At Transaction Processing Issues

Before you decide that transaction processing is the best thing since sliced bread, you should keep in mind several issues concerning transaction processing. These issues are outlined in this section.

Realizing That Transactions Occur in a Workspace

Transactions exist in a Workspace object and never are specific to a Connection or Database object. The BeginTrans, CommitTrans, and Rollback methods affect all operations on connections and databases in the workspace. If you want simultaneous, unrelated transactions to be in effect, you must create separate Workspace objects in which the transactions are applied.

Making Sure the Data Source Supports Transactions

Not all recordsets support transaction processing. FoxPro and dBASE files, for example, do not support transaction processing. Neither do certain back-end ODBC database servers. To make matters worse, no errors are encountered when using the transaction-processing methods on FoxPro or dBASE tables. It will appear as if everything were processed as planned, but all references to transactions actually are ignored. When in doubt, you can use the Transactions property of the Database or Recordset object to determine whether the data source supports transaction processing. The Transactions property is equal to True if the data source supports transaction processing and False if the data source does not support transaction processing. Listing 22.3 shows an example of how to determine whether an object supports transaction processing.

Listing 22.3. Determining whether a recordset supports transaction processing.

```
Sub SupportsTrans(strTableName)
   On Error GoTo SupportsTrans_Err
   Dim wrk As Workspace
   Dim db As DATABASE
   Dim rst As Recordset
   Dim fSupportsTrans As Boolean

   fSupportsTrans = False

   Set wrk = DBEngine(0)
   Set db = CurrentDb
   Set rst = db.OpenRecordset(strTableName, _
            dbOpenDynaset)

   'Begin the Transaction Loop Only if Recordset
   'Supports Transaction
   If rst.Transactions Then
      fSupportsTrans = True
      wrk.BeginTrans
   End If

   'Loop through recordset increasing Quantity field by 1
   Do Until rst.EOF
      rst.Edit
      rst!Quantity = rst!Quantity - 1
      rst.UPDATE
      rst.MoveNext
   Loop
   'Issue the CommitTrans if Everything went as Planned
   'and Recordset Supports Transactions
   If fSupportsTrans Then
      wrk.CommitTrans
   End If

SupportsTrans_Exit:
   Set wrk = Nothing
   Set db = Nothing
   Set rst = Nothing
   Exit Sub
```

continues

Listing 22.3. continued

```
SupportsTrans_Err:
   MsgBox "Error # " & Err.Number & ": " & Error.Description

   'Rollback the Transaction if An Error Occurred
   'and Recordset Supports Transactions
   If fSupportsTrans Then
      wrk.Rollback
   End If
   Resume SupportsTrans_Exit

End Sub
```

Notice that this code uses a Boolean variable called fSupportsTrans. The recordset is tested to see whether the SupportTrans property evaluates to True. If so, the BeginTrans is issued and the fSupportsTrans variable is set equal to True. The fSupportsTrans variable is evaluated two different times in the remainder of the routine. The CommitTrans method is issued only if fSupportsTrans evaluates to True. In the error handling, the Rollback method is issued only if the fSupportTrans variable is equal to True.

Nesting Transactions

Another issue to be aware of with transactions is that you can nest transactions up to five levels deep. The hierarchy for nesting is FIFO. The inner transactions always must be committed or rolled back before the outer transactions. After a CommitTrans occurs, you cannot undo changes made to that transaction unless that transaction is nested in another transaction that is itself rolled back. Furthermore, using Jet, nested transactions are not supported at all for ODBC data sources. Nested transactions are supported when using ODBCDirect. This is covered in the section "Using Transaction Processing in a Client/Server Environment," later in this chapter.

Neglecting to Explicitly Commit Transactions

When a transaction loop is executing, all updates are written to a log file in memory. If a CommitTrans is never executed, the changes are, in effect, rolled back. In other words, a Rollback is implicit if the changes are never explicitly written to disk with the CommitTrans method. This generally works to your advantage. If the power is interrupted or the machine hangs before the CommitTrans is executed, all changes are rolled back. This behavior can get you into trouble if you forget the CommitTrans method, however. If the workspace is closed without the CommitTrans method being executed, the memory log is flushed, and the transaction is implicitly rolled back.

Checking Available Memory

Another gotcha with transactions occurs when the physical memory on the computer is exhausted by the transaction log. Access first attempts to use virtual memory. The transaction log is written to the temporary directory specified by the TEMP environment variable of the user's machine. This method dramatically slows down the transaction process. If all memory and the TEMP disk space are exhausted by the transaction process, an error 2004 results. You must issue a Rollback at this point. Otherwise, you are in danger of violating the integrity of the database.

> **WARNING**
>
> If your code attempts to commit the transaction after a 2004 error has occurred, the Jet Engine commits as many changes as possible, leaving the database in an inconsistent state.

Using Forms with Transactions

Access handles its own transaction processing on bound forms. You cannot control this transaction processing in any way. If you want to use transaction processing with forms, you must create unbound forms.

Using Transaction Processing in a Multiuser Environment

In a multiuser environment, transaction processing has implications beyond the protection of data. By wrapping a process in a transaction loop, you ensure that you are in control of all records involved in the process. The cost of this additional control is reduced concurrency for the rest of the users of the application. Listing 22.4 illustrates this scenario.

Listing 22.4. A safe way to do transactions in a multiuser environment that sacrifices concurrency.

```
Sub MultiPessimistic()
    On Error GoTo MultiPessimistic_Err
    Dim wrk As Workspace
    Dim db As DATABASE
    Dim rst As Recordset
    Dim intCounter As Integer
    Dim intChoice As Integer
    Dim intTry As Integer

    Set wrk = DBEngine(0)
    Set db = CurrentDb
    Set rst = db.OpenRecordset("Select OrderId, ProductID, UnitPrice " & _
            "From tblOrderDetails Where ProductID > 50", _
                dbOpenDynaset)
    rst.LockEdits = True

    'Begin the Transaction Loop
    wrk.BeginTrans
```

continues

Listing 22.4. continued

```
'Loop through recordset increasing UnitPrice
Do Until rst.EOF
    'Lock Occurs Here for Each Record in the Loop
    rst.Edit
    rst!UnitPrice = rst!UnitPrice * 1.1
    rst.UPDATE
    rst.MoveNext
Loop
'Commit the Transaction; Everything went as Planned
'All locks released for ALL records involved in the Process
wrk.CommitTrans
Set wrk = Nothing
Set db = Nothing
Set rst = Nothing
Exit Sub

MultiPessimistic_Err:
    Select Case Err.Number
        Case 3260
            intCounter = intCounter + 1
            If intCounter > 2 Then
                intChoice = MsgBox(Err.Description, vbRetryCancel + vbCritical)
                Select Case intChoice
                    Case vbRetry
                        intCounter = 1
                    Case vbCancel
                        'User Selected Cancel, Roll Back
                        Resume TransUnsuccessful
                End Select
            End If
            DoEvents
            For intTry = 1 To 100: Next intTry
            Resume
        Case Else
            MsgBox "Error # " & Err.Number & ": " & Err.Description
    End Select

TransUnsuccessful:
    wrk.Rollback
    MsgBox "Warning: Entire Process Rolled Back"
    Set wrk = Nothing
    Set db = Nothing
    Set rst = Nothing
    Exit Sub

End Sub
```

The MultiPessimistic routine uses pessimistic locking. This means that each time the Edit method is issued, the record on which the edit is issued is locked. If all goes well and no error occurs, the lock is released when the CommitTrans is reached. The error-handling code traps for a 3260 error. This error means that the record is locked by another user. The user running the transaction processing is given the opportunity to retry or cancel. If the user chooses Retry, the code once again tries to issue the Edit method on the record. If the user chooses Cancel, a Rollback occurs. This cancels the changes made to all the records involved in the process.

Two key points should be made about the MultiPessimistic routine. First, as this routine executes, each record involved in the process is locked. This potentially means that all other users will be unable to edit a large percentage, or even any, of the records until the transaction process finishes. This is wonderful from a data-integrity standpoint, but it might not be practical in an environment where users must update data on a frequent basis. It therefore is a good idea to keep transaction loops as short in duration as possible. Second, if any of the lock attempts are unsuccessful, the entire transaction must be canceled. Once again, this might be what you want or need from a data-integrity standpoint, but it might require that all users refrain from editing data while an important process completes.

With optimistic locking, the lock attempt occurs when the Update method is issued rather than when the Edit method is issued. This does not make much of a difference; all the records involved in the transaction remain locked until the CommitTrans or Rollback occurs. An additional difference is in the errors for which you must trap. Listing 22.5 shows the code for using optimistic locking in a multiuser environment.

Listing 22.5. Optimistic locking in a multiuser environment.

```
Sub MultiOptimistic()
   On Error GoTo MultiOptimistic_Err
   Dim wrk As Workspace
   Dim db As DATABASE
   Dim rst As Recordset
   Dim intCounter As Integer
   Dim intChoice As Integer
   Dim intTry As Integer

   Set wrk = DBEngine(0)
   Set db = CurrentDb
   Set rst = db.OpenRecordset("Select OrderId, ProductID, UnitPrice " & _
             "From tblOrderDetails Where ProductID > 50", _
                dbOpenDynaset)
   rst.LockEdits = False

   'Begin the Transaction Loop
   wrk.BeginTrans
   'Loop through recordset increasing UnitPrice
   Do Until rst.EOF
      rst.Edit
      rst!UnitPrice = rst!UnitPrice * 1.1
      'Lock Occurs Here for Each Record in the Loop
      rst.UPDATE
      rst.MoveNext
   Loop
   'Commit the Transaction; Everything went as Planned
   'All locks released for ALL records involved in the Process
   wrk.CommitTrans
   Set wrk = Nothing
```

continues

Listing 22.5. continued

```
    Set db = Nothing
    Set rst = Nothing
    Exit Sub

MultiOptimistic_Err:
    Select Case Err.Number
        Case 3197  'Data Has Changed Error
            If rst.EditMode = dbEditInProgress Then
                intChoice = MsgBox("Overwrite Other User's Changes?", _
                    vbYesNoCancel + vbQuestion)
                Select Case intChoice
                    Case vbCancel, vbNo
                        MsgBox "Update Canceled"
                        Resume TransNotSuccessful
                    Case vbYes
                        rst.UPDATE
                        Resume
                End Select
            End If
        Case 3186, 3260   'Locked or Can't be Saved
            intCounter = intCounter + 1
            If intCounter > 2 Then
                intChoice = MsgBox(Err.Description, vbRetryCancel + vbCritical)
                Select Case intChoice
                    Case vbRetry
                        intCounter = 1
                    Case vbCancel
                        'User Selected Cancel, Roll Back
                        Resume TransNotSuccessful
                End Select
            End If
            DoEvents
            For intTry = 1 To 100: Next intTry
            Resume
        Case Else
            MsgBox "Error # " & Err.Number & ": " & Err.Description
    End Select

TransNotSuccessful:
    wrk.Rollback
    MsgBox "Warning: Entire Process Rolled Back"
    Set wrk = Nothing
    Set db = Nothing
    Set rst = Nothing
    Exit Sub

End Sub
```

Notice that, in the MultiOptimistic routine, the lock occurs each time the Update method is issued. All the locks are released when the CommitTrans is executed. Furthermore, the error handling checks for a 3197 (data has changed) error. The 3197 occurs when the data is changed by another user between the time the Edit method is issued and just before the Update method is issued.

Using Transaction Processing in a Client/Server Environment

When dealing with transactions in a client/server environment, you must consider several additional issues: when and how transactions occur, what types of transactions are supported, and what types of problems can occur.

Implicit Transactions

When explicit transactions are not used, the way in which transactions are committed on the database server depends on what types of commands are being executed. In general, every line of code has an implicit transaction around it. This means that there is not a way to roll back an action because it is committed immediately on the database server. The exceptions to this rule are any SQL statements issued that modify data. These SQL statements (UPDATE, INSERT, and APPEND) are executed in batches; a transaction loop is implicitly placed around the entire statement. If any records involved in the SQL statement cannot be updated successfully, the entire UPDATE, INSERT, or APPEND is rolled back.

Explicit Transactions

When explicit transactions are used, ODBC translates the BeginTrans, CommitTrans, and Rollback methods to the appropriate syntax of the back-end server and the transaction processes as expected. The main exception to this rule is when transactions are not supported by the specific back-end you are using. Listing 22.6 shows an example of transaction processing with an SQL server back-end.

Listing 22.6. Transaction processing with an SQL server back-end.

```
Sub TransSQLServer()
   Dim wrk As Workspace
   Dim db As DATABASE
   Dim qdf As QueryDef

   Set wrk = DBEngine(0)
   Set db = CurrentDb

   wrk.BeginTrans
   Set qdf = db.CreateQueryDef("")
   qdf.Connect = ("ODBC;Database=Pubs" & _
      ";DSN=PublisherData;UID=SA;PWD=")
   qdf.ReturnsRecords = False
   qdf.SQL = "UPDATE sales Set qty = qty + 1 " & _
      "Where Stor_ID = '7067';"
   qdf.Execute
   qdf.SQL = "Update titles Set price = price + 1 " & _
      "Where Type = 'Business'"
   qdf.Execute
   wrk.CommitTrans
```

Listing 22.6. continued

```
TransSQLServer_Exit:
    Set wrk = Nothing
    Set db = Nothing
    Set qdf = Nothing
    Exit Sub

TransSQLServer_Err:
    MsgBox "Error # " & Err.Number & ": " & Err.Description
    wrk.Rollback
    Resume TransSQLServer_Exit
End Sub
```

The `TransSQLServer` routine begins by creating `Workspace` and `Database` object variables. Next, it executes the BeginTrans method on the workspace. It creates a temporary query definition. Several properties are set for the query definition, including the Connect, ReturnsRecords, and SQL property. After these properties are set, the temporary query is executed. The SQL property of the query definition is modified, and the query is executed again. If both Execute methods complete successfully, the CommitTrans method is issued on the `Workspace` object. If any error occurs during processing, the Rollback method is issued.

Nested Transactions

One example of when transactions might not perform as expected is when your code uses nested transactions. When accessing an ODBC data source using Jet, nested transactions are not supported. If your code includes nested transactions, all but the outermost transaction loop are ignored. To avoid this problem, you can use ODBCDirect rather than Jet to process ODBC data. This subject is covered in Chapters 20, "Client/Server Techniques," and 21, "Client/Server Strategies."

Lock Limits

A potential pitfall when dealing with client/server databases involves lock limits. Many database servers impose strict limits on how many records can be locked concurrently. As you saw in Listings 22.2 and 22.3, a transaction loop can potentially lock a significant number of records. It is important to consider the maximum number of locks supported by your back-end when using transaction loops in your VBA code.

Negative Interactions with Server-Specific Transaction Commands

You should never use the server-specific transaction commands when building pass-through queries. These server-specific commands can conflict with the BeginTrans, CommitTrans, and Rollback methods, causing confusion and potential data corruption.

Practical Examples: Improving the Integrity of the Time and Billing Application Using Transaction Processing

As you continue to develop the Time and Billing application, you might find it necessary to use VBA code to accomplish certain tasks. These tasks might require that several processes complete successfully or not at all. As these situations arise, you should consider placing them in a transaction loop. An example of such a situation is the frmArchivePayments form, as shown in Figure 22.1. frmArchivePayments enables the user to specify a date range. This date range is used as the criterion to determine what data is sent to the tblPaymentsArchive table and removed from the tblPayments table. When this process is run, you want to ensure that the process runs in its entirety or not at all. Listing 22.7 shows transaction loop code suitable for Time and Billing.

Figure 22.1.

The frmArchivePayments form enables the user to specify a date range of payments to be archived.

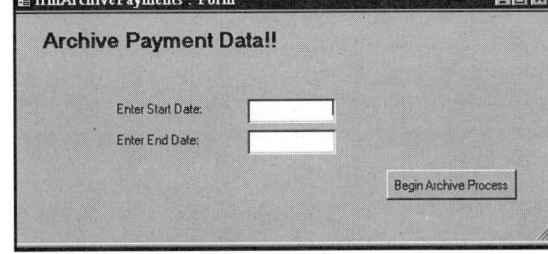

Listing 22.7. A transaction loop suitable for the Time and Billing application.

```
Sub cmdArchivePayments_Click()
On Error GoTo Err_cmdArchivePayments_Click

    Dim wrk As Workspace
    Dim db As DATABASE
    Dim strSQL As String

    Set wrk = DBEngine(0)
    Set db = CurrentDb

    wrk.BeginTrans
    strSQL = "INSERT INTO tblPaymentsArchive" & _
        " SELECT DISTINCTROW tblPayments.* " & _
        " FROM tblPayments " & _
        " WHERE tblPayments.PaymentDate Between #" & _
        Me!txtStartDate & _
        "# And #" & _
        Me!txtEndDate & "#;"
    db.Execute strSQL
    strSQL = "DELETE DISTINCTROW tblPayments.PaymentDate " & _
        "FROM tblPayments " & _
        " WHERE tblPayments.PaymentDate Between #" & _
```

continues

653

Listing 22.7. continued

```
            Me!txtStartDate & _
            "# And #" & _
            Me!txtEndDate & "#;"
    db.Execute strSQL
    wrk.CommitTrans

Exit_cmdArchivePayments_Click:
    Exit Sub

Err_cmdArchivePayments_Click:
    MsgBox Err.Description
    wrk.Rollback
    Resume Exit_cmdArchivePayments_Click

End Sub
```

This routine uses the BeginTrans method of the Workspace object to initiate a transaction loop. An SQL statement is built, using the values of the txtStartDate and txtEndDate controls on the form as criteria for the SQL statement. This SQL statement adds all records in the specified date range to the tblPaymentsArchive table. The Execute method is applied to the Database object, using the SQL string as an argument. The SQL string then is modified to build a statement that deletes all records in the specified date range from the tblPayments table. If both SQL statements execute successfully, the CommitTrans method is executed, committing both transactions. If an error occurs, the whole transaction is rolled back.

Summary

If transactions are used properly, you can gain many benefits from them. Transactions help ensure that all parts of a logical piece of work complete successfully or not at all. In some situations, they also can improve performance. You must be aware of several issues when using transactions. The potential pitfalls vary, depending on whether you are issuing a transaction in a multiuser Access environment or in a client/server environment. If you take all mitigating factors into account, you can ensure that transactions provide you with the data integrity you expect from them.

23

Optimizing Your Application

- Understanding Optimization, 656
- Modifying Hardware and Software Configurations, 656
- Understanding What Jet 3.5 Does to Improve Performance, 660
- Letting the Performance Analyzer Determine Problem Areas, 661
- Designing Tables to Optimize Performance, 662
- Designing Queries to Optimize Performance, 664
- Changing Code to Improve Performance, 664
- Designing Forms and Reports to Improve Performance, 673
- Practical Examples: Improving the Performance of the Time and Billing Application, 675

Understanding Optimization

In a world where hardware never seems to keep up with software, it is important to do everything you can to improve the performance of your application. This chapter will help you optimize your applications for speed and reduce the memory and hard disk space required by your applications.

Optimization is the process of reviewing your operating environment, VBA code, application objects, and data structures to ensure that they are providing optimum performance. In a nutshell, optimization is the process of making your application leaner and meaner.

Users become frustrated when an application runs slowly. In fact, if a user is not warned about a slow process, he or she often will reboot or shut down the power on the machine *while* a process is running. This can have dire results on the integrity of the data.

> **TIP**
>
> To help reduce the chance of users rebooting the computer during a lengthy process, it generally is a good idea to provide them with some sort of indication that a process will take a while. You can do this by using a message box that appears before processing begins, or by providing a status bar that shows the progress of the task being completed.

You can do many things to optimize an application's performance, ranging from using a front-end tool such as the Performance Analyzer to fastidiously adhering to certain coding techniques. This chapter highlights the major things you can do to optimize the performance of your applications.

Modifying Hardware and Software Configurations

The Access *environment* refers to the combination of hardware and software configurations under which Microsoft Access is running. These environmental settings can greatly affect the performance of an Access application.

The easiest way to improve the performance of an Access application is to upgrade the hardware and software configuration under which it is running. This form of optimization requires no direct intervention from the developer. A side benefit of most of the environmental changes you can make is that any improvements made to the environment are beneficial to users in all their Windows applications.

Improving the environment involves more than just adding some RAM. It also can mean optimally configuring the operating system and the Access application.

Hardware, Hardware, More Hardware Please!

The bottom line is that Windows 95 and Access 97 both crave hardware—the more, the better. The faster your users' machines and the more memory they have, the better. Additional hardware might not be the least expensive solution, but it certainly is the quickest and easiest thing you can do to improve the performance of your application.

RAM, RAM, That's All I Need!

Memory is what Access craves most, whether you are running under the full version of Microsoft Access or using the runtime version of the product. Microsoft Access requires 12M of RAM just to run under Windows 95, its standard operating environment. Although 12M of RAM is required, 16M of RAM is recommended by Microsoft. Under Windows NT, Access requires a minimum of 16M. Both requirements can climb dramatically if your user is running other applications or if your application uses OLE automation to communicate with other applications. Put in a very straightforward way, the more RAM you and the users of your application have, the better. 32M is a great environment for Access 97. In fact, if every one of your users has at least 32M of RAM, you can stop reading this chapter, because everything else covered here is going to provide you with minor benefits compared to adding more RAM. If you are like most of us, though, where not every one of your users has a Pentium 120 with 32M of RAM, read on.

> **NOTE**
>
> Developers should have a bare minimum of 24M of RAM installed on their machines. Remember that this is a minimum! Most developers agree that 32M of RAM is required if you intend to do any serious development work.

Defragment Your User's Hard Disk

As your computer writes information to disk, it attempts to find contiguous space on which to place data files. As the hard disk fills up, files are placed in fragmented pieces on the hard disk. Each time your application attempts to read data and programs, it must locate the information scattered over the disk. This is a very time-consuming process. It therefore is helpful to defragment the hard disk on which the application and data tables are stored, using a utility such as the Disk Defragmenter that ships with Windows 95.

TIP

The process of defragmenting a hard disk easily can be automated by using the System Agent, which is included as part of the Microsoft Plus! pack. The Microsoft Plus! package is sold as an add-on to Windows 95. The System Agent is a useful tool that enables you to schedule when and how often the defragmentation process occurs.

Compact Your Database

Just as the operating system fragments your files over time, Access itself introduces its own form of fragmentation. Each time you add and modify data, your database grows. The problem is that when you delete data or objects from your database, it does not shrink. Instead, Access leaves empty pages available in which new data will be placed. The problem is that these empty pages are not necessarily filled with data. You can free the empty space by using the Compact utility, which is part of the Microsoft Access software. The Compact utility frees excess space and attempts to make all data pages contiguous. You should compact your database frequently, especially if records or database objects (for example, forms and reports) are regularly added and deleted. You can access the Compact utility only when no database is open. To access the Compact utility, choose Tools | Database Utilities. Then choose the Compact Database option.

NOTE

It is worth noting that if you plan to distribute an Access application to other users, possibly via the runtime module, it is a good idea to include some means of compacting the database. Often, the runtime module does not allow access to the Compact menu item. The CompactDatabase method enables you to compact a database from within an Access database, but you cannot call this command from the current application. A second application must be created in order to use the CompactDatabase method on the original application.

Don't Use Compressed Drives

Regardless of the compression utility you are using, disk compression *will* significantly degrade performance with Access 97. This fact is documented in the README file.

Tune Virtual Memory: Tweak the Swap File

Although Windows 95 attempts to manage virtual memory on its own, you might find it useful to provide Windows 95 with some additional advice. To modify the size of the swap file, right-click My Computer. Choose Properties and then select the Performance tab. Click the Virtual Memory button. It might be useful to change the size of the swap file or to move it to a faster disk drive or a drive connected to a separate controller card. Any changes you make may *adversely* affect performance. It is important that you evaluate whether any changes you make will help the situation—or, perhaps, make things worse!

> **TIP**
>
> If Access 97 or Windows is running on a compressed drive, you can improve performance by moving the swap file to an uncompressed drive. If possible, the swap file should be located on a drive or partition solely dedicated to the swap file, or on a drive or partition that is accessed rarely by other applications. This helps to ensure that the swap file will remain in a contiguous location on disk.

Run Access and Your Application Locally

As covered in Chapter 18, "Developing for a Multiuser Environment," it is best to install both the Access software and your application objects on each user's local machine. Only the data tables should be stored on a network file server. Otherwise, you will be sending DLLs, OLE objects, help files, type libraries, executables, *and* database objects all over the network wire. If you want to get the *worst* possible performance out of an Access application, install it on a diskless workstation with 12M of RAM!

Do Everything You Can to Make Windows Itself Faster

It always amuses me that the users with the slowest machines and the least memory have the most accessories running. These accessories include multimedia, fancy wallpaper, and other nifty utilities. If performance is a problem, you might try to see whether eliminating some of the frivolous niceties improves the performance of your application. If it does, encourage the user to eliminate the frills, get more memory, or accept your application's performance.

Another tip to make Windows 95 run faster is to shut down and restart on a regular basis. Memory tends to get fragmented, and applications run more slowly. Although I can go weeks or months in Windows NT without rebooting, I find it beneficial to reboot my Windows 95 machine a couple of times a day.

Change Access's Software Settings

In addition to the more obvious measures just outlined, some minor software tweaking can go a long way toward improving performance. Adjusting several settings in the Windows Registry can dramatically improve performance. These changes involve the Registry's ISAM section. The properties you might want to change include MaxBufferSize and ReadAheadPages. Both these settings determine how the Jet Engine uses memory.

MaxBufferSize controls the maximum size of the Jet Engine's internal cache. By default, it is set to optimize performance on most machines. It does this by reading data in 2K pages, placing the data in a memory cache. The data in the cache is readily available to forms, reports, tables, and queries. Lowering the value for MaxBufferSize frees memory for other tasks. This might be helpful on a machine with a minimum memory configuration.

ReadAheadPages controls the number of 2K data pages that the Jet Engine reads ahead when performing sequential page reads. This number can range from 0 to 31, with the default at 16. The higher the number, the more efficient Access is at reading ahead so that data is available when you need it. The lower the number, the more memory is freed up for other tasks.

As you configure any of these settings, remember that what is good for one machine is not necessarily good for the next. The settings for each machine must be optimized with its unique hardware configuration in mind.

Understanding What Jet 3.5 Does to Improve Performance

Improvements have been made to the Jet 3.5 Engine to dramatically improve performance over its predecessors. Some of these improvements appeared with the Jet 3.0 Engine that shipped with Access 95, but many are new to Jet 3.5. The Jet 3.5 Engine is thoroughly 32-bit. It takes advantage of multiple execution threads, providing significant performance benefits.

Specific improvements to Jet 3.5 follow:

- Delete operations are faster. You can remove portions of a page at once, instead of removing data row by row.

- Jet 3.5 provides better multiuser concurrency on indexed columns. More users can read and update indexed columns without experiencing locking conflicts; indexed columns no longer contain read locks.

- Jet 3.5 offers implicit transaction processing. Whereas many people wrapped processing loops in the BeginTrans...CommitTrans construct in earlier versions of Access to limit the number of disk writes, the Jet 3.5 Engine handles this quite well on its own.

- Large queries run faster. This is due to improvements in the transactional behavior for SQL *data manipulation language* (DML) statements as well as new Registry settings that force transactions to commit when a certain lock threshold is reached.

- Queries containing the inequality operator (<>) run faster.

- Sequential reads are faster. Up to 64K of disk space can be allocated at a time.

- Temporary queries run faster.

- Deleting a table is faster when you use SQL DROP or SQL DELETE.

- The amount of space occupied by indexes is reduced.

- When you compact a database, all indexes are optimized for performance.

- Jet 3.5 offers an improved page allocation mechanism. This better ensures that data from a table is stored on adjacent pages and improves the read-ahead capability.

- The cache is configured dynamically. The cache is configured at startup based on the amount of system memory available and contains the most recently used data, thereby enhancing performance.

- ISAM support for HTML files is available.

- The MaxLocksPerFile registry setting enables you to force records to commit when a certain lock threshold is hit. This speeds up the completion of large queries when data is stored on NetWare and Windows NT-based servers.

Letting the Performance Analyzer Determine Problem Areas

You can do many things to improve the performance of an application. Most of them require significant attention and expertise on your part. The Performance Analyzer is a tool that does some of the work for you. This tool analyzes the design of an Access application. It suggests techniques you can use to improve the application's performance. Many of the techniques the Performance Analyzer suggests can be implemented automatically.

To use the Performance Analyzer, choose Tools | Analyze | Performance. The dialog box in Figure 23.1 appears.

Figure 23.1.
The Performance Analyzer dialog box.

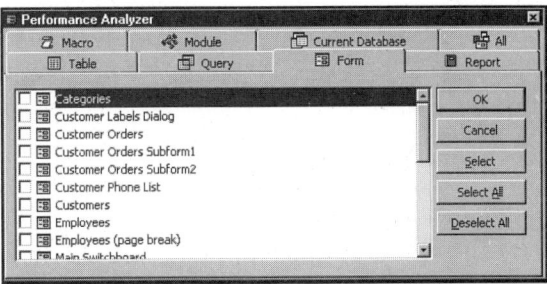

Select the individual tables, queries, forms, reports, macros, modules, and relationships you want the Performance Analyzer to scrutinize. After you click OK, the Performance Analyzer analyzes the selected objects. When it completes the analysis process, a dialog box appears, as shown in Figure 23.2. This dialog box provides you with a list of suggested improvements to the selected objects. The suggested improvements are broken down into recommendations, suggestions, ideas, and items that were fixed automatically. Suggested improvements will include things such as the addition of an index or the conversion of an OLE object. After analyzing the NorthWind database that ships with Access, for example, the Performance Analyzer suggested that the Customers form should use a stored query as the row source for the Country control. If you click on the suggestion and then click Optimize, Access prompts you for a name of the query and then performs the change for you.

Figure 23.2.
The second part of the Performance Analyzer dialog box.

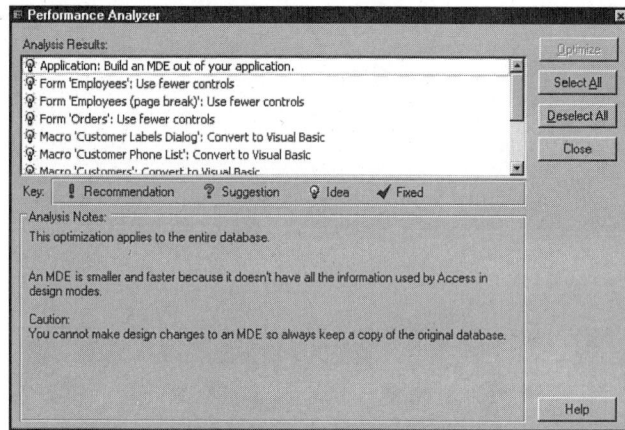

Designing Tables to Optimize Performance

Now that you have seen the changes you can make to your environment to improve performance, take a look at the changes you can make to your data structures to optimize performance. Such changes include eliminating redundant data, using indexes, selecting appropriate field data types, and using various query techniques.

Optimizing performance by tweaking the data structure is imperative for good performance. No matter what else you do to improve performance, poor data design can dramatically degrade the performance of your application. All other optimization attempts are futile without proper attention to this area.

You can spend days and days optimizing your data. These changes must be well thought out and carefully analyzed. Changes often are made over time as problems are identified. Such changes can include those in the following sections.

Why Be Normal?

In essence, this means that you should normalize your tables. Data that appears in multiple places can significantly slow down your application. Suppose that a company address appears in both the Customer table and the Orders table. This information should be included only in the Customer table. Queries should be used to combine the address and order data when needed.

I Thought You Just Told Me to Normalize

When it comes to performance, unfortunately, there are no hard-and-fast rules. Although, most of the time, you gain performance by normalizing your data structure, denormalizing your structure can help at times. This generally is the case when you find yourself creating a particular join over and over again. You can try denormalizing the data to see whether dramatic performance improvements result. Remember that there are definite downsides when you denormalize data; these affect data integrity and maintenance.

Index, Index, Index!

It is amazing how far an index can go in improving performance. Fields on both sides of a join should be indexed. Any fields or combination of fields on which you search also should be included in an index. You should create indexes for all columns used in query joins, searches, and sorts. You should create primary key indexes rather than unique indexes, and unique indexes rather than nonunique indexes. The performance improvements rendered by indexes are profound.

> **WARNING**
>
> Although indexes *can* dramatically improve performance, you should *not* create an index for every field in a table. Indexes do have their downsides. Besides taking up disk space, they also slow down the process of adding, editing, and deleting data.

> **TIP**
>
> In a multiple-field index, index on as few fields as possible. Multiple-field indexes can dramatically degrade performance.

> **NOTE**
>
> Client/server optimization strategies are covered in Chapter 21, "Client/Server Strategies."

Select the Correct Data Type

When defining a field, select the shortest data type available for the storage of the data. If you will be storing a code between 1 and 10 in the field, for example, there is no reason to select Double for a numeric field.

Designing Queries to Optimize Performance

Optimizing your queries requires a great deal of practice and experimentation. Some queries involving a one-to-many relationship run more efficiently if you place the criteria on the one side of the relationship, for example. Others run more efficiently if you place the criteria on the many side. Understanding some basics can go a long way toward improving the performance of your queries and your application as a whole:

- Include as few columns in the result set as possible.
- Try to reduce the number of complex expressions contained in the query. Although including a complex expression in a query eliminates the need to build the expression into each form and report, the performance benefits gained sometimes are worth the trouble.
- Use the Between operator instead of greater than (>) and less than (<).
- Use Count(*) rather than Count([column]).
- Group Totals queries by the field that is in the same table you are totaling. In other words, if you are totaling cost multiplied by price for each order in the Order Detail table, group by the order ID in the Order Detail table, not the order ID in the Orders table.

Now that you have seen what you can do with the design of your queries to improve performance, take a look at a couple of simple techniques you can use to improve the performance of your queries.

A simple but often neglected method of optimizing queries is to deliver your queries compiled. A query compiles when you open it in Datasheet view and then simply close it. If you modify a query and then save it, it is not compiled until the query runs. Delivering precompiled queries ensures that they run as quickly as possible.

Finally, it is important that you compile your queries using the same amount of data your application will contain. This is because Jet's Query Optimizer optimizes the query differently depending on the amount of data it finds. If you build a query using 100 records that will run on a live table containing 100,000 records, the query will not be optimized properly. You must rerun *and* resave your query using the correct quantity of data if you want the query to be optimized properly.

Changing Code to Improve Performance

No matter what you do to optimize the operating system environment and improve your data design, poor code can continue to bog you down. A properly optimized application is optimized in terms of the environment, data design, and code. Just as poor table design can degrade performance, poor coding techniques also can have a dramatic negative effect on performance. Changes to your code include eliminating variants and dead code, using built-in collections, and using specific object types. An important code-related optimization is to deliver your modules precompiled.

The following changes and techniques can help improve performance. It is important to recognize that any one change will not make much of a difference. However, an accumulation of all the changes, especially where code is being reexecuted in a loop, can make a significant impact on your application's performance.

Eliminate Variants and Use the Smallest Data Type Possible

Variant variables are the slowest; they carry a lot of overhead because they are resolved at runtime. Remember that this statement declares a variant type of variable:

```
Dim intCounter
```

To strong-type this variable as an integer, for example, you must modify your code to look like this:

```
Dim intCounter As Integer
```

Not only should you strong-type your variables, but you also should use the smallest data type possible. Remember that data types such as Boolean, Byte, Integer, and Long are the smallest and therefore the fastest. These are followed by Single, Double, Currency, and (finally) Variant. Of course, if you must store very large numbers with decimal points into a variable, you cannot pick Single. Just keep in mind that it is wise to select the smallest data type appropriate for the use of the variable.

Use Specific Object Types

Just as the General variant data type is inefficient, generic object variables also are inefficient. The MakeItBold subroutine uses a generic object variable, as shown in Listing 23.1.

Listing 23.1. The MakeItBold subroutine.

```
Private Sub cmdMakeBold_Click()
    Call MakeItBold(Screen.PreviousControl)
End Sub

Sub MakeItBold(ctlAny As Control)
    ctlAny.FontBold = True
End Sub
```

On the other hand, the SpecificBold subroutine uses a specific object variable, as Listing 23.2 shows.

Listing 23.2. The `SpecificBold` subroutine.

```
Private Sub cmdSpecificBold_Click()
    Call SpecificBold(Screen.PreviousControl)
End Sub

Sub SpecificBold(txtAny As TextBox)
    txtAny.FontBold = True
End Sub
```

The difference is that the `SpecificBold` routine expects to receive only text boxes. It does not need to resolve the type of object it receives and therefore is more efficient.

This code is contained in the CHAP23EX.MDB database on the accompanying CD-ROM. You can find the example in frmObjVar.

Use Inline Code

There is a tendency to call out to procedures for everything. This is good from a maintenance standpoint but not from an efficiency standpoint. Each time VBA calls out to a procedure, additional time is taken to locate and execute the procedure. This is particularly evident when the procedure is called numerous times. You need to decide how important maintainability is to you compared to speed.

Toggle Booleans Using Not

This code is very *inefficient*:

```
If bFlag = True Then
  bFlag = False
Else
    bFlag = True
End If
```

It should be modified to look like this:

```
bFlag = Not bFlag
```

Besides requiring fewer lines of code, this expression evaluates much more quickly at runtime.

Use the Built-In Collections

The built-in collections are there whether or not you use them. By using `For Each...Next` and a collection of objects, you can write very efficient code, as shown in Listing 23.3.

Listing 23.3. Using `For Each...Next`.

```
Sub FormCaption()
    Dim frm As Form
    For Each frm In Forms
        frm.Caption = frm.Caption & " - " & CurrentUser()
    Next
End Sub
```

In this example, you use the Forms collection to quickly and efficiently loop through each form, changing the caption on its title bar.

Use the Length Function

Using the `Len` function (as shown in Listing 23.5) is more efficient than testing for a zero-length string (as shown in Listing 23.4).

Listing 23.4. Testing for a zero-length string.

```
Sub SayNameZero(strName As String)
    If strName <> "" Then
        MsgBox strName
    End If
End Sub
```

Listing 23.5. Using the `Len` function.

```
Sub SayNameLen(strName As String)
    If Len(strName) Then
        MsgBox strName
    End If
End Sub
```

Listing 23.5 is easier for VBA to evaluate and therefore runs more quickly and efficiently.

Use `True` and `False` Instead of Zero

This example is very similar to the preceding one. It is better to evaluate for True and False (as shown in Listing 23.7) instead of 0 (as shown in Listing 23.6).

Listing 23.6. Evaluating for 0.

```
Sub SaySalaryZero(lngSalary As Long)
    If lngSalary <> 0 Then
        MsgBox "Salary is " & lngSalary
    End If
End Sub
```

Listing 23.7. Evaluating for `True` and `False`.

```
Sub SaySalaryTrue(lngSalary As Long)
    If lngSalary Then
        MsgBox "Salary is " & lngSalary
    End If
End Sub
```

The code in Listing 23.7 runs more efficiently.

Use Transactions... Sometimes?

In versions of Access prior to Access 95, transactions dramatically improve performance. Using explicit transactions, the data is written to disk only once, after the `CommitTrans`. All changes between a `BeginTrans` and a `CommitTrans` are buffered in memory. Because disk access has the slowest throughput on a computer, this technique offers you major performance benefits in versions of Access prior to Access 95. The difference with Access 95 and Access 97 is that the Jet 3.0 and 3.5 Engines implicitly buffer transactions. Most of the time, Jet's own transaction-handling offers better performance than your own. At other times, you can improve on what Jet does on its own. The only way you will know for sure is to do your own benchmarking. Each situation is different.

Eliminate Unused `Dim` and `Declare` Statements

As you modify your subroutines and functions, you often declare a variable and then never use it. Each `Dim` statement takes up memory, whether or not you are using it. Furthermore, `Declare` statements, which are used to call external library functions, also take up memory and resources. You should remove these statements if they are not being used.

Eliminate Unused Code

Most programmers experiment with various alternatives for accomplishing a task. This often involves creating numerous test subroutines and functions. The problem is that most people do not remove this code when they are done with it. This dead code is loaded with your application and therefore takes up memory and resources. Several third-party tools are available that can help you find both dead code and variable declarations. One tool that many people use is called Total Access Analyzer, by FMS, Inc. The Performance Analyzer, included as part of Access 97, also helps you eliminate dead code and variables.

Use Variables to Refer to Properties, Controls, and Data Access Objects

If you are going to repeatedly refer to an object, you should declare an object and refer to the object variable rather than the actual control, as shown in Listing 23.8.

Listing 23.8. Declaring an object and referring to the object variable.

```
Forms!frmAny!txtHello.FontBold = True
Forms!frmAny!txtHello.Enabled = True
Forms!frmAny!txtHello.Left = 1
Forms!frmAny!txtHello.Top = 1
```

This is a very scaled-down example, but if numerous properties are being changed, or if this code is being called recursively, you can use an object variable to make the code more efficient, as Listing 23.9 shows.

Listing 23.9. Using an object variable to make your code more efficient.

```
Private Sub cmdChangeObject_Click()
    Dim txt As TextBox
    Set txt = Forms!frmHello!txtHello1
    txt.FontBold = True
    txt.Enabled = True
    txt.Left = 100
    txt.Top = 100
End Sub
```

Use With...End With

Another way to optimize the code in the preceding example is to use a With...End With construct, as shown in Listing 23.10.

Listing 23.10. Using With...End With.

```
Private Sub cmdChangeObjectWith_Click()
    With Forms!frmHello!txtHello2
        .FontBold = True
        .Enabled = True
        .Left = 100
        .Top = 100
    End With
End Sub
```

Use the Me Keyword

In the preceding example, you used Forms!frmHello!txtHello to refer to a control on the current form. It is more efficient to refer to the control as Me!txtHello. This is because VBA searches only in the local name space. Although this makes your code more efficient, the downside is that the Me keyword only works in form modules. It will not work in code modules. This means that you cannot include the Me keyword in generic functions that are accessed by all your forms.

Use String Functions When Possible

Many of the functions come in two forms: one with a dollar sign ($) and one without. An example is `Left(sName)` versus `Left$(sName)`. It is more efficient to use the version with the dollar sign whenever possible. The functions with the dollar sign return strings rather than variants. When a string variable is returned, VBA does not need to perform type conversions.

Use Dynamic Arrays

Array elements take up memory, whether or not they are being used. It therefore is sometimes preferable to use dynamic arrays. You can increase the size of a dynamic array as necessary. If you want to reclaim the space used by all the elements of the array, you can use the `Erase` keyword, as in this example:

```
Erase aNames
```

If you want to reclaim some of the space being used by the array without destroying data in the elements you want to retain, use `Redim Preserve`:

```
Redim Preserve aNames(5)
```

This statement sizes the array to six elements. (It is zero-based.) Data in those six elements is retained.

> **WARNING**
>
> You need to be careful when using dynamic arrays with `Redim Preserve`. When you resize an array using `Redim Preserve`, the entire array is copied in memory. If you are running in a low-memory environment, this can mean that virtual disk space is used, which *slows* performance— or, worse than that, the application can fail if both physical and virtual memory are exhausted.

Use Constants When Possible

Constants improve *both* readability and performance. A constant's value is resolved after compilation. The value the constant represents is written to code. A normal variable has to be resolved as the code is running, because VBA needs to obtain the current value of the variable.

Use Bookmarks

A bookmark provides you with the most rapid access to a record. If you are planning to return to a record, set a variable equal to that record's bookmark. It is very easy to return to that record at any time. Listing 23.11 shows an example that uses a bookmark.

Listing 23.11. Using a bookmark.

```
Sub BookMarkIt()
    Dim db As DATABASE
    Dim rst As Recordset
    Dim strBM As String

    Set db = CurrentDb()
    Set rst = db.OpenRecordset("tblProjects", dbOpenSnapshot)
    strBM = rst.Bookmark
    Do Until rst.EOF
        Debug.Print rst!ProjectID
        rst.MoveNext
    Loop
    rst.Bookmark = strBM
    Debug.Print rst!ProjectID
End Sub
```

You can find this code in basOptimize of CHAP23EX.MDB. The bookmark is stored in a variable before the Do Until loop executes. After the Do Until loop executes, the recordset's bookmark is set equal to the value contained in the string variable.

Set Object Variables Equal to Nothing

Object variables take up memory and associated resources. You should set their values equal to Nothing when you are done using them. This conserves memory and resources. For example,

```
Set oObj = Nothing
```

Use Action Queries Instead of Looping Through Recordsets

Besides being easier to code, it is much more efficient to execute a stored query than to loop through a recordset, performing some action on each record. Listing 23.12 shows an example that loops through a recordset.

Listing 23.12. Looping through a recordset.

```
Sub LoopThrough()
    Dim db As DATABASE
    Dim rst As Recordset

    Set db = CurrentDb()
    Set rst = db.OpenRecordset("tblProjects", dbOpenDynaset)
    Do Until rst.EOF
        rst.Edit
        rst!ProjectTotalEstimate = rst!ProjectTotalEstimate + 1
        rst.UPDATE
        rst.MoveNext
    Loop
End Sub
```

This code, which is located in basOptimize of CHAP23EX.MDB, loops through a recordset, adding 1 to each project total estimate. Contrast this with the code in Listing 23.13.

Listing 23.13. Executing a stored query.

```
Sub ExecuteQuery()
    Dim db As DATABASE

    Set db = CurrentDb
    db.Execute "qryLowerEstimate"
End Sub
```

This code executes a stored query called qryLowerEstimate. The query runs much more efficiently than the Do Until loop.

Deliver Your Application with the Modules Compiled

Applications run more slowly when they are not compiled. Forms and reports load more slowly, and the application requires more memory. If you deliver your application with all the modules compiled, they do not need to be compiled on the user's machine before they are run.

To easily recompile all modules, choose Debug | Compile and Save All Modules with the Module window active. This command opens and compiles *all* code in the application, including the code behind forms and reports. It then saves the modules in the compiled state. This process preserves the compiled state of the application.

Retaining the Compiled State

Don't bother choosing the Run | Compile All Modules command if you plan to make additional changes to the application. An application becomes decompiled whenever the application's controls, forms, reports, or modules are modified. Even something as simple as adding a single control to a form causes the application to lose its compiled state. It therefore is important to choose the Debug | Compile and Save All Modules command immediately before you distribute the application.

> **WARNING**
>
> Renaming a database file causes the code contained in the database to decompile. It therefore is important to always choose the Compile and Save All Modules command after renaming a database.

Distribute Your Application as an MDE

The process of creating an MDE file compiles all modules, removes editable source code, and compacts the destination database. All Visual Basic code will run but cannot be viewed or edited. This improves performance, reduces the size of the database, and protects your intellectual property. Memory use also is improved. The process of saving an application as an MDE, and the implications of doing so, are covered in Chapter 37, "Distributing Your Application with ODE."

Organize Your Modules

VBA code theoretically can be placed in any module in your application. The problem is that a module is not loaded until a function in it is called. After a single procedure in a module is called, the *entire* module is loaded into memory. Furthermore, if a single variable in a module is used, the *entire* module is loaded into memory. As you might imagine, if you design your application without much thought, every module in your application will be loaded.

If you place *similar* routines all in one module, that module will be loaded and others will not. This means that if people are using only part of the functionality of your application, they will never be loading other code modules. This conserves memory and therefore optimizes your application.

Designing Forms and Reports to Improve Performance

You can do several things to forms and reports to improve your application's performance. These include techniques to quickly load the forms and reports, tips and tricks regarding OLE objects, and special coding techniques that apply only to forms and reports.

Designing Forms

Because forms are your main interface to your user, making them as efficient as possible can go a long way toward improving the user's perception of performance in your application. Additionally, many of the form techniques are extremely easy to implement.

Form-optimization techniques can be categorized in two ways: those that make the forms load more quickly, and those that enable you to more efficiently manipulate objects within the form.

The larger a form and the more controls and objects you have placed on it, the less efficient that form is. Make sure that controls on the form do not overlap. It also is extremely beneficial to group form data onto logical pages. This is especially important if your users have insufficient video RAM. Objects on subsequent pages should not be populated until the user moves to that page.

You should base forms and their controls on saved queries. Include only fields required by the form in the form's underlying query. Avoid using Select * queries. Because Access is so efficient at internally optimizing the manipulation of query results, this improves the performance of your forms. To further take advantage of the power of queries, reduce the number of records that the query returns, loading only the records you need to at a particular time.

If you will use a form solely to add new records, set the DataEntry property of the form to Yes so that it opens to a blank record. This is necessary because Access must read all records in order to display the blank record at the end of the recordset.

OLE objects take far more resources than images. If an OLE bitmapped object does not need to be changed, convert it to an image. To accomplish this, click on the object and choose Format | Change To.

Avoid the use of subforms whenever possible. Access treats a subform as a separate form. It therefore takes up significant memory. Make sure that all fields in a subform that are linked to the main form are indexed. If the data in the subform does not need to be edited, set its AllowEdits, AllowAdditions, and AllowDeletions properties to No, or set its RecordsetType property to Snapshot.

Make sure that the RowSource for a combo box includes only the columns needed for the combo box. Index on the first field that appears in the combo box. This has a dramatic effect on the speed at which a user can move to an element of the combo box. Also, whenever possible, make the first visible field of a combo box a text field. Access converts numeric fields to text as it searches through the combo box to find a matching value. Finally, don't base list boxes or combo boxes on linked data if that data rarely, if ever, changes. Instead, make the static table local, updating it whenever necessary.

A general rule regarding the performance of forms is to place all database objects, except data, on each user's machine. This eliminates the need for Access to constantly pull object definitions over the network.

Close forms that no longer are being used. Open forms take up memory and resources, degrading performance.

Another tip that can help you dramatically improve the performance of your forms is to use the default formatting and properties for as many controls as possible. This significantly improves performance, because only the form and control properties that differ from the default properties are saved with the form.

> **TIP**
>
> If most controls have a set of properties that are different from the default control for the form, you should change the default control for the form and then add controls based on the default. Access saves only the properties of the default control and does not need to store the properties for each control placed on the form. This can result in dramatic performance improvements.

Finally, eliminate the code module from forms that don't need it. A form without a form module loads more quickly and occupies less disk space. You still can call function procedures from an Event property using an expression, or you can navigate throughout your application from the form using hyperlinks. You can remove the module associated with a form by setting the HasModule property to No.

Designing Reports

Many of the report-optimization techniques are the same as the form-optimization techniques. Reducing the number of controls, avoiding overlapping controls, basing reports on queries, and avoiding OLE objects are all techniques that improve the performance of reports as well as forms.

You can use a few additional techniques to specifically improve the performance of reports. Eliminate any unnecessary sorting and grouping expressions, and index all fields on which you sort or group. Base subreports on queries rather than on tables, and include only necessary fields in the queries. Make sure that the queries underlying the report are optimized and that you index all fields in the subreport that are linked to the main report.

A special technique that you can use to improve the performance of reports was introduced with Access 95. It involves the No Data event and the HasData property. The No Data event is fired when a report is opened, and no data is returned by the record source of the report. The HasData property is used to determine whether a report is bound to an empty recordset. If the HasData property of a subreport is False, you can hide the subreport, thereby improving performance.

Practical Examples: Improving the Performance of the Time and Billing Application

To ensure that the Time and Billing Application is optimized, you can do several things:

- Make sure that the database is compacted.
- Use the Performance Analyzer to analyze the application and make recommendations for improvement.
- Choose Debug | Compile and Save All Modules before distributing the application.

Summary

The most attractive application can be extremely frustrating to use if its performance is less than acceptable. Because Access itself requires significant resources, you must make your code as lean and efficient as possible.

This chapter focused on several techniques for improving performance. Probably one of the easiest ways to improve performance is by modifying the hardware and software environment in which Access operates. You learned about adding RAM, defragmenting a hard disk, and tuning virtual memory and other settings to dramatically improve the performance of your applications. You also looked at using of the Performance Analyzer to quickly and easily identify problem areas in your application. Finally, the chapter focused on data-design fundamentals, coding techniques, and form- and report-optimization techniques.

By following the guidelines covered in this chapter, you can help ensure that you are not inadvertently introducing bottlenecks into your application. Although any one of the suggestions included in this chapter might not make a difference by itself, the combined effect of these performance enhancements can be quite dramatic.

24

Replication Made Easy

- What Is Replication?, 678
- Uses of Replication, 678
- Understanding When Replication Isn't Appropriate, 679
- An Overview of the Implementation of Replication, 680
- The Replication Architecture: What Makes Replication Tick?, 681
- Understanding Replication Topologies, 683
- Changes That Replication Makes to Your Database, 685
- Making a Database Replicable, 687
- Preventing Objects from Being Replicated, 690
- Creating Additional Replicas, 690
- Synchronizing Replicas, 691
- Resolving Replication Conflicts, 693
- Using the Replication Manager, 695
- Implementing Replication by Using Code, 705
- Practical Examples: Managing the Time and Billing Application with Replication, 708

What Is Replication?

Access 95 was the first desktop database that included built-in replication capabilities. Replication has further matured with the introduction of Access 97; it's a powerful feature that's becoming increasingly important in today's world of mobile and distributed computing. This chapter teaches you about replication and how to implement it through both the user interface and code.

Uses of Replication

Data replication is the ability of a system to automatically make copies of its data and application objects in remote locations. Any changes to the original or to the copies are propagated to all other copies. Data replication allows users to make changes to data offline at remote locations. Changes to either the original or the remote data are synchronized with other instances of the database.

To see an example of data replication at work, say you have a team of salespeople who are out on the road all day. At the end of the day, each salesperson logs on to one of the company's Windows NT servers through DUN (Dial-Up Networking) or RAS (Remote Access Services). Each salesperson's transactions are sent to the server. If necessary, any changes to the server data are also sent to the salesperson. In addition to data being replicated, if the developers in the organization are busily adding forms, reports, and modules to the database's master copy, any changes to the application components are also updated in the remote copies as users log on to the system.

This example illustrates just one of the several valuable uses of replication. In a nutshell, data replication is used to improve the availability and integrity of data throughout an organization or enterprise. The practical uses of data replication are many; they can be categorized into five general areas, explained in the following sections.

Sharing Data Among Offices

In today's global economy, it's the norm for companies to have many offices distributed throughout the country, or even the world. Before Access 95, it was difficult to implement an Access application that would support sharing data among several offices. However, with replication, each office can have a replica of the database. Periodically throughout the day, each office can synchronize its changes with corporate headquarters. How often the synchronization happens depends on the frequency required for data at each location to be current at any given moment.

Sharing Data Among Dispersed Users

Sharing data among dispersed users is illustrated by the salesperson example used earlier. This implementation of replication generally involves mobile users who connect to the network after modifying data out on the road. Because only incremental changes are transferred from the Design Master (the original) to the replicas (the copies), and from the replicas to the Design Master, this form of replication makes the mobile computing scenario economically feasible.

Reducing Network Load

Replication can be very effective in reducing network traffic loads. The Design Master can be replicated onto one or more additional servers. Distributed users can then make changes onto one of the additional servers, which significantly improves performance by distributing the processing load throughout the network. Changes made to the data on the additional servers can be synchronized with the main server periodically during the day. How often synchronization occurs depends on the need for data to be current at any moment in time.

Distributing Application Updates

Replication is an excellent vehicle for distributing application updates. Design changes can be made only to the Design Master; therefore, as users throughout the organization log on to synchronize with the Design Master, any structural changes to the application are sent to the user. This is much more efficient and effective than giving every user an entirely new copy of the application database each time a minor change is made to the application's schema.

Backing Up the Data in Your Application

Many people don't think of replication as a means of backing up application data, but replication is extremely well-suited for this task. Ordinarily, to back up an Access database, everyone must log off the system, but that's not necessary with replication. The synchronization process can occur periodically during the day while users are still logged on to the system, and all changes are replicated. Not only is this more efficient than backing up the entire database, but it also ensures that you can quickly be up and running on a backup server if there's a problem on a server.

Understanding When Replication Isn't Appropriate

Despite the many positive aspects of replication, replication is *not* appropriate in a couple of situations, such as when data consistency is critical. If an application requires that data be current at every given moment, then it isn't a good candidate for replication. Replication is also not effective when a large volume of *existing* records are modified throughout the day by many different users. In a situation like this, resolving conflicts that happen when multiple users update the same record wouldn't be practical.

An Overview of the Implementation of Replication

The following steps compose the replication process:

1. Making a database replicable.
2. Creating and distributing replicas.
3. Synchronizing replicas with the Design Master.
4. Resolving conflicts.

These steps can be done in the following ways:

- Through the Access user interface
- By using the Windows 95 Briefcase
- By using the Replication Manager
- By using DAO code

The steps needed for the replication process, and the alternatives for performing each step, are covered in this chapter. An overview of each alternative is outlined in the following sections.

The Access User Interface

The Access user interface gives you a series of menu items that allow you to perform all the steps of the replication process. The Tools | Replication menu has the following options: Create Replica, Synchronize Now, Resolve Conflict, and Recover Design Master. These menu options are covered throughout this chapter.

Briefcase Replication

The Windows 95 Briefcase supplies the foundation Access needs for the replication process. Users can simply drag a database file to the Briefcase to replicate it, make changes to the file while on the road, and synchronize the replica with the Design Master when they reconnect to the network. This is done because when Access 97 is installed, it registers a special class ID with the Windows 95 Briefcase. When a database is dragged to the Briefcase, the Briefcase's Reconciler code is called. When the user selects Update Selection or Update All from the Briefcase menu, the Merge Reconciler is called. Briefcase replication is available as an installation option through Windows 95, its successors, and Windows NT 4.0.

The Replication Manager

The Replication Manager is a sophisticated tool that's part of the Office Developer Edition. It's a mandatory player in the replication process when you're managing many replicas. Besides providing basic replication functionality, the Replication Manager lets you schedule the synchronization of replicas. In fact, the Replication Manager allows you to manage and intricately control all aspects of the replication process. The Replication Manager is covered in more detail in the section "Using the Replication Manager."

DAO Code

Most aspects of the replication process can also be done by using DAO code, which can be used to make a database replicable, create and synchronize replicas, and get and set properties of a replicable database. DAO can easily be integrated with the other methods of replication. Although requiring the most time and effort on your part, DAO code lets you base replication on events rather than time and give your users a custom user interface for the replication process.

Programs That Support Replication Using DAO

Visual Basic 4.0, Excel for Windows 95, Excel 97, and Visual C++ all support replication using data access objects. You can't perform replication with these products by using either the Briefcase or the Office Developer Edition, however, so it's easier to manage the replication process on a machine that has Access installed.

The Replication Architecture: What Makes Replication Tick?

Now that you know what replication is and what alternatives you have for implementing it, you're ready to learn about what makes it happen. Six components are responsible for the replication process:

- Tracking Layer
- Microsoft Replication Manager
- Synchronizer
- File System Transport
- Briefcase Reconciler
- Registry Entries

The Tracking Layer

The Tracking Layer refers to the part of the Jet Engine that's capable of tracking and recording all the changes made to the Design Master and to each of the replicas. It's responsible for making sure changes are available to be transmitted to other replicas.

The Microsoft Replication Manager

The Replication Manager gives you the tools needed to support the replication process. It can also be used to generate reports on synchronization activity.

The Synchronizer

If you use the Briefcase or the Access user interface to manage the replication process, Jet handles the exchange of information between the replicas. If you use the Replication Manager to manage the replication process, the Synchronizer is responsible for monitoring the changes and handling the exchange of data between replicas.

When you're using the Replication Manager, each replica is assigned a synchronizer. The Synchronizer performs either direct or indirect synchronization between the members of a replica set. When synchronization is initiated, the Synchronizer tries to make a direct connection with the target member of the replica set. If both members of the replica set can be opened simultaneously by the Synchronizer, direct synchronization occurs, which means that changes from one member of the replica set are applied directly to the other member.

If the Synchronizer determines that the target replica set member isn't available, then indirect synchronization takes place. There are many reasons why the target replica set member might be unavailable; some possible reasons why a direct connection can't be established include the following:

- The network server where the replica resides is down.
- The computer containing the other replica is logged off the network.
- The other member is currently involved in another synchronization.
- The other member is not in a shared folder.

Regardless of the cause of an indirect synchronization, the Synchronizer for the first member of the replica set leaves a message for the Synchronizer assigned to the member of the unavailable replica set. This message is stored in a shared folder on the network that acts as a drop-box location for the target member. All messages sent while a member of the replica set is unavailable are stored in the drop-box location.

> **NOTE**
>
> If you need to determine whether a direct or indirect synchronization occurred, you can browse the MSysExchangeLog system table.

The Synchronizer is configured through the Replication Manager user interface and is covered in more detail in the section "Using the Replication Manager."

File System Transport

The File System Transport is responsible for supplying messaging services to the Synchronizer.

The Briefcase Reconciler

The Briefcase Reconciler is another integral component of the replication architecture. As mentioned, it makes sure that a database is replicable and manages the merging of changes between the Briefcase replica and the Desktop replica.

Registry Entries

Several Windows Registry entries are responsible for helping with the replication process; a couple are shown in Figure 24.1. Notice the Replication Manager and Transporter subkeys under the `HKEY_LOCAL_MACHINE\SOFTWARE\Microsoft\Jet\3.5` key. These entries contain important path information used by the Replication Manager and the Synchronizer. The Briefcase Reconciler uses entries under `HKEY_CLASSES_ROOT\CLSID`. Note that although the name has changed to Synchronizer, the key in the registry remains Transporter.

Figure 24.1.

Replication and the Windows Registry.

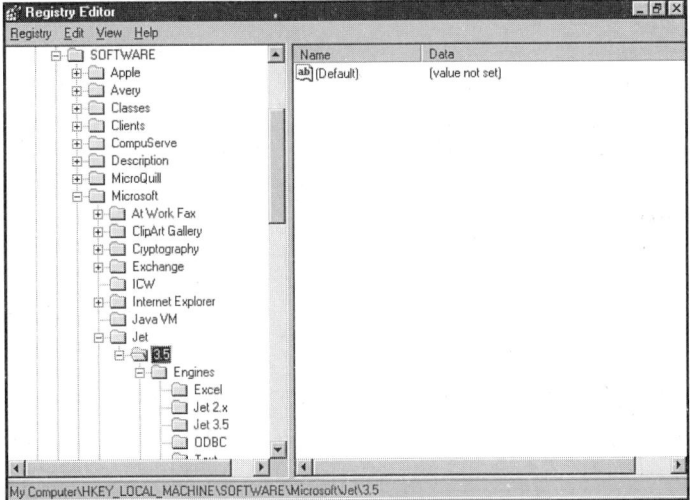

Understanding Replication Topologies

The topology for data synchronization determines which replicas synchronize with each other. The *topology* is essentially a blueprint for how the changes are merged between the members of the replica set. Different topologies are used for different situations, and the topology you choose is determined by your business needs and your organization's design. The synchronization topologies are Star, Ring, Fully Connected, Linear, and Hybrid. (See Figure 24.2.)

Figure 24.2.

Examples of replication topologies.

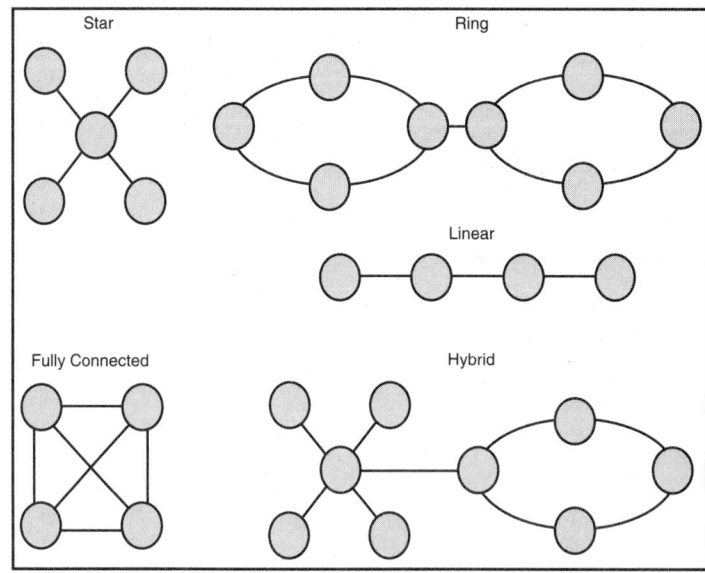

Star Topology

With the Star topology, a single hub periodically synchronizes with the rest of the replicas. The biggest advantage of this topology is simplicity and ease of programming. Another is that data doesn't have to travel very far. Each replica synchronizes with only one other database, the hub. However, this isn't particularly reliable. If the controlling replica is damaged or unavailable, the synchronization process can't take place. Another disadvantage of the Star topology is that the first replica to synchronize with the hub gets no data from the other replicas, but the last replica to synchronize with the hub receives all the data from the others. Issuing two rounds of synchronization can circumvent this problem. Finally, the Star topology can't be used with a large number of replicas because the entire load is placed on the hub.

> **NOTE**
>
> The Design Master must *never* be a hub. If you designate it as the hub, it's possible for partial design changes to be accidentally synchronized to the rest of the replicas. Instead, place the Design Master on one of the satellite machines and synchronize design changes with the controlling replica whenever they're complete and fully tested.

Ring Topology

With the Ring topology, each computer synchronizes with the next computer in the replication chain. There's no central point of synchronization in this scenario. The major advantage of the Ring topology is that the load is distributed throughout the satellite machines. The primary disadvantage is that it might take a long time for changes to be distributed throughout the replicas because there's no central point of synchronization. Furthermore, if one of the replicas in the chain is damaged or unavailable, the replication process stops, but this can be handled by using code that senses the problem and bypasses the unavailable machine.

Fully Connected Topology

When the Fully Connected topology is used, every replica synchronizes with every other replica. This topology offers several advantages. Its strongest point is that it makes sure data is the most current at any given moment because data is sent directly from each replica to all the other replicas in the replica set. For this reason, it's the best solution when the data *must* be as current as possible. Another benefit of the Fully Connected topology is its high level of redundancy. Also, because of the low level of *latency* (which means that at any given moment, it's likely the data isn't current) in the Fully Connected topology, the effect of any one of the replicas failing is minimal. The Fully Connected topology does have disadvantages, however. It requires the most overhead of any of the topologies because of the network traffic generated as each replica in the set synchronizes with all the others. Furthermore, the replication schedules must be staggered; otherwise, collisions will probably happen as more than one replica tries to synchronize with the same replica.

Linear Topology

The Linear topology is similar to the Ring topology except that the chain is never completed. For this reason, the Linear topology has the highest level of latency. The biggest advantage of the Linear topology is the low level of network traffic generated; however, this topology isn't practical for most applications because it takes more time for changes to reach all the replicas in the set.

Hybrid Topology

A Hybrid topology is any combination of the other topologies. In a complex application, it's usually not appropriate to use a single topology by itself. By combining the topologies, you can get exactly the results you need. Figure 24.2 illustrates just one example of a Hybrid topology—a Ring connected with a Star. You should experiment with the different configurations to see which topology best balances processing load, network traffic, and data latency.

Changes That Replication Makes to Your Database

Replication makes several changes to the database, but they're necessary to manage the demands of the replication process. The following changes are made to a database when it's replicated:

- Fields are added to each replicated table.
- Several system tables are added to the database.
- Properties are added to the database document objects.
- Sequential AutoNumber fields are changed to random AutoNumber fields.
- The size of the database increases.

Fields Added to Each Replicated Table

During the replication process, the Jet Engine determines whether each table has a field with an AutoNumber data type *and* a ReplicationID field size. If it doesn't find a field meeting these criteria, it adds a field called s_Guid to the table that uniquely identifies each record. It's identical across replicas.

The Jet Engine also adds two additional fields to each table in the database: s_Lineage and s_Generation. The s_Lineage field stores the IDs of replicas that have updated a record and the last version created by those replicas; the s_Generation field stores information about groups of changes. These fields are visible only if you opt to view system objects (use Tools | Options).

System Tables Added to the Database

The Jet Engine also adds several tables to your database that track conflicts, errors, and exchanges made between the replica databases. MSysSidetable, MSysErrors, MSysSchemaProb, and MSysExchangeLog are the most useful of these tables; they can be viewed if you have chosen to view system objects.

MSysSidetable tracks tables that have experienced a conflict during the synchronization process. It stores the name of the side table that has the conflicting records.

MSysErrors tracks all unresolved synchronization errors. It's empty when all errors have been resolved. This table can be found in all the replicas.

MSysSchemaProb identifies errors that happened while synchronizing a replica's *design*. It's visible only if a design conflict has occurred between the user's replica and another replica in the set.

MSysExchangeLog is a local table that stores information about synchronizations that have taken place between the local replica and other members of the replica set.

Properties Added to the Database Objects

Several new properties are added to a replicable database. The database's Replicable property is set to True, and this property *cannot* be modified after it's set to True. The ReplicaID property is a unique ID assigned to each replica. The DesignMasterID property can transfer the Design Master status to another database, which is generally done only if the original master becomes irreparably damaged.

In addition to the properties that apply to the database, two properties can be applied to the tables, queries, forms, reports, macros, and modules in the database: the KeepLocal and Replicable properties. The KeepLocal property, applied to an object *before* the database is replicated, prevents the object from being copied to the other replicas in the set. The Replicable property, used *after* a database is replicated, indicates that the object will be replicated.

Changes to Sequential AutoNumber Fields

Another important change made to your tables when replicating a database is that all the AutoNumber fields are changed from incremental to random. Existing records aren't affected, but new keys are generated randomly because that reduces conflicts when the databases are synchronized. If all the copies generate sequential keys, you can see that conflicts will happen when you try to merge changes. By randomly generating primary keys, this conflict is much less likely to take place.

Changes to the Size of the Database

When a database is replicated, its size increases because of the added fields and tables. Generally, this increase isn't a problem. If disk space is at a premium, you should consider this aspect of replication before you decide to build replication into your application.

Making a Database Replicable

A replicable database is simply a database whose Replicable property has been set to True. If a database hasn't been marked as replicable, you can't replicate it. However, when a database *has* been flagged as replicable, the Jet Engine makes several changes to it to render it replicable. Until these changes are made, the database isn't recognized as part of a replication set and can't be synchronized with other databases.

When you're ready to replicate a database, you should take the following steps:

1. Flag any objects in the database that you don't want replicated as local by setting their KeepLocal property to True.

2. Make a replication Design Master by setting the database's Replicable property to True.

3. Make copies—called *replicas*—of the Design Master.

You can make a database replicable by using the Access user interface, using the Windows 95 Briefcase, using the Replication Manager, or writing code. The following two sections cover using the Access user interface and the Windows 95 Briefcase. Making a database replicable by using the Replication Manager is covered in the section "Using the Replication Manager"; using code is covered in the section "Implementing Replication by Using Code."

Rendering a Database Replicable with the Access User Interface

Choose Tools | Replication | Create Replica. Microsoft Access gives you a warning that it must close the database before proceeding. (See Figure 24.3.)

Figure 24.3.

This dialog box warns you that Access must close the database before converting it to a Design Master.

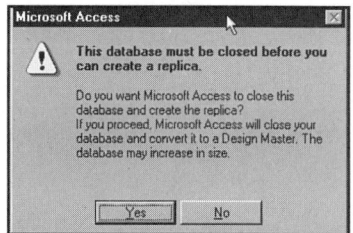

After selecting Yes, you see another dialog box asking whether you want Access to make a backup of the original database before continuing. (See Figure 24.4.) It's always a good idea to back up a database before replicating it because a database can't be returned to its nonreplicable state after it's flagged as replicable.

Figure 24.4.

This dialog box prompts you to have Access create a backup of the database before it's replicated.

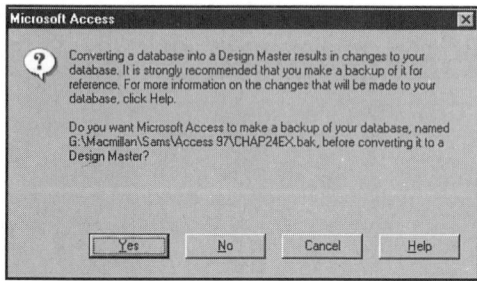

Next, you're prompted for the name and location of your new replica in the Location of New Replica dialog box. (See Figure 24.5.) After you click OK, the new replica is created and the process is finished.

Figure 24.5.
The Location of New Replica dialog box allows you to specify a location and name for the replica.

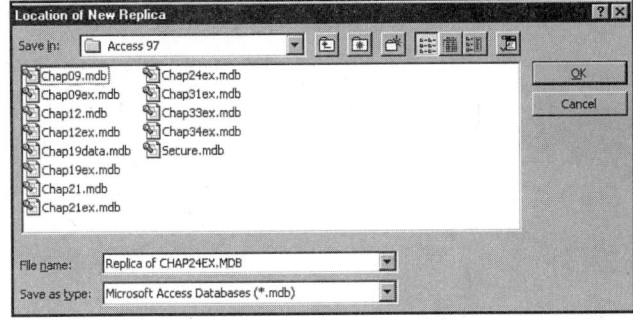

Your original database is converted to a Design Master, and the replica is assigned the name and location specified in the Location of New Replica dialog box. If the replication process is completed successfully, the dialog box shown in Figure 24.6 appears. Notice that only the Design Master can accept changes to the database structure (schema).

Figure 24.6.
This dialog box appears after successful replication of a database.

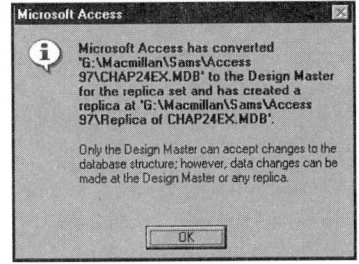

Rendering a Database Replicable with the Windows 95 Briefcase

Instead of using the Access user interface to replicate a database, you can use the Windows 95 Briefcase. All you need to do is drag and drop the database file from Windows Explorer to the Briefcase icon on your desktop; then you see the dialog box shown in Figure 24.7.

Figure 24.7.
This dialog box appears after you drag and drop a database to the Briefcase to be replicated.

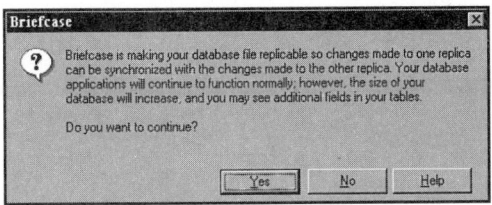

Except for the final message you get, you see the same series of messages as you do when you choose Replication from the Tools menu in the Access user interface. Only one database can be used to make design changes, such as modifying table structures. The Briefcase dialog box, shown in Figure 24.8, asks which database you want to keep as the Design Master. Generally, you select the Original Copy rather than the Briefcase Copy. You do this because the briefcase copy is generally used only as a means to add, edit, and delete data when on the road.

Figure 24.8.

The final dialog box you see during Briefcase replication offers you the choice of which copy you want to use for the Design Master.

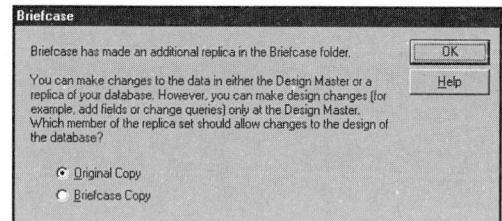

Preventing Objects from Being Replicated

You might want to *prevent* specific objects in a replicable database from being replicated if, for example, certain data in your database is confidential or it's unnecessary for most users to see certain data. An employee salary table, for example, might be maintained and used in the master but isn't necessary for any of the replicas. The fewer objects that are replicated, the more effective the synchronization process is.

Designating that an object won't be replicated can't be done by using the Access user interface; it can be done only by using VBA code or the Replication Manager. To do this, set the KeepLocal property of the specific objects to True. When you try to set the KeepLocal property to True with VBA code, you get an error unless you have already appended the property onto the object. You must, therefore, include error handling in your code to handle this problem. Using the Replication Manager to flag an object as nonreplicable is covered in the section "Replicating a Database with the Replication Manager." The code required to add the KeepLocal property to an object and set its value to True is covered in the section "Implementing Replication by Using Code."

Creating Additional Replicas

After you have made one replica, you'll probably want to make more. These additional replicas are copies that can be distributed throughout the organization. They can be created by using the Access user interface, the Windows 95 Briefcase, the Replication Manager, or VBA code.

A sales organization, for example, might use multiple replicas for sales reps who take copies of the database along on their notebook computers. Each of these copies must be a replica created by the replication process rather than a copy made by the operating system. Otherwise, the work of each salesperson can't be synchronized with that of the others.

Replicas can be made with any of the four methods mentioned, but additional replicas can also be made from any member of a replica set. Each replica set is independent from all other replica sets. Replicas from different sets can't be synchronized with one another.

Creating Additional Replicas with the Access User Interface

To create additional replicas with the Access user interface, follow these steps:

1. Open the database you want to replicate. You can open either the Design Master or any replica.
2. Choose Tools | Replication | Create Replica.
3. When prompted, supply a name for the new replica.

Creating Additional Replicas with the Windows 95 Briefcase

You can also make more replicas by dragging and dropping the Design Master—or any one of the replicas—to the Briefcase. If you drag and drop the Design Master to the Briefcase, you're prompted with a dialog box asking whether you want the Design Master or the replica to be placed in the Briefcase.

Synchronizing Replicas

To *synchronize* replicas means to reconcile all the changes between them. Modified records are changed in all the copies, deleted records are removed from all the replicas, and added records are appended to all the replicas.

The ability to synchronize is what makes data replication useful. Additions, modifications, and deletions are propagated among all the replicas in a set, which lets users see the changes other users made.

As with creating a replica, Access gives you four methods of synchronizing replicas: the Access user interface, the Windows 95 Briefcase, the Replication Manager, or VBA code.

Synchronizing Databases with the Access User Interface

To perform synchronization with the Access user interface, follow these steps:

1. Choose Tools | Replication | Synchronize Now.
2. The Synchronize Database dialog box opens. (See Figure 24.9.) Select the database you want to synchronize with and click OK.

Figure 24.9.

The Synchronize Database dialog box lets you select the database you want to synchronize with.

3. If no problems occur during the synchronization process, the dialog box shown in Figure 24.10 appears. You're warned that changes won't be visible until you close and reopen the database. If you select Yes, Access closes and reopens the database for you.

Figure 24.10.

This dialog box appears after a successful synchronization process.

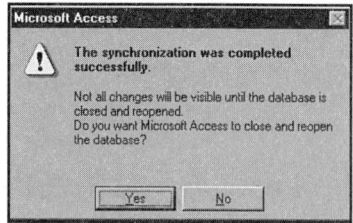

Synchronizing Databases with the Windows 95 Briefcase

The second way to synchronize replicas is by using the Windows 95 Briefcase. Simply open the Briefcase window and select the database file. On the Briefcase menu, click Update Selection. If you want to synchronize all the replicas in the Briefcase, click Update All to open the Update Briefcase dialog box. (See Figure 24.11.) Click Update, and the synchronization process is finished.

Figure 24.11.

The Update Briefcase dialog box appears when you're synchronizing from the Briefcase.

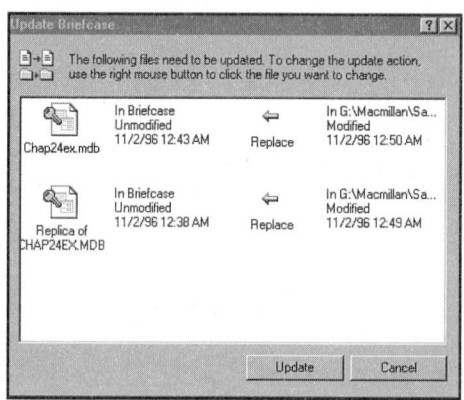

Resolving Replication Conflicts

When the Jet Engine tries to synchronize two databases, it might find that the same row has been changed in both databases, so a conflict results that must be handled. The rule is that the database in which the row has changed most often wins. If both rows have changed the same number of times, the winner is chosen randomly. This might sound frightening, but it isn't as bad is it seems because you can let the user know which changes were rejected.

You must know whether two members of the replica set contain conflicting information. Two users out in the field might have entered different information about a sale or a customer, so it's important that the program identify these inconsistencies and have a method for handling them.

If there are conflicts, you're warned about them when you try to open the database that has the conflicts. (See Figure 24.12.) Here, you're given the choice of whether to resolve the conflicts or not.

Figure 24.12.
This dialog box warns of synchronization conflicts.

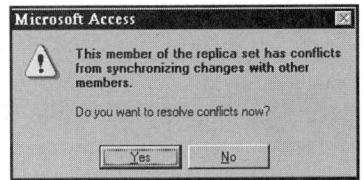

If the user selects Yes, the Jet Engine tries to identify the conflicts. After identifying the conflicts, the Resolve Replication Conflicts dialog box, shown in Figure 24.13, appears. Notice that in this example, the Jet Engine identified two conflicts in the tblClients table. The user can either resolve the conflicts or postpone the conflict resolution.

Figure 24.13.
Use the Resolve Replication Conflicts dialog box to resolve conflicts between tables.

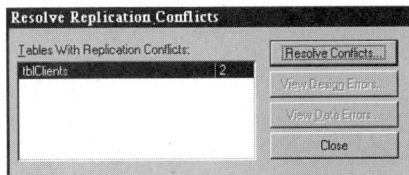

If the user clicks Resolve Conflict, another Resolve Replication Conflicts dialog box opens. (See Figure 24.14.) This dialog box shows the user each record that has a conflict, providing the opportunity to keep the existing record or overwrite with the conflict record.

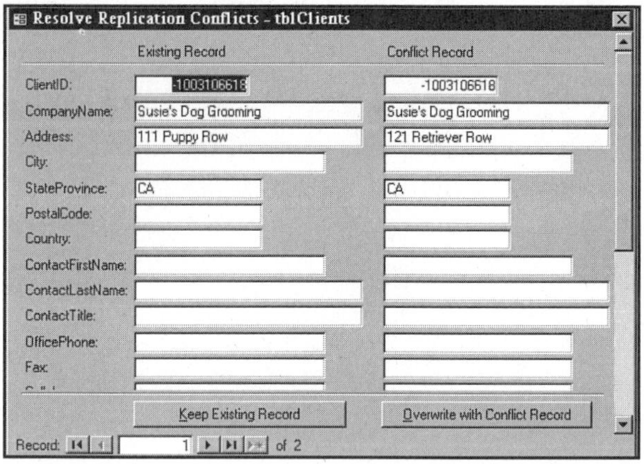

Figure 24.14.

In this Resolve Replication Conflicts dialog box, you view and resolve specific conflicts.

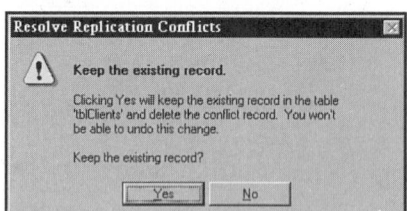

After you select Overwrite with Conflict Record, yet another Resolve Replication Conflicts dialog box opens. (See Figure 24.15.) This dialog box warns the user that data in the conflict record will overwrite data in the existing record. The user can proceed with or cancel the process. If the user selects Keep Existing Record, the warning dialog box shown in Figure 24.16 appears; it warns the user that the existing record will be maintained and the conflict record will be *permanently* deleted.

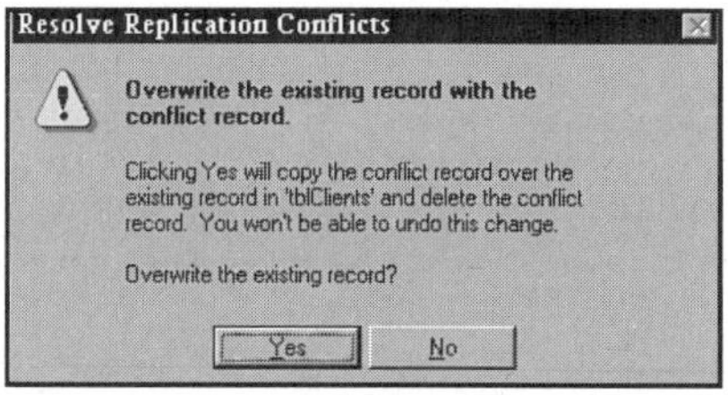

Figure 24.15.

This warning message appears when the user selects Overwrite with Conflict Record.

Figure 24.16.

This warning message appears when the user selects Keep Existing Record.

After the user resolves all conflicts, a message appears indicating that he or she successfully resolved all conflicts.

Using the Replication Manager

The Replication Manager is a powerful tool that lets you take full advantage of replication in Access 97. It's included only with the Microsoft Office 97 ODE. The Replication Manager's major benefits include the following:

- Lets you easily replicate a database
- Allows you to easily create additional replicas
- Gives you the ability to synchronize any replicas in the set
- Allows you to schedule automated synchronization
- Gives you the opportunity to view an object's replication history
- Lets you easily manage replication properties
- Offers a way to manage synchronization with replicas at remote sites
- Allows you to perform synchronization over a LAN, an intranet, or the Internet

Running the Replication Manager for the First Time

The Replication Manager can be opened by using a Desktop shortcut or through the Windows 95 Start menu. The first time you run the Replication Manager, the Configure Microsoft Replication Manager Wizard appears. (See Figure 24.17.)

Figure 24.17.
The Configure Microsoft Replication Manager Wizard.

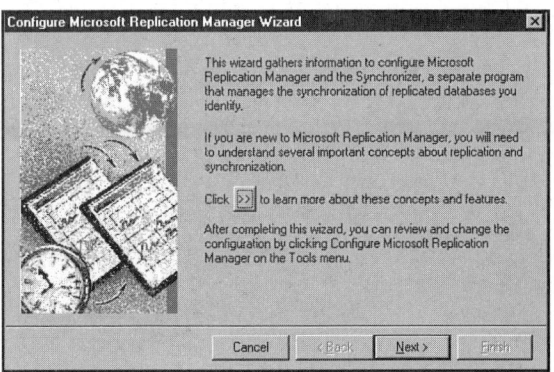

1. Click Next to start the configuration process and launch the Configure Microsoft Replication Manager Wizard.

2. This step of the Configure Microsoft Replication Manager Wizard asks whether you want to support indirect synchronization (See Figure 24.18.) With indirect synchronization, a Synchronizer for each of two replicas opens its own replica locally. A desktop computer leaves changes in a dropbox on the network. When the laptop connects to the network, the Synchronizer on the laptop finds the changes in its dropbox folder and applies them to the replica. The notebook leaves its changes in a dropbox folder of the desktop Synchronizer, which finds the changes and applies them. This is the preferred synchronization method for remote users who aren't always logged on to the network. Make your selection and click Next.

Figure 24.18.

Selecting a form of synchronization.

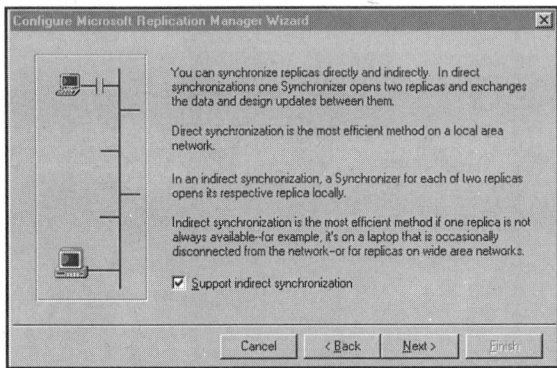

3. If you choose to support indirect synchronization, the next step of the wizard gives you some information about Synchronization types. After reading this, click Next, and the wizard prompts you for a location for the dropbox folder. (See Figure 24.19.) Select a folder and click Next.

Figure 24.19.

Selecting a location for the Synchronizer to store changes.

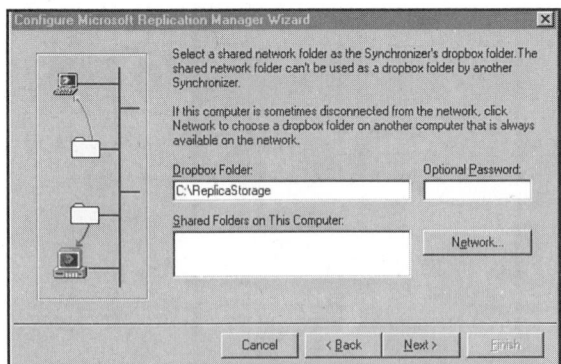

4. You're then asked whether the computer on which you're running the wizard is an Internet server. Make your selection and click Next.

5. If you indicate that the computer is an Internet server, the next step asks whether you want to use the Internet server to synchronize replicated databases. If you respond Yes and click Next, you're prompted for the name of the Internet server. Enter the name and click Next. (See Figure 24.20.) The next step asks you to provide a Shared folder and Share name used when synchronizing over the Internet. Click Next and you're prompted for an FTP alias name. Select the FTP alias name and click Next.

Figure 24.20.

If your computer is an Internet server, here's the place to tell the wizard its partial URL.

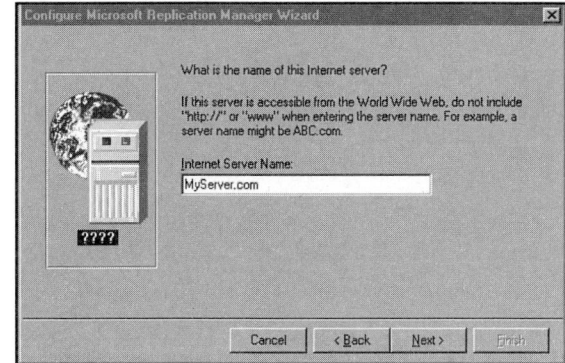

6. Select a location for the log file used to record significant events that happen during the synchronization process. (See Figure 24.21.) Click Next.

Figure 24.21.

Selecting the name and location for the log file.

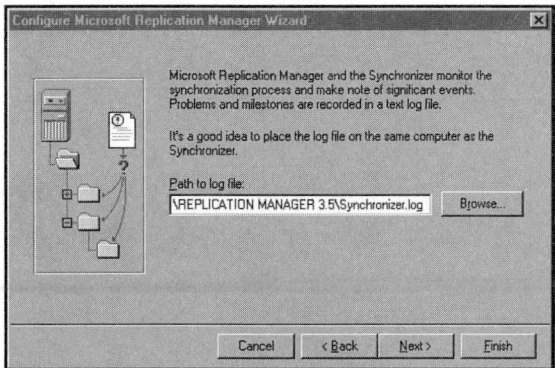

7. The next step of the wizard prompts you for a Synchronizer name. This name is used for an icon and as a descriptive name for the Synchronizer. This step of the wizard also asks whether you want to automatically start the Synchronizer when Windows starts. (See Figure 24.22.) The Synchronizer must be running for scheduled synchronization to take place, so you might want to select this option. Enter a Synchronizer name and indicate whether you want the Synchronizer to automatically start, then click Next.

Figure 24.22.
Selecting a name for the Synchronizer.

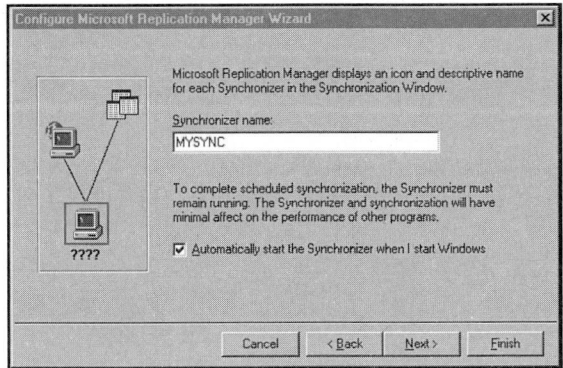

8. Click Finish to complete the process.

After the Configure Microsoft Replication Manager Wizard is finished, you can either convert a database to a Design Master or create a new replica. (See Figure 24.23.) You can perform these tasks any time, so you should click Close.

Figure 24.23.
The Replication Manager launches for the first time.

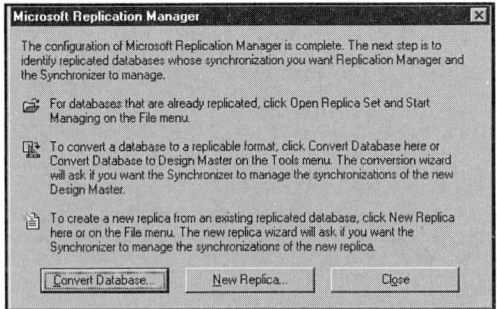

> **NOTE**
>
> If you opted to load the Synchronizer whenever you launch Windows, and you decide that you don't want the Synchronizer to be launched automatically, you must remove the Synchronizer icon from the Windows Startup folder.

Replicating a Database with the Replication Manager

In addition to using the Access user interface and the Briefcase to make a database replicable, you can also use the Replication Manager. It offers additional options, such as designating an object as local. Here are the steps:

1. From the Replication Manager, click the Convert Database to the Design Master toolbar button or choose File | Convert Database to Design Master. The Convert Database to Design Master Wizard appears. (See Figure 24.24.)

Figure 24.24.
Launching the Convert Database to Design Master Wizard.

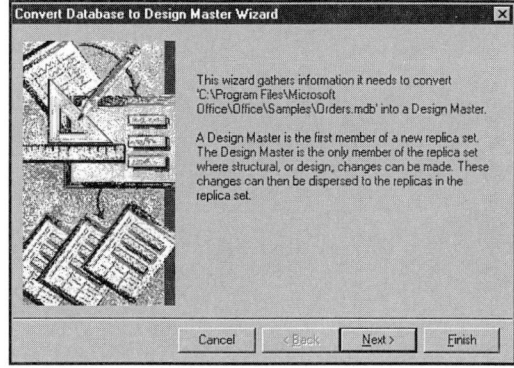

2. Select a file to convert and click Open.
3. Indicate whether you want to make a backup of the database before converting it to a Design Master, then click Next. It's always a good idea to keep a backup of the unreplicated database.
4. Enter a description for the new replica set and click Next. All replicas made from this Design Master will be members of the replica set you're creating. (See Figure 24.25.)

Figure 24.25.
Entering a description for the replica set.

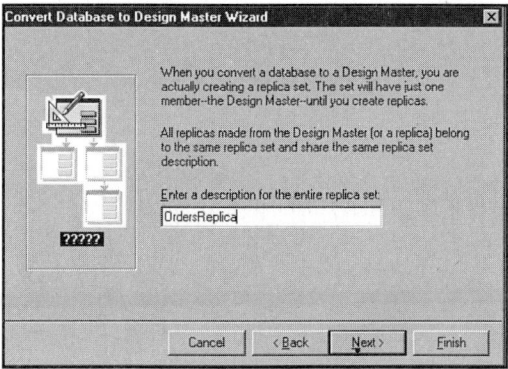

5. You're then asked whether you want to make all objects available to the replica set or flag some of them as local. (See Figure 24.26.) If you click "Make some objects available to the entire replica set," the Select Replicated Objects dialog box opens so you can designate selected objects as local. (See Figure 24.27.) To flag an object as local, clear its check box. Click OK when you're done.

Figure 24.26.

Designating whether you want all or just some objects to be replicated.

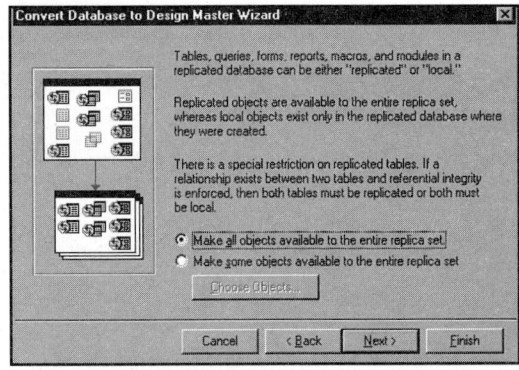

Figure 24.27.

Flagging objects as local or replicated.

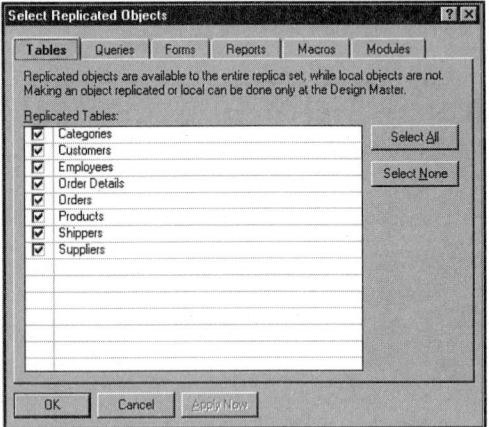

6. Next, indicate whether you want the replicas to be read-only. (See Figure 24.28.) The Design Master is the only place where you can make schema changes. If you want to limit data changes to the Design Master as well, select the option that makes all replicas read-only. In general, you should keep the default option of "I want to be able to create read-write replicas." Click Next after you make a selection.

Figure 24.28.

Indicating whether the database will allow read-write replicas to be created.

7. The next step of the wizard asks whether you want to manage synchronization of the Design Master with the Synchronizer found on the current machine. If you answer No, synchronization must originate by another managed member of the replica set. Make your selection and click Next.

8. Click Finish to complete the wizard; you're then notified of success or warned about any problems that happened during the conversion process.

> **NOTE**
>
> A table can't be designated as local if it's involved in a relationship with a replicated table.

> **NOTE**
>
> When you have more than one replica set, you must use the Managed Replicas tool on the Replication Manager toolbar to view a different replica set. Only one replica set can be viewed at a time.

Creating Replicas with the Replication Manager

Just as you can create replicas by using the Access user interface and the Windows 95 Briefcase, you can also create replicas with the Replication Manager. To do so, follow these steps:

1. Click New Replica on the toolbar, then click Next.

2. Select a Source and Destination for the replica. The Source is the name of the database you're replicating, and the Destination is the name of the replica. Click Next.

3. Indicate whether you want to be able to make data changes within the replica. Click Next.

4. Indicate whether you want the replica to be managed by the Synchronizer on the current machine. Click Next.

5. Click Finish.

> **NOTE**
>
> If you create a replica of a database managed by a different Synchronizer, you must use the Replication Manager on the other computer to configure the Synchronizer.

Partial Replication

Jet 3.5 and Access 97 have introduced *partial replication*, meaning that only a subset of the data is replicated. This is useful when you have, for example, several sales people and you want each salesperson to have just his or her own data. However, you want all the salespeople to be able to synchronize their changes with other databases on the network. Partial replicas can be created by using the Partial Replica Wizard (you can download it from the Microsoft Internet site) or by using VBA code. The procedure for using VBA code to create a partial replica is in the section "Creating a Partial Replica Using Code."

Synchronizing Replicas with the Replication Manager

Just as you can synchronize replicas with the Access user interface and the Windows 95 Briefcase, you can also use the Replication Manager by following these steps:

1. From the Replication Manager, click the Synchronize Now tool on the toolbar.
2. The Synchronize Now dialog box opens. (See Figure 24.29.) Here, you can designate details of the synchronization process. When you're done, click OK to finish the synchronization process.

Figure 24.29.
The Synchronize Now dialog box allows you to designate details of the synchronization process.

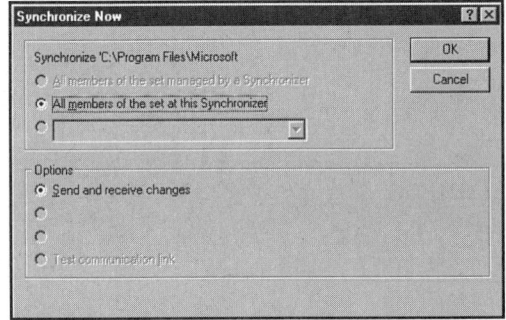

Remote Synchronizations

You might be surprised that the Replication Manager map shows only one machine, even though you have many replicas. One icon appears for each Synchronizer involved in the replica set. Figure 24.30 shows two Synchronizers involved in the replication process: TECRA and DELL. The second site was set up by installing the Replication Manager on the second machine. Any replica from the local site can then be moved to the remote site by establishing a connection to the remote site and choosing File | Move Replica. You can locate the Managed Folder at the remote site and move the replica to the remote site's Managed Folder.

Figure 24.30.

The Replication Manager map with two Synchronizers.

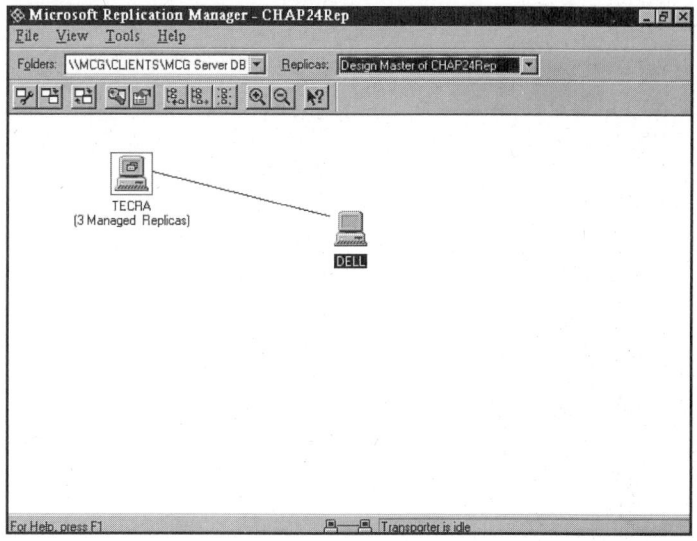

After both sites appear on the replication map, you can manage synchronizations by using the join line that connects them. You can right-click on the join line and select Synchronize Now or, to establish a schedule for synchronization, select Edit Schedule. Scheduling synchronization is covered in the next section.

Scheduled Synchronizations

Synchronizations can be scheduled between replicas managed by the same Synchronizer, or between replicas managed by two different Synchronizers. To schedule synchronization between replicas managed by the same Synchronizer, right-click on the icon representing the local Synchronizer and select Edit Locally Managed Replica Schedule. (See Figure 24.31.) From here, you can select the days and times when the replicas synchronize.

Figure 24.31.

Use the Edit Locally Managed Replica Schedule dialog box to select the days and times when the replicas synchronize.

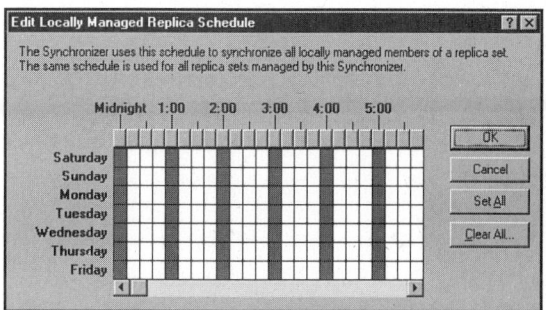

To schedule the synchronization process between two different Synchronizers, right-click on the join line and select Edit Schedule to open the Edit Schedule dialog box. Here you can schedule the specifics of the synchronization process between the two sites. The shading of each box indicates which Synchronizer initiates that exchange. If the connection can't be made when the exchange is initiated, the dropbox folder keeps a temporary log of the changes. Every 15 minutes, it retries the connection until it's successful.

Reviewing the Synchronization History

The synchronization history can be very useful. Besides giving you an audit trail, it helps you analyze the effectiveness of the topology and synchronization schedule you have selected. Three types of logs are kept by the Replication Manager:

- The local synchronization history
- The remote synchronization history
- The Synchronizer log

To view the local synchronization history, right-click the local machine icon and select View Local Synchronization History; this opens the Synchronization History dialog box. (See Figure 24.32.) It shows you details about the exchange of information between the local replicas.

Figure 24.32.
Viewing local synchronization history.

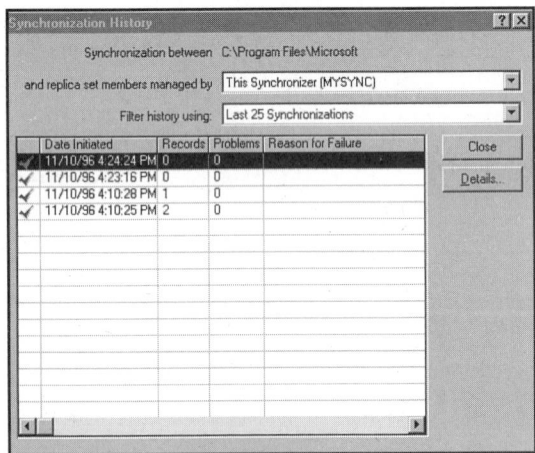

To view the remote synchronization history, select the line joining two Synchronizers and choose View | Synchronization History to open the Synchronization History dialog box. If you want more information about any of the log entries, click Details to open the Synchronization Details dialog box. (See Figure 24.33.)

Figure 24.33.
The Synchronization Details dialog box shows the details of a synchronization process.

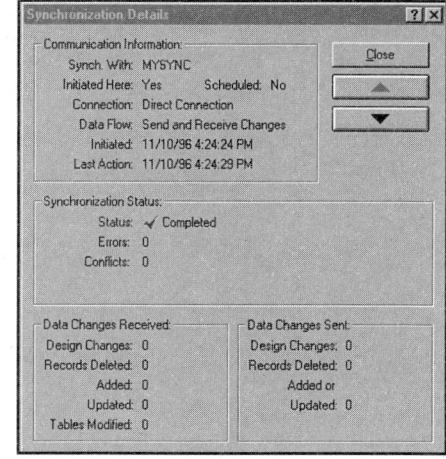

Working with Synchronization Properties

You can also view properties of the selected Synchronizer. To do this, double-click the Synchronizer and the Replica Properties window appears. This tabbed dialog box gives you important information about the selected Synchronizer.

> **NOTE**
>
> Jet 3.5 and Access 97 support synchronization over the Internet or an intranet. You place a replica on a server and use the Replication Manager to synchronize, using a standard HTTP connection. This process is covered in Chapter 27, "Access and the Internet."

Implementing Replication by Using Code

Most of the replication functions can be implemented by using code, but this isn't the easiest way to manage replication. However, sometimes you might want to implement aspects of the replication process with code so that you can better control the process, and its interface, from within your application.

Making a Database Replicable by Using Code

The following routine renders a database replicable by using code:

```
Sub MakeReplicable(strTargetDB As String)
    Dim db As Database
    Set db = DBEngine(0).OpenDatabase(strTargetDB, True)
    db.Properties.Append db.CreateProperty("Replicable", _
        dbText, "T")
    db.Close
End Sub
```

705

This routine accepts the path to any database as a parameter. It opens up the database exclusively, then appends the Replicable property to the database. This property contains a text value (dbText) set to True.

Flagging an Object as Local

Unless you do something special, all objects in a database are included in the replication process. The following code illustrates how to flag a database object as local. It sets the KeepLocal property of the tblEmployee table to True.

```
Sub MakeLocal()
    Const errPropNotFound = 3270
    Dim db As Database
    Dim tdf As TableDef
    On Error GoTo MakeLocal_Err

    Set db = CurrentDb
    Set tdf = db.TableDefs!tblEmployee
    tdf.Properties("KeepLocal").Value = "T"

    Exit Sub
MakeLocal_Err:
    If (Err = errPropNotFound) Then
        tdf.Properties.Append tdf.CreateProperty("KeepLocal", dbText, "T")
    Else
        MsgBox Error
    End If
End Sub
```

Notice that the code is set up to handle the error that occurs if the object, in this case the tblEmployee table, doesn't already have a KeepLocal property. The error handler appends the property to the object at runtime, and the code then sets the object's KeepLocal property to True.

Creating a Replica by Using Code

A new replica can be created with code by using the MakeReplica method. The code looks like this:

```
Sub MakeReplica(strRepCopy As String)
    Dim db As Database
    Set db = CurrentDb
    db.MakeReplica strRepCopy, ""
    db.Close
End Sub
```

This code accepts a parameter containing the path and filename for the replica. The MakeReplica method is executed on the database object, and the parameter name becomes the replica's name. The last parameter indicates whether the replica is created as read-only.

Creating a Partial Replica Using Code

You can also create a partial replica using VBA code, as follows:

Listing 24.1. Creating a partial replica.

```
Sub CreatePartialReplica(strOriginal As String, _
    strReplica As String, _
    strTable As String, _
    strFilter As String)

    Dim db As Database
    Dim tdf As TableDef
    Dim intCount As Integer

    'Open Original Database
    Set db = OpenDatabase(strOriginal)
    'Make Replica Database with dbRepMakePartial constant
    db.MakeReplica strReplica, "Great Replica", dbRepMakePartial
    'Close Original Database
    db.Close

    'Open Replica Database
    Set db = OpenDatabase(strReplica, True)
    Set tdf = db.TableDefs(strTable)
    tdf.ReplicaFilter = strFilter

    'Loop through each table definition
    'If table is a Foreign table then set its PartialReplica
    'property to True
    For intCount = 0 To db.Relations.Count - 1
        If db.Relations(intCount).ForeignTable = strTable Then
            db.Relations(intCount).PartialReplica = True
            Exit For
        End If
    Next intCount
    'Populate Partial Replica
    db.PopulatePartial strOriginal
    db.Close

End Sub
```

The code begins by creating an empty replica with no filters and no data records. It then sets a filter for a specific table in the database. The PartialReplica property of the table relationships between the selected table and the tables it's related to is set to get records only from the child tables that meet the parent filter. Finally, the partial replica is populated from the full replica.

Synchronizing a Database by Using Code

At times, you might want to finish the synchronization process by using VBA code. The following routine synchronizes the current database with the database whose name is passed as a parameter. The constant dbRepImpExpChanges indicates that you want to perform a two-way synchronization.

```
Sub Synchronize(strDBToSync As String)
    Dim db As Database
    Set db = CurrentDb
    db.Synchronize strDBToSync, dbRepImpExpChanges
    db.Close
End Sub
```

Handling Conflicts by Using Code

You can also handle conflicts by using code. What you do when a conflict is identified is determined by the business needs of your users.

```
Sub IdentifyConflicts()
    Dim db As Database
    Dim tdf As TableDef
    Dim rstErr As Recordset
    Set db = CurrentDb
    For Each tdf In db.TableDefs
        If Len(tdf.ConflictTable) Then
            Set rstErr = db.OpenRecordset(tdf.ConflictTable)
            Do While Not rstErr.EOF
                Debug.Print rstErr.Fields(0).Value
                rstErr.MoveNext
            Loop
            rstErr.Close
        End If
    Next td
End Sub
```

This routine goes through each table, determining whether something is in the table's ConflictTable property. If the ConflictTable property has something in it, a recordset is opened from the Conflict table. The routine loops through each record of the Conflict table, displaying the value of the first field in the Debug window.

Practical Examples: Managing the Time and Billing Application with Replication

You must make a decision about whether it's necessary to implement replication in the Time and Billing application. It could be very useful if, for example, you have many consultants who work in the field and need to enter client, project, billing, and expense information while on the road. Using what you've learned in this chapter, you can make sure all changes made to each consultant's copy of the database are sent to the main server database each time the consultant dials into the office.

Replication can also be used so that the data managed by the Time and Billing application is backed up during the day, which minimizes the chance of data loss or downtime. Finally, you might want to implement replication in the Time and Billing application to distribute the work load over a few servers in your organization.

The potential benefits of using replication with the Time and Billing application are many. With what you have learned in this chapter, you must decide whether replication is appropriate for your application and how it can best be used in your organization.

Summary

Replication is a very complex and robust Access feature. It can be used at the most basic level to synchronize changes between two databases, or, in an enterprise-wide application, to synchronize changes between many machines on a WAN (Wide Area Network). The easiest, but least robust, way to implement replication is by using the Access user interface or the Windows 95 Briefcase. However, with the Replication Manager, you can schedule and manage synchronization activity, as well as handle the most complex of replication topologies. Finally, by using code, you can customize the behavior of your application's synchronization activities.

Extending the Power of Access

25

CHAPTER

Automation: Communicating with Other Applications

- Understanding Automation, 714
- Defining Some Automation Terms, 714
- Declaring an Object Variable to Reference Your Application, 715
- Using `CreateObject` and `GetObject`, 717
- Manipulating an Automation Object, 719
- Controlling Excel from Access, 719
- Closing an Automation Object, 722
- Creating a Graph from Access, 723
- Controlling Word from Access, 726
- Controlling PowerPoint from Access, 728
- Controlling Access from Other Applications, 730
- Practical Examples: Using Automation to Extend the Functionality of the Time and Billing Application, 733

Understanding Automation

Windows users have come to expect seamless integration between products. They are not concerned with what product you use to develop their application; they just want to accomplish their tasks. Often, Microsoft Word, Microsoft Excel, or some other product is best suited for a particular task that your application must complete. It is your responsibility to pick the best tool for the job. This means that you must know how to communicate from your application directly to that tool.

All this means that you can no longer learn only about the product and language that you select as your development tool. Instead, you must learn about all the other available applications. You also must learn how to communicate with these applications—a challenging but exciting feat.

OLE automation is the capability of one application to control another application's objects. This means that your Access application can launch Excel, create or modify a spreadsheet, and print it—all without the user having to directly interact with the Excel application. Many people confuse automation with the process of linking and embedding. OLE 1.0 gave you the capability to create compound documents, meaning that you can embed an Excel spreadsheet in a Word document or link to the Excel spreadsheet from a Word document. This capability was exciting at the time and still is quite useful in many situations, but OLE 2.0 (in addition to everything that OLE 1.0 provides) introduced the capability for one application to actually control another application's objects. With Office 97, Microsoft changed the way users refer to OLE. It now is referred to as *automation* and is an industry standard and a feature of the *component object model* (COM).

Just as you can control other applications using automation, your Access application can be controlled by other applications, such as Excel or a Visual Basic application. This means that you can take advantage of Access's marvelous report writer from your Visual Basic application. In fact, you can list all the Access reports, allow your user to select one, and then run the report—all from a Visual Basic form.

Defining Some Automation Terms

Before you learn how automation works, you need to understand a few automation terms. Automation requires an automation client and an automation server. The *automation client* application is the one that is doing the talking. It is the application that is controlling the server application. Because this book is about Access, most of the examples in this chapter show Access as an automation client, meaning that the Access application is controlling the other application (Excel, Word, and so on). The *automation server* application is the application being controlled. It contains the objects being manipulated. Excel is acting as an automation server when Access launches Excel, makes it visible, creates a new worksheet, sends the results of a query to the worksheet, and graphs the spreadsheet data. It is Excel's objects that are being controlled, Excel's properties that are being changed, and Excel's methods that are being executed.

Another important component of automation is a *type library*; this is a database that lists the objects, properties, methods, and events exposed by an automation server application. Type libraries allow the server application's objects, properties, and methods to be syntax-checked by the Access compiler. You also can use a type library to get help on another application's objects, properties, and methods from within Access.

An *object model* of an automation server application contains the set of objects that are exposed to automation client applications. The objects in the object model are called *object types*. When you write automation code, you create and manipulate instances of an object type. These instances are called *objects*.

WARNING

It is important to be aware of the hardware that automation requires. It is common for a developer using a Pentium with 32M of RAM to create a really slick application, only to find that it won't run on the 12M 486s owned by users. Automation craves RAM. The more, the better! I recommend 24M of RAM or more for applications that use automation. It also is important to recognize that automation is not fast, even on the slickest of machines.

Declaring an Object Variable to Reference Your Application

Automation requires that you create object variables that reference application objects. After you create an object variable, you can query and change the object's properties as well as execute its methods.

You can learn about an object's properties and methods by using its object libraries. An *object library* contains a listing of all the properties and methods that an object exposes. To view foreign objects from Access, you first must establish a reference to that application. After a reference is established, you can view that object's properties and methods by using the Object Browser. You also can view any modules and classes that the parent object exposes.

To register an object, the Code window must be visible. With the Code window visible, choose Tools | References. The References dialog box appears, as shown in Figure 25.1.

Figure 25.1.

The References dialog box.

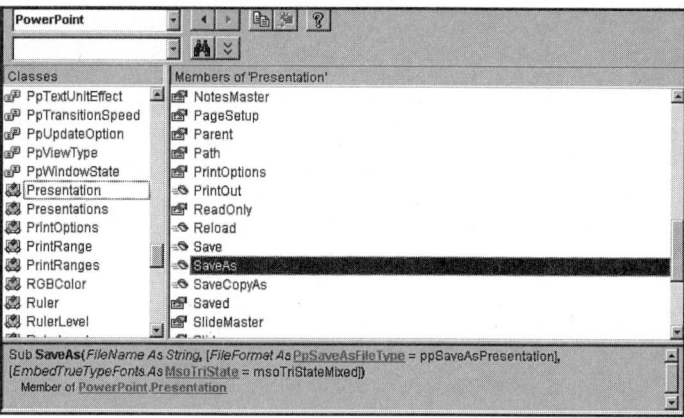

Each time you install a program, the Windows Registry is updated. The References dialog box shows you all the objects that are registered in Windows. (See Figure 25.2.) If you want to link to one of the available objects from within Access, you must enable the checkbox to the left of the object name. Choose OK. You can browse that object's properties and methods in the Object Browser, as shown in Figure 25.3. As covered in Chapter 10, "The Real Scoop on Objects, Properties, and Events," to access the Object Browser, you can choose View | Object Browser, press F2, or click the Object Browser tool while in the Module window. Notice that in Figure 25.3, the Object Browser displays all the classes that belong to the Access 8.0 object library. The Presentation class is selected. All the members of the Presentation class are displayed in the list box at the right. The SaveAs method is selected. Notice that the bottom half of the Object Browser shows all the arguments associated with the SaveAs method of the Presentation class.

Figure 25.2.

Registered automation server objects

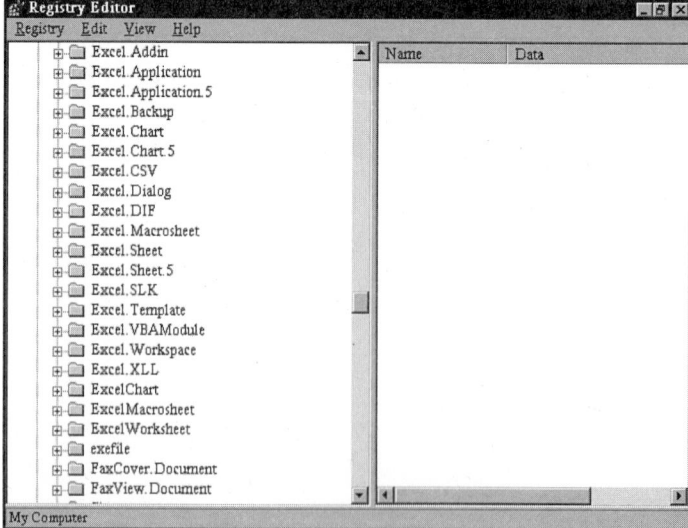

Figure 25.3.
The Object Browser.

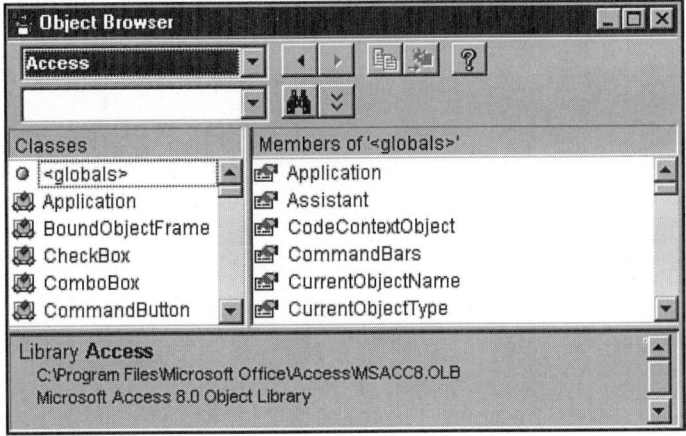

Using `CreateObject` and `GetObject`

Before you can talk to an application, you need to know the objects contained in it. You then can use `Dim`, `Private`, or `Public` statements to point to and control various application objects. Each product comes with documentation indicating which objects it supports. You also can view the objects that a product supports by using the Object Browser. After you create an object variable, you can manipulate the object without user intervention.

CreateObject

To create an instance of an object, you first must create a generic object variable that holds a reference to the object. You can do this by using a `Dim` statement:

```
Dim objExcel As Object
```

You then can use the `CreateObject` function to assign an automation server object to the object variable. The `CreateObject` function receives the class name for an application object as its parameter. This is the name the Windows Registry uses to reference the object. Here's an example:

```
Set objExcel = CreateObject("Excel.Application")
```

This code creates an object variable pointing to the Excel application object. A new instance of the Excel application is started automatically. This Excel object is part of the Excel application. It can be controlled by VBA using the object variable. Unless instructed otherwise, the instance of Excel is invisible. You can make it visible by using this statement:

```
objExcel.Visible = True
```

GetObject

The CreateObject function creates a new instance of the specified application, and the GetObject function points an object variable to an existing object. If the object does not exist, an error results. The GetObject function receives two parameters. The first is the full path to a file, and the second is the name of the application class. Here's an example:

```
objExcel = GetObject(,"Excel.Application")
```

This code points an existing occurrence of Excel to the objExcel object variable. If no instances of Excel are found, an error results. Because you did not specify a path name, the instance of Excel does not point to a specific file.

Certain applications register themselves as single-instance objects. This means that no matter how many times the CreateObject function is run, only one instance of the object is created. Microsoft Word is an example of a single-instance object. On the other hand, if the CreateObject function is used to launch Microsoft Excel, several instances of the application are created. The code in Listing 25.1 addresses this problem.

Listing 25.1. Starting Excel if it is not already running.

```
Sub LaunchExcel()
    On Error Resume Next
    'Sets Error Handling to Resume on the Line Following the Error
    Dim objExcel As Object    'Create Generic Object Variable
    'Attempt to Point an Occurrence of Excel to the Object Variable
    Set objExcel = GetObject(, "Excel.Application")
    If Err.Number Then    'Test to See if an Error Occurred
        'If an Error Occurs, Use CreateObject to Create an Instance of Excel
        Set objExcel = CreateObject("Excel.Application")
    End If
    objExcel.Visible = True
End Sub
```

This subroutine creates a generic object variable called objExcel. It uses the GetObject function to try to point the objExcel variable to an existing copy of Excel. If an error occurs, you know that Excel was not running. The CreateObject function then is used to create a new instance of Excel. Finally, the Excel object is made visible. This code ensures that only one copy of Excel is launched. You use CreateObject to launch Excel only if the GetObject function returns an error.

> **NOTE**
>
> It is important that you are aware of which objects register themselves as single-instance objects and which register themselves as multi-instance objects. You must take certain steps with multi-instance objects to ensure that you do not accidentally launch several instances of the application.

Manipulating an Automation Object

After you create an instance of an object, you are ready to set its properties and execute its methods. You can talk to the object through the object variable you created. By using this object variable, you can get and set properties and execute methods.

Setting and Retrieving Properties

The objects you will be talking to through automation all have properties. *Properties* are the attributes of the object—the adjectives you use to describe the objects. You can use VBA to inquire about the properties of objects and set the values of these properties. Here are some examples:

```
objExcel.Visible = True
objExcel.Caption = "Hello World"
objExcel.Cells(1, 1).Value = "Here I Am"
```

Each of these examples sets properties of the Excel application object. The first example sets the Visible property of the object to True. The second example sets the Caption of the object to "Hello World". The final example sets the Value property of the Cells object, contained in the Excel object, to the value "Here I Am".

Executing Methods

Properties refer to the attributes of an object, and *methods* refer to the actions you take on the object. Methods are the verbs that apply to a particular object type. Here's an example:

```
objExcel.Workbooks.Add
```

This code uses the Add method to add a workbook to the Excel object.

Controlling Excel from Access

Before you attempt to talk to Excel, you must understand its object model. Excel gives you an excellent overview of the Excel object model. You can find this model by searching for object model in Excel Help. Each object in the model has hypertext links that enable you to obtain specific help on the object, its properties, and its methods.

After you launch Excel, it launches as a hidden window with a Visible property of False. Destroying the Excel object variable does not cause Excel to terminate. To make things even more complicated, each time you use the CreateObject function to launch Excel, a new instance of Excel is launched. This means that it is possible for numerous hidden copies of Excel to be running on a user's machine, which can lead to serious resource problems. Therefore, you need to take several precautions when you want to communicate with Excel.

To begin, you must determine whether Excel is running before attempting to launch a new instance. If Excel already is running, you do not want to launch another copy of Excel, and you do not want to exit Excel when you are done working with it. If your application loads Excel, you will close it when you are done. The subroutine in Listing 25.2 launches Excel. As discussed earlier in the "GetObject" section, the GetObject function is used to point to an existing copy of Excel. If an error occurs, the CreateObject function points the object variable to a new instance of Excel. If the error occurs, the public variable gobjExcel is set to False, indicating that you are sure that Excel was not running before your application loaded it. This variable is used in the cleanup routine to determine whether the application exits Excel.

Listing 25.2. A subroutine to launch Excel.

```
Function CreateExcelObj()
    On Error Resume Next
    'Sets Error Handling to Resume on the Line Following the Error
    CreateExcelObj = False
    'Attempt to Point an Occurrence of Excel to the Object Variable
    Set gobjExcel = GetObject(, "Excel.Application")
    If Err.Number Then    'Test to See if an Error Occurred
        'If an Error Occurs, Use CreateObject to Create an Instance of Excel
        Set gobjExcel = CreateObject("Excel.Application")
        If gobjExcel Is Nothing Then
            gbExcelRunning = False
            CreateExcelObj = True
            MsgBox "Could Not Create Excel Object"
        Else
            gbExcelRunning = False
            CreateExcelObj = True
        End If
    Else
        gbExcelRunning = True
        CreateExcelObj = True
    End If
    Exit Function
End Function
```

NOTE

You can find this code and most other examples used in this chapter in the CHAP25EX.MDB database located on your sample code CD-ROM. This routine is located in basUtils.

WARNING

To take advantage of the exciting world of automation, all automation server applications must be installed on the user's machine, and the user must possess a full license to the server applications. In fact, you will be unable to compile and run the examples contained in the sample database for this chapter unless you have the server applications loaded on your development machine.

The CreatExcelObj function is called from the Click event of cmdFillExcel. The application attempts to talk to the Excel object only if the return value of the function is True, indicating that Excel was loaded successfully:

```
Private Sub cmdFillExcel_Click()
    gbExcelRunning = True
    If CreateExcelObj() Then
        Call FillCells
    End If
End Sub
```

If Excel launches successfully, the FillCells subroutine executes, as shown in Listing 25.3.

Listing 25.3. The FillCells subroutine.

```
Sub FillCells()
    Dim oWS As Object
    gobjExcel.Workbooks.Add
    Set oWS = gobjExcel.ActiveSheet
    oWS.Cells(1, 1).Value = "Schedule"
    oWS.Cells(2, 1).Value = "Day"
    oWS.Cells(2, 2).Value = "Tasks"
    oWS.Cells(3, 1).Value = 1
    oWS.Cells(4, 1).Value = 2
    gobjExcel.Range("A3:A4").SELECT
    gobjExcel.Selection.AutoFill gobjExcel.Range("A3:A33")
    gobjExcel.Range("A1").SELECT
    gobjExcel.Visible = True
End Sub
```

You can find this relatively simple routine in frmSimpleExcel, which is part of the CHAP25EX.MDB database file. (See Figure 25.4.) It begins by using the Add method on the Workbooks collection of the Excel object to add a new workbook to the instance of Excel. It then uses Set oWS = poExcel.ActiveSheet to provide a shortcut for talking to the active sheet in the new Excel workbook. Using the oWS object reference, the values of several cells are modified. The AutoFill method is used to quickly fill a range of cells with data. The cursor is returned to cell A1, and the Excel object is made visible. You might wonder what the AutoFill method is; it automates the process of filling a range of cells with a pattern of data. Figure 25.5 shows the results. I mention it here not just to tell you what it is, but also to illustrate an important point: You must know the product you are automating and its capabilities. If you are not familiar with the product from a user's perspective, you will find it extremely difficult to work with the product using automation.

Figure 25.4.

The form used to launch, communicate with, and close Excel.

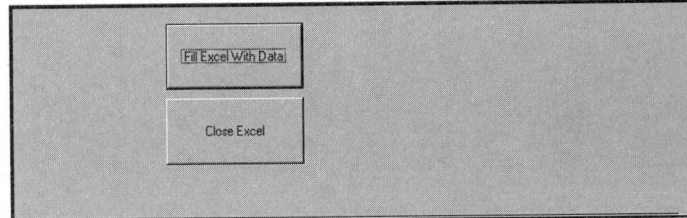

Figure 25.5.

Using the AutoFill method to populate a range of cells.

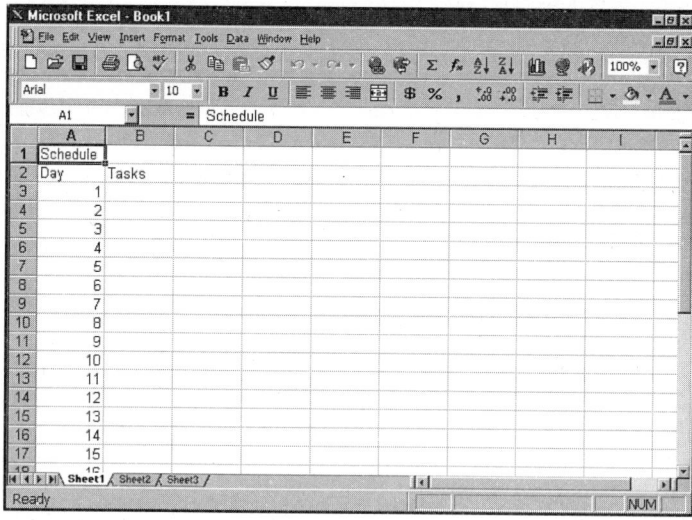

Closing an Automation Object

After the user clicks the CloseExcel command button, the CloseExcel subroutine is called, as shown in Listing 25.4. The CreateExcelObj routine determined whether the user was running Excel prior to launching your application. When the CloseExcel routine runs, it prompts the user to close Excel only if the public variable gbExcelRunning indicates that Excel was not running prior to your application. Otherwise, it prompts the user, warning that he or she must close Excel.

Listing 25.4. The CloseExcel routine.

```
Sub CloseExcel()
    On Error GoTo CloseExcel_Err
    Dim intAnswer As Integer
    Dim objWK As Object

    'Attempt to point to an active workbook
    Set objWK = gobjExcel.ActiveWorkbook
    'If Excel is Still Running and was NOT running before
    'this application executed it, prompt user to close
    If Not gbExcelRunning Then
        intAnswer = MsgBox("Do You Want to Close Excel?", vbYesNo)
        If vbYes Then
            objWK.Close False
            gobjExcel.Quit
        End If
    Else
        MsgBox "Excel Was Running Prior to This Application." & Chr(13) _
            & "Please Close Excel Yourself."
        gobjExcel.Visible = True
    End If
```

```
CloseExcel_Exit:
    Set gobjExcel = Nothing
    Set objWK = Nothing
    Exit Sub

CloseExcel_Err:
    MsgBox "Error # " & Err.Number & ": " & Err.Description
    Resume CloseExcel_Exit
End Sub
```

Creating a Graph from Access

Now that you have learned how to talk to Excel, you are ready to learn how to do something
a bit more practical. Figure 25.6 shows a form called frmCreateExcelGraph. The form shows
the result of a query that groups the result of price multiplied by quantity for each country.
The Create Excel Graph command button sends the result of the query to Excel and produces
the graph shown in Figure 25.7. (Listing 25.5 shows the code that produces this graph.)

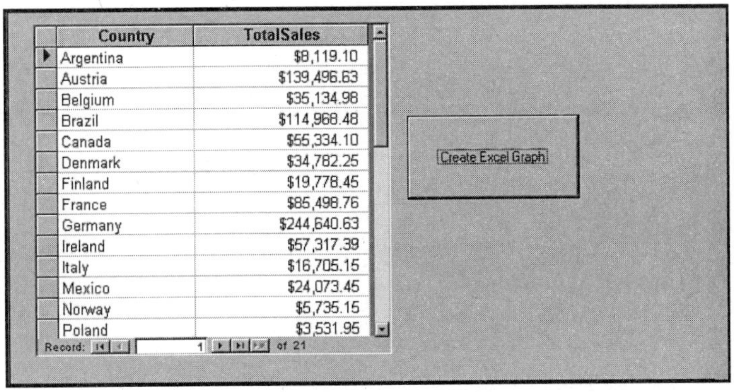

Figure 25.6.

*The form used to create
an Excel graph.*

Country	TotalSales
▶ Argentina	$8,119.10
Austria	$139,496.63
Belgium	$35,134.98
Brazil	$114,968.48
Canada	$55,334.10
Denmark	$34,782.25
Finland	$19,778.45
France	$85,498.76
Germany	$244,640.63
Ireland	$57,317.39
Italy	$16,705.15
Mexico	$24,073.45
Norway	$5,735.15
Poland	$3,531.95

Record: ◄◄ ◄ 1 ► ►► ►* of 21

[Create Excel Graph]

Listing 25.5. Creating a graph from Access.

```
Private Sub cmdCreateGraph_Click()
    On Error GoTo cmdCreateGraph_Err
    Dim db As DATABASE
    Dim rst As Recordset
    Dim fld As Field
    Dim objWS As Object
    Dim intRowCount As Integer
    Dim intColCount As Integer

    'Display Hourglass
    DoCmd.Hourglass True
    Set db = CurrentDb

    'Attempt to create Recordset and launch Excel
    If CreateRecordset(db, rst, "qrySalesByCountry") Then
        If CreateExcelObj() Then
```

Listing 25.5. continued

```
            gobjExcel.Workbooks.Add
            Set objWS = gobjExcel.ActiveSheet
            intRowCount = 1
            intColCount = 1
            'Loop through Fields collection using field names
            'as column headings
            For Each fld In rst.Fields
               If fld.Type <> dbLongBinary Then
                  objWS.Cells(1, intColCount).Value = fld.Name
                  intColCount = intColCount + 1
               End If
            Next fld
            'Loop through recordset, placing values in Excel
            Do Until rst.EOF
               intColCount = 1
               intRowCount = intRowCount + 1
               For Each fld In rst.Fields
                  If fld.Type <> dbLongBinary Then
                     objWS.Cells(intRowCount, intColCount).Value = fld.Value
                     intColCount = intColCount + 1
                  End If
               Next fld
               rst.MoveNext
            Loop
            gobjExcel.Columns("A:B").SELECT
            gobjExcel.Columns("A:B").EntireColumn.AutoFit
            gobjExcel.Range("A1").SELECT
            gobjExcel.ActiveCell.CurrentRegion.SELECT
            'Add a Chart Object
            gobjExcel.ActiveSheet.ChartObjects.Add(135.75, 14.25, 607.75, 301).SELECT
            'Run the Chart Wizard
            gobjExcel.ActiveChart.ChartWizard Source:=Range("A1:B22"), _
            Gallery:=xlColumn, _
            Format:=6, PlotBy:=xlColumns, CategoryLabels:=1, SeriesLabels _
            :=1, HasLegend:=1, Title:="Sales By Country", CategoryTitle _
            :="", ValueTitle:="", ExtraTitle:=""
            'Make Excel Visible
            gobjExcel.Visible = True
         Else
            MsgBox "Excel Not Successfully Launched"
         End If
      Else
         MsgBox "Too Many Records to Send to Excel"
      End If
      DoCmd.Hourglass False

cmdCreateGraph_Exit:
   Set db = Nothing
   Set rst = Nothing
   Set fld = Nothing
   Set objWS = Nothing
   DoCmd.Hourglass False
   Exit Sub

cmdCreateGraph_Err:
   MsgBox "Error # " & Err.Number & ": " & Err.Description
   Resume cmdCreateGraph_Exit
End Sub
```

Figure 25.7.

The result of a query graphed in Excel.

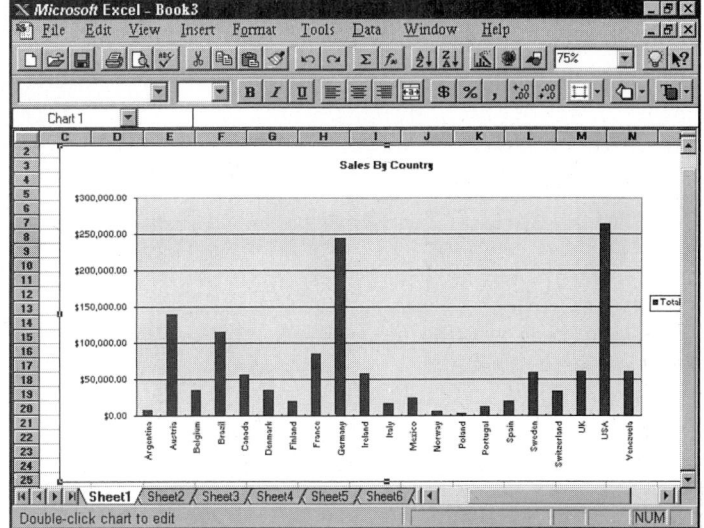

This routine begins by creating several object variables. It then points the db object variable to the current database. It calls a user-defined function called CreateRecordset. The CreateRecordset function receives three parameters: the database object variable, a recordset object variable, and the name of a query. Listing 25.6 shows the CreateRecordset function.

Listing 25.6. The CreateRecordset function.

```
Function CreateRecordset(dbAny As DATABASE, rstAny As Recordset, _
strTableName As String)
   Dim rstCount As Recordset
   On Error GoTo CreateRecordset_Err
   'Create recordset that contains count of records in query
   Set rstCount = dbAny.OpenRecordset("Select Count(*) As NumRecords _
   from " & strTableName)
   'If more than 500 records in query result, return false
   'Otherwise, create recordset from query
   If rstCount!NumRecords > 500 Then
      CreateRecordset = False
   Else
      Set rstAny = dbAny.OpenRecordset(strTableName, dbOpenDynaset)
      CreateRecordset = True
   End If

CreateRecordset_Exit:
   Set rstCount = Nothing
   Exit Function

CreateRecordset_Err:
   MsgBox "Error # " & Err.Number & ": " & Err.Description
   Resume CreateRecordset_Exit
End Function
```

This function begins by counting how many records are returned by the query name that is passed. If the number of records exceeds 500, the function returns a False; otherwise, the function opens a recordset based on the query name that is passed and returns a True. This function ensures that only a reasonable number of records is sent to Excel and that a recordset can be opened successfully.

If the CreateRecordset function returns a True, the remainder of the code in the Click event of the cmdCreateGraph command button executes. The routine uses the CreateExcelObj function to launch Excel. If Excel is opened successfully, a new workbook is created. The routine then loops through each field in the Fields collection of the recordset (the result of the query). The values of the cells in the first row of the worksheet are set equal to the names of the fields in the recordset. Next, the routine loops through each record in the recordset. The data from each row is placed in a different row in the spreadsheet. The data from each column in a particular row is placed in the various columns of the worksheet. OLE object fields (dbLongBinary) are excluded from the process.

After all the data in the recordset is sent to Excel, the routine is ready to create a chart. It moves the cursor to cell A1 and then selects the entire contiguous range of data. It adds a chart object to the worksheet and then uses the Chart Wizard to create a chart. Finally, Excel is made visible so that users can see the fruits of their efforts.

Controlling Word from Access

As you discovered in the preceding section, Excel exposes many objects. Each of these objects can be manipulated separately, using its own properties and methods. Prior to Office 97, this was not true for Word, because Word exposed only one object, called Word.Basic. With Microsoft Word 97, Visual Basic for Applications is available, and Word 97 exposes many objects just as Excel and other Microsoft products do.

Just like Excel, you can use the CreateObject function or GetObject function to launch Word. Like Excel, Word, launches as a hidden object. The Word application object has a Visible property, which makes the Word object visible. If you create a Word object using automation, Word will not automatically terminate, even if the object variable is destroyed.

Figure 25.8 shows the form called frmMergeToWord, which shows the results of running a query called qryMailMerge. After the user clicks the Merge to Word command button, all the records that are displayed are sent to a Word mail merge and printed. Figure 25.9 shows an example of the resulting document, and Listing 25.7 shows the code that generated this document.

Figure 25.8.

The data that will be merged to Word.

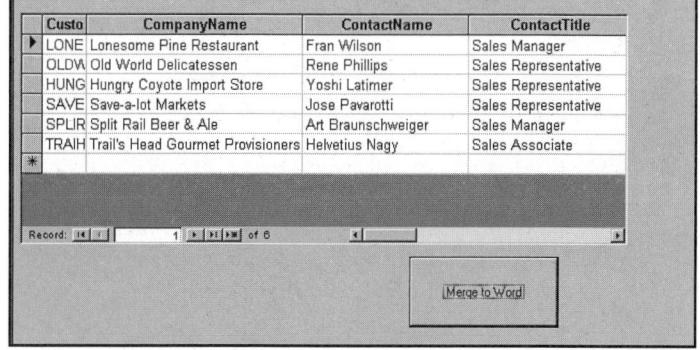

Figure 25.9.

The result of the mail merge.

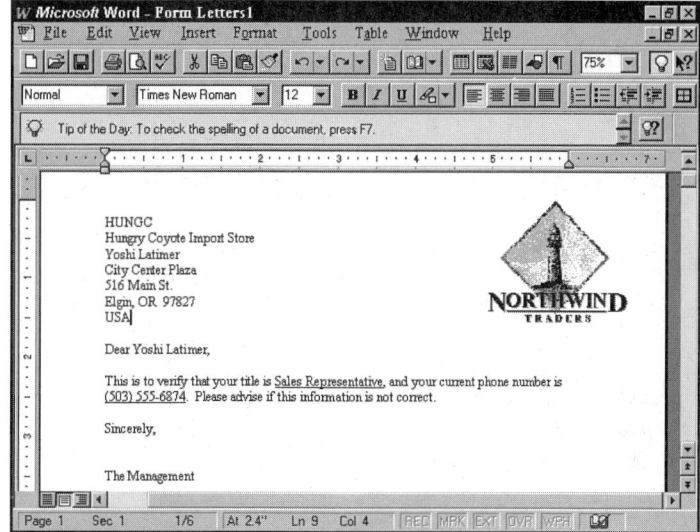

Listing 25.7. Generating a Word mail merge document.

```
Private Sub cmdMergeToWord_Click()

On Error GoTo cmdMergeToWord_Err
    DoCmd.Hourglass True
    If CreateWordObj() Then
        gobjWord.Documents.Open "c:\databases\customerletter.doc"
        With gobjWord.ActiveDocument.MailMerge
            .Destination = wdSendToNewDocument
            .SuppressBlankLines = True
            .Execute
        End With
        gobjWord.ActiveDocument.PrintPreview    'Preview
        gobjWord.Visible = True
    End If
```

continues

Listing 25.7. continued

```
cmdMergeToWord_Exit:
    DoCmd.Hourglass False
    Exit Sub

cmdMergeToWord_Err:
    MsgBox "Error # " & Err.Number & ": " & Err.Description
    Set gobjWord = Nothing
    Resume cmdMergeToWord_Exit
End Sub
```

The code begins by presenting an hourglass mouse pointer to the user. This ensures that if the process takes a while, the user knows that something is happening. It then calls the `CreateWordObj` routine to create a Word object. The `CreateWordObj` routine is very similar to the `CreateExcel` routine shown earlier in the chapter. The Open method is executed on the Documents collection of the Word object. It opens a document called customerletter in the databases directory. The customerletter document already has been set up to do a mail merge with the results of a query called qryMerge. The subroutine sets the Destination property of the `MailMerge` object to a new document. It sets the SuppressBlankLines property to True, and then executes the mail merge with the Execute method. This merges the results of qryMailMerge and creates a new document with the mail-merged letters. The PrintPreview method is executed on the `ActiveDocument` object so that the merged document is printed. Finally, the Visible property of the Word object is set to True, making Word visible, and the hourglass vanishes.

Controlling PowerPoint from Access

Believe it or not, even PowerPoint can be controlled using automation. You can create a presentation, print a presentation, or even run a slide show directly from Access.

PowerPoint launches as a hidden window. To make PowerPoint visible, you must set the Visible property of `AppWindow` to True. Destroying the PowerPoint object variable does not terminate the PowerPoint application.

> **NOTE**
>
> You can find details of the PowerPoint object model on the Microsoft Solutions Development Kit CD-ROM. You should review this object model before attempting to communicate with PowerPoint.

The code shown in Listing 25.8 is located under the `Click` event of the cmdChangePicture command button on frmOLEToPowerPoint, which is shown in Figure 25.10. Figure 25.11 shows the resulting PowerPoint slide.

Figure 25.10.

*The form used to create a
PowerPoint slide.*

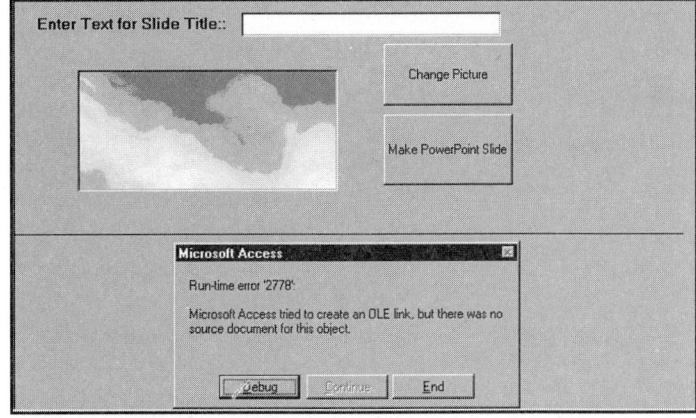

Figure 25.11.

The resulting PowerPoint slide.

Listing 25.8. Select Picture.

```
Private Sub cmdChangePicture_Click()
   dlgCommon.ShowOpen
   olePicture.SourceDoc = dlgCommon.FileName
   olePicture.Action = acOLECreateLink
End Sub
```

The code in the Click event of cmdChangePicture invokes the File Open common dialog box
so that the user can select a picture to be added to the slide. The FileName property returned
from this dialog box is used as the SourceDoc property for the automation object. The new
picture then is linked to the automation object.

Listing 25.9 shows the routine that creates the PowerPoint slide.

Listing 25.9. Creating the PowerPoint slide.

```
Private Sub cmdMakePPTSlide_Click()
    Dim objPresentation As Object
    Dim objSlide As Object
    'Create instance of PowerPoint application
    Set mobjPPT = CreateObject("PowerPoint.Application.8")
    'Make instance visible to user
    mobjPPT.Visible = True
    'Add a Presentation
    Set objPresentation = mobjPPT.Presentations.Add
    'Add a Slide
    Set objSlide = objPresentation.Slides.Add(1, ppLayoutTitleOnly)
    'Change the Slide Background
    objSlide.Background.Fill.ForeColor.RGB = RGB(255, 100, 100)
    'Modify the Slide Title
    With objSlide.Shapes.Title.TextFrame.TextRange
        .Text = Me!txtTitle
        .Font.Color.RGB = RGB(0, 0, 255)
        .Font.Italic = ppTrue
    End With
    'Add the OLE Picture
    objSlide.Shapes.AddOleObject _
        Left:=50, Top:=50, Width:=200, Height:=150, _
        FileName:=olePicture.SourceDoc, link:=True


cmdMakePPTSlide_Exit:
    Set objPresentation = Nothing
    Set objSlide = Nothing
    Exit Sub

cmdMakePPTSlide_Err:
    MsgBox "Error # " & Err.Number & ": " & Err.Description
    Resume cmdMakePPTSlide_Exit
End Sub
```

The routine begins by creating an instance of PowerPoint. The instance is made visible. A presentation then is added to the PowerPoint object, and a slide is added to the presentation. The background fill of the slide is modified. The Text, Color, and Italic properties of the title object are customized. Finally, the SourceDoc property of the olePicture object is used to create an automation object, which is added to the slide.

Controlling Access from Other Applications

Many times, you will want to control Access from another application. You might want to run an Access report from a Visual Basic or Excel application, for example. Just as you can tap into many of the rich features of other products (such as Excel) from Access, you can use some of Access's features from within another program. Fortunately, it is extremely easy to control Access from within other applications.

You can find an overview of the Access object model in Access Help. Unless you are very familiar with the Access object model, you should look at this graphical representation of Access's object model before you attempt to use automation to control Access. Access launches with its

Visible property set to False. You can change the Visible property of the application object to True to make Access visible.

The form shown in Figure 25.12 is a Visual Basic form. It is called frmReportSelect.frm and is part of a Visual Basic project called AutomateAccess.vbp. The form enables you to select any Access database. It displays a list of all reports in the selected database; you can use this list to preview an Access report or to print multiple Access reports.

Listing 25.10 shows how this Visual Basic form is created.

Figure 25.12.

The Visual Basic form that enables you to print Access reports.

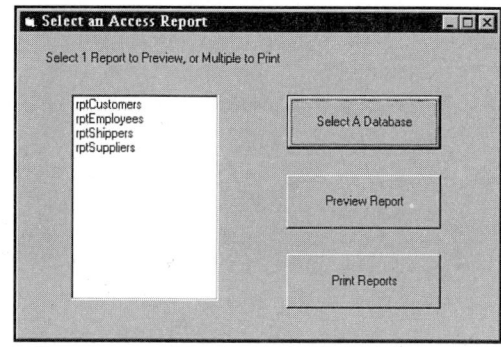

Listing 25.10. Creating a Visual Basic form to print reports.

```
Private Sub cmdSelectDB_Click()
    Call LoadReports
End Sub

Sub LoadReports()
    Dim ws As Workspace
    Dim db As Database
    Dim doc As Document
    Dim cnt As Container

    'Point at the Jet Engine
    Set ws = DBEngine(0)
    'Set a Filter and Initial Directory for the
    'Common Dialog Control
    dlgCommon.Filter = "Databases (*.mdb)¦*.mdb"
    dlgCommon.InitDir = App.Path
    'Display the File Open Common Dialog
    dlgCommon.ShowOpen
    'Open a Database using the selected Access file
    Set db = ws.OpenDatabase(dlgCommon.filename)
    'Look at the Reports collection
    Set cnt = db.Containers!Reports

    'Clear the List Box of previous entries
    lstReports.Clear
    'Loop through the collection of Reports
    'Add each report name to the List Box
    For Each doc In cnt.Documents
        lstReports.AddItem doc.Name
    Next doc
End Sub
```

The subprocedure begins by creating an instance of the Access application. It uses the OpenDatabase method of the Workspace object to open the Access database selected by the user in the File Open common dialog box. It then loops through the Reports collection of the selected database. The name of each report is added to the list box. So far, you have not launched Access. Instead, you have used *data access objects* (DAOs) to get at its objects.

The routine in Listing 25.11 creates a new instance of the Access application object.

Listing 25.11. Creating a new instance of the Access application object.

```
Private Sub cmdPreview_Click()
    Call RunReport
End Sub

Sub RunReport()
    On Error GoTo RunReport_Err
    'Create an Instance of the Access application
    Dim objAccess As New Access.Application

    'Open the selected Database
    objAccess.OpenCurrentDatabase (dlgCommon.filename)
    'Preview the Selected Report
    objAccess.DoCmd.OpenReport lstReports.Text, View:=acPreview
    'Set the Visible property of the Application to True
    objAccess.Visible = True

RunReport_Exit:
    Set objAccess = Nothing
    Exit Sub

RunReport_Err:
    MsgBox Err.Description
    Resume RunReport_Exit
End Sub
```

Dim objName As New is another way to create an instance of a registered application object. After the instance is created, the OpenCurrentDatabase method is used to open the selected database. The OpenReport method is used along with the constant acPreview. This causes the selected report to be previewed. Finally, the Access application object is made visible.

The Visual Basic application also gives the user the opportunity to send multiple Access reports to the printer. Listing 25.12 shows the code for this.

Listing 25.12. Sending multiple reports to the printer.

```
Private Sub cmdRunReport_Click()
    Call PrintReports
End Sub

Sub PrintReports()
    Dim intCounter As Integer
    On Error GoTo PrintReports_Err
```

```
    'Create an Instance of the Access Application
    Dim objAccess As New Access.Application

    'Open the Database that was selected in the
    'File Open Common Dialog
    objAccess.OpenCurrentDatabase (dlgCommon.filename)

    'Loop through the List Box
    'Print each report that is selected
    For intCounter = 0 To lstReports.ListCount - 1
        If lstReports.Selected(intCounter) Then
            objAccess.DoCmd.OpenReport lstReports.Text
        End If
    Next intCounter

PrintReport_Exit:
    Set objAccess = Nothing
    Exit Sub

PrintReports_Err:
    MsgBox Err.Description
    Set objAccess = Nothing
    Resume PrintReport_Exit

End Sub
```

This routine creates an instance of Access and then opens the selected database. It loops through the list box, identifying all the reports that have been selected. It then sends each report to the printer.

Practical Examples: Using Automation to Extend the Functionality of the Time and Billing Application

Many potential applications of automation exist for the Time and Billing application. One of them is discussed in this section.

The form in Figure 25.13 enables users to select a table or query to send to Excel. The form is called frmSendToExcel.

The list box on the form is populated with the Callback function shown in Listing 25.13. Notice that the function uses the TableDefs and QueryDefs collections to populate the list box, excluding all the system tables.

Figure 25.13.

*Exporting a table or query
to send to Excel.*

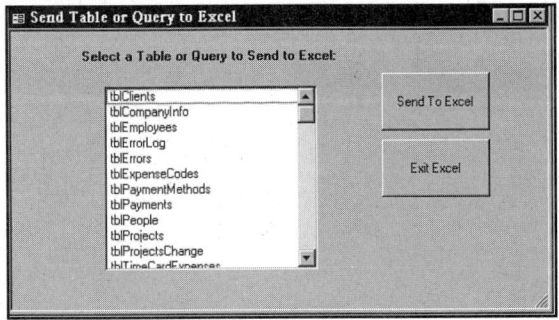

Listing 25.13. Using the `Callback` function to fill a list box.

```
Function FillWithTableList(ctl As Control, vntID As Variant, _
        lngRow As Long, lngCol As Long, intCode As Integer) _
        As Variant

    Dim db As DATABASE
    Dim tdf As TableDef
    Dim qdf As QueryDef
    Dim intCounter As Integer
    Static sastrTables() As String
    Static sintNumTables As Integer
    Dim varRetVal As Variant

    varRetVal = Null

    Select Case intCode
        Case acLBInitialize          ' Initialize.
            Set db = CurrentDb
            'Determine the Total Number of Tables + Queries
            sintNumTables = db.TableDefs.Count + db.QueryDefs.Count
            ReDim sastrTables(sintNumTables - 2)
            'Loop through each Table adding its name to
            'the List Box
            For Each tdf In db.TableDefs
                If Left(tdf.Name, 4) <> "MSys" Then
                    sastrTables(intCounter) = tdf.Name
                    intCounter = intCounter + 1
                End If
            Next tdf
            'Loop through each Query adding its name to
            'the List Box
            For Each qdf In db.QueryDefs
                sastrTables(intCounter) = qdf.Name
                intCounter = intCounter + 1
            Next qdf
            varRetVal = sintNumTables
        Case acLBOpen                 'Open
            varRetVal = Timer         'Generate unique ID for control.
        Case acLBGetRowCount          'Get number of rows.
            varRetVal = sintNumTables
        Case acLBGetColumnCount       'Get number of columns.
            varRetVal = 1
        Case acLBGetColumnWidth       'Get column width.
            varRetVal = -1            '-1 forces use of default width.
```

```
          Case acLBGetValue                  'Get the data.
              varRetVal = sastrTables(lngRow)
      End Select
      FillWithTableList = varRetVal
End Function
```

The Click event of the cmdSendToExcel command button sends the selected table or query to Excel. Listing 25.14 shows this code.

Listing 25.14. Sending a table or query to Excel.

```
Private Sub cmdSendToExcel_Click()
   On Error GoTo cmdSendToExcel_Err
   gbExcelRunning = True
   Dim objWS As Object
   Dim db As DATABASE
   Dim rst As Recordset
   Dim fld As Field
   Dim intColCount As Integer
   Dim intRowCount As Integer

   Set db = CurrentDb

   'Invoke Hourglass
   DoCmd.Hourglass True
   'Try to Create Recordset and Create Excel Object
   If CreateRecordset(db, rst, lstTables.Value) Then
       If CreateExcelObj() Then
           'Add a Workbook
           gobjExcel.Workbooks.Add
           'Create a Shortcut to the Active Sheet
           Set objWS = gobjExcel.ActiveSheet
           intRowCount = 1
           intColCount = 1
           'Loop through the Fields collection
           'Make each field name a column heading in Excel
           For Each fld In rst.Fields
               If fld.Type <> dbLongBinary Then
                   objWS.Cells(1, intColCount).Value = fld.Name
                   intColCount = intColCount + 1
               End If
           Next fld
           'Send Data from Recordset out to Excel
           Do Until rst.EOF
               intColCount = 1
               intRowCount = intRowCount + 1
               For Each fld In rst.Fields
                   If fld.Type <> dbLongBinary Then
                       objWS.Cells(intRowCount, intColCount).Value = fld.Value
                       intColCount = intColCount + 1
                   End If
               Next fld
               rst.MoveNext
           Loop
           gobjExcel.Range("A1").SELECT
```

continues

Listing 25.14. continued

```
            'Set up AutoFilter
            gobjExcel.Selection.AutoFilter
            gobjExcel.Visible = True
        Else
            MsgBox "Excel Not Successfully Launched"
        End If
    Else
        MsgBox "Too Many Records to Send to Excel"
    End If


cmdSendToExcel_Exit:
    DoCmd.Hourglass False
    Set objWS = Nothing
    Set db = Nothing
    Set rst = Nothing
    Set fld = Nothing
    Exit Sub

cmdSendToExcel_Err:
    MsgBox "Error # " & Err.Number & ": " & Err.Description
    Resume cmdSendToExcel_Exit
End Sub
```

The routine begins by creating a recordset object using the CreateRecordSet function shown in Listing 25.15. It then attempts to launch Excel. If it is successful, it loops through the Fields collection of the recordset resulting from the selected table or query. It lists all the field names as column headings in Excel. Next, it loops through the recordset, adding all the field values to the rows in the Excel worksheet. Finally, it issues the AutoFilter method so that the user easily can manipulate the data in Excel, filtering it as necessary. (See Figure 25.14.)

Figure 25.14.

Using AutoFilter to analyze data sent to Excel.

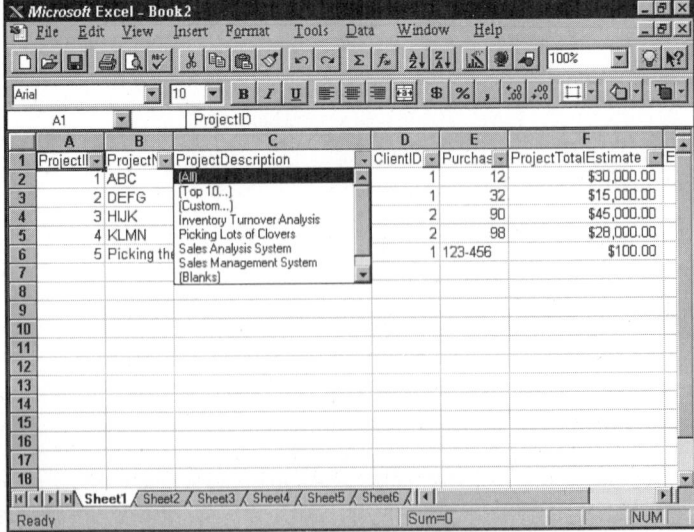

Listing 25.15. Checking recordset size.

```
Function CreateRecordset(dbAny As DATABASE, rstAny As Recordset, _
strTableName As String)
    Dim rstCount As Recordset
    On Error GoTo CreateRecordset_Err
    'Create recordset that contains count of records in query
    Set rstCount = dbAny.OpenRecordset("Select Count(*) As NumRecords from _
    " & strTableName)
    'If more than 500 records in query result, return false
    'Otherwise, create recordset from query
    If rstCount!NumRecords > 500 Then
        CreateRecordset = False
    Else
        Set rstAny = dbAny.OpenRecordset(strTableName, dbOpenDynaset)
        CreateRecordset = True
    End If

CreateRecordset_Exit:
    Set rstCount = Nothing
    Exit Function

CreateRecordset_Err:
    MsgBox "Error # " & Err.Number & ": " & Err.Description
    Resume CreateRecordset_Exit
End Function
```

This routine, found in basOLE, ensures that the recordset is not too large to send to Excel. If the size of the recordset is acceptable, it creates the recordset and returns `True`.

> **NOTE**
>
> This code worked with VB4, and it should work with future versions of Visual Basic.

Summary

Automation enables you to control other applications from your Access application, and it enables other programs to control your Access application. This chapter began by providing an overview of automation and why you might want to use it. It discussed creating an object variable to reference the application you are automating. After the ins and outs of the object variable were explained, you saw numerous examples of manipulating automation objects. You looked at detailed code showing automation involving Excel, Word, and PowerPoint. Finally, you learned about controlling Access from other applications.

The capability to communicate with other applications has become a prerequisite for successful software development. It is extremely important to be aware of the rich wealth of tools available. The capability to call on other applications' features is helping to make the world document-centric rather than application-centric. This means that users can focus on their tasks and not on how they are accomplishing those tasks. Although automation requires significant hardware and also is rather slow, the benefits it provides often are well worth the price.

26

CHAPTER

Using ActiveX Controls

- ActiveX Controls Explained, 740
- Incorporating ActiveX Controls in Access 97, 740
- Adding ActiveX Controls to Forms, 742
- Setting Properties of an ActiveX Control at Design Time, 745
- Coding Events of an ActiveX Control, 746
- The Calendar Control, 747
- The UpDown Object, 750
- The StatusBar Control, 751
- The Common Dialog Control, 753
- The Rich Textbox Control, 755
- The TabStrip Control, 758
- The ImageList Control, 760
- Licensing and Distribution Issues, 761
- Practical Examples: Implementing ActiveX Controls, 762

ActiveX Controls Explained

A powerful aspect of Access 97 is its ability to be extensible. In addition to the controls available as part of the product, you can incorporate ActiveX controls on your forms. This means you aren't limited by what Access supplies, only by the imaginations of third-party developers who design ActiveX controls.

> **NOTE**
>
> Microsoft has renamed *OLE controls* as *ActiveX controls*. You can expect to see these terms used interchangeably.

ActiveX controls support the OLE 2.0 custom control architecture and provide support for 32-bit operating systems. They have their own code, methods, events, and properties. An ActiveX control's functionality is stored in a file with an .OCX extension. This is why ActiveX controls are often referred to as OCXs. A Calendar OCX control comes with Microsoft Access, and additional OCX controls are included in the Microsoft Office Developer Edition (ODE) Tools for Windows 95 and are also available from third-party vendors, such as Crescent, Sheridan, Far Point, and many others.

Two types of ActiveX controls are available. The first is visible at both design time and runtime; after being placed on a form, it provides a front-end interface that allows the user to directly manipulate the object. One example is the Calendar control in Access 97. The second type of ActiveX control is visible at design time, but not at runtime; this type of control can, for example, give you access to all of Windows common dialog boxes, such as Open, Print, and so on. The control itself isn't visible to the user, but its functionality is available to the user at runtime. Another example is a timer control; it operates within the application, triggering event code to run, but isn't actually visible to the user.

With ActiveX controls, you can easily incorporate more functionality in your applications. For example, if you need to include a calendar on your form, you don't need to worry about how to build your own. Instead, you can include a custom calendar control and modify the calendar's behavior by changing its properties and executing its methods.

Incorporating ActiveX Controls in Access 97

Before you can incorporate an ActiveX control in your application, you must perform three steps:

1. Install the ActiveX control
2. Register the control
3. Add the control to a form

When you buy an ActiveX control, it generally has an installation program that copies the OCX file to your Windows system directory. The name of this directory can vary depending on whether you're running Windows 95 or Windows NT and what you named your Windows directory during your operating system installation.

Registering an ActiveX Control

After you have installed the control, you're ready to register it with Access. Often a control is automatically registered during installation, which is true of the Calendar OCX included with Access, as well as all the OCX controls that come with the Microsoft ODE Tools for Windows 95. OCX controls are registered in the HKEY_LOCAL_MACHINE\SOFTWARE class in the Windows Registry. (See Figure 26.1.) In the figure, the Image List control, registered as `ImagelistCtrl`, is selected.

Figure 26.1.

OCX controls in the Windows Registry.

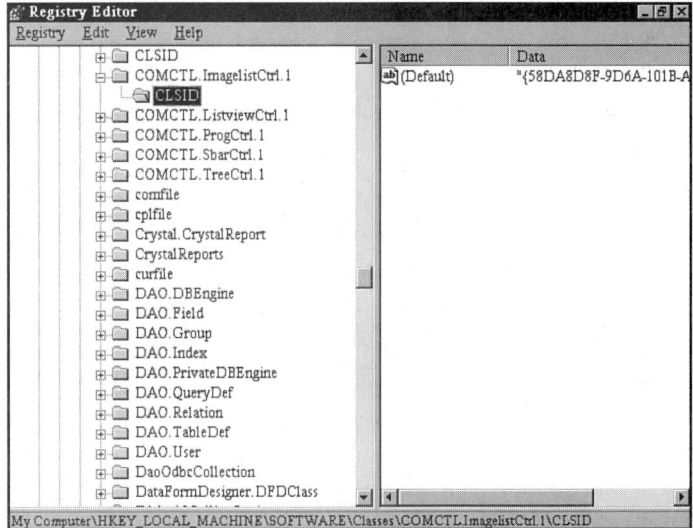

If an ActiveX control isn't registered, you can do so by using the ActiveX Controls dialog box. To open this dialog box, choose Tools | ActiveX Controls. (See Figure 26.2.)

The ActiveX Controls dialog box lists all the ActiveX controls currently registered in Access. To add an ActiveX control to the list, click Register. This opens the Add ActiveX Control dialog box. (See Figure 26.3.)

Figure 26.2.
Use the ActiveX Controls dialog box to register ActiveX controls.

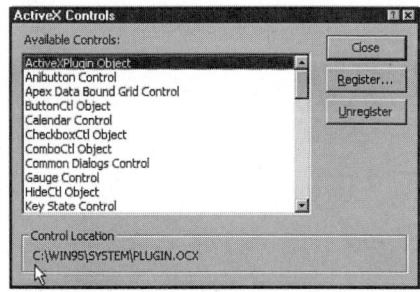

Figure 26.3.
The Add ActiveX Control dialog box allows you to locate the ActiveX control you want to register.

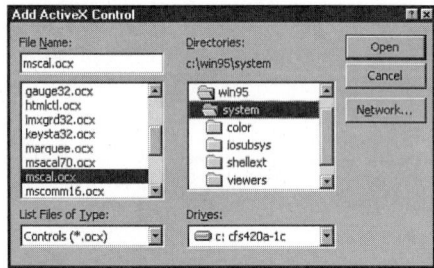

Make sure you're pointing to the directory containing the OCX you want to register. The control you're registering must already be installed; if it hasn't been installed, it won't be on the list. Select the OCX you want to register, and click OK. You then return to the ActiveX Controls dialog box, and the control you selected appears on the list of registered controls. You're ready to include the control on a form.

If you no longer plan to use an ActiveX control, you should use the Unregister function, which removes the Registry entries for controls you don't use.

Adding ActiveX Controls to Forms

Once you have registered an ActiveX control, you can include it on your forms. You do this in one of two ways:

- Select the ActiveX control from the toolbox by clicking the More Controls icon.
- Choose ActiveX Control from the Insert menu when you're in Form or Report Design view.

The More Controls tool shows you all ActiveX controls registered by your system. This in- cludes ActiveX controls that are part of Excel, Visual Basic, and any other application that uses ActiveX controls. Some of these controls won't work properly with Access. To determine which controls you can safely include in your application, read the Access Readme file or contact the vendor of the ActiveX control. The More Controls menu is shown in Figure 26.4.

Figure 26.4.

The More Controls menu shows all the ActiveX controls installed on the system.

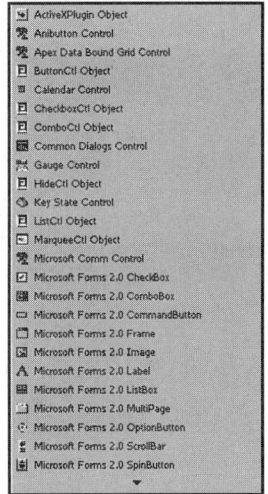

You can also use the Insert menu to select an ActiveX control from the Insert ActiveX Control dialog box. (See Figure 26.5.) After selecting a control from the Select an ActiveX Control list box, the control is placed on the form. You can move the control around the form and size it as needed.

Figure 26.5.

Use the Insert ActiveX Control dialog box to add an ActiveX control to a form.

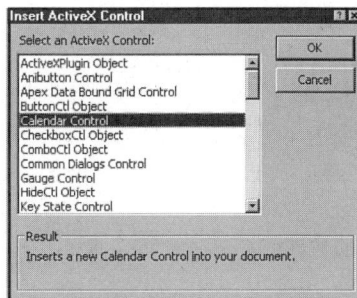

After you have placed an ActiveX control on a form, the control is ready to operate in its default format. If you insert the Calendar OCX control in a form and run the form, it looks like Figure 26.6.

The Calendar control can display all the months of the year, along with the corresponding days for each particular month. So far, you haven't set any properties for the calendar, nor have you written code to respond to any of the calendar's events. Setting an ActiveX control's properties, executing an ActiveX control's methods, and responding to an ActiveX control's events are covered in the following sections.

Figure 26.6.

A Calendar OCX, shown in Form view, with no properties explicitly set.

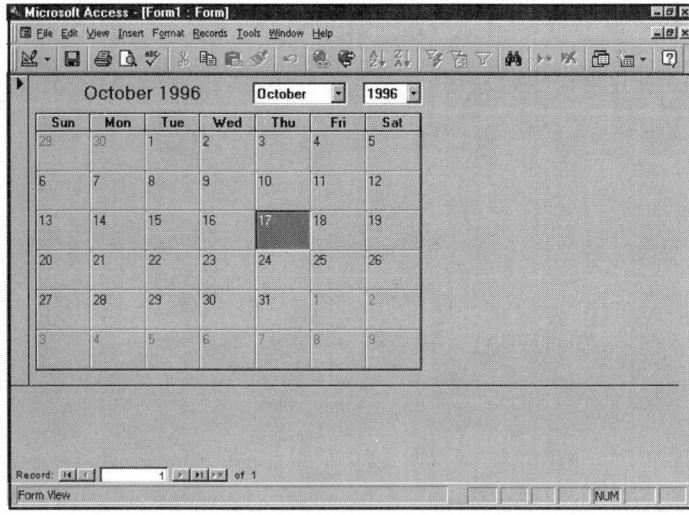

Understanding and Managing the Control Reference in Your Access Application

When you insert an ActiveX control on a form, Access automatically creates a reference to the control's Type Library that appears in the References dialog box. (See Figure 26.7.) To invoke the References dialog box, choose Tools | References with the Code window active. Note that the full path to the control is stored in this dialog box. For example, Figure 26.7 shows that the Calendar OCX is stored in C:\WIN95\SYSTEM. If the OCX is moved, VBA might not be able to resolve the reference. If this happens, you must open the References dialog box and manually remove the check from the reference marked as missing and set a reference to the ActiveX control in its new location.

Figure 26.7.

Use the References dialog box to add and remove library references.

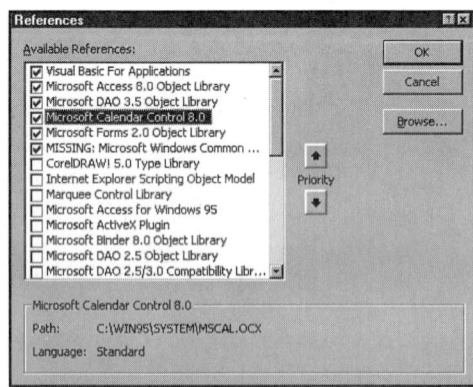

If you're distributing an application with ActiveX controls, the application may or may not work without problems. Access does its best to try to resolve references to ActiveX controls. If the controls are in the Windows\System directory or the directory Access is installed in, Access can automatically resolve the references, even if the application is installed in a different directory on the user's machine than it was on your machine.

Remember, not only do ActiveX controls need to be referenced, they need to be registered in the Windows Registry. If you use the Setup Wizard included with the Microsoft ODE Tools for Windows 95 to distribute your application, the OCXs are automatically registered when the user installs your application. If you don't use the Microsoft Office 97 ODE Setup program to distribute your application, you must write code to register the ActiveX control, or the user will have to manually register it.

Setting Properties of an ActiveX Control at Design Time

The methods, events, and properties associated with each ActiveX control differ. They're specific to that control and are determined by the control's author, and they are used to manipulate the control's appearance and behavior. Each control's methods, events, and properties are in a separate .OCX file.

If you don't modify a control's properties, it functions with its default appearance and behavior. Much of the richness of third-party controls comes from the ability to customize the controls by changing their properties at both design time and runtime. Some controls support *data binding*, which lets you store or display data in a control from an underlying field in a table. Furthermore, the ability to respond to an ActiveX control's events allows you to respond to the user's interaction with the control, and being able to execute the control's methods lets you manipulate the control.

Figure 26.8 shows some of the Calendar control's many properties. As with any control, most of its properties can be set at design time and modified or read at runtime.

Figure 26.8.

The Calendar control's Property sheet.

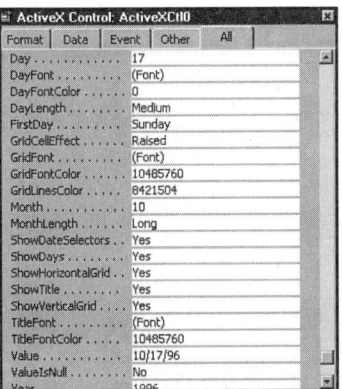

Another way to set properties for a control is to do it graphically by selecting the Custom property from the object's Property sheet, then clicking the build button. For example, if you select the Custom property from the Calendar control's Property sheet and click the build button, the Calendar Control Properties dialog box appears. (See Figure 26.9.) Here, you can modify many of the calendar's attributes, including the first day of the week, whether you want the days of the week to show, and the colors and fonts. The properties shown in this dialog box vary for each control.

Figure 26.9.
The Calendar Control Properties dialog box allows you to set some initial properties for the control.

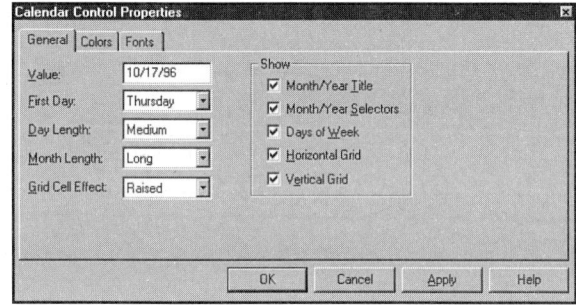

Coding Events of an ActiveX Control

Just as the properties of the control can be set or evaluated at runtime, the control's events can be coded, too. To get a list of all the events associated with an ActiveX control, open the Procedure box in the Module window. Make sure the control name for your ActiveX control is listed in the Object box. Figure 26.10 shows all the events for the Calendar control.

Figure 26.10.
Viewing the events of the Calendar control.

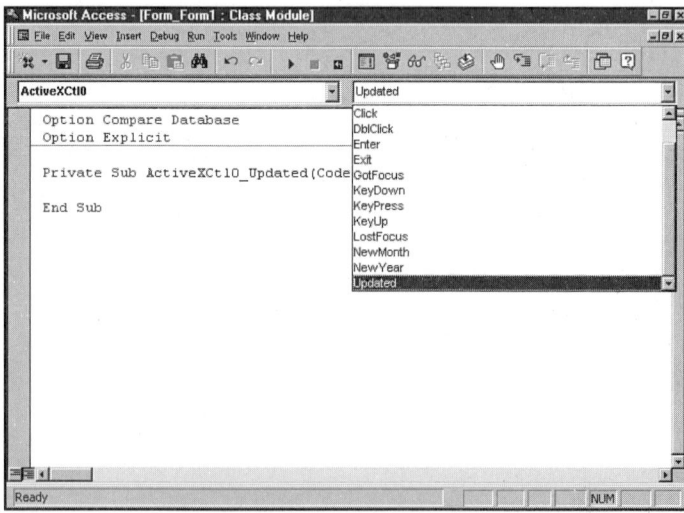

The Calendar control's `AfterUpdate` event is triggered when the user selects a date from the calendar. The following code changes the value of the txtDateSelected text box to the Value property of the calPickADay control. This code is placed in the Calendar control's `AfterUpdate` event so that it executes any time the user selects a date on the calendar.

```
Private Sub calPickADay_AfterUpdate()
    txtDateSelected.Value = calPickADay.Value
End Sub
```

This code—and most of the code in this chapter—is in the CHAP26EX.MDB file on the book's CD-ROM. This example is found in the frmPickADay form.

The Calendar Control

The Calendar control is one of the more powerful OCX controls available. Understanding its properties and methods makes it a lot easier to work with; they are covered in the following sections.

Properties of a Calendar Control

The Day, Month, and Year properties designate the day, month, and year displayed on the calendar. These properties are automatically changed at runtime as the user selects different dates on the calendar. You can modify the values programmatically by using macros or Visual Basic, thereby changing the day, month, or year that's selected.

The Value property is one of the Calendar control's most important properties. It retrieves the selected calendar date or moves the date highlight to a specific day. The following code uses the Value property to display the selected day in a message box:

```
Private Sub cmdDisplayDate_Click()
    MsgBox calSelectADay.Value
End Sub
```

The ValueIsNull property lets you indicate that no date is selected on the calendar. This property is used when you want to make sure the user explicitly selects a date.

The DayFont and DayFontColor properties specify the font and color for displaying the day titles. The DayFont property is further broken down into the properties Name, Size, Bold, Italic, Underline, and Strikethrough. An individual property can be modified like this:

```
calSelectADay.DayFont.Italic = True
```

You can use the `With...End With` construct to change several font properties at once:

```
With calSelectADay.DayFont
      .Bold = True
      .Italic = True
      .Name = "Arial"
End With
```

The DayFontColor property can be used to easily modify the color of the day titles:

```
calSelectADay.DayFontColor = 16711680
```

The GridFont and GridFontColor properties are similar to the DayFont and DayFontColor properties. GridFont determines the font type and size attributes for the text in the calendar, and GridFontColor indicates the text color in the calendar. For example, the following routine modifies the Bold, Italic, and Name properties of the GridFont property and changes the color of the days displayed on the calendar:

```
Private Sub cmdChangeGridFont_Click()
   With calSelectADay.GridFont
      .Bold = True
      .Italic = True
      .Name = "Arial"
   End With
   calSelectADay.GridFontColor = 8388736
End Sub
```

The DayLength and MonthLength properties designate how you want the day or month titles to be displayed. The available choices for DayLength are Short (0), Medium (1), and Long (2). Short displays the day as one character, Medium displays the day as a three-character abbreviation, and Long displays the full day (for example, Monday). The available choices for MonthLength are Short (0) and Long (2). Short displays the month as a three-character abbreviation, and Long displays the full month name. The following code specifies both the DayLength and MonthLength properties as Short:

```
Private Sub cmdChangeLength_Click()
   calSelectADay.DayLength = 0
   calSelectADay.MonthLength = 0
End Sub
```

The ShowDateSelectors property indicates whether combo boxes appear at the top of the calendar, allowing the user to select a month and year. This property can be set to True or False.

The ShowTitle property indicates whether the month and year are displayed at the top of the calendar.

The GridLinesFormat and GridLinesColor properties specify whether the gridlines are raised, sunken, or flat and what color they are.

Methods of a Calendar Control

The Calendar control also has several methods, or actions you can take on the Calendar object. The NextDay, PreviousDay, NextWeek, PreviousWeek, NextMonth, PreviousMonth, NextYear, and PreviousYear methods all move the control's Value property forward or backward by the specified period of time.

Other methods of the Calendar control include the following:

- The Refresh method repaints the Calendar control.
- The Today method sets the Value property to the current date.
- The AboutBox method displays the Calendar control's About box.

Figure 26.11 shows how the Calendar control works. As you can see, the form, called frmCalendar, lets the user move from day to day, month to month, or year to year. The user can also move to the current day, or even select a date, then click the Display Orders for Selected Date command button to view all the orders placed on the selected date.

Figure 26.11.

An example of using the Calendar control.

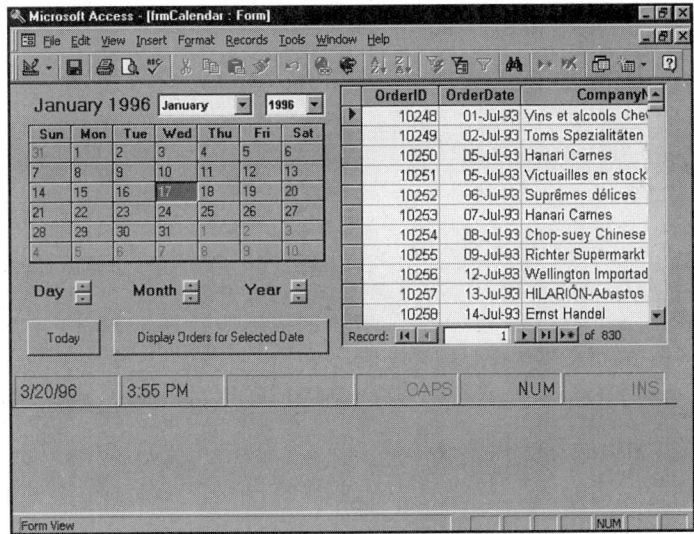

The code for the Today command button illustrates using the Today method:

```
Private Sub cmdToday_Click()
    calPickADay.Today
End Sub
```

Because the Today method is issued on the Calendar control, the selected day will become the current date. The code for the Display Orders for Selected Date command button looks like this:

```
Private Sub cmdOrders_Click()
    frmOrdersByDate.Form.RecordSource = _
        "Select * from qryOrdersByDate Where OrderDate = #" _
        & calPickADay.Value & "#"
End Sub
```

This code changes the subform's RecordSource to include only those records in which the OrderDate is equal to the selected calendar date. The remainder of the code for the frmCalendar form is discussed in the following section.

The UpDown Object

The UpDown object increments and decrements values. For example, on the frmCalendar form, UpDown objects increment and decrement the selected day, month, and year. Like the Calendar control, the UpDown object has its own built-in properties and methods. Although the properties can be modified on the Other tab of the Properties window, it's easier to modify them by using the UpDown properties dialog box.(See Figure 26.12.) To open it, double-click on the UpDown object whose properties you want to modify.

Figure 26.12.

The UpDown Properties dialog box.

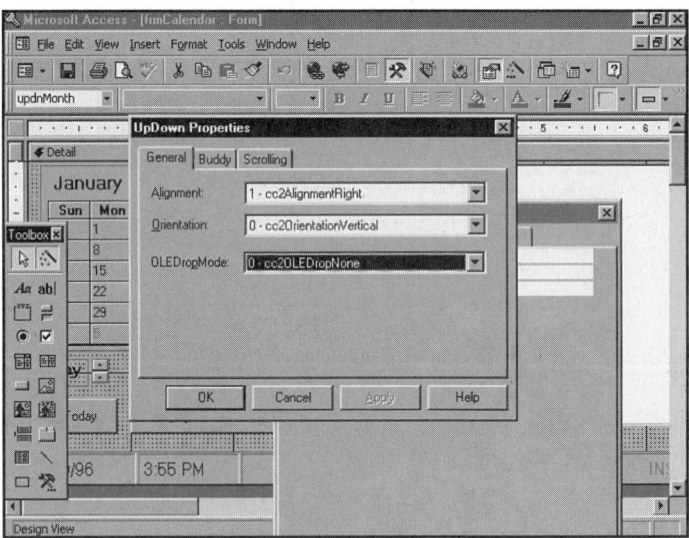

The Orientation property, one of the most important for the UpDown object, indicates whether you want the UpDown object to be displayed vertically or horizontally. The two most commonly used events of an UpDown object are the UpClick event and the DownClick event; they specify what happens when the user clicks either button of the control. The following code is placed in the DownClick event of the updnDay UpDown object on frmCalendar. Notice that the code executes a PreviousDay method on the calPickADay control, causing the Calendar control to set the focus to the previous day:

```
Private Sub updnDay_DownClick()
   calPickADay.PreviousDay
End Sub
```

The `UpClick` event of the updnDay control uses the `NextDay` method of the calPickADay control to cause the focus to shift to the next day:

```
Private Sub updnDay_UpClick()
   calPickADay.NextDay
End Sub
```

The `DownClick` event of the updnMonth control uses the Calendar control's `PreviousMonth` method to move focus to the same day in the previous month:

```
Private Sub updnMonth_DownClick()
   calPickADay.PreviousMonth
End Sub
```

The `UpClick` event of the updnMonth control uses the Calendar control's `NextMonth` method to move focus to the same day in the next month:

```
Private Sub spnMonth_UpClick()
   calPickADay.NextMonth
End Sub
```

The `DownClick` and `UpClick` events of the updnYear control use the Calendar control's `PreviousYear` and `NextYear` methods to move backward and forward a year in the calendar:

```
Private Sub spnYear_DownClick()
   calPickADay.PreviousYear
End Sub

Private Sub spnYear_UpClick()
   calPickADay.NextYear
End Sub
```

As you can see, by combining the different ActiveX controls, you can create exciting, user-friendly, utilitarian applications.

The StatusBar Control

You can use the StatusBar control to quickly and easily add professional-looking status bars to your forms, as shown in the frmCalendar form in Figure 26.12. The StatusBar in the figure has six panels; the first two have been configured to display the current date and time, and the last three display the status of the Caps, Num, and Ins keys.

Properties can be set for the StatusBar control as a whole or for the individual panels. (See Figure 26.13.) The Style property specifies whether you want the status bar to include multiple panels or only a single panel. The SimpleText property is used only for single-panel status bars; it specifies the text in the panel. Finally, the MousePointer property lets you select the type of mouse pointer that appears when it's placed over the StatusBar control.

Figure 26.13.

The general properties of the StatusBar control.

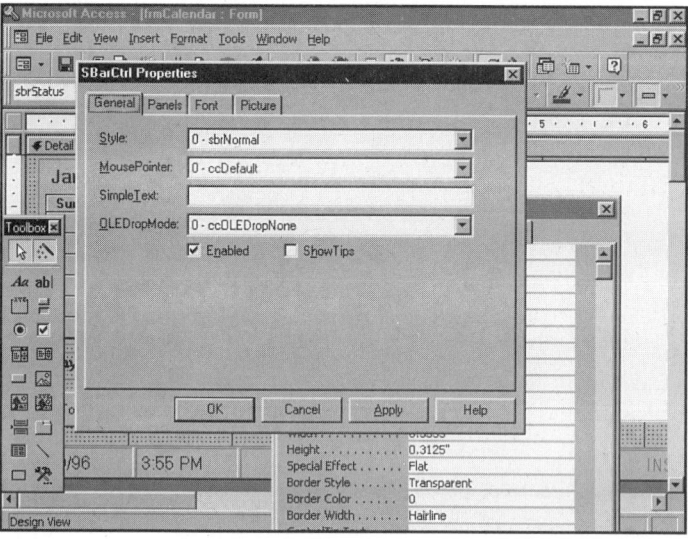

Each panel of the StatusBar control has properties that affect what that panel looks like and how it performs. The panel properties are shown in Figure 26.14. The Style property is an important one; it specifies what information is displayed in the panel. It can be set to Text, Caps, Num Lock, Ins, Scroll, Time, Date, or Kana Lock. Once set, the control can automatically sense whether the Caps Lock or other keys are active. The Text property indicates the text displayed in the panel when the Style property is set to Text. The value of this property is often modified at runtime to display a specific message to the user. The Alignment property determines whether the information is left-aligned, right-aligned, or centered in the panel, and the Bevel property can be set to None, Insert, or Raised.

Figure 26.14.

The StatusBar panel properties.

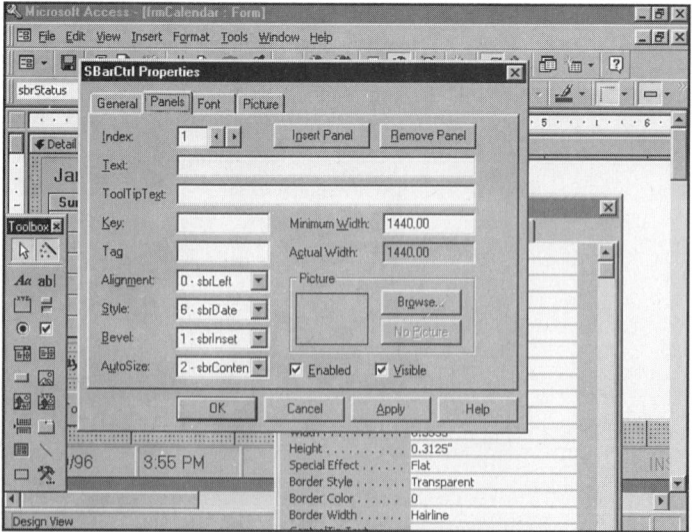

As you insert and remove panels, each panel is assigned an index, and the Index property is used to refer to a specific panel at runtime, as shown in this example:

```
Private Sub calPickADay_AfterUpdate()
    If calPickADay.Value = Date Then
        sbrStatus.Panels(3).Text = "TODAY!!!"
    Else
        sbrStatus.Panels(3).Text = ""
    End If
End Sub
```

This code evaluates the `calPickADay` value to see whether it's equal to the current date. If so, the text of the third panel is set to TODAY!!!. Otherwise, the third panel's text is set to a zero-length string.

> **WARNING**
>
> In the Access "world," almost everything is zero-based. Of course, there are exceptions to every rule. The StatusBar control is one of those exceptions—it's one-based. The code in the previous example really does modify the text in the third panel.

The Common Dialog Control

The Common Dialog control is actually like many controls in one. It's used to display the standard Windows File Open, File Save As, Font, Color, and Print common dialog boxes. It's a hidden control that doesn't appear at runtime but whose properties and methods can be manipulated by using VBA code. The frmCommonAndRich form, shown in Figure 26.15, illustrates using several of the common dialog boxes as well as the Rich Textbox control, covered in the next section.

Figure 26.15.
The form used to illustrate common dialog and rich text boxes.

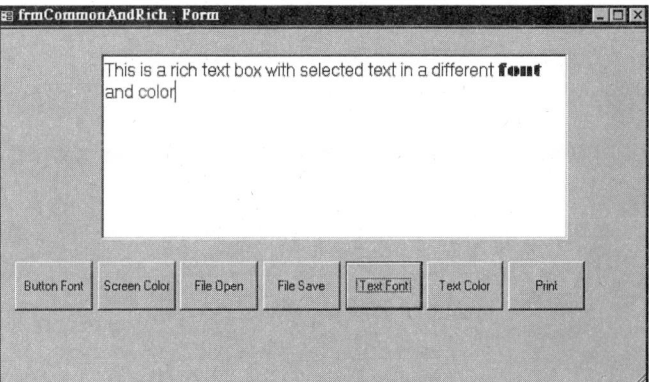

753

The Button Font and Screen Color command buttons illustrate using the Common Dialog control. They invoke the Color and Font common dialog boxes, respectively. The code for the Click event of the cmdColor command button looks like this:

```
Private Sub cmdColor_Click()
    dlgCommon.Flags = cdlCCFullOpen
    dlgCommon.ShowColor
    Me.Detail.BackColor = dlgCommon.Color
End Sub
```

The code begins by setting the Common Dialog control's Flags property, which is used to specify attributes of the common dialog box. The value of cdlCCFullOpen for the Color common dialog box indicates that the entire Color dialog box, including the portion that lets the user create custom colors, is displayed. The ShowColor method, when applied to the Common Dialog control, invokes the Color common dialog box. (See Figure 26.16.) The color the user selects is filled into the Color property of the Common Dialog control. This color is used to modify the BackColor property of the form's Detail section.

Figure 26.16.

The Color chooser is part of the common dialog box.

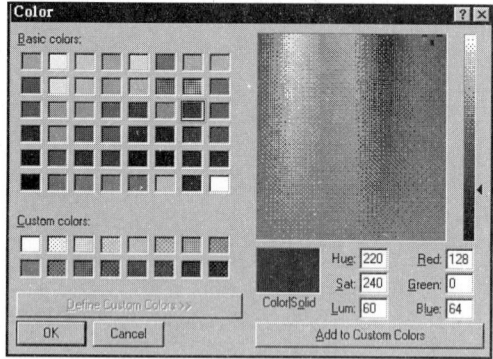

The following code uses the With...End With loop to change several properties from the Common Dialog box:

```
Private Sub cmdFont_Click()
    Dim ctl As Control
    dlgCommon.Flags = cdlCFScreenFonts
    dlgCommon.ShowFont
    For Each ctl In Controls
        If TypeOf ctl Is CommandButton Then
            With ctl
                .FontName = dlgCommon.FontName
                .FontBold = dlgCommon.FontBold
                .FontItalic = dlgCommon.FontItalic
                .FontSize = dlgCommon.FontSize
```

```
        End With
      End If
    Next ctl
End Sub
```

The Click event of cmdFont first sets the Common Dialog control's Flags property to cdlCFScreenFonts. For the Font common dialog box, the value of cdlCDFScreenFonts causes the dialog box to list only the screen fonts supported by the user's system. The ShowFont method is used to invoke the actual dialog box. (See Figure 26.17.) Using a With...End With construct, the code takes each property set in the common dialog box and uses it to loop through the form's Controls collection, modifying the font attributes of each command button.

Figure 26.17.

The Font part of the Common Dialog box allows you to set several font properties at one time.

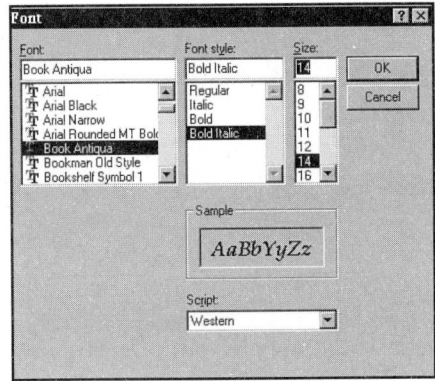

The File Open, File Save, and File Print common dialog boxes are covered in the next section.

The Rich Textbox Control

The Rich Textbox control allows you to design a text box for writing code that affects the selected text. Properties that can be specified for the selected text include the Font, Font Size, Bold, and Italic properties. You can even add bullet points to the selected text. Furthermore, you can save the contents of the Rich Textbox control in a rich text format (RTF) file and later retrieve it back into the control. Figure 26.18 shows the many properties that can be affected for the selected text.

Figure 26.18.

Properties that can be set for selected text in a rich text box.

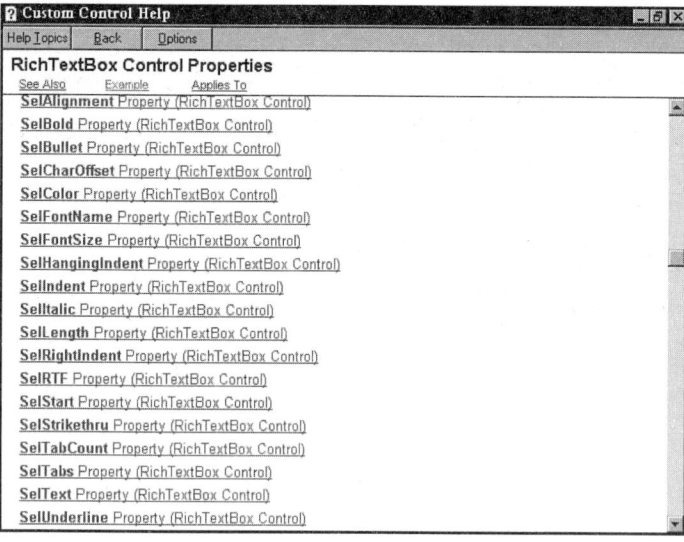

The following code illustrates using several of the Rich Textbox control's properties:

```
Private Sub cmdTextColor_Click()
    dlgCommon.ShowColor
    rtfDocument.SelColor = dlgCommon.Color
End Sub
```

This code uses the Color common dialog box to set the SelColor property of the Rich Textbox control. The selected text appears in whatever color the user selects from the common dialog box.

The Click event of the cmdTextFont command button sets the SelFontName, SelBold, SelItalic, and SelFontSize properties of the Rich Textbox control to the font, style, and size selected in the Font common dialog box:

```
Private Sub cmdTextFont_Click()
    dlgCommon.Flags = cdlCFScreenFonts
    dlgCommon.ShowFont
    With rtfDocument
        .SelFontName = dlgCommon.FontName
        .SelBold = dlgCommon.FontBold
        .SelItalic = dlgCommon.FontItalic
        .SelFontSize = dlgCommon.FontSize
    End With
End Sub
```

The selected attributes are applied only to the selected text.

The Rich Textbox control has a method called SaveFile that lets you save the contents of the Rich Textbox control to an RTF file. The code looks like this:

```
Private Sub cmdSave_Click()
    dlgCommon.Filter = "RTF Files (*.rtf)¦*.rtf"
```

```
    dlgCommon.ShowSave
    If dlgCommon.FileName = "" Then
        MsgBox "You Must Specify a File Name", vbExclamation, "File NOT Saved!"
    Else
        rtfDocument.SaveFile dlgCommon.FileName
    End If
End Sub
```

The code begins by setting the Common Dialog control's Filter property; this filters the filenames displayed in the File Save common dialog box. The ShowSave method invokes the Save common dialog box. (See Figure 26.19.) After the user types in or selects a filename, the Common Dialog control's FileName property is filled in with the name of the file that the user specified. If the user clicks Cancel, the FileName property contains a zero-length string, and the user is warned that the file wasn't saved.

Figure 26.19.

The Save As common dialog box allows you to enter a name, a location, and an extension to your file.

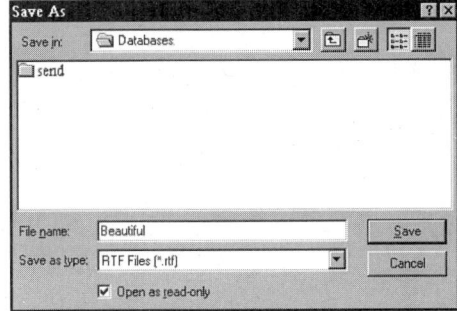

As mentioned, you can also retrieve the contents of an RTF file into the control. The code looks like this:

```
Private Sub cmdOpen_Click()
    dlgCommon.FileName = ""
    dlgCommon.Filter = "RTF Files (*.rtf)¦*.rtf"
    dlgCommon.InitDir = CurDir
    dlgCommon.ShowOpen
    If dlgCommon.FileName = "" Then
        MsgBox "You Must Specify a File Name", vbExclamation, "File Cannot Be
➡Opened!"
    Else
        rtfDocument.LoadFile dlgCommon.FileName
    End If
End Sub
```

The Click event of the cmdOpen command button uses the ShowOpen method to invoke the File Open common dialog box. (See Figure 26.20.) If the user selects a file, the Rich Textbox control's LoadFile method uses the Common Dialog control's FileName property as the name of the file to open.

Figure 26.20.

The Open common dialog box not only lets you specify which files to open, but also allows you to navigate around your computer and networks.

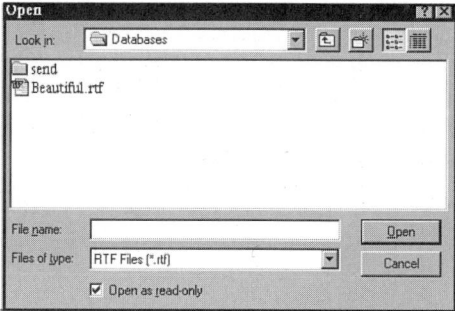

Besides being able to open and save the contents of a Rich Textbox control, you can print the control's contents. The `Click` event of the cmdPrint command button sets the Common Dialog control's Flags property to `cdlPDAllPages`:

```
Private Sub cmdPrint_Click()
    dlgCommon.Flags = cdlPDAllPages
    dlgCommon.ShowPrinter
    rtfDocument.SelPrint dlgCommon.hDC
End Sub
```

This selects the All option button in the Print dialog box (and deselects the Pages and Selection option buttons). The `ShowPrinter` method displays the Print common dialog box. (See Figure 26.21.) The `SelPrint` method of the Rich Textbox control is then used to print the selected text with the printer selected in the Print common dialog box.

Figure 26.21.

The Print common dialog box has several options for printing chores.

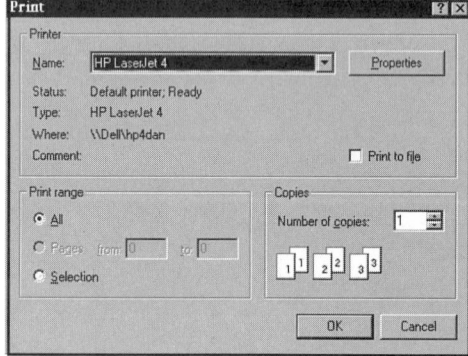

The TabStrip Control

You can use the TabStrip control to conserve screen real-estate by displaying data on different "pages" of the same form. The TabStrip control included in the ODE is the same control you're used to seeing in applications such as Microsoft Word and Microsoft Excel. It's easy to implement this control in your own forms. Figure 26.22 shows a form called frmTabbed that uses the TabStrip control.

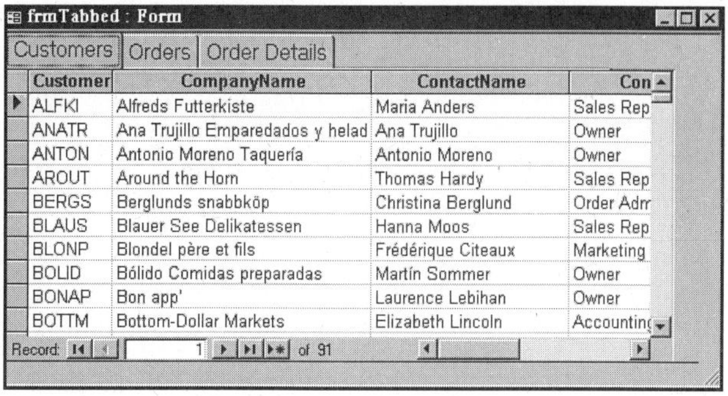

Figure 26.22.

A form that uses the TabStrip control.

As the user clicks on each tab, the appropriate information displays. For example, if the user selects a customer on the Customers tab, then clicks the Orders tab, all orders for the selected customer are displayed. If the user selects an order on the Orders tab, then clicks the Order Details tab, all details about the selected order are displayed. The code looks like this:

```
Private Sub tabSelect_Click()
    Select Case Me!tabSelect.SelectedItem.INDEX
        Case 1
            Me!fsubCustomers.Visible = True
            Me!fsubOrders.Visible = False
            Me!fsubOrderDetails.Visible = False
        Case 2
            Me!fsubOrders.Form.RecordSource = _
                "Select * from tblOrders Where CustomerID = '" _
                & Me!fsubCustomers.Form!CustomerID & "';"
            Me!fsubCustomers.Visible = False
            Me!fsubOrders.Visible = True
            Me!fsubOrderDetails.Visible = False
        Case 3
            Me!fsubOrders.Form.RecordSource = _
                "Select * from tblOrderDetails Where OrderID = " _
                & Me!fsubOrders.Form!OrderID & ";"
            Me!fsubCustomers.Visible = False
            Me!fsubOrders.Visible = False
            Me!fsubOrderDetails.Visible = True
    End Select
End Sub
```

Here's how the code works: After adding a TabStrip control to a form, you can double-click it to view its properties. (See Figure 26.23.) The TabStrip Control Properties dialog box allows you to set properties for the TabStrip control as a whole, as well as for each tab. Once the tabs have been added, you can code the TabStrip control's Click event to determine what will happen as the user clicks on each tab.

Figure 26.23.

The TabStrip control properties dialog box sets initial properties for the TabStrip control.

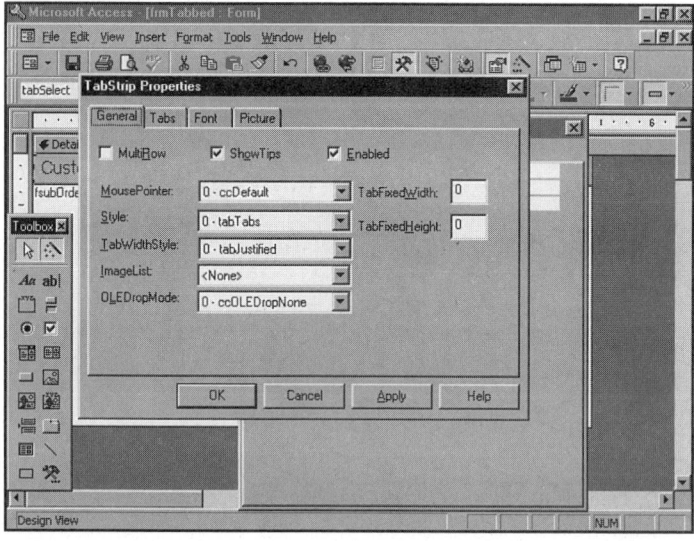

A Tab control is included as a standard control in the Access toolbox, so you don't need to use the ActiveX TabStrip control in your applications. Third-party vendors have Tab controls with more features than Microsoft's. These are all ActiveX-type controls.

Like the StatusBar control, the TabStrip control is one-based. A `Case` statement is used to evaluate which tab was selected. The frmTabbed form has three subforms: fsubCustomers, fsubOrders, and fsubOrderDetails. When the frmTabbed form is first displayed, only the fsubCustomers subform control is visible. As the user clicks on each tab in the TabStrip control, the appropriate subform is displayed, and the other two subforms are hidden. The RecordSource for fsubOrders is modified at runtime to show only orders for the selected customer from fsubCustomers, and the RecordSource for fsubOrderDetails is modified at runtime to show only the order detail items for the order selected on fsubOrders.

The ImageList Control

The TabStrip control can be enhanced by using an ImageList control, which stores images you'll be using in the form. It's populated at design time with these images. The ImageList control is hidden at runtime, but any of its images can be used in your form.

The frmImageList form, shown in Figure 26.24, is similar to the frmTabbed form, except that each tab has an image that comes from the ImageList control called imgPictures. The properties of the imgPictures ImageList control are shown in Figure 26.25. Notice that three pictures have been inserted. The General tab's size has been set to 16×16, and the tabSelect TabStrip control has been modified to include imgPictures as its ImageList under the General properties tab. The index of each picture in the imgPictures ImageList control has been added as the Image property for each tab in the TabStrip control; the Image property specifies which image in the bound ImageList control should be displayed in the particular tab.

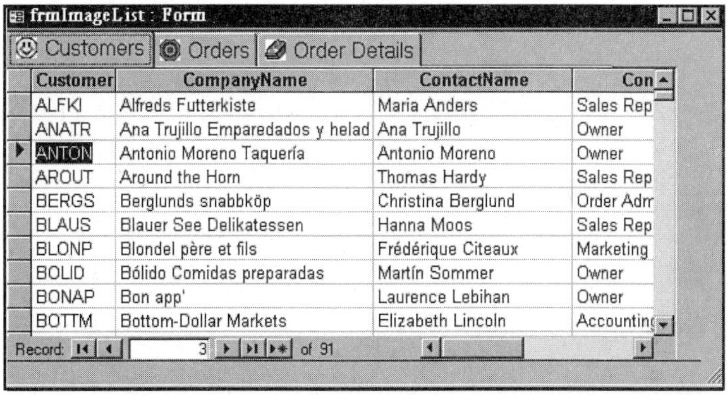

Figure 26.24.

The frmImageList form, with pictures for tabs.

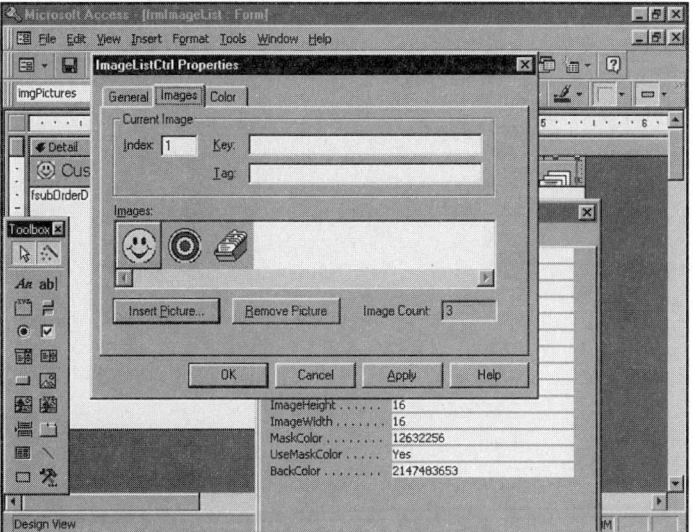

Figure 26.25.

The properties of the ImageList control.

Licensing and Distribution Issues

Some OCX controls can be distributed freely, but others have differing levels of restrictions. The licensing policies for a particular OCX control are determined by its vendor.

The licensing rules in effect for an OCX can be enforced by law, which means that improper distribution of the control is a crime. Distributing an OCX control without proper licensing is just like copying a software product illegally.

If you have any questions about licensing a third-party control, consult the vendor who created the control. A one-time fee might be required to freely distribute the OCX; in other cases, you might have to pay a royalty for each copy of the control that's distributed. If you aren't sure whether you want to buy a third-party control, you might want to consult the vendor. Many vendors let potential customers try out their products for a limited period of time. In fact, many of the demo versions are available online.

Practical Examples: Implementing ActiveX Controls

ActiveX controls can be used in many places in the Time and Billing application. Use your imagination to determine where controls will enhance the application's usefulness. The following examples illustrate a few potential uses of the ActiveX controls.

Adding a Calendar to the Report Criteria Dialog

One example of an ActiveX control is in the frmReportDateRange dialog box, shown in Figure 26.26. The Calendar control can be used to populate the Beginning Date and Ending Date text boxes.

Figure 26.26.

Adding the Calendar control to the Report Criteria form.

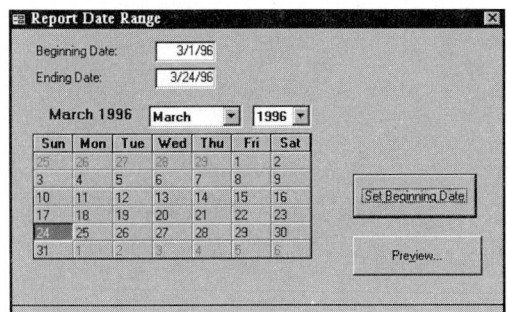

The code for adding the Calendar control looks like this:

```
Private Sub cmdSetDates_Click()
    On Error GoTo cmdSetDates_Error

    If cmdSetDates.Caption = "Set Beginning Date" Then
        BeginDate = calSetDates.Value
        cmdSetDates.Caption = "Set Ending Date"
    Else
        EndDate = calSetDates.Value
        cmdSetDates.Caption = "Set Beginning Date"
    End If

    Exit Sub
```

```
cmdSetDates_Error:
    MsgBox "Error # " & Err.Number & ": " & Err.Description
    Exit Sub

End Sub
```

Because the same calendar is used to populate the Beginning Date and Ending Date text boxes, the form has a command button with a caption that toggles. The user can select a date, then click Set Beginning Date. The BeginDate text box is populated with the value selected on the calendar, and the command button's caption is set to display Set Ending Date. If the command button's caption says Set Ending Date and the user clicks that button, the EndDate text box is filled with the value selected on the calendar, and the command button's caption changes to say Set Beginning Date.

Summary

ActiveX controls greatly extend the abilities of Access 97 and allow you to incorporate more functionality into your applications. These controls are easy to use and extremely powerful.

Each ActiveX control has its own properties, events, and methods. By modifying properties, reacting to events, and executing methods, you can take advantage of its rich features. Licensing for each ActiveX control varies, so you need to investigate that for each control you want to use to know whether—and under what conditions—you can distribute it to your users.

27

Access and
the Internet

- What's New with Access and the Internet, 766
- Saving Database Objects as HTML, 766
- Linking to HTML Files, 769
- Importing HTML Files, 771
- Static Versus Dynamic HTML Formats, 772
- The Publish to the Web Wizard, 773
- Working with HTML Templates, 775
- Sending Data to an FTP or HTTP Server, 776
- Taking Advantage of Hyperlinks, 777
- The Microsoft WebBrowser Control, 778
- The Web Toolbar, 778
- Replication Over the Internet, 779

What's New with Access and the Internet

Access 97 has many features that make it easier to develop Internet-aware applications—you can develop applications that publish dynamic or static information on the Internet or on your organization's intranet. The new Hyperlink field type allows you to store Internet and intranet addresses in your Access tables, and form hyperlinks make it easy to jump to Internet and intranet addresses directly from your forms. This chapter explores the power of Access and its integration with the Internet.

Saving Database Objects as HTML

Probably one of the more basic but powerful additions to Access is the ability to save database objects as HTML (HyperText Markup Language) documents. Table data, query results, form datasheets, forms, and reports can all be published as HTML. Each of these objects is covered in the following sections.

Saving Table Data as HTML

When saving table data to HTML, it's stored in the HTML file format so that it can be easily published on the Web; just follow these steps:

1. Click the Tables tab of the Database window.
2. Click to select the table whose data you want to save as HTML.
3. Choose File | Save As/Export to open the Save As dialog box.
4. Select "To an External File or Database" and click OK.
5. Use the Save As Type drop-down list to select HTML documents.
6. Select a filename and location for the HTML document.
7. Click Export to finish the process.

The file is exported to HTML and can be viewed from any Web browser. (See Figure 27.1.) You can also view the HTML source, as shown in Figure 27.2.

Figure 27.1.
The NorthWind Categories table saved as HTML.

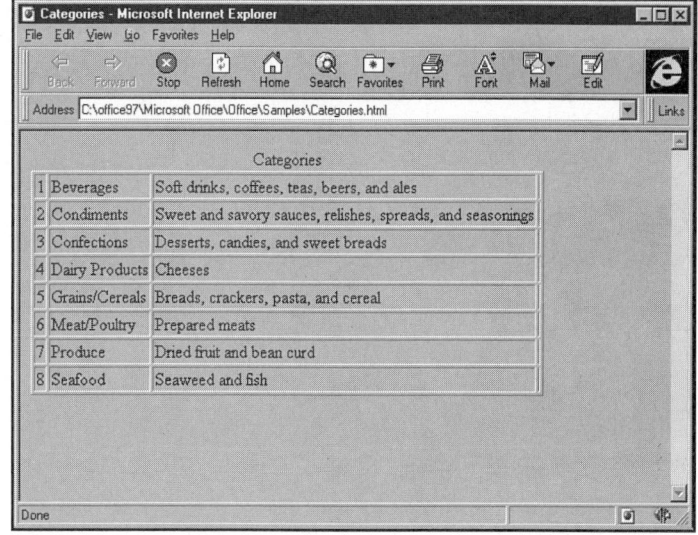

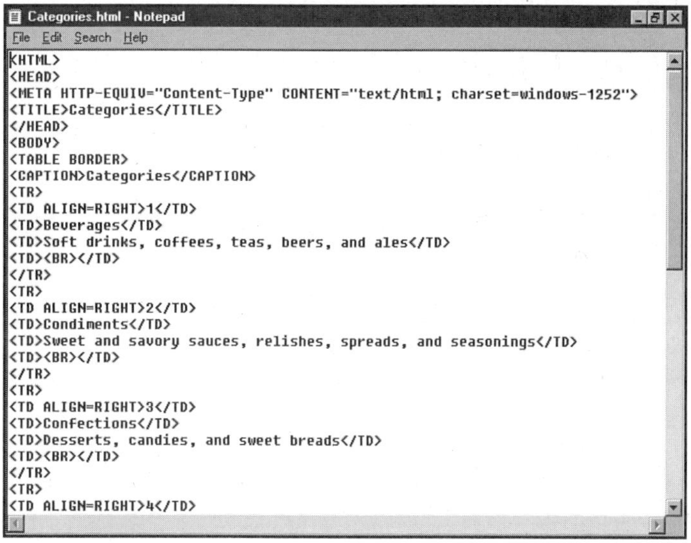

Figure 27.2.
Viewing the source of the Categories table's HTML file.

Saving Query Results as HTML

The ability to save query results as HTML means you don't need to save all fields and all records to an HTML file. In fact, you can even save the results of Totals queries and other complex queries as HTML. Saving the result of a query as HTML is similar to saving a table as HTML:

1. Click the Queries tab of the Database window.

2. Click to select the query whose results you want to save as HTML.

3. Choose File | Save As/Export to open the Save As dialog box.

4. Select "To an External File or Database" and click OK.

5. Use the Save As Type drop-down list to select HTML documents.

6. Select a filename and location for the HTML document.

7. Click Export to finish the process.

Saving Forms as HTML

Only a form's datasheet can be saved as HTML because an HTML file is a static file. It doesn't change as the data in the database changes, nor can the data in the HTML file be modified. To save a form's datasheet as HTML, follow these steps:

1. Click the Forms tab of the Database window.

2. Click to select the form whose results you want to save as HTML.

3. Choose File | Save As/Export to open the Save As dialog box.

4. Select "To an External File or Database" and click OK.

5. Use the Save As Type drop-down list to select HTML documents.

6. Select a filename and location for the HTML document.

7. Click Export; this opens the HTML Output Options dialog box.

8. Select an optional HTML template that's applied to the HTML document. By selecting an HTML template, you can easily maintain a consistent look for your Web publications.

Saving Reports as HTML

Reports and their formatting can be saved as HTML, too, which is an elegant way to publish data on an Internet or intranet site. To publish a report as HTML, just follow these steps:

1. Click the Reports tab of the Database window.

2. Click to select the report whose results you want to save as HTML.

3. Choose File | Save As/Export to open the Save As dialog box.

4. Select "To an External File or Database" and click OK.

5. Use the Save As Type drop-down list to select HTML documents.

6. Select a filename and location for the HTML document.

7. Click Export to open the HTML Output Options dialog box.

8. Select an optional HTML template that's applied to the HTML document.

Figure 27.3 shows a report published as HTML. Because the report is a multipage report, several HTML files were generated. Each page of the report is linked, and the user can easily navigate from page to page by using the First, Previous, Next, and Last hyperlinks automatically generated during the Save process.

Figure 27.3.
*Viewing the NorthWind
Catalog report as HTML.*

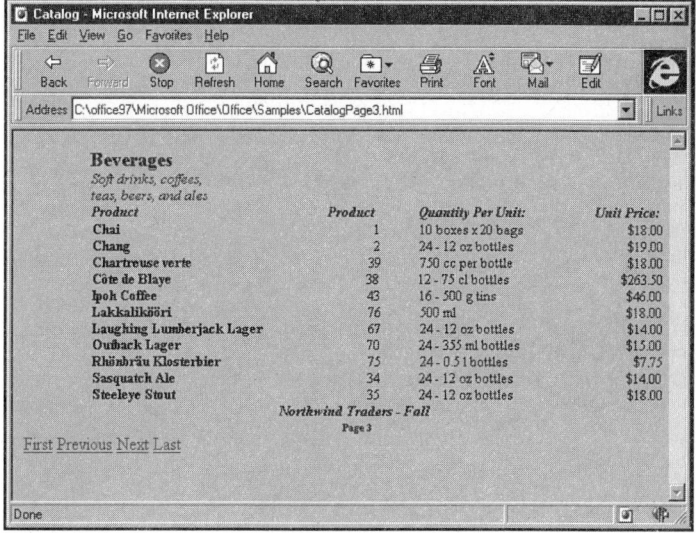

Linking to HTML Files

Just as you can link to FoxPro tables, Paradox tables, or ODBC data sources, you can also link
to HTML files by following these steps:

1. Right-click the Tables tab of the Database window and select Link Tables; this opens
   the Link dialog box.

2. Use the Files of Type drop-down list to select HTML documents.

3. Select the HTML file you want to link to and click Link. The Link HTML Wizard
   appears. (See Figure 27.4.)

4. In the wizard's first step, you indicate whether the first row of data contains column
   headings. You can also see Access's proposed layout for the linked table.

Figure 27.4.
*The first step of the Link
HTML Wizard.*

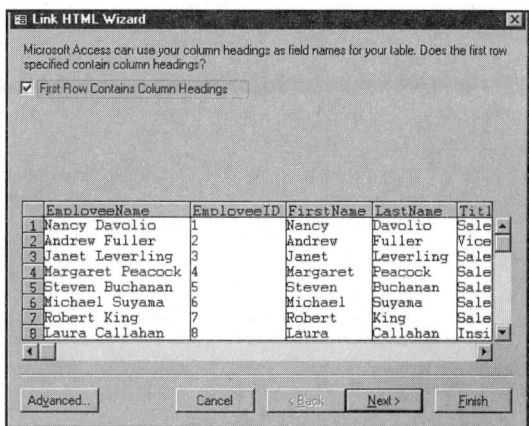

5. Click Advanced to designate specifics about the linked table. The Link Specification dialog box opens. (See Figure 27.5.) Here you can select which fields you want to include in the linked table, date delimiters, and other specifics of the linked file. Make your selections and click OK.

Figure 27.5.

In the Link Specification dialog box, you designate specifics about the linked table.

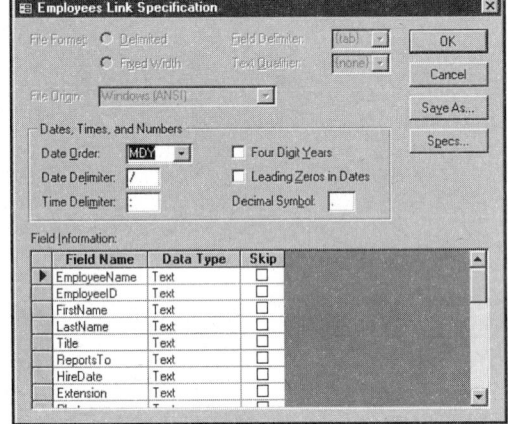

6. Click Next to proceed with the Link HTML Wizard. In the next step, you select a field name and data type for each field in the HTML file. Make your selections and click Next.

7. In the wizard's last step, you supply a table name for the linked table. Make your selection and click Finish.

8. You then see a message that the table linked successfully. The table appears in the Database window with a special icon indicating that it's an HTML file. (See Figure 27.6.)

Figure 27.6.

The Database window with a linked HTML document.

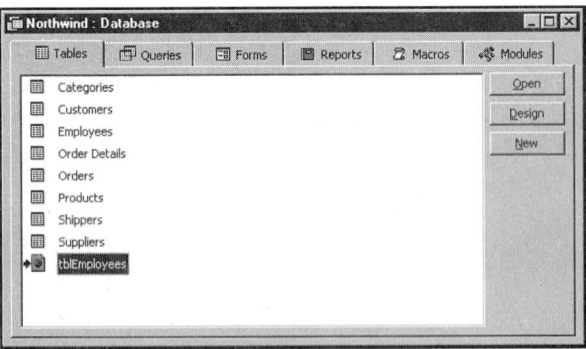

The linked HTML file can be browsed, queried, and reported on just like any other table. However, none of the data in the linked file can be modified.

Importing HTML Files

The data in an HTML file can be imported so that it becomes exactly like any other Access table; follow these steps to import an HTML file:

1. Right-click the Tables tab of the Database window and select Import; this opens the Import dialog box.

2. Use the Files of Type drop-down list to select HTML documents.

3. Select the HTML file you want to import and click Import to open the Import HTML Wizard. This wizard is almost identical to the Link HTML Wizard.

4. In the wizard's first step, you indicate whether the first row of data contains column headings. You can also see Access's proposed layout for the imported table.

5. Click Advanced to designate specifics about the imported table. The Import Specification dialog box opens. Here you can select which fields you want to include in the imported table, date delimiters, and other specifics of the imported file. Make your selections and click OK.

6. Click Next to go to the next step. Here, you have the choice of importing the data into a new table or adding it to an existing table. Make your selection and click Next.

7. In the next step, select a field name and data type for each field in the HTML file. You can also designate whether you want Access to create an index for the field and even whether you want to exclude the field entirely. Make your selections and click Next.

8. Next, the wizard lets you designate a primary key for the imported table. If you prefer, you can have Access supply the primary key. (See Figure 27.7.) Make your selection and click Next.

Figure 27.7.

Designating a primary key for your new table.

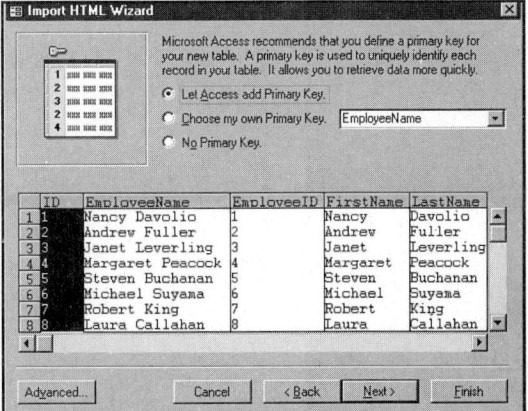

9. In the wizard's last step, supply a table name for the linked table. If you're concerned about whether the imported table is normalized, you can have Access launch the Table Analyzer after the import is finished. Make your selections and click Finish.

10. You then see a message that the table imported successfully; it appears in the Database window just as any other Access table does.

Static Versus Dynamic HTML Formats

Many people don't understand the differences between publishing static and dynamic data. *Static data* doesn't change. If you want to publish information that rarely, if ever, changes, you should create a static Web page; the techniques for doing so have been covered in the beginning of this chapter. The data output for each of the methods discussed so far is static and can be changed only by republishing the data and resubmitting it to the Web.

Dynamic data, on the other hand, does change. You should save your data in the dynamic format when you know it will change frequently and your Web application needs to store and retrieve live data from your application by using a form. To publish dynamic Web data, you must output the object to the IDC/HTX file format instead of an HTML file; this process creates two files. The .HTX file—an HTML extension file—has all the formatting tags and instructions needed so that the query's results can be formatted. The .IDC file—an Internet Database Connector file—contains an SQL statement and other information needed by the Microsoft Internet Information Server so that it can connect to an ODBC data source, such as your Access database file (.MDB). The ODBC data source name, user name, and password are all stored in the .IDC file, but no data is stored in it.

After you have published a database object and installed it on the Web by using a Web document publishing server, such as the Microsoft Internet Information Server (IIS), IIS opens the Access database by using the ODBC driver and the .IDC information file on request from a Web browser. It runs the query stored in the .IDC file and merges the result and the .HTX file into an HTML file that's sent back to the Web browser for display.

Another type of dynamic file is an ASP file; *ASP* stands for ActiveX Server Page. ActiveX Server is a component of Microsoft Internet Information Server 3.0 and later versions. The ASP file contains the following:

- ODBC connection information, such as the data source name, user name, and password
- One or more queries in the form of SQL statements
- Template directives for layout of the resulting HTML file
- VBScript code containing references to ActiveX Server controls

With an ASP file, you publish the object and install it. The Microsoft Internet Information Server, at the request of the Web browser, runs VBScript code and calls the ActiveX Server controls. It then opens up the database by using the ODBC driver and the .ASP file, runs the queries stored in the .ASP file, and merges the results and HTML tags in the .ASP file into an HTML file. The HTML file is then sent back to the Web browser for display.

The Publish to the Web Wizard

The Publish to the Web Wizard is a very powerful tool that allows you to easily publish Access objects on the World Wide Web; this wizard quickly and easily performs these tasks:

- Creates a Web publication from a table, query, form datasheet, form, or report
- Creates either a static or dynamic page
- Posts the Web publication to a Web server
- Creates a home page that ties together all published objects
- Allows you to use HTML templates so you can easily maintain consistency between your Web publications

The following steps are used to run the Publish to the Web Wizard:

1. Choose File | Save as HTML.
2. Click Next to leave the introductory screen.
3. Click to select each table, query, form, and report you want to publish to the Web, as shown in Figure 27.8, then click Next.

Figure 27.8.

The Publish to the Web wizard lets you designate the tables, queries, forms and reports you want to publish to the Web.

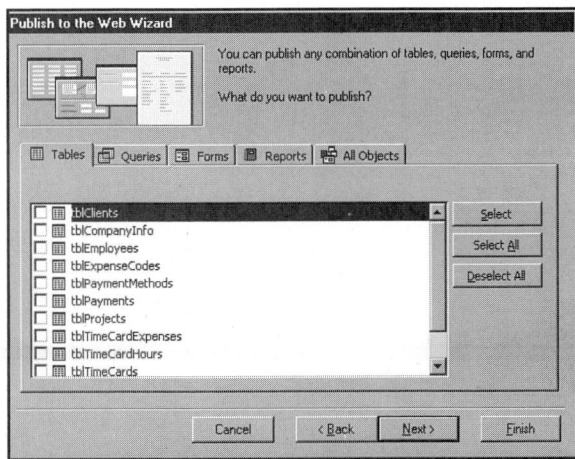

4. With HTML templates, you can produce consistent formatting in all your Web pages. If you have an HTML template you want to apply to the new publications, select it from the next step of the wizard and click Next.
5. Click to indicate whether you want to create pages in Static HTML (Microsoft Internet Information Server), Dynamic HTX/IDC, or Dynamic ASP (ActiveX Server). (See Figure 27.9.) Click Next to continue.

Figure 27.9.
You can publish a static format, dynamic HTX/IDC format, or dynamic ASP format.

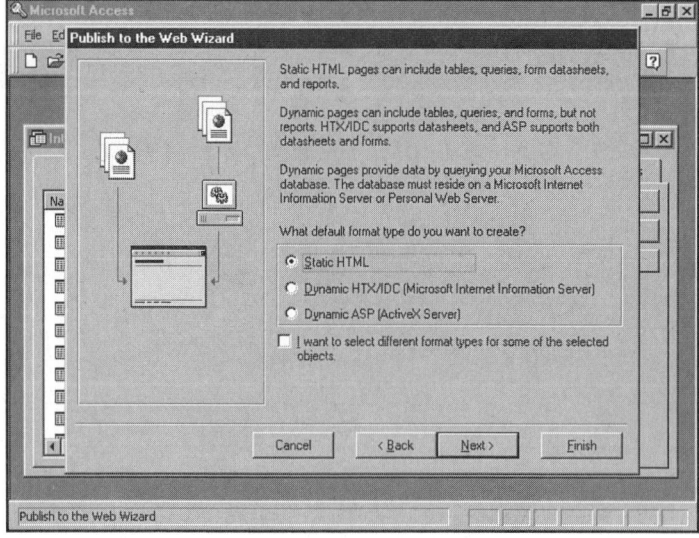

6. If you select Dynamic HTX/IDC or Dynamic ASP, you are prompted for Data Source and ActiveX Server information. (See Figure 27.10.) You must designate a valid data source name, and you can supply a user name and password, if you like. When you're done, click Next.

Figure 27.10.
When publishing dynamic HTX/IDC or dynamic ASP pages, you must designate the data source and ActiveX server information.

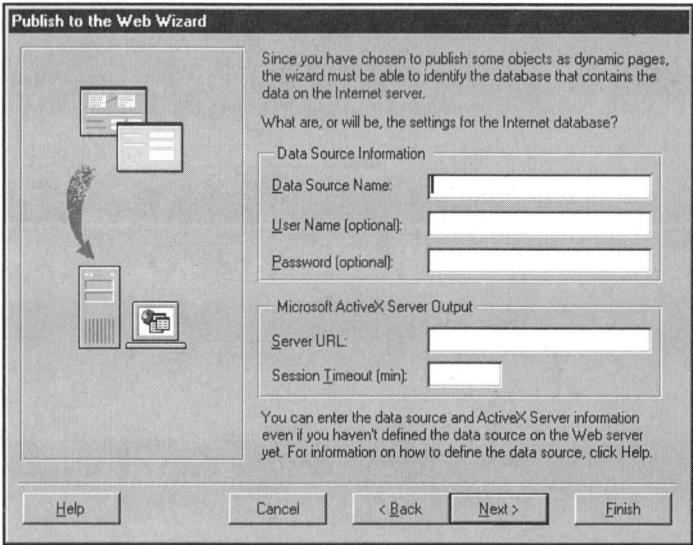

7. The next step of the wizard prompts you for a location where the publications will be placed. Remember that all files in the specified folder are published. Select a location and click Next.

8. If you like, Access can build a home page for you. In the wizard's next step, you choose whether you want the wizard to build the home page and supply a filename for it. (See Figure 27.11.) Fill in the required information and click Next.

Figure 27.11.
The Publish to the Web wizard can even build a home page for you.

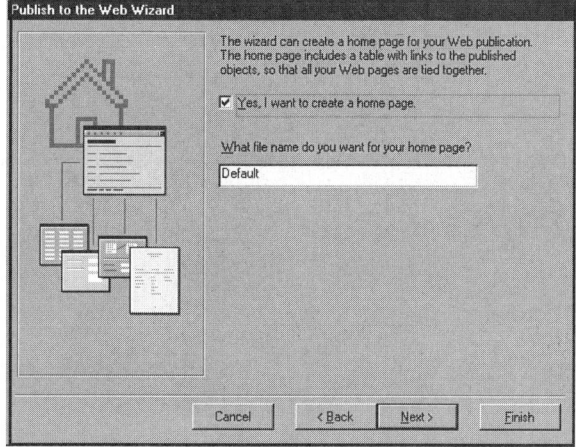

9. Finally, you can save all your answers so that you can use them again later. When you're done, click Finish.

Working with HTML Templates

HTML templates help give all your Web pages a consistent look. They allow you to effortlessly enhance the appearance of any Web page and add navigation to your Web application. HTML templates can include logos, background images, and standard navigation buttons.

An HTML template is a file that includes HTML tags and tokens unique to Access. These tags and tokens tell Access where to insert data. When you output a datasheet, form, or report to an HTML file, you can specify a template that's applied to the object. If you specify a template file when you output an object to a dynamic HTML format, it's merged with the HTX or ASP file during the output operation.

> **NOTE**
>
> By default, Access looks for template files in the \Program Files\Microsoft Office\Templates\Access folder. To change the default folder, choose Tools | Options and enter a different folder in the HTML Template box in the Hyperlinks/HTML tab of the Options dialog box.

Sending Data to an FTP or HTTP Server

Sometimes you need to import, link to, or export a database object to or from an FTP or HTTP server. *FTP*—File Transfer Protocol—is a protocol that allows you to transfer files over the Internet without a network server connection. *HTTP*—HyperText Transfer Protocol—is a behind-the-scenes Internet protocol that lets a client machine view documents written in HTML over the Internet. The techniques for importing, linking to, and exporting objects to an FTP server are covered in the following sections.

Importing or Linking to Data on FTP and HTTP Servers

The processes of importing and linking to FTP and HTTP servers are similar, so they're covered together in this section. Here's the steps to follow:

1. To import or link to data on an FTP server, right-click the Tables tab of the Database window.

2. Select Import to import data or Link Tables to link data; this opens the Import or Link dialog box.

3. To import or link to data on an HTTP server, type the Internet address—`http://www.mcgpc.com/employee.html`, for example—in the File Name box.

4. To import or link to data on an FTP server, you can either type the Internet address in the File Name box or click the arrow to the right of the Look In box, then click Internet Locations (FTP). You can then double-click to select the location of the item you want. The selected file is copied to the browser's cache folder.

> **NOTE**
>
> A linked table is actually a snapshot of the original data source, so you don't see any updates made to the original table while it's open. To refresh the local copy, you must close and reopen the table.

Exporting an Object to an FTP Server

Exporting a database object to a database server is essentially copying through the Internet; to do that, follow these steps:

1. Right-click the Tables tab of the Database window and select Save As/Export. The Save As dialog opens.

2. Select "To An External File or Database" and click OK.

3. Click to open the drop-down list to the right of the Save In box and select Internet Locations (FTP).

4. Click to select the FTP location, then click Export.

Taking Advantage of Hyperlinks

Hyperlinks in Access 97 are extremely powerful. They allow you to jump from your application to an Internet, intranet, or file location. Hyperlinks can be stored in table fields or placed directly on forms and reports.

Storing Hyperlinks in Tables

Using the new Hyperlink field type, you can easily store URLs (addresses to Internet or intranet sites) and UNCs (addresses to files on a local area network or a local hard disk) in your tables' records. To create a Hyperlink field, select Hyperlink from the Data Type drop-down list while viewing a table's design. Data stored in the field is used as a hyperlink address.

Placing Hyperlinks on Forms and Reports

Although the Hyperlink field type allows you to associate URLs and UNCs with each record in a table, the ability to place hyperlinks on forms and reports lets your users easily navigate from your forms and reports to other parts of your application and to URL and UNC locations. Hyperlinks can be added to command buttons, labels, and image controls because each of these controls has a Hyperlink Address and Hyperlink SubAddress property. (See Figure 27.12.) The Hyperlink Address property contains the actual URL or UNC, and the Hyperlink SubAddress property specifies a particular location in the URL or UNC. For example, if the UNC points to an Access database, the HyperLink SubAddress might point to a form in the database.

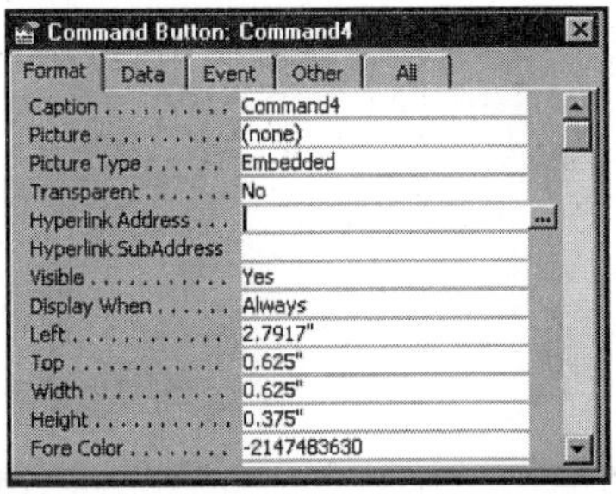

Figure 27.12.

Command buttons, labels, and image controls have Hyperlink Address and SubAddress properties.

The easiest way to specify the Hyperlink Address and SubAddress properties is to click in the Hyperlink Address property, then click the build button; this opens the Insert Hyperlink dialog box. Here, you can click Browse to find both the Hyperlink Address and Hyperlink SubAddress. The properties are automatically filled in for you. (See Figure 27.13.)

Figure 27.13.

Use the Insert Hyperlink dialog box to easily specify the Hyperlink Address and Hyperlink SubAddress properties.

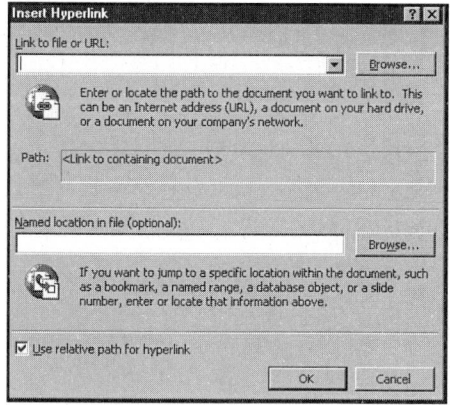

The Microsoft WebBrowser Control

The Microsoft WebBrowser control is an ActiveX control that lets you easily view Web pages and other documents from within your Access forms. You can find documentation about the WebBrowser control from Microsoft's Web site at `http://www.microsoft.com/intdev/sdk/docs/iexplore/`. If you bought Microsoft Office 97 on CD-ROM, you can also view a Help file in the Office 97 ValuPack, which has documentation about the WebBrowser control.

To add a WebBrowser control to a form, click More Controls in the toolbox and select Microsoft Web Browser control. Click and drag to add the control to the form. Once you've added the WebBrowser control to a form, you can use the control's `Navigate` method to open a Web site in the form. The following code opens a Web page in the WebBrowser control called wbrMarina:

```
Private Sub Form_Load()
    Me!wbrMarina.Navigate "http://www.mcgpc.com/"
End Sub
```

The Web Toolbar

The Web toolbar controls all the tools you need to navigate and allows you to quickly and easily do the following:

- Navigate from page to page
- Refresh the current page
- Search the Web
- Add items to favorites
- Navigate to favorites
- Move to a specific URL

It can be activated any time, just like any other toolbar, to make navigating the Web easier.

Replication Over the Internet

The Access 97 Replication Manager can be installed on an Internet or intranet server so that you can configure replicas to synchronize with replicas on the server. The replica on the Internet or intranet server is considered the *hub* since all other replicas synchronize with it.

During synchronization, each client machine makes an HTTP connection with an Internet or an intranet server. Direct synchronizations can't be performed over the Internet; instead, an FTP folder on the server acts as a dropbox folder for an indirect synchronization. It works like this: The client machine builds a message file containing all the design and data changes made since the replicas were last synchronized. This message file is placed in the FTP file location on the Internet or intranet server. The Synchronizer on the Internet or intranet server applies the changes to its local replica, then builds a message file with all the design and data changes made since the client and server replicas were last synchronized. These changes are also placed in the FTP file location. The server sends the message file's name and location back to the client workstation. The client then transfers the message file from the server to the client workstation by using FTP. All the changes specified in the message file are applied to the client replica. The client machine doesn't need to have a Synchronizer because Jet and Windows DLLs handle the synchronization.

Summary

It's easy to integrate Access and the Internet. Access allows you to easily publish database objects to the Web and import HTML data from the Web. In fact, you can even create dynamic Web pages! This means you can have a user fill out a form over the Internet that updates an Access database on your Web server. Access 97 helps bring your data to the continually evolving information superhighway—the possibilities are endless!

28

CHAPTER

Managing Application Development with Visual SourceSafe

- What Is Visual SourceSafe? 781
- How Do I Install Visual SourceSafe? 782
- Using Visual SourceSafe: An Overview 782
- The Logistics of Managing a Project with Visual SourceSafe 783
- Leveraging the Power of Visual SourceSafe 790
- Changes Visual SourceSafe Makes to Access's Behavior 791
- Understanding the Limitations of Visual SourceSafe 793
- Practical Examples: Putting the Time and Billing Application Under SourceSafe Control 793

What Is Visual SourceSafe?

Visual SourceSafe is a tool you can use to manage the development of an Access application being worked on by a team of developers. Once a database has been placed under SourceSafe control, each object must be checked out before it's modified. Once the changes to the object have been made, the object is checked in so that other developers can see the changes. At any time, you can get the following information about the objects in the database:

- Which objects are checked out
- A history of everything that has happened to an object
- The differences between two versions of an object

Using Visual SourceSafe, you can easily revert an object to a previous version or merge different versions of an object. Visual SourceSafe is not only a tool for teams of developers, but also for an individual developer who wants to keep every version of each object in an application. It's a phenomenal tool that helps make Access a serious developer environment.

How Do I Install Visual SourceSafe?

Visual SourceSafe can be used only with the Office Developer Edition of Access; however, it doesn't ship with the Office Developer Edition. It's included as part of the Enterprise edition of Visual Basic, or it can be bought as a standalone product. In fact, Visual SourceSafe isn't the only source-code control product that can be used with the Office Developer Edition. Instead, the Office Developer Edition supplies a software component, the Microsoft Access Source Code Control component, that can integrate various source-code control products into Access. To integrate Visual SourceSafe or another version control product into Access, you need to install both the ODE-supplied control and the client part of your version control product.

You integrate Visual SourceSafe with Access by running Netsetup.exe from the Visual SourceSafe directory. This sets up the Visual SourceSafe client. Until you do this, if you're running the Office Developer Edition of Access, you get an error message each time you launch Access, indicating that Access isn't under any source-code control application. Once you install Visual SourceSafe, you'll see a SourceSafe entry under the Tools menu:

- Create Database from SourceSafe Project
- Add Database to SourceSafe
- Run SourceSafe
- Options

The Create Database from SourceSafe Project menu item allows you to create a local database from an existing Visual SourceSafe project. The Add Database to SourceSafe option creates a Visual SourceSafe project from the open database. The Run SourceSafe option runs the Visual SourceSafe Explorer. Finally, the Options menu item lets you configure different Visual SourceSafe options. Each of these menu items is covered in the following sections.

Using Visual SourceSafe: An Overview

When you want to place a database under SourceSafe control, you create it from a SourceSafe project; this database becomes the master copy. Each developer works on a local copy of the database, and no objects in the database can be modified until they're checked out. When a developer checks out an object, it's copied from Visual SourceSafe into the local database. No other developers see changes made to the object until it's checked back in. When the developer checks the object back in, it's copied from the local database to the Visual SourceSafe project.

With the exception of modules, only one person can check out an object at a time. This means that two people can't make changes to any other types of objects under SourceSafe control simultaneously. Multiple developers, however, can check out modules. When you check a module back in, your changes are merged with any changes other developers have made since you checked the module out.

The Logistics of Managing a Project with Visual SourceSafe

The first step you must take when you decide to place an object under SourceSafe control is to add the host database to SourceSafe. You can then begin to check objects in and out and to use the product's features. The following sections explain in more detail how to work with Visual SourceSafe.

Adding a Database to Visual SourceSafe

When you're ready to place an application under SourceSafe control, take the following steps:

1. Choose Tools | SourceSafe | Add Database to SourceSafe.

2. A dialog box opens, indicating that Visual SourceSafe must close the database before it can be placed under SourceSafe control. (See Figure 28.1.) Click Yes to continue.

Figure 28.1.
This dialog box notifies you that the database must be closed for it to be added to SourceSafe control.

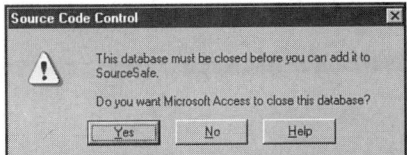

3. The Add SourceSafe Project dialog box appears. (See Figure 28.2.) The name of the database is selected as the name for the SourceSafe Project.

Figure 28.2.

Use the Add SourceSafe Project dialog box to select a project name.

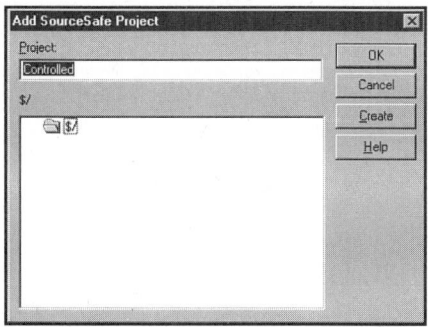

4. Click OK to accept the project name. You're then prompted to create the project. (See Figure 28.3.)

Figure 28.3.

The dialog box asking whether you want to create the project.

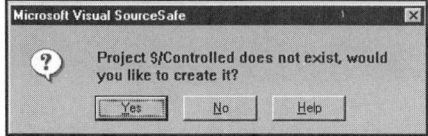

5. Click Yes to create the project; this opens the Add Object(s) to SourceSafe dialog box. (See Figure 28.4.) Here you can determine which database objects you want to place under SourceSafe control. By default, each object in the database is selected. You can deselect specific objects or deselect all objects, then select just the objects you want. When you're done, click OK.

Figure 28.4.

The Add Object(s) to SourceSafe dialog box lets you specify which objects you want to add to SourceSafe control.

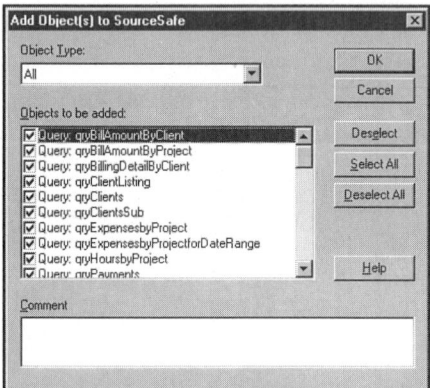

6. SourceSafe notifies you as it exports each object to SourceSafe. (See Figure 28.5.) When it's done, the warning shown in Figure 28.6 tells you that you don't have the Data and Misc. objects checked out. This means that any changes you make to local tables are lost the next time you check out or get the latest version of these objects.

Figure 28.5.

Including an object in Visual SourceSafe by exporting from the host database.

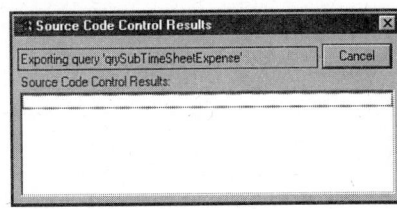

Figure 28.6.

This warning message tells you that you don't have the Data and Misc. objects checked out, so until you do, you can't proceed.

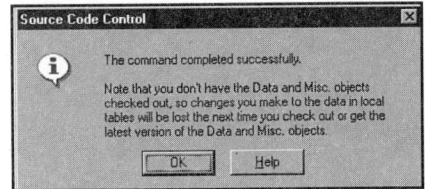

7. Click OK to complete the process. Looking at the Database window, you should see that each object has a lock that remains until you have checked out an object. (See Figure 28.7.)

Figure 28.7.

The Database window of a database under SourceSafe control with all objects locked.

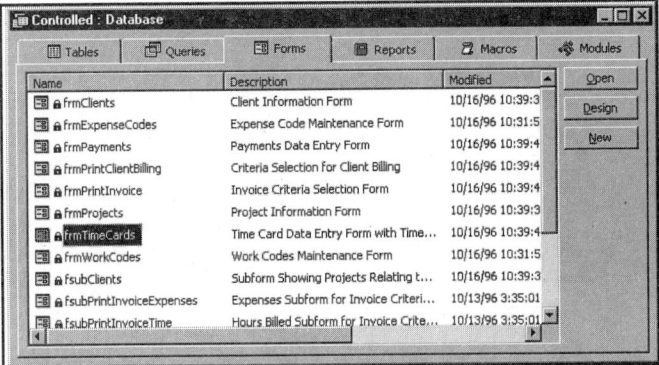

Once you add a database to SourceSafe control, the SourceSafe submenu expands to include many options needed to manage a SourceSafe project. (See Figure 28.8.) These options are covered throughout the remainder of this chapter.

Figure 28.8.

The Visual SourceSafe menu gives you several options for managing a Visual SourceSafe project.

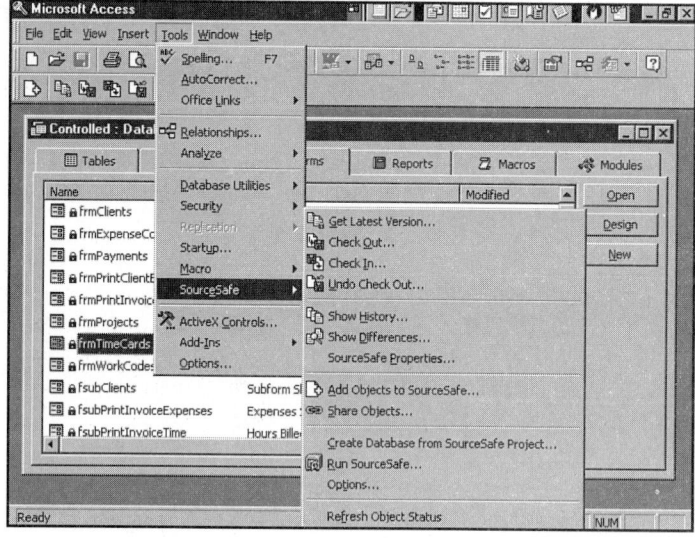

Understanding the Objects Placed Under SourceSafe Control

Each query, form, report, macro, and module is stored as a separate text file in Visual SourceSafe. When you add an object to SourceSafe control, it's exported to a text file and copied into the Visual SourceSafe project. When you check out an object, it's copied to a temporary location on your machine and then imported into the Access database on your machine as a query, form, report, macro, or module.

All other database objects (tables, relationships, command bars, database properties, startup properties, import/export specs, VBA project references, the VBA project name, and conditional compilation arguments) are stored in one Access MDB file that Visual SourceSafe treats as a binary file. These objects can't be checked out individually.

As mentioned, all queries, forms, reports, macros, and modules are stored as text files and the rest of the objects are stored in one binary file. Table 28.1 shows each object type and the extension the object is stored with when it gets added to Visual SourceSafe.

Table 28.1. File extensions for Visual SourceSafe files.

Object	Extension
Queries	ACQ
Forms	ACF
Reports	ACR
Macros	ACS
Modules	ACM
Tables, relationships, and miscellaneous objects	ACB

Creating a Database from a SourceSafe Project

The developer who adds a database to SourceSafe can continue to work on the original copy. Other developers who want to work on the application must create their own local copies of the database. To do that, follow these steps:

1. Choose Tools | SourceSafe | Create Database from SourceSafe Project from the menu to open the Open SourceSafe Project dialog box. (See Figure 28.9.)

Figure 28.9.

In the Open SourceSafe Project dialog box, you select a project used to create a local database copy.

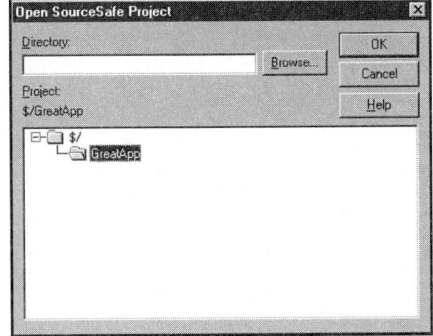

2. Select a project and click OK. You're prompted for a directory where your local copy of the database will be placed.

3. Select a directory and click OK; this returns you to the SourceSafe project dialog box.

4. Click OK to create the database. When Access is done creating the local objects, the Source Code Control Results window says Completed. (See Figure 28.10.)

Figure 28.10.

The Source Code Control Results window shows you the status of the database-creating process.

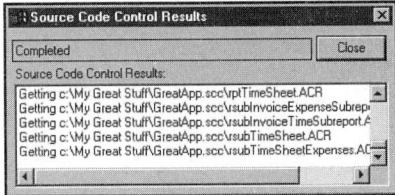

Checking in and Checking out Database Objects

Once a database has been added to Visual SourceSafe, you can't modify any of the objects you designated as controlled by SourceSafe without first checking them out. You check out the objects you want to modify, make changes to them, and check them back in when you're done. The easiest way to check out a single object is to right-click it and select Check Out. If you want to check out multiple objects, choose Tools | SourceSafe | Check Out; this opens the Check Out Object(s) from SourceSafe dialog box. (See Figure 28.11.) Here you can select all the objects you want to check out. When you return to the Database window, the objects you checked out have a checkmark next to them. (See Figure 28.12.)

787

Figure 28.11.

Use the Check Out Object(s) from SourceSafe dialog box to designate which database objects you want to check out.

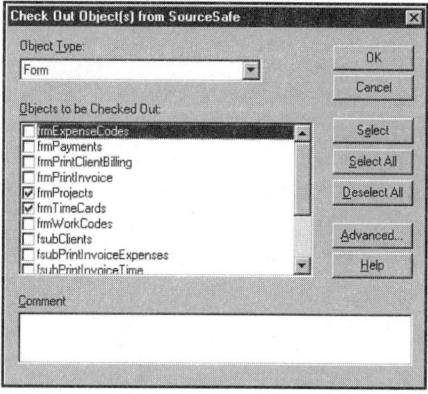

Figure 28.12.

The Database window adds an icon to show which objects in a database have been checked out.

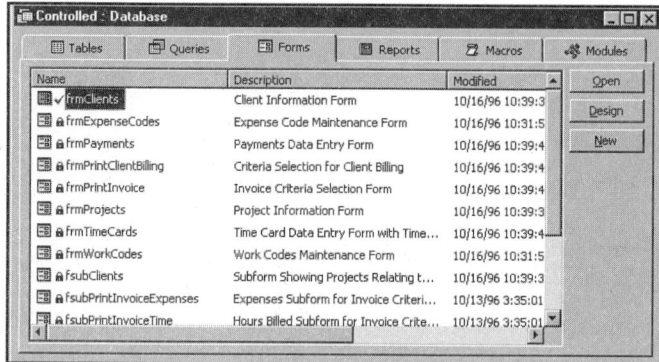

If you try to modify the design of an object that is *not* controlled by Visual SourceSafe, you don't get any error messages, so everything proceeds as usual. On the other hand, if you try to modify the design of an object that *is* controlled by Visual SourceSafe but hasn't been checked out, the error message in Figure 28.13 appears. As you can see, you're given the choice of checking out the object, opening the object as read-only and not checking it out, or canceling.

Figure 28.13.

The error message you see when you try to modify the design of an object that hasn't been checked out.

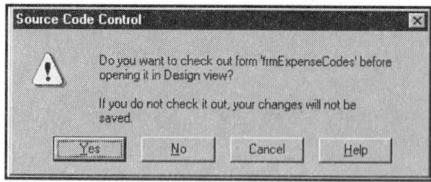

You can check in one object or check in several objects simultaneously. To check in objects, right-click any object that's checked out and select Check In; this opens the Check In Object(s) to SourceSafe dialog box. (See Figure 28.14.) Click to select any objects you want to check in, then click OK. The objects you checked in once again appear in the Database window with a lock, indicating that they can't be modified without being checked out.

Figure 28.14.

Use the Check In Object(s) to SourceSafe dialog box to designate which checked-out objects you want to check in.

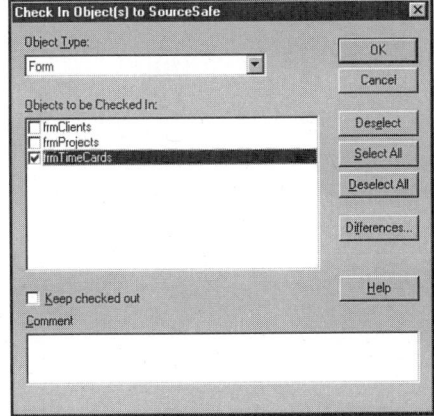

If you check out an object and realize that you made a mistake, you can right-click the object and choose Undo Check Out to quickly check it back in.

Getting the Latest Version

While you're working on the database, the objects in your local copy might not be updated with changes other users have made to the objects. To see these changes, you must get the object's latest version from the SourceSafe project. To do this with one object, right-click the object and select Get Latest Version; for multiple objects, choose Tools | SourceSafe | Get Latest Version. The Get Object(s) from SourceSafe dialog box appears, allowing you to select the objects you want.

Adding Objects to Visual SourceSafe

Depending on how you have configured Visual SourceSafe, you might be prompted to add new objects to SourceSafe control. If you add objects to your database and don't place them under SourceSafe control, you can always opt to add them later. To do this, choose Tools | SourceSafe | Add Object(s) to SourceSafe. The Add Object(s) to SourceSafe dialog box opens, showing you all the objects in your local database that haven't been added to SourceSafe control.

> **TIP**
>
> To control whether new objects are automatically placed under SourceSafe control, choose Tools | SourceSafe | Options. Pick the option you want from the "Add objects to source control when adding them to Microsoft Access" drop-down list.

Refreshing an Object's Status

When looking at the Database window, you can't be sure that the icons indicating an object's status accurately reflect the object's current state. To refresh the icons in the Database window, choose Tools | SourceSafe | Refresh Object Status.

Leveraging the Power of Visual SourceSafe

Not only does Visual SourceSafe help to manage the process of several developers working on an application simultaneously, but it also helps you manage versions of your application. It does this by showing you the differences between the checked-out version of an object and the version stored in the Visual SourceSafe project, by allowing you to view an object's history, and by letting you revert to an object's previous version.

Showing Differences Between Modules

One of the more powerful aspects of Visual SourceSafe is its ability to show the differences between the checked-out version of an object and the version in the SourceSafe project. These differences show you what you've done since you checked the object out. To view the differences, choose Tools | SourceSafe | View Differences. The Differences window opens, which lets you easily jump from difference to difference within the object. Deleted lines are blue, changed lines are red, and added lines are green.

Showing an Object's History

Often, it helps to view everything that's transpired in an object; for example, you might want to see who checked out each object and when. To see an object's history, first click to select the object, then choose Tools | SourceSafe | Show History. The History of File dialog box opens, which shows you the versions of the object, who performed each action on the object, the date the action was performed, and what the action was. From the History of File dialog box, you can do the following:

- View each version of the object
- See the details of each action taken on the object
- Get the object's current version from the Visual SourceSafe project

- See the differences between two versions of the object
- Pin a specific version of a file to the current project
- Roll back to a previous version of the object
- Get a report of everything that has transpired with the object

Reverting to an Object's Previous Version

Visual SourceSafe also gives you the ability to roll back to previous versions of an object. This is particularly useful if things have gone seriously awry and you want to start over in a version where conditions were more stable. You can revert to an object's previous version from the History of File dialog box. Select the version you want to roll back to and click Rollback. You're warned that your actions are irreversible. If you select Yes, the object is rolled back to the selected version.

Changes Visual SourceSafe Makes to Access's Behavior

Visual SourceSafe alters Access's behavior; the following sections explain these changes so they don't take you by surprise.

The Compact Command

Before you distribute a database, you should always compact it. When you try to compact a database that's under SourceSafe control, you're asked whether you want to remove the database from SourceSafe control. When you respond Yes, Access goes through each object in the database and removes all SourceSafe properties.

Opening a Database

When you open a database that's under SourceSafe control, it's always opened exclusively. This prevents more than one developer from modifying objects in the local database at a given time.

When you open a database, you can opt to have Access automatically refresh all objects from the SourceSafe project, you can be prompted on whether you want to refresh all objects, or you can opt not to have Access automatically refresh any objects. To modify this option, choose Tools | SourceSafe | Options and use the "Get latest checked in version of objects when opening a database" drop-down list to designate your choice.

Closing a Database

When closing a database, you can choose to have Access automatically check in all objects, to prompt you on whether you want to check in all objects, or not to have Access check in any objects. This option is found under Tools|SourceSafe|Options. Use the "Check in objects when closing the database" drop-down list to select your choice.

Opening an Object in Design View

Each time you check out an object, Access determines whether it has been checked out already. If the object hasn't been checked out by another user, you're asked whether you want to check it out. If you respond No, Access opens the object as read-only. If the object has been checked out by another user, and it's a module, you're warned that another user has the object checked out and you get the option of checking the object out. Your changes will be merged with the other user's changes later. If you try to check out any object other than a module, and it has already been checked out by another user, you're warned that you can just view the object as read-only in Design view.

Saving a New Object or Using Save As on an Existing Object

When you save a new object, or choose File | Save As for an existing object, you can designate whether the new object is placed under SourceSafe control by choosing Tools | SourceSafe | Options. You can have Access automatically place the object under SourceSafe control, you can have Access prompt you for your choice, or you can tell Access not to place the object under SourceSafe control. Use the "Add objects to source control when adding them to Microsoft Access" drop-down list to make your selection.

Renaming an Object

When you rename an object that's under SourceSafe control, Access automatically reflects the name change in the source control project. An object can't be renamed while checked out by another user.

> **NOTE**
>
> If you want to rename tables, command bars, and other objects that are part of the binary file, you must first check out Data and Misc. objects, since changes to the former objects will affect the latter.

Deleting an Object

When you delete an object, you can have Visual SourceSafe display a message box asking whether you want to remove the object from the SourceSafe project, you can have Access automatically remove the object from the SourceSafe project, or you can opt for Access not to remove the object from the SourceSafe project. This option can be configured by choosing Tool | SourceSafe | Options in the "Remove objects from source control when deleting them from Microsoft Access" drop-down list.

Understanding the Limitations of Visual SourceSafe

Although Visual SourceSafe is a powerful product, it does impose some limitations you should be aware of. Only Access 97 databases can be placed under Visual SourceSafe control, and user and group permissions can't be set when an object is under SourceSafe control. In fact, when you add a database to SourceSafe control, *all user and group permissions are removed! Furthermore, you can't put replicated databases under source code control, and you can't move, rename, or copy the local version of the database and continue working with it under SourceSafe control.* To move a database, you must first check in all objects, delete the local database, and then re-create it in the new location.

Practical Examples: Putting the Time and Billing Application Under SourceSafe Control

There are two reasons why you might want to place the Time and Billing application under SourceSafe control. First, multiple developers may be working on the project; second, you may want to keep track of changes made to each object to reserve the option of rolling back to a previous version of an object.

Summary

Visual SourceSafe is a powerful product for both the individual developer and members of a development team. It helps you manage group development and versioning of the objects in a database. Furthermore, it integrates seamlessly with Microsoft Access 97 and is fairly easy to use. In my opinion, most, if not all, Access databases should be placed under SourceSafe control while they're being developed.

29

Leveraging Your Application: Creating Your Own Libraries

- Understanding Library Databases, 796
- Preparing a Database To Be a Library, 796
- Creating a Reference, 798
- Debugging a Library Database, 805
- Securing an Access Library, 806
- Practical Examples: Building a Library for Your Application, 807

Understanding Library Databases

As your knowledge of the VBA language expands and you become more proficient as a VBA programmer, you probably will develop functions and subroutines that you would like all your databases to share. Without the use of library databases, the code in each of your databases is an island unto itself. Although the functions and subroutines within your code modules can be called from anywhere in the same database, these procedures cannot be called from a different database.

Without a shared library of code and other standard objects, you will find yourself copying routines and other database objects from one database to the next. The library database can be used by all your applications and distributed to all your users. A library database is just like any other database; it is simply a collection of procedures and objects that you want to share among numerous databases. The only difference between the library database and other databases is in the way the database is referenced. Instead of opening a library database to use it, you reference it from another database.

Access is highly dependent on library databases. The Table Wizard, Form Wizard, Report Wizard, Database Wizard, Database Splitter, Database Analyzer, and Database Documenter are all examples of tools that reside in library databases. In fact, all the wizards, builders, and menu add-ins you are accustomed to using while developing your applications are all contained in library databases. Wizards, builders, and menu add-ins are covered in Chapter 30, "Using Builders, Wizards, and Menu Add-Ins." This chapter focuses on creating library databases and placing generic functions in a library database to make them available to all your application databases.

Preparing a Database To Be a Library

Creating a library database involves three steps:

1. Writing the functions and creating the objects
2. Renaming the database with an MDA extension
3. Loading the database as a library

You begin by creating the generic objects you want to share among your applications. To follow standards, you should rename the database with the extension MDA, which is the naming standard for all Access library databases. To load the database as a library, you must reference it from another database. This process is covered in the next section.

Before you can reference a database as a library, you need to think about how to construct the database so that it best serves you as a library. Although a library database is just a normal database, planning the design of the library is integral to its success and usefulness. Improper planning can cause anything from extra memory being required to the database malfunctioning.

Structuring Code Modules for Optimal Performance

Library databases contain the general functions that you use in most of your applications. Because of the way Access loads code modules, you must structure your library databases effectively in order to achieve optimal performance.

Access 2.0 loaded all code modules the moment the application loaded. This meant that, when developing an Access 2.0 application, it was not particularly important how you structured your subroutines and functions within the various modules of the database. This situation changed dramatically with Access 95 and Access 97, which load code modules only if they are needed. In Access 95 and Access 97, if no procedures within a particular module are called, the module is never loaded into memory. On the other hand, if a single subroutine or function is called or if a public variable is referenced, the entire module loads. Therefore, it is crucial that you structure your modules to minimize what is loaded into memory.

These techniques help you structure your modules effectively:

- Separate frequently used procedures from those that are called infrequently.
- Place procedures that are used together in the same module.
- Place procedures that are called rarely in their own modules.
- If the same procedure is called by routines in more than one module, consider duplicating the routine and placing a copy of it in each module. This method prevents an entire module from loading just because a single routine within it is called.
- Place procedures within a call tree in the same module. This is necessary because Access looks at the potential call tree when it loads a module. If a procedure in one module is called from a procedure in another module, both modules are loaded into memory.

Although you generally want as little to load into memory as possible, the opposite is true for commonly used functions. By placing frequently used procedures in the same module, you ensure that they are loaded into memory and can be accessed quickly when they are called. This improves the performance of your application.

Writing Library Code that Runs

Code that runs perfectly in a normal database might not run as expected when it is part of a library database. One good example is the CurrentDB function. As you have seen throughout this book, the CurrentDB function is a commonly used function that enables you to reference the current database. You would think that the CurrentDB function references the database in which the code is running, but this is actually not the case. The CurrentDB function specifically references the database that is active in the user interface. If a library function refers to CurrentDB, it does not refer to itself; instead, it refers to the application database that is calling the library function. If you want to refer to the library database, you must use the CodeDB function. The CodeDB function always refers to the database in which the code is running. You must decide whether CurrentDB or CodeDB is applicable for each situation.

Compiling the Library

It is important to compile a library database before you distribute it. This ensures that it provides optimal performance. If library code is not compiled, it compiles each time it is accessed, which significantly degrades the performance of your application. The compilation process and its benefits are discussed in detail in Chapter 23, "Optimizing Your Application." After you complete all changes to the library database, you should choose Debug | Compile and Save All Modules. You must choose this command each time you make changes to the library database.

Creating a Reference

A *reference* is Access's way of locating a library database so that it can use the code in it. You can establish references in several ways:

- Create a library reference.
- Create a runtime reference.
- Create an explicit reference.
- Use VBA code.

Creating a Library Reference

You can create a library reference by adding the library to the Menu Add-Ins section of the Windows Registry, as shown in Figure 29.1. The Menu Add-Ins section is located in the HKEY_LOCAL_MACHINE\SOFTWARE\Microsoft\Office\8.0\Access\Menu Add-Ins subdirectory. This type of reference is limited, because it allows the functions of the library database to be invoked only as an add-in. Creating a library reference is covered in more detail in Chapter 30.

Figure 29.1.

Viewing the Menu Add-Ins section of the Windows Registry.

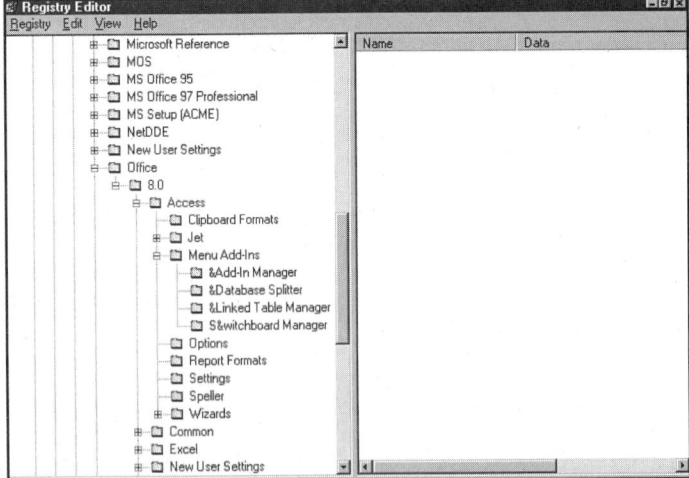

Creating a Runtime Reference

Creating a runtime reference involves establishing a reference to the library at runtime using the Run method of the `Application` object. This method of creating a reference actually opens the library database and executes the specified function. It uses OLE automation to accomplish this task.

The major advantage of this technique is that the library code is not loaded into memory until it is used. Furthermore, this technique does not require that additional modules in the call stack be loaded into memory unless they are called explicitly. Creating a runtime reference does have a few disadvantages, though:

- The library database must have an MDA extension.
- The library database must be located in the path specified in the AddInPath key in the Windows Registry. The AddInPath key is located in the HKEY_LOCAL_MACHINE\SOFTWARE\Microsoft\Office\8.0\Access\Wizards subdirectory, as shown in Figure 29.2.

Figure 29.2.

Viewing the AddInPath key of the Windows Registry.

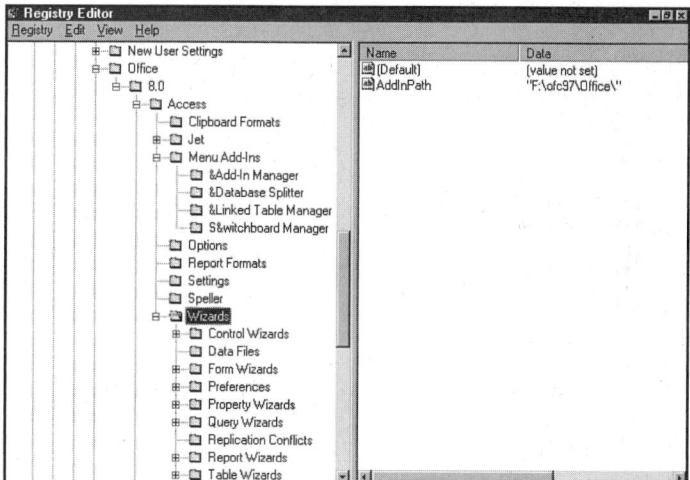

Calling a Function from a Library

The code in Listing 29.1 illustrates how to call a function in a library. Notice that the IsLoaded function is being called from the library. This code is located in the CHAP29EX.MDB database on the sample code CD-ROM.

Listing 29.1. Calling a function in a library.

```
Sub AppRun()
   If Application.Run("Chapter29Library.IsLoaded", "frmCustomers") Then
      MsgBox "Customers Form is Loaded"
   Else
      MsgBox "Customers Form is NOT Loaded!!"
   End If
End Sub
```

This code uses the Run method of the `Application` object to call the `IsLoaded` function, which is located in the CHAPTER29LIBRARY.MDA library. This file must be referenced with an explicit reference (see "Creating an Explicit Reference," later in this chapter) or be located in the directory specified in the AddInPath key of the Windows Registry. Notice the explicit reference to the name of the library in which the function is located. When using this method of loading a library (without an explicit reference), you must explicitly specify the library name.

Using the LoadOnStartup Key

You can add a LoadOnStartup key to the Windows Registry. This key provides a means for Access to load a type library when the database is loaded. A type library is not an actual module, but more a blueprint of what the module looks like. It displays the functions and constants for a specific module. This is helpful because Access can look up functions without having to actually load the module in which the function is located. This key is not automatically created for you. To create the LoadOnStartup key and add an entry to it, follow these steps:

1. Choose Run from the Windows Start menu.
2. Type **RegEdit** and click OK; this launches the Registry Editor.
3. Open the Registry tree until you see
   `HKEY_LOCAL_MACHINE\SOFTWARE\Microsoft\Office\8.0\Access\Wizards`.
4. Click the Wizards entry.
5. Choose Edit | New | Key. A new key is added.
6. Type **LoadOnStartup** as the name of the new key.
7. With LoadOnStartup selected, choose Edit | New | String Value.
8. Type the full name and path of the library.
9. Choose Edit | Modify.
10. Type **rw** for the value.

Figure 29.3 shows an example of a completed entry that references the library in the c:\Libraries directory: CHAPTER29LIBRARY.MDA.

Figure 29.3.

Referencing a library.

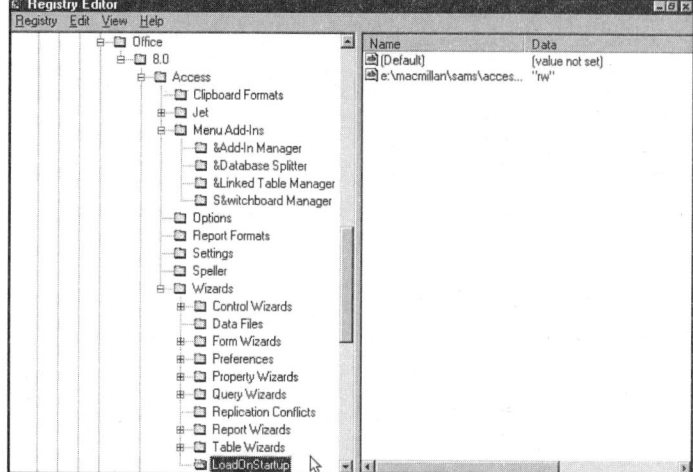

The module and procedure lists of library databases listed under the LoadOnStartup key are loaded when Access is started. When you use the Run method (discussed earlier in the "Creating a Library Reference" section), Access searches for the specified procedure in the loaded or referenced libraries. If it does not find the procedure, Access searches any databases listed in the LoadOnStartUp key. Because the module and procedure lists of databases listed under the key become available when Access is started, Access searches the list and then locates and loads the required library.

As you can see, the LoadOnStartUp key can reap the benefits of `Application.Run` by using the type library. This is beneficial because the functions can be checked without loading the actual module until it is referenced explicitly through code.

> **NOTE**
>
> The LoadOnStartUp key is not a panacea. Loading the type library when Access is loaded does slow down the initial load time for your application. Furthermore, the memory occupied by the type information is used regardless of whether the library functions actually are accessed. You must decide whether either of these facts is an issue.

Creating an Explicit Reference

The most common type of reference is an explicit reference. This type of reference is created from any code module in the database referencing the library. To create an explicit reference, follow these steps:

1. Choose a module from the database container window and click the Design button to open the Design view of the module.
2. Choose Tools | References. The References dialog box appears, as shown in Figure 29.4.

Figure 29.4.

The References dialog box.

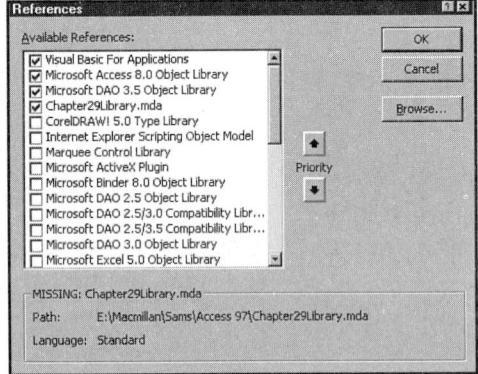

3. Click the Browse button.
4. Locate the library database you want to reference by scrolling in the Available References list box.
5. Click OK to close the References dialog box.

When you add a library database to the References dialog box, Access loads the database as a library when you make a call to the library from your code. You can call a library routine just as you would call any subroutine or function. You then can use code in the library database to open forms and other objects stored in the library. Access does not actually load the library database into memory until code in the active application database calls a function or subroutine that is located in the library.

Explicit library references impose a few limitations:

- The references you add in a database are available only to that database. Therefore, you must add the library reference to each application database that needs to use the library.

- The explicit path to the reference is stored in the database. This means that, if the library is moved, the reference cannot be resolved. Exceptions to this rule are covered later in this section.

When a function is called that is in a library that cannot be located, the message shown in Figure 29.5 appears. This box indicates that Access cannot find the project or library containing the procedure. The References dialog box shows the library as missing, as shown in the fourth line of the Available References list box in Figure 29.6.

Figure 29.5.

A warning message indicating that the library database cannot be located.

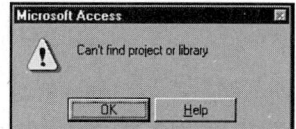

Figure 29.6.

The References dialog box with a library flagged as missing.

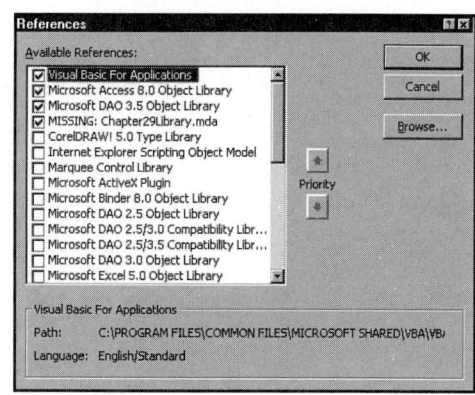

Although Access might not be able to find a library database that has been moved, it does its best to resolve library references. By default, Access looks in these places to attempt to resolve a library reference:

- The absolute path of the library
- The relative path to the library
- The directory where Access is installed
- The Windows path (Windows and Windows\System folders)
- The path located in the RefLibPaths key of the Windows Registry

Although most of these locations are self-explanatory, a couple of them require further explanation. If the library is not located in exactly the same location on the user's machine as it is on your machine, Access searches the relative path to the library next. This means that if the library is placed in the same directory as the database that is referencing it, or in the same relative location, the library database is found. Suppose that your application database is located in c:\AccessApps\Sales. The library database is located in c:\AccessApps\Sales\Libraries. The user installs the application in c:\SalesApp with the library installed in c:\SalesApp\Libraries. In this case, Access can resolve the reference to the library.

Another trick when dealing with library databases is to use the RefLibPaths key of the Windows Registry. If a key called RefLibPaths exists in the Windows Registry, Access also searches the paths specified under RefLibPaths in an attempt to resolve any references. To use this trick, follow these steps:

1. Create a RefLibPaths key under the HKEY_LOCAL_MACHINE\SOFTWARE\Microsoft\Office\8.0\Access subdirectory, if it does not already exist.

2. With the key selected, choose Edit | New | String Value.

3. Type the name of the library database.

4. Choose Edit | Modify.

5. Type the name of the path containing the library.

6. Repeat steps 2 through 5 for each library you are referencing.

This is a good method to use if you will be distributing an application containing several library databases. You can select a location for the library databases and then reference that location in the Windows Registry. You even can create the Registry entries programmatically by using Windows API calls or the VBA SaveSetting statement. Figure 29.7 shows the RefLibPath key with an entry for the Chapter29Library.mda library.

Figure 29.7.

The RefLibPath key of the Windows Registry.

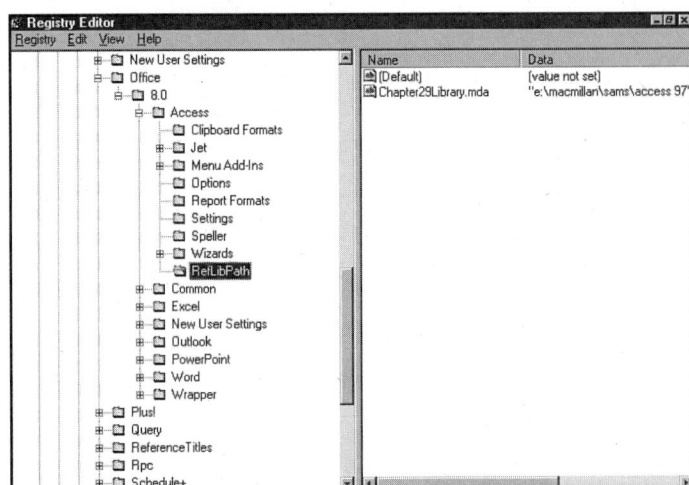

TIP

You can use the Setup Wizard to create the RefLibPaths key in the Windows Registry. This is the easiest way to create the RefLibPaths entry, but it requires that you distribute your application using the Setup Wizard.

Creating a Reference Using VBA Code

With Access 97 comes the capability to create library references using VBA code. The AddFromFile method accomplishes this task. The AddFromFile method is applied to the References collection. It accepts a string as a parameter, and the string contains the name of the library reference you are adding. Listing 29.2 shows the code to pass in a library name and then add a reference to it.

Listing 29.2. Locating and referencing libraries in code.

```
Function CreateLibRef(strLibName)
    Dim ref As Reference
    On Error GoTo CreateLibRef_Err
    ' Create new reference
    Set ref = References.AddFromFile(strLibName)
    CreateLibRef = True
Exit_CreateLibRef:
    Exit Function
CreateLibRef_Err:
    Dim intAnswer As Integer
    Dim strLocation As String
    intAnswer = MsgBox("Library Not Found, Attempt to Locate?", _
        vbYesNo, "Error")
    If intAnswer = vbYes Then
        strLocation = InputBox("Please Enter the Location of the Library")
        Resume
    Else
        CreateLibRef = False
        GoTo Exit_CreateLibRef
    End If

End Function
```

The routine begins by invoking an error handler. A reference object then is set to the result of the AddFromFile method being executed on the References collection. If the AddFromFile method executes successfully, the reference is created and the function returns a True condition. Otherwise, the user is asked whether he wants to locate the library database. If he responds affirmatively, he is prompted for the location of the library database and the code attempts once again to establish the reference. If he opts not to supply a location, the routine terminates, returning a False condition.

Debugging a Library Database

You can open a library database and test it just like any other database. Although you always should begin testing the library functions this way, it also is important that you give the database a test drive as a library. In other words, after you eliminate any bugs from the database, you should reference it from another database and test it as a library database.

If you need to make changes to a library database while accessing it from another database, you easily can do so by following these steps:

1. Make sure that the library database is referenced from Tools | References, as mentioned earlier in "Creating an Explicit Reference."

2. Click the Object Browser tool from the Module Design window.

3. From the Project/Library drop-down menu, select the library database that contains the code you want to modify. (See Figure 29.8.)

Figure 29.8.

Using the Object Browser to modify a library database.

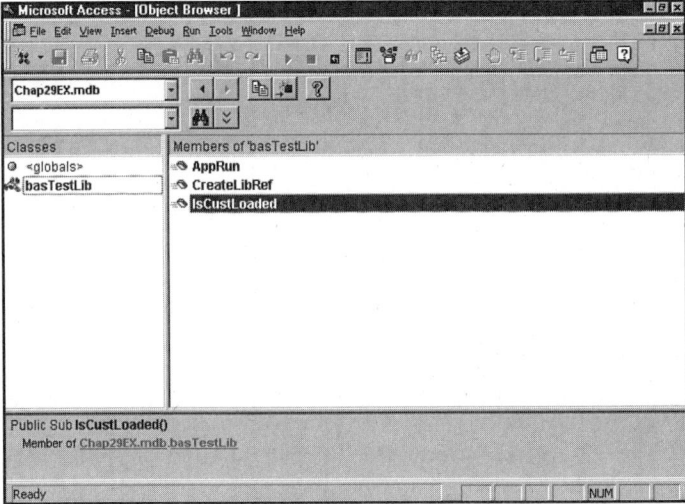

4. Select the class you want to modify from the Classes list box.

5. Select the member you want to modify from the Members list box.

6. Click Show Definition (the button with the arrow pointing toward the box). You are placed in the correct module and procedure of the library database. You now can make changes to the code in the database as required.

Securing an Access Library

Many people develop Access libraries for mass distribution in the retail market. Whether you are marketing a library database or just distributing it in your organization or to your clients, you should consider securing your library code. This protects the library code from being modified or copied by unauthorized individuals. It is highly advisable to secure your library if you plan on distributing your library—not only for the sake of securing your intellectual property, but to avoid the headache of some user who tries to alter the code and then calls you for support. Security issues are covered in detail in Chapter 32, "Database Security Made Easy."

Practical Examples: Building a Library for Your Application

Now that you are familiar with library databases and what they offer, try extracting all the generic functions from the Time and Billing application and placing them in a library database. This section presents a step-by-step roadmap to accomplishing this task.

> **NOTE**
>
> This process already has been completed for CHAP29.MDB. The associated library database is called CHAPTER29LIBRARY.MDA. If you want to complete this process as an exercise, copy CHAP26.MDB and complete the outlined steps.

To extract the generic functions from the Time and Billing application and place them in a library database, follow these steps:

1. Create a new database that will become the library database. Import the basUtils, basGenericErrorHandler, and basWinAPI modules as well as the frmError form into the library database.

2. Remove three routines from basUtils in the library database: `RunReport`, `GetCompanyInfo`, and `CreateInstances`. Assume that these routines are specific to the application database and should not be moved to become a part of the library.

3. Choose Debug | Compile and Save All Modules to ensure that you do not get any compile errors in the library database.

4. Open the application database.

5. Remove basGenericErrorHandler, basWinAPI, and frmError from the application database.

6. Remove six subroutines from basUtils in the application database: `IsLoaded`, `FlipEnabled`, `ImportantKey`, `AreTablesAttached`, `LastOccurence`, and `TryAgain`.

7. Choose Tools | References to reference the library database.

8. Choose Debug | Compile and Save All Modules to ensure that you do not get any compile errors in the application database.

9. Test the application to ensure that it runs successfully. To properly check all aspects of the application, you need to introduce an error to test the error-handling routines. Rename the CHAP19DATA.MDB database to test the linking routines.

You should move one more database element to the library database: the Report Selection Criteria form shown in Figure 29.9. This form is generic and can be used by many of the applications you create.

Figure 29.9.
The Report Date Selection form.

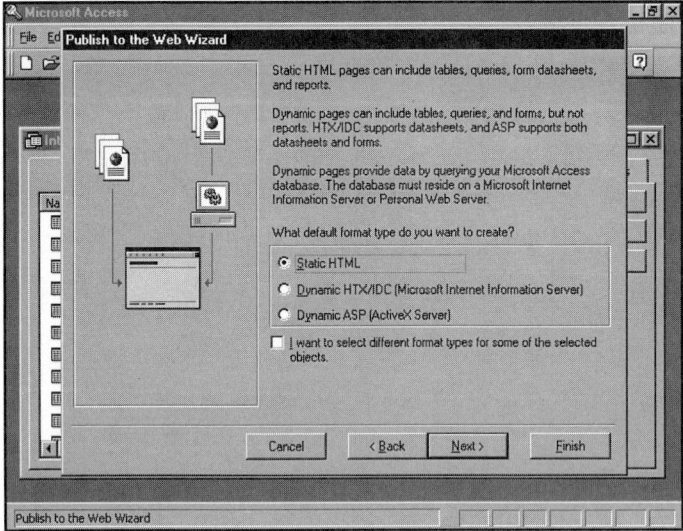

Follow these steps to move the frmReportDateRange form to the library database:

1. Open the library database and import the frmReportDateRange form.

2. Create a module called basGenericForms and add the OpenReportDateRange subroutine to the module. Because you cannot open a form in a library database directly, you must create a routine *within* the library database that opens the form.

3. Open the application database and remove the frmReportDateRange form.

4. Modify the appropriate objects within the application database like this:

```
Sub OpenReportDateRange(strOpenArg As String)
    DoCmd.OpenForm "frmReportDateRange", , , , , acDialog,
        strOpenArg
End Sub
```

You need to modify three reports in the application database to accommodate the movement of the frmReportDateRange form to a library database: rptProjectBillingsByWorkCode, rptClientBillingsByProject, and rptEmployeeBillingsByProject. The Open event of rptProjectBillingsByWorkCode should be modified to look like this:

```
Private Sub Report_Open(Cancel As Integer)
    Call OpenReportDateRange("rptProjectBillingsByWorkCode")
    If Not IsLoaded("frmReportDateRange") Then
        Cancel = True
    End If
End Sub
```

Instead of opening the form directly, which would not work because the form is in a library database, you must call the OpenReportDateRange library routine. The OpenReportDateRange library routine is responsible for opening the form. The strOpenArg parameter to the OpenReportDateRange subroutine is used as the OpenArgs parameter for the frmReportCriteria form. You must make similar changes to the rptClientBillingsByProject and rptEmployeeBillingsByProject reports. You should modify the Open event of the rptClientBillingsByProject report to look like Listing 29.3.

Listing 29.3. Modifying the Open event of the rptClientBillingsByProject report.

```
Private Sub Report_Open(Cancel As Integer)
    Call OpenReportDateRange("rptClientBillingsByProject")
    If Not IsLoaded("frmReportDateRange") Then
        Cancel = True
    Else
        Select Case Forms!frmReportDateRange!optDetailLevel.Value
            Case 1
                Me.Caption = Me.Caption & " - Summary Only"
                Me!lblTitle.Caption = Me.lblTitle.Caption & " - Summary Only"
                Me.Detail.Visible = False
            Case 2
                Me.Caption = Me.Caption & " - Detail Only"
                Me!lblTitle.Caption = Me.lblTitle.Caption & " - Detail Only"
                Me.GroupHeader0.Visible = False
                Me.GroupFooter1.Visible = False
                Me!CompanyNameDet.Visible = True
            Case 3
                Me.Caption = Me.Caption & " - Summary and Detail"
                Me!lblTitle.Caption = Me.lblTitle.Caption & " - Summary and Detail"
                Me!CompanyNameDet.Visible = False
        End Select
    End If
End Sub
```

You should modify the Open event of the rptEmployeeBillingsByProject report to look like this:

```
Private Sub Report_Open(Cancel As Integer)
    Call OpenReportDateRange("rptEmployeeBillingsByProject")
    If Not IsLoaded("frmReportDateRange") Then
        Cancel = True
    End If
End Sub
```

After you move the generic features of the application to the library database, you can try to build another application database and use the same library features.

Summary

Library databases enable you to create libraries of code, forms, reports, and other objects that will be shared by multiple databases. Library databases facilitate the application development process by enabling you to easily centralize the development of common code libraries. You also can use these databases to incorporate add-ins, wizards, and builders into your applications and development environment (covered in Chapter 28, "Managing Application Development with Visual SourceSafe").

This chapter began by defining a library database. It then walked you through all the steps required to prepare a database to become a library database. You can use several methods to reference a library database. The chapter discussed each method, highlighting the pros and cons of each. After you reference a library database, the debugging process begins. This chapter highlighted how easy it is to debug an Access 97 library database. Finally, it provided you with practical examples of how you can use library databases in your applications.

Library databases can greatly facilitate the application development process, enabling you to easily implement sophisticated functionality into all your applications. Although the process of designing library databases can be intimidating at first, a well-planned library database can shave hours off the application development and maintenance processes.

30

Using Builders, Wizards, and Menu Add-Ins

- Defining Builders, Wizards, and Menu Add-Ins, 812
- Using Builders, 812
- Using Wizards, 822
- Using Menu Add-Ins, 826
- Practical Examples: Designing Your Own Add-Ins, 829

Defining Builders, Wizards, and Menu Add-Ins

Add-ins are tools that extend the functionality of Access. They enhance the Access environment by making difficult tasks easier, automating repetitive tasks, and adding enhanced functionality. You can design add-ins for yourself or for others in your organization to use. You even might want to distribute add-ins as part of your application so that your users can build their own database objects. If you are really ambitious, you might decide to build an add-in for sale in the Access third-party market.

Microsoft Access supports three types of add-ins: builders, wizards, and menu add-ins. Each has its own advantages and uses. When you begin the process of designing an add-in, you must decide whether it will be a builder, wizard, or menu add-in. This decision affects how you design the add-in as well as how you install it. This chapter defines and shows you how to design and install each type of add-in.

Using Builders

A *builder* is an add-in that helps users construct an expression or another data element. Builders most often are used to help users fill in a property of a database object. Builders generally consist of a single dialog box that appears after the user clicks the ellipsis to the right of the property on the Property sheet. An example of a builder is the expression builder that appears when users are setting the control source of a text box on a form. Access supports three types of builders:

- Property builders
- Control builders
- Expression builders

Looking At Design Guidelines

When designing your own builder, you should be consistent with the builders that are part of Access. You therefore must learn about the standards for an Access builder. To design builders that are consistent with the built-in builders, keep a few guidelines in mind:

- Set the AutoCenter property of the Builder form to Yes.
- Remove record selectors and navigation buttons.
- Remove scroll bars.
- Be consistent about the placement of objects on the form. Place the OK and Cancel buttons in the same place in each builder you create, for example.
- Design the forms as dialog boxes.

Creating a Builder

Now that you are familiar with some general design guidelines for builders, you are ready to design your first builder. What a builder does is completely up to your imagination. For illustration, this section begins with a simple builder that prompts users to select the special effect for a text box. Three overall steps are required to create the builder:

1. Write a builder function.
2. Design a builder form.
3. Register the builder.

The following sections go over each of these steps in detail.

Writing a Builder Function

The *builder function* is the function Access calls each time the builder is launched. It launches the builder form and then returns a value to the appropriate property. Listing 30.1 is an example of a builder function. It is located in CHAP30LIB.MDA in the basBuilders module on the accompanying CD-ROM.

Listing 30.1. Using a builder function.

```
Function SpecialEffect(strObject As String, _
           strControl As String, _
           strCurrentValue As String)

  On Error GoTo SpecialEffect_Err
  DoCmd.OpenForm FormName:="frmSpecialEffect", _
              WindowMode:=acDialog, _
              OpenArgs:=strCurrentValue
  If SysCmd(acSysCmdGetObjectState, acForm, _
         "frmSpecialEffect") = acObjStateOpen Then
     Select Case Forms!frmSpecialEffect!optSpecialEffect.Value
        Case 1
           SpecialEffect = "Flat"
        Case 2
           SpecialEffect = "Raised"
        Case 3
           SpecialEffect = "Sunken"
        Case 4
           SpecialEffect = "Etched"
        Case 5
           SpecialEffect = "Shadowed"
        Case 6
           SpecialEffect = "Chiseled"
     End Select
     DoCmd.Close acForm, "frmSpecialEffect"
  Else
     SpecialEffect = strCurrentValue
  End If

SpecialEffect_Exit:
  Exit Function
```

continues

Listing 30.1. continued

```
SpecialEffect_Err:
    MsgBox "Error # " & Err.Number & ": " & Err.Description
    Resume SpecialEffect_Exit
End Function
```

A builder function must receive three preset arguments and must return the value that will become the value for the property being set. The three preset arguments follow:

- **strObject:** The name of the table, query, form, report, or module on which the builder is operating.
- **strControl:** The name of the control to which the property applies.
- **strCurrentValue:** The current property value.

Although the names of the arguments are arbitrary, their data types, positions, and content cannot be changed. Access automatically fills in the values for the three arguments.

The `SpecialEffect` function opens the form called frmSpecialEffect. It opens the form in Dialog mode, passing it the current value of the property as the `OpenArgs` value. Figure 30.1 shows the frmSpecialEffect form.

Figure 30.1.

The Special Effect builder form.

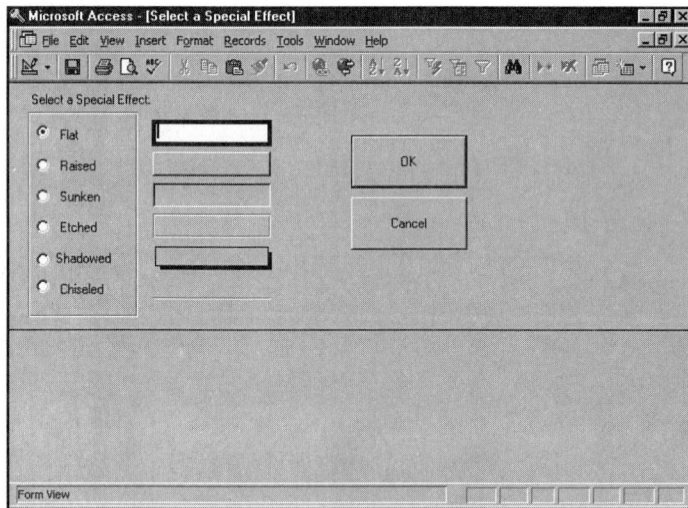

The following code is located in the `Click` event of the cmdOkay command button on the form:

```
Private Sub cmdOK_Click()
    Me.Visible = False
End Sub
```

Notice that the code sets the Visible property of the form to False. The code placed behind the cmdCancel command button looks like this:

```
Private Sub cmdCancel_Click()
   DoCmd.Close
End Sub
```

This code closes the frmSpecialEffect form.

After the user clicks OK or Cancel, the code in the SpecialEffect function continues to execute. The function uses the SysCmd function to determine whether the frmSpecialEffect form is loaded. You also can use the user-defined IsLoaded function to accomplish this task. If the frmSpecialEffect form still is loaded, the user must have selected a special effect and clicked OK. Because the form still is open, the function can determine which option button the user selected.

The Case statement in the SpecialEffect function evaluates the value of the optSpecialEffect option button found on the frmSpecialEffect form. It sets the return value for the function equal to the appropriate string, depending on the option button that the user of the builder selects. If the user of the builder selects the second option button (with a value of 2), for example, the SpecialEffect function returns the string "Raised". After the option button value is evaluated and the return value is set, the frmSpecialEffect form no longer is needed, so it is closed.

If the user chooses Cancel from the frmSpecialEffect form, the SysCmd function returns False, and the return value of the SpecialEffect function is set equal to strCurrentValue, the original property value. The property value therefore is not changed.

Designing a Builder Form

Although you have seen the code behind the Click event of the OK and Cancel buttons on the frmSpecialEffect form, you have not learned about the design of the form or the idea behind this builder. Ordinarily, when the Special Effect property is set from the Property window, no wizard exists to assist with the process. Although the process of setting the Special Effect property is quite simple, the main problem is that it is difficult to remember exactly what each special effect looks like. The custom special effect builder is designed with this potential problem in mind. It enables users of the builder to see what each special effect looks like before deciding which effect to select.

The properties of the form are quite simple. The Modal property of the form is set to Yes. The record selectors, navigation buttons, and scroll bars have been removed. The AutoCenter property of the form has been set to True. Six text boxes have been added to the form. The special effect of each text box has been set to a different style. An option group has been added to the form. This group has a different value, depending on which option button was selected. The Default property of the OK command button has been set to Yes, making the OK button the default choice. The Cancel property of the Cancel command button was set to Yes, ensuring that if the user presses Esc, the code behind the Cancel button executes. The code behind the Click events of the OK and Cancel buttons was shown in the preceding section. Listing 30.2 shows one more piece of code that enhances this builder.

815

Listing 30.2. Enhancing the builder.

```
Private Sub Form_Load()
    'Set the Value of the Option Group
    'To the Current Value of the Property
    Select Case Me.OpenArgs
           Case "Flat"
               Me!optSpecialEffect.Value = 1
           Case "Raised"
               Me!optSpecialEffect.Value = 2
           Case "Sunken"
               Me!optSpecialEffect.Value = 3
           Case "Etched"
               Me!optSpecialEffect.Value = 4
           Case "Shadowed"
               Me!optSpecialEffect.Value = 5
           Case "Chiseled"
               Me!optSpecialEffect.Value = 6
End Select
End Sub
```

This subroutine is placed in the Load event of the builder form. It sets the value of the option group to the current value of the property (passed in as an OpenArg).

Although the frmSpecialEffect form is not particularly exciting, it illustrates quite well that you can design a form of any level of complexity to facilitate the process of setting a property value. So far, though, you have not provided an entry point to the builder. If you select the Special Effect property, no ellipsis appears. You do not yet have access to the builder.

Registering a Builder

Before you can use a builder, you must register it. You can register a builder in two ways:

- Manually add the required entries to the Windows Registry.
- Set up the library database so that the Add-In Manager can create the Windows Registry entries for you.

Manually Adding Entries to the Windows Registry

Adding the required entries to the Windows Registry involves four steps:

1. If no Registry key exists for the property for which you are designing a builder, add the property as a subkey under Property Wizards.
2. Add an additional subkey for the builder.
3. Add four predefined Registry values for the key.
4. Set the proper data value for each value name.

The four value names that must be created for the subkey are Can Edit, Description, Function, and Library. Table 30.1 describes these value names for the Registry subkey.

Table 30.1. Values for the Registry subkey.

Value Name	Value Type	Purpose
Can Edit	DWORD	Allows the builder to operate on and modify an existing value.
Description	String	Specifies a description that appears in the dialog box, which is invoked automatically if more than one builder exists for a property.
Function	String	Name of the builder function.
Library	String	Name of the library containing the builder function.

Now that you have an overview of the steps involved in the process, you are ready to walk through the steps in detail. The following steps set up the builder called SpecialEffect, which is contained in the library database CHAP30LIB.MDA in the folder c:\AccessLibs:

1. To invoke the Registry Editor, choose Start | Run from the task bar. Type **regedit** and click OK. This invokes the Registry Editor.

2. Locate the HKEY_LOCAL_MACHINE\SOFTWARE\Microsoft\Office\8.0\ Access\Wizards\
Property Wizards key, as shown in Figure 30.2.

Figure 30.2.

The Property Wizards Registry key.

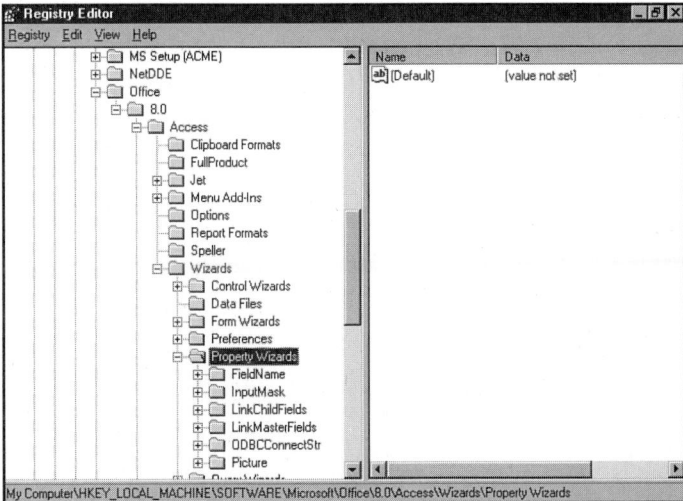

3. Determine whether a subkey exists with the name of the property for which you are creating a builder (in this case, SpecialEffect). If so, skip to step 6.

4. Choose Edit | New | Key.

5. Type the property name as the name for the new key (in this case, **SpecialEffect**).

6. With the new key selected, choose Edit | New | Key again.

7. Type a descriptive name for your builder (in this case, **SpecialEffectBuilder**).

8. Choose Edit | New | DWORD Value.

9. Type **Can Edit** as the value name.

10. Choose Edit | New | String Value.

11. Type **Description** as the value name.

12. Choose Edit | New | String Value.

13. Type **Function** as the value name.

14. Choose Edit | New | String Value.

15. Type **Library** as the value name.

16. Double-click the Can Edit value name. The Edit DWORD Value dialog box appears, as shown in Figure 30.3.

17. Enter **1** for the value data and click OK.

18. Double-click the Description value name. The Edit String dialog box appears, as shown in Figure 30.4.

Figure 30.3.
The Edit DWORD Value dialog box.

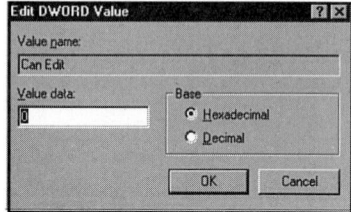

Figure 30.4.
The Edit String dialog box.

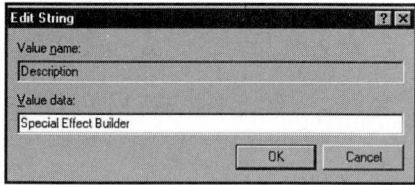

19. Enter the description you want the user of the builder to see if more than one builder is assigned to the property (in this case, **Special Effect Builder**).

20. Double-click the Function value name. Enter the name of the builder function (in this case, **SpecialEffect**).

21. Double-click the Library value name. Enter the name and location of the library database (in this case, **c:\AccessLibs\Chap30Lib.MDA**). You do not have to enter the path if the library is located in the Access folder.

Figure 30.5 shows the completed Registry entries. The builder now should be ready to use. To test the builder, you need to exit and relaunch Access. If all the Registry entries are created successfully, you can use the builder. To test the builder, open any database (not the library database), create a new form, and add a text box. Select Special Effect from the Format tab of the Properties window. An ellipsis appears to the right of the Special Effect drop-down list, as shown in Figure 30.6. If you click the ellipsis, the builder form appears. Select a special effect and click OK. The special effect you selected now appears in the Special Effect property.

Figure 30.5.
The completed Registry entries required to add the builder.

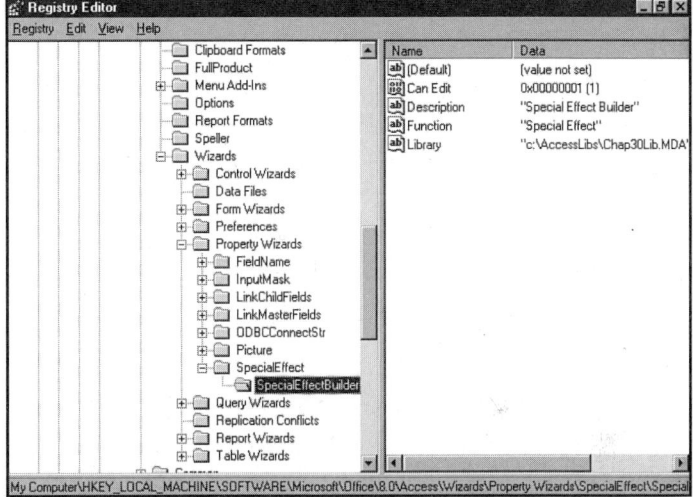

Figure 30.6.
Using the custom builder.

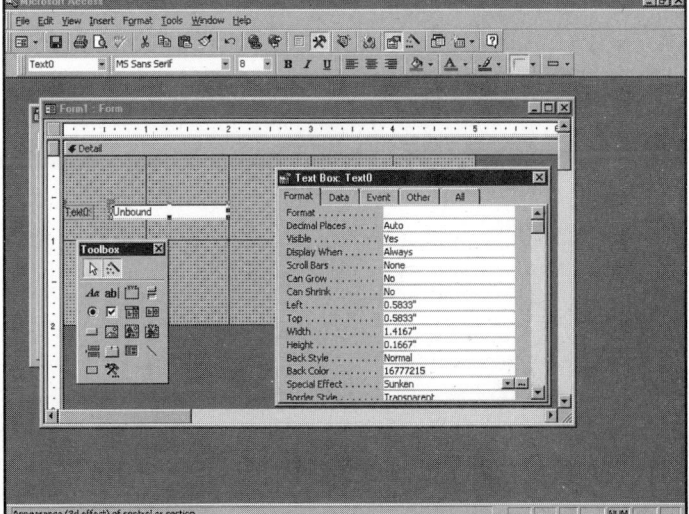

> **NOTE**
>
> If you do not follow exactly the format for the value names, the message `Invalid add-in entry for 'SpecialEffectBuilder'` appears, as shown in Figure 30.7. You must correct the Registry entry.

Figure 30.7.
This error message appears if the Registry entry is invalid.

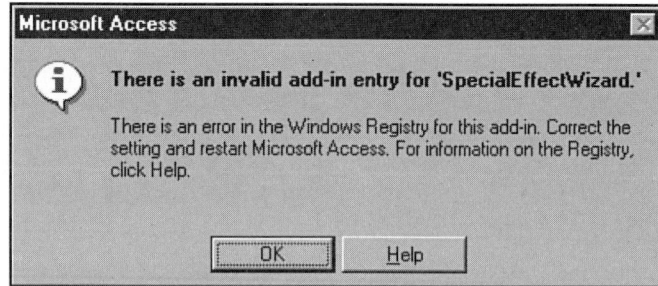

Automating the Creation of Registry Entries

The alternative to editing the Windows Registry manually is to set up the library database so that the Add-In Manager can create the Registry entries for you. This involves adding a table to the library database. The table must be called USysRegInfo. Follow these steps:

1. Tables that begin with USys or MSys are considered system tables and by default are hidden. The first step is to show system tables. With the library database open, choose Tools | Options. From the View tab, click System Objects. Click OK. Figure 30.8 shows the Tables tab.

Figure 30.8.
The Tables tab with system objects visible.

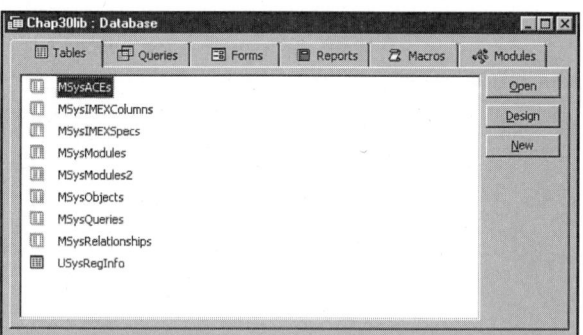

2. The next step is to import an existing USysRegInfo table. To do this, right-click the Tables tab in the Database window and select Import. Using the Import dialog box, move to the folder where Access is installed and locate the WZMAIN80.MDA file. This is a library file that ships with Access. Select the WZMAIN80.MDE file and click Import.

3. The Import Objects dialog box appears, as shown in Figure 30.9. Locate and select the USysRegInfo table and click OK. A copy of the USysRegInfo table is added to your library database.

Figure 30.9.

Using the Import Objects dialog box to add the USysRegInfo table to your library database.

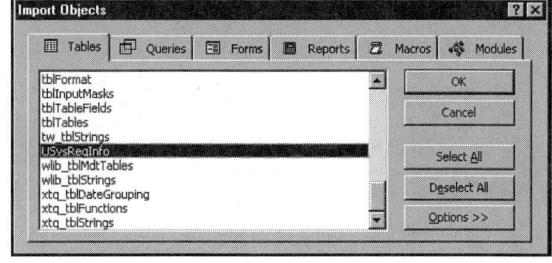

4. Double-click to open the USysRegInfo table in the Database window.

5. Delete any existing entries in the table.

6. Specific entries must be added to the USysRegInfo table. Figure 30.10 shows these entries, and Table 30.2 explains them. Add the entries and close the table.

7. Open the database that references the add-in.

8. Choose Tools | Add-Ins | Add-In Manager. The Add-In Manager dialog box appears, as shown in Figure 30.11.

9. Click the Add New button to launch the Open dialog box. Here, you can browse for your add-in.

10. Locate the add-in that you want to add and click OK. The add-in you select is added to the Add-In Manager dialog box and is selected for you.

11. Click Close. You now are ready to use the add-in.

Figure 30.10.

The completed table with entries for Registry.

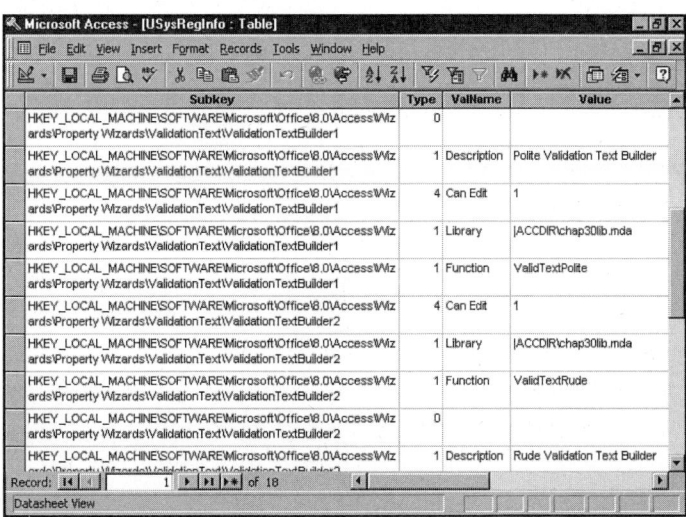

Figure 30.11.
The Add-in Manager dialog box.

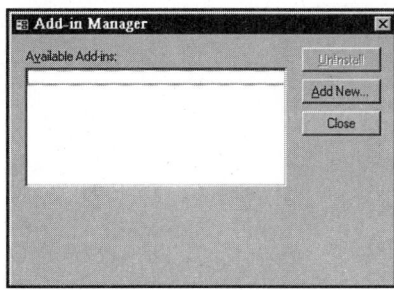

Table 30.2. The structure of the USysRegInfo table.

Field Name	Description
SubKey	Name of the subkey value in the Registry where the value you are adding is located.
Type	Type of subkey value you are creating (String, Binary, or DWORD).
ValName	Value name for the entry.
Value	Value associated with the value name.

Using Wizards

A *wizard* consists of a series of dialog boxes; it provides a step-by-step interface to creating a database object. The wizard shields users from the complexities of the process. You probably are familiar with wizards such as the Form Wizard, the Report Wizard, and the Database Wizard. Access 97 supports the development of several types of custom wizards:

- Table wizards
- Query wizards
- Form wizards
- Report wizards
- Property wizards
- Control wizards

Looking At Design Guidelines

Wizard design guidelines are almost identical to builder design guidelines. The main difference is that wizards generally present the user with multiple modal dialog boxes, whereas a builder generally consists of a single modal dialog box. All the data requirements for the wizard must be met before the user can close the last dialog box.

Creating a Wizard

Creating a wizard is more complex than creating a builder. Creating a wizard generally involves a multi-page form and is usually responsible for creating database objects. Consider a wizard that creates a simple form. The wizard consists of two modal dialog boxes, shown in Figures 30.12 and 30.13. The first dialog box asks the user for a form caption, form name, and message to appear on the new form. The second dialog box enables the user to add OK and Cancel buttons to the form. The multi-page form and all the code that enables it to work are in the CHAP30LIB.MDA database on the accompanying CD-ROM.

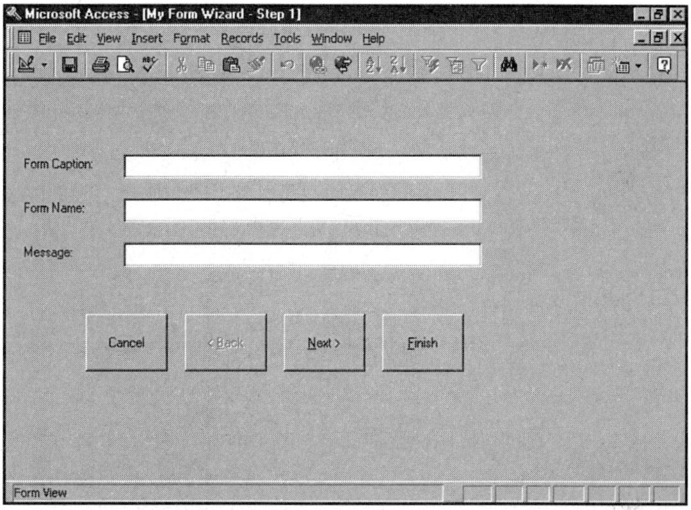

Figure 30.12.

Step 1 of the custom Form Wizard.

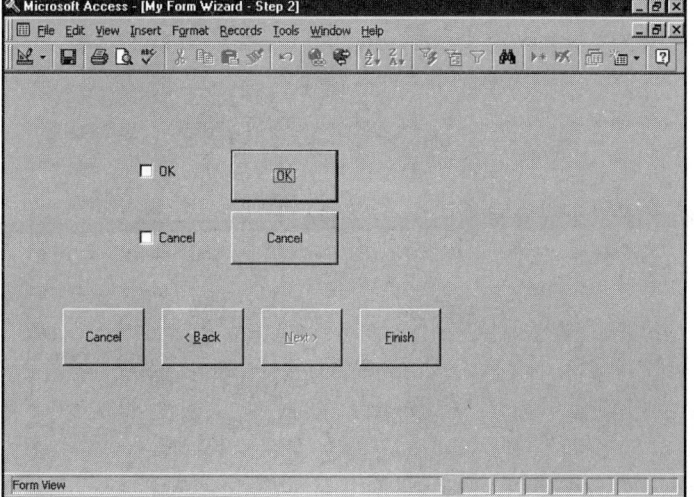

Figure 30.13.

Step 2 of the custom Form Wizard.

Each page of the wizard contains code to ensure that it operates successfully. The form is called frmGetFormInfo. The first page of this multi-page form gives the user the opportunity to choose Cancel, Next, or Finish. The code for the Cancel button looks like this:

```
Private Sub cmdCancel1_Click()
   DoCmd.Close
End Sub
```

This code closes the wizard form. No other actions are taken, because the process is being canceled. If the user clicks Next, this code executes:

```
Private Sub cmdNext1_Click()
   DoCmd.GoToPage 2
   Me.Caption = "My Form Wizard - Step 2"
End Sub
```

This code moves to the second page of the form and changes the caption of the form to indicate that the user is on step 2 of the wizard. The code under the Finish button looks like this:

```
Private Sub cmdFinish1_Click()
   If CreateCustomForm() Then
      MsgBox "Form Created Successfully"
      DoCmd.Close
   Else
      MsgBox "Unable to Create Form"
   End IfEnd Sub
```

This code calls a function called CreateCustomForm, which is responsible for building the actual form. The details of the CreateCustomForm function are discussed later in this section. If the function returns True, the wizard form is closed and a message is displayed indicating that the process was successful. Otherwise, a message is displayed indicating that the form was not created successfully, and the user remains in the wizard. The second page of the form contains similar subroutines. The code under the Back button looks like this:

```
Private Sub cmdBack2_Click()
   DoCmd.GoToPage 1
   Me.Caption = "My Form Wizard - Step 1"End Sub
```

This code moves back to the first page of the form. If the user chooses Cancel, this code executes:

```
Private Sub cmdCancel2_Click()
   DoCmd.CloseEnd Sub
```

This code closes the form, taking no further action. If the user clicks Finish, the Click event code of the cmdFinish2 command button executes:

```
Private Sub cmdFinish2_Click()
   Call cmdFinish1_ClickEnd Sub
```

This code calls the code under the Click event of the cmdFinish1 command button.

The CreateCustomForm function, as seen in Listing 30.3, contains the code that actually builds the new form.

Listing 30.3. The `CreateCustomForm` function builds the form.

```
Function CreateCustomForm() As Boolean

    On Error GoTo CreateCustomForm_Err

    Dim frmNew As Form
    Dim ctlNew As Control

    'Create a New Form and Set Several of Its Properties
    Set frmNew = CreateForm()
    frmNew.Caption = Forms!frmGetFormInfo.txtFormCaption
    frmNew.RecordSelectors = False
    frmNew.NavigationButtons = False
    frmNew.AutoCenter = True

    'Create a Label Control on the New Form
    'Set Several of Its Properties
    Set ctlNew = CreateControl(frmNew.Name, acLabel)
    ctlNew.Caption = Forms!frmGetFormInfo.txtLabelCaption
    ctlNew.Width = 3000
    ctlNew.Height = 1000
    ctlNew.Top = 1000
    ctlNew.Left = 1000

    'Evaluate to See if the User Requested an OK Command Button
    'If They Did, Add the Command Button and Set Its Properties
    'Add Click Event Code for the Command Button
    If Forms!frmGetButtons.chkOK.Value = -1 Then
        Set ctlNew = CreateControl(frmNew.Name, acCommandButton)
        ctlNew.Caption = "OK"
        ctlNew.Width = 1000
        ctlNew.Height = 500
        ctlNew.Top = 1000
        ctlNew.Left = 5000
        ctlNew.Name = "cmdOK"
        ctlNew.Properties("OnClick") = "[Event Procedure]"
        frmNew.Module.InsertText "Sub cmdOK_Click()" & vbCrLf & _
            vbTab & "DoCmd.Close acForm, """ & _
            Forms!frmGetFormInfo.txtFormName & _
            """" & vbCrLf & "End Sub"
    End If

    'Evaluate to See if the User Requested a Cancel Command Button
    'If They Did, Add the Command Button and Set Its Properties
    'Add Click Event Code for the Command Button
    If Forms!frmGetButtons.chkCancel.Value = -1 Then
        Set ctlNew = CreateControl(frmNew.Name, acCommandButton)
        ctlNew.Caption = "Cancel"
        ctlNew.Width = 1000
        ctlNew.Height = 500
        ctlNew.Top = 2000
        ctlNew.Left = 5000
        ctlNew.Name = "cmdCancel"
        ctlNew.Properties("OnClick") = "[Event Procedure]"
        frmNew.Module.InsertText "Sub cmdCancel_Click()" & vbCrLf & _
            vbTab & "MsgBox(""You Canceled!!"")" & vbCrLf & "End Sub"
    End If
```

continues **825**

Listing 30.3. continued

```
    'If the User Entered a Form Name, Save the Form
    If Not IsNull(Forms!frmGetFormInfo.txtFormName) Then
        DoCmd.Save , Forms!frmGetFormInfo.txtFormName
    End If

    'Return True If No Errors
    CreateCustomForm = True
    Exit Function

CreateCustomForm_Err:
    MsgBox "Error # " & Err.Number & ": " & Err.Description
    CreateCustomForm = False
    Exit Function
End Function
```

The code begins by creating both form and control object variables. The form object variable is set to the return value from the CreateForm function. The CreateForm function creates a new form object. Several properties of the new form object are set: Caption, RecordSelectors, NavigationButtons, and AutoCenter. Next, the function uses the CreateControl function to create a new label. A reference to the new label is called ctlNew. The Caption, Width, Height, Top, and Left properties of the new label are set. If the user indicated that he or she wanted an OK button, a new command button is created. The Caption, Width, Height, Top, Left, Name, and Properties properties are all set. The InsertText method is used to insert code for the Click event of the command button. If the user requested a Cancel button, the same properties are set. Finally, if the user indicated a name for the new form, the Save method is used to save the new form object.

> **NOTE**
>
> Several functions exist to create and delete forms, reports, form controls, and report controls. You can use DAO code to create, modify, and delete tables and queries. Using the functions and DAO code, you can manipulate database objects any way you want.

Getting the Wizard Ready to Go

Like a builder, a wizard needs to be added to the Windows Registry before it can be used. You can do this by modifying the Registry directly or by adding entries to the USysRegInfo table. Figure 30.14 shows the completed Registry entry for the custom Form Wizard.

Figure 30.14.

Registry entries for the custom Form Wizard.

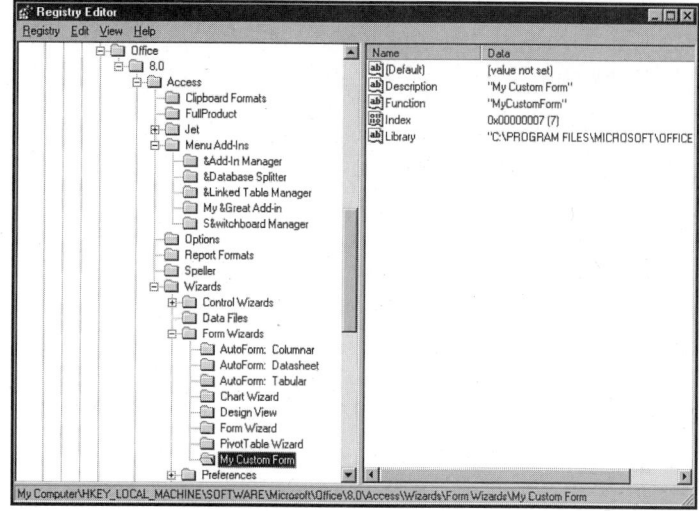

Notice that the function name is `MyCustomForm`. This is the entry point to the wizard. The Library key designates the name of the library add-in database containing the entry point function. The Description key specifies what appears in the New Object dialog box. Finally, the Index key designates the order in which the wizard is displayed in the list in the New Object dialog box. The `MyCustomForm` function simply calls the frmGetFormInfo form, initiating the wizard process:

```
Function MyCustomForm(strRecordSource As String) As Variant
   DoCmd.OpenForm FormName:="frmGetFormInfo", WindowMode:=acDialog
End Function
```

Using Menu Add-Ins

A *menu add-in* is a general-purpose tool that enables you to perform a task that generally affects multiple objects or Access itself. The Database Splitter and Database Documenter are examples of menu add-ins. You access menu add-ins through the Add-Ins submenu of the Tools menu.

Looking At Design Guidelines

Menu add-ins are available to the user whenever the Tools menu is available. Menu add-ins are not context-sensitive like wizards and builders. Therefore, they should in no way rely on what the user is doing at a particular moment.

Creating a Menu Add-In

Creating a menu add-in is just like creating a wizard. The difference is in how you install the add-in. The menu add-in must be registered under HKEY_LOCAL_MACHINE\SOFTWARE\ Microsoft\Office\8.0\Access\Menu Add-Ins. You can accomplish the registration process by modifying the Registry directly or by using the USysRegInfo table. Figure 30.15 shows the Registry with the correct entries to run the Form Wizard created earlier in this chapter. Figure 30.16 shows how you can automate the registration process by using the USysRegInfo table. Three entries are included in the USysRegInfo table. All three entries designate the proper place in the Registry tree to add the new key. The first entry contains the subkey and a type of zero. The second entry contains the value name Expression and the name of the entry-point function as the value. Notice that the expression name is preceded by an equals (=) sign and is followed by parentheses. The quotation marks within the parentheses are required because this particular entry-point function requires an argument. The third and final entry contains the value name Library and the name of the library as the value. This is all you need to do to turn a wizard into a menu add-in.

Figure 30.15.

Registry entries for the menu add-in.

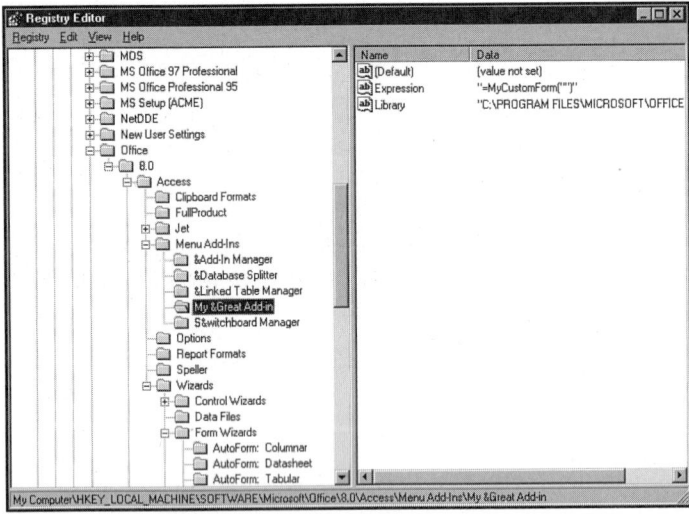

Figure 30.16.

The USysRegInfo entries for the menu add-in.

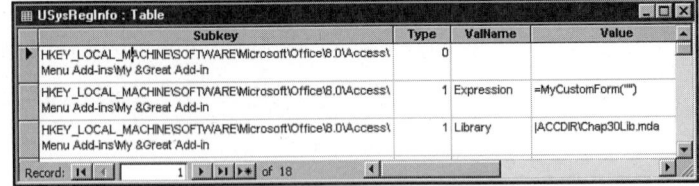

Practical Examples: Designing Your Own Add-Ins

The types of builders, wizards, and menu add-ins that you create depend on your specific needs. To reinforce what you have learned, this section includes the step-by-step process for creating a builder to help you add validation text messages. When you invoke the builder, the Choose Builder dialog box shown in Figure 30.17 appears. This dialog box appears because you will design two builders: one that enables the user to select from a list of polite messages and another that enables the user to select from rude messages. If the user selects Polite Validation Text Builder, the dialog box in Figure 30.18 appears. If the user selects Rude Validation Text builder, the dialog box in Figure 30.19 appears.

Figure 30.17.
The Choose Builder dialog box.

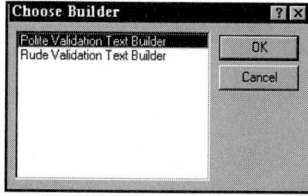

Figure 30.18.
The polite messages builder.

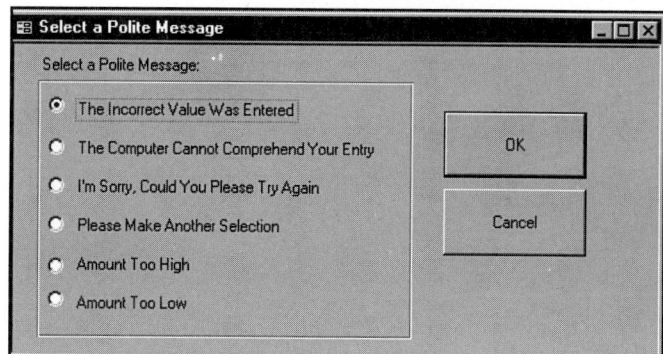

Figure 30.19.

The rude messages builder.

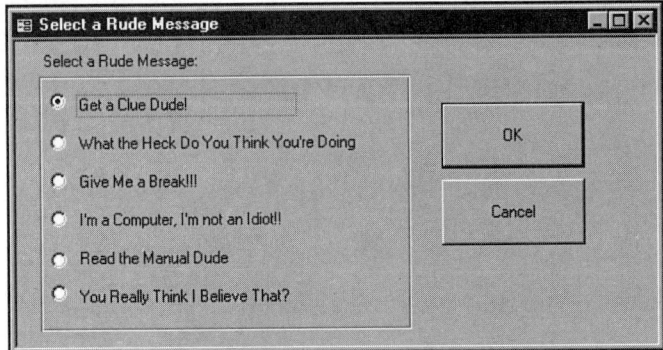

The first entry-point function is located in basBuilders and is shown in Listing 30.4.

Listing 30.4. The first entry-point function.

```
Function ValidTextPolite(strObject As String, _
            strControl As String, _
            strCurrentValue As String)

    On Error GoTo ValidTextPolite_Err
    DoCmd.OpenForm FormName:="frmPolite", _
                WindowMode:=acDialog, _
                OpenArgs:=strCurrentValue
    If SysCmd(acSysCmdGetObjectState, acForm, _
            "frmPolite") = acObjStateOpen Then
        Select Case Forms!frmPolite!optPolite.Value
            Case 1
                ValidTextPolite = "The Incorrect Value Was Entered"
            Case 2
                ValidTextPolite = "The Computer Cannot Comprehend Your Entry"
            Case 3
                ValidTextPolite = "I'm Sorry, Could You Please Try Again"
            Case 4
                ValidTextPolite = "Please Make Another Selection"
            Case 5
                ValidTextPolite = "Amount Too High"
            Case 6
                ValidTextPolite = "Amount Too Low"
        End Select
        DoCmd.Close acForm, "frmPolite"
    Else
        ValidTextPolite = strCurrentValue
    End If

ValidTextPolite_Exit:
    Exit Function

ValidTextPolite_Err:
    MsgBox "Error # " & Err.Number & ": " & Err.Description
    Resume ValidTextPolite_Exit
End Function
```

The `ValidTextPolite` function receives all the parameters required by a builder function. The function opens frmPolite modally, passing it the current validation text value of the selected control as the OpenArg. If the user selects a value from the frmPolite form and clicks OK, the value he or she selected is evaluated and the appropriate text is returned from the `ValidTextPolite` function. The return value is the value that becomes the validation text of the selected control. Listing 30.5 shows the Load event of frmPolite.

Listing 30.5. The Load event of frmPolite.

```
Private Sub Form_Load()
    'Set the Value of the Option Group
    'To the Current Value of the Property
    Select Case Me.OpenArgs
        Case "The Incorrect Value Was Entered"
            Me!optPolite.Value = 1
        Case "The Computer Cannot Comprehend Your Entry"
            Me!optPolite.Value = 2
        Case "I'm Sorry, Could You Please Try Again"
            Me!optPolite.Value = 3
        Case "Please Make Another Selection"
            Me!optPolite.Value = 4
        Case "Amount Too High"
            Me!optPolite.Value = 5
        Case "Amount Too Low"
            Me!optPolite.Value = 6
    End Select

End Sub
```

This code ensures that the value of the option button on the frmPolite form reflects the text that currently is entered in the Validation Text property of the current control. The `ValidTextRude` entry-point function is similar to `ValidTextPolite`. Listing 30.6 shows the `ValidTextRude` entry-point text function; it is located in basBuilders.

Listing 30.6. The ValidTextRude entry-point function.

```
Function ValidTextRude(strObject As String, _
            strControl As String, _
            strCurrentValue As String)

    On Error GoTo ValidTextRude_Err
    DoCmd.OpenForm FormName:="frmRude", _
                WindowMode:=acDialog, _
                OpenArgs:=strCurrentValue
    If SysCmd(acSysCmdGetObjectState, acForm, _
            "frmRude") = acObjStateOpen Then
        Select Case Forms!frmRude!optRude.Value
            Case 1
                ValidTextRude = "Get a Clue Dude"
            Case 2
                ValidTextRude = "What the Heck do You Think You're Doing?"
            Case 3
```

continues

Listing 30.6. continued

```
                ValidTextRude = "Give Me a Break!!"
            Case 4
                ValidTextRude = "I'm a Computer, I'm not an Idiot!!"
            Case 5
                ValidTextRude = "Read the Manual Dude"
            Case 6
                ValidTextRude = "You Really Think I Believe That?"
        End Select
        DoCmd.Close acForm, "frmRude"
    Else
        ValidTextRude = strCurrentValue
    End If

ValidTextRude_Exit:
    Exit Function

ValidTextRude_Err:
    MsgBox "Error # " & Err.Number & ": " & Err.Description
    Resume ValidTextRude_Exit
End Function
```

The Load event of frmRude is similar to the Load event of frmPolite, as Listing 30.7 shows.

Listing 30.7. The Load event of frmRude.

```
Private Sub Form_Load()
    'Set the Value of the Option Group
    'To the Current Value of the Property
    Select Case Me.OpenArgs
        Case "Get a Clue Dude!"
            Me!optRude.Value = 1
        Case "What the Heck Do You Think You're Doing"
            Me!optRude.Value = 2
        Case "Give Me a Break!!"
            Me!optRude.Value = 3
        Case "I'm a Computer, I'm not an Idiot!!"
            Me!optRude.Value = 4
        Case "Read the Manual Dude"
            Me!optRude.Value = 5
        Case "You Really Think I Believe That?"
            Me!optRude.Value = 6
    End Select

End Sub
```

To create the builder, design both forms so that they look like the ones in Figures 30.18 and 30.19. Include code for the `Load` event of each form as listed previously. The code behind the OK button of each form sets the Visible property of the form to False. The code behind the Cancel button on each form closes the form. Make sure that you name the option groups optPolite and optRude so that the code runs properly for each form. You can place the two entry-point functions, `ValidTextPolite` and `ValidTextRude`, in any code module in the library database. The last step involves registering the two builders. The entries in USysRegInfo, shown in Figure 30.20, accomplish the task of registering the builder the first time that the add-in is selected through the Add-Ins dialog box. This table is located in CHAP30LIB.MDA.

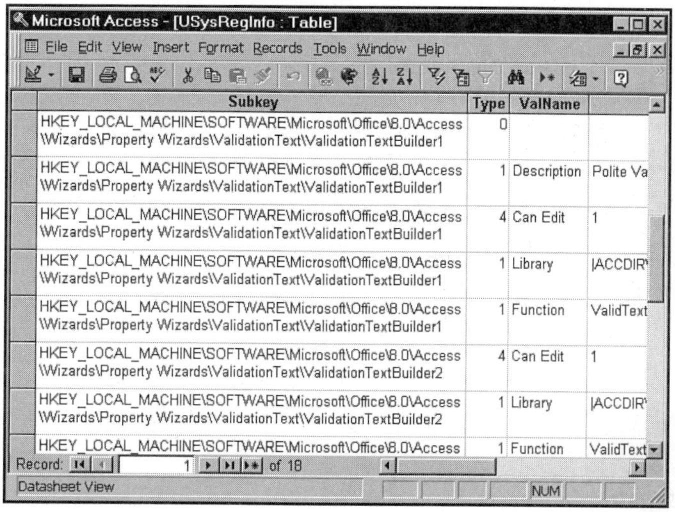

Subkey	Type	ValName	
HKEY_LOCAL_MACHINE\SOFTWARE\Microsoft\Office\8.0\Access \Wizards\Property Wizards\ValidationText\ValidationTextBuilder1	0		
HKEY_LOCAL_MACHINE\SOFTWARE\Microsoft\Office\8.0\Access \Wizards\Property Wizards\ValidationText\ValidationTextBuilder1	1	Description	Polite Va
HKEY_LOCAL_MACHINE\SOFTWARE\Microsoft\Office\8.0\Access \Wizards\Property Wizards\ValidationText\ValidationTextBuilder1	4	Can Edit	1
HKEY_LOCAL_MACHINE\SOFTWARE\Microsoft\Office\8.0\Access \Wizards\Property Wizards\ValidationText\ValidationTextBuilder1	1	Library	|ACCDIR\
HKEY_LOCAL_MACHINE\SOFTWARE\Microsoft\Office\8.0\Access \Wizards\Property Wizards\ValidationText\ValidationTextBuilder1	1	Function	ValidText
HKEY_LOCAL_MACHINE\SOFTWARE\Microsoft\Office\8.0\Access \Wizards\Property Wizards\ValidationText\ValidationTextBuilder2	4	Can Edit	1
HKEY_LOCAL_MACHINE\SOFTWARE\Microsoft\Office\8.0\Access \Wizards\Property Wizards\ValidationText\ValidationTextBuilder2	1	Library	|ACCDIR\
HKEY_LOCAL_MACHINE\SOFTWARE\Microsoft\Office\8.0\Access	1	Function	ValidText

Figure 30.20.
Registry entries for the polite and rude builders.

Summary

By creating builders, wizards, and add-ins, you can enhance the development environment for yourself and your users. You even can add wizards so that your users can build their own queries, forms, or reports on-the-fly without a full copy of Access. Your wizard simply needs to prompt the user for the appropriate information and then build the objects to your specifications. What you can do with wizards, builders, and add-ins is limited only by your imagination.

V

Putting the Final Polish on Your Application

31

Using External Functions: The Windows API

- Using the Win32 API, 838
- Declaring an External Function to the Compiler, 838
- Working with Constants and Types, 843
- Calling DLL Functions: Important Issues, 848
- Examining the Differences Between 16-Bit and 32-Bit APIs, 849
- Using API Functions, 849
- Getting Information about the Operating Environment, 849
- Determining Drive Types and Available Drive Space, 854
- Practical Examples: Applying What You Have Learned to the Time and Billing Application, 857

Using the Win32 API

One of the richest libraries of programming code functions is supplied by Windows itself. This function library commonly is referred to as the *Windows API* (Application Programming Interface). Fortunately, as VBA programmers, you can tap into the Windows function library by using these built-in Windows functions in your own VBA modules.

Furthermore, you might discover other *dynamic link libraries* (DLLs) that contain functions that would be useful in your applications. These DLLs also are available to you as long as you are properly licensed to use and distribute them.

A *DLL* is a library of procedures that applications can link to and use at runtime. Functions contained in the Windows API and other DLLs can provide your applications with significant added functionality. It is much more efficient to use an external DLL to accomplish a task than to attempt to write a VBA function to accomplish the same task.

Declaring an External Function to the Compiler

To use a DLL function, you must do the following:

- Declare the function to the VBA compiler.
- Call the function.
- Use the return value.

The VBA language is not intrinsically aware of the functions available in external libraries. Declaring a DLL function means making the VBA compiler aware of the name of the function, the library it is located in, the parameters it expects to receive, and the values it expects to return.

If you do not properly declare the library function to the VBA compiler, you receive an error message stating `Sub or Function Not Defined`. User-defined functions and subroutines written in VBA are declared using `Sub` or `Function` keywords. These keywords define the procedures so that VBA can locate the routines when they are called. Functions in a DLL are declared in the same way. After you declare a DLL function to the compiler, Access knows where to locate it, and you can use it throughout your application.

You declare an external function to VBA by using a `Declare` statement. You can place `Declare` statements in the Declarations section of a module, form, or report. A `Declare` statement placed in a module is immediately available to your entire application. If the `Declare` statement is explicitly declared as private, it is available only to the module in which it was declared. A `Declare` statement placed in the General Declarations section of a form or report is available only after the form or report is loaded. Furthermore, a `Declare` statement placed in the General Declarations section of a form or report can have only private scope.

You can use a `Declare` statement to declare both subroutines and functions. If the procedure returns a value, you must declare it as a function. If it does not return a value, you must declare it as a subroutine.

A `Declare` statement looks like this:

```
Private Declare Function GetKeyboardType Lib "user32" _
   (ByVal nTypeFlag As Long) As Long
```

This `Declare` statement declares a function called `GetKeyboardType`, which is located in the Windows 95 or Windows NT System folder in a DLL file called user32. It receives a long integer parameter by value and returns a long integer. Notice that this function was declared as private.

> **NOTE**
>
> Remember that the function name and library name are both case-sensitive. Unless you explicitly include the path as part of the `Declare` statement, the default system path, the Windows folder, and the Windows System folder are all searched for the library. Most Windows API functions are contained in the library files user32.exe, gdi32.exe, and kernel32.exe.

Passing by Reference versus Passing by Value

When a parameter is passed by *reference*, the memory address of the argument is passed to the function. When a parameter is passed by *value*, the actual value of the argument is passed to the function. Unless explicitly told otherwise, VBA passes all parameters by reference. Many library functions expect to receive parameters by value. If such a function is passed a reference to a memory location, it cannot function properly. If you want to pass an argument by value, the `ByVal` keyword must be placed in front of the argument in the `Declare` statement. When calling library functions, you must know the types of arguments a function expects to receive and whether the function expects to receive the parameters by reference or by value. Passing an argument by reference rather than by value, or passing the incorrect data type for an argument, can cause your system to become unstable and can even result in a General Protection Fault (GPF) error.

Passing String Parameters

String parameters require special handling when being passed to DLL functions. Windows has two ways of storing strings: the BSTR and LPSTR formats. Unless you are dealing with an API call specifically involving OLE, the string you are passing to the function is stored in the LPSTR format. DLL functions that receive strings in the LPSTR format cannot change the size of the string they are passed. This means that if a DLL function is passed a small string that it must fill in with a large value, the function simply overwrites another area of memory with the extra characters. This usually results in a GPF error. The following code demonstrates this point and handles the error that is generated:

```
Sub WinSysDir()
   Dim strBuffer As String
   Dim intLength As Integer
   Dim strDirectory As String

   strBuffer = Space$(160)

   intLength = GetSystemDirectory(strBuffer, Len(strBuffer))
   strDirectory = Left(strBuffer, intLength)
   MsgBox strDirectory
End Sub
```

> **NOTE**
>
> The code here, and most of the code in this chapter, is located in CHAP31EX.MDB on your sample code CD-ROM.

Notice that the Space$ function is used to store 160 spaces in the string variable strBuffer. Actually, the Space$ function stores 160 spaces, followed by a null character in the strBuffer variable.

The GetSystemDirectory Windows API function receives two parameters:

- The buffer that it will fill with the name of the Windows System folder—in this case, strBuffer.
- The length of the buffer that will be filled—in this case, Len(strBuffer). The key here is that the length of the buffer that is passed to the GetSystemDirectory function is more than sufficient to hold the name of the Windows System folder.

The GetSystemDirectory function fills the buffer and returns the length of the string that it actually found. By looking at the left intLength number of characters in the strBuffer variable, you can determine the actual location of the Windows System folder.

The Declare statement for the GetSystemDirectory function looks like this:

```
Declare Function GetSystemDirectory _
   Lib "kernel32" _
   (ByVal lpBuffer As String, ByVal nSize As Long) _
   As Long
```

Notice the ByVal keyword that precedes the lpBuffer parameter. Because the ByVal keyword is used, Visual Basic converts the string from BSTR to LPSTR format by adding a null terminator to the end of the string before passing it to the DLL function. If the ByVal keyword is omitted, Visual Basic passes a pointer to the function where the string is located in memory. This can cause serious problems.

> **WARNING**
>
> Windows API calls are fraught with potential danger. To reduce the chances of data loss or database corruption, always save your work before testing a procedure containing an external function call. If the Access application terminates, at least you won't lose your work. In addition, always make sure that your database is backed up. If the Access application terminates and your database is not closed properly, you risk the chance of damage to the database. Regularly backing up ensures that if the database becomes corrupted during testing, you can retrieve the last good version from a backup.

Aliasing a Function

When you declare a function to VBA, you are given the option to alias it. An *alias* is a substitute name that you can use to refer to a function. You might want to alias a Windows API function for several reasons:

- A DLL procedure has a name that includes an invalid character.
- A DLL procedure name is the same as a VBA keyword.
- You want to omit the *A* required by ANSI versions of the API call.
- You want to ensure that you have a unique procedure name in an Access library or application.
- You want to call a DLL procedure referenced by an ordinal number.

Reasons for aliasing an API function are discussed in more detail in the following sections.

Function Calls and Invalid Characters

It is not uncommon for a DLL procedure name to contain a character that is not allowed in VBA code. An example is a DLL procedure that begins with an underscore (_); VBA does not allow a procedure name to begin with an underscore. To use the DLL function, you must alias it, as this example shows:

```
Declare Function LOpen _
    Lib "kernel32" _
    Alias "_lopen" _
    (ByVal lpPathName As String, ByVal ReadWrite As Long) _
    As Long
```

Notice that the Windows API function _lopen begins with an underscore. The function is aliased as Lopen for use in the Access application.

DLL Functions with Duplicate Names

The DLL procedure name you want to use might share the same name as a VBA function. You can resolve this conflict only by aliasing the DLL function. The following code aliases a DLL function:

```
Declare Function GetObjectAPI _
    Lib "gdi32" _
    Alias "GetObject" _
    (ByVal hObject As Long, _
    ByVal nCount As Long, _
    lpObject As Any) As Long
```

The `GetObject` function is part of the Windows API and is a VBA function. When you alias the function, there is no confusion as to whether the API or VBA `GetObject` function is being called.

Eliminating the *A* Required by ANSI

Many API function calls have both ANSI and Unicode versions. The ANSI versions of the functions end with an *A*. You might want to call the ANSI version of a function but prefer to use the name of the function without the *A*. You can accomplish this by using an alias, as this code shows:

```
Declare Function FindWindow _
    Lib "user32" Alias "FindWindowA" _
    (ByVal lpClassName As Any, ByVal lpWindowsName As Any) As Long
```

This `Declare` statement creates an alias of `FindWindow` for the ANSI function `FindWindowA`.

> **NOTE**
>
> *Unicode* is a standard developed by the *International Standards Organization* (ISO). It was developed to overcome the 256-character limit imposed by the ANSI character standard. The ANSI standard uses only one byte to represent a character, limiting the number of characters to 256. This standard uses two bytes to represent a character, allowing up to 65,536 characters to be represented. Access uses Unicode for string manipulation, which can lead to problems with DLL calls. To overcome this problem, you always should call the ANSI version of the API function (the version of the function that ends with an *A*).

Unique Procedure Names in an Access Library or Module

Sometimes you simply want to ensure that a procedure name in a library you are creating is unique, or you might want to ensure that the code you are writing will not conflict with any libraries you are using. Unless you use the `Private` keyword to declare each procedure, external function declarations are global throughout Access's memory space. This can lead to potential conflicts, because Access does not allow multiple declarations of the same external routine. For this reason, you might want to place a unique identifier, such as your initials, at the beginning or end of the function declaration, as in this example:

```
Declare Function ABGetWindowsDirectory Lib "kernel32" _
Alias "GetWindowsDirectory" _
(ByVal lpBuffer As String, ByVal nSize As Long) As Long
```

This statement declares the Windows API function `GetWindowsDirectory` in the library kernel32. The function is aliased as `ABGetWindowsDirectory`. This function was aliased in order to differentiate it from other calls to the `GetWindowsDirectory` function that might share this procedure's scope.

Calling Functions Referenced with Ordinal Numbers

Every DLL procedure can be referenced by an ordinal number in addition to its name. In fact, some DLLs use only ordinal numbers and do not use procedure names at all, requiring you to use ordinal numbers when declaring the procedures. When you declare a function referenced by an ordinal number, you should declare the function with the `Alias` keyword, as in this example:

```
Declare Function GetAppSettings _
    Lib "Utilities" _
    Alias "#47" () As Long
```

This code declares a function with an ordinal number 47 in the library called Utilities. It now can be referred to as `GetAppSettings` whenever it is called in VBA code.

Working with Constants and Types

Some DLLs require the use of constants or user-defined types, otherwise known as *structures* or *parameters*. You must place these in the General Declarations section of your module, along with the `Declare` statements you have defined.

Working with Constants

Constants are used by many of the API functions. They provide you with an English-like way of sending required values to an API function. The constant is used as an alias for a specific value. Here's an example:

```
Global Const SM_CXSCREEN = 0
Global Const SM_CYSCREEN = 1
```

The constant declarations and function declarations are placed in the General Declarations section of a module. When the `GetSystemMetrics` function is called, the `SM_CXSCREEN` and `SM_CYSCREEN` constants are passed as arguments to the function:

```
Sub GetScreenInfo()
   MsgBox "Screen Resolution is : " & _
      GetSystemMetrics(SM_CXSCREEN) & _
```

843

```
      " By " & _
   GetSystemMetrics(SM_CYSCREEN)

End Sub
```

When the SM_CXSCREEN constant is passed to the GetSystemMetrics function, the horizontal screen resolution is returned; when the SM_CYSCREEN constant is passed to the function, the vertical screen resolution is returned.

Working with Types

When working with types, you first must declare the type in the General Declarations section of a module. You then can pass elements of a user-defined type, or you can pass the entire type as a single argument to the API function. The following code shows an example of a Type declaration:

```
Type OSVERSIONINFO
   dwOSVersionInfoSize As Long
   dwMajorVersion As Long
   dwMinorVersion As Long
   dwBuildNumber As Long
   dwPlatformId As Long
   strReserved As String * 128
End Type
```

The Type structure OSVERSIONINFO is declared in the General Declarations section of the module, as shown in Listing 31.1.

Listing 31.1. Declaring the Type structure OSVERSIONINFO in the General Declarations section of the module.

```
Function GetOSInfo()

   Dim OSInfo As OSVERSIONINFO
   Dim strMajorVersion As String
   Dim strMinorVersion As String
   Dim strBuildNumber As String
   Dim strPlatformId As String

   ' Set the length member before you call GetVersionEx
   OSInfo.dwOSVersionInfoSize = Len(OSInfo)
   If GetVersionEx(OSInfo) Then
       strMajorVersion = OSInfo.dwMajorVersion
       strMinorVersion = OSInfo.dwMinorVersion
       strBuildNumber = OSInfo.dwBuildNumber And &HFFFF&
       strPlatformId = OSInfo.dwPlatformId
       MsgBox "The Major Version Is:  " & strMajorVersion & Chr(13) & Chr(10) & _
              "The Minor Version Is:  " & strMinorVersion & Chr(13) & Chr(10) & _
              "The Build Number Is:  " & strBuildNumber & Chr(13) & Chr(10) & _
              "The Platform ID Is:   " & IIf(strPlatformId = 1, "Win 95", _
              "Win NT") & Chr(13) & Chr(10)
   End If
End Function
```

In this listing, the statement `Dim OSInfo As OSVERSIONIFO` creates a `Type` variable. The entire structure is passed to the `GetVersionEx` function. The `GetVersionEx` function fills in the elements of the structure with information about the operating system. This information then is retrieved and stored into variables that are displayed in a message box.

Using the Windows API Text Viewer

As you might imagine, `Declare` statements, constant declarations, and type structures can be time-consuming and difficult to add to your code modules. Fortunately, the Windows API Text Viewer, a tool that ships with the Microsoft Office Developer Edition Tools for Windows 95, helps you complete these tasks. It makes it easy for you to add `Declare` statements, types, and constants required by the Windows API function calls to your code. You can access the Windows API Text Viewer through the Windows 95 Start menu or by using a desktop shortcut. When you first launch the Windows API Text Viewer, it appears as shown in Figure 31.1. You can load a text file or a database file containing declares, types, and constants.

Figure 31.1.
The Windows API Text Viewer.

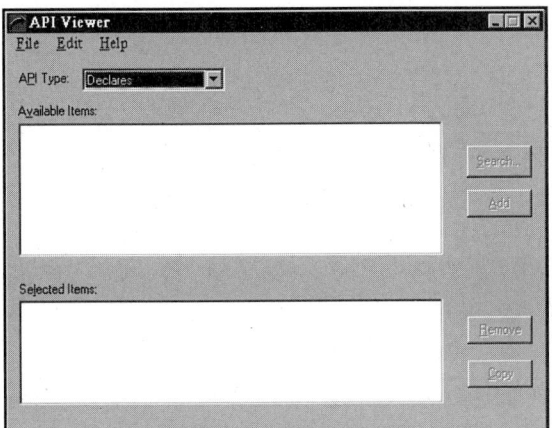

Loading a Text File

Microsoft Office Developer Edition Tools for Windows 95 ships with a file called WIN32API.TXT. You can load and browse this file so that you easily can obtain `Declare` statements, type structures, and constants. To load the WIN32API.TXT file into the Windows API Text Viewer, follow these steps:

1. Choose File | Load Text File. The Select a Text API File dialog box appears, as shown in Figure 31.2.
2. Select a text file to load into the viewer and click Open.
3. After the text file is loaded, the message shown in Figure 31.3 appears. It recommends that you convert the file to a database for better performance. If you click Yes, the Select a Name for the New Database dialog box appears, as shown in Figure 31.4.

Figure 31.2.
*The Select a Text API
File dialog box.*

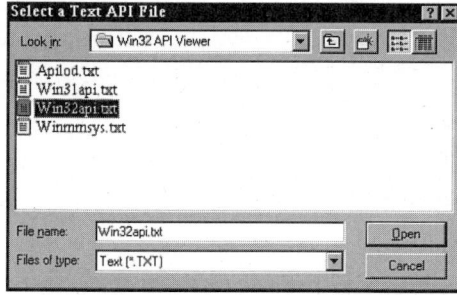

Figure 31.3.
*A message offering conversion of
a text file to an Access database.*

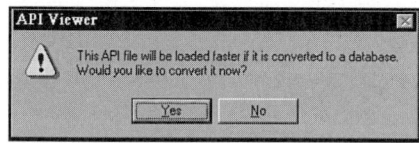

Figure 31.4.
*The Select a Name for This
New Database dialog box.*

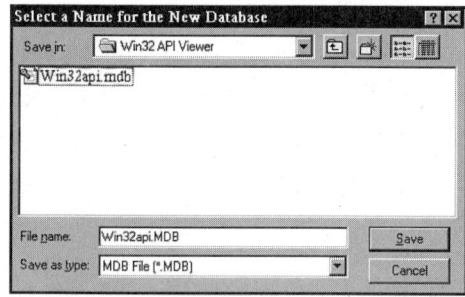

4. Select a name for the database and click Save.

Loading a Database File

After a text file is converted to a database, you should load the database each time you use the Windows API Text Viewer. To load the database file, follow these steps:

1. Choose File | Load Database File. The Select a Jet Database dialog box appears, as shown in Figure 31.5.

2. Select the database you want to load and click Open.

Figure 31.5.

You use the Select a Jet Database dialog box to specify the database you want to load into the Text Viewer.

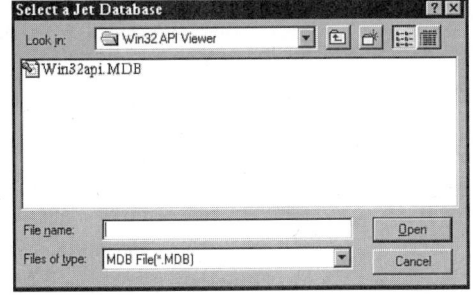

Pasting API Declares, Types, and Constants

Regardless of whether you have loaded a text or a database file, the Windows API Text Viewer appears as shown in Figure 31.6. All the declares for the 32-bit API appear in the Available Items list box. Select each `Declare` statement you want to add to your module and click Add. You can use the API Type drop-down list to view and select types or constants. In Figure 31.7, the `GetVersionEx` and `GetWindow` declares have been added to the Selected Items list. The `SM_CXSCREEN` and `SM_CYSCREEN` constants, as well as the `OSVERSIONINFO` type, also have been added.

Figure 31.6.

The Windows API Text Viewer after a file has been loaded.

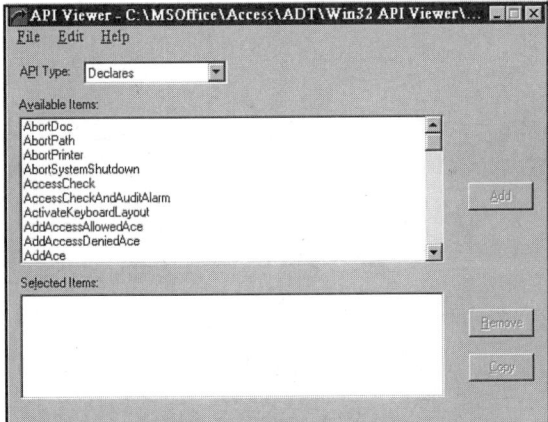

Follow these steps to add the selected items to a module:

1. In the API Text Viewer, click Copy. The selected declares, constants, and types are placed on the Windows Clipboard.

2. Place your cursor in the module where you want the selected declares, constants, and types to be placed.

3. Click Paste. The selected items are pasted into the module, as shown in Figure 31.8.

Figure 31.7.

The Windows API Text Viewer with several items in the Selected Items list.

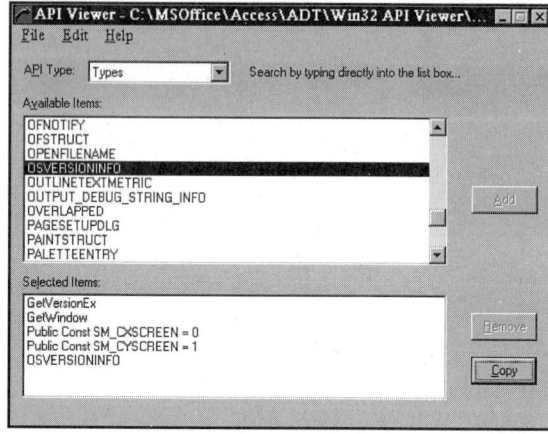

Figure 31.8.

A module after selected items are pasted into it.

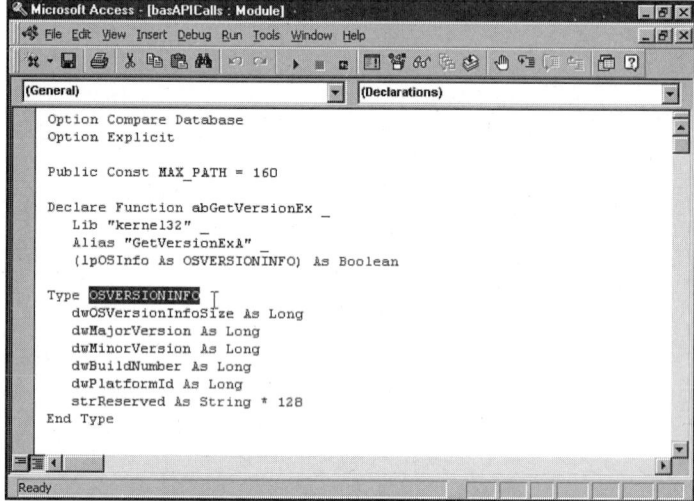

Calling DLL Functions: Important Issues

After a procedure is declared, you can call it just like any VBA function. The main issue is that you must ensure that you are passing correct values to the DLL. Otherwise, the bad call can cause your application to shut down without warning. In fact, external library calls are very tricky. You therefore should always save your work before you test the calls.

Most DLLs expect to receive standard C strings. These strings are terminated with a null character. If a DLL expects a null-terminated string, you must pass the string by value. The ByVal keyword tells VBA to pass the string as null-terminated.

Although you must pass strings by value, they actually are received by reference. The ByVal keyword simply means that the string is null-terminated. The DLL procedure actually can modify the value of the string, which can mean problems. As discussed in the "Passing String Parameters" section earlier in this chapter, if you do not preallocate space for the procedure to use, it overwrites any memory it can find, including memory currently being used by your application, another application, or even the operating system. You can avoid this problem by making the string argument long enough to accept the longest entry that you think will be placed into the parameter.

Examining the Differences Between 16-Bit and 32-Bit APIs

You might be familiar with the 16-bit API, but you need to be aware of some changes when working with the 32-bit API. These changes can cause you significant grief if you are not aware of them:

- Window handles (hWnd properties) now are *long integers* in the 32-bit API. They are *integers* in the 16-bit API.
- Function names are *not* case-sensitive in the 16-bit API. They *are* case-sensitive in the 32-bit API.
- When working with the 16-bit API, you should reboot whenever you get a GPF because it is likely that the memory of your computer is corrupted. With the 32-bit API, each program runs in its own virtual machine. It therefore often is unnecessary to reboot simply because a GPF occurs.
- Data types in the 32-bit API are exactly double what needs to be used in Visual Basic. This means that if you read C language documentation specifying that a particular API call requires a Double, you should use a Long with the Visual Basic call to the API function.

Using API Functions

The potential uses for API calls are endless. You can use API calls to modify the System menu, obtain system information, or even switch between running applications. In fact, you can accomplish so many things using API calls that entire books are devoted to the topic. The remainder of this chapter covers several of the common uses of API calls.

Getting Information about the Operating Environment

By using Windows API calls, you can get volumes of information about the system environment—including the type of hardware on which the application is running, the amount of memory that exists or is available, and the operating system version under which the application is running. This is just a sampling of the system environment information that you can get via the Windows API.

It is handy and professional to include system information in your application's Help About box. It also is important to include this system information in your error handling and logging because such information can help you diagnose problems. This is discussed in Chapter 17, "Handling Those Dreaded Runtime Errors."

Figure 31.9 shows a custom About dialog box that includes information about the system environment. This form uses several Windows API calls to get the system information displayed on the form.

Figure 31.9.

A custom About dialog box illustrating the capability to obtain system information from the Windows API.

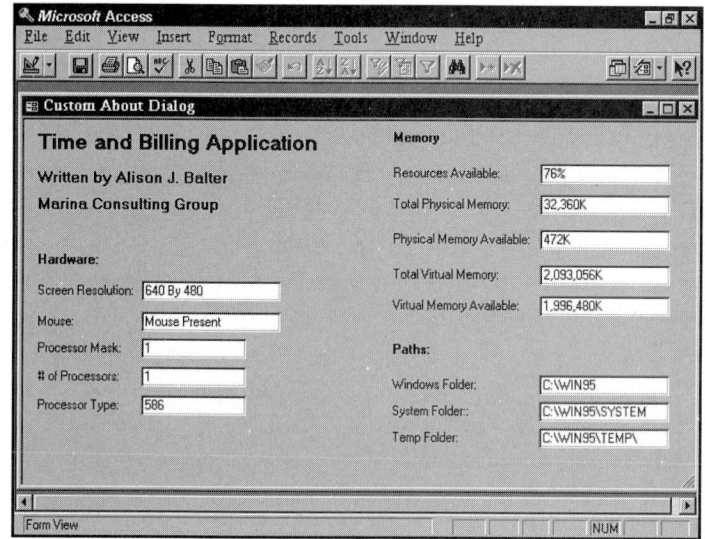

Before any of the DLL functions required to obtain this information can be called, all the functions need to be declared to the compiler. This is done in the General Declarations section of the module basUtils. Any constants and type structures used by the DLL calls also must be included in the General Declarations section. Listing 31.2 shows what the General Declarations section of basUtils looks like.

Listing 31.2. The General Declarations section of basUtils.

```
Option Compare Database
Option Explicit

Public Const MAX_PATH = 160

Declare Function abGetVersionEx _
    Lib "kernel32" _
    Alias "GetVersionExA" _
    (lpOSInfo As OSVERSIONINFO) As Boolean
```

```
Type OSVERSIONINFO
    dwOSVersionInfoSize As Long
    dwMajorVersion As Long
    dwMinorVersion As Long
    dwBuildNumber As Long
    dwPlatformId As Long
    strReserved As String * 128
End Type

'The function GetVersionEx gets information about
'the version of operating system that is currently
'running.  The information is filled into the type
'structure OSVERSIONINFO.

Const SM_CXSCREEN = 0
Const SM_CYSCREEN = 1
Const SM_MOUSEPRESENT = 19

Declare Function abGetSystemMetrics _
    Lib "user32" _
    Alias "GetSystemMetrics" _
    (ByVal nIndex As Long) As Long

'The GetSystemMetrics function uses three constants to
'determine whether a mouse is present, and to determine
'the width and height of the screen.

Type MEMORYSTATUS
    dwLength As Long
    dwMemoryLoad As Long
    dwTotalPhys As Long
    dwAvailPhys As Long
    dwTotalPageFile As Long
    dwAvailPageFile As Long
    dwTotalVirtual As Long
    dwAvailVirtual As Long
End Type

Declare Sub abGlobalMemoryStatus _
    Lib "kernel32" _
    Alias "GlobalMemoryStatus" _
    (lpBuffer As MEMORYSTATUS)

'The GlobalMemoryStatus function retrieves information
'about current available memory.  It points to a type
'structure called SYSTEM_INFO, filling in its elements
'with relevant memory information.

Type SYSTEM_INFO
    dwOemID As Long
    dwPageSize As Long
    lpMinimumApplicationAddress As Long
    lpMaximumApplicationAddress As Long
    dwActiveProcessorMask As Long
    dwNumberOrfProcessors As Long
    dwProcessorType As Long
    dwAllocationGranularity As Long
    dwReserved As Long
End Type
```

Listing 31.2. continued

```
Declare Sub abGetSystemInfo Lib "kernel32" _
    Alias "GetSystemInfo" _
    (lpSystemInfo As SYSTEM_INFO)

'The GetSystemInfo function returns information about
'the system.  It fills in the type structure SYSTEM_INFO
'with relevant information about the system.

Declare Function abGetWindowsDirectory _
    Lib "kernel32" _
    Alias "GetWindowsDirectoryA" _
    (ByVal lpBuffer As String, _
    ByVal nSize As Long) As Long

'The function GetWindowsDirectory retrieves the name of the
'directory within which Windows is running

Declare Function abGetSystemDirectory _
    Lib "kernel32" _
    Alias "GetSystemDirectoryA" _
    (ByVal lpBuffer As String, _
    ByVal nSize As Long) As Long

'The GetSystemDirectory function retrieves the name of the
'directory in which the Windows system files reside.

Declare Function abGetTempPath _
    Lib "kernel32" _
    Alias "GetTempPathA" _
    (ByVal nBufferLength As Long, _
    ByVal lpBuffer As String) As Long

'The GetTempPath function retrieves the name of the
'directory where temporary files are stored

Declare Function abGetCommandLine _
    Lib "kernel32" _
    Alias "GetCommandLineA" () _
    As String

'The GetCommandLine Function retrieves the command
'line for the current process
```

As you can see, several type structures, constants, and Declare statements are required to obtain all the information that appears on the form. When the form is opened, all the Windows API functions are called, and the text boxes on the form are filled with the system information. The Open event of the form calls a subroutine called GetSysInfo, which is shown in Listing 31.3.

Listing 31.3. The GetSysInfo subroutine.

```
Sub GetSysInfo(frmAny As Form)
    Dim intMousePresent As Integer
    Dim strBuffer As String
    Dim intLen As Integer
    Dim MS As MEMORYSTATUS
    Dim SI As SYSTEM_INFO
    Dim strCommandLine As String

    frmAny.txtScreenResolution = abGetSystemMetrics(SM_CXSCREEN) & _
    " By " & abGetSystemMetrics(SM_CYSCREEN)
    intMousePresent = CBool(abGetSystemMetrics(SM_MOUSEPRESENT))
    frmAny.txtMousePresent = IIf(intMousePresent, "Mouse Present", _
    "No Mouse Present")

    'Set the length member before you call GlobalMemoryStatus
    MS.dwLength = Len(MS)
    abGlobalMemoryStatus MS
    frmAny.txtMemoryLoad = MS.dwMemoryLoad & "%"
    frmAny.txtTotalPhysical = Format(Fix(MS.dwTotalPhys / 1024), "###,###") _
    & "K"
    frmAny.txtAvailablePhysical = Format(Fix(MS.dwAvailPhys / 1024), "###,###") _
    & "K"
    frmAny.txtTotalVirtual = Format(Fix(MS.dwTotalVirtual / 1024), "###,###") _
    & "K"
    frmAny.txtAvailableVirtual = Format(Fix(MS.dwAvailVirtual / 1024), _
    "###,###") & "K"

    abGetSystemInfo SI
    frmAny.txtProcessorMask = SI.dwActiveProcessorMask
    frmAny.txtNumberOfProcessors = SI.dwNumberOrfProcessors
    frmAny.txtProcessorType = SI.dwProcessorType


    strBuffer = Space(MAX_PATH)
    intLen = abGetWindowsDirectory(strBuffer, MAX_PATH)
    frmAny.txtWindowsDir = Left(strBuffer, intLen)

    strBuffer = Space(MAX_PATH)
    intLen = abGetSystemDirectory(strBuffer, MAX_PATH)
    frmAny.txtSystemDir = Left(strBuffer, intLen)

    strBuffer = Space(MAX_PATH)
    intLen = abGetTempPath(MAX_PATH, strBuffer)
    frmAny.txtTempDir = Left(strBuffer, intLen)

    strCommandLine = abGetCommandLine()
    frmAny.txtCommandLine = strCommandLine

End Sub
```

Now take a look at this subroutine in detail. The subroutine calls the function GetSystemMetrics. The GetSystemMetrics function is called three times. The first time, it is sent the constant SM_CXSCREEN, and the second time, it is sent the constant SM_CYSCREEN. These calls return the horizontal and vertical screen resolutions. The GetSystemMetrics function, when passed the constant SM_MOUSEPRESENT, returns a logical True or False indicating whether a mouse is present.

853

The GlobalMemoryStatus API call fills in a structure with several pieces of information regarding memory. The elements of the structure are filled with the memory load, total and available physical memory, and total and available virtual memory.

The GetSystemInfo API call also provides you with valuable system information. It fills in a structure with several technical tidbits, including the active processor mask, number of processors, and the processor type.

Next, your function calls GetWindowsDirectory, GetSystemDirectory, and GetTempPath. These three functions return the Windows folder, System folder, and temp file path, respectively. Notice that buffer space is preallocated before each call. Because each call returns the length of the folder name retrieved, you then take the characters on the left side of the buffer for the number of characters specified in the return value.

Finally, the function calls GetCommandLine. The GetCommandLine function returns the command link for the current process—in this case, Microsoft Access.

Determining Drive Types and Available Drive Space

Often, it is necessary to determine the types of drives available and the amount of space free on each drive. Fortunately, Windows API functions are available to help you to accomplish these tasks. The frmListDrives form lists the type of each drive installed on the system and the amount of free space on each drive, as shown in Figure 31.10. The declarations that are required for the APIs are shown in Listing 31.4.

Figure 31.10.

The frmListDrives form, showing the type of each drive installed on the system and the amount of free space on each drive.

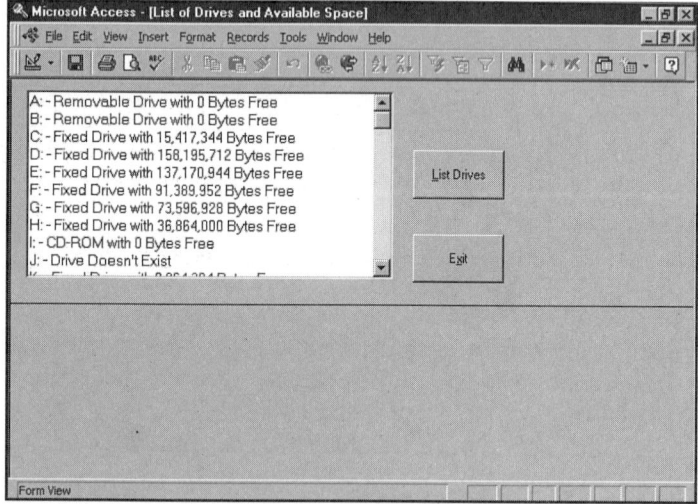

Listing 31.4. API declarations.

```
Public Const DRIVE_UNKNOWN = 0
Public Const DRIVE_UNAVAILABLE = 1
Public Const DRIVE_REMOVABLE = 2
Public Const DRIVE_FIXED = 3
Public Const DRIVE_REMOTE = 4
Public Const DRIVE_CDROM = 5
Public Const DRIVE_RAMDISK = 6

Declare Function abGetDriveType _
   Lib "kernel32" _
   Alias "GetDriveTypeA" _
   (ByVal nDrive As String) _
   As Long

'The GetDriveType Function returns an integer
'indicating the drive type

Declare Function abGetDiskFreeSpace _
   Lib "kernel32" _
   Alias "GetDiskFreeSpaceA" _
   (ByVal lpRootPathName As String, _
   lpSectorsPerCluster As Long, _
   lpBytesPerSector As Long, _
   lpNumberOfFreeClusters As Long, _
   lpTotalNumberOfClusters As Long) _
As Long

'The GetDiskFreeSpace Function determines the amount of
'free space on the active drive
```

The Click event of the cmdListDrives command button located on frmListDrives calls a subroutine called GetDriveInfo, sending it the txtDrives text box. Listing 31.5 shows the GetDriveInfo procedure.

Listing 31.5. The GetDriveInfo procedure.

```
Sub GetDriveInfo(ctlAny As Control)
   Dim intDrive As Integer
   Dim strDriveLetter As String
   Dim strDriveType As String
   Dim strSpaceFree As String

   'Loop through all drives
   For intDrive = 65 To 90 'A through Z
      strDriveLetter = (Chr(intDrive) & ":\")
      'Get Drive Type
      strDriveType = TypeOfDrive(strDriveLetter)
      'Get Space Free
      strSpaceFree = NumberOfBytesFree(strDriveLetter)
      ctlAny.Value = _
         ctlAny.Value & _
         Left(strDriveLetter, 2) & _
```

continues

Listing 31.5. continued

```
        " - " & strDriveType & _
        IIf(strDriveType <> "Drive Doesn't Exist", _
            strSpaceFree, "") & _
        vbCrLf
    Next intDrive

End Sub
```

The routine loops through all available drive letters. For each drive letter, two user-defined functions are called: TypeOfDrive and NumberOfBytesFree. Listing 31.6 shows the TypeOfDrive function.

Listing 31.6. The TypeOfDrive function.

```
Function TypeOfDrive(ByVal strDrive As String) As String
    Dim intDriveType As Integer
    Dim strDriveType As String

    intDriveType = abGetDriveType(strDrive)
    Select Case intDriveType
        Case DRIVE_UNKNOWN
            strDriveType = "Type Unknown"
        Case DRIVE_UNAVAILABLE
            strDriveType = "Drive Doesn't Exist"
        Case DRIVE_REMOVABLE
            strDriveType = "Removable Drive"
        Case DRIVE_FIXED
            strDriveType = "Fixed Drive"
        Case DRIVE_REMOTE
            strDriveType = "Network Drive"
        Case DRIVE_CDROM
            strDriveType = "CD-ROM"
        Case DRIVE_RAMDISK
            strDriveType = "RAM Disk"
    End Select
    TypeOfDrive = strDriveType
End Function
```

The TypeOfDrive function receives a drive letter as a parameter. It calls the Windows API function GetDriveType to determine the type of the drive whose drive letter was passed to the function. GetDriveType returns a numeric value that indicates the type of the specified drive. The return value is evaluated with a case statement, and text representing the drive type is returned from the function.

The NumberOfBytesFree function determines how many bytes are free on a particular drive, as shown in Listing 31.7.

Listing 31.7. The `NumberOfBytesFree` function.

```
Function NumberOfBytesFree(ByVal strDrive As String) As String
    Dim lngSectors As Long
    Dim lngBytes As Long
    Dim lngFreeClusters As Long
    Dim lngTotalClusters As Long
    Dim intErrNum As Integer

    intErrNum = abGetDiskFreeSpace(strDrive, lngSectors, _
    lngBytes, lngFreeClusters, lngTotalClusters)
    NumberOfBytesFree = " with " & _
        Format((lngBytes * lngSectors) * _
        lngFreeClusters, "#,##0") & _
        " Bytes Free"
End Function
```

This function receives a drive letter as a parameter. It then calls the `GetDiskFreeSpace` Windows API function, sending it the drive letter and several long integers. These long integers are filled in with the information required to determine the number of bytes free on the specified drive.

After the type of drive and number of bytes free are determined, the `GetDriveInfo` procedure concatenates the information with the text contained in a text box on the frmListDrives form. If the drive specified is unavailable, the amount of available disk space is not printed.

Practical Examples: Applying What You Have Learned to the Time and Billing Application

You can add some polish to the Time and Billing application by adding a custom About form to the application. You can add the form now and integrate it into the application in Chapter 37, "Distributing Your Application with ODE." The frmSystemInformation form has been added to the application, and the appropriate declares, constants, and types have been added to basWinAPI. The form and API functionality also can be added to a library so that they will be available to all applications.

Summary

External libraries, referred to as *dynamic link libraries*, open up the entire Windows API, as well as other function libraries, to your custom applications. Using external libraries, your applications can harness the power of functions written in other languages, such as C, Delphi, or Visual Basic 4.

32

CHAPTER

Database Security Made Easy

- Reviewing Your Options for Securing a Database, 860
- Implementing Share-Level Security: Establishing a Database Password, 860
- Encrypting a Database, 861
- Establishing User-Level Security, 863
- Providing an Additional Level of Security: Creating an MDE File, 877
- Looking At Special Issues, 878
- Practical Examples: Securing the Time and Billing Application, 880

Reviewing Your Options for Securing a Database

After you design and develop a sophisticated application, you should ensure that the integrity of the application and the data it maintains are not violated. Microsoft Access gives you several options for securing your database. These options range from a very simple method of applying a password to the entire database, to applying varying levels of security to each and every object in the database. The more intricate your security solution, the more difficult it is to implement. Fortunately, you can tailor the complexity of the security you implement to the level of security required by each particular application.

Implementing Share-Level Security: Establishing a Database Password

The simplest, yet least sophisticated, method of implementing security is to assign a password to the overall database. This means that every person who wants to gain access to the database must enter the same password. After a user gains access to the database, all the database's objects are available to that user. This type of security is referred to as *share-level security*.

Share-level security is the simplest and quickest security to set up. With almost no effort, the database and its objects are secured. This method of security is quite adequate for a small business where the users of the database want to ensure that no unauthorized people can obtain access to the data, but each person who *does* have access to the database has full access to all its objects.

To assign a database password, follow these steps:

1. Open the database to which you want to assign a password.
2. Choose Tools | Security | Set Database Password. The Set Database Password dialog box appears, as shown in Figure 32.1.
3. Type and verify the password and click OK. The password is case-sensitive.

Figure 32.1.
The Set Database Password dialog box.

After you assign a password to a database, users are prompted for a password each time they open the database. The Password Required dialog box appears each time the database is opened, as Figure 32.2 shows.

After users enter a valid password, they gain access to the database and all its objects. In fact, users even can remove the password by choosing Tools | Security | Unset Database Password. The Unset Database Password dialog box only requires that users know the original password. (See Figure 32.3.)

Figure 32.2.

The Password Required dialog box.

Figure 32.3.

The Unset Database Password dialog box.

This section outlines all there is to know about setting a database password. Although these passwords are extremely easy to understand and implement, they also are extremely unsophisticated. As you can see, users either have or do not have access to the database, and it is very easy for any user who has access to the database to modify or unset the password.

WARNING

If you forget the password associated with a database, there is absolutely no way that you will gain access to the database and its objects. It therefore is extremely important that you carefully maintain a list of the passwords associated with each database.

NOTE

In order to assign a password to a database, users must be able to open the database exclusively. You can grant or deny users the right to open a database exclusively by using the User and Group Permissions dialog box. Assigning rights that permit or deny users or groups exclusive open rights is covered in "Step 11: Assigning Rights to Users and Groups," later in this chapter.

Encrypting a Database

Before moving on to the more sophisticated methods of securing a database, it is important that you understand what *any* method of security does and does not provide for you. No matter how well you learn about and implement the techniques in this chapter, you will not be protected against someone attempting to read the data contained in your database. It is important that you are aware that even after you secure a database, someone with a disk editor can view the contents of the file. Although the data in the file will not appear in an easy-to-read format, the data is there and available for unauthorized individuals to see.

You might be feeling discouraged and asking yourself, "Why bother with security?" Do not despair! Fortunately, Access enables you to encrypt a database. The encryption process renders the data in the database indecipherable from data in word processors, disk utilities, and other products capable of reading text. When a database is encrypted, no one can decipher any of its data.

You can encrypt a database by using the standard Access menus or by writing a VBA subroutine. In either case, the database you are encrypting must not be open. To encrypt a database using Access's standard menus, follow these steps:

1. Make sure that no databases are open.
2. Choose Tools | Security | Encrypt/Decrypt Database.
3. Select the file you want to encrypt and click OK.
4. You are prompted for the name of the encrypted database. If you select the same name as the existing file, Access deletes the original decrypted file after it determines that the encryption process is successful.

> **NOTE**
>
> It is always a good idea to back up the original database before you begin the encryption process. This ensures that if something goes awry during the encryption process, you won't lose your data.

> **NOTE**
>
> You also can encrypt or decrypt a database file by using code. This is covered in Chapter 33, "Complex Security Issues."

When you encrypt a database, the entire database (not just the data) is encrypted. As you access the data and the objects in the database, Access needs to decrypt the objects so that users can use them and then encrypt them again when users are done accessing them. Regardless of the method of encryption you use, the encrypted database degrades performance by about 15 percent. Also, encrypted databases usually cannot be compressed by most disk-compression software utilities, because compression software usually relies on repeated patterns of data. The encryption process is so effective at removing any patterns that it renders most compression utilities ineffective. You need to decide whether this decrease in performance and the inability to compress the database file is worth the extra security that encryption provides.

Establishing User-Level Security

For most business environments, share-level security is not sufficient. Therefore, it is necessary to take a more sophisticated approach toward securing the objects in your database. User-level security enables you to grant specific rights to users and groups in a workgroup. This means that each user or group can have different permissions on the *same* object. With this method of security, each user begins by entering a user name and password. The Jet Engine validates the user name and password and determines the permissions associated with the user. Each user maintains his or her own password, which is unrelated to the passwords of the other users.

With this method of security, users belong to groups. You can assign rights at the group level, the user level, or both. Users inherit the rights of their least restrictive group. This is highlighted by the fact that security is always on. By default, all users get rights to all objects because every user is a member of the group called Users. By default, this group is given all rights to all objects. If you have not implemented security, all users are logged on as the Admin user, who is a member of the Users group and the all-powerful Admins group. The Jet Engine determines that the Admin user has no password and therefore does not display an opening logon screen. Because members of the Users and Admins groups get rights to all objects by default, it appears as though no security is in place.

With user-level security, you easily can customize and refine the rights to different objects. One set of users might be able to view, modify, add, and remove employee records, for example. Another set of users might be able to view only employee information. The last group of users might be allowed no access to the employee information, or they might be allowed access only to specific fields (such as name and address). The Access security model easily accommodates this type of scenario.

The major steps to implementing user-level security follow:

1. Use the Workgroup Administrator to establish a new system database.
2. Create a new user who will be the administrator of the database.
3. Make the user a member of the Admins group.
4. Change the logon for the group by adding an administrator password for the workgroup.
5. Remove the Admin user from the Admins group.
6. Exit and restart Access, logging on as the new system administrator.
7. Assign a password to the new system administrator.
8. Open the database you want to secure.

9. Run the Security Wizard, selecting the types of objects you want to be secured.

10. Create users and groups consisting of members of the workgroup defined by the system database.

11. Assign rights to users and groups for individual objects.

Step 1: Creating a Workgroup

The first step to establishing user-level security involves setting up a workgroup. Then you can define groups and users who belong to that workgroup and assign rights to those groups and users. Before you learn how to create groups and users, it is important for you to understand that groups and users are defined only in the context of a specific workgroup. Think of a workgroup as a group of users in a multiuser environment who share data and applications.

When you establish a new workgroup, Access creates a *workgroup information file*; this is where a unique identifier for the workgroup (called a WID), users, groups, and passwords are stored for a particular workgroup. All application databases can share the same workgroup file, or you can maintain separate workgroup files for different application databases.

Understanding the Workgroup: The System.mdw File

As mentioned in the preceding section, user and group security information is stored in a workgroup information file. The default name for this file is System.mdw. Each application database is associated with a specific workgroup information file. This combination of the information stored in the workgroup information file and the information stored in the database grants or denies individual users access to the database or to the objects in it. Multiple databases can share the same workgroup information file. The workgroup information file contains the following elements:

- The name of each user and group
- The list of users who make up each group
- The encrypted logon password for each user who is defined as part of the workgroup
- Each user's and group's unique *security identifiers* (SIDs)

An SID is a machine-generated binary string that uniquely identifies each user or group. The system database contains the names and SIDs of the groups and users who are members of that particular workgroup and, therefore, share a system database.

Actually, you can create many workgroup information files. The name of the workgroup information file currently being used is stored in the Windows Registry. You can view it under HKEY_LOCAL_MACHINE in the key called \HKEY_LOCAL_MACHINE\SOFTWARE\ Microsoft\Office\8.0\Access\Jet\3.5\Engines\.

Establishing a Workgroup

To establish a new workgroup, you must use the Workgroup Administrator. The Workgroup Administrator is a separate program that you execute outside of Microsoft Access. Under Windows NT 3.5*x*, you can access the Workgroup Administrator by clicking the Microsoft Access Workgroup Administrator icon in the Microsoft Access program group. Under Windows 95 and Windows NT 4.0, you must choose Run from the Start menu and browse to find the Wrkgadm.exe file. Of course, you can add a desktop shortcut to execute this file.

After you enter the Workgroup Administrator, you see the Workgroup Administrator dialog box, as shown in Figure 32.4.

From the Workgroup Administrator dialog box, you can create a new workgroup, or you can join one of the existing workgroups. If you click Create, you see the Workgroup Owner Information dialog box shown in Figure 32.5.

Figure 32.4.

The Workgroup Administrator.

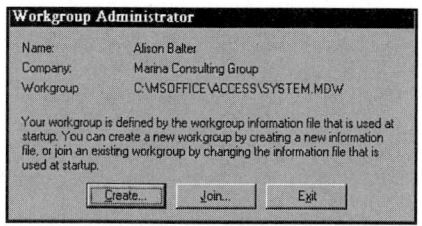

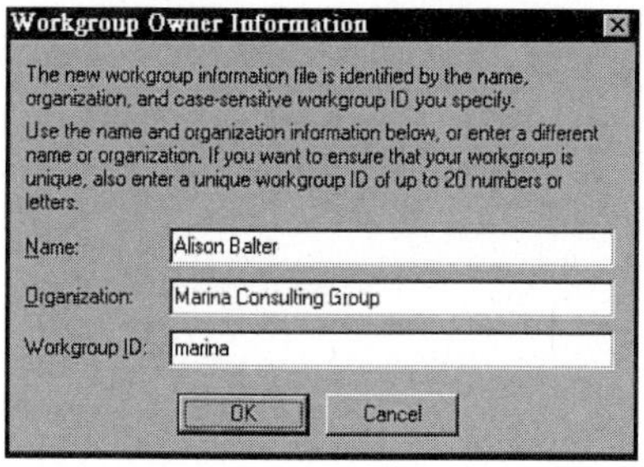

Figure 32.5.

The Workgroup Owner Information dialog box.

In the Workgroup Owner Information dialog box, you can enter a name, an organization, and a case-sensitive workgroup ID that will be used to uniquely identify the workgroup to the system. If you do not establish a unique workgroup ID, your database is not secure. As you will see, anyone can find out your name and organization. If you do not establish a workgroup ID, anyone can create a new system information file with your name and company, rendering any security that you implement totally futile.

It is important that you record and store all workgroup information in a very safe place, so that you can re-create it in the case of an emergency. After entering the workgroup owner information, click OK. The Workgroup Information File dialog box appears, prompting you for the name and location of the workgroup information file, as shown in Figure 32.6.

The Workgroup Information File dialog box enables you to enter the name and location of the workgroup file. After you type the name of a new workgroup file and click OK, you are asked to confirm the information, as shown in Figure 32.7. You are given one final opportunity to change any of the information. Click OK to confirm the information. Next, you are notified that the workgroup has been created successfully. You then can click Exit to close the workgroup administrator.

Figure 32.6.

The Workgroup Information File dialog box.

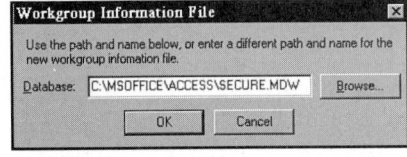

Figure 32.7.

The Confirm Workgroup Information dialog box.

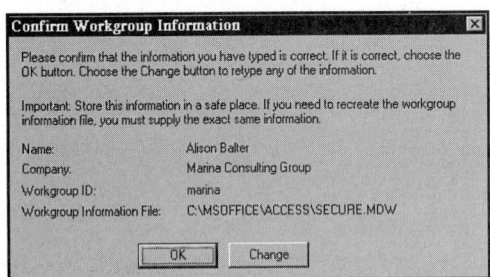

Joining a Different Workgroup

If different groups of users in your organization work with entirely different applications, you might find it appropriate to create multiple workgroup information files. In order to access a database that has been secured properly with a specific workgroup information file, the database must be accessed while the user is a member of that workgroup. If the same user requires access to more than one database, each associated with a different workgroup information file, it might be necessary for the user to join a different workgroup. This can be accomplished by using the Workgroup Administrator. To join a different workgroup, follow these steps:

1. Launch the Workgroup Administrator.

2. Click the Join button. The Workgroup Information File dialog box appears.

3. Locate the name of the workgroup file you want to join. You can click the Browse button to help you locate the workgroup file.

4. Click OK. You are notified that you successfully joined the workgroup, as Figure 32.8 shows.

Figure 32.8.
Confirmation that a workgroup was joined successfully.

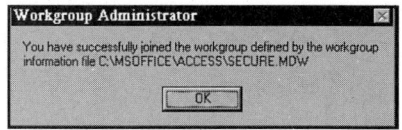

Step 2: Creating an Administrative User

After you join a workgroup, you are ready to create users and groups. You accomplish this from within Microsoft Access. Access comes with two predefined groups: the Admins group and the Users group. The Admins group is the System Administrator's group account. This group automatically contains a member called Admin. Members of this group have the irrevocable power to modify user and group memberships and to clear user passwords, so anyone who is a member of the Admins group is all-powerful within your system. The Admins group must contain at least one member at all times.

It is extremely important to create a unique workgroup ID from the Workgroup Administrator. Otherwise, members of other workgroups can create their own workgroup files and grant themselves permissions to your database's objects. Furthermore, it is important to ensure that the Admin user does not own any objects and is not given any explicit permissions. Because the Admin user is the same across all workgroups, all objects that Admin owns or has permissions to are available to anyone using another copy of Microsoft Access or Visual Basic.

The system also comes with a predefined Users group. This is the default group composed of all user accounts. All users automatically are added to the Users group and cannot be removed from this group. The Users group automatically gets all permissions to all objects. As with the Admin user, the Users group is the same across all workgroups. It therefore is extremely important that you take steps to remove all rights from the User's group, thereby ensuring that the objects in the database are secured properly.

The first step in this process is to create a new user who will be the Administrator for the database. To accomplish this, choose Tools | Security | User and Group Accounts. It does not matter which database you are in when you do this; it is only important that you are a member of the proper workgroup. Remember that you are defining users and groups for the workgroup—not for the database. The User and Group Accounts dialog box appears, as shown in Figure 32.9.

Figure 32.9.

The User and Group Accounts dialog box.

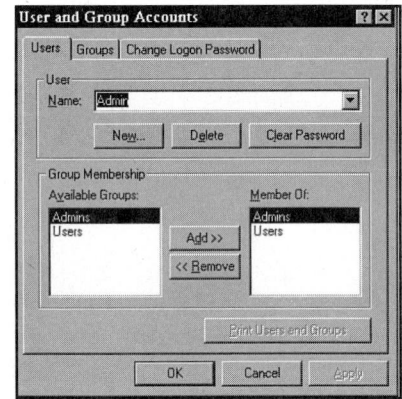

The User and Group Accounts dialog box enables you to create and delete users and assign their group memberships. It also enables you to create and delete groups and invoke a logon password for Microsoft Access. It is important to understand that even if you access this dialog box from a specific database, you are setting up users and groups for the *entire* workgroup. This means that if you assign a password while you are a member of the standard SYSTEM.MDW workgroup, and others on your network share the same system workgroup file, you will be extremely surprised when everyone on your network is prompted with a logon dialog box when they attempt to launch Microsoft Access. If you do not want this to occur, you must create a new system workgroup file before establishing security.

When you are sure that you are a member of the correct workgroup and are viewing the User and Group Accounts dialog box, you are ready to create a new user who will administrate your database. To establish a new administrative user, click New. The New User/Group dialog box appears, as shown in Figure 32.10.

Figure 32.10.

The New User/Group dialog box.

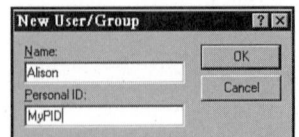

32

The New User/Group dialog box enables you to enter the user name and a unique personal ID. This personal ID is not a password. The user name and personal ID combine to become the encrypted SID that uniquely identifies the user to the system. Users create their own password when they log onto the system.

Step 3: Making the Administrative User a Member of the Admins Group

The next step is to make the new user a member of the Admins group. To do this, select the Admins group from the Available Groups list box, and then click Add with the new user selected in the Name drop-down list box. The new user should appear as a member of the Admins group, as shown in Figure 32.11.

Figure 32.11.
Adding the new user to the Admins group.

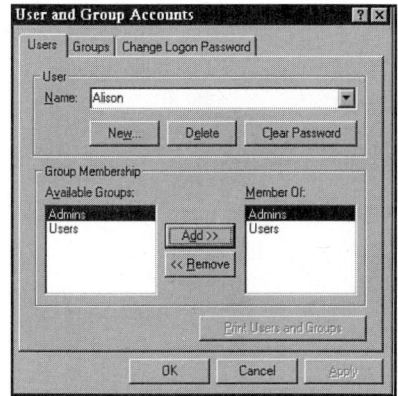

Step 4: Changing the Password for the Admin User

After creating the new user and making him or her a member of the Admins group, you are ready to change the logon for the workgroup by adding a password for the Admin user. This is necessary so that Access will prompt you with a Logon dialog box when you launch the product. If Admin has no password, the Logon dialog box never appears. Without a Logon dialog box, you will never be able to log on as the new user you just defined.

To change the password for the Admin user, click on the Change Logon Password tab of the User and Group Accounts dialog box to select it, as shown in Figure 32.12.

Assign a new password and verify it. (There is no old password unless you think of the old password as blank.) Then click Apply to establish a password for the Admin user. You cannot establish a password for the new user you just defined until you log on as that user.

Figure 32.12.

The Change Logon
Password tab.

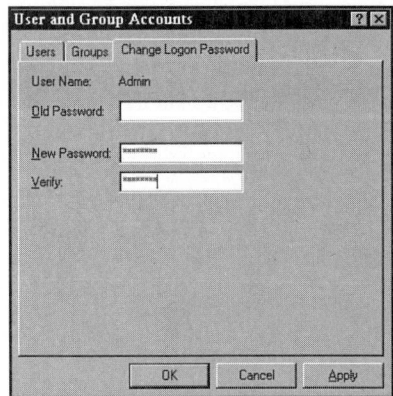

Step 5: Removing the Admin User from the Admins Group

Before you exit and reload Access, you should remove Admin from the Admins group. Remember that the Admin user is the same in *every* workgroup. Because the Admins group has all rights to all objects in the database (including the right to assign and remove permissions to other users and objects), if you do not remove Admin from the Admins group, your database will not be secure. To remove the Admin user from the Admins group, follow these steps:

1. Click to select the Users tab.

2. Select the Admin user from the Name drop-down list box.

3. Select Admins from the Member Of list box.

4. Click Remove. The User and Group Accounts dialog box now looks similar to the dialog box shown in Figure 32.13.

Figure 32.13.

Removing Admin from the
Admins group.

Step 6: Exiting Access and Logging On as the System Administrator

You now are ready to close the User and Group Accounts dialog box and exit Access. Click OK. Exit Access and attempt to run it again. You are prompted with the Access Logon dialog box shown in Figure 32.14.

Figure 32.14.

The Access Logon dialog box.

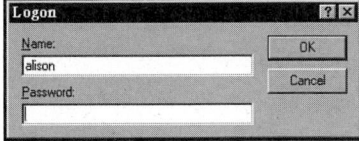

Log on as the new system administrator. You do not have a password at this point; only the Admin user has a password. At this point, it still does not matter which database is open.

Step 7: Assigning a Password to the System Administrator

After you log on as the new Administrator, you first should modify your password. Choose Tools | Security | User and Group Accounts. Click on the Change Logon Password tab. Remember that you can assign a password only for the user who you are logged on as.

Step 8: Opening the Database You Want to Secure

After all this work, you finally are ready to actually secure the database. Up to this point, it did not matter which database you had open. Everything you have done so far has applied to the workgroup rather than to a particular database. Open the database you want to secure. At the moment, the Admin user owns the database, and members of the Users group have rights to all objects in the database.

Step 9: Running the Security Wizard

The first thing you should do to secure the database is use the Security Wizard. The Security Wizard revokes the rights from all users and groups except for the user who currently is logged on. This wizard also creates a copy of the database in which the ownership of the database and all its objects are transferred to the user who is currently logged on.

To run the Security Wizard, choose Tools | Security | User Level Security Wizard. The Security Wizard dialog box appears, as shown in Figure 32.15.

In the Security Wizard dialog box, you select the objects you want to secure. Notice that you can secure all objects, or you can opt to secure just tables, queries, forms, reports, macros, or modules. After you click OK, the Destination Database dialog box appears, where you enter the name of the secured database, as shown in Figure 32.16. The owner of a database cannot be changed. The owner of a database *always* has rights to everything in the database. Because Admin is the owner of the database and Admin is the same in all workgroups, Access must copy all the database objects to a new, secure database owned by the new user. Access in no way modifies the existing, unsecured database. Type a name for the new secure database and click Save. Access creates the new database, copies all the objects to the new database, and removes all rights from all objects for the Users group in the new database. When the process is completed, the dialog box shown in Figure 32.17 appears.

Figure 32.15.

The Security Wizard dialog box.

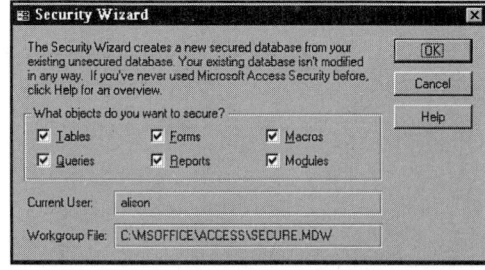

Figure 32.16.

The Destination Database dialog box.

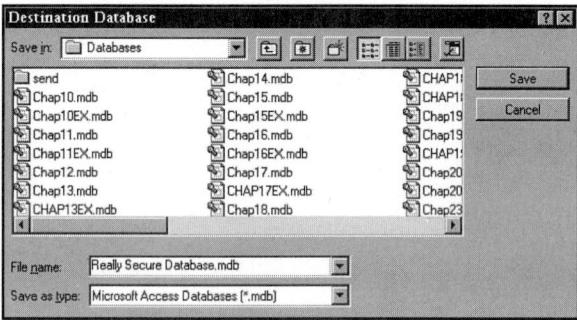

Figure 32.17.

A successfully completed Security Wizard process.

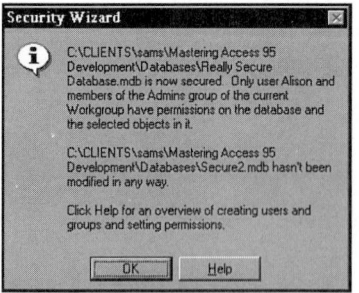

The Security Wizard dialog box warns you that the new database has been secured and that the original database has not been modified in any way. The new database is owned by the new System Administrator. All rights have been revoked from the Users group.

Step 10: Creating Users and Groups

After you establish and join a workgroup, you are ready to establish the users and groups who will be members of the workgroup. Users represent individual people who will access your database files. Users are members of groups. Groups are categories of users who share the same rights. Rights can be assigned at the user level or the group level. It is easier administratively to assign all rights at the group level. This involves categorizing access rights into logical groups and then assigning users to those groups.

If groups have been set up properly, the administration of the system is greatly facilitated. If the rights of a category of users need to be changed, you can change them at a group level. If a user is promoted and needs additional rights, you can make that user a member of a new group. This is much easier than trying to maintain separate rights for each user.

You can add, modify, and remove users and groups by using front-end interface tools, as well as through VBA code. This chapter covers how to maintain users and groups using the front-end interface tools. Chapter 33, "Complex Security Issues," covers how to maintain users and groups by using code.

Regardless of how you choose to define groups and users, you generally should create groups and then assign users to the appropriate groups. It is important to think through the design of the organization as well as your application before you begin the mechanical process of adding the groups and users.

Adding Groups

To add a new group, follow these steps:

1. Open the secured database and choose Tools | Security | User and Group Accounts.
2. Click the Groups tab of the User and Group Accounts dialog box.
3. Click New. The New User/Group dialog box appears.
4. Type the name of the group and enter a personal ID that uniquely identifies the group.
5. Click OK.
6. Repeat steps 3 through 5 for each group you want to add.

> **WARNING**
>
> The *personal identification* (PID) is a case-sensitive alphanumeric string that can be from four to 20 characters in length. In combination with the user or group name, the PID uniquely identifies the user or group in a workgroup. Personal identification numbers should be stored in a very safe place. In the hands of the wrong person, access to the PID can lead to a breach of security. On the other hand, if the database is damaged and an important PID is not available, the data and objects in the database will not be accessible, even to the most legitimate of users.

Adding Users

To add, delete, and modify users through the user interface, follow these steps:

1. Choose Tools | Security | User and Group Accounts.
2. Click the Users tab if it is not already selected.
3. Click New. The New User/Group dialog box appears.
4. Enter the name of the user and the personal ID associated with the user. Remember that this is not a password; instead, it combines with the user name to create a unique identifier for the user.
5. Click OK.
6. Repeat steps 3 through 5 for each user you want to define.

Assigning Users to the Appropriate Groups

Before you proceed with the final step, assigning rights to users and groups, you should make each user a member of the appropriate group. A user can be a member of as many groups as you choose, but remember that each user gets the rights of his or her most forgiving group. In other words, if a user is a member of both the Admins group and a group with read-only access to objects, the rights of the Admins group prevail. To assign each user to the appropriate groups, follow these steps:

1. Choose Tools | Security | User and Group Accounts.
2. Click the Users tab if it is not already selected.
3. From the Name drop-down list box, select the user for whom you want to create group membership.
4. Double-click the name of the group to which you want to add the user, or single-click the group and click the Add button.
5. Repeat steps 3 and 4 for each user to whom you want to assign group membership.

Figure 32.18 shows a user named Dan who has been added to the Managers group.

> **NOTE**
>
> Remember that the users and groups you create are for the workgroup as a whole—not just for a specific database.

Figure 32.18.

Assigning a user to the appropriate group.

Step 11: Assigning Rights to Users and Groups

So far, you have created groups and users, but you haven't given any of your groups or users rights to objects in the database. The key is to assign specific rights to each group, and then to make sure that all users are members of the appropriate groups. After that, you can assign each group specific permissions to the objects in your database. User and group information is maintained in the system database; permissions for objects are stored in system tables in the application database (MDB) file. After you establish a workgroup of users and groups, you must assign rights to specific objects in your database by following these steps:

1. Make sure that the database containing the objects you want to secure is open.

2. Choose Tools | Security | User and Group Permissions. The dialog box shown in Figure 32.19 appears. Notice that as you click on each user in the User/Group Name box, you see that only the Administrator has rights to any objects. If you select the Groups radio button, you see that only the Admins group has any rights.

Figure 32.19.

The User and Group Permissions dialog box.

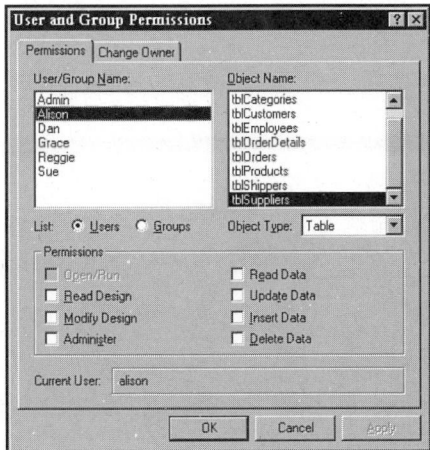

3. To assign rights to a group, select the Groups radio button. All the available groups appear in the User/Group Name box.

4. From the Object Type drop-down list, select the type of object you want to secure.

5. From the Object Name list box, select the names of the objects to which you want to assign rights. You can select multiple objects by pressing the Ctrl and Shift keys while you click the objects.

6. Enable the appropriate Permissions checkboxes to select permissions for the objects. The types of available permissions are listed in Table 32.1.

7. Repeat steps 4 through 6 for all objects to which you want to assign rights.

> **NOTE**
>
> It is recommended that you assign groups the rights to objects and then simply make users members of the appropriate groups. Notice that you can use the Object Type drop-down list to view the various types of objects that make up your database.

In order to assign permissions appropriately, it is important that you understand the types of permissions that are available in addition to what each type of permission allows the user to do.

Table 32.1. Assigning permissions.

Permission	Allows User To
Open/Run	Open a database, form, or report; or run a macro.
Open Exclusive	Open a database with exclusive access.
Read Design	View tables, queries, forms, reports, macros, and modules in Design view.
Modify Design	View and change the design of tables, queries, forms, reports, macros, and modules.
Administer	Set the database password, replicate the database, and change startup properties (when the user has administer permission of a database). Have full access to the object and its data (when the user has administer permission of a database object—such as a table, query, form, report, macro, or module). Assign permissions for that object to other users (when the user has administer permissions for an object).
Read Data	View the data in a table or query.
Update Data	View and modify table or query data. Cannot insert and delete records, however.
Insert Data	Add records to a table or query.
Delete Data	Delete records from a table or query.

Some of these permissions implicitly include associated permissions. A user cannot update data in a table if he or she does not have the rights to read the data and the design of the table in which that data is located, for example.

Providing an Additional Level of Security: Creating an MDE File

Access 97 offers an additional level of security through the creation of an MDE file. An *MDE file* is a database file with all editable source code removed. This means that all the source code behind the forms, reports, and modules contained in the database is eliminated. An MDE file offers additional security because the forms, reports, and modules in an MDE file cannot be modified. Other benefits of an MDE file include a reduced size and optimized memory usage. To create an MDE file, follow these steps:

1. Open the database on which the MDE file will be based.
2. Choose Tools | Database Utilities | Make MDE File. The Save MDE As dialog box appears.
3. Select a name for the MDE and click OK.

Before you dive into MDEs, it is important that you are aware of the restrictions they impose. If you plan ahead, these restrictions probably will not cause you too many problems. On the other hand, if you enter the world of MDEs unaware, they can cause you much grief. You should consider these restrictions:

- The design of the forms, reports, and modules in an MDE file cannot be viewed or modified. In fact, new forms, reports, and modules cannot be added to an MDE. It therefore is important to keep the original database when you create an MDE file. This is where you will make changes to existing forms, reports, and modules and add new forms, reports, and modules. When you are done, you simply rebuild the MDE.

- Because you must rebuild the MDE every time changes are made to the application, the front-end/back-end approach is best when dealing with MDE files. This means that the tables are contained in a standard Access database and the other objects are stored in the MDE file. You therefore can rebuild the MDE without worrying about the reconciliation of data.

- You cannot import or export forms, reports, or modules to or from an MDE.

- You cannot change code by using properties or methods of the Access or VBA object models, because MDEs contain no code.

- You cannot change the database's VBA project name.

- You cannot convert an MDE to future versions of Access. It will be necessary to convert the original database and then rebuild the MDE file with the new version.

- You cannot add or remove references to object libraries and databases from an MDE file. Also, you cannot change references to object libraries and databases.

- Every database that an MDE references must be an MDE. This means that if Database1 references Database2, which references Database3, all three databases must be stored as MDEs. You first must save Database3 as an MDE, reference it from Database2, and then save Database2 as an MDE. You then can reference Database2 from Database1, and finally save Database1 as an MDE.

- A replicated database cannot be saved as an MDE. The replication first must be removed from the database. This is accomplished by removing the replication system tables and properties from the database. The database then can be saved as an MDE, and the MDE can be replicated and distributed as a replica set. Any time changes must be made to the database, they must be made to the original database, resaved as an MDE file, and then redistributed as a new replica set.

- Any security that applies to a database will follow through to an MDE file created from it. To create an MDE from a database that already is secured, you first must join the workgroup information file associated with the database. You must have Open/ Run and Open Exclusive permissions to the database. You also must have Modify Design and Administer permissions to all tables in the database, or you must own all tables in the database. Finally, you must have Read Design permissions on all objects contained in the database.

- If you want to remove security from the database, you must remove the security from the original database and rebuild the MDE.

As long as you are aware of the restrictions associated with MDEs, they can offer you many benefits. In addition to the natural security they provide, the size and performance benefits they offer are significant.

Looking At Special Issues

Although the discussion of security so far has been quite thorough, a couple of issues surrounding the basics of security have not yet been covered. They include additional issues with passwords, understanding how security works with linked tables, understanding and working with object ownership, and printing security information. These topics are covered in this section.

Passwords

When you create a user, no password is assigned to that user. Passwords can be assigned to a user only when that user has logged onto the system. The system administrator cannot add or modify a user's password. It is important to encourage users to assign themselves a password the first time they log onto the system. By using VBA code, the users can be forced to assign themselves a password. This is covered in Chapter 33.

Although you cannot assign a password to a user or modify the user's password, you can remove a user's password. This is necessary when a user forgets his or her password. To clear a user's password, follow these steps:

1. Choose Tools | Security | User and Group Accounts.

2. From the Names drop-down list, select the user whose password you want to clear.

3. Click Clear Password to clear the user's password.

Security and Linked Tables

When you design your application with two databases (one for tables and the other for the remainder of the application objects), it is necessary for you to secure both databases. Securing only the linked tables is not sufficient!

A potential problem still exists. If a user has access to add, delete, and modify data from your application, that user can open the database containing the data tables from outside your application and modify the data without going through the forms and reports you designed. One solution to this problem is to revoke all rights from the tables. Base all forms and reports on queries that have the Run Permissions property set to Owner's. This provides users with the least opportunity to modify the data from outside your system.

Ownership

Remember that the user who creates the database is the database's owner. This user retains irrevocable rights to the database. You cannot change the owner of a database; you can change only the ownership of objects in the database. You can change the owner of the database if you have rights to its objects by creating a new database and importing all the objects from the other database. You can accomplish this by using the Security Wizard.

By default, the creator of each object in the database is its owner. To change the ownership of an object in the database, follow these steps:

1. Choose Tools | Security | User and Group Permissions.

2. Click the Change Owner tab to select it, as shown in Figure 32.20.

Figure 32.20.
Changing an object's ownership.

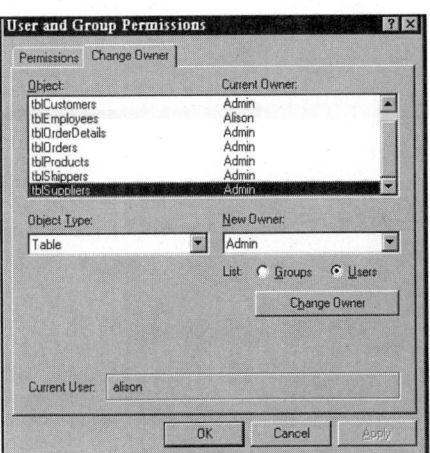

3. From the Object Type list box, select the objects whose ownership you want to change. You can press Ctrl and Shift while clicking to select multiple objects.

4. Select the Groups or Users option button.

5. Select the name of the group or user who will become the new owner of the objects.

6. Click Change Owner.

7. Repeat steps 3 through 6 for all objects for which you want to assign new ownership.

Printing Security

You can print a list of each user and the groups he or she is a member of by following these steps:

1. Choose Tools | Security | User and Group Accounts.

2. Click Print Users and Groups. The Print Security dialog box appears, as shown in Figure 32.21.

Figure 32.21.
The Print Security dialog box.

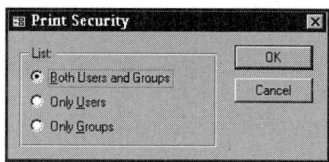

3. Select the Both Users and Groups, Only Users, or Only Groups option button.

4. Click OK.

> **NOTE**
>
> You can print the rights to different objects by using the Database Documenter. This is covered in Chapter 34, "Documenting Your System."

Practical Examples: Securing the Time and Billing Application

Now that you have learned the steps involved in properly securing an Access database, you can apply the steps to the Time and Billing application:

1. To begin, launch the Workgroup Administrator (Wrkgadm.exe). Click the Create button to create a new workgroup.

2. Call the workgroup ID TimeBillApp, as shown in Figure 32.22.

3. Call the workgroup Time.MDW. Click OK. Confirm the path to the new workgroup, as shown in Figure 32.23.

Figure 32.22.

*Entering information
for a new workgroup.*

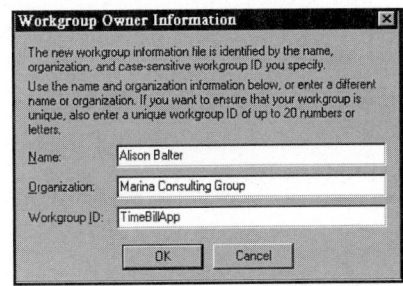

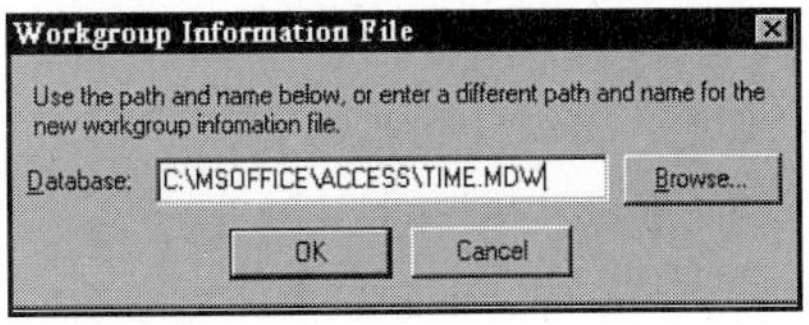

Figure 32.23.

*Specifying a name and
path for a new workgroup
information file.*

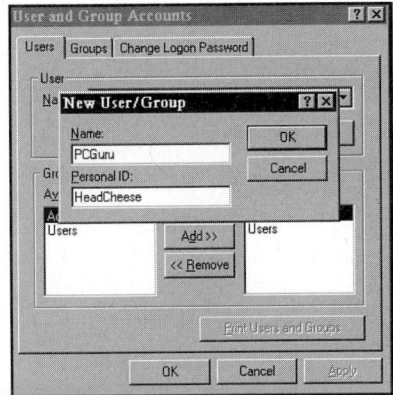

4. Exit the Workgroup Administrator and launch Access.

5. Choose Tools | Security | User and Group Accounts.

6. Click New and add a user named PCGuru. Give PCGuru a personal ID of HeadCheese, as shown in Figure 32.24.

Figure 32.24.

*Entering the name and
personal ID of a new user.*

7. Click Add >> to add PCGuru to the Admins group, as shown in Figure 32.25.

8. Click the Change Logon Password tab to select it.

9. Assign a new password of NoPower to the Admin user and click Apply.

10. Click the Users tab.

11. From the Name drop-down list, select Admin.

12. Remove Admin from the Admins group, as shown in Figure 32.26.

Figure 32.25.

Adding a user to a group.

Figure 32.26.

Removing a user from a group.

13. Exit and restart Access. Log on as PCGuru (with no password).

14. Choose Tools | Security | User and Group Accounts.

15. Click the Change Logon Password tab to select it.

16. Assign PCGuru the password of TheGuru.

17. Open the CHAP32 database. Don't forget to hold down the Shift key so that the AutoExec macro does not execute.

18. Choose Tools | Security | User-Level Security Wizard.

19. Click OK to secure all objects.

20. Select a folder location for the secured file and enter **CHAP32Secured** as the name of the database file. Click Save.

21. Hold down the Shift key and open CHAP32Secured.

22. Choose Tools | Security | User and Group Accounts.

23. Click the Groups tab to select it and add the following groups: Managers, Supervisors, and Staff. Assign any personal IDs you want.

24. Click the Users tab to select it and add the following users: Dan, Sue, Janet, Reggie, Maureen, and Paul. Assign any personal IDs you want.

25. Add Dan and Janet to the Managers group. Add Paul and Reggie to the Supervisors group. Add Sue and Maureen to the Staff group.

26. Choose Tools | Security | User and Group Permissions.

27. Select the Groups option button.

28. Select the Managers group. Assign the Managers group Update Data, Insert Data, and Delete Data permissions to the tblClients and tblProjects tables. Click the Apply button between each table. If you forget to click Apply, the dialog box shown in Figure 32.27 appears. Click Yes.

Figure 32.27.

This dialog box appears when you forget to apply rights to an object before moving to the next object.

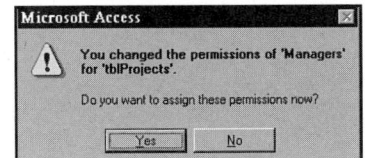

29. Select the Supervisors group. Assign the Supervisors group Update Data permissions to the tblClients and tblProjects tables.

30. Select the Staff group. Assign the Staff group Read Data rights to the tblClients and tblProjects tables.

31. Exit Access and log back on as each of the various users. Attempt to read, modify, add, and delete records from the tblClients and tblProjects tables. Ensure that security has been implemented as planned.

Don't forget that if the tables are linked, you need to go into the linked database to secure those tables.

Summary

The security system in Access 97 is quite robust but also somewhat complex. Using Access security, you can fully secure a database and all its objects. As a developer, you might want to prevent people from modifying the objects in your database. Furthermore, you might want to restrict certain users from viewing certain data, using specific forms, or running certain reports.

This chapter walked you through all the steps required to properly secure a database. It began by showing you how to set up a database password and how to encrypt a database. It then covered all the details of implementing user-level security.

Invoking user-level security first involves setting up a workgroup using the Workgroup Administrator. You then must create an administrative user and make that user a member of the Admins group. Next, you change the password for the Admin user and remove the Admin user from the Admins group. You then exit Access, log on as the System Administrator, and assign yourself a password. All these steps were covered in detail in this chapter. In addition, this chapter walked you through the process of using the Security Wizard to change the owner of the database from Admin to the new administrator and revoke all permissions from the Users group. This ensures that the database is truly secure. The final step is to assign permissions for groups and/or users to the objects that reside in your newly secured database. This chapter also covered this very powerful process.

33

Complex Security Issues

- Controlling Security Via Code, 886
- Maintaining Groups By Using Code, 886
- Maintaining Users By Using Code, 889
- Listing All Groups and Users, 894
- Working with Passwords, 896
- Assigning and Revoking Permissions to Objects By Using Code, 900
- Encrypting a Database By Using Code, 902
- Accomplishing Field-Level Security By Using Queries, 902
- Prohibiting Users from Creating Objects, 904
- Accomplishing Prohibited Tasks By Logging on as a Different User, 906
- Securing Client/Server Applications, 906
- Examining Security and Replication, 906
- Practical Examples: Applying Advanced Techniques to Your Application, 906

33

Controlling Security Via Code

You might not always be available to set up security for the users of your application. Of course, one alternative is to make sure that they purchase their own copy of Access and then to instruct them on how to maintain security using the user interface. Access security is very complex, though, so this solution is not particularly practical. In fact, if you are distributing your application to a large group of users, this option is an impossibility. Fortunately, you can build into your application code the capability to maintain all aspects of security directly. It is important that you give your administrative users the capabilities to establish and maintain security for their workgroups. This involves building a front-end interface to all the security functionality provided by Access. Behind the scenes, you can use DAO code to implement the security functionality.

Maintaining Groups By Using Code

Chapter 32, "Database Security Made Easy," discusses the importance of creating logical groups of users and then assigning rights to those groups. The administrator of your application might want to add or remove groups after you have distributed your application. You can use group data access objects to create and manage group accounts at runtime.

Adding a Group

You add a group by appending the Group object to the Groups collection. Figure 33.1 shows a form that enables users to add and remove groups.

Figure 33.1.
This form enables administrative users to add and remove groups.

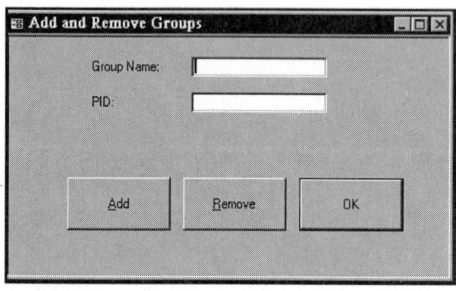

This form is called frmMaintainGroups and is included in the CHAP33EX.MDB database located on the sample code CD-ROM. Listing 33.1 shows the code behind the Add button.

Listing 33.1. Code behind the Add button.

```
Private Sub cmdAdd_Click()
    Dim fSuccess As Boolean
    If IsNull(Me!txtGroupName) Or IsNull(Me!txtPID) Then
        MsgBox "You Must Fill In Group Name and PID Before Proceeding"
```

```
        Else
            fSuccess = CreateGroups()
            If fSuccess Then
                MsgBox "Group Created Successfully"
            Else
                MsgBox "Group Not Created"
            End If
        End If
End Sub
```

This code tests to ensure that entries have been made for both the group name and PID. If so, the `CreateGroups` function is called. Based on the return value from `CreateGroups`, the user is notified as to whether the group was created successfully. Listing 33.2 uses the CreateGroup method of a workspace to add a new group to the workgroup.

Listing 33.2. The `CreateGroups` function.

```
Function CreateGroups() As Boolean

    On Error GoTo CreateGroups_Err

    Dim wrk As Workspace
    Dim grp As GROUP

    CreateGroups = True

    Set wrk = DBEngine.Workspaces(0)
    Set grp = wrk.CreateGroup(Me!txtGroupName, Me!txtPID)
    wrk.Groups.Append grp

CreateGroups_Exit:
    Set wrk = Nothing
    Set grp = Nothing
    Exit Function

CreateGroups_Err:
    MsgBox "Error # " & Err.Number & ": " & Err.Description
    CreateGroups = False
    Resume CreateGroups_Exit
End Function
```

The function uses a `Workspace` variable and a `Group` variable. The CreateGroup method of the `Workspace` object receives two parameters: the name of the group and the PID. The new group is referenced by the `Group` object variable, `grp`. The Append method, when applied to the `grp` object variable, adds a new group to the workspace. The function uses the value in `txtGroupName` as the name of the group to add and the value in `txtPID` as the PID for the group. After running this routine, you can verify that a new group has been added to the workgroup by choosing Tools | Security | User and Group Accounts. The newly created group should appear in the group drop-down list on the Group page.

Removing a Group

The code to remove a group is very similar to the code required to add a group. Listing 33.3 shows the code under the cmdRemove command button.

Listing 33.3. The cmdRemove command button code.

```
Private Sub cmdRemove_Click()
    Dim fSuccess As Boolean
    If IsNull(Me!txtGroupName) Then
        MsgBox "You Must Fill In Group Name Before Proceeding"
    Else
        fSuccess = RemoveGroups()
        If fSuccess Then
            MsgBox "Group Removed Successfully"
        Else
            MsgBox "Group Not Removed"
        End If
    End If
End Sub
```

This routine ensures that the group name has been filled in and then calls the RemoveGroups function. An appropriate message is displayed, indicating whether the group was removed successfully. Listing 33.4 shows the RemoveGroups function.

Listing 33.4. The RemoveGroups function.

```
Function RemoveGroups()
    On Error GoTo RemoveGroups_Err

    Dim wrk As Workspace

    RemoveGroups = True

    Set wrk = DBEngine.Workspaces(0)
    wrk.Groups.Delete Me!txtGroupName

RemoveGroups_Exit:
    Set wrk = Nothing
    Exit Function

RemoveGroups_Err:
    If Err.Number = 3265 Then
        MsgBox "Group Not Found"
    Else
        MsgBox "Error # " & Err.Number & ": " & Err.Description
    End If
    RemoveGroups = False
    Resume RemoveGroups_Exit

End Function
```

The `RemoveGroups` function performs the Delete method on the Groups collection of the workspace, using the value in `txtGroupName` as the name of the group to remove. If the group does not exist, an error number 3265 results. An appropriate error message appears.

Maintaining Users By Using Code

Not only might you want to maintain groups by using code, but you might also want to maintain users by using code. You can employ user data access objects to create and manage user accounts at runtime. The frmMaintainUsers form shown in Figure 33.2 illustrates this process.

Figure 33.2.
This form enables administrative users to add and remove users.

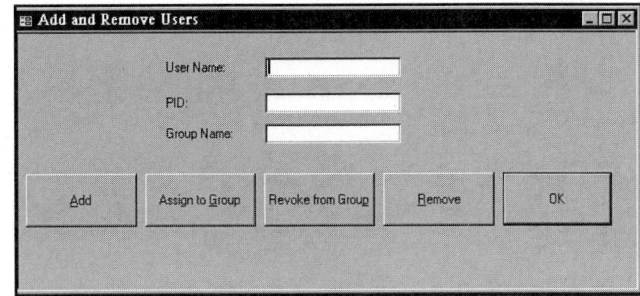

Adding Users

You add a user by appending the `User` object to the Users collection. The frmMaintainUsers form, also contained in CHAP33EX.MDB, contains a command button called cmdAddUsers that adds a user. Listing 33.5 shows the code for this.

Listing 33.5. The cmdAddUsers command button code.

```
Private Sub cmdAdd_Click()
    Dim fSuccess As Boolean
    If IsNull(Me!txtUserName) Or IsNull(Me!txtPID) Then
        MsgBox "You Must Fill In User Name and PID Before Proceeding"
    Else
        fSuccess = CreateUsers()
        If fSuccess Then
            MsgBox "User Created Successfully"
        Else
            MsgBox "User Not Created"
        End If
    End If
End Sub
```

This code checks to ensure that both the user name and PID have been filled in and then calls the `CreateUsers` function shown in Listing 33.6.

889

Listing 33.6. The `CreateUsers` function.

```
Function CreateUsers() As Boolean

    On Error GoTo CreateUsers_Err

    Dim wrk As Workspace
    Dim usr As User

    CreateUsers = True

    Set wrk = DBEngine.Workspaces(0)
    Set usr = wrk.CreateUser(Me!txtUserName, Me!txtPID)
    wrk.Users.Append usr

CreateUsers_Exit:
    Set wrk = Nothing
    Set usr = Nothing
    Exit Function

CreateUsers_Err:
    MsgBox "Error # " & Err.Number & ": " & Err.Description
    CreateUsers = False
    Resume CreateUsers_Exit
End Function
```

This routine creates Workspace and User object variables. It associates the Workspace object variable with the current workspace. It then invokes the CreateUser method to add the user to the workspace. The values in the txtUserName and txtPID are passed to the CreateUser function as arguments. The Append method then is applied to the Users collection of the workspace to add the user to the collection of users in the workspace.

Assigning Users to a Group

So far, you have added a user, but you have not given the user group membership. Next, take a look at how you can add a user to an existing group. Listing 33.7 shows the code behind the cmdAssign button on the frmMaintainUsers form.

Listing 33.7. The cmdAssign button code.

```
Private Sub cmdAssign_Click()
    Dim fSuccess As Boolean
    If IsNull(Me!txtUserName) Or IsNull(Me!txtGroupName) Then
        MsgBox "You Must Fill In User Name and Group Name Before Proceeding"
    Else
        fSuccess = AssignToGroup()
        If fSuccess Then
            MsgBox "User Successfully Assigned to Group"
        Else
            MsgBox "User Not Assigned to Group"
        End If
    End If
End Sub
```

This code ensures that both the `txtUserName` and `txtGroup` name are filled in and then calls the `AssignToGroup` function, which attempts to assign the user to the specified group. Listing 33.8 shows the `AssignToGroup` function.

Listing 33.8. The `AssignToGroup` function.

```
Function AssignToGroup()
   On Error GoTo AssignToGroup_Err

   Dim wrk As Workspace
   Dim grp As GROUP
   Dim usr As User

   AssignToGroup = True

   Set wrk = DBEngine.Workspaces(0)
   Set grp = wrk.Groups(Me!txtGroupName)
   Set usr = wrk.CreateUser(Me!txtUserName)
   grp.Users.Append usr

AssignToGroup_Exit:
   Set wrk = Nothing
   Set grp = Nothing
   Set usr = Nothing
   Exit Function

AssignToGroup_Err:
   If Err.Number = 3265 Then
      MsgBox "Group Not Found"
   Else
      MsgBox "Error # " & Err.Number & ": " & Err.Description
   End If
   AssignToGroup = False
   Resume AssignToGroup_Exit

End Function
```

This code creates three object variables: `Workspace`, `Group`, and `User`. The `Workspace` variable points to the current workspace. The `Group` variable points toward the group specified in the txtGroupName text box. The CreateUser method points the `User` object variable to the user specified in the text box. You might wonder why you should use a CreateUser method even though the user name already must exist in order for this code to run properly. This is because you must create another instance of the account before adding it to a group. Finally, the Append method is applied to the Users collection of the `Group` object to add the user to the group.

Removing Users from a Group

Just as you will want to add users to groups, you also will want to remove them from groups. The code in Listing 33.9 is located under the cmdRevoke command button on the frmMaintainUsers form.

Listing 33.9. The cmdRevoke command button code.

```
Private Sub cmdRevoke_Click()
    Dim fSuccess As Boolean
    If IsNull(Me!txtUserName) Or IsNull(Me!txtGroupName) Then
        MsgBox "You Must Fill In User Name and Group Name Before Proceeding"
    Else
        fSuccess = RevokeFromGroup()
        If fSuccess Then
            MsgBox "User Successfully Removed from Group"
        Else
            MsgBox "User Not Removed to Group"
        End If
    End If
End Sub
```

This code ensures that the name of the user and group are filled in on the form and then calls the RevokeFromGroup function, which is shown in Listing 33.10.

Listing 33.10. The RevokeFromGroup function.

```
Function RevokeFromGroup()
    On Error GoTo RevokeFromGroup_Err

    Dim wrk As Workspace
    Dim grp As GROUP

    RevokeFromGroup = True

    Set wrk = DBEngine.Workspaces(0)
    Set grp = wrk.Groups(Me!txtGroupName)
    grp.Users.Delete Me!txtUserName

RevokeFromGroup_Exit:
    Set wrk = Nothing
    Set grp = Nothing
    Exit Function

RevokeFromGroup_Err:
    If Err.Number = 3265 Then
        MsgBox "Group Not Found"
    Else
        MsgBox "Error # " & Err.Number & ": " & Err.Description
    End If
    RevokeFromGroup = False
    Resume RevokeFromGroup_Exit

End Function
```

This procedure establishes an object variable pointing to the group specified on the form. It then removes the specified user from the group by performing the Delete method on the Users collection of the group.

Removing Users

Sometimes you want to remove a user entirely. The cmdRemove command button on the frmMaintainUsers form accomplishes this task, as shown in Listing 33.11.

Listing 33.11. The cmdRemove command button code.

```
Private Sub cmdRemove_Click()
   Dim fSuccess As Boolean
   If IsNull(Me!txtUserName) Then
      MsgBox "You Must Fill In User Name Before Proceeding"
   Else
      fSuccess = RemoveUsers()
      If fSuccess Then
         MsgBox "User Removed Successfully"
      Else
         MsgBox "User Not Removed"
      End If
   End If
End Sub
```

This code needs only a user name to proceed. If a user name has been supplied, the RemoveUsers function is called, as shown in Listing 33.12.

Listing 33.12. The RemoveUsers function.

```
Function RemoveUsers()
   On Error GoTo RemoveUsers_Err

   Dim wrk As Workspace

   RemoveUsers = True

   Set wrk = DBEngine.Workspaces(0)
   wrk.Users.Delete Me!txtUserName

RemoveUsers_Exit:
   Set wrk = Nothing
   Exit Function

RemoveUsers_Err:
   If Err.Number = 3265 Then
      MsgBox "User Not Found"
   Else
      MsgBox "Error # " & Err.Number & ": " & Err.Description
   End If
   RemoveUsers = False
   Resume RemoveUsers_Exit

End Function
```

The RemoveUsers function issues the Delete method on the Users collection of the workspace. This removes the user from the workgroup.

Listing All Groups and Users

Figure 33.3 shows an enhanced version of the frmMaintainUsers form. It is called frmMaintainAll. The frmMaintainAll form, located in CHAP33EX.MDB, enables the user to add and remove users, assign users to groups, and assign passwords to users. The Groups and Users text boxes have been replaced with combo boxes so that the user can view and select from existing users and groups.

Figure 33.3.

This form enables administrative users to maintain users, groups, and passwords.

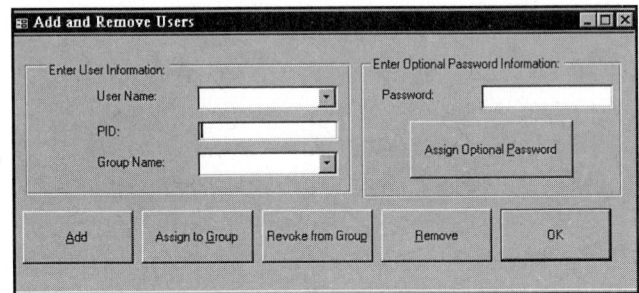

Listing All Groups

The ListGroups function is the callback function used to populate the cboGroups combo box. Callback functions are covered in detail in Chapter 13, "Let's Get More Intimate with Forms: Advanced Techniques." Listing 33.13 gathers a list of existing groups in the workgroup.

Listing 33.13. Creating a list of all groups.

```
Function ListGroups(ctl As Control, vntID As Variant, _
        lngRow As Long, lngCol As Long, intCode As Integer) _
        As Variant

    Dim wrk As Workspace
    Dim grp As GROUP
    Dim intCounter As Integer
    Static sastrGroups() As String
    Static sintNumGroups As Integer
    Dim varRetVal As Variant

    varRetVal = Null

    Select Case intCode
        Case acLBInitialize            ' Initialize.
            Set wrk = DBEngine(0)
            sintNumGroups = wrk.Groups.Count
```

```
          ReDim sastrGroups(sintNumGroups - 1)
          For Each grp In wrk.Groups
              sastrGroups(intCounter) = grp.Name
              intCounter = intCounter + 1
          Next grp
          varRetVal = sintNumGroups
      Case acLBOpen                    'Open
          varRetVal = Timer            'Generate unique ID for control.
      Case acLBGetRowCount             'Get number of rows.
          varRetVal = sintNumGroups
      Case acLBGetColumnCount          'Get number of columns.
          varRetVal = 1
      Case acLBGetColumnWidth          'Get column width.
          varRetVal = -1               '-1 forces use of default width.
      Case acLBGetValue                'Get the data.
          varRetVal = sastrGroups(lngRow)
   End Select
   ListGroups = varRetVal
End Function
```

The gist of the ListGroups function is that it uses the Count property of the Groups collection of the workspace to determine how many groups are contained in the workspace. This number is used by the callback function to designate how many rows will appear in the combo box. Notice the line For Each grp In wrk.Groups. This code loops through each group object in the Groups collection of the workspace. The Name property of the group object is added to the combo box.

Listing All Users

Listing all users is very similar to listing all groups, as Listing 33.14 shows.

Listing 33.14. Creating a list of all users.

```
Function ListUsers(ctl As Control, vntID As Variant, _
        lngRow As Long, lngCol As Long, intCode As Integer) _
        As Variant

   Dim wrk As Workspace
   Dim usr As User
   Dim intCounter As Integer
   Static sastrUsers() As String
   Static sintNumUsers As Integer
   Dim varRetVal As Variant

   varRetVal = Null

   Select Case intCode
      Case acLBInitialize            ' Initialize.
          Set wrk = DBEngine(0)
          sintNumUsers = wrk.Users.Count
```

continues

895

Listing 33.14. continued

```
        ReDim sastrUsers(sintNumUsers - 1)
        For Each usr In wrk.Users
            sastrUsers(intCounter) = usr.Name
            intCounter = intCounter + 1
        Next usr
        varRetVal = sintNumUsers
    Case acLBOpen                   'Open
        varRetVal = Timer           'Generate unique ID for control.
    Case acLBGetRowCount            'Get number of rows.
        varRetVal = sintNumUsers
    Case acLBGetColumnCount         'Get number of columns.
        varRetVal = 1
    Case acLBGetColumnWidth         'Get column width.
        varRetVal = -1              '-1 forces use of default width.
    Case acLBGetValue               'Get the data.
        varRetVal = sastrUsers(lngRow)
    End Select
    ListUsers = varRetVal
End Function
```

This code looks at the Count property of the Users collection of the Workspace object to determine how many users exist. The For Each usr In wrk.Users line loops through each user in the Users collection. The name of each user is added to an array that is used to populate the cboUsers combo box.

Working with Passwords

Many times, the administrative user needs to add, remove, or modify users' passwords. By using the user interface, you can modify only the password of the user currently logged on; by using code, however, you can modify any user's password, as long as you have administrative rights to do so.

Assigning Passwords to Users

The frmMaintainAll form enables the administrative user to assign a password to the user selected in the combo box. Listing 33.15 shows the code to assign a new password for a user.

Listing 33.15. Changing a user's password.

```
Private Sub cmdPassword_Click()
    Dim fSuccess As Boolean
    If IsNull(Me!cboUserName.Value) Then
        MsgBox "You Must Fill In User Name and Password Before Proceeding"
    Else
        fSuccess = AssignPassword()
        If fSuccess Then
            MsgBox "Password Successfully Changed"
```

```
        Else
            MsgBox "Password Not Changed"
        End If
    End If
End Sub
```

This routine ensures that a user name has been entered and then calls the `AssignPassword` function, as shown in Listing 33.16.

Listing 33.16. The `AssignPassword` function.

```
Function AssignPassword()
    On Error GoTo AssignPassword_Err

    Dim wrk As Workspace
    Dim usr As User

    AssignPassword = True

    Set wrk = DBEngine.Workspaces(0)
    wrk.Users(Me!cboUserName).NewPassword "", Nz(Me!txtPassword)

AssignPassword_Exit:
    Set wrk = Nothing
    Set usr = Nothing
    Exit Function

AssignPassword_Err:
    MsgBox "Error # " & Err.Number & ": " & Err.Description
    AssignPassword = False
    Resume AssignPassword_Exit

End Function
```

The `AssignPassword` function sets the NewPassword method of the `User` object specified in the cboUserName combo box, which is part of the Users collection. The first parameter, the old password, is left blank intentionally. Members of the Admins group can modify anyone's password but their own without having to know the old password. The second parameter, the new password, is the value entered in the txtPassword text box. The `Nz` function sets the new password to a zero-length string if the administrative user did not supply a new password.

Listing Users without Passwords

Many times, an administrative user simply wants to obtain a list of all users who do not have passwords. This list can be obtained quite easily by using VBA code and data access objects. Figure 33.4 shows the frmMaintainPasswords form, which is located in the CHAP33EX.MDB database.

Figure 33.4.

This form enables administrative users to view users without passwords.

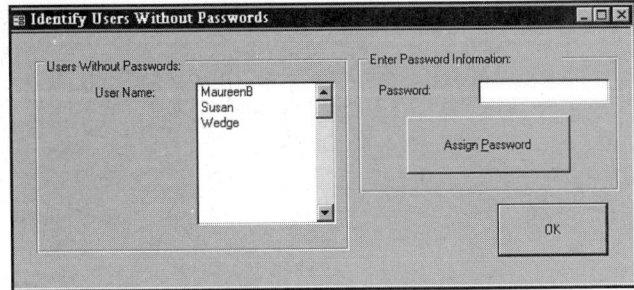

When the form is loaded, the list box uses a callback function to display a list of all users who do not have passwords. Listing 33.17 shows the code for the frmMaintainPasswords form.

Listing 33.17. Locating users without passwords.

```
Function ListUsers(ctl As Control, vntID As Variant, _
        lngRow As Long, lngCol As Long, intCode As Integer) _
        As Variant

    On Error GoTo ListUsers_Err

    Dim wrk As Workspace
    Dim wrkNew As Workspace
    Dim usr As User
    Dim intCounter As Integer
    Dim fNoPass As Boolean
    Static sastrUsers() As String
    Static sintNumUsers As Integer
    Dim varRetVal As Variant

    varRetVal = Null

    Select Case intCode
        Case acLBInitialize          ' Initialize.
            Set wrk = DBEngine(0)
            sintNumUsers = wrk.Users.Count
            ReDim sastrUsers(sintNumUsers - 1)
            For Each usr In wrk.Users
                fNoPass = True
                Set wrkNew = DBEngine.CreateWorkspace("NewWork", usr.Name, "")
                If fNoPass Then
                    sastrUsers(intCounter) = usr.Name
                    intCounter = intCounter + 1
                End If
            Next usr
            varRetVal = sintNumUsers
        Case acLBOpen                 'Open
            varRetVal = Timer         'Generate unique ID for control.
        Case acLBGetRowCount          'Get number of rows.
            varRetVal = sintNumUsers
        Case acLBGetColumnCount       'Get number of columns.
            varRetVal = 1
        Case acLBGetColumnWidth       'Get column width.
            varRetVal = -1            '-1 forces use of default width.
```

```
        Case acLBGetValue                 'Get the data.
            varRetVal = sastrUsers(lngRow)
    End Select
    ListUsers = varRetVal

ListUsers_Exit:
    Set wrk = Nothing
    Set usr = Nothing
    Exit Function

ListUsers_Err:
    If Err.Number = 3029 Then
        fNoPass = False
        Resume Next
    Else
        MsgBox "Error # " & Err.Number & ": " & Err.Description
        Resume ListUsers_Exit
    End If
End Function
```

The meat of the code is in the For...Each loop. The code loops through each user in the Users collection. It begins by setting the value of the fNoPass flag to True. It creates a new workspace and attempts to log onto the new workspace by using the Name property of the current user object and a password that is a zero-length string. If an error occurs, the error-handling code sets the fNoPass flag to False. The 3029 error means that the password was not valid, indicating that the user must have a password because the logon was not successful. If the logon was successful, the user must not have a password and therefore is added to the list box.

Ensuring That Users Have Passwords

You might want to ensure that users who log onto your application have a password. You can accomplish this by using the code shown in Listing 33.18.

Listing 33.18. Ensuring that your application's users have passwords.

```
Function AutoExec()
    Dim usr As User
    Dim strPassword As String

    Set usr = DBEngine(0).Users(CurrentUser)
    On Error Resume Next
    usr.NewPassword "", ""
    If Err.Number = 0 Then
        strPassword = InputBox("You Must Enter a Password Before Proceeding", _
                    "Enter Password")
        If strPassword = "" Then
            DoCmd.Quit
        Else
            usr.NewPassword "", strPassword
        End If
    End If
End Function
```

The `AutoExec` function can be called from the startup form of your application. It points a `User` object variable to `CurrentUser`. It accomplishes this by using the return value from the `CurrentUser` function as the user to look at in the Users collection. The `CurrentUser` function returns a string containing the name of the current user.

When an object variable is pointing at the correct user, the code attempts to set a new password for the user. When modifying the password of the current user, both the old password and the new password must be supplied to the NewPassword method. If the old password is incorrect, an error occurs. This indicates that the user has a password and nothing special needs to happen. If no error occurs, you know that no password exists, so the user is prompted for a password. If the user does not supply a password, the application quits. Otherwise, a new password is assigned to the user.

Assigning and Revoking Permissions to Objects By Using Code

Often, you will want to assign and revoke object permissions by using code. Once again, you easily can accomplish this by using DAO code. The form in Figure 33.5 is called frmTableRights and is located in the CHAP33EX.MDB database.

Figure 33.5.
This form enables administrative users to assign rights to groups.

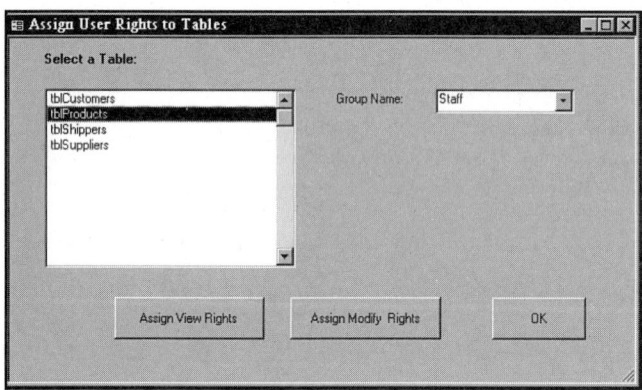

The code shown in Listing 33.19 assigns view rights for the table selected in the Select a Table list box to the group selected in the Group Name drop-down list.

Listing 33.19. Assigning view rights.

```
Private Sub cmdViewRights_Click()
    Dim db As DATABASE
    Dim doc As Document

    Set db = CurrentDb
```

```
        Set doc = db.Containers!Tables.Documents(lstTables.Value)
        doc.UserName = Me!cboGroupName.Value
        doc.Permissions = dbSecRetrieveData
End Sub
```

Notice that the code points a document variable to the table selected in the list box (lstTables.Value). The UserName property of the document is set equal to the group selected in the cboGroupName combo box. Then the Permissions property of the document is set equal to dbSecRetrieveData. The dbSecRetrieveData constant indicates that the user has rights to read the definition and data in the table. Table 33.1 lists the permission constants for queries and tables.

Table 33.1. The permission constants for queries and tables.

Permission Constant	Grants Permission To
dbSecDeleteData	Delete rows from the table or query.
dbSecInsertData	Insert new rows into the table or query.
dbSecReadDef	Read the definition of the table or query.
dbSecReplaceData	Modify table or query data.
dbSecRetrieveData	Read data stored in the table or query. Also, implicitly grants read permission to the definition of the table or query.
dbSecWriteDef	Alter the definition of the table or query.

Listing 33.20 shows an example in which the dbSecRetrieveData constant is combined with the dbSecReplaceData constant using a bitwise OR. The dbSecReplaceData constant does not imply that the user also can read the table definition and data. As you might guess, it is difficult to edit data if you cannot read it. You therefore must combine the dbSecRetrieveData constant with the dbSecReplaceData constant in order to allow the user or group to read and modify table data.

Listing 33.20. Modifying user rights.

```
Private Sub cmdModifyRights_Click()
    Dim db As DATABASE
    Dim doc As Document

    Set db = CurrentDb

    Set doc = db.Containers!Tables.Documents(lstTables.Value)
    doc.UserName = Me!cboGroupName.Value
    doc.Permissions = doc.Permissions Or _
        dbSecRetrieveData Or dbSecReplaceData
End Sub
```

Encrypting a Database By Using Code

Chapter 32 shows how you can encrypt a database by using the user interface. If a database is not encrypted, it is not really secure, because a savvy user can use a disk editor to view the data in the file. If you have distributed your application with the runtime version of Access and you want to give your user the capability to encrypt the database, you must write DAO code to accomplish the encryption process. The code looks like this:

```
Sub Encrypt(strDBNotEncrypted As String, strDBEncrypted As String)
    DBEngine.CompactDatabase strDBNotEncrypted, strDBEncrypted,_
        dbLangGeneral, dbEncrypt
End Sub
```

This subroutine receives two parameters. The first is the name of the database that you want to encrypt. The second is the name you want to assign to the encrypted database. The CompactDatabase method is issued on the Database Engine. This method receives five parameters: the name of the database to encrypt, the name for the new encrypted database, the collating order, option settings, and a database password. The last three parameters are optional. For the other option-settings parameter, you can use a constant to indicate that you want to encrypt the database.

Accomplishing Field-Level Security By Using Queries

In itself, Access does not provide field-level security. You can achieve field-level security by using queries, though. Here's how it works. You do not provide the user or group with any rights to the table that you want to secure. Instead, you give the user or group rights to a query containing only the fields that you want the user to be able to view. Ordinarily, this would not work, because if users cannot read the tables underlying a query, they cannot read the data in the query result.

The trick is in a query option called WITH OWNERACCESS OPTION. The WITH OWNERACCESS OPTION of a query grants the user running the query the rights possessed by the owner of the query. The Staff group, for example, has no rights to the tblEmployees table. The Supervisors group has Read Design and Modify permissions to the tblEmployees table. The qryEmployees query is owned by the Supervisors group, as shown in Figure 33.6. Figure 33.7 shows the query itself. Notice in Figure 33.7 that the Run Permissions property has been set to Owner's. Figure 33.8 shows the resulting SQL. Notice the WITH OWNERACCESS OPTION clause at the end of the SQL statement. When any member of the Staff group (who has no other rights to tblEmployees) runs the query, that member inherits the Supervisor group's capability to read and modify the table data.

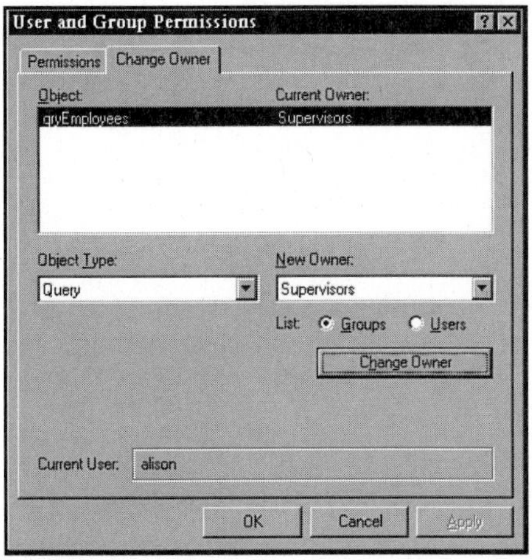

Figure 33.6.

The query owned by the Supervisors group.

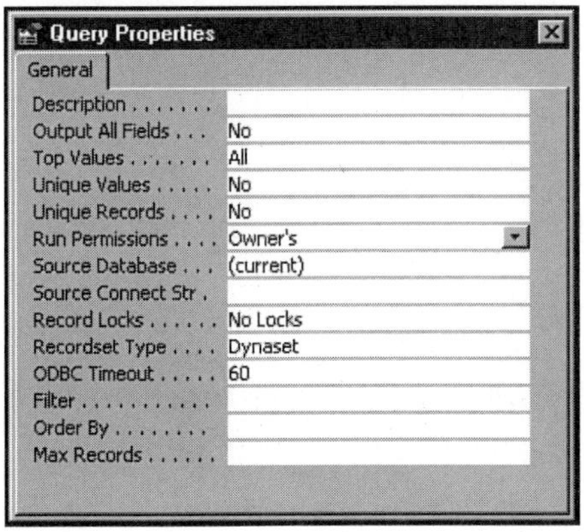

Figure 33.7.

The Design view of a query with Run Permissions set to Owners.

Figure 33.8.

*The SQL view of a query with
Run Permissions set to Owners.*

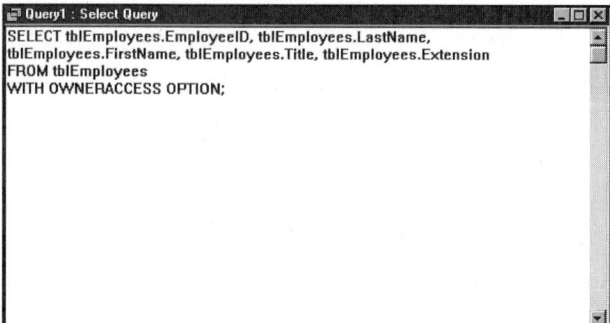

Prohibiting Users from Creating Objects

You might want to prevent the members of a workgroup from creating new databases or creating specific database objects. Preventing users from creating databases or other objects can be accomplished only by using VBA code.

Prohibiting Users from Creating Databases

By using data access objects, you can programmatically prohibit users from creating new databases. This is quite obviously a very powerful feature. Listing 33.21 shows the code you can use to accomplish this.

Listing 33.21. Prohibiting users from creating new databases.

```
Sub NoDBs(strGroupToProhibit)
   On Error GoTo NoDBs_Err
   Dim db As DATABASE
   Dim con As Container
   Dim strSystemDB As String

   'Obtain name of system file
   strSystemDB = SysCmd(acSysCmdGetWorkgroupFile)
   'Open the System Database
   Set db = DBEngine(0).OpenDatabase(strSystemDB)
   'Point to the Databases Collection
   Set con = db.Containers!Databases
   con.UserName = strGroupToProhibit
   con.Permissions = con.Permissions And Not dbSecDBCreate

NoDBs_Exit:
   Set db = Nothing
   Set con = Nothing
   Exit Sub

NoDBs_Err:
   MsgBox "Error # " & Err.Number & ": " & Err.Description
   Resume NoDBs_Exit
End Sub
```

The NoDBs routine receives the name of the user or group you will prohibit from creating databases. It opens the system database and points to the Containers collection. It then sets the permissions for the database to the existing permissions combined with Not dbSecDBCreate, thereby prohibiting the group or user from creating new databases.

Prohibiting Users from Creating Other Objects

You might not want to prohibit users from creating new databases. Instead, you might want to prevent them from creating new tables, queries, or other objects in *your* application or data database file. The code is similar to that required to prohibit users from creating new databases, as shown in Listing 33.22.

Listing 33.22. Prohibiting users or groups from creating other objects.

```
Sub NoTables(strGroupToProhibit)
    On Error GoTo NoTables_Err
    Dim db As DATABASE
    Dim con As Container
    Dim strSystemDB As String

    'Obtain name of system file
    strSystemDB = SysCmd(acSysCmdGetWorkgroupFile)
    'Point to the Current Database
    Set db = CurrentDb
    'Point to the Databases Collection
    Set con = db.Containers("Tables")
    con.UserName = strGroupToProhibit
    con.Permissions = con.Permissions And Not dbSecDBCreate

NoTables_Exit:
    Set db = Nothing
    Set con = Nothing
    Exit Sub

NoTables_Err:
    MsgBox "Error # " & Err.Number & ": " & Err.Description
    Resume NoTables_Exit

End Sub
```

The difference between this code and the code in Listing 33.21 (which prohibits users from creating new databases) is that this code points the database object variable to the current database instead of to the system database. It then points the Container object to the Tables collection. Other than these differences, the code is identical to the NoDBs routine.

Accomplishing Prohibited Tasks By Logging on as a Different User

Although you might not want particular users to be able to accomplish particular tasks, you might at times want to go "behind the scenes" and accomplish the task for them. As you saw in the preceding section, you can prohibit a user or group from creating new tables and queries. This is fine, except when you run into a situation in which your code requires that a temporary table be created. In this situation, you can temporarily log on as a different user, perform the process, and then log off.

Securing Client/Server Applications

It is important to understand that security for client/server applications must be applied on the back-end database server. You can request logon IDs and passwords from users at runtime and pass them to the database server as part of the connection string, but Access security itself does nothing in terms of interacting with client/server data. Any errors returned from the back-end must be handled by your application.

Examining Security and Replication

Database security cannot be implemented on replicated databases. Only user-level security can be implemented. All the replicas inherit the security applied to the Design Master. Replicate only the database file; never replicate the security information file (System.mdw). Instead, make sure that exactly the same security information file is available at each location where the replica is used. You can do this by copying the file to each location.

A user must have administer permission on a database in order to perform the following tasks:

- Converting a nonreplicable database into a replicable database
- Making a replica of the Design Master
- Making a local object replicable
- Making a replicable object local

Practical Examples: Applying Advanced Techniques to Your Application

The advanced techniques you build into the Time and Billing application depend on how much responsibility you want to give the application for implementing security. You might want to implement security from outside the application instead of building it directly into the application. You can add all the forms contained in CHAP33EX.MDB directly into the Time and

Billing application if you want. Also, you can add the code in the AutoExec routine (covered in the section "Ensuring That Users Have Passwords") into the Time and Billing application so that you force users running the application to assign themselves a password.

Summary

The security features available in Access are extremely rich and powerful. Being able to implement security using both code and the user interface gives you immense power and flexibility when implementing security in your application.

This chapter began by a look at maintaining users and groups using code. Next, you learned about using code to assign and maintain passwords, as well as determining whether a user has a password. You also learned about assigning and revoking permissions to objects by using code, as well as many other advanced techniques that give you full control over security in your application.

Security requires a lot of planning and forethought. You must make decisions about what groups to define and which rights you will assign to each group. Also, you must decide what features you will build into your application using VBA code. This chapter illustrated how you can build all aspects of security directly into the user interface of your application.

34

CHAPTER

Documenting Your System

- Understanding Why You Should Document, 910
- Preparing Your Application to Be Self-Documenting, 910
- Using Database Properties to Document the Overall Database, 914
- Using the Database Documenter, 916
- Writing Code to Create Your Own Documentation, 920
- Practical Examples: Applying What You Learned to the Time and Billing Application, 921

Understanding Why You Should Document

Back in the days of mainframes and very formal centralized *Management Information System* (MIS) departments, documentation was a mandatory requirement for the completion of an application. Today, it seems as though all types of people are developing applications: administrative assistants, CEOs, sales managers, MIS professionals, and so on. To make matters worse, many of us who consider ourselves MIS professionals never received any formal systems training. Finally, the demand to get an application up and running and then to move on to the next application is more prevalent than ever. As a result of all these factors, it seems that documentation has gone by the wayside.

Despite all the reasons why documentation doesn't seem to happen, it is as important to properly document your application today as it was in the mainframe days. Documentation provides you and your users with these benefits:

- It makes the system easy for you and others to maintain.
- It helps state the purpose and function of each object in the application.

Preparing Your Application to Be Self-Documenting

Fortunately, Access ships with an excellent tool to assist you with the process of documenting your database: the *Database Documenter*. Although this tool can be used without any special preparation on your part, a little bit of work as you build the components of your application can go a long way toward enhancing the value of the output supplied by the Database Documenter.

Documenting Your Tables

The Database Documenter prints all field and table descriptions entered in the design of a table. Figure 34.1 shows a table in Design view. Notice the descriptions for the ClientID and StateProvince fields. These descriptions provide additional information that is not obvious by looking at the field names. The Table Properties window also contains a Description property. This property is included in the documentation for the table when it is printed in the Database Documenter.

In addition to enhancing the output from the Database Documenter, entering a table description also assists you and the users of your database when working with the tables in the database. Figure 34.2 shows the Database window after descriptions are entered for the tables in the database. Notice that the description of each table appears in the Database window.

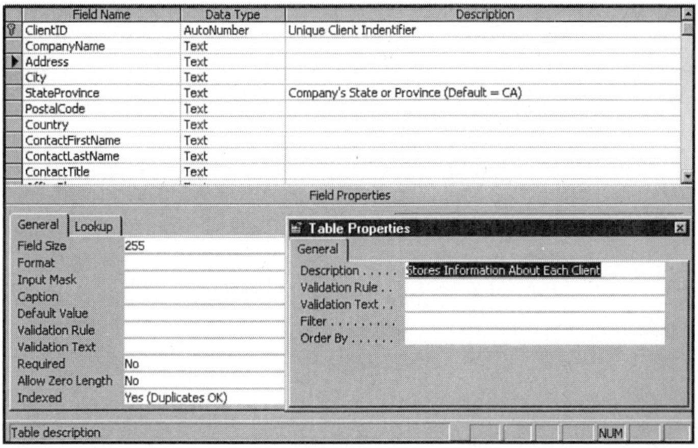

Figure 34.1.

Documenting a table by including descriptions of each field and using the Table Properties box.

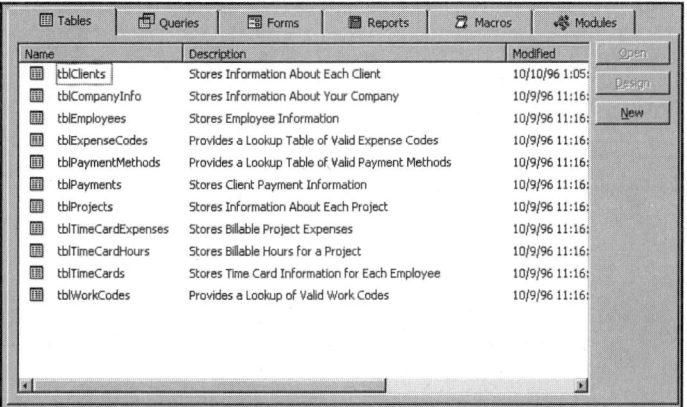

Figure 34.2.

The Database window with table descriptions.

Documenting Your Queries

Just as you can enhance the output the Database Documenter provides for tables, you also can enhance the output the Database Documenter provides for queries. Figure 34.3 shows the Query Properties window. As you can see, the Description property is filled in with a detailed description of the purpose of the query. Figure 34.3 shows the description of a query, and Figure 34.4 shows the description of an individual column in a query. Both the query and field descriptions are included in the output provided by the Database Documenter.

Figure 34.3.

Documenting a query using the Description property.

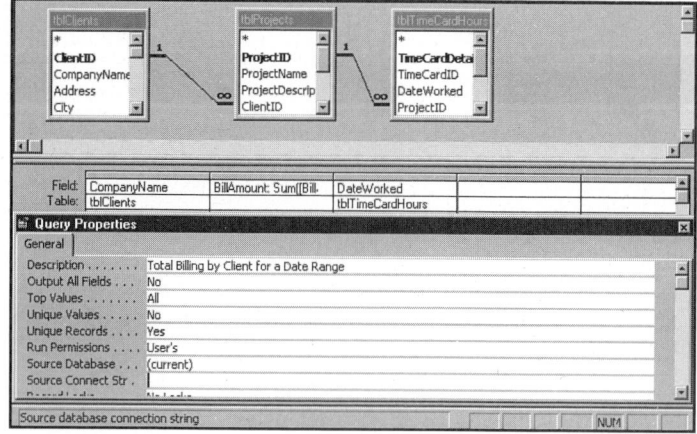

Figure 34.4.

Documenting a column in a query.

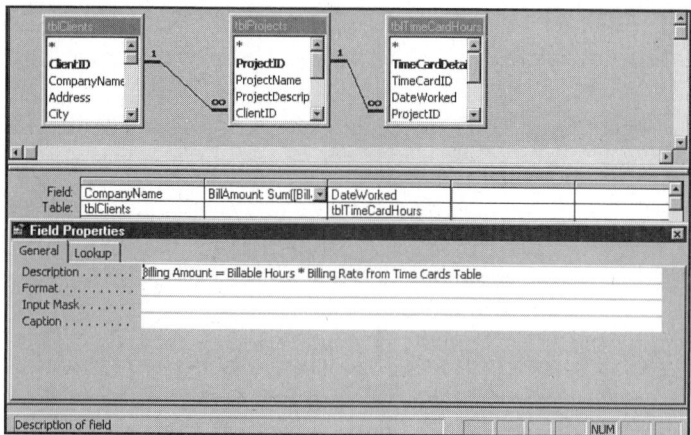

Documenting Your Forms

Documentation is not limited to table and query objects. A form has a Description property. It cannot be accessed from the Design view of the form, though. To view or modify the Description property of a form, follow these steps:

1. Make the Database window the active window.

2. Right-click on the form for which you want to add a description.

3. Choose Properties. The Object Properties dialog box appears, as shown in Figure 34.5.

4. Enter a description in the Description text box.

5. Click OK. The description you entered appears in the Database window, as shown in Figure 34.6, and it also appears in the output from the Database Documenter.

Figure 34.5.

You can use the Object Properties dialog box to document each object in the database.

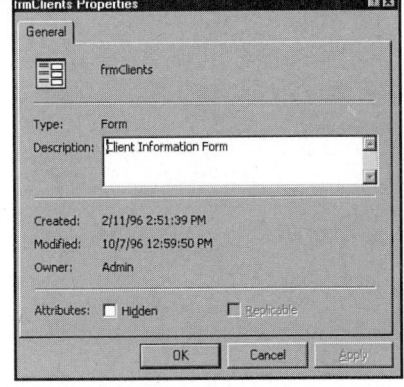

Figure 34.6.

The Database window with a description of a form.

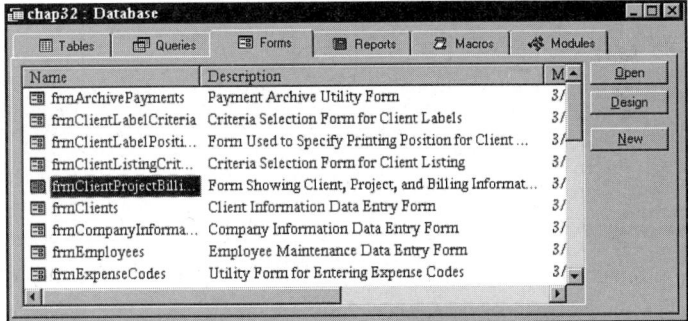

Documenting Your Reports

Reports are documented in exactly the same manner as forms. Reports have a Description property that must be entered in the Object Properties dialog box. Remember that to access this dialog box, you right-click on the object in the Database window and then choose Properties.

Documenting Your Macros

Macros can be documented in significantly more detail than forms and reports. You can document each individual line of the macro, as shown in Figure 34.7. Not only does this provide documentation in the Database Documenter, but macro comments become code comments when you convert a macro to a Visual Basic module. In addition to documenting each line of a macro, you can add a description to the macro. As with forms and reports, to accomplish this, right-click on the macro from the Database window and choose Properties.

Figure 34.7.

Documenting a macro by including a description of what each line of the macro does.

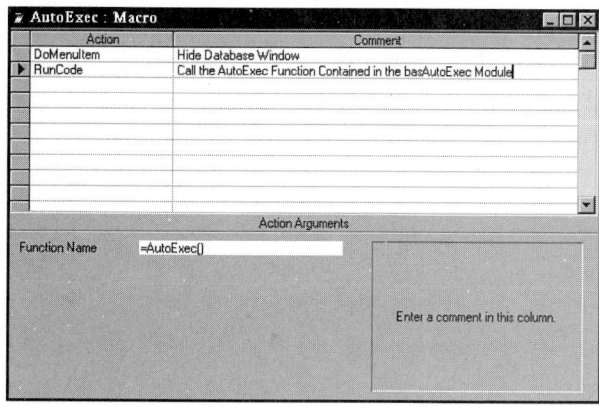

Documenting Your Modules

I cannot emphasize enough how important it is to document your modules. You accomplish this by using comments. Of course, not every line of code needs to be documented. I document all areas of my code that I feel are not self-explanatory. Comments help when I revisit the code to make modifications and enhancements. They also help anyone who is responsible for maintaining my code. Finally, comments provide the user with documentation about what my application is doing. Comments print with your code modules, as shown later in this chapter in the section "Using the Database Documenter." As with the other objects, you can right-click on a module to assign a description to it.

Using Database Properties to Document the Overall Database

In addition to enabling you to assign descriptions to the objects in the database, Microsoft Access enables you to document the database as a whole. You do this by filling in the information included in the Database Properties window. To access a database's properties, choose File | Database Properties or right-click the title bar of the Database window and choose Database Properties. The Database Properties dialog box appears, as shown in Figure 34.8. As you can see, it is a tabbed dialog box; tabs include General, Summary, Statistics, Contents, and Custom.

Descriptions of the tabs in the Database Properties dialog box follow:

- **General:** The General tab displays general information about your database. This includes the date the database was created, when it was last modified, when it was last accessed, its location, its size, its MS-DOS name, and its file attributes. None of the information on the General tab is modifiable.

Figure 34.8.

The Database Properties dialog box, showing the general properties of a database.

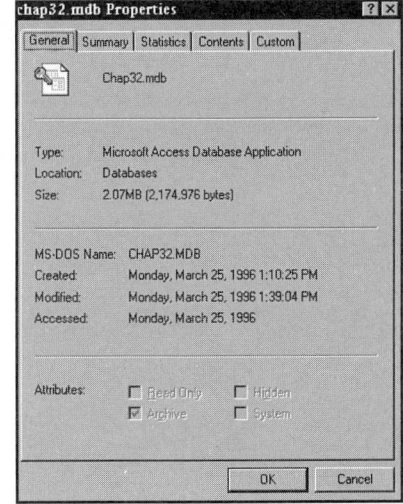

- **Summary:** The Summary tab, shown in Figure 34.9, contains modifiable information that describes the database and what it does. This tab includes the database title, its subject, and comments about the database. It also includes the *hyperlink base*—a base address used for all relative hyperlinks inserted in the database. The base address can be an Internet address (URL) or a filename path (UNC).

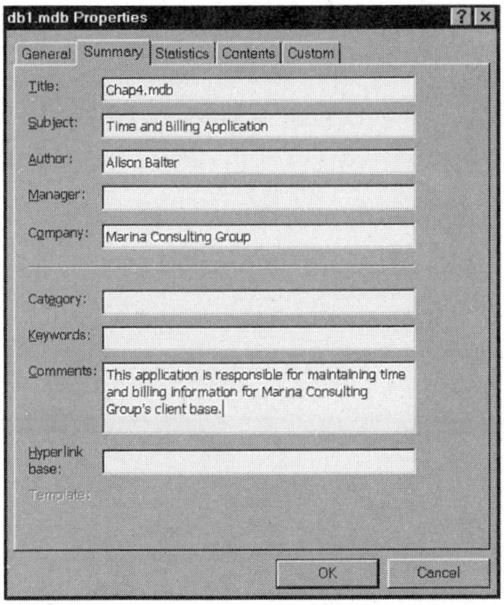

Figure 34.9.

The Summary tab of the Database Properties dialog box.

- **Statistics:** The Statistics tab contains statistics of the database, such as when it was created, last modified, and last accessed.
- **Contents:** The Contents tab, shown in Figure 34.10, includes a list of all the objects contained in the database.

34

Figure 34.10.

The Contents tab of the Database Properties dialog box.

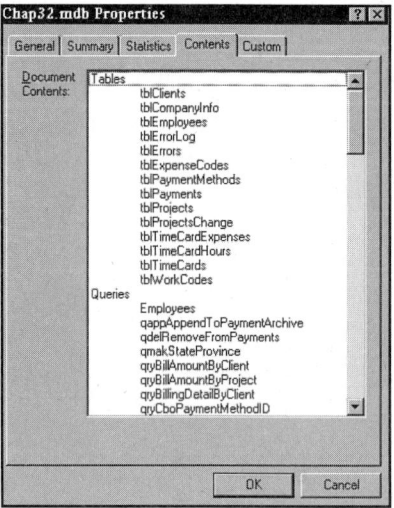

- **Custom:** The Custom tab enables you to define custom properties associated with the database. This is useful when you are dealing with a large organization with numerous databases, and you want to be able to search for all the databases containing certain properties.

Using the Database Documenter

The *Database Documenter* is an elegant tool that is part of the Access application. It enables you to selectively produce varying levels of documentation for each of the objects in your database. Here's how it works:

1. Make sure that the Database window is the active window.

2. Choose Tools|Analyze|Documenter. The Documenter dialog box appears, as shown in Figure 34.11.

Figure 34.11.

You can use the Documenter dialog box to designate which objects you want to document.

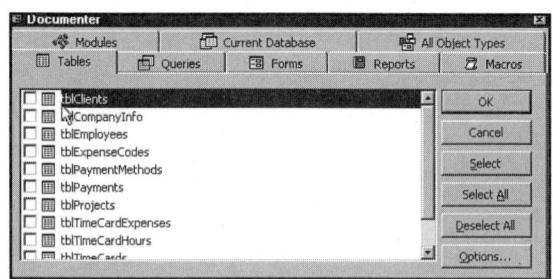

3. Click the appropriate tab to select the type of object you want to document. To document a table, for example, click the Tables tab.

4. Enable the checkbox to the left of each object that you want to document. You can click the Select All command button to select all objects of the selected type.

5. Click the Options button to refine the level of detail provided for each object. Depending on which object type is selected, different options are displayed. Database Documenter options are covered in the next section of this chapter.

6. Repeat steps 3 through 5 to select all database objects that you want to document.

7. Click OK when you are ready to produce the documentation.

TIP

To document all objects in the database, click the All Object Types tab and then click Select All.

WARNING

Access can take quite a bit of time to produce the requested documentation, particularly if numerous objects are selected. For this reason, you should not begin the documentation process if you will soon need your computer to accomplish other tasks. This is because, while Access is processing this task, switching to another application becomes difficult if not impossible—how difficult depends on the amount of RAM installed on your system.

NOTE

To document the properties of the database or the relationships between the tables in the database, click the Current Database tab and select Properties or Relationships.

After you select all the desired objects and options and click OK, the Object Definition window appears. You can use this Print Preview window to view the documentation output for the objects you selected. (See Figure 34.12.) This Print Preview window is just like any other Print Preview window; you can view each page of the documentation and send the documentation to the printer.

Using the Documenter Options

By default, the Database Documenter outputs a huge volume of information for each selected object. Each control on a form is documented, for example, including every property of the control. It is easy to produce 50 pages of documentation for a couple of database objects.

Besides being a tremendous waste of paper, though, this volume of information is overwhelming to review. Fortunately, you can refine the level of detail provided by the Documenter for each category of object you are documenting. Just click the Options button in the Documenter dialog box.

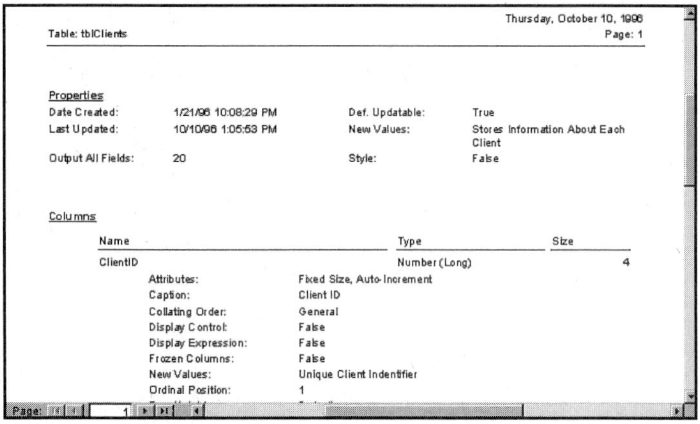

Figure 34.12.
The Object Definition Print Preview window.

Figure 34.13 shows the Table Definition options. Notice that you can specify whether you want to print table properties, relationships, and permissions by user and group. You also can indicate the level of detail you want to display for each field: nothing; names, data types, and sizes; or names, data types, sizes, and properties. For table indexes, you can opt to include nothing; names and fields; or names, fields, and properties.

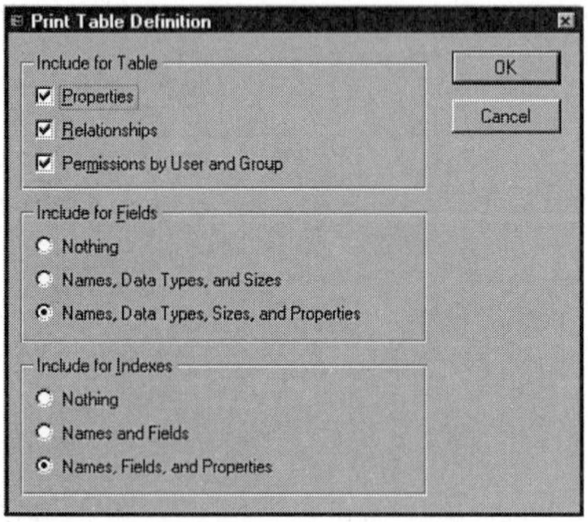

Figure 34.13.
You can use the Print Table Definition dialog box to designate which aspects of a table's definition are documented.

If you select the Queries tab and then click Options, the Print Query Definition dialog box appears, as shown in Figure 34.14. Here, you can select the level of detail to be output for the selected queries. You can choose whether to include properties, SQL, parameters, relationships, and permissions by user and group for the query. You also can select the level of detail to include for each column of the query and for the indexes involved in the query.

Figure 34.14.

You use the Print Query Definition dialog box to designate which aspects of a query's definition are documented.

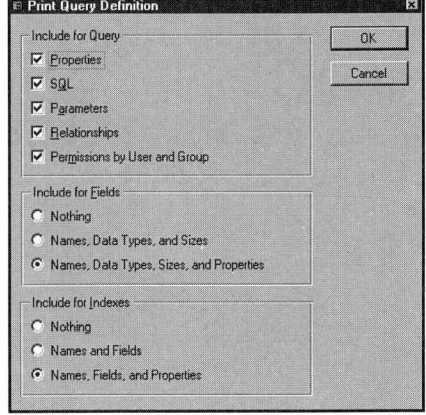

The Form and Report options are similar. Figure 34.15 shows the Print Form Definition dialog box. Here, you can specify whether you want to print properties, code, and permissions by user and group for the form. For each control on the form, you can choose to print nothing, the names of the controls, or the names and properties of the controls. The Print Report Definition dialog box offers the same options.

Figure 34.15.

You use the Print Form Definition dialog box to designate which aspects of a form's definition are documented.

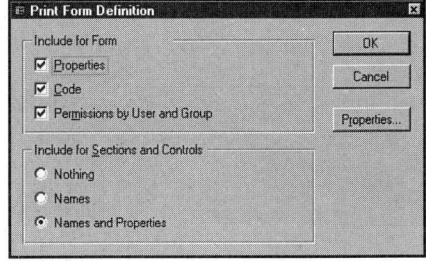

For macros, you can choose whether you want to print macro properties, actions and arguments, or permissions by user and group. For modules, you can choose to view properties, code, and permissions by user and group.

As you can see, the Database Documenter gives you great flexibility in the level of detail it provides. Of course, if you haven't filled in the properties of an object (for example, the description), it does you no good to ask the Documenter to print those properties.

Producing Documentation in Other Formats

After you produce the documentation and it appears in the Object Definition Print Preview window, you can output it to other formats. From the Print Preview window, choose File | Output To. The Output To dialog box appears, as shown in Figure 34.16. Notice that you can output the documentation to HTML, Microsoft Excel, a Rich Text Format file, or an

MS-DOS text file. After you select the format and click OK, Access prompts you for a name for the new file. If you select the AutoStart checkbox from the Output To dialog box that follows the screen shown in Figure 34.16, the Documenter creates the file and then launches you into the appropriate application. The application launched depends on your Registry entries. If Microsoft's *Internet Explorer* (IE) is the application associated with the file extension HTML, for example, AutoStart launches IE with your Documenter output loaded when you output to an HTML file. Similarly, if you choose a Microsoft Excel file format and Excel is associated through the Registry with XLS file types, AutoStart launches Excel with your output loaded on file output. The same holds true for the other file types—RTF and TXT and their respective Registry associations, which usually are Word and Notepad.

Figure 34.16.
You use the Output To dialog box to designate the type of file to which the object definition will be output.

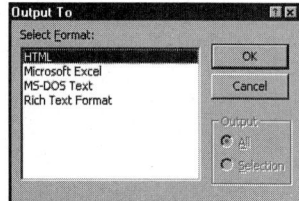

Writing Code to Create Your Own Documentation

Most of the time, the options provided by the Database Documenter are sufficient. At times, you won't like the format the Database Documenter selects—or, more important, you might want to document properties of the database objects not available through the user interface. In these situations, you can choose to enumerate the database objects by using code and then output them to a custom report format.

Using data access objects, you can enumerate any of the objects in your database. Listing 34.1 shows an example.

Listing 34.1. Using DAOs to enumerate the table objects in a database.

```
Sub EnumerateTables()
    Dim db As DATABASE
    Dim tdf As TableDef
    Dim fld As Field
    Dim fSystem As Boolean
    Dim fAttached As Boolean

    Set db = CurrentDb
    DoCmd.SetWarnings False
    For Each tdf In db.TableDefs
        fSystem = tdf.Attributes And dbSystemObject
        fAttached = tdf.Attributes And dbAttachedTable
        DoCmd.RunSQL "INSERT INTO tblTableDoc" _
            & "(TableName, DateCreated, LastModified, " _
            & "SystemObj, AttachedTable ) " _
            & "Values (""" & tdf.Name & """, #" _
```

```
            & tdf.DateCreated & "#, #" _
            & tdf.LastUpdated & "#, " _
            & fSystem & ", " & fAttached & ")"
    Next tdf
    DoCmd.SetWarnings True
End Sub
```

The `EnumerateTables` routine, located in the basDocument module of CHAP34EX.MDB on your sample code CD-ROM, documents various information about the tables in the database. It uses a `For..Each` loop to loop through all the table definitions in the database. For each table in the TableDefs collection, `EnumerateTables` determines whether the table is a system table or a linked table. It then executes an SQL statement, inserting all the requested information about the table definition into a table called tblTableDoc. This table then can be used as the foundation for a report. Of course, when you use appropriate `For..Each` loops and properties, *any* information about *any* of the objects in the database can be obtained by using the same technique.

Practical Examples: Applying What You Learned to the Time and Billing Application

Practice using various options in the Database Documenter for the Time and Billing application. As you change the options for each object type, view the output differences. If you are particularly ambitious, try writing some DAO code to enumerate the objects of the database.

Summary

Documentation is a necessary part of the application-development process; fortunately, Microsoft Access makes it very easy. This chapter covered the object Description properties Access provides, as well as the extremely powerful Database Documenter. This chapter also highlighted how you can create your own documentation using data access objects and custom reports. By using any combination of the techniques covered in this chapter, you can produce very complete documentation for all aspects of your application.

35

CHAPTER

Database
Maintenance
Techniques

- Understanding What Database Maintenance Is All About, 924
- Compacting Your Database, 924
- Repairing Your Database, 928

35

Understanding What Database Maintenance Is All About

Although you don't need to do too much to maintain an Access database, you must know a couple of important techniques in order to ensure that your databases are maintained as effectively as possible. The two techniques you should be familiar with are compacting and repairing. *Compacting* a database means removing unused space, and *repairing* a database involves repairing a damaged database (MDB) file. Both these processes and the ways you can accomplish them are covered in this chapter.

Compacting Your Database

As you and the users of your application work with a database, the database grows in size. In order to maintain a high state of performance, Access defers the removal of discarded pages from the database until you explicitly compact the database file. This means that, as you add data and other objects to the database and remove data and objects from the database, the disk space that was occupied by the deleted objects is not reclaimed. This results not only in a very large database (MDB) file, but it also ultimately means a degradation in performance as the physical file becomes fragmented on disk. Compacting a database accomplishes these tasks:

- Reclaims all space occupied by deleted data and database objects.

- Reorganizes the database file so that the pages of each table in the database are contiguous. This improves performance because, as the user works with the table, the data in the table is located contiguously on the disk.

- Resets counter fields so that the next value will be one more than the last *undeleted* counter value. If, while testing, you add many records that you delete just prior to placing the application in production, compacting the database resets all the counter values back to 1.

- Re-creates the table statistics used by the Jet Engine when queries are executed and marks all queries to be recompiled the next time they are run. These are two very important related benefits of the compacting process. If indexes have been added to a table or the volume of data in the table has been dramatically changed, the query won't execute efficiently. This is because the stored query plan that Jet uses to execute the query is based on inaccurate information. When the database is compacted, all table statistics and the query plan for each query are updated to reflect the current state of the tables in the database.

> **TIP**
>
> It is a good idea to repair a database and defragment the hard drive it is stored on before performing the compact process. The repair process ensures that there are no lurking database errors that may be exacerbated by the compact process. This follow-up defragmentation process ensures that as much contiguous disk space as possible is available for the compacted database.

To compact a database, you can use one of three methods:

- Use commands provided in the user interface.
- Click on an icon you set up for the user.
- Use the CompactDatabase method.

Regardless of which method you select for the compact procedure, the following conditions must be true:

- The user performing the compact procedure must have the rights to open the database exclusively.
- The user performing the compact procedure must have Modify Design permission for all tables in the database.
- The database must be available to be opened for exclusive use. This means that no other users can be using the database.
- Enough disk space must be available for both the original database and the compacted version of the database. This is true even if the database is compacted to a database with the same name.

> **WARNING**
>
> It is a bad idea to compact a database to the same name. If the compact process fails, the original database may be destroyed. For this reason, you always should compact a database to a new name.

Using the User Interface

The Access user interface gives users a fairly straightforward interface to the compact operation. To compact the currently open database, choose Tools | Database Utilities | Compact Database. The current database then is closed, compacted, and reopened.

To compact a database other than the currently open database, follow these steps:

1. Close the open database.
2. Choose Tools | Database Utilities | Compact Database. The Database to Compact From dialog box appears, as shown in Figure 35.1.

925

Figure 35.1.

The Database To Compact From dialog box.

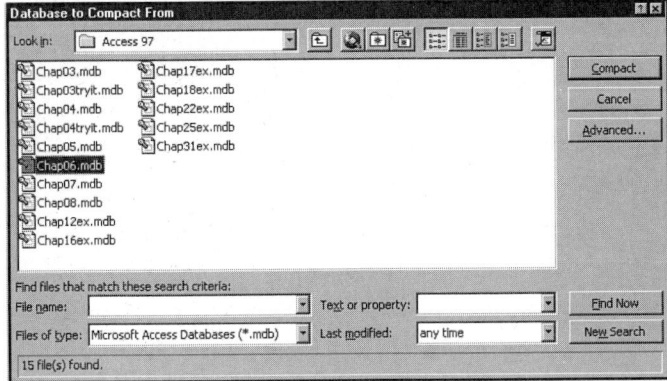

3. Select the database you want to compact and click Compact. The Compact Database Into dialog box appears, as shown in Figure 35.2.

Figure 35.2.

The Compact Database Into dialog box.

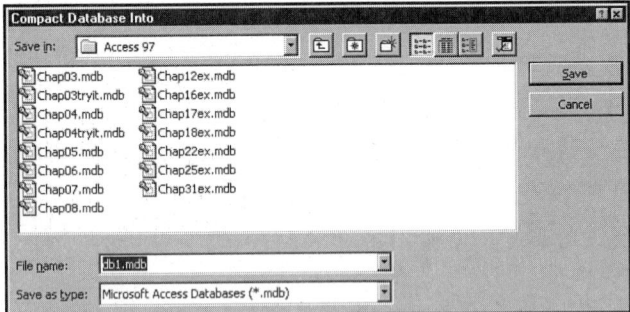

4. Select the name for the compacted database. This can be the same name as the original database name, or it can be a new name (see the preceding warning about compacting a database to the same name). Click Save.

5. If you select the same name, you are prompted to replace the existing file. Click Yes.

Using a Shortcut

A very simple way to give users a way to compact a database is to create an icon that performs the compact process. This is accomplished by using the /Compact command-line option. The /Compact command-line option compacts the database without ever opening it. The shortcut looks like this:

```
c:\MSOffice\Access\Msaccess.exe c:\Databases\TimeAndBilling.MDB /Compact
```

This syntax can be followed by a space and the name of a destination database if you do not want the current database to be overwritten by the compacted version. If you do not include a path for the destination database, it is placed in the My Documents folder by default. The shortcut can be created automatically for you by using the Setup Wizard that ships with the Microsoft Office Developer Edition Tools for Windows 95. This is covered in Chapter 37, "Distributing Your Application with ODE."

To create a shortcut yourself, follow these steps:

1. Open the folder where your application is installed.
2. Right-click on the application (MDB) icon for your database.
3. Choose Create Shortcut.
4. Right-click on the shortcut you just created.
5. Choose Properties.
6. Click the Shortcut tab.
7. In the Target box, click to the right of the command line and add the /Compact option.

Using Code

By using the CompactDatabase method, you can compact a database using code. The CompactDatabase method is performed on the DBEngine object. It receives the old database and new database as parameters. In addition, it receives these optional parameters:

- Locale
- Options
- Password

The Locale is an optional string that determines the collating order in which the data in the compacted database will be sorted. This option is used when you are working with a database in which the data is stored in another language and you want the data to be collated in a particular language.

The Options argument is used to specify whether you want the compacted database to be encrypted as well as into what version you want the database to be compacted. The two constants you can use for encryption are dbEncrypt and dbDecrypt. If you do not specify either of these constants, the compacted database will have the same encryption status as the original source database. You can specify an additional constant in the Options argument. This constant determines the version of the data in the compacted database. The available options are dbVersion10, dbVersion11, dbVersion20, and dbVersion30. The CompactDatabase method converts only data—not the objects in the database.

Finally, the Password argument enables you to supply the password for a database that is password protected.

The following code, contained in the basUtils module of Chap35Ex.MDB, compacts and encrypts a database called Chap35Big.MDB:

```
Sub CompactDB()
   DBEngine.CompactDatabase "c:\databases\Chap35Big.MDB", _
        "c:\databases\Chap35Small.MDB", _
        dbLangGeneral, dbEncrypt
End Sub
```

This uses the dbLangGeneral locale, which is appropriate for English, German, French, Portuguese, Italian, and Modern Spanish. The compacted database will be called Chap35ExSmall.MDB.

In order for this code to execute successfully, remember that the Chap35Big database must be closed and that the user running the code must have the right to open the database exclusively. Furthermore, the user must have Modify Design permissions for all tables in the database.

Repairing Your Database

The repair process is used when a database has been damaged. Damage can occur to a database because the power is interrupted while the database is open, or for several other reasons. Regardless of the cause of the damage, a damaged database often can be salvaged using the repair utility. As with the compact process, the repair process can be executed from the Access interface, by using a desktop shortcut, or by using *Data Access Object* (DAO) code.

To perform the repair process, these conditions must be met:

- The user performing the repair process must have the rights to open the database exclusively.
- The database must be available to be opened for exclusive use. This means that no other users can be using the database.

It is a good idea to back up the database before attempting to repair it, because it is possible for the repair process to do further damage to the database. Also, do not use the repair process as a substitute for carefully following backup procedures. The repair process is not always successful. Nothing is as foolproof as a fastidiously executed backup process.

> **NOTE**
>
> If, at any time, Access detects that a database is damaged, you are prompted to repair the database. This occurs when you attempt to open, compact, encrypt, or decrypt the damaged database. At other times, Access might not detect the damage. Instead, you might suspect that damage has occurred because the database behaves unpredictably. This is when you should perform the repair process, using one of the methods covered in this chapter.

Using the User Interface

As with the compact process, the Access interface provides a fairly straightforward interface to the repair operation. To repair the current database, choose Tools | Database Utilities | Repair Database. The current database is closed, repaired, and reopened.

Follow these steps to repair a database other than the currently open database:

1. Close the open database.
2. Choose Tools | Database Utilities | Repair Database. The Repair Database dialog box appears, as shown in Figure 35.3.

Figure 35.3.

The Repair Database dialog box.

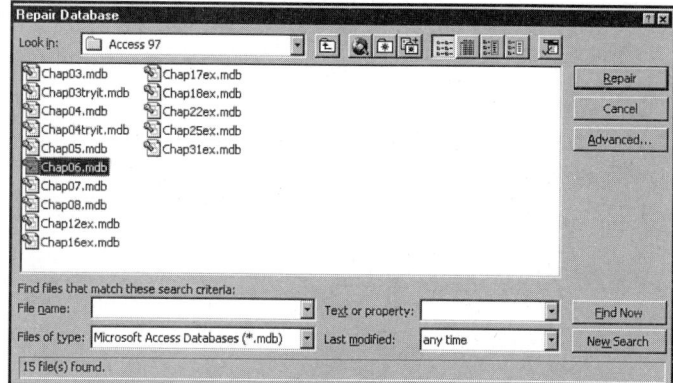

3. Select the database you want to repair and click Repair. If the repair process is successful, the message box shown in Figure 35.4 appears. Otherwise, you are notified that the repair process could not complete successfully.

Figure 35.4.

This message appears when the repair process is successful.

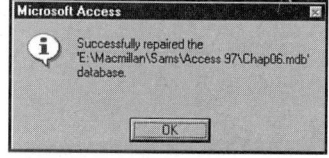

Using a Shortcut

Just as you can use the /Compact command-line switch to compact a database, you can use the /Repair command-line switch to repair a database. The format follows:

```
c:\MSOffice\Access\Msaccess.exe c:\Databases\TimeAndBilling.MDB /Repair
```

You can create this shortcut using exactly the same method covered in "Using a Shortcut," earlier in this chapter.

929

> **NOTE**
>
> When a database is repaired, it might increase in size. This is due to indexes that are created to assist with the repair process. It therefore is a good idea to compact a database after you repair it. You can do this by using the combination of the `/Repair` and `/Compact` switches. When you specify both command-line switches, Access always repairs the database before compacting it.

Using Code

Just as you can compact a database using code, you also can repair it using code. The subroutine in Listing 35.1 illustrates this process.

Listing 35.1. Repairing a database using code.

```
Sub RepairDB()
    Dim db As DATABASE
    On Error Resume Next
    Set db = OpenDatabase("c:\databases\Chap35Damaged.MDB")
    If DBEngine.Errors.Count > 0 Then
        If Err = 1000 Then 'Database Corrupt
            MsgBox "Database is Corrupt..Attempting to Repair"
            DBEngine.RepairDatabase "c:\databases\Chap35Damaged.MDB"
        End If
    End If
End Sub
```

The `RepairDB` subroutine attempts to open the Chap35Damaged database. If an error occurs on the OpenDatabase method, the `On Error Resume Next` statement causes the next line of code to execute. The next line of code evaluates to see whether the error was number 1000, indicating that the database is corrupt. If so, the code executes the RepairDatabase method on the `DBEngine` object using the name of the damaged database as an argument.

Summary

The compact process should be performed regularly—especially on databases containing your application data. The compact process provides major benefits in terms of both performance and conservation of disk space. The more activity that occurs on a database, the more frequently it should be compacted.

It is a good idea to occasionally repair a database just to ensure that no insidious damage has occurred. If a database is damaged, it might be repairable. This chapter covered issues surrounding the process of repairing a database, as well as the three methods you can use to repair any Access database. The important thing to remember is that the repair utility is in no way a substitute for proper backup techniques.

36

CHAPTER

Developing a Help File

- Deciding To Create a Help File, 932
- Looking At Help from a User's Perspective, 932
- Planning the Help File, 936
- Building the Help Components, 937
- Adding Custom Help to Your Applications, 952
- Getting Help with Help: Authoring Tools, 953
- Practical Examples: Adding Help to the Time and Billing Application, 954

Deciding To Create a Help File

In a perfect world, you could create an application that would not require any explanation. In this perfect world, your user simply could view any form in your application and *instantly* know how to use it. No assistance would be required. Unfortunately, the world is not perfect. Even with the elegant graphical user interface that Windows provides, you must give users guidance in using your application. You can accomplish this task in a relatively easy manner by including Help files with your application.

Looking At Help from a User's Perspective

Before you venture into the process of creating a custom Help file, it is important that you become familiar with the basics of working with Windows 95 Help. This provides you with a context in which to develop your own Help files. Your own Help files should provide your users with the same look and feel as the Help files included with Access, Word, Excel, and the other standard products with which your users already are familiar.

Figure 36.1 shows the Access Help dialog box. Notice the Contents, Index, and Find tabs. These tabs are standard for many Windows applications. Each tab of the Help dialog box provides users with a different interface for obtaining the help they need. There is also a new Office Assistant.

Figure 36.1.
The Microsoft Access 97 Help Topics dialog box.

The Contents Tab

The Contents tab of the Help dialog box provides an expandable/collapsible table of contents for the Help file. Using the Contents tab, users can peruse the available topics, learning about all aspects of your application. Users can double-click the item on which they want help, and Access displays help on the selected topic. (See Figure 36.2.)

Figure 36.2.

*Viewing help information on
an item selected from the
Contents tab.*

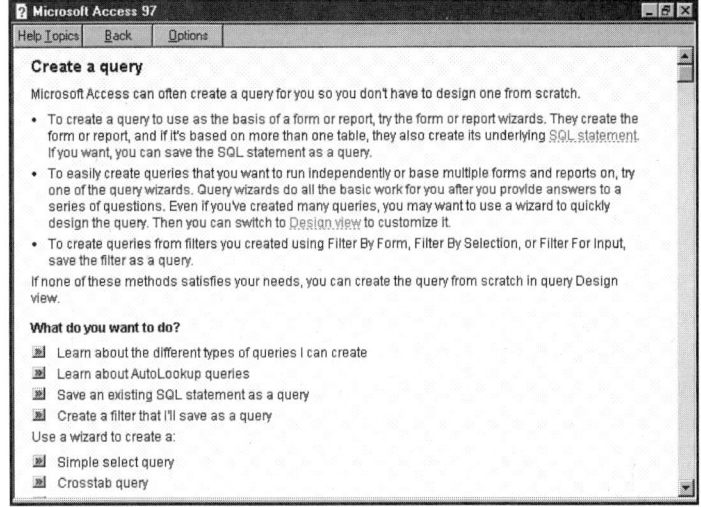

The Index Tab

The Index tab replaces the Search dialog box available in previous versions of Windows. It enables users to search for Help topics using keywords, as shown in Figure 36.3. After the keyword is found, users can double-click the entry for which they want help. A Topics Found dialog box appears if more than one entry is found on the selected Help topic, as shown in Figure 36.4. Otherwise, the user is immediately provided with help on the selected topic. The help can appear in the main Help window or in a secondary Help window. Usually, overviews are displayed in the main window, and step-by-step instructions for accomplishing specific tasks are provided in a secondary window.

Figure 36.3.

*Using the Index tab
to search for a keyword.*

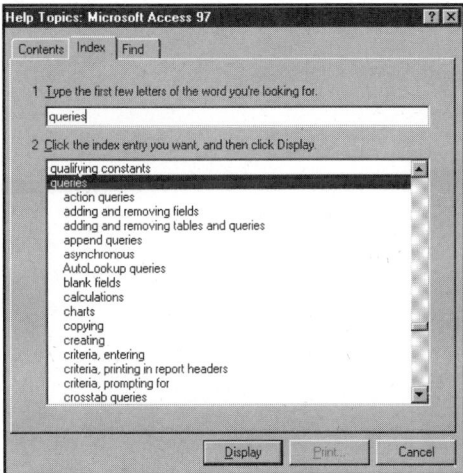

Figure 36.4.
The Topics Found dialog box.

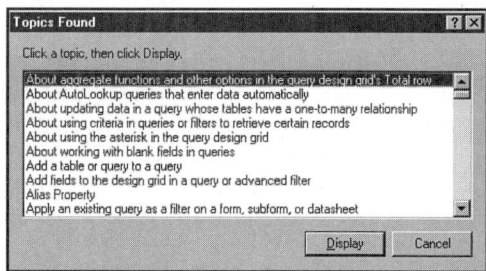

The Find Tab

The Find tab enables users to search for a particular word or phrase. After typing the selected word or phrase, users see a list box that enables them to refine their search. After users select a matching word from the list box, a list of topics associated with the matching word is displayed, as shown in Figure 36.5. Users then can double-click the entry they want to learn about.

Figure 36.5.
Using the Find tab.

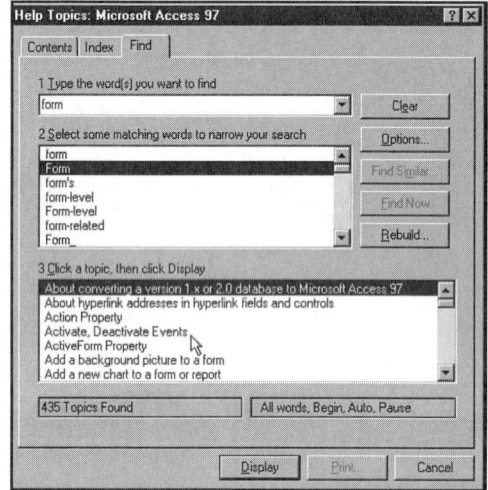

The Office Assistant

One of the more subtle changes between Access 95 and Access 97 is the Office Assistant. In Access 95, this was known as the Answer Wizard; for Office 97, Microsoft has renamed the Answer Wizard to the Office Assistant and included it in Word, Excel, Access, and PowerPoint. It still operates the same as the Answer Wizard. Users enter English-like questions and obtain a list of topics associated with their question. Users simply enter a question in the text box and then press the Search button; the related topics then are displayed for the users to choose.

Button Bars

The button bar on the Help window enables users to easily navigate through Help. The secondary Help window shown in Figure 36.6 enables users to view Help topics, move back to the previous Help topic, or view available options. Button bars are fully customizable so that you can provide your users with the appropriate options.

Figure 36.6.
Using the button bar.

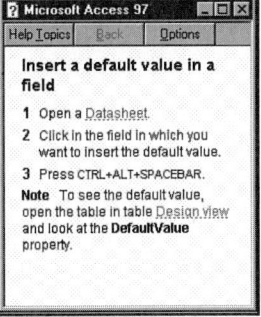

Hotspots

The underlined words, phrases, or sentences that appear in green in the Help topic are called *hotspots*. When users place the mouse over a hotspot, the mouse pointer turns into a hand. If users click over a hotspot underlined with a dotted line, a pop-up window appears with specific information about the hotspot item, as shown in Figure 36.7. This pop-up window disappears after users click anywhere else on-screen. When users clicks over a hotspot underlined with a solid line, help is displayed about a related topic.

Figure 36.7.
A topic popped up from a hotspot.

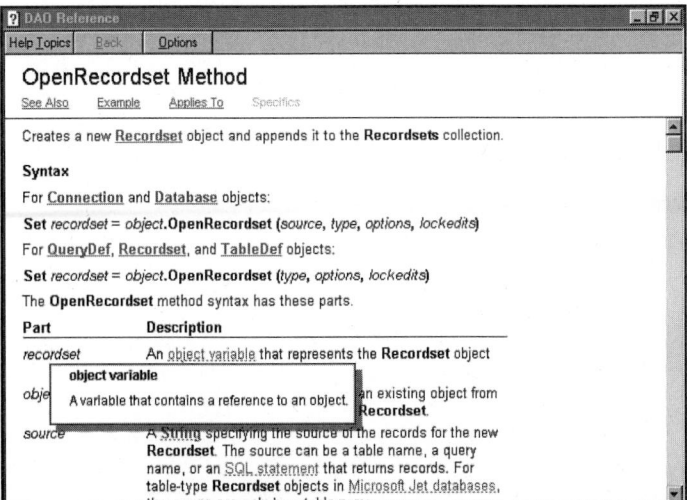

Hypergraphics

Help topics can contain pictures (images) set up to operate as hotspots. When users place the mouse over the picture, the mouse pointer appears as a hand. After users click the hypergraphic, a pop-up window appears, providing additional information about the picture. The hypergraphic in Figure 36.8 shows the Query Type tool. After users click the picture of the tool, a pop-up window appears with additional information about the Query Type tool.

Figure 36.8.

Using hypergraphics.

Authorable Buttons

Figure 36.9 shows an example of *authorable* buttons. These buttons perform an action, such as displaying a secondary window, after users click them.

Planning the Help File

Before you worry about *how* to build a Help file, you should plan what it will look like. What you provide in a Help file is determined by the type of users who will be working with your application. If your application will be distributed to a wide range of users (including those new to Windows), for example, your Help file should include the most basic information. On the other hand, if your application is directed toward power users who are extremely adept at Windows and maybe even Access, your Help file should focus on assisting users with the more complex aspects of your application. In general, your Help file should contain the following:

- An introduction to your application
- A description of each form and report that comprises your application
- Instructions on how to use the various controls on your forms
- A description of each toolbar and each tool contained on the toolbar
- Instructions for carrying out tasks such as adding a client, deleting a client, or adding projects related to a client

Depending on the level of the users, you might want to provide additional detail, such as a description of terms, concepts, or Windows 95 or Access skills required for the use of your application.

Figure 36.9.

Using authorable buttons.

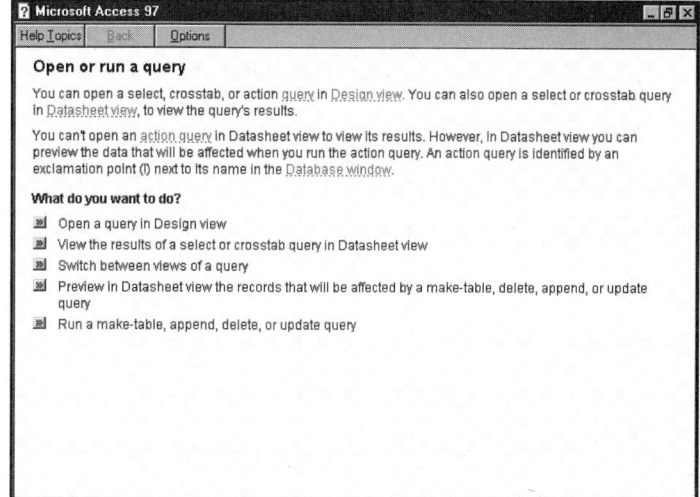

Building the Help Components

After you decide what to include in the Help file that will accompany your application, you are ready to begin the process of creating the actual file. The following is an overview of the tasks required to build a custom Help file:

- Build a Help topic file (RTF).
- Create a map file (MAP).
- Create a contents file (CNT).

- Create the Help project file (HPJ).
- Prepare the Help file to be compiled.
- Compile the Help project file (HLP).
- Add the Help file to your application.

Each of these steps is covered in detail in the following sections.

Creating a Topic File

The first step in creating a Help file is to create a topic file. The *topic file* is a *Rich Text Format* (RTF) file containing all the text and formatting codes that will appear in the Help file. A Help project must contain at least one topic file. It can contain more than one topic file if you choose. You can create Help topic files in Microsoft Word or by using any tool that enables you to build a file in the RTF format. This file format contains special characters and formatting that the Help compiler uses to build the custom Help file.

Several Help-authoring tools are available to assist you with the process of building a topic file. These include RoboHelp, Doc-To-Help, and ForeHelp, just to name a few. These valuable tools (discussed in the "Getting Help with Help: Authoring Tools" section of this chapter) assist you with the process of building the RTF file. Even if you plan to use one of these tools, it is a good idea to understand how the RTF file is built. This section provides you with the knowledge and tools to build and work with an RTF file.

Creating an RTF File

This section covers how to build a topic file using Microsoft Word for Windows 95. You easily can modify the steps to work with other versions of Microsoft Word or with other tools that enable you to save a file in the RTF format. To begin the process of building the Help topic file, follow these steps:

1. Create a new Microsoft Word document.
2. Choose Save.
3. In the Save As Type drop-down list, select Rich Text Format as the file type, as shown in Figure 36.10.
4. Enter a filename for the Help topic file and click Save.

Figure 36.10.

Selecting Rich Text Format from the Save As Type drop-down list.

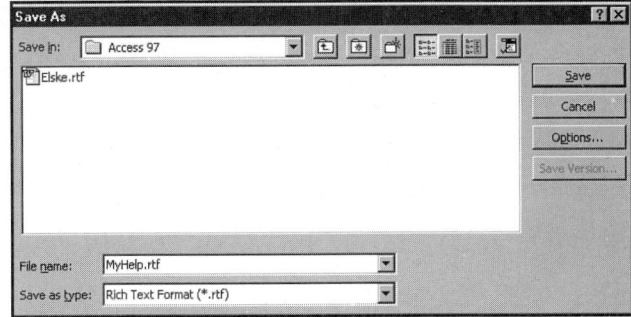

Adding a Help Topic

You now are ready to begin the process of entering the text and formatting codes that dictate the content, appearance, and functionality of your custom Help file. The Help compiler uses various footnotes as codes to designate the role that each portion of the RTF file will serve. In other words, each footnote communicates the function of the text to the Help compiler. The pound sign (#), for example, is used to designate a unique topic ID for the text that it precedes. You add each Help topic with the appropriate footnote codes. Here's how it works:

1. Insert a hard page break indicating that you are starting a new Help topic. You do not need to insert a hard page break before the first Help topic.

2. Choose Insert | Footnote from the Word menu.

3. Choose Custom Mark, as shown in Figure 36.11.

Figure 36.11.

Inserting a special footnote code.

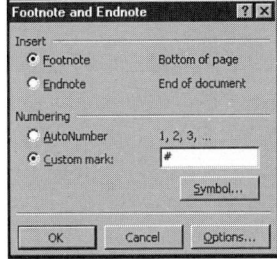

4. Type one of the special footnote characters covered in the sections that follow.

5. Click OK.

6. Repeat steps 2 through 5, adding all the special characters required for the Help topic you are adding.

7. Type the Help topic title as it should appear on the Help window's title bar.

8. Press Enter and type all the text for the topic.

Before you walk through the step-by-step process of building a Help topic, it is important that you understand the meaning of the more commonly used footnote codes. These are covered in the following sections.

Creating Topic IDs: The # Footnote

The pound sign (#) footnote is required for every Help topic. It identifies a unique topic ID. This is the name that WINHELP uses to identify the topic. The topic ID must be unique within the Help project.

Creating Titles: The $ Footnote

The dollar sign ($) footnote also is required for every Help topic. It specifies the Help topic's title as it will appear in the Topics Found dialog box, the Bookmark dialog box, and the History window. This title should match the topic title that appears in the Help window.

Specifying Search Keywords: The K Footnote

The letter K specifies search keywords for the topic. These are the keywords the user can employ when searching for the topic. Remember that users do not always remember the correct terms for the topic on which they need help. It is important to be creative when designating search keywords so that you supply your users with a variety of terms that will bring them to the correct Help topic.

Using Other Tags

Several other tags exist that enable you to build extremely complex Help files. The asterisk (*) footnote, for example, enables you to create Build tags. These Build tags enable you to create several versions of a Help file using the same Help topic file. This is an excellent option if you want to provide different Help files to the different levels of users to whom you will distribute your application. Other tags enable you to specify the window in which a Help topic is displayed, designate entry-point macros, and so on. These more advanced tags are not covered in this text.

Giving It a Test Run: Building Some Help Topics

All this might seem rather confusing to you. The best way to learn how it really works is to build your own topic file. With a new RTF file open (see the "Creating an RTF File" section earlier in this chapter), follow these steps:

1. Select the Insert menu and choose Footnote.

2. After the dialog box opens, click Custom Mark.

3. Type a pound sign (#) in the Custom Mark text box and click OK. This designates the text that you type in the footnote as a unique topic ID.

4. Notice that the cursor drops to the Footnote window. Type the unique identifier in the Footnote window. In this case, type `ProjectForm`.

5. Press F6 to move back to the text-editing window, or click after the pound sign.

6. Select the Insert menu and choose Footnote.

7. Type a dollar sign ($) in the Custom Mark text box and click OK. This designates the text that you type in the footnote as the Help topic title that will appear in the Topics Found, Bookmark, and History dialog boxes.

8. Type `Using the Project Form` in the Footnote window.

9. Press F6 to move back to the text-editing window, or click after the $.

10. Select the Insert menu and choose Footnote.

11. Type the letter K (in uppercase) in the Custom Mark text box and click OK. This designates the text that you type in the footnote as search keywords. Each search keyword must be separated by a semicolon. In this case, type `Project;Client Projects;Work Completed`.

12. Press F6 to move back to the text-editing window, or click after the letter K.

13. Type the text that will appear as the Help title. This should match the text you specified for the $ footnote.

14. Press Enter and type the Help text the user will see.

15. Insert a hard page break and repeat all the steps for each Help topic you want to add.

Figure 36.12 illustrates the RTF file as it should appear after following these steps. You can continue adding additional topics as desired.

Figure 36.12.
An RTF file with a Help topic.

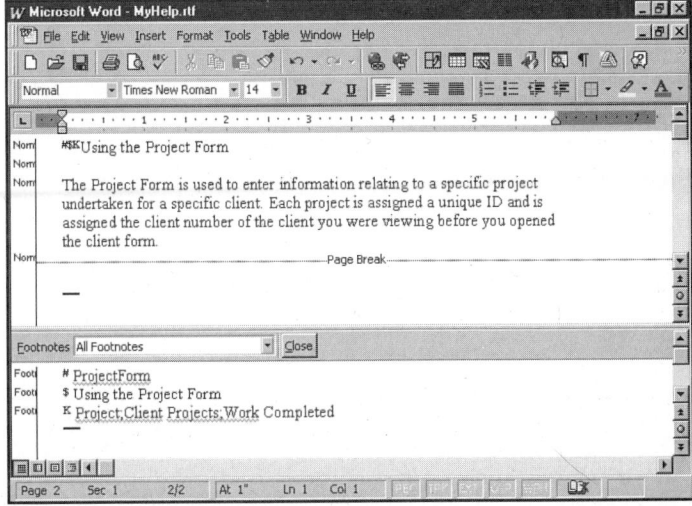

Adding Nonscrolling Regions

Access Help and the Help provided with many other products contain nonscrolling regions. These regions often include the hotspots See Also or Example, as shown in Figure 36.13. The nonscrolling region for the Help topic in Figure 36.13 includes hotspots for See Also, Example, Applies To, and Specifics. You can have only one nonscrolling region per Help topic. It must include the first paragraph of the Help topic (the one with the footnotes).

To create a nonscrolling region, follow these steps:

1. Select the paragraphs that you want to include in the nonscrolling region.
2. Choose Format│Paragraph; a dialog box opens.
3. Click to select the Text Flow tab.

Figure 36.13.

A nonscrolling region with hotspots.

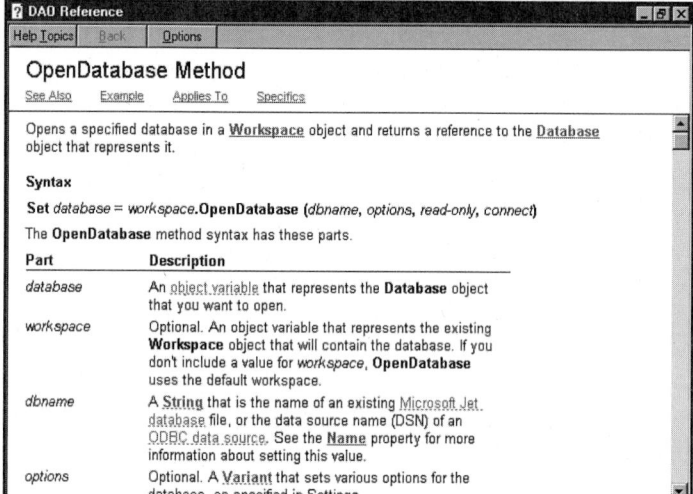

4. Enable the Keep with Next checkbox.
5. Click OK.

Adding Hotspots

One of the wonderful aspects of Windows Help is the capability to quickly jump from one topic to another related topic or to obtain more information about an entry in the text. Hotspots enable you to provide this functionality to the users of your application. There are three types of hotspots:

- *Jumps* send the user from one related topic to another.
- *Pop ups* display a Help topic in a pop-up window and usually provide some sort of definition or additional explanation.

- *Macro hotspots* run a Winhelp macro. There are several built-in macros for Help. For a complete listing, see the Help compiler tools.

Follow these steps to create a jump hotspot:

1. Type the hotspot text in your RTF Word document.
2. Without pressing the spacebar, type the topic ID of the topic to which you want to jump.
3. Select the hotspot text and double-underline it by pressing Ctrl+Shift+D.
4. Select the topic ID and hide it by pressing Ctrl+Shift+H.

> **NOTE**
>
> To view hidden text in Microsoft Word for Windows 95, choose Tools I Options and then click the View tab. Then enable the Hidden Text checkbox.

To create a pop-up hotspot, follow these steps:

1. Type the hotspot text in your RTF Word document.
2. Without adding any spaces, type the topic ID of the Help topic you want the hotspot to display in the pop-up window.
3. Select the hotspot text and single-underline it by pressing Ctrl+U.
4. Select the topic ID and mark it as hidden by pressing Ctrl+Shift+H.

Figure 36.14 shows a pop-up hotspot with the word ID that pops up a window with the Help text with the associated topic ID of UniqueIdentifier.

Figure 36.14.

A pop-up hotspot.

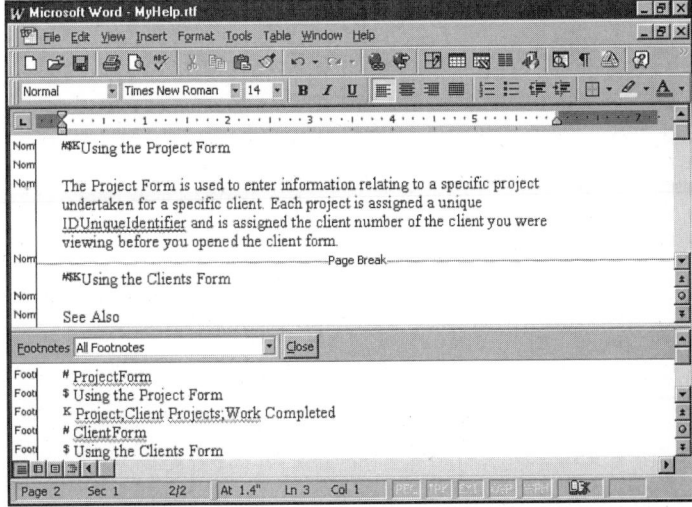

Adding Graphics

The WinHelp Engine supports the following types of graphics files:

- **Bitmaps:** BMP or DIB extensions
- **Windows metafiles:** WMF extensions
- **Shed graphics:** SHG extensions
- **Multiresolution bitmaps:** MRB extensions

Graphics files can be embedded in the topic file, or they can be referenced. It is almost always best to reference a graphics file instead of embedding it in the topic file. Embedded graphics require a significant amount of memory and generally are not practical. To reference a graphics file, insert the following statement where you want the graphic to appear:

```
{bmx[t] filename}
```

The `bm` is hard-coded text. The `x` is a variable that can be set to one of the following:

- **c:** Indicates that the graphic is like a character and will flow with the text.
- **l:** Indicates that the graphic will appear as if it were in a left-justified frame; text will flow around the picture.
- **r:** Indicates that the graphic will appear as if it were in a right-justified frame, and again, the text will flow around the picture.

The `t` parameter is optional. If it is used, the background color of the graphic is replaced with the background color of the Help topic containing the graphic.

Figure 36.15 shows the bitmap called contacts.bmp as it flows with the paragraph in which it is inserted.

Figure 36.15.

Inserting a graphic.

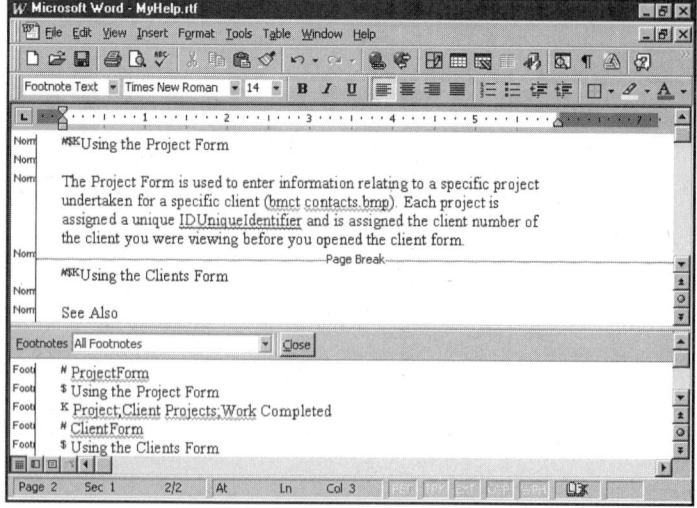

Adding Hypergraphics

A *hypergraphic* is a picture that functions like a hotspot. When users place the mouse over the hypergraphic, a hand appears. If users click the graphic, a pop-up window appears. To add a hypergraphic, follow these steps:

1. Add a graphic reference as described in the "Adding Graphics" section of this chapter.

2. Without pressing the spacebar, add a hotspot as explained in the "Adding Hotspots" section of this chapter.

Figure 36.16 shows an example in which the contacts.bmp bitmap is used as a hotspot to display a window containing help with the topic ID of ClientForm. The name of the graphic is underlined, and the topic ID is hidden.

Figure 36.16.

Inserting a hypergraphic.

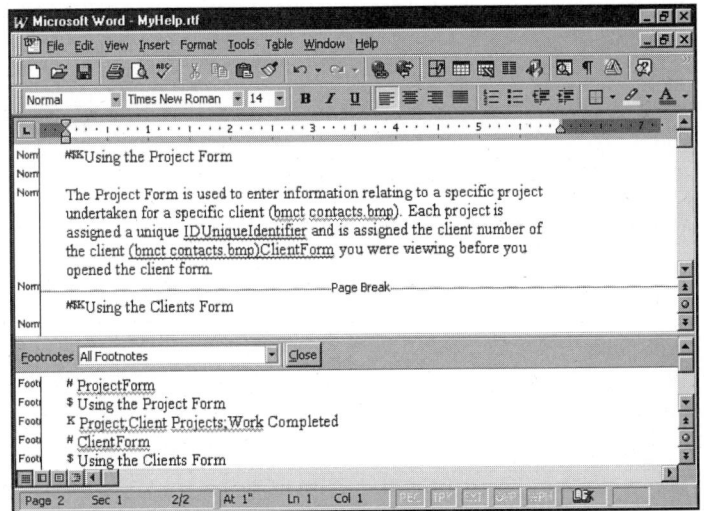

Creating a Map File

A *map file* is an optional ASCII text file that contains a context number for each topic ID. These context IDs ultimately will be used to associate a particular Help topic with a specific form, report, or control. Associating a Help topic with a specific form, report, or control is covered in the "Adding Custom Help to Your Applications" section, later in this chapter.

Although the map file is optional, it is highly recommended. You can map Help topics to context numbers directly in the Help project file, but this can become unwieldy even with the smallest of Help files. A map file is very easy to create, so there is really no reason to refrain from creating one.

To create a map file, follow these steps:

1. Launch a text editor such as Notepad.
2. Add a `#define topic-ID context-number` statement to each line of the map file.
3. Save the file as ASCII text with a MAP extension.

A context number must be created for each topic ID in the Help file. When assigning context numbers, you should leave extra room between each topic number. This enables you to easily insert additional related items at any time. The idea is that you want your topic numbers to be logically sequenced and you do *not* want to change a topic number after it has been associated with an Access object.

Creating a Contents File

A *contents file* is an ASCII text file that is used to determine the table of contents that appears on the Contents tab of the Help Topics dialog box. The contents file must be distributed along with your application and the compiled Help file (HLP). To create a contents file, follow these steps:

1. Launch a text editor such as Notepad.
2. Begin with a `:Base` statement. This statement specifies the name of the compiled Help file.
3. Use the `:Title` statement to specify a title for the Help Topics dialog box.
4. Use an `:Index` statement to identify the Help file containing the keywords you want to include in the Index tab.
5. Add a topic paragraph for each topic you want to include in the table of contents. Use 1 for first-level headings, 2 for second-level headings, and so on.
6. Save the file as an ASCII text file with a CNT extension.

Creating the Help Project File

The Help project file brings everything about the Help file together, including the following:

- A list of topic files associated with the Help project
- A list of map files associated with the Help project
- The name of the contents file associated with the project
- A reference to the location of graphics files required by the project
- Definitions of the Help project windows
- Title of the Help file

The easiest way to build the Help project file is to use the Help Workshop. You can get the Help Workshop in one of these ways:

- As part of the Office 97 Developer Edition Tools
- In the Windows SDK (System Development Kit)
- On the Microsoft Developer Network Level 2 CD-ROM

You can launch the Help Workshop by using the Start menu or by using a desktop shortcut. Figure 36.17 shows the window that appears after the Help Workshop is launched.

Figure 36.17.
The Help Workshop window.

To create a new project file, follow these steps:

1. Choose File|New. The New dialog box appears, asking whether you are creating a new project file or a contents file, as shown in Figure 36.18. Instead of creating the contents file using the techniques covered in the "Creating a Contents File" section of this chapter, you can use the Help Workshop to create a contents file.

Figure 36.18.
Selecting the type of file you are creating.

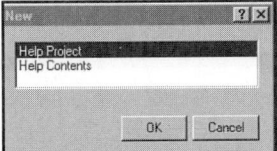

2. Select Help Project and click OK. The Project File Name dialog box appears, as shown in Figure 36.19.

3. Select a name and location for the Help project file and click Save. The Help Workshop window appears, as shown in Figure 36.20.

Figure 36.19.

The Project File Name dialog box.

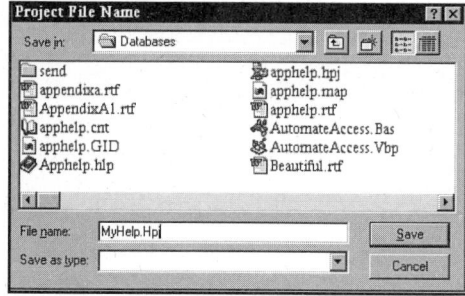

Figure 36.20.

The Help Workshop window after creating a project.

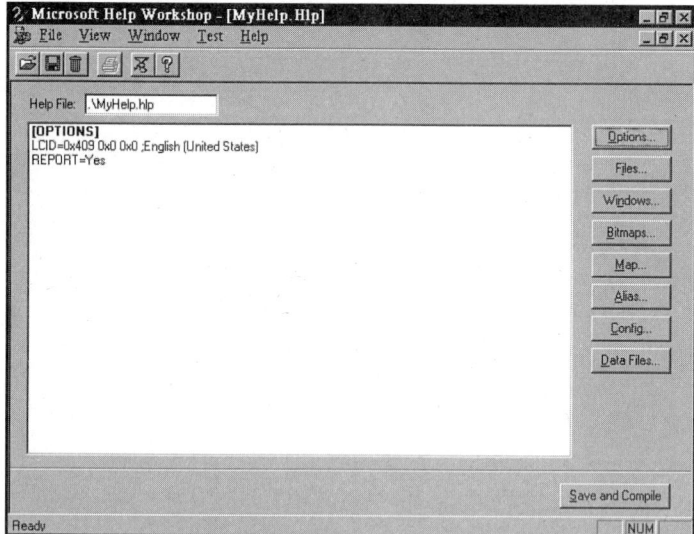

Preparing the Help Project to be Compiled

After you create a Help file, you must perform several tasks to prepare the Help project to be compiled. You must specify the Help topic file, the map file, and the location of graphics files. You also probably should customize the Help window and specify other optional settings. The steps involved in performing each of these tasks are covered in the sections that follow.

Specifying the Help Topic File

The first step is to locate the Help topic file. This is the RTF file you created in the "Creating a Topic File" section of this chapter. Follow these steps:

1. Click the Files button on the right side of the Help Workshop window. The Topic Files dialog box appears.

2. Click Add to add a topic file.

3. Select an RTF file and click Open. The Topic Files dialog box appears, as shown in Figure 36.21.

4. Click OK to close the Topic Files dialog box.

Figure 36.21.
The Topic Files dialog box.

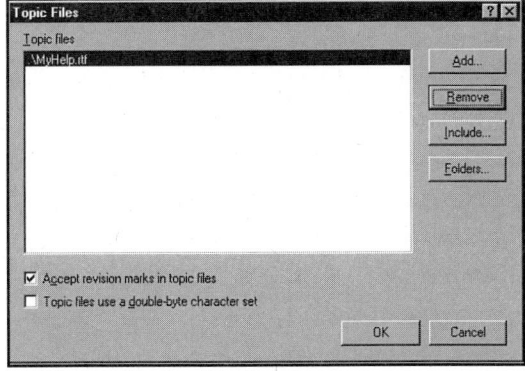

Specifying the Map File

The next step in the process is to designate the location of the map file, which is accomplished with these steps:

1. Click the Map button on the right side of the Help Workshop window.

2. Click the Include button to include an existing map file.

3. Click Browse in the Include file dialog box. Locate a map file and click Open. Then click OK. The Map dialog box appears, as shown in Figure 36.22.

4. Click OK to close the Map dialog box.

Figure 36.22.
The Map dialog box.

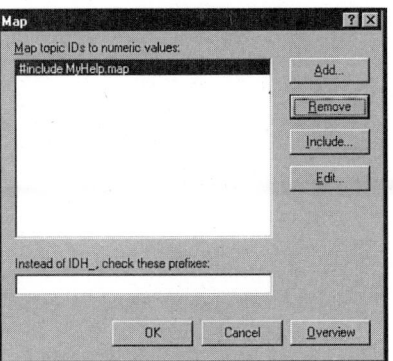

Locating Graphics Files

You do not need to specify a bitmaps folder if the bitmaps are in the same folder as the Help project. If the bitmaps are in a different location, you must follow these steps:

1. Click the Bitmaps button on the right side of the Help Workshop window.

2. Click Add and select a bitmaps folder.

3. Click OK to close the Bitmap Folders dialog box.

Adding and Customizing Help Windows

The Help Workshop gives you the opportunity to create secondary Help windows. Secondary Help windows give the user step-by-step guidance in completing a process. To add new Help windows, click the Windows button on the right side of the Help Workshop window. The Window Properties dialog box appears, as shown in Figure 36.23.

Figure 36.23.

The Window Properties dialog box.

From the Window Properties dialog box, you can add and customize new Help windows. To add a new Help window, follow these steps:

1. Click Add. The Add a New Window Type dialog box appears, as shown in Figure 36.24.

2. Type a name for the new Help window.

3. From the Based on This Standard Window drop-down list, select a style for the new Help window.

4. Click OK to return to the Add a New Window Type dialog box.

5. Select the General tab. Fill in the title bar text for the new window. You also can indicate that you want to keep the Help window on top. This is standard for step-by-step Help windows so that they remain on top while the user performs a task.

6. Click the Position tab and specify a custom position for the new Help window.

7. Click the Buttons tab, where you can select the buttons that you want to appear on the button bar of your new window. (See Figure 36.25.)

Figure 36.24.

The Add a New Window
Type dialog box.

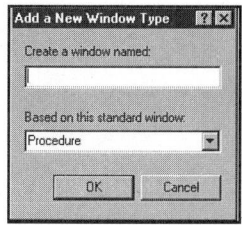

Figure 36.25.

The Buttons tab of the
Window Properties dialog box.

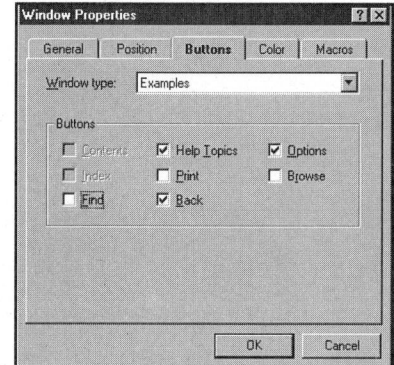

8. Click the Color tab to specify custom colors for both the nonscrolling and topic areas of the Help window.

9. Click the Macros tab if you want to instruct the Help Compiler to run a macro when the Help window opens.

10. Click OK to add the new window.

The new window can be used in the following ways:

- When a user selects the Help topic from the Index tab or Find tab
- As a jump from a hotspot

To display the new Help window after users select the Help topic from the Index tab or Find tab, you must use the greater than (>) footnote when adding the Help topic.

To display the new Help window after users click a jump hotspot, you must follow the topic ID with a greater than (>) symbol and then the name of the window. The hotspot New Projects jumps to a topic called AddNewProject, opening it in the AddProj window.

Using Other Options

The Help Workshop offers some final options. To access these additional features, click the Options button fron the main screen. The Options dialog box appears, as shown in Figure 36.26. This dialog box has several tabs. Each tab enables you to define different aspects of your Help project. The General tab, for example, enables you to specify a default Help topic and define a title for the Help window. The Compression tab enables you to select a level of compression for the compiled Help file. The higher the level of compression, the longer the Help file takes to compile, but the less space the Help files require. Also, if you use Maximum compression, the Help file loads more quickly and operates better on users' machines.

Figure 36.26.

The Options dialog box.

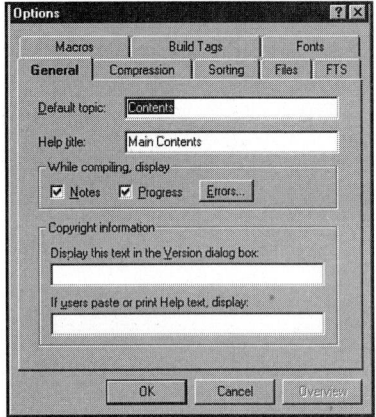

Compiling the Project

After you select a Help topic file, specify the map file, define the location of your graphics files, add and customize any additional Help windows, and indicate any special options for the Help project, you are ready to compile the project into an HLP file. This is the file that your Access application will use.

To save all changes to the Help file and then compile it, click the Save and Compile buttons. After the project is compiled and saved, notice that five topics, five jumps, 15 keywords, and one bitmap have been defined. The Help file compiled with no errors or warnings. The file MyHelp.hlp now is compiled and ready to be attached to an Access database.

Adding Custom Help to Your Applications

After you create a compiled Help file, you need to let your application know that it is available. You also must associate different objects in your application with various Help topics in the Help file. Each form and report has a Help File property and a Help Context ID property. The Help File property must be filled in with the name of a compiled Help file. The Help context ID is the number that you defined in the map file. Each control on a form contains a Help context ID property. If you fill in this property with a context ID as specified in the map file, the Help topic that has the topic ID associated with the specified context ID appears whenever that control has focus and the user presses F1. The number 150, for example, found in the Help Context ID field of the frmClients form shown in Figure 36.27, is associated via the map file with the Help topic ID ClientForm.

Figure 36.27.

Associating a form, report, or control with a specific Help topic.

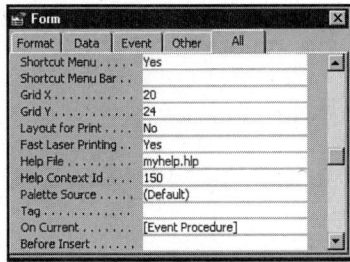

Getting Help with Help: Authoring Tools

Many people feel that the process of creating the RTF topic file in Microsoft Word (or using another word processor) is tedious and difficult. Fortunately, several third-party tools are on the market to assist you with this process.

RoboHELP is one of the more popular help-authoring tools. Available from Blue Sky Software, this excellent tool adds user-friendly toolbars, menu commands, and dialog boxes to Microsoft Word, significantly easing the process of creating the RTF file. Creating the footnotes and jumps as well as adding graphics to the RTF file becomes a matter of pointing and clicking. RoboHELP also facilitates the process of building help into your application by automatically creating and maintaining the Help project and map files for you!

> **NOTE**
>
> For more information, or to purchase RoboHELP, you can contact Blue Sky Software at (619) 459-6365 or by fax at (619) 459-6366.

Another popular help-authoring tool is Doc-To-Help. This product, offered by WexTech Systems, enables you to create a printed manual and online help at the same time. Like RoboHELP, Doc-To-Help provides templates that add buttons and menu commands to Microsoft Word, making the process of developing the RTF file a matter of pointing and clicking.

> **NOTE**
>
> For more information, or to order Doc-To-Help, contact WexTech Systems, Inc. at (212) 949-9595 or by fax at (212) 949-4007.

Practical Examples: Adding Help to the Time and Billing Application

The MyHelp.rtf file, included on the sample code CD-ROM, contains Help topics that assist you with the following tasks:

- Using the Clients form
- Using the Projects form
- Viewing multiple projects simultaneously
- Adding a new project

The MyHelp.rtf topic file was compiled along with the MyHelp.map map file to build the MyHelp.hlp Help file. The MyHelp.cnt contents file also is included on the sample code CD-ROM. The resulting Help file has been associated with the CHAP36.MDB database. The AddNewProject topic ID and the UniqueIdentifier topic ID can be accessed by using hotspots included in the ProjectForm topic, as shown in Figure 36.28. The Help project is complete; it has standard Windows Help context, index, and built-in printing capabilities.

Figure 36.28.

Help in the Time and Billing Application.

954

Summary

Most Windows products today ship with extremely elegant and effective Help systems. Windows users are accustomed to pressing their F1 keys to obtain the assistance they need even to accomplish the most complex tasks. To provide the professional polish that your users expect in an application and to assist them with getting the most out of the product you provide, you should include a custom Help system as part of your application. By using the tools that ship with Microsoft Access and the Office 97 Developer Edition Tools, or by using third-party tools, you can provide your users with very elegant (and often expected) online help documentation at their fingertips.

37

Distributing Your Application with ODE

- Distributing Your Application: An Introduction, 958
- Looking At the ODE, 958
- Distributing Your Application to Run with a Full Copy of Access, 960
- Using Full Versions versus Runtime Versions of Access, 961
- Preparing Your Database for Use with the Access Runtime Version, 964
- Looking At Other Issues, 984
- Practical Examples: Distributing the Time and Billing Application, 989

Distributing Your Application: An Introduction

Many developers are responsible for designing applications that will be distributed to many users. The most basic distribution option is to require each user to purchase a copy of Access and then simply provide each user with a copy of the database (MDB) files required for the application. The developer then can go to each user and configure the application appropriately.

Although distributing an application by copying it to each user's machine does not require much specialized knowledge on the part of the developer, it generally is not very practical. For one thing, it often is prohibitively expensive for each user of the application to own a copy of Access. Furthermore, in many situations, the developer is distributing an application to users who are dispersed throughout the country or even the world. Many Access applications are mass-marketed to hundreds or even thousands of users. It is very impractical to require such a user base to own Microsoft Access or to properly install the application without a professional setup program. Finally, without the Microsoft *Office Developer Edition* (ODE), it is much more difficult for you as a developer to provide the user with the professional look and feel you want your application to have. For these reasons, most developers must purchase ODE and learn how to take advantage of what it offers.

Looking At the ODE

The ODE is a version of Microsoft Office that enables you to package and distribute professional-looking applications without requiring your users to purchase the Access application software. The ODE is like several products in one. The ODE is targeted toward developers and includes these tools:

- A royalty-free runtime license
- The Setup Wizard
- The Replication Manager
- A two-volume language reference
- The Office-Compatible Basic Toolkit Style Guide
- Several 32-bit ActiveX controls
- The Win32 API Text Viewer
- The Help Workshop for Windows 95
- The Microsoft Access Developer Sample CD-ROM
- The Microsoft Graph Runtime Executable

Each of these components is discussed in the sections that follow.

Royalty-Free Runtime License

The royalty-free runtime license provided with the ODE enables your users to take advantage of your application and all that it provides without owning their own copy of Access. As you will see later in this chapter, your users cannot directly create new database objects with the Access runtime version. Nor do they have access to the Database window, built-in toolbars, numerous menu items, and several other features that are part of the full Access product. In many situations, you don't want the user to have access to all these features. Instead, you want to provide your users with a very complete, fully integrated application that only you will be responsible for modifying. Furthermore, you want to provide all this to your users without requiring them to purchase Access. The ODE, with its royalty-free runtime license, enables you to do exactly that.

Setup Wizard

The Setup Wizard enables you to easily create distribution disks containing all the files necessary to run your application. The Setup Wizard creates a highly professional-looking setup program that your users will run when they want to install your application. Using the Setup Wizard, you can customize what is included with your application. You can even provide your users with the familiar Standard, Compressed, and Custom options they have come to know from installing other Microsoft products. The Setup Wizard is covered in detail in the "Running the Setup Wizard" section of this chapter.

Replication Manager

The Replication Manager is a tool that enables you to manage replication in your custom application. This highly powerful, very sophisticated tool contains a runtime version that can be distributed with your applications. The Replication Manager is covered in detail in Chapter 24, "Replication Made Easy."

Two-Volume Language Reference

To many people's surprise, Access does not include a Language Reference or a Data Access Reference as "standard equipment." Although such documentation is available online, many developers prefer to view their documentation in print. Both the Access Language Reference and the Data Access Reference are included as hard copy with the ODE.

32-Bit ActiveX Controls

ActiveX controls give your application significant functionality with little work on your part. Only one ActiveX control ships with Access: the Calendar control. The ODE ships with 12 additional, extremely utilitarian custom controls. They include the Common Dialog control,

Rich Text Box control, Status Bar control, and Data Outline control, just to mention a few. These controls help you to build highly professional applications with minimal effort. ActiveX custom controls are covered in detail in Chapter 26, "Using ActiveX Controls."

Win32 API Text Viewer

The Win32 API Text Viewer facilitates the process of including the `Declare` statements, `Type` declarations, and `Constant` declarations required for you to use DLL functions in your applications. The ODE ships with Win32API.txt. This file, when loaded into the Win32 API Text Viewer, enables you to select `Declare` statements, `Type` declarations, and `Constant` declarations and then copy them into your modules with the click of a mouse. This time-saving tool is discussed in detail in Chapter 31, "Using External Functions: The Windows API."

Help Workshop for Windows 95

The Help Workshop for Windows 95 significantly eases the pain associated with the process of building custom Help into your applications. It assists with the process of creating the Help project, enabling you to easily specify all the components of the project. The Help Workshop for Windows 95 Help Compiler is covered in detail in Chapter 36, "Developing a Help File."

Microsoft Access Developer Sample CD-ROM

The Microsoft Access Developer Sample CD-ROM contains information about the Microsoft Developer Network. It also includes numerous articles and white papers that can assist you with the completion of many complex tasks.

Microsoft Graph Runtime Executable

The Microsoft Graph Runtime Executable enables you to distribute the Graphing Engine with your application. This means that you can add graphing functionality to your applications without mandating that your users own some other product that includes Microsoft Graph.

Distributing Your Application to Run with a Full Copy of Access

Many developers distribute their applications to end-users who own and have installed Microsoft Access. These users might be responsible for designing their own ad hoc queries and reports. For these users, it is important that you properly secure your application, provide the users of your application with only the functionality you want included in your application, and give professional polish to your application.

Many of the topics in this chapter apply to your application whether you are distributing the application to users with the Access runtime version or with the full copy of Access. You probably should include a switchboard, custom menu bars, and custom toolbars in your application, for example, whether you are distributing your application with the runtime version or for use under the full version of Access.

Using Full Versions versus Runtime Versions of Access

Many people have the misconception that using the Setup Wizard and distributing your application using the Access runtime version somehow means that the application is compiled. This is not the case at all! In fact, if the database is not secured properly, anyone can install his or her own copy of Access and modify the application's data and other objects just as you can. Using the Setup Wizard and distributing your application with the Access runtime version does not modify the database in any way. It simply gives you the license to freely distribute the engine required to run your application.

Actually, the engine is not even a modified version of the Access executable! The MSACCESS.EXE that you distribute is the same as the MSACCESS.EXE that you use to build your application. When you use the Setup Wizard to create installation disks for your users, the same MSACCESS.EXE that you use is copied to the installation disks. So how can there be any difference between the retail and runtime versions of Access?

When the user installs your application, the MSACCESS.EXE is copied to the user's machine. During this process, the installation program checks a Windows Registry licensing key to see whether the user owns a copy of Access. If the licensing key indicates that the user does not own a copy of Access, or if the key does not exist, the licensing key (which is a set of numbers and letters) is updated to indicate that the user will be using the runtime version of the product. When Access executes and the runtime licensing key is found, the product launches in runtime mode.

When the runtime licensing key is found, Access behaves differently than when the full licensing key is found. If you are not aware of the differences, you will be quite surprised when certain aspects of your application no longer function as expected. Differences between the full and runtime versions of the product follow:

- The Database window is hidden.
- Design views are hidden.
- Built-in toolbars are not supported.
- Some menu items are not available.
- Certain keys are disabled.

Hidden Database Window

When users launch your application using the runtime version of Access, the Database window is not visible. It's actually there, but it is hidden because its colors are set to the same colors as the Windows background color. This means that you can interact with the Database window using code, but the users of your application will be unable to interact with the Database window directly.

The fact that the Database window is hidden tends to be a double-edged sword. On one hand, it prevents most users from modifying the objects in your application. On the other hand, it puts the responsibility on you to build a complete interface for your application. Remember that, for you as a developer, the Database window is a starting point. You must provide a different starting point and navigational tools for your users to maneuver throughout your application.

Hidden Design Views

The users of your application won't have direct access to any design views, which means that they are unable to create or modify tables, queries, forms, reports, macros, or modules. You still can get to all this functionality through code, though. You can build a wizard that enables your users to define all aspects of a query or some other object, for example, and then build the query (or other object) by using DAO code. Again, this helps protect your application from novice users, but it puts the pressure on you to ensure that your application provides its users with all the functionality they need.

Built-In Toolbars Not Supported

All built-in toolbars are completely unavailable with the runtime version of Access, which means that you must design your own toolbars and attach them to your forms and reports as appropriate. This is covered in the "Adding Custom Menus and Toolbars" section of this chapter.

Unavailable Menu Items

Built-in toolbars are not supported at all when using the runtime version of Access, but menus are simply modified after the runtime key is found. Many menu items are hidden in the runtime version. These hidden menu items prevent users from making changes to your application. The easiest way to obtain a list of hidden menu items is to look in the ODE Help file. The Help file contains a topic called Hidden Menu Commands in the Run-Time Environment, as shown in Figure 37.1. This Help topic shows each hidden menu command, which menu it is contained in, and from which windows it is removed.

Figure 37.1.
Help on hidden menu commands in the runtime environment.

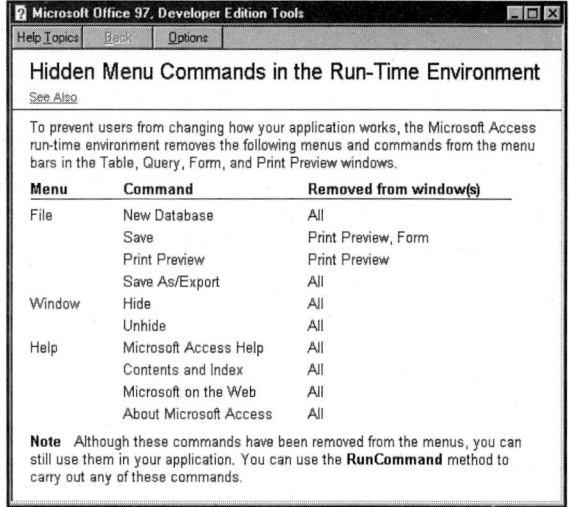

Although many of the menu commands are hidden from the user, they can be accessed by using the DoMenuItem command. In other words, the functionality is there, but it is simply hidden from your users.

Disabled Keys

Several keystrokes are unavailable to your users when they run your application with the runtime version of Access. Table 37.1 lists these keystrokes.

Table 37.1. Disabled keys.

Keys	Function
Ctrl+Break	Halts macro and code execution
Shift (when opening the database)	Prevents execution of the AutoExec macro and ignores Startup properties
Alt+F1/F11	Displays the Database window
F12	Displays the Save As dialog box
Shift+F12	Saves a database object
Ctrl+G	Displays the Debug window
Ctrl+F11	Toggles between custom and built-in toolbars

As you can see, these are keys that you would rarely, if ever, want your users to use. You might consider the disabling of these keystrokes a positive side effect of using the runtime version of the product.

Preparing Your Database for Use with the Access Runtime Version

Several steps are required to prepare your database for use with the Access runtime version. Although many of these steps are mandatory when distributing your application with the runtime version, they also are good as a general practice when developing a polished application. To prepare your application for use with the Access runtime version, follow these steps:

- Create the application.
- Test and debug the application.
- Create Help files and associate the Help topics with the application's objects.
- Run and test the application with the /Runtime command line argument.
- Run the Setup Wizard.
- Package and distribute the application.

Creating the Application

You need to be concerned about several things when designing an application for use with the Access runtime version. Although the following items are niceties in any application, they are a mandatory aspect of developing an application for use with the Access runtime version:

- Build the application around forms.
- Build error handling into the application.
- Build custom menus and toolbars into the application.
- Set startup options for the application.
- Properly secure the application.

Building the Application Around Forms

The first step when creating the application with runtime distribution in mind is to build the application around forms. This means that everything in the application needs to be forms-driven. Your application generally should begin by displaying a Main Switchboard. The Main Switchboard then can direct the user to additional switchboards, such as a Data Entry Switchboard, Reports Switchboard, Maintenance Switchboard, and so on. The easiest way to create such a switchboard is by using the Switchboard Wizard. Here's how it works:

1. Choose Tools | Add-ins | Switchboard Manager. If you have not yet created a switchboard for your application, the Switchboard Manager message box appears, as shown in Figure 37.2.

2. Click Yes. The Switchboard Manager dialog box appears, as shown in Figure 37.3. Notice that a Main Switchboard is created.

3. Begin by adding additional switchboard pages. To do this, click New. The Create New dialog box appears, as shown in Figure 37.4.

4. Type a name for the new switchboard page and click OK.

Figure 37.2.
The Switchboard Manager message box..

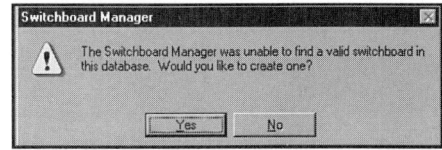

Figure 37.3.
Creating a switchboard.

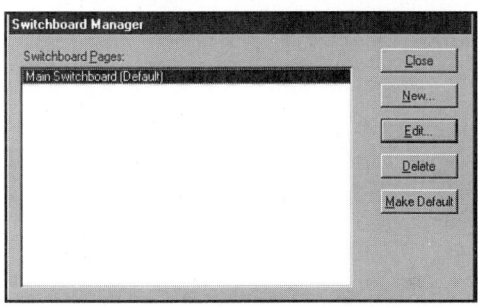

Figure 37.4.
The Create New dialog box.

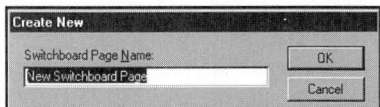

5. Repeat steps 3 and 4 for each switchboard page you want to add.

6. When you are done adding pages, the Switchboard Manager window should look something like the one in Figure 37.5. You now are ready to add items to each switchboard page. To add items to the Main Switchboard, click the Main Switchboard entry and click Edit. The Edit Switchboard Page dialog box appears, as shown in Figure 37.6.

7. Click New to add a new item to the Main Switchboard. The Edit Switchboard Item dialog box appears, as shown in Figure 37.7.

Figure 37.5.

The Switchboard Manager dialog box after adding pages.

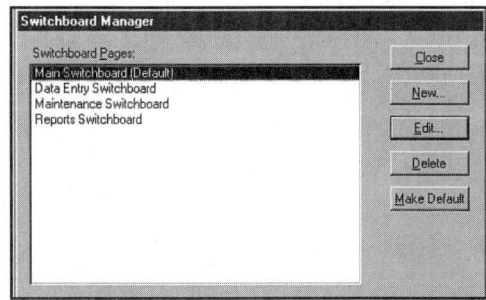

Figure 37.6.

The Edit Switchboard Page dialog box.

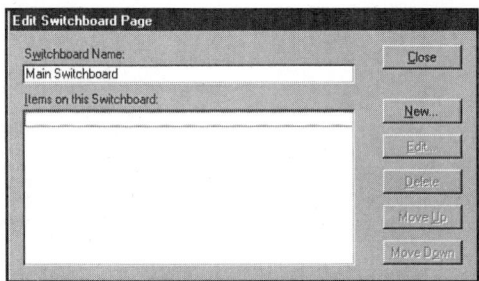

Figure 37.7.

The Edit Switchboard Item dialog box.

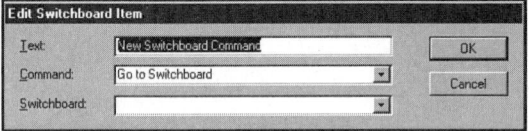

8. In the Text box, enter the text for the new switchboard item.

9. Select an appropriate command from the Command drop-down list. Available commands control the capability to go to another switchboard, open a form, or open a report.

10. The third item in the Edit Switchboard Item dialog box varies, depending on which command you select from the Command drop-down list. If you select Go to Switchboard from the Command drop-down list, for example, the third option enables you to select from available switchboards. If you select Open Form in Edit Mode, the third option enables you to select from available forms. Select the third option and click OK.

11. Repeat steps 6 through 10 to add each item to the Main Switchboard.

12. After adding entries to the Main Switchboard, the Edit Switchboard Page dialog box should look similar to the one in Figure 37.8. Click Close to return to the main Switchboard Manager dialog box.

Figure 37.8.

The Edit Switchboard Page dialog box after adding several entries.

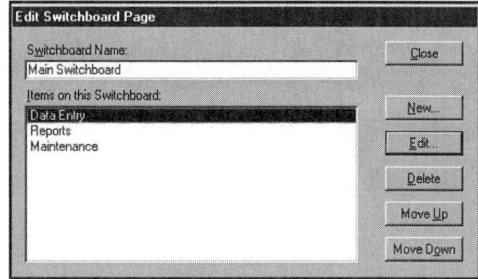

13. Repeat steps 6 through 12 for each switchboard page.

14. When you are ready to generate the switchboard, click Close from the main Switchboard Manager window. The switchboard then is generated.

Follow these steps to add, remove, or edit items from an existing switchboard:

1. Choose Tools | Add-ins | Switchboard Manager. The Switchboard Manager dialog box appears.

2. Select the Switchboard page you want to affect. Click Delete to delete the page, or click Edit to make changes to the page. If you want to add a new page, click Add.

3. If you click Edit, the Edit Switchboard Page dialog box appears. You can click the Move Up and Move Down buttons to move items up and down on the Switchboard page. You also can add, edit, and delete items from the page.

4. When you are finished, click OK. The changes take effect immediately.

Figure 37.9 shows a completed switchboard.

Figure 37.9.

A completed switchboard.

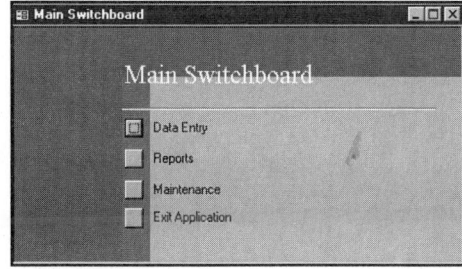

Building Error Handling into the Application

It is imperative that you build error handling into your application. If an error occurs when someone is using the runtime version of Access and no error handling is in place, an error message is displayed and the user instantly is returned to the Windows desktop. Therefore, it is crucial that you build error handling into all your routines. Creating a generic error handler to assist you with this task is covered in Chapter 17, "Handling Those Dreaded Runtime Errors."

Adding Custom Menus and Toolbars

As mentioned earlier in this chapter, limited versions of the standard Access menus are available under the Access runtime version, but toolbars are not available at all. You therefore must provide your users with whatever menu bar and toolbar functionality the application requires.

As discussed in Chapter 13, "Let's Get More Intimate with Forms: Advanced Techniques," you can attach a menu bar to a form by using the Menu Bar property of the form. (See Figure 37.10.) When a specific menu bar is associated with a particular form or report, the menu appears whenever the form or report becomes the active window. It generally is easier to base a form or report's menu on one of the standard Access menus and then add or remove menu items as appropriate.

Figure 37.10.

The Menu Bar property of a form.

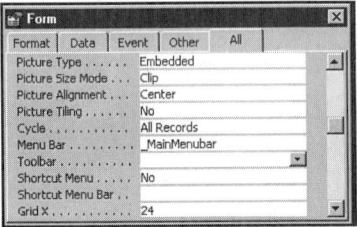

You must build each toolbar that you want to use with your application. As covered in Chapter 13, you can specify the toolbar that you want to be visible with your form or report by using the Toolbar property of the form or report. At times, you might prefer to control the toolbars that display by using code. By using this method, you can give the users access to your own toolbars or custom toolbars at will. Listing 37.1 shows the code placed in the `Activate` event of the form or report.

Listing 37.1. Code for the `Activate` event.

```
Private Sub Form_Activate()
On Error GoTo Err_Form_Activate
    Call ToolBarShow("tbrMainForm", True)
    Me![fsubClients].Requery

Exit_Form_Activate:
    Exit Sub

Err_Form_Activate:
    MsgBox Err.Description
    Resume Exit_Form_Activate
End Sub
```

The `Activate` event of the frmClients form calls a user-defined procedure called `ToolbarShow`. It passes the `ToolbarShow` routine two parameters: the name of the toolbar it will affect and a Boolean variable indicating whether the specified toolbar should be shown or hidden. Listing 37.2 shows the `ToolbarShow` routine.

Listing 37.2. The `ToolbarShow` routine.

```
Sub ToolBarShow(strToolbar As String, fShow As Boolean)
    DoCmd.ShowToolbar strToolbar, _
        IIf(fShow, acToolbarYes, acToolbarNo)
    DoCmd.ShowToolbar "Form View", _
        IIf(fShow, acToolbarNo, acToolbarWhereApprop)
End Sub
```

The `ToolBarShow` routine is one routine that handles both the showing and hiding of custom toolbars. It receives a string and a Boolean variable. The Showtoolbar method, contained in the `DoCmd` object, sets the toolbars to visible or hidden. The command does this by taking the name of the toolbar and a Boolean value (both are passed in as parameters) and toggling the Visible property for that toolbar to True for visible or False for hidden, depending on which was passed into the function. If the `ToolBarShow` routine is passed the string `tbrMainForm` and the Boolean True, for example, it shows the tbrMainForm toolbar.

In case the application will run in both the retail and runtime versions of Access, you should ensure that the standard toolbar is hidden when the form is active. The second ShowToolbar method indicates that the Form View toolbar will be hidden if you are displaying the custom toolbar and will be shown, where appropriate, if you are hiding the custom toolbar. The Deactivate event of the form looks like this:

```
Private Sub Form_Deactivate()
    Call ToolBarShow("tbrMainForm", False)
End Sub
```

This routine hides the tbrMainForm toolbar and shows the Form View toolbar where appropriate.

Clearly, it is important that you perform all the menu and toolbar handling required by your application. This ensures that all menu bars and toolbars are available when they should be, and *only* when they should be.

Setting Startup Options

Access 97 provides you with several startup options that enable you to control what happens to your application when it is loaded. Figure 37.11 shows the Startup dialog box, which includes the Advanced options. Table 37.2 lists each option in the Startup dialog box.

Figure 37.11.

The Startup dialog box.

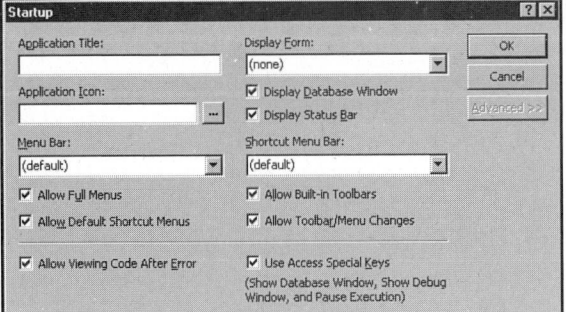

Table 37.2. Startup options.

Option	Function
Application Title	Sets the AppTitle property, which displays a custom title in the application title bar.
Application Icon	Sets the AppIcon property, which displays a custom icon in the application title bar.
Menu Bar	Sets the StartupMenuBar property, which specifies the custom menu bar displayed by default when the application is loaded.
Allow Full Menus	Sets the AllowFullMenus property, which allows or restricts the use of Access menus.
Allow Default Shortcut Menus	Sets the AllowShortcutMenus property, which allows or restricts the use of standard Access shortcut menus.
Display Form	Sets the StartupForm property, which specifies the form displayed when the application is loaded.
Display Database Window	Sets the StartupShowDBWindow property, which determines whether the Database window is visible when the application is opened.
Display Status Bar	Sets the StartupShowStatusBar property, which determines whether the status bar is visible when the application is opened.
Shortcut Menu Bar	Sets the StartupShortcutMenuBar property, which specifies a menu bar displayed by default as the shortcut menu bar.

Option	Function
Allow Built-in Toolbars	Sets the AllowBuiltInToolbars property, which indicates whether built-in toolbars are available to your users.
Allow Toolbar/Menu Changes	Sets the AllowToolbarChanges property, which determines whether your users can customize toolbars in the application.
Allow Viewing Code After Error	Sets the AllowBreakIntoCode property, which indicates whether Ctrl+Break places the user in the Code window after an error.
Use Access Special Keys	Sets the AllowSpecialKeys property, which determines whether the user can use keys such as F11 to display the Database window, Ctrl+F11 to toggle between custom and built-in toolbars, and so on.

As you might have guessed, many of these options apply only when you are running the application under the retail version of Access. You do not need to set the Display Database Window property, for example, if your application will be running only under the runtime version of Access. The Database window is never available under the runtime version of the product, so this property is ignored when the application is run under the runtime version. Regardless, I like setting these properties to ensure that the application behaves as I want it to under *both* the retail and runtime versions of the product.

All the properties can be set by using the Startup dialog box or by using code. If you use code, you must make sure that the property exists for the Database object before you set it. If the property does not exist, you must append the property to the Database object.

Only users with Administer permission for the database can modify the Startup properties. If you want to ensure that certain users cannot modify the startup options of the database, you must ensure that they do not have Administer permissions.

As part of the startup options for your database, you should determine what code, if any, is run when the application is loaded. You can accomplish this in one of two ways. You can start the application with an AutoExec macro and then issue a RunCode action to execute a VBA procedure. Or, you can designate a Startup form for the application and then call a custom AutoExec routine from the Open event of the Startup form. The code shown in Listing 37.3 is called from the Open event of the Startup form for the Time and Billing application. This code, and the rest of the code in this chapter, is located in the CHAP37.MDB database file on the sample code CD-ROM.

Listing 37.3. Setting options from a Startup form routine.

```
Sub AutoExec(frmAny As Form)
    On Error GoTo AutoExec_Err:

    Dim fAnswer As Boolean
    DoCmd.OpenForm "frmSplash"
    DoEvents
    DoCmd.Hourglass True
    fAnswer = AreTablesAttached(frmAny)
    If Not fAnswer Then
        MsgBox "You Cannot Run This App Without Locating Data Tables"
        DoCmd.Close acForm, "frmSplash"
        DoCmd.Quit
    End If
    Call GetCompanyInfo
    DoCmd.Hourglass False
    If IsLoaded("frmSplash") Then
        DoCmd.Close acForm, "frmSplash"
    End If
    Exit Sub

AutoExec_Err:
    DoCmd.Hourglass False
    MsgBox "Error # " & Err.Number & ": " & Err.Description
    Exit Sub
End Sub
```

This generic routine receives any form as a parameter. It uses the OpenForm method to open a form called frmSplash. Then it issues a DoEvents command to give the form time to open. An hourglass mouse pointer is displayed, and the routine calls a user-defined function that ensures that the database tables are linked successfully. This AreTablesAttached routine is covered in the "Automating the Process of Linking Tables" section of this chapter. If the AreTablesAttached function returns False, users are warned that they cannot run the application. The frmSplash form is closed and the application is exited. As long as the tables links were established successfully, the AutoExec routine proceeds to call a routine called GetCompanyInfo, where it loads frequently used information into an array. The hourglass mouse pointer is removed, and the splash screen is unloaded.

Securing the Application

Don't fool yourself! Remember that the runtime version of Access in no way secures your application. It simply provides you with royalty-free distribution. You must perform all the same measures to secure your application under the runtime version of Access that you perform under the retail version of the product. The bottom line is that you must take measures to secure your application if you want it and its data to be secure. The basics of security are covered in Chapter 32, "Database Security Made Easy," and the intricacies of security are covered in Chapter 33, "Complex Security Issues." Distributing your application as an MDE provides an additional level of security while improving performance and decreasing the size of the database file. MDE files are covered in the next section.

Distributing Your Application as an MDE

The process of creating an MDE file compiles all modules, removes all source code from your database, and compacts the destination database. All code will run, but the user will be unable to modify forms, reports, and modules. Besides protecting the objects in your database, this process reduces the size of the database and some of the overhead associated with it, thereby improving application performance. Creating and distributing an MDE file is not as simple as it might appear at first glance. Chapter 32 covers the process of creating an MDE file and the important issues that surround this new Access file format.

Adding Custom Help to the Application

To add polish to your application and ensure that the help you provide to your users applies to what they are looking at in your application, you must provide a custom Help file. Adding help to your application is covered in detail in Chapter 36. In essence, it involves creating an RTF file and other supporting files and using the Windows 95 Help Workshop to build a compiled Help file. You then must add help to the various objects in your application.

Testing and Debugging the Application

Before you even bother trying to run your application under the runtime version, you should fully test and debug the application under the retail version of the product. When you are fairly confident that you have all the kinks worked out of the application, you are ready to test it in the runtime environment.

Running and Testing the Application with the `/Runtime` Command Line Switch

Microsoft provides you with a very easy way to test an application to see how it will perform under the runtime version of Access without having to actually create distribution disks. You can do this by using the `/Runtime` command-line switch. The `/Runtime` switch forces Access to load in runtime mode. Here's how it works:

```
c:\msoffice\access\msaccess.exe c:\clients\sams\master~1\databases\chap37.mdb
➥/runtime
```

After you load the application with the `/Runtime` switch, you should once again test all aspects of the application. At times, you might want to test to see whether the application has been launched with the runtime or retail version of the product. You can accomplish this with the following code:

```
If Not SysCmd(acSysCmdRuntime) _
    And CurrentUser <> "Admin" Then
    MsgBox "You aren't allowed here"
End If
```

The SysCmd function, when passed the constant acSysCmdRuntime, checks to see whether the application was launched by using the runtime version of Access. In this case, if the program was run with the retail version of Access and CurrentUser is not Admin, a message is displayed indicating that the user is not allowed. Of course, you easily could modify this routine to check for other users and to quit the application if an unauthorized person attempts to launch the application without the runtime version of the product.

Running the Setup Wizard

After you have fully tested and prepared your application for distribution, you are ready to run the Setup Wizard. The Setup Wizard walks you through all the steps required to build distribution disks that include all the components your application needs to run. You can launch the Setup Wizard from the Windows 95 Startup menu or by using a desktop shortcut. When you launch the Setup Wizard, the Setup Wizard Welcome dialog box appears, as shown in Figure 37.12.

Figure 37.12.

The Setup Wizard Welcome dialog box.

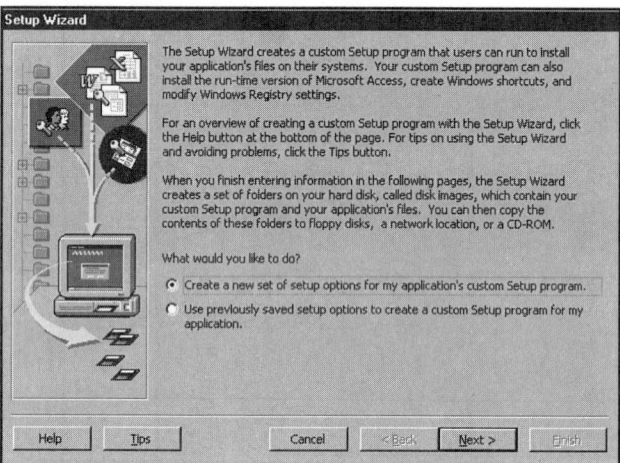

Viewing the Introductory Screen

The Setup Wizard Welcome dialog box enables you to create a new set of Setup options or to use a previously saved set of options. If you select Create a New Set of Setup Options for My Application's Custom Setup Program and click Next, the next step of the Setup Wizard appears.

Adding Files to be Included on the Distribution Disks

The second step of the Setup Wizard enables you to specify files that you want to add to the Setup disks, as shown in Figure 37.13. The types of files you will add from this dialog box follow:

- Application databases
- Data databases
- Library files
- OCX files
- Icon files
- Splash screens
- Help files
- Any other special files that you need to distribute

Figure 37.13.
Adding files to the Setup disks.

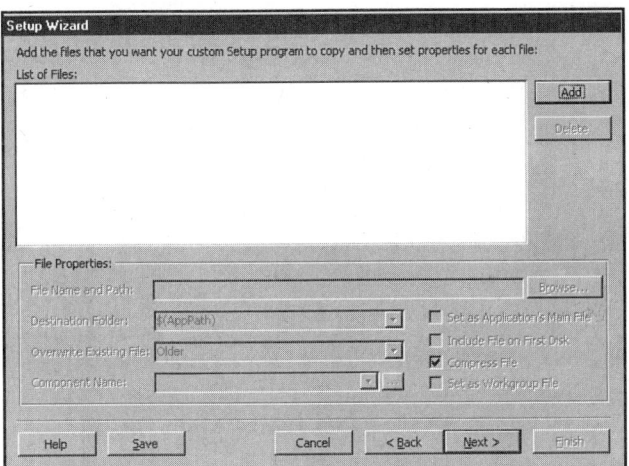

Follow these steps to add a file:

1. In the Setup Wizard dialog box, click Add. The Select Files dialog box appears.
2. Locate the file you want to add and click Add. After you add several files, the Setup Wizard dialog box looks like the one in Figure 37.14.
3. Set the options for each file included on the distribution disks. Table 37.3 lists these options.
4. When you are done setting the options for all the files, click Next.

Figure 37.14.

The Setup Wizard dialog box after adding several files.

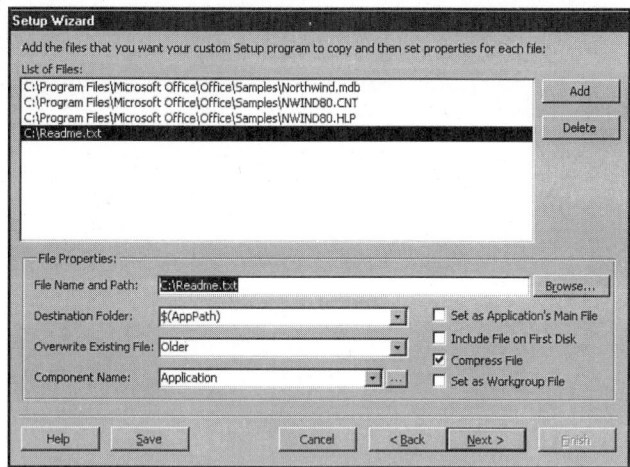

Table 37.3. Options available for files you add to the distribution disks.

Property	Function
File Name and Path	Specifies the location and path of the component being included.
Destination Folder	Specifies where the file will be placed when the Setup program is executed. The options are `$(AppPath)`, `$(AppPath)\subfolder`, `$(WinPath)`, or `$(WinSysPath)`. These specify the application path, a subpath to the application path, the Windows folder, and the Windows System folder, respectively.
Overwrite Existing File	Applies when the user has installed a copy of your application. Indicates whether the new file only overwrites an existing file if the existing file is older, always overwrites the existing file, or never overwrites the file.
Component Name	By default, all files belong to the Application component. You can define custom components and specify when and how those components will be installed (see the next section, "Adding Components").
Set as Application's Main File	Indicates that the selected file is your application database.

Property	Function
Include File on First Disk	Enables you to designate that the selected file always will be found on the first Setup disk.
Compress File	Indicates whether the selected file should be compressed on the Setup disks.
Set as Workgroup File	When distributing an MDW file, designates the file as the system workgroup file.

Adding Components

By default, the only type of component is Application; anything that is an Application component is defined to install under Typical, Compact, and Custom installations. By defining additional components, you can categorize Application components and set their properties as a group. You can create a component called HelpFiles, for example, and install anything with a component name of HelpFiles only under typical and custom installations, as shown in Figure 37.15. After you define components, you assign to a specific component category each file you are including with your application.

Figure 37.15.
Creating component categories.

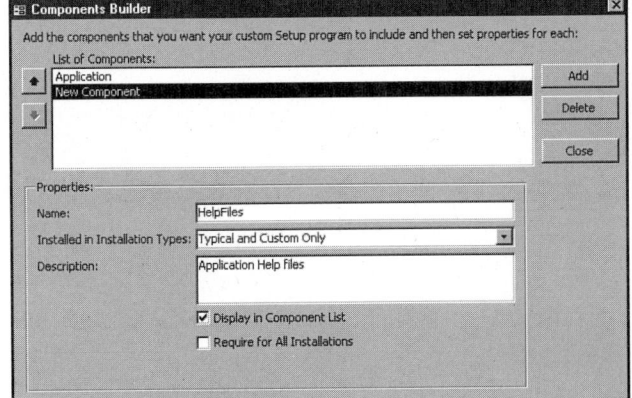

Defining Shortcuts

The third dialog box of the Setup Wizard is a tabbed dialog box that enables you to define desktop shortcuts that your application will create. Figure 37.16 shows the Shortcut step of the Setup Wizard. You use the first tab to define general shortcut properties, and the second tab enables you to define database shortcut properties. You generally should establish shortcuts for your application and for the compact and repair processes. Table 37.4 lists the properties included in this dialog box.

Figure 37.16.

Defining shortcuts.

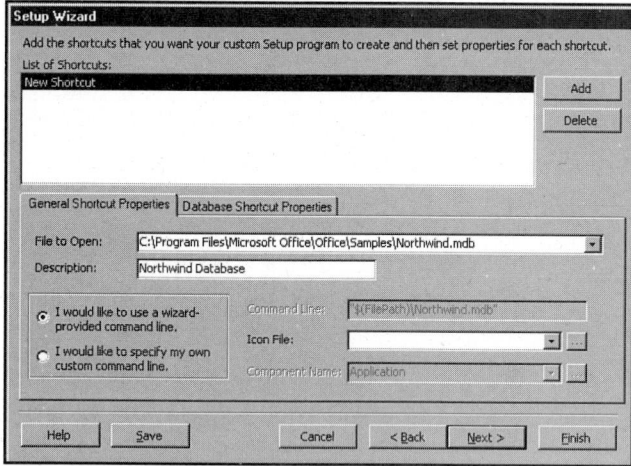

Table 37.4. Properties for shortcuts.

Property	Function
File to Open	Specifies the file that the shortcut opens.
Description	Specifies the text that appears for the desktop shortcut.
Command-Line Style	Determines whether you want the wizard to build the command line or you want to type your own command line.
Command Line	Specifies the command line that runs after the user selects the shortcut.
Icon File	Selects the icon that appears on the desktop.
Component Name	Selects in which component category the shortcut is included.
Database Shortcut	Determines what you want the shortcut Action Options to do.
Database Command-Line	Specifies how you want the application Options to work. Selecting the Workgroup option, for example, causes the application to run with a custom MDW (workgroup information file).

Adding Registry Values

The next step of the Setup Wizard enables you to add Registry values when your application is installed. You can add Registry values for anything you want. A predefined Registry value used by an application is the AppHelpFile key, for example. Using the AppHelpFile key, you can specify a Help file that you want your application to use. Figure 37.17 illustrates the process of defining a Registry entry.

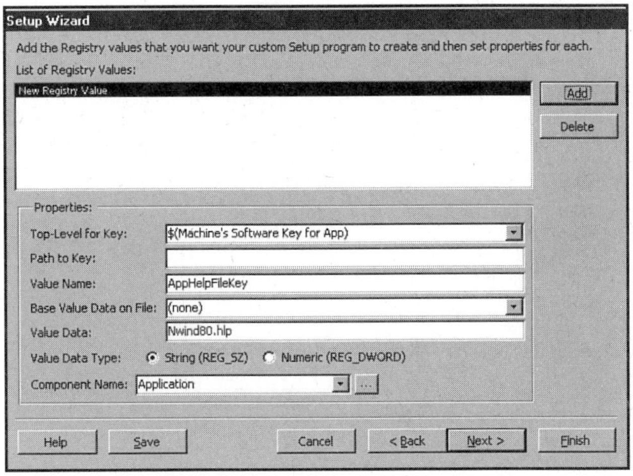

Figure 37.17.
Defining a Registry entry.

Designating Access Components

The next step of the Setup Wizard enables you to designate Access components that you want to include with your application. (See Figure 37.18.) It is imperative that you select all ISAM drivers and other runtime components that your application requires to run. Otherwise, your application won't run properly.

Figure 37.18.
Designating Access components.

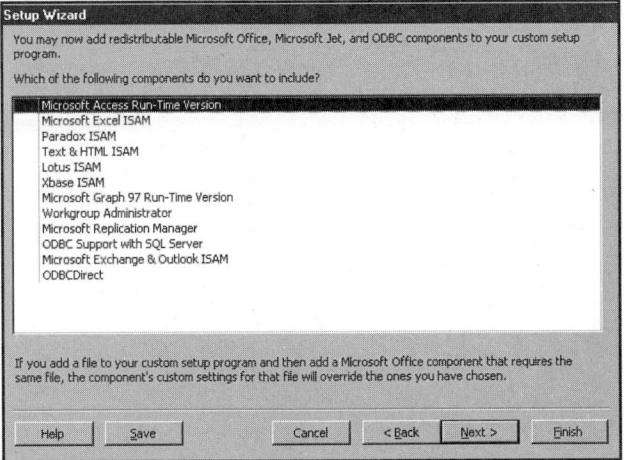

Reordering Components and Setting Their Properties

The next step of the Setup Wizard enables you to reorder the various components of the application and set their properties. (See Figure 37.19.) All custom categories have the properties you defined when you added the component. You can override those properties here.

Figure 37.19.
Reordering components and setting their properties.

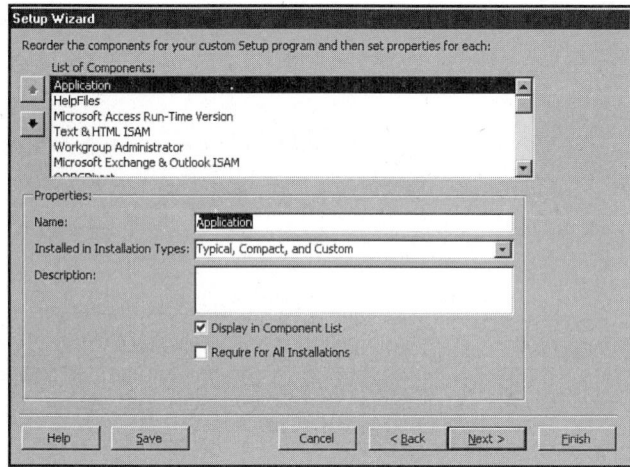

Setting Key Attributes of the Application

The next step in the Setup Wizard enables you to specify some key attributes of your application. (See Figure 37.20.) These attributes include the name of the application, the version number, the name of your company, and the suggested folder for the installation.

Figure 37.20.
Specifying key attributes of the application.

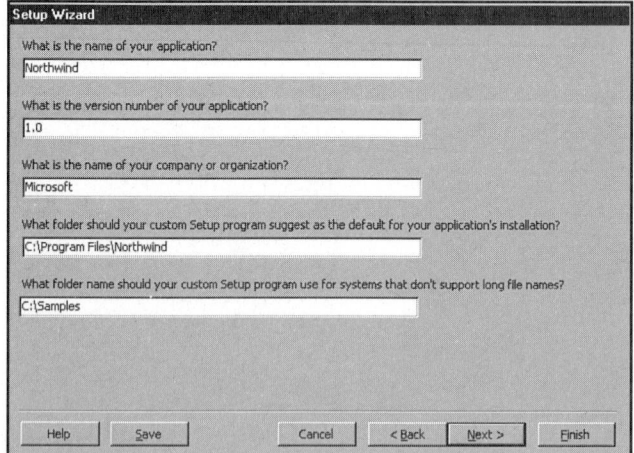

Specifying That a Program Execute After Setup is Completed

The next step in the Setup Wizard enables you to designate the name of an executable that will run after the Setup program is complete. (See Figure 37.21.) You can use this step to run Notepad.exe and load a designated Read.Me file, for example.

Figure 37.21.

Specifying a program that will execute after setup is completed.

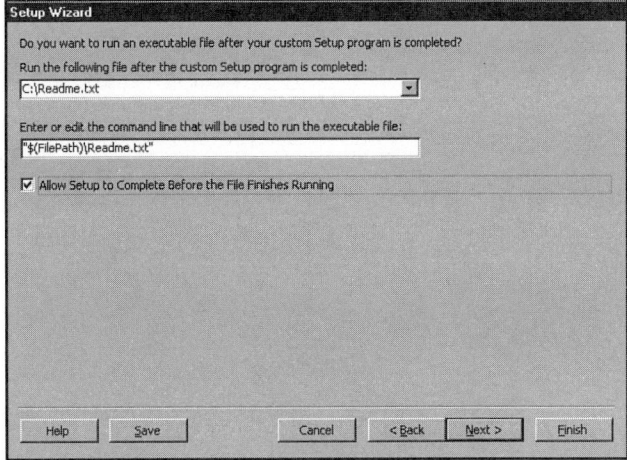

Specifying a Location for the Setup Files

Finally, you can determine where the installation files will be located when the wizard creates them. (See Figure 37.22.) It is a good idea to create a network setup from which your users can install the application. You also can specify whether the files will be compressed on the network server.

Figure 37.22.

Telling the Setup Wizard where to store its output files.

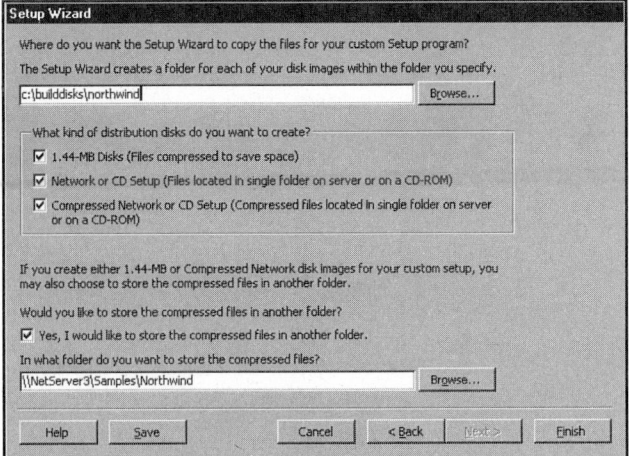

> **WARNING**
>
> Always save the Setup template when prompted. (See Figure 37.23.) This ensures that if the Setup process does not complete successfully or if you need to rerun the Setup process at a later time, you won't have to redefine all the options.

Figure 37.23.

Saving the Setup options as a template.

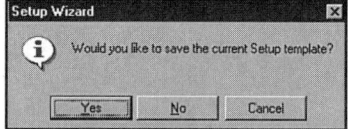

Packaging and Distributing the Application

The most important thing you must do when packaging and distributing your application is to test the application on a machine that has never had a copy of Access or any Access runtime application installed. This ensures that your application includes all required components. I like to keep a clean machine available for testing my application setups. Here's what I do:

1. Back up the Windows and Windows\System folders on the machine.
2. Install my application.
3. Test my application.
4. Delete my application.
5. Delete everything in the Windows\System folder.
6. Restore the Windows System folder from backup.

By following these steps, I ensure that I always have a machine on which to test my application. Obviously, it is imperative that you test *all* aspects of your application on the machine on which you performed the installation from your Setup disks.

When you are ready to test the Setup process, follow these steps:

1. Choose Run from the Windows 95 Start menu.
2. Locate the Setup files that the Setup Wizard created in the Run dialog box, as shown in Figure 37.24.
3. Click OK. The Application Setup dialog box appears, as shown in Figure 37.25.
4. Click Continue.
5. Select a location for the application installation. (See Figure 37.26.)

Figure 37.24.

Selecting Run from the Start menu.

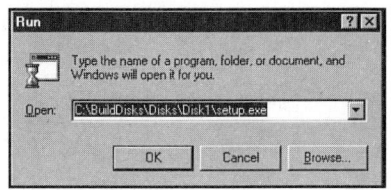

Figure 37.25.

The Application Setup Welcome dialog box.

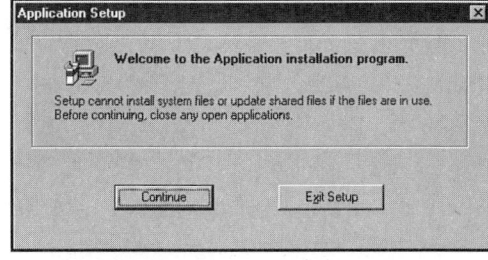

Figure 37.26.

Selecting a location for the program installation.

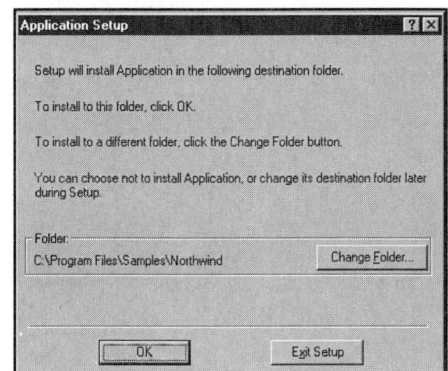

6. Click OK. The Application Setup dialog box appears.

7. Select the type of installation that you want: Typical, Custom, or Compact. (See Figure 37.27.) If you select Typical or Compact, you are asked no further questions and the installation process proceeds. If you select Custom, the Application - Custom dialog box appears, where you can select the components you want to install, as shown in Figure 37.28.

Figure 37.27.

Selecting a typical, compact, or custom installation.

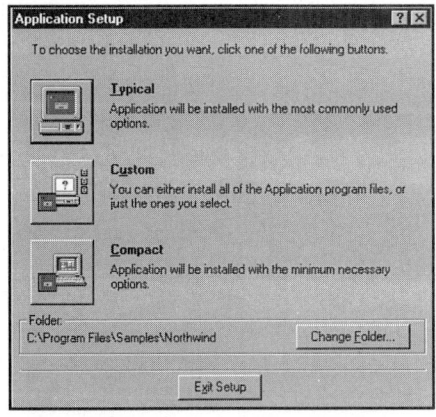

Figure 37.28.

Custom installation.

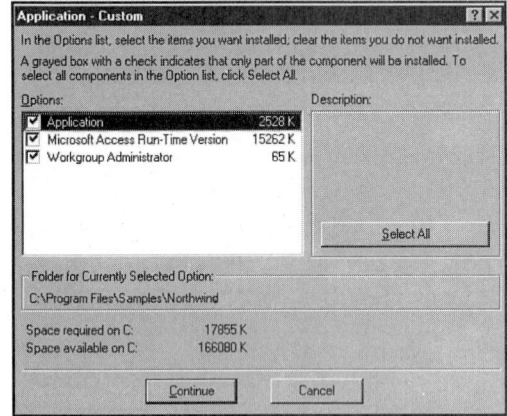

The installation process is completed. If you opted during the Setup Wizard to create desktop shortcuts, they are created automatically when the Setup program is executed.

Looking At Other Issues

Two additional issues have not yet been covered regarding the distribution of your application. The first issue involves ensuring that the application database can establish any links that it has to external tables. The second issue involves the prospect of using replication to effectively distribute changes to your application.

Automating the Process of Linking to Tables

Access hard-codes locations for table links. This means that if you install your application on another machine, unless the other machine has exactly the same folder structure as you do on your machine, the tables will not link successfully. The code shown in Listing 37.4 checks to see whether the required tables are available. If they are not found in the expected location, the routine attempts to locate them in the same folder as the application database. If they still cannot be found, the user is given an opportunity to locate the files. If they *still* cannot be found, the application terminates.

Listing 37.4. The Auto Attach function.

```
Function AreTablesAttached(frmAny As Form) As Boolean
    'Update connection information in linked tables.

    'Set up required constants
    Const MAXTABLES = 8
    Const NONEXISTENT_TABLE = 3011
    Const DB_NOT_FOUND = 3024
    Const ACCESS_DENIED = 3051
    Const READ_ONLY_DATABASE = 3027

    'Declare required variables
    Dim intTableCount As Integer
    Dim strFilename As String
    Dim vntReturnValue As Variant
    Dim tdf As TableDef
    Dim db As DATABASE
    Dim rst As Recordset
    Dim strAppDir As String

    'Point Database object variable at the current database
    Set db = CurrentDb

    'Set default return value of True
    AreTablesAttached = True

    ' Continue if links are broken.
    On Error Resume Next
    'Open one linked table to see if connection
    'information is correct.
    Set rst = db.OpenRecordset("tblClients")
    'Exit if connection information is correct.
    If Err.Number = 0 Then
      rst.Close
      Exit Function
    Else
      'Otherwise, determine location of current database
      strAppDir = Left(db.Name, LastOccurrence(db.Name, "\"))
      'Try to establish the connection searching for the linked
      'tables in the same folder as the application database
      If TryAgain(strAppDir) Then
          rst.Close
          Exit Function
      End If
      'If connection still cannot be established, continue
      'Warn the user
```

continues

Listing 37.4. continued

```
        MsgBox "You Must Locate the Data Tables"
        'Set the DialogTitle property of the Common dialog control
        frmAny!dlgCommon.DialogTitle = "Please Locate Data File"
        'Invoke the File Open common dialog
        frmAny!dlgCommon.ShowOpen
        'Store the name and location the user selected
        strFilename = frmAny!dlgCommon.filename
    End If


    'If the user did not select a file, bail out
    If strFilename = "" Then
        GoTo Exit_Failed ' User pressed Cancel.
    End If


    'Initialize progress meter.
    vntReturnValue = SysCmd(SYSCMD_INITMETER, "Attaching tables", MAXTABLES)


    ' Loop through all tables, relinking those with nonzero-length Connect strings.
intTableCount = 1  ' Initialize TableCount for status meter.
    For Each tdf In db.TableDefs
        If tdf.Connect <> "" Then
            tdf.Connect = ";DATABASE=" & strFilename
            Err.Number = 0
            tdf.RefreshLink
            If Err.Number <> 0 Then
                If Err.Number = NONEXISTENT_TABLE Then
                    MsgBox "File '" & strFilename & _
                        "' does not contain required table '" & _
                        tdf.SourceTableName & "'", 16, "Can't Run This App"
                ElseIf Err.Number = DB_NOT_FOUND Then
                    MsgBox "You can't run Time and Billing App " & vbCrLf & _
                        "Until you locate Data File", 16, "Can't Run Application"
                ElseIf Err.Number = ACCESS_DENIED Then
                    MsgBox "Couldn't open " & strFilename & _
                        " because it is read-only or it is located " & _
                        "on a read-only share.", 16, "Can't Run This App"
                ElseIf Err.Number = READ_ONLY_DATABASE Then
                    MsgBox "Can't reattach tables because Data File " & _
                        "is read-only or is located on a read-only share.", _
                        16, "Can't Run This App"
                Else
                    MsgBox Error, 16, "Can't Run This App"
                End If
intResponse = MsgBox(tdf.Name & " Not Found. " & _
                    vbCrLf & "Would You Like to Locate it?", _
                    vbQuestion + vbYesNo)
                If intResponse = vbYes Then
                    Forms!frmLogon!dlgCommon.DialogTitle = "Please Locate " & _
                        tdf.Name
                    Forms!frmLogon!dlgCommon.ShowOpen
                    strFilename = Forms!frmLogon!dlgCommon.filename
                Else
                    AreTablesAttached = False
                    GoTo Exit_Final
                End If
            End If
            intTableCount = intTableCount + 1
            vntReturnValue = SysCmd(SYSCMD_UPDATEMETER, intTableCount)
```

```
        End If
    Next tdf

    GoTo Exit_Final

Exit_Failed:
    MsgBox "You can't run this example until " & _
        "you locate Data File", 16, "Can't Run This Example"
    AreTablesAttached = False

Exit_Final:
    vntReturnValue = SysCmd(SYSCMD_REMOVEMETER)

End Function
```

The routine begins by declaring several required constants and variables. It then points a database object variable to the current database. It establishes a default return value of True and then uses the On Error Resume Next statement to instruct Access to resume on the next line if an error occurs. Next, the routine attempts to base a recordset on the tblClients table. If no error occurs, you know that the link was successfully established, and you can exit the function. Otherwise, the routine uses the LastOccurrence function (found immediately after this explanation), along with the VBA Left function to locate the folder in which the application database resides. It uses the TryAgain function (also found later in this section) to attempt to link to the files, looking in the same location for the data database as the application database. If the tables still cannot be linked successfully, the user is prompted for the location of the data tables. If the user cancels, or if the routine is still unsuccessful at locating the tables, a value of False is returned from the function.

The LastOccurrence routine receives two parameters: the string you want to search and the string for which you want to search. It proceeds to find the last occurrence of the string you want to search for in the string you are searching. For your purposes, you want to search the db.Name string (the name and location of the current database) for the last backslash. By doing this and then looking at everything *before* the last backslash, you can obtain the path in which the application database is located. Listing 37.5 shows the Find String function.

Listing 37.5. The Find String function.

```
Function LastOccurrence(strSearchString As String, _
            strLastOccurrence As String) As Integer

    Dim intVal As Integer, intLastPos As Integer

    'Find the first occurrence of the specified character
    intVal = InStr(strSearchString, strLastOccurrence)

    'Find each next occurrence of the specified character
    Do Until intVal = 0
```

continues

Listing 37.5. The `Find String` function.

```
        'Keep track of the last position found
        intLastPos = intVal
        intVal = InStr(intLastPos + 1, strSearchString, strLastOccurrence)
    Loop

    'Return the last position found
    LastOccurrence = intLastPos

End Function
```

The `TryAgain` function uses the `strAppDir` variable, which contains the path that the application database is running in, to once again attempt to locate the linked tables. (See Listing 37.6.) If it is successful, it returns True. Otherwise, it returns False.

Listing 37.6. The `TryAgain` function.

```
Function TryAgain(strAppDir As String)

    'Invoke Error Handling
    On Error GoTo TryAgain_Err

    'Declare Required Variables and Constants
    Dim db As DATABASE
    Dim tdf As TableDef
    Dim vntReturnValue As Variant
    Dim intTableCount As Integer

    Const MAXTABLES = 8

    'Initialize Progress Meter
    vntReturnValue = SysCmd(SYSCMD_INITMETER, "Attaching tables", MAXTABLES)

    'Point to the current database
    Set db = CurrentDb

    intTableCount = 1
    'Set default return value of True
    TryAgain = True
    'Loop through each table in the database
    For Each tdf In db.TableDefs
        'If the connection string is bad, attempt to locate
        'the data tables in the same folder as the application
        'database
        If tdf.Connect <> "" Then
            tdf.Connect = ";DATABASE=" & strAppDir & "CHAP19DATA.MDB"
            tdf.RefreshLink
            'Update Progress Meter
            intTableCount = intTableCount + 1
            vntReturnValue = SysCmd(SYSCMD_UPDATEMETER, intTableCount)
        End If
    Next tdf

TryAgain_Exit:
    Set db = Nothing
```

```
      Set tdf = Nothing
      vntReturnValue = SysCmd(SYSCMD_REMOVEMETER)
      Exit Function

TryAgain_Err:
      TryAgain = False
      Resume TryAgain_Exit
End Function
```

Using Replication to Efficiently Distribute Your Application

You might not want to rebuild and redistribute Setup disks each time you change the design of your application database. Not only is this time-consuming, but it is difficult to ensure that each user runs the Setup process in order to obtain the application database. If your organization is networked, it generally is much more effective to distribute application updates using replication. This involves making design changes to the Design Master and then synchronizing with a hub after the changes are completed and tested properly. Replication is covered in detail in Chapter 24.

Practical Examples: Distributing the Time and Billing Application

The completed Time and Billing application, found on your sample code CD-ROM as CHAP37.MDB, has been modified to prepare it for distribution. Switchboards have been added to assist the user with the process of navigating throughout the application. Error handling has been built into most of the application's routines. Custom toolbars and menu bars have been added to the application's forms and reports. Startup options have been set. The application has been fully tested under the runtime version of the product. All that is left is to properly secure the application to meet the specific needs of your organization and to build the Setup disks.

Summary

The process of preparing an application for distribution actually starts in the planning of the application. It involves everything from providing a means by which the users of the application can navigate from task to task, to preparing the distribution disks. It also involves important steps, such as properly securing the application to ensure that the integrity of its data and objects are maintained, and building in a solid error handler to ensure that all errors are handled gracefully. Remember that, whether your users will be running your application using the retail or runtime version of Access, by using the techniques you learned in this chapter, you can add professional polish and pizzazz to any application.

VI

PART

Appendixes

Table Structures

This appendix gives you a complete listing of all the tables included in the Time and Billing application. Each table includes the following:

- A list of the field names, types, and lengths of each field in the table
- A detailed list of the properties associated with each field in the table

The tblClients table

This table stores pertinent information about each client, such as the company name, contact name, and phone numbers.

Table A.1. The tblClients table.

Field Name	Type	Size (Bytes)
ClientID	Number (Long)	4
CompanyName	Text	50
Address	Text	255
City	Text	30
StateProvince	Text	20
PostalCode	Text	20
Country	Text	20
ContactFirstName	Text	30
ContactLastName	Text	50
ContactTitle	Text	50
OfficePhone	Text	30
Fax	Text	30
Cellular	Text	30
Home	Text	30
EMailAddress	Text	30
ReferredBy	Text	30
AssociatedWith	Text	30
IntroDate	Date/Time	8
DefaultRate	Currency	8
Notes	Memo	(Varies)
HomePage	Hyperlink	

Table A.2. The field properties for each field in the tblClients table.

Property	Value
ClientID	**Number (Long)**
Allow Zero Length	False
Attributes	Fixed Size, Auto-Increment
Caption	Client ID
Collating Order	General
Column Hidden	False
Column Order	Default
Column Width	Default
Ordinal Position	0
Required	False
Source Field	ClientID
Source Table	tblClients
CompanyName	**Text**
Allow Zero Length	False
Attributes	Variable Length
Caption	Company Name
Collating Order	General
Column Hidden	False
Column Order	Default
Column Width	Default
Display Control	Text Box
Ordinal Position	1
Required	True
Source Field	CompanyName
Source Table	tblClients
Address	**Text**
Allow Zero Length	False
Attributes	Variable Length
Collating Order	General
Column Hidden	False

continues

Table A.2. continued

Property	Value
Column Order	Default
Column Width	Default
Display Control	Text Box
Ordinal Position	2
Required	False
Source Field	Address
Source Table	tblClients
City	**Text**
Allow Zero Length	False
Attributes	Variable Length
Collating Order	General
Column Hidden	alse
Column Order	Default
Column Width	Default
Display Control	Text Box
Ordinal Position	3
Required	False
Source Field	City
Source Table	tblClients
StateProvince	**Text**
Allow Zero Length	False
Attributes	Variable Length
Caption	State/Province
Collating Order	General
Column Hidden	False
Column Order	Default
Column Width	Default
Default Value	"CA"
Display Control	Text Box
Ordinal Position	4
Required	False

Property	Value
Source Field	StateProvince
Source Table	tblClients
PostalCode	**Text**
Allow Zero Length	False
Attributes	Variable Length
Caption	Postal Code
Collating Order	General
Column Hidden	False
Column Order	Default
Column Width	Default
Display Control	Text Box
Ordinal Position	5
Required	False
Source Field	PostalCode
Source Table	tblClients
Country	**Text**
Allow Zero Length	False
Attributes	Variable Length
Collating Order	General
Column Hidden	False
Column Order	Default
Column Width	Default
Display Control	Text Box
Ordinal Position	6
Required	False
Source Field	Country
Source Table	tblClients
ContactFirstName	**Text**
Allow Zero Length	False
Attributes	Variable Length

continues

Table A.2. continued

Property	Value
Caption	Contact First Name
Collating Order	General
Column Hidden	False
Column Order	Default
Column Width	Default
Display Control	Text Box
Ordinal Position	7
Required	False
Source Field	ContactFirstName
Source Table	tblClients
ContactLastName	**Text**
Allow Zero Length	False
Attributes	Variable Length
Caption	Contact Last Name
Collating Order	General
Column Hidden	False
Column Order	Default
Column Width	Default
Display Control	Text Box
Ordinal Position	8
Required	False
Source Field	ContactLastName
Source Table	tblClients
ContactTitle	**Text**
Allow Zero Length	False
Attributes	Variable Length
Caption	Contact Title
Collating Order	General
Column Hidden	False
Column Order	Default

Property	Value
Column Width	Default
Display Control	Text Box
Ordinal Position	9
Required	False
Source Field	ContactTitle
Source Table	tblClients
OfficePhone	**Text**
Allow Zero Length	False
Attributes	Variable Length
Caption	Office Phone
Collating Order	General
Column Hidden	False
Column Order	Default
Column Width	Default
Display Control	Text Box
Input Mask	!\(999\)000\-0000
Ordinal Position	10
Required	False
Source Field	OfficePhone
Source Table	tblClients
Fax	**Text**
Allow Zero Length	False
Attributes	Variable Length
Collating Order	General
Column Hidden	False
Column Order	Default
Column Width	Default
Display Control	Text Box
Input Mask	!\(999\)000\-0000
Ordinal Position	11
Required	False

continues

Table A.2. continued

Property	Value
Source Field	Fax
Source Table	tblClients
Cellular	**Text**
Allow Zero Length	False
Attributes	Variable Length
Collating Order	General
Column Hidden	False
Column Order	Default
Column Width	Default
Display Control	Text Box
Input Mask	!\(999\)000\-0000
Ordinal Position	12
Required	False
Source Field	Cellular
Source Table	tblClients
Home	**Text**
Allow Zero Length	False
Attributes	Variable Length
Collating Order	General
Column Hidden	False
Column Order	Default
Column Width	Default
Display Control	Text Box
Input Mask	!\(999\)000\-0000
Ordinal Position	13
Required	False
Source Field	Home
Source Table	tblClients

Property	Value
EMailAddress	**Text**
Allow Zero Length	False
Attributes	Variable Length
Caption	E-Mail Address
Collating Order	General
Column Hidden	False
Column Order	Default
Column Width	Default
Display Control	Text Box
Ordinal Position	14
Required	False
Source Field	EMailAddress
Source Table	tblClients
ReferredBy	**Text**
Allow Zero Length	False
Attributes	Variable Length
Caption	Referred By
Collating Order	General
Column Hidden	False
Column Order	Default
Column Width	Default
Display Control	Text Box
Ordinal Position	15
Required	False
Source Field	ReferredBy
Source Table	tblClients
AssociatedWith	**Text**
Allow Zero Length	False
Attributes	Variable Length
Caption	Associated With
Collating Order	General

Table A.2. continued

Property	Value
Column Hidden	False
Column Order	Default
Column Width	Default
Display Control	Text Box
Ordinal Position	16
Required	False
Source Field	AssociatedWith
Source Table	tblClients
IntroDate	**Date/Time**
Allow Zero Length	False
Attributes	Fixed Size
Caption	Intro Date
Collating Order	General
Column Hidden	False
Column Order	Default
Column Width	Default
Default Value	=Date()
Ordinal Position	17
Required	True
Source Field	IntroDate
Source Table	tblClients
Validation Rule	<=Date()
Validation Text	Date Entered Must Be On Or Before Today
DefaultRate	**Currency**
Allow Zero Length	False
Attributes	Fixed Size
Caption	Default Rate
Collating Order	General
Column Hidden	False
Column Order	Default
Column Width	Default

Property	Value
Decimal Places	255
Default Value	125
Format	Currency
Ordinal Position	18
Required	False
Source Field	DefaultRate
Source Table	tblClients
Validation Rule	Between 75 And 150
Validation Text	Rate Must Be Between 75 and 150

Notes	**Memo**
Allow Zero Length	False
Attributes	Variable Length
Collating Order	General
Column Hidden	False
Column Order	Default
Column Width	Default
Ordinal Position	19
Required	False
Source Field	Notes
Source Table	tblClients

HomePage	**Hyperlink**
Allow Zero Length	False
Attributes	Variable Length
Caption	Home Page
Collating Order	General
Column Hidden	False
Column Order	Default
Column Width	Default
Ordinal Position	20
Required	False
Source Field	HomePage
Source Table	tblClients

The tblCompanyInfo Table

This table stores information about your company, including address and default payment terms.

Table A.3. The tblCompanyInfo table.

Field Name	Type	Size (Bytes)
SetupID	Number (Long)	4
Company Name	Text	50
Address	Text	255
City	Text	50
StateProvince	Text	20
PostalCode	Text	20
Country	Text	50
PhoneNumber	Text	30
FaxNumber	Text	30
DefaultPayment Terms	Text	255
DefaultInvoiceDescription	Memo	(varies)

Table A.4. The properties of each field included in the tblCompanyInfo table.

Property	Value
SetupID	**Number (Long)**
Allow Zero Length	False
Attributes	Fixed Size, Auto-Increment
Caption	SetupID
Collating Order	General
Column Hidden	False
Column Order	Default
Column Width	Default
Ordinal Position	0
Required	False
Source Field	SetupID
Source Table	tblCompanyInfo

Property	Value
CompanyName	**Text**
Allow Zero Length	False
Attributes	Variable Length
Caption	Company Name
Collating Order	General
Column Hidden	False
Column Order	Default
Column Width	Default
Display Control	Text Box
Ordinal Position	1
Required	False
Source Field	CompanyName
Source Table	tblCompanyInfo
Address	**Text**
Allow Zero Length	False
Attributes	Variable Length
Collating Order	General
Column Hidden	False
Column Order	Default
Column Width	Default
Display Control	Text Box
Ordinal Position	2
Required	False
Source Field	Address
Source Table	tblCompanyInfo
City	**Text**
Allow Zero Length	False
Attributes	Variable Length
Collating Order	General
Column Hidden	False
Column Order	Default

Table A.4. continued

Property	Value
Column Width	Default
Display Control	Text Box
Ordinal Position	3
Required	False
Source Field	City
Source Table	tblCompanyInfo
StateProvince	**Text**
Allow Zero Length	False
Attributes	Variable Length
Caption	State/Province
Collating Order	General
Column Hidden	False
Column Order	Default
Column Width	Default
Display Control	Text Box
Ordinal Position	4
Required	False
Source Field	StateProvince
Source Table	tblCompanyInfo
PostalCode	**Text**
Allow Zero Length	False
Attributes	Variable Length
Caption	Postal Code
Collating Order	General
Column Hidden	False
Column Order	Default
Column Width	Default
Display Control	Text Box
Input Mask	00000\-9999
Ordinal Position	5

Property	Value
Required	False
Source Field	PostalCode
Source Table	tblCompanyInfo
Country	**Text**
Allow Zero Length	False
Attributes	Variable Length
Collating Order	General
Column Hidden	False
Column Order	Default
Column Width	Default
Display Control	Text Box
Ordinal Position	6
Required	False
Source Field	Country
Source Table	tblCompanyInfo
PhoneNumber	**Text**
Allow Zero Length	False
Attributes	Variable Length
Caption	Phone Number
Collating Order	General
Column Hidden	False
Column Order	Default
Column Width	Default
Display Control	Text Box
Input Mask	!\(999") "000\-0000
Ordinal Position	7
Required	False
Source Field	PhoneNumber
Source Table	tblCompanyInfo

continues

Table A.4. continued

Property	Value
FaxNumber	**Text**
Allow Zero Length	False
Attributes	Variable Length
Caption	Fax Number
Collating Order	General
Column Hidden	False
Column Order	Default
Column Width	Default
Display Control	Text Box
Input Mask	!\(999") "000\-0000
Ordinal Position	8
Required	False
Source Field	FaxNumber
Source Table	tblCompanyInfo
DefaultPaymentTerms	**Text**
Allow Zero Length	False
Attributes	Variable Length
Caption	Default Payment Terms
Collating Order	General
Column Hidden	False
Column Order	Default
Column Width	Default
Display Control	Text Box
Ordinal Position	9
Required	False
Source Field	DefaultPaymentTerms
Source Table	tblCompanyInfo
DefaultInvoiceDescription	**Memo**
Allow Zero Length	False
Attributes	Variable Length

Property	Value
Caption	Default Invoice Description
Collating Order	General
Column Hidden	False
Column Order	Default
Column Width	Default
Ordinal Position	10
Required	False
Source Field	DefaultInvoiceDescription
Source Table	tblCompanyInfo

The tblEmployees Table

This table includes relevant employee information, such as name, address, and billing rate.

Table A.5. The tblEmployees table.

Field Name	Type	Size (Bytes)
EmployeeID	Number (Long)	4
FirstName	Text	50
LastName	Text	50
Title	Text	50
EmailName	Text	50
Extension	Text	30
Address	Text	255
City	Text	50
StateOrProvince	Text	20
PostalCode	Text	20
Country	Text	50
HomePhone	Text	30
WorkPhone	Text	30
BillingRate	Currency	8

Table A.6. The properties of each field included in the tblEmployees table.

Property	Value
EmployeeID	**Number (Long)**
Allow Zero Length	False
Attributes	Fixed Size, Auto-Increment
Caption	Employee ID
Collating Order	General
Ordinal Position	0
Required	False
Source Field	EmployeeID
Source Table	tblEmployees
FirstName	**Text**
Allow Zero Length	False
Attributes	Variable Length
Caption	First Name
Collating Order	General
Ordinal Position	1
Required	False
Source Field	FirstName
Source Table	tblEmployees
LastName	**Text**
Allow Zero Length	False
Attributes	Variable Length
Caption	Last Name
Collating Order	General
Ordinal Position	2
Required	False
Source Field	LastName
Source Table	tblEmployees
Title	**Text**
Allow Zero Length	False
Attributes	Variable Length

Property	Value
Collating Order	General
Ordinal Position	3
Required	False
Source Field	Title
Source Table	tblEmployees
EmailName	**Text**
Allow Zero Length	False
Attributes	Variable Length
Caption	Email Name
Collating Order	General
Ordinal Position	4
Required	False
Source Field	EmailName
Source Table	tblEmployees
Extension	**Text**
Allow Zero Length	False
Attributes	Variable Length
Collating Order	General
Ordinal Position	5
Required	False
Source Field	Extension
Source Table	tblEmployees
Address	**Text**
Allow Zero Length	False
Attributes	Variable Length
Collating Order	General
Ordinal Position	6
Required	False
Source Field	Address
Source Table	tblEmployees

continues

Table A.6. continued

Property	Value
City	**Text**
Allow Zero Length	False
Attributes	Variable Length
Collating Order	General
Ordinal Position	7
Required	False
Source Field	City
Source Table	tblEmployees
StateOrProvince	**Text**
Allow Zero Length	False
Attributes	Variable Length
Caption	State/Province
Collating Order	General
Ordinal Position	8
Required	False
Source Field	StateOrProvince
Source Table	tblEmployees
PostalCode	**Text**
Allow Zero Length	False
Attributes	Variable Length
Caption	Postal Code
Collating Order	General
Input Mask	00000-9999
Ordinal Position	9
Required	False
Source Field	PostalCode
Source Table	tblEmployees
Country	**Text**
Allow Zero Length	False
Attributes	Variable Length

Property	Value
Collating Order	General
Ordinal Position	10
Required	False
Source Field	Country
Source Table	tblEmployees
HomePhone	**Text**
Allow Zero Length	False
Attributes	Variable Length
Caption	Home Phone
Collating Order	General
Input Mask	!(999) 000-0000
Ordinal Position	11
Required	False
Source Field	HomePhone
Source Table	tblEmployees
WorkPhone	**Text**
Allow Zero Length	False
Attributes	Variable Length
Caption	Work Phone
Collating Order	General
Input Mask	!(999) 000-0000
Ordinal Position	12
Required	False
Source Field	WorkPhone
Source Table	tblEmployees
BillingRate	**Currency**
Allow Zero Length	False
Attributes	Fixed Size
Caption	Billing Rate
Collating Order	General

Table A.6. continued

Property	Value
Decimal Places	2
Format	Currency
Ordinal Position	13
Required	False
Source Field	BillingRate
Source Table	tblEmployees

The tblErrorLog Table

This table logs all application errors encountered while using the Time and Billing application, including error number and the name of the routine and module where the error occurred.

Table A.7. The tblErrorLog table.

Field Name	Type	Size (Bytes)
ErrorSeq	Number (Long)	4
ErrorDate	Date/Time	8
ErrorTime	Date/Time	8
UserName	Text	30
ErrorNum	Number (Integer)	2
ErrorString	Text	30
Module	Text	50
Routine	Text	50

Table A.8. The properties and values associated with each field in the tblErrorLog table.

Property	Value
ErrorSeq	**Number (Long)**
Allow Zero Length	False
Attributes	Fixed Size, Auto-Increment
Collating Order	General
Column Hidden	False

Property	Value
Column Order	Default
Column Width	Default
Description	Unique Identifier for the Error
Ordinal Position	0
Required	False
Source Field	ErrorSeq
Source Table	tblErrorLog

ErrorDate	**Date/Time**
Allow Zero Length	False
Attributes	Fixed Size
Collating Order	General
Column Hidden	False
Column Order	Default
Column Width	Default
Description	Date that the Error Occurred
Format	Medium Date
Ordinal Position	1
Required	False
Source Field	ErrorDate
Source Table	tblErrorLog

ErrorTime	**Date/Time**
Allow Zero Length	False
Attributes	Fixed Size
Collating Order	General
Column Hidden	False
Column Order	Default
Column Width	Default
Description	Time that the Error Occurred
Format	Long Time
Ordinal Position	2

continues

1015

Table A.8. continued

Property	Value
Required	False
Source Field	ErrorTime
Source Table	tblErrorLog
UserName	**Text**
Allow Zero Length	False
Attributes	Variable Length
Collating Order	General
Column Hidden	False
Column Order	Default
Column Width	Default
Description	Name of the User
Display Control	Text Box
Ordinal Position	3
Required	False
Source Field	UserName
Source Table	tblErrorLog
ErrorNum	**Number (Integer)**
Allow Zero Length	False
Attributes	Fixed Size
Collating Order	General
Column Hidden	False
Column Order	Default
Column Width	Default
Decimal Places	255
Default Value	0
Description	VBA Error Code
Display Control	Text Box
Ordinal Position	4
Required	False
Source Field	ErrorNum
Source Table	tblErrorLog

Property	Value
ErrorString	**Text**
Allow Zero Length	False
Attributes	Variable Length
Collating Order	General
Column Hidden	False
Column Order	Default
Column Width	Default
Description	VBA Error Description
Display Control	Text Box
Ordinal Position	5
Required	False
Source Field	ErrorString
Source Table	tblErrorLog
Module	**Text**
Allow Zero Length	False
Attributes	Variable Length
Collating Order	General
Column Hidden	False
Column Order	Default
Column Width	Default
Description	Module in Which the Error Occurred
Display Control	Text Box
Ordinal Position	6
Required	False
Source Field	Module
Source Table	tblErrorLog
Routine	**Text**
Allow Zero Length	False
Attributes	Variable Length
Collating Order	General

continues

Table A.8. continued

Property	Value
Column Hidden	False
Column Order	Default
Column Width	Default
Description	Routine in Which the Error Occurred
Display Control	Text Box
Ordinal Position	7
Required	False
Source Field	Routine
Source Table	tblErrorLog

The tblErrors Table

This table gives you information about how your application should respond to error numbers.

Table A.9. The tblErrors table.

Field Name	Type	Size (Bytes)
ErrorNum	Number (Long)	4
Response	Number (Long)	4

Table A.10. The properties and values associated with each field in the tblErrors table.

Property	Value
ErrorNum	**Number (Long)**
Allow Zero Length	False
Attributes	Fixed Size
Collating Order	General
Column Hidden	False
Column Order	Default
Column Width	Default
Decimal Places	255

Property	Value
Default Value	0
Description	Number of the Error
Display Control	Text Box
Ordinal Position	0
Required	False
Source Field	ErrorNum
Source Table	tblErrors
Response	**Number (Long)**
Allow Zero Length	False
Attributes	Fixed Size
Collating Order	General
Column Hidden	False
Column Order	Default
Column Width	Default
Decimal Places	255
Default Value	0
Description	Action to Take
Display Control	Text Box
Ordinal Position	1
Required	False
Source Field	Response
Source Table	tblErrors

The tblExpenseCodes Tables

This table contains all the valid expense codes used in the Time and Billing application.

Table A.11. The tblExpenseCodes.

Field Name	Type	Size (Bytes)
ExpenseCodeID	Number (Long)	4
ExpenseCode	Text	30

Table A.12. The field properties of the tblExpenseCodes table.

Property	Value
ExpenseCodeID	**Number (Long)**
Allow Zero Length	False
Attributes	Fixed Size, Auto-Increment
Caption	Expense Code ID
Collating Order	General
Ordinal Position	0
Required	False
Source Field	ExpenseCodeID
Source Table	tblExpenseCodes
ExpenseCode	**Text**
Allow Zero Length	False
Attributes	Variable Length
Caption	Expense Code
Collating Order	General
Ordinal Position	1
Required	False
Source Field	ExpenseCode
Source Table	tblExpenseCodes

The tblPaymentMethods Table

This table lists the valid payment methods.

Table A.13. The tblPaymentMethods table.

Field Name	Type	Size (Bytes)
PaymentMethodID	Number (Long)	4
PaymentMethod	Text	50
CreditCard	Yes/No	1

Table A.14. The field properties of the tblPaymentMethods table.

Property	Value
PaymentMethodID	**Number (Long)**
Allow Zero Length	False
Attributes	Fixed Size, Auto-Increment
Caption	Payment Method ID
Collating Order	General
Ordinal Position	0
Required	False
Source Field	PaymentMethodID
Source Table	tblPaymentMethods
PaymentMethod	**Text**
Allow Zero Length	False
Attributes	Variable Length
Caption	Payment Method
Collating Order	General
Ordinal Position	1
Required	False
Source Field	PaymentMethod
Source Table	tblPaymentMethods
CreditCard	**Yes/No**
Allow Zero Length	False
Attributes	Fixed Size
Caption	Credit Card?
Collating Order	General
Format	Yes/No
Ordinal Position	2
Required	False
Source Field	CreditCard
Source Table	tblPaymentMethods

The tblPayments Table

This table stores client payment information, such as the amount and date of payment for particular projects.

Table A.15. The tblPayments table.

Field Name	Type	Size (Bytes)
PaymentID	Number (Long)	4
ProjectID	Number (Long)	4
PaymentAmount	Currency	8
PaymentDate	Date/Time	8
CreditCardNumber	Text	30
CardholdersName	Text	50
CreditCardExpDate	Date/Time	8
PaymentMethodID	Number (Long)	4

Table A.16. The field properties of the tblPayments table.

Property	Value
PaymentID	**Number (Long)**
Allow Zero Length	False
Attributes	Fixed Size, Auto-Increment
Caption	Payment ID
Collating Order	General
Column Hidden	False
Column Order	Default
Column Width	Default
Ordinal Position	0
Required	False
Source Field	PaymentID
Source Table	tblPayments
ProjectID	**Number (Long)**
Allow Zero Length	False

Property	Value
Attributes	Fixed Size
Caption	Project ID
Collating Order	General
Column Hidden	False
Column Order	Default
Column Width	Default
Decimal Places	255
Display Control	Text Box
Ordinal Position	1
Required	False
Source Field	ProjectID
Source Table	tblPayments
PaymentAmount	**Currency**
Allow Zero Length	False
Attributes	Fixed Size
Caption	Payment Amount
Collating Order	General
Column Hidden	False
Column Order	Default
Column Width	Default
Decimal Places	2
Format	Currency
Ordinal Position	2
Required	False
Source Field	PaymentAmount
Source Table	tblPayments
PaymentDate	**Date/Time**
Allow Zero Length	False
Attributes	Fixed Size
Caption	Payment Date

continues

Table A.16. continued

Property	Value
Collating Order	General
Column Hidden	False
Column Order	Default
Column Width	Default
Format	Short Date
Input Mask	99/99/00
Ordinal Position	3
Required	False
Source Field	PaymentDate
Source Table	tblPayments
CreditCardNumber	**Text**
Allow Zero Length	False
Attributes	Variable Length
Caption	Credit Card #
Collating Order	General
Column Hidden	False
Column Order	Default
Column Width	Default
Display Control	Text Box
Ordinal Position	4
Required	False
Source Field	CreditCardNumber
Source Table	tblPayments
CardholdersName	**Text**
Allow Zero Length	False
Attributes	Variable Length
Caption	Cardholder Name
Collating Order	General
Column Hidden	False
Column Order	Default

Property	Value
Column Width	Default
Display Control	Text Box
Ordinal Position	5
Required	False
Source Field	CardholdersName
Source Table	tblPayments

CreditCardExpDate **Date/Time**

Allow Zero Length	False
Attributes	Fixed Size
Caption	Card Exp. Date
Collating Order	General
Column Hidden	False
Column Order	Default
Column Width	Default
Format	Short Date
Input Mask	99/99/00
Ordinal Position	6
Required	False
Source Field	CreditCardExpDate
Source Table	tblPayments

PaymentMethodID **Number (Long)**

Allow Zero Length	False
Attributes	Fixed Size
Bound Column	1
Caption	Payment Method ID
Collating Order	General
Column Count	3
Column Heads	False
Column Hidden	False
Column Order	Default

continues

Table A.16. The field properties of the tblPayments table.

Property	Value
Column Width	Default
Column Widths	0;1440;0
Decimal Places	255
Display Control	Combo Box
Limit To List	True
List Rows	8
List Width	1
Ordinal Position	7
Required	False
Row Source Type	Table/Query
Row Source	SELECT DISTINCTROW tblPaymentMethods.* FROM tblPaymentMethods ORDER BY tblPaymentMethods.PaymentMethod;
Source Field	PaymentMethodID
Source Table	tblPayments

The tblProjects Table

This table stores information about each project, including a cost estimate and important dates.

Table A.17. The tblProjects table.

Field Name	Type	Size (Bytes)
ProjectID	Number (Long)	4
ProjectName	Text	50
ProjectDescription	Memo	-
ClientID	Number (Long)	4
PurchaseOrderNumber	Text	50
ProjectTotalEstimate	Currency	8
EmployeeID	Number (Long)	4
ProjectBeginDate	Date/Time	8
ProjectEndDate	Date/Time	8

Table A.18. The field properties of the tblProjects table.

Property	Value
ProjectID	**Number (Long)**
Allow Zero Length	False
Attributes	Fixed Size, Auto-Increment
Caption	Project ID
Collating Order	General
Column Hidden	False
Column Order	Default
Column Width	Default
Ordinal Position	0
Required	False
Source Field	ProjectID
Source Table	tblProjects
ProjectName	**Text**
Allow Zero Length	False
Attributes	Variable Length
Caption	Project Name
Collating Order	General
Column Hidden	False
Column Order	Default
Column Width	Default
Display Control	Text Box
Ordinal Position	1
Required	True
Source Field	ProjectName
Source Table	tblProjects
ProjectDescription	**Memo**
Allow Zero Length	False
Attributes	Variable Length
Caption	Project Description

continues

1027

Table A.18. continued

Property	Value
Collating Order	General
Column Hidden	False
Column Order	Default
Column Width	Default
Ordinal Position	2
Required	False
Source Field	ProjectDescription
Source Table	tblProjects
ClientID	**Number (Long)**
Allow Zero Length	False
Attributes	Fixed Size
Bound Column	1
Caption	Client ID
Collating Order	General
Column Count	2
Column Heads	False
Column Hidden	False
Column Order	Default
Column Width	Default
Column Widths	;14400
Decimal Places	255
Default Value	0
Display Control	Combo Box
Limit To List	True
List Rows	8
List Width	1
Ordinal Position	3
Required	True
Row Source Type	Table/Query

Property	Value
Row Source	SELECT DISTINCTROW [tblClients].[ClientID], [tblClients].[CompanyName] FROM [tblClients];
Source Field	ClientID
Source Table	tblProjects

PurchaseOrderNumber	**Text**
Allow Zero Length	False
Attributes	Variable Length
Caption	Purchase Order Number
Collating Order	General
Column Hidden	False
Column Order	Default
Column Width	Default
Display Control	Text Box
Ordinal Position	4
Required	False
Source Field	PurchaseOrderNumber
Source Table	tblProjects

ProjectTotalEstimate	**Currency**
Allow Zero Length	False
Attributes	Fixed Size
Caption	ProjectTotalEstimate
Collating Order	General
Column Hidden	False
Column Order	Default
Column Width	Default
Decimal Places	255
Default Value	0

continues

Table A.18. continued

Property	Value
Format	Currency
Ordinal Position	5
Required	False
Source Field	ProjectTotalEstimate
Source Table	tblProjects
EmployeeID	**Number (Long)**
Allow Zero Length	False
Attributes	Fixed Size
Caption	Employee ID
Collating Order	General
Column Hidden	False
Column Order	Default
Column Width	Default
Decimal Places	255
Default Value	0
Display Control	Text Box
Ordinal Position	6
Required	False
Source Field	EmployeeID
Source Table	tblProjects
ProjectBeginDate	**Date/Time**
Allow Zero Length	False
Attributes	Fixed Size
Caption	Project Begin Date
Collating Order	General
Column Hidden	False
Column Order	Default
Column Width	Default
Ordinal Position	7
Required	False

Property	Value
Source Field	ProjectBeginDate
Source Table	tblProjects
ProjectEndDate	**Date/Time**
Allow Zero Length	False
Attributes	Fixed Size
Caption	Project End Date
Collating Order	General
Column Hidden	False
Column Order	Default
Column Width	Default
Ordinal Position	8
Required	False
Source Field	ProjectEndDate
Source Table	tblProjects

The tblTimeCardExpenses Table

This tables stores necessary information for billable project expenses, such as the date and amount of the expense.

Table A.19. The tblTimeCardExpenses table.

Field Name	Type	Size (Bytes)
TimeCardExpenseID	Number (Long)	4
TimeCardID	Number (Long)	4
ExpenseDate	Date/Time	8
ProjectID	Number (Long)	4
ExpenseDescription	Text	255
ExpenseAmount	Currency	8
ExpenseCodeID	Number (Long)	4

Table A.20. The field properties of the tblTimeCardExpenses table.

Property	Value
TimeCardExpenseID	**Number (Long)**
Allow Zero Length	False
Attributes	Fixed Size, Auto-Increment
Caption	Time Card Expense ID
Collating Order	General
Column Hidden	False
Column Order	Default
Column Width	Default
Ordinal Position	0
Required	False
Source Field	TimeCardExpenseID
Source Table	tblTimeCardExpenses
TimeCardID	**Number (Long)**
Allow Zero Length	False
Attributes	Fixed Size
Caption	Time Card ID
Collating Order	General
Column Hidden	False
Column Order	Default
Column Width	Default
Decimal Places	255
Display Control	Text Box
Ordinal Position	1
Required	False
Source Field	TimeCardID
Source Table	tblTimeCardExpenses
ExpenseDate	**Date/Time**
Allow Zero Length	False
Attributes	Fixed Size
Caption	Expense Date

Property	Value
Collating Order	General
Column Hidden	False
Column Order	Default
Column Width	Default
Format	Short Date
Input Mask	99/99/00
Ordinal Position	2
Required	False
Source Field	ExpenseDate
Source Table	tblTimeCardExpenses
ProjectID	**Number (Long)**
Allow Zero Length	False
Attributes	Fixed Size
Bound Column	1
Caption	Project ID
Collating Order	General
Column Count	3
Column Heads	False
Column Hidden	False
Column Order	Default
Column Width	Default
Column Widths	0;1020;3156
Decimal Places	255
Display Control	Combo Box
Limit To List	True
List Rows	8
List Width	3
Ordinal Position	3
Required	False
Row Source Type	Table/Query

continues

1033

Table A.20. continued

Property	Value
Row Source	SELECT DISTINCTROW tblProjects.* FROM tblProjects ORDER BY tblProjects.ProjectName;
Source Field	ProjectID
Source Table	tblTimeCardExpenses
ExpenseDescription	**Text**
Allow Zero Length	False
Attributes	Variable Length
Caption	Expense Description
Collating Order	General
Column Hidden	False
Column Order	Default
Column Width	Default
Display Control	Text Box
Ordinal Position	4
Required	False
Source Field	ExpenseDescription
Source Table	tblTimeCardExpenses
ExpenseAmount	**Currency**
Allow Zero Length	False
Attributes	Fixed Size
Caption	Expense Amount
Collating Order	General
Column Hidden	False
Column Order	Default
Column Width	Default
Decimal Places	2
Format	Currency

Property	Value
Ordinal Position	5
Required	False
Source Field	ExpenseAmount
Source Table	tblTimeCardExpenses
ExpenseCodeID	**Number (Long)**
Allow Zero Length	False
Attributes	Fixed Size
Bound Column	1
Caption	Expense Code ID
Collating Order	General
Column Count	2
Column Heads	False
Column Hidden	False
Column Order	Default
Column Width	Default
Column Widths	0;2880
Decimal Places	255
Display Control	Combo Box
Limit To List	True
List Rows	8
List Width	2
Ordinal Position	6
Required	False
Row Source Type	Table/Query
Row Source	SELECT DISTINCTROW tblExpenseCodes.* FROM tblExpenseCodes ORDER BY tblExpenseCodes.ExpenseCode;
Source Field	ExpenseCodeID
Source Table	tblTimeCardExpenses

The tblTimeCardHours Table

This table stores a record of billable hours for a project, including dates and billing rates.

Table A.21. The tblTimeCardHours table.

Field Name	Type	Size (Bytes)
TimeCardDetailID	Number (Long)	4
TimeCardID	Number (Long)	4
DateWorked	Date/Time	8
ProjectID	Number (Long)	4
WorkDescription	Text	255
BillableHours	Number (Double)	8
BillingRate	Currency	8
WorkCodeID	Number (Long)	4

Table A.22. The field properties of the tblTimeCardHours table.

Property	Value
TimeCardDetailID	**Number (Long)**
Allow Zero Length	False
Attributes	Fixed Size, Auto-Increment
Caption	Time Card Detail ID
Collating Order	General
Column Hidden	False
Column Order	Default
Column Width	Default
Ordinal Position	0
Required	False
Source Field	TimeCardDetailID
Source Table	tblTimeCardHours
TimeCardID	**Number (Long)**
Allow Zero Length	False
Attributes	Fixed Size

Property	Value
Caption	Time Card ID
Collating Order	General
Column Hidden	False
Column Order	Default
Column Width	Default
Decimal Places	255
Display Control	Text Box
Ordinal Position	1
Required	False
Source Field	TimeCardID
Source Table	tblTimeCardHours

DateWorked	**Date/Time**
Allow Zero Length	False
Attributes	Fixed Size
Caption	Date Worked
Collating Order	General
Column Hidden	False
Column Order	Default
Column Width	Default
Format	Short Date
Input Mask	99/99/00
Ordinal Position	2
Required	False
Source Field	DateWorked
Source Table	tblTimeCardHours

ProjectID	**Number (Long)**
Allow Zero Length	False
Attributes	Fixed Size
Bound Column	1

continues

Table A.22. continued

Property	Value
Caption	Project ID
Collating Order	General
Column Count	3
Column Heads	False
Column Hidden	False
Column Order	Default
Column Width	Default
Column Widths	0;1020;3156
Decimal Places	255
Display Control	Combo Box
Limit To List	True
List Rows	8
List Width	3
Ordinal Position	3
Required	False
Row Source Type	Table/Query
Row Source	SELECT DISTINCTROW tblProjects.* FROM tblProjects ORDER BY tblProjects.ProjectName;
Source Field	ProjectID
Source Table	tblTimeCardHours
WorkDescription	**Text**
Allow Zero Length	False
Attributes	Variable Length
Caption	Work Description
Collating Order	General
Column Hidden	False
Column Order	Default
Column Width	Default
Display Control	Text Box
Ordinal Position	4

Property	Value
Required	False
Source Field	WorkDescription
Source Table	tblTimeCardHours
BillableHours	**Number (Double)**
Allow Zero Length	False
Attributes	Fixed Size
Caption	Billable Hours
Collating Order	General
Column Hidden	False
Column Order	Default
Column Width	Default
Decimal Places	255
Display Control	Text Box
Ordinal Position	5
Required	False
Source Field	BillableHours
Source Table	tblTimeCardHours
BillingRate	**Currency**
Allow Zero Length	False
Attributes	Fixed Size
Caption	Billing Rate
Collating Order	General
Column Hidden	False
Column Order	Default
Column Width	Default
Decimal Places	2
Format	Currency
Ordinal Position	6
Required	False
Source Field	BillingRate
Source Table	tblTimeCardHours

continues

Table A.22. continued

Property	Value
WorkCodeID	**Number (Long)**
Allow Zero Length	False
Attributes	Fixed Size
Bound Column	1
Caption	Work Code ID
Collating Order	General
Column Count	2
Column Heads	False
Column Hidden	False
Column Order	Default
Column Width	Default
Column Widths	0;2880
Decimal Places	255
Display Control	Combo Box
Limit To List	True
List Rows	8
List Width	2
Ordinal Position	7
Required	False
Row Source Type	Table/Query
Row Source	SELECT DISTINCTROW tblWorkCodes.* FROM tblWorkCodes ORDER BY tblWorkCodes.WorkCode;
Source Field	WorkCodeID
Source Table	tblTimeCardHours

The tblTimeCards Table

This table stores time card information for each employee.

Table A.23. The tblTimeCards table.

Field Name	Type	Size (Bytes)
TimeCardID	Number (Long)	4
EmployeeID	Number (Long)	4
DateEntered	Date/Time	8

Table A.24. The field properties of the tblTimeCards table.

Property	Value
TimeCardID	**Number (Long)**
Allow Zero Length	False
Attributes	Fixed Size, Auto-Increment
Caption	Time Card ID
Collating Order	General
Column Hidden	False
Column Order	Default
Column Width	Default
Ordinal Position	0
Required	False
Source Field	TimeCardID
Source Table	tblTimeCards

continues

Table A.24. continued

Property	Value
EmployeeID	**Number (Long)**
Allow Zero Length	False
Attributes	Fixed Size
Bound Column	1
Caption	Employee ID
Collating Order	General
Column Count	3
Column Heads	False
Column Hidden	False
Column Order	Default
Column Width	Default
Column Widths	0;2000;700
Decimal Places	255
Display Control	Combo Box
Limit To List	True
List Rows	8
List Width	2
Ordinal Position	1
Required	False
Row Source Type	Table/Query
Row Source	SELECT tblEmployees.EmployeeID, [LastName] & ", " & [FirstName] AS EmployeeName, tblEmployees.BillingRate FROM tblEmployees ORDER BY [LastName] & ", " & [FirstName];
Source Field	EmployeeID
Source Table	tblTimeCards
DateEntered	**Date/Time**
Allow Zero Length	False
Attributes	Fixed Size
Caption	Date Entered

Property	Value
Collating Order	General
Column Hidden	False
Column Order	Default
Column Width	Default
Format	Short Date
Input Mask	99/99/00
Ordinal Position	2
Required	False
Source Field	DateEntered
Source Table	tblTimeCards

The tblWorkCodes Table

This table supplies valid work codes for the application.

Table A.25. The tblWorkCodes table.

Field Name	Type	Size (Bytes)
WorkCodeID	Number (Long)	4
WorkCode	Text	30

Table A.26. The field properties of the tblWorkCodes table.

Property	Value
WorkCodeID	**Number (Long)**
Allow Zero Length	False
Attributes	Fixed Size, Auto-Increment
Caption	Work Code ID
Collating Order	General
Ordinal Position	0
Required	False
Source Field	WorkCodeID
Source Table	tblWorkCodes

continues **1043**

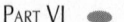
Table A.26. continued

Property	Value
WorkCode	**Text**
Allow Zero Length	False
Attributes	Variable Length
Caption	Work Code
Collating Order	General
Ordinal Position	1
Required	False
Source Field	WorkCode
Source Table	tblWorkCodes

B

Naming Conventions

This appendix gives you suggestions for naming variables and other database objects. The suggested standards are based on the Leszynski Naming Conventions (LNC) for Microsoft Access. If you want more information about these standards, or want to get the full copy provided by Kwery Corporation, call Kwery's order line at 1-800-ATKWERY or the product information line at 206-644-7830. Kwery can also be reached by CompuServe at 71573,3261 or by fax at 206-644-8409.

When creating variable names, it's important for you to make the type and intended use of each variable clear and self-documenting. Here are a few rules to follow:

- Remember to always make variable names mixed case, with each word or abbreviation in the variable name capitalized.
- Don't use underscore characters in your variable names.
- Abbreviate variables names only when it's necessary.
- Make the beginning of each variable name describe the type of data it contains.

Following these conventions will go a long way toward keeping your code concise and readable. Table B.1 recommends prefixes for Access object tags.

Table B.1. Access object-naming conventions.

Prefix	Control Type	Example
app	Application	appInfoBase
chk	CheckBox	chkReadOnly
cbo	ComboBox	cboLanguages
cmd	CommandButton	cmdRefreshTable
ctl	Control	ctlAny
ctls	Controls	ctlsAll
ocx	CustomControl	ocxCalendar
dcm	DoCmd	dcmOpenForm
frm	Form	frmDataEntryView
frms	Forms	frmsClientsAndOrders
img	Image	imgHeadShot
lbl	Label	lblShowAllCheckBox
lin	Line	linDivider
lst	ListBox	lstLastTenSites
bas	Module	basErrorControl
ole	ObjectFrame	oleWorksheet
opt	OptionButton	optReadOnly

Prefix	Control Type	Example
fra	OptionGroup (frame)	fraColorSchemes
brk	PageBreak	brkTopOfForm
pal	PaletteButton	palBackgroundColor
prps	Properties	prpsActiveForm
shp	Rectangle	shpHidableFrame
rpt	Report	rptOrders
rpts	Reports	rptsTodaysChanges
scr	Screen	scrSecondSplashScreen
sec	Section	secOrderDetail
fsub	Subform	fsubBillableHours
rsub	SubReport	rsubTopFiveSales
txt	TextBox	txtAdditionalNotes
tgl	ToggleButton	tglShowFormatting

Table B.2 lists prefix tags for standard variable types, as well as the storage space required by each.

Table B.2. Standard variable data type prefixes.

Prefix	Data Type	Storage	Example
byt	Byte	1 byte	byteArray
f	Boolean	2 bytes	fSecurityClear
int	Integer	2 bytes	intLoop
lng	Long	4 bytes	lngEnv
sng	Single	4 bytes	sngValue
dbl	Double	8 bytes	dblValue
cur	Currency	8 bytes	curCostPerUnit
dat	Date and Time	8 bytes	datStartTime
obj	Object	varies	objActiveObject
str	String	1 byte per character	strFirstName
stf	String (fixed length)	10 bytes + 1 byte per char	stfSocNumber
var	Variant	16 bytes + 1 byte per char	varInput

The Jet Engine uses objects you might need to refer to in VBA code. Table B.3 lists the Data Access Objects' (DAO) object types and their standard naming prefixes.

Table B.3. Jet object/collection prefixes.

Prefix	Object Type
cnt	Container
cnts	Containers
db	Database
dbs	Databases
dbe	DBEngine
doc	Document
docs	Documents
err	Error
errs	Errors
fld	Field
flds	Fields
grp	Group
grps	Groups
idx	Index
idxs	Indexes
prm	Parameter
prms	Parameters
pdbe	PrivDBEngine
prp	Property
prps	Properties
qry (or qdf)	QueryDef
qrys (or qdfs)	QueryDefs
rst	Recordset
rsts	Recordsets
rel	Relation
rels	Relations
tbl (or tdf)	TableDef
tbls (or tdfs)	TableDefs

Prefix	Object Type
usr	User
usrs	Users
wrk	Workspace
wrks	Workspaces

In addition to the standard notations for variables, there are variable notations for scope and lifetime. These should be placed at the beginning of the variable, before any other prefix. Table B.4 lists the scope and lifetime prefixes.

Table B.4. Prefixes for scope and lifetime.

Prefix	Description
(none)	Local variable, procedure-level lifetime
s	Local variable, program-level lifetime (static variable)
m	Private (module) variable, program-level lifetime
g	Public (global) variable, program-level lifetime

Table B.5 lists general naming convention tags for the Database window objects.

Table B.5. Tags for Database window objects.

Prefix	Object Type
tbl	Table
qry	Query
frm	Form
rpt	Report
mcr	Macro
bas	Module

There are two sets of naming conventions you can use when naming specific Database window objects: Either use the prefix for the general object prefix from the table, or supply one of the more descriptive tags listed in Table B.6.

Table B.6. Tags for specific Database window objects.

Prefix	Suffix	Object Type
tlkp	Lookup	Table (lookup)
qsel	(none)	Query (select)
qapp	Append	Query (append)
qxtb	XTab	Query (crosstab)
qddl	DDL	Query (DDL)
qdel	Delete	Query (delete)
qflt	Filter	Query (filter)
qlkp	Lookup	Query (lookup)
qmak	MakeTable	Query (make table)
qspt	PassThru	Query (SQL pass-through)
qtot	Totals	Query (totals)
quni	Union	Query (union)
qupd	Update	Query (update)
fdlg	Dlg	Form (dialog)
fmnu	Mnu	Form (menu)
fmsg	Msg	Form (message)
fsfr	Subform	Form (subform)
rsrp	SubReport	Form (subreport)
mmnu	Mnu	Macro (menu)

Index

Symbols

' (apostrophe), comments, VBA, 222

! (exclamation point) bang, 290

(pound sign)
  Help files, 939-940
  Const directive, VBA, 225

$ footnote (Help files), 940

( ) (parentheses), VBA functions, 463

; (semicolon), input masks, 53

< (less than sign), query criteria operator, 92

<= (less than or equal to sign), query criteria operator, 92

<> (not equal to sign), query criteria operator, 92

= (equal sign), query criteria operator, 92

> (greater than sign), query criteria operator, 92

>= (greater than or equal to sign), query criteria operator, 92

[ ] (square brackets), expressions, 103

\ (backslash), input masks, 53

_ (underscore), line continuation character, VBA, 222

16-bit APIs, compared to 32-bit, 849

32-bit APIs, compared to 16-bit, 849

2004 errors, transaction processing, 647

3167 errors, 555

3186 errors, 558

3197 errors, 555, 558, 650

3260 errors, 555, 558

3260 errors, 555, 558, 648

A

About option, ODBC Data Source Administrator, 613

AbsolutePosition property, records, 474-475

accelerator keys, control events, 386

Access
  controlling from other applications, 730-733
  Internet compatibility, 766
  runtime version compared to standard version, 30-31

Access 2.0, transaction processing benefits, **640**
Access Object Model, **280**
accessing the properties of the DBEngine object (listing), **463**
accommodating for missing parameters in your code (listing), **262**
accounts, user, **456**
acDataErrAdded argument, NotInList event, **411**
acDataErrContinue argument, NotInList event, **411**
acDataErrDisplay argument, NotInList event, **411**
action queries, **332**
  append, creating, 336
  compared to VBA code, 340
  delete, creating, 334-335
  make table, creating, 337-339
  results, previewing, 335
  update, creating, 332-333
  warning messages, 339-340
  warnings, 334
actions (macros), **306-308**
  copying, 320-321
  deleting, 319
  inserting, 318
  moving, 319-320
  overwriting, 320
Activate event
  forms, 378
  reports, 427
ActiveControl property, **301**
ActiveForm property, **301**
ActiveReport property, **301**
ActiveX
  ASP file format, 772
  Calendar control, 747
    methods, 748-750
    properties, 747-748
  controls, 740, 959
    adding to applications, 740

adding to forms, 742-743
Calendar, 743
coding events, 746-747
Common Dialog, 753-758
compatibility, 742
data binding, 745
dialog boxes, 740
examples, 762-763
ImageList, 760-761
licensing, 761-762
ODE, 29
references, 744-745
registering, 741-742
setting properties, 745-746
StatusBar, 751-753
Tab, 760
TabStrip, 758-760
types, 740
Unregister function, 742
UpDown object, 750-751
ActiveX Controls dialog box, **741**
Add ActiveX Control dialog box, **741**
Add command button, creating, **487**
Add method, **295**
Add New button, **821**
Add Object(s) to SourceSafe dialog box, **784**
Add SourceSafe Project dialog box, **783**
Add-In Manager
  command (Add-Ins menu), 821
  configuring Registry entries, 820-822
  dialog box, 821
add-ins
  builders, 812
    builder functions, 813-815
    creating, 813
    designing, 812, 829-833
    forms, 815-816

    registering, 816-822
    testing, 819
  defined, 812
  menus
    creating, 828
    defined, 827
    designing, 827
  wizards
    creating, 823-826
    defined, 822
    designing, 822
    registering, 826-827
Add-Ins command (Tools menu), **821**
Add-Ins menu commands, Add-In Manager, **821**
add-ons, Microsoft Plus! package, **658**
adding records to a recordset (listing), **479**
AddNew method, recordsets, **479-480**
Administer permission, **876**
administrative user
  accounts, creating, 867-869
  Admin group, joining, 869
After Error option, **971**
AfterDelConfirm event, forms, **376**
AfterInsert event, forms, **375**
AfterUpdate event, **635**
  controls, 383-384
  forms, 375
Alias property, queries, **111**
aligning
  objects
    forms, 127-128
    limitations, 177
    reports, 177
  text, objects, 128
ALL clause, SQL, **359**
All Records option, data locking, **551**
Allow Additions property, forms, **143**
Allow AutoCorrect property, controls, **149**

Allow Built-in Toolbars option, 971
Allow Default Shortcut Menus option, 970
Allow Deletions property, forms, 143
Allow Edits property, forms, 143
Allow Filters property, forms, 143
Allow Full Menus option, 970
Allow Toolbar/Menu Changes option, 971
Allow Viewing Code option, 971
Allow Zero Length property
  coordinating with Zero Length property, 58
  tables, 57
altering a form's record source at runtime (listing), 409-410
alternative for establishing a link to an external table (listing), 582
Analyze command (Tools menu), 661
Analyze menu commands, Performance, 661
and (query criteria operator), 92
ANSI functions, renaming, 842
Answer Wizard, *see* **Office Assistant**
APIs
  16-bit compared to 32-bit, 849
  calls, declaring, 535
  declarations (listing), 855
  functions, 849
  Windows API Viewer, 30
apostrophe ('), comments, VBA, 222
app prefix, 1046
Append method, adding tables to databases, 483

append queries, creating, 336
Application Icon option, 970
Application Title option, 970
applications
  ActiveX controls, adding, 740
  attributes, setting, 980
  client/server
    converting, 36
    developing, 6
    security, 906
    system performance, 28
  components, adding, 977
  controlling Access, 730-733
  databases, organization, 26-27
  debugging, 973
  designing
    multiuser issues, 542
    options, 605-607
  developing
    corporations, 5-6
    data analysis, 17
    designing, 17
    financial considerations, 4
    initial implementation, 21
    maintenance, 21
    normalization, 18-19
    personal, 4
    prototypes, 20
    requirements, 17-22
    small business, 4
    strategies, 26
    task analysis, 17
    testing, 20
  development, managing with Visual SourceSafe, 790-791
  distributing, 31-33
    Access full version, 960-961
    ActiveX controls, 959
    adding files to disks, 975-977
    adding Registry values, 979

  creating for runtime version, 964, 972
    defining shortcuts, 977
    designating Access components, 979
    examples, 989
    Graph Runtime Executable, 960
    Help Workshop, 960
    location of setup files, 981
    MDE files, 973
    preparing for runtime version, 984
    replication, 989
    Replication Manager, 959
    requirements, 958
    running after setup, 981
    runtime license, 959
    security, 972
    setting component properties, 980
    Setup Wizard, 29, 959, 974-977
    startup options, 969-972
    testing, 982-984
  example designs, 21-22
  expandability, 6-7
  forms, creating for runtime version, 964-967
  front-ends, designing, 35
  Help
    adding, 973
    custom files, 952-954
  installing, 33
  launching, creating macros, 422-423
  licensing, ODE, 29
  monitors, performance considerations, 16
  multiuser
    designing, 542
    installing, 543-544
    installing Access, 542-543
  navigating, forms, 118
  optimization, 656, 664
    arrays, 670

bookmarks, 670-671
Boolean expressions, 666
built-in collections,
  666-667
compiling, 672
constants, 670
data structures, 662-663
Declare statements, 668
defined, 656
Dim statements, 668
distribution, 673
hardware configuration,
  657-659
inline code, 666
Jet 3.5, 660-661
Len function, 667
loops, 671-672
me keyword, 669
network settings, 659
object references, 668-669
object types, 665-666
organization, 673
Performance Analyzer,
  661-662
queries, 664
Registry settings, 659-660
string functions, 670
transactions, 668
true/false evaluations,
  667-668
unused code, 668
variants, 665
Windows 95, 659
With...End With, 669
optimizing, adding version
  fields, 633
performance, organizing
  database objects, 26
referencing, object variables,
  715-716
runtime versions, testing
  before distributing, 33
security
  assigning rights, 34-35
  preventing alterations, 34
server connections,
  reducing, 633

source code, removing, 32
system performance
  indexes, 62
  limiting factors, 5
testing, 973
  Runtime command-line
    switch, 973-974
Time and Billing, see Time
  and Billing application
ApplyFilter event, forms, 381
architecture, replication, 681
  Briefcase Reconciler, 683
  File System Transport, 683
  Registry settings, 683
  Replication Manager, 682
  Synchronizer, 682
  Tracking Layer, 681
archiving records, append
  queries, 336
AreTablesAttached routine
  (listing), 596-597
arguments
  Callback function, 413
  dbAppendOnly, 467
  dbConsistent, 467
  dbDenyRead, 467
  dbDenyWrite, 467
  dbForwardOnly, 467
  dbInconsistent, 467
  dbReadOnly, 467
  dbSeeChanges, 467
  dbSQL PassThrough, 468
  macros, 306-310
  NotInList event, responses,
    411
  recordsets, arguments,
    467-468
  TransferDatabase method,
    573
  TransferSpreadsheet
    method, 575
  TransferText method, 574
  see also parameters
arrays, 257
  declaring, 257-258
  dynamic, declaring,
    258-259
  fixed, 257

optimization, 670
scope, 257
As String keyword, 231
ascending sorts, queries, 90
ASCII files, external data
  issues, 591
ASP file format, 772
assigning permissions,
  900-901
AssignToGroup function,
  891
attributes (applications),
  setting, 980
authorable buttons, 936
authoring tools (Help files),
  938, 953
Auto Attach function
  (listing), 985-987
Auto Center property, forms,
  141
Auto Data Tips feature, 508
  Code window, 275
Auto Indent feature, Code
  window, 275
Auto List Members feature,
  Code window, 275
Auto Quick Info feature,
  Code window, 275
Auto Repeat property,
  controls, 149
Auto Resize property, forms,
  141
Auto Syntax Check feature,
  Code window, 275
Auto Tab property, controls,
  149
AutoExec macros, 325-328
AutoKeys macros, 326-327
automation, 714
  client, 714
  objects, 715
    closing, 722-723
  OLE automation, 714
  servers, 714
    object models, 715
  type libraries, 715

AutoNumber fields, 48-50, 687
    creating custom, 564
    upsizing to client/servers, 610
avoiding bugs, 494-495
    naming standards, 494
    Option Explicit, 494
    strong typing, 494
    variable scoping, 495

B

Back Color property, controls, 147, 185
back-ends
    compared to front-ends, 605
    tables, linking to front-end applications, 605
Back Style property, controls, 147, 185
backslash (\), input masks, 53
backups
    backup/recovery capability, Access compared to client/servers, 603
    database replication, 679
bang (!), 290
bas prefix, 1046, 1049
BeforeDelConfirm event, forms, 376
BeforeInsert event, forms, 374-375
BeforeUpdate event
    controls, 383
    forms, 375
BeginTrans method, transaction processing, 643
between (query criteria operator), 92
between date and date (expression), queries, 95
bitmaps (graphics), 944
    multiresolution, 944

BOF property, recordsets, 469-470
bookmarks, 670-671
    adding, 249
    bookmark usage listing, 670
    dynasets, 630
    LastModified property, 480
    property
        listing, 475
        records, 475-476
    retrieving, servers, 630
    Variant variables, 476
Border Color property, controls, 147, 185
Border Style property
    controls, 147, 185
    forms, 141
Border Width property, controls, 147, 185
borders, forms, 141
Bound Column property, combo boxes, 134
bound controls, 150, 187
Bound Object Frame tool, 179
bound objects
    frames
        events, 384
        reports, 179
    forms, 406-407
breaking Watch expressions
    at changes, 511
    when true, 510-511
breakpoints, 500-502
    removing, 501, 504
    setting, 500
    stepping through code, 503-504
        executing to, 504
breaks (page), inserting in reports, 187
Briefcase
    Reconciler, 683
    menu commands
        Update All, 680
        Update Selection, 680, 692

brk prefix, 1047
bugs
    Access debugger, 500
        breakpoints, 500-502
        invoking, 500
        Stop statements, 500
        watches, 500
    application examples, 513
    avoiding, 494-495
        naming standards, 494
        Option Explicit, 494
        strong typing, 494
        variable scoping, 495
    Calls window, 506
    continuing after runtime errors, 512-513
    Debug window, 495-499
        clearing, 497
        executing functions, 498
        executing methods, 498
        executing subroutines, 498
        immediate pane, 496
        Locals pane, 507
        opening, 495-496
        printing to, 499
        setting property values, 497, 503
        setting variable values, 497, 503, 507
        testing functions, 498
        testing property values, 496
        testing variable values, 496
    debugging problems, 513
        GotFocus events, 513
        LostFocus events, 513
        resetting code, 513
    logic errors, 495
    Set Next Statement, 505
    stepping through code, 502-505
        breakpoints, 503-504
        Step Into, 502-503
        Step Out, 505
        Step Over, 504

Watch expressions,
507-511
adding, 508-510
Auto Data Tips, 508
breaking at changes, 511
breaking when true,
510-511
editing, 510
quick watch, 508
builders
builder functions, 813
preset arguments,
814-815
program listing, 813-814
creating, 813
defined, 812
designing, 812, 829
Load events, 831-833
ValidTextPolite function,
830-831
ValidTextRude function,
831-832
forms, 815-816
Modal property, 815
registering, 816
Add-In Manager,
820-822
manual entries, 816-819
testing, 819
building a query (listing),
483
building expressions, macros,
310
bulk changes using a
predefined action query
(listing), 478
business tables, 41
businesses, developing
applications
corporations, 5-6
small, 4
button bars, Help window,
935
buttons
Add New, 821
authorable, 936
Virtual Memory, 658

byt data-type prefix, 1047
ByVal keyword, 839

C

calculated controls, 150, 187
Immediate If (IIF)
statements, 224
calculated fields, nested
queries, 345
calculating
field types (selecting), 47
fields
examples, 102
queries, 101-103
null values, 109
Calendar control, 743, 747
methods, 748-750
properties, 747-748
Calendar Control Properties
dialog box, 746
Call keyword, 214
Call LoopThroughCollection
subroutine, 499
Call Stack button, 506
Callback function, 734
arguments, 413
combo/list boxes,
populating, 412-415
callback function listing all
reports in the database
(listing), 485-486
calling
functions
invalid characters, 841
libraries, 799
ordinal number
references, 843
procedures, 214
public procedures, name
conflicts, 215
Calling a function in a
library (listing), 800
Calls window, 506
Can Edit subkey value
(Registry), 817

Can Grow property
controls, 146, 185
reports, 197
Can Shrink property
controls, 146, 185
reports, 197
subreports, 193
Cancel property, controls,
149
Can Grow property,
subreports, 193
Caption property
controls, 146, 185
forms, 140
reports, 182
tables, 54
captions
command buttons, 185
labels, 185
default, 131
option groups, 136
Cascade Delete Related
Records option, 78-79
Cascade Update Related
Fields option, 77
Cascade Update Related
Fields Referential, Integrity
setting
action queries, 334
delete queries, 335
cascading error effect,
523-524
case sensitivity
function names, 839
library names, 839
passwords, 860
upsizing to client/servers,
611
CBF (Code Behind Forms),
210
cbo prefix, 1046
centralizing error handling,
520
Change event, controls, 384
Change To command
(Format menu), 674

characters
  fields, naming, 44
  literals, input masks, 53
charts, reports, 168
  see also graphics
Check Box tool, 135
**Check In Object(s) to
  SourceSafe dialog box, 789**
**Check Out Object(s) from
  SourceSafe dialog box, 787**
checkboxes
  forms, adding, 135
  Hide Key Column, 60
**checking for an empty
  recordset using
  RecordCount (listing), 471**
chk prefix, 1046
**Choose Builder dialog box,
  829**
Class modules, 210
  compared to Standard, 217
  creating, 265-268
  procedures, declaring, 215
clauses, SQL
  ALL, 359
  FROM, 357
  GROUP BY, 359
  HAVING, 360
  JOIN, 358-359
  ORDER BY, 358
  SELECT, 357
  WHERE, 358
clearing errors, 523
Click event
  controls, 385-386
  forms, 379
client/servers, 600
  Access, integrating,
    605-607
  accessing, ODBCDirect,
    624-627
  applications
    developing, 6
    security, 906
  compared to Access,
    600-601

compared to file servers, 6
connecting, 615
connections, reducing, 633
converting, 36
  considerations, 36-37
dynasets, 630
evaluating needs, 604
explicit transactions, 651
field names, compatibility,
  44
forms
  optimizing, 633-637
  unbound, 635
implementing, strategies,
  630
implicit transactions, 651
nested transactions, 652
ODBCDirect, 607
  *performance
    considerations, 632*
pass-through queries, 606,
  620-623
  creating, 621
  executing, 621-622
pass-through queries,
  performance
  considerations, 631
queries
  optimizing, 633-634
  system performance, 28
recordsets, selecting types,
  630-631
stored procedures,
  executing, 622-623
strategies, 37
  examples, 637-638
tables
  linking, 616-617
  opening, 624
terminology, 608-609
transactions
  lock limits, 652
  processing, 651-652
upsizing
  AutoNumber fields, 610
  case-sensitivity, 611

  default values, 610
  indexes, 610
  *ODBC data sources,
    612-615*
  ODBC drivers, 612
  preparation, 612
  properties, 612
  relationships, 611
  reserved words, 611
  security, 611
  table names, 611
  validation rules, 610
  VBA, 612
upsizing tables, 609
views
  *compared to queries,
    619-620*
  linking, 619-620
clients, automation, 714
**Clients form, creating,
  160-161**
**Close Button property,
  forms, 142**
Close event
  forms, 378
  reports, 426
CloseExcel routine, 722
closing
  databases, Visual
    SourceSafe, 791
  forms, events, 377-378, 382
  windows, designing forms,
    124
cmd prefix, 1046
**cmdFinish1 command
  button, 824**
**cmdFinish2 command
  button, 824**
**cnt object-naming prefix,
  1048**
**cnts object-naming prefix,
  1048**
code
  compacting databases,
    927-928
  compiling, 672
  optimizing, 664

arrays, 670
bookmarks, 670-671
Boolean expressions, 666
built-in collections, 666-667
constants, 670
Declare statements, 668
Dim statements, 668
distribution, 673
inline code, 666
Len function, 667
loops, 671-672
me keyword, 669
object references, 668-669
object types, 665-666
organization, 673
string functions, 670
transactions, 668
true/false evaluations, 667-668
unused code, 668
variants, 665
With...End With, 669
repairing databases, 930
Code Behind Forms, see CBF
code for the Activate event (listing), 968
code for the Add button (listing), 487
code for the Find button (listing), 488
code for the Move Next button (listing), 487
code for the Move Previous button (listing), 486
code to list and display ODBCDirect properties (listing), 626-627
Code window
Auto Data Tips feature, 275
Auto Indent feature, 275
Auto List Members feature, 275
Auto Quick Info feature, 275
Auto Syntax Check feature, 275

customizing, 274
style features, 275
Require Variable Declaration feature, 275
Tab width, 275
VBA, 244
splitting, 248-249
viewing multiple, 249
collections
commands, 293-294
compared to containers, 294-295
compared to objects, 293
controls, 288
custom
adding items, 295-296
creating, 295
defining, 295
loops, 296
removing items, 296
Forms, 280
items
referencing, 297
returning, 299-300
Modules, 281
objects, 288
properties, Key, 299
Reports, 281
colors
forms, selecting palettes, 143
reports, properties, 182
Column Count property, combo boxes, 134
Column Width property, combo boxes, 134
columns (queries)
moving, 89-90
selecting, 357
columns (client/servers), 608
COM (component object model), 714
Combo Box tool, 132
Combo Box Wizard, 132
combo boxes, 410-415
converting to list boxes, 139
forms, adding, 132-135

labels, 134
NotInList event, handling, 410-411
populating, Callback function, 412-415
properties, 134-135
command bars, programming, 404
see also menus
Command Button Wizard, 151-153
command buttons
Calendar control, Today, 749
captions, 185
control events, 386
creating
Add, 487
Find, 488
Move Next, 487
Move Previous, 486
displaying, MsgBox function, 398
enabling/disabling, 302-304
forms, adding, 151
hyperlinks, adding, 158
command-line switches, Runtime, testing applications, 973-974
commands
Add-Ins menu, Add-In Manager, 821
Analyze menu, Performance, 661
Briefcase menu
Update All, 680
Update Selection, 680, 692
collections, 293-294
Compact, Visual SourceSafe, 791
Debug menu, Compile, 672
Edit menu, New, 818
File menu, Save As/Export, 63
Format menu, Change To, 674

hidden, runtime version, 963
menus, adding, 403
multiple objects, 293
New menu
  DWORD Value, 818
  Key, 818
  String Value, 818
objects, 293
Option Explicit, 494
Replication menu
  Create Replica, 688, 691
  Synchronize Now, 691
Run menu, Compile All Modules, 672
Start menu, Run, 817
Tools menu, 782
  Add-Ins, 821
  Analyze, 661
  Database Utilities, 658
  Options, 686, 820
  Relationships, 72
  Replication, 680, 688
VBA, viewing code, 245-246
comments
macros, 321
VBA, 222
CommitTrans method, transaction processing, 643
Common Dialog
ActiveX control, 400, 753-755
properties, 754
Compact command, Visual SourceSafe, 791
Compact utility, 658
compacting databases, 924-928
comparison query criteria operator, 92
compilation objects, 273-274
Compile All Modules command (Run menu), 672
Compile All Modules feature, 274

Compile and Save All Modules feature, 274
Compile command (Debug menu), 672
Compile Loaded Modules tool, 273
compile on demand feature, disabling, 273
compiler constants
declaring, 225
Public, 225
compiling, 273-274
Compile All Modules feature, 274
Compile and Save All Modules feature, 274
compile on demand feature, 273
libraries, 798
loaded modules, 273
queries, 344
Complete Word, modules, 238
Component Name option, 976
component object model, *see* **COM**
components
applications, adding, 977
properties, setting, 980
Compress File option, 977
compressing drives, 658
concatenating strings, compared to adding values, 271
concurrency (transaction processing), multiuser systems, 647-650
conditional compilation, *see* **conditional If control structure**
conditional constants, compared to constants/ variables, 226
conditional If control structure, 225-226
conditions, macros, 306, 312

Configure Microsoft Replication Manager Wizard, 695-698
configuring Replication Manager, 695-698
conflict resolution (data replication), 693-695
connection strings (external tables), opening, 585
Const keyword, 254
constants
compiler, declaring, 225
declaring, 843
DLLs, 843-847
efficiency, 670
errors, 255
functions, 843
intrinsic, 254-256
  examples, 276-277
naming, 256
  conventions, 254
Object Browser, 233
optimization, 670
permissions, 901
scope, 255
strong typing, 254
Symbolic, 254
  defining, 254
system-defined, 254
VBA, 253, 256
viewing, 256
Container objects, 483-484
Document objects, 484
containers, compared to collections, 294-295
Containers object, data access object model, 460
containers: listing all in a database (listing), 460
contents files (Help files), 946
Contents tab
Database Properties dialog box, 915
Help dialog box, 932
context-sensitive help, VBA, 247

Continue buttons, 512
continuous forms
creating, 390
properties, Dividing Lines, 141
Control Box property, forms, 142
Control Panel
currency fields, 50
date/time fields, 49
Control properties, forms, 145-150
Control Source property
combo boxes, 134
controls, 147, 186
control sources, Expression Builder, 150
control structures
conditional If, 225-226
If...Then...Else, 223-224
Immediate If (IIF), 224-225
loops, 227-230
breaking, 228
VBA, 223-230
see also statements
Control Wizard, combo boxes, adding to forms, 132
controls, 131
ActiveX, 740
adding to applications, 740
adding to forms, 742-743
Calendar, 743
coding events, 746-747
Common Dialog, 753-755
compatibility, 742
data binding, 745
dialog boxes, 740
examples, 762-763
ImageList, 760-761
licensing, 761-762
ODE, 29
references, 744-745
registering, 741-742
Rich Textbox, 755-758

setting properties, 745-746
StatusBar, 751-753
Tab, 760
TabStrip, 758-760
types, 740
Unregister function, 742
UpDown object, 750-751
bound, 150, 187
calculated, 150, 187
Immediate If (IIF) statements, 224
Calendar, 747
methods, 748-750
properties, 747-748
checkboxes, 135
collections, 288
combo boxes, 132-135
converting to list boxes, 139
Common Dialog Box, 400
dialog boxes, 753
events
AfterUpdate, 383-384
BeforeUpdate, 383
Change, 384
Click, 385-386
DblClick, 386-387
Enter, 384
Exit, 385
GotFocus, 385
KeyDown, 387
KeyPress, 387
KeyUp, 387
LostFocus, 385
MouseDown, 387
MouseMove, 387
MouseUp, 387
NotInList, 384
sequence, 388
Updated, 384
focus, events, 388
forms
converting types, 138-139
events, 383
hyperlinks, adding, 158
labels, 131-132

list boxes, 135
naming, conflicts, 186
option buttons, 136
option groups, 136-138
Page Break, inserting in forms, 391
properties, 184-186
Allow AutoCorrect, 149
Auto Repeat, 149
Auto Tab, 149
Back Color, 147, 185
Back Special Effect, 147
Back Style, 147, 185
Border Color, 147, 185
Border Style, 147, 185
Border Width, 147, 185
Can Grow, 146, 185
Can Shrink, 146, 185
Cancel, 149
Caption, 146, 185
Control Source, 147, 186
ControlTip, 150
Data, 147-148, 186
Decimal Places, 146, 185
Default, 149
Default Value, 148
Display When, 146
Enabled, 148
Enter Key Behavior, 149
Filter Lookup, 148
Font Color, 185
Font Italic, 147, 185
Font Name, 147, 185
Font Size, 147, 185
Font Underline, 147, 185
Font Weight, 147, 185
Fore Color, 147
Format, 145-147, 185
Height, 146, 185
Help Context ID, 150
Hide Duplicates, 185
Hyperlink Address, 146, 185
Hyperlink SubAddress, 146, 185

Input Mask, 147
Left, 146, 185
Locked, 148
Name, 149, 186
Running Sum, 186
Scroll Bars, 146
Shortcut Menu Bar, 149
Status Bar Text, 149
Special Effect, 185
Tab Index, 149
Tab Stop, 149
Tag, 150, 186
Text Align, 147, 186
Top, 146, 185
Validation Rule, 148
Validation Text, 148
Visible, 146, 185
Width, 146, 185
reports, 178-181
  bound object frames, 179
  image, 181
  labels, 178
  lines, 179
  rectangles, 179
  text boxes, 178
  unbound object frames,
    180
subforms, referencing, 416
Tab, 393
  adding controls to tab
    pages, 394
  adding to forms, 393
  changing properties, 394
text boxes, 132
  converting to combo
    boxes, 138-139
toggle buttons, 136
transparent, 147
TypeOf keyword, 300
types, determining,
  300-301
unbound, 150, 187
uninitialized, testing, 269
updating data, events, 388
WebBrowser, 778
ControlTip property,
  controls, 150

Convert Database to Design
  Master Wizard, 699
converting
  macros to VBA code,
    324-325
  OLE objects to images, 674
copying
  databases, Visual
    SourceSafe, 787
  macro actions, 320-321
  records, controlling user
    access, 141
counter fields, resetting, 924
  see also AutoNumber fields
cover sheet, reports, 171
CPU, system requirements,
  16
Create New Data Source
  dialog box, 614
Create Replica command
  (Replication menu), 688,
  691
CreateControl function, 826
CreateCustomForm function,
  824-826
  code listing, 824-826
CreateForm function, 826
CreateGroups function, 887
CreateObject function, 717
CreateQueryDef method,
  483
CreateRecordset function,
  725
CreateTableDef method, 483
CreateUsers function, 890
CreatExcelObj function, 721
creating
  databases, prohibiting,
    904-905
  errors, user-defined, 526
  graphs, Excel, 723-726
  Help files
    building components,
      937-952
    reasons, 932
  macros, 306-313
  RTF files, 938

creating a foreign table
  (listing), 588
creating a link to an Access
  table stored in another
  database (listing), 582
creating a partial replica
  (listing), 707
creating a table, adding
  fields, and adding a primary
  key index (listing), 481
creating an ODBCDirect
  workspace (listing),
  625-626
criteria (queries)
  dates, 94-95
  functions, 365-366
  Like, 346
  sorting, 92-94
  specifying at runtime,
    112-114, 476-477
Cross Tabulation reports,
  167
crosstab queries, 347
  columns, fixed headings,
    352-353
  creating, 348-350
    Design view, 351-352
  parameters, 353
  reports, creating, 440-446
Crosstab Query Wizard,
  348-350
crosstab reports, printing,
  448-449
ctl prefix, 1046
ctls prefix, 1046
cur data-type prefix, 1047
currency field type, 48-50
Current event, forms, 374
CurrentDB( ) function,
  462-463
Custom Print Preview
  toolbar, displaying, 442
Custom tab (Database
  Properties dialog box), 916
customizing swap files, 658
Cycle property, forms, 144

D

DAO (Data Access Objects)
code
*compared to
ODBCDirect code, 626*
*integrating with
replication, 681*
naming conventions,
1048-1049
dat data-type prefix, 1047
data
analysis (applications),
developing, 17
binding, ActiveX controls,
745
backing up, database
replication, 679
data access object model,
454
Container objects, 460
Database objects, 456
Document objects, 461
Error objects, 462
Field objects, 458
Group objects, 456
Index objects, 458
Parameter objects, 459
Properties objects, 461
QueryDef objects, 458
Recordset objects, 460
Relation objects, 460
TableDef objects, 457
User objects, 456
Workspace objects, 456
entry forms (recordset
methods), examples,
486-489
locking, 546-547
conflicts, 555-561
*error dialog boxes,
overriding, 552*
examples, 565-566
forms, 548-552
OLE objects, 552
options, 547
queries, 548
recordsets, 552-555

reports, 548
testing, 562
*transaction processing,
553*
users, locating, 561
partial replication,
programming, 707
replicating
local objects, 706
programming, 705-706
replication
architecture, 681-683
benefits, 678-679
*conflict resolution,
693-695*
*database changes,
685-687*
defined, 678
enabling, 687-690
implementing, 680-681
limitations, 679
partial, 702
preventing, 690
replica creation, 690-691
*replica synchronization,
691-692*
*Replication Manager,
695-705*
topologies, 683-685
sharing, database
replication, 678-679
sources, defining, DLLs,
615
structures, optimization,
662-664
types
dBASE, mapping, 590
prefixes, 1047-1048
variables, 219-220
**Data Entry property, forms,
143**
**Data Grouping property,
reports, 183**
Data properties
controls, 147-148, 186
forms, 143-144
reports, 183

**Database Documenter,
910-920**
objects, printing rights, 880
options, 917-919
Database keyword, 585
Database locking, 547
Database objects
creating, 480-483
modifying, 480-483
variables, creating, 466
**Database Properties dialog
box, 914-916**
Database Splitter
examples, 595
external data, linking,
575-578
Database Splitter Wizard, 27
**Database Utilities command
(Tools menu), 658**
Database window
runtime version, 962
tables, viewing, 8
**Database window objects,
naming conventions,
1049-1050**
databases
closing, Visual SourceSafe,
791
compacting, 345, 658,
924-928
Visual SourceSafe, 791
counter fields, resetting,
924
creating, prohibiting,
904-905
defined, 7
documentation, 914-916
encrypting, 902
libraries
code, 797
compiling, 798
creating, 796
debugging, 805-806
referencing, 798-805
security, 806
maintenance, 924-930
objects, 7
checking in/out, 787-789
organizing, 26-27

saving in HTML format,
766-768
opening, Visual SourceSafe,
791
performance considerations
application types, 603
backup/recovery
capability, 603
file size, 602
security, 604
user base, 602
properties, documentation,
914-917
repairing, 928-930
replicating
Internet, 779
security, 906
start-up options, 32
Visual SourceSafe
adding, 783-786
creating local copies, 787
running, 783
Databases object, data access
object model, 456
datasheets
converting to tables
entering field data, 45
naming fields, 45
tables, creating, 44-46
date( ) expression, queries, 94
date/time field type, 48-49
DateAdd function, 233
DateDiff function, 233
DatePart function, 233
datepart (date, interval)
expression, queries, 95
dates, query criteria, 94-95
Day property, Calendar
control, 747
day (date) expression,
queries, 94
DayFont property, Calendar
control, 747
DayFontColor property,
Calendar control, 747
DayLength property,
Calendar control, 748
db object-naming prefix,
1048

dbAppendOnly argument,
recordsets, 467
dBASE external data issues,
589-590
dbConsistent argument,
recordsets, 467
dbDenyRead argument,
recordsets, 467
dbDenyWrite argument,
recordsets, 467
dbe object-naming prefix,
1048
DBEngine object, 454, 462
dbForwardOnly argument,
recordsets, 467
dbInconsistent argument,
recordsets, 467
dbl data-type prefix, 1047
DblClick event
controls, 386-387
forms, 379
dbReadOnly argument,
recordsets, 467
dbs object-naming prefix,
1048
dbSeeChanges argument,
recordsets, 467
dbSQLPassThrough
argument, recordsets, 468
dcm prefix, 1046
DDL (Data Definition
Language), client/servers,
608
Deactivate event
forms, 378-379
reports, 427
Debug menu commands,
Compile, 672
Debug window, 495-499
clearing, 497
executing functions, 498
executing methods, 498
executing subroutines, 498
functions, testing, 498
immediate pane, 496
Locals pane, 507
columns, 507

updating information,
507
opening, 495-496
printing to, 499
Call
LoopThroughCollection,
499
problems, 513
properties
setting values, 497, 503
testing values, 496
variables
setting values, 497, 503
testing values, 496
Watch expressions,
507-511
adding, 508-510
Auto Data Tips, 508
breaking at changes, 511
breaking when true,
510-511
editing, 510
quick watch, 508
Debug window pane
variables, setting values,
507
Debug.Print statements,
form events, determining
sequence, 381
debugger, 500
breakpoints, 500-502
removing, 501
setting, 500
invoking, 500
problems, 513
GotFocus events, 513
LostFocus events, 513
resetting code, 513
Stop statements, 500
watches, 500
debugging
Access debugger, 500
breakpoints, 500-502
invoking, 500
Stop statements, 500
watches, 500
application examples, 513
applications, 973

avoiding bugs, 494-495
  naming standards, 494
  Option Explicit, 494
  strong typing, 494
  variable scoping, 495
Calls window, 506
continuing after runtime
  errors, 512-513
libraries, 805-806
logic errors, 495
problems, 513
  GotFocus events, 513
  LostFocus events, 513
  resetting code, 513
Set Next Statement, 505
stepping through code,
  502-505
  breakpoints, 503-504
  Step Into, 502-503
  Step Out, 505
  Step Over, 504
Watch expressions,
  507-511
  adding, 508-510
  Auto Data Tips, 508
  breaking at changes, 511
  breaking when true,
    510-511
  editing, 510
  quick watch, 508
Decimal Places property,
  controls, 146, 185
declarations, API calls, 535
Declare statement, 838
declaring
  arrays, 257-258
    dynamic, 258-259
  compiler constants, 225
  constants, 843
  functions
    aliasing, 841
    DLLs, 838-839
  procedures
    Class modules, 215
    private, 216
  types, 844-845

variables, 218
  modules, 210
  object, 291
  Option Explicit
    statement, 212
  performance
    considerations, 218
  user-defined types, 252
declaring objects & referring
  to variables (listing), 668
declaring the type structure
  OSVERSIONINFO in the
  General Declarations
  section (listing), 844
Default Open Mode option
  (data locking), 549
Default property, controls,
  149
Default Record Locking
  option, 548
Default Value property
  controls, 148
  tables, 54
Default View property,
  forms, 140
defaults, properties, 291
defining
  collections, custom, 295
  constants, Symbolic, 254
  data sources, DLLs, 615
  relationships, 8
Definition feature, modules,
  238
defragmentation, 657-658
Delete Confirm dialog box,
  376
Delete Data permission, 876
Delete event, forms, 376
Delete method, recordsets,
  478-479
Delete queries, 479
  creating, 334-335
deleting
  fields, tables, 44
  files, from disk, 520
  groups (security), 888-889
  macro actions, 319

menus, custom, 404
objects, Visual SourceSafe,
  792
records, 478-479
  action queries, 334-335
  controlling user access,
    141
  form events, 376
relationships, 75
deleting a record (listing),
  488
deleting records with the
  Delete method (listing),
  479
denormalization, 663
descending sorts, queries, 90
Description property
  queries, 112
  tables, 61
Description subkey value
  (Registry), 817
Design view
  forms, 12
    creating, 122-123
  reports, 12
    creating, 174
  runtime version, 962
  tables, 8, 43
designing
  applications, options,
    605-607
  builders, 812, 829
    Load events, 831-833
    ValidTextPolite function,
      830-831
    ValidTextRude function,
      831-832
  forms
    toolbars, 123-124
    windows, 124
  menu add-ins, 827
  wizards, 822
DesignMasterID property,
  687
Destination Folder option,
  976
Detail reports, 166

Detail section
Format event, reports, 443
forms, 120
Print event, reports, 444
reports, 171
**determining whether a record
is locked before editing
(listing), 562**
dialog boxes, 397
ActiveX controls, 740
Add ActiveX Control, 741
Add Object(s) to
SourceSafe, 784
Add SourceSafe Project,
783
Add-In Manager, 821
Calendar Control
Properties, 746
Check In Object(s) to
SourceSafe, 789
Check Out Object(s) from
SourceSafe, 787
Choose Builder, 829
controls, 753
Create New Data Source,
614
creating, 118, 142
examples, 484-486
data locking, overriding,
552
Database Properties,
914-916
Delete Confirm, 376
Edit DWORD Value, 818
Edit String, 818
Edit Switchboard Page,
966-967
Field Builder, 43
Help Topics, properties,
283
History of File, 790
Import, 820
external data, 571
Import Objects, 821
Insert ActiveX Control, 743
Insert Hyperlink, 62
Insert Object, 180

Link, 576
Link Tables, 616
Location of New Replica,
688
Login, 616
message boxes, 397
Modal property, 144
New Form, 120
New Object, 827
New Query, 86
New Report, 171
New Table, 40
New User/Group, 868
Open, 821
Password Required, 860
Performance Analyzer, 661
Pop Up property, 144
queries, prompting for
criteria, 113
Query Parameters, 114
References, 716, 744
libraries, 802
Relationships, 73
Report Selection Form,
creating, 484-486
Resolve Replication
Conflicts, 693
Save MDE As, 877
Select Data Source, 616
Select Unique Record
Identifier, 617
*linking other table
formats, 578*
Set Database Password, 860
Show Table, designing
queries, 86
Show Tables, 74
self join queries, 355
SQL Server Login, 616
Startup, 32, 969
Synchronization Details,
704
Synchronization History,
704
Synchronize Database, 691
Synchronize Now, 702
Tab Order, 131

Topics Found, properties,
283
Unset Database Password,
860
Update Briefcase, 692
User and Group Accounts,
868
User and Group
Permissions, 34, 861, 875
Workgroup Information
File, 866
Workgroup Owner
Information, 865
dialog forms, creating, 397
Dim statement, 717
variables, 218
**directives (VBA), #Const,
225**
**discovering who has locked
the page (listing), 561**
disks
compression, 658
defragmenting, 657-658
**Display Control property,
lookups, 60**
**Display Database Window
option, 970**
Display Form option, 970
**Display Status Bar option,
970**
**Display When property,
controls, 146**
displaying
command buttons, MsgBox
function, 398
help forms, 142
icons, MsgBox function,
398
records
form events, 377
forms, 28
Screen object, 281
toolbars, 427
*Custom Print Preview,
442*
**displaytext hyperlink field
type, 48**

distributing
ActiveX controls, 761-762
applications, 31-33, 673
Access full version, 960
*Access full version
compared to runtime
version, 961*
ActiveX controls, 959
*adding files to disks,
975-977*
*adding Registry values,
979*
*creating for runtime
version, 964, 972*
defining shortcuts, 977
*designating Access
components, 979*
examples, 989
*Graph Runtime
Executable, 960*
Help Workshop, 960
location of setup files, 981
MDE files, 973
*preparing for runtime
version, 964, 984*
replication, 989
*Replication Manager,
959*
requirements, 958
running after setup, 981
*running Setup Wizard,
974-977*
runtime license, 959
security, 972
setting attributes, 980
*setting component
properties, 980*
Setup Wizard, 29, 959
startup options, 969-972
testing, 982-984
updates, database
replication, 679
**distribution disks, adding
files, 975-977**
**Dividing Lines property,
forms, 141**

DLLs, 838
constants, 843-847
data sources, defining, 615
functions
declaring, 838-839
issues, 848
types, 844-845
Do loops, 227-228
**doc object-naming prefix,
1048**
DoCmd object, 281
examples, 276-277
external data, importing,
572-575
macros, executing, 250-251
OpenForm method, 251
DoCmd object (macros), 328
**docs object-naming prefix,
1048**
Document objects
Container objects, 484
data access object model,
461
documentation, 910
Database Documenter,
916-920
databases, 914-916
objects, 917
properties, 917
formats, 919-920
forms, 912
macros, 321, 913
modules, 914
queries, 911
reports, 913
self-documentation,
910-916
tables, 46, 910
writing code, 920-921
documents
compared to collections,
294-295
HTML
exporting, 592-594
importing, 592-594
linking, 592-594

locating, Insert URL dialog
box, 62
**drivers (video), system
requirements, 16**
drives, compression, 658
DSN keyword, 585
**DWORD Value command
(New menu), 818**
dynamic arrays
declaring, 258-259
efficiency, 670
**dynamic HTML format,
772-773**
dynasets, 10, 464
bookmarks, 630
client/servers, 630
opening, 466, 469
preventing writing, 467
records, appending, 467
updating, 467

E

**Edit DWORD Value dialog
box, 818**
**Edit menu commands, New,
818**
Edit String dialog box, 818
**Edit Switchboard Page dialog
box, 966-967**
**Edited Record option, data
locking, 552**
editing
forms, preventing, 148
macros, 318-321
Switchboard forms, 967
Watch expressions, 510
editors, registry, 643
invoking, 817
ElseIf statements, 223
embedded graphics, *see*
graphics
embedding objects
compared to linking,
406-407
in-place activation, 406

embedding a database password in code (listing), 586

Empty value
testing, 268
Variant variables, 268-269

Enabled property, controls, 148

enabling
command buttons, 302-304
replication, 687-688
Access user interface, 688-689
Windows 95 Briefcase, 689-690

encryption, 861-862
backups, 862
databases, 902
performance considerations, 862

enforced referential integrity, queries, 99-100

Enhancing the builder (listing), 815-816

Enter event, controls, 384

Enter Key Behavior property, controls, 149

EOF property
recordsets, 469-470
with MoveNext (listing), 470

equal sign (=), query criteria operator, 92

Err object, 524-525

err object-naming prefix, 1048

Error event, 517-518
forms, 380
reports, 428

error forms, 534-536
printing, 536

error handling, 516-517, 537-538
applications, distributing, 32
centralizing, 520
creating, 967

handlers
description, 519-520
generic, 527, 536
number, 519-520
invoking (preventing), 537

error messages, optimistic locking, 554

Error object, data access object model, 462

ErrorHandler function, 529, 532

errors
calculations, null values, 109
cascading error effect, 523-524
clearing, 523
constants, 255
error 3167, 555
error 3186, 558
error 3197, 555, 558
error 3260, 555, 558
functions, 838
generating, 525
Immediate If (IIF) statements, 224
Invalid add-in entry message, 820
libraries, loading, 802
listing, 518
logging, 530-531
On_Error statements, 518-520
optimistic locking, 558-560
pessimistic locking, 555-558
properties, Validation Rule, 55
raising, 525-526
recordsets, updating, 467
responding to, 531-534
transaction processing, 646-650
memory, 646
user-defined, creating, 526

Errors collection, 526-527

errs object-naming prefix, 1048

establishing a link to an external table (listing), 581

establishing relationships between database objects (listing), 482

Evaluating for 0 (listing), 667

Evaluating for True and False (listing), 668

evaluating which items are selected in the multi-select list box (listing), 415

events
ActiveX controls, coding, 746-747
AfterUpdate, 635
bound object frames, 384
controls
AfterUpdate, 383-384
BeforeUpdate, 383
Change, 384
Click, 385-386
DblClick, 386-387
Enter, 384
Exit, 385
focus, 388
GotFocus, 385
KeyDown, 387
KeyPress, 387
KeyUp, 387
LostFocus, 385
MouseDown, 387
MouseMove, 387
MouseUp, 387
NotInList, 384
sequence, 388
Updated, 384
updating data, 388
defined, 284
error events, 517-518
forms
Activate, 378
AfterDelConfirm, 376
AfterInsert, 375
AfterUpdate, 375
ApplyFilter, 381
BeforeDelConfirm, 376
BeforeInsert, 374-375

BeforeUpdate, 375
Click, 379
Close, 378
closing, 382
controls, 383
Current, 374
DblClick, 379
Deactivate, 378-379
Delete, 376
Error, 380
Filter, 381, 405-406
focus, 382
GotFocus, 379
KeyDown, 380
KeyPress, 380
keystrokes, 382
KeyUp, 380
Load, 377
LostFocus, 379
mouse, 382
MouseDown, 379
MouseMove, 380
MouseUp, 380
Open, 376
opening, 381
order of occurrence, 376
Resize, 377
sections, 383
sequence, 381-382
sizing, 382
Timer, 381
Unload, 377-378
GotFocus, debugging
  problems, 513
LostFocus, debugging
  problems, 513
NotInList, handling,
  410-411
procedures
  creating, 213
  modules, 212
reports, 426
  Activate, 427
  Close, 426
  Deactivate, 427
  Error, 428
  Format, 429-431

NoData, 428
Open, 426
Page, 428
Print, 431-432
Retreat, 432
running macros, 315-318
sections, 429-433
sequence, 429-433
Rich Textbox, 756
UpDown object, 750
viewing, 284
**example of the Format event
on report layout (listing),
429-430**
**example of the Print event to
calculate column and row
totals (listing), 431-432**
Excel
  controlling from Access,
  719-721
  graphs, creating from
  Access, 723-726
**exclamation point (!) bang,
290**
**ExclusiveAsyncDelay
Registry setting, transaction
processing, 642**
executing
  functions, Debug window,
  498
  methods, Debug window,
  498
  subroutines, Debug
  window, 498
  see also running
**executing a pass-through
query using code (listing),
621**
**executing a stored query
(listing), 672**
**executing the sp_columns
stored procedure (listing),
623**
Exit event, controls, 385
**explicit references, libraries,
801**

exporting
  data, FTP servers, 776
  HTML documents,
  592-594
Expression Builder, 150
  queries, 103
expressions
  between date and date,
  queries, 95
  building, macros, 310
  date( ), queries, 94
  datepart (date, interval),
  queries, 95
  day (date), queries, 94
  forms, 150-151
  month (date), queries, 94
  null values, converting to
  zero, 109
  properties, 289
  queries, 346
    calculated fields, 101
    Rushmore, 346
  weekday (date), queries, 95
  year (date), queries, 94
external data, 568
  compatibility, 568
  connection information,
  troubleshooting, 591
  defined, 568
  examples, 594-598
  hard drive requirements,
  591
  HTML documents,
  592-594
  importing, 568-571
    DoCmd object, 572-575
    Import dialog box, 571
  linking, 545-569, 575-582
    creating links, 581
    Database Splitter,
    575-578
    ISAM formats, 580
    other Access tables, 576
    other tables, 577
  opening, 569-570, 582-584
    connection information,
    583

passwords, 585-586
performance considerations, 591
refreshing links, 586-588
removing links, 586-588
storage, 568
tables
ASCII files, 591
creating, 588-589
dBASE, 589-590
FoxPro, 590
troubleshooting, 591

F

f data-type prefix, 1047
Fast Laser Printing property
forms, 145
reports, 184
fdlg object-naming prefix, 1050
Field Builder dialog box, 43
Field List properties (queries), 111
Field List window, 125
availability, 143
field properties (queries), 110-111
Field Size property (tables), 51
field-level security (queries), 902
fields
AutoNumber, creating custom, 564
calculated
creating, 101-103
nested queries, 345
combo boxes, setting width, 133
entering data, converting datasheets to tables, 45
entries, zero-length compared to null, 57
excluding (queries), 107

forms
adding, 125
preventing editing, 148
Hyperlink, 62-63, 766
storing, 777
indexing
queries, 345
searching tables, 58
selecting field types, 47
multifield indexes, creating, 58
naming
cautions, 44
client/server compatibility, 44
converting datasheets, 45
legal characters, 44
length, 44
normalization, 18
optimizing, 663
primary keys, 59
printing
methods, 469
properties, 470
properties, 51
Allow Zero Length, 57
Caption, 54
Default Value, 54
Field Size, 51
Format, 52
Indexed, 58
Input Mask, 52-53
queries, 110
Required, 57
Validation Rule, 55
Validation Text, 55-56
queries
adding, 87
counting, 108
creating parameters, 114
inserting, 89
moving, 89-90
removing, 88
selecting, 86-88
sorting multiple, 91
reports, adding, 175

selecting
creating forms, 121
reports, 172
size
AutoNumber fields, 50
currency fields, 50
date/time fields, 49
hyperlink fields, 51
memo fields, 49
number fields, 49
OLE Object fields, 50
text fields, 49
yes/no fields, 50
sorting, selecting field types, 47
space requirements, 47
tables
defining, 43
deleting, 44
descriptions, 44
inserting, 44-46
selecting in Table Wizard, 41
selecting types, 46-48
types, 43
types
AutoNumber, 48-50
calculations, 47
currency, 48-50
date/time, 48-49
hyperlink, 48, 51
memo, 48-49
number, 48-49
OLE Object, 48-50
text, 47-49
yes/no, 48-50
uninitialized, testing, 269
updating (queries), 332
values, lookups, 59-60
version, adding, 633
Fields collection: getting information (listing), 458
Fields object (data access object model), 458

File DSN option (ODBC Data Source Administrator), 613
File menu commands, Save As/Export, 63
File Name and Path option, 976
file servers
 applications, installing, 543
 compared to client/ servers, 6
 installing Access, 542
File System Transport, 683
File Transfer Protocol (FTP), 776
files
 ASP format, 772
 deleting from disk, 520
 distribution disks, adding, 975-977
 extensions, Visual SourceSafe, 786
 formats, supported, 570
 Help files
  # (pound sign), footnotes, 939-940
  authoring tools, 938, 953
  contents files, 946
  creating, 932
  custom, 952
  graphics, 944
  hotspots, 942-943
  hypergraphics, 945
  jump hotspots, 942-943
  K footnote, 940
  macro hotspots, 943
  map files, 945-946
  nonscrolling regions, 942
  planning, 936-937
  pop up hotspots, 942-943
  tags, 940
  titles, 940
  topic files, 938-941
 Help Project file, compiling, 948-952
 Help project file, 946-947
 HTX format, 772

IDC format, 772
importing, HTML, 771-772
LDB, networks, 563-564
linking, HTML, 769-770
logs, synchronization history (replicated data), 704
map files, 945-946
MDE
 distributing files, 973
 restrictions, 877
 security, 877-878
 setup, location after distribution, 981
 workgroup information, 864
 WZMAIN80.MDE, importing, 820
FillCells subroutine, 721
filling a listbox by using a Callback function (listing), 412
Filter event (forms), 381, 405-406
Filter Lookup property (controls), 148
Filter On property (reports), 183
Filter property
 forms, 143
 queries, 112
 reports, 183
 tables, 62
Filtering an existing recordset (listing), 472
filters
 forms, 143
  controlling behavior, 405-406
 records (table recordset objects), 465
 recordsets, 472-473
 reports, 183
find and replace feature (VBA), 246
Find command button, creating, 488

Find String function (listing), 987-988
Find tab (Help dialog box), 934
FindFirst method
 listing, 474
 recordsets, 473
finding recordsets, 473-474
FindLast method (recordsets), 473
FindNext method (recordsets), 473
FindPrevious method (recordsets), 473
first entry-point function (listing), 830-831
fixed arrays, 257
fld object-naming prefix, 1048
flds object-naming prefix, 1048
fmnu object-naming prefix, 1050
fmsg object-naming prefix, 1050
focus
 control events, 388
 form events, 378-382
 records (form events), 374
Font Color property (controls), 185
Font Italic property (controls), 147, 185
Font Name property (controls), 147, 185
Font Size property (controls), 147, 185
Font Underline property (controls), 147, 185
Font Weight property (controls), 147, 185
footer section
 forms, 120
 Page Footers, 171
For Each...Next loops, 229-230
 listing, 666

For...Next loops, 228-229

Force New Page property (reports), 187, 196

Fore Color property (controls), 147

foreign keys, 71
client/servers, 608
Required property, 57

foreign tables, *see* **external data**

Form and Report Class modules, 210

Form Design toolbar, 123-124

Form Design window, 123-131

Form property, 301

Form view, 11

Form Wizard
forms, creating, 121-122
launching, 122
one-to-many forms, 153-154

Format event
compared to Print event, 432
reports, 429-431

Format function, 231

Format menu (forms)
aligning objects, 127
commands, Change To, 674
sizing objects, 129
Snap to Grid, 128
spacing, 129

Format properties
controls, 145-147, 185
forms, 140-143
reports, 182
tables, 52

FormatCount property (reports), 434

formats
documentation, 919-920
files, supported, 570

Formatting toolbar, 123-124
reports, 175

forms, 11, 118
ActiveX controls, 740
adding, 742-743
Allow Additions property, 143
Allow Deletions property, 143
Allow Edits property, 143
Allow Filters property, 143
applications
creating for runtime version, 964-967
distributing, 31
navigating, 118
Auto Center property, 141
Auto Resize property, 141
Border Style property, 141
borders, 141
bound objects, 406-407
builder forms, 815-816
Modal property, 815
Callback function, 414
Caption property, 140
class modules, 417
Close Button property, 142
closing, events, 377-378, 382
colors, selecting palettes, 143
combo boxes
NotInList event handling, 410-411
record sources, 132
command buttons, adding, 151
components, 119-120
continuous
creating, 390
Dividing Lines property, 141
Control Box property, 142
Control properties, 145-150
controls, 131
checkboxes, 135
combo boxes, 132-135
converting types, 138-139

events, 383
labels, 131
list boxes, 135
option buttons, 136
option groups, 136-138
text boxes, 132
toggle buttons, 136
creating, 120, 389-397
Design View, 122-123
examples, 160-164
fields, selecting, 121
Form Wizard, 121-122
layouts, selecting, 122
queries, 121
styles, selecting, 122
titles, 122
custom menus, adding to forms, 400-404
Cycle property, 144
data entry, recordset method examples, 486-489
Data Entry property, 143
data locking, 548-552
Data properties, 143-144
Default View property, 140
designing
prototypes, 20
toolbars, 123-124
detail section, 120
dialog, creating, 397
Dividing Lines property, 141
documentation, 912
emulating with reports, 169
error
creating, 534-536
printing, 536
event procedures, 212
events, 374
Activate, 378
AfterDelConfirm, 376
AfterInsert, 375
AfterUpdate, 375
ApplyFilter, 381
BeforeDelConfirm, 376
BeforeInsert, 374-375

BeforeUpdate, 375
Click, 379
Close, 378
Current, 374
DblClick, 379
Deactivate, 378-379
Delete, 376
Error, 380
Filter, 381
GotFocus, 379
KeyDown, 380
KeyPress, 380
KeyUp, 380
Load, 377
LostFocus, 379
MouseDown, 379
MouseMove, 380
MouseUp, 380
Open, 376
order of occurrence, 376
Resize, 377
sequence, 381-382
Timer, 381
Unload, 377-378
expressions, 150-151
Fast Laser Printing
  property, 145
fields
  adding, 125
  preventing editing, 148
Filter event, 405-406
Filter property, 143
filters, 143
  controlling behavior,
  405-406
focus, events, 378-382
footer section, 120
Format properties, 140-143
Forms collection, 280
frmGetFormInfo, 824
frmSpecialEffect, 814-816
Grid X property, 142
Grid Y property, 142
Has Module property, 145
header section, 120
help, displaying, 142

Help Context ID property,
  145
Help File property, 145
hyperlinks, adding,
  158-159, 777
Internet, compatibility,
  158-160
keystrokes, events, 382
labels
  captions, 54
  sizing, 129
Layout for Print property,
  143
Menu Bar property, 144
menus
  creating, 400
  designing, 402-404
methods, creating custom,
  421-422
Min Max Buttons property,
  142
modal, 119
Modal property, 144
mouse events, 382
multipage, creating,
  391-393
navigating, setting
  properties, 141
Navigation Buttons
  property, 141
objects
  aligning, 127-128
  linking compared to
    embedding, 406-407
  moving, 126-127
  selecting, 125-126
  sizing, 128-129
  spacing, 129-130
one-to-many, 153
  creating, 153-156
opening, 376
  events, 381
  macros, 307
optimization, 673-675
  client/servers, 633-637
Order By property, 143

Palette Source property,
  143
parameter queries, 476
passing values (parameter
  queries), 367
Picture properties, 142
Pop Up property, 144
primary keys, fetching from
  servers, 631
printing, 119, 143-145
properties, 139-145
  creating custom, 417-421
  creating public variables,
    418-419
  Default Value, 54
  OpenArgs, 408
  Validation Rules, 56
Properties window, 140
queries, 157
Record Locks property, 144
Record Selectors property,
  141
Record Source property,
  143
record sources, 125
  changing, 408-410
  changing at runtime, 143
  system reports, 28
records
  displaying, 28
  locking, 144
  ordering, 143
Recordset Type property,
  144
RecordsetClone property,
  476
recordsets, synchronizing,
  417
running macros, 315-318
saving
  HTML format, 159
  Microsoft IIS format, 160
Scroll Bars property, 141
sections, events, 383
Short Menu Bar property,
  145

Short Menu property, 145
single, creating, 389
sizing, events, 382
Snap to Grid, 128
 adjusting grid, 142
 disabling, 128
splash screen, creating, 396, 423
styles, 119
subforms, 390, 416
 adding, 156
switchboard, 118, 395
 creating, 964-967
 editing, 967
Tab controls, adding, 393
tab order, changing, 130, 394
tabbed, creating, 393-394
Tag property, 145
titles, Caption property, 140
Toolbar property, 145
transaction processing, 647
Type variables, storing data, 253
types, 389-397
unbound objects, 407
 data locking, 564
viewing, 11
 options, 140
Views Allowed property, 141
What is This Button property, 142
Width property, 142
windows, Form Design, 123-131
Forms collection, compared to Forms container, 461
FoxPro, external data issues, 590
fra prefix, 1047
frm prefix, 1046, 1049
frmGetFormInfo form, 824
frms prefix, 1046
frmSpecialEffect form, 814-816

FROM clause (SQL), 357
front-ends
compared to back-ends, 605
designing, 35
file format compatibility, 604
tables, linking from back-end servers, 605
fsfr prefix, 1050
fsub prefix, 1047
FTP (File Transfer Protocol), 776
Full Module View (VBA), 211, 249
Fully Connected topology, 685
Function subkey value (Registry), 817
functions, 210, 259
ANSI, renaming, 842
APIs, 849
AssignToGroup, 891
builder functions, 813
 arguments, 814-815
Callback, 734
 arguments, 413
 populating combo/list boxes, 412-415
calling
 invalid characters, 841
 libraries, 799
 ordinal number references, 843
code, viewing, 245-246
constants, 843
CreateControl, 826
CreateCustomForm, 824-826
CreateForm, 826
CreateGroups, 887
CreateObject, 717
CreateRecordset, 725
CreateUsers, 890
CreatExcelObj, 721
creating, 213-214

CurrentDB( ), 462-463
DateAdd, 233
DateDiff, 233
DatePart, 233
declaring, aliasing, 841
DLLs
 declaring, 838-839
 issues, 848
error messages, 838
ErrorHandler, 529, 532
examples, 239-240
executing, Debug window, 498
Format, 231
GetObject, 718
InputBox, 400
Instr, 232
IsEmpty, 268
IsLoaded, 815
IsNull, 269
Left, 232
libraries
 DLLs, 838
 Win32 API, 838
List, 413
ListGroups, 894
Mid, 232
modules, 14, 210
MsgBox, 397-399
MyCustomForm, 827
names, resolving conflicts, 842
Object Browser, 233
objects, passing, 298
parameters, 230-231
 optional, 261-263
 passing by reference compared to value, 260-261
queries, criteria, 365-366
RemoveGroups, 888
RemoveUsers, 893
RevokeFromGroup, 892
Right, 232
SpecialEffect, 814
stepping over, 504

strings, 231-232
SysCmd, 815
testing, Debug window, 498
UCase, 232
Unregister (ActiveX controls), 742
values, returning, 230-231
VBA, 231-234
parentheses, 463
viewing, Full Module View, 211 .

G

g scope prefix, 1049
General Declarations sections
compiler constants, 225
modules, 210
statements, Option Explicit, 212
General Declarations section of basUtils (listing), 850-852
General tab (Database Properties dialog box), 914
generating errors, 525
generic error handler, 527-536
generic object variables, compared to specific, 292
GetDriveInfo procedure (listing), 855
GetErrorInfo subroutine, 536
GetObject function, 718
GetSysInfo subroutine (listing), 853
GetSystemInfo subroutine, 534
global variables, 210, 221-222
creating, form properties, 418-419

GotFocus event
controls, 385
debugging problems, 513
forms, 379
Graph Runtime Executable, 960
graphics
bitmap files, creating splash screen forms, 397
bitmaps, 944
Help files, 944
Help Project file, 950
metafiles, 944
multiresolution bitmaps, 944
reports, 168
Shed graphics, 944
see also charts; hypergraphics
graphs (Excel), creating from Access, 723-726
greater than or equal to sign (>=), query criteria operator, 92
greater than sign (>), query criteria operator, 92
Grid X property
forms, 142
reports, 182
Grid Y property
forms, 142
reports, 182
GridFont property (Calendar control), 748
GridFontColor property (Calendar control), 748
GridLinesColor property (Calendar control), 748
GridLinesFormat property (Calendar control), 748
GROUP BY clause (SQL), 359
Group Footer property (reports), 171, 195
Group Header property (reports), 171, 195

Group Interval property (reports), 195
group levels (reports), adding, 172
Group On property (reports), 195
Group variable, 887
grouping data (reports), 193-194
properties, 195-196
groups (security), 456, 886-889
adding, 886-887
deleting, 888-889
listing, 894-896
maintenance, 889-894
users
adding, 889-890
assigning, 890-891
removing, 891-894
Groups object (data access object model), 456
Grp Keep Together property (reports), 182
grp object-naming prefix, 1048
grps object-naming prefix, 1048

H

handling optimistic locking errors (listing), 558-559
handling pessimistic locking errors (listing), 556
handling pessimistic locking errors in transactions (listing), 557-560
hard disks
compression, 658
defragmentation, 657-658
hard drives
external data, space requirements, 591
free space, determining, 854

hardware, system requirements, 16-17
Has Module property
  forms, 145
  reports, 184
HasContinued property (reports), 435
HAVING clause (SQL), 360
header section
  forms, 120
  page headers, 171
headings, crosstab queries, 352-353
Height property (controls), 146, 185
help
  adding to applications, 973
  creating, 30-32
  forms, displaying, 142
  hotspots, 935
  hypergraphics, 936
  properties, 282
  users' perspective, 932, 936
  VBA, context-sensitive, 247
Help About dialog box (operating system information), 850
Help Context ID property
  controls, 150
  forms, 145
  reports, 184
Help dialog box
  Contents tab, 932
  Find tab, 934
  Index tab, 933
Help File property
  forms, 145
  reports, 184
Help files
  $ (dollar sign), footnotes, 940
  # (pound sign), footnotes, 939-940
  authoring tools, 938, 953
  contents files, 946

  creating, 932
    building components, 937-952
  custom, 952
  graphics, 944
  hotspots, 942-943
  hypergraphics, 945
  jump hotspots, 942-943
  K footnote, 940
  macro hotspots, 943
  map files, 945-946
  nonscrolling regions, 942
  planning, 936-937
  pop-up hotspots, 942-943
  tags, 940
  titles, 940
  topic files, 938
  topics
    inserting, 939-940
    keywords, 940
    sample, 940-941
Help project file, 946-947
  compiling, 948-952
Help Topics dialog box, properties, 283
Help window
  button bars, 935
  customizing, 950-951
Help Workshop, 950-951, 960
hidden text, 943
Hide Duplicates property (controls), 185
Hide Key Column checkbox, 60
hiding toolbars, 427
History of File dialog box, 790
hotspots, 935
  Help files, 942-943
HTML (Hypertext Markup Language)
  exporting, 592-594
  formats, static compared to dynamic, 772-773

  forms, saving in HTML format, 159, 768
  importing, 592-594, 771-772
  linking, 592-594, 769-770
  objects, saving in HTML format, 766-768
  queries, saving in HTML format, 767
  reports, saving in HTML format, 199, 768
  tables
    converting data, 63-65
    saving in HTML format, 766
  templates, 775
HTTP (Hypertext Transfer Protocol) servers, 776
HTX file format, 772
Hybrid topology, 685
hypergraphics (Help files), 936, 945
Hyperlink Address property (controls), 146, 185
hyperlink field type, 48, 51, 62-63, 766
  Internet, publishing table data, 62
Hyperlink SubAddress property (controls), 146, 185
hyperlinks
  adding
    forms, 158-159, 777
    reports, 777
  labels (reports), 198-199
  storing in fields, 777

I

icons, displaying (MsgBox function), 398
IDC file format, 772
IDE (interactive development environment), 274

idx object-naming prefix, 1048

idxs object-naming prefix, 1048

If statements, 223
  compared to Select Case statements, 224
  conditional, 225-226

If...Then...Else control structure, 223-224

image controls, compared to unbound object frames, 180

ImageList (ActiveX control), 760-761

images
  bitmap files, creating splash screen forms, 397
  reports, 181
  see also graphics

img prefix, 1046

Immediate If (IIF) control structure, 224-225

immediate pane (Debug window), 496
  clearing, 497

implicit transactions (Registry settings), modifying, 642

ImplicitCommitSync Registry setting (transaction processing), 642

Import dialog box, 820
  external data, 571

Import HTML Wizard, 592-594

Import Objects dialog box, 821

importing data
  external data, 568-571
    DoCmd object, 572-575
    Import dialog box, 571
  file formats, supported, 570
  FTP servers, 776
  HTML documents, 592-594, 771-772

HTTP servers, 776
USysRegInfo tables, 820

in (query criteria operator), 93

in-place activation (bound objects), 406

Include File on First Disk option, 977

Index tab (Help dialog box), 933

Indexed property (tables), 58

indexes
  advantages, 663
  multifield, creating, 58
  performance considerations, 58, 62
  primary key, 59
  relationships, 80
  tables, adding, 481
  upsizing to client/servers, 610

Indexes object (data access object model), 458

indexing fields
  queries, 345
  selecting field types, 47

infinite loops, 228

InitVars routine (reports), 442-443

input boxes, creating, 400

input devices, system requirements, 16

Input Mask property
  controls, 147
  tables, 52-53

Input Mask Wizard, 52

input masks, literal characters, 53

InputBox function, 400

Insert ActiveX Control dialog box, 743

Insert Data permission, 876

Insert Hyperlink dialog box, 62

Insert Object dialog box, 180

inserting
  fields
    queries, 89
    tables, 44
  OLE objects (reports), 180
  Page Break controls (forms), 391
  page breaks (reports), 187

inserting default values when parameters are missing (listing), 262

installing
  Access, multiuser applications, 542-543
  ActiveX controls, registering, 741
  applications
    creating setup disks, 33
    networks, 33
  menu add-ins, 828
  multiuser applications, 543-544
  Registry, restoring, 33
  testing, 33
  Visual SourceSafe, 782

Instr function, 232

int data-type prefix, 1047

interactive development environment (IDE), 274

Internet
  Access, new features, 766
  compatibility, 766
  databases
    replicating, 779
    synchronization, 705
  forms, compatibility, 158-160
  hyperlinks, 777
  reports, compatibility, 198-199
  tables, hyperlink field type, 62

intrinsic constants, 254-256
  examples, 276-277

Invalid add-in entry error messages, 820

invoking
error handling, preventing, 537
Registry Editor, 817
is not (query criteria operator), 93
is null (query criteria operator), 93
ISAM
drivers, Registry keys, 584
formats, supported (linking data), 580
IsEmpty function, 268
IsLoaded function, 815
IsNull function, 269
calculations, eliminating errors, 110

J

Jet 3.5, optimization, 660-661
Jet Engine
data access object model, 454
objects, naming conventions, 1048-1049
queries, optimizing, 344-347
query plan, 28
SQL statements, passing through, 468
tables, adding/removing, 481
tracking layer, 681
user interfaces, Container objects, 483
JOIN clause (SQL), 358-359
joins (queries)
outer, 353-354
tables, 358-359
jump hotspots (Help files), 942-943
junction tables, 72

K

K footnote (Help files), 940
Keep Together property (reports), 196
KeepLocal property, 687, 690
Key command (New menu), 818
Key property (collections), 299
KeyDown event
controls, 387
forms, 380
KeyPress event (forms), 380
keystrokes
forms, events, 382
runtime version, 963-964
KeyUp event
controls, 387
forms, 380
keywords
As String, 231
ByVal, 839
Call, 214
Const, 254
Database, 585
DSN, 585
Help topics, 940
Me
efficiency, 669
referencing, 388-389
New, creating objects, 297-298
Preserve, 259
Public, 215
PWD, 585
TypeOf
control structures, 224
controls, 300
UID, 585
Kill statement, 520
Kwery Corporation, 1046

L

Label tool, 131, 178
Label Wizard, mailing labels, 169
labels
captions, 54, 185
default, 131
combo boxes, 134
forms
adding, 131-132
sizing, 129
hyperlinks, adding, 158
mailing labels, 169
printing multiple, 438-440
reports, 178
cutting from fields, 175
hyperlinks, 198-199
sizing automatically, 178
language reference, 959
Last Position (modules), 239
LastModified property, 480
LastModified property after AddNew (listing), 480
launching
Form Wizard, 122
macros, creating, 422-423
Report Wizard, 174
Word, 726
Layout for Print property
forms, 143
reports, 182
layouts
reports, 173
selecting, creating forms, 122
lbl prefix, 1046
LDB files, security, 563-564
Left function, 232
Left Outer Joins, 354
Left property (controls), 146, 185
Len function (listing), 667
less than or equal to sign (<=), query criteria operator, 92

less than sign (<), query criteria operator, 92
Leszynski Naming Conventions (LNC), 15, 217, 1046
libraries
  compiling, 798
  creating, examples, 807-809
  databases
    code, 797
    creating, 796
  debugging, 805-806
  explicit references, 801
  functions
    calling, 799
    DLLs, 838
    Win32 API, 838
  loading
    error messages, 802
    LoadOnStartup Registry key, 800-801
  modules, designing, 797
  objects, viewing, 287
  procedures, unique names, 842
  referencing, 798-805
  Registry, creating references, 798
  runtime references, creating, 799
  security, 806
  type libraries, 715
  VBA, 796
    creating references, 805
Library subkey value (Registry), 817
licensing
  ActiveX controls, 761-762
  applications (ODE), 29
  runtime, 959
like (query criteria operator), 92
Like criteria (queries), 346
lin prefix, 1046
line continuation character (VBA), 222

Line tool, 179
Linear topology, 685
lines (reports), 179
Link Child Fields property
  subforms, 156
  subreports, 193
Link dialog box, 576
Link Master Fields property
  subforms, 156
  subreports, 193
Link Tables dialog box, 616
linking
  back-end tables to front-end applications, 605
  data
    FTP servers, 776
    HTTP servers, 776
  external data, 545-546, 568-569, 575-582
    creating links, 581
    Database Splitter, 575-578
    ISAM formats, 580
    other Access tables, 576
    other tables, 577
  file formats, supported, 570
  HTML documents, 592-594, 769-770
  objects, compared to embedding, 406-407
  tables
    accessing in networks, 546
    automation, 984-989
    code, 618
    examples, 595-598
    security, 879
    UI, 616-617
    updating, 776
  views, client/servers, 619-620
linking to an external table (listing), 579
links, refreshing/removing, 586-588
List Box Wizard, 135

list boxes, 410-415
  forms, adding, 135
  multi-select property, 414-415
  populating, Callback function, 412-415
List Constants (modules), 236
List function (values), 413
List Properties and Methods (modules), 235-236
ListGroups function, 894
listing each Container object and its associated Document objects (listing), 484
listing errors in the current database (listing), 463
listings
  Access application object instance, 732
  accessing the properties of the DBEngine object, 463
  accommodating for missing parameters in your code, 262
  adding records to a recordset, 479
  altering a form's record source at runtime, 409-410
  alternative for establishing a link to an external table, 582
  API declarations, 855
  AreTablesAttached routine, 596-597
  assigning view rights, 900
  AssignPassword function, 897
  AssignToGroup function, 891
  Auto Attach function, 985-987
  bookmark property, 475

bookmark usage, 670
Builder function, 813-814
building a query, 483
bulk changes using a predefined action query, 478
Call stack for previous error handler, 524
Callback function, 734
Callback function listing all reports in the database, 485-486
calling a function in a library, 800
changing passwords, 896
checking for an empty recordset using RecordCount, 471
checking recordset size, 737
CloseExcel routine, 722
cmdAddUsers command button code, 889
cmdAssign button code, 890
cmdRemove command button code, 888, 893
cmdRevoke command button code, 892
code behind the Add button, 886
code for the Activate event, 968
code for the Add button, 487
code for the Find button, 488
code for the Move Next button, 487
code for the Move Previous button, 486
code to list and display ODBCDirect properties, 626-627
code with no error handling example, 516

containers: listing all in a database, 460
CreateCustomForm function, 824-826
CreateGroups function, 887
CreateRecordset function, 725
CreateUsers function, 890
creating a foreign table, 588
creating a link to an Access table stored in another database, 582
creating a partial replica, 707
creating a table, adding fields, and adding a primary key index, 481
creating an ODBCDirect workspace, 625-626
creating Excel graphs from Access, 723
creating PowerPoint slides, 730
declaring the type structure OSVERSIONINFO in the General Declarations section, 844
declaring objects and referring to variables, 668
declaring Windows API calls, 535
deleting a record, 488
deleting records with the Delete method, 479
determining whether a record is locked before editing, 562
discovering who has locked the page, 561
embedding a database password in code, 586
enhancing the builder, 815-816
enumerating database table objects w/DAO, 920

EOF property with MoveNext, 470
error handling w/ On_Error_GoTo statement, 519
error-handling routine, 517
ErrorHandler function, 529-532
ErrorHandler function return value, 533
establishing a link to an external table, 581
establishing relationships between database objects, 482
evaluating for 0, 667
evaluating for True and False, 668
evaluating which items are selected in the multi-select list box, 415
example of the Format event on report layout, 429-430
example of the Print event to calculate column and row totals, 431-432
executing a pass-through query using code, 621
executing a stored query, 672
executing the sp_columns stored procedure, 623
Fields collection: getting information, 458
FillCells subroutine, 721
filling a listbox by using a Callback function, 412
filtering an existing recordset, 472
Find String function, 987-988
FindFirst method, 474
first entry-point function, 830-831

For Each...Next, 666
General Declarations section of basUtils, 850-852
generating Word mail merge document, 727
generic error handler, 527
generic error-handling type structure, 528
GetDriveInfo procedure, 855
GetErrorInfo subroutine, 536
GetSysInfo subroutine, 853
Getting system information through code, 534
groups (security), 894-896
handling optimistic locking errors, 558-559
handling pessimistic locking errors, 556
handling pessimistic locking errors in transactions, 557-560
ignoring error and continuing execution, 520
inserting default values when parameters are missing, 262
LastModified property after AddNew, 480
Len function, 667
linking to an external table, 579
listing all groups, 894
listing each Container object and its associated Document objects, 484
listing errors in the current database, 463
listing users, 895
Load event of frmPolite, 831
Load event of frmRude, 832-833

loading the application and checking table attachments, 595
locating users without passwords, 898
LogError routine, 530
looping through a recordset, 671
MakeItBold subroutine, 665
methods for clsRecordsets, 266-267
modifying user rights, 901
Move methods, 469
object variables for code efficiency, 669
OpenDatabase method, 583
OpenDatabase to connect a remote server database, 624
opening a dynaset type of recordset on a table, 466
opening a recordset, 465
opening a recordset based on a query, 466
OpenRecordset argument code, 468
optimistic locking in a multiuser environment, 649-650
overriding default error handling under a form, 565-566
parameter queries, 477
preconnecting to the server, 632
printing error forms, 536
printing every property of Document objects, 462
printing query information with the QueryDefs collection, 458
printing the names of Document objects, 461

printing the name of each database in a workspace, 456
prohibiting database creation, 904
prompting the user for database path and name, 587
queries: listing all parameters, 459
raising an error, 525
RecordCount property limitations, 471
recordset support for transaction processing, 645-646
RecordsetClone property, 476
refreshing a link, 587
Relations collection, 460
RemoveGroups function, 888
RemoveUsers function, 893
removing a link, 588
removing a table, 482
repairing database using code, 930
requiring password validation, 586
Resume_Next statement, 522
RevokeFromGroup function, 892
Seek method, 473
select picture, 729
sending multiple reports to the printer, 732
sending table as query to Excel, 735
setting options from a Startup form routine, 972
sorting an existing recordset, 472
SpecificBold subroutine, 665

specifying where a record was found, 474

subroutine to launch Excel, 720

testing for a zero-length string, 667

ToolbarShow routine, 969

transaction loop suitable for the Time and Billing application, 653-654

transaction processing using Access Basic as seen in Access 2.0, 640

transaction processing with an SQL server back-end, 651-652

transactions in a multiuser environment, sacrificing concurrency, 647-648

TransferDatabase method, 572

TransferSpreadsheet method, 574

TransferText method, 574

TryAgain function, 988-989

TypeOfDrive function, 856

updating records that meet a set criteria, 477

user-defined error creation, 526

using the TableDefs and Indexes collections, 457

ValidTextRude entry-point function, 831-832

VBA code for linking to an external table, 618

viewing errors in Errors Collection, 527

viewing Sub_Form_Error from frmOrders, 518

Visual Basic form to Print Reports, 731

With…End With, 669

writing to an error log, 531

LNC (Leszynski Naming Conventions), 15, 217, 1046

lng data-type prefix, 1047

Load event (forms), 377

Load event of frmPolite (listing), 831

Load event of frmRude (listing), 832-833

loading
  libraries
    error messages, 802
    LoadOnStartup Registry key, 800-801
  modules, 797

loading the application and checking table attachments (listing), 595

LoadOnStartup key (Registry), 800-801

local variables, 220

Locals pane
  columns, 507
  updating information, 507

Location of New Replica dialog box, 688

Locked property (controls), 148

locking
  data, 546-547
    conflicts, 555-561
    examples, 565-566
    forms, 548-552
    locating users, 561
    options, 547
    queries, 548
    recordsets, 552-555
    reports, 548
    testing, 562
    unbound forms, 564
  optimistic, transaction processing, 649-650
  pessimistic, transaction processing, 648
  records (forms), 144
  tables, creating reports, 183

LogError routine, 530

logging errors, 530-531

logic errors, 495

Login dialog box, 616

Lookup Wizard, 59-60

lookups
  Display Control property, 60
  Hide Key Column checkbox, 60
  performing, 59

looping through a recordset (listing), 671

loops, 227-230
  breaking, 228
  custom collections, 296
  Do, 227-228
  efficiency of, 671-672
  For Each…Next, 229-230
  For…Next, 228-229
  infinite, 228
  With…End With, 229

LostFocus event
  controls, 385
  debugging problems, 513
  forms, 379

lst prefix, 1046

M

m scope prefix, 1049

Macro Design window, 13, 306
  adding actions, 307
  running macros, 314

macro hotspots (Help files), 943

macros, 13
  actions, 306
    copying, 320-321
    deleting, 319
    inserting, 318
    moving, 319-320
    overwriting, 320

arguments, 306, 309-310
AutoExec, 325-328
AutoKeys, 326-327
comments, 321
compared to VBA, 208-209
conditions, 306, 312
converting to VBA code,
 324-325
creating, 306-313
 launching applications,
 422-423
designing, 13
DoCmd object, 281, 328
documenting, 321, 913
editing, 318-321
executing, DoCmd object,
 250-251
forms, opening, 307
names, 306, 311-312
queries, opening, 307
reasons for use, 323-324
reports, opening, 307
running, 13, 306-318
 from forms, 315-318
 Macro Design window,
 314
 Macros tab, 315
 from report events,
 315-318
 subroutines, 314
stepping through, 323
tables, opening, 307
testing, 322-323
Macros tab, running macros,
315
mailing labels, 169
maintenance of applications,
21
 organizing database objects,
 26
make table queries, creating,
337-339
MakeItBold subroutine
listing, 665
Managed Replicas tool, 701

Management Information
System (MIS), 910
many-to-many relationships,
72
map files
 Help files, 945-946
 Help Project file, 949
mapping dBASE data types,
590
MaxBufferSize Registry
settings, 660
mcr prefix, 1049
MDE files, 673
 applications, distributing,
 973
 restrictions, 877
 security, 877-878
Me keyword
 efficiency, 669
 referencing, 388-389
Me property, 301
memo field type, 48-49
memory
 freeing variables, 292
 modules, loading, 797
 optimization, 657
 RAM, system requirements,
 16
 records, retrieving from
 servers, 630
 transaction processing, 646
 variables, 292
 virtual, optimizing,
 658-659
menu add-ins
 creating, 828
 defined, 827
 designing, 827
 installing, 828
Menu Bar option, 970
Menu Bar property
 forms, 144
 reports, 184
menus
 commands, adding, 403

custom
 adding to forms, 400-404
 creating for runtime
 version, 968-969
 deleting, 404
 renaming, 404
Format
 aligning form objects, 127
 sizing form objects, 129
 Snap to Grid (forms),
 128
 spacing form objects, 129
forms
 creating, 400
 designing, 402-404
 items, runtime version, 962
 View, changing tab order,
 131
message boxes, 397
messages, warning
 action queries, 339-340
 suppressing, 340
metafiles (graphics), 944
methods, 719
 Add, 295
 AddNew, 479-480
 Append, adding tables to
 databases, 483
 BeginTrans, transaction
 processing, 643
 bookmarks, retrieving from
 servers, 630
 CommitTrans, transaction
 processing, 643
 compared to properties,
 289-290
 CreateQueryDef, 483
 CreateTableDef, 483
 custom, creating, 421-422
 data locking, 546
 defined, 285
 Delete, 478-479
 executing, 289-290
 Debug window, 498
 fields, printing, 469
 FindFirst, 473

FindLast, 473
FindNext, 473
FindPrevious, 473
Move, 468
MoveFirst, 468
MoveLast, 468
MoveNext, 468
MovePrevious, 468
objects (object library), 715
OpenDatabase, 583
  client/servers, 622
OpenForm, DoCmd
  object, 251
OpenRecordSet, 465, 637
Raise, 525-526
recordsets, 468-469
  examples, 486-489
Remove, 296
Requery, 563
Rich Textbox, 756
Rollback, transaction
  processing, 643
Seek, 473-474
SetOption, modifying
  Registry settings at
  runtime, 643
SetWarnings, 339
TransferDatabase,
  importing external data,
  572-573
TransferSpreadsheet,
  importing external data,
  574-575
TransferText, importing
  external data, 573-574
methods for clsRecordsets
(listing), 266-267
Microsoft Access Language
Reference, 29
Microsoft IIS, saving forms
in IIS format, 160
Microsoft Office 97 Data
Access Reference, 29
Microsoft Plus! package, 658
Microsoft Replication

Manager, 29
Mid function, 232
Min Max Buttons property
(forms), 142
MIS (Management
Information System), 910
mmnu object-naming prefix,
1050
modal forms, 119
Modal property, 815
  forms, 144
Modify Design permission,
876
Module Design window, 14
Module property, 301
Module window, executing
procedures, 250
module-level variables, 210,
221
modules, 14-15
  CBF, 210
  Class, 210
    compared to Standard,
    217
    creating, 265-268
    declaring procedures, 215
  comparing versions (Visual
    SourceSafe), 790
  compiling loaded, 273
  Complete Word, 238
  constants, intrinsic, 256
  Definition feature, 238
  documentation, 914
  event procedures, 212
  Form and Report Class,
    210
  functions, 210
    creating, 213-214
  General Declarations
    sections, 210
  Last Position, 239
  libraries, designing, 797
  List Constants, 236
  List Properties and
    Methods, 235-236
  loading, 797

Modules collection, 281
  Parameter Info, 238
  Quick Info, 237
  standard, 210
  statements, Option Explicit,
    212
  subroutines, 210
    creating, 213-214
  Text Viewer, 845
    adding elements, 847
  tools, 235-239
  variables, declaring, 210
  VBA, 210-218
  viewing, 14
    Full Module View, 211
monitors
  drivers, system
    requirements, 16
  resolution, performance
    considerations, 16
Month property (Calendar
control), 747
month (date) expression,
queries, 94
MonthLength property
(Calendar control), 748
More Controls tool, 742
mouse
  forms, events, 382
  objects
    moving, 126-127
    selecting, 125-126
    sizing, 129
  reports, selecting objects,
    176
MouseDown event
  controls, 387
  forms, 379
MouseMove event
  controls, 387
  forms, 380
MousePress event (controls),
387
MouseUp event
  controls, 387
  forms, 380

Move method
 listing, 469
 recordsets, 468
**Move Next command button,
 creating, 487**
**Move Previous command
 button, creating, 486**
**MoveFirst method
 (recordsets), 468**
MoveLast method
 bookmarks, retrieving from
  servers, 630
 recordsets, 468
**MoveLayout property
 (reports), 433**
**MoveNext method
 (recordsets), 468**
**MovePrevious method
 (recordsets), 468**
moving
 macro actions, 319-320
 objects, forms, 126-127
MS Office 97 (VBA), 208
MsgBox function, 397-399
MSysErrors tables, 686
**MSysExchangeLog tables,
 686**
MSysSchemaProb tables, 686
MSysSidetable tables, 686
**multi-select property (list
 boxes), 414-415**
**multipage forms, creating,
 391-393**
**multiresolution bitmaps
 (graphics), 944**
multithreading, support, 603
multiuser applications
 designing, 542
 installing, 543-544
  Access, 542-543
**MyCustomForm function,
 827**

N

**Name property (controls),
 149, 186**
named parameters, 251, 263
**naming conventions, 494,
 1046**
 constants, 254-256
 controls, conflicts, 186
 fields
  cautions, 44
  converting datasheets, 45
  legal characters, 44
  length, 44
 macros, 306, 311-312
 menus, custom, 404
 objects, 15, 1046-1047
  DAOs, 1048-1049
  *Database window objects,
   1049-1050*
  Visual SourceSafe, 792
 procedures, Leszynski
  Naming Conventions,
  217
 tables, 41
 update queries, 333
 variables, 1046
  changing, 246
  Private, 221
  Public, 222
navigating
 forms
  applications, 118
  setting properties, 141
 switchboard forms, 395
 VBA, 244
**Navigation Buttons property
 (forms), 141**
**nested queries, calculated
 fields, 345**
nesting transactions, 646
networks
 applications, designing, 542
 data locking, 546-547
 linked tables, accessing, 546

 load reduction, 679
 performance considerations,
  replication, 565
 security
  LDB files, 563-564
  share-level, 860
 servers
  installing Access, 542
  *installing applications,
   543*
 workstations
  installing Access, 543
  *installing applications,
   544*
 see also workgroups
**New command (Edit menu),
 818**
New Form dialog box, 120
**New keyword, creating
 objects, 297-298**
New menu commands
 DWORD Value, 818
 Key, 818
 String Value, 818
New Object dialog box, 827
New Query dialog box, 86
New Report dialog box, 171
**New Row or Col property
 (reports), 196**
New Table dialog box, 40
**New User/Group dialog box,
 868**
**NextRecord property
 (reports), 433**
No Data events, 675
 reports, 428
No Locks option, 551
normalization
 applications, developing,
  18-19
 calculated fields, creating,
  101-103
 queries, 96
 relationships, 42
 tables, 662-663

**not (query criteria operator),
93**
**not equal to sign (<>), query
criteria operator, 92**
notes (memo fields), 49
NotInList event
  combo boxes, handling,
    410-411
  controls, 384
**null (query criteria operator),
93**
**null entries, compared to
zero-length, 57**
null values
  calculations, 109
  converting to zero, 109
  examples, 276-277
  queries, 364
  query results, 108-109
  variables, 219
  Variant variables, 269-273
number field type, 48-49
**Number of Update Retries
option (data locking), 549**
**NumberOfBytesFree
function (listing), 857**

O

obj data-type prefix, 1047
Object Browser, 233, 286
  intrinsic constants, 256
  running, 287-288
**object libraries, methods/
properties, 715**
object models, 715
object types, 715
object variables
  assigning, 291
  compared to variables,
    291-292
  declaring, 291
  generic compared to
    specific, 292

objects, creating, 297
referencing applications,
  715-716
**object variables for code
efficiency (listing), 669**
objects, 280, 715
  ! (bang), 290
  Access Object Model, 280
  aligning, limitations, 177
  automation objects, closing,
    722-723
  bound (forms), 406-407
  checking in/out (Visual
    SourceSafe), 782,
    786-789
  collections, 288
    adding items, 295-296
    commands, 293-294
    creating custom, 295
    defining custom, 295
    loops, 296
    referencing items, 297
    removing items, 296
    *returning to items,
      299-300*
  commands, 293
  compared to collections,
    293
  compilation, 273-274
  Container, 483-484
    *data access object model,
      460*
    Document objects, 484
  creating
    New keyword, 297-298
    *prohibiting users,
      904-905*
  DAOs, naming
    conventions, 1048-1049
  data access, 454
  Database
    creating, 480-483
    creating variables, 466
    *data access object model,
      456*

    modifying, 480-483
Database window objects,
  naming, 1049-1050
databases, 7
  documentation, 917
  organizing, 26-27
DBEngine, 454, 462
defined, 282
deleting, Visual SourceSafe,
  792
DoCmd, 281
  examples, 276-277
  *executing macros,
    250-251*
  *importing external data,
    572-575*
  OpenForm method, 251
Document
  Container objects, 484
  *data access object model,
    461*
embedded, in-place
  activation, 406
Err, 524-525
Error (data access object
  model), 462
event procedures, 212
  creating, 213
events, viewing, 284
examples, 302-304
Fields (data access object
  model), 458
forms
  aligning, 127-128
  moving, 126-127
  selecting, 125-126
  sizing, 128-129
  spacing, 129-130
Forms collections, 280
Groups (data access object
  model), 456
Indexes (data access object
  model), 458
libraries, viewing, 287
linking compared to
  embedding, 406-407

methods, 285
  object library, 715
Modules collections, 281
naming, 15, 1046-1047
Object Browser, 233, 286
  running, 287-288
OLE
  data locking, 552
  inserting in reports, 180
opening in Design view
  (Visual SourceSafe), 792
ownership, changing, 879
Parameter (data access
  object model), 459
passing to functions/
  subroutines, 298
permissions, assigning, 35,
  900-901
procedures, calling, 214
properties, 282-283,
  301-302
  creating, 264-265
  data access object model,
  461
  defaults, 291
  object library, 715
  viewing, 283
publishing (WWW), 773
QueryDefs (data access
  object model), 458
Recordset, 463
  creating variables, 465
  data access object model,
  460
  properties, 465-467
  selecting types, 465
referencing, 288-289
registering, 715
Relations (data access object
  model), 460
renaming (Visual
  SourceSafe), 792
replicating, keeping local,
  706
reports
  aligning, 177
  moving, 176-177

selecting, 175-176
sizing, 177
Snap to Grid, 177
spacing, 178
Reports collections, 281
reverting (Visual
  SourceSafe), 782, 791
rights (Database
  Documenter), 880
saving
  HTML format, 766-768
  Visual SourceSafe, 792
Screen, 281
security (Security Wizard),
  871
TableDefs (data access
  object model), 457
unbound (forms), 407
User (data access object
  model), 456
variables, creating, 463
viewing development
  history (Visual
  SourceSafe), 790
Visual SourceSafe
  adding, 789-790
  getting latest version, 789
  refreshing, 790
Workspace
  data access object model,
  456
  transaction processing,
  643-644
ocx prefix, 1046
ODBC (Open Database
  Connectivity)
  client/servers, 608
  data sources, upsizing to
    client/servers, 612-615
  drivers, upsizing to client/
    servers, 612
  servers, connecting, 632
  translating SQL statements,
    606
ODBC Data Source
  Administrator, 612

ODBC Drivers option
  (OBDC Data Source
  Administrator), 613
ODBC Refresh Interval
  option (data locking), 550
ODBCDirect, 607
  client/servers
    accessing, 624-627
    performance
      considerations, 632
  code compared to DAO
    code, 626
ODE (Office Developer
  Edition), 28, 958
  ActiveX controls, 959
  applications, licensing, 29
  Graph Runtime Executable,
    960
  Help Workshop, 960
  language reference, 959
  Replication Manager, 959
  runtime license, 959
  sample CD-ROM, 960
  Setup Wizard, 959
  tools, 958
  Win32 API Text Viewer,
    960
Office Assistant, 934
OLE (Object Linking and
  Embedding)
  bound objects (forms),
    406-407
  controls, *see* ActiveX
    controls
  data locking, 552
  objects
    converting to images, 674
    inserting in reports, 180
  unbound objects (forms),
    407
OLE Automation, 714
OLE Object field type, 48-50
ole prefix, 1046
On_Error statement,
  518-520

On_Error_Goto statement, 519

On_Error_Goto_0 statement, 520

On_Error_Resume_Next statement, 520

one-to-many forms, 153
 creating, 153-156

one-to-many relationships, 9, 70-71
 lookups, 59-60
 queries, updating, 98

one-to-one relationships, 71-72

Open dialog box, 821

Open event
 forms, 376
 reports, 426
  crosstab queries, 441

Open Exclusive permission, 876

Open/Run permission, 876

OpenArgs property (forms), 408

OpenDatabase method, 583
 pass-through queries
  (client/servers), 622

OpenDatabase method (listing), 583

OpenDatabase to connect a remote server database (listing), 624

OpenForm method (DoCmd object), 251

opening
 databases
  user level security, 871
  Visual SourceSafe, 791
 dynasets, 469
 external data, 569-570, 582-584
  connection information, 583
 file formats, supported, 570
 forms, 376
  events, 381
  macros, 307

queries, macros, 307
 recordsets, dynasets, 466
 reports, 197
  macros, 307
 tables
  client/servers, 624
  macros, 307
 windows, designing forms, 124

opening a dynaset type of recordset on a table (listing), 466

opening a recordset (listing), 465

opening a recordset based on a query (listing), 466

OpenRecordset argument code (listing), 468

OpenRecordSet method, 465, 637

operating systems, system requirements, 16

operators (queries), criteria, 92-93

opt prefix, 1046

optimistic locking, 144, 554-555
 errors, 558-560
 transaction processing, 649-650

optimistic locking in a multiuser environment (listing), 649-650

optimization, 656
 applications, adding version fields, 633
 code, 664
  arrays, 670
  bookmarks, 670-671
  Boolean expressions, 666
  built-in collections, 666-667
  compiling, 672
  constants, 670
  Declare statements, 668
  Dim statements, 668

distribution, 673
  inline code, 666
  Len function, 667
  loops, 671-672
  me keyword, 669
  object references, 668-669
  object types, 665-666
  organization, 673
  string functions, 670
  transactions, 668
  true/false evaluations, 667-668
  unused code, 668
  variants, 665
  With...End With, 669
 data structures, 662
  data types, 663
  indexes, 663
  normalization, 662-663
 defined, 656
 forms, 673-675
  client/servers, 633-637
 hardware, 657
  Compact utility, 658
  defragmentation, 657-658
  disk compression, 658
  RAM, 657
  virtual memory, 658-659
 Jet 3.5, 660-661
 networks, 659
 Performance Analyzer, 661-662
 queries, 344-347, 664
  client/servers, 633-634
 reports, 675
 software
  Registry settings, 659-660
  Windows 95, 659
 Time and Billing application, 675
 see also system performance

option buttons (forms), adding, 136

Option Explicit command, 494
modules, 212
Option Group Wizard, 136-138
option groups
captions, 136
forms, adding, 136-138
optional parameters, 261-263
Options command (Tools menu), 686, 820
optSpecialEffect option button, 815
or (query criteria operator), 92
ORDER BY clause (SQL), 358
Order By On property (reports), 183
Order By property
forms, 143
queries, 112
reports, 183
Orientation property (UpDown object), 750
outer joins (queries), 353-354
Output All Fields property (queries), 112
overriding data-locking error dialog boxes, 552
overriding default error handling under a form (listing), 565-566
Overwrite Existing File option, 976
Overwrite with Conflict Record option (replication), 694
overwriting macro actions, 320

P

Page Break controls (forms), inserting, 391
Page Break tool, 187
Page event (reports), 428
Page Footer Format event (reports), 447
Page Footer property (reports), 171, 182
Page Header property (reports), 171, 182
page headers (reports), printing, 446-448
Page locking, 547
page numbers, printing, 171
PageHeader Format event (reports), 443
pal prefix, 1047
Palette Source property
forms, 143
reports, 182
Parameter Info (modules), 238
Parameter object (data access object model), 459
parameter queries, 476-477
creating, 112-114
listing, 477
passing values (forms), 367
parameters
crosstab queries, 353
functions, 230-231
named, 251, 263
optional, 261-263
passing
by reference, 839
by reference, compared to by value, 260-261
by value, 839
queries, defining, 113
strings, passing, 839-840
subroutines, 230-231
see also arguments

Parent property, 301
parentheses (VBA functions), 463
Partial Replica Wizard, 702
partial replication, 702
pass-through queries, 362-363
client/servers, 606, 620-623
creating, 621
executing, 621-622
performance considerations, 631
compared to ODBCDirect, 607
creating, 363
transaction processing, 652
passing objects (subroutines/functions), 298
Password Required dialog box, 860
passwords, 896-899
administrative user, 869-871
assigning, 860, 896-897
case-sensitivity, 860
ensuring, 899
external tables, 585-586
linking external data, 581
lost, 861
security, 878
share-level security, 860-861
user rights, 861
user-level security, 863
pasting code into applications, 288
Payments form, creating, 162-163
pdbe object-naming prefix, 1048
Performance Analyzer, 661-662
queries, 345
Performance Analyzer dialog box, 661

Performance command (Analyze menu), 661
permissions
  assigning, 34-35
  constants, 901
  objects, assigning/revoking, 900-901
  workgroups, types, 876-877
personal identification (workgroups), 873
personal tables, 41
pessimistic locking, 144, 553
  errors, 555-558
  transaction processing, 648
Picture properties
  forms, 142
  reports, 182
PKZIP, 34
pop-up hotspots (Help files), 942-943
Pop Up property (forms), 144
pop-up windows (hotspots), 935
pound sign (#) in Help files, 939
PowerPoint
  controlling from Access, 728-730
  slides, 730
precedence of procedures, 216-217
preconnecting to the server (listing), 632
predefined tables, 41
Preserve keyword, 259
preventing
  data replication, 690
  error handling, 537
previewing reports, 12
PreviousControl property, 301
primary keys, 18, 41, 59
  append queries, 337
  client/servers, 608

forms, fetching from servers, 631
  normalization, 18
Print event
  compared to Format event, 432
  reports, 431-432
PrintCount property (reports), 435
printing
  crosstab reports, 448-449
  to Debug window, 499
    Call LoopThroughCollection, 499
  error forms, 536
  fields, methods, 469
  forms, 119, 143-145
  labels, multiple, 438-440
  page headers (reports), 446-448
  page numbers, 171
  reports, 184
    inserting page breaks, 187
    properties, 182, 434
  security permissions, 880
printing every property of Document objects (listing), 462
printing query information with the QueryDefs collection (listing), 458
printing the name of each database in a workspace (listing), 456
printing the names of Document objects (listing), 461
PrintSection property (reports), 433
private procedures, 216
private variables, 210, 221
prm object-naming prefix, 1048

prms object-naming prefix, 1048
Procedure view (VBA), 249
procedures
  calling, 214
    name conflicts, 215
  declaring, Class modules, 215
  event
    creating, 213
    modules, 212
  executing, Module window, 250
  libraries, unique names, 842
  naming, Leszynski Naming Conventions, 217
  private, 216
  public, 215
  scope, 215-217
    precedence, 216-217
  static, 217
programming
  bookmarks, adding, 249
  code
    customizing style features, 275
    Full Module view, 249
    pasting into applications, 288
    Procedure view, 249
  Code window, Tab width, 275
  command bars, 404
  database replication, 705-706
    keeping objects local, 706
    partial, 707
  importing external data, 572-575
  linking external data, 579
    connection information, 579-581
  replication
    synchronization, 707
    troubleshooting, 708

VBA
   constants, 253, 256
   environment, 244
   find and replace feature,
      246
   viewing code, 245-246
Projects form
   creating, 163-164
   multiple instances, 302
**prompting the user for
   database path and name
   (listing), 587**
properties
   AbsolutePosition, 474-475
   ActiveControl, 301
   ActiveForm, 301
   ActiveReport, 301
   ActiveX controls, setting at
      design time, 745-746
   Alias (queries), 111
   BOF, 469-470
   bookmark, records,
      475-476
   Bound Column (combo
      boxes), 134
   Calendar control
      Day, 747
      DayFont, 747
      DayFontColor, 747
      DayLength, 748
      GridFont, 748
      GridFontColor, 748
      GridLinesColor, 748
      GridLinesFormat, 748
      Month, 747
      MonthLength, 748
      ShowDateSelectors, 748
      ShowTitle, 748
      Value, 747
      ValueIsNull, 747
      Year, 747
   collections, Key, 299
   Column Count (combo
      boxes), 134
   Column Width (combo
      boxes), 134

combo boxes, 134-135
Common Dialog control,
   754
compared to methods,
   289-290
components, setting, 980
Control (forms), 145-150
Control Source (combo
   boxes), 134
controls, 184-186
   Allow AutoCorrect, 149
   Auto Repeat, 149
   Auto Tab, 149
   Back Color, 147, 185
   Back Style, 147, 185
   Border Color, 147, 185
   Border Style, 147, 185
   Border Width, 147, 185
   Can Grow, 146
   Can Shrink, 146, 185
   Cancel, 149
   Caption, 146, 185
   Control Source, 147, 186
   ControlTip, 150
   Data, 147-148, 186
   Decimal Places, 146, 185
   Default, 149
   Default Value, 148
   Display When, 146
   Enabled, 148
   Enter Key Behavior, 149
   Filter Lookup, 148
   Font Color, 185
   Font Italic, 147, 185
   Font Name, 147, 185
   Font Size, 147, 185
   Font Underline, 147,
      185
   Font Weight, 147, 185
   Fore Color, 147
   Format, 145-147, 185
   Height, 146, 185
   Help Context ID, 150
   Hide Duplicates, 185
   Hyperlink Address, 146,
      185

   Hyperlink SubAddress,
      146, 185
   Input Mask, 147
   Left, 146, 185
   Locked, 148
   Name, 149, 186
   Running Sum, 186
   Scroll Bars, 146
   Shortcut Menu Bar, 149
   Special Effect, 147, 185
   Status Bar Text, 149
   Tab Index, 149
   Tab Stop, 149
   Tag, 150, 186
   Text Align, 147, 186
   Top, 146, 185
   Validation Rule, 148
   Validation Text, 148
   Visible, 146, 185
   Width, 146, 185
data replicas, 705
databases, documentation,
   914-917
defaults, 291
defined, 282-283
Description
   queries, 112
   tables, 61
DesignMasterID, 687
Display Control (lookups),
   60
EOF, 469-470
Err object, 524
expressions, 289
Field List (queries), 111
fields, 51
   Allow Zero Length, 57
   Caption, 54
   Default Value, 54
   Field Size, 51
   Format, 52
   Indexed, 58
   Input Mask, 52-53
   printing, 470
   queries, 110-111
   Required, 57

Validation Rule, 55
Validation Text, 55-56
Filter
  queries, 112
  tables, 62
Force New Page (reports),
  187
Form, 301
forms, 139-145
  Allow Additions, 143
  Allow Deletions, 143
  Allow Edits, 143
  Allow Filters, 143
  Auto Center, 141
  Auto Resize, 141
  Border Style, 141
  Caption, 140
  Close Button, 142
  Control Box, 142
  creating custom, 417-421
  *creating public variables,
    418-419*
  Cycle, 144
  Data, 143-144
  Data Entry, 143
  Default View, 140
  Dividing Lines, 141
  Fast Laser Printing, 145
  Filter, 143
  Format, 140-143
  Grid X, 142
  Grid Y, 142
  Has Module, 145
  Help Context ID, 145
  Help File, 145
  Layout for Print, 143
  Menu Bar, 144
  Min Max Buttons, 142
  Modal, 144
  Navigation Buttons, 141
  OpenArgs, 408
  Order By, 143
  Palette Source, 143
  Picture, 142
  Pop Up, 144
  Record Locks, 144

Record Selectors, 141
Record Source, 143
Recordset Type, 144
Scroll Bars, 141
Shortcut Menu, 145
Shortcut Menu Bar, 145
Tag, 145
Toolbar, 145
Views Allowed, 141
What is This Button, 142
Width, 142
help, 282
KeepLocal, 687, 690
LastModified, 480
Me, 301
modifying, 289-290
Module, 301
multi-select list boxes,
  414-415
Object Browser, 233
objects, 301-302
  creating, 264-265
  object library, 715
Order By (queries), 112
Orientation (UpDown
  object), 750
Output All Fields (queries),
  112
Parent, 301
PreviousControl, 301
queries, 110, 911
  viewing, 340
Record Locks (queries), 112
RecordCount, 470-471
Recordset objects, 465-467
RecordsetClone, 301
  forms, 417, 476
recordsets, 469-471
Replicable, 687
ReplicaID, 686
Report, 301
reports, 181-184
  Caption, 182
  Data, 183
  Data Grouping, 183
  Fast Laser Printing, 184

Filter, 183
Filter On, 183
Format, 182
FormatCount, 434
Grid X, 182
Grid Y, 182
Grp Keep Together, 182
Has Module, 184
HasContinued, 435
Help Context ID, 184
Help File, 184
Layout for Print, 182
Menu Bar, 184
MoveLayout, 433
NextRecord, 433
Order By, 183
Order By On, 183
Page Footer, 182
Page Header, 182
Palette Source, 182
Picture, 182
PrintCount, 435
PrintSection, 433
Record Locks, 183
Record Source, 183
runtime, 433-435
Shortcut Menu Bar, 184
*sorting/grouping data,
  195-196*
Tag, 184
Toolbar, 184
Width, 182
WillContinue, 435
retrieving, 719
Rich Textbox, 756
Row Source Type (combo
  boxes), 134
Run Permissions (queries),
  112
Section, 301
setting, 719
setting values, Debug
  window, 497, 503
Source (queries), 111
Startup, modifying, 971
StatusBar control, 751

subforms
Link Child Fields, 156
Link Master Fields, 156
Source Object, 156
subreports
Can Grow, 193
Can Shrink, 193
Link Child Fields, 193
Link Master Fields, 193
Source Object, 193
SupportTrans (transaction processing), 646
Tab control, changing, 394
tab pages, changing, 394
tables, 61-62
testing values, Debug window, 496
TimerInterval (form events), 381
toolbars, viewing, 401
Top Values (queries), 112, 342-343
Unique Records (queries), 112, 342
Unique Values (queries), 112, 341
UpDown object, 750
upsizing to client/servers, 612
Validation Rule (tables), 61
Validation Text (tables), 61
viewing, 283
Properties object (data access object model), 461
Properties window
forms, 140
reports, 182
Property Get routine, 264-265
custom properties, 419, 421
Property Let routine, 264
custom properties, 419, 421
property procedures, 264-265
prototypes, developing applications, 20

prp object-naming prefix, 1048
prps object-naming prefix, 1047-1048
Public keyword, 215
public procedures, 215
public variables, 210, 221-222
creating, form properties, 418-419
Publish to the Web Wizard, 64, 773-775
PWD keyword, 585

Q

qapp object-naming prefix, 1050
qddl object-naming prefix, 1050
qdel object-naming prefix, 1050
qflt object-naming prefix, 1050
qlkp object-naming prefix, 1050
qmak object-naming prefix, 1050
qry object-naming prefix, 1048
qry prefix, 1049
qrys object-naming prefix, 1048
qsel object-naming prefix, 1050
qspt object-naming prefix, 1050
qtot object-naming prefix, 1050
queries, 10-11
action, 332
append, 336-339
delete, 334-335
previewing results, 335
update, 332-333

warning messages, 339-340
warnings, 334
Alias property, 111
analyzing, 344-345
improving performance, 345-346
calculated fields, creating, 101-103
client/servers, compared to views, 619-620
columns, selecting, 357
compiling, 344
creating, 482-483
examples, 97, 115-116
multiple tables, 96-97
selecting fields, 86-88
criteria
dates, 94-95
functions, 365-366
Like, 346
specifying at runtime, 112-114
crosstab, 347
creating, 348-350
creating in Design view, 351-352
fixed column headings, 352-353
parameters, 353
data locking, 548
Delete, 479
Description property, 112
designing, 10
documentation, 911
dynasets, 464
examples, 368-370
Expression Builder, 103
expressions, 346
dates, 94-95
Field List properties, 111
field properties, 110-111
fields
adding, 87
counting, 108

excluding, 107
 indexing, 345
 inserting, 89
 moving, 89-90
 removing, 88
Filter property, 112
forms, 157
 combo boxes, 133
 creating, 121
 record sources, 125
multiple tables
 displaying records, 99
 enforced referential
  integrity, 99-100
 limitations, 98-99
 updating, 98
nested, calculated fields,
 345
null values, 364
opening (macros), 307
optimizing, 344-347, 664
 client/servers, 633-634
Order By property, 112
outer joins, 353-354
Output All Fields property,
 112
parameters, 112-114,
 476-477
 creating, 112-114
 defining, 113
 passing values from forms,
  367
pass-through, 362-363
 client/servers, 606,
  620-623
 compared to
  ODBCDirect, 607
 creating, 363
 servers, 631
 transaction processing,
  652
Performance Analyzer, 345
performance considerations,
 344-345
 improving performance,
  345-346

properties, 110, 911
 Default Value, 54
 Top Values, 342-343
 Unique Records, 342
 Unique Values, 341
 Validation Rules, 56
 viewing, 340
Query Plan, 344
Record Locks property, 112
records, counting, 346
recordsets, 463
reports
 creating, 440-446
 efficiency considerations,
  172
results
 null values, 108-109
 sorting, 90-91
 updating, 95-96
row fix-up, 99
Run Permissions property,
 112
running, 10, 88
Rushmore, 346-347
saving, 90
security, field-level, 902
select, defined, 86
self joins, 355-356
snapshots, 630-631
sorting
 criteria, 92-94
 multiple fields, 91
Source property, 111
SQL, 356-361
 creating, 360
stored
 compared to embedded
  SQL statements, 157
 reports, 197-198
subqueries, 364
system performance, 28
table recordset objects, 465
tables
 joining, 358-359
 removing, 97
 selecting, 357

temporary, creating, 483
Top Values property, 112
Totals
 creating, 105
 examples, 107
totals, 104-107
union, creating, 362
Unique Records property,
 112
Unique Values property,
 112
update, 478
windows, SQL View, 360
queries designing, examples,
 93
queries: listing all parameters
 (listing), 459
Query Design window, 10
Query Parameters dialog
 box, 114
Query Plan, 28, 344
QueryDefs object (data
 access object model), 458
Quick Info, modules, 237
quick watch, toolbar button,
 508
quni object-naming prefix,
 1050
qupd object-naming prefix,
 1050
qxtb object-naming prefix,
 1050

R

Raise method, 525-526
RAM (random access
 memory), 16
 optimization, 657
 system requirements, 16
Read Data permission, 876
Read Design permission, 876
ReadAheadPages Registry
 settings, 660
recompiling, modules, 672

Reconciler (Briefcase), 683
Record Locks property
　forms, 144
　queries, 112
　reports, 183
Record Selectors property
　forms, 141
Record Source property
　forms, 143
　reports, 183
record sources
　forms, 125
　　changing, 408-410
　　changing at runtime, 143
　　combo boxes, 132
　reports, changing, 435-437
RecordCount property,
　470-471
　limitations (listing), 471
records
　AbsolutePosition property,
　　474-475
　adding queries, 336
　appending dynasets, 467
　archiving append queries,
　　336
　bookmark property,
　　475-476
　copying/deleting,
　　controlling user access,
　　141
　counting
　　queries, 346
　　recordsets, 470-471
　creating form events, 374
　deleting, 478-479
　　form events, 376
　　queries, 334-335
　displaying
　　form events, 377
　　forms, 28
　dynasets, 10, 464
　filtering (table recordset
　　objects), 465
　focus (form events), 374

forms
　locking, 144
　ordering, 143
memory (retrieving from
　servers), 630
normalization, 18
refreshing, 550
reports (sorting), 183
saving (form events), 375
snapshots, 630-631
　forward-scrolling, 631
sorting, table recordset
　objects, 465
static, 464
updating
　form events, 375
　queries, 332-333
viewing, creating forms,
　389-394
**Recordset objects (data access
　object model), 460-463**
　properties, 465-467
　selecting types, 465
　variables, creating, 465
**recordset support for
　transaction processing
　(listing), 645-646**
**Recordset Type property,
　forms, 144**
**RecordsetClone property,
　301**
　forms, 417, 476
**RecordsetClone property
　(listing), 476**
recordsets
　AddNew method, 479-480
　BOF property, 469-470
　client/servers, selecting
　　types, 630-631
　creating
　　arguments, 467-468
　　*backward compatibility,
　　467*
　data locking, 552-555
　Delete method, 478-479
　dynasets, 464

EOF property, 469-470
filtering, 472-473
FindFirst method, 473
finding, 473-474
FindLast method, 473
FindNext method, 473
FindPrevious method, 473
forms, synchronizing, 417
LastModified property, 480
methods, 468-469
　examples, 486-489
Move method, 468
MoveFirst method, 468
MoveLast method, 468
MoveNext method, 468
MovePrevious method, 468
opening, dynasets, 466
preventing writing, 467
properties, 469-471
RecordCount property,
　470-471
records, counting, 470-471
refreshing compared to
　requerying, 550
requerying, 563
Seek method, 473-474
snapshots, 464
sorting, 472
tables, 464
　preventing reading, 467
transaction processing,
　compatibility, 645-646
types, efficiency
　considerations, 464
updating, 467
　multiple records, 478
　single records, 477-478
Rectangle tool, 179
rectangles
　reports, 179
　transparent, 179
**reducing, network load,
　database replication, 679**
**references, ActiveX controls,
　744-745**

References dialog box, 716,
744
  libraries, 802
referencing
  controls, subforms, 416
  custom collections, items,
  297
  libraries, 798-805
  Me keyword, 388-389
  objects, 288-289
  parameters, 839
referencing applications,
object variables, 715-716
referential integrity, 75-77
  enforced, queries, 99-100
RefLibPaths key (Registry),
803
Refresh Interval option (data
locking), 550
refreshing
  records, 550
  recordsets, compared to
  requerying, 550
refreshing a link (listing),
587
registering
  ActiveX controls, 741-742
  builders, 816
    Add-In Manager,
    820-822
    manually, 816-819
  wizards, 826-827
Registry
  builder configuration
    Add-In Manager,
    820-822
    manual, 816-819
  Editor, 643
    invoking, 817
  keys, ISAM drivers, 584
  libraries, creating references,
  798
  LoadOnStartup key,
  800-801

modifying settings,
  transaction processing,
  642-643
RefLibPaths key, 803
replication settings, 683
restoring (installing
  applications), 33
server connections,
  timeouts, 633
settings
  ExclusiveAsyncDelay, 642
  ImplicitCommitSync,
  642
  modifying at runtime,
  643
  SharedAsyncDelay, 642
  UserCommitSync, 642
subkeys, creating, 818
values, adding to
  applications, 979
wizard configuration, 826
workgroup information
  files, 864
rel object-naming prefix,
1048
Relations object (data access
object model), 460
relationships, 70
  benefits, 80
  defining, 8
  deleting, 75
  establishing, 73
    guidlines, 73-74
  indexes, 80
  joins, outer, 353-354
  many-to-many, 72
  modifying, 75
  normalizing, 42
  one-to-many, 9, 70-71
  one-to-one, 71-72
  referential integrity, 75-77
  self, defining, 356
  tables
    Cascade Delete Related
    Records option, 78-79

    Cascade Update Related
    Fields option, 77
    creating, 482
    creating tables, 42
  time and billing database
    example, 81-83
  unhiding, 9
  upsizing to client/servers,
  611
  window, 72
Relationships command
(Tools menu), 72
Relationships dialog box, 73
Relationships window, 8
rels object-naming prefix,
1048
remote synchronization,
replicated data, 702
Remove method, 296
RemoveGroups function, 888
RemoveUsers function, 893
removing a link (listing), 588
removing a table (listing),
482
repairing databases, 928-930
Repeat Section property,
reports, 197
Replicable property, 687
ReplicaID property, 686
replicas
  creating, 690-691
    Access user interface, 691
    Windows 95 Briefcase,
    691
  synchronizing, 691
    Access user interface,
    691-692
    Windows 95 Briefcase,
    692
replication
  applications, distributing,
  989
  architecture, 681
    Briefcase Reconciler, 683
    File System Transport,
    683

Registry settings, 683
Replication Manager,
  682
Synchronizer, 682
Tracking Layer, 681
conflict resolution, 693-695
databases
  Internet, 779
  security, 906
database changes, 685
  additional fields, 686
  AutoNumber fields, 687
  object properties, 686-687
  size, 687
  system tables, 686
defined, 678
enabling, 687-688
  Access user interface,
    688-689
  Windows 95 Briefcase,
    689-690
examples, 708-709
implementing, 680
  Briefcase, 680
  DAO code, 681
  Replication Manager,
    680-681
  Replication menu
    commands, 680
limitations, 679
management,
  synchronizers, 701
Microsoft Replication
  Manager, 29
networks, performance
  considerations, 565
objects, keeping local, 706
partial, 702
  programming, 707
preventing, 690
programming, 705-706
replicas
  creating, 690-691
  synchronizing, 691-692
Replication ID field type,
  50

Replication Manager
  benefits, 695
  configuring, 695-698
  creating replicas, 701
  options, 698-701
  synchronization logs, 704
  synchronization
    properties, 705
  synchronizing, 702-704
synchronization,
  programming, 707
topologies, 683
  Fully Connected, 685
  Hybrid, 685
  Linear, 685
  Ring, 684-685
  Star, 684
troubleshooting,
  programming, 708
uses
  backups, 679
  data sharing, 678-679
  load reduction, 679
  update distribution, 679
Replication command (Tools
menu), 680, 688
Replication ID field type, 50
Replication Manager,
680-682, 779, 959
  benefits, 695
  configuring, 695-698
  options, 698-701
  replicas, creating, 701
  synchronization, 702-704
    logs, 704
    properties, 705
Replication menu
commands, 680
  Create Replica, 688, 691
  Synchronize Now, 691
Report Builder, 169
Report Design toolbar, 175
Report Design window,
reports, creating, 174-178
Report Footer Format event,
reports, 445

Report Footers, 171
Report Headers, 171
Report property, 301
Report Selection Form dialog
box, creating, 484-486
Report Wizard, 172-174
  launching, 174
reports, 12
  charts, 168
  class modules, 417
  color, properties, 182
  controls, 178-181
    bound object frames, 179
    image, 181
    labels, 178
    lines, 179
    rectangles, 179
    text boxes, 178
    unbound object frames,
      180
  cover sheets, 171
  creating, 171, 435-449
    Design view, 174
    locking tables, 183
    multiple tables, 187-193
    queries, 440-446
    Report Design window,
      174-178
    tools, 174
  Cross Tabulation, 167
  crosstab, printing, 448-449
  data
    grouping, 182-183,
      193-196
    locking, 548
  Detail, 166, 171
  dialog boxes, creating,
    484-486
  documentation, 913
  efficiency, normalization,
    19
  emulating forms, 169
  events, 426
    Activate, 427
    Close, 426

Deactivate, 427
Error, 428
Format, 429-431
NoData, 428
Open, 426
Page, 428
Print, 431-432
Retreat, 432
running macros, 315-318
sequence, 429, 433
examples, 199-204, 450
fields
   adding, 175
   cutting labels, 175
   selecting, 172
graphics, 168
Group Footers, 171
Group Headers, 171
group levels, adding, 172
hyperlinks, adding, 777
Internet, compatibility,
   198-199
labels
   captions, 54
   hyperlinks, 198-199
   printing, 438-440
layouts, 173
mailing labels, 169
objects
   aligning, 177
   moving, 176-177
   selecting, 175-176
   sizing, 177
   Snap to Grid, 177
   spacing, 178
opening, 197
   macros, 307
optimization, 675
page breaks, inserting, 187
Page Footers, 171
Page Headers, 171
   printing, 446-448
previewing, 12
printing, 182-184
   properties, 434

properties, 181-184
   Can Grow, 197
   Can Shrink, 197
   Caption, 182
   Data, 183
   Data Grouping, 183
   Fast Laser Printing, 184
   Filter, 183
   Filter On, 183
   Force New Page, 187,
    196
   Format, 182
   Grid X, 182
   Grid Y, 182
   Group Footer, 195
   Group Header, 195
   Group Interval, 195
   Group On, 195
   Grp Keep Together, 182
   Has Module, 184
   Help Context ID, 184
   Help File, 184
   Keep Together, 196
   Layout for Print, 182
   Menu Bar, 184
   New Row or Col, 196
   Order By, 183
   Order By On, 183
   Page Footer, 182
   Page Header, 182
   Palette Source, 182
   Picture, 182
   Record Locks, 183
   Record Source, 183
   Repeat Section, 197
   runtime, 433, 435
   Shortcut Menu Bar, 184
   Tag, 184
   Toolbar, 184
   Visible, 196
   Width, 182
Properties window, 182
queries, efficiency
  considerations, 172

record sources, 183
   changing, 435-437
   system reports, 28
Report Footers, 171
Report Headers, 171
Reports collection, 281
saving, HTML format, 199
sections, 170
   events, 429-433
   hiding/displaying,
    437-438
sorting, 193-194
   levels, selecting, 173
   properties, 195-196
stored queries, 197-198
styles, selecting, 173
subreports, 193
Summary, 167
   Detail section, 171
titles, 173
   Caption property, 182
totals, 171
types, 166
wizards, 171
Requery method, 563
requerying, recordsets, 563
Require Variable Declaration
  feature, Code window, 275
Required property
  coordinating with Allow
    Zero Length property, 58
  tables, 57
requiring password
  validation (listing), 586
reserved words, upsizing to
  client/servers, 611
Reset button, 513
resetting code, debugging
  problems, 513
Resize event, forms, 377
resolution, monitors,
  performance
  considerations, 16
Resolve Replication Conflicts
  dialog box, 693

resolving replication conflicts, 693-695
responding to errors, 531-534
Resume statements, 521-522
Retreat event, reports, 432
RevokeFromGroup function, 892
revoking permissions, 900-901
RFT (Rich Text Format), 938
Rich Textbox
  ActiveX control, 755-758
  events, 756
  methods, 756
  properties, 756
Right function, 232
Right Outer Joins, 354
rights (users), modifying, 901
Ring topology, 684-685
Rollback method, transaction processing, 643
routines, CloseExcel, 722
row fix-up, queries, 99
Row Source Type property, combo boxes, 134
rows (client/servers), 608
rpt prefix, 1047-1049
rptClientListing report, creating, 199
rpts prefix, 1047
rptTimeSheet report, creating, 202
rsrp object-naming prefix, 1050
rst object-naming prefix, 1048
rsts object-naming prefix, 1048
rsub prefix, 1047
RTF files, creating, 938
rulers, forms, selecting objects, 126
Run command (Start menu), 817

Run menu commands, Compile All Modules, 672
Run Permissions property, queries, 112
running
  macros, 13, 306-318
    from forms, 315-318
    from report events, 315-318
    Macro Design window, 314
    Macros tab, 315
    subroutines, 314
  Object Browser, 287-288
  queries, 10, 88
  Setup Wizard, 974-977
  Visual SourceSafe, 783
Running Sum property, controls, 186
Runtime command line switch, applications, testing, 973-974
runtime
  errors
    continuing after, 512-513
    resetting code after, 513
  license, 959
  version
    compared to standard version, 30-31
    Database window, 962
    Design view, 962
    forms, creating applications, 964-967
    keystrokes, 963-964
    menu items, 962
    toolbars, 962
Rushmore, 346-347

S

Save As/Export command, File menu, 63
Save MDE As dialog box, 877
saving
  forms
    HTML format, 159, 768
    Microsoft IIS format, 160
  objects, Visual SourceSafe, 792
  queries, 90
    HTML format, 767
  records, form events, 375
  reports, HTML format, 199, 768
  Setup template, 982
  tables, HTML format, 766
scalability, 6-7
  databases, organizing database objects, 27
scheduled synchronization, replicated data, 703
schema (client/servers), 609
scope
  arrays, 257
  constants, 255
  procedures, 215-217
    precedence, 216-217
  variables, 220-222
scr prefix, 1047
Screen object, 281
Scroll Bars property
  controls, 146
  forms, 141
scrolling, snapshots, 467
searches, Help topics, 933
searching, tables, indexing fields, 58
sec prefix, 1047
Section property, 301
sections
  forms, events, 383

reports, 170
  events, 429-433
  hiding/displaying,
    437-438
security, 32
  Access compared to client/
    servers, 604
  applications
    assigning rights, 34-35
    distributing, 972
    preventing alterations, 34
  client/servers
    applications, 906
    views, 619-620
  controlling with code, 886
  encryption, 861-862
  examples, 88-883
  field-level, queries, 902
  groups, 886-889
    adding, 886-887
    adding users, 889-890
    assigning users, 890-891
    deleting, 888-889
    listing, 894-896
    maintenance, 889-894
    removing users, 891-894
  libraries, 806
  MDE files, 877-878
  networks, LDB files,
    563-564
  options, 860
  ownership, changing, 879
  passwords, 878, 896-899
  printing permissions, 880
  replicated databases, 906
  share-level, 860-861
  tables, linked, 879
  upsizing to client/servers,
    611
  user groups, 863
  user level
    administrative user,
      867-869
    administrative user
      passwords, 869-871

changing workgroup
  membership, 866
creating users/groups, 873
creating workgroups,
  864-866
logging in as
  administrative user,
  871
opening databases, 871
removing administrative
  user, 870
security Wizard, 871
user-level, 863-877
workspaces, creating
  multiple, 456
Security Wizard, 871
Seek method
  listing, 473
  recordsets, 473-474
Select Case statement,
  226-227
Select Case statements,
  compared to If statements,
  224
SELECT clause, SQL, 357
Select Data Source dialog
  box, 616
select queries, 10
  defined, 86
Select Unique Record
  Identifier dialog box, 617
  linking other table formats,
    578
selecting, objects, forms,
  125-126
selection handles, 125
  objects, sizing, 128
self joins, queries, 355-356
self-documentation, 910-916
self-relationships, defining,
  356
semicolon (;), input masks,
  53
servers
  applications, installing, 543
  automation server, 714

bookmarks, retrieving, 630
connecting, 615
connection timeouts, 633
FTP
  exporting data, 776
  importing data, 776
  linking data, 776
  sending data, 776
HTTP
  importing data, 776
  linking data, 776
  sending data, 776
installing Access, 542
ODBC, connecting, 632
Set as Applications Main File
  option, 976
Set as Workgroup File
  option, 977
Set Database Password dialog
  box, 860
Set Next Statement, 505
SetOption method, registry,
  modifying at runtime, 643
setting properties, 719
setting options from a
  Startup form routine
  (listing), 972
setup disks, creating, 33
setup files, location,
  specifying, 981
Setup template, saving, 982
Setup Wizard, 959
  applications, distributing,
    29
  introductory screen, 974
  RefLibPaths key, creating,
    804
  running, 974-977
SetWarnings method, 339
share-level security, 860-861
SharedAsyncDelay Registry
  setting, transaction
  processing, 642
sharing, data
  database replication, 678
  dispersed users, 678-679

Shed graphics, 944
Shift+F2 command, VBA,
    viewing code, 245-246
Shortcut Menu Bar option,
    970
Shortcut Menu Bar property
    controls, 149
    forms, 145
    reports, 184
Shortcut Menu property,
    forms, 145
shortcuts
    defining, distributing
        applications, 977
    repairing databases,
        929-930
Show Tables dialog box, 74
    queries, designing, 86
    self-join queries, 355
ShowDateSelectors property,
    Calendar control, 748
ShowTitle property,
    Calendar control, 748
shp prefix, 1047
Simple Query Wizard, 86
single forms, creating, 389
sizing forms, events, 382
slides (PowerPoint), 730
Snap to Grid
    disabling, 177
    forms, 128
        adjusting grid, 142
        disabling, 128
    objects, reports, 177
snapshots, 464, 630-631
    forward-scrolling, 631
    preventing writing, 467
    scrolling, 467
sng data-type prefix, 1047
software
    Microsoft Plus! package,
        658
    optimizing
        Jet 3.5, 660-661
        Performance Analyzer,
            661-662

Registry settings, 659-660
    Windows 95, 659
sorting
    fields, selecting field types,
        47
    queries
        criteria, 92-94
        multiple fields, 91
        results, 90-91
    records
        reports, 183
        table recordset objects,
            465
    recordsets, 472
    reports, 193-194
        properties, 195-196
sorting an existing recordset
    (listing), 472
sorting levels, reports,
    selecting, 173
source code, removing, 32
Source Object property
    subforms, 156
    subreports, 193
Source property, queries, 111
source-code control products,
    782
Special Effect property, 815
    controls, 147, 185
SpecialEffect function, 814
specific object variables,
    compared to generic, 292
SpecificBold subroutine
    listing, 665
specifying where a record was
    found (listing), 474
splash screen forms, creating,
    396, 423
SQL (Structured Query
    Language), 28
    ALL clause, 359
    client/servers, 609
    FROM clause, 357
    GROUP BY clause, 359
    HAVING clause, 360

history, 356
    JOIN clause, 358-359
    ORDER BY clause, 358
    queries, 356-359, 361
        creating, 360
    SELECT clause, 357
    statements
        append queries, 337
        compared to stored
            queries, 157
        delete queries, 335
        executing from VBA,
            360-361
        implicit transactions, 651
        left outer joins, 354
        linking back-end tables to
            front-end applications,
            605
        make table queries, 339
        queries, 28
        reports, 197-198
        saving as queries, 198
        storing queries, 334
    syntax, 357
    translating for ODBC, 606
    WHERE clause, 358
SQL Server, converting
    applications, 36
SQL Server Login dialog box,
    616
SQL View window, queries,
    360
square brackets ([ ]),
    expressions, 103
Standard modules, compared
    to Class, 217
standard modules, 210
standard version, compared
    to runtime version, 30-31
Star topology, 684
Start menu commands, Run,
    817
start-up options, databases,
    32
Startup dialog box, 32, 969

startup options (applications), setting, 969-972
Startup properties, modifying, 971
statements
  Debug.Print, form events sequence, 381
  Declare, 838
  Dim, 717
    variables, 218
  ElseIf, 223
  If, 223
    compared to Select Case statements, 224
  Kill, 520
  MsgBox, 397
  On_Error, 518-520
  On_Error_Goto, 519
  On_Error_Goto_0, 520
  On_Error_Resume_Next, 520
  Option Explicit, modules, 212
  Resume statements, 521-522
  Resume_Next, 522
  Select Case, 226-227
    compared to If statements, 224
  SQL
    append queries, 337
    delete queries, 335
    executing from VBA, 360-361
    implicit transactions, 651
    left outer joins, 354
    linking back-end tables to front-end applications, 605
    make table queries, 339
    queries, 28
    reports, 197-198
    saving as queries, 198
    storing queries, 334

Type, 252
  see also control structures
static HTML format, 772-773
Static procedures, 217
Static variables, 220
Statistics tab (Database Priorities dialog box), 915
Status Bar Text property, controls, 149
StatusBar
  ActiveX control, 751-753
  properties, 751
Step Into, 502-503
Step Out, 505
Step Over, 504
  selecting functions, 504
stepping through code, 502-505
  breakpoints, 503-504
    executing to, 504
  macros, 323
  Step Into, 502-503
  Step Out, 505
  Step Over, 504
stf data-type prefix, 1047
Stop statements, 500
stored procedures, executing (client/servers), 622-623
stored queries, reports, 197-198
str data-type prefix, 1047
strControl argument (builder functions), 814
strCurrentValue argument (builder function), 814
String Value command (New menu), 818
strings
  compiler constants, 225
  connection, open external tables, 585
  functions, 231-232
  Null value, concatenation compared to addition, 271

parameters, passing, 839-840
workgroups, identifying users/groups, 864
strObject argument (builder functions), 814
stored procedures (client/servers), 609
Structured Query Language, *see* SQL
styles, selecting, creating forms, 122
subaddress, hyperlink field type, 48
Subform/Subreport Wizard, 193
  one-to-many forms, 155-156
subforms, 390, 416
  adding, 156
  controls, referencing, 416
  efficiency of, 674
  modifying, 156
  properties, 156
  tab order, altering datasheet columns, 156
  viewing, 156
SubKey field (USysRegInfo table), 822
subkeys, creating, 818
subqueries, 364
subreports, 193
  Link Can Grow property, 193
  Link Can Shrink property, 193
  Link Child Fields property, 193
  Link Master Fields property, 193
  modifying, 193
  Source Object property, 193
subroutines, 210
  Call LoopThroughCollection, 499

code, viewing, 245-246
creating, 213-214
examples, 239-240
executing, Debug window, 498
FillCells, 721
GetErrorInfor, 536
GetSystemInfo, 534
macros, 314
modules, 14, 210
objects, passing, 298
parameters, 230-231
stepping over, 504
viewing, Full Module View, 211
Summary reports, 167
Detail section, 171
Summary tab (Database Properties dialog box), 915
SupportTrans property, transaction processing, 646
swap files, customizing, 658
Switchboard forms, 31, 395
creating, 964-967
editing, 967
Switchboard Manager, 118, 395
Switchboard Wizard, 964-967
switchboards, creating, 118
switches, Runtime, testing applications, 973-974
Symbolic constants, defining, 254
synchronization, programming, 707
troubleshooting, 708
Synchronization Details dialog box, 704
Synchronization History dialog box, 704
Synchronize Database dialog box, 691
Synchronize Now command (Replication menu), 691

Synchronize Now dialog box, 702
Synchronize Now tool, 702
Synchronizer, 682
synchronizers, replicas, managing, 701
synchronizing
data
history logs, 704
properties, 705
replicated, 702-704
forms, recordsets, 417
replicas, 691
Access user interface, 691-692
Windows 95 Briefcase, 692
syntax, SQL, 357
SysCmd function, 815
System Agent, 658
System DSN option, ODBC Data Source Administrator, 613
system performance
application types, 603
backup/recovery capability, 603
database size, 602
databases, organization, 27
encryption, 862
external data, 591
forms, record sources, 28
image controls compared to unbound object frames, 181
limiting factors, 5
modules, 797
network demands, 603
networks, replication, 565
queries, 344-345
improving performance, 345-346
reports, record sources, 28

security, 604
server connections, reducing, 633
transaction processing, 641
user base, 602
variables, declaring, 218
see also optimization
system requirements
client/server applications, 6
developers, 16
hardware, 16-17
minimum, 16
system-defined constants, 254

T

Tab controls, 393, 760
forms, adding, 393
tab pages
adding controls, 394
properties, changing, 394
Tab Index property, controls, 149
tab order
forms
changing, 130
Cycle property, 144
modifying, tab pages, 394
Tab Order dialog box, 131
Tab Stop property, controls, 149
tabbed forms, creating, 393-394
Table and Recordset locking, 547
Table Wizard, 41-42
TableDefs object, data access object model, 457
tables, 8-10
adding, 481
to databases, 483
Application database, 27

back end, linking to front
end applications, 605
business, 41
creating, 40
  datasheets, 44-46
  designing, 43-44
  queries, 337-339
  Table Wizard, 41-42
data
  *converting to HTML,
  63-65*
  updating in queries, 95
databases, organizing, 26-27
Description property, 61
Design view, 8, 43
designing, examples, 65-68
documentation, 910
documenting, 46
dynasets, 10, 464
external
  ASCII files, 591
  creating, 588-589
  dBASE, 589-590
  FoxPro, 590
  opening, 569-570
fields
  defining, 43
  deleting, 44
  descriptions, 44
  inserting, 44-46
  *selecting in Table
  Wizard, 41*
  selecting types, 46-48
  types, 43
Filter property, 62
forms, 11
  combo boxes, 133
  *creating one-to-many,
  153-156*
  HTML format, 768
  one-to-many, 153
  record sources, 125
indexes, adding, 481
Internet, hyperlink field
type, 62
joining, queries, 358-359

joins, outer, 354
junction, 72
linked
  client/servers, 616
  searching, 474
  security, 879
  updating, 776
linking
  accessing in networks, 546
  automation, 984-989
  examples, 595-598
locking, creating reports,
  183
MSysErrors, 686
MSysExchangeLog, 686
MSysSchemaProb, 686
MSysSidetable, 686
multiple
  creating queries, 96-97
  creating reports, 187-193
names, upsizing to client/
  servers, 611
naming conventions, 41
normalization, 18-19
notes, memo fields, 49
opening
  client/servers, 624
  macros, 307
optimizing, 662
  data types, 663
  indexes, 663
  normalization, 662-663
  queries, 664
personal, 41
predefined, 41
primary keys, 41, 59
properties, 61-62
queries
  HTML format, 767
  removing, 97
  selecting, 357
  specifying attributes, 111
  system performance, 28
recordsets, 463-464
  preventing reading, 467

relationships, 70
  benefits, 80
  *Cascade Delete Related
  Records option, 78-79*
  *Cascade Update Related
  Fields option, 77*
  creating, 482
  creating tables, 42
  defining, 8
  deleting, 75
  establishing, 73-74
  indexes, 80
  many-to-many, 72
  modifying, 75
  one-to-many, 9, 70-71
  one-to-one, 71-72
  *referential integrity,
  75-77*
removing, 481
replicated, designating as
local, 701
reports, HTML format,
768
saving, HTML format, 766
searching, indexing fields,
58
self joins, 355-356
TableDefs objects, 457
temporary, location, 27
Time and Billing
application
  tblClients, 994-1003
  *tblCompanyInfo,
  1004-1009*
  tblEmployees, 1009-1013
  tblErrorLog, 1014-1018
  tblErrors, 1018-1019
  *tblExpenseCodes,
  1019-1020*
  *tblPaymentMethods,
  1020-1021*
  tblPayments, 1022-1026
  tblProjects, 1026-1031
  *tblTimeCardExpenses,
  1031-1035*

tblTimeCardHours,
1036-1040
tblTimeCards,
1041-1043
tblWorkCodes,
1043-1044
upsizing to client/servers,
609
USysRegInfo
importing, 820
structure, 822
Validation Rule property,
61
Validation Text property,
61
viewing, 8
creating tables, 42
workstations, installing
locally, 544
TabStrip, ActiveX control,
758-760
Tag property
controls, 150, 186
forms, 145
reports, 184
tags, Help files, 940
task analysis, applications,
developing, 17
tbl object-naming prefix,
1048
tbl prefix, 1049
tblClients table, Time and
Billing application
field properties, 995-1003
fields, 994
tblCompanyInfo table, Time
and Billing application
field properties, 1004-1009
fields, 1004
tblEmployees table, Time
and Billing application
field properties, 1010-1014
fields, 1009

tblErrorLog table, Time and
Billing application
field properties, 1014-1018
fields, 1014
tblErrors table, Time and
Billing application
field properties, 1018-1019
fields, 1018
tblExpenseCodes table, Time
and Billing application
field properties, 1020
fields, 1019
tblPaymentMethods table,
Time and Billing
application
field properties, 1021
fields, 1020
tblPayments table, Time and
Billing application
field properties, 1022-1026
fields, 1022
tblProjects table, Time and
Billing application
field properties, 1027-1031
fields, 1026
tblTimeCardExpenses table,
Time and Billing
application
field properties, 1032-1035
fields, 1031
tblTimeCardHours table,
Time and Billing
application
field properties, 1036-1040
fields, 1036
tblTimeCards table, Time
and Billing application
field properties, 1041-1043
fields, 1041
tblWorkCodes table, Time
and Billing application
field properties, 1043-1044
fields, 1043

templates
HTML, 775
Setup, saving, 982
testing
applications, 20, 973
distribution, 982-984
Runtime command-line
switch, 973-974
builders, 819
data locking, 562
Empty value, 268
functions, Debug window,
498
installing, 33
macros, 322-323
property values, Debug
window, 496
runtime applications, before
distributing, 33
transaction processing, 642
variable values, Debug
window, 496
Testing for a zero-length
string listing, 667
text, aligning, objects, 128
Text Align property,
controls, 147, 186
Text Box tool, 132, 178
text boxes
converting to combo boxes,
138-139
forms, adding, 132
input boxes, creating, 400
reports, 178
text field type, 47-49
Text Viewer
database file, loading, 846
modules, 845
adding elements, 847
WIN32API.TXT, loading,
845
tgl prefix, 1047
Relations collection (listing),
460

Time and Billing application
converting to client/server, 38
data locking: examples, 565-566
distributing, examples, 989
libraries, examples, 807-809
linking tables, 595-598
objects, examples, 302-304
optimizing, 675
queries, examples, 115-116, 368-370
reports, examples, 450
replication, examples, 708-709
reports, examples, 199-204
security, examples, 880-883
subroutines/functions, examples, 239-240
tables, 994
  designing, 65-68
  tblClients, 994-1003
  tblCompanyInfo, 1004-1009
  tblEmployees, 1009-1013
  tblErrorLog, 1014-1018
  tblErrors, 1018-1019
  tblExpenseCodes, 1019-1020
  tblPaymentMethods, 1020-1021
  tblPayments, 1022-1026
  tblProjects, 1026-1031
  tblTimeCardExpenses, 1031-1035
  tblTimeCardHours, 1036-1040
  tblTimeCards, 1040-1043
  tblWorkCodes, 1043-1044
transaction processing, examples, 653-654
VBA, examples, 276-278
Visual SourceSafe, 793

Time Cards form, creating, 162
timeouts, server connections, setting, 633
Timer event, forms, 381
timestamps, adding, 633
titles
forms, Caption property, 140
Help files, 940
reports, 173
  Caption property, 182
selecting, creating forms, 122
see also page headers
tlkp object-naming prefix, 1050
Today command button, Calendar control, code, 749
toggle buttons, forms, adding, 136
toolbar buttons
Call Stack, 506
Continue, 512
Quick Watch, 508
Reset, 513
Toolbar property
forms, 145
reports, 184
toolbars
creating, 32
custom, creating for runtime version, 968-969
Custom Print Preview, displaying, 442
Form Design, 123-124
Formatting, 123-124
  reports, 175
forms, designing, 123-124
hiding/showing, 427
properties, viewing, 401
Report Design, 175
runtime version, 962
Web, 778

ToolbarShow routine (listing), 969
tools
Bound Object Frame, 179
Check Box, 135
Combo Box, 132
Compile Loaded Modules, 273
Label, 131, 178
Line, 179
Managed Replicas, 701
modules, 235-239
More Controls, 742
ODE, 28-29, 958
Page Break, 187
Rectangle, 179
reports, creating, 174
Synchronize Now, 702
Text Box, 132, 178
Unbound Object Frame, 180
Visual SourceSafe, 782
  installing, 782
Tools menu commands, 782
Add-Ins, 821
Analyze, 661
Database Utilities, 658
Options, 686, 820
Relationships, 72
Replication, 680, 688
Top property, controls, 146, 185
Top Values property, queries, 112, 342-343
topic files (Help files), 938
Topics Found dialog box, properties, 283, 933
topologies, 683
Fully Connected, 685
Hybrid, 685
Linear, 685
Ring, 684-685
Star, 684
totals
queries, 104-107
reports, 171

Totals queries
  creating, 105
  examples, 107
Tracing option, ODBC Data Source Administrator, 613
Tracking Layer (Jet), 681
transaction (client/servers), 609
transaction loop suitable for the Time and Billing application (listing), 653-654
transaction processing, 640
  benefits, 640-642
  client/servers, 651-652
  data locking, 553
  errors, 646-650
    memory, 646
  examples, 653-654
  explicit, client/servers, 651
  forms, 647
  implemeting, 643-644
  implicit, client/servers, 651
  issues, 644-647
  lock limits, client/servers, 652
  methods, 643
  multiuser systems, concurrency issues, 647-650
  nested transactions, client/servers, 652
  optimistic locking, 554, 649-650
  pessimistic locking, 648
  properties, SupportTrans, 646
  queries, pass-through, 652
  recordsets, compatibility, 645-646
  Registry
    modifying settings, 642-643
    modifying settings at runtime, 643
  speed considerations, 641

testing, 642
transactions, nesting, 646
Workspace objects, 644
transaction processing using Access Basic as seen in Access 2.0 (listing), 640
transaction processing with an SQL server back-end (listing), 651-652
transactions, 640
  client/servers
    explicit, 651
    implicit, 651
    lock limits, 652
    nested, 652
  nesting, 646
transactions in a multiuser environment, sacrificing concurrency (listing), 647-648
TransferDatabase method, external data, importing, 572-573
TransferDatabase method (listing), 572
TransferSpreadsheet method, external data, importing, 574-575
TransferSpreadsheet method (listing), 574
TransferText method, external data, importing, 573-574
TransferText method (listing), 574
transparent controls, 147
triggers (client/servers), 609
troubleshooting
  external data, 591
  replication, 708
TryAgain function (listing), 988-989
txt prefix, 1047
Type field (USysRegInfo table), 822

type libraries, 715
Type statement, 252
Type variables
  creating, 252
  data
    retrieving, 253
    storing, 253
  examples, 277-278
TypeOf keyword
  control structures, 224
  controls, 300
TypeOfDrive function (listing), 856
types, DLLs, 844-845
typing, variables, declaring, 218

U

UCase function, 232
UID keyword, 585
unbound controls, 150, 187
unbound forms
  client/servers, 635
  data locking, 564
Unbound Object Frame tool, 180
unbound objects
  frame reports, 180
  forms, 407
UNC
  Hyperlink Address control property, 146
  hyperlink field type, 51
  linking external data, 580
  tables, hyperlink field type, 62
underscore (_), line continuation character, VBA, 222
Unicode, 842
Uniform Resource Locators, *see* URLs
union queries, creating, 362

Unique Records property, queries, 112, 342
Unique Values property, queries, 112, 341
Universal Naming Convention, *see* UNC
Unload event, forms, 377-378
Unregister function, ActiveX controls, 742
Unset Database Password dialog box, 860
Update All command (Briefcase menu), 680
Update Briefcase dialog box, 692
Update Data permission, 876
update queries, 478
    creating, 332-333
    naming, 333
Update Retry Interval option (data locking), 550
Update Selection command (Briefcase menu), 680, 692
Updated event, controls, 384
updates, distributing, 679
updating
    data, control events, 388
    dynasets, 467
    queries
        multiple tables, 98
        results, 95-96
    records
        form events, 375
        queries, 10
    recordsets, 467
        errors, 467
        multiple records, 478
        single records, 477-478
    tables, linked, 776
updating records that meet a set criteria (listing), 477
UpDown object
    ActiveX control, 750-751
    events, 750

upsizing, issues, 601-612
Upsizing Wizard, 36
URLs (Uniform Resource Locators), 51
    Hyperlink Address control property, 146
    hyperlink field type, 51
    tables, hyperlink field type, 62
Use Access Special Keys option, 971
user accounts, 456
User and Group Accounts dialog box, 868
User and Group Permissions dialog box, 34, 861, 875
User DSN option, ODBC Data Source Administrator, 613
user groups, permissions, assigning, 34
user interface
    compacting databases, 925-927
    repairing databases, 929
user interfaces, Container objects, 483
user-level security, 863-877
    administrative user
        logging on, 871
        passwords, 869-871
        removing, 870
    databases, opening, 871
    Security Wizard, 871
    workgroups
        administrative user, 867-869
        changing membership, 866
        creating, 864-866
        creating users/groups, 873
User object, data access object model, 456
user-defined errors, 526

user-defined variable types, declaring, 252
UserCommitDelay Registry setting, transaction processing, 642
users
    assigning passwords, 896-897
    creating objects, prohibiting, 904-905
    listing, 894-896
    passwords, ensuring, 899
    rights, modifying, 901
Users group, 867
using the TableDefs and Indexes collections (listing), 457
usr object-naming prefix, 1049
USysRegInfo table structure, 822
USysRegInfo tables, importing, 820
utilities, Compact, 658

V

Validation Rule property
    controls, 148
    tables, 55, 61
validation rules, upsizing to client/servers, 610
Validation Text property
    controls, 148
    tables, 55-56, 61
ValidTextRude entry-point function (listing), 831-832
ValName field (USysRegInfo table), 822
Value field (USysRegInfo table), 822
Value property, Calendar control, 747
ValueIsNull property, Calendar control, 747

values
default, upsizing to client/
servers, 610
Empty, Variant variables,
268-269
List function, 413
Null
examples, 276-277
Variant variables,
269-273
null, queries, 364
parameters, passing, 839
properties
assigning, 264
retrieving, 264-265
returning
functions, 230-231
MsgBox function, 399
var data-type prefix, 1047
variables
compared to object
variables, 291-292
data types, 219-220
prefixes, 1047-1048
Database objects, creating,
466
declaring, 218
modules, 210
Option Explicit
statement, 212
performance
considerations, 218
Dim statement, 218
Group, 887
local, 220
memory, 292
freeing, 292
naming, 221
changing, 246
Public, 222
naming conventions, 1046
null values, 219
object
application references,
715-716

assigning, 291
creating objects, 297
declaring, 291
generic compared to
specific, 292
objects, creating, 463
Private, 221
private, 210
Public, 221-222
public, 210
form properties, 418-419
Recordset objects, creating,
465
scope, 220-222
scoping, 495
setting values
Debug window, 497, 503
Locals pane, 507
Static, 220
strong typing, 494
testing values
Debug window, 496
Type
creating, 252
examples, 277-278
retrieving data, 253
storing data, 253
types
declaring user-defined,
252
user-defined, 252
Variant, 268
bookmarks, 476
Empty value, 268-269
Null value, 269-273
variants, 219
VBA, 218-222
viewing, Locals pane, 507
Workspace, 887
Variant variables, 268
bookmarks, 476
Empty value, 268-269
Null value, 269-273
variant variables, 219

**VBA (Visual Basic for
Applications), 13, 208-209,
463**
#Const directive, 225
bookmarks, adding, 249
code
compared to action
queries, 340
converting from macro,
324-325
viewing, 245-246
Code window, 244
splitting, 248-249
viewing multiple, 249
command bars,
programming, 404
comments, 222
compared to macros,
208-209
constants, 253, 256
control structures, 223-230
DLL functions, declaring,
838
executing macros, DoCmd
object, 250-251
find and replace feature,
246
Full Module view, 249
functions, 231-234
parentheses, 463
help, context-sensitive, 247
libraries, 796
creating references, 805
line continuation character,
222
loops, 227-230
macros, 13
Module window, executing
procedures, 250
modules, 210-218
MsgBox function, 397-399
MsgBox statement, 397
named parameters, 251
navigating, 244
Procedure view, 249

programming,
environment, 244
SQL statements, executing,
360-361
upsizing to client/servers,
612
variables, 218-222
declaring user-defined
types, 252
user-defined types, 252
VBA code for linking to an
external table (listing), 618
Version fields, adding, 633
video, display, system
requirements, 16
View menu, forms, changing
tab order, 131
viewing
code
Full Module view, 249
Procedure view, 249
VBA, 245, 246
constants, 256
events, 284
forms, 11
options, 140
properties, 139
hidden text, 943
modules, 14
Full Module View, 211
object libraries, 287
properties, 283
queries, 340
toolbars, 401
Relationships window, 8
reports, previewing, 12
subforms, 156
tables, 8
creating tables, 42
views
client servers, linking,
619-620
client/servers, compared to
queries, 619-620

Design, creating forms,
122-123
Full Module, 211
Views Allowed property,
forms, 141
virtual memory, optimizing,
658-659
Virtual Memory buttons, 658
Visible property
controls, 146, 185
reports, 196
Visual Basic for Applications
see VBA
Visual SourceSafe, 782
Compact command, 791
databases
adding, 783-786
closing, 791
opening, 791
file extensions, 786
installing, 782
limitations, 793
modules, comparing
versions, 790
objects
adding, 789
adding automatically,
790
checking in/out, 786-789
deleting, 792
getting latest version, 789
opening in Design view,
792
refreshing, 790
renaming, 792
reverting, 791
saving, 792
running, 783
Visual SourceSafe
Access, behavioral
modifications, 791-792
databases, creating local
copies, 787
objects, viewing
development history, 790

W-X-Y-Z

warning messages
Action queries, 339-340
suppressing, 340
Watch expressions, 507-511
adding, 508-510
Auto Data Tips, 508
breaking at changes, 511
breaking when True,
510-511
editing, 510
quick watch, 508
watches, 500
Web sites
PKZIP, 34
WebBrowser control, 778
Web toolbar, 778
WebBrowser control, 778
weekday (date) expression,
queries, 95
What is This Button
property, forms, 142
WHERE clause, SQL, 358
Width property
controls, 146, 185
forms, 142
reports, 182
WillContinue property,
reports, 435
Win32 API, 838
data loss, preventing, 841
hard drives, determining
free space, 854
operating environment, 849
Text Viewer, 960
WIN32API.TXT, loading,
Text Viewer, 845
Windows, Registry keys,
ISAM drivers, 584
windows
Calls, 506
Code
Auto Data Tips feature,
275

Auto Indent feature, 275
Auto List Members
feature, 275
Auto Quick Info feature,
275
Auto Syntax Check
feature, 275
customizing, 274
customizing style features,
275
Required Variable
Declaration feature,
275
splitting, 248-249
Tab width, 275
VBA, 244
viewing multiple, 249
Database
runtime version, 962
viewing tables, 8
Debug, 495-499
clearing, 497
executing functions, 498
executing methods, 498
executing subroutines,
498
immediate pane, 496
Locals pane, 507
opening, 495-496
printing to, 499
problems, 513
setting property values,
497, 503
setting variable values,
497, 503, 507
testing functions, 498
testing property values,
496
testing variable values,
496
Watch expressions,
507-511
Field List, 125
availability, 143
Form Design, 123-131

form events, 378
forms, designing, 124
Help, customizing,
950-951
Macro Design, 13, 306
Module, executing
procedures, 250
Module Design, 14
Properties
forms, 140
reports, 182
Query Design, 10
Relationships, 8, 72
Report Design, creating
reports, 174-178
reports, designing, 175
SQL View, queries, 360
Windows 95
add-ons, Microsoft Plus!
package, 658
Help Compiler, 30
optimizing, 659
Windows API Viewer, 30
With...End With listing, 669
With...End With loops, 229
wizards
Combo Box, 132
Command Button,
151-153
Configure Microsoft
Replication Manager,
695-698
Control, adding combo
boxes to forms, 132
Convert Database to
Design Master, 699
creating, 823-826
CreateControl function,
826
CreateCustomForm
function, 824-826
CreateForm function,
826
Crosstab Query, 348-350

Database Splitter, 27
defined, 822
designing, 822
Form
creating forms, 121-122
launching, 122
one-to-many forms,
153-154
Import HTML, 592-594
Input Mask, 52
List Box, 135
Lookup, 59-60
Option Group, 136-138
Partial Replica, 702
Publish to the Web,
64, 773-775
registering, 826-827
Report, 172-174
launching, 174
reports, 171
Security, 871
Setup
distributing applications,
29
introductory screen, 974
running, 974-977
Simple Query, 86
Subform/Subreport, 193
one-to-many forms,
155-156
Switchboard, 964-967
Table, 41-42
Upsizing, 36
Word, controlling from
Access, 726-728
Workgroup Administrator,
865
Workgroup Information File
dialog box, 866
workgroup information files,
864
Workgroup Owner
Information dialog box,
865
workgroups, 456

Access 97 Unleashed, Second Edition

—Dwayne Gifford, et al.

This book enables current and new users to quickly and easily find the information they need on Access's new features. It also serves as a complete reference for database programmers new to Access. Readers learn advanced techniques for working with tables, queries, forms, and data. They also learn how to program Access and integrate the database with the Internet. CD-ROM includes Access utilities and applications, as well as an electronic Access reference library. Covers Access.

Price: $49.99 USA/$70.95 CDN
ISBN 0-672-30983-1   1,100 pp.

Teach Yourself Microsoft Office 97 in 24 Hours

—Greg Perry

This entry-level book includes numerous illustrations and screen shots to assist readers in a step-by-step plan for learning Office 97. Focuses on using the most widely requested features of Office. Readers also learn about creating documents in Word that include hypertext links to files created with other Office products. Covers Office 97.

Price: $19.99 USA/$28.95 CDN
ISBN 0-672-31009-0   450 pp.

Microsoft Office 97 Unleashed, Second Edition

—Sue Charlesworth & Paul McFedries, et al.

Microsoft has brought the Web to its Office suite of products. Hyperlinking, office assistants, and active document support enable users to publish documents on the Web or an intranet site. Readers learn to completely integrate with Microsoft FrontPage and to point-and-click a Web page into existence. This book also covers each of the Office products—Excel, Access, Powerpoint, Word, and Outlook—and shows users how to create presentations and Web documents. Readers learn to extend Office to work on a network; they also look at the various Office Solution Kits and how to use them. CD-ROM includes powerful utilities and two best-selling books in HTML format.

Price: $35.00 USA/$49.95 CDN
ISBN 0-672-31010-4   1,200 pp.

Teach Yourself Access 97 in 14 Days, Fourth Edition

—Paul Cassel

Through the examples, workshop sessions, and Q&A sections in this book, users will master the most important features of Access. In just two weeks, they'll be able to develop their own databases and create stunning forms and reports. Covers wizards, tables, data types, validation, forms, queries, artificial fields, macros, and more. Readers learn how to program with Access Basic and Access lingo.

Price: $29.99 USA/$42.95 CDN
ISBN 0-672-30969-6   700 pp.

Microsoft FrontPage 97 Unleashed, Second Edition

—William Stanek

FrontPage 97 works directly with the Microsoft Office 97 suite of products. Its built-in WYSIWYG editor is the best and most popular Web-authoring tool on the market. New and experienced FrontPage users will find this book a valuable tool for learning to use the new version's power to add multimedia, sound, animation, and Office 97 documents to a Web site. CD-ROM contains all the examples, built-in templates, Web publishing resources, and more. Covers FrontPage 97.

Price: $49.99 USA/ $70.95 CDN
ISBN 1-57521-226-9   1,000 pp.

Microsoft SQL Server 6.5 Unleashed, Second Edition

—David Solomon & Daniel Woodbeck, et al.

This comprehensive reference details the steps needed to plan, design, install, administer, and tune large and small databases. In many cases, readers will use the techniques in this edition to create and manage their own complex environments. CD-ROM includes source code, libraries, and administration tools. Covers programming topics such as SQL, data structures, programming constructs, stored procedures, referential integrity, large table strategies, and more. Offers updates covering all new features of SQL Server 6.5, including the new transaction processing monitor and Internet/database connectivity through SQL Server's new Web Wizard.

Price: $59.99 USA/$84.95 CDN
ISBN 0-672-30956-4   1,100 pp.

World Wide Web Database Developer's Guide

—Mark Swank & Drew Kittel

This book teaches readers how to quickly and professionally create a database and connect it to the Internet. Real-world database problems and solutions explain how to manage this information. Includes HTML, Java, and the newest Netscape 2.0 features to help organize information. CD-ROM explores ways to convert and present database information quickly and professionally. Readers discover how to use the latest Java and Netscape 2.0 features. Covers the World Wide Web.

Price: $59.99 USA/$84.95 CDN
ISBN 1-57521-048-7   800 pp.

Intranets Unleashed

—David Garrett, et al.

Intranets, internal Web sites that can be accessed within a company's firewalls, quickly are becoming the status quo in business. This book shows IS managers and personnel how to effectively set up and run large or small intranets. Everything from design to security is discussed. CD-ROM contains source code and valuable utilities. Readers learn how to develop intranets for corporate use. Covers intranets.

Price: $59.99 USA/$84.95 CDN
ISBN 1-57521-115-7   900 pp.

Add to Your Sams Library Today with the Best Books for Programming, Operating Systems, and New Technologies

The easiest way to order is to pick up the phone and call

1-800-428-5331

between 9:00 a.m. and 5:00 p.m. EST.
For faster service please have your credit card available.

ISBN	Quantity	Description of Item	Unit Cost	Total Cost
0-672-30983-1		Access 97 Unleashed, Second Edition (Book/CD-ROM)	$49.99	
0-672-31009-0		Teach Yourself Microsoft Office 97 in 24 Hours	$19.99	
0-672-31010-4		Microsoft Office 97 Unleashed, Second Edition (Book/CD-ROM)	$35.00	
0-672-30969-6		Teach Yourself Access 97 in 14 Days, Fourth Edition	$29.99	
1-57521-226-9		Microsoft FrontPage 97 Unleashed, Second Edition (Book/CD-ROM)	$49.99	
0-672-30956-4		Microsoft SQL Server 6.5 Unleashed, Second Edition (Book/CD-ROM)	$59.99	
1-57521-048-7		World Wide Web Database Developer's Guide (Book/CD-ROM)	$59.99	
1-57521-115-7		Intranets Unleashed (Book/CD-ROM)	$59.99	
❏ 3 ½" Disk		Shipping and Handling: See information below.		
❏ 5 ¼" Disk		TOTAL		

Shipping and Handling: $4.00 for the first book, and $1.75 for each additional book. Floppy disk: add $1.75 for shipping and handling. If you need to have it NOW, we can ship product to you in 24 hours for an additional charge of approximately $18.00, and you will receive your item overnight or in two days. Overseas shipping and handling adds $2.00 per book and $8.00 for up to three disks. Prices subject to change. Call for availability and pricing information on latest editions.

201 W. 103rd Street, Indianapolis, Indiana 46290

1-800-428-5331 — Orders   1-800-835-3202 — Fax   1-800-858-7674 — Customer Service

ISBN 0-672-30999-8